Ke
Gerry Hampson
Saud Al-Mishari
Greg Ramsey
Kenneth van Surksum
Michael Wiles

System Center Configuration Manager Current Branch

with Byron Holt and Garth Jones

UNLEASHED

System Center Configuration Manager Current Branch Unleashed

ISBN-13: 978-0-672-33790-1

ISBN-10: 0-672-33790-8

Library of Congress Control Number: 2018932443

Printed in the United States of America

1 18

Trademarks

Warning and Disclaimer

Bulk Sales

Senior Acquisitions Editor
Trina MacDonald

Development Editor
Mark Renfrow

Managing Editor
Sandra Schroeder

Senior Project Editor
Lori Lyons

Copy Editor
Kitty Wilson

Project Manager
Dhayanidhi Karunanidhi

Indexer
Kenneth D. Johnson

Proofreader
Abigail Manheim

Technical Editor
Steve Rachui

Cover Designer
Chuti Prasertsith

Compositor
codemantra

Contents at a Glance

E   (**Online Only**) Extending Hardware Inventory

        You can find Appendix E at informit.com/title/9780672337901.

        Click the Downloads tab to access the PDF file.

Table of Contents

E   (Online Only) Extending Hardware Inventory

You can find Appendix E at informit.com/title/9780672337901.
Click the Downloads tab to access the PDF file.

About the Authors

Kerrie Meyler, Cloud and Datacenter Management MVP, is the lead author of numerous System Center books in the *Unleashed* series, including *Microsoft Hybrid Cloud Unleashed* (2018), *System Center 2012 R2 Configuration Manager Unleashed Supplement* (2014), *System Center 2012 Configuration Manager Unleashed* (2012), and *System Center Configuration Manager 2007 Unleashed* (2009). She also coauthored *System Center Configuration Manager Reporting* (2016). Kerrie is an independent consultant with more than 20 years of information technology experience. She was responsible for evangelizing Systems Management Server (SMS) while a Senior Technology Specialist at Microsoft and has presented on System Center technologies at TechEd and MMS.

Gerry Hampson, Enterprise Mobility MVP, is a senior consultant with Ergo Group, based in Dublin. He has 20 years of technology experience and specializes in deploying Microsoft solutions. Gerry has a bachelor of engineering degree and numerous Microsoft, HP, and Cisco certifications (MCSE, MCITP, ASE, CCNA). He previously coauthored *Troubleshooting System Center Configuration Manager* (Packt, 2016). Gerry has a popular blog where he shares device management tips and tricks (gerryhampsoncm.blogspot.com). He is an active member of the Windows Management Users Group and regularly presents at user group meetings and conferences in Ireland and the UK. Gerry has worked with SMS and Configuration Manager since SMS 2003.

Saud Al-Mishari is a 15-year Microsoft veteran and a Program Manager with the Enterprise Mobility and Management (EMM) group, which owns Microsoft Intune and System Center Configuration Manager. He is part of EMM's Customer Experience Team (CXP) organization and helps Microsoft's largest customers deploy and adopt Microsoft Intune. Saud's career has focused on systems and device management, along with enterprise operations across various roles in consulting and support. He has worked across Europe, the Middle East, and Africa; he has spent significant time working with industry-leading companies in the UK and Saudi Arabia.

Greg Ramsey, Enterprise Mobility MVP, is the Enterprise Tools Strategist at Dell, Inc. He has a B.S. in computer sciences and engineering from Ohio State University. Greg coauthored *System Center Configuration Manager 2012 R2 Unleashed*, *System Center Configuration Manager 2012 Unleashed*, *Microsoft System Center 2012 Configuration Manager: Administration Cookbook* (Packt, 2012), and *System Center Configuration Manager 2007 Unleashed*. Greg is a cofounder of the Ohio SMS Users Group and the Central Texas Systems Management User Group.

Kenneth van Surksum, MCT and former MVP, is a trainer and managing consultant at insight24, a company based in the Netherlands. With almost 20 years of experience, Kenneth has worked with SMS 1.2 and successive versions of the product and specializes in OS deployment. Kenneth was a contributing author for *System Center 2012 R2 Configuration Manager Unleashed*, *System Center 2012 Configuration Manager Unleashed*, *System Center 2012 Service Manager Unleashed*, and coauthored *Mastering Windows 7 Deployment* (Sybex, 2011).

Michael Wiles begin working with SMS 1.1 as a Microsoft support engineer in 1997 and was a Senior Premier Field Engineer (PFE) from 2005 to 2012. He now works for NTT Data, as a Configuration Specialist Advisor, leading the infrastructure team and working on transitions and transformations with new customers at NTT Data Services. Michael was a contributing author on *System Center 2012 R2 Configuration Manager Unleashed Supplement* (2014).

About the Contributing Authors

Byron Holt, CISSP and an IT professional for over 20 years, has been a lead SMS and Configuration Manager engineer for several Global 5000 corporations and was part of the Active Directory and Enterprise Manageability support teams while working at Microsoft. Byron's experience includes software development, security architecture, and systems management. He currently works for McAfee as an infrastructure and process security architect. Byron coauthored *System Center Configuration Manager 2012 Unleashed* (2014).

Garth Jones, Enterprise and Client Manager MVP, is Chief Architect at Enhansoft, an Ottawa-based company that develops products and services to extend the value of System Center Configuration Manager. Garth started working with the product in 1996, when it was known as SMS. He is the founder of the Ottawa Windows Server User Group and its associated study group. Garth was the lead author of *System Center Configuration Manager Reporting Unleashed* (2016).

Dedication

To our families, who have supported us through the long process of writing this book, and to the Configuration Manager community for its continued support.

Acknowledgments

Writing a book is an all-encompassing and time-consuming project, and this book certainly meets that description. Configuration Manager is a massive topic, and this book benefitted from the input of many individuals. The authors and contributors would like to offer their sincere appreciation to all those who helped with this book, including the team at Enhansoft, John Joyner and ClearPointe Technology Group, Paul Saukko, Steve Thompson, Jason Sandys, and Steve Rachui.

We would also like to thank our spouses and significant others for their patience and understanding during the many hours spent on this book.

Thanks also go to the staff at Pearson, in particular to Trina MacDonald, Mark Renfrow, and Lori Lyons.

Foreword

Microsoft System Center Configuration Manager Current Branch—it's a whole new ball-game from what you have known from previous versions of Configuration Manager. New features, like the easy method for keeping the environment up to date with new builds, to new features for managing Windows 10, to new integration features with Microsoft Azure services, make this the best version of Configuration Manager ever released. And as you know, it is also constantly evolving. New features are being added three times a year, increasing the need to be constantly learning to remain up to date with what the product has to offer. In order to do so, learning from others who know those features is a great way to help you remain "in the know."

I would certainly expect that this book will prove to be an extremely valuable resource for you in your efforts of learning what is new in Configuration Manager Current Branch—at least at the time of writing the book. No book is going to be able to always be up to date, as by the time it is published, a new build of Configuration Manager may have already been released. However, to get you up to speed on what the product provides that can potentially benefit your organization, this book would be a great addition to your learning path.

No one is going to be able to be an expert in the entire product—it is just too huge of a product. That's why having a book with numerous authors is a great way to get many various perspectives and experiences shared quickly and easily. And knowing the majority of the authors, I'm sure that you will find this a fantastic addition in your collection of Configuration Manager resources.

All the best to you in your learning and use of Configuration Manager—as you know, I love the product, and trust that you will too once you get it firmly entrenched in your environment.

Wally Mead
(former) Senior Program Manager, Configuration Manager Product Group
Microsoft Corporation
Now at Cireson

Reader Services

Register your copy of *System Center Configuration Manager Current Branch Unleashed* at informit.com for convenient access to downloads, updates, and corrections as they become available. To start the registration process, go to informit.com/register and log in or create an account*. Enter the product ISBN, **9780672337901**, and click **Submit**. When the process is complete, you will find any available bonus content under Registered Products.

*Be sure to check the box that you would like to hear from us to receive exclusive discounts on future editions of this product.

INTRODUCTION

Microsoft's *System Center Configuration Manager Current Branch* represents the software company's continuing maturation of its systems management platform. As Microsoft has moved to updating Windows at an ever-faster cadence, software that interacts with it must also adopt a faster pace to remain aligned with the operating system. This is certainly true of Configuration Manager (ConfigMgr), which previously incorporated the year of its release as part of its name but now goes by *Current Branch*, with updates approximately three times a year. Microsoft designed Configuration Manager Current Branch to be part of its Software as a Service (SaaS) platform, which enables it to keep pace with Windows 10 updates and provide support for new Windows features as they become available. This book discusses Configuration Manager Current Branch as of version 1710.

Configuration Manager provides a total solution for systems management in a people-centric world. Beginning with ConfigMgr 2012, ConfigMgr can deploy applications to users rather than devices. Applications are not limited to those running on Windows; they can also be deployed to Linux, UNIX, OS X, iOS, Windows Phone, Symbian, and Android operating systems. Configuration Manager enables unified management to large groups of computers across on-premise, service provider, and Microsoft Azure environments, enabling administrators to manage deployments and security of devices and applications across an enterprise in an automated fashion. While its most frequently used feature is software deployment, ConfigMgr also encompasses operating system deployment (OSD), patch management for operating system and other software updates, mobile device management, endpoint management, and more.

Part I: Configuration Manager Overview and Concepts

This book begins with an introduction to configuration management, including initiatives and methodology. This includes Dynamic System Initiative (DSI), the IT Infrastructure Library (ITIL), and Microsoft Operations Framework (MOF). Although some to consider this to be more of an alphabet soup of frameworks than constructive information, these strategies and approaches give a structure to managing one's environment—from system configuration and inventory management to proactive management and infrastructure optimization. More importantly, implementing Configuration Manager is a project, and as such, it should include a structured approach with its own deployment. Chapter 1, "Configuration Management Basics," starts with the big picture and brings it down to the pain points that system administrators deal with on a daily basis, showing how Configuration Manager plans to address these challenges.

Chapter 2, "Configuration Manager Overview," shows how Configuration Manager has evolved from its first days in 1994 as Systems Management Server (SMS) 1.0, and introduces key concepts and feature dependencies. In Chapter 3, "Looking Inside Configuration Manager," the book begins to peel back the layers of the onion, discussing the design concepts behind Configuration Manager Current Branch, major ConfigMgr components, its relationship with Windows Management Instrumentation (WMI), the ConfigMgr database, and more.

Part II: Planning and Installation

Before installing any software, you need to spend time planning and designing its architecture. ConfigMgr is no exception. Chapter 4, "Architecture Design Planning," begins this discussion with developing a solution architecture and assessing your environment; it covers licensing, hierarchy and site planning, planning considerations for specific ConfigMgr services, and implementation considerations. Chapter 5, "Network Design," steps through the network concepts to consider when planning a ConfigMgr architecture and deployment.

When it is time to implement your design, read Chapter 6, "Installing and Updating System Center Configuration Manager," which steps through the installation and update process; and Chapter 7, "Upgrading and Migrating to ConfigMgr Current Branch," which discusses how to move from a Configuration Manager 2012 to a ConfigMgr Current Branch environment.

Part III: Configuration Manager Operations

The third part of this book focuses on ConfigMgr operations in your environment, which is where you will spend the bulk of your time. This includes navigating through the console, discussed in Chapter 8, "Using the Configuration Manager Console." Using ConfigMgr requires an installed client on managed systems, as covered in depth in

Chapter 9, "Client Management." Day-to-day operations include managing compliance settings, covered in Chapter 10, "Managing Compliance," and software distribution, discussed in Chapter 11, "Creating and Managing Applications," Chapter 12, "Creating and Using Deployment Types," Chapter 13, "Creating and Managing Packages and Programs," and Chapter 14, "Distributing and Deploying Applications and Packages." ConfigMgr operations include activities such as patch management (discussed in Chapter 15, "Managing Software Updates"), integrating Intune with ConfigMgr (Chapter 16, "Integrating Intune Hybrid into Your Configuration Manager Environment"), managing mobile devices (Chapter 17, "Mobile Device Management"), and conditional access (Chapter 18, "Conditional Access in Configuration Manager"). Also covered are endpoint management (Chapter 19, "Endpoint Protection"), running queries (Chapter 20, "Configuration Manager Queries"), reporting (Chapter 21, "Configuration Manager Reporting"), and operating system deployment (Chapter 22, "Operating System Deployment"). These chapters discuss those key functionalities and their use in System Center Configuration Manager.

Part IV: Configuration Manager Administration

This last part of the book discusses administration of your ConfigMgr environment. This includes security requirements (Chapter 23, "Security and Delegation in Configuration Manager") and backups and maintenance (Chapter 24, "Backup, Recovery, and Maintenance").

Part V: Appendixes

By this time, you should have at your disposal all the tools necessary to become a hybrid cloud expert. The last part of the book includes five appendixes:

▶ Appendix A, "Configuration Manager Log Files," discusses the myriad log files used by Configuration Manager that are helpful when trying to troubleshoot assorted issues.

▶ Appendix B, "Co-Managing Microsoft Intune and ConfigMgr," discusses how you might move workloads from ConfigMgr to Microsoft Intune, functionality first available with ConfigMgr Current Branch 1710.

▶ Appendix C, "Reference URLs," incorporates useful references you can access for further information about Configuration Manager, which is also included as live links available for download under the Downloads tab at Pearson's InformIT website, at http://www.informit.com/title/9780672337901.

▶ Appendix D, "Available Online," discusses value-added content available for download under the Downloads tab at Pearson's InformIT website, at http://www.informit.com/title/9780672337901.

▶ (Online Only) Appendix E, "Extending Hardware Inventory," takes a deep dive into how to extend hardware inventory. This appendix is available at Pearson's InformIT website at http://www.informit.com/title/9780672337901, under the Downloads tab.

Lab Environment

While developing this book, the authors used a lab environment provided by ClearPointe Technology. The ConfigMgr site hierarchy, installed in the odyssey.com domain, consisted of a CAS (Armada), two primary site servers (Athena and Ambassador), and a secondary site server under Athena (Charon). See Chapter 2 for a diagram of the hierarchy used in the Odyssey lab.

Disclaimers and Fine Print

The authors want to offer several disclaimers. While the authors of this book have made every attempt to present information that is accurate and current as known at the time, they are not infallible. Any updates and corrections will be provided as errata on the InformIT website at http://www.informit.com/title/9780672337901.

Thank you for purchasing *System Center Configuration Manager Current Branch Unleashed*. The authors hope it is worth your while.

PART I

Configuration Management Overview and Concepts

IN THIS PART

CHAPTER 1

Configuration Management Basics

System Center Configuration Manager (ConfigMgr) is the latest evolution of Microsoft's continuing maturation of its systems management platform. Microsoft initially released ConfigMgr's predecessor, Systems Management Server (SMS), in 1994, along with Windows NT Server 3.5, to help support managing MS-DOS, Windows for Workgroups, Windows NT, Mac, and OS/2 desktops on Windows NT Server, NetWare, LAN Manager, and Pathworks networks. As they say, "You've come a long way, baby!"

Configuration Manager provides a total solution for systems management in a people-centric IT environment, including the ability to catalog hardware and software, deliver new software packages and updates, and deploy Windows operating systems with ease. You can also use it to manage mobile devices, OS X, and Linux/UNIX clients. ConfigMgr gives you the resources you need to get and stay in control of your on-premise and mobile environments and helps with managing, configuring, and securing devices and applications. For example, Configuration Manager Current Branch includes the following new capabilities over Configuration Manager 2012 R2:

▶ **Windows 10 Support:** Updates that help you quickly deploy, upgrade, and configure Windows 10.

▶ **Servicing Model:** A new ConfigMgr servicing model keeps you current with continuous innovations delivered through Windows as a Service.

▶ **Mobile Device Management (MDM):** Building on unified management of on-premise and cloud-based mobile devices introduced with ConfigMgr 2012 R2, this version includes Android and iOS innovations through MDM when integrated with Microsoft Intune, including the ability to impose conditional access on devices and on-premise MDM support.

▶ **Monitoring:** Configuration Manager enables you to see clients that are online and view the health of Windows 10 devices.

▶ **Office 365 Management:** You can manage Office 365 clients using ConfigMgr's software update management workflow.

▶ **Application Management:** Software Center has a new, modern look, with increased capabilities.

This chapter introduces System Center Configuration Manager. To avoid constantly repeating that very long name, this book uses the Microsoft-approved abbreviations of this System Center component, Configuration Manager and ConfigMgr. This sixth edition of Microsoft's systems management platform includes numerous additions in functionality as well as security and scalability improvements over its predecessors, and it builds on the people-centric IT capabilities introduced in ConfigMgr 2012 R2.

The chapter discusses Microsoft's approach to information technology (IT) operations and systems management, including an explanation of the Microsoft Operations Framework (MOF), which incorporates and expands on the concepts contained in the Information Technology Infrastructure Library (ITIL) standard. It also examines Gartner Group's Infrastructure & Operational (I&O) Maturity Model, which is used in the assessment of the maturity of organizations' IT operations.

10 Reasons to Use Configuration Manager

Why should you consider using Configuration Manager in the first place? How does Configuration Manager make your daily life as a systems administration easier? This book describes the features and benefits of Configuration Manager in detail. To give you a quick idea of why ConfigMgr is worth a look, the following is a list of 10 scenarios in which you might want to use Configuration Manager:

▶ The bulk of your department's budget goes toward paying for teams of contractors to perform operating system (OS) and software upgrades rather than paying talented people like you the big bucks to implement the platforms and processes to automate and centralize management of company systems and user devices.

▶ You realize systems management would be much easier if you had visibility and control of all your systems and devices—regardless of the platform or technology they are using—from a single management console.

▶ Your new full-time job is keeping auditors happy by proving that your organization is compliant with an increasing number of government regulations.

► When you try to install Windows 10 for the accounting department, you discover it cannot run on half the computers because they do not have enough RAM. (It would have been nice to know that when submitting your budget requests!)

► You spent your last vacation on a trip from desktop to desktop, installing Microsoft Office 2016.

► You lack the internal resources to apply software updates manually to your systems every month.

► The laptops used by the sales team are still running Windows XP because salespeople never come to the home office. Meanwhile, the team is closing sales using iPads and other mobile devices while connecting to the cloud.

► Within days of updating system configurations to meet corporate security requirements, you find that several have already drifted out of compliance.

► Your software environment is so diverse and distributed that you can no longer keep track of which software versions should be installed on which system.

► By the time you update your documentation, everything has changed, and you have to start all over again!

While trying to bring some humor to the discussion, these topics represent very real problems for many systems administrators. If you are one of those individuals, you owe it to yourself to explore how your organization might leverage Configuration Manager to solve numerous problems. The pain points just listed are common to most users to some degree, and System Center Configuration Manager holds solutions for all of them.

However, perhaps the most important reason for using Configuration Manager is the peace of mind it gives you, as an administrator, to know that you have complete visibility and control of your IT systems. The stability and productivity this can bring to your organization is a great benefit as well.

The Evolution of Systems Management

Systems and configuration management has evolved significantly since the first release of SMS, and this landscape continues to experience great advancements today. Consider the proliferation of compliance-driven controls, movement toward the cloud, and explosion of devices; all these factors add significant complexity and exciting new functionality to the management picture.

NOTE: DEFINING THE CLOUD

What does *cloud* mean? Cloud can be a nebulous term and concept to some. It is many things and seems to be everywhere, being mentioned in blogs, magazine articles, commercials, books, user groups, IT conferences, and everywhere in between—in the halls of almost every organization and within the ranks of IT. While you may even hear the term cloud mentioned in movies, to many, the meaning of the term cloud is hazy.

Explained in the simplest of terms, cloud is a metaphor for hosted technology resources and applications. Hosted technology is nothing new; in the 1960s, companies used time-sharing services provided by service bureaus. You could consider hosted technology as offering technology as a service to which businesses and consumers subscribe. Technology as a service can be defined as data storage, hosted applications, and IT resources such as computers, networks, virtual servers, data processing, backups, and many other types of technology workloads. Examples of cloud services include Google Drive, Microsoft Office 365, and Oracle's Salesforce CRM.

System Center Configuration Manager is a software solution that delivers end-to-end management functionality for systems administrators. It provides configuration management, patch management, software and operating system distribution, remote control, asset management, hardware and software inventory, cloud integration via Microsoft Intune, and a robust reporting framework to make sense of the variety of available data for internal systems tracking and regulatory reporting requirements.

These capabilities are significant because today's IT systems are prone to a number of problems from the perspective of systems management, including the following:

▶ Hurdles in the distributed enterprise

▶ Automation challenges

▶ Configuration "shift and drift"

▶ Lack of security and control

▶ Timeliness of asset data

▶ Lack of automation and enforcement

▶ Proliferation of cloud computing

▶ Lack of process consistency

This list should not be surprising, as these types of problems manifest themselves to varying degrees in IT shops of all sizes. In fact, in a 2012 report, Forrester Research estimates that 82% of large IT organizations are pursuing service management, and 67% are planning to increase Windows management (see https://www.forrester.com/report/Sustain+Service+Management+And+Automation+Funding/-/E-RES61499). The next sections look at these issues from a systems management perspective.

Hurdles in the Distributed Enterprise

You may encounter a number of challenges when implementing systems management in a distributed enterprise, including the following:

▶ **Increasing Threats:** According to the SANS Institute, the threat landscape is increasingly dynamic, making efficient and proactive update management more important than ever before (see https://www.computerworld.com/article/2565944/security0/sans-unveils-top-20-security-vulnerabilities.html). Symantec's 2017 Internet Security

Threat Report concluded that cyber criminals revealed new levels of ambition in 2016, causing unprecedented levels of disruption with relatively simple IT tools and cloud services (https://www.symantec.com/security-center/threat-report).

▶ **Regulatory Compliance:** Sarbanes-Oxley, HIPAA, and many other regulations have forced organizations to adopt and implement fairly sophisticated controls to demonstrate compliance.

▶ **OS and Software Provisioning:** Rolling out the OS and software on new workstations and servers, especially in branch offices, can be both time-consuming and logistically challenging.

▶ **Methodology:** With the bar for effective IT operations higher than ever before, organizations are forced to adapt a more mature implementation of IT operational processes to deliver the necessary services to the organization's business units more efficiently.

With increasing operational requirements unaccompanied by linear growth in IT staffing levels, organizations must discover ways to streamline administration through the use of tools and automation.

Automation Challenges

As functionality in client and server systems has increased, so too has complexity. Both desktop and server deployments can be very time-consuming when performed manually. With the number and variety of security threats increasing every year, timely application of security updates is of paramount importance. Regulatory compliance issues add an additional burden, requiring IT to demonstrate that system configurations meet regulatory requirements.

These problems have a common element: All beg for some measure of automation to ensure that IT can meet expectations in these areas at the expected level of accuracy and efficiency. To get IT operational requirements in hand, organizations must implement tools and processes that make OS and software deployment, update management, and configuration monitoring more efficient and effective.

Configuration "Shift and Drift"

Even in IT organizations with well-defined and well-documented change management, procedures can fall short of perfection. Unplanned and unwanted changes frequently find their way into the environment, sometimes as an unintended side effect of an approved, scheduled change.

You may be familiar with an old philosophical saying "If a tree falls in a forest and no one is around to hear it, does it make a sound?" Here is the configuration management equivalent: "If a change is made on a system and no one knows about it, does identifying it make a difference?"

The answer to this question is absolutely *yes*. Every change to a system has some potential to affect the functionality or security of a system or that system's adherence to corporate or regulatory standards.

For example, adding a feature to a web application component may affect the application binaries, potentially overwriting files or settings replaced by a critical security patch. Alternatively, perhaps the engineer implementing the change sees a setting he or she thinks is misconfigured and decides to just "fix" it while working on the system. In an e-commerce scenario with sensitive customer data involved, this could have potentially devastating consequences.

At the end of the day, your selected systems management platform must bring a strong element of baseline configuration monitoring to ensure that configuration standards are implemented and maintained with the required consistency.

Lack of Security and Control

Managing systems becomes much more challenging outside the realm of the traditional LAN-connected desktop or server. Traveling users who rarely connect to the trusted network (other than to periodically change their password) can really make this seem an impossible task. Just keeping these systems up to date on security patches can easily become a full-time job. Maintaining patch levels and system configurations to corporate standards when your roaming users only connect via the Internet can make this activity exceedingly painful. In reality, remote sales and support staff make this an everyday problem. To add to the quandary, these users are frequently among those installing unapproved applications from unknown sources, putting the organization at greater risk when they finally do connect to the network.

Point-of-Sale (POS) devices running embedded operating systems pose unique challenges, thanks to their specialized operating systems that can be difficult to administer and—for many systems management solutions—are completely unmanageable. Frequently these systems perform critical functions within the business (as cash registers, automated teller machines, and so on), making the need for visibility and control from configuration and security perspectives an absolute necessity.

Mobile devices have moved from a role of high-dollar phone to a mini-computer used for everything: Internet access, Global Positioning System (GPS) navigation, and storage for all manner of potentially sensitive business data. From the chief information officer's perspective, ensuring that these devices are securely maintained (and appropriately password protected) is somewhat like gravity: It's a more than a good idea—it's the law!

But seriously, as computing continues to evolve and more devices release users from the structures of office life, the problem only gets larger.

Cloud computing adds additional challenges to security and control. The question becomes how to best share these controls among the different stakeholders while maintaining strong oversight. This is discussed further in the "Proliferation of Cloud Computing" section, later in this chapter.

Timeliness of Asset Data

Maintaining a current picture of what is deployed and in use in your environment is a constant challenge due to the ever-increasing pace of change. However, failing to maintain an accurate snapshot of current conditions comes at a cost. Many organizations utilize a manual process involving Excel spreadsheets and custom scripting, and asset data is often obsolete by the time a single pass at the infrastructure is complete.

Without this data, organizations can over-purchase (or, worse yet, under-purchase) software licensing. Having accurate asset information can help you get a better handle on your licensing costs. Likewise, without current configuration data, areas including incident and problem management may suffer, as troubleshooting incidents will be more error prone and time-consuming.

Lack of Automation and Enforcement

With the perpetually increasing and evolving technology needs of a business, the need to automate resource provisioning, standardize, and enforce standard configurations becomes increasingly important.

Resource provisioning of new workstations or servers can be a very labor-intensive exercise. Installing a client OS and required applications may take a day or longer if performed manually. Ad hoc scripting to automate these tasks can be a complex endeavor. Once deployed, ensuring that the client and server configuration is consistent can seem an insurmountable task. With customer privacy and regulatory compliance at stake, consequences can be severe if this challenge is not met head on.

Proliferation of Cloud Computing

There is an old saying: "If you fail to plan, you plan to fail." In no area of IT operations is this truer than when considering cloud technologies.

When dealing with systems management, you have to consider many different functions, such as software and patch deployment, resource provisioning, and configuration management. Managing server and application configuration in an increasingly "cloudy" world, where boundaries between systems and applications are not always clear, requires consideration of new elements of management not present in a purely on-premise environment.

Cloud computing—whether private, public, or hybrid cloud—is a very exciting concept to IT operations. The potential for dramatic increases in process automation and efficiency and reduction in deployment costs is very real. Cloud technology makes it possible to provision new servers and applications in a matter of minutes. However, this newfound agility comes with a potential downside, which is the reality that cloud computing can increase the velocity of change in your environment. The tools used to manage and track changes to a server often fail to address new dynamics that come when cloud computing is introduced into a computing environment.

Many organizations make the mistake of taking on new tools and technologies in an ad hoc fashion, without first reviewing them in the context of the process controls used to manage the introduction of change into the environment. These big gains in efficiency can lead to a completely new problem: inconsistencies in processes not designed to address the new dynamics that come with the cloud.

Lack of Process Consistency

When it comes to identifying and resolving problems, many IT organizations still "fly by the seat of their pants." Using standard procedures and a methodology helps minimize risk and solve issues more quickly.

A *methodology* is a framework of processes and procedures used by those who work in a particular discipline. It is a structured process that defines the who, what, where, when, and why of operations and the procedures to use when defining problems, solutions, and courses of action.

When employing a standard set of processes, it is important to ensure that the framework being adopted adheres to accepted industry standards or best practices and that it takes into account the requirements of the business—ensuring continuity between expectations and the services delivered by the IT organization. Consistently using a repeatable and measurable set of practices allows organizations to more accurately quantify their progress, facilitating adjustment of processes as necessary to improve future results.

The most effective IT organizations build an element of self-examination into their IT service management (ITSM) strategy to ensure that processes can be incrementally improved or modified to meet the changing needs of the business. With IT's continually increased role in running successful business operations, it is critical to have a structured and standard way to define IT operations aligned to the needs of the business and enable IT to meet expectations of business stakeholders. This alignment results in improved business relationships where business units engage IT as a partner in developing and delivering innovations to drive business results.

The Bottom Line

Systems management can be intimidating when you consider that the problems described to this point in the chapter could happen even in an ostensibly "managed" environment. However, these examples serve to illustrate that the very processes used to manage change must themselves be reviewed periodically and updated to accommodate changes in tools and technologies employed from the desktop to the datacenter.

Likewise, meeting the expectations of both business and compliance regulation can seem an impossible task. As technology evolves, so must IT's thinking, management tools, and processes. This makes it necessary to embrace continual improvement in methodologies used to reduce risk while increasing agility in managing systems to keep pace with the increasing velocity of change.

Systems Management Defined

Systems management is a journey, not a destination. That is to say, it is not something you achieve at a point in time. Systems management encompasses all points in the IT service triangle, as shown in Figure 1.1, including a set of processes and the tools and people implementing them. Although the role of each varies at different points within the IT service life cycle, the end goals do not change. How effectively these components are utilized determines the ultimate degree of success, manifesting in the outputs of productive employees producing and delivering quality products and services.

Technology   Quality and Productivity   People

Process

FIGURE 1.1   The IT service triangle includes people, process, and technology.

At a process level, systems management touches nearly every area of IT operations. It can continually manage a computing resource, such as a client workstation, from the initial provisioning of the OS and hardware to end-of-life, when user settings are migrated to a new machine. The hardware and software inventory data collected by your systems management solution can play a key role in incident and problem management, providing information that facilitates faster troubleshooting.

As IT operations grow in size, scope, complexity, and business impact, the common denominator at all phases is efficiency and automation, based on repeatable processes that conform to industry best practices. Achieving this necessitates capturing subject matter expertise and business context into a repeatable, partially or fully automated process. At the beginning of the service life cycle is service provisioning, which from a systems management perspective means OS and software deployment. Automation at this phase can save hours or days of manual deployment effort in each iteration.

After resources are in production, the focus expands to include managing and maintaining systems via ongoing activities IT uses to manage the health and configuration of systems. These activities may touch areas such as configuration management by monitoring for unwanted changes in standard system and application configuration baselines.

As the service life cycle continues, systems management can affect release management in the form of software upgrades. Activities include software metering activities, such as reclaiming unused licenses for reuse elsewhere. If you are able to automate these processes to a great degree, you achieve higher reliability and security, greater availability, better asset allocation, and a more predictable IT environment. These factors translate into business agility, more efficient and less expensive operations, and a greater ability to respond quickly to changing conditions.

Reducing costs and increasing productivity in IT service management are important because efficiency in operations frees up money for innovation and product improvements. Information security is also imperative because the price tag of compromised systems and data recovery from security exposures can be large, and those costs continue to rise each year.

Microsoft's Strategy for Systems Management

Microsoft utilizes a multifaceted approach to ITSM. This strategy includes advancements in the following areas:

▶ **Adoption of a model-based management strategy to implement synthetic transaction technology:** Such a strategy is a component of the Dynamic Systems Initiative, discussed in the next section, "Microsoft's Dynamic Systems Initiative (DSI)." Configuration Manager delivers Service Modeling Language (SML)-based models in its Compliance Settings feature, allowing administrators to define intended configurations.

▶ **Incorporating the Infrastructure & Operational (I&O) Maturity Model as a framework for aligning IT with business needs:** As discussed in the "Judging Your IT Organization's Maturity" section, later in this chapter, the five levels of infrastructure and operational maturity help identify your organization's capability to take on new challenges.

▶ **Supporting a standard web services specification for systems management:** WS-Management is a specification of a SOAP-based protocol, based on web services, used to manage servers, devices, and applications. (SOAP stands for *Simple Object Access Protocol*.) The intent is to provide a universal language that all types of devices can use to share data about themselves, which in turn makes them easier to manage.

▶ **Integrating infrastructure and management into OS and server products:** This requires exposing services and interfaces that management applications can utilize.

▶ **Building complete management solutions on this infrastructure:** This can be done either by making them available in the operating system or by using management products such as Configuration Manager.

▶ **Continuing to drive down the complexity of Windows management:** Providing core management infrastructure and capabilities in the Windows platform itself allows business and management application developers to improve their infrastructures and capabilities. Microsoft believes that improving the manageability of solutions built on Windows Server will be a key driver in shaping the future of Windows management.

▶ **Updating regularly:** Recognizing the rapid rate of software changes as systems move to the cloud, Microsoft has aligned Configuration Manager to have updates multiple times each year, as introduced using the Current Branch model with ConfigMgr's release in late 2015. Using this model, ConfigMgr's regular updates are designed to support the faster pace of updates for Windows 10 and Microsoft Intune.

Microsoft's Dynamic Systems Initiative (DSI)

Reducing costs and increasing productivity in IT service management are important because efficiency in operations frees up money for innovation and product improvements. Information security is also imperative because the price tag of compromised systems and data recovery from security exposures can be large, and these costs continue to rise each year.

A large percentage of departmental budgets and resources typically focus on mundane maintenance tasks, such as applying software patches or monitoring network health, without leaving staff time or energy to focus on more exhilarating and productive strategic initiatives.

DSI, a Microsoft and industry strategy, is intended to enhance the Windows platform, delivering a coordinated set of solutions that simplify and automate how businesses design, deploy, and operate distributed systems. DSI helps IT and developers create operationally aware platforms. By designing platforms that are more manageable and automating operations, organizations can reduce costs and proactively address priorities.

DSI is about building software that enables knowledge of an IT system to be created, modified, transferred, and operated on throughout the life cycle of that system. It is a commitment from Microsoft and its partners to help IT teams capture and use knowledge to design systems that are more manageable and to automate operations, which in turn reduces costs and gives organizations additional time to focus proactively on what is most important. By innovating across applications, development tools, the platform, and management solutions, DSI results in the following:

▶ Increased productivity and reduced costs across all areas of IT

▶ Increased responsiveness to changing business needs

▶ Reduced time and effort spent developing, deploying, and managing applications and software systems

Microsoft is positioning DSI as the connector of the entire system and service life cycles.

Microsoft Product Integration

DSI focuses on automating datacenter operational jobs and reducing associated labor though self-managing systems. Following are several examples where Microsoft products and tools integrate with DSI:

▶ Configuration Manager uses model-based configuration baseline templates in its Compliance Settings feature to automate identification of undesired shifts in system configurations.

▶ Visual Studio is a model-based development tool that leverages SML, enabling operations managers and application architects to collaborate early in the development phase and ensure that applications are modeled with operational requirements in mind.

▶ Windows Server Update Services (WSUS) enables greater and more efficient administrative control through modeling technology that enables downstream systems to construct accurate models representing their current state, available updates, and installed software.

> **SDM AND SML: WHAT'S THE DIFFERENCE?**
>
> Microsoft originally used the System Definition Model (SDM) as its standard schema with DSI. SDM was a proprietary specification put forward by Microsoft. The company later decided to implement SML, which is an industrywide published specification used in heterogeneous environments. Using SML helps DSI adoption by incorporating a standard that Microsoft's partners can understand and apply across mixed platforms. SML is discussed later in this chapter, in the section "The Role of Service Modeling Language in IT Operations."

DSI focuses on automating datacenter operations and reducing total cost of ownership (TCO) though self-managing systems. Can logic be implemented in management software so the software can identify system or application issues in real time and then dynamically take actions to mitigate the problem? Consider the scenario where, without operator intervention, a management system moves a virtual machine running a line-of-business application because the existing host is experiencing an extended spike in resource utilization. DSI aims to extend this type of self-healing and self-management to other areas of operations.

In support of DSI, Microsoft has invested heavily in three major areas:

- ▶ **Systems Designed for Management:** Microsoft is delivering development and authoring tools, such as Visual Studio, that enable businesses to capture the knowledge of everyone from business users and project managers to the architects, developers, testers, and operations staff using models. By capturing and embedding this knowledge into the infrastructure, organizations can reduce support complexity and cost.

- ▶ **An Operationally Aware Platform:** The core Windows operating system and its related technologies are critical when solving everyday operational and service challenges. This requires designing operating system services for manageability. In addition, the operating system and server products must provide rich instrumentation and hardware resource virtualization support.

- ▶ **Cloud Applications:** Utilizing public and hybrid cloud functionality improves the agility of an organization by simplifying the effort involved in modifying, adding, or removing the resources a service uses in performing work.

The Importance of DSI

There are three architectural elements behind the DSI initiative:

- ▶ Developers have tools (such as Visual Studio) to design applications such that they are easier for administrators to manage after they are in production.

- ▶ Microsoft products can be secured and updated in a uniform way.

- ▶ Microsoft server applications are optimized for management.

DSI represents a departure from the traditional approach to systems management. It focuses on designing for operations from the application development stage rather than taking a more customary operations perspective that concentrates on automating task-based processes. This strategy highlights the fact that Microsoft's DSI is about building software that enables knowledge of an IT system to be created, modified, transferred, and used throughout the life cycle of a system. DSI's core principles of knowledge, models, and the life cycle are key in addressing the challenges of complexity and manageability faced by IT. By capturing knowledge and incorporating health models, DSI can facilitate easier troubleshooting and maintenance and, thus, lower TCO.

The Role of Service Modeling Language in IT Operations

A key underlying component of DSI is the eXtensible Markup Language (XML)-based specification called Service Modeling Language (SML). SML is a standard developed by several leading IT companies that defines a consistent way for infrastructure and application architects to define how applications, infrastructure, and services are modeled.

SML facilitates modeling systems from a development, deployment, and support perspective with modular, reusable building blocks that eliminate the need to reinvent the wheel when describing and defining a new service. The end result is systems that are easier to develop, implement, manage, and maintain, resulting in reduced TCO for the organization. SML is a core technology that plays a prominent role in future products developed to support the ongoing objectives of DSI.

NOTE: SML RESOURCES ON THE WEB

SML functionality and configuration management within Configuration Manager is implemented using Compliance Settings. For more information about SML, view the latest draft of the SML standard, at http://www.w3.org/TR/sml/. For additional technical information about SML from Microsoft, see https://technet.microsoft.com/library/bb687996.aspx.

ITIL and MOF

ITIL is widely accepted as an international standard of best practices and guidelines for IT services. MOF is closely related to ITIL; both describe best practices for IT service management processes. The next sections introduce you to ITIL and MOF. Warning: Fasten your seat belt because this is where the acronym fun really begins!

What Is ITIL?

As part of Microsoft's management approach, the company relied on an international standards-setting body as its basis for developing an operational framework. The British Office of Government Commerce (OGC) provides best practices advice and guidance on using IT in service management and operations. The OGC also publishes the IT Infrastructure Library, commonly known as ITIL.

ITIL provides a cohesive set of best practices for ITSM. These best practices include a series of books that provide direction and guidance on provisioning quality IT services and facilities needed to support IT. The documents are maintained by the OGC and supported by publications, qualifications, and an international users group.

Started in the 1980s, ITIL is under constant development by a consortium of industry IT leaders. ITIL covers a number of areas and is primarily focused on ITSM; in fact, ITIL is considered to be the most consistent and comprehensive documentation of best practices for ITSM worldwide. ITSM is a business-driven, customer-centric approach to managing IT. It specifically addresses the strategic business value generated by IT and the need to deliver high-quality IT services to a business organization. Following are the key objectives of ITSM:

▶ Align IT services with current and future needs of the business and its customers

▶ Improve the quality of IT services delivered

▶ Reduce long-term costs of providing services

MORE ABOUT ITIL

The core books for ITIL version 3 (ITIL v3) were published on June 30, 2007. With v3, ITIL adopted an integrated service life cycle approach to ITSM, as opposed to organizing itself around the concepts of IT service delivery and support.

ITIL v2 was a targeted product, explicitly designed to bridge the gap between technology and business, with a strong process focus on effective service support and delivery. The v3 documents recognize the service management challenges brought about by advancements in technology, such as virtualization and outsourcing, and emerging challenges for service providers. The v3 framework emphasizes managing the life cycle of the services provided by IT and the importance of creating business value rather than just executing processes.

ITIL v3 has five core volumes:

▶ **Service Strategy:** This volume identifies market opportunities for which services could be developed to meet a requirement on the part of internal or external customers. Key areas here are service portfolio management and financial management.

▶ **Service Design:** This volume focuses on the activities that take place to develop the strategy into a design document that addresses all aspects of the proposed service and the processes intended to support it. Key areas of this volume are availability management, capacity management, continuity management, and security management.

▶ **Service Transition:** This volume focuses on implementing the output of service design activities and creating a production service (or modifying an existing service). There is some overlap between this volume and the next one, Service Operation. Key areas of the Service Transition volume are change management, release management, configuration management, and service knowledge management.

▶ **Service Operation:** This volume involves the activities required to operate services and maintain their functionality, as defined in service level agreements (SLAs) with customers. Key areas here are incident management, problem management, and request fulfillment.

▶ **Continual Service Improvement:** This volume focuses on the ability to deliver continual improvement to the quality of the services that the IT organization delivers to the business. Key areas include service reporting, service measurement, and service level management.

Philosophically speaking, ITSM focuses on the customer's perspective of IT's contribution to the business, which is analogous to the objectives of other frameworks in terms of their consideration of alignment of IT service support and delivery with business goals in mind.

While ITIL describes the *what*, *when*, and *why* of IT operations, it stops short of describing *how* a specific activity should be carried out. A driving force behind its development was the recognition that organizations are increasingly dependent on IT for satisfying their corporate objectives relating to both internal and external customers, which increases the requirement for high-quality IT services. Many large IT organizations realize that the road to a customer-centric service organization runs along an ITIL framework.

ITIL also specifies keeping measurements or metrics to assess performance over time. Measurements can include a variety of statistics, such as the number and severity of service outages, along with the amount of time it takes to restore service. These metrics, or key performance indicators (KPIs), can be used to quantify to management how well IT is performing. This information can prove particularly useful for justifying resources during the budget process!

What Is MOF?

ITIL is generally accepted as the "best practices" for the industry. Being technology agnostic, it is a foundation that can be adopted and adapted to meet the specific needs of various IT organizations. Although Microsoft chose to adopt ITIL as a standard for its own IT operations for its descriptive guidance, Microsoft designed MOF to provide prescriptive guidance for effective design, implementation, and support of Microsoft technologies.

MOF is a set of publications that provide both descriptive (*what to do*, *when*, and *why*) and prescriptive (*how to do*) guidance on ITSM. The key focus in developing MOF was providing a framework specifically geared toward managing Microsoft technologies. Microsoft created the first version of MOF in 1999. The latest iteration of MOF (version 4) is designed to do the following:

▶ Update MOF to include the full end-to-end IT service life cycle

▶ Let IT governance serve as the foundation of the life cycle

▶ Provide useful, easily consumable best practice-based guidance

▶ Simplify and consolidate service management functions (SMFs), emphasizing workflows, decisions, outcomes, and roles

MOF v4 now incorporates Microsoft's previously existing Microsoft Solutions Framework (MSF), providing guidance for application development solutions. The combined framework provides guidance throughout the IT life cycle, as shown in Figure 1.2.

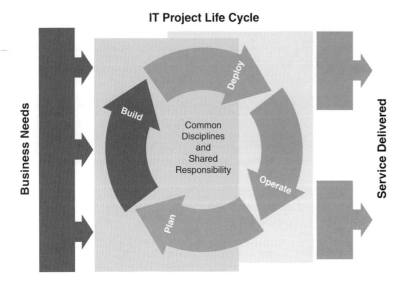

FIGURE 1.2   The IT life cycle.

At its core, MOF is a collection of best practices, principles, and models. It provides direction to achieve reliability, availability, supportability, and manageability of mission-critical production systems, focusing on solutions and services using Microsoft products and technologies. MOF extends ITIL by including guidance and best practices derived from the experience of Microsoft's internal operations groups, partners, and customers worldwide. MOF aligns with and builds on the ITSM practices documented in ITIL, thus enhancing the supportability built on Microsoft's products and technologies.

MOF uses a model that describes Microsoft's approach to IT operations and the service management life cycle. The model organizes the ITIL volumes Service Strategy, Service Design, Service Transition, Service Operation, and Continual Service Improvement and includes additional MOF processes in the MOF components, as illustrated in Figure 1.3.

It is important to note that the activities pictured in Figure 1.3 can occur simultaneously within an IT organization. Each area has a specific focus and tasks, and within each area are policies, procedures, standards, and best practices that support specific service management-focused tasks.

Configuration Manager can be employed to support tasks in the different top-level MOF components. Let's look briefly at each of these areas and see how you can use Configuration Manager to support MOF:

▶ **Plan:** This phase covers activities related to IT strategy, standards, policies, and finances. This is where the business and IT collaborate to determine how IT can most effectively deliver services, enabling the overall organization to succeed.

   Configuration Manager delivers services that support the business, enabling IT to change to meet business strategy and support the business in becoming more efficient.

FIGURE 1.3   The IT life cycle, as described in MOF v4, has three life cycle phases and one functional layer operating throughout all the other phases.

▶ **Deliver:** This phase represents activities related to envisioning, planning, building, testing, and deploying IT service solutions. It takes a service solution from vision through deployment, ensuring a stable solution that is in line with business requirements and customer specifications.

Inventory management enables you to keep a handle on your hardware and software inventory, assisting with managing costs and planning for operating system and software upgrades.

Configuration Manager uses a connector to provide configuration item data about the computer from System Center Service Manager, enabling that information to be used in the Service Manager configuration management database (CMDB).

▶ **Operate:** This phase focuses on activities related to operating, monitoring, supporting, and addressing issues with IT services. It ensures that IT services function in line with SLA targets.

You can incorporate a structure into the software updates capability to assess the current situation, identify new updates, evaluate and plan for deployment, and put the actual update deployment into effect, reducing the support and operations costs of implementation by using a process.

▶ **Manage:** This layer, which operates continuously though the three phases, covers activities related to managing governance, risk, compliance, changes, configurations, and organizations. It promotes consistency and accountability in planning and delivering IT services, and providing the basis for developing and operating a flexible and durable IT environment.

The Manage layer establishes an approach to ITSM activities that helps coordinate the work of the SMFs in the three life cycle phases.

Configuration Manager's Compliance Settings feature enables you to manage compliance of your systems and identify noncompliant systems so you can take actions for remediation.

You can find additional information about MOF at https://msdn.microsoft.com/en-us/library/ms959769(v=cs.70).aspx.

MOF Does Not Replace ITIL

Microsoft believes that ITIL is the leading body of knowledge of best practices. For that reason, it uses ITIL as the foundation for MOF. Instead of replacing ITIL, MOF complements it and is similar to ITIL in several ways:

▶ MOF (incorporating MSF) spans the entire IT life cycle.

▶ Both MOF and ITIL are based on best practices for IT management, drawing on the expertise of practitioners worldwide.

▶ The MOF body of knowledge is applicable across the business community (from small businesses to large enterprises). MOF also is not limited only to those using the Microsoft platform in a homogenous environment.

▶ As is the case with ITIL, MOF has expanded to be more than just a documentation set.

Microsoft and its partners provide a variety of resources to support MOF principles and guidance, including self-assessments, IT management tools that incorporate MOF terminology and features, training programs and certification, and consulting services.

Total Quality Management (TQM)

The goal of TQM is to continuously improve the quality of products and processes. It functions on the premise that the quality of products and processes is the responsibility of everyone involved with the creation or consumption of the products or services offered by the organization. TQM capitalizes on the involvement of management, workforce, suppliers, and even customers to meet or exceed customer expectations.

Six Sigma

Six Sigma is a business management strategy, originally developed by Motorola, that seeks to identify and remove the causes of defects and errors in manufacturing and business processes. Six Sigma process improvement originated in 1986 from Motorola's drive toward reducing defects by minimizing variation in processes through metrics measurement. Applications of the Six Sigma project execution methodology have since expanded to incorporate practices common in TQM and supply chain management (for example, customer satisfaction, developing closer supplier relationships).

Service Management Mastery: ISO 20000

You can think of ITIL and ITSM as providing a framework for IT to rethink the ways in which it contributes to and aligns with the business. ISO 20000, which is the first international standard for ITSM, institutionalizes these processes. ISO 20000 helps companies align IT services and business strategy, creates a formal framework for continual service improvement, and provides benchmarks for comparison to best practices.

ISO 20000 was developed to reflect the best-practice guidance contained within ITIL. The standard also supports other ITSM frameworks and approaches, including MOF, Capacity Maturity Model Integration (CMMI), and Six Sigma. ISO 20000 consists of two major areas:

▶ Part 1 promotes adoption of an integrated process approach to deliver managed services effectively to meet business and customer requirements.

▶ Part 2 is a "code of practice" that describes the best practices for service management within the scope of ISO 20000-1.

These two areas—basically what to do and how to do it—have similarities to the approach taken by the other standards, including MOF.

ISO 20000 goes beyond ITIL, MOF, Six Sigma, and other frameworks in providing organizational or corporate certification for organizations that effectively adopt and implement the ISO 20000 code of practice.

Judging Your IT Organization's Maturity

If there is one thing constant about information technology, it is that it is continuously evolving; and as it evolves, IT departments try to keep up with it by jumping on the latest technology trends. No one wants to be left off the bandwagon, be it BYOD, cloud technology, or the various trends/fads of the moment.

Continually reinventing the environment requires your IT organization to have the maturity to make the leap. If you are constantly fighting fires, it is hard to find the time or develop the skill sets necessary to take on something new, particularly if it may require re-architecting the way you do things. In addition, adapting new technologies and architectures requires funding and CxO support; being a trusted business partner helps, but that will not happen if your IT department is caught in a reactionary loop.

Loosely defined, the Infrastructure & Operational (I&O) Maturity Model applies to an organization's capability to take on new challenges. Gartner recognizes five levels of infrastructure and operations maturity, and has developed a self-assessment tool (available at https://www.gartner.com/doc/2481415/itscore-overview-infrastructure-operations) that organizations can use to understand their level of maturity. These are the five levels:

1. **Aware:** Realizing that infrastructure and operational maturity is business critical and beginning to take actions to gain operational control and visibility. These actions are across people, process, and technologies—the three elements for a successful organizational transformation—and affect quality and productivity.

2. **Committed:** Moving to a managed environment to become more customer-centric and increase customer satisfaction levels.

3. **Proactive:** Gaining efficiencies and service quality through standardization, policy development, and governance and implementing proactive/cross-departmental processes. This could include change and release management.

4. **Service-Aligned:** Managing IT as though it is a business. Industry best practices are in place, and the organization is customer-focused, proven, competitive, and a trusted provider.

5. **Business Partner:** Realizing that IT is a critical strategic player and business partner for the organization.

Most organizations do not make it to level 5. For a more complete discussion of this model, see https://www.savision.com/resources/blog/how-mature-your-it-department.

Bridging the Systems Management Gap

Configuration Manager is Microsoft's software platform for addressing systems management issues. It is a key component of Microsoft's management strategy that can be used to bridge many of the gaps in service support and delivery. Configuration Manager was designed around the following key themes:

▶ **Security:** Role-based administration secures the access needed to administer Configuration Manager. You can also secure access to the objects that you manage, such as collections, deployments, and sites.

▶ **Simplicity:** ConfigMgr delivers a simplified user interface with limited top-level icons, organized in a way that makes resources easier to locate. Improvements in branch office support also serve to not only simplify management of the branch office but also reduce ConfigMgr infrastructure costs in these scenarios.

▶ **Manageability:** Offline OS and driver packages can be created to support OS deployment in scenarios with no or low-bandwidth connectivity. The Updates and Servicing service method makes it easy to locate and install recommended updates. Native Wake On LAN support makes patching workstations after-hours more hands-off.

The Value Proposition of Configuration Manager

By November 2016, more than 50 million devices were actively being managed by Configuration Manager Current Branch (see https://blogs.technet.microsoft.com/enterprisemobility/2016/11/18/configmgr-current-branch-surpasses-50m-managed-devices/). Configuration Manager helps you empower your employees to use the devices and applications they need to be productive while maintaining corporate compliance and control. With blurred boundaries between work and life, on-premise and the cloud, people expect consistent access to corporate services from wherever they are, on any device they are using—including desktops, laptops, smart phones, and tablets.

Configuration Manager helps you embrace this trend without giving up the control needed to protect your corporate assets. User experiences can be delivered and managed based on corporate identity, network connectivity, and device type—enabling you to meet the demand for consistent, anywhere access to corporate services. By providing a unified infrastructure for mobile, physical, and virtual environments, ConfigMgr helps you manage everything in one place, using processes you already have established. This infrastructure also extends to include critical endpoint security and service management technologies necessary to protect and support your workers; at the same time, it provides simplified administrative tools and improved compliance enforcement mechanisms to help make IT more efficient and effective.

The value of Configuration Manager lies in these areas:

▶ **Empowering individuals to be productive from anywhere on whatever device they choose:** The application model empowers you to deliver the best application experience to the user, based on his or her identity, device, and connection.

▶ **Supporting the faster pace of updates:** This applies to Windows 10 and Microsoft Intune, with regular updates to Current Branch.

▶ **Streamlining operations with a unified infrastructure, integrating client management and protection across mobile, physical, and virtual environments:** Role-based administration, Intune hybrid integration, and virtualization scenario support can simplify both infrastructure and processes for IT.

▶ **Driving organizational efficiency for IT with improved visibility and enforcement options for maintaining system compliance:** This means fewer mouse clicks to accomplish tasks and more automation in activities such as patch management and settings enforcement.

Summary

This chapter introduced the challenges of systems and configuration management and discussed what System Center Configuration Manager brings to the table to meet those challenges. Systems management is a process that touches many areas within ITIL and MOF, such as change and configuration management, asset management, security management, and, indirectly, release management. This chapter discussed the functionality delivered in Configuration Manager that you can leverage to meet these challenges more easily and effectively.

This chapter also discussed ITIL, which is an internationally accepted framework of best practices for IT service management. ITIL identifies what should be described in IT operations, although not actually how to accomplish it, and how the processes are related and affect one another. To provide additional guidance for its own IT and other customers, Microsoft uses ITIL as the foundation of its own operations framework, MOF. The objective of MOF is to provide both descriptive (what to do and why) and prescriptive (how to do it) guidance flow for IT service management as it relates to Microsoft products.

Microsoft's management approach, which incorporates the processes and software tools of MOF, is a strategy or blueprint intended to build automation and knowledge into datacenter operations. Microsoft's investment includes building systems designed for operations, developing an operationally aware platform, and establishing a commitment to intelligent management software.

Configuration Manager is a tool for managing systems in a way that increases the quality of service that IT delivers while reducing the operational cost of service delivery. Configuration Manager is a critical component in Microsoft's approach to systems management that can increase your organization's agility in delivering on its service commitments to the business.

Systems management is a key component in an effective service management strategy. Throughout this book, you will see this functionality described and demonstrated, and you will come to understand the full value of Configuration Manager as a platform for improving the automation, security, and efficiency of service support and delivery in your IT organization.

Chapter 2, "Configuration Manager Overview," provides an overview of Configuration Manager terminology and discusses key concepts, feature dependencies, history, and what is new in Configuration Manager Current Branch.

Configuration Manager Overview

Chapter 1, "Configuration Management Basics," discusses the challenges of systems and configuration management. This chapter covers the history of System Center Configuration Manager (ConfigMgr). This chapter also discusses key concepts and terminology used in later chapters of this book to help you as a ConfigMgr administrator become familiar with the lexicon.

The current version of System Center Configuration Manager, Current Branch, includes a significant number of changes. Even seasoned ConfigMgr administrators will discover that concepts they were once familiar with are now different. This chapter covers those changes. To assist in planning a new ConfigMgr implementation or migration of an existing infrastructure, this chapter also outlines feature dependencies.

A Journey Through Time: SMS to ConfigMgr Current Branch

Starting with Systems Management Server (SMS) 1.0 and ending with System Center Configuration Manager Current Branch, Microsoft has released six major versions of its systems and configuration management product. After SMS 1.0 (code-named Hermes) came versions 1.1, 1.2, 2.0, and—as Microsoft moved to incorporating the release year as part of the name of the product—SMS 2003. Microsoft rebranded the following version, 2007, as System Center Configuration Manager. Microsoft next released System Center Configuration Manager 2012 in 2012. The most current release, System Center Configuration Manager Current Branch, was first released in November 2015 to support Windows 10 and new Windows servicing options. Since this initial release, additional updates are made available approximately three times a year. Different update versions are identified by year and month (such as version 1710), but the release is still known as Configuration Manager Current Branch.

Systems Management Server 1.x

Microsoft began its journey into the configuration management space in 1994 with the SMS 1.0 release. Subsequent releases in the 1.x product line were versions 1.1 and 1.2, released in 1995 and 1996, respectively. Though these two "dot" releases were planned initially as service packs, the added features were significant enough to become product releases.

However, version 1.x of the product failed to receive wide adoption. Requirements such as installing the site server on a Windows NT backup domain controller (BDC) made deployment cumbersome. In addition, the management scope of SMS 1.x only supported control of an entire domain. Inventory functions were executed using login scripts. Administrators received numerous complaints from end users about prolonged logon times—yet another reason for the product's slow adoption.

Systems Management Server 2.0

Microsoft released SMS 2.0 in early 1999, complete with a new user interface (UI) utilizing the Microsoft Management Console (MMC). The first service pack (SP) became available eight months later. SMS 2.0 was a complete rewrite of Microsoft's configuration management product, and it unfortunately did not pass through the quality control gates it should have. The product was plagued with bugs and only became a relatively stable platform with SP 2, released in 2000. By the time Microsoft released a third service pack, in 2001, the SMS 2.0 platform had truly stabilized.

SMS 2.0 addressed many concerns Microsoft's customers had with SMS 1.x. It allowed installation of a site server on a member server instead of a domain controller. The inventory process was moved to agent components rather than running in login scripts. In addition, the management scope was defined by subnets instead of the entire domain. Despite these enhancements, the product had several significant failings:

▶ The client agent was not designed for a mobile workforce and did not consider low-bandwidth situations, and at this time, laptops were becoming prevalent.

▶ It did not allow for Active Directory (AD) integration, even though the product was released just before Active Directory became available with Windows 2000.

Neither SP 4 (released in 2002) nor SP 5 (2003) addressed these areas, as they primarily provided bug fixes rather than new functionality. However, the shortcomings in SMS 2.0 positioned Microsoft to release a product that addressed them: SMS 2003.

Systems Management Server 2003

Microsoft released the next major version of SMS in November 2003. The release was so late in 2003 that it could have been named SMS 2004! This release added integration with Active Directory, along with functionality supporting a mobile workforce.

The SMS server infrastructure remained largely the same, with the inclusion of Internet Information Server (IIS), which arguably raised complexity but brought significant benefits (such as communication over HTTP and the use of the Background Intelligent Transfer System [BITS]). In addition, SMS 2003 included significant improvements to the SMS agent, as discussed in the section "Configuration Manager Agent" later in this chapter. A legacy client was maintained to support older operating systems, such as Windows 98 and Windows NT 4.0. Windows 95 support was dropped entirely. Another significant change was a revamp of the reporting interface into SMS Web Reporting, which removed the complicated and obtuse Crystal reports.

Most of the changes in this version were not noticeable in the console. The UI looked almost identical to that of SMS 2.0.

Active Directory Integration

Organizations willing to extend their schema for SMS could leverage AD to optimize the way SMS 2003 operated in addition to taking advantage of AD's capabilities (such as being able to discover AD clients). This was known as *Active Directory integration*. There were numerous benefits from extending the schema, such as AD site boundaries, global roaming, and advanced security (meaning the large number of service accounts previously required was no longer necessary). While most of these capabilities were minor, they improved the overall administrative experience.

One substantial change in SMS 2003 from its predecessor was the introduction of a concept called *roaming*. Roaming came in two flavors:

▶ **Global Roaming:** Clients could retrieve site information from AD, enabling them to know the site they were in, communicate with the resident management point (MP) for that site, and receive information pertaining to the distribution points (DPs) of that site. Global roaming was only available to organizations that extended the AD schema.

▶ **Regional Roaming:** Clients were unaware of any site they may have roamed into and continued speaking to their default MP. As long as the client had roamed into a site lower in the hierarchy than its assigned site, the default MP could inform the client of the closest DPs.

Additional Functionality Releases

To stay competitive, Microsoft continued to release functionality incrementally into SMS 2003 with service packs and a new branding called R2 (Release 2).

The first two service packs (released in 2004 and June 2006), were largely hotfix rollups with performance optimization. Functional changes were minor, adding support for newer operating systems. Microsoft announced that rather than adding new capabilities in service packs, it would include new functionality in *feature packs*, an example being the Operating System Deployment (OSD) Feature Pack released as a free download in November 2004.

Microsoft released the first full update to SMS 2003 with an R2 release in late 2006. SMS 2003 R2 was built on SMS 2003 SP 2, with two additional features:

▶ Scan Tool for Vulnerability Assessment

▶ Inventory Tool for Custom Updates (ITCU)

SMS 2003 SP 3, released in 2007, was the last maintenance release for the product. Along with another hotfix rollup, SP 3 included Asset Intelligence (a product developed from Microsoft's acquisition of AssetMatrix). Asset Intelligence normalized more than 400,000 software titles into a legible format, easing the burden of tracking and reporting on licensing data. SP 3 also included an extension to OSD for deploying the Vista operating system, though considering the adoption rate of Vista, that is hardly worth noting!

System Center Configuration Manager 2007

The next release of the product saw a change in branding. No longer called Systems Management Server, the software was aligned into the System Center product line and renamed Configuration Manager. ConfigMgr 2007 was released in August 2007.

In this version, the legacy client was finally dropped, along with support for operating systems prior to Windows 2000. All of the familiar feature packs released for SMS 2003 were included as part of ConfigMgr 2007, removing the requirement to layer installation after installation to get all the features.

ConfigMgr 2007 was the first version to use public key infrastructure (PKI) for securing client-to-server communications. This security mode was known as *native mode*. With the use of native mode and PKI, it was possible to manage clients that rarely connected over virtual private networks (VPNs) or came into the office. The utilization of Internet-based client management (IBCM) enabled management of ConfigMgr 2007 clients over a regular Internet connection.

Out-of-band (OOB) management and improved asset intelligence functionality were the highlights of the first service pack, released in May 2008. Just a year after the release to manufacturing (RTM) of ConfigMgr 2007, Microsoft released ConfigMgr 2007 R2, which included a number of changes:

▶ **Application Virtualization:** This feature supported running virtual applications sequenced through the Application Virtualization (App-V) platform.

▶ **Client Status Reporting (CSR):** This separate tool analyzed and reported on client health.

▶ **OSD Improvements:** OSD enhancements included support for unknown computers, improvements to task sequences that allowed alternate credentials for running command lines, and network bandwidth efficiency gains with multicast deployments.

▶ **SQL Server Reporting Services (SSRS) Support:** This enhancement enabled the use of SSRS for ConfigMgr reports, including the ability to convert most reports to the SSRS format.

Microsoft released ConfigMgr 2007 R3 in late 2010, introducing another wave of new features and improvements. This release included power management, eliminating the need to use third-party products to manage and report on computer power consumption. There were also several other improvements:

▶ **Performance:** Performance in scalability was improved to support up to 100,000 clients per primary site and 300,000 clients in a hierarchy.

▶ **Delta Discovery:** AD discovery was modified to provide a delta discovery method that only picked up changes such as additions, deletions, and modifications, reducing the load on the site server running the discovery.

▶ **Dynamic Collection Updates:** Under certain conditions (first-time discovery, OSD provisioned, initial hardware inventory scan, or ConfigMgr client upgrade), collections can be enabled to dynamically add new resources as they are discovered.

▶ **Prestaged Media:** Prestaging media allows a PC manufacturer to load a custom image to a PC during the build process in the manufacturing facility.

In December 2010 (post R3), Microsoft released Forefront Endpoint Protection 2010 and integrated it into ConfigMgr to provide malware and security protection.

ConfigMgr is a system that continuously improves and evolves. The requirement to support every new Windows operating system is difficult enough to manage; in addition, a configuration management system developed by Microsoft is expected to manage (to some extent) every product Microsoft ever released! From the 1.x releases that installed software and ran inventory by login script to the most advanced agent capable of installing the latest security updates, delivering whole operating systems, and self-healing, ConfigMgr has had a long career managing the rich Microsoft ecosystem.

The product has grown immensely complex over the years. At one point, it was expected that a ConfigMgr administrator could learn the entire product to an expert level. Today, with all the features that extend ConfigMgr beyond simple inventory management and software delivery, it is easy to become buried in the details.

System Center 2012 and 2012 R2 Configuration Manager

System Center 2012 Configuration Manager, released in the first part of 2012, brought waves of changes to the systems management platform, injecting new life into a product whose legacy now dated back over 15 years. This version included some radical changes that required adoption of new concepts and thinking. By understanding relationships of users to devices and following the intent of managing software, ConfigMgr finally aimed to optimize both the administrative experience and the end user experience. Following is a brief list of the top changes for 2012:

▶ **Central Administration Site (CAS):** The CAS, introduced for large environments, was primarily used for reporting and facilitating communication between primary sites in the hierarchy. Using the CAS requires a bit more SQL skills because database replication occurs between the CAS and primary sites.

▶ **Administration Console:** The new administration console was a welcome update to the old MMC-style console. This new console allowed more flexible add-ins, a ribbon bar, objects filtered by role-based administration, search capabilities, and temporary nodes to help with navigation.

▶ **Improved IBCM:** IBCM kicked up a notch or two, supporting user-based policies, task sequences (external to OSD), and smarter software updates downloads.

▶ **Software Center and Application Catalog:** Previously, Run Advertised Programs was the only end-user interface for installing optional programs (other than a hook on Add/Remove Programs). Software Center (machine-based) and Application Catalog (user-based) provided a two-stop shop, which improved the end-user experience.

▶ **Multiple Management Points per Site:** Multiple management points allow the client to select a MP based on network location, enabling a larger number of clients per site, as well as redundancy that was previously available only with a network load balancing (NLB) cluster.

▶ **Boundary and Boundary Group Improvements:** Boundaries were no longer site specific, and connection speeds could be configured at the boundary group as a content location server.

▶ **Fallback Site for Client Assignment:** As an optional setting for the hierarchy, you could set a fallback site so that if a client was not in a boundary group, automatic site assignment would assign the client to the fallback site.

▶ **Discovery Improvements:** Discovery is processed only one time, at the primary sites, and shared among all primary sites. Active Directory Forest Discovery was also added, allowing discovery of subnets and AD sites and optionally allowing them to be added as boundaries.

▶ **Client Settings:** Previously, client settings were configured per site. With ConfigMgr 2012, client agent settings could be grouped into centrally configured client settings groups and applied to collections with precedence.

▶ **Role-Based Administration (RBA):** RBA enabled simpler configuration of rights, based on roles, scopes, and collections. RBA settings apply across the entire hierarchy.

▶ **Collection Improvements:** ConfigMgr 2012 brought multiple improvements to collections. Include and exclude rules enabled easy alteration of collection membership based on other collections. Incremental collection member evaluation significantly improved software delivery by populating query-based collections with new members much faster than previously. Collection limiting was required on every collection, reducing risk and simplifying RBA.

▶ **Application Management:** Applications were introduced, allowing for requirement rules, along with multiple deployment types to add enhanced detection and deployment, as well as a simplified end-user experience.

▶ **OSD Enhancements:** OSD improvements included applying offline updates, prestart command files, mandatory deployment, cross-hierarchy media, relating of users to computers during operating system deployment for proper software delivery, and more.

▶ **Distribution Point Enhancements:** The content library provided a single-instance store for content on distribution points. Distribution point groups allowed logical grouping and management of content. In-console monitoring of distribution status and content validation simplified the administrative experience. BranchCache was also integrated so that it became possible to manage BranchCache settings and configure per-deployment type for applications and per-deployment type for packages.

▶ **Reporting:** The Reporting Point was removed, encouraging administrators to learn more about SSRS. Leveraging SSRS for reporting is more extensible, provides graphical capabilities, and allows for easier integration of data from other sources than with the old Reporting Point.

System Center 2012 R2 Configuration Manager brought support for new devices as well as improvements in the core platform, including the following:

▶ **OSD:** Support for the latest Windows operating systems (Windows 8.1 and Server 2012 R2) was added, as well as some features inherited from the Microsoft Deployment Toolkit (MDT), such as Run PowerShell Script, Check Readiness, and Set Dynamic Variables. Also, new task sequence variables were added to improve resiliency and improve status.

▶ **Mobile Device Management (MDM):** Support was added for enrollment of Android and iOS for MDM with Intune Extensions.

▶ **Profile Management:** Support included remote connection profiles, certificate profiles, VPN profiles, Wi-Fi profiles, and email profiles to simplify the end-user experience.

▶ **Content Management:** R2 included enhancements in pull-distribution points, such as support for prioritization of source DPs, improved status reporting, and much-requested support in the Monitoring node to redistribute failed distributions. The Distribution Point Usage Summary report helped in understanding how each distribution point was being utilized.

▶ **Role-Based Administration Reporting:** Report data could now be automatically filtered for content based on RBA configurations.

Configuration Manager Terminology

Microsoft has added many new terms in the past two versions of Configuration Manager, and it is important that you become familiar with them. In addition, the meanings of some terms have changed. Before you try to understand how to deploy and operate ConfigMgr, you should familiarize yourself with the terminology and concepts related to Configuration Manager that are discussed in the following sections.

Configuration Manager Site

A *site* is the core role in Configuration Manager. Depending on the organization's requirements, the architecture may be as simple as a single primary site. Large enterprises may require starting with a central administration site and at least one primary site. Figure 2.1, which is a diagram view in the ConfigMgr console, complete with site status, shows how a typical hierarchy might look.

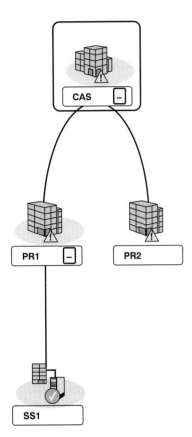

FIGURE 2.1   Hierarchical view of the Odyssey lab hierarchy used throughout this book. For more information, see the Introduction to this book.

Site Hierarchy

Any organization with more than one site connected together by definition has a site hierarchy. Every site hierarchy includes at least one primary site. A site hierarchy with more than one primary site must include a CAS. Hierarchies can also include secondary sites.

Previous versions of ConfigMgr gave the site hierarchy the flexibility to be immensely deep and complex (although this was not recommended). ConfigMgr 2012 enabled using a simplistic, flat hierarchy, and ConfigMgr Current Branch takes that even further, improving scalability. Starting from the top, the hierarchy for a large organization generally goes three tiers deep, as shown in Figure 2.2.

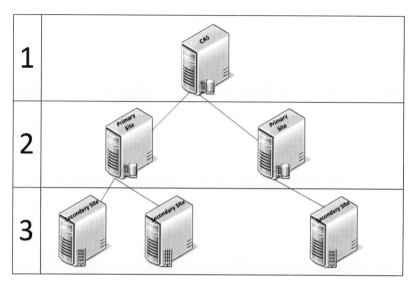

FIGURE 2.2   Site hierarchy depth diagram.

It is important to note that a secondary site can exist in a tiered hierarchy with another secondary site, effectively creating more than three tiers. However, all secondary sites communicate with their primary site for database replication. While you can adopt this topology, there are very few reasons for secondary sites in ConfigMgr. Chapter 4, "Architecture Design Planning," provides details on creating an optimized hierarchy.

> **NOTE: COMPLEX HIERARCHY CONS**
>
> Complex hierarchies are generally not recommended due to the amount of time administrative functions (such as setting up applications and packages) take to reach the client at the very bottom of the hierarchy. Data sent from the client at the bottom of the hierarchy also takes a long time to reach the very top of the hierarchy.

Central Administration Site

The *central administration site* was introduced with System Center 2012 Configuration Manager. A CAS is used to manage all other sites, facilitate site-to-site communication, and manage reporting. The CAS does not support clients or process any client data. The CAS is a required site whenever you are connecting multiple primary sites.

In versions of the product previous to System Center 2012 Configuration Manager, this concept was known as a *central site*, although it was not technically restricted from supporting clients. A central site was the top-level primary site of a site hierarchy.

Primary Site

Every implementation of Configuration Manager requires at least one *primary site*. This is a site to which clients can be assigned and that can be administered using the Configuration Manager console. Because this is a required site, the real question is whether multiple primary sites are needed.

> **NOTE: START WITH A SINGLE PRIMARY SITE**
>
> There are very few exceptions for when a CAS is necessary. If you feel you require a CAS, work with your favorite consultant or MVP for insight. If you are not sure if you need a CAS, remember that you can always start with a single primary site and add a CAS later, as needed.

Following are areas to consider when planning for additional primary sites:

▶ **Scale:** A standalone primary site supports 150,000 desktops/laptops, plus 25,000 devices running Mac and Windows CE 7.0. A primary site under a CAS supports 150,000 total clients and devices. A secondary site supports 15,000 desktops/laptops. Review the current scaling numbers at https://docs.microsoft.com/sccm/core/plan-design/configs/size-and-scale-numbers.

▶ **Complexity:** When using a CAS, additional troubleshooting steps are required for database replication.

Secondary Site

Secondary sites in Configuration Manager Current Branch perform the same role as in ConfigMgr 2012:

▶ A secondary site requires a SQL Server database. You can install SQL prior to installing the secondary site, or SQL Express will automatically install during secondary site installation.

▶ Secondary sites automatically receive the proxy management point and distribution point roles.

▶ Scalability has increased to 15,000 devices in ConfigMgr Current Branch.

A secondary site is always a child site of a primary site and can only be administered by a primary site. Clients cannot be assigned directly to secondary sites. Because the administration consoles can only connect to a CAS or a primary site, secondary sites are typically used in locations that do not have administrators.

Secondary sites can help control bandwidth utilization by managing the flow of client information sent up the hierarchy. In addition, secondary sites can be tiered to help control content distribution to remote sites. The Software Update Point (SUP) role can be positioned on a secondary site server to provide local access to clients scanning for compliance without needing to talk to a primary site server. However, a hierarchy with secondary sites adds a layer of complexity that often is not necessary.

NOTE: FEWER SITES IS MORE!

Generally speaking, the simpler your environment, the better. Bandwidth savings for a secondary site are often negated due to SQL replication that must occur from primary site to secondary site. Before adding secondary sites, consider adding remote management points, distribution points, and software update points, as needed.

Carefully consider whether to use a secondary site. Simplicity is best when designing your hierarchy. More information on secondary sites is available in Chapter 4.

Site Systems

Each site can perform a wide variety of roles, based on the site type. Any computer, whether server or workstation, hosting a site system role is referred to as a *site system server*. Some site system roles are required for operation of the site. While roles can be transferred to other site servers in some cases, following is a list of site system roles that must exist in each primary site:

▶ **Component Server:** This is any server running the ConfigMgr Executive service.

▶ **Site Database Server:** This is a server with Microsoft SQL Server installed, hosting the ConfigMgr site database.

▶ **Site Server:** This main role contains components and services required to run a central administration, primary, or secondary site.

▶ **Site System:** This role supports both required and optional site system roles. Any server (or share) with an assigned role automatically receives this role.

▶ **SMS Provider:** This is a Windows Management Instrumentation (WMI) provider operating as an interface between the ConfigMgr console and the site database.

In addition to default roles, System Center Configuration Manager includes optional roles to support other capabilities:

▶ **Application Catalog Web Service Point:** This role relays software information from the Software Library to the Application Catalog website.

▶ **Application Catalog Website Point:** This is an optional role required for presenting available software to users.

▶ **Asset Intelligence Synchronization Point:** This role synchronizes Asset Intelligence data from System Center Online by downloading Asset Intelligence catalog data and uploading custom catalog data.

▶ **Distribution Point:** The DP holds application source files for clients to access.

▶ **Fallback Status Point (FSP):** The FSP provides an alternate location for clients to send up status messages during installation when they are unable to communicate with their management point.

▶ **Management Point:** The MP facilitates communication between a client and a site server by storing and providing policy and content location information to the client and receiving data from the client, such as status messages and inventory.

▶ **Mobile Device Enrollment Proxy Point:** This role allows the management of mobile device enrollment through ConfigMgr.

▶ **Service Connection Point (SCP):** This role enables the ConfigMgr hierarchy to send anonymous usage data to Microsoft, as well as provide the channel for downloading and installing updates to Current Branch.

▶ **Reporting Services Point:** This role is used to integrate reporting through SSRS and is required if you are using reports.

▶ **Software Update Point:** The SUP provides software update management for ConfigMgr clients by integrating with Windows Server Update Services (WSUS).

▶ **State Migration Point:** When using OSD, the state migration point holds the user state data for migration to the new operating system.

▶ **System Health Validator Point:** This role previously validated Network Access Protection (NAP) policies from the ConfigMgr client. Although it is still visible in the console, the role is no longer used. See https://docs.microsoft.com/sccm/core/plan-design/hierarchy/plan-for-site-system-servers-and-site-system-roles for more information.

Senders

Senders are installed as a part of the ConfigMgr site server to manage connectivity to other sites and ensure data integrity and error recovery during transmissions. Senders operate multiple threads in parallel to boost the transfer of data (assuming that the sender is not throttled). You can change the concurrent threads and retry settings, displayed in Figure 2.3, for each site.

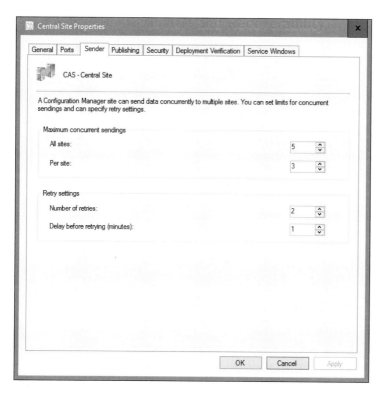

FIGURE 2.3   Changing concurrent threads and retry settings for the sender.

NOTE: UNDERSTANDING MAXIMUM CONCURRENT THREADS

When the number of connected sites exceeds the maximum concurrent threads default of five, data queues up, and ConfigMgr will wait for an available thread to free up before sending to the next site. Increasing this value increases the throughput of data between sites, which also increases the demand for more network bandwidth.

Managing Content (File) Replication

File replication (which was updated in ConfigMgr 2012 SP 1 to use replication routes rather than addresses to configure replication between sites) helps manage communication between two sites by controlling data flow through schedules and bandwidth rate limits. By default, an entry (shown in Figure 2.4) is created from the parent to child and child to parent whenever a site server is added to the hierarchy.

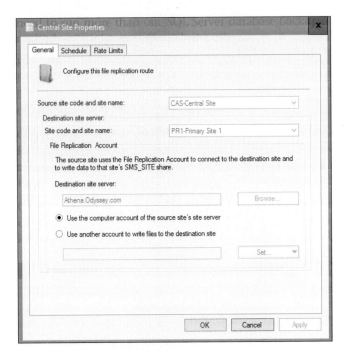

FIGURE 2.4   Addresses used in the Odyssey hierarchy.

Discovering Resources

Knowing the available resources in a network is one of the benefits of having a configuration management system. Configuration Manager uses a variety of discovery methods to gather resource information. Following are the seven types of discovery methods:

▶ Active Directory Forest Discovery

▶ Active Directory Security Group Discovery

▶ Active Directory System Discovery

▶ Active Directory System Group Discovery

▶ Active Directory User Discovery

▶ Heartbeat Discovery

▶ Network Discovery

The Active Directory Forest Discovery method, the newest type of discovery and introduced in ConfigMgr 2012, discovers trusted forests, AD sites, and Internet Protocol (IP) subnets. In addition, this discovery method can automatically create Active Directory site boundaries as well as IP subnet boundaries as they are discovered.

Active Directory discovery methods can target specific LDAP paths, and can be configured to recursively search those paths. Optionally, ConfigMgr can expand groups and discover members of groups. With certain Active Directory object types, you can specify attributes of the discovered resources as part of the information to retrieve.

Polling schedules are defined to run at set intervals. By default, most discovery methods run once a week. Active Directory discovery methods also support delta discovery to help get newly discovered resources into the ConfigMgr database quickly.

> **TIP: HEARTBEAT DISCOVERY IS THE ONLY REQUIRED DISCOVERY**
>
> When a device installs the ConfigMgr client, it sends a heartbeat discovery record and brings the new resource into the database. Other discovery methods are not required and should be enabled with caution. For example, if computer records are not well maintained in Active Directory, enabling any of the Active Directory discovery methods may fill the ConfigMgr database with records of computers that might not exist. To mitigate the risk of discovering "stale" records in Active Directory, the authors recommend leveraging discovery filters to exclude devices with old login times or last password resets.

Figure 2.5 shows the available discovery methods in the Details pane.

Icon	Name	Status	Site	Description
	Active Directory Forest Discovery	Enabled	CAS	Configures settings that Configuration Manager uses to find A...
	Active Directory Forest Discovery	Enabled	PR1	Configures settings that Configuration Manager uses to find A...
	Active Directory Group Discovery	Enabled	PR1	Configures settings that Configuration Manager uses to find g...
	Active Directory System Discovery	Enabled	PR1	Configures settings that Configuration Manager uses to find c...
	Active Directory User Discovery	Enabled	PR1	Configures settings that Configuration Manager uses to find u...
	Heartbeat Discovery	Enabled	PR1	Configures interval for Configuration Manager clients to perio...
	Network Discovery	Disabled	PR1	Configures settings and polling intervals to discover resources...
	Network Discovery	Disabled	SS1	Configures settings and polling intervals to discover resources...

FIGURE 2.5   Discovery methods listed in the System Center Configuration Manager console.

Configuration Manager Agent

The System Center Configuration Manager agent, known as the *client*, resides on managed systems, servers, and workstations. The client checks in on a defined interval with the ConfigMgr MP to determine if new policies are available. This interval is 60 minutes by default, although you can expand it to 1440 minutes (24 hours).

You can deploy the client in a number of ways. A common method of deployment is to prestage the client into an operating system image. However, many other methods also exist, such as manually installing, automatically pushing installs with the ConfigMgr server, using software updates, using group policy, and using scripts (logon or machine).

The ConfigMgr client performs a wide range of actions. It is responsible for collecting computer inventory, checking for security update compliance, facilitating remote control, managing the computer's power state, managing application state (installing or uninstalling software), reimaging the computer, and managing computer settings. The client also downloads and applies policies received from the ConfigMgr server and sends up status and state messages. The client is discussed further in Chapter 9, "Client Management."

Configuration Manager Console

Using the System Center framework, the Configuration Manager console features an intuitive interface complete with navigational shortcuts, temporary nodes, and rich search functionality.

The console has a Navigation pane to help you navigate quickly between the following operational groupings:

▶ Administration

▶ Software Library

▶ Monitoring

▶ Assets and Compliance

An Outlook-style ribbon provides access to common administrative tasks (see Figure 2.6). As the object focus changes, the options available on the ribbon bar adapt to the object type, displaying relevant tasks in the console.

FIGURE 2.6   Ribbon bar with context focused on Software Updates.

When you select an object that contains details, the Details pane displays tabs pertinent to the object that help further categorize information to reduce overall clutter. Furthermore, the entire console is security context aware. Role-based administration uses the assigned role and scope to display only the features available to the user. The Details pane in Figure 2.7 shows details and statistics for a security update.

For additional information on security and role-based administration, see Chapter 23, "Security and Delegation in Configuration Manager." The console is discussed in Chapter 8, "Using the Configuration Manager Console."

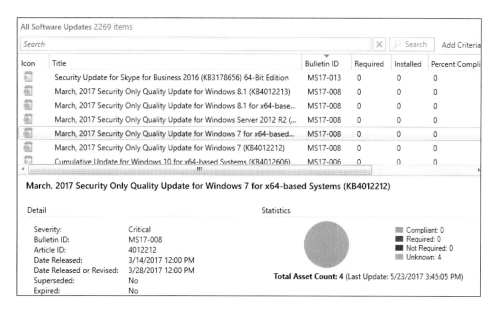

FIGURE 2.7   Details pane information for a security update.

Collections for Targeting Users and Devices

A *collection* is a logical grouping of either users or devices. A collection is used to target a group of objects for management, such as security boundaries, client settings, or deployments. During a collection evaluation cycle, if a schedule is specified, the membership of the collection is updated with any new objects that match the criteria specified by a collection rule.

NOTE: COLLECTIONS ARE EITHER USER OR DEVICE SPECIFIC

Prior to ConfigMgr 2012, a collection could contain both users and devices in the same collection. The new collection paradigm prevents mixing users and devices in the same collection. If you attempt to migrate a mixed collection from ConfigMgr 2007, you will receive a warning and must manually remediate the collection migration. See Chapter 7, "Upgrading and Migrating to ConfigMgr Current Branch," for more information.

A collection rule defines the membership of a collection. There are several different types of rules:

▶ **Direct Rule:** An object is added directly to the collection.

▶ **Query Rule:** An object is added to the collection, based on the result of a query.

▶ **Include Rule:** Objects in other collections can be can be added using this rule.

▶ **Exclude Rule:** Objects in other collections can be excluded using this rule.

In addition to collection rules, every collection requires a *limited collection*, which is basically a global filter for a collection. Collections eventually roll up to one of the built-in collections; however, you can (for example) create a collection named

All Test Servers and leverage role-based administration to limit a team's scope to that collection. If you do this, any collection the team creates is limited to All Test Servers (or any child collection of All Test Servers). Collections are discussed further in Chapter 14, "Distributing and Deploying Applications and Packages."

Querying Client Data

Queries, which are discussed in Chapter 20, "Configuration Manager Queries," request information from the ConfigMgr database through the WMI provider. If you specify criteria in a query, you get a filtered result of objects. Queries in ConfigMgr are written in WMI Query Language (WQL) and can return results from hundreds of different attribute classes, ranging from inventory data to sites. Following is an example of a typical query to return devices with 4GB of RAM or greater:

```
SELECT
    SMS_R_System.Name,
    SMS_G_System_X86_PC_MEMORY.TotalPhysicalMemory
FROM
    SMS_R_System
    INNER JOIN SMS_G_System_X86_PC_Memory ON
    SMS_G_System_X86_PC_Memory.ResourceID = SMS_R_System.ResourceId
WHERE
    SMS_G_System_X86_PC_Memory.TotalPhysicalMemory > 4192000
```

Using Alerts to Respond to Problems Quickly

System Center Configuration Manager provides near-real-time monitoring, with alerts displaying in the console. The alerts are state based, automatically updating as conditions change and covering technologies such as client health, deployments, and software updates. Figure 2.8 shows a replication link down error alert with supporting information in the Details pane.

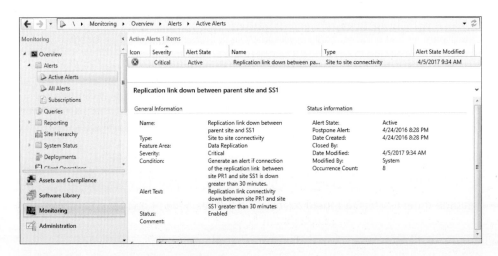

FIGURE 2.8   Replication link down error.

Using Packages

A package can contain source files and programs. Programs are instructions telling the client how to execute a script; they range from shell commands to full scripts. In some cases, source files do not have to be included if they are not required by the executing program. For example, a package to defragment a hard drive would not require any source files because the program calls an existing executable.

Packages were used as the primary tool for software deployment in ConfigMgr 2007 and SMS. With the introduction of applications in System Center 2012 Configuration Manager, the intent for packages was to be legacy functionality, used predominantly for scripting situations. However, many companies still use packages for software deployment. Packages are described in Chapter 13, "Creating and Managing Packages and Programs."

Managing Applications

As users become increasingly more technically savvy, their expectations of the user experience when interacting with IT also change. Previously, it was feasible to manage an environment as a collection of computers with a one-to-one relationship between users and computers: You could rely on each user having only a single device. Users now have multiple devices and tend to be extremely mobile. To support these changes, the concept of software distribution has evolved into a state-based system that has the intelligence of understanding the user-to-device relationship. These concepts are discussed in Chapter 14.

The application model of Configuration Manager Current Branch significantly improves software deployment and the life cycle compared to the traditional packages and programs model (the only software distribution model used in versions of ConfigMgr and SMS prior to ConfigMgr 2012). For example, the evaluation processing that occurred in ConfigMgr 2007 operated at the collection level, with complex queries driving the intelligence behind targeting software to the right devices. With ConfigMgr applications, much of that intelligence occurs at the client, via requirement rules. Collections are still a necessary part of targeting; however, because the evaluation is no longer at the collection level, complex collection queries are not required for application management.

Applications are models of software that contain far more than source files and program execution instructions. Models define the properties of software. They contain the deployment types to support local installations, virtual applications, and mobile applications. Because these models are state based, the "state" of the application can be detected. This means ConfigMgr can detect if the software is installed before attempting an installation and can detect whether the software has been uninstalled and needs to be reinstalled. The inverse is also true if the requirement is to uninstall software.

Deployment Types

Deployment types exist within applications to facilitate different installation methods. A *deployment type* specifies installation files, commands, and programs, based on established criteria, which are used to install the correct type of software. The following information is typically held by a deployment type:

▶ Application dependencies

▶ Command for installation

▶ Command for uninstallation

▶ Content source location

▶ Detection method for verifying whether the application is installed

▶ Installation method

▶ Requirement rules

Configuration Manager uses the following deployment types:

▶ Windows Installer (MSI)

▶ Windows App Package

▶ Application Virtualization

▶ Window Phone App Package

▶ Windows Mobile Cabinet (CAB)

▶ App Package for iOS

▶ App Package for iOS from App Store

▶ App Package for Android (.apk file)

▶ App Package for Android on Google Play

▶ Mac OS X

▶ Web Application

▶ Windows Installer through MDM

Global Conditions and Requirement Rules

Requirement rules, which are contained in applications, instruct the client to evaluate properties in real time. Before the client even begins to download content, it first runs through the evaluation to determine which deployment type applies (if any).

A *global condition* is the foundation of a requirement rule. It can be defined by script, WMI query, registry, and much more. ConfigMgr comes with a handful of defined global conditions, such as CPU speed, operating system, total physical memory, and AD site.

For example, let's say an application requires a minimum of 500MB to install. You could add a requirement rule that uses the provided Free disk space global condition. The rule would specify the condition as requiring at least 500MB. When the client is instructed to install the software, it first evaluates its available drive space, and, if it meets the conditions, it installs the software. Figure 2.9 illustrates how a requirement rule is constructed.

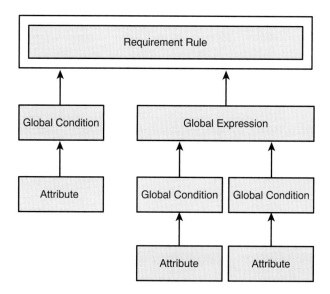

FIGURE 2.9   Requirement rule relationship with global conditions and global expressions.

Global Expressions

A *global expression* contains a logical grouping of different global conditions and their associated values. Instead of repeating the same core global conditions in each application, you could create a global expression that defines those core conditions and use it in a requirement rule.

For example, if all the computers in your finance department were in the same OU, you could create a global expression named Finance Dept, require the device to belong to the Finance Dept OU, and require the device to be the primary device. Following is what this expression would look like:

```
Organizational unit (OU) One of {OU=Finance,DC=odyssey,DC=com} AND Primary device
Equals True
```

Dependencies

As you begin to develop a software library, you might find that one application relies on (that is, has a *dependency* upon) another application. If, for example, an application were dependent on Java Runtime 6, a dependency could specify that before installing the application, Java Runtime 6 must first be installed. The choice of whether to automatically install a dependency is optional and is configured as part of the dependency.

Deployments

A *deployment* is a set of instructions for the ConfigMgr client to evaluate and execute. Deployments typically refer to applications or packages, although they can include task sequences, software updates, and configuration baselines. Because application deployments are state based, administrators need only deploy to a collection once, leveraging requirement rules to manage the installation state.

Available deployment types are constrained based on the type of collection targeted. For example, if the target collection is a user collection, the software update deployment type is not an available option because software updates are targeted to devices.

Content Management

Content management refers to the technologies in ConfigMgr responsible for storing, distributing, and maintaining content (for example, installation source files and operating system images).

Distribution Points

A *distribution point* (DP), as discussed in Chapter 14, is a site role that stores content and facilitates the transfer of content to devices. A site could contain multiple DPs to help offset a large volume of content transfer to devices or situate content closer to a group of devices, reducing impact on traffic over the WAN.

In bandwidth-sensitive locations, content distribution to a DP can be throttled. In addition, you can schedule DPs to transfer content during optimal times of day. You can also prestage content to the distribution point.

Branch DPs, PXE shares, and DP shares from previous versions of ConfigMgr no longer exist. However, the standard DP is now much more robust, supporting additional options that to enable it to handle PXE, multicast, and pull DPs, which can pull content from one or more other DPs. Cloud DPs (in Microsoft Azure) are also a new feature; they help your clients access content from around the globe and outside your corporate network.

Distribution Point Groups

A logical grouping of distribution points is a *distribution point group*. For ease of administration, you can send content to a DP group instead of individually selecting DPs. This way, you send the content to all members of the DP group. Any new members of a DP group will automatically receive the distributed content. Figure 2.10 shows how three distribution points are managed as a single distribution group.

Collections can also be associated to distribution point groups. Whenever content is distributed to the collection, all associated DPs of the DP group receive the content. See Chapter 14 for additional information.

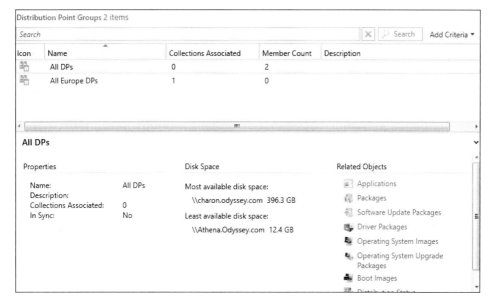

FIGURE 2.10   Distribution point group with three members.

Content Library

A *content library* is a single-instance storage file structure that stores all content on a DP. Because it leverages single-instance storage, all unique files are stored only once, no matter how many times the same file is referenced by a package, an application, a software update, or an operating system deployment.

> **NOTE: THE SMSPKG SHARE IS STILL REQUIRED FOR THE RUN FROM DISTRIBUTION POINT OPTION**
>
> Earlier versions of ConfigMgr stored content in SMSPKG folders. Even with a content library, ConfigMgr relies on the SMSPKG folder when a deployment for a legacy package is set to the Run program from distribution point option.

Software Update Management

Configuration Manager allows you to manage client software update compliance, much as you would with WSUS. However, ConfigMgr offers greater capability to control and manage the deployment of software updates, providing a rich console to manage compliance through monitoring and reporting. See Chapter 15, "Managing Software Updates," for additional information.

Compliance Settings

Compliance settings assess the configuration compliance of devices such as the service pack level of the OS, whether applications are installed, whether specific software updates have been applied, and so on. Compliance settings also enable management of mobile devices (via policies), Windows Hello settings, and Windows Information Protection. Option-ally, some configuration settings can be remediated to return settings back to the correct value, thereby providing true configuration drift management. Chapter 10, "Managing Compliance," discusses how this works in detail.

Configuration Items

A *configuration item* is a unit of compliance that defines the required value of a specified setting. It can contain multiple settings and multiple rules to evaluate settings. The follow-ing are the high-level categories for configuration item types with the ConfigMgr client installed:

▶ Windows 10

▶ Mac OS X

▶ Windows Desktops and Servers (with optional application-specific filters)

In addition, the following configuration item types are also supported through a hybrid connection to devices managed in Intune:

▶ Windows 8.1 and Windows 10

▶ Windows Phone

▶ iOS and Mac OS X

▶ Android and Samsung Knox

▶ Android for Work

Configuration Baselines

A *configuration baseline* is a collection of configuration items as well as other configuration baselines that define an overall compliance status. A configuration baseline is deployed to a collection, instructing the devices in the collection to assess compliance based on the specified conditions. In order for the configuration baseline to evaluate as compliant, all the included items must be compliant.

Content Transfer via BITS

BITS is a component of IIS that manages file transfers in a more advanced manner than a standard copy job. When the ConfigMgr client requests files from BITS, BITS handles the transfer asynchronously, freeing the ConfigMgr client to move on to other tasks. Being bandwidth sensitive, BITS continuously monitors the available bandwidth during the transfer and throttles the transfer as required. Although BITS can help manage bandwidth, it does not manage the bandwidth of the network—only the local NIC.

In addition, BITS supports checkpoint restarts. If a network connection is lost during transfer, BITS stops the transfer and resumes where it left off when the connection is avail-able again.

Measuring Software Usage

Software metering is a component of the ConfigMgr client that passively collects software usage statistics based on a defined rule set. Rules are defined either manually or automatically, based on ConfigMgr inventory data. The usage statistics from software metering can be used in reports to help administrators understand the following:

▶ The count of a software program actively in use

▶ The most active time of day for software use

▶ The regular users of software

▶ Whether software is still in use

Using BranchCache and Peer Cache to Reduce WAN Consumption

BranchCache is a software-based wide area network (WAN) optimization technology designed to reduce bandwidth usage. Environments composed of supported operating systems can leverage the data-caching benefits of BranchCache. ConfigMgr can utilize BranchCache on applications, packages, and task sequences.

Say you are deploying an application to a group of computers in a remote office. When BranchCache is utilized, the first client to retrieve the application content from a Branch-Cache-enabled DP caches it locally, making it available to other clients in its local subnet. Whenever another client requests the same content, it refers to the first client for the application, reducing the requirement to traverse the WAN to retrieve the same content. Once that client retrieves the content, it caches the content for other local clients.

Peer Cache is another software-based WAN optimization technology used to reduce bandwidth usage. It supports standard application and software deployments, as well as OSD.

Reporting

Reporting in System Center Configuration Manager is fully integrated into SSRS. Reports and subscriptions can be managed directly from the ConfigMgr console. Outside the console, ConfigMgr uses Report Builder for authoring reports. Visual Studio remains an option for authoring reports, and it offers the greatest flexibility. With Configuration Manager Current Branch, Microsoft introduced an integrated data warehouse. See Chapter 21, "Configuration Manager Reporting," for additional information.

What's New in Current Branch (Through the 1710 Release)

System Center Configuration Manager Current Branch is a moving target. As described in Chapter 1, ConfigMgr Current Branch is a live and ever-changing product, updated multiple times per year. Following is a high-level list of significant changes since ConfigMgr 2012, based on currently released versions.

What's New in Baseline Version 1511

ConfigMgr Current Branch version 1511, released in December 2015, was the first release of ConfigMgr Current Branch, and it contains the most significant changes since ConfigMgr 2012. For more details, review https://docs.microsoft.com/sccm/core/plan-design/changes/what-has-changed-from-configuration-manager-2012.

In-Console Updates for ConfigMgr

The Updates and Servicing node allows you to easily identify hotfixes and new releases of Current Branch. You simply right-click and follow the wizard to perform the update. See Chapter 6, "Installing and Updating System Center Configuration Manager," for more information.

Service Connection Point Role

The SCP role replaces the Microsoft Intune Connector from ConfigMgr 2012 R2 and provides the following functionality:

▶ Replaces the Microsoft Intune Connector for mobile device management integration with Intune

▶ Uploads usage data (described in the next section)

▶ Makes updates for ConfigMgr Current Branch available for download and installation

Usage Data Collection

Usage Data Collection is used to collect data about your sites and infrastructure and submit it through the SCP. During installation, you specify the level of data to be collected. This anonymous data collection provides priceless insight to the ConfigMgr product group, allowing better understanding of how ConfigMgr is being used. It also helps the product group ensure that its testing cycles emulate real-world scenarios. For more information, review usage data levels and settings at https://docs.microsoft.com/sccm/core/servers/deploy/install/setup-reference#bkmk_usage.

Support for Intel Active Management Technology (AMT)

While native support for AMT-based computers has been deprecated in ConfigMgr Current Branch, you can still fully manage AMT-based computers with the Intel Add-on for ConfigMgr, available at http://www.intel.com/content/www/us/en/software/setup-configuration-software.html.

Client Deployment

ConfigMgr Current Branch provides a new capability for testing new versions of the Configuration Manager client. Simply create a pre-production collection to pilot the new client. When you are satisfied, you can promote the pre-production client to production, which automatically upgrades the rest of the clients in your hierarchy with the new version.

Operating System Deployment

ConfigMgr Current Branch version 1511 includes three significant changes to OSD:

▶ **Operating System Upgrade Task Sequence:** This task sequence is used to upgrade from previous versions of Windows to Windows 10.

▶ **Windows Preinstallation Environment (WinPE) Peer Cache:** WinPE Peer Cache can be used with OSD to enable systems to pull content from a local peer instead of downloading from a DP. This is a great alternative to placing a DP in each remote office.

▶ **Windows as a Service Visibility:** You can track and manage the servicing plans for Windows 10 in your environment and create deployment rings as well as alerts to be notified when you have versions of Windows 10 that are nearing end-of-support.

Application Management

The following significant changes are new to application management in ConfigMgr Current Branch version 1511:

▶ **Universal Windows Platform (UWP) Support:** You can deploy UWP apps to Windows 10 devices.

▶ **Improved Software Center:** Software Center now displays both machine- and user-targeted software, allowing you to (finally) have one location for all available software in your environment. As an added bonus, Silverlight is no longer required for Software Center.

▶ **Install Windows Installer-based Software through the MDM Channel:** The title says it all: You can now deploy MSI files to MDM devices that support Windows Installer. Note that currently this feature only supports installation through the logged-in user context.

▶ **Browse the Windows Store for Approved Applications:** Previously, you had to specify a direct link to an application or browse to a computer that already had the application installed. Now, you can easily browse the Windows Store to obtain the application link.

Software Updates

Two significant changes were made for software updates:

▶ **Support for Windows Update for Business (WUfB):** You can use this client setting to target a collection to remove clients from using WSUS for software update management.

▶ **WSUS Clean-up Task:** The WSUS Clean-up task is now available directly in the ConfigMgr console. It sets expired software updates to a status of declined on the WSUS server, which prevents the Windows Update Agent from scanning for these old updates.

Compliance Settings

Many new configuration item types are available in ConfigMgr Current Branch:

▶ Windows 10 devices managed with the ConfigMgr client

▶ Mac OS X devices managed with the ConfigMgr client

▶ Windows desktop and server computers managed with the ConfigMgr client

▶ Windows 8.1 and Windows 10, Windows Phone, iOS, and Mac OS X devices managed *without* the ConfigMgr client (These are managed with the MDM client.)

▶ Android and Samsung Knox devices without the ConfigMgr client (These are also managed with the MDM client.)

▶ Support for managing settings on Mac OS X enrolled in either Intune or ConfigMgr

Protecting Data and Site Infrastructure

ConfigMgr supports management of Windows Hello for Business through client agent settings.

Mobile Device Management with Microsoft Intune

ConfigMgr 1511 introduced the following improvements to the mobile device management experience:

▶ The ability to set a limit for the number of devices a user can enroll

▶ The ability to set the terms and conditions that a user must accept in the company portal in order to use the portal

▶ A new Device Enrollment Manager role

On-Premise Mobile Device Management

Also new to version 1511 is support for managing mobile devices with the on-premise Configuration Manager infrastructure. This feature is currently limited to support for Windows 10 and Windows 10 mobile devices.

What's New in Version 1602

ConfigMgr Current Branch version 1602, released in March 2016, was the first in-console update experience (from version 1511 to version 1602). Version 1602 was not a baseline update, so for a fresh install or upgrade, you must have first installed the previous baseline version (in this case, version 1511).

Support for SQL Server AlwaysOn Availability Groups

You can now leverage SQL Server AlwaysOn availability groups to support high availability and disaster recovery solutions for central and primary sites.

Windows 10 Servicing Improvements

Servicing improvements allow you to filter on Language, Required, and Title criteria, which significantly reduces the content that needs to be downloaded for servicing. Also, a new console node, Windows 10 Servicing -> All Windows 10 Updates, contains all servicing updates (rather than being in the Software Updates node).

Version 1602 also introduced features to caution administrators with high-risk deployments, such as operating system deployments. (Review https://docs.microsoft.com/sccm/protect/understand/settings-to-manage-high-risk-deployments for more information.) This version improved the end-user experience for operating system upgrades, providing more visibility into what is occurring.

Application Management

Version 1602 introduced features for iOS application configuration policies for settings such as port number, security, and branding, as well as the ability to manage volume-purchased iOS applications. ConfigMgr imports licensing information from the App Store and tracks usage.

Software Updates

ConfigMgr now supports the ability to manage Office 365 updates through the Software Updates node of the console.

Compliance Settings Enhancements

New settings are available for Windows 8.1 and Windows 10 to help you control new devices, such as the Surface Hub device. You can also enable Kiosk mode on Android Samsung Knox devices.

Conditional Access Improvements

PCs managed by ConfigMgr can now be managed with conditional access policies, which means you can restrict access to Exchange Online and SharePoint based on compliance with company policy. Also, new compliance policy rules allow you to ensure that automatic updates are enabled and password policies are in place before allowing a user to unlock a device.

Client Management Improvements

Client online status is a new indicator on a device in a collection, signaling whether the device is currently online. In addition, you can trigger new actions on a device (or collection of devices) to download machine and user policy. Software Center branding has been expanded to allow you to change color, the organization name, and the icon.

What's New in Version 1606

ConfigMgr Current Branch version 1606 was released in July 2016 and became available as an in-console update from version 1511. Version 1606 was not a baseline update, so for a fresh install or upgrade, you must have installed the previous baseline version first (in this case, version 1511).

Updates and Servicing Node

Several changes were made to the Updates and Servicing node, including:

▶ More installation status details are available, allowing you to view separate details for the download, replication, prerequisite check, and installation stages.

▶ A retry option was added for prerequisite check failures.

▶ The admin console was updated to provide a cleaner view of updates by showing only the most recent (by simply clicking the History button to see the update history). The pre-production client upgrade feature was also renamed Promote Pre-production Client.

Pre-release Features

You can now give consent to use pre-release features and can then select and enable their use.

NOTE: PRE-RELEASE FEATURES ARE FULLY SUPPORTED!

Conventional wisdom may tell you that pre-release = not supported, but that is not the case with ConfigMgr Current Branch. Pre-release versions are fully supported but are in active development and, based on feedback, may change significantly in subsequent releases. Microsoft wants you to use pre-release features, even if only in your test environment, so that you can give feedback to the product team to help shape the feature. And if there is a pre-release feature you really love, have no fear in moving it to production for your environment (after fully testing, of course); just be sure to fully test future updates to that feature. For more information on pre-release features, visit https://docs.microsoft.com/sccm/core/servers/manage/pre-release-features.

More Intelligent Distribution Point Update Behavior

With the original release of version 1511, all distributions points would go offline at the same time during the upgrade process. With version 1606, ConfigMgr manages upgrades to subsets of DPs at any given time, which allows existing DPs to service content download requests.

Accessibility

You can now navigate between different nodes of a workspace by typing the first letter of the node name.

Administration Node

Multiple changes were made in the Administration node, including the ability to connect ConfigMgr to Microsoft Operations Management Suite (OMS) to make collection data, as well as the ability to configure the size of the cache folder on client computers with new options in Client Settings.

On-Premise Mobile Device Management

Expanding on the on-premise mobile device management feature released in version 1511, you can now support multiple device management points.

Application Management

Several new updates were made to application management, including the following:

▶ You can now connect to the Windows Store for Business to synchronize the list of apps purchased with ConfigMgr, as well as view and deploy them from ConfigMgr.

▶ The Software Center interface was improved so that the Installed Software tab is collapsed to the Installation Status tab. Also, Updates, Operating Systems, and Applications have been separated onto three separate tabs. Another sorely missed feature from ConfigMgr 2012 that was restored in ConfigMgr Current Branch version 1606 is the ability to install all software updates with a simple selector.

▶ From the properties of an application or package, you can now click on a link to show the content status for the object.

Software Updates

Multiple features were added to improve the software update process:

▶ Client settings were introduced to support management of the Office 365 client agent.

▶ You can now manually trigger clients to switch to a new software update point on the next scan.

▶ Two new well-requested features were added for update behavior starting with Windows 10. You can now choose Update and Restart or Update and Shutdown, which provide an experience similar to the native Windows Update experience.

▶ A new option for software update deployments (on the User Experience tab) allows you to choose the option to perform a new scan and deployment evaluation after patch restart. This is helpful for patching newly applicable updates (based on the updates just installed) in the same patch window.

Operating System Deployment

OSD also received several updates, based on user feedback:

▶ You now have the option to perform a full scan during the Install Software Updates step instead of using cached results.

▶ You can customize the RamDisk TFTP window size for PXE-enabled DPs, which enables you to optimize TFTP traffic on your network.

New Compliance Setting

A new compliance setting for Android and Samsung Knox devices enables you to allow smart lock and other trust agents, which means you can disable or bypass a lock screen password based on NFC tags or connected Bluetooth devices. You can also use this setting to prevent users from configuring smart lock.

Device Configuration and Protection

Several updates were made in this area, including the following:

▶ You can manage the iOS Activation Lock feature, with which you can require the user's Apple ID and password before erasing or reactivating the device.

▶ Support for Windows Defender Advanced Threat Protection was added.

▶ Devices with IMEI or iOS serial numbers can be predeclared.

▶ On-premise support for health attestation was added.

Remote Control

Remote control received an update, allowing the end user to accept or deny file transfers from a remote control session.

What's New in Version 1610

Just five months after the release of version 1606, another release of goodness was received with version 1610. The following sections list the most notable updates.

In-Console Monitoring of Update Installation Status

A new phase called Post Installation was added to the site update monitoring process. During this phase, you can now see status for tasks like restarting services, replication, and more.

Improvements for Boundary Groups

Version 1610 introduced a new model for boundary groups, removing the old, familiar Fast and Slow and focusing more on fallback and precedence.

Peer Cache for Content Distribution to Clients

Another welcome addition is Peer Cache, which helps you manage deployment of content to clients in remote locations. You first deploy client settings to a collection to enable Peer Cache, and then clients in that collection can act as a peer content source for other clients in the same boundary group.

Cloud Management Gateway

The cloud management gateway (CMG) service is deployed to Microsoft Azure, and your on-premise infrastructure can connect to it (using the CMG connection point). This lays the groundwork for a simpler way to manage clients than the old Internet-based client management process.

Policy Sync for Intune-Enrolled Devices

You can now request a policy sync for an Intune-enrolled device from the ConfigMgr console.

Compliance Settings for Configuring Windows Defender Settings

You can now configure Windows Defender client settings on Intune-enrolled Windows 10 computers with compliance settings.

Software Center Improvements

Version 1610 incorporates the following improvements to Software Center:

▶ Users can now request apps from Software Center (which is similar to the Application Catalog experience).

▶ Indicators in Software Center identify new software.

▶ Customizable branding for all Software Center dialog boxes provides a more consistent experience.

▶ The Snooze and remind me option allows a user to defer software until Later or until a fixed time.

Enforcement Grace Period for Required Application and Software Update Deployments

You can now grant additional grace periods for newly deployed software or updates. This scenario is helpful for when users return from vacation, so that they are not inundated with updates and reboots.

Software Updates Dashboard

The new dashboard helps you easily track compliance of software updates. You can access the dashboard from **Monitoring -> Overview -> Security -> Software Updates**.

Office 365 Client Management Dashboard

The Office 365 Client Management dashboard provides charts that show information such as the number of Office 365 clients, installed versions, languages, and channels.

Task Sequence Steps to Manage BIOS-to-UEFI Conversion

This is another top-requested item: You can now customize a task sequence step to prepare the disk to support the Unified Extensible Firmware Interface (UEFI).

New Compliance Settings for Configuration Items

There are dozens of new settings in ConfigMgr that previously existed only in standalone Intune but now are supported with **ConfigMgr -> Intune Hybrid**.

What's New in Baseline Version 1702

In addition to being an update to Current Branch, version 1702 is also a new baseline for Current Branch (so when installing a new site, you can start with version 1702).

ConfigMgr Administration Console Features

The following are a few new features of the administration console:

▶ Most objects now support a column named Object Path, which is helpful when performing searches as it allows you to see the full path to the object.

▶ Search text is preserved when you switch between the current node and sub-nodes.

▶ The setting to search sub-nodes is also preserved when you switch to a new node.

Sending Feedback from the Configuration Manager Console

You can now click Send feedback to ConfigMgr Product Group from the Home tab of the ribbon or any right-click menu.

Changes for Updates and Servicing

The following are the major updates to Updates and Servicing:

▶ The Updates and Servicing node is now a top-level node under Administration.

▶ There are two new update states in the console, Available for Install and Ready for Download.

▶ Update choices have been simplified. By default, ConfigMgr shows the latest update available instead of all potential updates. (Most of the time, you want to install the latest update.)

▶ Support is now provided for improved cleanup of older updates, with a new automatic cleanup function that deletes unneeded downloads from the EasySetupPayload folder on the site server.

Data Warehouse Service Point Role

Data Warehouse Service Point is a new role in ConfigMgr that enables you to store and report on long-term historical data.

Peer Cache Improvements

Peer Cache is getting smarter; it now rejects requests for less-desired peers that are in a state of high CPU, high disk I/O, low battery, and more.

Content Library Cleanup Tool

You can use the new content library cleanup tool to remove content from DPs where the content is no longer related to an application.

Software Update Points Added to Boundary Groups

Software update points have been added to boundary groups. This long-awaited feature helps you make software update points smarter, based on boundary group locations.

Application Management

A significant update to application management is that you can now check the status of a running executable before installing an application. For example, on a deployment type, you could specify java.exe as a file to detect (and ensure that it is not running) prior to running your application installation.

Operating System Deployment Updates

The following are several long-awaited (and frequently requested) feature updates to OSD:

▶ **Expiration of standalone media:** This functionality allows you to optionally set start and end dates for your media.

▶ **New content in standalone media:** Previously, only content referenced in the TS could be included. Now you can specify additional packages, driver packages, and applications to be staged.

▶ **Improvements to Software Center warning messages for high-impact task sequences:** You can now configure any task sequence as a high-risk deployment. You can also choose the default notification message or create your own custom notification message.

▶ **Returning to the previous page when a task sequence fails:** Previously, this required you to completely restart OSD. Now you can simply click the Back button.

▶ **Support for pre-caching of content for available deployments and task sequences.**

▶ **Support to convert from BIOS to UEFI during an in-place upgrade to Windows 10.**

▶ **Improvements to the Install Applications task sequence step:** You can now allow up to 99 applications in the Install Applications step. The wizard also supports multi-select, which simplifies the administrative experience.

▶ **New variables for the Auto Apply Drivers task sequence:** New variables available allow you to control the timeout for resolving, connecting, sending, and receiving driver requests.

Software Updates Features

Software Updates supports the following two new features:

▶ You can now deploy Office 365 applications to clients. You can configure installation settings, download Office 365, and deploy Office 365 as an application from ConfigMgr.

▶ You can now manage express installation files for Windows 10 updates.

You can now set ConfigMgr to smartly download only the changes between the current month's cumulative update for Windows 10 and the previous month's update. The express installation files significantly reduce the amount of content required to be downloaded each month for Windows 10 Updates.

Mobile Device Management Updates (for Hybrid MDM)

The following new features are available:

▶ You can now create version-agnostic installations for Intune-managed devices. Simply choose Android, Samsung Knox, iPhone, or iPad for a simplified administrative experience.

▶ Enrollment and management in Android for Work is now supported. You can enroll devices, approve and deploy work applications, create and deploy configuration items, perform selective wipe, configure email profiles, and configure compliance policies.

▶ Deploying volume-purchase iOS apps to device collections is another long-awaited feature that is now supported.

▶ Support for the iOS Volume Purchase Program for Education allows you to track applications purchased through the education program.

▶ Support for multiple volume-purchase program tokens has been added.

▶ You can now synchronize custom line-of-business apps from the Windows Store for Business.

▶ Improvements to conditional access include blocking access to corporate resources (that support conditional access) when users are using applications that are part of a noncompliant list of applications. This helps mitigate data leakage through unsecured applications.

Protecting Devices

Multiple features have been added or improved to help you protect devices:

▶ You can detect outdated antimalware client versions by configuring alerts to identify when Endpoint Protection clients are out-of-date.

▶ Updates to device health attestation updates allow on-premise clients to now be configured and managed from the management point.

▶ Windows Hello for Business enhancements enable you to manage certificate profiles, as well as provide additional notification to end users when additional actions are required to be completed for Windows Hello for Business configuration.

What's New in Baseline Version 1706

Once again, the ConfigMgr team delivered a stellar set of features with the 1706 release. Version 1706 is an in-console update available to sites currently running version 1606, 1610, or 1702. The next sections present the highlights of changes with version 1706.

Site Infrastructure Changes

Following are several new features in the infrastructure:

▶ Peer Cache supports express installation files for Windows 10 and Office 365. Also, Peer Cache no longer uses the Network Access account to download requests from peers (except while in WinPE).

▶ Data Warehouse is now a fully released product, and it supports SQL Server AlwaysOn availability groups, as well as failover clusters.

▶ SQL Server AlwaysOn availability groups includes new features such as asynchronous commit replicas, which can be used in disaster recovery scenarios.

▶ The Update Reset Tool (CMUpdateReset.exe) can reset any failed attempts in downloading or replicating content.

▶ Improved boundary groups for software update points provide the ability to configure a time for fallback to neighbor boundary groups, as well as shorter cycles to quickly select the next server from the pool of available servers.

▶ Azure integration includes multiple improvements with Azure AD:

   ▶ Azure Services Wizard simplifies configuration for Cloud Management, OMS Connector, Upgrade Readiness, and Windows Store for Business.

   ▶ Azure AD authentication can be used for clients on the Internet to access ConfigMgr sites. With this feature, client authentication certificates are no longer required.

▶ Azure AD User Discovery is a new discovery method to support users in Azure AD. Both full and delta synchronizations are supported.

Compliance Settings Changes

The following are some new features in compliance settings:

▶ There are new configuration item settings for Windows 10 devices enrolled with Intune, such as regional settings, power and sleep, language, store, and Microsoft Edge.

▶ New device compliance policy rules specify password types and restrictions, blocking of USB debugging, blocking of apps from unknown sources, and more.

Application Management Changes

The following are several few new features in application management:

▶ The ability to run PowerShell scripts from the ConfigMgr console means you can import and edit scripts, require approval for deployment, and run scripts on collections or devices and quickly examine the results.

▶ Mobile application management policy settings allow you to block screen capture (Android), disable contacts synchronization, and disable printing.

Operating System Deployment Changes

The following are new features in OSD:

▶ Secure boot status is collected in hardware inventory and enabled by default.

▶ Task sequences can be very long; you can now collapse sub-areas as desired. This is a long-requested feature request from the community.

▶ You can now reload boot images with the current Windows PE version, which previously could only be accomplished by calling a WMI method. Now you can choose to reload whenever you update DPs.

Software Updates Changes
The following are new features in Software Updates:

▶ The download time for Express Updates has been significantly improved.

▶ Microsoft Surface drivers can be updated through the Software Updates process.

▶ You can now configure Windows Update for Business deferral policies for Windows 10 Feature Updates or Quality Updates for Windows 10 devices that are managed by Windows Update for Business.

▶ ConfigMgr now leverages the Office Click-to-Run user experience for Office 365 updates, including pop-up and in-app notifications and countdowns.

What's New in Version 1710

Once again, the ConfigMgr team continues to deliver at a fantastic pace, with a great set of features (again) with this release. Version 1710 is an in-console update available to sites currently running version 1610, 1702, or 1706. The next sections present the highlights of changes with version 1710.

Site Infrastructure Changes
The following are new features in the infrastructure:

▶ Peer Cache is now a fully released product. It has been a pre-release product for the past several releases but is now fully released.

▶ Cloud distribution points are now available in the Azure government cloud.

Client Management Changes
The following are new features for client management:

▶ **Co-management for Windows 10 devices:** Starting with ConfigMgr Current Branch version 1710 and Windows 10 1607, devices joined to hybrid Azure AD can be co-managed with both Intune and ConfigMgr. This is a significant milestone that enables ConfigMgr customers to migrate from ConfigMgr to Intune on a per-feature level instead of making a single cutover from ConfigMgr to Intune. For additional information, see Appendix B, "Co-Managing Microsoft Intune and ConfigMgr."

▶ **Identifying and restarting computers:** You can add the column Pending Restart to the device collection view to show systems requiring a restart and then use the client notification channel to restart systems.

Application Management Changes
The following are new features for application management:

▶ Improvements to the new Scripts node support security scopes, real-time monitoring, and better visibility for parameters.

▶ New mobile application management policies enable you to disable printing and synchronization of contacts.

Operating System Deployment Changes

The one significant change for OSD in the 1710 release is the long-awaited feature to support child task sequences in a task sequence. You now can basically include one task sequence inside another task sequence.

Software Center Changes

Version 1710 enables you to control enterprise branding and tab visibility for Software Center. You can choose the visible tabs as well as color, theme, and logo.

Windows Telemetry Changes

You can now limit Windows 10 enhanced telemetry to only send data relevant to Windows Analytics Device Health.

Mobile Device Management

Hybrid MDM scenarios are supported on ARM64 devices running Windows 10. You can enroll devices, perform full and selective wipes, manage settings and compliance policy, and manage applications and various profiles (email, certificate, and Wi-Fi).

Device Protection Changes

Following are several new features for device protection:

▶ By using Endpoint Protection, you can create and deploy the Windows Defender Application Guard policy.

▶ Policy changes for Device Guard let you set devices to automatically run software that is trusted by the Intelligent Security Graph.

> **TIP: HOW TO STAY INFORMED OF NEW UPDATES**
>
> The list of what's new continues to grow multiple times per year. To keep informed of new updates, review the article at https://docs.microsoft.com/sccm/core/plan-design/changes/whats-new-incremental-versions.

Deprecated Features, Software, and Operating Systems

In addition to the new features listed in the previous sections, the following features and support have been deprecated as of version 1702:

▶ SQL Server 2008 R2 is no longer supported.

▶ Windows Server 2008 R2 is no longer supported as a site system, and site roles have also been deprecated (except the Distribution Point role, which is still supported in 2008 R2). 2008 R2 continues to be supported as a managed client.

▶ Windows Server 2008 is no longer supported as a site system or site role but is still supported as a managed client.

▶ Windows XP Embedded is no longer supported.

▶ Network Access Protection has been deprecated.

▶ OOB management has been deprecated.

▶ Older versions of Software Center (those that are dependent on Silverlight) are in the process of being deprecated.

▶ The capability to create virtual hard disks (.vhds) has been deprecated.

▶ The System Center Configuration Manager Upgrade Assessment Tool (which uses the Application Compatibility Toolkit) has been deprecated.

As ConfigMgr Current Branch is a living release, check out https://docs.microsoft.com/sccm/core/plan-design/changes/removed-and-deprecated-features to see new information on deprecated items.

Summary

System Center Configuration Manager Current Branch is a continuously evolving product. This chapter provided some history about ConfigMgr and described some of the terminology related to it. This chapter also detailed what's new in ConfigMgr Current Branch, as well as what has been deprecated.

CHAPTER 3

Looking Inside Configuration Manager

This chapter explores some of the internals of System Center Configuration Manager Current Branch, also referred to as ConfigMgr. It describes the architecture and how ConfigMgr is designed, at both site and hierarchy levels. It dives into components that make up ConfigMgr and external components that ConfigMgr depends on—such as Windows Management Instrumentation (WMI), SQL Server, and Internet Information Services (IIS)—and reviews site-to-site and client-to-site communication methods.

This chapter includes an overview of WMI for those unfamiliar with this venerable technology, which powers Windows manageability. The chapter discusses the infrastructure architecture of WMI and the logical WMI object model, as well as how ConfigMgr leverages WMI to provide a stable automation and development interface for both clients and servers.

This chapter also explores the ConfigMgr database, discussing its data store and data access, as well as the types of client information stored and represented in the database. It introduces ConfigMgr's status and state message systems and the role these play in relaying client and server status throughout the hierarchy.

This chapter discusses site-to-site replication for administrators and architects considering implementation of a hierarchy. It reviews the major replication methods provided by ConfigMgr to move data and content between sites. The last section covers Active Directory (AD) integration for those implementing Configuration Manager for the first time or planning to publish site data to AD.

Understanding the ConfigMgr Architecture

Configuration Manager is a highly scalable client management solution capable of supporting over a million client devices in a single hierarchy. Part of its capability to scale is due to its internal architecture. This chapter discusses ConfigMgr internals, providing information on how it operates and laying a foundation for further learning about ConfigMgr.

A combination of scalability of the various components, including sites, enables support of up to 175,000 clients in a standalone primary site or 150,000 clients in a primary site in a hierarchy. ConfigMgr therefore provides a distributed solution that scales depending on the function of each server. For example, a management point (MP), which is primarily a web service, scales up to 25,000 clients. A distribution point (DP) supports up to 4,000 client connections.

At its core, ConfigMgr is a three-tiered application:

▶ **Web Server Tier:** At the front of client and user connections are web servers that host websites and web services along with servers hosting content for applications and servers. These servers are the most numerous in a site, supporting large-scale environments.

▶ **Site Server Tier:** The middle tier is the site server, which performs data processing for client data along with site and site system status data. The site server also manages the site systems within the site and performs and initiates intersite communication. The site server provides servicing for the site by installing and updating other site systems and the site itself.

▶ **Site Database Tier:** The third tier is the site database tier, hosted on Microsoft SQL Server. Since ConfigMgr 2012, the amount of processing performed by the database tier has steadily increased. The trend of the database tier tacking on more processing responsibilities continues in the latest version of ConfigMgr, with additional processing occurring in the site database rather than the site server or site systems.

External Components to ConfigMgr

The following sections describe components that are crucial to the functioning of ConfigMgr. While these are not the only underlying components leveraged, they are the most crucial and are the ones you will come across most regularly.

The Role of WMI

WMI is used heavily throughout ConfigMgr. Used by the SMS provider on the server side, it provides a software development kit (SDK) interface to the site database. All administrative write and, optionally, read access to the site database is performed via WMI. This includes the ConfigMgr console itself. Every change made in the console is sent via remote procedure call (RPC) to the SMS provider. This WMI provider provides a stable platform to build applications and a gating mechanism to control access. ConfigMgr's PowerShell cmdlets also leverage the SMS provider for access.

The site server uses WMI to install new and manage existing site systems. WMI determines whether prerequisites are met and installs bootstrap services that perform the actual installations of the site systems.

WMI is also used with various functions on the client side. It is used to store client information and configuration and to provide client-side automation and SDK support for client activities, along with older component object model (COM) interfaces. The ConfigMgr client uses WMI to gather hardware/software inventory, using built-in providers to gather the information required from the operating system (OS). Hardware inventory information is gathered directly from WMI.

Knowledge of WMI is crucial to troubleshooting various ConfigMgr processes on both the client and server sides. It is also useful if you are interested in scripting, automating, or developing applications to run on top of ConfigMgr.

The Role of IIS

IIS is a built-in component of Windows Server that enables Windows to host websites and services. ConfigMgr uses IIS to enable the platform to build its websites and services. ConfigMgr uses IIS to host a range of site system roles, including the following:

▶ Management Point

▶ Distribution Point

▶ Software Update Point

▶ Application Catalog

IIS is used to support .NET-based web services and ASP.NET websites (such as in the Application Catalog website and service), as well as Internet Server Application Programming Interface (ISAPI) filters and extensions (for example, in the MP). It also includes simpler file publishing capabilities for the DP. Understanding IIS is essential to troubleshooting client-side issues.

The Role of SQL Server

Microsoft SQL Server is the only database engine supported for hosting the ConfigMgr site database. Its database engine also provides the core components that enable ConfigMgr's database replication service between sites. As discussed in the earlier section "Understanding ConfigMgr Architecture," the site database of ConfigMgr has been performing an increasing amount of computation and processing of data since the 2012 release.

Even the ConfigMgr client contains a SQL Server Compact Edition (SQL Server CE) database for various internal functions. Microsoft does not document the database structure; ConfigMgr client automation should use the WMI Client SDK provider, discussed further in the section "The Configuration Manager Client WMI Namespace," later in this chapter. Knowledge of SQL Server is useful for creating custom reports and troubleshooting advanced performance issues.

ConfigMgr Communication Methods

ConfigMgr uses a variety of communication methods between clients and servers. Understanding these methods can assist with troubleshooting as well as designing environments with complex network security requirements.

Server Message Block Protocol

Server Message Block (SMB), the protocol powering Windows Server file servers and file shares, has been used for file sharing since the early days of Windows. While the protocol has changed greatly over the years, these changes are not critical to ConfigMgr's usage of SMB.

ConfigMgr uses SMB and file shares for content replication and intrasite communication, and clients may use it to access content. For additional information regarding client behavior and content replication, see the chapters that discuss software distribution functions: Chapter 11, "Creating and Managing Applications," Chapter 12, "Creating and Using Deployment Types," Chapter 13, "Creating and Managing Packages and Programs", and Chapter 14, "Distributing and Deploying Applications and Packages." Content includes application installation source files and OS images.

> **NOTE: THE SMB ROLE IN REPLICATION HAS CHANGED**
>
> ConfigMgr uses SMB to initialize intersite data replication, otherwise known as Data Replication Service (DRS). Prior to ConfigMgr 2012, SMB was used for all intersite client and site data replication. This is no longer the case, and it is now used only to jumpstart or reset database information. All subsequent replication occurs via DRS. See the next section for more information.

When installing site systems, you use SMB to place ConfigMgr site system installation files on the destination server to allow installation to start. This process uses administrative shares in Windows—that is, shares created automatically by Windows to enable easier remote administration of the Windows folder (%*windir*%) and the root folder of the hard drive. Push installation of ConfigMgr clients by the site server also uses SMB to place client installation binaries on Windows systems.

SMB also replicates information from remote site systems to the site server. The SMB connection is initiated by the site system server to the site server by default; you can override this in the site system properties in the console. Information replicated in this manner includes client-generated inventory and status and state messages received by the MP. The MP receives this information via its IIS web service and forwards it to the site server for processing.

Data Replication Service

DRS is a communication method first introduced in Configuration Manager 2012. It replaced the file-based replication methods previously used, removing the need to reprocess those files at each site in a hierarchy. All non-content replication between sites uses this method of replication.

DRS is both initialized and invoked by the site server. Replication occurs directly between the SQL Server database engine instances hosting the site database at each site and is built on a combination of SQL Server change tracking and the SQL Server Service Broker (SSB). Outside of invocation by the site server, all other work occurs inside the SQL Server database engine.

ConfigMgr Client Communications

Client communications in ConfigMgr primarily occur via HTTP or optionally HTTPS between the client and the MP, DP, and software update point (SUP). Several exceptions include clients accessing legacy package/program content from DPs and booting to Windows Preinstallation Environment (WinPE) via the Preboot eXecution Environment (PXE) protocol from a PXE-enabled DP.

The client does not communicate directly with the site server; it communicates with site system roles. You may install site system roles on the site server, which is common in smaller ConfigMgr environments. Note that except for client push installation, the client always initiates communication to the site system from a network point of view and never vice versa. This does not imply that ConfigMgr does not push software, updates, or general instructions to clients; it refers to the network traffic and how ports are opened.

While this may appear to be an architectural limitation, it is a key design component that enables ConfigMgr to scale to the level it does. Instead of the server consuming its own Transmission Control Protocol/Internet Protocol (TCP/IP) ports making outbound connections, clients connect to a single port and pull policy. That policy might be an instruction to "push" software or updates.

This method of communication includes client notifications, used to run an immediate policy retrieval or endpoint protection scan. Here the client establishes an outbound TCP connection to the server and attempts to keep that port open. The server can then reply on the same TCP session to instruct the client to immediately perform an operation. This means the server does not have to establish an outbound connection, and no open ports are required on the client. This is very similar to the architecture Exchange ActiveSync uses to push email to mobile phones, as well as the push notification infrastructures used by Apple and Google for their respective mobile platforms.

ConfigMgr's Internal Components

A site server has several core internal components, each with a specific function. The most important ConfigMgr process is SMSExec, the SMS Executive, which is the main service on the site server. All major site server functions exist as threads underneath this process. The ConfigMgr console refers to these threads as *components*. A single component often consists of multiple threads responsible for initializing all types of intersite replication, processing of client information, processing of ConfigMgr site system information, and installation of site system roles.

Information and messaging within a site are routed through a series of folders and file shares called *inboxes*. Each inbox is located under *<ConfigMgr install directory>*\inboxes and exists at each type of site, although some inboxes are dormant as the data they receive is not processed at that type of site. (For example, hardware inventory is not processed at the central administration site [CAS] or secondary sites.)

Another critical component is the SMS Agent Host, ccmexec.exe. This component or service, often known as the ConfigMgr client component, also serves critical functions on site system role holders such as the MP. These threads and their log files have names starting with MP_ (such as MP_Ddr.log or MP_Location.log). The MP runs primarily within IIS. Internally to IIS, it is hosted within a set of ISAPI components, which rely on ccmexec.exe threads to pull information from the site database. The components both respond to ConfigMgr client requests for policy and receive client data for eventual processing by the site server.

ccmexec.exe is also responsible for pushing client inventory, status, and state messages to the site server. You can override this in secure environments where it may be desirable to have the site server pull from a lower-trust Internet-facing MP than have that MP reach out to the site server.

Key Site Components

The following are some of the key site components and their functions:

▶ **Configuration Manager Update:** This standalone process and Windows service is responsible for handling upgrades of sites when initiated via the Updates and Servicing node of the console. It runs prerequisite checks and initiates setup.

▶ **Discovery Data Manager:** This is a set of threads of SMSExec and is responsible for processing discovery information gathered by the various discovery methods available in ConfigMgr.

▶ **Hierarchy Manager:** This thread of SMSExec services various functions. It ensures that information about the site is published to AD for clients and other sites in the hierarchy. It monitors for configuration errors that could block DRS. It also serves a critical role in replicating mobile device data from Intune (see the sidebar "A Replication Exception: Hybrid MDM with Microsoft Intune," later in this chapter). The Hierarchy Manager is integral to the site and hierarchy upgrade process in ConfigMgr Current Branch, coordinating the upgrade process and packaging upgrade content binaries/files for replication through the hierarchy.

▶ **Inventory Data Loader:** This SMSExec thread is responsible for processing hardware inventory data from clients at primary site servers. It does not provide a direct function on the CAS or secondary sites.

▶ **LAN Sender:** LAN Sender is a set of threads of SMSExec. This component is confusingly named, as it is responsible for replication of information between sites—and sites often reside across WAN links. This naming has to do with legacy data protocols that are no longer supported, such as X.25 and ISDN. The LAN Sender uses SMB to transmit files to file shares hosted on a destination site, and it uses certain capabilities of the SMB protocol to make these copies capable of restarting and throttling.

▶ **Replication Configuration Monitor:** This SMSExec thread is responsible for handling DRS replication between ConfigMgr sites. It handles both setup and repair of replication through initialization and regular initiation of replication in SQL Server itself by executing a stored procedure (spDRSActivation). This component runs all on types of ConfigMgr sites to support DRS across the hierarchy. If this component or SMSExec is not running, the site cannot use DRS to replicate and is considered offline.

▶ **Site Component Manager:** This is hosted as a separate Windows process named SiteComp.exe and is responsible for servicing and updating within a site. While Configuration Manager Update updates the site by running setup in the background, Site Component Manager is responsible for updating SMSExec and all remote site systems and also for initial installation of those site systems. If this component is stopped, servicing operations cannot successfully complete, and no new remote site system roles can be installed or removed.

This list is not exhaustive. For a more comprehensive list of components and their log files, see Appendix A, "Configuration Manager Log Files."

ConfigMgr's Use of Inboxes

Inboxes in ConfigMgr have a long history. Although still crucial, their criticality to the operation of a ConfigMgr site and its hierarchy has been reduced over the years. All client data passes through the inboxes located in the *<ConfigMgr install directory>*\inboxes folder on the site server.

For example, say that the MP pulls information from the site database. Instead of writing information there, it pushes that information to one of the site server's inboxes, based on the type of data. The major client information inboxes include auth\dataldr.box (hardware inventory), auth\sinv.box (software inventory), and auth\statesys.box (state messages).

Discovery information processing also leverages inboxes. The various discovery methods write the discovery data records (DDR, or .ddr files) to auth\ddm.box for processing by Data Discovery Manager, which inserts this information into the site database. This is then made available via the SMS provider over WMI and SQL Server views for Transact-SQL (T-SQL) access.

Inboxes also handle the flow of information for the purposes of content replication to support application management and operating system deployment (OSD).

Basically, all ConfigMgr client and server data touches an inbox at some point—to be forwarded (for processing), replicated (if content), or processed. The key design difference from ConfigMgr 2007 and earlier is that information now traverses inboxes as seldom as possible. Information and data is no longer processed and forwarded up the hierarchy for reprocessing at a higher level or down the hierarchy (in the case of content metadata and configuration information). The newer versions of ConfigMgr process information once and rely on DRS to move data between site databases.

A REPLICATION EXCEPTION: HYBRID MDM WITH MICROSOFT INTUNE

As discussed in this section, a key objective of the replication model is to process once and avoid forwarding information in files around the hierarchy. One exception is mobile device information from Intune, which takes a slightly different path in a hierarchy. Messages are synced from Intune via the service connection point (SCP). Chapter 16, "Integrating Intune Hybrid into Your Configuration Manager Environment," and Chapter 17, "Managing Mobile Devices," provide additional information on hybrid mobile device management (MDM). These messages are processed and then sent to their respective client data processing components (Data Discovery Manager [DDM], Data Loader, and StateSys) for processing into the site database, as with any other client data on a standalone primary site.

In a hierarchy, the SCP is installed at the CAS, and messages are sent to Hierarchy Manager for routing to the mobile device's assigned site or the default mobile device site for the hierarchy (as defined in the Microsoft Intune Subscription properties). This is unusual because Hierarchy Manager does not normally route messages, even on a primary site, and because this client data is replicated down the hierarchy using file replication to transmit the data via SMB. As discussed in this section, client data has not been replicated via SMB and file replication since ConfigMgr 2012.

After the assigned or default mobile device (primary) site processes the client data, that information is replicated *back* to the CAS via DRS. This round trip is needed to have a single point of contact with Intune while continuing to offload the CAS from processing client data (as opposed to message routing).

A WMI Primer

WMI is Microsoft's implementation of Web-Based Enterprise Management (WBEM), an industrywide initiative that provides a common technology for accessing management information across a heterogeneous enterprise estate. The group behind the standard is the Distributed Management Task Force (DMTF); for information on the DMTF and WBEM, see http://www.dmtf.org/standards/wbem. WBEM is a discovery, access, and manipulation methodology. The data model it provides access to is the Common Information Model (CIM). WMI implements CIM and provides access in accordance with WBEM.

> **NOTE: ABOUT THE WMI PRIMER**
>
> This section is intended for those who are unfamiliar with or want a better understanding of WMI. WMI has been part of Windows since Windows 2000 and continues to be available in Windows 10 and Windows Server 2016. If you are familiar with WMI, CIM, and WBEM in Windows, you can skip this section of the chapter.
>
> This section also largely remains unchanged from the *System Center 2012 Configuration Manager Unleashed* (Sams Publishing) version of this book, as the information has not changed since that book was published in 2013.

Understanding the WMI Architecture

WMI provides a method to write programs and scripts that interact with local resources on Windows systems. It is frequently supplanted by PowerShell, which often leverages WMI to perform some of these functions. PowerShell is discussed further in the section "Interaction Between WMI and PowerShell," later in this chapter, which discusses how ConfigMgr now allows access to its WMI interfaces via PowerShell.

WMI exposes managed resources through a COM API. Programs written in C/C++ can call these resources directly, or you can access them through intermediate layers with applications such as scripts, .NET code, Windows forms, or web forms. WMI presents a consistent and extensible object model to represent a wide variety of system, network, and other resources. Using WMI, which has been available since Windows 2000, ensures that the scripts you write will run on the widest variety of systems, although PowerShell is becoming equally ubiquitous for supported Microsoft operating systems. PowerShell has the added benefit of supporting Microsoft's cloud services, and PowerShell itself can use WMI.

Following are examples of what you can do with WMI:

▶ Obtain a list of all accounts on a system and rename one of them

▶ Get a list of running processes on the system

▶ Extract the network configuration of a system

Using an object model removes much of the complexity that is otherwise required to access and manipulate these resources. Examples of resources that are manageable through WMI include hardware devices, running processes, the Windows file system and Registry, applications, and databases.

You can use several methods to access WMI's services and object model, including the following:

▶ Directly on the local machine

▶ Remotely through a Distributed COM (DCOM) network connection

▶ Remotely using WinRM (Windows Remote Management)

▶ Remotely using PowerShell Remoting

ConfigMgr also relies on DCOM access for remote access and calls WMI directly on systems running ConfigMgr code.

NOTE: WINDOWS REMOTE MANAGEMENT

While newer access methods such as WinRM exist, the original access method, DCOM, remains available. WinRM is Microsoft's implementation of the DMTF's WS-Man (Web Services Management) web services standard. WS-Man is a SOAP-based specification published by the DMTF. Simple Object Access Protocol (SOAP) is a standard for invoking objects remotely over an Hypertext Transfer Protocol (HTTP) or Hypertext Transfer Protocol over Secure Socket Layer (HTTPS) connection. Its main advantage is that it works across many existing network firewalls without additional configuration. For a complete description of WS-Man and related specifications, see http://www.dmtf.org/standards/wsman.

WMI supports requests from management applications to do the following:

▶ Retrieve or modify individual data items (properties) of managed objects

▶ Invoke actions (methods) supported by managed objects

▶ Execute queries against the data set of managed objects

▶ Register to receive events from managed objects

TIP: ABOUT WMI QUERY LANGUAGE

WMI provides its own query language that allows you to query managed objects as data providers. WMI Query Language (WQL) is a subset of T-SQL with minor semantic changes. Unlike T-SQL, WQL does not provide statements for inserting, deleting, or updating data, and it does not support joins. WQL includes extensions that support WMI events and other features specific to WMI. ConfigMgr also has specific extensions to WQL that are available only in the ConfigMgr SMS provider. WQL is the basis for ConfigMgr queries in the administration console (because console connections use WMI to the SMS provider), whereas T-SQL is used for ConfigMgr reports, as reports run in SQL Server Reporting Services (SSRS). These languages are discussed in Chapter 20, "Configuration Manager Queries," and Chapter 21, "Configuration Manager Reporting."

An important advantage of WQL is that a WQL query can return WMI objects as well as specific properties. Because management applications such as the ConfigMgr console interact with WMI objects, WQL queries can return result sets that you can use within the ConfigMgr infrastructure. For example, ConfigMgr collection query rules are based on WQL queries. See https://docs.microsoft.com/sccm/develop/core/understand/extended-wmi-query-language for more information about WQL.

WMI handles requests from management applications as follows:

1. A management application submits a request to the WMI infrastructure, which passes the request to the appropriate provider. (The next section of this chapter describes WMI providers.)

2. The provider handles the interaction with the system resources and returns the resulting response to WMI.

3. WMI passes the response back to the calling application. This may be actual data about the resource or the result of a request operation.

Figure 3.1 shows this basic data flow in WMI.

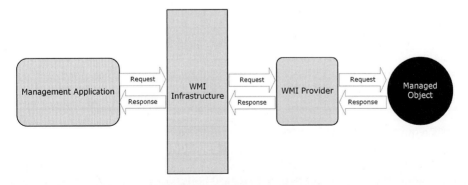

FIGURE 3.1   Basic WMI data flow.

WMI Providers

WMI providers are similar to device drivers in that they know how to interact with a particular resource or set of resources. Like a device driver, a provider must implement certain interfaces that WMI expects every provider to have, along with some additional ones. Microsoft supplies several built-in providers as part of Windows, such as the Event Log provider and the BitLocker Drive Encryption provider. A list of Microsoft-supplied providers is available at https://msdn.microsoft.com/library/aa394570.aspx. You will see providers implemented in the following ways:

- ▶ As dynamic link libraries (DLLs)

- ▶ As Windows processes and services

The idea behind creating a provider is to relieve management applications and scripts from having to be coded specifically to use an interface or a method that a developer provides. WMI providers are translation layers between management/administrative tools and applications, and they enable applications to be easily integrated in an enterprise information technology (IT) operations environment.

Just as the WMI infrastructure serves management applications through a COM interface, providers act as COM servers to handle requests from the WMI infrastructure. When a provider loads, it registers its location and the classes, objects, properties, methods, and events it provides with WMI. WMI uses this information to route requests from management/administrative tools to the proper providers. Providers are then responsible for interacting with the underlying managed object, using whatever custom method the developer chose to implement.

About the WMI Infrastructure

Figure 3.2 displays the main logical components of the WMI infrastructure. The core is Common Information Model Object Manager (CIMOM), described in the "Inside the WMI Object Model" section, later in this chapter. CIMOM handles requests between management applications and WMI providers, communicating with management applications through the COM API, as described earlier, in the "Understanding the WMI Architecture" section. CIMOM also manages the WMI Repository, an on-disk database that WMI uses to store certain types of data. Dynamic data is pulled on demand from the provider when requested. Static data is stored in the WMI Repository. Providers can compile static information into this repository as part of registration; the information can be flagged for automatic recompilation.

Most files that WMI uses are stored by default on the file system in the %*windir*%\system32\wbem folder. The WMI Repository is a set of files located by default in %*windir*%\System32\wbem\repository. The exact file system structure varies slightly depending on the Windows version.

The Winmgmt executable contains the WMI service components. The physical implementation of the WMI infrastructure varies depending on the version of Windows. Beginning with Windows Vista, Microsoft introduced several significant enhancements in WMI security and stability, including the ability to specify process isolation levels, security contexts, and resource limits for provider instances.

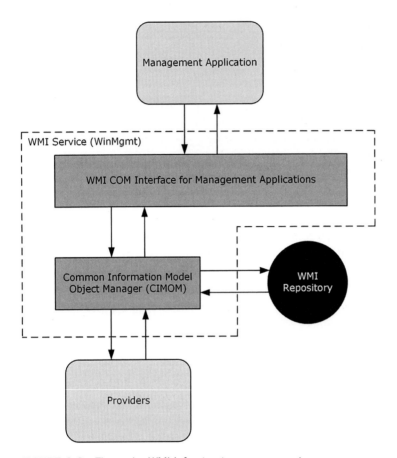

FIGURE 3.2   The major WMI infrastructure components.

Configuration parameters for the WMI service are stored in the Windows Registry subtree HKEY_LOCAL_MACHINE\Software\Microsoft\WBEM. The keys and values in this section of the Registry specify WMI file locations, logging behavior, the list of installed providers, the default namespace for scripts, and other WMI options. You rarely need to edit these options directly. As with any changes to the Registry, use extreme caution as such changes can destabilize your system.

WMI also provides detailed logging of its activities. Prior to Windows Vista, log entries were written in plain text to files in the %*windir*%\system32\wbem\logs folder. Most of these logs no longer exist; Event Tracing for Windows (ETW) makes log data available to event data consumers, including the Event Log Service. Event tracing for WMI is not enabled by default. The "Managing WMI" section, later in this chapter, discusses logging and event tracing options for WMI and configuration of tracing for WMI.

Some WMI providers, such as the ConfigMgr provider, also log their activity. Appendix A discusses logging by the ConfigMgr WMI provider.

Inside the WMI Object Model

Understanding the WMI object model is essential for writing programs or scripts that interact with WMI. It is also helpful for ConfigMgr administrators who want a better understanding of ConfigMgr objects such as collections and client settings. CIM is the basis for the WMI object model. It defines a core model that provides the basic semantics for representing managed objects and describes several common models representing specific areas of management, such as systems, networks, and applications. Third parties develop extended models, which are platform-specific implementations of common classes. You can categorize the class definitions used to represent managed objects as follows:

▶ Core classes represent general constructs that are applicable to all areas of management. Core classes are part of the core model and are the basic building blocks from which other classes are developed.

▶ Common classes represent specific types of managed objects and are generalized representations of a category of objects, such as a computer system or an application. These classes are not tied to a particular implementation or technology. The CIM_ManagedSystemElement class is the most basic and general class, and is at the root of the CIM class hierarchy.

▶ Extended classes are technology-specific extensions of common classes, such as a Win32 computer system or ConfigMgr.

WMI classes support inheritance, meaning you can derive a new class from an existing class. The derived class is often referred to as a *child*, or subclass, of the original class. The child class has a set of attributes available from its parent class. Inheritance saves developers the effort of needing to create definitions for all class attributes from scratch. Developers of a child class can optionally override the definition of an inherited attribute with a different definition better suited to that class. A child class can also have additional attributes that are not inherited from the parent.

Typically, core and common classes are not used directly to represent managed objects; they are used as base classes from which other classes are derived. The "The Configuration Manager Client WMI Namespace" section of this chapter presents an example of how a class inherits attributes from its parent class.

A special type of WMI class is SystemClass. WMI uses system classes internally to support its operations. They represent things such as providers, WMI events, and inheritance metadata about WMI classes.

WMI classes support three types of attributes:

▶ *Properties* are characteristics of managed objects, such as the name of a computer system or the current value of a performance counter.

▶ *Methods* are actions that a managed object can perform on your behalf. As an example, an object representing a Windows service may provide methods to start, stop, or restart the service.

▶ *Associations* are links to a special type of WMI class, an association class, which represents a relationship between other objects.

You can also modify WMI classes, properties, and methods by using qualifiers. A qualifier on a class may designate it as abstract, meaning the class is used only to derive other classes, and no objects of that class will be created. Two important qualifiers designate data as static or dynamic:

▶ **Static data:** This data is supplied in the class or object definition and stored in the WMI Repository.

▶ **Dynamic data:** This data is accessed directly through the provider and represents live data on the system.

The CIM specification includes a language for exchanging management information. Managed Object Format (MOF) provides a way to describe classes, instances, and other CIM constructs in textual form. In WMI, MOF files are included with providers to register the classes, properties, objects, and events they support with WMI. The information in the MOF files is compiled and stored to the WMI Repository. Examples of information in MOF format are included in the next section.

Namespaces organize WMI classes and other elements. A namespace is a container, much like a folder in a file system. Developers can add objects to existing namespaces or create new namespaces. The `root` namespace defines a hierarchy organizing the namespaces on a system. The "Managing WMI" section, later in this chapter, describes the WMI Control tool, which allows you to specify the default namespace for connections to WMI. Generally, the default namespace is `root\CIMv2`. This namespace defines most of the major classes for Windows management, and the next section looks at several classes in that namespace. Because ConfigMgr is all about Windows management, it is not surprising that it uses this namespace extensively. ConfigMgr also defines its own namespaces, discussed in the section "Configuration Manager and WMI."

If you are familiar with relational databases such as SQL Server, you may find it useful to consider an analogy between WMI and a database system. Table 3.1 presents some corresponding WMI and database concepts. Table 3.1 is useful when you are attempting to correlate between SMS provider information in WMI and database views in SQL Server.

TABLE 3.1   Corresponding WMI and Database Concepts

WMI Concept	Database Concept
WMI infrastructure	Database engine
Namespace	Database
Class	Table
Instance	Row
Attribute	Column

This section discussed the major concepts of WMI and the CIM model, which are essential to understanding ConfigMgr WMI activity. To learn about other aspects of CIM, you might start with the tutorial at http://www.wbemsolutions.com/tutorials/CIM/index.html. The full CIM specification is at http://www.dmtf.org/standards/cim. Documentation for WMI is available at http://msdn.microsoft.com/library/aa394582.aspx.

Managing WMI

This section illustrates options available for configuring WMI; it is not a "how-to" guide for administering WMI. You should seldom need to modify the WMI settings directly during day-to-day ConfigMgr administration. However, understanding WMI's options can help you understand its inner workings and functionality.

WMI Control is a graphical tool for managing the most important properties of the WMI infrastructure. Only members of the local Administrators group can use WMI Control. To run this tool, perform the following steps:

1. Launch the Computer Management MMC snap-in (compmgmt.msc). The exact procedure varies depending on the version of Windows you are running. Generally, you can right-click **Computer** or **My Computer** and choose **Manage**.

2. Expand the **Services and Applications** node in the console tree. For server operating systems, expand the **Configuration** node.

3. Right-click **WMI Control** and choose **Properties**.

WMI Control opens to the General tab. As shown in Figure 3.3, the properties on this tab confirm that you have successfully connected to WMI on the local machine, display some basic properties of your system, and specify the installed version of WMI.

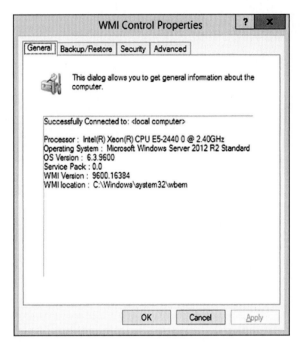

FIGURE 3.3   The General tab for WMI Control shows a successful connection to WMI on the local machine.

TIP: ABOUT MANAGING WMI ON A REMOTE MACHINE

You can use the WMI Control tool to manage WMI locally or on a remote machine. To connect to WMI on a remote machine, follow the same procedure previously described in this section, with one additional step. Immediately after step 1, right-click the **Computer Management** node at the top of the tree, choose **Connect to Another Computer**, enter the name or IP address of the computer you want to manage, and click **OK**. After connecting to the remote machine, complete steps 2 and 3 of the procedure.

In addition to needing administrative privileges on the remote machine, you need appropriate DCOM permissions, described later in this section. In addition, DCOM network protocols must not be blocked on the remote machine or any intermediary devices.

You manage WMI security from the Security tab of the WMI Control tool. WMI uses standard Windows ACLs to secure each WMI namespace existing on a machine. A namespace, as described further in the "Inside the WMI Object Model" section of this chapter, is a container that holds other WMI elements. The tree structure in the Security tab shows the WMI namespaces (see Figure 3.4).

FIGURE 3.4   The Security tab of the WMI Control tool, displaying the top-level WMI namespaces.

The namespace is the most granular level for applying ACLs in WMI. The process of setting security on WMI namespaces, and the technology behind it, is similar to the process of setting NT File System (NTFS) security. If you click a namespace to select it and click **Security**, you see a dialog box similar to the one displayed in Figure 3.5.

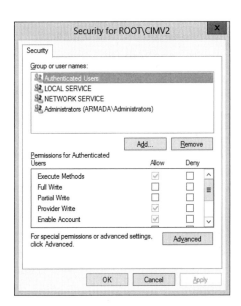

FIGURE 3.5   The WMI ACL entries for `root\CIMv2`, the main WMI namespace.

NOTE: ABOUT THE CONFIGMGR ADMINS GROUP

ConfigMgr automatically creates a local group named ConfigMgr Admins on each computer where you install the SMS provider, and it assigns appropriate WMI permissions to this group. All administrative users configured as part of role-based administration are added to this group automatically, as is the site server computer account. The name ConfigMgr Admins does not imply anything about the permissions related to role-based administration. If you grant your help desk staff members read-only access to the ConfigMgr console via role-based administration, they appear in the ConfigMgr Admins group. The ConfigMgr provider provides an additional security layer above the WMI namespace ACL supplied by Windows, down to the ConfigMgr object class and object instance level.

The dialog box in Figure 3.6 allows you to add security principals to the discretionary ACL (DACL) of the WMI namespace. The DACL specifies who can access the namespace and the type of access. Windows Vista enhancements to WMI, mentioned earlier in this chapter, in the section "Understanding the WMI Architecture," include a system access control list (SACL) for WMI namespaces, which specifies the actions audited for each security principal.

TIP: ABOUT AUDITING

As with other auditing of object access in Windows, to audit access to WMI namespaces, you must enable the effective value of the Audit Object Access group policy setting. The Windows Security event log records the events specified in the auditing settings.

To specify auditing on a WMI namespace, follow these steps:

1. In the Security dialog box, shown in Figure 3.5, click **Advanced**.

2. In the Advanced Security Settings dialog box, click the **Auditing** tab.

3. Click **Select a Principal** and then enter the name of the user group or built-in security principal, as shown in Figure 3.6. Click **OK**.

4. Select **Fail** from the **Type** dropdown menu.

5. Click **Show Advanced Permissions** to display a list of specific types of events to audit.

6. In the Advanced dialog box, check the desired types of events from the selection of check boxes and click **OK**.

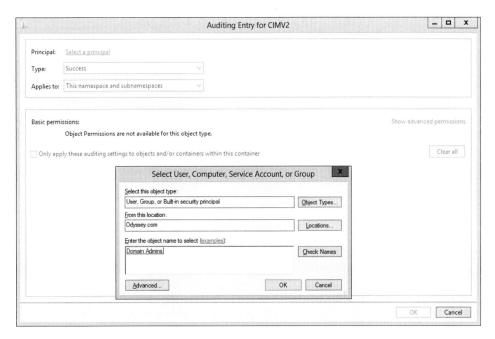

FIGURE 3.6   Adding permissions for a security principal.

REAL WORLD: USING AUDITING TO TROUBLESHOOT WMI CONNECTIONS

You can use auditing as a troubleshooting tool in the following ways:

▶ You can audit for access failures to help determine if security problems are causing a WMI problem.

▶ You can audit for access success to help determine whether there is a successful connection.

Be judicious in auditing; excessive auditing consumes unnecessary system resources and generates noise in the Security event log.

Figure 3.7 shows the entries to enable auditing for all access failures by members of the Domain Admins group.

The remaining tabs of the tool allow you to change the default namespace for WMI connections and provide several methods for backing up the WMI Repository. Windows system state backups also back up the repository. To enable tracing in Windows Vista and newer operating systems, enable logging and configure log options in the Windows Event Viewer.

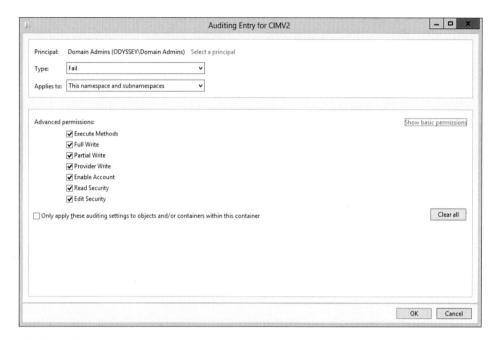

FIGURE 3.7   Adding permissions for a security principal.

Follow these steps to enable WMI Trace Logging in Windows Vista and later:

1. Open the Event Viewer (eventvwr.exe).

2. From the **View** menu, select **Show Analytic and Debug Logs**.

3. In the tree control, expand **Applications and Service Logs -> Microsoft -> Windows -> WMI-Activity**.

4. To enable the Trace event log, right-click **Trace** and select **Enable Log** from the context menu. Choose **Log Properties** from that menu to configure logging properties for WMI. You can now view, filter, and manage the WMI log from this node in the Event Viewer tree.

Enabling WMI activity tracing causes three different types of events to be generated in the WMI activity. These logs show the start, middle, and end of a single sequence (or WMI session). Following are the possible event IDs for these events:

▶ **Event ID 1:** This event shows the start of the WMI session. The key event fields are User and Namespace. The User event field allows you to focus on only the operation sessions that you are looking for (as do the Operation and GroupOperationId fields if that user account is making multiple connections). The Namespace event field is important when similarly named classes are in two different namespaces, as the next event does not provide you with details of the namespace used.

▶ **Event ID 2:** This event shows the actual operations performed. There may be one or more Event ID 2 events generated, depending on the behavior of the application or script using WMI. These events contain `ProviderName` and `Path` fields. The `Path` field indicates the path to the WMI object called.

▶ **Event ID 3:** This event shows the end of the WMI session. The only event field that this event contains is `GroupOperationId`, and it is used to indicate the session or sequence being closed.

Read more about WMI logging at http://msdn.microsoft.com/library/aa394564.aspx.

Note that User Account Control applies to privileged WMI operations. This can affect some scripts and command-line utilities. For a discussion of User Account Control and WMI, see http://msdn.microsoft.com/library/aa826699.aspx.

Additional command-line tools are available for managing WMI; see http://msdn.microsoft.com/library/aa827351.aspx.

Configuration Manager and WMI

ConfigMgr leverages WMI heavily. At its simplest, the client uses WMI to extract information about the hardware, OS, and installed software of the client machine. ConfigMgr also uses WMI to enable client agent and server-side functions. It is important for anyone working on ConfigMgr to understand WMI and its leverage by ConfigMgr. If you are already familiar with ConfigMgr and considering getting a deeper understanding of ConfigMgr's internals, WMI is one of the best areas to focus on. If you are considering automating ConfigMgr via scripts and applications, the following sections are critical for understanding when and where to leverage WMI, as they show how ConfigMgr uses WMI on its servers and look at the client-side elements. They also take a brief look at how PowerShell and WMI interact in the context of ConfigMgr.

WMI on Configuration Manager Servers

The SMS provider is a WMI provider that exposes all the editable objects in the ConfigMgr site database as WMI-managed objects. The ConfigMgr console leverages the SMS provider to perform all administrative actions. Ancillary ConfigMgr tools such as Resource Explorer and Service Manager leverage the SMS provider to provide information. Chapter 8, "Using the Configuration Manager Console," discusses the ConfigMgr console.

The SMS provider is typically deployed alongside the site server or site database server at each site, as discussed in Chapter 4, "Architecture Design Planning." The provider also implements the ConfigMgr role-based administration (RBA) security model; ConfigMgr requires more granular administration controls than those provided by the WMI infrastructure. Chapter 23, "Security and Delegation in Configuration Manager," covers RBA and security in detail.

The SMS provider has existed since Systems Management Server (SMS) was released. While the internals of the provider have changed, and object types have come and gone, its function remains unchanged. MSDN (Microsoft Developer Network) documentation sometimes refers to it as the SDK provider. The provider provides a translation layer between ConfigMgr console and the underlying SQL Server database, as shown in Figure 3.8. As SDKs tend to be stable to ensure backward compatibility and avoid breaking developer applications, the translation function of the SMS provider is critical. As Microsoft changes the database to support alterations to ConfigMgr, the SMS provider's internal implementation also changes to talk to the altered components, keeping the public side of the interface intact. When entire features are deprecated and removed from ConfigMgr, the SMS provider removes the public interfaces.

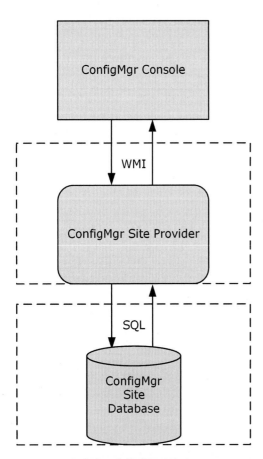

FIGURE 3.8   Diagram of the SMS provider architecture.

An important gating and control mechanism used by the SMS provider is a locking mechanism called Serialized Editing of Distributed Objects (SEDO), which helps ensure that objects are locked across the ConfigMgr hierarchy or within a site.

This is all handled for the user by the console and the SMS provider. When the same object is edited in one site while open in another site (even by the same user), an error is thrown by the console, allowing the user to either view the object as read-only or retry accessing the same object. Figure 3.9 shows an example of the error message.

FIGURE 3.9   An error message generated by a failure to lock a remote object via SEDO.

SEDO: SERIALIZED EDITING OF DISTRIBUTED OBJECTS

The SEDO locking mechanism is built on the same architecture as ConfigMgr's DRS (see the "Site-to-Site Replication" section, later in this chapter), removing the need for complex collision detection logic in a multi-master model like the ConfigMgr hierarchy model, as each primary site could in theory have the same object edited in parallel. There is no need for "last write wins" logic and/or overwritten objects to be saved with a temporary name. SEDO also saves ConfigMgr administrators from attempting to unwind these collisions.

These locks can be implicit or explicit in nature, depending on where the object is assigned. An implicit lock is always attempted. If the object is not assigned to the current site where the user is attempting to edit the object, an explicit lock request for the transfer of the lock from the assigned site must be requested.

Editing a SEDO-enabled object causes a SEDO message to be replicated immediately to the site where the object is assigned via DRS. If positive acknowledgement is not received from the assigned site, object editing cannot occur. This means editing *can* occur on the site where the object is assigned while replication is down—but not on other sites.

For more information about SEDO, see the ConfigMgr SDK at https://msdn.microsoft.com/library/hh949794.aspx.

This section uses ConfigMgr collections to illustrate how to walk through the capabilities provided by the SMS provider. (For information regarding collections, see Chapter 11 and Chapter 13.) It also walks through various SMS provider methods of extracting data. It assumes that these commands are local on the server hosting the SMS provider (usually the site server or the site database server) and that the site code of the ConfigMgr site is *CAS*. The commands are native PowerShell methods of interacting with WMI and not ConfigMgr-specific cmdlets, discussed in the "Interaction Between WMI and PowerShell" section, later in this chapter.

The following PowerShell command pulls all collection objects from the SMS provider:

```
Get-WmiObject -class SMS_Collection -namespace "root\SMS\site_CAS"
```

This command should return a number of collections. The following is an example of the output, showing a selection of important properties:

```
CollectionID              : SMS00001
Comment                   : All Systems
LastChangeTime            : 20160424145345.500000+***
LastMemberChangeTime      : 20160425182902.723000+***
LastRefreshTime           : 20160530110058.993000+***
MemberClassName           : SMS_CM_RES_COLL_SMS00001
MemberCount               : 11
Name                      : All Systems
```

This output includes the `MemberClassName` property, which returns the class for all members of the collection. Use the following command to determine what devices are members of the All Systems collection:

```
Get-WmiObject -class SMS_CM_RES_COLL_SMS00001 -namespace "root\SMS\site_CAS"
```

This returns all instances of the `SMS_CM_RES_COLL_SMS00001` class, which itself inherits the `SMS_CollectionMember` class (a generic definition of what any collection member should look like). There is one instance of the `SMS_CM_RES_COLL_xxxxxxxx` class per member of a collection. Each instance contains information about a member device or user (jointly referred to as a *resource*). Following are examples of properties that appear in the output:

```
DeviceOS                       : Microsoft Windows NT Server 10.0
Domain                         : ODYSSEY
IsClient                       : False
Name                           : PANTHEON
ResourceID                     : 2097152003
ResourceType                   : 5
```

Next, a `ResourceID` property is obtained. Every resource in the database has a `ResourceID` property that uniquely identifies it. You can use this property to find details about the client. These client details are intrinsic to that client and not related to its membership in one or more collections. The following command (which you can modify to match your client machine's `ResourceID`) retrieves that information:

```
Get-WmiObject -class SMS_R_System -namespace "root\SMS\site_CAS" -filter
"ResourceID=2097152003"
```

Some of the object types introduced with ConfigMgr 2012 contain string properties that store eXtensible Markup Language (XML). While the role of the provider remains intact, using these XML properties allows for complex object models, such as the application model, and any objects based on compliance settings to be represented easily without massively extending the SMS provider object model. (Chapters 11 and 12 discuss the application model, and Chapter 10, "Managing Compliance," covers compliance settings.) Storing this level of detail in distinct properties would mean a lot of inflexibility in regard to changes. The "Interaction Between WMI and PowerShell" section, later in this chapter, discusses how to read this information. You would write to these XML attributes by using .NET code (which is what the console does) published in the ConfigMgr SDK or Power-Shell cmdlets specifically written to support these XML properties. You can see one of these XML elements by running the command in Listing 3.1 to return the XML definition of a ConfigMgr application object. (In this code, replace '7-Zip 15.14 (x64 edition)' with the name of an application in your environment.)

LISTING 3.1   Returning the XML Definition of a ConfigMgr Application Object

```
$app = Get-WmiObject -Class SMS_Application -Namespace "root\SMS\site_CAS"
  -Filter "LocalizedDisplayName='7-Zip 15.14 (x64 edition)'"
$app.Get()
$app.SDMPackageXML
```

The script returns a single string containing the XML definition of the application object. The $app variable shows very little specific information about the application, as all the critical information is stored in the SDMPackageXML property in XML.

The script has an intermediary step of calling $app.Get(). This is an important step, as the SDMPackageXML property is defined as a "lazy" property in WMI by the SMS provider. Marking a property lazy denotes that it is expensive to return relative to the other properties in an object. This may only be noticeable when a large number of instances of the class are returned. Because lazy properties are not returned using the default instantiation process for a class, these properties are returned null by default when queried. Using Get() tells WMI to return all lazy properties for a given instance of a class.

The Configuration Manager Client WMI Namespace

The ConfigMgr client heavily leverages WMI internally and externally. It creates its own additional classes in the root\CIMv2 namespace and creates its own distinct namespaces to support client activities. These namespaces begin with root\CCM. This namespace is actually shared between clients and the MP, as they share the same core process, ccmexec.exe. Underneath root\CCM are multiple additional namespaces supporting various client operations. As shown in Figure 3.10, you can see some of the additional namespaces via wbemtest (Windows Management Instrumentation Tester). Launch the wbemtest tool from any machine by running wbemtest.exe from the command prompt or the Windows Run dialog. Follow these steps to view the namespaces:

1. Run wbemtest.exe with elevated administrative rights.

2. Click **Connect**.

3. Under Namespace, enter **root\CCM**.

4. Click **Connect**.

5. Click **Enum Instances**.

6. Type **__NAMESPACE** and click **OK**.

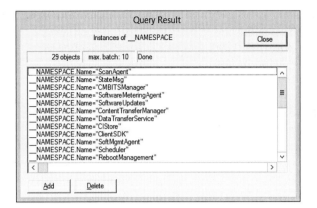

FIGURE 3.10   Using wbemtest to view namespaces under the `root\CCM` namespace.

TIP: TOOLS TO VIEW WMI

The remainder of this section uses wbemtest to interact with WMI and view various ConfigMgr namespaces. wbemtest was selected because it is universally available by default on all systems where WMI is installed (Windows 2000 and up). This makes the tool useful for troubleshooting issues on live production systems without the need to install other tools. The following are some other tools you might consider:

▶ **WMI Explorer (PowerShell version):** Written by Marc van Orsouw, http://powershell.org/wmi-explorer/

▶ **WMI Explorer (.NET version):** https://wmie.codeplex.com/

Some of the most interesting namespaces are `root\CCM\Policy` and its child namespaces `root\CCM\Policy\Machine\actualconfig` and `root\CCM\Policy\<User SID>\actualconfig`, which show machine and user policies targeted to that ConfigMgr agent. (Replace `<User SID>` with the Windows account security identifier [SID] for that user.) A policy is a combination of client settings, deployment, and schedules sent to the client by the ConfigMgr site, as discussed in the next section.

Other interesting namespaces are `root\CCM\SoftwareUpdates` and `root\CCM\ClientSDK`. The `SoftwareUpdates` namespace is used to store information returned from the Windows Update Agent (WUA) API calls performed by the ConfigMgr agent as part of software update management. (See Chapter 15, "Managing Software Updates," for information on software updates.) The `ClientSDK` namespace allows you to automate client-side activities. The "Automating the ConfigMgr Client via WMI" section, later in this chapter, discusses combining these two classes.

Obtaining Hardware Inventory Through WMI

The ConfigMgr client agent gathers hardware inventory data by querying WMI. The client agent settings determine what object classes were queried and sent to the server as the client's inventory data. Most types of data gathered by hardware inventory are defined under the client agent settings in the ConfigMgr console. You can add or modify the total set of potential inventory collected by editing the default client agent settings or creating a custom client setting and deploying it to a collection of the systems from which you need to gather that information. Chapter 9, "Client Management," describes client settings and inventory customizations through the ConfigMgr console.

> **NOTE: HARDWARE INVENTORY BY ANY OTHER NAME**
>
> *Hardware inventory* is a bit of a misnomer. While it does collect information about a client system's hardware, it also collects far more information than just hardware. It also collects OS configuration information such as logical network configuration, services, features enabled on Windows Server, logged-in user information, and general OS information. It also collects information about installed applications and is the primary method of gathering Registry information from clients. Hardware inventory performs all these non-hardware-related operations because it is the method for gathering WMI information from clients. All the information listed is stored in WMI. For these resources, a more technically accurate though acronym-heavy and jargon-laced name for hardware inventory could be *WMI inventory*.

The Default Settings client settings ship out of the box with a number of preconfigured classes to gather. In some cases, you might require a custom data class. For example, you might need to gather information about an application or a specific OS configuration exposed in WMI. There may also be some Registry information you want to gather as a part of hardware inventory. (You can also determine how the Registry is configured via compliance settings; see Chapter 10.) In these cases, you import a .mof file into the default client settings or a custom client setting to gather this additional information.

To apply inventory settings from a custom .mof file, navigate to **Administration -> Client Settings** and either select Default Client Settings or create a Custom Client Device Settings object. On the Properties page, choose **Hardware Inventory**, click **Set Classes**, and click **Import**.

ConfigMgr clients download client settings as part of their machine policy retrieval cycle. Any changes are compiled and loaded into the WMI Repository. The ConfigMgr client stores its machine policy in the `root\CCM\Policy\Machine\actualconfig` WMI namespace. Use wbemtest to examine some of the inventory-related objects in this namespace. Follow these steps to launch wbemtest:

1. Run wbemtest.exe with elevated administrative rights.
2. Click **Connect**.
3. Under Namespace, as shown in Figure 3.11, enter `root\CCM\Policy\Machine\actualconfig`.
4. Click **Connect**.

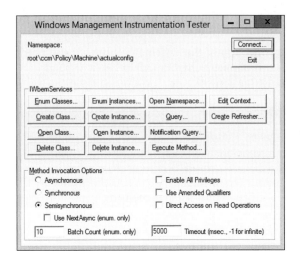

FIGURE 3.11   Using wbemtest to connect to the `root\CCM\Policy\Machine\actualconfig` namespace.

To return a list of available classes in this namespace, click **Enum Classes**. You can double-click any of the returned classes to show their definitions. Then, to return all instances of a class, click **Instances**. Alternatively, if you know the name of the class you want to view, use Enum Instances instead of Enum Classes on the main page of wbemtest. Use either method to view the instances of the `InventoryDataItem` class.

`InventoryDataItem` is the class that represents inventory items defined in machine policy. At first, the list looks quite intimidating, with a bunch of globally unique identifiers (GUIDs) returned in a list. However, if you scroll to the right, you see the `ItemClass` property and much more human-readable information. Double-clicking the row for `Win32_Service` returns a list of all Windows services.

The `Namespace` and `ItemClass` properties tell the InventoryAgent thread of CCMExec.exe (the main ConfigMgr client process) what to inventory and its location. InventoryAgent is the component of the client responsible for gathering inventory. The Properties property contains a comma-separated list of properties to gather for each instance of `Win32_Service` under the `root\CIMv2` namespace. These properties follow:

`DisplayName, Name, PathName, ServiceType, StartMode, StartName, Status`

Instances of the `Win32_Service` class have additional properties beyond those listed. To add additional properties to be gathered as part of hardware inventory, modify the client settings (either default or custom ones). To view these settings, open the ConfigMgr console and navigate to **Administration -> Default Client Agent Settings -> Properties -> Hardware Inventory -> Set Classes**. Classes that are checked are collected along with any checked properties. Figure 3.12 shows the properties for the `Win32_Service` class, which represents Windows background services.

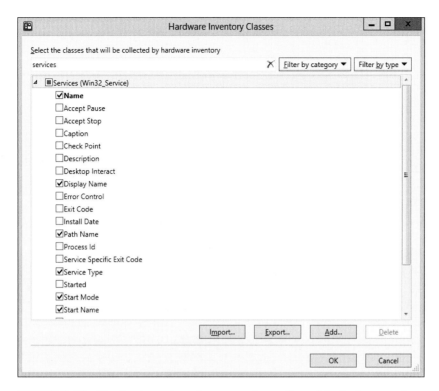

FIGURE 3.12   The hardware inventory properties gathered for instances of `Win32_Service` on ConfigMgr clients.

Following is a list of the key ConfigMgr client namespaces:

▶ ScanAgent

▶ StateMsg

▶ SoftwareUpdates

▶ ContentTransferManager

▶ DataTransferService

▶ CIStore

▶ ClientSDK

▶ Scheduler

▶ RebootManagement

▶ Messaging

- ▶ DCMAgent
- ▶ dcm
- ▶ Policy
- ▶ InvAgt
- ▶ LocationServices

Automating the ConfigMgr Client via WMI

One of the most significant namespaces mentioned in the preceding section is the `root\`
`CCM\ClientSDK` namespace. This namespace provides a wealth of classes, with information
and methods that allow you to write client-side scripts or automation using WMI. While
the other classes are useful for understanding some of the internal behaviors of the
ConfigMgr client, the `ClientSDK` namespace has practical, everyday applications.

For example, if you want to automate software update management, you can use the
`CCM_SoftwareUpdatesManager` and `CCM_SoftwareUpdate` classes to interact with and get the
status of software updates, respectively. You can do the same for software distribution by
using `CCM_Program` and `CCM_ProgramManager` and/or `CCM_Application`, `CCM_Application-
Actions`, and `CCM_ApplicationPolicy`, depending on the type of software distribution used.

A simple example of how to use `ClientSDK` is to get and set business hours defined on
the client system. These business hours are designed to allow end users some self-service
determination of when ConfigMgr client activity will occur (although ConfigMgr administrators can override this at will). Some customers want to modify or preconfigure these
settings for end users. This section uses PowerShell to call out to WMI to get information
about the configured business hours and change them.

You can start with getting the currently configured business hours by running the
following command (run with elevated administrative rights), which invokes the
`GetBusinessHours` method of the `CCM_ClientUXSettings` class:

```
Invoke-WmiMethod -Class CCM_ClientUXSettings -Namespace "root\ccm\clientsdk"
   -Name GetBusinessHours
```

This command returns something similar to the following (though internal WMI properties that start with __ and `PSComputerName` have been removed for readability):

```
EndTime         : 22
ReturnValue     : 0
StartTime       : 5
WorkingDays     : 62
```

These results show that on the test client, business hours start at 5 AM (05:00) and end at
10 PM (22:00). Figure 3.13 displays this in the Software Center.

FIGURE 3.13   The default Software Center business hours match what is found via the
`ClientSDK` namespace.

You can alter this setting to set working hours to start at 6 AM (06:00) and end at 7 PM
(19:00). Start by retrieving the order of the parameters for the `SetBusinessHours` method
of the `CCM_ClientUXSettings` class. The `Invoke-WmiMethod` PowerShell cmdlet expects that
input parameters are specified in a specific order. The following command finds the order:

```
([wmiclass]'root\ccm\clientsdk:CCM_ClientUXSettings').GetMethodParameters
  ('SetBusinessHours')
```

This command returns something similar to the following (though internal WMI properties that start with __ and `PSComputerName` have been removed for readability):

```
EndTime         :
StartTime       :
WorkingDays     :
```

This shows that the order of the input parameters is `EndTime`, `StartTime`, and `WorkingDays`.
Leave `WorkingDays` as it is (on the test client, it is 62, which maps to Mon–Tue–Wed–Thu–
Fri). The following command allows you to invoke the `SetBusinessHours` method to alter
the client's business hours to 6 AM to 7 PM (06:00 to 19:00):

```
Invoke-WmiMethod -Class CCM_ClientUXSettings -Namespace "root\ccm\clientsdk"
  -Name SetBusinessHours -ArgumentList 19,6,62
```

You should get a result with a `ReturnValue` property set to zero (success). Now if you re-invoke `GetBusinessHours`, you get the following (though internal WMI properties that start with __ and `PSComputerName` have been removed for readability):

```
EndTime        : 19
ReturnValue    : 0
StartTime      : 6
WorkingDays    : 62
```

This matches Figure 3.14, which shows the new Software Center business hours settings.

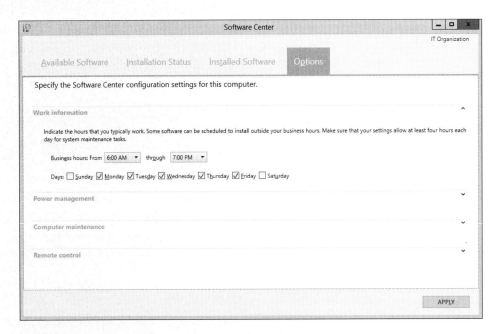

FIGURE 3.14   The changed Software Center business hours after invoking the `SetBusinessHours` method.

Further information on the `ClientSDK` namespace is available in the ConfigMgr SDK in MSDN at https://msdn.microsoft.com/library/jj874139.aspx.

Interaction Between WMI and PowerShell

ConfigMgr has been based on WMI since its SMS days. For IT pros, this meant using Visual Basic scripts to automate tedious ConfigMgr tasks or using alternative scripting languages such as Perl. With the advent of PowerShell, which has become the standard scripting interface across Microsoft's products, ConfigMgr administrators faced a gap compared to the proliferation of PowerShell skills across other teams in their organizations. Power-Shell can make calls to WMI, meaning it has always been possible to use PowerShell to make calls to the SMS provider to both get and set (read/write) data. However, it was not always straightforward, given some of the more niche capabilities of WMI that the SMS provider leverages. In addition, there were few samples of this from Microsoft, although the community generated many good examples and samples.

Starting with ConfigMgr Current Branch version 1610, Microsoft has integrated PowerShell cmdlets into each release of ConfigMgr Current Branch. This negates the need to update the cmdlet module in addition to the console with each release. The latest information on the changes in each release can be found at https://docs.microsoft.com/powershell/sccm/overview.

One of the most important capabilities of the PowerShell module is that it introduces the ability to handle XML data types. ConfigMgr 2012 and later rely heavily on XML data types of compliance settings and related objects (software update, application management, and MDM). When these features are accessed via WMI, critical data is stored only in string WMI properties as XML. Reading this data is therefore challenging if you do not have knowledge of the data types, and writing becomes a dangerous operation to codify.

The ConfigMgr console achieves reading and writing of these XML documents via specific .NET libraries, documented in the ConfigMgr SDK. The PowerShell module requires the console to be installed so it can leverage the full suite of the .NET libraries to enable access to the SMS provider.

Compare the results of this PowerShell WMI cmdlet:

```
$app = Get-WmiObject -Namespace "root\sms\site_CAS" -Class SMS_Application
  -Filter "LocalizedDisplayName='Microsoft Outlook'"
Get-WmiObject -Namespace "root\sms\site_CAS" -Class SMS_DeploymentType
  -Filter ("AppModelName='" + $app.ModelName + "'")
```

with the results of this ConfigMgr PowerShell module cmdlet:

```
Get-CMDeploymentType -ApplicationName "<application name>"
```

The ConfigMgr PowerShell method is simpler, and you can also easily create deployment types by using Add-CMDeploymentType, whereas with WMI, you would need to build the XML in PowerShell or use PowerShell to call out to .NET, neither of which is a trivial task.

Inside the ConfigMgr Database

The ConfigMgr database stores all information about your ConfigMgr environment. This includes information about all agent-managed clients, Intune-managed mobile devices, site information, and discovery information. ConfigMgr supports only Microsoft SQL Server for hosting its database. By default, the database is named CM_ followed by the three-digit alphanumeric code for the ConfigMgr site in question.

Microsoft does not publish the database schema, as it can change without notice. Instead, Microsoft publishes information about the views and works to keep these views static between releases.

ConfigMgr Tables and Views

ConfigMgr's database, like any other SQL Server database, contains information in a series of tables. Tables store information in two dimensions. One dimension of each table is defined by a set of columns. The other dimension is the rows or instances of the column sets.

As discussed in the previous section, Microsoft does not publicly document these tables. SQL Server provides another method of accessing information: using *views*. Consider views as virtual tables; a view is essentially a query exposing data from one or more tables. Microsoft publishes information about these views, and every built-in report in ConfigMgr is based on these views. The idea is not to isolate information from customers but rather to provide a stable platform for them to build reports and solutions. In the event that a table needs to be changed, Microsoft modifies the associated view to ensure that existing reports are not impacted. Chapter 21 provides more details on views and their usage along with other methods of reporting on ConfigMgr data.

NOTE: THE DYNAMIC NATURE OF THE CONFIGMGR DATABASE SCHEMA

The ConfigMgr schema is not documented, and it is subject to change with each release and also changes dynamically. Specifically, when you modify the data collected by discovery or inventory methods in ConfigMgr, the tables and views supporting discovery and inventory are modified automatically.

In the case of discovery, adding an attribute to a discovery method causes DDM to request the addition of a column to the underlying table for the resource (user or system) where the attribute is added. An example of this is adding an AD attribute to AD User Discovery or AD System Discovery in the console, which triggers the change on the process of the .ddr files by the DDM thread of the SMSExec process.

Modifying hardware inventory by collecting an additional WMI property or class causes changes in the tables supporting hardware inventory. Specifically, when the resulting .mif files are processed by Data Loader (the dataldr thread of SMSExec), one of two changes occurs. In the case of an additional property to an existing class, an additional column is added to the table holding instances of this class across clients, along with the table's corresponding view. In the case of an additional WMI class being inventoried, an additional table and view are created.

Using SQL Server Management Studio

While most day-to-day ConfigMgr administration does not require accessing the site database, it is useful to know how to view information in the database. This can be helpful for support purposes and to quickly view information to support creating scripts (or other applications) or reporting. The following steps walk you through using SQL Server Management Studio, the SQL Server administrative interface. (See Chapter 21 for additional information on SQL Server Management Studio and the basics of T-SQL.)

To access the ConfigMgr views, perform the following steps:

1. Open SQL Server Management Studio by going to **Start -> All Programs -> Microsoft SQL Server <*version*> -> SQL Server Management Studio**.

2. After the console launches, enter the name of the SQL Server hosting the ConfigMgr site database.

3. After the connection completes, expand the *<servername>*\database\CM_*<site code>*\ views in the left-hand pane.

CAUTION: DO NOT CHANGE THE CONFIGMGR DATABASE

Microsoft does not support modifying the ConfigMgr site database, as doing so can cause unpredictable results and may affect the stability of the database's site or even the hierarchy. Do not add, delete, or change objects in the database. Do not modify any data stored in any objects.

Microsoft Support professionals may request a change as part of a workaround or resolution to an issue, based on guidance from the ConfigMgr development team. Prior to making any changes, under guidance from Microsoft Support, the authors recommend always making a backup of the database (and confirm restorability).

Exploring the ConfigMgr Database

The following sections discuss how to view various types of data stored in the ConfigMgr database and show how this information appears in the sample environment used by this book. Chapter 21 includes a more comprehensive list of various object types and their corresponding views in the database.

Collections

Let's start with one of the most critical ConfigMgr object types, the collection. (You glimpsed the use of collections with WMI in the "WMI on Configuration Manager Servers" section, earlier in this chapter.) In WMI, the ConfigMgr collection class is named `SMS_Collection`. In the site database, the view is very similarly named `v_Collection`, with the only change in naming being the move from `SMS_` to `v_`. (This is covered further in the tip "Finding Other Views in the Database Schema Dynamically," later in this chapter.) Figure 3.15 shows what `v_Collection` looks like. These columns match up nicely with the information you see when looking at `SMS_Collection` properties. You will see this pattern repeated frequently when moving between WMI and SQL.

	CollectionID	Name	MemberCount	MemberClassName
1	SMS00001	All Systems	11	v_CM_RES_COLL_SMS00001
2	SMS00002	All Users	0	v_CM_RES_COLL_SMS00002
3	SMS00003	All User Groups	0	v_CM_RES_COLL_SMS00003
4	SMS00004	All Users and User Groups	0	v_CM_RES_COLL_SMS00004
5	SMSOTHER	All Custom Resources	0	v_CM_RES_COLL_SMSOTHER
6	SMS000US	All Unknown Computers	2	v_CM_RES_COLL_SMS000US
7	SMSDM001	All Mobile Devices	0	v_CM_RES_COLL_SMSDM001
8	SMSDM003	All Desktop and Server Clients	2	v_CM_RES_COLL_SMSDM003
9	CAS00014	Test Client Coll	2	v_CM_RES_COLL_CAS00014
10	CAS00015	Web Servers	1	v_CM_RES_COLL_CAS00015

FIGURE 3.15   `v_Collection` displayed using SQL Server Management Studio.

Figure 3.15 shows the `CollectionID` column as the unique (within the hierarchy) identifier for the collection. This is an important column when you want to link `v_Collection` to other views. You can also use this column with `v_FullCollectionMembership` to return devices or users in a given collection.

In addition, there are views created dynamically for each collection, named `v_CM_RES_COLL_<collectionID>`. For example, the view `v_CM_RES_COLL_SMS00001` represents the default All Systems collection. As you create collections, more of these dynamic collections are created, each containing the member users or devices of that collection. This is useful when you are writing scripts or queries that need to access collection members and you need to use a specific collection every time. If you need to parameterize, or take the collection as input to the script/query you are writing, using `v_FullCollectionMembership` provides a better view.

Hardware Inventory

Hardware inventory views are interesting for several reasons. They follow a similar naming standard as collection views, where their WMI name (for example, `SMS_G_System_PC_BIOS`) has the `SMS_G_System` turned into `v_GS` (for example, `v_GS_PC_BIOS`). These views are also dynamically created and modified in several different scenarios. When processing hardware inventory for a newly added class, when adding a new property, or when the value of property is too long to fit into the existing column for the property in the site database, SMSExec automatically alters the table schema to fit the new incoming data. The corresponding view to that table is created or modified to accommodate the newly defined table definition.

Client Settings

Client settings are also found in the site database views and stored in `v_SMSMClientAgentConfig_Base`. Note that settings are quite often stored in XML-typed columns in the client settings view. This can make reporting or reading a query difficult in some instances. SQL Server natively supports handling XML data in T-SQL queries; Listing 3.2 shows an example of how to extract the endpoint protection definition update fallback source and order it using the T-SQL `CROSS APPLY` command.

LISTING 3.2   Extracting the Endpoint Protection Definition Update Fallback Source

```
SELECT AMSettings.Name, CliSettings.PropertyName,

   AMSettingsValue.FallbackSource.value('.', 'nvarchar(max)') AS 'FallbackSource'
FROM vSMS_AntimalwareSettings AS AMSettings

JOIN vSMS_ClientAgentConfig_Base AS CliSettings
ON AMSettings.ID = CliSettings.SettingsID

CROSS APPLY CliSettings.XmlValue.nodes('/StringArrayXML/Value') AS
AMSettingsValue(FallbackSource)

WHERE CliSettings.PropertyName = 'FallbackOrder'
```

This should return something similar to the information shown in Figure 3.16, with readable information for each endpoint protection policy defining the fallback order to use.

	Name	PropertyName	FallbackSource
1	SCEP Performance-Optimized	FallbackOrder	AMDefinitionFallbackOrderFromCM
2	SCEP Performance-Optimized	FallbackOrder	InternalDefinitionUpdateServer
3	SCEP Performance-Optimized	FallbackOrder	MicrosoftUpdateServer
4	SCEP Performance-Optimized	FallbackOrder	MMPC

FIGURE 3.16   Query results showing how XML data is presented when handled via T-SQL.

TIP: FINDING OTHER VIEWS IN THE DATABASE SCHEMA DYNAMICALLY

There are multiple ways to find additional views and methods of extracting data from the site database:

▶ You can look at a built-in report that contains the information you are looking for or as a start on that information.

▶ You can use the `v_SchemaViews` view, which contains a list of all other views defined in the site database and their general types, including Status, Inventory, and Inventory History. A key type is the Schema type, which defines the other helper views besides `v_SchemaView`. Looking at these views is useful as the views sometimes contain late-breaking views that have not yet been documented elsewhere. Use the following query to find them:

```
SELECT [Type],[ViewName] FROM [v_SchemaViews] WHERE [Type]='Schema'
```

▶ You can trawl the definitions of views looking for particular column names. This can be useful when you have a certain column that you want to join to another view but do not know what other views contain the same column that might be useful as joins. This method is the most complex and relies on querying the SQL Server system views to extract information about the schema. Such a query can also be modified to search for other objects.

In the sample query shown in Listing 3.3, you can replace `ResourceID` to search for a different string, but be sure to retain the `%` symbols.

LISTING 3.3   Searching the Definitions of All Database Views for a Particular String

```
DECLARE @varObjectToSearchFor varchar(max)

SET @varObjectToSearchFor = '%ResourceID%'

SELECT
udf.name AS [Name]

FROM
sys.objects AS udf
LEFT OUTER JOIN sys.sql_modules AS smudf ON smudf.object_id = udf.object_id
```

```
LEFT OUTER JOIN sys.system_sql_modules AS ssmudf ON ssmudf.object_id = udf.object_id
WHERE
(udf.type = 'V') AND
(ssmudf.definition LIKE @varObjectToSearchFor OR smudf.definition
   LIKE @varObjectToSearchFor)


ORDER BY
[Name] ASC
```

Status and State Messages Overview

The following sections discuss status and state messages and their use within ConfigMgr. Status messages have existed in ConfigMgr since SMS 2.0. State messages are a newer concept, introduced with ConfigMgr 2007, and their usage has expanded since that time.

Using Status Messages

A status message represents an event and is similar to messages in the Windows Event Log. Each status message type has a defined message template and variables populated by the component generating the message. These messages are not stateful, in that they do not designate the particular state of a client or a client operation or deployment. However, each process (such as legacy software distribution via packages and programs, discussed in Chapters 13 and 14) has a process defined in code that it goes through and certain status messages it generates. From that defined process, it is possible to infer statefulness. For example, if a package-based software distribution deployment goes through six steps, each with its own message, you can infer that if you see the message from step 6 that it has completed the process. The issue is that if a seventh step is added in an update to ConfigMgr, reports and processes would need to be rewritten to support the new definition of the final message in the process.

Conversely, status messages are useful for task sequences in OSD. Because a task sequence (TS) is a custom set of steps defined by an administrator, generating a hard-coded set of state messages would not be useful as these messages could only define known stages (such as starting, processing, and ending a TS). Status messages are generated for each step in the TS during task sequence execution. (For more information about OSD, see Chapter 22, "Operating System Deployment.")

Status messages are also useful for picking up specific events from site servers and site systems for methods of eventing as data from clients is processed and internal processes occur. For example, if the Data Loader (DataLdr) is unable to process a delta inventory because it has yet to receive a full inventory (usually because a client was deleted manually from the console), it generates a status message to reflect that. If the Site Component Manager (SiteComp) cannot install or reinstall a site system role, it generates a status message for each failed attempt.

Client status messages are sent via the MP to the primary site server for processing. Both client and server status messages are written to the statmgr.box inbox for processing and are processed by the Status Manager component of SMSExec on the site server and inserted into the site database.

How State Messages Work

In contrast to status messages, state messages (as their name implies) are stateful. Each state message refers to a specific activity, compliance item, or operation. These messages have distinctly defined topics that they relate to (for example, application management). Each topic has multiple corresponding state message IDs that define the state for the instance of the topic.

For example, a certain topic type defines some state messages as relating to application management. Within that topic type are state message IDs that correlate to the various states of an application deployment, including Success, In Progress, Unknown, Requirements Not Met, or Error. The instance of the topic type in this case is an application deployment to a user or device. Each message reflects a state of the deployment and overwrites the last reported state. Conceptually, an application deployment may go from Unknown to In Progress and then to either Success or Error, depending on whether the application installer succeeded or failed.

State messages are used primarily to support client operations and reduce the need for repeated messages and are generally less noisy than status messages. For example, if an application repeatedly fails, it may simply stay in the Error state unless the specific type of error changes. Contrast this with status messages, which are generated for each attempt, with potentially more than one status message per attempt. A client also maintains a list of the various activities and deployments for which it has sent a state message; wherever possible, it attempts to send delta state messages to reduce the load on the site infrastructure.

State messages are sent via the MP to the primary site server for processing. They are written to the auth\statesys.box inboxes for processing and are in turn processed by the State System component of SMSExec on the site server and inserted into the site database.

Site-to-Site Replication

The following sections cover the two primary methods of site-to-site replication in ConfigMgr: database replication (handled by DRS) and content replication (or file replication). These replication methods have been the cornerstone of ConfigMgr since the 2012 release.

About Configuration Manager Database Replication

Database replication replaces the file-based replication methods previously used. It removes the need to reprocess these files at each site in the hierarchy.

These files contained client data (status and state messages along with inventory and discovery) and server data (status messages and discovery data). These were processed at each site, which had an impact on the scalability of the site as the messages had to be processed at each site they traversed to ensure that each site's database contained the correct information. This lack of scalability led to bloated hierarchies with additional sites just to distribute (scale out) processing load.

This method was inefficient because information was processed *at least* twice in a hierarchy—once at the primary site and again at the central site. In complex and large hierarchies with multiple tiers of primary sites (which was possible with ConfigMgr 2007 and earlier versions), this could cause the same file to be processed numerous times. Each processing incurred write costs into the site database for each site, along with inbox processing by ConfigMgr components. The event of a flood of data to process at any one site resulted in a flood of data to every site above that flooded site.

ConfigMgr 2012 removed this issue by introducing database replication. *Database replication* is a slightly confusing term as transactional database replication is one of the most common methods of database replication used by SQL Server database administrators. This term was also used in early beta versions of ConfigMgr 2012. For this reason, this book refers to it as DRS from here on, as DRS has nothing to do with transactional database replication in SQL Server.

DRS uses SQL Server change tracking to monitor for table changes and store them. With each activation of DRS by SMSExec's Replication Control Manager (RCM), changes since the last activation are reviewed and bundled into compressed XML messages and passed to the SSB. The SSB provides a guaranteed transmission method between SQL Server database engine instances for an SQL Server-based application, in this case ConfigMgr. The term *guaranteed* is used from a developer point of view to refer to a transmission method that the developer is not responsible for maintaining; rather, the SSB provides a resilient transmission method for atomic messages where the developer can fire messages and assume that they were delivered.

As part of creating a ConfigMgr site in a hierarchy, asymmetric keys are exchanged for authentication of each SQL Server database engine instance for use with the SSB. Setup also initializes the database on each end of the replication. The initialization extracts from the database information that is authoritative for that type of data. The CAS is authoritative for global data, which includes all console objects. Primary sites are authoritative for site data, which includes client data (inventory, state/status, and discovery) along with site-specific information (state and status messages). In addition, some types of data could be conceptually viewed as being shared—in the sense that the CAS and its child primary sites both write different information to the same table. For the purposes of DRS, authority is defined at the table layer and not within a table. This is an important distinction, as DRS is used to recover a site outside its change-tracking interval.

For these reasons, if you implement a hierarchy, it is important to monitor DRS replication between your ConfigMgr sites to ensure that any outage is resolved as quickly as possible. Furthermore, while it is *possible* to increase the data retention value to 14 days, doing so has an impact on the performance of the site database and SQL Server because almost three times the amount of data for the changes must be stored in the site database.

DRS CRASH COURSE

As discussed earlier in this section, change tracking detects changes within a site database for the purposes of DRS. These changes must be stored somewhere for subsequent use. There are scenarios where a transmission outage between two sites could occur: There could be a transitory network issue, or one of the site servers (or a site database server) could be down. Change tracking has a rolling buffer to cater for these sorts of outages. By default, this rolling buffer is configured to store 5 days' worth of data. You can configure the data retention value from 1 to 14 days via the Database properties for the site database in the ConfigMgr console under **Monitoring -> Database Replication -> Parent Database Properties** (or **Child Database Properties**, depending on the server you are changing). Figure 3.17 shows the default configuration for a CAS database.

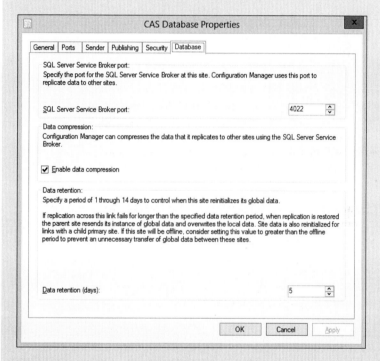

FIGURE 3.17   Data retention setting on a CAS's database properties in the ConfigMgr console.

Notice the lengthy text describing this setting in Figure 3.17. By default, there is potential data loss in scenarios where an outage lasts longer than 5 days. Changes that occurred more than 5 days ago are lost, as SQL Server change tracking has a default retention of 5 days. DRS therefore knows it has some missing data (that occurred after the 5-day mark) and cannot trust any of the data sent or received since that truncation occurred (even if only a single day). When this occurs, the site goes through a process of reinitialization. Much as with initial setup, data is extracted from the parent and child database, sent via the file replication (SMB) method to each site, and inserted in bulk into the receiving database. Replication can continue from there via DRS.

As each site is authoritative for its own data and the CAS is authoritative for global data, there is minimal potential for overlap. There is a *potential for* data loss in scenarios where administrators begin editing global data or objects (applications, client settings, software update deployments, and so on) at the child primary site. In practice, administrators may unknowingly do this to allow client operations to continue to function during a replication outage. It is necessary to do so only when you are sure you can restore communication via the two sites within the data retention period. If this is not possible and the replication between the two sites is down for over 5 days, any changes to global data made at the primary site are overwritten by changes from the CAS. This overwriting occurs because ConfigMgr reinitialized DRS between the two sites, and the CAS's export overwrites all global data at the primary site, regardless of who modified the data (because the CAS is authoritative for global data).

About Content Replication

To enable content replication, ConfigMgr uses SMB to copy files from one site server to another site server. This is generally from the CAS to its child primary sites. You could create content directly on a child primary site and have it replicate up, although using this method causes additional replication lag and is less efficient due to replication up to the CAS and back down again to the other child primary sites in the hierarchy. Chapter 5, "Network Design," and Chapter 14 cover content replication in more detail.

Active Directory Integration with ConfigMgr

AD (or, more formally, Active Directory Domain Services [ADDS]) is the central information store used by Windows Server to maintain entity and relationship data for a wide variety of objects in a networked environment. It provides a set of core services, including authentication, authorization, and directory services. ConfigMgr utilizes ADDS to support many of its features.

> **NOTE: SCHEMA EXTENSIONS AND CONFIGMGR UPDATES**
>
> The ConfigMgr 2007 and ConfigMgr 2012 schema extensions are unchanged. If you extended the AD schema for ConfigMgr 2007 or ConfigMgr 2012, you do not need to run the ConfigMgr Current Branch schema extensions.

ConfigMgr uses ADDS implicitly to support authentication and authorization through the use of computer accounts, primarily through use of the Local System account, and optionally with service accounts to perform certain operations. ConfigMgr can also use published information about its sites and services, making that information easily accessible to ADDS clients. ConfigMgr clients treat AD as a trusted location for obtaining information to confirm the identity of a site's MPs. To take advantage of these capabilities, you must extend the AD schema to create classes of objects specific to ConfigMgr.

While it is not necessary to extend the schema for ConfigMgr operations, it is required for certain ConfigMgr features. Extending the schema greatly simplifies ConfigMgr deployment and operations. The following section discusses the process of extending the AD schema. Chapter 4 discusses the benefits and feature dependencies of the extended schema and why you might want to include schema extensions in your design.

Implementing Schema Extensions

All objects in ADDS are instances of classes defined in the ADDS schema. The schema provides definitions for common objects such as users, computers, and printers. The schema also defines attributes used to describe objects. The schema is extensible, allowing administrators and applications to define new object classes and modify existing classes for an organization's instance of AD. The ConfigMgr schema extensions are relatively low risk, involving only a specific set of classes with specific object and attribute names that are not likely to cause conflict. However, you should test any schema modifications before applying them to your production environment.

CAUTION: ABOUT CHANGING THE SCHEMA

Schema modifications are a one-way operation and cannot be reversed. At best, schema modification can be deactivated. It is important to have a *working* (that is, *restorable*) backup of AD in case you need to perform an authoritative restore. For more information on the impact of AD schema extensions and modifications, see https://msdn.microsoft.com/library/ms677103.aspx.

You may want to suspend replication on the schema master while performing a schema modification; in the event of an error during schema application, another server can seize the schema master role, and the old schema master can be rebuilt from backup. For this reason, you should avoid performing schema modifications over unreliable connections.

Before actually extending the schema for ConfigMgr, run the dcdiag and repladmin commands included as part of the Domain Controller role in Windows Server. These tools validate that all domain controllers are replicating and healthy. Because it may be difficult to validate the output of these tools, output the results to a text file by using the following syntax:

```
dcdiag > %temp%\dcdiag.log
```

In the case of repladmin, the following syntax (all on one line) helps to validate the state of replication:

```
repadmin /replsum /bysrc /bydest /sort:delta > %temp%\repladmin.log
```

Review the output of the repladmin command to ensure that all domain controllers show no replication failures (that is, 0 in the `Fails` column). For more information on how to perform schema changes, see https://msdn.microsoft.com/library/windows/desktop/ms676929.aspx.

After you extend the ADDS schema and perform the other steps necessary to publish site information to ADDS, ConfigMgr sites can publish information to ADDS. The next sections describe the process for extending the schema and configuring sites to publish to AD, as well as the AD objects and attributes created by the schema extensions.

Tools for Extending a Schema

You can extend a schema in either of two ways:

▶ Running the ExtADSch.exe utility from the ConfigMgr installation media

▶ Using the LDIFDE (Lightweight Directory Access Protocol [LDAP] Data Interchange Format Directory Exchange) utility included with Windows Server to import the ConfigMgr_ad_schema.ldf LDIF file

To use all the features of ConfigMgr, you must use AD with a Windows Server 2008 or later domain functional level. All site systems must be members of a Windows Server AD domain that meets that domain functional level (though it does not need to be the same domain or in some cases the same forest). ConfigMgr clients may be joined to a workgroup or a domain. For a complete list of Active Directory support requirements, see https://docs.microsoft.com/sccm/core/plan-design/configs/support-for-active-directory-domains.

Using ExtADSch

Using ExtADSch.exe is the simplest way to extend a schema. Simply run it with the appropriate permissions, and ExtADSch.exe creates a log file called extadsch.log, located in the root of the system drive (*%systemdrive%*), which lists all schema modifications it has made and the status of the operation. Following the list of attributes that have been created, the log should include the entry `Successfully extended the Active Directory schema.`

Using LDIFDE

LDIFDE is a powerful command-line utility for extracting and updating directory service data on ADDS domain controllers. LDIFDE provides command-line switches that allow you to specify a number of options, including some you may want to use when updating the schema for ConfigMgr.

Find detailed information about using LDIFDE at https://docs.microsoft.com/previous-versions/windows/it-pro/windows-server-2012-R2-and-2012/cc731033(v=ws.11) and ConfigMgr-specific instructions at https://docs.microsoft.com/sccm/core/plan-design/network/extend-the-active-directory-schema. The following example is a typical command to update the schema for ConfigMgr:

```
LDIFDE -i -f - ConfigMgr_ad_schema.ldf -v -j %temp%\SchemaUpdate.log
```

The verbose logging available with LDIFDE includes more detail than the log file generated by ExtADSch.exe. The ConfigMgr_ad_schema.ldf file allows you to review all intended changes before they are applied, or you can provide the ConfigMgr_ad_schema.ldf to your Active Directory administrators for them to review if required.

Extending a Schema

Each AD forest has a single domain controller with the role of schema master. All schema modifications are made on the schema master. To modify the schema, log on using an account in the forest root domain that is a member of the Schema Admins group.

NOTE: ABOUT THE SCHEMA ADMINS GROUP

The built-in Schema Admins group exists in the root domain of your forest. Normally there should not be any user accounts in the Schema Admins group. To protect the schema from any accidental modifications, only add accounts to Schema Admins temporarily when you need to modify the schema.

The ConfigMgr schema modifications create 4 new classes and 14 new attributes used with these classes. The classes represent the following:

▶ **Management Points (MS-SMS-Management-Point):** Clients can use this information to find a management point and confirm the identity of a management point in case the policy signing key changes (for example, during a site recovery).

▶ **Roaming Boundary Ranges (MS-SMS-Roaming-Boundary-Range):** Clients can use this information to locate ConfigMgr services based on their network location.

▶ **Server Locator Points (MS-SMS-Server-Locator-Point):** This legacy class is created but not used as part of ConfigMgr Current Branch schema extensions. It was used in ConfigMgr 2007 to enable clients to find an SLP and determine their assigned site. The SLP role no longer exists; its functionality has been integrated into the MP.

▶ **ConfigMgr Sites (MS-SMS-Site):** Clients can retrieve important information about the site from this AD object.

Objects and attributes in the ConfigMgr schema modification are prefixed with MS-SMS, which helps minimize the risk of collisions with other custom or application-specific schema extensions. In addition, all objects and attributes in the schema have the isMemberOfPartialAttributeSet flag set to True. This flag causes instances of these objects and attributes to be included as part of the partial attribute set and marked for replication to all global catalog domain controllers in the forest. This allows a site server that is a member of a domain to advertise its existence to all clients in the forest instead of just that domain.

Summary

This chapter provided a view into the internals of Configuration Manager. It described the architecture along with external components that ConfigMgr relies on. It discussed the communication protocols used to move information around the site and the hierarchy, and it reviewed the internal components to provide an understanding of the key components of a ConfigMgr site.

The chapter discussed WMI and ConfigMgr's utilization of WMI at the server and client levels. This chapter also looked at the ConfigMgr database in depth, providing information on how to view the various SQL Server views available to administrators. A review of replication of content and DRS explains how information is moved through a hierarchy. The chapter also provided a summary of the ConfigMgr schema extensions to ADDS.

PART II

Planning and Installation

IN THIS PART

Architecture Design Planning

This chapter continues the discussion in Chapter 2, "Configuration Manager Overview," and Chapter 3, "Looking Inside Configuration Manager." It covers the requirements gathering, planning, and operational transition required to deliver a successful System Center Configuration Manager (ConfigMgr) deployment and provides a starting point and overview for later chapters. The chapter discusses all areas required for a new deployment and contains helpful information for those upgrading to ConfigMgr Current Branch.

Developing the Solution Architecture

ConfigMgr Current Branch is designed to continue the flexibility and configurability of Microsoft's flagship change and configuration management product, while dealing with a rapidly evolving world. Like any other technology, ConfigMgr must be delivered as a solution to your business and technical requirements. You must determine your organization's goals, the current state of your environment, and current constraints of your information technology (IT) service delivery capability. You can then fit ConfigMgr into your solution rather than fitting your solution to technology. Figure 4.1 summarizes the planning and design process. Note that the "Test and Stabilize" phase in Figure 4.1 is not covered in this chapter, but testing should be included as part of a ConfigMgr deployment project to ensure technical readiness and that the design meets functional requirements.

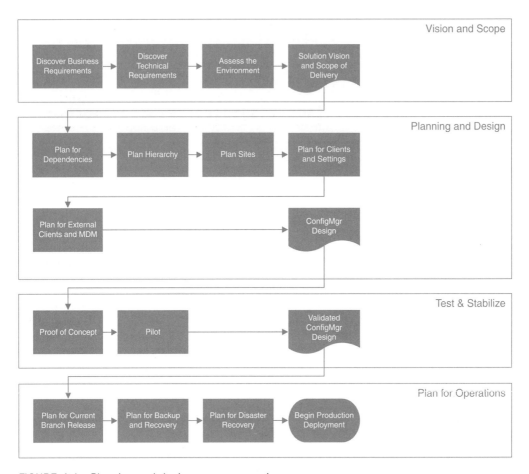

FIGURE 4.1   Planning and design process overview.

Discovering Business Requirements

The most important requirements to consider are those of the business. These vary from one organization to another and are heavily dependent on the business's industry alignment. For example, the needs of a university vary from those of a retail bank or a consumer packaged goods manufacturer. Attitudes to risk, willingness to adopt new ways of working, and overall views of technology also differ between industries.

It may be difficult to determine business requirements for a management product such as ConfigMgr. Business requirements are often IT or technical requirements masquerading as requirements for the business. For example, security requirements are not business requirements. While adhering to the compliance and regulatory environment in which the business operates is a business requirement and security requirements may underpin that, implementing security updates is not something the business may even care about.

Following are areas to explore with your business representatives as potential sources of requirements:

▶ **User Experience:** User experience is often overlooked in requirements. There could be requirements around availability. For example, an emergency 911 call center might require that no more than 15% of users be offline at any time. For an investment bank, the requirement could be that trading desk devices are online during market hours plus one hour before and one hour after trading. Another requirement could be whether there are minimal prompts or whether prompts are always provided, putting the user in control. Formally tracking these requirements helps counterbalance them against software updates compliance and other requirements.

▶ **Speed of Delivery or Availability of (Other) Services:** Certain businesses require speed of delivery for various functions of ConfigMgr. A business relying heavily on field sales staff may require that operating system deployments be completed in two hours to refresh a laptop or tablet, minimizing the time spent by sales staff in the office away from customers. This objective may then be tied to requiring infrastructure in field offices to be capable of delivering images at appropriate speeds.

▶ **Cost Controls:** Business pressures may force IT to minimize capital expenditures or costs in general; factor this into the solution architecture as a business requirement. While these pressures are often mentioned during project discussions, you should call them out with the nature of the required cost controls. If reducing capital expenditures is a priority, hosting ConfigMgr in Microsoft Azure Infrastructure as a Service (IaaS) might be ideal.

Alternatively, the business might consider a special capital expenditure but may want to avoid fixed/regular operational expenditures. Perhaps your networks are charged based on bandwidth consumption (4G/3G) or with bandwidth caps (satellite links); understanding the business impact of exceeding those limits and corresponding costs for more bandwidth and possible lost business due to an outage is another important cost control business requirement.

These constraints might manifest themselves as enabling a line manager to manage software asset management expenditures; having ConfigMgr feed an asset management system could help with that requirement.

▶ **Compliance and Regulatory Issues:** Most businesses are subject to some compliance or regulatory requirements, which might impact the ConfigMgr solution. Payment Card Industry (PCI) compliance comes into play in retail companies, banks, and other service organizations processing payment cards. PCI requires that you address security vulnerabilities either through vendor-supplied (for example, operating system) updates or compensating controls. Government and public-sector organizations may have regulatory requirements, such as those placed on local governments to access state/provincial or federal systems. These could include validation of security configuration and updates.

▶ **Consumerization of IT:** Over time, business users and the public have become increasingly tech savvy, and new employees' expectations of IT service are drastically different from what they once were. Depending on the industry of the business or parts of the business, there could be expectations of a highly user-centric service where end users "pull" services when required or convenient rather than having those services pushed on them. The business may need to have a consumer model of IT services to ensure that it can hire the best and brightest. If the competition provides a better IT service that enables an employee to be more productive, the employee may go there instead.

Discovering IT Requirements

After you capture business requirements, focus on IT requirements. These should include technical requirements such as delivering 98% patch compliance. They also should encompass service delivery or IT/information systems (IS) business requirements, such as minimizing the number of help desk tickets raised during deployment of a key line of business (LOB) application. IT requirements should be distinct from business requirements, although there may be overlap or a certain business requirement could lead to an IT requirement. As an example, PCI compliance as a business key requirement to continue allowing customers to buy your products with a credit card may lead to IT security requiring a 99.9% patch compliance level on servers. These could also be in direct conflict with one another—patching all systems in 48 hours while the business demands that no more than 5% of staff be unable to work at any one time due to IT processes.

Conflicting or complementary requirements are not issues; they are points of discussion in a design workshop. These key discussions should occur up front and should be ratified to ensure that the project continues smoothly through to delivery.

The following are some suggested areas to explore for requirements:

▶ **IT Security:** This may include health attestation prior to resource access (conditional access), update compliance requirements, antimalware, or security configuration management.

▶ **Service Availability:** This may include the availability of the solution itself as well as the need for the solution to not affect availability of other solutions (for example, do not take more than 50% of a cluster offline for patching).

▶ **Cloud Consumption/Adoption:** This is an IT requirement, but it is an important one. Cloud adoption tends to manifest itself in various ways. It includes consumption of services using in-house private cloud or via private cloud service providers, as well as consumption of public cloud IaaS models such as Amazon Web Services (AWS) and Microsoft Azure (particularly with ConfigMgr Current Branch's support for Microsoft Azure). This is typically reflected in a requirement around hosting ConfigMgr infrastructure in a cloud-based (private or public) fabric.

▶ **Desktop OS Supportability:** A ConfigMgr deployment is often tied to an upgrade to the standard operating system (OS) offering. Previously this might have been moving from Windows XP supported by ConfigMgr 2007 to Windows 7 supported by ConfigMgr 2012. This also holds true with Windows 10, as Windows 10 Semi-Annual Channel after release 1511 requires use of ConfigMgr Current Branch. There is a saying that "if you want to go fast with Windows, you need to go fast with ConfigMgr." The platform being managed cannot outpace the product that manages it.

Assessing Your Environment

The last set of requirements are implicit environmental ones. These are the realities of delivering the solution, and they include the following:

▶ **Organizational Structure:** Is your IT organization centrally managed or delivered via a service provider model that requires centralized administrative oversight? Alternatively, is your business split into separate companies, each with its own discrete IT organization that requires complete autonomy?

▶ **IT Service Delivery Processes:** Does your IT organization have existing configuration management processes in place? Does that include a configuration management database (CMDB)? Are there change and release management processes in place? What information must be provided to those processes and associated systems?

▶ **Service Level Agreements (SLAs):** What SLAs have been agreed upon and must continue to be delivered? Is there scope to change them if needed? Are there underpinning agreements with associated teams, vendors, suppliers, or service providers?

▶ **Dependent IT Teams:** What teams will you depend on to deliver the solution and ultimately the service itself once operational? What teams are dependent on your solution and service?

▶ **Datacenters and Server Infrastructure:** Where are your datacenters or computing centers? Are there different classes of datacenters? What defines these classes? Are there known limitations within the datacenters (for example, limited network speed), or is the storage area network (SAN) running out of disk enclosure space?

▶ **Virtualization and Cloud Computing:** Is this used? If so, how is storage subsystem performance ensured for virtual machines (VMs)? Are there any limits on VM size in terms of memory or CPU?

▶ **Operating Systems and Device Types:** What supported operating systems are in use? What types of Windows devices are used, and what is the ratio of desktops, laptops, and tablets? Are mobile devices being managed? What platforms are used? What are your device usage scenarios? This might include kiosk usage, shared devices with one device for multiple users, personal devices, shift workers, and embedded systems.

▶ **Network Topology:** Does your network operate a hub-and-spoke model for wide area network (WAN) connectivity? Are there regional network hubs? Are there common contention points, meaning areas of the WAN where multiple point-to-point connections converge onto a single link that is a lower speed than the sum of the individual point-to-point links? How is Internet access provided to mobile devices? Are there Internet-connected offices? Chapter 5, "Network Design," discusses additional network planning considerations for ConfigMgr.

▶ **Active Directory Configuration:** What does your Active Directory Domain Services (ADDS) look like? Do you have a single forest with multiple domains? A single domain? Multiple forests? Are cross-forest trusts in place? Is Active Directory Certificate Services (ADCS) deployed to provide a public key infrastructure (PKI)? Is it an enterprise ADCS deployment?

▶ **Enterprise Storage:** Is there a centralized storage solution? What tiers of storage are provided in terms of capacity versus performance? What information does the storage team require to provision storage?

▶ **Server Management and Monitoring:** What backup solution is available for ConfigMgr? Does this include SQL Server backup capabilities? Is an enterprise monitoring solution available? Does that solution provide its own monitoring definition, or is an off-the-shelf definition available for ConfigMgr?

As part of the solution delivery, once the high- and low-level designs are in place, you may want to map the service in the context of the overall IT environment. Understand and diagram the dependent services, software, infrastructure, and teams that support them. At a basic level, when these underpinning components fail or are degraded, ConfigMgr as a service fails or is degraded. Include the services and solutions that depend on ConfigMgr; that is, if ConfigMgr fails or is degraded, the services or solutions that will also fail.

Defining these environmental requirements in advance ensures a smooth transition from project delivery into service delivery or production operations, with a clear set of roles and responsibilities for problem and incident management.

Envisioning the Solution and Scope of Delivery

The next element of delivery is packaging the requirements together in a vision and scope document. This document is a first attempt for an architecture and strategy and addresses the remainder of the design and planning phases. It should rationalize the requirements discussed in a design workshop and highlight those requiring additional discussion and investigation. An example might be that the document could establish key priorities and preferences for the solution, such as whether user-centric computing is a priority or whether minimal prompts and interaction are preferred.

Planning for Infrastructure Dependencies

This section looks at infrastructure dependencies for the ConfigMgr solution, specifically around Active Directory (AD). The section is an important early step in your architectural design, as you should understand what external dependencies exist prior to working on the solution. These constraints affect how you can meet the requirements. After establishing the dependencies, you can begin to look at how to architect the ConfigMgr solution, as discussed in the "Hierarchy Planning in ConfigMgr" section, later in this chapter. Chapter 5 provides information about network infrastructure dependencies.

ADDS Considerations

ADDS is required for ConfigMgr, which does not install unless the site server is a member of an AD domain. The following sections discuss other AD requirements.

Deciding Whether to Extend the AD Schema

For a new ConfigMgr deployment, you should decide whether to extend the AD schema. Chapter 3 discusses these schema changes. This chapter looks at reasons for making a substantive change to your AD forest(s). The decision workflow in Figure 4.2 summarizes the reasons to extend the AD schema.

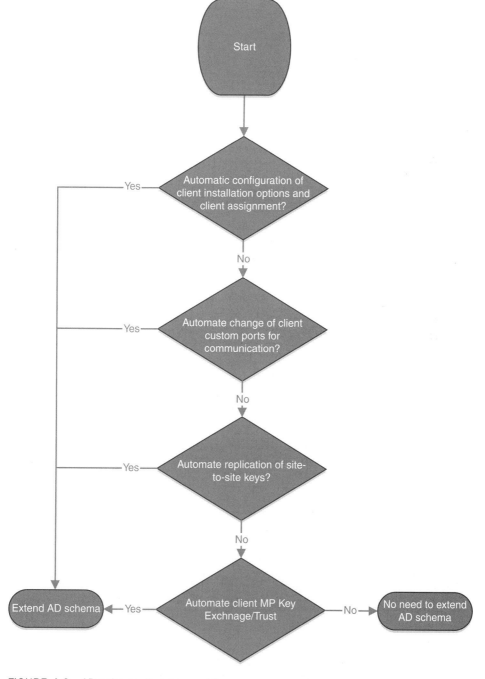

FIGURE 4.2   AD schema decision workflow.

The schema extensions, which enable AD integration with ConfigMgr, allow clients to use a trusted source to look up information. When the clients are newly installed or there has been a significant servicing operation (usually recovery of a site), having this information can significantly ease deployment or recovery. The client may use AD in the following ways:

▶ **Client Installation and Site Assignment:** Clients can query ADDS to determine configurations specific to initial installation, such as log information, initial download cache size, and site assignment information.

NOTE: SITE ASSIGNMENT WITHOUT EXTENDING THE SCHEMA

If the schema is not extended, site assignment requires specifying a site code as a command line parameter, either by supplying a management point (MP) or Domain Name System (DNS) domain name. Specifying the DNS domain name requires enabling publishing site information to DNS in the site configuration.

You also cannot customize the command line parameters for the Windows Server Update Services (WSUS) client installation method, which is useful as it does not require pushing to clients—as the client machines pull the ConfigMgr agent.

▶ **Custom Port Configurations for Clients:** Custom configurations can allow a client to obtain a port number from ADDS at installation time. If the port changes later, the client can find the new configuration in ADDS. Not publishing site information would require deploying a script to these devices to change their port configuration or reinstalling the client with a new port configuration.

▶ **Client MP Key Exchange:** This allows clients to obtain the site server's public key to confirm the signature on policies from the MP and occurs automatically during installation. However, when the site server's public key changes, such as when the site server is reinstalled, the client cannot verify the re-signed policies. This is security feature is meant to prevent injecting policy from an untrusted source. Not publishing this information to ADDS means you must reinstall any clients installed before the key changed.

ConfigMgr site servers also use the AD schema extensions for content file-based replication key exchange, which allows site servers in a hierarchy to read public key information for the source site server that replicated content to it. If not published to ADDS, site public keys are manually exchanged using the preinst.exe (hierarchy maintenance) tool. This key is reset whenever a site is recovered (specifically, when the site server is reinstalled as part of a recovery operation), which means preinst.exe must be run to exchange the new keys in order for content to replicate.

Multi-Forest and Workgroup Considerations

A ConfigMgr site can manage workgroup clients and clients in trusted and untrusted AD forests. By default, workgroup clients require manual approval in the console, as—unlike domain member computers—they do not have a computer account and cannot be authenticated by the MP. You can also configure clients to be approved without authentication, but this means potentially sensitive policies (such as task sequences with domain joint credentials stored with reversible encryption) would be delivered to clients that cannot first be authenticated. In addition, if you plan to use packages and programs from a file share directly on a workgroup client, you must have one or more network access accounts (NAAs) configured. This is because the Local System security principal on a workgroup client, which is the context under which the ConfigMgr agent runs, would not have permissions to access Internet Information Services (IIS) or file shares on distribution points (DPs) that are domain member servers. The NAA allows this to occur.

For clients in other forests, client communications depend on whether site systems are installed in that forest or whether a cross-forest trust is in place. If neither is the case, the clients in the untrusted forest are effectively treated as workgroup clients, as the ConfigMgr site systems cannot authenticate the computer accounts. Authentication occurs using a specific subpath on the MP website, even though the rest of the MP website allows anonymous access. This is done to validate whether a client is from a trusted domain and thus known to AD. When a cross-forest trust is in place, the clients have their authentication to the site systems routed through the trust to domain controllers (DCs) in the clients' forest via the trust.

If you cannot establish a trust, ConfigMgr supports placing site systems in a remote untrusted forest. This is possible for most site systems and all client-facing site systems.

Clients prefer talking to MPs and DPs in their own forest. You can install remote site systems in an untrusted forest to enable clients to authenticate against site systems in their own forest. The site server uses a site system connection account to connect to the remote site system in the untrusted forest; this domain account is in the untrusted forest. If the remote site system requires database access (for example, MP, Software Catalog, or Preboot eXecution Environment [PXE]-enabled DP), the remote site system must be provided with a site database access account, which would be created in the forest of the site server. This configuration allows the remote site system to authenticate to SQL Server and read information from the site database.

> **NOTE: UNTRUSTED FORESTS AND CONFIGMGR**
>
> AD forests are the security boundary for AD, completely isolating one forest from another. In and of itself, a trust does not breach that trust boundary, as enterprise administrators in one forest cannot affect a trusted forest, and users from the trusted forest must still be granted permissions to a resource in order to access the resource.
>
> Deploying a single ConfigMgr hierarchy may implicitly bridge a security boundary, depending on where the ConfigMgr agent is deployed in the untrusted forest. When the ConfigMgr agent is installed on DCs or most clients in a domain, it provides ConfigMgr with administrative control over systems where the agent is installed (using Local System privileges). This control implies a level of trust of the ConfigMgr administrators and domain admins of the AD domain to which the ConfigMgr site servers belong. If you are not able to create a cross-forest trust in your environment, consider the security implications of a single hierarchy between those two forests and determine whether creating the trust would be less of a security concern.

In addition to remote site systems, ConfigMgr can publish information to trusted and untrusted AD forests. Add the forest to your hierarchy from **Administration -> Hierarchy Configuration**, right-click **Active Directory Forests**, and choose **Add Forest**. Figure 4.3 shows the Add Forest dialog, which allows you to configure both forest discovery and publishing. For trusted forests, you can use the site server's computer account to write to the trusted forest, assuming that the appropriate permissions are granted to the System Management container. You can also specify an account in the forest being configured for publishing or discovery. By configuring publishing to remote forests, you allow clients in those forests (both trusted and untrusted) to discover hierarchy resources.

When deploying to a user collection or using user device affinity, ensure that AD User Discovery is configured. AD User Discovery is required for these two features to work, as it allows ConfigMgr to match up client- and server-side user information. This means you cannot use these features for users with devices in workgroups. You must use an LDAP query to discover users with devices in untrusted forests. This is also necessary with computers when using AD System Discovery. If you plan to use ConfigMgr's on-premise mobile device enrollment capabilities and have users in untrusted forests, configure an enrollment point in the user's forest to support this feature.

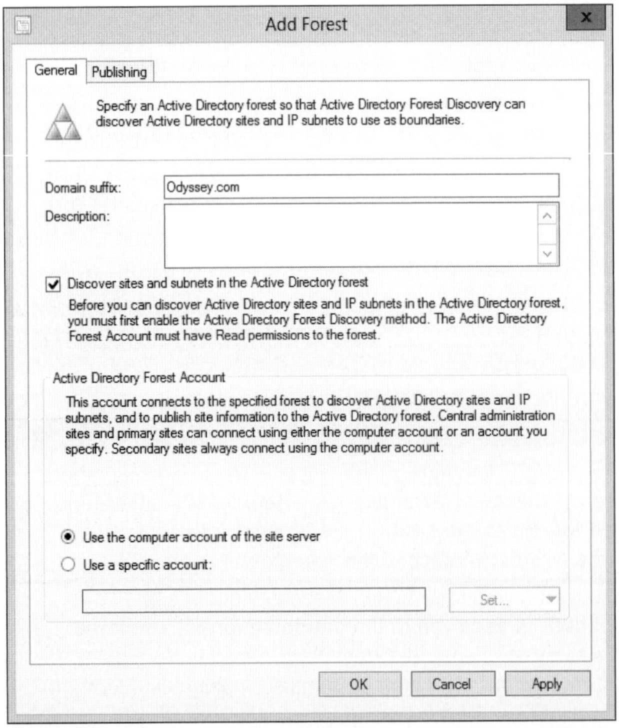

FIGURE 4.3   The Add Forest dialog.

TIP: AD DISCOVERY METHODS AND NAME RESOLUTION

AD User Discovery and AD System Discovery have several name resolution requirements when dealing with remote untrusted forests. One is the ability to resolve the DCs in that forest; in addition, for AD System Discovery, the site server must be able to resolve the IP address of the computer being discovered (that is, the client PC).

For each AD location, you can specify an account to perform the AD queries. For untrusted forests, this can be an account in that forest. However, if name resolution does not work, discovery will fail even with a valid account, as the site server cannot find a DC to run the query against. DNS name resolution may not have been configured for the untrusted forest. Configure DNS in the site server's domain to forward to the untrusted forest's domain's DNS or configure the hosts file on the site server to resolve one of the DCs in the remote forest. The authors do not recommend using a hosts file, as it is a static mapping, must be manually maintained, and breaks if the IP address of the chosen DC changes.

Installing the ConfigMgr Agent on Workgroup Clients   Workgroup clients cannot utilize the AD schema extensions or use group policy. However, these clients must be able to find and trust an MP. You can use the command line to configure workgroup clients to trust a specific MP and site; or you can publish a site's MPs to DNS, enabling them to be located by clients. MP lookup occurs automatically when the Publish Selected Intranet Management Points in DNS check box is checked in the Management Point Component properties, which causes records to be published to the MP's DNS server if it supports dynamic registration of DNS SRV records. An SRV record can be manually registered when dynamic publishing is not possible or if the workgroup client uses a different DNS infrastructure. For information on configuring these DNS records, see https://docs.microsoft.com/sccm/core/plan-design/hierarchy/ understand-how-clients-find-site-resources-and-services.

You must use the DNSSUFFIX command-line switch during client installation, which limits the client installation methods available in your design. If DNS cannot be configured (for example, if you have a client in the demilitarized zone [DMZ] of a network using an ISP's DNS servers), use the SMSMP command-line switch during client installation to tell the client which MP to use for its initial connection.

Establishing client trust of the MP and site to which it is assigned occurs automatically when the client communicates to the MP during installation, as the MP returns a trusted root key for the hierarchy. The client can then verify the signatures on all policies subsequently sent to it from this MP or other MPs. The client implicitly trusts the first MP it communicates with when the AD schema is not extended or AD is not accessible (for example, workgroup clients). This may be undesirable in secure or high-risk environments; in this case, use the SMSROOTKEYPATH property to hard-code the key as part of the installation command-line.

For more information on command-line options, see https://docs.microsoft.com/sccm/core/clients/deploy/about-client-installation-properties. For information on client installation and management, see Chapter 9, "Client Management."

Installing the ConfigMgr Agent on Azure AD Join Systems   Windows 10 introduces a new computer membership option outside of workgroup or AD domain join, known as Azure AD Join (AADJ). Using AADJ is an alternative to joining a computer to on-premise AD. It is similar to Workplace Join in Windows 8.1 (called the Add a Work or School Account feature in Windows 10), except it replaces a workgroup or domain join and provides a method for the end user to directly log in to Azure AD rather than to a local computer user account or an on-premise domain user account. There are also differences in terms of single sign-on to Azure AD protected Software as a Service (SaaS) applications. AADJ is primarily designed for use with the built-in mobile device management (MDM) components of Windows 10 and, thus, management through Microsoft Intune.

You can install the ConfigMgr agent on an AADJ device. In this scenario and based on the current release of ConfigMgr when this book was published, the client should be treated as a workgroup client for the purposes of AD discovery methods, deployments, and the other capabilities listed in the "Installing the ConfigMgr Agent on Workgroup Clients" section, earlier in this chapter.

Active Directory Certificate Services Considerations

Certain ConfigMgr Current Branch features and capabilities require PKI-issued certificates. You may use any x.509 PKI implementation that supports version 3 certificates; however, Internet-based client management (IBCM) requires issuing certificates to all your client computers. For this reason, using a Microsoft Enterprise PKI based on Windows Server ADCS is the simplest approach as auto enrollment can be configured using AD group policy. Third-party certificates services and managed PKI offerings also support client computer-initiated certificates, which often mimic ADCS certificate authorities.

The following ConfigMgr features depend on PKI-issued certificates:

▶ **HTTPS Encryption and Authentication of Client Communication:** See Chapter 9 for more information.

▶ **Management of Client Devices on the Internet without Using a VPN:** Client certs are used to authenticate Internet-based clients when connecting to ConfigMgr without the use of a virtual private network (VPN). This applies to both IBCM and the cloud management gateway (CMG). As an alternative, if you have deployed Azure AD, clients can authenticate to CMG with their Azure identity as of ConfigMgr Current Branch 1706.

▶ **On-Premise MDM:** MDM supports Windows 10 and legacy embedded systems. It requires an enrollment certificate on each device for mutual authentication and SSL communication with the site systems.

▶ **Certificate Deployment Profiles:** These profiles require a PKI to issue certificates either via Simple Certificate Enrollment Protocol or distribution of a Public-Key Cryptography Standards #12 (PKCS #12) file. On Windows, a PKCS #12 file is also known as Personal Information Exchange (PFX) file.

ConfigMgr also leverages various cryptographic functions to support various internal processes, including the following:

▶ **Client Policy Signing:** All client policies are signed by the site server. The self-generated key is created at site installation and re-created during a site recovery. The key is called the *trusted root key*; the public portion of the key is published to AD. See Chapter 3 for more details.

▶ **Custom Update Signing:** Custom software updates must be signed by a publisher. The certificate must be trusted for installation of updates by the Windows Update Agent (implemented using the Trusted Publisher certificate store); ConfigMgr clients require a valid digital certificate for installation.

▶ **Inventory Signing:** Clients by default sign their inventory and state messages with a self-signed certificate unless enabled for HTTPS, when they utilize the PKI-issued certificate used to communicate with the MP. Clients can be configured to encrypt their inventory and state messages; this is independent of encryption at the transport layer using HTTPS.

▶ **Site-to-site Communication:** Site servers use keys to ensure the integrity of intersite file replication. DRS uses certificates stored in SQL Server to authenticate SQL Server Service Broker (SSB) endpoints.

For a comprehensive list of cryptographic controls maintained by Microsoft, see https:// docs.microsoft.com/sccm/protect/deploy-use/cryptographic-controls-technical-reference.

If you are planning to leverage HTTPS for client communication or Internet-based clients using IBCM, review Microsoft's published list of required certificate properties at https://docs.microsoft.com/sccm/core/plan-design/security/plan-for-security#BKMK_PlanningForCertificates.

It may be that your organization's PKI was not designed to accommodate deploying client authentication certificates to a large number of client machines. Reasons may include the following:

▶ **High-Assurance PKI:** The PKI may be designed for high assurance. High-assurance PKI is designed to provide parties accepting certificates with a high level of confidence over identity validation that occurs as part of their issuance. These types of PKI may have a manual certificate approval process that requires a human approver to approve each certificate. This prevents the bulk issuance of certs to computer systems, as the same level of confidence and assurance cannot be provided, and manual overhead would be prohibitive.

▶ **Manual Review of Certificate Requests:** There may be operational processes that require manual review of all certificate requests. This would significantly hamper issuing one certificate per PC.

▶ **Scalability of the PKI:** The PKI may have been architected to support hundreds and not thousands of requests. Windows systems where the ConfigMgr client runs not only need an initial certificate but must renew certificates regularly.

▶ **Costs of Certificate Issuance:** The PKI may be provided as a managed service or outsourced, meaning there may be fixed contractual costs associated with certificate issuance and management, which would make use of the PKI very expensive and completely invalidate any value from ConfigMgr features that rely on those certificates (especially ConfigMgr client certificates).

Consider deploying a low-assurance PKI designed specifically to issue bulk certificates for computer systems and integrated with AD. This PKI could be limited to only issuing client authentication certificates and could be automatically trusted only by internal AD domain-joined systems. This approach allows you to leverage the features of ConfigMgr that require PKI certificates (such as IBCM and HTTPS client communication) without impacting the existing PKI, reducing that PKI's assurance level, and incurring per-certificate costs.

Hierarchy Planning in ConfigMgr

After establishing your objectives, constraints, and infrastructure prerequisites, you can start working on the ConfigMgr design tasks. The first design consideration should be determining how to structure your hierarchy. A hierarchy may be as simple as a single site with associated site systems or as complex as a central administration site (CAS) with over a dozen primary sites. ConfigMgr does not allow logically removing or moving primary sites within a hierarchy, so you should spend some time up front determining what structure meets your organization's requirements. Do not configure a CAS simply because you might need it in the future; ConfigMgr allows you to add a CAS to a standalone primary site and add new primary sites.

Chapter 2 introduced the concept of ConfigMgr hierarchies. Sites in a hierarchy share replicated data, security policy, and administrator-created objects (software updates, boundaries, and so on). A single primary site can be a hierarchy, as it may have secondary sites underneath it. Within a hierarchy are certain site system roles that are hierarchywide and support hierarchywide functions, such as the service connection point (SCP).

ConfigMgr Current Branch supports migration from ConfigMgr 2007. Like ConfigMgr 2012, it cannot support 2007 sites in its hierarchy. ConfigMgr Current Branch also supports migration from ConfigMgr 2012 SP 2 or 2012 R2 SP 1. For these versions, it also supports in-place upgrading to Current Branch. It is more common to upgrade from these versions than to migrate to Current Branch. For more information on migration, see Chapter 7, "Upgrading and Migrating to ConfigMgr Current Branch."

Microsoft regularly updates ConfigMgr Current Branch. Microsoft currently plans to release updates three times a year. Each update is supported for 12 months, and the latest critical (but non-security) updates always go into the latest updates. This means you should take care in your design to keep your ConfigMgr hierarchies and site infrastructure as simple as possible, as the team operating ConfigMgr in your organization must regularly update them. This is similar to the approximately quarterly release cycle of cumulative updates in ConfigMgr 2012; while the cumulative updates did not define support, as part of a support case, Microsoft Support would likely request that you upgrade to the latest cumulative update.

About Configuration Manager Sites

Every site system and client is part of a site. Each site has a site server, a site database, an SMS provider, and an alphanumeric three-character site code. The site code must be unique throughout the hierarchy and across hierarchies where multiple hierarchies share the same AD forest. There are three different types of sites in ConfigMgr: the CAS, primary sites, and secondary sites. The next sections describe these different types of sites.

CAUTION: RESTRICTIONS AND REUSE OF SITE CODES

You should avoid certain names when selecting site codes. These include reserved names such as AUX, CON, NUL, PRN, and SMS. For more information and a list of reserved names, see https://msdn.microsoft.com/library/aa365247.aspx. You can also use WinObj from Windows Sysinternals (http://technet.microsoft.com/sysinternals) to view reserved names (listed under \GLOBAL in WinObj).

In addition, you should avoid reusing site codes from decommissioned hierarchies, as doing so can lead to issues if references to the old site codes were not removed from AD, DNS, or WINS. Client-side troubleshooting can be complicated if a client tries to talk to a now-decommissioned site and the site code is reused.

The Central Administration Site

The CAS acts as the replication hub for primary sites in a hierarchy and is required only when you have multiple primary sites. You can connect up to 25 primary sites to a single CAS, though in practice this number is much smaller in all but the largest ConfigMgr environments that have hundreds of thousands of clients. The CAS does not manage clients directly, clients cannot be assigned to it, and it cannot have secondary sites directly beneath it.

A CAS should not be used as a "future proofing" mechanism in a design unless there is clear data supporting a future increase in client counts, such as an impending merger or acquisition. You can always add a CAS to a single primary site later.

Primary Sites

Every ConfigMgr client is assigned to a primary site and receives policy from its assigned site. Primary sites are used to scale out managing clients, as each primary site can support up to 150,000 clients per primary site or 175,000 for a standalone primary. Microsoft regularly tests Configuration Manager and may revise these figures; for the latest supported client numbers, see https://docs.microsoft.com/sccm/core/plan-design/configs/supported-operating-systems-for-site-system-servers.

Secondary Sites

A secondary site is a form of proxy site for a primary site. Secondary sites are installed directly from the ConfigMgr console using the site server permissions and are upgraded from the console. These sites have a database like the CAS and primary sites, but it is much smaller, given the relatively limited functionality this site type provides. It does, however, mean that data replication between the site databases must be factored into the decision about whether to deploy a secondary site. The secondary site database can be hosted on SQL Server or, more commonly, SQL Server Express, which is installed automatically by the primary site server during secondary site installation.

A secondary site installs an MP (termed a proxy MP) site system role and commonly also has DP and software update point (SUP) roles. These roles are installed to proxy client requests locally. The secondary site's proxy MP uses the secondary site's database and the Linked Server feature of SQL Server's database engine to query the primary site's database. The proxy MP can then cache client policy requests. The primary design capability a secondary site provides is the ability to host the SUP and allow software update metadata queries to occur locally, which is significant as the results from software update metadata queries may be up to tens of megabytes per client, depending on the OS and software installed.

Chapter 5 provides more information on determining when to opt for a secondary site over a DP.

Hierarchywide Site System Roles

Certain site systems provide services to the entire hierarchy. The following site system roles synchronize with Microsoft services on the Internet, and you can configure them at the top-level site in your hierarchy, either at the CAS or a standalone primary site:

▶ **Asset Intelligence Synchronization Point:** This site system role allows you to request software asset classification data that helps improve reporting on software assets in your environment.

▶ **Endpoint Protection Point:** This role uses System Center Endpoint Protection (SCEP) installation to pull metadata to help populate SCEP reports. It also defines the default Microsoft Active Protection Service (MAPS) participation level. MAPS allows the Endpoint Protection agent to send telemetry data on suspicious behavior to Microsoft and receive dynamic micro-definitions in response. For more information on SCEP, see Chapter 19, "Endpoint Protection."

▶ **Service Connection Point:** The SCP role provides two key functions:

   ▶ For customers using Microsoft Intune integrated with ConfigMgr, the SCP provides the data channel to send and receive information from Intune. For more information on Microsoft Intune, see Chapter 16, "Integrating Intune Hybrid into Your Configuration Manager Environment," and Chapter 17, "Managing Mobile Devices."

   ▶ The SCP is used as the channel to obtain information from Microsoft regarding new releases of ConfigMgr, individual hotfixes/updates, and new features. It is also used to send telemetry information to Microsoft.

▶ **Software Update Point (top-level):** This SUP role pulls metadata from Microsoft Update, and all other SUPs in the hierarchy connect to this SUP to pull metadata. Chapter 15, "Managing Software Updates," discusses the operation of SUPs in more detail.

You should assign these four site system roles to a server with good Internet connectivity. All four roles support communication via web proxy (including authentication) and do not require direct access to the Internet.

You may install other roles at multiple locations throughout the hierarchy. These hierarchywide roles do not have to be deployed at each primary site and can be installed centrally:

▶ **Data Warehouse Service Point:** This role underpins the data warehouse capabilities released in ConfigMgr Current Branch version 1706. The role installs and configures the data warehouse database. It also adds reports that surface the data stored in the data warehouse. The data warehouse stores up to three years' worth of data, up to 2TB.

▶ **Application Catalog Website Point:** This role provides users with access to the software in the application catalog. This is used as a backup location in Current Branch, with the new Software Center (part of the ConfigMgr client) now the primary location for user self-service.

▶ **Application Catalog Web Service Point:** This role provides the middle-tier web services between the application catalog website point and the site database.

▶ **Fallback Status Point:** The Fallback Status Point (FSP) role provides a way for ConfigMgr clients to report communication failures with their assigned MP(s).

The last two roles are hierarchywide and may be deployed to the CAS as well as primary sites:

▶ **System Health Validator Point:** This role helps support Network Access Protection (NAP). NAP is still supported in Configuration Manager Current Branch, although it is deprecated in Windows Server.

▶ **Reporting Services Point:** The Reporting Service Point (RSP) role uses SQL Server Reporting Services (SSRS) to provide reports using data from the ConfigMgr site database. It is commonly installed at the top-level site (that is, the CAS or standalone primary site). You can deploy multiple RSPs within a single site to facilitate administrator access to reporting, allowing certain administrators to be granted additional control over SSRS custom reports. You can also deploy RSPs to lower-level primary sites, restricting access to client-generated data only available at that primary site's site database (in which case all administrator-created objects are accessible). For more information on reporting, see Chapter 21, "Configuration Manager Reporting."

Planning Your Hierarchy Structure

Similar to ConfigMgr 2012, Configuration Manager Current Branch allows a single site to span multiple geographic locations separated by WANs more efficiently than earlier versions of Configuration Manager. The "Planning for Content Management" section, later in this chapter, discusses content distribution, and Chapter 5 explains how to design for various network architectures. ConfigMgr sites no longer serve as boundaries for security, client settings, or network locations.

A well-designed ConfigMgr Current Branch hierarchy is likely to contain far fewer sites than ConfigMgr 2007 or even ConfigMgr 2012. Aim for a design that leverages sites to scale up management until client support numbers force adding more sites. The smaller and flatter a hierarchy, the less complex and easier it is to manage.

A CAS introduces inherent complexities in designs. These include lag in both the downward propagation of object creations and modification, as well as the upward propagation of client information. This means there is up to a 5-minute lag on the creation/modification of an object (deploying an application or update) due to replication. It also means the change of a dynamic or static rule on a collection incurs a minimum delay of up to 10 minutes—5 minutes to replicate the new rule down, and 5 minutes to replicate the changes in the collection backup. There is also collection evaluation time on the primary site to factor into to the end-to-end timing.

In addition to delays introduced by replication, replication between the CAS and all primary sites must remain active and healthy, which introduces additional operational overhead. This differs from a hierarchy composed of a single standalone primary site with secondary sites, which while requiring replication to support content replication and site status reporting, does not require the same level of replication. By default, an outage of more than five days means that replication must be reinitiated and all data synchronized between the two sites experiencing an outage. See Chapter 3 for more details on replication.

Once you determine whether your hierarchy will consist of a CAS and child primary sites or a standalone primary site, you need to determine what the underlying site structure, if any, will look like. Many organizations choose to use a single primary site with remote

DPs. However, there are reasons you might want to have multiple primary sites in your hierarchy, such as the following:

▶ A single primary site supports up to 175,000 clients. If you anticipate having more than 175,000 clients, plan for more primary sites. A single primary site in a hierarchy supports only 150,000 clients. Check the latest client support numbers at https://docs.microsoft.com/sccm/core/plan-design/configs/supported-operating-systems-for-site-system-servers. These numbers are determined using client defaults for policy polling, software update evaluation, and inventory reporting.

▶ Additional primary sites distribute client assignment across those sites, reducing the risks associated with the failure of a single primary site. However, these sites should not be used for disaster recovery (DR) or backup and recovery processes. For information on backup and recovery, see Chapter 24, "Backup, Recovery, and Maintenance."

▶ You may choose to install an additional site to support Internet-based clients if there is a discrete group of Internet-only clients. The "Planning for Internet-Based Clients" section, later in this chapter, discusses single-site and multiple-site options to support Internet-based clients.

▶ You may choose to install an additional site to support Intune-managed MDM devices. Generally, this is required only when the total of Intune MDM and ConfigMgr agent-managed devices exceeds 175,000. This additional site has a very small site system footprint, with no need for MP, DP, SUP, or other roles that support the ConfigMgr agent. The "Planning for Mobile Device Management" section, later in this chapter, discusses this further from a design point of view. See Chapters 16 and 17 for additional details.

Planning Boundaries and Boundary Groups

ConfigMgr *boundaries* define network locations in which clients may reside. As discussed in Chapter 2, boundaries are defined at the hierarchy level and are globally replicated by the CAS to all primary sites in the hierarchy. *Boundary groups* aggregate boundaries for efficient management. A boundary may define a single network subnet; a boundary group may then represent a branch office. A boundary group could also represent a metropolitan area network or a region rather than a single building. Boundaries and boundary groups serve two key functions:

▶ **Selection of Protected Site Systems:** Site systems are associated with boundary groups; design your boundary groups to support this mapping function. These site systems are the MP, DP, and state migration point (SMP).

▶ **Automatic Site Assignment:** If using automatic site assignment, you must configure one or more boundary group(s) for automatic site assignment. During automatic site assignment, the client determines whether its current network location corresponds to a boundary configured for site assignment. If the client is within such a boundary, it assigns itself to the appropriate site; otherwise, automatic assignment fails. Automatic site assignment is no longer the default in Configuration Manager. Depending on the client installation method used and the number of primary sites, automatic site assignment may not be required. See Chapter 9 for more details on client installation.

Boundaries must be added to a boundary group before they can be used. Site assignment is configured on boundary groups rather than individual boundaries. Similarly, protected site systems are associated with boundary groups. The following boundary types are defined:

▶ Active Directory site

▶ Internet Protocol (IP) subnet

▶ IP range

▶ Internet Protocol version 6 (IPv6) prefix

These individual boundary types can be combined in a boundary group. All boundary types are determined by the client and then sent to the MP to locate content or site systems. The only exception is the IP range boundary type, where the client sends up its IP address, and the MP determines the IP range to which the client belongs.

NOTE: SUPERNETS AND CIDR

Supernets, subnets, and classless interdomain routing (CIDR) are subtly different. This is important to understand, as it causes AD sites and IP subnet boundaries to not work correctly with the CIDR method commonly used in network administration today. CIDR uses variable-length subnet masking (VLSM) to provide more flexible addressing and simpler administration than older Class A, B, and C IP subnets. However, network hosts (desktops or laptops running the ConfigMgr client in the case of ConfigMgr) are unaware of CIDR—as only network routers or layer 3 switches understand it for the purpose of routing packets. A network host only needs to know when to send a packet to the network gateway or about the first router in the route to the destination host.

For this reason, in combination with the fact that the ConfigMgr agent determines its subnet based on host OS information, IP subnets must be defined *per* client subnet and not based on the supernets used by network administrators to define routing within the network. Following is an example of how this works:

▶ A network team defines four buildings in the same region, using the supernet 10.10.8.0/22, and each building with a subnet from this list: 10.10.8.0/24, 10.10.9.0/24, 10.10.10.0/24, and 10.10.11.0/24.

▶ A client located in subnet 10.10.10.0/24 with IP address 10.10.10.100 sends up these two pieces of information to the MP.

▶ The subnet matched by the MP in the site database is 10.10.10.0/24 and not 10.10.8.0/22.

If subnet ID 10.10.8.0 is configured, this client does not fall into that subnet. This is because the client thinks it is in subnet ID 10.10.10.0 and knows nothing about supernet 10.10.8.0/22 or subnet 10.10.8.0 in this case. To support supernet 10.10.8.0/22 using

IP subnets, you must define the following subnet IDs: 10.10.8.0, 10.10.9.0, 10.10.10.0, and 10.10.11.0. This configuration supports the individual clients in each subnet and the configuration of each underlying subnet by the network team.

An additional constraint is that over the past decade, AD sites have converged into larger AD sites, covering more network locations. This has occurred as network links have improved while AD client-to-DC traffic has largely remained constant. ConfigMgr content delivery consumes more bandwidth than AD policy and authentication traffic. It is important to understand how your AD teams use AD sites and the AD site topology's correlation to actual network links. You will want to ensure your AD team knows that your ConfigMgr design and operations depend on their configuration of AD sites.

Microsoft recommends that you create as few boundaries as possible to meet your requirements based on the constraints of your network topology. The following guidelines will help you consider how to minimize the overall number of boundaries in your site or hierarchy:

▶ Do not use a small IP range that matches one or a handful of IP subnets.

▶ Do use IP ranges to handle exceptions such as networks used for VPN connections.

▶ Do use single IP ranges to replace a large number of IP subnets or AD sites.

Boundary groups are used in content distribution to control the DPs from which a client retrieves content. Because boundaries are hierarchywide, DP boundaries are independent of sites, and a DP can be shared between sites. This allows you to optimize content delivery based on network considerations. When clients are not within the boundaries of a DP with the required content, they use the deployment option specified for slow or unreliable networks.

Chapter 5 discusses network considerations for the placement of protected site systems. Chapter 14, "Distributing and Deploying Applications and Packages," discusses content deployment.

Overlapping boundaries are boundaries that include the same network locations. Overlapping boundaries were explicitly unsupported in Configuration Manager 2007; however, this is no longer the case:

▶ **Automatic Site Assignment:** Overlapping boundaries remain unsupported for automatic site assignment. If you use boundaries for automatic site assignment, plan and maintain boundaries appropriate to your network topology and do not overlap. Automatic site assignment can have unpredictable results when a client is located within the boundaries of more than one site.

▶ **Content Location:** Overlapping boundaries are supported for content distribution. For clients that fall into multiple boundary groups, the MP returns a complete list of all DPs associated with content requested by the client, based on all boundaries and boundary groups in which the client is located. The client then follows its normal DP location rules to select the best DP from that list.

Microsoft significantly modified boundary groups in the 1610 release, introducing the ability to define relationships between boundary groups. Each relationship can have a defined timeout before failover occurs. This allows for designs where one remote location can fail over to an intermediary or a regional datacenter prior to failover to the core datacenter where the site server is located. Alternatively, relationships can be built to fail over to another boundary group at the same physical location instead of traversing a WAN link. Microsoft also made changes in ConfigMgr Current Branch version 1706 to the fallback behavior of SUPs within and between boundary groups, allowing for more predictable behavior and, in the case of repeat failovers, a more aggressive failover cycle. The objective of these changes is to reduce the need to leverage network load balancing for SUPs.

For more information on the version 1610 and later boundary models (including version 1706 SUP failover changes), see https://docs.microsoft.com/sccm/core/servers/deploy/configure/define-site-boundaries-and-boundary-groups. For legacy information on ConfigMgr behavior prior to version 1610, refer to https://docs.microsoft.com/sccm/core/servers/deploy/configure/boundary-groups-for-1511-1602-and-1606.

Site Planning for Configuration Manager

After determining the number of sites and their scope, the next step is to plan how to design each site. This is a significant element of the design. It involves determining the number of site systems to deploy and their hardware specifications. This phase tends to be the lengthiest part of a ConfigMgr design and may force some reevaluation of your overall site count and hierarchy structure.

Site Servers and Site Systems Planning

The site server and site system servers are the foundation of a hierarchy or standalone primary site. Chapter 2 introduced site system roles; this section helps you determine what site system roles are required and the server infrastructure necessary to deliver those roles. Site system roles may be hosted on the site server itself or remotely on another server. Following is a listing of key considerations for site system role placement:

▶ **Network Topology:** Place DPs at each physical site if the site spans a WAN link or is a large metropolitan campus with backbone LAN links (that act as points of congestion). This proximity to the clients may be ideal as it allows them to obtain content locally, albeit at increased server infrastructure costs. Chapter 5 discusses network considerations for DP placement. This should also factor in the bandwidth savings that client peer caching introduces (introduced with ConfigMgr Current Branch version 1610 and improved in version 1706). For more information, see https://docs.microsoft.com/sccm/core/plan-design/hierarchy/client-peer-cache.

▶ **Security:** Moving client-facing roles away from the site server allows you to move client network connections away from the site server as well. Client-facing roles include the MP, DP, SUP, and Application Catalog roles. Moving these roles also allows you to remove the need for IIS on the site server, which is more secure when supporting clients on untrusted networks. An untrusted network could be the Internet, a perimeter network, or a DMZ. For clients on the Internet, IBCM may warrant having duplicate sets of MPs, DPs, and SUPs just to support those clients, depending on a company's internal security policies and risk assessments.

▶ **Scalability:** For large sites, moving site system roles off the site server and scaling out may be crucial to achieving software delivery requirements. The MP and SUP no longer support Windows Server network load balancing in ConfigMgr Current Branch via the console. (The SUP supports this via the SMS provider for scripting.) The ConfigMgr client can now automatically switch servers hosting those roles as new instances are added. The DPs continue to provide scalability as clients randomly select from the available list of DPs returned by their assigned MP. If a site needs to scale to the supported limit or close to that limit, multiple site systems (DP/MP/SUPs) are required.

▶ **Management:** If a separate team manages SQL Server, corporate policy often says that this team must manage all instances of SQL Server. This can mean that a remote site database must be deployed on an existing instance of SQL Server managed by that team. Note that the ConfigMgr site server's computer account requires sysadmin rights to the SQL Server instance and local administrative rights to the Windows server where the SQL Server instance is running. Ensure that the SQL Server team is familiar with supporting the SSB and certificate-based authentication. These requirements may make the ConfigMgr site database out of scope for that team.

▶ **Availability:** The only supported way to increase ConfigMgr site availability is by adding additional client-facing site system servers (MP, DP, and SUP). For the database layer to be highly available, it must be deployed with a failover cluster or SQL Server Always On availability groups. Neither of these SQL Server high-availability topologies can be leveraged when the site server is colocated with SQL Server, as the site server does not support running on a clustered server.

▶ **Performance:** In general, the best performance in larger sites is achieved with dedicated site database servers with hardware profiles specifically designed with SQL Server performance in mind. It also includes having a large amount of system memory dedicated to SQL Server. SQL Server regularly polls the operating system to determine how much free memory is available, with the intention of preventing the OS from paging. If SQL Server is on a dedicated server, these checks allow it to consume the most amount of memory without impacting the OS. When colocated with the site server, it is important for the SQL Server maximum memory to be between 80% and 90% of the system memory (depending on the total amount of system memory). This helps prevent starving of various other components, including Windows Management Instrumentation (WMI), the SMS Executive, IIS, and the file system cache of memory.

The SMS provider role is considered a special case. As discussed in Chapter 3, this is a WMI provider that serves as an interface to the database for the ConfigMgr console, scripts, PowerShell cmdlets, third-party tools, and custom-built applications. The CAS and each primary site require one instance of the SMS provider, although they support additional instances. The decision to deploy additional SMS providers is primarily based on one of the following requirements:

▶ **The ConfigMgr console has an increased level of availability:** When there are multiple providers, the console nondeterministically selects a provider to use, enabling the site to sustain a single provider outage. While console errors would occur, a connection can eventually be made. This may be useful in an emergency.

▶ **You need to support many ConfigMgr console connections:** You can support an increased number of console connections by increasing site server resources or moving the SMS provider to a dedicated server.

The SMS provider is automatically installed on the site server during site setup. It can also be installed on the site database server or another server. You can change its location by rerunning setup on the site server. Setup is also used to add additional instances of the provider to a site. Following are requirements for a server to host an SMS provider instance:

▶ The provider must be installed on a server joined to an AD domain that has a two-way trust with the site database and site server's domain.

▶ The server cannot host any other site system roles from another site.

▶ The server cannot host any other SMS providers for any site.

▶ The server must be running a version of Windows Server supported for a site server. At the time this book was published, this included Windows Server 2012 and later versions. Windows Server 2008/2008 R2 are deprecated and unsupported for all roles other than the state migration point and DP roles. Windows Server 2008 was deprecated in version 1511, and Windows Server 2008 R2 was deprecated in version 1702. ConfigMgr Current Branch version 1602 introduced support for in-place upgrade of the site server from Windows Server 2008 R2 to Windows Server 2012 R2. (For more information, see https://docs.microsoft.com /sccm/core/plan-design/changes/whats-new-in-version-1602#bkmk_UpgradeOS.) For the latest information on ConfigMgr removed and deprecated features, see https://docs.microsoft.com/sccm/core/plan-design/changes/removed-and-deprecated-features.

▶ The server must have the Windows Assessment and Deployment Kit (ADK) components installed. These components to be installed on a SMS provider are the same components selected when installing the ADK as a prerequisite when installing a site server.

Following are points to consider regarding a location for the SMS provider:

▶ **Site Server:** Using a site server is the simplest approach as there are no network connectivity issues. However, the server resources of the site server must be shared between the site server and the provider.

▶ **Site Database Server:** Placing the provider here may yield the best performance, as all provider-to-database communication occurs on the server. This option is not available if the site database is on a clustered instance of SQL Server. Note that placing the SMS provider here consumes server resources that would otherwise be dedicated to the SQL Server instance, which may complicate SQL Server performance troubleshooting.

▶ **Any Other Server:** This is the only option that allows you to increase availability of the SMS provider function, as discussed previously in this section. The server must have a high-speed network connection to the site server and site database server. This placement requires additional server hardware resources.

Capacity Planning for ConfigMgr Sites

This section focuses on the scalability of sites and site system roles, which plays a role in determining the topology of the hierarchy and of individual sites. Use this section in conjunction with the network guidance found in Chapter 5. Specific guidance is produced by Microsoft and updated regularly based on performance changes made to new releases of ConfigMgr Current Branch and availability of new hardware; see https://docs.microsoft .com/sccm/core/plan-design/configs/recommended-hardware for additional information. Following are certain guiding principles to consider when looking at performance of the site system roles:

▶ **DPs:** These servers require the ability to serve large amounts of data to clients via IIS and file shares, resulting in heavy disk read operations and the capability to quickly move data to clients over the network. Even when clients are on the same LAN, you may completely consume larger amounts of bandwidth from storage and network subsystems on the server. This is also true with a virtualized DP, as host storage and network infrastructures are often shared across VMs, with little to no isolation between VMs.

▶ **MPs:** These servers tend to be CPU-bound for calculation processes. The MP also requires a relatively quick storage subsystem in large environments, as client data is temporarily stored there before being sent to the site server for final processing.

▶ **Site Server:** The site server requires a large amount of CPU and memory resources, second only to the site database. The memory is necessary for the SMS provider and SMSExec process, the core Windows service of ConfigMgr. The CPU is used for processing required for discovery, hash calculations for content, client data, and general information processing. However, the most critical resource to a site server is the storage subsystem, which should support a large number of small random-write operations. These types of storage operations are the most difficult to handle on hard drives. RAID 10 (mirroring and striping) is often recommended to provide the best performance. In the largest ConfigMgr environments, storage controller bandwidth and caches are important considerations.

▶ **Site Database:** The site database should have the highest proportion of server resources allocated, including CPU, memory, and storage resources. To support the highest level of scalability, these can be four to six times the memory and twice the processing power of the site server. SQL Server best practices regarding storage also apply, including isolating data and log files from each other and splitting those files to allow SQL Server to perform parallel operations. Microsoft suggests that customers with large deployments use a remote site database instead of colocating it with the site server. This is a change from previous versions, where the guideline was to keep both roles on the same server, largely due to lower-capacity network links within datacenters at that time.

▶ **SUPs:** A SUP consumes the most server resources of the key client-facing site systems (DP, SUP, and MP). This can be twice the memory and processor resources of an MP. The SUP is essentially an IIS web service and background WSUS service.

TIP: TWEAKING THE IIS CONFIGURATION OF THE SUP

SUPs require modifications to the WSUS IIS Application Pool configuration, stored in WsusPool Application Pool. Find the setting by right-clicking **WsusPool** under **Application Pools** in IIS and selecting **Advanced Settings**. Within the Advanced Settings dialog, set the following:

▶ Double the value of **(General)** -> **Queue Length**, from **1000** to **2000**.

▶ Quadruple **Recycling** -> **Private Memory Limit (KB)**, from 1,843,200 to **7,372,800** or set to **0** (unlimited).

These settings allow the SUP's WSUS components to meet the more complex nature of WSUS metadata queries used by the ConfigMgr software update feature. For the latest guidance, see https://docs.microsoft.com/sccm/core/plan-design/configs/recommended-hardware.

Specific guidance is produced by Microsoft and updated regularly based on performance changes made to new releases of ConfigMgr Current Branch and availability of new hardware; see https://docs.microsoft.com/sccm/core/plan-design/configs/recommended-hardware.

Configuration Manager on Microsoft Azure

ConfigMgr Current Branch fully supports hosting ConfigMgr servers in Microsoft Azure IaaS VMs. When hosting servers in Azure, it is important to follow the TechNet documentation regarding server sizing (see the "Capacity Planning for ConfigMgr Sites" section, earlier in this chapter, and the "ConfigMgr Scalability Limits" section, later in this chapter). You should also follow Microsoft's guidance regarding Azure storage, which provides limited throughput for standard disks. This can be anywhere from 300 to 500 I/O operations per second (IOPS) depending on VM size. For information about Azure storage scalability and performance, see https://azure.microsoft.com/documentation/articles/storage-scalability-targets/.

Azure Premium Storage provides increased storage throughput but with fixed disk sizes and higher cost. You could use the Storage Pools feature of Windows Server inside an Azure VM to combine multiple lower-cost P10 premium storage disks and provide increased storage. At the other extreme, you could combine multiple P30 disks, the highest specification of Premium Storage, to provide even higher levels of performance, especially to SQL Server. Premium Storage also requires specific types of Azure VMs. For information on Premium Storage, see https://azure.microsoft.com/documentation/articles/storage-premium-storage/.

Not all processor resources are created equal in Azure. Azure VMs have different series, denoted by the alphabetic prefixes A, D, F, GS, and N. The size of a VM in a series is denoted by the numeric suffix (for example, A0, D13, F8, GS5, and N24). VMs supporting Premium Storage are denoted by S (for example, GS5, DS13). Finally, certain series of VMs have a second release; for example, D13_v2 is the second version of the D-series VM.

The series is important, as it alters the underlying processor type used by the host. For example, the Dv2, F, and G series and their xS Premium Storage counterpart all feature Intel Xeon E5-2673 v3 (Haswell) processors, which provide increased compute power over the A and D series VMs. For a complete list of the current Azure VM sizes, processor performance, and VM-level network bandwidth limits, see https://azure.microsoft.com/documentation/articles/virtual-machines-windows-sizes/. Network bandwidth is an important consideration when hosting a ConfigMgr infrastructure in Azure. Azure charges for outbound data when using the site-to-site VPN option to provide connectivity between on-premise networks and Azure virtual networks. The ConfigMgr site server and core roles often push data to clients and ConfigMgr servers in remote locations such as branch offices, which can result in a very large amount of outbound data (from Azure to on-premise). Azure site-to-site VPNs occur over an Internet link, which may not have the capacity to support a large amount of content replication.

Azure offers ExpressRoute as an alternative to using VPNs over the Internet. ExpressRoute, which is provided by your company's network service provider, supplies a dedicated amount of bandwidth, up to a 10Gbps dedicated fiber link between your corporate network and your Azure virtual networks. It includes unlimited inbound and outbound data transfer costs and can be critical to a successful ConfigMgr deployment on Azure. Note that ExpressRoute is not available in all Azure locations, and not all network service providers globally support ExpressRoute circuits. For information about ExpressRoute, including costs and availability, see https://azure.microsoft.com/services/expressroute/.

Ultimately, consider the option of using Azure in a similar manner to how you would consider hosting VMs in a service provider's or outsourcer's datacenter. Take into account the site-to-site connectivity between the two networks and ensure that your provider's storage subsystem offers adequate performance and throughput for your ConfigMgr environment.

ConfigMgr Scalability Limits

Certain scalability requirements are crucial for determining when to add additional site systems and sites. Consider the following:

▶ **Overall Client Limits:** A standalone primary site supports up to 175,000 clients, a child primary site in a hierarchy supports up to 150,000 clients, and a hierarchy supports up to 1,025,000 devices. Those clients are composed of devices types grouped based on the following resource requirements:

   ▶ Devices running the ConfigMgr agent (Windows, Linux, or UNIX)

   ▶ Devices running the ConfigMgr device agent (Mac or Windows CE 7.0)

   ▶ Devices managed via the Microsoft Intune MDM channel (Windows, iOS, Android, or Mac)

   ▶ Devices managed via the on-premise MDM channel (Windows 10)

For a complete list of the device type limits for each type of site, see https://docs .microsoft.com/sccm/core/plan-design/configs/size-and-scale-numbers#bkmk_ clientnumbers. Secondary sites support up to 15,000 devices running the ConfigMgr agent (Windows, Linux, or UNIX).

▶ **Hierarchy Limits:** A CAS can support up to 25 primary sites. Few environments, if any, hit this limit, and such a large number of primary sites should be avoided whenever possible due to the complexity of database replication with that many primary sites. Each primary site can have up to 250 secondary sites.

▶ **MP Limits:** Each MP can support 25,000 clients, and each primary site can support 15 MPs. MPs should not be installed across a WAN link from the primary site server or site database. A secondary site can have only one MP, which must be installed on the secondary site server.

▶ **DP Limits:** Each DP supports 4,000 client connections. Primary and secondary sites support 250 DPs. If a DP is configured as a pull-DP, an additional 2,000 pull-DPs can be added to the primary or secondary site. Those pull-DPs count against the 4,000 client connections of the DP they pull from. A primary site supports a combined total of 5,000 DPs across itself and all of its child secondary sites. Each DP can have a total of 10,000 applications or packages.

▶ **SUP Limits:** Each SUP supports up to 25,000 clients when installed on the primary site server. When deployed remotely from its primary site server and on dedicated hardware, the SUP supports up to 150,000 clients. While there is no documented maximum number of SUPs per site, scalability is not a concern. Because a single SUP role can easily scale to the number of clients supported by a primary site, often two SUPs are all that is required to provide increased availability.

See https://docs.microsoft.com/sccm/core/plan-design/configs/size-and-scale-numbers for a complete list of the various limits. This list is regularly updated based on changes to ConfigMgr and further testing performed by the ConfigMgr product team.

Meeting Availability Requirements

Availability in ConfigMgr has always posed challenges due to lack of support for clustering or other high-availability methods for the site server. However, the other site system roles provide multiple methods for increasing the availability of the site and the services it offers. This section provides a breakdown of key components and how their availability may be increased:

▶ **Site Database:** As with previous versions, ConfigMgr Current Branch provides support for Windows Failover Clustering for SQL Server. This helps to ensure that the various operations that rely on the site database can continue to function. ConfigMgr Current Branch version 1602 and later support SQL Server AlwaysOn availability groups, which allow two SQL Server instances to be highly available without using shared storage. An added benefit is that there is no single point of failure in the shared storage subsystem in the cluster, where data corruption can impact availability. Having a highly available database helps ensure the following:

   ▶ The site's MPs can continue to serve existing policy to clients. Clients can install software, run task sequences, and deploy software updates.

   ▶ The site's SUPs can continue to serve metadata for software update scans and deployment evaluations for existing deployments to clients. This requires that the SUP's WSUS database be stored on the highly available SQL Server instance.

▶ **MPs:** ConfigMgr Current Branch allows you to install multiple MPs in the same site, which enables clients to automatically fail over from one MP to another and is critical for enabling client functions to continue without impact. Failover is handled automatically by clients without requiring any load balancing solutions. It is important to deploy additional MPs to provide for availability in addition to scalability. For example, if you are going to support 50,000 clients in a site, you should deploy three MPs. Because the support scalability limit for an MP is 25,000 clients, the additional MP allows a single MP failure to be handled automatically. MPs depend on the site database server to function, so this should be factored into their availability.

▶ **SUPs:** ConfigMgr Current Branch allows multiple SUPs to be installed in the same site, which enables clients to continue with software update processes in the event of a failure by a single SUP. Failover is handled automatically by clients, without requiring any load balancing solutions.

▶ **DPs:** ConfigMgr allows for multiple DPs in a single site. Clients select DPs nondeterministically after initially grouping fast and slow clients. This helps ensure that content is available for the client to install software, software updates, and operating systems as they are deployed.

▶ **SMS Provider:** ConfigMgr allows for multiple SMS providers to be deployed in a single site. These do not provide instance failover or dynamic routing. Instead, all providers are tried nondeterministically, which means you may see errors in the ConfigMgr console when the console attempts to connect to a provider that is offline. The console will eventually reach an online provider. This allows you to avoid a complete console outage; instead, there is a degradation to the console experience in the event of an outage.

As with the availability of any solution, consider your need for a highly available solution in the context of your business requirements. Do not invest in additional infrastructure and associated complexity if your target for speed of software delivery to end users does not warrant that level of availability.

Planning for Content Management

Content in the context of ConfigMgr refers to the files for applications, packages, software updates, and operating system deployments. One of ConfigMgr's most important functions is its ability to efficiently deliver content to varied network locations. This section provides guidance on planning for content management. Chapter 5 discusses planning for content distribution.

Content distribution starts with the content source location(s). The site server pulls content to the content library on the site server itself and then distributes it to a set of DPs associated with the site. In the case of the content source location, you can choose to specify existing locations where source files are stored or establish a new source location. The choice largely depends on the integrity and ease of management of the existing locations. If these are not secured or are exceedingly complex, take this opportunity to establish a new unified location. Source file locations should be subject to additional technical and operational controls around changes to the sources. Anyone who can modify source files can potentially deliver content to client systems.

ConfigMgr Current Branch leverages the content library feature/architecture introduced in ConfigMgr 2012. This allows for file-level single-instance storage and minimizes duplicate distribution of source files between sites. The content library is stored in a custom format due to the single instancing used.

Following is a set of high-level planning elements to consider in your design for DPs:

▶ **Add DPs for Redundancy:** Deploy one or more DPs in the same network as your site server. Adding DPs provides a level of redundancy (see the "Meeting Availability Requirements" section, earlier in this chapter).

▶ **Leverage BranchCache:** BranchCache provides peer-to-peer distribution of content at locations with a single subnet, as ConfigMgr only supports BranchCache in distributed mode. Distributed mode uses subnet broadcast to find peer nodes, which means every subnet must have at least one download of the content. Using BranchCache also helps reduce the load on DPs by allowing clients to share content.

▶ **Leverage Peer Cache:** ConfigMgr's Peer Cache feature provides peer-to-peer caching inside the Windows Preinstallation Environment (WinPE). Peer Cache is available for all ConfigMgr Current Branch version 1610 and above client operations and can be used to enable clients to share content for app deployment and software updates.

Peer Cache has enjoyed significant improvements with each release of ConfigMgr Current Branch, and the aim is to reduce the need to deploy DPs at every branch office. See https://docs.microsoft.com/sccm/core/plan-design/hierarchy/client-peer-cache for more information.

▶ **Consider DPs for Larger Remote Locations:** Deploy protected DPs at larger remote network locations such as branch offices. Associate these DPs with the boundary groups containing boundaries of network locations where that DP is located. If a client is inside a boundary group served by a protected DP, it will prefer the protected DPs first.

▶ **Content for Internet Clients:** If you support Internet-based clients, place HTTPS-enabled DPs in locations accessible to these clients. Consider leveraging the Cloud DP role in Microsoft Azure to reduce the Internet connectivity demands of content downloads from Internet clients, serving them from Azure datacenter(s), albeit at a charge per megabyte served and stored.

▶ **Leverage Pull-DPs at Branch Offices:** Pull-DPs allow for environments with many branch locations. Using pull-DPs also permits you to support a large number of locations without additional primary or secondary sites. Configure content replication based on your network topology. For example, if you have a single unified Multiprotocol Label Switching (MPLS) network, you may not need to chain content replication to regional or hub locations and instead can leverage the "flat" nature of your network topology.

▶ **Use Distribution Point Groups (DPGs) to Simplify Content Distribution Administration:** DPGs allow you to streamline targeting of similar DPs. For example, branch offices often have identical requirements for content. Group all your branch offices together to enable targeting them once rather than multiple times. DPGs can be used to group DPs logically and physically. You could leverage a DPG to identify DPs that serve a particular business unit. Keep in mind that when a DP is added to a group, it automatically receives all content assigned to the group.

▶ **Use Prestaged Content for Sites with Very Slow Links:** When WAN connectivity provides limited bandwidth, consider configuring the DP in that location to use prestaged content. This enables you to replicate content out of band of ConfigMgr, enabling you to use postal or package delivery services to distribute content in bulk. This does require additional administrative overhead and cost but can be key to enabling timely services to those locations.

See Chapter 5 for more detailed discussion of content distribution and network design planning. Chapter 14 discusses the operational elements of content management.

Planning for Client Deployment and Settings

The ConfigMgr client is delivered as a single client, with components enabled based on the settings defined by the assigned site. The client must be installed on systems that are to be managed. Installation often requires the discovery of client systems via a discovery method prior to deployment. Discovery can also be helpful in planning.

This section focuses on deploying the ConfigMgr client to Windows desktops and laptops. It does not cover the deployment of the Linux, UNIX, or Mac OS X clients or MDM capabilities provided by Microsoft Intune. For more information on MDM capabilities, see Chapter 16.

The client feature components you enable and their configuration directly affect the user experience, including performance, scalability, and security of the managed environment. This section provides an overview of the considerations for designing and planning around client settings. Chapter 9 provides additional detail related to client settings and their configuration.

Planning Client Discovery and Installation

Before using ConfigMgr to manage a system, you must install the ConfigMgr client, and often you must discover the client. This section introduces some basic considerations to include in planning and design. Chapter 9 provides more details on client deployment and configuring installation methods. Following are methods you can use to install the ConfigMgr client:

▶ **Client Push Installation:** This method involves using WMI, remote administration calls, and administrative file shares for the site server to install the ConfigMgr client to potential client systems and invoke the client installation process. Before you can push the client to a remote system, the system must first be discovered. You can enable client push installation on a sitewide basis or selectively install individual or groups of systems in collections. Client push installation has a number of configurable dependencies, and properties are defined sitewide. Client push allows you to control installation entirely within ConfigMgr, which may simplify administration if collaborating with AD administrators requires additional time or effort. Client push requires certain prerequisites, firewall exceptions, and the use of administrative rights, all of which make it less secure. This installation method supports workgroup clients if they are discoverable and you meet access and permissions requirements for those clients (that is, knowing a local administrator account on those devices and that the admin shares are accessible).

▶ **SUP-Based Installation:** This method involves using the SUPs throughout your hierarchy to install the client. SUP-based installation does not require discovering a system before installing the client on it. It is best to use group policy preferences (GPP) to set required WSUS client settings, as this allows the ConfigMgr agent to override those GPP settings. This method is a good choice if you already use WSUS for software updates. GPP settings for the WSUS client can be targeted using any controls available with group policy object (GPO) assignment and filtering (that is, organizational units [OUs], the Deny Application security right, or WMI filtering). Bandwidth consumption can be minimized by using Background Intelligent Transfer Service (BITS), but you cannot control when the installation occurs, as it uses a

WSUS update with a deadline in the past. You can also use this method with work-group clients, but you must be able to remotely configure a client's Registry in order to define its WSUS server as one of the SUPs in its nearest site. Figure 4.4 shows how to configure SUP-based installation. Note that after checking the check box, you must use one of the previously mentioned methods to tell clients to use the SUP as their WSUS server.

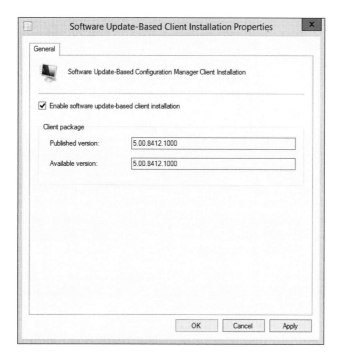

FIGURE 4.4   Enabling SUP-based client installation.

▶ **Group Policy Installation:** This method involves using group policy software installation to invoke a special Windows Installer package designed for this installation method. Like SUP-based installation, this method also provides control over targeting, as it also leverages GPO assignment. Similarly, there are no controls over when installation occurs, as it is only during device startup.

▶ **Manual Installation:** An administrator can log on to a system and manually run the CCMSetup.exe client installation program. This does not require prior discovery of the system, has few dependencies, and is a great way to install several test clients; however, it is not scalable.

▶ **Logon/Startup Script Installation:** It is possible to automate manual installation by scripting CCMSetup.exe to install the client. This provides an extremely high level of control because you use a custom-developed script to control CCMSetup.exe. There is limited control on when the logon or startup script is invoked, as it is tied to either user logon (in the case of a logon script) or system startup (if a startup script). The same targeting capabilities are available as with GPOs, discussed earlier in this section with SUP-based installation. You can use this method with workgroup machines by leveraging PsExec from Windows Sysinternals (http://technet.microsoft.com/sysinternals) or any method that allows remote execution of a script on a target system. There is no requirement for client discovery prior to using this installation method.

▶ **Installation via Intune MDM-Managed Windows Devices:** You can deploy the ConfigMgr client when Windows 10 devices are enrolled in MDM. This is particularly important if automatic MDM enrollment is configured in Azure AD as part of the join process. For more information on the automatic MDM process, see https://docs.microsoft.com/intune/windows-enroll#enable-windows-10-automatic-enrollment. This method helps ensure that devices can be joined to Azure AD as part of a user-initiated modern device provisioning in Windows 10 over the Internet, while maintaining existing management capabilities and methodologies. It is especially suited to use with the CMG configured with Azure AD authentication. For more information about this method, see https://docs.microsoft.com/sccm/core/clients/deploy/deploy-clients-to-windows-computers#how-to-install-clients-to-intune-mdm-managed-windows-devices. For more information on how to use Intune and ConfigMgr together to manage Windows 10 devices, see Appendix B, "Co-Managing Microsoft Intune and ConfigMgr."

▶ **Installation via Windows AutoPilot:** Similar to the previous bullet point, you can use Windows AutoPilot to automate the Azure AD Join process. Automating this process will trigger enrollment in Intune and using the previous bullet point's installation method will trigger the installation of the ConfigMgr agent. This allows you automatically to bring machines under management straight from the factory. For more information on Windows Autopilot and its use with Intune, see https://docs.microsoft.com/intune/enrollment-autopilot.

▶ **Upgrade Installation:** You can use your existing software distribution infrastructure to upgrade the client. This requires an older version of the ConfigMgr client to be installed on the system and communicating with the site. This is useful if upgrading from ConfigMgr 2012/2012 R2.

Chapter 2 described available discovery methods. Two discovery methods are available to discover potential clients:

▶ **Active Directory System Discovery:** This method involves using Lightweight Directory Access Protocol (LDAP) to access AD to extract information about computers in the domain. It also uses DNS queries to resolve IP addresses. If you use this method of discovery, ensure that your AD database is well maintained and that obsolete computer accounts are regularly purged. Alternatively, you can use settings available in the Active Directory System Discovery Options tab to filter out computers that have not logged in (which occurs as part of system startup) or that have updated their computer password, which occurs every 30 days implicitly. Configure this on each primary site managing on-premise clients with the ConfigMgr site needing to discover clients. Determining whether discovery is required should be based on two considerations:

▶ Whether you are using a client installation method that requires systems first be discovered, such as client push installation.

▶ When you need to obtain information from AD computer objects to extend the ConfigMgr database. Where possible, scope AD System Discovery at each primary site to minimize unnecessary discovery.

▶ **Network Discovery:** This method involves using various network protocols to enumerate IP subnets and hosts, discussed in Chapter 5. The key network discovery method is Dynamic Host Configuration Protocol (DHCP), which is available if you have Microsoft DHCP servers. This method is particularly useful as network discovery does not rely on pulling dynamic data from the network or individual systems. The DHCP method pulls DHCP address lease information directly from specific DHCP servers you define, providing a more predictable method of network discovery. You can configure multiple DHCP servers, as shown in Figure 4.5.

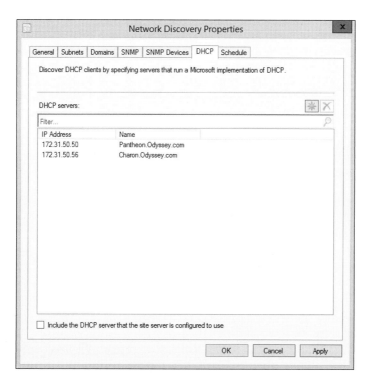

FIGURE 4.5 DHCP server configuration in Network Discovery.

You can configure each discovery method at one or more sites in your hierarchy. When an object is discovered, the discovery method creates a data discovery record (DDR), which is placed in the auth\DDM.box inbox with basic information about the object. The DDR file is processed by the CAS or primary site generating the DDR, causing the information in the file to be inserted in the database and replicated up the hierarchy as part of site data.

ConfigMgr provides additional AD discovery methods for finding information about users and your environment:

▶ **Active Directory Forest Discovery:** This method involves obtaining information about AD sites and AD-defined subnets and creating IP range boundaries based on these subnets. This method is useful for small environments as it reduces manual configuration. For larger environments, review the "Planning Boundaries and Boundary Groups" section, earlier in this chapter.

▶ **Active Directory Group Discovery:** This method involves obtaining information about security and distribution groups. It appends group membership information, which becomes a string array property of the user object in the ConfigMgr database and can be used to target deployments using rule-based collections. You can also define one or more groups in AD Group Discovery, causing discovery of the members of those groups. This is useful when you cannot scope discovery by another method. In the case of security groups, the actual group is returned as a group object. These objects enable targeting of deployments, specifically software distribution and applications, to groups without requiring rule-based dynamic collection evaluation. Evaluation is performed on the client side, based on the user's access token group membership, which creates a very efficient method of targeting software deployment via group membership. The user's access token needs to be updated with each membership change, but this occurs on the user's system based on logon/logoff or lock (Windows 8.1 and later).

▶ **Active Directory User Discovery:** This method involves obtaining information about users in AD.

All Active Directory discovery methods should be run at the site with the best possible connectivity to a DC. Each has delta discovery capabilities, meaning it uses change notification queries to obtain changes that have occurred on the DC since the last delta discovery pass. Delta discovery makes the process extremely efficient and occurs every five minutes by default (compared to every seven days for full discovery). Avoid changing the full discovery cycle if possible, as doing so causes all records to be extracted from AD based on the search criteria defined for that discovery method.

NOTE: DELTA DISCOVERY IS TIED TO A SPECIFIC DC

When delta discovery first runs, it obtains a DC using normal AD client application programming interfaces (APIs). This lookup of the nearest DC is based on the AD site of the site server. Delta discovery next runs LDAP queries against the DC based on the particular discovery method and queries the DC for the highest usnChanged attribute for the objects returned by the LDAP query used by that discovery method. The value of the `usnChanged` attribute is then persisted.

The `usnChanged` attribute is specific to a given DC and tracks changes written to the AD database instance on that DC. As new changes are replicated in or made locally on the DC, the `usnChanged` attribute value is incremented. Subsequent executions of the delta discovery run the same LDAP query as before but only look for objects with a higher `usnChanged` value than the last delta discovery.

The `usnChanged` attribute is specific to that DC. If that DC goes offline, the next delta discovery will be a full discovery to ensure that all changes are captured and a new `usnChanged` value is captured. In large environments where full discovery can take hours, arrange for the AD administrators to notify you of any outages—specifically outages in AD sites that have site servers performing AD discovery. You can then notify teams that depend on AD discovery for software distribution or other ConfigMgr functions.

You can configure the AD User Discovery and AD System Discovery methods to discover any AD attributes of the discovered objects. As you plan your user-centric management, consider attributes that can help you deliver appropriate content to your users. You can also include AD extension attributes, which allow free-form strings to be written to computer objects in AD. This way you can easily add attributes to client systems in the ConfigMgr database without using a custom-developed discovery method.

Planning Your Client Settings

Client settings in ConfigMgr Current Branch are controlled by a default sitewide settings policy and optional custom client settings policies. Custom client settings policies are targeted to collections of users or systems, enabling you to control the behavior or experience of those systems or users.

Core Client Settings for Systems

The following settings areas affect core client behavior or critical elements of the user experience:

▶ **Client Policy:** These settings control how frequently the ConfigMgr client polls for machine policy, which are policies targeted to the system rather than to a user. Increasing the frequency at which clients poll for policy decreases the scalability of MPs and the site database. If you need to distribute policy immediately, consider using client notification to push policy retrieval requests to collections. Client policy also controls whether the ConfigMgr client polls for user policy and whether user policy is triggered from Internet clients.

REAL WORLD: USING CLIENT NOTIFICATION

You might use client notification in an emergency security update distribution or Endpoint Protection/Defender definition update in response to zero-day malware, where the ability to trigger immediate policy retrieval is key to speedy security incident response. Using client notification means that policy retrieval can occur more quickly than even a 10-minute policy polling cycle, without incurring the constant scalability impact of a sixfold increase in the frequency at which clients poll the MP and database for policy. Client notification can also evaluate software updates or application deployments and trigger hardware and software inventory.

▶ **Computer Agent:** These core settings allow you to control most end-user experience elements of the ConfigMgr client. These settings include end-user deployment deadline reminders, organization name in the Software Center, whether the new Current Branch Software Center is enabled, who has installation permissions on the system (all users, administrators, primary users, or no users), and whether notifications are displayed for new deployments.

This area also controls the Additional software manages the deployment of application and software update settings; if enabled, the client never triggers software updates or application installs. You can use the ConfigMgr SDK and client-side WMI calls to write scripts or applications that trigger application and/or update installations using custom logic or rules.

Another important setting, Disable deadline randomization, causes all schedules to trigger exactly when they are defined to occur, assuming that the client received the policy prior to the deadline. Leaving this setting disabled in large environments helps distribute the load of incoming state and status messages from clients. It also allows you to determine in which systems deadline randomization is desired. You should also enable this setting where there is a shared storage system, such as Virtual Desktop Infrastructure (VDI), and server virtualization environments (Microsoft Hyper-V or EMC VMware), to help ensure that storage I/O is randomized, preventing all clients from triggering their schedules at the same time. See the "Using a Simple Schedule Versus a Full Schedule" section, later in this chapter, for information on ConfigMgr client schedules.

▶ **Computer Restart:** The two settings in this section allow you to control the restart user experience, as shown in Figure 4.6:

 ▶ Display a temporary notification to the user controls the first notification that the user receives of a pending restart. The user can close this dialog box, and the default is a 90-minute countdown.

 ▶ Display a dialog box that the user cannot close controls the final countdown presented to a user prior to restart. The end user cannot dismiss this dialog box, and there is a 15-minute countdown by default.

Depending on your user requirements, you may want to extend one or both of these time-outs to best suit your desired user experience.

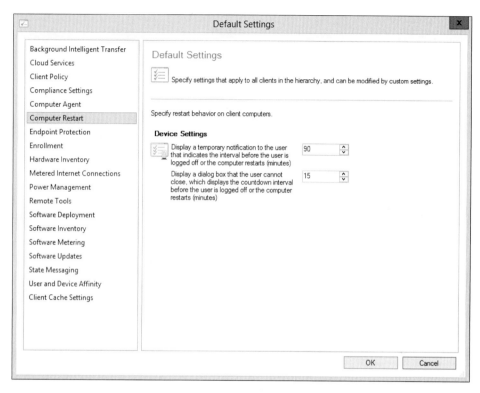

FIGURE 4.6   Computer Restart section of the client settings.

▶ **Hardware Inventory:** These settings allow you to control hardware inventory enablement and configuration. Hardware inventory occurs every seven days by default. Running this more frequently has a negative impact on site performance, as there is more inventory to process and history to maintain. The Hardware Inventory section also allows you to control the hardware inventory classes (WMI classes and registry values) collected by the client. MIF file collection can be toggled selectively per client rather than across the entire hierarchy, as with ConfigMgr 2007 and earlier, allowing you to restrict MIF file collection to only those clients where administrators are trusted not to generate unneeded MIF files that affect the size and schema of the site database.

▶ **Remote Tools:** These settings allow you to control whether remote control is enabled and the level of user interaction required for remote control. Disabling the requirement for user permissions prior to taking control of the device may cause privacy, regulatory, and legal concerns, depending on the local laws where the system resides. This section also allows you to configure Remote Assistance and Remote Desktop local policy settings; these are overridden by group policy for domain-joined systems.

▶ **Software Deployment:** This setting allows you to control how often application deployment reevaluation occurs; the default is seven days. ConfigMgr triggers deployment reevaluations to determine the current state of all required applications targeted to the system and user. The process is designed to address scenarios where a process external to ConfigMgr changes the state of the system. For example, the user might uninstall/install software, or a group policy startup script may change the system. Reevaluations occur after the initial evaluation to determine whether applications need to be installed on the system. The initial evaluation occurs immediately after policy is received by the client.

▶ **Software Inventory:** This settings area allows you to control software inventory. By default, software inventory runs every seven days. You can control the types of files searched for and the folder paths where those searches occur. You can also trigger file collection and send files back to the ConfigMgr site for storage and later review, which is useful when you need to pull critical log files from client systems. These files should be small both for transmission and data storage reasons. Review these settings to ensure that user privacy and any local privacy laws are not violated.

Software inventory is actually file inventory. Add/Remove Programs (Programs and Features) data and installed MSI information is gathered by hardware inventory from the Registry and WMI. Hardware inventory is far more efficient for the client and ConfigMgr site infrastructure. Reserve software inventory or tightly scoped searches for certain files that occur infrequently. By default, software inventory is enabled but with no rules, which means it is effectively disabled.

CAUTION: PERFORMANCE IMPACT OF SOFTWARE INVENTORY

Software inventory can have a large impact on site performance. The information is written to several very large tables in the site database. In larger environments, these tables can contain tens of millions of rows, and because there is no logical place to partition data such as a WMI class or Registry key, these tables cannot be partitioned into separate tables, as with hardware inventory.

▶ **Software Metering:** This settings area allows you to specify whether the software metering component is enabled and the frequency at which metering information is reported. Rules are not configured; they are in the console under Assets and Compliance -> Software Metering. By default, the client reports metering information every seven days. Software metering is often confused with inventory, as the terms *inventory* and *metering* are sometimes used interchangeably. In ConfigMgr, metering is the act of measuring how often, for how long, and by whom software is run. Installations of software are best tracked via hardware inventory and asset intelligence or, less efficiently, via software inventory.

▶ **Software Updates:** This area allows you to define the configuration of the Software Update component of the ConfigMgr client. It controls the frequency of software update scans and deployment reevaluations.

Software update scans detect the compliance state for software update products and categories configured in the Software Update component settings of the site or hierarchy. Deployment reevaluation is only concerned with the installation and compliance information for updates deployed to the system rather than with all metadata stored on the SUP that applies to the system.

The other crucial setting in this area is for installing other software update deployments, when any software update deployment deadline is reached, install other software update deployments. This setting allows you to configure the ConfigMgr client to bring forward deadlines for any updates to be installed in the future, so you can minimize the impact on end users by reducing the number of restarts. Enabling the setting generally results in a more positive experience for users.

Additional Client Settings for Systems

The following additional settings areas are available for systems (see Chapter 9):

▶ Background Intelligent Transfer

▶ Cloud Services

▶ Client Cache Settings

▶ Compliance Settings

▶ Endpoint Protection

▶ Enrollment

▶ Metered Internet Connections

▶ State Messaging

▶ User and Device Affinity

You can also define client settings that can be targeted to users. This allows additional flexibility over targeting systems for these settings areas. Only a subset of the available settings areas can be deployed to users—specifically Cloud Services, Enrollment, and User and Device Affinity.

Using a Simple Schedule Versus a Full Schedule

Schedules are defined throughout ConfigMgr for various recurring activities. A full or custom schedule is usually represented as a reoccurrence pattern and an effective date for the schedule to start. For example, the following is a default full schedule in the console: "Occurs every 7 days effective 2/1/1970 12:00 AM." To define a simple schedule, you select the Simple Schedule radio button. Simple schedules are useful because they are relative. They trigger when the defined time has elapsed and are relative to the last time each client performed an activity. A full schedule causes client activity to coalesce, assuming that clients are online when the schedule is due to occur.

Use simple schedules wherever possible to help distribute client load. Combine this with setting Disable Deadline Randomization to No in the Computer Agent settings area to further ensure distributing client load. In specific scenarios that require precision, use a full schedule and select Disable Deadline Randomization.

Defining the User Experience

A key element of a ConfigMgr design is determining how ConfigMgr interacts with end users. This is often forgotten in the rush to meet IT requirements such as application distribution SLAs and security requirements such as security update compliance. Some assume that ConfigMgr should not interact with end users and should remain in the background, with the best user experience being no user experience.

Getting feedback about your business users' expectations of how their devices should be managed is critical to a successful ConfigMgr implementation and operations. While this does not have to include direct engagement with end users, having stakeholders provide input and sign off on the user experience ensures business buy-in about how their devices are managed.

User interaction is not necessarily the goal. However, you do want to apply a level of user choice and consent; it should not override governance and policies that maintain the security and compliance of a user's device. If there is no direct conflict between choice and security, allowing end users to decide and allowing them to opt in or out of default behavior can go a long way toward improving satisfaction with IT.

REAL WORLD: USER EXPERIENCE MODELING

Consider choosing whether a user should be prompted to install software updates or whether they should install silently. IT typically wants to install silently, without user prompting. The issue with a silent install is that software updates almost always require a restart, and users often request incredibly long restart countdowns. aEven for updates that do not request a restart, installation may impact the device's performance.

An alternative to silent forced installs and long restart counters is to allow a user to have a grace period prior to the deployment deadline, enabling the user to choose the most convenient time for servicing to occur on the device. This is a simple way to improve the end-user experience with ConfigMgr—as well as perceived control. Security is maintained as the deadline is still enforced, but the user could choose to opt in early. Users who do not want to receive a prompt can define business hours and allow ConfigMgr to automatically install outside those hours.

In some cases, the nature of the overall business or a specific department can help determine the optimal user experience. Consider a call center with shift workers, where there is a threshold of the minimum number of desktops required to run a shift that could be used to define maintenance windows in ConfigMgr. Such maintenance windows allow installations and restarts to occur without impacting the business function of the call center. Each shift could also determine machines not to use because they will be restarted and when that will occur. Communication is critical, as otherwise the behavior may appear random to a user.

ConfigMgr provides various powerful methods for configuring and controlling devices. Those capabilities should not be used to the detriment of the end-user experience. Ultimately, ConfigMgr should not get in the way of doing work; careful consideration during the design and planning phase can help mitigate the risk of impacting business departments.

Planning for External Device Management

This section discusses the components that deliver additional capabilities to a device management solution. These components do not in themselves provide service capability; they extend the reach and capability of ConfigMgr to provide those service capabilities to remote PCs and mobile devices. In the case of mobile devices, these capabilities can help consolidate systems into a single solution. Internet-based client management enables you to continue managing devices after they leave your organization and to manage devices that never enter your network. The following sections cover the high-level planning that goes into a Configuration Manager design. Details of these capabilities can be found in Chapters 9 and 16.

Planning for Internet-Based Clients

IBCM provides a secure connection between the ConfigMgr client and the ConfigMgr client-facing site systems (MP, DP, SUP, and so on) while that client is on the Internet. IBCM has been available since ConfigMgr 2007. ConfigMgr Current Branch has fewer requirements than ConfigMgr 2007 for IBCM.

IBCM allows the ConfigMgr infrastructure to communicate with a client on an untrusted network. While its name implies that this is purely the Internet, IBCM has uses outside pure Internet-connected scenarios. It can support clients on untrusted networks, such as servers in a perimeter network or DMZ. This includes partner or cross-organization networks. IBCM can also support clients on networks where client authentication is not possible.

Figure 4.7 provides a high-level network topology view of a typical IBCM deployment. For the sake of clarity, the diagram does not show the following communication methods:

▶ Site server-to-site system file replication (TCP/445)

▶ Site server-to-site system role installation (TCP/445 and WMI over RPC)

▶ IBCM SUP to intranet SUP communication (TCP/8530, TCP/8531, TCP/443, or TCP/80, depending on WSUS and IIS installation configuration)

It also does not show IBCM site system to AD domain controller traffic.

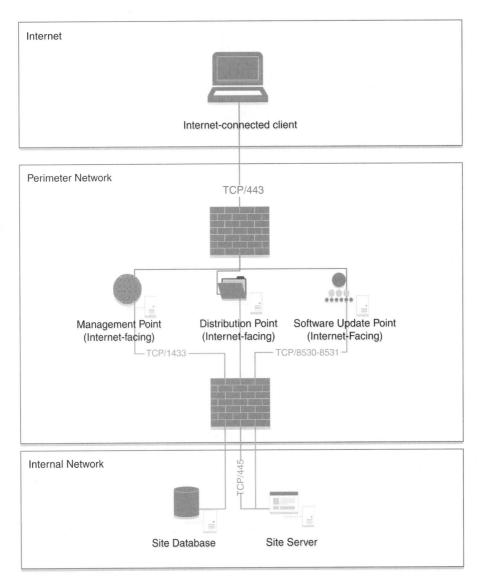

FIGURE 4.7   IBCM high-level network architecture.

The network and site system topology required to support IBCM was often a limiting factor in its use. In ConfigMgr Current Branch version 1610, Microsoft introduced the CMG, which eliminates the need to deploy dedicated servers in your DMZ. The CMG is deployed as one or more Azure VMs (using Azure's Platform as a Service [PaaS] model rather than its IaaS model). A CMG connector point role is deployed on-premise and communicates with CMG VMs in Azure. You can create multiple CMGs for improved availability.

There is currently a list of unsupported features when using the CMG. For more information on the CMG, the latest information on supported scenarios, its costs, and Azure requirements, see https://docs.microsoft.com/sccm/core/clients/manage/plan-cloud-management-gateway.

IBCM Requirements

Client connections from the Internet or an untrusted network require a higher level of security than intranet-based clients. For this reason, IBCM requires client authentication certificates issued by a PKI. Using a PKI-issued certificate allows ConfigMgr to increase the security of the connection, as the default behavior of intranet-based ConfigMgr clients is to generate a self-signed certificate for authentication to the MP. In contrast, a PKI certificate is issued by an independent authority (the PKI) and helps ensure that the client is trustworthy. The issuing authority of the client authentication certificate must be trusted by the site system servers.

IBCM requires that client-facing site systems—such as the MP, DP, and SUP—be published on the Internet, which you can achieve by enabling existing site system servers to accept Internet connections. This requires that the site system be configured to use HTTPS for both Internet and intranet client communication.

Alternatively, in large and/or secure environments, you might deploy dedicated Internet-facing site systems that are configured to only support HTTPS and only accept connections from Internet-based clients; they would actively reject intranet-based clients. These site systems are often deployed into DMZs or perimeter networks. While the site systems must still be joined to an AD domain, that domain can be specifically created for the DMZ or perimeter network and potentially only to support those site systems. In addition, this domain/forest does not have to be trusted by the primary site's domain/forest. You can configure the site server and site system to each use service accounts from the other server's domain for communication.

As an additional security precaution, you could configure the site server to pull information from the Internet-facing site systems, which would allow you to configure any intervening firewalls or router access control lists (ACLs) to prevent the site system from making inbound connections to the site server. Core communication occurs over Server Message Block (SMB, TCP/445) and Remote Procedure Call (RPC, random high value TCP port and TCP/135). Instead, the site server can be configured to initiate outbound connections to the site system, which enables you to configure intervening networks to allow outbound connections from a high-trust network (your intranet) to a lower-trust network (your DMZ/perimeter network).

The site system's HTTPS port (TCP/443 by default) must be open to the Internet or published via reverse proxy; exact publishing methods vary based on your organization's network. Discuss the publishing methods available in your environment with your network team.

The Internet-based MP requires a read-only connection to the site database. This requires that a SQL Server connection port (TCP/1433 by default) be open inbound from your DMZ/perimeter network into your corporate network. If this is not acceptable to your network and/or security teams, you can deploy a replica database into the DMZ/perimeter network, although that increases costs. Alternatively, you can deploy a reverse proxy in the DMZ/perimeter network to proxy and perform SSL bridging while keeping the MP within your corporate network (or an intermediate network, if one is available).

The HTTPS connection's SSL/TLS tunnel may be bridged or tunneled if published; if the port is opened directly, the tunnels are established directly to the server. Microsoft recommends publishing IBCM systems via reverse proxy or a similar publishing solution and using TLS/SSL bridging rather than tunneling. This is recommended because connections only reach the site system server after authentication at the network edge instead of authentication of the connection occurring at the site system server. See https://docs.microsoft.com/sccm/core/clients/manage/plan-internet-based-client-management for additional information.

Client Roaming Behavior with IBCM

IBCM does not support roaming between primary sites. Networks providing Internet connectivity often use network address translation (NAT), a web proxy server (transparent or explicit), or other translation/proxy methods to protect client systems and reduce the number of IPv4 addresses used. This translation makes it impossible for the ConfigMgr client to determine the actual IP address or subnet of the IP address making the network connection, which means ConfigMgr cannot accurately determine its physical location and closest primary site.

You must provision Internet-facing site systems at the primary site. Determine if you can publish servers to the Internet from all your datacenters. If not, you could host each site's site systems in the same location, but they would have to traverse datacenter-to-datacenter WAN links to access the site server and site database. Alternatively, you could use Microsoft Azure to host the Internet-facing site system; this is an especially viable option when your organization has an ExpressRoute connection per datacenter. If you do not need multiple primary sites for scalability and require IBCM, it might be simpler to design for a single primary site than for multiple primary sites.

Using the CMG and Cloud DP in Place of IBCM

As discussed in the introduction to this section on IBCM, ConfigMgr Current Branch version 1610 includes the CMG. CMG vastly simplifies managing Internet-based ConfigMgr clients. CMG can be combined with cloud DPs to provide an Azure-based footprint to provide services to your Internet-based clients, removing the need for both on-premise servers in your DMZ and open inbound ports on your network. It also eliminates the need to use your Internet bandwidth to serve content and policy for ConfigMgr. Conversely, it requires paying Microsoft to both host the needed PaaS VMs and any outbound traffic from Azure to the Internet.

Prior to ConfigMgr Current Branch version 1706, to use the CMG, you had to issue client certificates to authenticate clients. In ConfigMgr Current Branch versions 1706 and later, you can configure the CMG to leverage Azure AD identity as an alternative to client certs for Windows 10 clients. This simplifies the prerequisites for utilizing the CMG, ultimately making the CMG the simplest ConfigMgr method for providing management to external clients.

Leveraging Azure AD for client authentication requires that your Windows 10 clients be Azure AD joined or domain joined and hybrid Azure AD joined. For more information on Azure AD Join and hybrid Azure AD Join, see https://docs.microsoft.com/azure/active-directory/device-management-introduction.

If you are upgrading an environment and IBCM is not deployed, using the CMG and cloud DPs can be a simple way to rapidly provide services to Internet-based clients. For more information, see the following sources:

- **CMG:** https://docs.microsoft.com/sccm/core/clients/manage/plan-cloud-management-gateway

- **Using Azure AD with the CMG:** https://docs.microsoft.com/sccm/core/clients/deploy/deploy-clients-cmg-azure

- **Cloud DPs:** https://docs.microsoft.com/sccm/core/plan-design/hierarchy/use-a-cloud-based-distribution-point

Planning for Mobile Device Management

MDM is becoming a crucial requirement for supporting mobility services. It is therefore important to determine whether you will include MDM in your ConfigMgr deployment design. In addition to its legacy MDM capabilities for Windows Embedded/CE, ConfigMgr has two key methods that support modern MDM:

- **MDM support for customers with Windows 10 devices without an Internet connection:** On-premise MDM was added to ConfigMgr to support customers with Windows 10 devices without an Internet connection. For Internet-connected devices, on-premise MDM provides a subset of the capabilities provided by Microsoft Intune and is not the Microsoft recommended approach. Devices without Internet-connectivity might include devices such as barcode scanners that run Windows 10 IoT Mobile Enterprise, which replaced Windows Embedded Handheld.

- **Microsoft Intune integration in a "hybrid" deployment topology:** ConfigMgr supports Microsoft Intune integration in a hybrid deployment topology. (See Chapter 16 for more details on setting up this topology.) With Intune hybrid, ConfigMgr is responsible for creating and deploying policy to users and devices. Intune delivers mobile device discovery, inventory, compliance, and application installation status to ConfigMgr; ConfigMgr supports managing Apple iOS, Google Android, and Microsoft Windows mobile devices (including Windows 10 PCs via the MDM channel). Using Intune also enables cloud-only features such as app protection policies (APP), formerly known as Intune mobile application management (MAM), that do not rely on device enrollment. APP is accessed via the Azure portal (https://portal.azure.com), under the Microsoft Intune resource type.

If you are planning to deploy Intune, a key consideration is whether to leverage Intune in a hybrid topology or keep it decoupled from ConfigMgr (known as Intune on Azure). This decision is crucial as it affects the speed at which you receive updates, with Intune standalone being updated monthly (at the time this book was published). With

ConfigMgr Current Branch 1610, Microsoft has enabled customers to switch from Intune hybrid to Intune on Azure by removing the SCP. Currently, changing topologies also requires that all MDM configuration be reimplemented in Intune on Azure but does not require device reenrollment.

If you are upgrading from ConfigMgr 2012 or an older version of ConfigMgr Current Branch, you can find information on how to switch to Intune on Azure using the steps at https://docs.microsoft.com/sccm/mdm/deploy-use/change-mdm-authority. If you want to switch authorities but are not ready to move all users over at one time, Microsoft provides a mixed authority mode that allows you to transition user by user from hybrid to Intune on Azure. For details on how to use this method, see https://docs.microsoft.com/sccm/mdm/deploy-use/migrate-mixed-authority.

Microsoft recommends the Intune on Azure topology for Microsoft Intune implementations over hybrid with ConfigMgr. This is especially true as the new co-management capabilities in ConfigMgr Current Branch 1710 are not supported with hybrid (see Appendix B for more information on co-management). Microsoft has stated that it is committed to continuing to support customers on Intune hybrid. With that said, Microsoft actively asks customers to consider Intune on Azure first and provide feedback if they decide to use Intune hybrid. For a complete breakdown of the latest on choosing between hybrid and Intune on Azure, see https://docs.microsoft.com/sccm/mdm/understand/choose-between-standalone-intune-and-hybrid-mobile-device-management.

Planning for Continuous Updates

This section discusses the new servicing model in ConfigMgr Current Branch. It is important that the design and any associated deployment project consider this model as part of transitioning into operations. Understanding why Microsoft chose this approach along with strategies to manage changes helps ensure that your organization can get the most out of the new model. The model includes a completely rewritten updating process for ConfigMgr that automates replication and installation of updates.

Servicing and Updates in Current Branch

ConfigMgr Current Branch includes a new Updates and Servicing node that is available under the Cloud Services node of the Administration workspace. This is not only a notification area for new updates and releases; it is a front end to a completely rewritten servicing model for ConfigMgr that allows one-click upgrades of hierarchies with control over client behavior. This feature provides a quicker and more robust upgrade experience, which is important with the more frequent release cycle for ConfigMgr. Instead of waiting years for new features in a service pack or product release, a smaller set of updates is available multiple times a year. There are two primary reasons for the new servicing model:

▶ **Windows 10 Servicing Model:** Microsoft is constantly updating Windows 10, with updates currently released approximately twice a year. This speed of release is a massive change for enterprise IT. The primary OS that ConfigMgr manages is the Windows client OS. To manage an OS that is constantly updating, ConfigMgr itself must be updated at a similar frequency. There is little point in a management solution that cannot manage the latest capabilities of the devices it is managing.

▶ **Hybrid Intune MDM:** Microsoft Intune is updated monthly, including both back-end service updates and, for Intune standalone, updates to the web console. For hybrid customers to access these changes, ConfigMgr must release both console and server code changes.

Updates to Current Branch are delta updates, which makes them different from service packs in previous versions. A ConfigMgr service pack was often the same size as the full product and frequently contained several years of SQL Server database changes for modifying the database schema to support the cumulative updates and any new features. Current Branch releases contain several months of changes and only those since the last update. It therefore takes far less time to actually apply these releases.

In addition, Current Branch releases, unlike historic service packs and cumulative updates, are installed directly in the console. ConfigMgr is constantly polling Microsoft web services for new releases and automatically downloads them as they become available. Selecting Install from the Updates and Servicing node of the console causes the content to be replicated throughout the hierarchy. A prerequisite check runs; after each site reports that the prerequisite check has passed, the installation begins in top-down order from the CAS.

Each release includes a list of new features available with that release. You can choose to make those features available throughout your hierarchy, enable only a subset of features, or not make new features available; this gives you control and additional testing time for new features, if required. Microsoft occasionally adds pre-release features, which are not meant for production usage but are features Microsoft believes require testing in production with a pilot to fully validate the feature. You do not have to enable these features or use them until they exit the pre-release stage. Usually the transition from pre-release to release occurs during the next release, though Intune features may be released in response to an Intune service change.

At the time this book was published, configuration Manager Current Branch had had six major versions since its 1511 release in November 2015. These are listed in Table 4.1:

TABLE 4.1   ConfigMgr Current Branch Releases and Dates

Release	Date	Includes...
ConfigMgr Current Branch 1602	February 2016	▶ First major update to Current Branch
ConfigMgr Current Branch 1606	June/July 2016	▶ Support for Windows 10 Anniversary Update (version 1607)
ConfigMgr Current Branch 1610	October/ November 2016	▶ New boundary model ▶ Cloud management gateway ▶ Peer Cache

Release	Date	Includes...
ConfigMgr Current Branch 1702	March/ April 2017	▶ Windows 10 Creators Update support ▶ Office 365 ProPlus update management ▶ Conditional Access ▶ Enhancement to deployment management ▶ Android for Work support and other MDM hybrid parity features
ConfigMgr Current Branch 1706	June/July 2017	▶ Added data warehouse feature ▶ Azure AD integration ▶ Peer Cache & SQL Server availability group enhancements ▶ Ability to run PowerShell scripts directly from the console ▶ Management of Microsoft Surface driver updates ▶ Integration with Windows Analytics ▶ Enhancements to Device Guard policies ▶ Intune hybrid MDM capability enhancements
ConfigMgr Current Branch 1710	November/ December 2017	▶ Support for co-management of Windows 10 devices by both ConfigMgr and Microsoft Intune simultaneously (see Appendix B) ▶ Support for configuration of Windows Defender Application Control, Application Guard, and Exploit Guard

As Table 4.1 shows, Microsoft has followed a release schedule of approximately three times a year. It is critical that you have a plan for handling these updates as part of an operational procedure to get the most value out of your investment in ConfigMgr. Also keep in mind that Microsoft supports each release only for a single year. For example, version 1602 was not supported as of March 2017.

In comparison, ConfigMgr 2012 R2 had a quarterly release cycle of cumulative updates. These updates were not required for supportability but were often recommended as part of standard troubleshooting by Microsoft Support. The installation of urgent hotfixes required installing the most recent cumulative update. These updates were released more frequently than Current Branch releases. Cumulative updates were more difficult to deploy as the updates had to be distributed and installed on each site server in order, and client updates had to be deployed. Generally, it should take less time overall to deploy a Current Branch release than a cumulative update. It is important to take all this into consideration as part of your operational plans for Current Branch.

Testing and Release Management of Current Branch Releases

Considering how to manage the regular release schedule of Current Branch is a crucial element of your ConfigMgr design. Previously, this planning could be left to operational teams, given its infrequency. Those teams would know that a service pack release meant that a 12-month countdown had started, giving them a year to upgrade before they lost support.

With ConfigMgr Current Branch, each release includes a one-year supportability countdown similar to a service pack, but these releases occur approximately three times a year. Working with your operational teams and making the operational procedures associated with servicing part of your handover to your operational teams is key to both keeping in line with Microsoft's support policies and leveraging the most value out of ConfigMgr Current Branch (and potentially Windows 10 and/or Intune hybrid investments). Read Microsoft's support policy for ConfigMgr Current Branch versions at https://docs.microsoft.com/sccm/core/servers/manage/current-branch-versions-supported.

The most common model for release and change management is the test and production environments, where all changes go through testing and then are released to production. Some environments have multiple stages of test environments, referred to as development, staging, pre-product, integration, and user acceptance testing. Ultimately, ConfigMgr Current Branch releases should cascade from your test environment(s) to production like any other changes.

It is also important to determine whether you will enable a feature as part of deploying a new update. Just because a feature exists does not mean you must enable it. It makes sense to get on the latest build as a first priority and then determine if and when you will make those features available, especially in a large organization where you operate the ConfigMgr infrastructure on behalf of other teams.

The Updates and Servicing node also allows you to configure pre-production collection of clients that automatically receive the new ConfigMgr client. After performing any additional testing required by your change and release management processes, the updated client can be released to production clients (all clients not in the pre-production collection). ConfigMgr provides in-console monitoring for the entire process, including the server upgrade and client upgrade elements.

Microsoft often provides first-wave and general access for the same release, which means you can select the speed at which you receive access to a release. You could place your test environment on the first wave to provide additional time to test new releases. (The amount of time varies with every release.) The scripts that enable access to the first wave are published with the announcement of each release on Microsoft's Enterprise Mobility and Security Blog, at https://cloudblogs.microsoft.com/enterprisemobility/?content-type=announcements&product=system-center-configuration-manager.

You may also want to consider ConfigMgr Current Branch Technical Preview. This is similar to the old open betas for ConfigMgr 2007 and 2012, except Technical Preview is a discrete branch of updates that are released as a perpetual 90-day evaluation (with each update resetting the timer). This is similar to the Windows Insider program for Windows 10. Updates are released monthly or every other month, and Technical Preview enables you to experiment with features before they are released and provide feedback to Microsoft through the Configuration Manager UserVoice page (https://configurationmanager.uservoice.com/). Sites that are installed from Technical Preview media are updated from the console directly, like sites installed from production media. It is not possible to move from production to

Technical Preview or vice versa. Features included in Technical Preview may not be included in the next production release; something being included in Technical Preview does not imply a release schedule.

CAUTION: DO NOT USE TECHNICAL PREVIEW FOR PRODUCTION TESTING

Avoid using Technical Preview in test labs where you test production changes. Technical Preview is almost a completely isolated branch of releases, with features that may not be available for several public production releases. Deploying Technical Preview to the lab where you perform production testing would invalidate that environment, as it would no longer be representative of production.

It also would not make for a good test, as you would not be testing the same thing. If you do not have an environment available for Technical Preview, either run it on a single VM or skip using Technical Preview.

The following is an example of a release cycle plan for Current Branch:

▶ Include an agreed-upon and pre-planned process for handling Current Branch releases for your operational team once in production.

▶ Cascade ConfigMgr Current Branch releases through your test environments and into production.

▶ If you need to carefully manage your environment, do not enable new features; follow change and release management processes for each feature.

▶ Keep in mind that you can use the pre-production clients feature to phase out the rollout of the new ConfigMgr client included in each ConfigMgr Current Branch release. This allows you to perform production pilots, which can be useful even in test environments.

▶ Where possible, use Technical Preview to get continuous insight into what is coming with the new releases. You will then have fewer surprises with each ConfigMgr Current Branch release.

Planning for Restorability and Recoverability

The following sections discuss planning for backup, restoration, and recovery, discussing the various supported backup methods. The sections explain how to build a design that includes restorability and recoverability in addition to availability. A design lending itself to restoration and/or recovery from a serious outage is as critical as one that is highly available. It is also important to plan for a supported restoration/recovery method, as you do not want to face limited support from Microsoft during an outage.

For information on configuring backups and performing restores, see Chapter 24.

Availability, Restorability, and Recoverability

It is important to differentiate between several similar and interlinked terms related to backup and recovery:

▶ **Availability:** Availability relates to how available the service or solution is. This can be achieved both proactively and reactively. They can be proactive in the sense that SQL Server databases may be clustered and multiple MPs can be deployed; these architectural decisions are designed to improve the fault tolerance of your ConfigMgr infrastructure. Reactively refers to what you can do to quickly recover from a fault to ensure availability.

▶ **Restorability:** Restorability relates to the ability to restore stateful elements of the service from backup. Stateful is an important consideration, as stateless elements of the service (such as a MP) can be rebuilt without data loss. Restorability is specifically called out because it is different from recoverability, as you may be dealing with corruption or human error rather than rectifying a fault. The ability to restore is equally important to disaster recovery. You are more likely to need to restore from backup than you are to perform a complete disaster recovery. You need the ability to recover data if data corruption or human error occurs.

▶ **Recoverability:** Recoverability relates to the ability to recover from a disaster. This could be the loss of a datacenter or another major event. Having a restorable service does not imply recoverability, but restorability is often critical to recoverability. Recoverability also implies having processes and procedures in place that allow someone unfamiliar with the service to recover it.

These three elements should be considered in your ConfigMgr design to ensure the following:

▶ Preventing or mitigating faults by planning for availability

▶ Restoring after corruption and human error by planning for backup and restorability of those backups

▶ Recovering from serious disasters by planning for recoverability

Do not neglect any element, or you risk being unprepared for a low-risk but high-impact disaster or a higher-risk but lower-impact human error.

Determining Your Recovery Time and Point Objectives

An important step in planning any recovery process is determining your recovery time objective (RTO) and recovery point objective (RPO). These objectives determine the requirements your design needs to meet. Your RPO defines the data and time your organization is willing to lose as part of recovery. For example, if backups occur only once a day, your RPO is up to a single day. If you only replicate backup to your alternate datacenter once a week, your DR RPO is one week. You should consider how much work you are willing to lose during a recovery. Perhaps for the duration of a critical global project that relies on ConfigMgr with globally distributed delegated administration, you need to run more than one SQL Server database backup a day to ensure that the work of multiple administrators is not lost in the event of an outage.

Recovery time is how quickly service can be restored. You may have different RTOs for normal faults (disk failure, human error) versus DR scenarios. In general, your RTO for normal fault is the shortest time possible, while a DR is necessarily more complex and often has a higher RTO.

Consider the business and IT importance and impact of ConfigMgr when determining RTO and RPO. Do not adopt objectives for your business-critical systems simply because they can be met. Justify the objectives with empirical data to support the funding needed to perform the backup recovery testing and other operational procedures.

ConfigMgr can be used to underpin recovery of other systems. For example, it might be used to build PCs shipped to an alternate site to recover a business-critical system. This increases that business system's RTO as it cannot be quicker than ConfigMgr's RTO.

REAL WORLD: AVOID USING UNSUPPORTED BACKUP METHODS

Alternative DR and service continuity methods are often used to speed up server recovery, particularly with VMs. These methods utilize storage snapshots of the entire server and data replication to move the data between geographic sites. These methods are not supported by Microsoft's Configuration Manager product team. This does not mean that they do not work but rather that they have not been tested. For this reason, it is always a good idea to use a supported backup method (see "Planning for Backup" in this chapter and Chapter 24).

There are good reasons to use supported methods: They have been extensively tested by Microsoft, and they are what Microsoft Support is familiar with. This is important for DR scenarios where the ConfigMgr administrator might not be available and your organization may be relying on someone unfamiliar with ConfigMgr to recover a system requiring Microsoft Support's assistance. There are other considerations if you have a hierarchy, as your sites are replicating data sequentially at the database level. If any site reverts to an older version of the database, it is likely to break replication. In addition, you need to use supported backup methods to provide for scenarios where there is database corruption or human error (for example, a deletion of a large number of systems or objects from the database). Replicating server storage between geographic sites would just replicate an error in the database.

In some scenarios, using an unsupported backup or storage replication option may be unavoidable due to organizational standards or RTO requirements. In such situations, it is still a good idea to have a backup process to provide a safety net and address the concerns highlighted in the previous paragraph.

Planning for Backup

There are two main supported backup methods in ConfigMgr:

▶ **ConfigMgr Backup:** This is conducted by the site server and backs up the file system, Registry, and site database into a folder that can then be backed up normally using any file backup tool.

▶ **SQL Server Backup:** Introduced with ConfigMgr 2012, SQL Server backups are not specific to ConfigMgr, and open up the ability to use any Microsoft-supported SQL Server backup method.

ConfigMgr backup is most commonly used and has the fewest dependencies on other technologies and the teams that run those technologies. No one needs to configure SQL Server to perform backups, and all Windows storage snapshots are handled by the site server. However, this method often results in very large backups, especially in environments with hundreds of thousands of clients. Also, the information stored in the file system under the ConfigMgr installation folder is not critical to the recovery of the site.

SQL Server backup provides several key benefits over traditional ConfigMgr backup. It gives your SQL Server database administrators flexibility to choose the database backup model that suits them best. SQL Server backups can be heavily compressed in large environments, reducing time to replicate the backup and allowing more backups to be maintained. You can also use features such as SQL Server Managed Backup if hosting your ConfigMgr infrastructure in Microsoft Azure. If you use SQL Server backup, you will lose any files being processed in the ConfigMgr inboxes at the time of a failure. In general, this is not a major concern unless you regularly have backup logs in those inboxes. (A backlog that is so persistent should be addressed separately anyway.)

Certain items cannot be recovered using either method. These include certificates and passwords stored in the database, which are backed up by both ConfigMgr backup and SQL Server backup but are stored encrypted. The encryption key is not backed up for security reasons, which means any certificates and passwords must be reentered after the site is restored. Package and application source files are not backed up; however, if stored on a remote file server, that file server should have its own backup. If you are using Intune hybrid, the authors recommend opening a support case so that Microsoft Support can assist with recovering the site and ensure that the connectivity between your tenant and the restored site is healthy.

Summary

This chapter discussed the key elements for developing a ConfigMgr design. It covered requirements gathering and the scoping of the technical elements of a design. It also provided an overview of the key elements of both client and server design elements, including site and site system scalability and placement, along with client discovery and settings. (For further details, see Chapter 9.) Content management and network design were also briefly covered; for a full discussion, see Chapters 14 and 5. The chapter also discussed how to maintain and manage ConfigMgr Current Branch, given the new release schedule and evergreen/always-updating servicing model. To gain a better understanding of co-management and how it helps to modernize the management of Windows 10, see Appendix B. This chapter should be followed up with the various in-depth chapters based on your requirements and planning for deploying ConfigMgr.

CHAPTER 5

Network Design

Configuration Manager (ConfigMgr) makes extensive use of your organization's network to manage Windows systems and other supported devices. This can include any form of long-haul or global circuits, wide area network (WAN) links, local area network (LAN) connections, and even the Internet. If a system or device can reach your ConfigMgr site over some type of network connection, ConfigMgr can help manage it.

This chapter does not cover network design; it discusses how to design and configure ConfigMgr for your organization's network. Similarly, this chapter assumes that basic network services required for any network application are working properly. This includes, but is not limited to, the following:

▶ Name resolution and Domain Name System (DNS) services

▶ Internet Protocol (IP) routing

▶ IP addressing and Dynamic Host Configuration Protocol (DHCP)

▶ Firewall and proxy configuration

Network considerations affect your site design and operations. The following key concepts are covered in this chapter:

▶ **Network Utilization:** ConfigMgr needs to live within your network without adversely affecting it or other applications using it. In short, ConfigMgr must be a good citizen of your network, while providing its services within an acceptable time frame.

▶ **Service Location:** Managed systems must be able to find the services provided by ConfigMgr, regardless of where in the network the services or managed systems are located.

▶ **Security:** If compromised, the data and systems managed by ConfigMgr could pose a serious risk to your network and to your organization. Protecting ConfigMgr includes protecting the network communication that is integral to ConfigMgr's operations.

Knowing how ConfigMgr uses the network helps you deploy and configure ConfigMgr correctly, as well as optimize its use of the network and available bandwidth. Without this knowledge and proper planning, ConfigMgr can become a costly endeavor, failing to live up to its potential or even its basic capabilities. This chapter discusses what you need to know, including information regarding communication and data flows, ports and protocols, and site design considerations.

Configuration Manager and the Network

Designing and configuring ConfigMgr for your network is primarily about the location of your managed clients and connecting these locations. *Location* in this context refers to the network location and not the geographic location. While designating network locations by geographic location is helpful for identification purposes, it tells you nothing about how systems at those locations traverse the network or how well they are connected to each other.

When designing a ConfigMgr-efficient network, you should identify and map the locations where managed systems exist or will exist and where the primary ConfigMgr services will be hosted. The latter is generally a decision already made based on the location of your organization's main datacenter. If your organization has multiple datacenters, you must choose which will host your core ConfigMgr services. The main or chosen datacenter should have good connectivity to all locations that will have managed systems. Direct connectivity is not required as long as the clients can reach this datacenter over the network.

If the size of your organization dictates that you will be using a central administration site (CAS) and multiple primary sites, this main or chosen datacenter is where you should locate the CAS and the first primary site's site server.

For each client location, compile the following information:

▶ Name

▶ Number of managed clients

▶ Available bandwidth

▶ Expected management activities

▶ Current network usage patterns

▶ IP addresses used

▶ Ability to place servers at location

▶ Network path

Gathering this data is not a trivial task; however, it is important to be thorough and accurate, as nearly all of your design and configuration stems from this information.

Use the collected information to determine the placement and location of additional ConfigMgr servers, including primary site servers (if using a CAS), secondary site servers, and site systems within any site. In general, you want to add and place these additional servers to minimize WAN usage and maximize local connectivity. This doesn't mean every location requires its own ConfigMgr server, just that you should consider placing one at every location with a larger number of managed clients or limited bandwidth. This determination is subjective and organization specific.

Network Considerations for Server Placement

For all but the simplest of organizations, you most likely will support client systems at remote locations or need to add additional site systems for scalability or availability reasons. Optimally placing the ConfigMgr roles on site systems to support these clients prevents them from having to reach across WAN links that could be slow, congested, expensive, or all of these.

The ConfigMgr client agent communicates with only six specific site roles. These are often categorized as the *client-facing roles*:

- ▶ Application Catalog Web Service Point
- ▶ Distribution Point
- ▶ Fallback Status Point
- ▶ Management Point
- ▶ Software Update Point
- ▶ State Migration Point

NOTE: ENROLLMENT PROXY POINTS

Enrollment proxy points are also technically client-facing roles, although they are only used for legacy mobile device management and Mac OS X management. However, they are used sparingly at best, typically at device enrollment time only, as indicated by their name.

All other site roles support site-centric operations and do not directly support clients. To ensure the best and fastest possible network connection, place these roles in close proximity to the site server for the site to which they belong. In general, the site server is usually the best location for these roles and is required for the Endpoint Protection Point role, which must exist on the top-level site server in the hierarchy if System Center Endpoint Protection (SCEP) will be used and managed by ConfigMgr. The service connection point (SCP) also must exist on the top-level site server.

Of the six client-facing roles just introduced, one role handles a vast majority of client traffic: the Distribution Point (DP) role. Place this role in close proximity to the managed clients to minimize WAN usage and support clients at remote locations. You can implement this in one of two ways: by directly placing site systems hosting the DP role at or near the client locations or by placing secondary site servers at or near the locations. Using a DP that is part of a primary site is generally preferred as it is simpler to deploy and maintain.

Secondary sites provide an intermediary between a client's assigned site and the site that manages the client. Clients are never directly assigned to a secondary site but can use the roles attached to a secondary site. This includes the following client-facing roles:

▶ Distribution Point

▶ Management Point

▶ Software Update Point

▶ State Migration Point

When you attach these client-facing roles to a secondary site that is close to its clients, a client does not need to communicate with its assigned primary site, which may be across a WAN link. Clients can use these roles based on the boundaries and boundary groups configured in the hierarchy, discussed in the "Using Boundaries and Boundary Groups" section, later in this chapter.

Using Distribution Points and Secondary Sites

The choice between using a DP and a secondary site is somewhat subjective, and there are no hard-and-fast guidelines. Table 5.1 summarizes the pros and cons of each.

TABLE 5.1   Using DPs Versus Secondary Sites

Site Role	Pro	Con
Distribution point	Simple Can be hosted on Windows workstations	Only handles content distribution to clients
Secondary site	Handles content distribution to clients using its own DP role Handles policy, inventory, and client messaging using its own Management Point (MP) role Handles Windows Server Update Services (WSUS) catalog distribution with its own software update point role Handles state migration data during operating system deployment using its own state migration point (SMP)	Complex Requires a local instance of SQL Server Express (or SQL Server) Uses SQL replication to exchange information with the primary site Must be hosted on Windows Server 2008 R2 or above No availability options

As Table 5.1 shows, secondary sites handle nearly all client traffic while keeping it local. This makes it appear that a secondary site is the preferred approach, but secondary sites increase complexity in the hierarchy and also create the possibility of orphaned clients. Clients could become orphaned if the secondary site server is unavailable for some reason, as clients using roles at that site would be unable to obtain policy or download content until boundaries were manually changed at the primary site. Changing the boundaries would enable the clients to use different MPs and DPs until the secondary site was repaired.

How do you choose between secondary sites and DPs without any strict guidelines? The authors recommend weighing the available bandwidth to a location—which should include factors such as existing congestion and usage patterns—against the number of client systems to be managed at that location.

Understanding Data Flows

The most important aspect of network design related to ConfigMgr is understanding how data flows inside ConfigMgr. Understanding this concept allows you to place servers with site roles in locations that can help keep your network from being overutilized. It also enables you to simplify the network so you can avoid using server roles where they are unnecessary. There are three types of data flow to consider:

▶ Communication to the client

▶ Communication from the client

▶ Communication between ConfigMgr site servers and sites

The following sections take an in-depth look at the first two data flows; the third is covered in the "Designing Intrasite Communication" section, later in this chapter.

Communication Going to the Client

Communication that flows to the client consists of policies and content:

▶ **Policies:** Policies tell a client that something needs to be done. A client policy is created when an administrator using the ConfigMgr console makes a change to the client. Policies can be as simple as a change to the client settings that tells the client how often to check for new policy or as complex as informing the client that during hardware inventory, it must query the Windows Registry for new keys to include in inventory.

The SMS provider, ConfigMgr console, and policy provider component work together to create policies and update the collection of clients to which to distribute the policies. Usually when clients check for new policies, there is no policy to download. However, in a busy environment, a client could receive 5 to 10 policies each time it checks, which could potentially cause communication congestion on the network.

Clients contact an MP to download new policy. In the ConfigMgr back-end engine, the MP contacts the SQL Server database and runs a query for that client. The MP also writes the time and date that the client checked for the policy. When the MP has the policy, the client downloads it and stores the policy in its Windows

Management Instrumentation (WMI) namespace. You can view these activities in the client's policy agent log file.

▶ **Content:** Content is the source files for applications, software packages, operating systems, updates, and anything else that you want the client to execute. Content is first sent to a DP. Once a client gets a policy that involves content, it makes a content location request to the MP, which queries the database using Active Directory (AD) and IP information provided by the client. The MP determines where the content is located and returns that information to the client. The client then connects to the DP's web page and uses Background Intelligent Transfer Service (BITS) to download the content it needs.

Content downloads to the client or DP comprise the most significant network use by ConfigMgr, and you will spend the bulk of your time collecting information about network bandwidth and the number of clients at a location and determining the best location to place the DP. This information can help you determine how many DPs are necessary and where to place them. If you plan your DPs correctly, content download should not cause network issues.

Communication from the Client

The ConfigMgr client can collect a wealth of information about itself and the deployments it has run, as well as whether they were successful. This information is stored on the client after it is collected, and, when possible, it is sent to the MP, where it is stored in the local database or, in the case of a multisite hierarchy, forwarded to the parent site. This information can then be used for reporting, exported into other databases, reviewed by local admins for hierarchy health reasons, and so on. Most of this information falls into three areas:

▶ **Inventory Information:** This consists of hardware inventory, software inventory, discovery data, and metering data. These items are collected by components running under the SMS Agent Host service and sent to the MP.

▶ **Client Health Information:** When the client is installed, a scheduled task is created to run the CCMEval.exe program, which reads the CCMEval.xml file and runs tests against the different health items in the eXtensible Markup Language (XML) file. For example, it verifies whether the SMS Agent Host service is running; if the service is not running, CCMEval.exe starts the service. The results of all these tests are compiled and forwarded to the MP to be added to the client health section of the ConfigMgr database.

▶ **Messages and Alerts:** The client service and its components generate a series of state messages, status messages, and alerts. For example, when the client runs a deployment, a status message is created that tells ConfigMgr the program is running. Another message is created for a success or failure when that program finishes. These are again stored locally and sent to the MP for processing into the ConfigMgr database.

All client communication is web based, uses HTTP or HTTPS, and is encrypted for security.

Designing Intrasite Communication

A ConfigMgr environment can be a single site with all site roles on one machine or, more commonly, it can include a single site with multiple remote site server roles or multiple sites with multiple server roles. *Intrasite communication* is communication between these multiple remote server roles within the same site. This section focuses on communication between the site and the remote site server roles.

Whether simple or complex, all ConfigMgr Current Branch sites have the following core components that communicate with each other: the site server, the SMS provider, and the site database. All site server roles communicate with one or more of these components. Most of these site servers fall into the following communication groups:

▶ SQL Server communication

▶ Remote Procedure Call (RPC) communication

▶ Server Message Block (SMB) communication

The following sections discuss these communication methods.

Understanding SQL Server Communication

The heartbeat of every ConfigMgr hierarchy is SQL Server, as almost every component of ConfigMgr communicates in some way with the SQL Server site database. SQL Server communication is usually set up in one of two ways: as a default instance that uses a static port or as a named instance that uses a dynamic port.

The default instance uses the standard port 1433. ConfigMgr Current Branch does not support using dynamic ports. If you use a named instance, you must set SQL to use a static port. As 1433 is a well-known port for SQL, the authors suggest using a different port for security reasons. Ensure that you open the firewall for that port number.

Once the port number is defined, SQL Server communicates using Transmission Control Protocol/Internet Protocol (TCP/IP). ConfigMgr Current Branch also supports using named pipes to connect to SQL Server; however, you should use this communication only to troubleshoot SQL Server connection issues.

> **NOTE: POTENTIAL SECURITY ISSUES WITH NAMED PIPES SQL CONNECTIONS**
>
> Named pipes use an older authentication method called NT LAN Manager (NTLM). NTLM only authenticates the client during communication, which could cause a security issue by allowing a rogue server to intercept the communication between client and server. NTLM does not support the new and more secure Kerberos authentication method, which provides mutual authentication of both the client and the server. For more information on Kerberos, see https://msdn.microsoft.com/library/bb742516.aspx.

The SMS provider is a tool used to communicate with the SQL database. This is a WMI provider that you can access through WMI or managed classes. The ConfigMgr console makes extensive use of the SMS provider to communicate with the SQL database. Most site roles include code to communicate directly with SQL Server and bypass the SMS provider.

Using RPC Communication

RPC is an interprocess communication method that clients and servers use to communicate with each other. A program can use the RPC protocol to request a service from a program located on another computer in the same network. RPC follows the client/server model, where the requesting program is the client and the service-providing program is the server. The request goes over TCP or UDP port 135. The RPC service uses an endpoint mapper, which is the service responsible for responding to client requests to determine which dynamic endpoints or ports to use for communication. This method allows programs to not use the same port at the same time. When the service starts, it registers with the RPC service and requests the assignment of one or more dynamic port numbers for its use.

Consider an example of a ConfigMgr site server that needs to install an MP on a remote server. The site server uses the RPC client to connect to the endpoint mapper on port 135 and identify the service to which it wants to connect. The endpoint mapper service replies with the port number for the client to use. The client disconnects and reconnects to the server using the assigned port number; then the communication starts, the MP files are copied, and installation begins.

The dynamic port range used changed beginning with Windows Server 2008; it is now between 49152 and 65535. For security reasons, you may want to use something besides the default range, and you may want to change that range value. This can be accomplished with the netsh command:

```
netsh int ipv4 set dynamicport tcp start=number num=range
netsh int ipv4 set dynamicport udp start=number num=range
netsh int ipv6 set dynamicport tcp start=number num=range
netsh int ipv6 set dynamicport udp start=number num=range
```

If you are unsure of the dynamic port range, you can use the following commands to view that port range:

```
netsh int ipv4 show dynamicport tcp
netsh int ipv4 show dynamicport udp
netsh int ipv6 show dynamicport tcp
netsh int ipv6 show dynamicport udp
```

Using SMB Communication

SMB is a protocol for sharing files, printers, ports, interprocess communication mechanisms such as named pipes, and mail slots between computers on a network. SMB is an older protocol that dates back to the mid-1980s and has gone through several changes over the years, typically as new versions of the Windows Server operating system (OS) have been released. Windows Server 2016 uses version SMB 3.1.1. Each new version or update adds enhancements to the protocol; these are known as *dialects*. Most Windows clients support at least six different dialects of the Microsoft SMB protocol. SMB works over TCP port 445. This is a very common port and should be open at all firewalls and routers on your internal network. The SMB protocol follows the client/server model.

To illustrate an example of SMB communication for ConfigMgr, consider when the package transfer manager needs to copy a package to a DP. One of the first steps is to determine the dialect with the highest level of functionality that both the client and the server can support. Once this dialect protocol is established, the site server can connect or log in as needed to the DP. The site server can then proceed to connect to the tree (share name) on the DP. Once connected successfully, the site server gets a tree ID (TID) it can use when connecting to that share name in the future. The site server now can open, read, and write files using that TID.

Because this process occurs across multiple computers in a networked environment, network performance can affect SMB and cause failures. If network bandwidth is highly utilized, the file copy can slow down or even fail. Network latency also causes SMB file copies and connections to fail or stop partway into the connection.

NOTE: NETWORK LATENCY AND BANDWIDTH

Latency and bandwidth are the two primary measures of network performance. *Network latency* is delay in transmitting data from one point to another. Several factors can contribute to latency. For example, delays might be introduced by packets queuing up on network devices for long distances such as round trips to satellites. The quickest way to measure latency is to ping a remote node and note the response time in the reply. *Bandwidth* is the total amount of data that a network can handle in a given amount of time, and it is determined by the capacity of components such as network cards, cabling, and switches. You can use tools such as netperf, available at http://www.netperf.org/netperf/, to measure bandwidth.

Using External Communication

Most of ConfigMgr's communication is internal, or within the confines of the network it is installed in; however, some site roles and features require external communication. Those roles/features are not installed by default, and you must manually choose to install them. The following require external communication:

▶ **Software Update Point (SUP):** The SUP component interfaces with WSUS. One of the SUP's components configures the WSUS server, and another component tells WSUS when to synchronize with Microsoft Updates. Communication between the WSUS server and Microsoft Update occurs over the HTTP and HTTPS protocols. The information is logged in the WCM.log, Wsyncmgr.log, WSUSCtrl.log, and SoftwareDistribution.log files.

▶ **Service Connection Point (SCP):** This new component provides several functions, including helping manage your on-premise and off-premise mobile devices, upload ConfigMgr usage data, and download updates to your ConfigMgr infrastructure. This communication occurs over the HTTPS protocol. The information is logged in the CMUpdate.log file.

▶ **Asset Intelligence Synchronization Point (AI):** AI provides two-way communication to Microsoft regarding your AI information. This information is mainly a download of new updates to the AI catalog, stored in the ConfigMgr database. Uploads consist of custom software title information for categorization. This communication occurs over the HTTPS protocol. Information is logged in the Aiupdatesvc.log file.

▶ **Downloading Software Updates:** The console is used to create the software update deployment package. Software updates are downloaded from Microsoft Update into the deployment package. The component PatchDownloader performs this task over the HTTPS protocol. This component logs its information in the PatchDownloader.log file.

HTTPS is used for all ConfigMgr external communication, which occurs over TCP port 443. The firewall should be opened to allow port 443 traffic. A proxy account or server may be needed, and each of these components includes areas to specify proxy information.

Using Intersite Communication

When there is more than one site in a ConfigMgr hierarchy, whether it be primary or secondary, the sites need to communicate with each other. Information such as client inventory, status messages, state messages, content, collection information, packages, applications, metadata, and other items must be passed from site to site. ConfigMgr uses two types of communication for this information:

▶ File-based replication

▶ SQL Server–based replication

Intersite communication describes these two forms of replication and how they are used by sites to communicate with each other. It is important that both types of replication work correctly in a multisite hierarchy. Consider an example of a package created at the CAS. The metadata for that package is sent to the lower-tiered sites via SQL Server–based replication, and the actual content is sent using file-based replication. If either method is not working or is impacted by network issues, the package deployment will be unsuccessful.

File-Based Replication in ConfigMgr

File-based replication has not changed much in the last few versions of ConfigMgr; it is all SMB-based traffic. ConfigMgr continues to use file-based replication for the following data types:

▶ **Content:** It doesn't matter what type of content is involved; package, application, and software updates all use file-based replication to move from site to site or from site to DP.

▶ **Status Messages from a Client that are for the Fallback Status Point (FSP):** These messages are sent to the client's assigned site.

▶ **Data from a Secondary Site:** Most secondary site data is sent to the parent site via SQL Server–based replication, but some data from components running on the secondary site server use file-based replication.

▶ **Data Discovery Records (DDRs):** DDRs are sent to the discovery site via file-based replication the first time they are discovered, and after that, they are processed at their assigned site. If DDRs are sent to a different site than the assigned site, file-based replication is used to send them to the correct assigned site for that client.

File-based replication can occur in both directions: from the parent site to the child site and from the child site to the parent site. Two key threads of the SMSExec service perform these services:

▶ **Scheduler Thread:** The scheduler works off a job file. This file is usually created by the thread wanting to do file-based replication. The scheduler reads the job file, which contains the destination site code, the path to the instruction file and the data file, and the job ID. The scheduler then creates a send request file for the sender to act on. The scheduler updates a log file called schedule.log that is located in the Logs folder.

▶ **Sender Thread:** The sender works off the sender request file created by the scheduler. This file can be found in the inboxes\schedule.box\outboxes\LAN folder and generally ends with a SRQ file extension. The file contains the destination site code, the job file ID, the path to the instruction file, and the path to the data file. The sender reads this file, makes a network connection to the destination site, and uses the SMB protocol to copy the instruction and data files. The sender logs its information in Logs\sender.log.

The sender has settings that control how it functions, located on the Sender tab of the site properties. Figure 5.1 shows these settings:

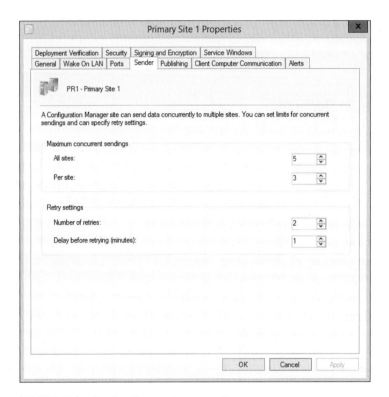

FIGURE 5.1   Configuring sender properties.

▶ **Maximum Concurrent Sendings**

    ▶ **All Sites:** Senders can use multiple threads to send more than one job at a time. This setting controls the maximum number of sendings (1 to 999) the sender can execute simultaneously. Increasing this number speeds up site-to-site communications but could potentially consume more bandwidth.

    ▶ **Per Site:** This is the number of sendings (1 to 999) that could execute simultaneously to a single site. Always set this setting to a lower value than Maximum Concurrent Sendings (All Sites) to avoid the possibility that all of a sender's threads will be occupied sending to a site that is unavailable.

▶ **Retry Settings**

    ▶ **Number of Retries:** Specifies the number of times (1 to 99) that the sender will retry a failed sending.

    ▶ **Delay Before Retrying (Minutes):** Specifies the delay (1 to 99 minutes) before retrying a failed sending attempt.

NOTE: THE NUMBER OF THREADS

When changing the number of concurrent sending threads, do not increase the number of threads so much that you cause a performance issue rather than a gain. The default values of 5 (All Sites) and 3 (Per Site), shown in Figure 5.1, should work well for most hierarchies; if you need to change the values for performance reasons, start with 7 and 5 and then move up from there in increments of 2 until you find the right settings for your hierarchy.

The sender uses a file replication route to understand how to connect to the destination site. Each route includes a source site and a destination site, the security account to use when making the connection, and the fully qualified domain name (FQDN) of the destination site server. The route has several configurable settings to help with a slow network or to limit bandwidth to certain hours. These are located in the ConfigMgr console under **Administration -> Hierarchy Configuration -> File Replication**, which lists all the file replication routes. You can then choose a route and look at its properties (see Figure 5.2).

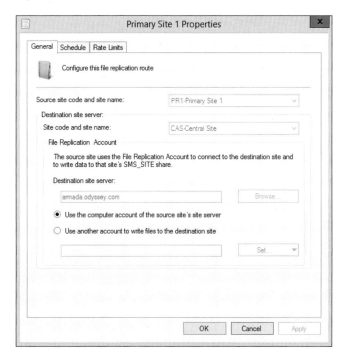

FIGURE 5.2   Configuring a file replication route.

The Schedule tab allows you to choose the hours of the day and night the sender can use to send data to the destination site. This is based on the priorities that have been set for the data. Three priorities can be set for the data:

▶ High

▶ Medium

▶ Low

The Rate Limits tab allows you to set the percentage of available network capacity to use when sending data to the destination site. Figure 5.3 provides an example.

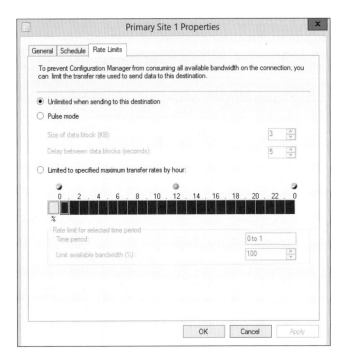

FIGURE 5.3   Configuring rate limits.

When implementing rate limits, there are three options to choose from:

▶ **Unlimited When Sending to This Destination:** This option allows an unlimited data transfer rate.

▶ **Pulse Mode:** Using Pulse mode allows you to limit the amount of data sent by specifying the size of the data blocks sent in kilobytes and the delay in seconds for how often the blocks should be sent. For example, say that you set up Pulse mode for 50KB and the delay is 5, meaning ConfigMgr will send 50KB across the network, wait 5 seconds, and then send another 50KB and wait 5 seconds, and so on. When you have a slow network between sites, this is an efficient way to avoid overutilizing the network.

▶ **Limited to Specified Maximum Transfer Rates by Hour:** This setting is often misunderstood. It allows you to set a time period and a percentage amount to use during that time period. An example would be to set the time period from 8 AM to 10 AM and the percentage amount to 50%. This means that during the hours of 8 AM to 10 AM, ConfigMgr would use 100% of the bandwidth 50% of the time and 0% of the bandwidth the other 50% of the time. This is accomplished by dividing out the time into time periods. You can configure this setting for every hour of the day.

Utilizing this setting is useful if you have a network on the edge of being overutilized during the day, and you need to make sure ConfigMgr doesn't consume all your bandwidth when sending data. Because this setting can be set for only daytime hours, at night ConfigMgr could send 100% of the data 100% of the time.

NOTE: ONE COMMUNICATION AT A TIME

When either of the options on the Rate Limits tab is enabled, the sender overrides any settings it has for concurrent sendings. Only one data item will be sent to the site at one time.

Using SQL Server–Based Replication

ConfigMgr 2012 introduced SQL Server–based replication (also known as *database replication*), which works with two types of data:

▶ **Global Data:** This is data intended to be shared with all ConfigMgr sites and includes any data generated by the ConfigMgr console. Global data is present and replicated at the CAS and all primary sites. Secondary sites also contain a small subset of global data, such as MP and DP lookup information. Following are examples of global data:

  ▶ Collection rules and counts

  ▶ Package, program, and application metadata

  ▶ All deployments

  ▶ Configuration items metadata

  ▶ Software update metadata

  ▶ Task sequence metadata

  ▶ Site control file information (now stored in the ConfigMgr database)

  ▶ System resource lists

  ▶ Site security objects

  ▶ Alert rules

Global data can be created at the CAS or a primary site. If created at a primary site, it is replicated to the CAS, which replicates it to all primary sites. Primary sites replicate needed information to the secondary sites.

▶ **Site Data:** This is data generated by clients and the local site systems. Site data is replicated up the hierarchy and not across the hierarchy. This means a client's hardware inventory is sent to the local site and then replicated up to the CAS but not replicated to any other primary site. Following are examples of site data:

▶ Collection membership results

▶ Alert messages

▶ Hardware and software inventory

▶ Software metering data

▶ Asset intelligence client access license track data

▶ Status messages

▶ Software distribution status details

▶ Status summary data

▶ Component and site status summarizers

▶ Client health data and history

▶ Wake on LAN

▶ Software updates site data

Data is replicated through the hierarchy (or, in the case of site data, up the hierarchy) every one to seven minutes to ensure that anyone looking at the CAS has the most accurate view of what is occurring in the hierarchy. The CAS and all primary sites contain the same global data. This helps with disaster recovery when a site crashes; because the same data is at the CAS, it can be recovered faster, leading to less downtime for the hierarchy.

Database replication has several components that work together inside and outside SQL to move the data from the database of a site server to the database of other site servers. The following components replicate the data:

▶ **Data Replication Service (DRS):** DRS is the name given to the overall process and service ConfigMgr uses to replicate data through SQL Server to other sites. DRS was written partly in SQL and partly in ConfigMgr. This is not to be confused with SQL replication, which is a feature of SQL Server. ConfigMgr uses DRS instead of SQL replication.

▶ **SQL Server Service Broker (SSB):** SSB is a feature of SQL Server that was first introduced with SQL Server 2005. It is an integrated part of the database engine and provides queuing and reliable direct asynchronous messages between itself and other service brokers. This is accomplished by exchanging messages in a dialog conversation between the two service brokers. SSB is used to send the data from one database to another.

▶ **Replication Configuration Monitor (RCM):** RCM is a thread of the SMSExec service. This thread is responsible for interacting with the SQL side of DRS. RCM monitors and configures different items of DRS. RCM writes to the rcmctrl.log file in the Logs folder. This log file should be the first place you look when DRS is not working properly.

▶ **Replication Group:** Replication includes global and site data. That data is broken down further into replication groups. A replication group is a group of database tables that are similar in nature. An example of a replication group is the Alerts group, which contains information from all the alert tables.

▶ **Replication Pattern:** Once you have a replication group, the data is further segregated using replication patterns. Three patterns are used:

> ▶ **Global:** This pattern is any data that is created by the administrator using the ConfigMgr console or PowerShell scripts that need to be replicated between the CAS and primary sites.

> ▶ **Global_Proxy:** This subset of the global pattern contains data that is shared across the primary sites and their respective secondary sites.

> ▶ **Site:** This pattern is the same as the site data previously mentioned in this section. This is data shared between the primary site and the CAS and is created primarily by the clients.

▶ **Article Names:** Replication groups are further divided into article names based on a `replicationID` assigned to the replication group. It is the grouping of the `replicationID` that creates the article name.

DRS has two modes:

▶ **Site Initialization Mode:** It is important to understand how a site is initialized, as that can affect your network traffic. Consider an example with a CAS and two primary sites. Say that you are adding a third primary site to your hierarchy. When the site installation is complete, the site will begin to initialize.

The new primary site creates a message sent through DRS to the CAS, telling the CAS that the primary site is new and has no SQL data. The rcmctrl component on the CAS uses the Bulk Copy Program (BCP) to extract the data from the database and store it in encrypted files. The data is extracted according to the replication groups previously discussed in this section. Once extracted, the rcmctrl component compresses all the files into a single file. File-based replication then starts, and the file is transferred to the new primary site, where the rcmctrl component uncompresses the files and uses BCP to copy the data into the primary site's database.

This process continues until the primary site has all the data from the CAS. For a medium to large environment, this involves transferring gigabytes of data using file-based replication, which can create some network traffic issues even in the best of bandwidth situations. Be aware of the potential impact to network traffic and bandwidth when bringing a new primary site into the hierarchy.

▶ **Site Active mode:** Once a site is initialized, the global data is ready to be used and shared. The site goes into active mode, where DRS is the source of data replication. An example of this would be a user at the CAS creating a new package using the ConfigMgr console. The SMS provider would write that package's metadata into several tables at the CAS, one being the SMSPackages table. SQL change tracking notes that the SMSPackages table has changed; this changed data is gathered up, and DRS is used to replicate it to all primary sites in the hierarchy.

NOTE: MAINTENANCE MODES

While a site is installed, it is in site maintenance mode until initialization is complete. This means that the site is read-only; the console is active but does not allow you to make changes. When a site is active and DRS is working, it is possible that replication can break or be delayed because of network issues. When this occurs, the site is placed into replication maintenance mode until the issue is fixed or the delayed network issue is resolved. While in replication maintenance mode, the site is usable, and changes can be made, but no replication occurs until the site is active again. The changes are stored and released to DRS when the site is active.

Designing Client Communication

Part of the process of understanding what the network design needs to look like is being aware of how ConfigMgr Current Branch clients will communicate across the network. Client communication has not changed in this version; ConfigMgr Current Branch still uses HTTP and HTTPS for connections to site server roles. Clients initiate communication to site system roles such as MPs to get policies and to DPs to download content. Table 5.2 shows the default ports and protocols used for the various communication methods.

TABLE 5.2   Default Ports and Protocols for Client Communication

Client Service	Port Number	Protocol Used
Client request	80	HTTP
Client request	443	HTTPS
Client notification	10123	TCP
Wake on LAN	9	UDP

An organization may want to change the port numbers so that they are different from those listed in Table 5.2 for security reasons; this could be related to network firewall policies or perhaps a custom IIS website. The client spends the majority of time communicating with the MP and the DP; because these are websites, they may not be installed on the IIS default website and may require access using a custom port number. ConfigMgr Current Branch allows you to change the port numbers used for HTTP and HTTPS communication. Figure 5.4 shows the Ports tab for the site properties, where you can add a custom port.

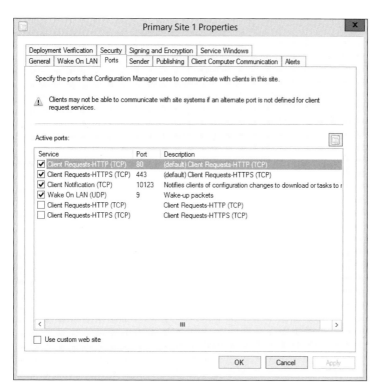

FIGURE 5.4   Configuring a custom client port.

TIP: USING A CUSTOM PORT

You should determine whether to use a custom port for the client during the planning stages of your ConfigMgr hierarchy, as this allows all site roles that have websites to be initially installed using the correct port number. You can then install the clients using the new custom port. It is easier to implement custom ports at the beginning than to go back and add them later.

If using a custom port, ensure that the client knows the port number and uses that port when communicating. You accomplish this by using a command-line option when installing or reinstalling the client. The full set of command-line options for client installation is at https://technet.microsoft.com/library/mt489016.aspx. The following is a sample command to install the client to use the custom port 8080:

```
CCMSetup.exe /mp:armada.odyssey.com SMSSITECODE=PR1 CCMHTTPPORT=8080
```

The command-line option `CCMHTTPPORT=8080` tells the client that when communicating using HTTP, it should use port 8080.

If the client is already installed, and you need to change the port number used for communication, you have three options:

▶ Reinstall the client using a command line specifying the correct port number to use.

▶ Run a dual configuration for a period of time. However, you must have both the default and custom ports enabled at the same time. The client obtains the new port number from Active Directory Domain Services (ADDS); you can disable the old port number when all the clients have the new port number.

▶ Use the portswitch.vbs script. This sample script is provided in the tools folder of the ConfigMgr installation media and is designed to be run with software distribution. You can use a deployment to have the clients run the script, which sets the new port number. If you use this script, both the current port number and the new port number must be enabled, as the client downloads the policy and continues to run this deployment with the old port.

> **TIP: CHANGING THE PORT ON SITE SYSTEM ROLES**
>
> If you change a client port after the site system roles are installed, when the clients start to communicate on the new port, you should change the site system roles to also communicate using the new port. Not doing this in the proper order can be an issue, as it can leave clients in an unmanaged state. You should designate any custom port usage before installing your ConfigMgr hierarchy.

Using the Service Location

ConfigMgr Current Branch clients use the service location to find the sites and site system roles they need to use. A client uses a service request to get this information. The service request is a query of different items. The client makes a service location request under the following conditions:

▶ Every 25 hours of continuous operation

▶ When the client detects a change to its network configuration or location

▶ When the ccmexec.exe service starts or is restarted

▶ When the client must locate a site system role providing a required service

The client uses the following three options to complete the service request:

▶ **ADDS:** The client uses ADDS as its primary method of service location. This requires the AD schema to be extended, ConfigMgr Current Branch to publish its site information in ADDS, the AD forest to be enabled for publishing inside ConfigMgr, and the computer to be a member of the domain.

▶ **DNS:** If you cannot publish the ConfigMgr information into ADDS, you can publish the MPs' information into DNS. The client will query DNS to find any published MPs.

▶ **WINS:** When all else fails, ConfigMgr falls back to using Windows Internet Name Service (WINS) to find an MP.

When a client successfully locates and contacts an MP from one of these resources, it downloads a current list of available MPs and updates its local MP list. This list is sorted by client, based on network location, and the list is stored locally in WMI. The MP list is sorted by the following classifications:

▶ **Proxy:** This is an MP at a secondary site.

▶ **Local:** This is any MP associated with the client's current network location, defined by the site boundaries. If the client falls into multiple boundary groups, the local MP list is a union of all MPs within the boundary groups.

▶ **Assigned:** This is any MP that is a site system for the client's assigned site.

The client uses an MP based on this MP list; if multiple MPs are within the same classification, it chooses the most secure MP available. If all the MPs in the list use the same security method, the client randomly chooses an MP to use.

> **TIP: NETWORK TRAFFIC TO MPS**
>
> Understanding how a client chooses an MP can help with MP placement during hierarchy design. It allows you to place MPs in the optimal location for network traffic and prevent clients from going across a slow link to talk to an MP.

About Background Intelligent Transfer Service

BITS is a component of Windows that allows asynchronous, prioritized, and throttled transfers of files between machines using idle network bandwidth. Following are some aspects of the BITS feature set:

▶ BITS transfers files on behalf of applications requesting its service. A transfer occurs in the background as long as there is a network connection. If the network connection is lost, the transfer is suspended; when the network connection becomes available, the transfer restarts where it was suspended.

▶ BITS constantly monitors network traffic so it uses only idle bandwidth. This makes BITS a perfect choice for networks with slow connection links or high bandwidth utilization.

▶ BITS works by having the application that needs a transfer create a job that is placed into the BITS queue. BITS reads the queue and starts to schedule the job for transfer to the destination URL.

▶ BITS used round-robin scheduling to process jobs in the same priority and prevent large transfer jobs from holding up smaller jobs.

▶ BITS has a built-in error-handling mechanism. Errors are either fatal or transient. If an error is fatal, BITS transfers control of the job to the application that created it. Transient errors are temporary errors that usually resolve themselves over time. BITS works with transient errors by retrying the transfer at the point where the error happened.

▶ BITS transfers occur over SMB, HTTP, and HTTPS.

Configuration Manager makes extensive use of BITS to efficiently use network bandwidth and deal with network connections that are unreliable or not always available. BITS 2.5 or higher is a required ConfigMgr Current Branch component. BITS supports downloads over both HTTP and HTTPS.

BITS Versions for ConfigMgr Clients

Microsoft has released several versions of BITS, each with added functionality. ConfigMgr Current Branch supports the following versions:

▶ **BITS 2.5:** Included on all systems running Windows Server 2008, Windows Vista, and Windows XP Service Pack (SP) 3, version 2.5 can also be installed on machines running Windows Server 2003 SP 1 or SP 2 or Windows XP SP 2 64 bit. The QMgr.dll version is 6.7.xxxx.xxxx.

▶ **BITS 3.0:** This version is available on Windows Server 2008 and Windows Vista operating systems only. The QMgr.dll version is 7.0.xxxx.xxxx.

▶ **BITS 4.0:** Available natively in Windows 7 and Windows Server 2008 R2, this version can be downloaded and installed on Windows Vista SP 1 or SP 2 and Windows Server 2008 SP 2. The QMgr.dll version is 7.5.xxxx.xxxx.

▶ **BITS 5.0:** This version is included in Windows Server 2012, 2012 R2, Windows 8, and Windows 8.1. The version of QMgr.dll is 7.7.xxxx.xxxx. Windows 10 also includes BITS 5.0 but with some new features that allow the use of PowerShell cmdlets. The QMgr.dll version in Windows 10 is 7.8.xxxx.xxxx.

More information about the new features added with each version of BITS is available at https://msdn.microsoft.com/library/aa363167.aspx.

TIP: FINDING THE BITS VERSION

Some versions of BITS were included natively in different operating systems, while some versions were available as separate installs. To determine the version of BITS that is installed, check the version of the file %*windir*%\System32\Qmgr.dll. You can compare this version information with the Qmgr.dll file information at https://msdn.microsoft.com/library/aa363167.aspx to determine what version is installed.

A problem with earlier versions of BITS is that the system is only aware of the traffic passing through the network interface card (NIC). Even when the network segment to which the machine is connected is congested, if there is little or no network activity on the local machine, it appears to BITS that most of the bandwidth supported by the card is available. Under these conditions, BITS transmits data at a high rate, potentially causing additional network congestion problems. BITS 2.5 and higher versions get around this limitation by pulling usage statistics from the Internet gateway device (IGD). Certain conditions must be met to pull statistics from the IGD:

▶ Universal Plug and Play (UPnP) must be enabled.

▶ The device must support UPnP byte counters.

▶ UPnP traffic (TCP 2869 and UDP 1900) is not blocked by any firewall device or software.

▶ The device must respond to `GetTotalBytesSent` and `GetTotalBytesReceived` in a timely fashion.

▶ The file transfer must traverse the gateway.

BITS does an excellent job of intelligently managing the use of network bandwidth with its default settings. To tweak those settings to have BITS use only a certain amount of bandwidth or reserve extra bandwidth for other mission-critical applications, you can use one of the following methods to fine-tune BITS:

▶ Active Directory Group Policy

▶ ConfigMgr Client Settings for BITS

The next sections discuss these methods.

Using Group Policy

AD group policy provides the ability to target groups of machines with a certain policy setting or a group of policy settings. Machines must be joined to the domain to receive the policy. Policies are typically applied at the domain or organizational unit (OU) level but could be applied at the site level, if appropriate. The policy template containing settings for BITS is located under **Computer Configuration -> Policies -> Administrative Templates -> Network -> Background Intelligent Transfer Service (BITS)**. Figure 5.5 shows the settings that are available to edit.

Some of the settings are self-explanatory; for more information, see https://msdn.microsoft.com/library/aa362844(v=VS.85).aspx.

TIP: FINER CONTROL OF SETTINGS

You can achieve more granular control of the settings by using security groups and/or WMI filtering. With filtering, you can selectively apply the group policy objects to users or computers, based on the results of WMI queries or AD security group membership. More in-depth information about group policy and filtering is available at https://docs.microsoft.com/windows/access-protection/windows-firewall/create-wmi-filters-for-the-gpo.

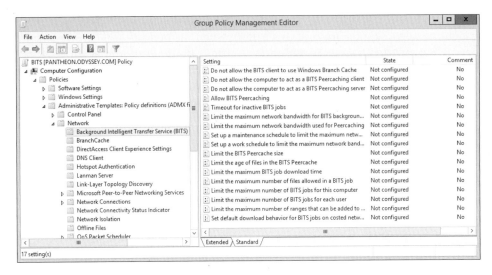

FIGURE 5.5   BITS group policy settings.

ConfigMgr Client Settings for BITS

ConfigMgr provides for setting limited control over BITS. Following is a list of what you can set using ConfigMgr:

▶ Start and stop times for throttling

▶ Maximum transfer rates during and outside the throttle times

▶ The ability to allow BITS downloads outside the throttle window

You can find these settings in the client agent settings, located under **Administration -> Client Settings -> Default Client Settings**. Figure 5.6 shows the available settings.

Once these settings are changed, a policy is created for the collection to which the settings are deployed; if the default collection, the policy is created for all machines. Clients download these settings as a policy when they check again for policy at the MP. Once the client downloads the policy, it is applied to that machine.

CAUTION: CONFLICTING SETTINGS FOR BITS

Group policy allows more settings than ConfigMgr for fine-tuning BITS, but you may find yourself in a situation where you need to use both to control BITS settings at a site or multiple locations. In this case, avoid applying the same settings using both methods. Settings from group policy override ConfigMgr settings and may cause issues with BITS. With both methods, test the settings before implementing them in production.

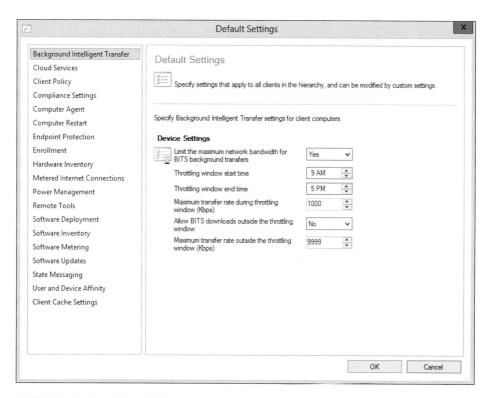

FIGURE 5.6   ConfigMgr BITS settings.

Understanding BranchCache

BranchCache is a technology that optimizes WAN bandwidth between the main location and remote locations. When users at a remote location access content on remote servers, BranchCache copies the content from the main location and caches it at the remote locations, allowing client computers at the remote locations to access the content locally rather than over the WAN. BranchCache is included in some editions of Windows Server beginning with 2008 R2 and in Windows 7 and later versions. BranchCache has two modes of operation:

▶ **Distributed Cache Mode:** The content cache at a branch office is distributed among client computers.

▶ **Hosted Cache Mode:** The content cache at a branch office is hosted on one or more server computers, which are called *hosted cache servers*.

BranchCache is a function of the operating system and ConfigMgr; however, ConfigMgr only works with BranchCache in distributed mode, taking advantage of HTTP and BITS as the protocol. The first client to pull the requested content does so across the WAN link from a DP. When other clients request the same content, they first attempt to locate the content in the BranchCache of a peer computer on the same subnet. If the content is available on the peer, it is pulled from there; otherwise, the clients go across the WAN to the DP for content. Using BranchCache in this fashion allows two important advantages for users located at sites across a WAN link:

▶ **Reduced Client Latency**: Downloading content from the local subnet greatly reduces the time needed for retrieval. BranchCache also downloads content in 64KB blocks and makes each block available after it is downloaded and verified rather than waiting for the entire download to complete.

▶ **Improved WAN Utilization**: WAN traffic is reduced because content may be downloaded to the local site once and used by many clients. In addition, BranchCache utilizes BITS 4.0, providing network-friendly optimizations such as bandwidth throttling and resumption of interrupted transfers.

BranchCache is easy to set up to use with ConfigMgr, with two items to configure:

▶ **Server Side**: Because BranchCache is a feature of the operating system, it is installed from Server Manager on the DP used at the main location. ConfigMgr makes this easy by including a check box on the General tab of the properties of the DP. You can check this box to have ConfigMgr install BranchCache for you. Figure 5.7 shows the check box to install BranchCache. This is all that is required to install Branch-Cache on the server side.

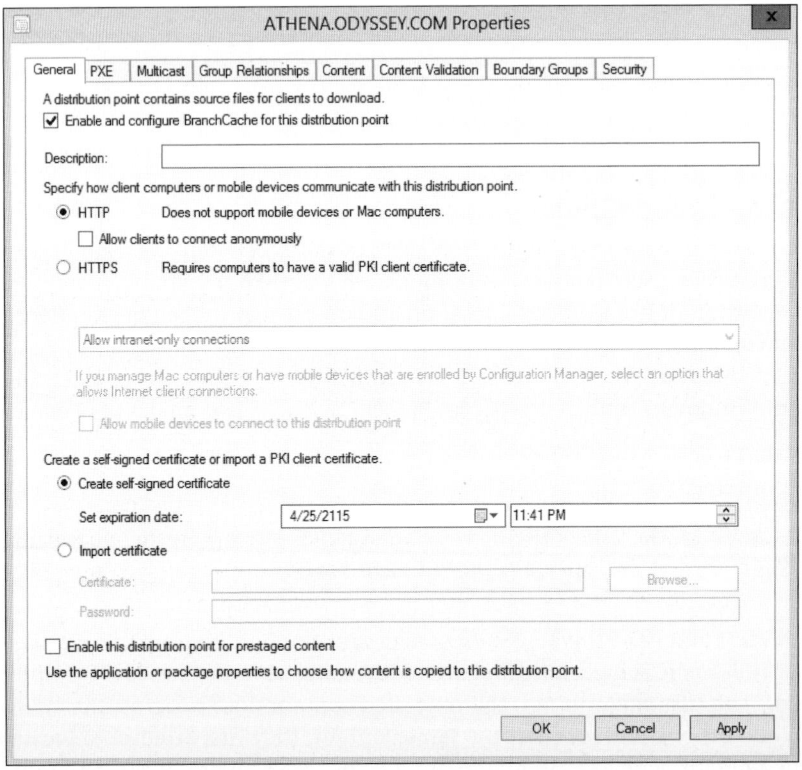

FIGURE 5.7   Specifying to install BranchCache on a DP.

▶ **Client side:** Configuring the client side is somewhat more difficult. The client machines must have a group policy enabled to turn on BranchCache for them. Find the group policy at **Computer Configuration -> Policies -> Administrative Templates -> Network -> BranchCache.** Figure 5.8 shows the group policy settings for BranchCache.

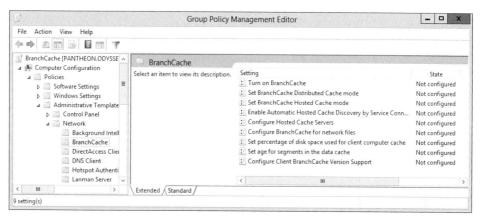

FIGURE 5.8   BranchCache group policy settings.

At a minimum, you need to enable these two settings in group policy:

▶ Turn on BranchCache

▶ Set BranchCache Distributed Cache Mode

The authors also recommend you set the following two options:

▶ **Configure BranchCache for Network Files:** This setting specifies the minimum latency for caching to occur. The client uses the BranchCache feature when it does not receive content from a remote source within the specified interval. The default value is 80ms. Setting a higher value causes more WAN downloads to occur but uses less disk space, I/O, and network throughput on the client systems acting as cache repositories.

▶ **Set Percentage of Disk Space Used for Client Computer Cache:** The default setting allows up to 5% of the client disk space for caching. The cache is located under *%systemroot%*\ServiceProfiles\NetworkService\AppData\Local\PeerDistRepub.

You must also configure Windows Firewall or third-party firewall software to allow BranchCache transfers and the Web Services Dynamic Discovery (WS-Discovery) protocol to discover cached content.

The last step in getting BranchCache to work with ConfigMgr is to configure your packages or applications to enable BranchCache. For applications, check the **Allow Clients to Share Content with Other Clients on the Same Subnet** box on the Content tab for the application properties. For packages, the same check box appears on the Distribution Point tab for the deployment properties.

When a BranchCache-enabled client attempts to access content from a server that is not on the local subnet, the client first determines the latency of the connection. If the latency exceeds the configured threshold, the client attempts to discover the content on the local subnet. The first BranchCache-enabled client on the subnet to access the content learns that it is not available locally and retrieves it from the remote DP. The client then caches the content and makes it available to other clients on the same subnet. When other clients later try to access the content, local clients respond that it is available in cache, and the content is sourced locally.

For more in-depth information on BranchCache, see http://technet.microsoft.com/network/dd425028.aspx.

Understanding Peer Cache

New to ConfigMgr Current Branch is Peer Cache for ConfigMgr clients, added with version 1610. Peer Cache is nothing new; it has been around for years as an add-on to ConfigMgr from various manufacturers. What is new is that it is now built into the ConfigMgr client from the ground up. Peer Cache helps you manage deployment of content to clients that have this feature enabled. It enables clients to share the content they have already downloaded with other clients on the same subnet that need the content. In ConfigMgr Current Branch version 1706, Peer Cache supports the distribution of content express installation files for Windows 10 and update files for Office 365. No configurations are needed; this support is automatically built in.

TIP: CONFIGMGR PRE-RELEASE FEATURES

Pre-release features are items in ConfigMgr that have had some testing but not the rigorous extensive testing that production code has been through. They are a new item to ConfigMgr. You should use them in a lab environment until they are released as production features. To enable the use of a pre-release feature, you must consent to using it in the console.

Navigate to **Administration** -> **Overview** -> **Site Configuration** -> **Sites** and choose **Hierarchy Settings** either from the ribbon bar or by right-clicking **Sites**. On the General tab, check the box **Consent to Use Pre-release Features**, which enables you to turn on pre-release features in the console. Then navigate to **Administration** -> **Overview** -> **Cloud Services** -> **Updates and Servicing** -> **Features**, where you can see the list of features for the version of ConfigMgr you have installed. Some of the features will say release, and some will say pre-release. By right-clicking a pre-release feature, you get the option to turn on that pre-release feature. When you turn on a pre-release feature, it appears in the console, so it can be configured and used. The console may need to be restarted before you can see the feature.

Requirements for Peer Cache

As with other features in ConfigMgr, you must consider some requirements in order for Peer Cache to work correctly:

▶ **The network access account (NAA) has full rights to the client cache folder:** This is a big requirement because in the past, the NAA has always been a domain user with basic permissions on client systems. The NAA must have Full Control permission to the %*windir*%\ccmcache folder. The NAA is used to access the cache folder and allow clients to download the content. Starting with the version of Peer Cache used with ConfigMgr Current Branch version 1706, the NAA is no longer used unless the client is running a task sequence that reboots the machine into Windows Preinstallation Environment (WinPE); in this case, the NAA is still needed to access content from a peer.

▶ **Peer Cache is only used by clients in the same boundary group:** A client can only download content from the peer cache of a machine in the same boundary. When clients request machines that have content for it, peer cache clients with content in the same boundary are returned to the client.

▶ **Hardware inventory must be up to date:** The current boundary of a peer cache content source is determined by the last hardware inventory the client has sent to the database. If a peer cache content source roams to a different boundary but does not submit an updated hardware inventory, a client could download content across a slow network. You should consider whether the machine is prone to roaming or is stationary when choosing what machines will become content peers.

▶ **The type of content does not matter:** Any type of content that is in the cache of a peer source can be given out to clients requesting the content. Software updates, packages, applications, and any other content types are all available for download.

▶ **The requesting client does not have to have Peer Cache enabled:** Clients without Peer Cache enabled can download content from a Peer Cache–enabled source. This means you can designate several peer cache source content clients in each boundary from which clients can download content.

Configuring Peer Cache

Configuring Peer Cache is fairly straightforward. You need to first determine who will become a peer cache content source. While you can set up every client to become a peer cache sources, the authors recommend considering the following:

▶ **Whether the machine is a desktop or stationary machine:** The best machine to act as a peer cache source is one that does not move or change boundaries. The last hardware inventory reported by the machine is used to determine the boundary for which it can serve as a peer cache source. If the machine roams to different boundaries, content might be delivered across a slow network link. You can find out what machines are desktop units by querying their chassis type in the v_GS_System_Enclosure database view. You end up with a number that corresponds to a chassis type (see https://msdn.microsoft.com/library/aa394474(v=vs.85).aspx). The value for a desktop is 3.

▶ **Free disk space:** Choose machines with a lot of free disk space, which enables you to have designated machines in boundaries that might have all or a great amount of your content stored in the content cache. The more content you store, the greater the disk space needed. On these machines, increase the client cache amount from the default size so the content is stored longer and is not removed when you need more space in the cache. You can collect this information in hardware inventory, but it is not turned on by default. Enable the `Free Space (MB)` item in the `Logical Disk (SMS_LogicalDisk)` class so that it can be returned in hardware inventory. This allows you to query the `v_GS_Logical_Disk` database view for that information.

▶ **Active clients:** When searching for a machine, check that it is an active client. You may find the perfect machine to be a peer content source but then learn that it is only turned on once a week. When checking the machine, verify that it is an active client that stays powered on all the time.

When you have found the machines you want to use as peer cache content sources, create a collection and add them to the collection. This allows you to group the machines together. Now you are ready to configure the Peer Cache settings. Because you only want the machines in the collection to receive the Peer Cache policies, you need to create a new custom client device setting. Therefore, navigate to **Administration -> Overview -> Site Configuration -> Client Settings** and choose **Create Custom Client Device Settings** either from the ribbon bar or after right-clicking Client Settings. You then see a dialog box that allows you to name the custom device settings and choose the client settings you want to apply to this custom setting. Choose **Client Cache Settings**, and a new section is added to the dialog box, where you can configure the settings, as shown in Figure 5.9.

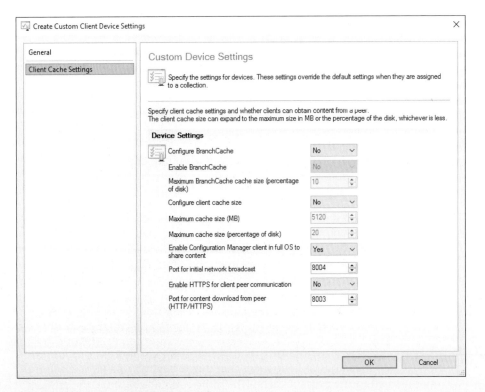

FIGURE 5.9   Peer client cache settings.

Use the last four settings on this page to configure the peer client cache settings:

▶ **Enable Configuration Manager Client in Full OS to Share Content:** This drop-down box allows you to choose Yes or No. Choosing Yes enables this setting and also shows a popup dialog box on the screen. This popup explains that it will auto-matically configure Windows Firewall on clients to open the ports that you choose to use but that any third-party firewall must have the ports opened manually.

▶ **Port for Initial Network Broadcast:** This option allows you to choose the port to use for the broadcast. When clients are trying to find a peer cache content source machine, they will broadcast on this port and wait for any machines to answer. Port 8004 is used by default. This port must be opened on any third-party firewalls and routers for communication to work correctly.

▶ **Enable HTTPS for Client Peer Communication:** This dropdown box allows you to choose Yes or No. If you choose Yes, all peer communication occurs across HTTPS.

▶ **Port for Content Download from Peer (HTTP/HTTPS):** You specify the port num-ber the client will use to download content from the peer cache content source machine. This port is used for HTTP and HTTPS communication, and it must be open on any firewalls or routers.

After configuring these settings, deploy the custom client settings to the collection you created for your peer cache content source machines.

When these machines get the policy to be peer content sources, a hidden IIS web page is installed on each one, and the ports are opened in Windows Firewall to allow incoming connections. This is visible inside the CAS.log file on the peer content source machines. You can also see references to a new service thread for the client, known as the Super Peer service, as well as the website that peer clients will use to connect, called SCCM_Branch-Cache$. (That is just the name Microsoft used; it has nothing to do with BranchCache itself.) When monitoring the CAS log, you also see references to impersonating the NAA access account credentials. This is how the Super Peer service thread gets access to the Cache folder on the peer source.

Understanding How Peer Cache Works

The next step in the process is getting the content on the peer cache content sources. At this time, there is no pre-cache option; the only way to accomplish this is to deploy the content to the peer cache content source machines by using a deployment task (DT) in ConfigMgr. The authors recommend utilizing the collection used for deploying the custom client device settings or creating a new collection and then creating your deployment and targeting it to that collection. This should occur ahead of time so that when deployment to other systems occurs, the peer content sources already have the content stored in their cache. At this point, when the peer content source machines download the content, it will be from a DP, so ensure that your content is distributed to the correct DPs for the boundaries that your peer content sources are in.

When the peer sources have the content in their cache folders, create your deployment to other systems. When the clients receive the deployment and begin downloading content, a request is made to the MP, asking for DPs in this boundary with the content. The MP queries the database and returns a list of DPs and peer content sources. The client tries to use the peer content sources first and falls back to a DP if it cannot get the content from a peer source. When the download starts, you can monitor the Content Transfer Manager log (ContentTransferManager.log) for an overview of the download. To see detailed information about the download, follow the Data Transfer Service log file (DataTransferService.log). This log file shows information about the machine being connected to for the download, the files being downloaded, the job number used to download the files, errors that might occur during the download, and a success message with the start time, ending time, and amount of time for the download.

On the peer content source side, you can monitor the CAS log file to see the connections and the downloads that are occurring. If you see issues with a download, be sure to view both sides of the download: the client and the peer content source. You typically should not notice a difference between using a peer content source or a DP.

TIP: AUTHENTICATION REQUIRED ERROR

When reviewing DataTransferService.log on the client trying to download content from a peer content source, you will see an error stating that authentication is required. This is because when the client makes a connection to the peer content source, it uses its local machine account first. That machine account does not have any rights on the peer content source.

When this error happens, a few lines later in the log file, you will see that it reverts back to using the NAA. This is why that account needs to have full control permissions on the peer content source's cache folder.

After the download completes and the applications, packages, or software updates have been installed, the download information is aggregated and sent back to the MP for inclusion into the database once every 24 hours. The data that is sent back is used to populate the new Client Data Sources dashboard, shown in Figure 5.10.

The dashboard has several tiles that display information that tells users what content has been downloaded using DPs, Peer Cache, BranchCache, and cloud DPs. You can also hover over the graphic tiles for a breakdown by size of the downloads of each of the content servers. Remember that this data is sent back from the clients only every 24 hours, which means it may take a day or so for the dashboard to be updated with new data.

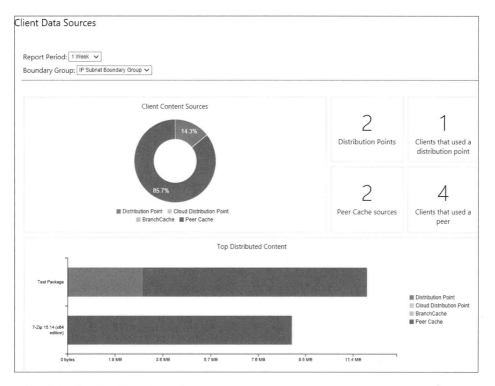

FIGURE 5.10   The Client Data Source dashboard.

Using Boundaries and Boundary Groups

ConfigMgr needs a way to organize together machines that have a common relationship. The machines may be in the same AD site or the same IP subnet. A *boundary* allows these machines to be grouped together for purposes of content and policy. Boundaries by themselves are not used but become active when added to a boundary group. Boundaries and boundary groups provide the following uses:

▶ **Site Assignment:** When you choose to use automatic site assignment, the client determines if its current network location (AD site and/or IP subnet/address) falls within a defined boundary. If it does, the client is assigned to the site defined within the boundary group of which the boundary is a member. This is an automatic site assignment process.

▶ **Site Systems:** A boundary group contains a list of site systems to be used by clients falling within the boundaries of the group. These could be MPs, DPs, or even SMPs. When a site system is added to the boundary group, it can only be used by the clients that fall within the boundaries assigned to the boundary group; this is known as a *protected site system*.

A boundary is defined by using one of the following methods:

▶ Active Directory site

▶ IP subnet

▶ IP address range

▶ IPv6 prefix

In small to medium-sized networks, you should be able to use only the AD site method or perhaps a combination of AD sites and IP subnets. In larger networks, network administrators may be using classless interdomain routing (CIDR) and/or supernetting to define IP subnets (see https://technet.microsoft.com/library/cc958837.aspx for additional information). Note that ConfigMgr does not support these methods. The boundary methods expect AD sites and IP subnets to use a specific subnet mask, based on legacy class assignments. When using CIDR and/or supernetting, you may find that you are using a third boundary type, IP address ranges. Ranges allow you to define a group of IP addresses without being concerned about the type of subnetting that is in place.

If your hierarchy includes workgroup machines or clients residing in a different forest where there is no trust relationship, you must use a boundary method other than AD sites because workgroup machines cannot query AD to retrieve site information.

TIP: IP ADDRESS RANGES AND PERFORMANCE

It is a best practice to use IP address ranges only when all other boundary methods are not an option. This is because the site periodically evaluates boundary members; queries required to access members of an IP address range require a substantially larger use of SQL Server resources than queries accessing members of other boundary types. This is more of an issue with medium to large hierarchies that mostly use IP address ranges.

If a site includes multiple MPs, the client gets a list of all the MPs and randomly chooses one to communicate with to retrieve policies. This could lead to clients across a slow network link communicating with an MP on the other side of the slow link instead of communicating with a local MP. Adding the local MP to the boundary group of the clients across that slow link lets them get a list of preferred MPs; the client then communicates with the preferred MP in its boundary group first, falling back to the MP list only if it cannot communicate with the preferred MP. This can help prevent network congestion on the slow link. The same boundary groups can also contain DPs, providing the client with a location or locations for downloading content.

NOTE: OVERLAPPING BOUNDARIES

Overlapping boundaries are boundaries that include the same network locations and are members of different boundary groups with different site roles assigned to the boundary group. Overlapping boundaries are supported only for content distribution. When a client falls into overlapping boundaries, it receives a complete list of DPs with the content it is requesting, regardless of the site the client is in. This allows the client to randomly choose a DP from which it would like to download content. Auto-site assignment is not supported with overlapping boundaries.

Starting with version 1610, ConfigMgr Current Branch changed how boundary groups work. Previous versions used the concept of fast and slow network links. When adding a site system to a boundary group, you could assign that system as a fast or slow link. You could also assign a DP as a fallback DP, meaning that if the client could not find the content on a DP or was not in the boundaries of a DP, it could use the fallback DP to look for content. This sometimes meant a client might go across a slow network link to pull content from the fallback DP, but at least it could get the content.

In ConfigMgr Current Branch version 1610, Microsoft removed the ability to use fast and slow links when adding site systems to a boundary group. ConfigMgr now automatically adds a default boundary group named Default-Site-Boundary-Group<*site code*>, which is used when a site upgrades to version 1610. To ensure that the current fallback behavior from the previous version remains available until the new boundary groups and relationships are configured, DPs that are enabled for fallback are added to this new default boundary group.

Adding site systems to a boundary group is the same as with previous versions; you just no longer have a fast or slow link to configure. There is a new tab in the properties of a boundary group called Relationships (see Figure 5.11).

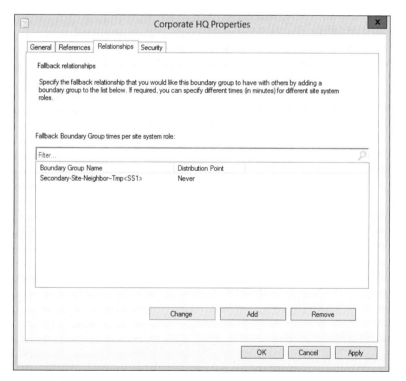

FIGURE 5.11   The Relationships tab of the boundary group properties.

You can use this tab to define the relationship between this boundary group and another boundary group, and you can allow the client to fall back if it cannot find content in its own boundary group. This relationship, called *neighbor boundary groups*, enables you to create a one-way link between the current boundary group and neighbor boundary groups you add. The client searches for content in its own boundary group and falls back to neighbor boundary groups if the content is not found. You can assign a time value to each neighbor, telling the client how long to wait before falling back to that neighbor to search for content; you can also define a priority list for the neighbors the client will search.

TIP: LINKS BETWEEN A NEW BOUNDARY GROUP AND THE DEFAULT BOUNDARY GROUP

When you create a new boundary group, an implied link is created to the default boundary group for the site. This allows the client to fall back to site systems defined in that default boundary group when it is not in a boundary. It also allows clients to fall back and use these site systems when they cannot find any content in their neighbor boundary groups. When defining neighbors, ensure that you set the time value to something less than the default 120 minutes defined for the default site boundary group. If you don't, clients will use the default site boundary group before using their neighbors.

For detailed information on these changes to boundary groups, see https://docs.microsoft .com/sccm/core/servers/deploy/configure/define-site-boundaries-and-boundary-groups#a-namebkmkboundarygroupsa-boundary-groups.

About Client Communication Security

This chapter discusses client communication in earlier sections but has not mentioned how to secure that communication. The communication between a client and a site server is secure by default by using a self-signed certificate; however, you might want or need more secure methods of communication. ConfigMgr provides the following methods to enhance client-to-server communications:

▶ **Signed Client Data:** To protect data sent from clients, you can require a client to sign the data before sending it. To enhance the security even further, you can require the data to be signed using the SHA-256 algorithm.

▶ **Encryption:** While signing the data helps protect it from tampering, encryption protects the data from information disclosure, which means it is not vulnerable to network sniffing devices. 3DES is the encryption technology used when encryption is enabled. It protects inventory data and state messages.

▶ **PKI Certificates and HTTPS:** When using HTTPS, the client must present a valid authentication certificate issued by the trusted root certificate authority to both the IIS server and the client. When using HTTPS for all client communications, you do not need to use the signing or encryption methods.

When ConfigMgr clients request policy, they first get a policy assignment so they know which policies apply to them, and then they request only those policy bodies. Each policy assignment contains the calculated hash for the corresponding policy body. The client retrieves the applicable policy bodies and then calculates the hash on each body. If the hash on a downloaded policy body does not match the hash in the policy assignment, the client discards the policy body.

In-depth information about cryptographic controls for ConfigMgr can be found at https://technet.microsoft.com/library/mt629331.aspx.

Troubleshooting Network-Related Issues

A prerequisite for ConfigMgr to operate correctly is that the underlying network must be working properly. Troubleshooting a network involves several different items, including the following:

▶ Basic connectivity to network services

▶ DNS resolution

▶ Routers and firewall ports

▶ Congested or slow network links

▶ MPs and DPs

▶ Service Principal Names

TIP: BE PATIENT WHEN TROUBLESHOOTING NETWORK PROBLEMS

Network issues can be difficult to troubleshoot as they can be intermittent and may return after you think they have been solved. The best plan of attack for these types of issues is to start with a known good baseline and work forward from there. The authors find that they often go back to the very basics of how ConfigMgr works with the network to get that good working baseline. Take your time and be patient when dealing with these types of issues.

The following sections briefly describe some of these issues and tools for troubleshooting these items.

Troubleshooting Basic Network Connectivity

Basic network connectivity refers to the ability to connect to network services such as printers, file shares, and internal and external websites. These services should work correctly without any user intervention; a user should be able to open a browser and connect to any website or print a document on the network printer without issues. The network protocol used to make such connections is TCP/IP.

To troubleshoot basic network connectivity, open a CMD window (by selecting **Start -> Run** and then typing **cmd**) and run the following commands (which work much better when you have administrator rights on the workstation):

▶ **ipconfig /all**—This command provides a considerable amount of information about the TCP/IP configuration on your workstation.

Check whether you have a valid IP address from your DHCP server or, if you're using a static IP address, whether it is correct. An IP address beginning with 169 is an auto-configuration address assigned when the machine cannot communicate with the DHCP server. This would be the first issue to resolve.

Next, check the DNS server address, which needs to be configured to point to the correct DNS server for name resolution.

Another item is the default gateway. This device allows the packets to leave your local network and travel to its destination. If it is not set correctly, your network traffic will not go past local resources.

Figure 5.12 shows the results of running `ipconfig /all`.

```
C:\Windows\system32\cmd.exe                                    —   □   ×

Microsoft Windows [Version 10.0.10586]
(c) 2015 Microsoft Corporation. All rights reserved.

C:\Users\mwiles>ipconfig /all

Windows IP Configuration

    Host Name . . . . . . . . . . . . : Albert
    Primary Dns Suffix  . . . . . . . : Odyssey.com
    Node Type . . . . . . . . . . . . : Hybrid
    IP Routing Enabled. . . . . . . . : No
    WINS Proxy Enabled. . . . . . . . : No
    DNS Suffix Search List. . . . . . : Odyssey.com

Ethernet adapter Ethernet:

    Connection-specific DNS Suffix  . :
    Description . . . . . . . . . . . : Microsoft Hyper-V Network Adapter
    Physical Address. . . . . . . . . : 00-15-5D-E8-78-36
    DHCP Enabled. . . . . . . . . . . : No
    Autoconfiguration Enabled . . . . : Yes
    Link-local IPv6 Address . . . . . : fe80::d912:cef:fbd0:2c62%3(Preferred)
    IPv4 Address. . . . . . . . . . . : 172.31.50.57(Preferred)
    Subnet Mask . . . . . . . . . . . : 255.255.255.0
    Default Gateway . . . . . . . . . : 172.31.50.252
    DHCPv6 IAID . . . . . . . . . . . : 50337117
    DHCPv6 Client DUID. . . . . . . . : 00-01-00-01-1E-83-8F-CB-00-15-5D-E8-78-36
    DNS Servers . . . . . . . . . . . : 172.31.50.50
    NetBIOS over Tcpip. . . . . . . . : Enabled

Tunnel adapter isatap.{BCC3629A-CA63-4726-B806-9200A0364B95}:

    Media State . . . . . . . . . . . : Media disconnected
    Connection-specific DNS Suffix  . :
    Description . . . . . . . . . . . : Microsoft ISATAP Adapter
    Physical Address. . . . . . . . . : 00-00-00-00-00-00-00-E0
    DHCP Enabled. . . . . . . . . . . : No
    Autoconfiguration Enabled . . . . : Yes

C:\Users\mwiles>_
```

FIGURE 5.12   `ipconfig /all` results.

TIP: MULTIPLE IP ADDRESSES

It is possible to see results of several IP addresses. If a workstation has a wired connection, a wireless connection, and maybe a VPN connection, you will see multiple IP addresses and other information for IP addresses. You also will see IPv6 information if that is enabled. In these cases, it might be easier to pipe the results to a text file for easier reading. You can do this by running `ipconfig /all > ipconfig.txt`. The config.txt text file is created in the same folder where you are running the command.

▶ **ping**—If you determine that the machine has an IP address and the other items check out, you can next test TCP/IP connectivity by performing a ping test. When you use the `ping` command, your machine sends a ping packet to another IP address and waits for a result. If the other machine answers, you see reply messages; if it doesn't, you see a request timed out message. You can also perform a ping test on your local machine to verify its connectivity: Use the machine's IP address, which you obtain from the ipconfig command, or the industry standard 127.0.0.1 address, known as a *loopback address*. If you suspect that the local machine's IP stack is not working correctly, you should ping the loopback address. Following are the commands for those tests:

```
ping 127.0.0.1
ping <Remote IP Address that you want to connect to>
```

Both of these commands should return something similar to the following:

```
Pinging 127.0.0.1 with 32 bytes of data:
Reply from 127.0.0.1: bytes=32 time<1ms TTL=128
Reply from 127.0.0.1: bytes=32 time<1ms TTL=128
Reply from 127.0.0.1: bytes=32 time<1ms TTL=128
Reply from 127.0.0.1: bytes=32 time<1ms TTL=128
Ping statistics for 127.0.0.1:
Packets: Sent = 4, Received = 4, Lost = 0 (0% loss),
Approximate round trip times in milli-seconds:
Minimum = 0ms, Maximum = 0ms, Average = 0ms
```

Testing DNS Resolution

To this point, the chapter has discussed pinging an IP address. ConfigMgr only uses FQDNs as a method to communicate; for example, when the client wants to talk to the MP, it starts with the FQDN name of the MP and tries to connect. ConfigMgr relies on the workstation's underlying network connectivity to perform DNS resolution, resolving that FQDN to an IP address so the network connection can be made. You can test this name resolution by using the ping command; instead of pinging an IP address, though, you ping the machine name. Figure 5.13 shows an example.

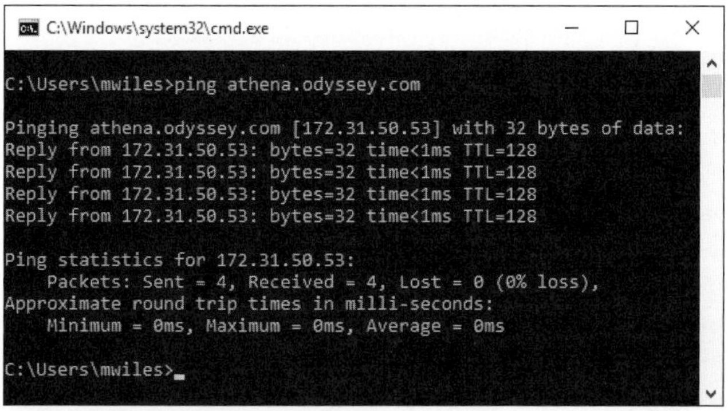

FIGURE 5.13 Pinging a machine by name.

Figure 5.13 shows that the ping started with the FQDN, Athena.odyssey.com, which resolved to the IP address 95.211.219.66. The information returned then looks just like the ping in the previous section. Name resolution turns a name into an IP address, and the machine knows how to connect to that IP address. If name resolution is not working, you see results similar to the following:

```
ping athena.odyssey.com
Ping request could not find host athena.odyssey.com. Please check the name and
try again.
```

Results such as these indicate a problem with DNS, which you can troubleshoot by using the NSlookup command, described at http://support.microsoft.com/kb/200525. To troubleshoot NetBIOS name resolution using Nbtstat and other methods, see http://support.microsoft.com/kb/323388. It is also useful to ping the known IP address of the target machine; if that works, the issue is narrowed to some type of name resolution–related issue.

An additional DNS problem that may arise is an incorrect referral. Incorrect referrals occur when a hostname is used instead of a FQDN and the wrong domain name is appended due to the DNS suffix search order. Incorrect referrals typically result in access denied errors. If you see unexpected access denied errors, ping the site system using both the hostname and FQDN to verify that they resolve to the same address.

TIP: USING THE HOSTS FILE

To further test a DNS issue or to temporarily work around that issue, edit the HOSTS file on the machine you are testing. This file is located at *%systemroot%*\system32\drivers\etc and does not have a file extension. Use an administrator account to run Windows Notepad and then open the file. At the end of the file, enter the IP address and FQDN of the machine you cannot resolve, save the file, and exit Notepad. A machine always reads the HOSTS file for the FQDN of the name before trying to resolve it with another method. When you get a successful ping, fix the DNS issue. Remember to go back and remove the HOSTS file entry.

Troubleshooting Routers and Firewall Ports

When you can get a packet outside the local network, it must pass through a router. A router is a software or hardware device that connects different networks together and allows packets to pass from one network to the other. If a router drops packets or doesn't allow them to cross networks, your network connection is broken at that particular point. tracert (short for trace route), is a tool you can use to determine if a packet is making it across the routers to its final destination. The program traces the route from where the packet started to its final destination, if it can get that far. The point at which the packet crosses a router is called a *hop*. tracert shows you the hops to get to the final destination. For a real-world example, Figure 5.14 shows a trace route from the ConfigMgr Unleashed lab to a live website.

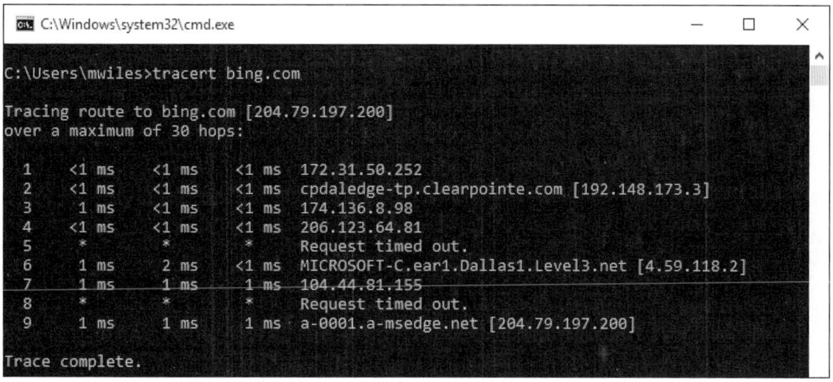

FIGURE 5.14   Tracing the route to the bing.com website.

Figure 5.14 shows that the name is resolved and then traces a route to it. There are nine hops, meaning the packet goes over nine routers to get to the address. Hops 5 and 8 show request timed out messages, but hops 6 and 9 look good. It might be that the router could not provide information at the hops where the messages occurred. If you see continuous request timed out messages, it means the packet got lost at that last hop.

If tracert shows that the packet makes it to the final destination, but `ping` still fails, you may have a port or firewall issue. The firewall could be set so that the machine doesn't respond to incoming pings, which would cause your pings to fail. Ports blocked by firewalls and routers are common sources of connectivity problems. In other cases, a port may simply not be listening on the system to which you are trying to connect. You can attempt to connect to the specific port on the target system with the telnet command. For example, to verify that you can connect to the Trivial File Transfer Protocol (TFTP) daemon service (port 69) on PXE-enabled DP Charon.Odyssey.com, open a command prompt (by selecting **Start** -> **Run** and then typing **cmd**) and enter the following:

```
telnet Charon.Odyssey.com 69
```

If telnet is successful, it will open the telnet screen with a cursor. If the connection fails, you will receive an error message.

When a connection to a port fails, first verify that the service is listening on the appropriate port. On the machine that should receive the connections, enter the command `netstat –a` to list all connections and listening ports and then check the following:

▶ If the port is not shown, verify that all system requirements and prerequisites are met.

▶ If the port displays as enabled, check all network firewall logs for dropped packets.

Refer to your network team or vendor firewall documentation for procedures to check firewall logs. Also, check the Windows Firewall logs and settings (see http://technet.microsoft .com/network/bb545423.aspx) and any third-party security software that performs intrusion detection and prevention.

Additional tools are available to troubleshoot port status issues. Consider these examples:

▶ The PortQry command-line utility, downloadable from http://www.microsoft .com/downloads/details.aspx?familyid=89811747-C74B-4638-A2D5-AC828BDC6983&displaylang=en.

▶ PortQryUI, which you can download from http://www.microsoft.com/downloads/ details.aspx?FamilyID=8355E537-1EA6-4569-AABB-F248F4BD91D0&displaylang=en. PortQryUI provides equivalent functionality to PortQry through a graphical user interface (GUI).

You can go to http://www.microsoft.com/downloads and search for PortQry to bring up links for these tools.

Congested or Slow Network Links

You may experience slowness with ConfigMgr and networks, meaning that things don't happen as fast as they once did. This is often seen with content downloads on clients. You can test slowness with the `ping` command. From the client, ping the DP from which ConfigMgr is trying to download the content. In the results of the command, notice an item called `time`. It is written this way in the ping results:

```
Reply from 172.31.50.53: bytes=32 time=50ms TTL=128
```

`time=50ms` means it took 50 milliseconds to get the reply from the destination site. The higher the number, the slower the network. A high value may also be returned if a network is congested. Sometimes the ping times out because the network is slow. In these cases, you can change the `ping` command line to insert a time to wait before timing out, like this:

```
Ping -w 3000 <IP address of target system>
```

In this example, `3000` is the number of milliseconds for the `ping` command to wait for a reply before timing out.

Testing MPs and DPs

A network issue could be the MP or DP to which you are trying to connect. In ConfigMgr, both the MP and the DP are websites. ConfigMgr provides some commands to test the connectivity to these websites. In your browser, type the following commands to connect to the MP website for testing:

```
http://<FQDN of the MP>sms_mp/.sms_aut?mplist
http://<FQDN of the MP>/sms_mp/.sms_aut?mpcert
```

`mplist` returns a list of the MPs in the same site, and `mpcert` returns a string of characters corresponding to the MP certificate.

If you are using HTTPS for the MPs, enter the following:

```
https://<FQDN of the MP>sms_mp/.sms_aut?mplist
https://<FQDN of the MP>/sms_mp/.sms_aut?mpcert
```

You may run into issues where the client is not downloading the complete package or perhaps cannot find the package on the DP. In such a case, you can test the DP to verify package contents or see if the package is on the DP. Run the following command in your browser window (if using HTTPS, change HTTP to HTTPS):

```
http://<FQDN of the DP>/SMS_DP_SMSPKG$/<Package ID you want to test>
```

After entering this command, you are prompted to enter your user ID and password to verify that you have permissions to the content store where the package is located. Once access is granted, a list of package files is returned. Figure 5.15 shows an example of this, using the built-in ConfigMgr client package.

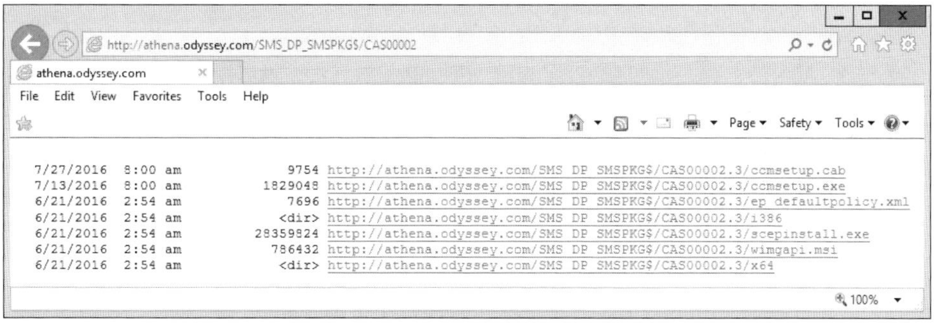

FIGURE 5.15   Testing the contents of a package on a DP.

Troubleshooting Service Principal Names

Service principal names (SPNs) provide information that clients use to identify and mutually authenticate with services using Kerberos authentication. Services use Active Directory SPN registration to make the required information available to clients. Missing or incorrect SPN registration is a common cause of problems with client communications with site systems, such as failure to download content or client approval problems. HTTP 401 errors in client log files, including Datatransferservice.log and ccmexec.log, may indicate problems with SPN registrations. To register the required SPNs properly, consider the following:

▶ If running the SQL Server service using a domain account on the site database server or other roles requiring SQL Server, follow the instructions at http://technet.microsoft.com/library/bb735885.aspx to register the SPN. If the SQL Server service is configured to run under the local system account, the SPN does not need to be manually registered. However, running SQL Server as local system is not recommended for security reasons.

▶ For site systems that require IIS, if the system is registered in DNS using a CNAME (a DNS alias rather than the actual computer name), you must register the SPN by using the procedure described at http://technet.microsoft.com/library/bb694288.aspx.

Summary

This chapter provided an in-depth look at one of the underlying prerequisites for Config-Mgr: the network. It discussed how ConfigMgr communicates with its site servers, other sites, and external resources. It talked about the ways clients communicate with site roles such as the MP and DP. It covered where to place servers for the best client performance and how clients use boundaries and boundary groups, BranchCache, and Peer Cache. It discussed communication security, how clients use that security, and other site roles that use that security. The chapter discussed the ports used for communication and the protocols for those ports. It discussed troubleshooting issues, including in-depth information on pings, ping tests, and how to verify that an MP and DP are working correctly.

Chapter 6, "Installing and Updating System Center Configuration Manager," covers installing and updating ConfigMgr.

Installing and Updating System Center Configuration Manager

As indicated in Chapter 4, "Architecture Design Planning," and Chapter 5, "Network Design," installing Configuration Manager (ConfigMgr) properly is much more than mounting the .iso on a server and running a setup program. ConfigMgr is a wide and deep product, meaning it has many in-depth capabilities that you must properly plan for as well as properly implement. Should you fail in these activities, you will run into immediate issues, and your expectations of ConfigMgr may truly fall short.

The Configuration Manager installation experience has been vastly improved and simplified from previous versions of the product. The authors strongly recommend reviewing Chapters 4 and 5 as a prerequisite to reading this chapter. Chapter 4 provides in-depth information and guidance on planning activities and decisions that will influence the choices you make during the installation steps this chapter discusses. Chapter 5 thoroughly covers the network requirements of ConfigMgr, discussing items such as firewalls, ports, client communications, and more. This chapter takes you through the foundational steps of installing a site hierarchy, primary standalone sites, site servers, and required components and performing the initial site configuration.

NOTE: CONFIGMGR CURRENT BRANCH BASELINE BUILD

Microsoft plans to release a "baseline build" of ConfigMgr Current Branch every year. A baseline build is required for initial installation. At the time this book was published, build (version) 1702 was the latest baseline build. Identify the latest baseline build and support life cycle at https://docs.microsoft.com/sccm/core/servers/manage/updates#a-namebkmkbaselinesa-baseline-and-update-versions.

Performing Preinstallation Tasks

Successfully installing Configuration Manager sites depends on the correct installation and configuration of all required external components.

The preceding chapters of this book provide extensive information on the dependencies and requirements you need to consider prior to performing the installation. The authors recommend creating a checklist of requirements based on the information in those chapters.

TIP: CHECKING DEPENDENCIES FOR INSTALLATION

Chapter 2, "Configuration Manager Overview," outlines the dependencies required for each role in Configuration Manager.

The following sections provide a summary of the requirements specific to the installation tasks for ConfigMgr sites and the roles that can be installed during setup. The Management Point (MP) and Distribution Point (DP) roles are the only supported roles available for selection during installation of a primary site.

Required Windows and Hardware Components

Before you start the System Center Configuration Manager setup wizard, consider the following prerequisites:

▶ **Minimum hardware requirements:** Minimum hardware requirements, which in addition to the supported hardware requirements of the operating system, are specified at https://docs.microsoft.com/sccm/core/plan-design/configs/recommended-hardware.

▶ **Operating systems:** All site roles support the following Windows operating systems (both Standard and Datacenter editions):

  ▶ Windows Server 2012

  ▶ Windows Server 2012 R2

  ▶ Windows Server 2016

▶ **Operating system roles and features:** Table 6.1 lists roles and features that may be required, depending on the ConfigMgr site system being used. Be sure to review the latest information at https://docs.microsoft.com/sccm/core/plan-design/network/prepare-windows-servers.

TABLE 6.1   Operating System Roles and Features

Feature/Role	Component
Features	.NET Framework:
	▶ ASP.NET
	▶ HTTP activation
	▶ Non-HTTP activation
	▶ Windows Communication Foundation (WCF) services
	Background Intelligent Transfer Services (BITS)
	BranchCache
	Data Deduplication
	Remote Differential Compression
Roles	Network Device Enrollment Service
	Web server (IIS):
	▶ Common HTTP features:
	▶ HTTP redirection
	▶ Application development:
	▶ .NET extensibility
	▶ ASP.NET
	▶ ISAPI extensions
	▶ ISAPI filters
	▶ Management tools:
	▶ IIS 6 Management compatibility
	▶ IIS 6 Metabase compatibility
	▶ IIS 6 Windows Management Instrumentation (WMI) compatibility
	▶ Security
	▶ Request filtering
	▶ Windows authentication

To prepare your Windows servers to support ConfigMgr, review the latest information at https://docs.microsoft.com/sccm/core/plan-design/network/prepare-windows-servers. A frequent setup mistake is neglecting to configure IIS request filtering on DPs. By default, IIS filters specific filenames and extensions from download, which makes a lot of sense for websites. However, for a DP, you may need to download a folder named bin or a file with a .PCK extension—which requires configuring IIS filters. Also be sure to run the Prerequisite Checker (as discussed in the "Using the Prerequisite Checker" section, later in this chapter) on each server that will install a site role to ensure that all required components are installed.

TIP: CONFIGMGR PREREQUISITES

As ConfigMgr is an ever-changing product, so are the prerequisites. The prerequisites listed in this book were accurate at the time this book was published, but you should be sure to review the latest prerequisite information at https://docs.microsoft.com/sccm/core/plan-design/configs/supported-operating-systems-for-site-system-servers.

During planning, consider creating a matrix of your site systems by role and plan to configure the prerequisites by role type. Also, realize that Microsoft's hardware requirements are for a minimum installation; plan to add additional resources based on the production demands of your ConfigMgr site(s).

The authors recommend that you plan to baseline a proof of concept (POC) site and scale it based on scenario testing in a controlled environment.

SQL Server Requirements

Every ConfigMgr site has a database engine requirement. Following are supported database requirements for the server assigned the site database role (review the latest information at https://docs.microsoft.com/sccm/core/plan-design/configs/support-for-sql-server-versions):

▶ **SQL Server version:** The following versions and editions are required and supported:

   ▶ SQL Server 2016 Standard and Enterprise

   ▶ SQL Server 2014 Standard and Enterprise

   ▶ SQL Server 2012 Standard and Enterprise

NOTE: MANAGING MORE THAN 50,000 CLIENTS

To be supported by Microsoft when you need to manage more than 50,000 clients, use SQL Server Enterprise edition. If SQL Server Standard edition is installed for the central administration site (CAS), the hierarchy is limited to managing a maximum of 50,000 clients. Upgrading the database server to Enterprise edition after site installation does not change this limit. Plan to install the Enterprise edition of SQL Server if your hierarchy needs to support more than 50,000 clients.

Microsoft also recommends using at least four TempDB data files, which should be of equal size.

▶ **SQL Server requirements:** Following is the required configuration for the supported editions and versions of SQL Server (for additional information, see Chapter 4):

   ▶ **Database collation:** SQL_Latin1_General_CP1_CI_AS. Each site must use the same collation.

   ▶ **SQL Server features:** Database Engine Services is the only required feature for each database site server.

   ▶ **Authentication method:** Windows authentication is required.

   ▶ **SQL Server instance:** Install a dedicated instance of SQL Server for each site.

   ▶ **SQL Server memory:** In implementation scenarios with the site server role and the database role colocated, dedicate at least 50% of the memory to SQL Server.

▶ **SQL Server Reporting Service (SSRS):** SSRS is optional but must be installed for the Reporting Services point role.

▶ **SQL Server Ports:** Configuration Manager supports only static ports (default or custom). In the case of SQL Server named instances, which use dynamic ports by default, you must manually configure a static port. Information on static ports for a named instance is available at https://docs.microsoft.com/sql/database-engine/configure-windows/configure-a-server-to-listen-on-a-specific-tcp-port.

▶ **SQL Server Memory:** You must set a memory limit for the SQL Server instance; a warning is displayed during the prerequisite check if the default configuration is unlimited. This setting is very important, and failing to configure it normally leaves SQL Server consuming nearly all the available memory by default. The authors recommend setting this limit to a value that leaves the operating system and other applications co-hosted on the server with enough memory to function at their recommended levels.

▶ **SQL TempDB:** The out-of-the-box configuration will lead to fragmentation issues as TempDB grows, so you must configure SQL TempDB. For information on best practice, see Steve Thompson's excellent post on configuring TempDB size for ConfigMgr at https://stevethompsonmvp.wordpress.com/2016/02/05/proper-tempdb-creation-for-configuration-manager/.

TIP: ACCOUNT TYPE FOR SQL SERVICE

You can configure the SQL Server service to use an Active Directory (AD) domain account or the local system account. Microsoft's SQL product team recommends using a domain account as a security best practice. Using a domain account requires you to register the service principal name (SPN) manually for the account. Information on SPN registration is available at https://docs.microsoft.com/sccm/core/servers/manage/modify-your-infrastructure#bkmk_SPN. Using the local system account option registers the SPN automatically. If the SPN is not configured properly for the AD account assigned as the SQL service account, Configuration Manager may not function correctly. The authors recommend ensuring that the SPN registration is configured properly before proceeding with your ConfigMgr installation.

Active Directory Requirements

A Configuration Manager installation has mandatory and optional Active Directory requirements, documented at https://docs.microsoft.com/sccm/core/plan-design/configs/support-for-active-directory-domains:

▶ **Mandatory:** All site systems must be members of an AD domain. You must use a domain user account that is a local administrator on the site server for the installation.

▶ **Optional:** You can extend the AD forest schema to support publishing ConfigMgr data. Though the schema extension is optional, there are many benefits, as discussed in Chapter 2, which covers the schema extension steps in detail. (There are no changes in the schema if you previously extended it for ConfigMgr 2007 and newer versions.) A recommended best practice is to use an AD security group for the delegation required after extending the schema.

Windows Server Update Services

You must install the Windows Server Update Services (WSUS) role on each server that will be a software update point (SUP). You must also install the WSUS administration console on the ConfigMgr site server when the SUP will be installed on a remote site system. Simply install the WSUS role; there is no need to configure it, as ConfigMgr configures WSUS when you install the SUP. Review the latest prerequisites for the SUP at https:// docs.microsoft.com/sccm/sum/plan-design/prerequisites-for-software-updates.

TIP: KEEP WSUS VERSIONS CONSISTENT

The WSUS version on the site server must be the same as the WSUS version on the SUP for the site server.

Install the WSUS role on each server that will be a SUP. You must also install the WSUS administration console on the ConfigMgr primary site server when the SUP is on a different server from the primary site.

Using the Prerequisite Checker

The Prerequisite Checker is crucial to ensuring a safe and smooth installation of ConfigMgr. Selecting **Assess Server Readiness** on the ConfigMgr Installation splash screen, displayed in Figure 6.1, redirects you to the latest prerequisite information at https://docs.microsoft.com/sccm/core/servers/deploy/install/prerequisite-checker.

NOTE: ADDITIONAL OPTIONS ON THE INITIAL SPLASH SCREEN

The splash screen contains additional options that allow you to do the following:

▶ Install the admin console

▶ Download System Center Updates Publisher (SCUP), which is used for detection/deployment of third party patches

▶ Download clients for additional operating systems such as Linux and Mac OS X

Configuration Manager has two options for running a prerequisite check:

▶ Invoke the Prerequisite Checker as part of the setup routine

▶ Use the standalone Prerequisite Checker

FIGURE 6.1   ConfigMgr installation splash page.

ConfigMgr uses the same executable to perform the prerequisite checks. The tool generates three log files in the root of the system drive. The primary log file with the full check details is ConfigMgrPrereq.log.

The following sections discuss the differences in these two approaches.

Invoking the Prerequisite Checker as Part of the Setup Routine

The Prerequisite Checker runs by default for any new installation. While it is important for this check to run during installation, many ConfigMgr administrators prefer to run it separately first to avoid any surprises or excess work while attempting installation.

Using the Standalone Prerequisite Checker

The other option available with the Prerequisite Checker is to run it from a command prompt. This option provides the most flexibility and additionally allows you to target a remote computer. The Prerequisite Checker verifies the minimum requirement of each site type listed in the relevant installation. Following are the checks you can either run on the local machine or use on a remote machine:

▶ Configuration Manager console

▶ SQL and SQL Express

▶ SMS provider

▶ CAS

▶ Primary site

▶ Secondary site

▶ Upgrade to secondary site

▶ Management point

▶ Distribution point

The tool requires you to use the fully qualified domain name (FQDN) of the targeted machine. Run the tool at the command prompt with a /? switch to invoke the help menu and view correct syntax, illustrated in Figure 6.2. Table 6.2 lists all the command-line options.

```
G:\SMSSETUP\BIN\X64>prereqchk.exe /?
Invalid arguments were specified. Please see the command-line options usage.
Usage:
--------------------------------
PREREQCHK.EXE [/NOUI] /PRI /SQL <FQDN of SQL Server>
              /SDK <FQDN of SMS Provider>
              [/JOIN <FQDN of central administration site>]
              [/MP <FQDN of management point>]
              [/DP <FQDN of distribution point>]

PREREQCHK.EXE [/NOUI] /CAS /SQL <FQDN of SQL Server>
              /SDK <FQDN of SMS Provider>
              [/EXPAND <FQDN of expand primary site>]

PREREQCHK.EXE [/NOUI] /SEC <FQDN of secondary site> [/INSTALLSQLEXPRESS]

PREREQCHK.EXE [/NOUI] /SECUPGRADE <FQDN of secondary site> [/SQL]

PREREQCHK.EXE /ADMINUI
```

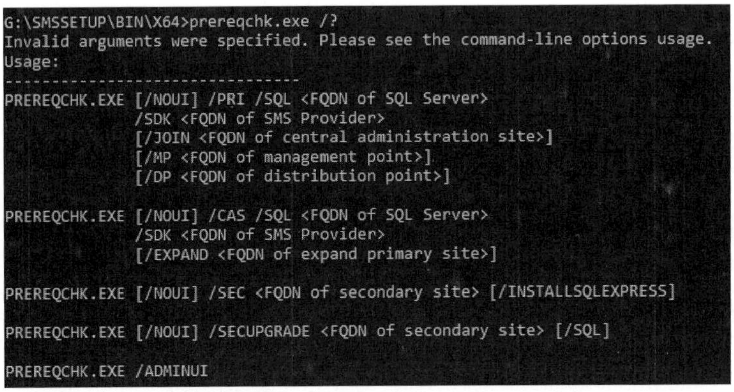

FIGURE 6.2   ConfigMgr Prerequisite Checker command-line options.

TABLE 6.2   Prerequisite Checker Command-Line Options and Usage

Usage Switch	Description
/NOUI	Runs the Prerequisite Checker without displaying the user interface. Specify this option before any other options.
/PRI or /CAS	Verifies that the local computer meets the requirements for the primary site or CAS. You can specify only one option; it cannot be combined with the /SEC option.
/SEC <FQDN of secondary site>	Verifies that the specified computer meets the requirements for the secondary site. This option cannot be combined with the /PRI or /CAS option.
[/INSTALLSQLEXPRESS]	Verifies whether SQL Express can be installed on the specified computer. This option can be used only after the /SEC option.
/SQL <FQDN of SQL Server>	Verifies that the specified computer meets the requirements for SQL Server to host the ConfigMgr site database. This option is required when using the /PRI or /CAS option.
/SDK <FQDN of SMS provider>	Verifies that the specified computer meets the requirements for the SMS provider. This option is required when you use the /PRI or /CAS option.

Usage Switch	Description
`/JOIN <FQDN of central administration site>`	Verifies that the local computer meets the requirements for connecting to the central administration site. This option is valid only when you use the `/PRI` option.
`/MP <FQDN of management point>`	Verifies that the specified computer meets the requirements for the MP site system role.
`/DP <FQDN of distribution point>`	Verifies that the specified computer meets the requirements for the DP site system role.
`/ADMINUI`	Verifies that the local computer meets the prerequisites for the ConfigMgr console. This option cannot be combined with any other option.

TIP: PREREQUISITE CHECKER STANDALONE

In the unlikely event that you cannot run the Prerequisite Checker remotely, copy the Prerequisite Checker files to the remote computer. Review the directions at https://docs.microsoft.com/sccm/core/servers/deploy/install/prerequisite-checker#copy-prerequisite-checker-files-to-another-computer.

Using the Prerequisite Files Downloader Tool

A mandatory part of ConfigMgr installation via the setup wizard is checking for updated prerequisite components. The updated prerequisite components check requires an Internet connection to download files required by the setup routine. An option exists to download the prerequisite components from a local drive and specify the location of the files without an Internet connection requirement during the installation.

Perform the following steps to download the files to a local folder:

1. Create a folder on a local drive.

2. Open the command prompt as administrator.

3. Navigate to the SMSSETUP\Bin\X64 folder and run setupdl.exe.

4. Follow the wizard to download the files to the desired folder. (Review c:\ConfigMgrSetup.log for download progress and troubleshooting.)

5. Browse to the folder you created for the prerequisite files and start the download.

Performing Site Installation Tasks

The "Performing Preinstallation Tasks" section, earlier in this chapter, discusses prerequisites and dependencies you must consider and perform before invoking the System Center Configuration Manager Setup Wizard. The remainder of this chapter discusses installing ConfigMgr sites and initial postinstallation configurations.

You can install and implement ConfigMgr two different ways:

▶ By creating a hierarchy

▶ By creating a standalone site

These two methods require you to install specific Configuration Manager site types and with a specific installation order.

A hierarchy supports the CAS, child primary, and secondary site types. In a hierarchy, a primary site must always join an existing CAS. Note that in a design where you have one primary site, you can add a CAS in the future as needed. (See the note "Do You need a Central Administration Site?" for more information.) This is discussed further in Chapter 4. Following is the order in which you must install a hierarchy:

1. Install a CAS by following the steps discussed in the next section, "Installing a Central Administration Site."

2. Install one or more child primary sites by following the steps in the "Installing a Primary Site" section, later in this chapter.

3. Based on your design and needs, optionally install secondary sites under the child primary sites, as described in the "Installing a Secondary Site" section, later in this chapter.

A standalone site supports one primary site and one or more secondary sites under the primary site. Following is the order in which you must handle a standalone site implementation:

1. Install a primary site by following the steps discussed in the "Installing a Primary Site" section, later in this chapter.

2. Based on your design and needs, optionally install secondary sites under the primary site by following the steps in the "Installing a Secondary Site" section, later in this chapter.

NOTE: DO YOU NEED A CENTRAL ADMINISTRATION SITE?

In most cases, a CAS is not necessary. ConfigMgr has very granular role-based administration and very high scale numbers to support a single primary site. (Review the latest scale numbers at https://docs.microsoft.com/sccm/core/plan-design/configs/size-and-scale-numbers.) At the time this book was published, a single primary site could support 150,000 total clients. If you have more than 150,000 clients, or have other reasons you think you need a CAS, the authors recommend engaging a consultant to confirm hierarchy design. Chapter 4 discusses site planning in more detail.

TIP: USING THE CMTRACE LOG FILE READER FOR CONFIGMGR

The ConfigMgr installation includes an updated standalone log file reader, CMTrace.exe, which is located in \SMSSETUP\TOOLS. CMTrace.exe is great for reading the log files generated by the installation and configuration process. CMTrace is also installed to the \TOOLS folder during installation, and it occasionally receives updates with ConfigMgr updates.

If you copy CMTrace to alternate locations (as is commonly done), be sure to look for newer versions of CMTrace after upgrading any primary site.

Installing a Central Administration Site

If you plan to build a hierarchy with more than one primary site, you must install a central administration site first. Following is a list of activities you must perform before starting the installation:

1. Install a supported operating system.

2. Install and configure the prerequisites for the CAS.

3. Optionally extend the AD schema and configure the delegation required.

4. Document the site code and site name for the CAS.

5. Optionally run the standalone Prerequisite Checker.

The authors recommend installing the prerequisites relevant to the CAS on the server or servers allocated to the CAS site installation. The supported roles on a CAS are listed in Chapter 4.

NOTE: ABOUT PREREQUISITES

The database server and SSRS requirements apply only if the CAS server is hosting the SQL Server components. Also, the minimum WSUS installation required on a CAS is the WSUS console. If you perform a full installation of WSUS, remember to cancel the Windows Server Update Services Configuration Wizard, as running it is not required.

With the prerequisites successfully installed, it is time to install the CAS. Perform the following steps:

1. Log on to the server (Armada in this example) using a domain user account with local administration privileges.

2. Start the installation from the System Center Configuration Manager splash screen. Double-click splash.hta and click **Install**.

3. Work through the following significant wizard pages:

   ▶ **Before You Begin:** This page lists the items you must check before you begin the installation. Click **Next**.

   ▶ **Getting Started:** Select **Install a Configuration Manager Central Administration Site**, shown in Figure 6.3, and then click **Next**.

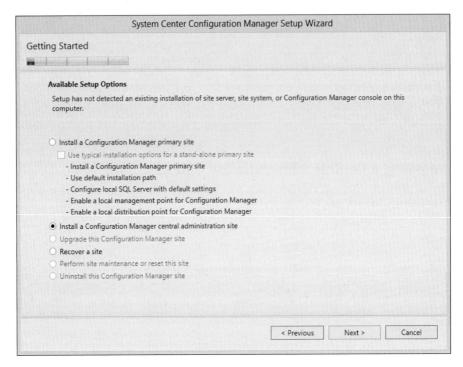

FIGURE 6.3   Getting started with the CAS installation.

▶ **Product Key and Select for Current Branch (CB) or Long Term Servicing Branch (LTSB):** Enter your product code and select **Current Branch**, and then click **Next**.

▶ **Prerequisite Licenses:** Accept the terms to continue with the installation, and then click **Next**.

▶ **Prerequisite Downloads:** You have two options: Download Required Files or Use Previously Downloaded Files. Specify either a UNC file path or a local file path to an existing folder. With the second option, you can use setupdl.exe in advance to download the prerequisite files to a local folder. This option is useful in situations where there is no Internet access during the installation process. Click **Next**.

▶ **Server Language Selection:** Select the supported languages that are appropriate for your environment. (You can change this setting after installation by rerunning setup and selecting the Site Maintenance option.) Click **Next**.

▶ **Site and Installation Settings:** Type a unique three-character site code, provide a site name, and specify the installation folder. You cannot change these settings without reinstallation. Review Chapter 4 for information. Figure 6.4 shows the Site and Installation Settings page. Click **Next**.

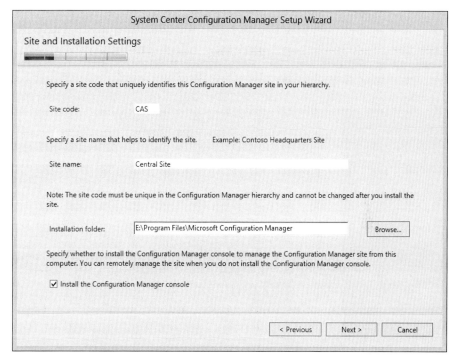

FIGURE 6.4   Specifying site and installation settings.

▶ **Central Administration Site Installation:** Choose the first option when installing a new hierarchy; choose the second option when adding a CAS to a standalone primary site, and then click **Next**.

▶ **Database Information:** Type the server name, instance name, and database name for the site server hosting the CAS database role. Figure 6.5 shows the default selection when the database server is colocated on the site server. It also shows the SQL Server service broker port (which is the service used for replication in the hierarchy). Click **Next**.

▶ **Database File Information:** Enter the paths to the locations of the SQL Server data file and transaction log. The default locations are entered by default. Click **Next**.

▶ **SMS Provider Settings:** Accept or specify the SMS provider settings, and then click **Next**.

▶ **Usage Data:** This page provides basic information about usage data collected by Microsoft. After installation, you can change the level of data collected through the ConfigMgr console. Click **Next**.

▶ **Service Connection Point Setup:** This is your connection to the cloud and performs many functions in your hierarchy. Read full details about the service connection point at https://docs.microsoft.com/sccm/core/servers/deploy/configure/about-the-service-connection-point. Click **Next**.

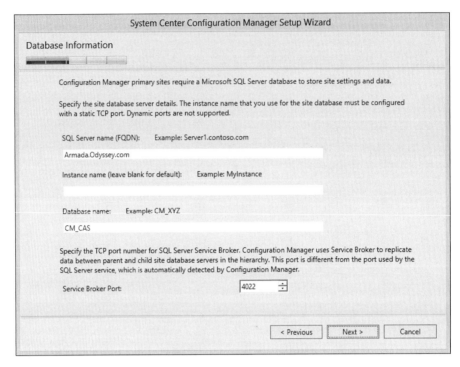

FIGURE 6.5   Providing database configuration information.

▶ **Settings Summary:** Review the summary of settings selected and then click **Next** to begin the built-in prerequisite check.

▶ **Prerequisite Check:** During installation, the prerequisite check automatically runs. There should be no surprises at this point if you ran the Prerequisite Checker separately. Click **Next**.

▶ **Installation Progress:** During installation you get the **View Log** option, which conveniently uses CMTrace.

▶ **Complete Installation:** The final wizard page includes a link to the installation log files. Click **Finish**.

For more information, review the documentation for using the setup wizard at https://docs.microsoft.com/sccm/core/servers/deploy/install/use-the-setup-wizard-to-install-sites.

Installing a Primary Site

There are two modes of installation for a primary site:

▶ **Create a standalone primary site:** This is used for a single primary site installation.

▶ **Join the primary site to an existing hierarchy:** You can install this primary site type only if you previously installed a CAS as part of a hierarchy deployment.

The two modes of primary sites differ in the type of roles you can enable. The supported roles on a primary site are listed in Chapter 4.

Following is a list of steps you must perform before starting the installation of either type of primary site:

1. Install a supported operating system.

2. Install and configure the minimum prerequisites for a primary site.

3. Optionally extend the AD schema and configure the delegation required.

4. Document the site code and site name for the primary site.

5. Optionally run the standalone Prerequisite Checker.

6. Document the CAS site code and FQDN of the CAS site provider.

7. Verify that the SQL collation on the child primary assigned database server is the same as the CAS database.

8. Ensure that the user account running the installation has the following rights:

   ▶ Local administrator rights on the CAS site server

   ▶ Local administrator rights on the CAS database server

   ▶ Local administrator rights on the primary site server

   ▶ Local administrator rights on the primary site database server

   ▶ User-assigned rights with the Infrastructure Administrator or Full Administrator role on the CAS

TIP: ABOUT PREREQUISITES

The authors recommend installing all the prerequisites for the primary role based on the design of the environment. In scenarios where all roles are hosted on a single server, installing the prerequisites in advance reduces errors during additional site role installation. Review the complete list of prerequisites at https://docs.microsoft.com/sccm/core/plan-design/configs/site-and-site-system-prerequisites.

With the prerequisites successfully installed, you can install a primary site that will join to the existing CAS. (The standalone primary site installation uses a very similar process, so this chapter shows the more complex scenario of connecting to an existing CAS in detail.) Perform the following steps:

1. Log on to the server (Athena in this example) with a domain user account with local administration privileges.

2. Start the installation from the System Center Configuration Manager splash screen. Double-click splash.hta and click **Install**.

3. Work through the following significant wizard pages to install a standalone primary site:

▶ **Getting Started:** Select **Install a Configuration Manager Primary Site**, and then click **Next**.

▶ **Prerequisite Downloads:** You have two options: Download Required Files or Use Previously Downloaded Files. Specify either a UNC file path or local file path to an existing folder, and then click **Next**.

▶ **Server Language Selection:** Select the supported languages that are appropriate for your environment. This setting can be changed postinstallation, by rerunning setup and selecting the Site Maintenance option. Click **Next**.

▶ **Client Language Selection:** Select the Configuration Manager client-supported languages appropriate for your environment, and then click **Next**. You can change this setting after installation by rerunning setup and selecting the Site Maintenance option.

▶ **Site and Installation Settings:** Type a unique three-character site code, provide a site name, and specify the installation folder. You cannot change these settings without a reinstallation. Figure 6.6 shows the Site and Installation Settings page. Click **Next**.

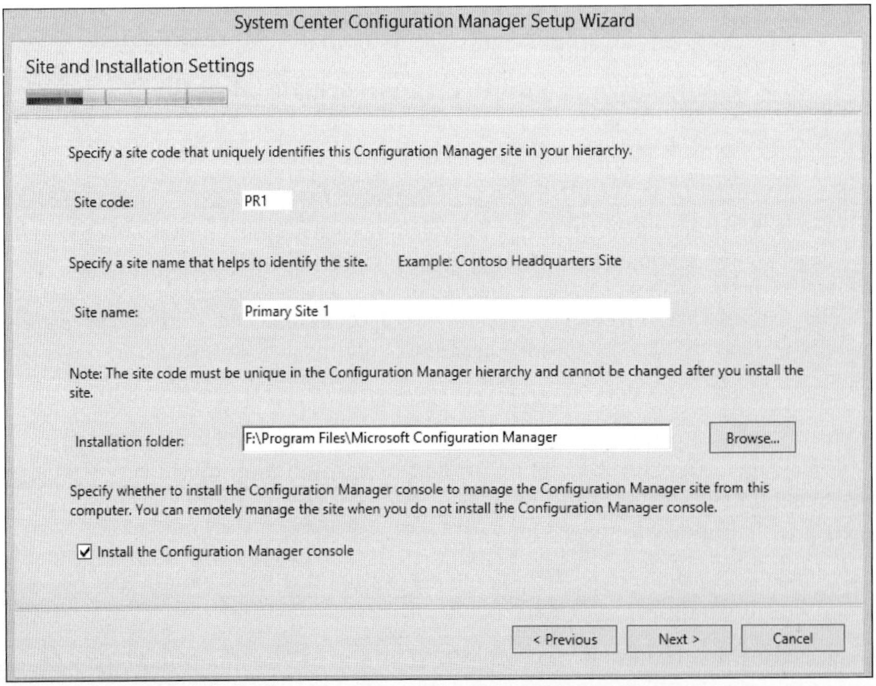

FIGURE 6.6   Selecting the site code and site name.

▶ **Primary Site Installation:** Select **Join the Primary Site to an Existing Hierarchy** and specify the FQDN of the CAS. Click **Next**.

▶ **Database Information:** Type the server name, instance name, and database name for the site server hosting the primary site database role. Figure 6.6 shows the default selection when the database server is colocated on the site server. It also shows the SQL Server service broker port (which is the service used for replication in the hierarchy). Click **Next**.

▶ **Database File Information:** Enter the path to the location for the SQL Server data file and transaction log. The default locations are entered by default. Click **Next**.

▶ **SMS Provider Settings:** Accept or specify the SMS provider settings and click **Next**. Chapters 4 and 5 discuss aspects of the SMS provider.

▶ **Client Computer Communication Settings:** Select whether clients communicate over HTTPS only (which requires PKI certificate authentication to be configured) or whether to use a particular communication protocol on each site system. Click **Next**.

▶ **Site System Roles:** You can install the MP and DP roles. Select the required roles and click **Next**. Figure 6.7 shows both optional roles selected.

▶ **Settings Summary:** Review the summary of settings selected and click **Next** to begin the built-in prerequisite check.

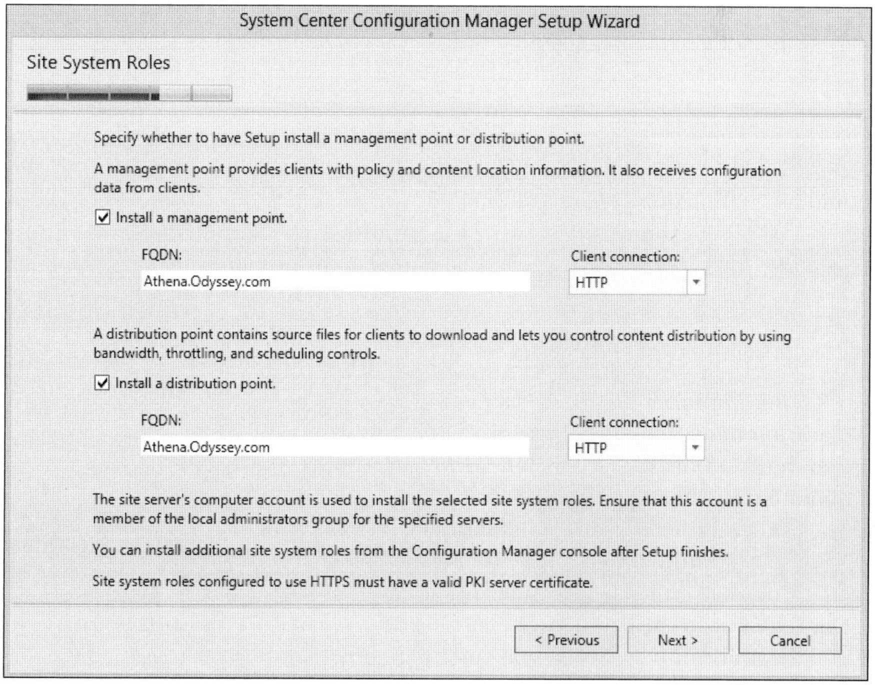

FIGURE 6.7 Configuring the MP and DP site system roles.

▶ **Prerequisite Check:** Review and resolve any blocking issues and click **Begin Install**.

▶ **Complete Installation:** The final wizard page is the completion page. There is a link to the installation log files on this page.

▶ **Review Logs:** When the installation dialog shows that the process is complete, the fun is just beginning. Review C:\ConfigMgrSetup.log for additional information. Click **Finish**.

Installing a Secondary Site

The final site type you can install is a secondary site. You must connect to a primary site or a CAS to initiate the installation from the administration console. A DP and an MP are automatically enabled as part of installing a secondary site.

Following is the list of additional prerequisite activities you must perform before starting the Create Secondary Site Wizard:

▶ Document the secondary site code and site name.

▶ Add the primary site provider server computer account to the local administrators group on the secondary site server.

▶ Optionally assign the secondary site provider server computer account security rights to publish to the system management folder in the case where the Active Directory schema has been extended.

▶ Ensure that the user account running the installation has the following rights:

  ▶ Local administrator rights on the secondary site server

  ▶ Local administrator rights on the primary site server

  ▶ Local administrator rights on the primary site database server

  ▶ User-assigned rights with the Infrastructure Administrator or Full Administrator role on the CAS or secondary site parent primary site

▶ Install and configure the required prerequisites, as documented at https://docs .microsoft.com/sccm/core/plan-design/configs/site-and-site-system-prerequisites.

▶ Optionally run the standalone Prerequisite Checker with the SEC option.

With the prerequisites successfully installed, it is time to install the secondary site. Perform the following steps:

1. Launch the Configuration Manager console and connect to the secondary site's parent primary site (for a standalone primary) or the CAS.

2. Connect to the ConfigMgr console and navigate to **Administration -> Site Configuration -> Sites**. Select the parent primary site in the middle pane and then click **Create Secondary Site** on the ribbon bar.

3. Configure the following significant wizard pages to create a secondary site:

> **General:** Type a unique three-character site code, the fully qualified domain name, and a site name and specify the installation folder for the secondary site. You cannot change these settings without a reinstallation. Figure 6.8 shows the general page with configuration details for the secondary site SS1 in the Odyssey lab. Click **Next**.

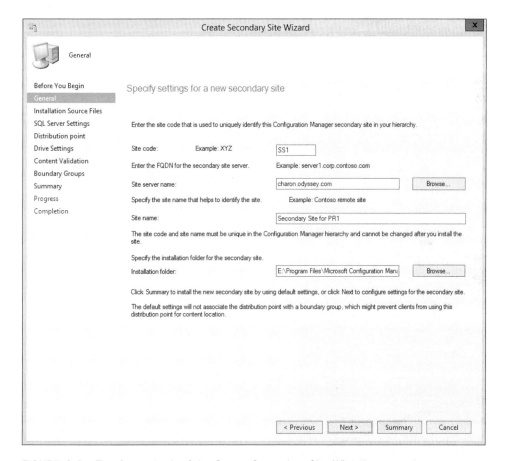

FIGURE 6.8   The General tab of the Create Secondary Site Wizard.

> **Installation Source Files:** You have three options:
>
>> ▶ Copy installation files over the network from the parent site server
>>
>> ▶ Use the source files at the following location
>>
>> ▶ Use the source files at the following location on the secondary site server (most secure)
>
> The default option is to copy the source files from the parent site. Accept the default or provide details for the alternative choice, and then click **Next**.

▶ **SQL Server Settings:** Accept the default option to install SQL Server Express using the default ports or provide the details for a full supported SQL Server instance for the secondary site. Click **Next**.

▶ **Distribution Point:** Review the distribution point options on this page. The authors recommend selecting the option to install IIS if required, as shown in Figure 6.9. Note that you can have IIS and BranchCache installed on the new server by enabling the check boxes. Click **Next**.

▶ **Drive Settings:** You have two configurable options: Drive Space Reserve and Content Placement Options. Specify the minimum space to reserve on the distribution point drive(s). You can also select the logical drives to use and a secondary location. The default is to allow automatic configuration where the drive with the most free space is selected. Click **Next**.

▶ **Content Validation:** Specify content validation configuration by enabling the check box **Validate Content on a Schedule** and selecting the desired schedule time. Click **Next**.

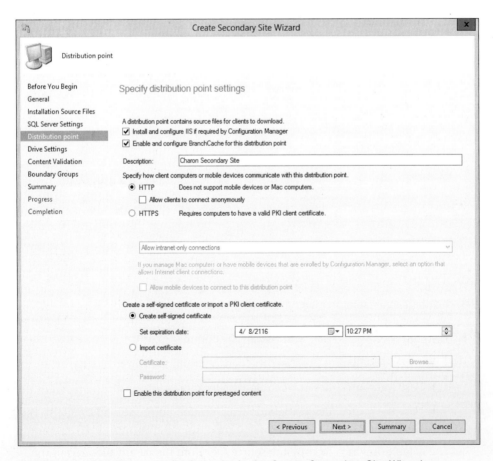

FIGURE 6.9   Installing a distribution point in the Create Secondary Site Wizard.

▶ **Boundary Group:** Select or create boundary groups you want to assign to the distribution point of the secondary site and whether clients outside the assigned boundary groups can use the DP as a fallback. Click **Next**.

▶ **Summary:** Review the Summary page to verify the configuration and then click **Next** to begin the installation.

▶ **Complete Installation:** The final wizard page completes the wizard and shows success if all you have completed all mandatory sections. The installation process is not complete, however; when you click **Finish**, the wizard gathers your secondary site installation properties and initiates the installation process. Monitor the state and status of the installation by selecting the secondary site in the console and selecting **Show Install Status**. Use the status window to track the installation of the secondary site. Click **Finish**.

Installation Validation

The installation wizard eventually reports either success or failure. Investigate failures by using the log files listed in Appendix A, "Configuration Manager Log Files." You must also validate reported success status, as discussed in the next sections.

Validation Using the Console

You can validate the successful installation of a ConfigMgr site by using the ConfigMgr console. Two nodes can be used to validate the status of the site and components selected during the installation of the site:

▶ Site Status

▶ Component Status

These status nodes are located under **Monitoring -> System Status -> Site Status** and **Monitoring -> System Status -> Component Status**. These two status nodes are illustrated in Figure 6.10.

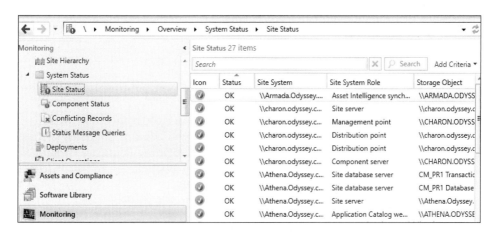

FIGURE 6.10   Viewing site status.

A healthy functioning site shows a status of OK for all configured and active components for the site. Review warnings and errors in the status nodes and resolve them before making the site available for use.

Validation with Log Files

ConfigMgr provides extensive logging of processes and installation. For a list of Configuration Manager log files, see Appendix A.

The installation log files also provide a detailed look at the installation steps performed by the installation process.

Configuring Site Properties

The "Performing Preinstallation Tasks" and "Performing Site Installation Tasks" sections of this chapter discussed preparing and installing the supported site types in Configuration Manager. The remainder of this chapter discusses basic configurations you must perform before managing clients.

Initial ConfigMgr Configurations

After successfully installing your Configuration Manager site, the authors recommend that you perform some initial configurations. The customizations discussed in the following sections focus on ensuring that you can provide the following basic functionality:

▶ Establishing reporting functionality

▶ Preparing ConfigMgr for client management

Establishing Reporting Functionality

ConfigMgr addresses the saying "You can't manage what you don't measure." ConfigMgr reporting capabilities provide the means to see and measure the various features and functionality of the product. The Reporting Point (RP) role is an optional installation and highly recommended. The RP is typically installed and enabled on a CAS for the hierarchy implementation and on the primary site for a standalone implementation. For a detailed discussion on the reporting functionality, see Chapter 21, "Configuration Manager Reporting."

Preparing Configuration Manager for Client Management

The basic client management functionality of a Configuration Manager implementation requires you to configure and enable core infrastructure settings after installation.

ConfigMgr has simplified the creation of boundaries and separated the two functions associated with them. Separation of boundaries is implemented by using boundary groups. Boundary groups, discussed later in this chapter, in the "Configuring Boundary Groups" section, have a dependency on creating standard boundaries. Boundaries can be created manually as well as through Active Directory Forest Discovery.

Configuring Active Directory Forest Discovery

Active Directory Forest Discovery is a newer discovery method for Configuration Manager. Chapter 9, "Client Management," discusses discovery methods in depth. This section discusses the use of AD Forest Discovery in relation to site boundary creation. Figure 6.11 shows the properties of the Active Directory Forest Discovery for the hierarchy. (This discovery method is configurable at all primary sites, as well as the CAS.) You must enable this discovery method and select one or both automatic boundary creation methods if you want AD sites and subnets in your environment created as site boundaries in ConfigMgr.

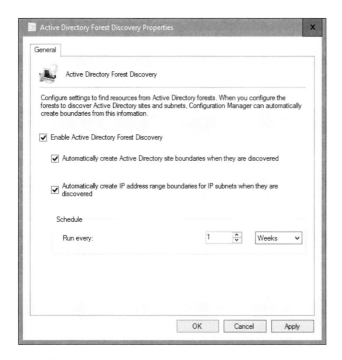

FIGURE 6.11   Active Directory Forest Discovery Properties.

Configuring Boundary Groups

In Configuration Manager, boundaries—whether manually created or automatically created by Active Directory Forest Discovery—are not in use until you create a boundary group. ConfigMgr Current Branch version 1610 reinvigorated boundary groups to support boundary group relationships, which control fallback and time intervals to fallback. For more information, see https://docs.microsoft.com/sccm/core/servers/deploy/configure/boundary-groups. Also, clients can now use boundary groups for SUP and MP selection.

The authors recommend that you create a boundary group for site assignments before deploying ConfigMgr agents. You can optionally create a boundary group for content required by clients.

Follow these steps to create a boundary group for site assignment:

1. In the console, navigate to **Administration -> Hierarchy Configuration -> Boundary Groups** and click **Create Boundary Group** on the ribbon bar.

2. In the General section, type a name and a description for the boundary group. Click **Add** in the Boundaries section and select the relevant boundary/boundaries. Figure 6.12 shows an example.

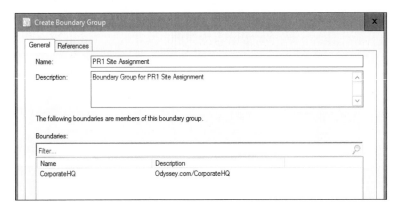

FIGURE 6.12   The General tab of the Create Boundary Group dialog.

3. To configure the boundary group type and association with a site, configure the properties on the References tab:

   ▶ **Site Assignment:** Select **Use this boundary group for site assignment** and select the site associated with the boundary group, as illustrated in Figure 6.13.

   ▶ **Content:** In the case of a content-only boundary group configuration, make sure **Use this boundary group for site assignment** is not selected. Under the content location section, click **Add** and select a content role site system(s). Figure 6.14 illustrates a boundary group configured for content only.

NOTE: SITE ASSIGNMENT BOUNDARY GROUPS

You must configure a site assignment boundary group for a primary site before you install a ConfigMgr client in the scenario where only one primary site is installed in the hierarchy or in a standalone primary site implementation. Client deployment will not complete if the site you try to assign the client to does not have a site assignment boundary group configured or a fallback site configured for hierarchy implementations with more than one primary site.

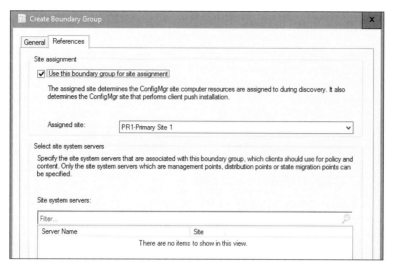

FIGURE 6.13   Creating a boundary group for site assignment.

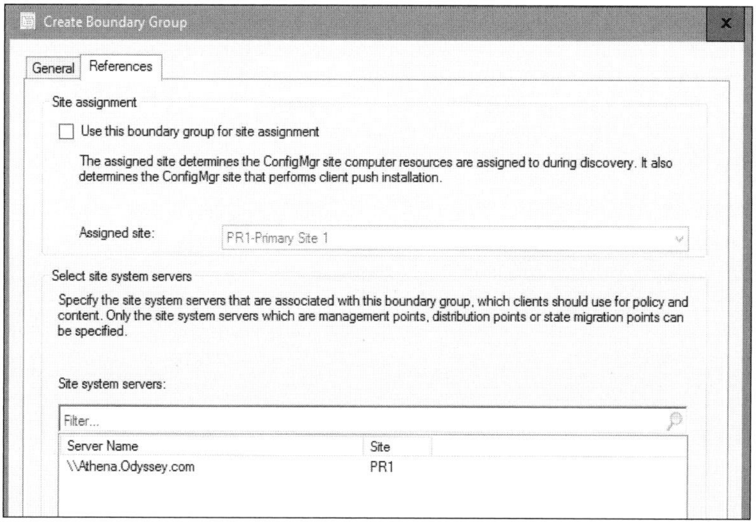

FIGURE 6.14   Creating a boundary group for content.

TIP: SEPARATE BOUNDARY GROUPS

You can combine site assignment and content location into a single boundary group; how-ever, when you do, you lose flexibility and better separation. In addition, site assignment boundary groups cannot have overlapping boundaries, whereas content boundary groups support overlapping boundaries. The authors recommend planning for and implementing boundary groups for site assignment and having separate boundary groups for content location only.

Connecting ConfigMgr to Cloud Services

ConfigMgr now has the capability to connect to various Microsoft cloud services. Each cloud service provides different capabilities, and each can be configured independently, except for the cloud management gateway (CMG) that is optimally used with Azure AD authentication. Once you establish connectivity to a given cloud service, you can use that service for one or more ConfigMgr features.

Authenticating to Azure Active Directory

By connecting to Azure AD, you enable ConfigMgr to authenticate to various cloud services and also delegate ConfigMgr permissions to access those services. This is done by using two different Azure AD app types:

▶ A *web app* is basically an identity (a client ID) along with a credential (a secret key) that allows an application to authenticate to Azure AD by relying on a user account that maps to the OAuth standard's definition of a private or confidential client.

▶ A *native app* is basically an identity without credentials that is used with user or device authentication to access resources; this maps to the OAuth standard's definition of a public client.

ConfigMgr uses one or both types of apps to access Microsoft cloud services, depending on the requirements of the cloud service to which you are establishing connectivity.

You must have an Azure AD tenant to connect to Azure AD. This is included automatically with a subscription to Office 365 or Microsoft Intune. A Microsoft Enterprise Mobility + Security (EMS) subscription also includes Azure Active Directory Premium.

If you have global admin rights to your tenant, you can use ConfigMgr to create the necessary web app and/or native app directly from the ConfigMgr console. However, if another team owns global admin rights in your organization, you can request that they create a web app and/or native app for you and send you that information, which you can then import into the ConfigMgr wizard. The following information must be collected from that team:

▶ Web app:

   ▶ Friendly name of the app

   ▶ Friendly name of the tenant

   ▶ Tenant ID (a GUID)

   ▶ Client ID (a GUID)

   ▶ Secret key (a random string value)

▶ Native app:

   ▶ Friendly name of the app

   ▶ Client ID (a GUID)

For more information on how to create a web app in the Azure AD portal, see the Azure AD documentation at https://docs.microsoft.com/azure/active-directory/develop/ active-directory-integrating-applications. The ConfigMgr apps do not require an actual sign-on URL (for web apps) or redirect URI (for native apps). Any value may be supplied.

The following sections explain how to use the Azure services wizard to establish connectivity between ConfigMgr and each respective cloud service. To launch the Azure services wizard, follow these steps:

1. In the ConfigMgr console, navigate to **Administration -> Cloud Services -> Azure Services**.

2. Expand the **Azure Services** group in the **Home** tab on the ribbon bar and click **Configure Azure Services**.

3. When the Azure services wizard launches, select the Azure service to which you want to connect.

Connecting to Cloud Management

Connecting ConfigMgr to the CMG enables you to configure Azure AD user discovery and authentication. Azure AD user discovery can be used to target software to users with Azure AD Join (AADJ) Windows 10 devices. You can also allow the CMG to authenticate Azure AD Join Windows 10 clients. This removes a common hurdle to Internet-based client management (IBCM), which required client certificates to authenticate to Internet-facing MPs. Instead, the CMG leverages Azure AD and the Azure AD device identity on an Azure AD Join Windows 10 device to authenticate clients on the Internet.

Follow these steps to connect to cloud management:

1. In the ConfigMgr console, launch the Azure service wizard, as discussed in the "Authenticating to Azure Active Directory" section, earlier in this chapter.

2. On the Azure Services page, select **Cloud Management Gateway**.

3. On the General page, provide a name and a description.

4. On the App page, create a web app or a native app by clicking **Browse**.

   For a web app, either import the information from your Azure AD team (see the "Authenticating to Azure Active Directory" section) or click **Create** and follow the rest of the steps in the Server App window:

   ▶ Supply a friendly name for the app, a home page URL, an app ID URI, and the secret key validity period (which is like a password expiration date for a service account).

   ▶ Sign in with an account that has permissions to create web apps in Azure AD.

For a native app, either import the information from your Azure AD team (see the "Authenticating to Azure Active Directory" section) or click **Create** and follow the remainder of the steps in the Client App window:

▶ Supply a friendly name for the app and a redirect URI.

▶ Sign in using an account that has permission to create native apps in Azure AD.

5. In the Discovery page of the wizard, click **Enable Azure Active Directory User Discovery** and optionally configure the discovery schedule by clicking **Settings**.

Refer to Chapter 9 for additional information on Azure AD User Discovery.

Connecting to OMS Connector

Connecting to the Microsoft Operations Management Suite (OMS) cloud service allows you to sync your ConfigMgr collections to the OMS portal, enabling you to use collections as OMS computer groups. You can then use those computer groups to scope/filter your OMS Log Analytics searches. For information on how to import ConfigMgr information to OMS, see the OMS documentation at https://docs.microsoft.com/azure/log-analytics/log-analytics-sccm.

To configure the OMS connection, ensure that the following prerequisites are met:

▶ The OMS connector does not support creating web apps via the Azure services wizard; instead, you must pre-create the web app by following the steps in the "Authenticating to Azure Active Directory" section, earlier in this chapter. Once those steps are complete, grant the web app contributor rights in the Azure resource group that contains the OMS Log Analytics workspace. For details on how to delegate permissions, see the OMS documentation at https://docs.microsoft.com/azure/log-analytics/log-analytics-sccm#provide-configuration-manager-with-permissions-to-oms.

▶ The OMS connector must be installed on the computer hosting the service connection point (SCP), and the SCP must be in online mode.

▶ You must also install the Microsoft Monitoring Agent (MMA) for OMS on the SCP, as the MMA and the OMS connector must use the same OMS workspace. To install the agent, see the OMS documentation at https://docs.microsoft.com/azure/log-analytics/log-analytics-sccm#download-and-install-the-agent.

When you have met all the prerequisites for connecting the OMS connector, use the procedure documented at https://docs.microsoft.com/sccm/core/clients/manage/sync-data-microsoft-operations-management-suite to establish a connection to OMS.

Connecting to Upgrade Readiness

The procedure at https://docs.microsoft.com/sccm/core/clients/manage/upgrade/upgrade-analytics discusses how to connect to Upgrade Readiness (formerly known as Upgrade Analytics).

Deploying a CMG in Microsoft Azure

To set up a CMG for ConfigMgr, follow the documentation at https://docs.microsoft.com/sccm/core/clients/manage/setup-cloud-management-gateway. The CMG is hosted in Azure App Services (Azure's Platform as a Service offering). This means that the virtual machines hosted in Azure are designed to be headless and managed by Azure itself, similar to a cloud DP.

The CMG also requires that you select an Azure cloud service domain name (*<name>*. cloudapp.net). This name can be any format or even random text, but it must be globally unique. The FQDN of the CMG is then associated with a CNAME DNS record (for example, myCMG.contoso.com). The FQDN of the CNAME DNS record is then used to point your clients to the CMG and to require an SSL server certificate. Having the CNAME associated with your registered domain name allows you to obtain a certificate from a public certificate authority such as DigiCert. You can use the *<name>*.cloudapp.net format directly, but because Microsoft owns the cloudapp.net domain, you must use a private/internal certificate authority.

The CMG requires an on premise HTTPS MP to allow secure communication. Clients on your network automatically obtain a primary site's CMG's name for use when they are on the Internet. You can either leverage client authentication certificates (like IBCM) or, if using Windows 10 devices in ConfigMgr Current Branch version 1710, you can have those clients leverage Azure AD authentication to the CMG to further simplify deployment. Appendix B, "Co-Managing Microsoft Intune and ConfigMgr," provides additional information.

Installing Optional Site Systems

This portion of the chapter discusses site system installation and uses the fallback status point (FSP) as an example of site roles you can install for your Configuration Manager primary site or hierarchy.

Installing the Fallback Status Point

The FSP is the ConfigMgr clients' emergency system. The FSP is typically used during client installation and during postinstallation when clients cannot communicate with their management points. You must assign an FSP to a client during the client installation; so plan to install an FSP role before deploying clients. To install and enable an FSP for a ConfigMgr site, follow these steps:

1. In the console, navigate to **Administration -> Site Configuration -> Sites**. In the middle pane, select the desired site on which to enable the FSP and click **Add Site System Roles** on the ribbon bar.

2. Configure the following options on the General page:

   ▶ **Name:** This option is preselected. (You must specify a fully qualified domain name if you initiate the role creation by selecting the Add Site system option.)

   ▶ **Site Code:** This is the site on which you will be enabling the role.

   ▶ **Specify an FQDN for This Site System for Use on the Internet:** The FQDN is used in the case where a supported site system role will be accessed from the Internet.

▶ **Require the Site Server to Initiate Connections to This Site System:** With this security option, communication is controlled and initiated by the site provider.

▶ **Site System Installation Account:** Use the site system computer account to install the role or specify a domain user account.

Click **Next** to proceed to the role selection page.

3. On the Proxy page of the wizard, enter any proxy information that is required for your site server to connect to Microsoft.

4. Select **Fallback status point** on the System Role Selection page, as shown in Figure 6.15.

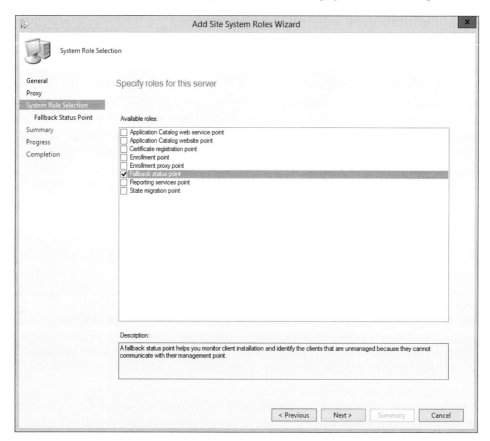

FIGURE 6.15   Selecting the Fallback Status Point role in the Add Site System Roles Wizard.

5. On the next page, set the FSP-specific settings by either accepting the default configuration or modifying the number of state messages and throttle interval, in seconds, from their defaults (which are 10000 and 3600, respectively).

6. On the summary page, review the settings and click **Next** to proceed with role installation.

7. Review the FSPMSI.log file for the installation status.

TIP: FSP LOCATION AND CLIENT INSTALLATION

The FSP is the site role clients send messages to if communication to their assigned management point fails. Plan to install the FSP role on a different site server from the MP. In addition, specify the FSP property in the client installation options of the site. If an FSP is installed, the client push installation method automatically assigns an FSP to a client during installation. Other installation methods require you to specify the FSP property, although this is not required if it is already specified in the client installation properties and the AD schema is extended.

Configuring Hierarchy Settings

Hierarchy settings are sitewide settings that are managed from the top site (the CAS if you have a CAS; otherwise, your single primary site). The following sections look at some of the most popular settings.

Fallback Site   Clients that do not fall within a site assignment boundary group are assigned to the fallback site if one is configured for the hierarchy. This option is specific to hierarchies only. Perform the following steps to enable a primary site in a hierarchy as a fallback site:

1. In the console, navigate to **Administration -> Site Configuration -> Sites**. Click the **Sites** node and then click **Hierarchy Settings** on the ribbon bar.

2. Check the option **Use a fallback site** (see Figure 6.16), select a primary site from the hierarchy, and click **OK** to complete the configuration.

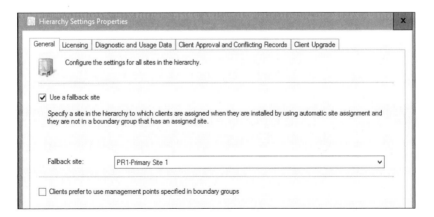

FIGURE 6.16   Enabling the fallback site.

Diagnostics and Usage Data   Choose the level of diagnostics data wisely; don't simply choose Basic. You can help the ConfigMgr product team's cause by encouraging your attorneys and security/privacy consultants to submit the right level of diagnostics data for your company. The more you give, the more you help the product team build the right features, identify and fix the most popular bugs, and give you a better product. Review the diagnostics data at https://docs.microsoft.com/sccm/core/plan-design/diagnostics/how-diagnostics-and-usage-data-is-used and the diagnostics data FAQ at https://docs.microsoft.com/sccm/core/understand/frequently-asked-questions-about-diagnostics-and-usage-data.

To view and modify diagnostics and usage data, return to **Hierarchy Settings** (as described in the previous section) and select the **Diagnostics and Usage Data** tab. Review the options.

Troubleshooting Site Installation

Generally, installations complete flawlessly, although you may occasionally have the need to troubleshoot. Table 6.3 provides information on troubleshooting resources, known issues, and resolutions.

TABLE 6.3   Troubleshooting Resources and Known Issues

Resource/Issue	Notes
Log file	Configuration Manager provides detailed logging of the installation process. The logs specific to installation are listed in Appendix A.
Incorrect or missing dependency component configuration	Most of the common troubleshooting issues are associated with missing or incorrectly configured dependencies. You must ensure that you have installed and configured the required prerequisites. Run the Prerequisite Checker and plan to resolve issues identified before proceeding with the installation. Review the latest supported configuration information at https://docs.microsoft.com/sccm/core/plan-design/configs/supported-configurations.
Firewalls	You must ensure that the required ports used by Configuration Manager during and after the installation process are configured properly on firewalls (operating system or external appliances).
User and computer account rights	You must ensure that the required rights have been assigned to users or computer accounts used in the installation and configuration processes.
SQL non-default instances	Ensure that you configure static ports for SQL Server instances. The default instance is configured with a static port (the default is 1433). All other instances are configured by default with a dynamic port.
Publishing in Active Directory	You must delegate the required security rights to the System Management container. The installation process for hierarchies uses published data in this folder for the initial replication configuration.

Resource/Issue	Notes
Replication issues during hierarchy primary and secondary site installation.	A primary site installation when joined to a hierarchy must perform an initial replication with the CAS. This replication process is also required for a secondary site. If this initial replication process is unsuccessful, the site indicates a pending state, and the console shows a read-only status.
	You must ensure that all site provider servers have the right to publish to the System Management container using the computer account and are also in the local administrators group of both child and parent sites before starting the installation.
	Sites in a read-only or pending state may require a full reinstallation.

TIP: USER FORUMS AND BLOGS

Troubleshooting information on Configuration Manager is available on Internet user forums. Use the ConfigMgr Current Branch Forum at https://social.technet.microsoft.com/Forums/en-US/home?category=ConfigMgrCB as well as search engines such as Bing and Google to aid in your troubleshooting, as the product has many community leaders discussing the most up-to-date issues and how they have been resolved.

Updating Configuration Manager

After you have deployed ConfigMgr Current Branch, prepare to update! Updates are normally released three times per year. Even if you install ConfigMgr with the latest baseline version, odds are you will have an update already available, or one will become available soon after you complete the installation.

NOTE: KNOW THE DIFFERENCE BETWEEN *INSTALL*, *UPGRADE*, AND *UPDATE*

Note the difference between *install*, *upgrade*, and *update*. Initially, you either *install* ConfigMgr Current Branch or *upgrade* (also called in-place upgrade) from ConfigMgr 2012 to ConfigMgr Current Branch. Once you have ConfigMgr Current Branch up and running, you then *update* ConfigMgr, usually by triggering in-console updates, but sometimes out-of-band updates may also need to be installed. Read more at https://docs.microsoft.com/sccm/core/understand/upgrade-update-install.

Most updates arrive and are initiated in the console. Following are the significant wizard pages you must configure to perform an in-console update. (The images here show an update of build 1706 with a hotfix. The process is the same for a new version of Current Branch.) Navigate to **Administration Updates and Servicing** and follow these steps:

1. From the Updates and Servicing node, select the desired update and click **Install Update Pack**.

2. On the General page, review the information about what is included in the update and choose whether to ignore prerequisite checks. As always, a best practice is to perform the prerequisite check separately, prior to running an update.

3. On the Features page, review and choose the desired features. Note that you can later enable these features from the Updates and Servicing node.

4. On the Client Update Settings tab, choose whether to validate in a pre-production collection or upgrade the client without validating, as shown in Figure 6.17. (For more information on updating clients, see Chapter 9.)

5. Review and accept the license terms.

6. Confirm the settings on the Summary tab.

7. Review the progress and completion message to verify that the wizard completes successfully.

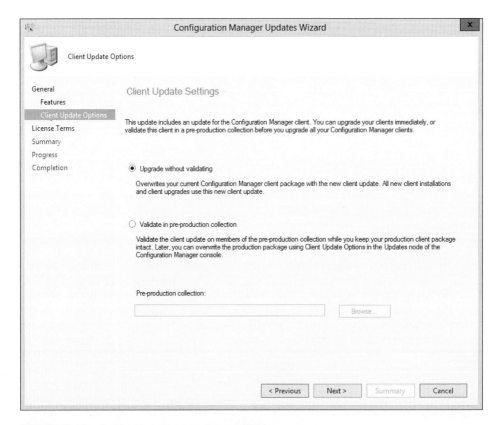

FIGURE 6.17   Configuring client update settings.

Congratulations! You have successfully started the update process. A common misconception is that the update is complete at this point, but it is really just getting started. Depending on the type of update, the process could take from one to multiple hours, so be patient and let the process continue.

8. Review the status of the update from the Updates and Servicing node. In the Details pane, click **Show Status** to monitor the process in more detail. The wizard takes you to **Monitoring -> Overview -> Updates and Servicing** status and filters the view to show the details of the update you are currently installing (see Figure 6.18).

9. Click **Show Status** to launch the detailed installation status dialog shown in Figure 6.19. Then click on the various statuses in the upper pane to see the details in the lower pane. Click **Refresh** to receive updated information in the dialog. Click the **View Post-Setup Configuration Tasks** link to go to a web page with generic post-setup tasks that you may need to perform, depending on your environment.

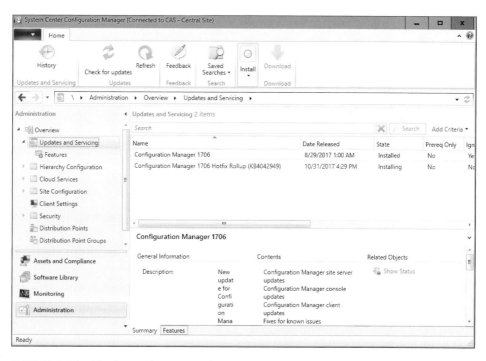

FIGURE 6.18   Viewing update status from the Updates and Servicing node.

FIGURE 6.19 Detailed update status.

As these figures show, the update process is fairly painless. So update well and update often. If you encounter issues, review CMUpdate.log in the site server log file folder. Review Appendix A for additional log file information.

Scheduling Updates

By default, the entire hierarchy is automatically updated immediately (in proper order) after success of the top-level site (either a CAS or a single primary site). For many environments, this process is acceptable. You may have a requirement from your customers or users for different downtime windows, based on location or other operational needs. You can configure service windows that are specific to the update process; when you do this, standard ConfigMgr service windows do not impact the site update process. You can configure service windows for each site by using the following process:

1. Navigate to **Administration -> Overview -> Sites**, select the desired site, and click **Properties** on the ribbon bar.

2. In the properties dialog, chose the Service Windows tab, as shown in Figure 6.20, and click the starburst icon to create a new service window.

FIGURE 6.20   Configuring the site service window.

Using CD.Latest

When you install an update, your base installation changes, and it should be considered unique to your environment. A folder on your site server named CD.Latest is basically a source installation folder with up-to-date files (based on the last update installed to your environment). The following are supported scenarios for using the CD.Latest installation files:

▶ **Site Recovery:** When you need to reinstall the site, you must use CD.Latest, which contains the binaries that match the ConfigMgr database. If you do not have CD.Latest, you cannot recover the site.

▶ **Installing a Child Primary Site:** Use the CD.Latest files from the CAS as source files for installing each child primary site.

▶ **Expanding a Standalone Primary Site:** You currently have a standalone primary site, so you must use the source files from the CD.Latest folder on your primary site.

Never use CD.Latest for a fresh standalone installation. Always use the latest ConfigMgr baseline build and update using the process described in the "Updating Configuration Manager" section of this chapter. Read more about CD.Latest at https://docs.microsoft .com/sccm/core/servers/manage/the-cd.latest-folder.

Summary

This chapter discussed and provided guidance on preparing for System Center Configuration Manager Current Branch installation, installation of supported sites, postinstallation configuration, upgrading, and troubleshooting of installation issues.

Chapter 7, "Upgrading and Migrating to ConfigMgr Current Branch," provides a detailed discussion of how to migrate from previous versions of the product to ConfigMgr Current Branch.

Upgrading and Migrating to ConfigMgr Current Branch

System Center Configuration Manager (ConfigMgr) has evolved and continues to evolve with technological advances and organizational strategies for managing a diverse and dynamic environment. ConfigMgr Current Branch includes numerous changes to the product since ConfigMgr 2012 R2, as discussed in Chapter 2, "Configuration Manager Overview."

Chapter 6, "Installing and Updating System Center Configuration Manager," discussed installing a new Configuration Manager hierarchy. As Microsoft releases new versions of the systems management software, those responsible for existing installations must determine how to best move to the most recent version of the product. If you have an existing ConfigMgr deployment, you will almost certainly want to preserve much of the work put into that implementation when you move to the newest version. Unlike the previous version, ConfigMgr Current Branch supports in-place upgrades as well as migration.

This chapter discusses and provides guidance on the upgrade and migration process. It also discusses pre-migration considerations, the process of migrating your old ConfigMgr infrastructure, migration of features and objects, client migration, and troubleshooting of migration issues.

Deciding Whether to Upgrade or Migrate to Current Branch

No two environments are alike, so unless you do not have an existing ConfigMgr environment, you should weigh the options of upgrading versus migrating. Following are some thoughts and considerations for each method:

▶ *Upgrading* is generally the easiest method for moving to ConfigMgr Current Branch. If you are happy with your current ConfigMgr infrastructure design and are running on a supported operating system, upgrading is almost as easy as clicking Next, Next, and Finish. You can also upgrade the operating system and SQL version. And you can always upgrade the server hardware with a backup and restore, as long as the new server has the same name, domain, and operating system (OS).

If you want to preserve existing data in ConfigMgr (such as inventory history, application and package deployments, and so on), you *must* use the upgrade method.

▶ *Migration* supports additional scenarios. Migrating involves creating a new site, often with a new structure, and moving objects from the old site to the new site. As long as you can route from the new site to the old site (and have valid credentials in both), you can selectively migrate desired objects. Migration is also a great option if you want to reduce your ConfigMgr infrastructure. The number of supported clients has significantly increased since ConfigMgr 2012, and many companies no longer need a central administration site (CAS) and multiple primary sites. Migration is the best way to preserve your existing objects (such as collections, packages, and applications) and still change your ConfigMgr infrastructure design.

The following scenarios *require* that you use the migration method:

▶ You want to change the name of any of the site servers.

▶ You want to change the installation folder for the site installation files.

▶ You want to join the site server to a different domain.

▶ Your ConfigMgr 2012/2012 R2 infrastructure includes a CAS, and you want to remove it.

▶ You have ConfigMgr 2007 installed and want to go directly to ConfigMgr Current Branch.

▶ You currently have a ConfigMgr Current Branch site or hierarchy and want to move to a new ConfigMgr Current Branch site or hierarchy.

Upgrading to ConfigMgr Current Branch

Upgrading from a supported version of ConfigMgr 2012 or 2012 R2 is generally the most efficient approach. Even if your hardware or operating system is approaching end-of-life, you can still work through a process to back up/restore to new hardware and a different operating system. This section does not go into the backup/restore details; see Chapter 24, "Backup, Recovery, and Maintenance," for more information on that process.

As with any other software upgrade, you need to first clean house and make sure you have a firm foundation. Spend the time to clean up old items (packages, applications, software updates, and so on) and also ensure that both ConfigMgr and the operating system are healthy: Review logs, the event viewer, and site component status to avoid preventable failures.

Preparing for Upgrade

Preparation is key to success! Before upgrading your production instance, test the entire process in a lab environment that is similar to a production environment. While this may seem like it takes a lot of time, it will build your confidence in the process and give you an opportunity to learn in a safe environment.

Verifying Supported Current Branch Baseline Version, OS, SQL Version, and Windows Automated Installation Kit (AIK)

The supported versions of ConfigMgr Current Branch will change faster than a book can be published. Always refer to the latest Microsoft documentation to verify the following:

▶ **Ensure that you have the latest baseline version of ConfigMgr Current Branch.** The baseline is updated approximately once a year, so start with the latest supported version. You can identify the latest baseline version at https://docs.microsoft.com/sccm/core/servers/manage/updates#baseline-and-update-versions.

▶ **Verify that you have a fully patched and supported Windows operating system.** Now is the time to get your operating system up to date. As always, ensure that you have a good backup and then ensure that your OS is fully patched. The supported operating systems for ConfigMgr Current Branch are a moving target. Review the supported operating systems for ConfigMgr at https://docs.microsoft.com/sccm/core/plan-design/configs/supported-operating-systems-for-site-system-servers.

▶ **Ensure that SQL Server is up to date.** SQL Server is foundational to ConfigMgr, and it is in your best interest to get to the latest supported version of SQL. Verify that you have a supported version of SQL Server for ConfigMgr Current Branch at https://docs.microsoft.com/sccm/core/plan-design/configs/support-for-sql-server-versions.

▶ **Ensure that the AIK is up-to-date.** The AIK is backward compatible with Windows 7. Ensure that you are on a supported version of the AIK for Current Branch, based on the information provided at https://docs.microsoft.com/sccm/core/plan-design/configs/support-for-windows-10. Also, be sure to back up all customized boot images before upgrading.

NOTE: FINDING THE OVERLAP

ConfigMgr Current Branch fully supports in-place upgrades from 2012 and 2012 R2; the key is to find the supported overlap. For example, ConfigMgr 2012 may not support SQL 2016, but it supports SQL 2014, and so does ConfigMgr Current Branch. Therefore, if you are planning to upgrade, spend the time to get your current infrastructure up to the latest supported version and verify that ConfigMgr Current Branch also supports those versions. After upgrading to Current Branch (with the latest updates) with your "overlap configuration," proceed to upgrade SQL Server and the ADK to the latest version. See the following three-part blog series by a Microsoft Premier Field Engineer that discusses the details: https://blogs.technet.microsoft.com/systemcenterpfe/2017/08/16/lift-shift-configmgr-2012-to-configmgr-1702-current-branch-part-1-the-upgrade/.

Performing a Test Upgrade of the SQL Database

Upgrading your ConfigMgr database is a one-way street—if you encounter problems during the upgrade process and the upgrade to ConfigMgr Current Branch is unsuccessful, you may be in an unsupported configuration where the database is upgraded but the site is not. If the upgrade is not successful, you can revert to your backup (you know, that one you made immediately before upgrading).

To lessen the chance of problems, the authors recommend testing the database upgrade first: Restore your most recent backup of the database to a new SQL Server instance (one that has absolutely nothing to do with ConfigMgr). Launch the process with `smssetup.exe /testdbupgrade`, specifying the database instance and database name. View c:\ConfigMgrSetup.log to monitor the status and verify the success of the upgrade. Review this process at https://docs.microsoft.com/sccm/core/servers/manage/test-database-upgrade.

> **NOTE: MAINTAINING CURRENT BRANCH, NO TEST DATABASE UPGRADE NECESSARY**
>
> While testing the database upgrade is essential when moving from ConfigMgr 2012 or 2012 R2 to ConfigMgr Current Branch, this test is no longer required on Current Branch, as you can now retry the database upgrade when upgrading from one version of Current Branch to the next.

Performing the Upgrade

After taking the time to perform the process in a lab and verifying a successful database upgrade, it's show time! Launch smssetup.exe from the latest Current Branch baseline build (located in the smssetup\bin\x64 folder of the installation source files) and use the wizard to perform the following steps:

1. The first dialog you see is Before You Begin. Read the detail, and click **Next**.

2. Figure 7.1 shows the Getting Started page, which lists the available options. Notice that because a version of ConfigMgr is currently installed, you only get options to upgrade, recover a site, or uninstall the existing site. Select **Upgrade This Configuration Manager Site** and click **Next**.

3. On the Product Key page, shown in Figure 7.2, enter your license key, select the Software Assurance expiration date, and choose **Current Branch**. (There are very few, rare cases in which you should consider selecting Long Term Servicing Branch. Plan to use Current Branch unless you have identified an unconquerable hurdle to doing so.) Click **Next**.

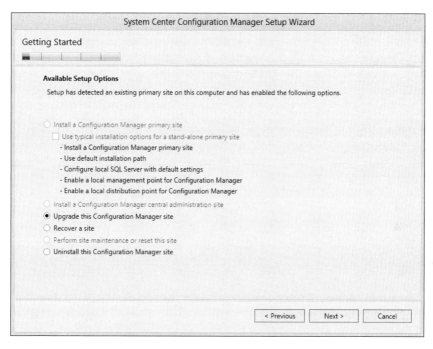

FIGURE 7.1   The Getting Started page of the installation/upgrade wizard.

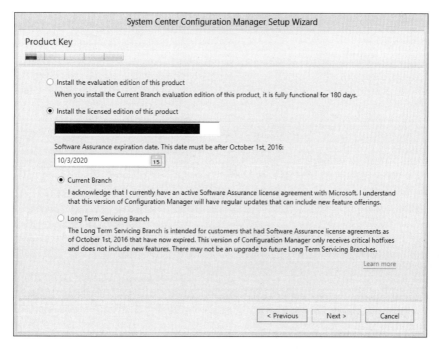

FIGURE 7.2   The Product Key page of the installation/upgrade wizard.

4. Carefully read each End User License Agreement and accept the license agreement, and then click **Next**.

5. On the Prerequisite Downloads page, shown in Figure 7.3, either download the current prerequisite files or set the location path of the prerequisites (if they were downloaded previously).

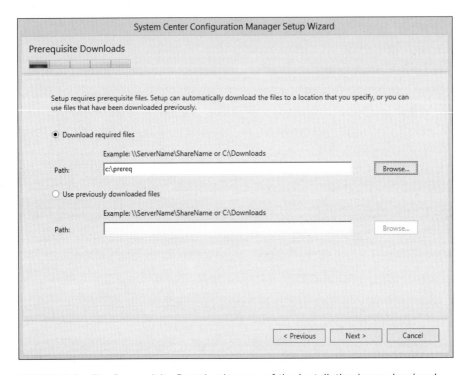

FIGURE 7.3   The Prerequisite Downloads page of the installation/upgrade wizard.

6. After the ConfigMgr Setup Downloader downloads all files to the desired location, click **Next**.

7. Choose the language(s) that can be used in the ConfigMgr console and reports and then click **Next**.

8. Select the language(s) that will be supported on the ConfigMgr client and click **Next**.

9. Review the Diagnostic and Usage information and click **Next** to proceed to the Service Connection Point setup.

10. In the screen shown in Figure 7.4, review the settings for the service connection point (SCP) setup, which is a critical component of ConfigMgr Current Branch in that almost all updates are sent through this channel. Telemetry data is also sent through the SCP. Click **Next**.

For more information about the SCP, see Chapter 6.

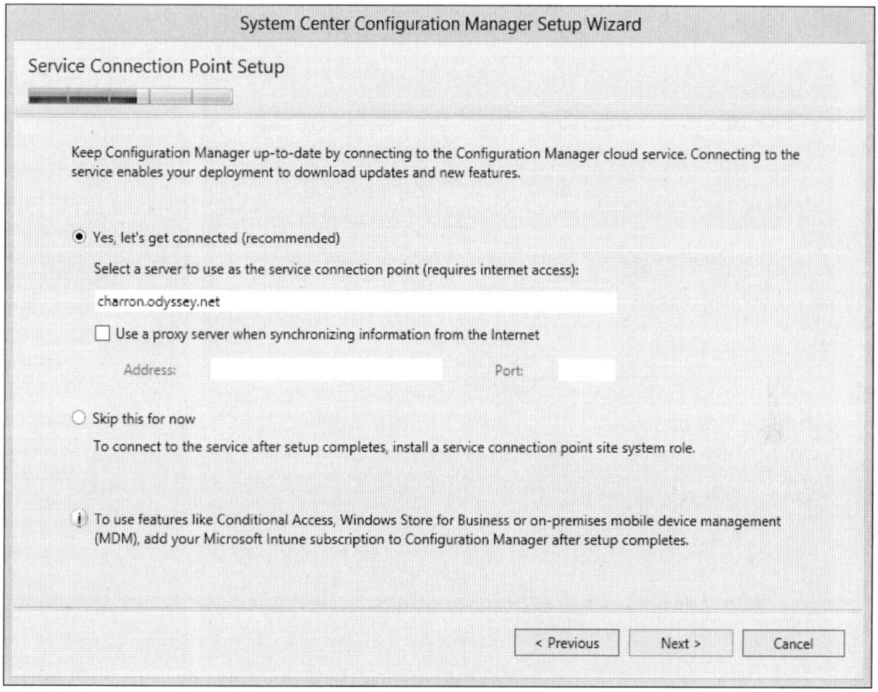

System Center Configuration Manager Setup Wizard

Service Connection Point Setup

Keep Configuration Manager up-to-date by connecting to the Configuration Manager cloud service. Connecting to the service enables your deployment to download updates and new features.

◉ Yes, let's get connected (recommended)

Select a server to use as the service connection point (requires internet access):

charron.odyssey.net

☐ Use a proxy server when synchronizing information from the Internet

Address: Port:

○ Skip this for now

To connect to the service after setup completes, install a service connection point site system role.

ⓘ To use features like Conditional Access, Windows Store for Business or on-premises mobile device management (MDM), add your Microsoft Intune subscription to Configuration Manager after setup completes.

[< Previous] [Next >] [Cancel]

FIGURE 7.4   The Service Connection Point Setup screen.

11. Review the Settings Summary page, which summarizes the type of setup that is running (an upgrade in this case), and click **Next**.

12. In the Prerequisite Check screen, shown in Figure 7.5, review all the warnings and failures presented. Click each row to view the details; you will find that many of them include links to the Internet for relevant information.

13. After reviewing the prerequisite warnings and fixing all errors, the text of the **Next** button will change to **Begin Install**. Click **Begin Install** to start the installation process. Review c:\ConfigMgrPrereq.log for detailed information regarding prerequisite checks.

14. After the installation begins, review the information in the setup wizard and look in the root of the C:\ drive at the various ConfigMgr logs that are used for initial deployment. Figure 7.6 shows the wizard, which says **Core Setup Has Completed**. More work is still occurring in the background, and clicking **View Log** allows you to monitor the rest of the configuration. If you leave the wizard page open, you can watch the icons change from in progress to complete.

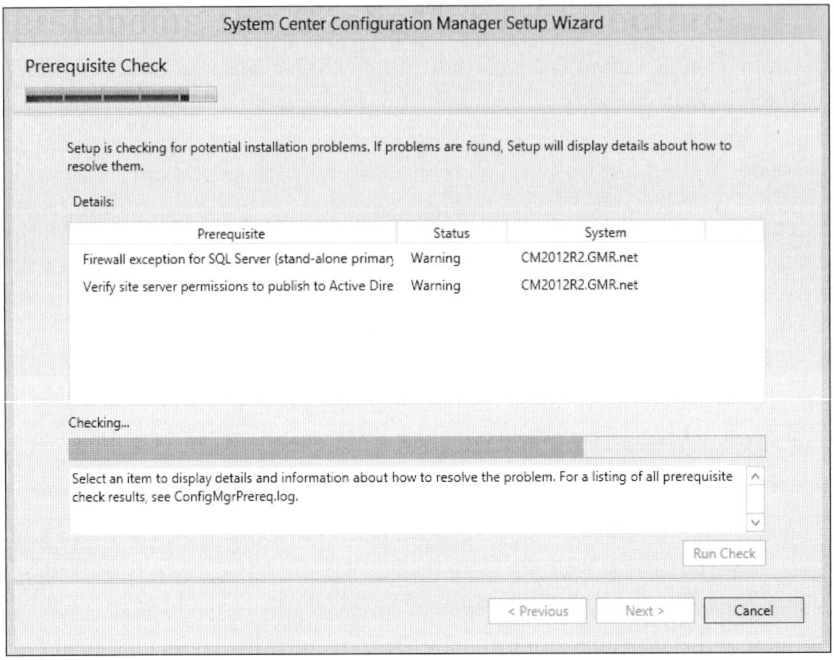

FIGURE 7.5   The Prerequisite Check screen.

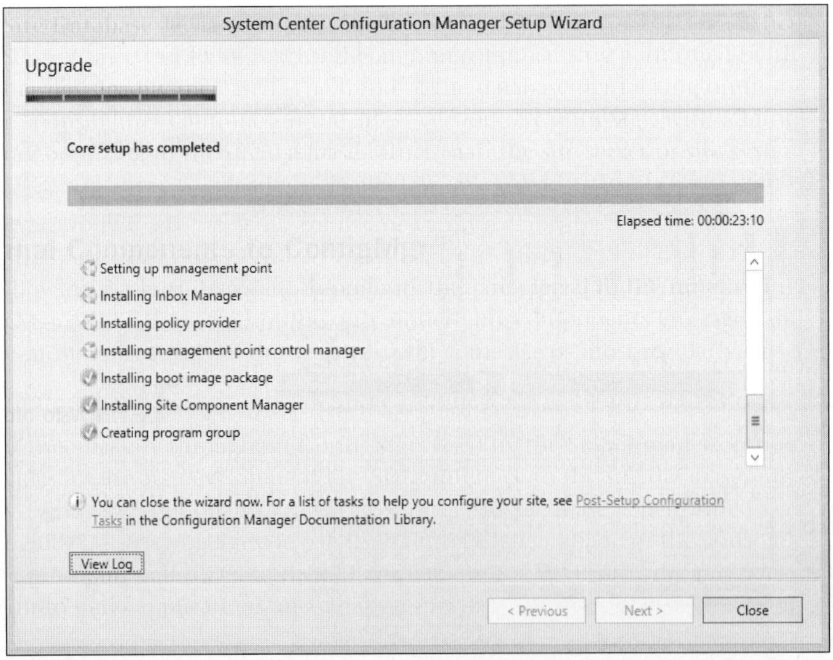

FIGURE 7.6   The ConfigMgr Current Branch upgrade is complete.

Migrating to ConfigMgr Current Branch

The migration process is like moving to a new house from your current home. Moving to a new house provides both opportunities and challenges:

▶ Opportunities:

> ▶ Clearing out the old stuff you don't really use
>
> ▶ Getting new fixtures and furniture
>
> ▶ Acquiring more space and better scenery

▶ Challenges:

> ▶ Organizing and coordinating the move
>
> ▶ Packing and labeling what you are taking to the new house
>
> ▶ Enlisting friends to help or paying to use a moving company

Migrating to Configuration Manager Current Branch from ConfigMgr 2007, 2012, or 2012 R2 is, in effect, a new implementation followed by a migration of supported objects from the existing ConfigMgr implementation. (Implementation planning is covered extensively in Chapter 4, "Architecture Design Planning," and is a prerequisite to the overall migration process.)

A successful migration to ConfigMgr Current Branch relies on a combination of art (design, planning, and installation) and science (the technical mechanism used to move objects). The remainder of this chapter discusses using these two methodologies when migrating to Configuration Manager Current Branch.

Migration, Not an Upgrade

The primary goal of migrating to a new version of an established platform is to preserve functional settings and configurations. Microsoft makes this possible with ConfigMgr Current Branch by including migration tools built into the product. Using these tools enables you to safely export and preserve previous configurations and objects from your existing ConfigMgr site or hierarchy.

The migration process centers on the capability to share distribution points (DPs) between your existing site and the new ConfigMgr Current Branch site.

The following is the supported approach for migrating from previous versions of ConfigMgr to Configuration Manager Current Branch:

1. Provision the new server(s) for your Configuration Manager Current Branch site or hierarchy. The authors recommend using a new site or hierarchy design specific to ConfigMgr Current Branch, as discussed in Chapter 4.

2. Perform initial configuration specific to Configuration Manager Current Branch.

3. Establish a migration link to your existing ConfigMgr site or hierarchy.

4. Optionally share site roles (DPs); for information on this, see the "Performing Migration Jobs" section, later in this chapter.

5. Create migration jobs to migrate supported objects.

6. Upgrade the ConfigMgr client agents and assign them to the Configuration Manager Current Branch site.

7. Decommission the old ConfigMgr site and site systems. Optionally, you could rebuild servers and reuse them for Configuration Manager Current Branch site roles.

If your current site server is running directly on physical hardware, migration presents a great opportunity to leverage virtualization. Using virtualization enables you to reduce one significant life cycle element: server hardware. ConfigMgr Current Branch is supported on virtualized systems, and implementing virtualization can remove the challenge of provisioning new physical hardware associated with side-by-side migrations.

> **NOTE: VIRTUAL VERSUS PHYSICAL SERVERS**
>
> The use of virtual servers for site roles introduces flexibility and, in most cases, reduces operational costs in management and maintenance. While Configuration Manager Current Branch is highly scalable, using a virtualization platform requires that you test and plan for performance impact with large environments. The authors recommend testing on a small scale and measuring performance.
>
> Performing a detailed test provides you with factual data, which you can use to model requirements for a medium or large deployment. It also assists with making a decision between using virtualization or physical machines for Configuration Manager Current Branch roles.
>
> ConfigMgr Current Branch is also supported in Microsoft Azure. For more information, review https://docs.microsoft.com/sccm/core/understand/configuration-manager-on-azure.

Planning the Migration

Microsoft does not support migrating from versions of the product prior to ConfigMgr 2007. The migration functionality of Configuration Manager Current Branch is discussed in the "Performing Migration Jobs" section, later in this chapter. Although ConfigMgr 2007 is past its end-of-life date, you can still leverage the migration tool to move from ConfigMgr 2007 to ConfigMgr Current Branch, if needed. Note that the migration feature is also used to migrate objects from one Current Branch environment to another.

What Is Migrated

The migration process involves new terms and concepts. Table 7.1 provides an overview of the terms and concepts specific to migration in Configuration Manager Current Branch.

TABLE 7.1 Migration-Specific Terms and Concepts

Concept or Term	Notes
Source hierarchy	This is the source ConfigMgr hierarchy. Start with the top site (central site or CAS) in a full hierarchy or the primary site in cases where only one primary site is installed.
Source sites	These sites are identified after querying the source hierarchy. A source site would be a primary site below the ConfigMgr central site or CAS in a hierarchy.
Data gathering	This process, which is an ongoing process once a source hierarchy has been configured, identifies data you can migrate to ConfigMgr Current Branch.
Migration jobs	You can configure specific jobs to migrate supported discovered objects from the data gathering process.
Client migration	This is the process of migrating the old ConfigMgr client to ConfigMgr Current Branch. (Note that you need to use a supported client installation method to upgrade the ConfigMgr client. Review Chapter 9, "Client Management," for more information.)
Monitoring migration	This is the process of monitoring migration activities. Most monitoring is performed in the ConfigMgr Current Branch console. You can also use the log file generated by the migration process to monitor migration activities.
Stop Gathering Data	This task stops or suspends data gathering from the source site.
Clean Up Migration Data	This task involves cleaning up the migration metadata. It does not clean up the data you have migrated but rather the configuration used to migrate the data in the first place (that is, it clears the source hierarchy and starts again).
Shared distribution points	Configuration Manager Current Branch can use DPs from ConfigMgr during the migration phase. The content metadata is migrated, but the actual content can be accessed by clients using the ConfigMgr DP until all clients have migrated. When migration is complete, you can upgrade the DPs.

The following are the supported objects the migration wizard can migrate from ConfigMgr:

▶ Collections

▶ Advertisements

▶ Boundaries

▶ Software distribution packages

▶ Applications

▶ Virtual application packages

▶ Software updates

▶ Deployments

▶ Deployment packages

▶ Templates

▶ Software update lists

▶ Operating system deployment (OSD) images

▶ Boot images

▶ Driver packages

▶ Drivers

▶ Images

▶ Packages

▶ Task sequences

▶ Configuration items

▶ Configuration baselines

▶ Asset Intelligence customizations

▶ Custom catalogs

▶ Custom hardware requirements

▶ Software metering rules

What Is Not Migrated

Some constraints and rules apply to the supported objects for migration. Table 7.2 lists the constraints and rules around the supported migrated objects.

TABLE 7.2   Migration Object Constraints and Rules

Migrated Object(s)	Constraints and Rules
Collections	Empty collections without objects associated are migrated as organization folders. ▶ Site code references in collections are flagged. ▶ Users and devices cannot be part of the same collection. ▶ Nested empty collections are converted to folders.
Packages	All package source locations have to use a universal naming convention (UNC) path.
OSD	The ConfigMgr 2007 client installation package is not migrated.
Deployments	Deployments (advertisements) are available for selection only when using collection migration.

The following objects cannot be migrated from ConfigMgr 2007 using the migration wizard:

▶ Queries

▶ Security rights and instances for the site and objects

▶ Configuration Manager 2007 reports from SQL Server Reporting Services (SSRS)

▶ Configuration Manager 2007 web reports

▶ Client inventory and history data

▶ Active Management Technology (AMT) client provisioning information

▶ Files in the client cache

Performing Pre-Migration Activities

A successful migration to Configuration Manager Current Branch requires you to perform several activities before invoking the migration wizard. A high-level overview of these steps follows:

1. Complete the installation and configuration of the Configuration Manager Current Branch hierarchy (as a standalone site or CAS-installed hierarchy).

2. Ensure that the old ConfigMgr source site(s) is at a supported version.

3. Prepare the old ConfigMgr sources site(s) and Configuration Manager Current Branch destination site(s) for migration.

4. Provision and configure the migration user account for the old ConfigMgr source sites.

5. Assign the old ConfigMgr source site database access rights to the migration account.

6. Assign the Full Administrator role to the migration account in the destination Configuration Manager Current Branch hierarchy.

These activities are discussed in the following sections.

Installing and Configuring the Configuration Manager Hierarchy

The destination Configuration Manager Current Branch hierarchy should be fully configured before you start the migration process. You should test and validate the full functionality in scope for the implementation before invoking any of the migration wizards.

The migration process assumes that a fully configured site is in place. Chapters 4, 5, and 6 cover planning and installation in depth, and the authors recommend that you review those chapters to ensure that the Configuration Manager Current Branch site is ready to receive migrated data. The Configuration Manager Current Branch online documentation

is an excellent source of information; review the migration section at https://docs
.microsoft.com/sccm/core/migration/migrate-data-between-hierarchies for additional
information.

Ensuring That the Old ConfigMgr Source Site(s) Is at a Supported Version

The only supported ConfigMgr 2007 version is ConfigMgr 2007 with Service Pack (SP) 2.
If you are on ConfigMgr 2007, upgrade to SP 2 and validate that the site is fully
operational before attempting to migrate to Configuration Manager Current Branch.
For ConfigMgr 2012 and 2012 R2, ensure that the latest service pack is installed prior to
attempting to migrate.

Preparing the Old ConfigMgr Site(s) for Migration

The migration process is an opportunity to "clean house." You should plan to perform an
audit of supported migration objects (see the "What Is Migrated" section, earlier in this
chapter). The following are examples of some recommended activities:

▶ Review ConfigMgr objects and plan to remove (or exclude) redundant non-
applicable objects.

  ▶ Delete redundant and unnecessary deployments.

  ▶ Create placeholder collections for redundant deployments and avoid keeping
  old deployments linked to live collections.

  ▶ Clean up packages, applications, software updates, and other ConfigMgr
  objects. Over time, everyone accumulates a bit of dust in the closets.

▶ Review collections in scope.

  ▶ Avoid mixed collections for ConfigMgr 2007 (that is, user and device
  combined collections); this is not an issue in ConfigMgr 2012 and later,
  as mixed collections are not permitted.

  ▶ As a best practice, only mark query-based collections for migration.

  ▶ Review advertisements or deployments linked to collections.

  ▶ Avoid using site codes in query-based collections.

▶ Review the software updates catalog synchronization settings. Determine whether all
the synchronized categories are still relevant to your environment today.

Preparing Source and Destination Sites for Migration

The migration process has a dependency on security credentials and infrastructure
configuration, as described in Table 7.3.

TABLE 7.3   Migration User Account and Infrastructure Prerequisites

Site/Infrastructure	Required Settings
Configuration Manager Current Branch destination site (CAS or primary site)	This should be a migration user account with the Full Administration role. A security best practice is to use the computer account instead of a user account.
Old ConfigMgr source sites (site provider)	This should be a migration user account with Read permission to all source site objects. The account must optionally have Delete permission to the old ConfigMgr Site class if you plan to upgrade the distribution point.
Old ConfigMgr source sites (site database)	Assign Read and Execute permissions to the source site database. In SQL, this is equivalent to assigning the following to the Windows Login account: db_datareader and smsschm_users on the site database for the source site. A security best practice is to use the computer account instead of a user account.
Shared distribution points	The old ConfigMgr source site and the Configuration Manager Current Branch primary site or CAS must use the same client port number.
Firewall/network protocols	The following network protocols are used when gathering data to communicate between the source and destination sites: ▶ NetBIOS/SMB: 445 (TCP) ▶ RPC (WMI): 135 (TCP) ▶ SQL Server: 1433 (TCP)
DCOM security group on the source site provider	The migration user must be a member of the Distributed COM Users local group.

Coexistence Considerations

This section examines coexistence considerations specific to migration. Chapter 4 provides details on coexistence when considering the implementation of Configuration Manager Current Branch. As discussed in the following sections, there are two main areas of focus during the migration:

▶ Shared infrastructure

▶ Client management

Shared Infrastructure

Configuration Manager Current Branch allows you to use a DP from your old ConfigMgr site during the migration phase for clients. When the migration is complete, you can upgrade the DP. This shared infrastructure functionality minimizes data storage requirements and network bandwidth utilization.

Your previous version of Configuration Manager and ConfigMgr Current Branch publish information into the same Active Directory (AD) system folder when implemented in the same domain. As a part of the migration process, you must plan for new site codes for your ConfigMgr Current Branch hierarchy.

Client Management

You need to complete your infrastructure migration before migrating clients from your old ConfigMgr site. The authors recommend migrating a small set of clients to validate the process and assure the functionality of the migration. A best practice is to use Internet Protocol (IP) range or exclusive subnet boundaries for site assignment, as doing so avoids boundary overlaps between the old infrastructure and the new sites. Upgraded ConfigMgr clients can access DPs that are configured as shared distribution points as long as their original site is still configured as the active source site.

The following sections discuss the technical process of moving objects, which is the science of migration.

Performing the Migration

The "Planning the Migration" section, earlier in this chapter, discusses activities and considerations that are required before you invoke the Configuration Manager Current Branch migration wizards. The remainder of the chapter discusses configuration and execution of the migration jobs, migration of the old ConfigMgr clients, and migration troubleshooting.

Migrating by Features and Dependencies

Configuration Manager Current Branch presents the migration job wizards by collection or by object. A structured approach to migration is to organize the process by infrastructure-only objects such as boundaries and then by the features linked to collections.

The first migration configuration required is data gathering from the active source hierarchy, which is the top site of your old ConfigMgr hierarchy.

Migrating Dependencies Configuration

You must complete several prerequisites for the migration jobs before invoking the built-in wizards in the ConfigMgr Current Branch console:

> ▶ **ConfigMgr Migration Account Configuration:** This includes delegation rights in a local security group, the console, and SQL Server database access rights for the old ConfigMgr site.

> ▶ **ConfigMgr Current Branch Migration Account Configuration:** This configuration consists of delegation rights to the migration account either on the CAS or a standalone primary site.

Configuring the Configuration Manager Migration User Account

A migration account is a service account used to connect from your new ConfigMgr site to your old ConfigMgr site in order to retrieve and import objects to the new site. Perform the following steps when a dedicated account is used for the migration tasks:

1. Create a dedicated Active Directory domain user—for example, a user named CMMigration.

2. Add the migration user account to the Distributed COM Users group on each primary site server provider (a.k.a. SMS provider) in your hierarchy. In Server Manager, navigate to **Configuration -> Groups -> Distributed COM Users -> Properties** and add the migration user created in step 1.

3. Grant the migration user Read and Execute rights in the database for all primary sites in scope in the old ConfigMgr hierarchy.

4. Grant a minimal number of read object rights to the migration user account in the old ConfigMgr primary sites in scope of the migration. Add a new user by specifying the migration user you created in step 1.

5. When you add a new user, copy rights from an existing ConfigMgr user or user group if you have one already configured appropriately for the site.

Configuring the Active Source Site

After you configure the migration user credentials and have appropriate rights for the old ConfigMgr and Configuration Manager Current Branch environments, you are ready to configure the migration wizard components. Start with the active source site, which is the top site of the old ConfigMgr hierarchy. The authors recommend that you perform a health check and clean up your old ConfigMgr source site(s) before starting this process. Perform the following steps to configure this site:

1. Connect to the ConfigMgr Current Branch console and navigate to **Migration -> Active Source Hierarchy**. Click **Specify Source Hierarchy** on the ribbon bar. The Specify Source Hierarchy page appears, and on it you can specify these settings (see Figure 7.7):

   ▶ **Source Hierarchy:** The default value is **New Source Hierarchy** for a new site with no migration settings configured. Changing this setting cancels all existing migration jobs for the current configured active source site.

   ▶ **Top-Level Configuration Manager Site Server:** Specify the fully qualified domain name (FQDN) value to the top site of the old ConfigMgr site (for example, **BLUEBONNET.ODYSSEY.COM**).

   ▶ **Specify Source Site Access Account to Use to Access the SMS Provider:** Select a new or existing user account that has been granted minimal read rights in the old ConfigMgr site. Only user accounts are supported for this configuration.

▶ **Specify the Source Site Database Account:** Select a new or existing user account that has been granted minimal read and execute rights to the old ConfigMgr SQL database. You can use the same account as specified for the provider access to simplify management of migration user credentials.

▶ **Enable Distribution Point Sharing for the Source Site Server:** Enable this check box to allow clients in the new environment to access content from the old DPs.

2. Click **OK.** The initial data gathering process begins. The time the process takes to complete depends on the size of your old ConfigMgr hierarchy. Review migmctrl.log in the site server logs folder for detailed progress.

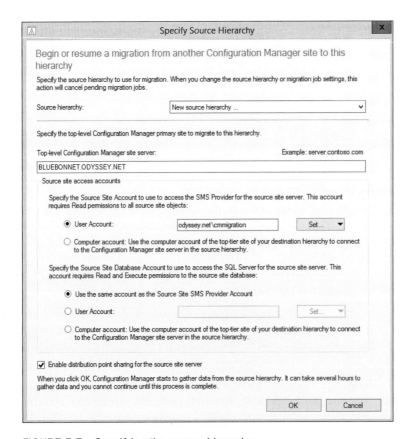

FIGURE 7.7   Specifying the source hierarchy.

Configuring Child Sites for Data Gathering (ConfigMgr 2007 Only)

If you have a ConfigMgr 2007 site hierarchy with multiple child primary sites, you must configure credentials as a separate step before you can migrate objects from the child sites. The active source site configuration only allows you to migrate objects from that site. Perform the following steps for the child site(s) before attempting to configure migration jobs for objects configured at the child site(s):

1. Connect to the ConfigMgr Current Branch console and navigate to **Migration ->
   Active Source Hierarchy**. Select the child site and click **Configure Credentials** on
   the ribbon bar. You are shown the same settings required for the active source site
   configuration except for the requirement for the hierarchy and FQDN settings.

2. If you have configured the same account for all sites, select **Existing Account**.

3. Select the user account specified for the active source site. (Note that this is the
   scenario where you are using the same migration user account for the child sites in
   your hierarchy.) Use the same account for the site database access. Click **OK** to begin
   the process of gathering data for the child site.

Performing Migration Jobs

There are two types of migration jobs, each of which addresses a specific migration
scenario:

▶ **Object Migration:** Migrates supported objects

▶ **Objects Modified after Migration:** Migrates objects that have changed since either
  object migration or collection migration

You specify the migration job type on the first page of the Create Migration Job Wizard.

Object Migration Jobs

Use an object migration job to migrate the supported objects from your previous ConfigMgr
sites. Most object types are supported by this job type, as shown in Figure 7.8.

To configure and run an object migration job, connect to the Configuration Manager Current Branch console and navigate to **Migration -> Migration jobs -> Create Migration Job**.
Provide a name and, optionally, a description, and under Job type select **Object Migration**.

As you come to each of the following wizard pages after the object migration selection,
make the appropriate selections:

▶ **Select Objects:** This page presents a list of objects available for selection.

▶ **Content Ownership:** You must assign ownership of the content associated with
  deployment objects. The CAS owns the metadata for the content, but you must
  select a primary site as the content owner. A best practice to minimize network traffic associated with content transfer is to select the closest available site in the destination hierarchy.

▶ **Site Code Replacement:** This page lists selected collections with query-based rules
  that include site codes in the WMI Query Language (WQL) query. You can replace
  the source site code with a destination site code.

▶ **Security Scope:** The authors recommend that you plan and create security scopes
  before running the object migration job. For example, if Dallas client administrators are responsible for operating system deployment objects, you can select Dallas
  Clients as the security scope.

▶ **Settings:** This page has three parts:

  ▶ **Scheduling:** You can specify not to run the job and effectively save the job for manual execution, run the job now (default), or schedule the job to run on a specified date and time (destination server time or UTC).

  ▶ **Object Conflict Resolution:** Specify the behavior for overwriting updated previously migrated objects. The default is not to overwrite updated objects.

  ▶ **Additional Object Behavior Settings:** This is where you can enable or disable the option to transfer the organizational folder structure for objects from the source Configuration Manager site to the destination site.

▶ **Summary:** This is the final verification page before you complete the wizard. The migration job is now started if you selected the Run the Migration Job option on the Settings page. After closing the wizard, monitor the progress of the job from the Migration Jobs node, as shown in Figure 7.9.

The built-in migration capabilities are designed to support a continual migration process. Objects and collections in your ConfigMgr source sites may change after a migration job has completed. The next section, "Objects Modified After Migration Job," discusses the built-in migration capabilities used to update migration objects that have changed at the ConfigMgr source site since the last successful migration.

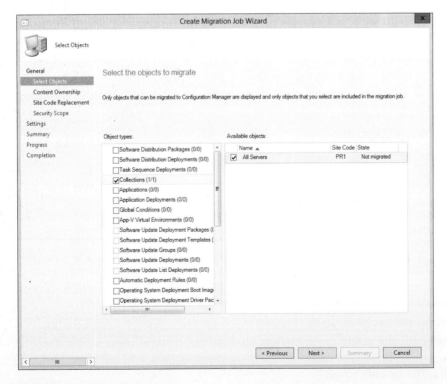

FIGURE 7.8   Object migration.

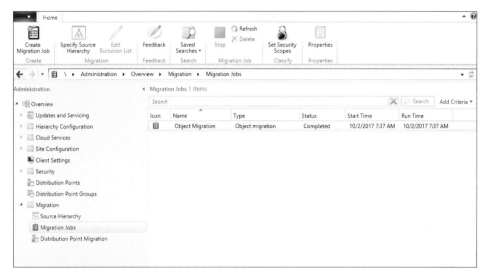

FIGURE 7.9   Migration job status.

Objects Modified After Migration Jobs

The objects modified after migration job type depend on a successful completion of the data gathering from the ConfigMgr source site after an object change. The data gathering job runs every four hours by default. You can initiate the data gathering process outside the schedule set by using the Gather Data Now option for the source site.

To configure a job to migrate objects modified after a migration job, connect to the Configuration Manager Current Branch console and navigate to **Migration -> Migration jobs -> Create Migration Job**. Provide a name and, optionally, a description, and under Job type select **Objects Modified After Migration**.

Next, as you come to each of the following wizard pages, make the appropriate selections:

- ▶ **Select Objects:** This page presents a list of objects available for selection. Only migrated objects that have changed at the source site are listed for selection. The State column of modified objects shows the value **Modified at Source Site**, as shown in Figure 7.10.

- ▶ **Content Ownership:** You must assign ownership of the content associated with deployment objects. You can change the content owner for the modified object.

- ▶ **Site Code Replacement:** This page lists selected collections with query-based rules that include a site code in the WQL query. You can replace the source site code with a destination site code.

- ▶ **Security Scope:** Assign a security scope.

▶ **Review Information:** This page provides information on the behavior of objects being migrated. The information on this page gives you an additional checklist. For example, it reminds you that custom boot images will be replaced with the default Configuration Manager Current Branch boot images. You also have the option to save the review information to a text file.

▶ **Settings:** The settings page has three parts:

  ▶ **Scheduling:** You can specify not to run the job and effectively save the job for manual execution, run the job now (default), or schedule the job to run on a specified date and time (destination server time or UTC).

  ▶ **Object Conflict Resolution:** The only option available for this job type is Overwrite All Objects.

  ▶ **Additional Object Behavior Settings:** You can enable or disable the option to transfer the organizational folder structure for objects from Configuration Manager source site to the destination site.

▶ **Summary:** This is the final verification page before you complete the wizard. The migration job is started if the Run the Migration Job option was selected on the Settings page.

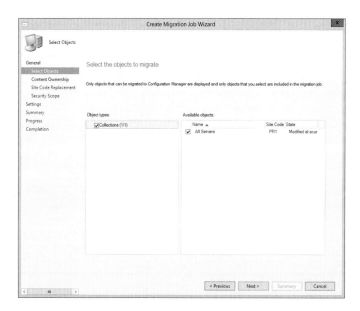

FIGURE 7.10   Selecting updated objects to migrate.

The content that migrated objects depend on is not automatically distributed to DPs in the destination site. After migration, you must assign either a distribution point or a distribution point group. Assigning a distribution point or distribution point group involves copying content from the source location to the DPs or distribution point groups. The built-in migration capabilities provide a means for upgraded ConfigMgr and new Configuration Manager Current Branch clients to access content on the original ConfigMgr DPs from the active source hierarchy. This capability is called *shared distribution points*.

Shared Distribution Points

You can use the source ConfigMgr DPs during and after migration to access content. The migration process offers three options:

▶ **Share Distribution Points:** You can configure one or more distribution points from your source hierarchy to be shared DPs to minimize content traffic during the migration phase. Migrated ConfigMgr clients can use shared DPs after they have been upgraded.

▶ **Upgrade ConfigMgr Distribution Points:** You can upgrade the shared distribution points as part of the migration process. Configured shared DPs are listed under the Shared Distribution Points tab for the configured ConfigMgr source site upgrade possibility status. ConfigMgr distribution points can be upgraded only if the site server meets the following criteria:

  ▶ Can be any type of ConfigMgr distribution point

  ▶ Must meet the supported requirements for a ConfigMgr Current Branch distribution point

  ▶ Can be a secondary site but with no other site system roles

  ▶ Cannot have a ConfigMgr client agent installed

  ▶ Cannot be a ConfigMgr primary site

▶ **Upgrade ConfigMgr Secondary Sites:** During the migration process, you can upgrade a shared DP that is colocated with a secondary site. The upgrade process removes the secondary site but preserves the original distribution point content. Configuration Manager Current Branch distribution points have built-in scheduling and thus are excellent replacements for secondary sites that were established for the sole purpose of being content bandwidth managers.

TIP: SHARED DISTRIBUTION POINTS ACCESS

The migration process allows you to migrate from multiple hierarchies. After a hierarchy is migrated, you can change the source hierarchy. Shared DPs from other hierarchies are no longer available if you change the source hierarchy.

Migration Cleanup

To complete the migration, you must perform the built-in Clean Up Migration Data migration function. Cleanup is required if you want to migrate data from a different ConfigMgr hierarchy.

The cleanup process comprises two tasks:

▶ **Stop Gathering Data:** You must stop gathering data for all ConfigMgr source sites configured under the active source sites. The Clean Up Migration Data process will fail if this step is not performed.

▶ **Clean Up Migration Data:** This process deletes all migration jobs and removes all ConfigMgr source hierarchy information. You must stop data gathering from the lowest child site configured in the active source hierarchy and repeat the process up the configured active source hierarchy. This process does not delete migrated objects; migration configuration and jobs are deleted for the configured active source hierarchy.

Migrating Reports and Clients

Reports and clients are the two types of objects that you can migrate to Configuration Manager Current Branch from your ConfigMgr sites without using the built-in migration function. How to migrate reports and clients is discussed in the "Migrating Reports" and "Client Migration and Methods" sections, later in this chapter.

Migrating Reports

If your ConfigMgr source environment uses a reporting service point with no customized reports, you can review the new ConfigMgr Current Branch reports as part of your migration planning. These reports have been reengineered to query the latest schema of the product. The default ConfigMgr SSRS reports cannot be migrated to ConfigMgr Current Branch.

Migrating Custom Reports

To migrate a custom SSRS-based report, first review the ConfigMgr Current Branch reports to see if your reporting criteria are in an existing default report. If your criteria are not met, test your report queries against the new database schema. If your report queries run with the correct results, you have the option of saving your RDL file and importing it into ConfigMgr Current Branch (see Chapter 21, "Configuration Manager Reporting," for additional information on this topic).

Client Migration and Methods

Configuration Manager Current Branch supports an in-place upgrade of the existing ConfigMgr client. The supported methods for upgrade are the same as for a standard installation of the client:

▶ Client push

▶ Group policy

▶ Manual installation

▶ Software distribution

▶ Software update based

Regardless of the client upgrade method, you must ensure that the ConfigMgr clients to be upgraded meet the minimum requirements for a ConfigMgr Current Branch client.

Background and Client Migration Concepts

The goal of migrating ConfigMgr clients to ConfigMgr Current Branch is to retain as much existing client management information as possible.

The following information is retained when a ConfigMgr client is upgraded:

- ▶ Unique identifier (GUID)
- ▶ Deployment history

The following information is not retained:

- ▶ Files in the client cache
- ▶ Information about "advertisements/deployments" that have not yet run
- ▶ Desired configuration management (DCM) compliance data
- ▶ Inventory information
- ▶ Information stored in the Configuration Manager client registry, such as power schemes, logging settings, and local policy settings

Plan to migrate the information the client will depend on, such as deployments, collections, and packages. The "Performing Migration Jobs" section, earlier in this chapter, provides information on how to migrate the supported objects that the upgraded client depends on.

REAL WORLD: CLIENT AUDIT AND CLIENT HEALTH

A migration is an excellent opportunity to audit the environment and validate the health of existing clients. Plan to perform an audit with the aim of validating that you have full coverage for all clients in scope; while you do this, check the health state of existing clients. Upgrading an unhealthy client will not necessarily resolve an underlying external issue (for example, Windows Management Instrumentation [WMI] corruption). While Configuration Manager Current Branch has significantly improved client health monitoring and remediation of built-in functions, an upgrade will not fix existing issues with the ConfigMgr client. You should plan to resolve issues with existing clients before attempting to upgrade.

Client Migration Strategies for the Network

Client migration typically involves two considerations:

- ▶ How the migration occurs
- ▶ When and how many clients you migrate

The ConfigMgr client migration methods are discussed in the "Client Migration and Methods" section. To determine when and how many clients to migrate at a time, you must plan and execute the upgrade process with minimal disruption to your existing operating environment.

The major impact is on the network infrastructure, due to the initial traffic generated by client activities after the upgrade of the ConfigMgr client. Consider the following strategies when executing the client migration phase:

▶ **Upgrade in Batches:** Migrate in batches in line with the available bandwidth of your network infrastructure. The authors recommend performing a pilot migration coordinated with the network team to obtain a measurement of the traffic that is generated. Use the actual measured network impact as a guide.

▶ **Minimize Active Targeted Deployments to the Devices Migrated and Users Aligned with the Migrated Devices:** An industry best practice during this phase is to freeze the deployment for all but essential activities.

Troubleshooting Migration Issues

The migration process can present some technical challenges and issues. Table 7.4 provides information on troubleshooting resources, known issues, and resolutions.

TABLE 7.4   Troubleshooting Resources and Known Issues

Resource/Issue	Notes
Log file	The migration process is logged in the log file migmctrl.log (in the <ConfigMgrInstallPath>\LOGS folder on the site server). This file is automatically overwritten, so check it as soon as you encounter any issues.
Migration reports	Enable the Reporting Services role for ConfigMgr Current Branch in order to have access to the migration reports.
Migration workspace	Monitor individual migration jobs in the ConfigMgr Current Branch console, at **Administration -> Migration -> Migration jobs**.
Gathering data failure for a ConfigMgr source site	Check the security delegation for the configured migration account.
Content access failure for a shared DP	Ensure that the source hierarchy for the shared DP is still the active source site.
Inability to delete migration jobs after migration	Stop all data gathering for all sites configured under the active source site. Run the Clean Up Migration Data task. You must stop data gathering from the lowest child site configured and work your way up the hierarchy to the top site.

Summary

This chapter covered the two options to move from an older version of ConfigMgr to ConfigMgr Current Branch: upgrading and migrating. It walked through the upgrade process and provided guidance on the migration process. It included background on why to consider upgrading versus migration as well as on migrating custom reports and clients.

Chapter 8, "Using the Configuration Manager Console," provides a detailed discussion of the Configuration Manager Current Branch console.

PART III

Configuration Manager Operations

IN THIS PART

Using the Configuration Manager Console

Configuration Manager's console historically used the Microsoft Management Console (MMC) framework. The console has evolved over the years, receiving little touches to enhance the administrative experience with each product version.

Starting with System Center 2012 Configuration Manager (ConfigMgr), the console utilizes the System Center framework, bringing a fresh and intuitive look to the platform. By building the ConfigMgr console on this common framework, Microsoft aligned the console with the familiar look and feel of the other System Center products. In addition, role-based security controls the console experience, giving each security role a common set of views, tasks, and objects.

The ConfigMgr console is the administrative interface for managing all facets of the ConfigMgr infrastructure, applications, deployments, software updates, monitoring, and users and devices. As a key element of any ConfigMgr environment, the console is also the interface used to maintain the site and hierarchy; you use it to perform daily tasks to manage and configure sites, the site database, and clients and to monitor the status of the hierarchy.

The console sports some very nice features, which this chapter covers in detail. The highlights follow:

▶ Similar operations are grouped together into intuitive, administrative workspaces.

▶ ConfigMgr now has Outlook-style navigation, coupled with context-sensitive ribbon tabs that display only the relevant actions.

▶ Supporting role-based administration (RBA), the console displays only what you have rights to see, removing much of the clutter and confusion often associated with a very busy console.

▶ Search bars in nearly every facet of the console enable instant filtering to narrow down the scope of data to a manageable view.

▶ PowerShell integration allows you to quickly launch a PowerShell command prompt or the Integrated Scripting Environment (ISE) and automatically load the ConfigMgr module for PowerShell.

▶ Temporary nodes help track various objects used in the console, allowing quick reference to objects you have already visited.

▶ Just as in your favorite web browser, a temporary history is available of the areas you have visited while navigating the console, making it easy to go back to a previous view.

▶ In-console alerts bring near-real-time status information, providing light monitoring functionality without requiring you to leave the console.

This chapter describes the core areas of the console and its many features. It also covers console installation and deployment, including console prerequisites, security considerations, and troubleshooting.

Touring the Console

As you open the System Center Configuration Manager console, you will notice that it is divided into four main quadrants, reminiscent of previous versions of Outlook:

▶ Navigation

▶ Lists

▶ Detail

▶ Bars

In addition, the console contains functionality that is similar in behavior to Outlook. The Navigation pane and ribbon bar are key elements of Outlook that you will immediately recognize in the ConfigMgr console.

Configuration Manager Console Panes

Console panes are areas that are themed to contain certain types of objects. There are three panes in the console, as shown in Figure 8.1:

▶ **Navigation:** The left side of the console is known as the Navigation pane (sometimes referred to as the WunderBar). The workspaces at the bottom allow you to move quickly between administrative areas, and you can use the folder list at the top to select specific nodes.

▶ **List:** Depending on the selected node, the List pane on the right side displays charts, dashboards, or lists of objects.

▶ **Details:** When you select certain items in the List pane, the Details pane dynamically shows additional information about the selected item. Often, the Details pane is broken out into multiple tabs that provide more information.

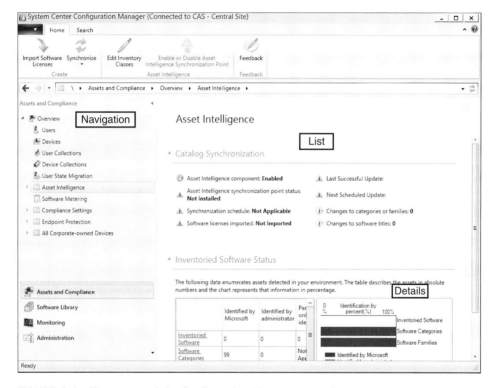

FIGURE 8.1   The panes of the Configuration Manager console.

NOTE: WUNDERBAR TRIVIA

Did you ever wonder where the name WunderBar originated? Before the WunderBar term was used, the Navigation pane was known as the "Combined Outlook Bar and Folder List." To learn how it got this name, as well as how the ribbon bar got its name, see http://blogs.msdn.com/b/jensenh/archive/2005/10/07/478214.aspx.

Configuration Manager Console Bars

The ConfigMgr console also includes three bars, displayed in Figure 8.2:

▶ **Ribbon:** The ribbon bar, situated along the top of the console, is a context-sensitive list of commands available based on the selected object.

▶ **Address:** The address bar, shown as in Figure 8.2, shows the node on which the console is currently focused. It is primarily designed to make navigation easier by providing a history of places already visited.

▶ **Search:** The search bar provides a means of isolating the objects in the List pane by matching them against criteria to help you quickly find information.

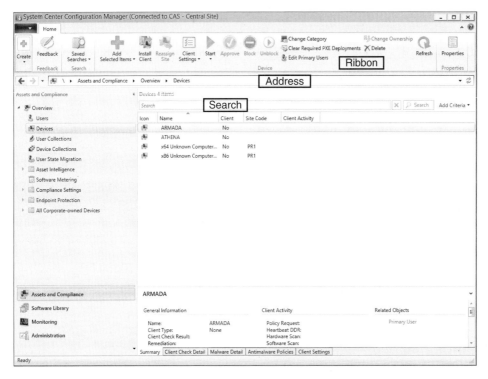

FIGURE 8.2   The ribbon, address, and search bars of the Configuration Manager console.

Using the Backstage

The tab on the far-left section of the ribbon bar is referred to as the *backstage*. The backstage contains a common set of commands that are available no matter where the focus is in the ConfigMgr console, providing a consistent set of commands. As shown in Figure 8.3, the backstage contains the following commands:

▶ **Connect to a New Site:** Displays the Site Connection dialog box for connecting to a different site server.

▶ **Connect via Windows PowerShell:** Launches a PowerShell command prompt and loads the ConfigMgr module.

▶ **Connect via Windows PowerShell ISE:** Launches the PowerShell ISE and loads the ConfigMgr module.

▶ **About Configuration Manager:** Displays the About System Center Configuration Manager dialog box.

▶ **Help:** Displays the help file.

▶ **Customer Experience Improvement Program:** Launches the Customer Experience Improvement Program dialog box, which you can use to enable or disable participation in that program.

▶ **Exit:** Closes the ConfigMgr console.

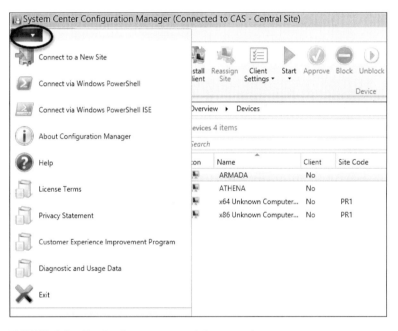

FIGURE 8.3   The backstage area of the console.

Configuration Manager Workspaces

The Configuration Manager console has four different workspaces:

▶ Assets and Compliance

▶ Software Library

▶ Monitoring

▶ Administration

Each workspace is designed for a specific purpose, and similar functions are grouped together. When you select a workspace, the Navigation pane displays a particular set of nodes in the folder list. The next sections discuss these four workspaces.

Using Assets and Compliance

The Assets and Compliance workspace, shown in Figure 8.4, includes collections for managing users and devices. In addition, you can use this workspace to manage user state migration, asset intelligence, and software metering.

FIGURE 8.4   The Assets and Compliance workspace.

You can use this workspace to manage baselines and configuration items for compliance settings. You can also manage endpoint protection policies for configuring antimalware and firewall settings in this workspace.

Following are the main nodes in the Assets and Compliance workspace:

▶ Users

▶ Devices

▶ User Collections

▶ Device Collections

▶ User State Migration

▶ Asset Intelligence

▶ Software Metering

▶ Compliance Settings

▶ Endpoint Protection

▶ All Corporate-owned Devices

Functions of the Software Library

The Software Library workspace, shown in Figure 8.5, shows all the elements for managing applications, software updates, and operating system deployments. However, this node is not just about organizing content; it includes other activities, such as managing the global conditions and requirement rules that drive the stateful behavior of applications, managing automatic deployment rules for software updates, and managing task sequences—which provides a means for performing multiple steps on a client system (typically when using Operating System Deployment [OSD]). In addition, when users request applications through Software Center, these approval requests populate the Approval Requests node. You can use this workspace to approve or deny application requests.

FIGURE 8.5   The Software Library workspace.

You can use this workspace to manage all software updates, including synchronizing software updates and managing automatic deployment rules to update and deploy software updates. All drivers, images, and task sequences that comprise operating system deployments exist in this workspace.

The Software Library workspace has four main nodes:

▶ Application Management

▶ Software Updates

▶ Operating Systems

▶ Windows 10 Servicing

Capabilities of the Monitoring Workspace

The Monitoring workspace, as the name suggests, monitors information. You can view the status of the ConfigMgr infrastructure (site, component, distribution, replication, and so on) in various nodes. Client health information is also available. When these types of statuses are set for alerting, the alert data populates the Alerts node, enabling you to manage these alerts (by commenting, postponing, disabling, and so on). You can view status information in more ways than just text. This workspace includes diagram views that display status, alert, and configuration data over a hierarchy diagram or geographic view. Figure 8.6 shows a site hierarchy diagram view that graphically shows the status of the hierarchy.

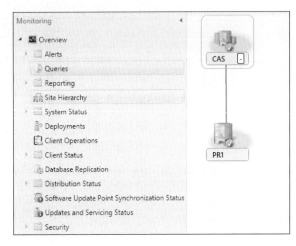

FIGURE 8.6   Hierarchy diagram view.

You might typically think of monitoring in terms of alerts and statuses, but the Monitoring workspace contains far more. For example, you can manage reports and create subscriptions from this workspace.

You also manage and execute queries from the Monitoring workspace. Although collections and queries are often viewed as interrelated, it is important to note that they exist in different workspaces in the console.

The following are the main nodes in this workspace:

▶ Alerts

▶ Queries

▶ Reporting

▶ Site Hierarchy

▶ System Status

▶ Deployments

▶ Client Operations

▶ Client Status

▶ Database Replication

▶ Distribution Status

▶ Software Update Point Synchronization Status

▶ Updates and Servicing Status

▶ Security

Managing ConfigMgr Through the Administration Workspace

The Administration workspace, shown in Figure 8.7, contains the nodes necessary for managing the ConfigMgr infrastructure, security, and settings. ConfigMgr infrastructure management consists of tasks such as managing distribution points, site boundaries, resource discoveries, and migration of objects from separate ConfigMgr hierarchies. You can create, assign, and edit custom ConfigMgr client settings in this workspace.

FIGURE 8.7   The Administration workspace.

You can use this workspace to add administrative users to System Center Configuration Manager. You can assign new roles, create scopes, and apply permissions. In addition, you can manage certificates used in various components of ConfigMgr in the Administration workspace.

This workspace consists of the following main nodes:

▶ Updates and Servicing

▶ Hierarchy Configuration

▶ Cloud Services

▶ Site Configuration

▶ Client Settings

▶ Security

▶ Distribution Points

▶ Distribution Point Groups

▶ Migration

Deploying the Console

The ConfigMgr console can be installed as a part of the central administration site (CAS) or primary site server installation. Unlike earlier versions of ConfigMgr, with Current Branch this is a choice and not a requirement. Most organizations do not have a single person manage the administration and operation of ConfigMgr. This is especially true in enterprises where management resides with entire teams.

Console Placement

Regardless of whether administration is by one administrator or a group of administrators scattered around the globe, the authors recommend installing the console locally on the administrator's desktop.

However, depending on your hierarchy, there could be potential challenges with local console installations. For example, if the hierarchy is designed such that a site database server and SMS provider are not physically near the administrator and WAN latency is an issue, the console may perform poorly as it must retrieve content over a slow link.

You might want to install the console on a server with the SMS provider and allow administrators access to the console over Remote Desktop Services (RDS). The SMS provider can be installed on the ConfigMgr site server, the database server, or an entirely separate server. Installing additional SMS providers in a site distributes the workload and provides high availability for console connections. If bandwidth is a factor, the console could be loaded on the primary site server, allowing administrators to use RDS to manage the site.

Regardless of the number of providers, if the SMS provider is not on the same server as the database server, there will be impacts to console performance from the speed and latency of the connection from the SMS provider to the database.

> **NOTE: THE ROLE OF THE SMS PROVIDER**
>
> When a ConfigMgr console connects to a ConfigMgr site server, it is important to recognize that the console is connecting to the database. To be more specific, the console connects to the SMS provider, a Windows Management Instrumentation (WMI) provider that handles all reads and writes to the site database.

Often those using ConfigMgr are not administrators. For example, help desk staff might use the console as a means to view a device's configuration data or connect through remote control to assist an end user. In situations such as these, it is far safer and easier to provide a local console than to allow help desk staff to log on to the server directly.

Supported Platforms

The ConfigMgr console can run on any currently supported Windows operating system, either workstation or server, x86 or x64.

Installation Prerequisites

System Center Configuration Manager includes the Prerequisite Checker, which can help determine whether a computer meets the requirements to run the ConfigMgr console. You can find the prereqchk.exe utility located under SMSSETUP\BIN\X64 of the ConfigMgr source files or the *%ProgramFiles%*\Microsoft Configuration Manager\bin\x64 folder of an installed server.

When you run prereqchk.exe with the ADMINUI switch, it runs through a scan of the specified system to determine if it meets the requirements for installing the console. You run the utility to scan for console prerequisites by issuing the following command:

```
prereqchk.exe /ADMINUI
```

After the utility runs, you can find the log of the prerequisite scan in the root of the system drive named ConfigMgrPrereq.log. Following are the required components for the ConfigMgr console:

▶ .NET Framework 4.2 or higher

▶ Microsoft XML Core Services 6.0 (MSXML60)

▶ Windows Remote Management (WinRM) v1.1

For further information about the Prerequisite Checker, see https://docs.microsoft.com/sccm/core/servers/deploy/install/prerequisite-checker.

Installation Using the Configuration Manager Setup Wizard

When all prerequisites are met, you can install the ConfigMgr console by launching the System Center Configuration Manager Setup Wizard. Start the wizard by opening the splash.hta file, found in the root of the installation media.

> **TIP: LAUNCHING THE CONSOLE INSTALLATION WIZARD WITHOUT THE SETUP WIZARD**
>
> It is not necessary to use the System Center Configuration Manager Setup Wizard to install the console, as the console install is now separate from the rest of the product. Navigate to the \SMSSETUP\BIN\I386 folder and click **consolesetup.exe** to launch the console installation program.

8

To install the console using the System Center Configuration Manager Setup Wizard, perform the following steps:

1. In the Tools and Standalone Components section, click the **Install Configuration Manager Console** link.

2. The Configuration Manager Console Setup Wizard launches, indicating This Wizard Will Install the Configuration Manager Console. When you are ready, click **Next** to continue.

3. On the Site Server page, enter the site server fully qualified domain name (FQDN) for the ConfigMgr console to connect to on its first launch. Click **Next**.

4. The Installation Folder page displays the default path where the installation will occur. Choose the default or select a new path by clicking **Browse**, and then click **Next**.

5. On the Ready to Install screen, which displays all settings required for setup, select **Back** to review or change the settings, if necessary. Then click **Install**. The Please Wait page appears, showing a progress bar that provides a visual indicator of the installation. The wizard also displays the installation steps on this page.

6. When installation completes, leave the option **Start the Configuration Manager Console After You Close the Setup Wizard Is Displayed** checked and click **Finish** to complete the wizard.

Unattended Console Installation

In situations in which multiple individuals will manage administration and operation of the ConfigMgr infrastructure, it may be beneficial to automate the console installation.

Before installing the console, verify that the target systems meet the prerequisites identified earlier in this chapter, in the "Installation Prerequisites" section, including the supported platform (though this should not be a problem in most scenarios). The supported method for installing the ConfigMgr console uses the executable consolesetup.exe mentioned in the "Launching the Console Installation Wizard Without the Setup Wizard" tip in the previous section.

The executable accepts the following switches:

▶ `/q`: Indicates a silent install of the ConfigMgr console. Requires specifying ENABLESQM and DEFAULTSITESERVERNAME.

▶ `/uninstall`: Uninstalls the ConfigMgr console.

▶ `DEFAULTSITESERVERNAME`: Specifies the site server FQDN to which the console will connect upon launch.

▶ `ENABLESQM`: Indicates the acceptance of joining the Customer Experience Improvement Program (CEIP)—0 for no or 1 for yes.

▶ `TARGETDIR`: Specifies a different folder if the default folder, *%ProgramFiles%*\Microsoft Configuration Manager\AdminConsole, is not acceptable.

▶ `LangPackDir`: Specifies a folder where the language pack files are located if you wish to install a language pack.

The switches that do not begin with a slash (/) all require the use of an equal sign (=) between the switch and the value. Following are some examples of using the switches with consolesetup.exe:

▶ `consolesetup.exe /q DEFAULTSITESERVERNAME=armada.odyssey.com ENABLESQM=0`

▶ `consolesetup.exe /q DEFAULTSITESERVERNAME=armada.odyssey.com ENABLESQM=1`
  `LangPackDir=c:\LangPacks`

▶ `consolesetup.exe /uninstall`

Using Role-Based Administration

The Configuration Manager console is context sensitive, based on the security of each administrative user. As you begin to assign permissions to other users, you will notice that the console displays only what the user is allowed to manage.

The console is designed to reflect only what the administrative user is assigned to do. This behavior means specialized console customization is not necessary, as the console automatically displays what is pertinent. You therefore need to deploy only a single version of the console and can let the assigned security do the rest.

How Content Is Displayed

For an administrative user to use the ConfigMgr console, that user must be assigned to at least one role, or the console will fail to connect. Once a role is defined, when the console is opened, the objects that fall under the management of the administrative user are displayed and accessible. All other objects are hidden from view. The console displays content based on the assigned roles, scopes, and collections:

▶ **Roles:** Visible workspaces, nodes, folders, objects, and actions are defined by the administrative user's associated role.

▶ **Scopes:** Only the objects associated with assigned scopes can be managed.

▶ **Collections:** Only assigned collections can be viewed and managed.

The Three States of Objects Interaction

Objects in the console exist in three states: shown, hidden, and disabled. Objects in a shown state do just as the name implies: If a user has permission to manage these objects, they display in the console. If the object is a folder or a node, the parent objects are also displayed.

By default, objects are hidden. Only when users are granted access to them do objects appear. Hidden behavior is determined by the following rules:

▶ **Actions:** If an administrative user does not have permissions to perform the action, the action is not displayed.

▶ **Objects:** If an object does not belong to a security scope assigned to the administrative user, the object is not displayed.

▶ **Nodes:** Without access to manage items in the node, the node will not be displayed.

▶ **Workspaces:** Without access to manage at least one node in the workspace, the workspace itself will not be displayed.

Objects that are disabled display as grayed-out objects in the console and do not allow full interaction. This is typical whenever a user is granted read access to an object.

Connecting to a Site

During installation of the Configuration Manager console, a default site server is specified; the console will connect to this server upon opening. If no default is specified during installation, you are prompted to specify the default on first launch. You are free to connect to any site server to which you have access. By accessing the backstage, you can use the Connect to a New Site dialog to provide a site server name. You can launch multiple instances of the admin console to connect to different sites simultaneously.

Personalizing the Console

There are few options for customizing the console, as an administrative user's security context drives what is available for view and use. The ConfigMgr console allows for limited personalization to suit your taste, and it all has to do with the Navigation pane.

The default order of workspaces in the Navigation pane is Assets and Compliance, Software Library, Monitoring, and Administration. You can arrange this order to something that makes more sense for you. Perform the following steps to rearrange workspaces:

1. Click the arrow below the last workspace in the Navigation pane (see Figure 8.8).

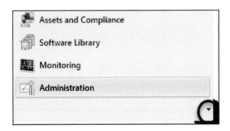

FIGURE 8.8   Navigation pane arrow.

2. When the menu opens, choose **Navigation Pane Options**.

3. In the Navigation Pane Options window (see Figure 8.9), click the workspace to move and then click either Move Up or Move Down as many times as needed to get the workspace where you want it.

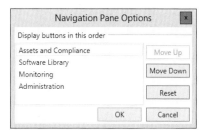

FIGURE 8.9   Navigation pane options.

4. When all the workspaces are arranged in your order of preference, click **OK**.

TIP: RESETTING WORKSPACES

If you need to reset the workspaces to their original order, follow the preceding steps to open the Navigation Pane Options dialog and select **Reset**. This places the workspaces back into their original order.

If the Workspaces pane overlaps the node list, you can collapse it. When it is collapsed, the workspaces are represented by only icons. Collapse the Workspaces pane by moving the separator bar down. Using the Show More Buttons and Show Fewer Buttons selections (see Figure 8.10) is the equivalent of using the separator bar.

FIGURE 8.10   Console separator bar with the Show More Buttons and Show Fewer Buttons selections.

A vertical separator bar also exists between the Navigation pane and the List and Detail panes. The List and Detail panes have a horizontal separator bar as well; it is used for resizing.

The In-Console Alert Experience

In-console alerts allow an administrator to configure basic monitoring for the health of the ConfigMgr environment, as well as note the success of deployments. Alerts are state-based (meaning they update automatically as the condition changes), providing a near real-time monitoring experience and subscription capability. However, ConfigMgr alerts are limited in functionality and should not be considered a monitoring solution as robust as is provided by other tools, such as System Center Operations Manager, which is designed to handle enterprise-level alerting, notification, and performance metric gathering. Microsoft Operations Management Suite (OMS) can also be used to capture data from the application log and forward events to your favorite IT service management tool.

Viewing Alerts

Alerts are located in the Monitoring workspace of the Configuration Manager console. The Overview node provides a list of recent alerts. If you click the Alerts node, you can see the list of available alerts in the List pane, along with details of any highlighted alert in the Details pane.

Available actions are based on the state of the alert. ConfigMgr assigns the following five states for alerts:

- ▶ **Active:** A specified condition is met.
- ▶ **Canceled:** A specified condition is no longer met.
- ▶ **Disabled:** The condition of an alert is not evaluated while in this state.
- ▶ **Never Triggered:** An alert has been created, but no condition has yet been met.
- ▶ **Postponed:** The same as disabled, with an expiration period to revert to an active state.

Figure 8.11 shows configured alerts that have not yet been triggered.

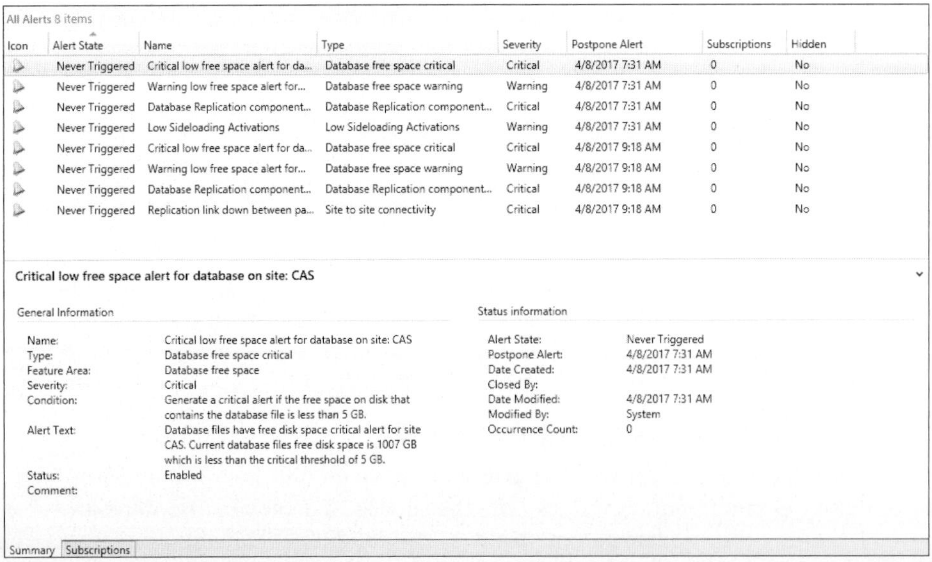

FIGURE 8.11   The Alerts pane.

Managing Alerts

Alerts that bubble up in the ConfigMgr console support a variety of actions. As mentioned in the previous section, available actions are dependent on the state of the alert. For example, the Enable action is not available on an enabled alert. The available alert actions are as follows (see Figure 8.12):

▶ **Postpone:** Postponing an alert essentially ignores the alert for a specified period of time. When the time period has lapsed, the alert is updated to its current state. You can only postpone active alerts.

▶ **Edit Comments:** You can add or modify comments to provide additional context about an alert.

▶ **Configure:** Configuring an alert provides the ability to change the name, severity, and definition.

▶ **Enable:** You can enable the selected alert.

▶ **Disable:** You can disable the selected alert.

▶ **Refresh:** Refresh is not for a specified alert but rather refreshes the entire list of alerts.

▶ **Delete:** Deleting an alert removes it from the Alerts node and the list of recent alerts.

FIGURE 8.12   Available alert actions.

CAUTION: USING THE DELETE ACTION

The three states—Postpone, Disable, and Delete—might be confusing at first since their descriptions are somewhat similar. Postpone and Disable are most alike; disabling an alert is much like postponing an alert without a time period. Delete, however, is very different from either Postpone or Disable. Deleting an alert modifies the alert configuration, turning off the alert. This is quite different from disabling an alert since the disabled alert configuration remains the same and can be reenabled. If you want to reestablish a deleted alert, you must create and configure it again.

Configuring Alerts

Whereas you can view alerts in a single area of the ConfigMgr console (the Alerts node of the Monitoring workspace), alert configuration pages are scattered around the console. This creates a challenge because you need to know the locations of all the configuration areas for creating alerts. Table 8.1 shows the locations and functions of the alerts you can create.

TABLE 8.1   Alert Locations

Workspace	Node	Function
Administration	Sites	Low free disk space alerts on the site database server. See Chapter 24, "Backup, Recovery, and Maintenance," for additional information.
Software Library	Applications	Alerts about deployment success or failure percentage meeting a specified threshold. More information is available in Chapter 14, "Distributing and Deploying Applications and Packages."
	Software Updates Groups	Alerts about deployment compliance failing to meet a specified threshold. More information is available in Chapter 15, "Managing Software Updates."
Monitoring	Database Replication	Alerts about a replication link not working for a specified duration. Additional information is available in Chapter 24.
Assets and Compliance	Device Collections	Alerts about a value falling below a specified client check, remediation, or activity threshold. Chapter 9, "Client Management," contains additional information for setting up alerts.
		Antimalware alerts for Endpoint Protection from client systems. You can find more detail in Chapter 19, "Endpoint Protection."
	Compliance Settings	Alerts about baseline deployment compliance falling below a specified threshold. Additional information is available in Chapter 10, "Managing Compliance."

The configuration of each is slightly different, but overall configuration uses the same basic concept: You need to enable an alert and specify a threshold value. Refer to the chapters listed in Table 8.1 for additional information.

Subscribing to Alerts

Subscriptions specifically refer to malware alerts. An alert subscription sends an email whenever a malware condition is met.

This section provides an example of setting up a subscription for System Center Endpoint Protection. Perform the following steps:

1. Navigate to **Monitoring -> Alerts -> Subscriptions**.

2. On the ribbon bar, click **Create Subscription**.

3. In the New Subscription window, provide a name for the subscription.

4. Specify the email address of the alert recipient. If there are multiple recipients, separate the email addresses with semicolons (;).

5. Select the email language.

6. Select the appropriate alerts and click **OK**.

Figure 8.13 shows a fully configured alert subscription.

FIGURE 8.13   Alert subscription.

Configuration Manager Service Manager

The Configuration Manager Service Manager console assists in managing the state of ConfigMgr components. The console, shown in Figure 8.14, can check component status, set logging, and control the running state.

While nearly all components should be in a running state, a handful of components run only when initiated. For example, the SMS_SITE_BACKUP service remains stopped until the backup operation for ConfigMgr is initiated.

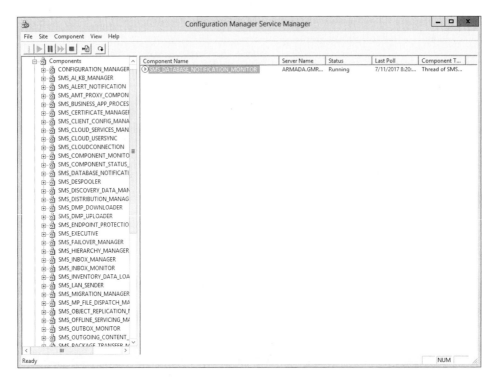

FIGURE 8.14   Viewing the Service Manager console.

Initiating the Configuration Manager Service Manager Console

Configuration Manager Service Manager can be launched either through the ConfigMgr console or directly by running the proper executable.

To launch Service Manager from the ConfigMgr console, follow these steps:

1. Navigate to **Monitoring -> System Status -> Component**.

2. On the ribbon bar, click **Start** and then select **Configuration Manager Service Manager**.

To start Configuration Manager Service Manager outside the ConfigMgr console, navigate to the *%ProgramFiles%*\Microsoft Configuration Manager\AdminConsole\bin\i386 folder and open the compmgr.exe file. To make this easier in the future, create a shortcut to the file, as the Start menu does not include a shortcut for this file.

Unlike when launching the Configuration Manager Service Manager console from the ConfigMgr console, you must provide a site server name to connect to when the Service Manager console initially opens. If you prefer to launch the console directed at a specific server, simply add the name of the site server after compmgr.exe. The following example shows how to open Configuration Manager Service Manager connecting to the Athena site server:

```
%ProgramFiles%\Microsoft Configuration Manager\AdminConsole\bin\i386\
compmgr.exe Athena
```

Operating the Configuration Manager Service Manager Console

You can perform several actions within the Configuration Manager Service Manager console. Configuration Manager components are managed in a similar fashion to standard Windows services: They can be started, stopped, paused, resumed, and queried.

Following are the options Configuration Manager Service Manager offers for managing components, listed in the order displayed on the toolbar shown in Figure 8.15:

▶ **Query:** Use this action to detect the current status of a component.

▶ **Start:** Use this action to start a component that is in a stopped state.

▶ **Pause:** If you want to preserve a component's runtime environment, pause the service. Data in the component log file will persist when paused. Keep in mind that certain components do not support pausing.

▶ **Resume:** This action can be applied to any component in a paused state.

▶ **Stop:** When there is no concern for the preservation of a component's runtime environment or data in the component's log file, use this action to shut down the component.

▶ **Logging:** This action displays the log control dialog to control whether logging is enabled or disabled, the name and location of the log file, and the size of the log file.

FIGURE 8.15   Service Manager console toolbar.

NOTE: COMPONENT ACTIONS NOT AVAILABLE UNTIL AFTER QUERY

Unlike with Windows services, to perform an action against a component, you must first query. Actions are available based on the component's status. For example, the resume action is available only when a component is paused.

The Configuration Manager Service Manager console supports the following general actions:

▶ **Clear status:** This action simply blanks the component status.

▶ **Site refresh:** This action refreshes the list of components.

▶ **Connect:** This action displays the Connect to Site dialog. The Service Manager console supports connecting to multiple sites.

▶ **Disconnect:** This action displays the Disconnect from Sites dialog. This dialog box supports selecting multiple sites and disconnecting from multiple sites at once.

TIP: PERFORMING ACTIONS AGAINST MULTIPLE COMPONENTS

While the Components node is selected, you can select multiple components by using Ctrl+click; or you can select all components by using Ctrl+A. When multiple components are selected, you can use the query action to check the status of the selected components.

In addition, the logging action displays a slightly modified log control dialog that allows the use of a same filename for all selected components.

Using PowerShell with ConfigMgr

PowerShell integration is a new addition to the admin console, starting with this version of Configuration Manager. You can launch a PowerShell command window or the Power-Shell ISE from the top-left dropdown, as shown in Figure 8.16.

FIGURE 8.16   Launching PowerShell.

The first time you launch the window to connect to PowerShell, you are prompted about whether to run software from an untrusted publisher, as shown in Figure 8.17. Choose the appropriate answer for your organization, and a command prompt appears that includes the site code of the site to which you are connected.

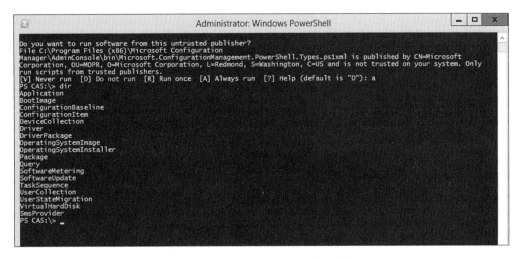

FIGURE 8.17   The PowerShell prompt, connected to the site CAS.

When you launch the PowerShell ISE option, the ISE window loads a file with code to load the ConfigMgr module and connect to the site server. You can reuse this code in your automation scripts to eliminate the need to launch the ConfigMgr console. Figure 8.18 shows the .ps1 file.

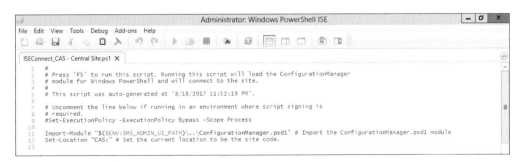

FIGURE 8.18   The PowerShell ISE with code to load the ConfigMgr module and connect to the site.

Review the ConfigMgr cmdlet documentation at https://docs.microsoft.com/powershell/sccm/overview?view=sccm-ps.

Security Considerations

By default, a local group called SMS Admins is granted the permissions required to access the SMS provider and the Common Information Model (CIM) repository. Whenever an administrative user is granted access to Configuration Manager, the user is added to the SMS Admins group and inherently receives these permissions.

> **NOTE: SMS ADMINS GROUP DOES NOT PROVIDE ADMINISTRATIVE ACCESS**
>
> Although the name SMS Admins might sound as if it grants full administrative rights to ConfigMgr, this is not the case. Even when you are a member of the SMS Admins group, you cannot access a database unless you have been granted administrative user database access as well. Think of it as an office building: The SMS Admins group is the key to the front, public space. Once inside, you must be given access to the individual office suites.

SMS Provider Permissions

When you run the ConfigMgr console locally (on the same server where the SMS provider exists), it uses WMI to connect to the SMS provider, and in turn the SMS provider allows access to the site database. This is made slightly more complicated for remote connections with the added requirement for Distributed Component Object Model (DCOM) permissions.

Because Configuration Manager still uses WMI, and WMI relies on DCOM, it is vital that you understand the requirements for WMI. For information about remote WMI security requirements, see https://docs.microsoft.com/sccm/core/plan-design/hierarchy/plan-for-the-sms-provider.

DCOM Permissions

Administrative users running the console from their workstations, where the SMS provider does not exist, require the Remote Activation DCOM privilege on any computer where the SMS provider is installed and providing access to the ConfigMgr database. (In most cases, the SMS provider is installed on the same server as the site server.)

By default, the local SMS Admins group has the following permissions applied:

▶ Local Launch

▶ Remote Launch

▶ Local Activation

▶ Remote Activation

It is important to note that for remote console access, only the Remote Activation privilege is required. Figure 8.19 shows a custom local group provided this privilege.

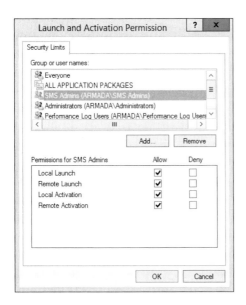

FIGURE 8.19   DCOM permissions with the Remote Activation privilege.

WMI Permissions

Along with DCOM permissions, WMI permissions are also required for ConfigMgr console access. By default, the SMS Admins group is given the permissions necessary to provide operability.

Permissions are applied to two different namespaces. The following privileges are granted to the SMS Admins group in the `Root\SMS` WMI namespace:

- ▶ Enable Account
- ▶ Remote Enable

Figure 8.20 shows the permissions assigned to the same custom group as in Figure 8.19 (SMS Admins), with the appropriate permissions granted to the `Root\SMS` namespace.

The SMS Admins group is provided a slightly different set of permissions than the `Root\SMS\site_<site code>` WMI namespace:

- ▶ Enable Account
- ▶ Execute Methods
- ▶ Provider Write
- ▶ Remote Enable

Figure 8.21 shows the same custom group (SMS Admins) with the appropriate permissions for this namespace.

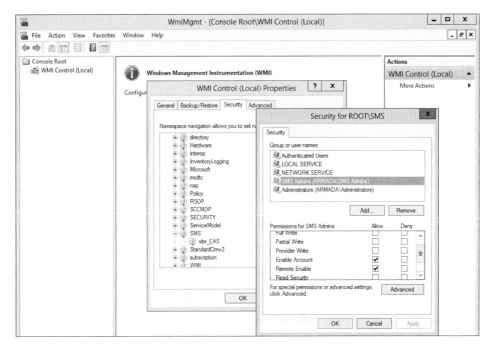

FIGURE 8.20   WMI permissions required on the `Root\SMS` namespace.

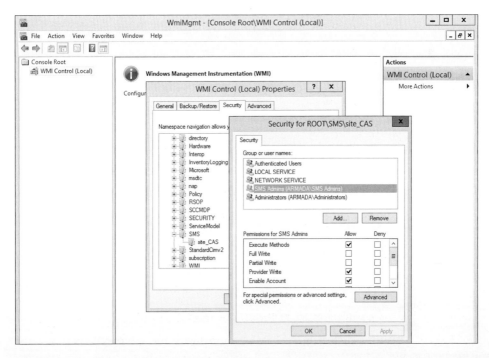

FIGURE 8.21   WMI permissions required on the `Root\sms\site_<site code>` WMI namespace.

Troubleshooting Console Issues

With the role-based ConfigMgr console, the expected behavior may not always be the out-come. Console problems often are due to insufficient or inappropriately assigned security privileges. The following sections describe how to troubleshoot issues with the ConfigMgr console.

Console Logging

Administrators cherish the rich, detailed logging provided in ConfigMgr. This detailed log-ging is available for the ConfigMgr console. Use the log to gain valuable insight and detail about console-related issues. The console logs to the SMSAdminUI.log file located in the following path:

```
<%ProgramFiles%>\Microsoft Configuration Manager\AdminConsole\AdminUILog
```

If the default logging level in SMSAdminUI.log does not provide sufficient detail, you can increase the logging verbosity. To enable verbose logging, follow these steps:

1. Navigate to the following path:

   ```
   <%ProgramFiles%>\Microsoft Configuration Manager\AdminConsole\bin
   ```

2. Open the file Microsoft.ConfigurationManagement.exe.config.

3. Search for the line `<source name="SmsAdminUISnapIn" switch-Value="Error" >` and change `Error` to `Verbose`.

4. If the ConfigMgr console is open, restart the console to cause the setting to take effect.

> **CAUTION: DO NOT LEAVE LOGGING SET TO VERBOSE**
>
> When logging levels are increased, the log size and activity to write logs also increase. If you enable verbose logging, be sure to change the logging level back to its default when you are finished.

Active Directory Integration

At a minimum, the required DCOM permission is Remote Activation. To verify the Remote Activation permission, perform the following steps:

1. On the site server (and any SMS provider computer), start the Component Services console by clicking **Start** -> **Run** and then typing **dcomcnfg.exe**.

2. Expand **Component Services** -> **Computers**.

3. Right-click **My Computer** and select **Properties** from the menu.

4. Switch to the COM Security tab.

5. In the lower section, titled Launch and Activation Permissions, click **Edit Limits**. At this point, if permissions are correct (refer to Figure 8.19 in the "Security Considerations for the Console" section), the remaining steps are not necessary. If permissions are missing, proceed to step 6.

6. Click **Add** and specify the interested account or group. Click **OK**.

7. In the permissions area, deselect all other values and select **Remote Activation**.

8. Click **OK** to close the Launch and Activation Permission dialog box and click **OK** to close the My Computer Properties dialog box.

9. In the permissions area, deselect all other values and select **Remote Activation**.

10. Close the Component Services console.

Verifying WMI Permissions

Validating WMI permissions occurs at two different WMI namespaces. Even though the namespaces are along the same path, the privileges differ for the two namespaces, and therefore the child namespaces do not inherit from the parent. Note that the screenshots shown earlier in this chapter illustrate providing access to a custom local group (SMS Admins).

To verify WMI permissions, perform the following steps:

1. On the site server (and any SMS provider computer), start the Component Services console by selecting **Start -> Administrative Tools -> Computer Management**.

2. Expand the Services and Applications node and right-click **WMI Control**.

3. Select **Properties** in the menu to launch the WMI Control Properties dialog.

4. Switch to the Security tab and expand the Root node. Select **SMS** and click **Security**.

5. Verify that the following permissions are listed:

   ▶ Enable Account

   ▶ Remote Enable

6. Expand the SMS node and select the site_<*site code*> node below it.

7. Click **Security**.

8. Select **Properties** in the menu and verify that the following permissions are listed:

   ▶ Enable Account

   ▶ Execute Methods

   ▶ Provider Write

   ▶ Remote Enable

9. Close all dialog boxes as necessary.

Refer to Figures 8.20 and 8.21, earlier in this chapter, for an illustration of the permissions applied properly.

Connectivity Issues

Console connection status messages are often vague, providing very little help for determining issues. Even the SMSAdminUI.log might not provide much value. Situations like these may leave you wondering in which layer the permissions issue is occurring.

It is helpful to filter out whether a problem is occurring both locally and remotely. Knowing this information helps isolate where to look for problems. To test this scenario, launch the console from the administrative user's desktop and record the results. When you are done with that, launch the console under the administrative user's context on the ConfigMgr server. Table 8.2 lists the components to examine.

TABLE 8.2   Testing Console Behavior

If Local Console Fails	And Remote Console Fails	Check These Components
×	×	WMI, ConfigMgr
	×	WMI, DCOM

Common Problems

Table 8.3 describes issues you might experience while using the ConfigMgr console.

TABLE 8.3   Console Problems and Resolutions

Error	Description
Error: Configuration Manager cannot connect to the site.	If the SMSAdminUI.log contains "Insufficient privilege to connect, error: Access is denied." and an administrative user does not have local administrator privileges to the ConfigMgr site server, he or she is most likely missing DCOM privileges. Ensure that the user is a member of the Distributed COM Users local group.
	If the SMSAdminUI.log contains "Transport error; failed to connect, message: 'The SMS Provider reported an error'"
	▶ Ensure that the user is a member of the SMS Admins local group.
	▶ If the user is a member of the SMS Admins local group, ensure that an administrative user context has been created for that user with at least one role assigned.
Expected objects are not displayed in the console.	Ensure that the administrative user has the correct security scopes and collections assigned.
Expected workspaces, nodes, or actions are not displayed in the console.	Ensure that the administrative user is assigned the correct security role that grants access to the correct objects.

Summary

This chapter introduced the System Center Configuration Manager console and covered the console's panes and other features. It stepped through a console installation and discussed automating the console installation. This chapter described how to use the secondary console, Configuration Manager Service Manager, and actions to control the various ConfigMgr components.

The chapter ended with a troubleshooting section to help diagnose common console problems. Chapter 9 discusses managing clients.

Client Management

With a working System Center Configuration Manager (ConfigMgr) environment, you can begin managing remote devices in a process referred to as *client management*. A *client* is the end device managed by ConfigMgr; this can be any system with agent software installed and configured or managed through its built-in management capabilities (based on the Open Mobile Alliance Device Management [OMA DM] standard). Clients can be mobile devices, workstations, server operating systems, or cash registers using Windows Embedded systems. While they are not required to be ConfigMgr clients, site servers typically have the client agent software installed. By using mobile device management (MDM) to manage clients, ConfigMgr leverages its hybrid Intune or on-premise MDM functionality. This chapter discusses clients that have the client agent software installed.

This chapter describes ConfigMgr client requirements and installation, discovery, updating and configuration, client settings, inventory, client management, client health, and Wake on LAN (WOL). Configuring clients managed through ConfigMgr's MDM capabilities is covered in Chapter 16, "Integrating Intune Hybrid into Your Configuration Manager Environment," and Chapter 17, "Managing Mobile Devices."

Configuration Manager has the ability to execute tasks on clients, which requires agent software, running the agent as a background service. Once installed and configured, the ConfigMgr client, which communicates with the ConfigMgr back-end infrastructure, can execute commands for tasks such as running hardware inventory or installing software.

When ConfigMgr is implemented in environments that have devices already in place, its discovery functionality can find potential clients in the network.

ConfigMgr Client Agent Requirements

Before installing or pushing the ConfigMgr client agent, establish whether the client devices are supported in terms of hardware and installed operating systems. Microsoft provides guidelines for supported hardware and supports ConfigMgr clients on a specific list of defined platforms running Microsoft Windows, Apple Mac OS X, Linux, and UNIX.

The authors recommend inventorying your systems to help plan client agent deployment. A free tool to assist with this task is the Microsoft Assessment and Planning (MAP) Toolkit. This solution accelerator provides extensive hardware and software information, utilizing an inventory, assessment, and reporting tool designed for technology migration projects such as Windows 10 migrations or migrations toward Microsoft Azure. The MAP Toolkit is available at http://www.microsoft.com/download/details.aspx?id=7826.

For frequently asked questions on MAP, see http://social.technet.microsoft.com/wiki/contents/articles/1643.aspx.

Agent Hardware Dependencies

Microsoft publishes hardware requirements for the ConfigMgr client agent; these requirements can change with each new ConfigMgr build. Microsoft publishes both minimal and recommended requirements; however, running on a minimal hardware configuration does not provide optimal performance. To check the recommended hardware specifications for Current Branch, see https://docs.microsoft.com/sccm/core/plan-design/configs/recommended-hardware.

Supported Operating Systems for the Client Agent

ConfigMgr currently supports installing client agent software on the following:

▶ Windows 7 and higher versions

▶ Windows Server 2008 and higher versions

▶ Windows Embedded and Windows CE

▶ Mac OS X 10.9 and higher

▶ AIX, CentOS, Debian, HP-UX, Oracle Linux, Red Hat Enterprise Linux (RHEL), Solaris, SUSE Linux Enterprise Server (SLES), and Ubuntu UNIX and Linux distributions

Supported OS versions may change with each new build; check https://docs.microsoft.com/sccm/core/plan-design/configs/supported-operating-systems-for-site-system-servers#bkmk_ClientOS for current information.

Agent Software Dependencies

Before installing the ConfigMgr client agent on Windows devices, verify that the device meets the following prerequisites:

▶ The Microsoft Task Scheduler service is enabled.

▶ Microsoft Background Intelligent Transfer Service (BITS) version 2.5 or higher is installed.

▶ The Windows Installer version is at least 3.1.4000.2435.

The ConfigMgr client agent installation process automatically installs necessary prerequisites, although you may want to preinstall if a reboot is required. Find the prerequisite software at https://docs.microsoft.com/sccm/core/clients/deploy/prerequisites-for-deploying-clients-to-windows-computers.

You can install the ConfigMgr mobile device legacy client on supported mobile devices such as Windows Mobile and Windows CE. Available features depend on the platform and client type (discussed in Chapter 17).

Other Agent Dependencies

Besides hardware, supported operating systems, and software dependencies, there are other dependencies to address before your ConfigMgr environment can be installed or used. See Chapter 5, "Network Design," for information. The authors recommend regularly checking supported configurations for ConfigMgr at https://docs.microsoft.com/sccm/core/plan-design/configs/supported-configurations.

Installing, Upgrading, and Uninstalling ConfigMgr Client Agents

There are several approaches for installing the ConfigMgr client agent; select one that fits your particular rollout scenario. For example, you could use your legacy non-Microsoft software distribution environment to roll out the ConfigMgr agent, and then you can use the agent to remove legacy agent software.

The next sections discuss the different ways to install the ConfigMgr client agent. Chapter 17 discusses installing the mobile client and enrolling your mobile device for MDM.

Manually Installing on Windows Computers

Manually installing the ConfigMgr client agent on Windows systems requires only the ConfigMgr client installation binaries, which are located on any site server and management point (MP) in the client subfolder of the SMS-<*site code*> share or provided using CD, DVD, or USB media. The CCMSetup.exe program copies all necessary installation prerequisites to the client computer, installs software prerequisites, and starts the Client.msi Windows Installer package to install the client. You cannot run Client.msi directly; run CCMSetup with administrative permissions for a manual installation.

CCMSetup.exe and Client.msi support command-line options and properties to change installation behavior. Specify CCMSetup.exe command-line properties and then Client.msi MSI properties, using the format `CCMSetup.exe </CCMSetup properties>` `<Client.msi properties>`. CCMSetup properties always start with /.

See https://docs.microsoft.com/sccm/core/clients/deploy/about-client-installation-properties for a complete overview of installation properties, options, and usage examples.

Following is sample syntax to install a ConfigMgr client agent manually in a site that has its properties published to Active Directory (AD):

```
CCMSetup.exe /MP:APOLLO SMSSITECODE=AUTO FSP=APOLLO
```

This example installs the ConfigMgr client agent using the MP installed on the Apollo system. The PR1 site code is determined by querying AD. The fallback status point (FSP), also installed on the Apollo system, is used to send state messages until the client successfully joins the PR1 site. /MP:APOLLO is a CCMSetup property, and SMSSITECODE and FSP are Client.msi properties.

Manually Installing on Mac Computers

Managing and installing the client on Mac systems requires certificates for mutual authentication and encrypted data transfers, necessitating a public key infrastructure (PKI) environment. The ConfigMgr enrollment and enrollment proxy site system roles support PKI and requesting and installing computer certificates.

Chapter 6, "Installing and Updating System Center Configuration Manager," discusses installing and configuring ConfigMgr to support agent installation and configuration. The "Understanding Client Settings" section of this chapter describes how to configure the default client settings for enrollment and how to configure the enrollment profile.

You can manually install a certificate if the certificate meets ConfigMgr requirements. Mac clients always check for certificate revocation, requiring certificate revocation list (CRL) functionality.

Creating and issuing a Mac client certificate template on a certificate authority (CA) is described at https://docs.microsoft.com/sccm/core/plan-design/network/example-deployment-of-pki-certificates. You must also configure default client settings related to enrollment, including the following:

▶ Setting Allow users to enroll mobile devices and Mac computers to **Yes**

▶ Configuring an enrollment profile

Before installing the agent, download the program installation files and make them available on the Mac system. Obtain these files by installing the ConfigMgrMacClients.msi file on a Windows system. Download the .msi from https://www.microsoft.com/download/details.aspx?id=47719.

Run the ConfigMgrMacClient.msi file on a Windows system and then extract the Macclient.dmg file to the folder %*ProgramFiles*%\Microsoft\System Center Configuration Manager for Mac Client. A DMG file is a Mac OS X Disk Image File, comparable to an ISO file, which contains program installation files for Apple applications. Run Macclient.dmg locally to extract its contents and then perform the following steps to install the agent on Mac OS X:

1. Navigate to the folder where the installation files were extracted.

2. Enter the following command:

```
sudo ./ccmsetup
```

Wait for the Completed Installation message to appear. Ignore the message asking to restart and continue with the next step to install the certificate.

3. Run the following command line from the tools subfolder to install the certificate:

```
sudo ./CMEnroll -s <name of the enrollment proxy server>
-ignorecertchainvalidation -u <user name>
```

sudo allows you to run installation programs using security privileges of another user (superuser by default).

For the name of the enrollment proxy server, use the computer name in the fully qualified domain name (FQDN) format: *<domain>\<username>* or *<username>@<domain name>* notation. For this example, use the following command line:

```
sudo ./CMEnroll -s Athena.Odyssey.com -ignorecertchainvalidation
-u odyssey\ksurksum
```

The message Successfully enrolled indicates a successful installation.

4. Use the Mac Computer Enrollment Wizard to enroll the client. This opens when you finish installing the client or click **Enroll** in the Configuration Manager preference page. The wizard asks for the username, password, and server name of the enrollment proxy point server, as provided at the command line when running CMEnroll.

Restart the Mac system to complete the installation.

NOTE: LIMITING THE ENROLLED CERTIFICATE FOR USE BY CONFIGMGR

You can modify the keychain access, as described at https://docs.microsoft.com/sccm/core/clients/deploy/deploy-clients-to-macs. This article also describes renewing the client certificate using the Renew Certificate Wizard and renewing it manually, as well as how to use a certificate request and installation method independent of ConfigMgr.

Verify a successful installation by finding the client in the All Systems collection or by opening the Configuration Manager item in the System Preferences on the Mac. If there are any issues, use CMDiagnostics to determine the cause. This program creates a .zip file saved to the computer's desktop.

Manually Installing on UNIX and Linux Computers

Download client installation files for UNIX/Linux systems from https://www.microsoft.com/download/details.aspx?id=47719.

Install the ConfigMgr client agent on UNIX/Linux computers by using the install script, which is included in the client installation files. The agent uses root credentials to collect hardware inventory and deploy software. After downloading the client installation files and extracting them on a Windows system, copy the install script and .tar file to the UNIX/Linux system. Before running the install script, modify its rights with the following command:

```
chmod +x install
```

Start the install script by using the following syntax:

```
./install -mp <MP name> -sitecode <site code> <command line properties>
<client installation package filename>
```

The following is an example:

```
./install -mp athena.odyssey.com -sitecode PR1 ccm-Universalx64.tar
```

Specify command-line properties for the install script after the -sitecode option. These properties are described at https://docs.microsoft.com/sccm/core/clients/deploy/deploy-clients-to-unix-and-linux-servers.

Review the scxcm.log file at /var/opt/microsoft to determine whether the client installed successfully. The client should also become visible under **Assets and Compliance -> Devices** in the console.

Using Logon Scripts to Install on Windows Devices

Login scripts install the ConfigMgr client agent when a user logs on. If you specify the /logon switch for the CCMSetup.exe installer, the client is installed only if it is not already installed. Use the /source property to specify an installation source or use the /MP parameter to specify a management point. If /MP is not provided, CCMSetup searches AD, DNS, or WINS to find published MP information.

Following is sample syntax to install the client agent from a logon script:

```
CCMSetup.exe /logon /MP:APOLLO SMSSITECODE=PR1
```

Installing Using Group Policy for Windows Devices

You can install the ConfigMgr client by using the publish or assign functionality provided by AD:

▶ When you assign the ConfigMgr client, the software is installed the first time the computer starts.

▶ When you publish the client, it appears in the Control Panel Programs and Features applet, from where it can be installed.

As group policy software installation supports only .msi files, you can only specify the CCMSetup.msi file, found in the *<ConfigMgrInstallPath>*\bin\i386 folder on the site server, without providing additional parameters. Following is how to provide those parameters:

▶ When the AD schema is extended for ConfigMgr and ConfigMgr publishes site information to AD, the client can query AD for installation properties; these are pushed to AD based on the settings specified in the Client Push Installation Properties.

▶ If the schema is not extended, use group policy to populate the ConfigMgr client properties in the Registry by using a group policy object (GPO). These properties are used during ConfigMgr client installation. Use the ConfigMgrInstallation.adm template located in *<ConfigMgrInstallPath>*\Tools to make the necessary properties available in the GPO management console.

CAUTION: BE CAREFUL WHEN USING ADM TEMPLATES

ADM templates are the old format of templates used to distribute group policy settings; the new format is ADMX. ADM files tattoo their settings in the Registry, which means to remove those settings, you would have to explicitly delete them from the client's Registry.

Installing Using Software Update Point (SUP) for Windows Devices

You can leverage a Windows Server Update Services (WSUS) infrastructure to install the ConfigMgr client agent on target computers and publish the client software as an additional software update. Point clients without an installed ConfigMgr client to the SUP, which runs WSUS using a GPO. Publish the ConfigMgr client to the SUP by configuring the software update-based client installation properties. Follow these steps:

1. In the ConfigMgr console, navigate to **Administration -> Overview -> Site Configuration -> Sites**.

2. In the navigation tree, select *<site code> - <site name>* in the Details pane, select **Client Installation Settings** from the ribbon bar and select **Software Update-Based Client Installation** to enable ConfigMgr to publish the ConfigMgr client to the SUP.

This method precludes directly providing any installation properties. Have ConfigMgr push the settings to AD or use a GPO to populate the properties in the Registry, as in a ConfigMgr client deployment using group policy.

Use the SUP to update ConfigMgr clients after they are installed; this occurs using the software updates functionality in ConfigMgr. For additional information, see Chapter 15, "Managing Software Updates."

Installing and Assigning Windows 10 Clients Using Azure AD for Authentication

If your clients are running Windows 10 and are Azure AD joined, and if users log in to the device using their Azure AD identity, you can install the ConfigMgr agent software on the Internet by making use of the cloud management gateway (CMG).

Before you can install the ConfigMgr agent on an Azure AD-joined Windows 10 device, you must do the following:

▶ Set up Configuration Manager cloud services

▶ Set up the CMG

Chapter 6 discusses installing Configuration Manager cloud services and the CMG.

Once cloud services and the CMG are set up, you must configure the cloud services client settings to allow the use of a cloud distribution point (DP) to automatically register new Windows 10 domain-joined devices with Azure AD and to enable the use of a CMG in case you want to enroll clients when Windows 10 clients are residing on the Internet.

To enroll clients while within the network boundaries of ConfigMgr, at least one MP must be configured with HTTPS.

To install the ConfigMgr client agent on a Windows 10 device meeting this scenario, use the following command-line options for CCMSetup.exe or CCMSetup.msi with the `CCMSETUPCMD` parameter:

▶ `/MP`: The download source, which can be set to the CMG if bootstrapping from the Internet.

▶ `CCMHOSTNAME`: The name of your Internet MP. You can find this by running `gwmi -namespace root\ccm\locationservices -class SMS_ActiveMPCandidate` from a command prompt on a managed client.

▶ `SMSSiteCode`: The site code of your Configuration Manager site.

▶ `SMSMP`: The name of your lookup MP; this can be on your intranet.

▶ `AADTENANTID, AADTENANTNAME`: The ID and name of the Azure AD tenant you linked to ConfigMgr. You can find this by running `dsregcmd.exe /status` from a command prompt on an Azure AD-joined device.

▶ `AADCLIENTAPPID`: The Azure AD client app ID.

▶ `AADResourceUri`: The URI of the onboarded Azure AD server app.

TIP: FINDING THE CLIENT APP ID AND IDENTIFIER URI

The app ID can be found in the App registrations section of Azure AD. More information on how to find the ID is available at https://docs.microsoft.com/azure/azure-resource-manager/resource-group-create-service-principal-portal#get-application-id-and-authentication-key. The URI of the onboarded Azure AD server app can be found on the properties page of the Cloud Management Azure Service.

Following is an example of how a CCMSetup command line could look:

```
ccmsetup.exe /mp: https://UNLEASHED.CLOUDAPP.NET/
CCM_Proxy_MutualAuth/72057594037928100
CCMHOSTNAME=UNLEASHED.CLOUDAPP.NET/CCM_
Proxy_MutualAuth/72057594037928100 SMSSiteCode=PR1
SMSMP=https://Athena.Odyssey.com
AADTENANTID=72F988BF-86F1-41AF-91AB-2D7CD011DB47 AADTENANTNAME=unleashed
AADCLIENTAPPID=bef323b3-042f-41a6-907a-f9faf0d17026
AADRESOURCEURI=https://unleashedserver
```

When deploying the agent using Intune, the command line should be built as follows:

```
ccmsetup.msi CCMSETUPCMD="/mp:<URL of cloud management gateway mutual auth
endpoint>
CCMHOSTNAME=<URL of cloud management gateway mutual auth endpoint>
SMSSiteCode=<site code> SMSMP=https://<FQDN of MP> AADTENANTID=<AAD tenant ID>
AADTENANTNAME=<Tenant name> AADCLIENTAPPID=<Server AppID for AAD Integration>
AADRESOURCEURI=https://<Resource ID>"
```

Approving Clients

ConfigMgr automatically approves a computer belonging to a trusted domain by default. You can change the default and instead specify configuring each computer manually or automatically approving all computers. This last option is not recommended, as it means that every computer with a ConfigMgr client can assign itself to a ConfigMgr site.

To configure the client approval settings, perform the following steps:

1. In the ConfigMgr console, navigate to **Administration -> Overview -> Site Configuration -> Sites**.

2. Click **Hierarchy Settings** from the ribbon bar to open the Hierarchy Settings Properties page.

3. On the Client Approval and Conflicting Records tab of this page, displayed in Figure 9.1, specify the approval method for the site.

Following is what you need to know about client approval:

▶ Clients communicating using HTTP and self-signed certificates must be approved before they can participate in the ConfigMgr hierarchy.

▶ AD clients from local and trusted forests are approved automatically.

▶ Client approval is not necessary when configuring clients to always use HTTPS to communicate with your site or if the clients use a PKI certificate to communicate to site systems, as they are already trusted by means of the installed certificate.

To approve a client, navigate to Assets and Compliance and select the client from the Devices node or from a device collection. Then click **Approve** on the ribbon bar.

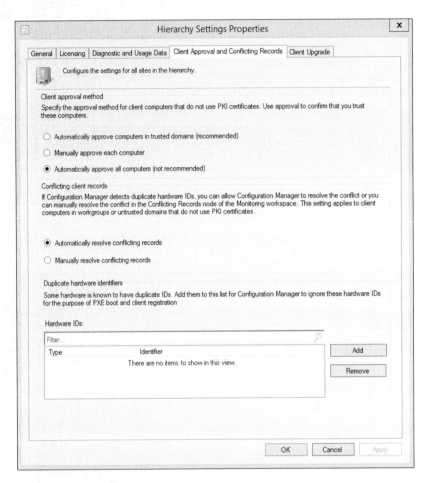

FIGURE 9.1   Configuring client approval settings.

Pushing the Client

You can push the client to computer objects known to ConfigMgr. Begin by enabling Active Directory System Discovery or Network Discovery to find potential clients, as described in the section "Finding Potential ConfigMgr Clients in Your Network," later in this chapter. ConfigMgr can then send the necessary installation files to the target machine and begin remotely executing client installation. The only requirement is to configure the client push installation agent account.

> **TIP: INSTALLATION PROPERTIES THAT ARE PUBLISHED TO AD**
>
> For information about installation properties published to AD, see https://docs.microsoft.com/sccm/core/clients/deploy/about-client-installation-properties-published-to-active-directory-domain-services.

Enabling Client Push for Windows Devices

Once a client appears under Assets and Compliance -> Devices, you can specify how to push the ConfigMgr client to those devices by enabling client push on a site-wide basis or triggering the client for specific collections or individual systems using manual push. Following are several prerequisites to meet before you can successfully push a client to a remote computer:

▶ One of the specified client push installation accounts must be a member of the local administrators group.

▶ The remote computer must have the ADMIN$ share enabled.

▶ The computer must be found by the site server and vice versa, using Domain Name System (DNS) name resolution.

▶ The computer must be discovered.

▶ The computer must be reachable by the site server.

▶ The computer must be able to contact an MP to download supporting files.

With client push, the ConfigMgr site server connects to the client computer and verifies its OS information, based on the information stored in the entry for the client in the ClientPushMachine_G table in the site database, which contains the computer name and other information. The site server then connects to the ADMIN$ share on the client and its Registry via Windows Management Instrumentation (WMI) to gather information about the client. It copies CCMSetup.exe and MobileClient.tcf from *<ConfigMgrInstallPath>*\bin\ i386 to *%windir%*/ccmsetup on the client. CCMSetup.exe uses this file to locate the installation files on the site server and initiates a local installation of the client. Listing 9.1 shows a sample file, with all options configured for the client to install to the Odyssey PR1 site.

LISTING 9.1   Sample MobileClient.tcf File

```
[WINNT CLIENT FILES]
    bin\%cli_cpu%\MobileClient.tcf=MobileClient.tcf
    bin\%cli_cpu%\ccmsetup.exe=ccmsetup.exe

[SERVER PATHS]
    Server1=\\ATHENA.ODYSSEY.COM\SMSClient
    MP1=Athena.Odyssey.com
    ServerRemoteName1=\\Athena.Odyssey.com\SMSClient

[Site]
    Last TCF Update=09/26/2016 00:20:09
    SMSMPLIST=Athena.Odyssey.com
    IISSSLState=224
    IISPreferedPort=80
    IISSSLPreferedPort=443
```

```
   IISPortsList=80
   IISSSLPortsList=443

SMSPublicRootKey=0602000000A4000052534131000800000 1000100C1D526FA058D04BED2FCE230B6CB435
8C14E2CEB3342AC1C9D8349074D18B9C3B10271A6263347FD8B845328B5726A79A9017F088F3722D903AB29A
8B35419A3EB0620493B0D99B555D7180E52403FC4FF5E013A1CD3D0E4282C140C258F0157049F9408F2D6127
98AFCF52A4CAD4694109E5EA2EBFF4771874D58BD34DCAF320AB9AFCAA5DF868E1899EC249E6A38F81F2F2FD
4972FA48701D34D1EE0126B03BB4A1AC59B23A712626CA8D4D791DA952C170916B482519A2724841107698FB
2AED05E7AF394C2AAC6A6AC294D761AD3824F7211986BBE4E20C9CF449B68F5CFD3E0E255C3C0B3C2B22F965
B29EB86575619DE2026E7FCB7AFB90584818FF8AC
   SelectFirstCertificate=1


[Client Install]
   Install=INSTALL=ALL SMSSITECODE=PR1


[IDENT]
   TYPE=Target Configuration File
```

When ConfigMgr determines that the CCMSetup.exe service started successfully and the agent is running, the `ClientPushMachine_G` table entry is updated for verification. The entry is deleted after a second verification. If something goes wrong, ConfigMgr retries the installation every 60 minutes for 7 days and then discards the installation.

Enabling Automatic Site-Wide Client Push for Windows Devices
You can enable automatic side-wide client push for client records newly added to the database. A client with an existing database record is not pushed. Enable automatic site-wide client push by configuring the Client Push Installation properties. Follow these steps:

1. In the ConfigMgr console, navigate to **Administration -> Overview -> Site Configuration -> Sites**.

2. In the navigation tree, select *<site code>* - *<site name>* in the Details pane, click **Client Installation Settings** from the ribbon bar, and then select **Client Push Installation Properties**.

3. Select **Enable automatic site-wide client push installation** on the General tab, as displayed in Figure 9.2.

4. Specify parameters for client push, selecting server, workstations, and ConfigMgr site system servers. Stipulate whether to install the client software on domain controllers (DCs) or prevent that unless specified in the wizard.

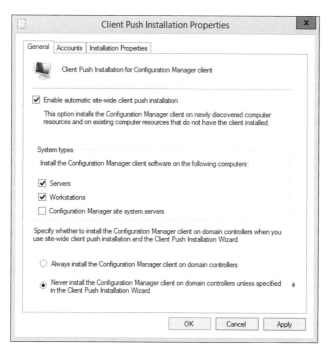

FIGURE 9.2   Configuring client push installation properties.

Following is information on the other tabs of the Client Push Installation Properties dialog:

▶ **Accounts:** Specify one or more accounts for ConfigMgr to use to initiate installation; these should be local administrators. ConfigMgr tries each account until it finds a local administrator.

Select an account specified previously in ConfigMgr or provide a new account to use by keying it in or clicking **Browse**. Click **Verify** to confirm that the account and password are correct.

Provide the location of a network share; click **Test connection** to verify that the account is valid by using it to connect to the network share.

▶ **Installation Properties:** Specify the installation properties used by the Client.msi Windows Installer file when installing the ConfigMgr client software. By default, `SMSSITECODE=<site code>` is already available.

To prevent individual systems from receiving the client with site-wide client push enabled, add the computer names of these systems to a Registry key on the primary site server. You may want to do so for temporary systems you do not want to manage or systems where you may not install any additional client software for legal reasons. See https://technet.microsoft.com/library/bb693996.aspx for additional information.

Manually Pushing the Agent

To manually push the ConfigMgr client to a collection or to an individual system, specify a client push installation account or verify that the computer account is a local administrator on those systems. Then perform the following steps:

1. In the ConfigMgr console, navigate to **Assets and Compliance -> Devices** and select a device in the Details pane. Alternatively, navigate to **Device Collections** and select one of the collections.

2. Click **Install Client** from the ribbon bar or from the right-click context menu to start the Install Configuration Manager Client Wizard, which provides three installation options you can select individually before continuing the installation:

   ▶ Whether to install the client software when the computer is a DC.

   ▶ Whether to always install the client software, even if it is already installed.

   ▶ Whether a site server other than the site server in the assigned site for the resource can perform the installation. When this is enabled, you can choose a site server from a dropdown list.

3. Click **Next** on the Installation Options page.

4. Review the Summary page and click **Next** to install the ConfigMgr client on the target system.

5. On the Completion page that displays when installation completes, click **Close** to close the wizard.

An empty .ccr file matching the MachineID value in the database entry is created in the *<ConfigMgrInstallPath>*\inboxes\ccr.box\inproc folder and triggers the client installation. If the installation fails, the .ccr record is moved to the *<ConfigMgrInstallPath>*\inboxes\ ccrretry.box folder, where ConfigMgr retries the installation every 60 minutes for 7 days.

Blocking and Unblocking Clients

When you no longer want a client to participate in the ConfigMgr infrastructure—for example, when the computer is stolen or missing—you can block the client. Select the client from the Devices node or in a device collection and then click **Block** on the ribbon bar. Click **Unblock** to allow the client to participate in the ConfigMgr hierarchy again.

Automatically Upgrading the Client on Windows

The automatic client upgrade feature upgrades an older version of the ConfigMgr client agent assigned to a ConfigMgr site. Until it is upgraded, features such as client settings, applications, and software updates are unavailable or unreliable. The upgrade automatically creates a client upgrade package and program that is distributed to all available DPs in the hierarchy. It respects maintenance windows, does not upgrade agents running on non-persistent virtual desktop infrastructure (VDI) images, and runs only when the site to which the ConfigMgr client agent is assigned is at the same version as the top-level site in the hierarchy. Perform the following steps to configure this feature:

1. In the ConfigMgr console, navigate to **Administration -> Overview -> Site Configuration -> Sites**.

2. On the ribbon bar, select **Hierarchy Settings** to open the Hierarchy Settings Properties dialog.

3. On the Client Upgrade tab, shown in Figure 9.3, specify whether you want to enable automatic upgrading of clients when new updates are available.

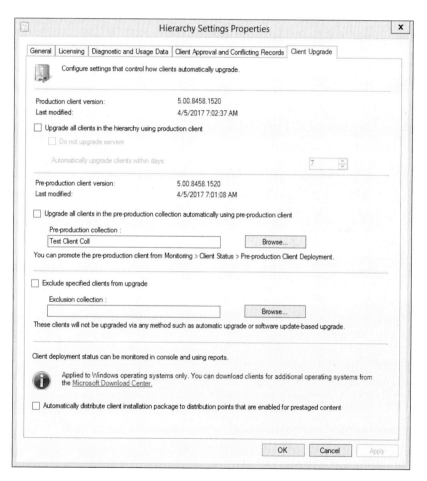

FIGURE 9.3   Configuring client upgrade hierarchy settings.

You can automatically upgrade the client on Windows operating systems by using a two-phased approach:

▶ Upgrade clients in a pre-production collection (enabled by default). ConfigMgr client agents belonging to the Test Client Coll collection automatically update to the latest version of the ConfigMgr client agent. To promote the pre-production client to production status, browse to **Monitoring -> Client Status**, right-click **Pre-Production Client Deployment**, and select **Promote Pre-production** client.

▶ After verifying functionality for the client agent deployed to the pre-production collection, enable automatic client upgrading for all other client agents by promoting that client and enabling the check box **Upgrade all clients in the hierarchy using the production client**. Exclude servers by selecting the **Do not upgrade servers** option.

▶ If necessary, specify an exclude collection. All clients belonging to that collection will be excluded from automatic client upgrade and therefore must be updated manually.

Configure when to begin upgrading; the default is 7 days by default, and 31 days is the maximum. You can specify whether to automatically distribute the ConfigMgr client installation package with its updates to DPs that are enabled for prestaged content.

When updating ConfigMgr using the Updates and Servicing functionality discussed in Chapter 6, the ConfigMgr administrator can also update the ConfigMgr client software; choose to upgrade without validating, causing the client package to be overwritten with the new version used by every new client installation or client upgrade; or validate the new ConfigMgr client package first in a pre-production collection. The pre-production package can then be promoted to production.

Monitoring the Automatic Client Upgrade Feature

Use the Monitoring workspace to monitor the status of the Automatic Client Upgrade feature. Perform the following steps to monitor this feature:

1. In the ConfigMgr console, navigate to **Monitoring -> Overview -> Client Status**.

2. Select **Pre-Production Client Deployment** to review the client deployment status to the defined pre-production collection.

3. Select **Production Client Deployment** to review the client deployment status as configured in the Hierarchy settings. Click **Browse** and select a production collection to see the status.

Selecting a slice in the pie chart of the client deployment status page creates a temporary device collection containing the clients that are compliant, in progress, not started, failed, or of unknown status.

Troubleshooting Client Agent Installation on Windows Devices

Client installation can be problematic for many reasons; much depends on how you are installing the client, whether it is reachable, and whether all software prerequisites are installable.

When using client push, ensure that all prerequisites are met, ensure that the site server can connect to the client machines, and ensure that one of the configured Client Push Installation accounts can reach the machine on its ADMIN$ share. Test by performing a `net use` to a client using the Client Push Installation account credentials. Following are some issues that can prevent the ConfigMgr infrastructure from connecting to the client:

▶ The firewall is incorrectly configured.

▶ The ADMIN$ share is unavailable.

▶ The installation account does not have the required administrative rights.

▶ The Client Push Installation account is locked out or has an expired password.

▶ A pending reboot initiated by another software installation is preventing installation of the client software.

▶ There is a nonworking or corrupted DCOM or WMI configuration.

TIP: TROUBLESHOOTING CLIENT INSTALLATION AND WMI

Following are several blogs to assist with troubleshooting:

▶ See the in-depth article at http://blogs.technet.com/b/sudheesn/archive/2010/05/31/troubleshooting-sccm-part-i-client-push-installation.aspx. Although it was written for ConfigMgr 2007, the concepts are still valid.

▶ The System Center Configuration Manager team blog article on WMI troubleshooting provides tips for solving WMI issues. See https://cloudblogs.microsoft.com/enterprisemobility/2009/05/08/wmi-troubleshooting-tips/.

If the site server can connect to the client, ConfigMgr copies necessary files to *%windir%* ccmsetup, and the installation begins from there. CCMSetup.log provides installation progress, showing information about each step and what went wrong if the client does not install successfully.

Problems could be caused by incorrectly configured site boundaries and boundary groups, or the CCMSetup bootstrapper may be unable to find the necessary files to install the software prerequisites from an MP. ConfigMgr provides reports to assist with failing client installations. Follow these steps to access the reports:

1. In the ConfigMgr console, navigate to **Monitoring -> Overview -> Reporting -> Reports -> Client Push**. You now see several reports available regarding client push installation:

   ▶ Client Push Installation Status Details

   ▶ Client Push Installation Status Details For a Specified Site

   ▶ Client Push Installation Status Summary

   ▶ Client Push Installation Status Summary For a Specified Site

   The reports provide guidance on where client push installation is failing and where to investigate the issue. For example, if a prerequisite software installation is failing, you could start by examining what occurs when manually installing that software on a failing machine. Use verbose logging to check the log file to determine the root cause.

2. Select a report and click **Run** from the ribbon bar to open a page where you can provide criteria before running the report.

For additional information regarding ConfigMgr reporting, see Chapter 21, "Configuration Manager Reporting."

Problems may also occur with client push installation or client assignment after installing the client, leaving the client in an unmanaged state.

> **TIP: MORE TROUBLESHOOTING INFORMATION**
>
> Although written for ConfigMgr 2007, KB925282 (http://support.microsoft.com/kb/925282) includes a good overview of the client push installation process and what can go wrong.

Uninstalling the ConfigMgr Client Agent

To remove the ConfigMgr client agent on Windows systems, open a command prompt as administrator and browse to the CCMSetup folder in the OS installation folder (%*systemdrive*%\windows).Type `CCMSetup.exe /uninstall` to remove the client agent.

On Mac OS X computers, use the CMUnistall program in the DMG file extracted to the Mac OS X client. Start a command line in the program location and type `sudo ./CMUninstall -c`.

On UNIX and Linux computers, use the `uninstall` utility installed during ConfigMgr client agent installation. Uninstall the ConfigMgr client agent by typing `/opt/microsoft/configmgr/bin/uninstall` at the command line.

Finding Potential ConfigMgr Clients in Your Network

Discovery is the process of locating potential clients prior to installing client software on these systems. You must discover systems before you can remotely install the client. The next sections discuss different methods for discovering clients.

System Center Configuration Manager currently offers six discovery types:

- ▶ Active Directory Forest Discovery
- ▶ Active Directory Group Discovery
- ▶ Active Directory User Discovery
- ▶ Active Directory System Discovery
- ▶ Heartbeat Discovery
- ▶ Network Discovery

CAUTION: NEED FOR A CLEAN ACTIVE DIRECTORY

If you use one of the AD discovery methods and your AD contains objects no longer used, such as obsolete groups, computers, and user accounts, these objects will also be imported into ConfigMgr. Although some discovery methods provide methods to prevent pollution, the authors recommend that you clean up AD on a regular basis.

Using Active Directory Forest Discovery

Active Directory Forest Discovery lets you discover Internet Protocol (IP) subnets and AD sites that you can automatically add as boundaries. You can also find remote forests to which you can publish ConfigMgr site information for clients in that forest to use. You must discover a remote forest before publishing information to it.

This discovery method is disabled by default, and it runs weekly by default when enabled. It can be configured for the central administration site (CAS) and primary sites. Follow these steps:

1. In the ConfigMgr console, navigate to **Administration -> Overview -> Hierarchy Configuration -> Discovery Methods**. Select **Active Directory Forest Discovery** and **choose Properties**.

2. On the General tab, shown in Figure 9.4, check the box **Enable Active Directory Forest Discovery**. Also specify whether to create site boundaries from AD and whether you want to create IP address range boundaries for IP subnets.

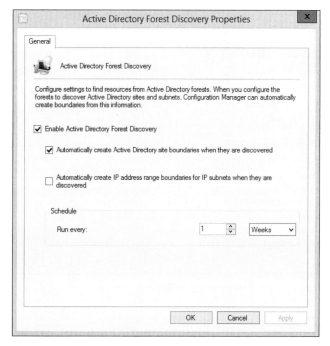

FIGURE 9.4   Enabling Active Directory Forest Discovery.

You can modify the default discovery schedule from 1 week to between 1 hour and 4 weeks. A weekly schedule is usually sufficient. For some scenarios—for example, in the midst of a huge migration that affects AD—you may want to use a different value.

Follow these steps to configure publishing to an AD forest:

1. Navigate to **Administration -> Overview -> Hierarchy Configuration -> Active Directory Forests**. Select a forest and choose **Properties**.

2. On the General tab, select whether to discover sites and subnets in that forest. You can also specify the discovery account (which is, by default, the computer account of the site server).

3. On the Publishing tab, select the sites to publish to the remote forest. By default, information is published to the root of that forest; to override the default, specify a particular domain or server.

To configure a new forest in the Active Directory forests configuration, perform the following steps:

1. Navigate to **Administration -> Overview -> Hierarchy Configuration -> Active Directory Forests**. Click **Add Forest** in the upper-left corner of the ribbon bar.

2. Provide the domain suffix of the forest you want to add. You can also make all the changes described in the previous procedure in this section for configuring an already added forest.

3. Click **OK** to save the newly added forest configuration.

Using Active Directory Group Discovery

Active Directory Group Discovery lets you discover AD groups and their memberships. It inventories groups, group membership, group membership relationships, and basic information about the objects in these discovered groups if those resources are not already discovered using other discovery methods.

You can specify a location in AD to search for groups in a specific container, or you can specify a specific group. These are security groups by default.

> **TIP: ABOUT DELTA DISCOVERY**
>
> *Delta discovery* discovers changes since the last inventory and uses fewer resources than full discovery. It is available for Active Directory Group, User, and System Discovery. Delta discovery searches AD every five minutes by default for attributes changed since the last full discovery. However, delta discovery cannot detect removal of resources from AD; this is detected only by a full discovery cycle.

Perform these steps to configure Active Directory Group Discovery:

1. Navigate to **Administration -> Overview -> Hierarchy Configuration -> Discovery Methods**.

2. Select **Active Directory Group Discovery** and choose **Properties**.

3. On the General page, shown in Figure 9.5, check the box **Enable Active Directory Group Discovery**, which is disabled by default.

4. To add a location or group, click **Add** and select one of the following:

   ▶ **Groups**: Select **Groups** to open the Add Groups dialog. Specify the group to add or click **Browse** to select one. The site server's computer account is used for searching; specify another account if necessary (such as to specify a group in another AD domain). You can also select a specific DC to search to lessen the burden on other DCs serving users and devices; the default domain and forest is used by default.

   ▶ **Location**: Select **Location** to open the Add Active Directory Location dialog. Specify a name to reflect the location you want to add and click **Browse** to search for an AD container. The search is recursive by default, meaning child objects of the selected container are included. The site server's computer account is used by default to search AD.

5. On the Polling Schedule tab, specify the full discovery polling schedule, which is set as every 7 days. Specify whether to use delta discovery, which is enabled by default with a 5-minute interval and can be set from 5 to 60 minutes.

6. Use the Options tab to exclude certain computers from discovery. These could be computers that have not logged on to a domain for a certain amount of time (90 days by default) or computers for which the computer account was not updated for a certain amount of time (also 90 days by default). You can also enable discovery of members of distribution groups. For this option to work for systems that have not logged on to a domain for a certain amount of time, your AD domain functional level must be Windows Server 2003 or later.

6

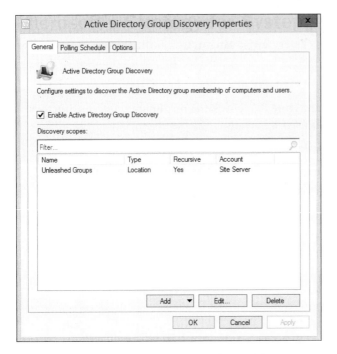

FIGURE 9.5   Enabling Active Directory Group Discovery.

Using Active Directory User Discovery

Active Directory User Discovery discovers user accounts and their AD attributes. Config-
Mgr discovers some attributes by default, such as username, unique username, domain,
and AD container; you can specify others. Synchronizing these attributes can help with
creating queries or collection queries that leverage these user attributes. Follow these steps
to configure Active Directory User Discovery:

1. In the ConfigMgr console, navigate to **Administration -> Overview -> Hierarchy
   Configuration -> Discovery Methods**.

2. Select **Active Directory User Discovery** and choose **Properties**.

3. On the General tab, shown in Figure 9.6, check the box **Enable Active Directory
   User Discovery**. Click the starburst icon and specify an AD container to search by
   providing the Lightweight Directory Access Protocol (LDAP) path manually or by
   clicking **Browse** and searching for a container. This search is recursive by default.
   Specify if you want to discover users that reside within groups. By default, the site
   server's computer account is used to search AD; specify another account as needed.

4. On the Polling Schedule tab, specify the full discovery polling schedule, which
   is set to every 7 days. Specify whether you want to use delta discovery, which is
   enabled by default.

5. On the Active Directory Attributes tab, add specific attributes belonging to the user object to include with the discovery. Select an attribute and click **Add**. For other attributes, select **Custom** and type the attribute name.

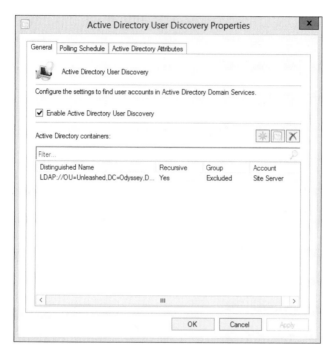

FIGURE 9.6   Enabling Active Directory User Discovery.

Using Active Directory System Discovery

Active Directory System Discovery polls the specified AD containers, such as domains and sites in a DC, to discover computers. This method can also recursively poll specified AD containers and connect to each discovered system to retrieve details about the computer. Follow these steps to enable Active Directory System Discovery:

1. In the ConfigMgr console, navigate to **Administration -> Overview -> Hierarchy Configuration -> Discovery Methods**.

2. In the navigation tree, select **Active Directory System Discovery** and choose **Properties** from the ribbon bar.

The following are the different tabs for Active Directory System Discovery:

▶ **General:** The General tab, shown in Figure 9.7, allows you to enable System Discovery for the site. Specify AD containers to include in the discovery by clicking the starburst icon or modify an already provided container by clicking the edit icon to its right. Delete a container by selecting it and clicking the red X.

Click the starburst icon to open the Active Directory Container page. Specify a container to search during discovery. Provide an LDAP query or click **Browse** and select a container from a hierarchy list. You can also specify a global catalog (GC) query to find an AD container within multiple domains. Next, specify the search options, which include recursively searching AD child containers and discovering AD group objects. Recursively searching child containers searches any child container within the specified path. Discovering objects within AD groups also discovers objects within groups in the search path.

Specify a service account to use for the discovery process. By default this is the site server's computer account, which should at least have read permissions for the specified location. Alternatively, specify a specific domain account with the same user rights.

Click **OK** after configuring the Active Directory container properties to return to the Active Directory System Discovery Properties dialog.

▶ **Polling Schedule:** Use this tab to modify how often ConfigMgr polls AD to find computer data. By default, full discovery polling occurs every 7 days starting Thursday 1/1/1998, and delta discovery runs every 5 minutes. These settings are modifiable.

▶ **Active Directory Attributes:** Specify the AD properties of discovered objects to discover. Attributes discovered by default include name, sAMAccountName, and primaryGroupID. Specify additional attributes, such as adminCount, department, and division, by selecting them from the available attributes list and clicking **Add**.

▶ **Options:** Use this tab to exclude computers from discovery—for example, to discover only computers that have logged on or updated their computer account password with the domain within a given period (90 days by default). This lets you keep the ConfigMgr environment clean even if Active Directory is not. These settings are disabled by default.

When enabling options to exclude computers from discovery, the default values are set to 90 days and are modifiable. These settings could depend on the value you configured for clients to update their computer password (30 days by default) and on the number of days within which a client must contact the key management server (KMS) if KMS is the activation mechanism.

Once you enable Active Directory System Discovery or discover clients using Active Directory Group Discovery, clients begin to appear in the Devices node of the Assets and Compliance workspace; these clients do not yet have the ConfigMgr client installed. It is easy to determine whether a client is not installed as the Client column in the Devices view is set to No.

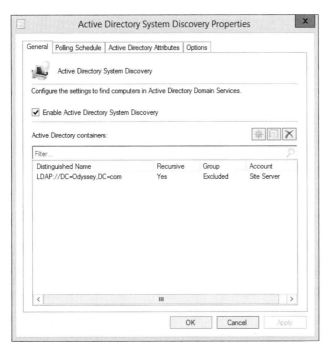

FIGURE 9.7   Enabling Active Directory System Discovery.

Using Heartbeat Discovery

Heartbeat Discovery is enabled by default when a ConfigMgr site is installed. This discovery method should always be enabled, as it is used to determine if clients are healthy and reachable. This discovery method runs on every ConfigMgr client and creates discovery data records (DDRs) that contain information about the client, including network location, NetBIOS name, and operational status. The DDR is copied to the MP, where it is processed by the client's primary site. Heartbeat Discovery lets ConfigMgr determine whether clients are reachable and healthy.

The ConfigMgr client sends a DDR for Heartbeat Discovery every 7 days by default. Using Heartbeat Discovery with the Delete Aged Discovery Data setting in the Site Maintenance task lets you configure when to delete an inactive client from the site database. (Site maintenance tasks are discussed in Chapter 24, "Backup, Recovery, and Maintenance.") The ConfigMgr client logs Heartbeat Discovery actions in the InventoryAgent.log file, found in the %*windir*%\CCM\Logs folder.

To configure Heartbeat Discovery, follow these steps:

   1. In the ConfigMgr console, navigate to **Administration -> Overview -> Hierarchy Configuration -> Discovery Methods**.

2. In the navigation tree, select **Heartbeat Discovery** for the site code for which you want to enable Heartbeat Discovery and then select **Properties**.

3. On the General tab, specify whether to disable Heartbeat Discovery and the schedule to use.

With site-wide client push installation, discussed in the "Pushing the Client" section, configure the heartbeat schedule to run less frequently than the client rediscovery period for the Clear Install Flag site maintenance task, discussed in Chapter 24. If the Clear Install Flag task is set to a lower value than the client rediscovery value, ConfigMgr reinstalls the client even if it is running as expected.

The MP of mobile devices managed by an agent generates a DDR for those devices. Disabling Heartbeat Discovery does not disable generating the DDR.

Using Network Discovery

Network Discovery allows you to discover resources you cannot find with any other discovery methods. It enables you to search domains, Simple Network Management Protocol (SNMP) services, and Dynamic Host Configuration Protocol (DHCP) servers to find resources. Network Discovery is unique because, in addition to finding computers, it finds network devices such as printers, routers, and bridges. It is disabled by default and can be configured per primary and secondary site. Follow these steps to enable it:

1. In the ConfigMgr console, navigate to **Administration -> Overview -> Hierarchy Configuration -> Discovery Methods**.

2. In the navigation tree, select **Network Discovery** under the site code for which you want to enable Network Discovery and then choose **Properties** from the ribbon bar. Following is information on each tab:

   ▶ **General:** You can select a check box to enable network discovery. You can specify one of the following discovery types:

      ▶ **Topology:** Topology (which is the default) finds the topology of your network by discovering IP subnets and routers using SNMP, although it does not discover potential clients. The number of subnets and routers discovered is dependent on the specified router hops on the SNMP tab.

      ▶ **Topology and client:** Selecting this option also allows you to discover potential client devices.

      ▶ **Topology, client, and client operating system:** Selecting this option causes operating systems and versions to be discovered.

   Specifying that you have a slow network speed causes ConfigMgr to make automatic adjustments such as doubling the SNMP time-out value and reducing the number of SNMP sessions.

▶ **Subnets:** You can specify the subnets to search. By default only the subnet of the server running discovery is searched; you can disable this by deselecting the check box Search local subnets. Click the starburst icon to specify a new subnet and provide its subnet address and subnet mask. Modify subnet settings or disable a subnet by clicking the edit icon (which is next to the starburst). You can also delete subnets or switch the order of appearance.

▶ **Domains:** Use this tab to specify domains to search. Only the local domain is searched by default; disable this by deselecting the Search local domain check box. Add additional domains by clicking the starburst icon to specify a domain name. Click the edit icon to modify the domain properties or (temporarily) disable this option by deselecting Enable domain search. You can also delete domains from being searched or switch the order in which they are searched.

▶ **SNMP:** This tab specifies SNMP community names and the maximum number of router hops for the discovery process. The public community name is included by default. To specify additional SNMP community names, click the starburst icon and specify a name. You can modify the search order for the SNMP communities and delete previously provided community names. Specify maximum hops to indicate the number of hops used to search for discovered objects. Hops lets you specify how many routers the process will pass through.

▶ **SNMP Devices:** Specify specific SNMP devices to discover. If you know the IP address or device name to be discovered, click the starburst icon to provide that information.

▶ **DHCP:** Specify one or more Microsoft DHCP servers to use to discover clients receiving their IP address from a Microsoft DHCP server. You can also specify using the DHCP server that gave the site server its IP address by clicking the check box Include the DHCP server that the site server is configured to use.

▶ **Schedule:** Identify one or more schedules by specifying when Network Discovery will run. Click the starburst icon to create a schedule by identifying a start time and duration and a recurrence schedule, which can be none, monthly, weekly, or a custom interval.

CAUTION: DETERMINE WHETHER YOU REALLY WANT TO ENABLE NETWORK DISCOVERY

Use Network Discovery as a last resort to find ConfigMgr clients. Depending on the specified Network Discovery settings, you will get a considerable amount of information that ends up in the All Systems collection; determine whether you want to use that information within ConfigMgr. If not, do not use this discovery method.

Manually Importing Clients into ConfigMgr

You can manually import clients into ConfigMgr by using the console or scripts that automatically create DDR files. The main use case for manual import is when you are not using unknown client support during operating system deployment. Follow these steps to manually import a client:

1. Navigate in the console to **Assets and Compliance -> Devices**.

2. Select **Import Computer Information** on the ribbon bar to open the Import Computer Information Wizard.

3. Select to import a single computer or to import computers using a file.

   If you select **Import Single Computer**, provide at least the computer name and either the media access control (MAC) address or SMBIOS GUID of the machine (see Figure 9.8). You can also specify whether to provide a reference computer for use in operating system deployment when migrating settings from an old computer to this new computer.

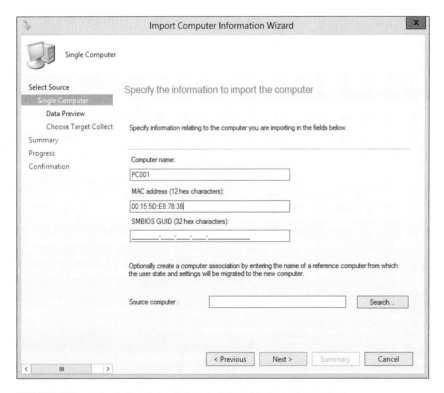

FIGURE 9.8   Import Computer Wizard dialog for a single computer.

CAUTION: DYNAMIC MAC ADDRESSES CAN CAUSE ISSUES

When importing computers by using their MAC addresses, make sure that the MAC address of a computer doesn't change. In virtual environments, MAC addresses may be provided dynamically to virtual machines (VMs). In addition, sometimes multiple computers have the same MAC address, as when they are deployed from a docking station with NICs embedded or using a USB dongle for the network adapter. You can specify MAC addresses or SMBIOS GUIDs on the Client Approval and Conflicting Records tab of the Hierarchy Settings Properties dialog box.

If you select **Import computers using a file**, browse for a comma-separated values (CSV) file you can create with Microsoft Excel. The minimum information to supply in this file is the computer name and SMBIOS GUID or MAC address of the machine. You can provide additional information, such as specific variables. If using column headings in the CSV file, check **This file has column headings** to ignore the first line of the file.

Map the values in the CSV file to the corresponding ConfigMgr fields. If you supplied the CSV fields in the order Name, SMBIOS GUID, MAC Address, Source Computer, Variable1, Variable 2, the most important information is mapped automatically; all you should do is map the provided variables to a ConfigMgr variable. If you don't make this mapping, these values are ignored.

After supplying the computer information using a CSV file or the wizard, a data preview page indicates the expected result of the import. Click **Next** to supply the collection to which you want to add the computer resources (All Systems by default).

4. On the Summary page, which shows what will be imported and where, click **Next** to begin the import. When the import is complete, close the wizard to see the new computers displayed in the specified collection.

Using Azure AD User Discovery

Starting with version 1706, you can discover Azure AD users with Configuration Manager. For Azure AD user discovery to work, Azure Services for cloud management must be set up. This is discussed in Chapter 6.

Azure AD User Discovery is available in the console as one of the properties of Azure cloud management services. Find the cloud management properties by navigating to **Administration -> Overview -> Cloud Services -> Azure Services**. From the Azure AD User Discovery tab of the Cloud Management Properties dialog box, you can initiate a full discovery, configure delta discovery, and set the schedule on which the discovery should run.

What to Know About Client Agent Assignment

When the ConfigMgr client agent is successfully installed, it must assign itself to a ConfigMgr site so it can be managed. ConfigMgr clients can be assigned only to primary sites, not secondary sites or the CAS. If a client does not assign itself to a site, it becomes unmanaged and stays unmanaged until it successfully assigns itself to a site. Client assignment is attempted every 10 minutes. Once assigned, the client remains assigned to that site even if it roams to another site; it never automatically switches to a different site. Following are the two ways for a client to assign itself to a ConfigMgr site:

▶ **Manually, Based on Provided Parameters:** You can manually assign a client by using the SMSSITECODE property during client installation or by providing the site code in the Configuration Manager Control Panel applet. Manual assignment is necessary when a client is already assigned, when it resides on the Internet, when DNS publishing is used to find the MP, or when the client's network location does not fall within a boundary group configured for site assignment and a fallback site is not configured. When a client is installed using a task sequence, the SMSSITECODE property is also provided as a client installation property.

▶ **Automatically, Based on Information the Client Finds in AD:** This occurs by default when you install the client manually and provide SMSSITECODE=AUTO during installation. It requires the MP to be either discoverable or provided as an option.

   You can also initiate automatic client assignment by clicking **Discover** in the Configuration Manager Control Panel applet. The client uses its AD site and IP address to look up its site boundary configured in ConfigMgr and published to AD (or from an MP, if the necessary schema changes to AD for ConfigMgr have not occurred). If the IP falls within a boundary group specified for site assignment on the ConfigMgr site, the client assigns itself to that site. If the client does not fall within a ConfigMgr site boundary group and a fallback site is specified in the hierarchy, the client is assigned to the fallback site. Chapter 6 discusses configuring fallback site assignment.

After an intranet-based ConfigMgr client completes site assignment, it performs a site compatibility check to verify that it is assigned to a ConfigMgr site and has a supported OS and version. Assignment fails if the site is ConfigMgr 2007 or 2012 or if the OS or version is not supported. The compatibility check verifies that the client can access an MP when applicable and can access the site information in AD when published. The check does not occur if the client is configured for Internet-based client management. Assignment succeeds if an older ConfigMgr client agent is assigned to a newer site. The client can then be upgraded via automatic client upgrade.

The configmgrassignment.adm Group Policy template file is also available to configure client assignment. This file is located on the site server in the *<ConfigMgrInstallPath>*\Tools folder and can be used to set these settings using GPO:

▶ Assigned Site by Specifying a Site Code

▶ Site Assignment Retry Interval in Minutes

▶ Site Assignment Retry Duration in Hours

After it is assigned to a site, the client uses the site's initial MP and composes a list of available MPs (the MP list), stored locally in WMI. This list contains MPs specified during setup and MPs matching the client's site code, available in AD. The client sorts the list; HTTPS-capable MPs are first if configured with a PKI certificate based on random order or by boundary group configuration if the option Clients prefer to use management points specified in boundary groups is enabled in the hierarchy settings. The list is extended with HTTP-capable MPs in random order or MPs specified by boundary group settings, if enabled. If it has a PKI certificate, the client tries all HTTPS-capable MPs first.

The client updates the MP list every 25 hours, when CCMExec is restarted, and when it receives a new IP address that resets the order of MPs to use. If the client cannot contact an MP from the MP list, it uses an alternative method to search for an MP, in the following order:

▶ **Active Directory:** The ConfigMgr site server publishes MP information to the Active Directory domain to which the client belongs.

▶ **DNS:** DNS information is published by the ConfigMgr site automatically if allowed or to DNS manually if automatic publishing is not allowed. For clients to use DNS as a location mechanism for finding the MP, the DNS domain suffix must be provided during client installation with the `DNSSUFFIX` parameter.

▶ **WINS:** When the site server is configured to use WINS, it uses this information to publish the MP information.

DNS and WINS are used when an MP was not specified during client setup and the AD schema is not extended for ConfigMgr. The ConfigMgr client consults DNS or WINS and adds the MPs published in DNS or WINS to its MP list.

You can also configure clients such that MPs assigned to a boundary group are preferred over other available MPs. This requires enabling the option Clients prefer to use management points specified in boundary groups on the General tab of the Hierarchy Settings Properties dialog box and adding MPs as a site system server in the References tab of the Boundary Groups dialog box.

When a client may only communicate with a specific MP or specific MPs, you can define these MPs in the client's Registry. This scenario could be useful for clients in a demilitarized zone (DMZ) environment that are allowed to communicate only with MPs in that same DMZ. Define the MPs for a client to use by specifying the FQDN of the MP(s) as a `Reg_Multi_SZ` value for the `AllowedMPs` key in the `HKLM\SOFTWARE\Microsoft\CCM` Registry path. You can specify multiple MPs, one per line.

Monitoring Client Agent Health and Activity Status

ConfigMgr can only manage healthy clients, which means the client agent's health is essential. Your support organization must consider monitoring the health of agents and remediating problems as a must-have operational task. In addition to monitoring client health, you can monitor client agent activity.

Each client agent runs the Configuration Manager Health Evaluation scheduled task, scheduled at the primary site level. If the client is powered off or in sleep mode, the task runs when the computer is booted or comes out of sleep mode. This scheduled task calls ccmeval.exe, evaluates client health status, and sends results to the site server by using state messages. If it cannot deliver a message, it uses an FSP if one is deployed. ccmeval.exe loads the ccmeval.xml evaluation file, found in the *%windir%*\CCM folder, which contains the client health evaluation rules. Open this file to see the checks and actions that occur. Microsoft does not support modifying ccmeval.xml to include custom checks. For information about the health checks performed, see https://docs.microsoft.com/sccm/core/clients/manage/monitor-clients#BKMK_ClientHealth.

The Configuration Manager Health Evaluation scheduled task also provides remediation by checking important WMI namespaces, classes, and instances, and it reinstalls the ConfigMgr client if missing. It tests whether it can read and write to WMI; if not, it rebuilds the repository and reinstalls the ConfigMgr client.

You can configure the client health mechanism to only perform checks rather than attempt to remediate. To configure health-only scanning, open the Registry and navigate to `HKLM/Software/Microsoft/CCM/CCMEval` to change the `NotifyOnly` value from `FALSE` to `TRUE`.

Results are displayed in the console under **Monitoring -> Client Status -> Client Check**. From there you can configure client status settings, which specify evaluation periods for client activity and retention of client status history from 0 to 90 days. You can also schedule client status updates to recur between 1 (default) and 31 days.

You can modify the evaluation periods between 1 and 30 days for the following settings:

- ▶ Client policy request (by default set to 4 days)
- ▶ Heartbeat discovery (by default set to 7 days)
- ▶ Hardware inventory (by default set to 7 days)
- ▶ Software inventory (by default set to 7 days)
- ▶ Status messages (by default set to 7 days)

For example, when the software inventory evaluation period is set to 7 days and the site server has not received software inventory data from a client in that time, it considers that client inactive for software inventory. The ConfigMgr client is considered inactive when it is inactive for all listed activities.

Each primary site runs the `CH_UpdateAll` stored procedure, which summarizes client health and client activity information and provides the schedule for when clients run the Configuration Manager Health Evaluation scheduled task; this is every day by default but is configurable. Follow these steps to change the schedule:

1. In the ConfigMgr console, navigate to **Monitoring -> Client Status**.

2. Select **Schedule Client Status Update** on the ribbon bar.

3. Configure the recurrence schedule that by default is set to every 1 day, but can be set to a value between 1 hour and 31 days.

You can also update client status by selecting **Refresh Client Status** on the ribbon bar; this triggers the stored procedure and refreshes the charts with the latest information, as shown in Figure 9.9.

FIGURE 9.9 Client status monitoring.

Look at the Results panes of the Client Status, Client Activity, and Client Check nodes for an overview of statistics and recent alerts. Clicking the corresponding regions in the chart or hyperlinks in the Results pane creates a temporary collection that contains the computer objects belonging to that selection. The Statistics node uses the All Desktop and Server Clients collection by default; change this to any other device collection by clicking **Browse** and selecting another collection.

Understanding Client Settings

Client settings are defined centrally, accessible through the Administration workspace, and apply to all deployed ConfigMgr client agents. They allow a ConfigMgr administrator to control the client's functionality and behavior.

ConfigMgr lets you specify client settings at the collection level, meaning you can define different settings as necessary. Note that this can lead to conflicts if a client belongs to multiple collections with client settings. You can set priorities to help manage these settings; the lowest number wins. Design these priorities carefully to maintain consistent client behavior, as you would when designing group policy in AD.

Client settings also assist with VDI scenarios. Each client randomizes scheduled times for hardware inventory, software inventory, software update scans, software update deployment evaluations, compliance settings evaluations, application deployment evaluations, and endpoint protection scans on VMs sharing the same host.

Each ConfigMgr installation has default settings, which are configured at the hierarchy level and applicable to every user and device that does not have custom settings. You can apply other (custom) settings to override the defaults. Default client settings have a priority of 10,000, which means you could theoretically define 9,999 custom client device and user settings. Custom device settings are deployed to device collections; custom user settings are deployed to user collections. When creating custom settings, keep them at a minimum and provide meaningful names so you know what each one does.

Configure default settings by selecting **Administration -> Client Settings -> Default Client Settings** and then double-click or choose **Properties** from the right-click context menu or the ribbon bar to open the Default Settings dialog box. Some settings cannot be set through custom device or user settings (for example, the Enrollment profile in the Enrollment section or hardware inventory classes in the Hardware section).

Some settings can use a simple or custom schedule, as shown in Figure 9.10. Following is information about each:

▶ **Simple Schedule:** A simple schedule allows you to specify an action that runs regularly each specified number of days, hours, minutes, and so on. The client determines when to run this action based on its installation date and coded randomization that distributes the load on ConfigMgr. This option is preferred with VDI clients, as it minimizes the load on the host hosting the VMs—because not all VMs run the same client action at exactly the same time.

▶ **Custom Schedule:** Use a custom schedule to specify exactly the time to launch the action. This means each client receiving the schedule initiates that action at exactly the same time, which could put a high load on ConfigMgr. Consider using a custom schedule when other processes running at specified intervals require current information.

FIGURE 9.10   Setting a schedule for client settings.

Client Settings Priority

Defining a priority lets you specify which settings apply when a client receives multiple custom settings. Settings with a lower priority number take precedence over those with higher numbers. Since the default client settings have the highest priority count (10,000), custom settings have precedence over default client settings.

Use custom client settings to provide specific settings to apply to members of one or more specific collections. For example, you can define another hardware inventory schedule for specific servers managed with ConfigMgr. The first custom client setting defined receives priority 1, the second priority 2, and so on. You can make adjustments to this schedule by increasing or decreasing the priority, by using the right-click context menu or ribbon bar to select **Priority**.

You can deploy custom settings to one or more collections. Select a setting and choose **Deploy** from the ribbon bar and specify the collection to which to apply the settings.

To view the result of client settings applied to a device or user, use the resultant client settings capability provided in the Assets and Compliance workspace. Right-click a device, user, or group and select **Client Settings -> Resultant Client Settings** to open the Resultant Client Settings panes, which display the effective client settings for that device, user, or group.

TIP: DO NOT MODIFY DEFAULT CLIENT SETTINGS

The authors recommend not modifying the default client settings. Keeping the default client settings at their original values allows you to refer back to the settings supplied out of the box.

Configurable Client Settings

The following sections describe available client settings for devices and users.

Background Intelligent Transfer Device Settings

Use the Background Intelligent Transfer device settings to configure the behavior of BITS. BITS provides bandwidth throttling to control the transfer of packets between ConfigMgr clients and their MPs. There are several options, including start and stop times for a throttling window, allowing BITS downloads outside a defined throttling window, and maximum transfer rate during and outside the window. After enabling BITS with the setting Limit the maximum network bandwidth for BITS background transfers, you can modify the following:

▶ Specify the time frame for enabling BITS bandwidth throttling by specifying a start and end time window.

▶ If throttling should always be enabled, set the start and stop times for throttling to the same value.

▶ Specify the maximum transfer rate during the throttling window (in kilobytes per second).

▶ Select **Yes** for the Allow BITS downloads outside the throttling window option to specify whether to use bandwidth throttling outside the specified throttling window. You can specify the maximum transfer rate (in kilobytes per second) when BITS downloads are allowed outside the window.

CAUTION: DO NOT SET CONFLICTING BITS GROUP POLICY OBJECTS

If you also configure BITS settings by using group policy, GPO settings could overwrite the settings coming from ConfigMgr and vice versa, leading to unpredictable results when those settings differ.

Client Cache Settings Device Settings

Client Cache Settings device settings allow you to control the ConfigMgr cache size and specify settings concerning BranchCache and Peer Cache on the client.

ConfigMgr clients can leverage BranchCache, a Windows feature that enables clients in remote locations to obtain content from local clients caching that content. Enable BranchCache by setting the option Allow clients to share content with other clients on the same subnet; this is available for packages, application deployment types, and software updates. Chapter 5 discusses setting up BranchCache. The device settings allow you to specify whether to configure BranchCache on clients. When enabling the Configure BranchCache option, specify whether to enable BranchCache and the percentage of disk space to use for the cache.

Peer Cache is similar in functionality but does not require a BranchCache infrastructure. In contrast to BranchCache (which is enabled for any file transfer), Peer Cache only caches ConfigMgr-related file transfers; see Chapter 5 for additional information. Enable Peer Cache by setting the Enable Configuration Manager client in full OS to share content setting to Yes and specifying whether to use HTTP or HTTPS to communicate between client peers. You can also specify the port for initial network broadcast (port 8004 by default) and the port for content download from peer (8003 by default).

Each ConfigMgr client agent also has a cache folder where software distribution-related files are downloaded before executing. This folder is normally in *%windir%*\ccmcache and defaults to 5120MB. If the cache size is too small, the client cannot download the files necessary for a certain task, which then fails. Configure client cache size in the Configuration Manager Control Panel applet on individual clients or by setting the Configure client cache size setting in the Client Cache Settings device settings to Yes. You then can specify the maximum size (in megabytes) or a percentage of disk space to use for the client cache.

Client Policy Device Settings

Client policy device settings relate to how the client deals with its received policy, which comes from its MP. By default, a client requests policy every 60 minutes, which is typically sufficient. You can modify the policy refresh interval to between 3 minutes and 24 hours (1440 minutes).

When the Enable user policy polling on clients setting is set to No, users do not receive required applications or any other operations contained in user policies, they do not receive revisions and updates for applications published in the application catalog, and they do not see notifications about application approval requests.

User policy requests from Internet clients work only when the Enable user policy setting is set to True and the Internet-based MP can successfully authenticate the user using Windows authentication.

Cloud Services Device and User Settings

Use Cloud Services device and user settings to allow or disallow access to a cloud distribution point. Allow Windows 10 domain-joined devices to automatically register with Azure Active Directory and enable clients to use a CMG. The setting to use a cloud DP is disabled by default, while the other two options are enabled by default. Refer to Chapter 5 for information about the use and use cases of a cloud DP and CMG.

Compliance Settings Device Settings

Use Compliance Settings device settings to enable or disable the functionality provided, as discussed in Chapter 10, "Managing Compliance."

The capability to report and alert on compliance helps monitor and manage configuration drift. You can apply Compliance Settings device settings to desktops, servers, mobile devices, and users; you can also use these settings to remediate WMI, Registry, and script settings that are not natively compliant in ConfigMgr. Automated remediation can drastically reduce the amount of time a noncompliant configuration stays out of compliance.

You can also enable the use of User Data and Profiles management, which is disabled by default. Prior to using this functionality, which is described in Chapter 10, enable it using a client device setting.

Computer Agent Device Settings

Use Computer Agent device settings to define settings related to software distribution on the agent. These settings include specifying the notification interval for deployments, the default Application Catalog website point, and more. Following is information on these settings:

▶ **Deployment Deadline:** Specify the notification intervals before a deployment deadline is reached. By default, users are notified 48 hours in advance when the deployment deadline is greater than 24 hours; you can set this value between 1 and 999 hours.

   If the deployment deadline is less than 24 hours but over 1 hour, users are reminded every 4 hours; this is modifiable from 1 to 24 hours.

   If the deployment deadline is less than 1 hour, users are notified every 15 minutes; this can be changed to between 5 and 25 minutes.

▶ **Application Catalog:** Following are settings related to the default Application Catalog website point:

   ▶ **Specify the Server That Hosts the Application Catalog Website by Clicking Set Website:** Configuring this setting requires that the application catalog website point be installed. The authors recommend using a NetBIOS name to prevent clients from receiving a credentials prompt when connecting to the website. You must specify the NetBIOS name on the website point properties and have a name resolution mechanism in place that supports short names; this could be specifying the necessary DNS domain suffix search list on the client or using the DNS GlobalNames Zone (GNZ) feature.

▶ **Using Automatic Detection, Allowing Clients to Receive the Closest Application Catalog:** Automatic detection makes a service location request to a MP every 25 hours, returning an application catalog website based on the client's location and pointing clients automatically to the application catalog website from their own sites. You can specify different catalogs for clients residing on the intranet and those on the Internet; those configured for HTTPS take precedence over HTTP. You may decide not to use automatic detection if you want to manually specify which clients connect to what server or do not want to wait 25 hours when the application catalog website point changes.

▶ **Specifying the URL to a Customized Application Catalog, Allowing You to Specify a URL to a Custom Website Hosting Application Catalog Functionality:** If the application catalog website is not added to the trusted sites zone in Internet Explorer (IE) on the client, IE Protected Mode may not allow you to install applications from the catalog. In this case, add the application catalog website to the trusted sites zone in IE by using a GPO. When you use the Add default Application Catalog website to Internet Explorer trusted sites zone setting, ConfigMgr ensures that only the current application catalog is added to the zone. If using other mechanisms to populate the trusted sites zones or other security zones for IE, verify that they do not conflict with ConfigMgr settings.

▶ **Allow Silverlight Applications to Run in Elevated Trust Mode:** Version 1511 included a new Software Center combining the functionality of the old Software Center and the Application Catalog. The Application Catalog website point and Application Catalog web service point site system roles are still required for user-available applications to appear in the new Software Center.

Microsoft Silverlight is required for the old Software Center. For more information about the old and new versions of Software Center, see the "Use New Software Center" bullet in this list.

▶ **Organization Name Displayed in Software Center:** This name appears in the Software Center, which can help users identify whether it is from a trusted source.

▶ **Use New Software Center:** The new Software Center does not require Microsoft Silverlight. Enable use by setting this to **Yes**. For more on using the new software catalog, see Chapter 14, "Distributing and Deploying Applications and Packages."

▶ **Enable Communication with Health Attestation Service:** You can specify whether the client on which the ConfigMgr client agent is running should use the Health Attestation service.

The Health Attestation feature was introduced with Windows 10. It ensures that client computers have a trustworthy BIOS, TPM, and boot software configuration by turning on and using the following options:

▶ Secure Boot

▶ BitLocker

▶ Code Integrity

▶ Early-Launch Antimalware (ELAM)

The client can report its health attestation status to ConfigMgr; information is shown in the console. The status could be used to define rules for conditional access in compliance policies for devices.

You can find health attestation information by navigating to **Monitoring ->
Security -> Health Attestation**. In the Health Attestation results pane, the following information is available:

▶ Health Attestation Status

▶ Devices Reporting Health Attestation

▶ Noncompliant Devices by Client Type

▶ Top Missing Health Attestation Settings

More information about Windows 10 health attestation is available at https://docs.microsoft.com/windows/device-security/protect-high-value-assets-by-controlling-the-health-of-windows-10-based-devices.

▶ **Install Permissions:** Specify which users can initiate software installation, software updates, and task sequences; it is set to All Users by default. If it is set to No Users, required deployments are always installed at the deadline, and users cannot initiate software installation from the Software Center or Application Catalog. You can also enable this for administrators and primary users only, or for administrators only.

▶ **Suspend BitLocker PIN Entry on Restart:** Enable suspension of the BitLocker PIN during restart if BitLocker with PIN is enabled on the client by setting the Suspend BitLocker PIN entry on restart to Always.

▶ **Additional Software Manages the Deployment of Applications and Software Updates:** Set Agent extensions manage the deployment of applications and software updates to True when using a third-party solution or the ConfigMgr software development kit (SDK). You can also use this option on a collection of VDI clients sharing the same master VM, where you want regular ConfigMgr options to work but don't want those clients to download and apply any updates as those updates are typically applied to the master VM only.

▶ **PowerShell Execution Policy:** If your clients run PowerShell 2.0 or higher, you can specify the PowerShell execution policy to apply during ConfigMgr actions. This is set to Restricted by default, meaning the current PowerShell restriction settings on the client are used. Setting it to Bypass allows ConfigMgr to use unsigned scripts during ConfigMgr actions.

▶ **Show Notifications for New Deployments:** Enable notifications for new deployments by setting this to Yes.

▶ **Disable Deadline Randomization:** If this setting is enabled, the agent delays installing required software for up to two hours when the deadline is reached. This setting is especially useful in VDI environments where you don't want all VDI clients to start a certain action at the same time, possibly causing a drop in performance for the entire VDI environment.

Computer Restart Device Settings
Computer Restart device settings allow you to specify the countdown interval for ConfigMgr-initiated restarts:

▶ **Display Countdown Interval Before Log Off and Restart:** This is set to 90 minutes by default and can be between 1 minute and 24 hours (1440 minutes).

▶ **Display Countdown Interval Before Final Log Off and Restart in Minutes:** This is set to 15 minutes by default and can be set between 1 minute and 24 hours.

Ensure that the intervals specified are shorter in duration than the shortest maintenance window so the computer will restart during the window.

Endpoint Protection Device Settings
Endpoint Protection device settings are available after you configure endpoint protection in ConfigMgr. Chapter 19, "Endpoint Protection," discusses configuring endpoint protection and setting corresponding device settings.

Enrollment Device and User Settings
The Enrollment device and user settings allow you to specify the polling interval for modern devices, mobile devices, and Mac computers; the interval is 1440 minutes (24 hours) by default. The following settings are available:

▶ **Allow Users to Enroll Mobile Devices and Mac Computers:** This setting, which is No by default, allows you to specify whether users can enroll older-style mobile devices, such as Windows Mobile and Windows CE and Mac computers. If this is set to Yes, set the Enrollment profile by clicking Set Profile to open the Enrollment Profile dialog.

▶ **Allow Users to Enroll Modern Devices:** Specify if users are allowed to enroll modern devices using on-premise MDM. The default is No. If it is set to Yes, you can set the Enrollment profile by clicking Set Profile to open the Enrollment Profile dialog.

Chapter 17 discusses setting up enrollment for modern devices. It also covers configuring corresponding user settings.

Hardware Inventory Device Settings

The Hardware Inventory device settings allow you to enable or disable hardware inventory and define related settings. When enabled (default), you can specify a schedule (which is every 7 days by default). You can also specify if you want to collect specific MIFs (management information files), identify a maximum MIF file size, and define hardware inventory classes.

Client settings can define other Hardware Inventory settings for laptops versus for traditional desktop systems. Configure the items you want to inventory by modifying hardware inventory settings at the Default Client Agent settings level. Perform the following steps:

1. Navigate to **Administration -> Overview -> Client Settings**.

2. Select **Default Client Settings** and choose **Properties** from the ribbon bar.

3. Select **Hardware Inventory settings** and then **Set Classes** to open a new dialog box, where you can enable or disable those inventory classes (see Figure 9.11). If a class is checked with a black checkmark in this window, the class and all its properties are inventoried.

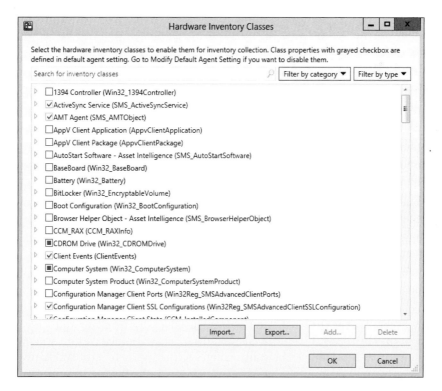

FIGURE 9.11   Enabling Hardware Inventory classes.

If a class has a gray box, the class and some of its properties are inventoried; it is not inventoried if it is not checked. Modify this list by defining custom client devices settings, which enable you to specify different selections for specific collections.

There are several ways to extend inventoried items:

▶ Import a Managed Object Format (MOF) file by using the import functionality, which allows you to browse for MOF files (Chapter 3, "Looking Inside Configuration Manager," discusses MOF files and their structure.)

▶ Export the settings to a MOF file, which can be imported into another ConfigMgr environment

MIF files can extend hardware inventory information or collect information that is not available in the system. You could write a tool that collects information from an end user, with output in MIF format ready to be picked up by ConfigMgr inventory. MIF file information is sent to and stored in the site database with the default client inventory data. There are two types of MIF files:

▶ **NOIDMIF:** These files are automatically associated with the client where the NOIDMIF file is inventoried. To have ConfigMgr process a NOIDMIF file, place it in the *%windir%*\CCM\Inventory\noidmifs (default) folder.

▶ **IDMIF:** IDMIF files are not associated with the computer they are collected from. This means you can collect inventory about non-ConfigMgr devices. These files are collected only if they meet the maximum custom MIF file size specified value, which is less than 250KB by default. Store IDMIF files in the *%windir%*\CCM\Inventory\ idmifs folder to be picked up by hardware inventory.

CAUTION: BE CAREFUL WHEN USING MIF FILES

Data collected from NOIDMIF and IDMIF files is not validated and could overwrite valid data stored in the database, potentially breaking ConfigMgr site functionality. Microsoft makes MIF file functionality available to customers still leveraging it. The authors do not recommend using MIF files unless no other option meets your requirements.

Modify MIF storage locations in the Registry by changing the values that specify the locations of the NOIDMIF and IDMIF files. The single Registry key is located under HKLM\ Software\Microsoft\SMS\Client\Configuration\Client Properties, and you need to modify the NOIDMIF Directory and IDMIF Directory values.

The ConfigMgr client scans the hardware currently installed on the client and sends that information to the site server. Inventory takes hardware changes (deltas) into account, letting administrators determine if there are changes to hardware. Inventoried hardware is defined centrally in the ConfigMgr settings—which you can adjust to include or omit specific hardware. If the client is not connected to the network during inventory, inventory occurs, and the data is uploaded when connectivity resumes. If the client is offline, inventory starts once the client is available.

Hardware inventory also inventories the software listed in the Programs and Features Control Panel applet, which typically suffices to determine software installed on a client. However, not all software is advertised in that applet; use software inventory for a full inventory of your software.

If standard hardware inventory does not provide the needed information, it may be that what is inventoried is not configured in the applied client settings, or new hardware may be available but unknown to ConfigMgr. You can modify ConfigMgr to enable inventory of extra or additional hardware, as discussed in online-only Appendix E, "Extending Hardware Inventory," which you can download from the book's companion website, at http://www.informit.com/title/9780672337901, on the Downloads tab.

Metered Internet Connections Device Settings

Use the Metered Internet Connections device settings to specify whether you want to allow client communication when the client is connected to ConfigMgr over a metered Internet connection; this is blocked by default. The setting Allow allows communication, and Limit only allows the following types of client communications:

▶ Client policy retrieval

▶ Client state messages to send to the site

▶ Software installation requests using Application Catalog functionality

▶ Required deployments

User-initiated software installation from Software Center or the Application Catalog is always permitted, regardless of metered Internet connection settings. If the data transfer limit specified on the client is reached, site communication is no longer initiated.

Power Management Device Settings

The Power Management device settings specify whether ConfigMgr power management is enabled and whether users can exclude their devices from those settings. You can also specify whether wake-up proxy functionality is used and the wake-up proxy (default 25536 UDP) and Wake On LAN (default 9 UDP) port numbers. Specify whether to create a Windows Firewall exception for wake-up proxy; clicking Configure opens the Wake-up Proxy and Windows Firewall Client Settings dialog to enable this for the Domain, Private, and Public firewall profiles. You can also specify one or multiple IPv6 prefixes, comma-separated, to specify prefixes, if required, for DirectAccess or other devices. The "Using Wake on LAN and Power Management" section, later in this chapter, provides additional information.

Remote Tools Device Settings

Use the Remote Tools device settings to specify whether client remote control is enabled. Indicate whether users can change the remote control policy and notification settings in the Software Center applet, whether remote control of an unattended computer is permitted, whether to prompt a user for remote control permission, and whether local administrators on the client may use remote control. You can also configure an allowed access level of Full Control, View Only, or No Access. Specify permitted viewers by listing an AD group or user.

Remote Tools settings can remotely manage client desktops for troubleshooting purposes. This functionality enables remote control from a central point, providing logging capabilities and report functionality. Remote Tools leverages the Windows Remote Desktop Protocol (RDP) functionality. You can use it in several ways—to completely take over the desktop using Remote Desktop or to assist the end user by using the Remote Assistance functionality, where both the end user and help desk view the same desktop.

Remote control behavior depends on the client's effective default or client device settings. Modify client settings by navigating to **Administration -> Overview -> Client Settings** and selecting **Default Client settings** and then modifying custom device settings or creating new settings. Open the Remote Tools section and click **Configure** to open the Remote Control and Windows Firewall Client Settings dialog. Enable the check box **Enable Remote Control on client computers** to be able to configure other settings:

▶ Whether ConfigMgr can configure Windows Firewall on the destination computer automatically with the correct rules to allow it to be remotely controlled. Enable rules for the Domain, Private, or Public firewall profile or a combination of these.

▶ Whether users can modify the policy or notification settings in Software Center. If enabled, users can specify whether to use the remote access settings specified by the ConfigMgr administrator or to override these settings with their own values.

▶ Whether to enable remote control of an unattended computer.

▶ Whether the user is prompted for remote control permission and presented with a dialog box to allow remote control.

▶ Whether the user is asked for permission when content is transferred from the shared clipboard.

▶ Whether remote control permissions are granted to members of the local administrators group and the type of access allowed. Available options are None, View Only, and Full Control.

▶ Who can initiate remote control by configuring permissions, allowing AD users or groups.

▶ The types of notifications a user receives when Remote Control is active, enabling a notification icon in the taskbar or a connection bar during a remote session. You can also configure a sound to play on the client, either at the beginning and end of the session or repeatedly.

▶ Manage solicited and unsolicited Remote Assistance settings; if True, ConfigMgr manages Remote Assistance settings. You can also specify the level of access for Remote Assistance; the None, View Only, and Full Control options are available.

▶ Whether ConfigMgr manages the Remote Desktop settings of the client receiving the client settings (set If Manage Remote Desktop to True).

▶ Whether permitted viewers are allowed to connect; use the Remote Desktop connection for users specified in the Permitted viewers list to set up a remote connection.

▶ Requiring network level authentication (NLA) on computers that run Windows Vista and later to configure the Remote Desktop connection to use NLA to connect to the remote computer.

For more information about the Remote Tools settings, see the "Using Remote Control" section, later in this chapter.

Software Center Device Settings

Use Software Center device settings to configure the behavior of the new Software Center. You can provide a company name and color scheme, and select a logo for Software Center. You can also choose to hide the Applications, Updates, Operating Systems, Installation Status, Device Compliance, and Options tabs.

Software Deployment Device Settings

Use Software Deployment device settings to specify when software deployments are reevaluated on clients for required deployments. Select Schedule to change the default value (every 7 days effective 2/1/1970 12:00 AM) and whether it is a simple or custom schedule. Chapter 14 discusses software deployment.

Software Inventory Device Settings

The Software Inventory device settings allow you to enable or disable software inventory. Software inventory is a file inventory; you inventory certain files based on predefined search strings. You could inventory all executables to complement hardware inventory. Information in the file header of inventoried files is available in the console, allowing a ConfigMgr administrator to report on software inventory or create dynamic collections for software distribution. Software inventory reflects the latest uploaded data and does not include deltas. You also can upload specified files to the ConfigMgr hierarchy. You could scan for .ini files matching a certain search query and upload those files to become part of that inventory, which you could then query using the Resource Explorer, as discussed in the "Using the Resource Explorer" section, later in this chapter.

To configure software inventory, navigate to **Administration -> Overview -> Client Settings**. Select **Default Client setting** or **Custom Device Settings**. You can also create new custom device settings.

Configure software inventory in the Software Inventory section:

▶ Enable inventory by setting the **Enable software inventory on clients value** to **True** and specifying a schedule that defines when clients should execute software inventory.

▶ Select **Set inventory reporting detail** to specify what to report about the inventoried files: inventory details about the file only, the product associated with the file, or all information (using the **Full Details** option).

9

▶ Click **Set Types**, which is part of the Inventory these file types option, to configure the types of files to inventory by opening the Configure Client Setting page:

  ▶ Click the starburst icon to specify the files to inventory. Specify a specific file-name or use the * or ? wildcard characters, as shown in Figure 9.12.

  ▶ Specify where to look for the file, which is set to All client hard disks by default, and whether to search subfolders of the specified location. You can also specify to search encrypted and compressed files, which is disabled by default, and to exclude the Windows folder from searches.

FIGURE 9.12   Inventoried file properties for software inventory.

▶ Select **Set Files** to collect files and open the Configure Client Setting dialog. Click the starburst icon to open the Collected File Properties dialog box, where you can specify files to collect. Specify the filename, optionally using the * and ? wildcard characters, location, and whether to search subfolders. You can include encrypted and compressed files (which are excluded by default), and the total volume of files collected, which is 128KB by default. Collecting too many files can negatively impact network bandwidth capacity and your ConfigMgr infrastructure.

Software Metering Device Settings

Software Metering device settings measure software usage rather than just inventorying it. Software metering rules can collect file usage data. Select **Schedule** to change the default value (every 7 days, effective 2/1/1970 12:00 AM) and specify a simple or custom schedule.

Software Metering device settings collect file usage data. Enable software metering by using default client settings or custom client device settings, described earlier in this section. To view data from software metering, navigate to **Monitoring -> Reporting -> Software Metering**.

After enabling software metering, you can create software metering rules. Follow these steps:

1. Navigate to **Assets and Compliance -> Software Metering**. ConfigMgr automatically creates a (disabled) software metering rule when 10% of computers in the hierarchy use a program and stopping automatic creation once 100 rules are created, by default. Click **Software Metering Properties** in the ribbon bar to modify these settings and data retention. To enable a rule, select it and click **Enable** on the ribbon bar.

2. Select **Create Software Metering Rule** on the ribbon bar to open the Create Software Metering Rule Wizard, which you can use to create a custom software metering rule.

3. Provide a name for the rule; type the name of the file to monitor or click **Browse** to browse to it. By browsing, ConfigMgr reads the details of the file from the file header and automatically fills in the file information.

4. Click **Next** to continue to the Summary page to review the software metering rule settings, and click **Next** again to create the rule. Click **Close** in the Completion page to close the wizard.

Use reports to view the information from software metering and create collections based on the information they provide. These collections are based on the `Software Usage Data` attribute class. Chapter 14 discusses creating collections.

TIP: MORE INFORMATION ABOUT SOFTWARE METERING

Minfang Lv, a ConfigMgr sustained engineer at Microsoft, provides insight into software metering at https://blogs.msdn.microsoft.com/minfangl/2011/04/28/step-by-step-on-how-to-use-software-metering/. Although written for ConfigMgr 2007, the article is still valid for ConfigMgr Current Branch.

Software Updates Device Settings

Software Updates device settings allow you to specify how the client handles software updates coming from ConfigMgr (see Chapter 15).

State Messaging Device Setting

State messaging reflects point-in-time conditions on the client, and the State Messaging setting enables you to track data flow through the hierarchy. There is a single setting for state messaging, the State message reporting cycle, which defaults to 15 minutes and can be set between 1 and 43200 minutes (12 days).

State messages sent by ConfigMgr clients to their MP or FSP report the current state of ConfigMgr client operations. The result of these messages is shown in reports. Various data in the console depends on the state messages received, such as software updates and settings management.

For more information about state messaging, see Steve Rachui's article at https://blogs. msdn.microsoft.com/steverac/2011/01/07/sccm-state-messagingin-depth/, and Chapter 3.

User and Device Affinity Device and User Settings

Use User and Device Affinity settings, available in custom device settings and custom user settings, to specify settings that relate to the affinity between the user and the device being used.

You can use device affinity when defining deployment types in applications. Chapter 11, "Creating and Managing Applications," covers user and device affinity and using this information when deploying applications. Using default settings, a user device affinity mapping is created after the device is used for 48 hours (2880 minutes) within 30 days. For ConfigMgr to automatically create user device affinities based on the specified data, set Automatically configure user device affinity from usage data to True.

User and Device Affinity settings for users allow you to specify whether to enable a user to define their primary device. There is only one setting for user and device affinity for users—if it is set to True, users can set their own device affinity in the Application Catalog.

Windows Analytics Device Settings

Use Windows Analytics device settings to configure the behavior of Windows telemetry on Windows clients. Once enabled, you need a unique commercial ID key to map your data to the Operations Management Suite (OMS) workspace for your organization. For Windows 10 you can specify the telemetry level to use: Basic, Enhanced (Limited), Enhanced, or Full. For more information about what the telemetry levels provide, see https://docs.microsoft.com/windows/configuration/ configure-windows-telemetry-in-your-organization#telemetry-levels.

For Windows 7 and 8.1, telemetry can only be enabled or disabled. The following options are available for Internet Explorer data:

▶ Disable

▶ Enable for local internet, trusted sites, and machine local only

▶ Enable for Internet and restricted sites only

▶ Enable for all zones

Information about Windows 7 and 8.1 telemetry is available at https://go.microsoft.com/ fwlink/?LinkID=822965. See https://msdn.microsoft.com/library/ms537183(v=vs.85).aspx for additional information about IE telemetry.

Using Remote Control

Many organizations provide remote support to end users; Windows includes Remote Desktop sessions and Remote Assistance functionality. However, many companies require that remote control of workstations be managed and logged centrally.

Start the Remote Control viewer from the Windows Start menu or the ConfigMgr console. ConfigMgr also lets you start a Remote Assistance or Remote Desktop session to the remote computer.

The notification bar in Figure 9.13 is quite visible on the remotely controlled computer and displays the account name of the user remotely controlling the computer. Remote control uses TCP port 2701; ports 2702 and 135 are no longer used. If Kerberos authentication fails when you want to control a computer remotely, the system prompts whether to use the less secure NT LAN Manager (NTLM) authentication mechanism. If the connection to the remotely controlled machine is disconnected, the remote computer is locked. Remote Control supports multiple monitors.

FIGURE 9.13   Configuration Manager remote control example.

Remotely Administering a Client Computer

Remotely administer a client computer from the Assets and Compliance workspace by selecting it from the Devices node or one of the device collections and then selecting **Start -> Remote Control** to start the Remote Control viewer window to administer the client computer remotely. Permissions set using the Remote Tools client settings determine whether you can view or take control of the machine's keyboard and mouse.

Start the Remote Control viewer from the command line with CmRcViewer.exe, located in the *<%ConfigMgrInstallPath%>*\AdminConsole\Bin\x64 folder. Supply two values when connecting to a client computer with this utility:

▶ The NetBIOS or FQDN of the client you want to administer remotely

▶ The site server to which you want to send state messages

An example of the use of CmRcViewer.exe is `CmRcViewer.exe albert.odyssey.com`
`\\ambassador.odyssey.com`.

Providing Remote Assistance

Provide remote assistance to a client computer from the Assets and Compliance workspace. Select the client computer from the Devices node or one of the device collections and then select **Start -> Remote Assistance** to start the Remote Assistance client.

NOTE: PREREQUISITE FOR PROVIDING REMOTE ASSISTANCE

To use the Remote Assistance functionality, install the Remote Assistance feature on the machine running the ConfigMgr console.

Using Remote Desktop

Use Remote Desktop to connect to a client computer from the Assets and Compliance workspace by selecting the client computer from the Devices node or one of the device collections. Then select **Start** from the ribbon bar and click **Remote Desktop Client** to start a RDP session to the client.

TIP: AUDITING REMOTE CONTROL

Using remote control from ConfigMgr is advantageous as its actions are audited by ConfigMgr and can be retrieved using two reports:

▶ All computers remotely controlled by a specific user

▶ All remote control information

Using the Resource Explorer

The Resource Explorer, which is executed from the ConfigMgr console, provides insight into hardware inventory, software inventory, and file collections. To start the Resource Explorer, navigate to **Assets and Compliance**, select **Devices**, or locate the device in one of the available collections. Select the device for which you want to see information and then select **Start -> Resource Explorer** from the ribbon bar or from the right-click context menu.

The following nodes appear in the Resource Explorer:

▶ **Hardware:** Hardware shows hardware from the last hardware inventory. Extend the list by enabling extra classes or properties or add extra data to hardware inventory by extending it, as described in online-only Appendix E.

▶ **Hardware History:** Hardware History shows what changed between hardware inventory scans, providing information about changes to inventory.

▶ **Software:** Software provides insight into data coming from software inventory. It provides an overview of collected files, file details of inventoried files, when the last software scan was performed on the client, and information about which products were inventoried.

Using Wake on LAN and Power Management

One challenge of updating a system is its power status; the system must be powered on to be maintained. Generally, the best time to update or deploy software to systems is at night, when the systems are not in use. However, many users turn off their desktops at the end of the day, and some systems go into a power-saving hibernation mode when not used. These systems present a problem with no easy workaround and may end up being unpatched or slammed with patches when users log in to the network in the morning. To alleviate this, implement Wake on LAN or configure the Wakeup time (desktop computers) setting in the Power Management tab of the collection properties.

Using Wake on LAN

Wake on LAN is an industry standard to send a remote signal over the network to a system to wake it when it is powered off or hibernating. The signal is a *magic packet*, a specially crafted network packet. The network interface card (NIC) of the destination system receives this packet (referred as a wake-up packet in the ConfigMgr console) and wakes up the system.

WOL Prerequisites

There are two ConfigMgr-specific and three external prerequisites to fully enable WOL capabilities in ConfigMgr. Following are the ConfigMgr prerequisites:

▶ Enable hardware inventory.

▶ Install the ConfigMgr agent on destination systems.

These are the external prerequisites:

▶ Ensure that NICs support WOL and the use of magic packets.

▶ Enable WOL on NICs and in the BIOS of destination systems.

▶ If using subnet-directed broadcasts (discussed in the next section), configure the network infrastructure to forward these broadcasts.

6

Configuring WOL

ConfigMgr has several WOL configuration options. Use the Wake On LAN tab of the *<site>* Properties dialog, which is accessible from **Administration -> Overview -> Site Configuration -> Sites**. Right-click *<site code>* - *<site name>* in the Details pane and select **Properties**.

The Wake On LAN tab provides several approaches to how the site wakes up computers. When enabling WOL on this tab, you must configure how to power on your clients. The following options are available:

▶ Subnet-directed broadcast

▶ Unicast

To view the port used for the magic packet, select the Ports tab of the *<site>* Properties dialog box. The default is UDP port 9; change it by double-clicking the Wake On Lan (UDP) entry in the list box or select it and click **Properties** to launch the Port Details dialog. A single port number is supported. Click **Advanced** to access advanced options, which are mainly network and ConfigMgr throttling controls; change these only if issues occur.

Two Types of WOL

ConfigMgr supports two types of WOL:

▶ **Unicast:** Unicast WOL sends a single magic packet to the IP address of the system, taken from the hardware inventory of the destination system. This is a specially crafted UDP packet sent directly to the destination's IP address. Some network adapters might not respond to wake-up packets when using unicast, depending on their configured sleep state.

The magic packet includes the system's MAC address. The destination NIC compares the MAC address to its own before waking up the system; if it does not match, the NIC does not signal the system to wake up. Unicast is supported in both IPv4 and IPv6 environments.

CAUTION: WOL RELIES ON ARP CACHE

A major weakness of unicast is its reliance on the Address Resolution Protocol (ARP) cache of the last layer 3 device in the path to the targeted system. While the device usually is a router or layer 3 switch, it could be the primary site server if both systems are on the same subnet.

If the ARP cache of the device no longer contains the MAC address of the target, it uses an ARP request to discover the MAC address. However, because responding to an ARP request is a function of a running OS, the magic packet cannot be delivered to the target. An exception is when the network card and driver installed on a system have a feature called ARP Offload and the feature is enabled.

▶ **Subnet Directed:** ConfigMgr broadcasts the magic packet to the IP subnet of the destination system, where each NIC compares the MAC address in the magic packet to its own, waking up its system if there is a match and enabling ConfigMgr to wake up those systems with changed IP addresses still on that subnet. Subnet-directed WOL utilizes subnet-directed broadcasts, requiring support from your network infrastructure. These broadcasts are often disabled due to overhead or security concerns, as enabling them opens the network to possible distributed denial-of-service (DDoS) attacks such as Smurf attacks. Mitigate this by changing the default port used by subnet-directed WOL packets and configuring the network to allow only subnet-directed broadcasts from your site server.

Using Wake-up Proxy

Supplement the Wake on LAN wake-up packet method by implementing a wake-up proxy, which uses a peer-to-peer protocol. Selected computers check whether other computers on the subnet are awake and wake them if necessary. The online peers, called *manager computers*, send each other TCP/IP pings every five seconds. Computers not responding to these pings are considered asleep.

For wake-up proxy to work correctly, at least three computers should be awake and receive guardian computer functionality, meaning they stay awake and ignore any settings related to power management.

The computers in the subnet that are powered on request that the network switch redirect broadcast traffic to themselves and keep the ARP cache for the sleeping computers populated. This issue, known as *MAC flap*, can cause network monitoring or network intrusion to create alerts or shut down ports. The authors recommend consulting your network group prior to implementing this feature.

For more information about implementing wake-up proxy, refer to https://docs.microsoft.com/sccm/core/clients/deploy/plan/plan-wake-up-clients.

Using WOL

ConfigMgr manages all the details for actually implementing WOL. You simply tell the system when to use it. ConfigMgr supports WOL for these activities:

▶ Application management package/program mandatory deployments

▶ Task sequence mandatory deployments

▶ Software update mandatory deployments

A check box appears on the Deployment Settings page of the deployment wizard for each object if the deployment is set to Required; this cannot be changed after you create the deployment. ConfigMgr then sends the WOL request to the destination system at its scheduled mandatory time. Magic packets are sent only from the primary site server. When the destination system wakes up, it initiates any applicable mandatory deployments.

If a deployment becomes mandatory on a system after the time scheduled for the deployment—such as by being added to a collection where a deployment is past its mandatory time—that system will not have a magic packet sent to it.

WOL is a great addition to the ConfigMgr toolset, although third-party tools can enhance its functionality. The two primary third-party alternatives (Green Planet from Adaptiva and Night Watchman from 1E) fill some gaps and enable greater flexibility for both WOL and power management by providing peer-to-peer capabilities, where peer systems harvest MAC addresses and send WOL magic packets based on ConfigMgr and other events.

Configuring Power Management

After enabling power management, discussed in the "Understanding Client Settings" section, configure its settings at the collection level. Follow these steps:

1. Navigate to **Assets and Compliance -> Device Collections**. Select the collection and choose **Properties**.

2. On the Power Management tab, select the **Specify power management settings for this collection** radio button.

Indicate peak hours by specifying the start and end times of the peak hours time frame. You can then specify the power plan to use during and outside specified peak hours. Select a plan by choosing it from a list. The following plans are available by default:

▶ Customized Peak (ConfigMgr)

▶ Customized Non-peak (ConfigMgr)

▶ Balanced (ConfigMgr)

▶ High Performance (ConfigMgr)

▶ Power Saver (ConfigMgr)

Select **View** to open the power plan's properties. Selecting the Customized Peak (ConfigMgr) or Customized Non-peak (ConfigMgr) power plan changes this option to Edit, allowing you to modify that plan, as shown in Figure 9.14, or create a plan by providing a new name and description. Power plan settings can be set for when a device is on battery or plugged in.

You can enable the option Wakeup time (desktop computers) and specify a time when a desktop computer will wake from sleep or hibernation to install software or updates.

Click **Browse** to copy power plan settings from a collection and then select a device collection from the Select Collection dialog.

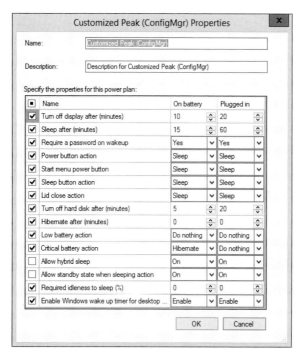

FIGURE 9.14   Customized Peak (ConfigMgr) Properties.

When a device is a member of a collection where the power management option Never apply power management settings to computers in this collection is set, the computer does not apply power management settings even if it belongs to another collection with power settings. If it belongs to multiple collections with power settings configured, the least restrictive value is the effective value. Wake up is the time closest to midnight. Configuring power settings using a GPO overrides ConfigMgr settings.

Many reports analyze power consumption and check applied power settings. See https://docs.microsoft.com/sccm/core/clients/manage/power/monitor-and-plan-for-power-management for more information.

Summary

This chapter discussed importing ConfigMgr clients by using discovery methods or a manual process. It discussed client requirements to install the ConfigMgr client agent, as well as the different ways to install the agent. When ConfigMgr is installed in an Active Directory environment, you can use discovery methods to find clients that need the agent. Once the client is installed, it must assign itself to a ConfigMgr site and stay healthy.

The chapter discussed using different client device and user settings, allowing you to granularly define those settings. It discussed managing the client, leveraging WOL using ConfigMgr to wake up clients, and configuring power plans to control the power settings configuration on ConfigMgr client agents.

CHAPTER 10

Managing Compliance

Microsoft introduced compliance settings functionality to System Center Configuration Manager (ConfigMgr) with ConfigMgr 2007, at which point it was called Desired Configuration Management (DCM). ConfigMgr 2012 added some new functions and changed the name to Compliance Settings. ConfigMgr Current Branch improves the Compliance Settings feature set with an improved workflow to create configuration items, showing only settings relevant to the platform you choose, and adds new configuration items for Windows 10, Mac OS X, and Windows desktop and server systems with an installed ConfigMgr client. Current Branch also includes updated support for devices (Windows 8.1, 10, Phone, iOS, Mac OS X, Android, and Samsung Knox) managed without the ConfigMgr client through Microsoft Intune.

Compliance Settings provides the capability to manage the configuration and compliance of devices in a single pane of glass. This ConfigMgr component allows you to define, monitor, enforce, remediate, and report configuration compliance, as well as handle the following four factors that all information technology (IT) organizations must deal with:

▶ **Regulatory Compliance:** Given the impact of regulatory laws in the United States that cover privacy and corporate responsibility, regulatory compliance is a key scenario for many IT organizations. Examples include the Sarbanes-Oxley (SOX) Act of 2002, the Gramm-Leach-Bliley Act (GLBA), and the Health Insurance Portability and Accountability Act (HIPAA).

These regulations require IT organizations to set specific security and privacy standards for corporate and user data, along with IT systems. The difficult part for IT is trying to enforce and report on the enforcement of these standards. Most organizations have no way to enforce these policies and rely on custom scripts or tools to provide on-demand results. As these laws are not technical in nature, the technical requirements to fulfill the standards become subject to interpretation and vary between organizations: SOX for you is not necessarily SOX for someone else.

Even if your organization is not subject to specific regulatory compliance laws, it should still be subject to internal policies and standards. Validating your infrastructure's compliance against internal governance is the same as validating it against government standards.

▶ **Pre- and Post-Change Verification:** An organization must verify the configuration of a system before and after planned changes are made. It is generally useful to verify that you are only applying changes to systems in a specific state, that the planned changes occurred, and that unintended changes did not take place.

▶ **Configuration Drift:** Configuration drift starts the moment a system goes into production and is difficult to control. No matter how set in stone your build process is, systems begin to drift from the standard as soon as multiple administrators or users log in to a system to install applications, troubleshoot issues, or tweak performance. Drift for a particular system is unpredictable and, over time, has the potential to cause technical issues.

▶ **Time to Resolution:** An overwhelming number of problems are due to human error. These problems ultimately become the dreaded problem tickets that every on-call administrator loathes, particularly when they occur in the middle of the night. Stopping human error is all but impossible; however, identifying human error quickly so it can be resolved is key to reducing the impact of such errors.

Settings management does not instantly fix these issues, but it helps in managing them and reducing the amount of time spent trying to achieve compliance. It also allows you to incorporate the issues into your current set of processes.

This chapter covers settings management, including compliance settings, client configuration for compliance settings, configuration items, how to create items and baselines, strategies for compliance, and troubleshooting when things go wrong.

Configuring Compliance Settings

Compliance Settings differs from other ConfigMgr features in that you do not configure it; you simply enable or disable it. There are two areas to configure: enabling or disabling user data and profiles and scheduling compliance evaluation. These are all client-based settings, located in the ConfigMgr console under **Administration -> Client Settings -> Default Settings**; look for the Compliance Settings section, displayed in Figure 10.1. The settings follow:

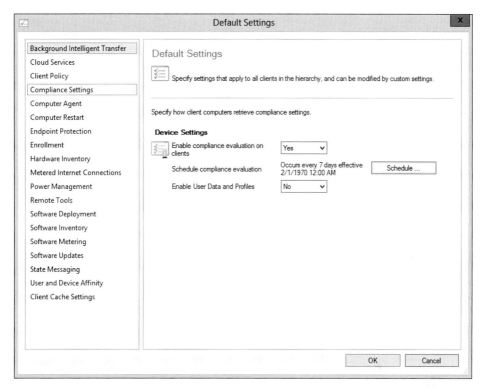

FIGURE 10.1   Client Compliance Settings.

▶ **Enable Compliance Evaluation:** Choose Yes to enable or No from the dropdown menu to disable compliance evaluation on the client.

▶ **Schedule Compliance Evaluation:** Choose a simple or a custom schedule. Use a simple schedule to set how often the compliance evaluation runs, in days, hours, and minutes. A custom schedule lets you choose down to the day, hour, and minute when a compliance evaluation runs on the client.

▶ **Enable User Data and Profiles:** Choose Yes or No. User data and profiles configuration items contain settings that allow you to manage folder redirection, offline files, and roaming profiles on Windows 8, 8.1, 10, Server 2012 R2, and Server 2016 clients.

NOTE: CHOOSING A SIMPLE OR COMPLEX SCHEDULE

With a simple schedule, the ConfigMgr client uses its installation date and a random off-set built into the code to determine when the evaluation will run; this minimizes the load so all clients do not return results at the same time.

A custom schedule provides more flexibility in choosing a specific time for the clients to run the evaluation. All clients run the evaluation at the same time, according to the time zone they are in. This may cause network congestion across slower links.

10

The only prerequisite for Compliance Settings is that the ConfigMgr client must be installed on the machine. Compliance settings evaluation is completed by the compliance and settings management component on the client, which is installed during ConfigMgr client installation. It is then enabled on the client when the Enable compliance evaluation on clients setting shown in Figure 10.1 is set to **Yes**.

Understanding Compliance Settings

Four types of objects comprise the compliance settings the client evaluates:

▶ **Configuration Items:** These settings, values, and criteria are compared, checked, evaluated, and possibly remediated on the clients.

▶ **Configuration Baselines:** These collections of items are put together in a group called a *baseline*, and the baseline is sent to the client for evaluation. Items cannot be evaluated until they are part of a baseline.

▶ **User Data and Profiles:** These can manage folder redirection, offline settings, and roaming profiles for clients running Windows 8 and above.

▶ **Remote Connection Profiles:** You use profiles to set up connections for devices to remotely connect to your corporate network. See https://docs.microsoft.com/sccm/compliance/deploy-use/create-remote-connection-profiles for in-depth information.

Each organization's needs and wants around settings management vary, which is why Microsoft created and continues to tune this component so that it can handle many different situations users may need to evaluate or check on.

Using Configuration Items

At the heart of settings management are configuration items (CIs). CIs are the rules and settings you create for evaluation on a client system. CIs are very flexible, depending on the type of device to which they are sent. Windows-based PCs with the ConfigMgr client have the most options. With the explosion of devices in the workplace, Microsoft has updated CIs to handle a greater variety of devices with and without the ConfigMgr client installed on them. Table 10.1 shows the devices and the types of settings available with each device.

TABLE 10.1   Devices and Settings

Device	Settings
Windows PCs with the ConfigMgr client	Creating custom CIs ranging from Registry values to Windows Management Instrumentation (WMI) queries, file versions, AD attributes, and so on
Microsoft Intune-enrolled devices (Windows PCs, iOS, Android, Windows Phone, Macs without ConfigMgr client)	Settings from a predefined list only
Macs with ConfigMgr client	Creating custom CIs to evaluate Mac OS X property lists and results that would be returned by a script

Microsoft Intune allows you to greatly enhance the number of devices you can support with settings management. Information on Microsoft Intune is available at https://www.microsoft.com/cloud-platform/microsoft-intune.

TIP: MICROSOFT INTUNE TRIAL

Because using Intune is an additional cost, the authors recommend researching it and conducting a 30-day trial to evaluate the service. This can help you understand what Intune can provide and whether your use would justify its cost. Information about getting started with a free 30-day evaluation is available at https://docs.microsoft.com/intune/understand-explore/get-started-with-a-30-day-trial-of-microsoft-intune.

A CI is a container that holds objects added to it for use in evaluations. The objects you add depend on what you want to evaluate; however, the following objects are always in a CI:

▶ **Detection Method Information (for Windows CIs Containing Application Settings Only):** Lets you determine where an application is installed on the client by detecting the Windows installer file for the application, using a custom script, or allowing you to specify that the application is always installed on the client.

▶ **Settings:** Used for compliance checking. Some settings are predefined, depending on the device selected for compliance settings. A setting for Windows Phone could be the setting for password expiration. For a Windows system with the ConfigMgr client, an example might be the value of a Registry key or results of a Windows Query Language (WQL) query.

▶ **Compliance Rules:** Lets you determine whether the setting meets compliance. Using the example in the previous bullet of settings with a Registry key, the compliance rule could be whether the Registry key exists on the client; if so, the client is compliant, and if not, the client is noncompliant.

▶ **Supported Platforms:** Specifies the operating systems (OSs) for the devices to which you are allowed to send the CIs for evaluation. If the client is running an unsupported OS and receives the CIs, it does not evaluate them for compliance and returns a `requirements not met` status message.

You can create a child CI if you need to make the properties of a CI more restrictive or different in some way but want to maintain a relationship with the original CI. A child CI inherits the properties of its parent. You cannot change those properties, but you can add new information to the child CI. Create a child CI by right-clicking an existing CI and selecting **Create child configuration item**.

Using Configuration Baselines

A large hierarchy may have hundreds of CIs to track many different things on clients. A configuration baseline is the organization of these CIs into a logical group that makes sense for your organization. A baseline can include an unlimited number of CIs and even other baselines.

10

Baselines can contain software updates, which are not defined as CIs for the purpose of adding them to baselines. You can add a software update by selecting it when creating a baseline. When the client evaluates the baseline, the software update is evaluated and then installed or not installed. Consider an example of a hierarchy that receives updates in a variety of ways: via ConfigMgr, Windows Server Update Services (WSUS), and the Internet. One way to determine if a software update is installed on all your systems is by creating a configuration baseline that contains the software update and having clients evaluate the baseline.

As with CIs, there may be times when you have created so many baselines that you need to filter them. ConfigMgr's built-in filtering and search capabilities inside the console can help limit the baselines shown or can help find a particular baseline of interest. Following are some criteria specific to filtering configuration baselines:

▶ **Revision:** Indicates the highest revision number of the configuration baseline. Editing a baseline increments the revision number, which can become lost in environments with many changes. Use the revision number to confirm that you are using the correct version.

▶ **Compliance Count:** Counts the systems reporting being compliant with the settings in the baseline. Choose the operator that fits best to return the correct results you need.

▶ **Noncompliance Count:** Counts the systems reporting being noncompliant with the settings in the baseline. Choose the operator that fits best to return the correct results you need.

▶ **Failure Count:** Counts the systems reporting failures while running or trying to run the evaluation on the baseline. Again, choose the operator that fits best to return the correct results you need.

▶ **Categories:** Allows you to search by category in that baseline.

▶ **Relationships:** If configuration baselines are nested inside one another, relationships can help you find those nested baselines. This is good for troubleshooting baselines nested inside each other.

When your configuration baseline is built with all the items added to it, you are ready to deploy that baseline to a collection of clients. You cannot directly deploy CIs to clients; they must be assigned to a configuration baseline to be deployed.

Use the ConfigMgr console to import and export configuration baselines. If someone has created a baseline with CIs and posted it to the Internet, you can download that baseline and import it into your console for testing. Make sure to import these baselines only into your lab until they are thoroughly tested and verified as safe for your production environment.

NOTE: VULNERABILITY ASSESSMENT

The Configuration Manager Vulnerability Assessment configuration pack contains several baselines for Windows operating systems, SQL Server, and Internet Information Services (IIS), which you can import into your ConfigMgr console for testing. Find the download of this configuration pack at https://www.microsoft.com/download/details.aspx?id=51948.

Using User Data and Profiles

User data and profiles can help with configuring some user settings. This settings management component is rarely used, as these settings typically are set by Active Directory (AD) group policy objects (GPOs), which provide more granularity.

You might want to use these settings with a virtual desktop infrastructure (VDI) environment. Use user data and profiles to control the following settings:

▶ **Folder Redirection:** You can change where files are stored for the desktop, start menu, documents, music, videos, favorites, contacts, downloads, links, searches, saved games, application data, and pictures. You can redirect these folders to remote or local devices. With remote, you can choose a specified folder or use the user's home folder.

▶ **Offline Files:** You can enable or disable the use of offline files. If enabling, you can set the background synchronization and whether to use metered network connections. You can also enable slow links and set the latency threshold and synchronization interval.

▶ **Roaming Profiles:** You can specify redirection of the entire user's profile to a file share. This occurs at user login and synchronizes all changes to the profile at logoff. Options include excluding folders from roaming profiles, managing slow links and network settings, and managing access settings.

User data and profile settings deal with user settings and thus can only be deployed to a collection of users. The target systems for these users must be Windows 8.x and above. Use any or all of these settings for the best experience for your users.

Using Remote Connection Profiles

The Remote Connection Profiles feature allows users to remotely connect to work computers when not connected to the corporate domain or when their personal computers are connected over the Internet. Use profiles to deploy Remote Desktop Connection settings to users in device collections. Users can then use the company portal to access their primary work computers through Remote Desktop, utilizing the Remote Desktop Connection settings provided by the portal. Windows Intune is required to use the company portal. If the company portal is not available, users can still use remote connection profile information to connect to work computers with a remote desktop connection over a virtual private network (VPN) connection.

> **NOTE: GPO OVERRIDES CONFIGMGR SETTINGS**
>
> Settings from remote connection profiles created with ConfigMgr are stored in the policy of the local machine. These settings can override remote desktop settings configured by other applications. However, Windows GPOs used to set remote desktop settings override the ConfigMgr settings. Understanding this precedence is important to ensure that conflicts do not arise.

10

The following devices can be used to access a work computer:

▶ Computers running Windows 7 and above; if using the company portal, Windows 8.1 and above

▶ Devices running iOS

▶ Devices running Android

A Windows Intune subscription along with the service connection point (SCP) is required to use iOS and Android devices.

Remote connection profiles have several prerequisites that are both internal ConfigMgr dependencies and external dependencies:

▶ **Remote Desktop (RD) Gateway Server:** A connection to an RD gateway server must be in place for users outside the company network to connect to work computers.

▶ **Firewall Settings:** Any host-based firewall system must be configured to allow the Mstsc.exe program through it.

▶ **Service Connection Point:** ConfigMgr must have a configured connection to Microsoft Intune.

▶ **User Device Affinity:** For a user to connect to a work computer, that computer must be a primary device of the user who is trying to connect.

▶ **Compliance Settings Manager Role:** If using role-based management in the ConfigMgr console, the user creating the remote connection profiles must be assigned the compliance settings manager security role.

When remote connection profiles are first deployed to a client system and evaluated, the Remote PC Connect local security group is created on that machine. This security group is populated with the primary users of the computer to which the profile is deployed. Members of the local administrators group can add or remove users to the group; however, when the ConfigMgr client next evaluates the remote connection profile (by default every seven days on a simple schedule), it removes any users that are not primary users of the machine and adds any users previously removed that are primary users of the machine, as defined by ConfigMgr.

If the device affinity relationship between a user and the device changes, ConfigMgr disables the remote connection profile and Windows Firewall settings to prevent connecting to the computer.

Creating Configuration Items

As stated in the previous section, CIs are the settings, values, and criteria that are compared, checked, evaluated, and possibly remediated on client systems. CIs are added to a baseline and then deployed to a collection of clients. The ConfigMgr console is used to create these CIs. To view, edit, or create CIs, navigate to **Assets and Compliance -> Compliance Settings -> Configuration Items**. Create a new CI by selecting **Create Configuration Item** from the ribbon bar or from the right-click context menu to start the Create Configuration Item Wizard. Figure 10.2 shows the default state of the CI in the wizard.

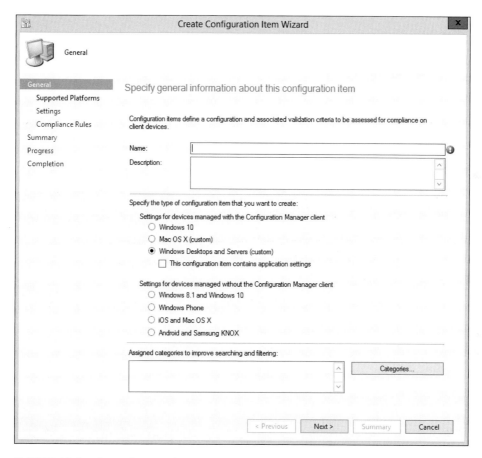

FIGURE 10.2   General page of the Create Configuration Item Wizard.

The pages of the wizard differ depending on the type of CI you are creating; however, the General page is the same for all types. Provide a name that describes what the CI is about and optionally add a description. If there are many CIs, it is easier to find the correct one if the name is descriptive. Then choose between the following types of CIs:

▶ **Settings for Devices Managed with the ConfigMgr Client:** This type of system has an installed ConfigMgr client—typically desktops and server type operating systems. There are several different types:

  ▶ **Windows 10:** This option allows you to leverage the mobility features built in to Windows 10. It does not provide the full set of options you find for Windows workstations and servers.

  ▶ **Mac OS X (Custom):** Use this option to check compliance with Mac OS X preferences for an application or to run a custom shell script on a Mac.

10

▶ **Windows Desktops and Servers (Custom):** The most used option to create a CI, this is for Windows 7, 8.x, and 10, and Server 2008 R2, 2012 R2, and 2016.

▶ **This Configuration Item Contains Application Settings:** This check box that goes with the Windows Desktops and Servers option lets you check settings for an application using the product code.

▶ **Settings for Devices Managed Without the ConfigMgr Client:** For these mobile systems, such as iPads, phones, tablets, and so on, you can access the mobility settings on the devices using Microsoft Intune.

▶ **Windows 8.1 and Windows 10:** Use this option for tablets running Windows 8.1 and 10; it allows you to check mobility settings for these tablets.

▶ **Windows Phone:** This option is for Windows Phone versions 8.0 and 8.1.

▶ **iOS and Mac OS X:** Use this option to access the settings for any of the iOS devices, such as an iPad or iPhone, as well as Mac OS X mobility profiles.

▶ **Android and Samsung Knox:** This option is for mobility settings for Android tablets and phones and the Samsung Knox family of devices.

Devices with a ConfigMgr Client

Installing a ConfigMgr client on a device provides the most flexibility in terms of the options you can choose and the CIs you can create. While all the devices have some similar items, there are also very different items to use with settings management.

Windows 10 Configuration Items

You can create CIs based on the mobility features built in to Windows 10, but you cannot use the full feature set of settings management for Windows 10 desktops or laptops.

REAL WORLD: USING GPOS WITH WINDOWS 10 INSTEAD OF CIS

CIs allow you to configure many settings for Windows 10. With the ability to create custom CIs using scripts, you might think that you can configure all Windows 10 settings using CIs. However, the authors recommend considering using GPOs for some of the settings. An example would be setting the option for Windows 10 to defer upgrades. While you could set this with a CI, a much easier and better approach is to use a GPO and, if needed, use a CI to monitor the setting and report on noncompliance.

Use the Supported Platforms section of the Create Configuration Item Wizard to choose Windows 10 64-bit, 32-bit, or both operating systems. The Device Settings page of the wizard displays next; Figure 10.3 shows the available options.

Each option you select creates a new menu item in the Create Configuration Item Wizard. Each item has several different settings; for in-depth information on these settings, see https://docs.microsoft.com/sccm/compliance/deploy-use/create-configuration-items-for-windows-10-devices-managed-with-the-client#windows-10-configuration-item-settings-reference.

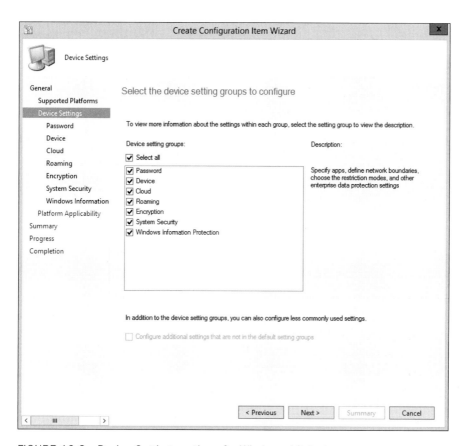

FIGURE 10.3   Device Settings options for Windows 10 devices.

The last option listed in Figure 10.3 is Windows Information Protection (WIP), formally known as Enterprise Data Protection. WIP includes new settings found only on Windows 10 version 1607 and above and Windows 10 Mobile. WIP settings help combat accidental data leakage, which occurs when employees send corporate data from personal email accounts or save corporate documents out to a public cloud; basically, this is when corporate-owned data is transmitted on networks outside the corporate enterprise network. WIP provides the following benefits:

▶ Separation between personal and corporate data, without requiring employees to switch environments or apps

▶ Additional data protection for existing line-of-business apps without a need to update the apps

▶ Ability to wipe corporate data from devices while leaving personal data untouched

▶ Audit reports for tracking issues and remedial actions

▶ Integration with your existing management system (Microsoft Intune and ConfigMgr Current Branch)

Figure 10.4 shows the many properties that you can set for WIP:

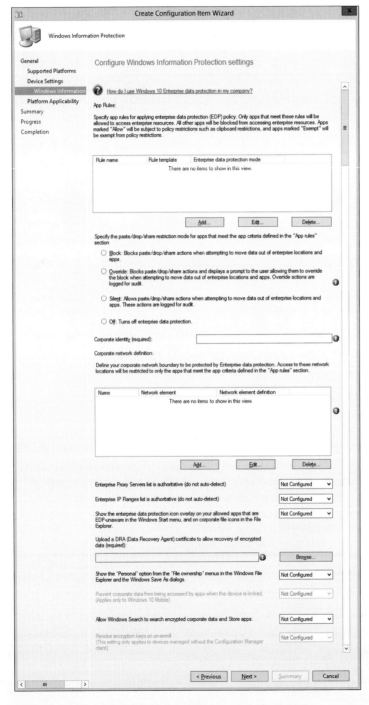

FIGURE 10.4   Windows Information Protection properties.

▶ **App Rules:** Use this section of the wizard page to create rules that set the enterprise data protection mode for an application. You can set a rule to allow protection for the application or make it exempt. You can use wildcards for the product name, binary name, or version.

▶ **Paste/Drop/Share Restriction Mode:** Set the mode you want enforced for apps that meet the criteria previously defined in the App Rules section. There are four modes to choose from:

  ▶ **Block:** When inappropriate data sharing is found, the employee is blocked from completing the action.

  ▶ **Override:** Blocks inappropriate data sharing but allows the user to override the block and share the data. If a user chooses to override the block, the action is logged into the audit log.

  ▶ **Silent:** Runs in the background and logs inappropriate actions in the audit log.

  ▶ **Off:** Turns off the restriction mode and does not protect your data or log any information in the audit logs.

▶ **Corporate Identity (Required):** Use this field to define your domain or domains. If you have multiple domains, the first one defined is considered your corporate identity and the others as being owned by the first one. Use a | as a separator between domains.

▶ **Corporate Network Definition:** Use this box to define the network boundaries for WIP to protect. You can define boundaries in several ways:

  ▶ Enterprise cloud resources

  ▶ Enterprise network domain names

  ▶ Enterprise proxy servers

  ▶ Enterprise internal proxy servers

  ▶ Enterprise IPv4 ranges

  ▶ Enterprise IPv6 ranges

  ▶ Neutral resources

▶ **Enterprise Proxy Servers List Is Authoritative (Do Not Auto-Detect):** Use this dropdown to treat the list of proxy servers defined in the corporate network definition box as the complete list of proxy servers. If not configured, Windows searches the immediate network for additional servers.

▶ **Enterprise IP Ranges List Is Authoritative (Do Not Auto-Detect):** Use this dropdown to treat the list of IP ranges in the corporate network definition box as the complete list of ranges. If not configured, Windows searches for additional IP ranges on any domain-joined devices connected to your network.

10

▶ **Show the WIP Icon Overlay on Your Allowed Apps That Are WIP-Unaware in the Windows Start Menu and on Corporate File Icons in the File Explorer:** Use this dropdown to overlay an icon on the corporate files or Start menu so the user knows that they are not WIP-aware applications or files.

▶ **Upload a Data Recovery Agent (DRA) Certificate to Allow Recovery of Encrypted Data (Required):** Once your WIP policy is deployed to clients, Windows begins encrypting corporate data on the local device. If the local encryption keys are lost or revoked, the data is unrecoverable. Use this option to include a public key for encrypting the data while you hold the private key in case it is needed for decryption.

▶ **Show the Personal Option in the "File Ownership" Menus in the Windows File Explorer and the Windows Save As Dialogs:** Use this dropdown to allow a user to choose whether a file is for personal or work use when it is saved. Not Configured is the same as Yes. Selecting No turns off the setting and does not provide the user with an option to save the file as personal.

▶ **Prevent Corporate Data from Being Accessed by Apps When the Device Is Locked (Applies Only to Windows 10 Mobile):** Use this option to add a PIN code on a Windows 10 mobile locked device that protects the key used to encrypt the enterprise data on the device. Yes turns this on, and No or Not Configured turns it off.

▶ **Allow Windows Search to Search Encrypted Corporate Data and Store Apps:** Use this option to toggle the ability for Windows Search to index encrypted data and Windows Store apps. Yes turns this on, and No or Not Configured turns it off.

▶ **Revoke Encryption Keys on Un-enroll:** This option allows you to revoke the user's local encryption keys from the device when it is removed from WIP. When the keys are revoked, the user cannot access that data. Yes is the same as Not Configured and turns on the process of revoking the keys.

Mac OS X (Custom) Configuration Items

You can manage settings for devices running version 10.9 through 10.11 of Mac OS X. Mac OS X uses a property list (plist) to store settings for applications, much as Windows uses the Registry to store settings. Apple developers explain that property lists organize data into named values and lists of values, using several object types. These types provide the means to produce data that is meaningfully structured, transportable, storable, and accessible—and also as efficient as possible. ConfigMgr compliance settings allow you to look at the plist and confirm that existing values are set correctly; if a value is not correct, a remediation script can be launched to set a property to its correct value. You can also run a shell script that returns a value to evaluate and remediate, if necessary.

Selecting Mac OS X (custom) on the General tab opens the Supported Platforms page, where you have the option to select what version of the OS applies to this CI. You next are presented with the Settings page, which is blank by default. Click **New** to add a setting. Figure 10.5 shows the page that appears, which includes the following settings:

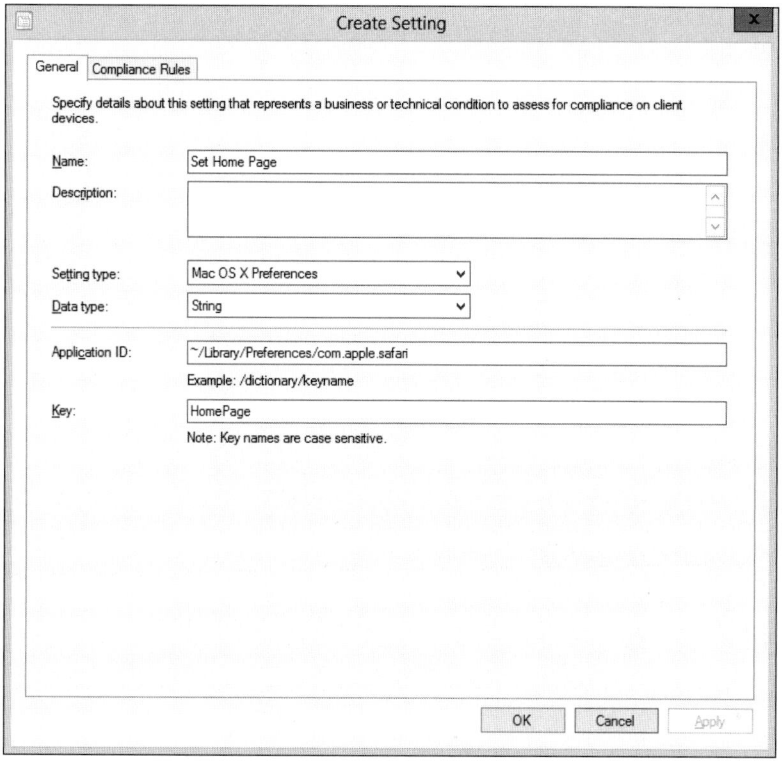

FIGURE 10.5   Create Setting page.

▶ **Name:** (Required) Provide a meaningful name so when you are reviewing the results, you know from the name what the setting is for.

▶ **Description:** Explain the setting in detail.

▶ **Setting Type:** (Required) The dropdown has two options to choose from:

   ▶ **Mac OS X Preferences:** Set the keys within property lists for an application.

   ▶ **Script:** Use this to run a script. Choosing this option changes the bottom part of the page so that it offers two options:

      ▶ **Discovery Script:** (Required) This shell script is used to find and return the value of a setting you want to view. This usually occurs in two steps: Find the current user and store in a variable for later use and then gather the current setting of the value that you want to change.

      ▶ **Remediation Script:** Once the values are compared and a machine is determined to be noncompliant, the remediation script can be run to fix the value and return the machine to compliance. This is a shell script.

▶ **Data Type:** (Required) Identify the type of data for the value you want to compare. The dropdown menu choices are as follows:

    ▶ String

    ▶ Date and time

    ▶ Integer

    ▶ Floating point

    ▶ Boolean

▶ **Application ID:** (Required) Points to the location of the plist file to use.

▶ **Key:** (Required) The name of the item holding the value you will check for.

CAUTION: THE KEY IS CASE-SENSITIVE

The key name in Figure 10.5 is case-sensitive. If it is not exactly the same key as in the plist file on the Mac client, it is not evaluated. You cannot edit the key after it is created. If you need to change the key, delete this compliance setting and create a new one.

The Compliance Rules tab defines the conditions used to determine compliance or noncompliance. Click **New** to open the Create Rule page, which allows you to create a rule to define your conditions. Figure 10.6 shows the Create Rules page, which offers the following settings:

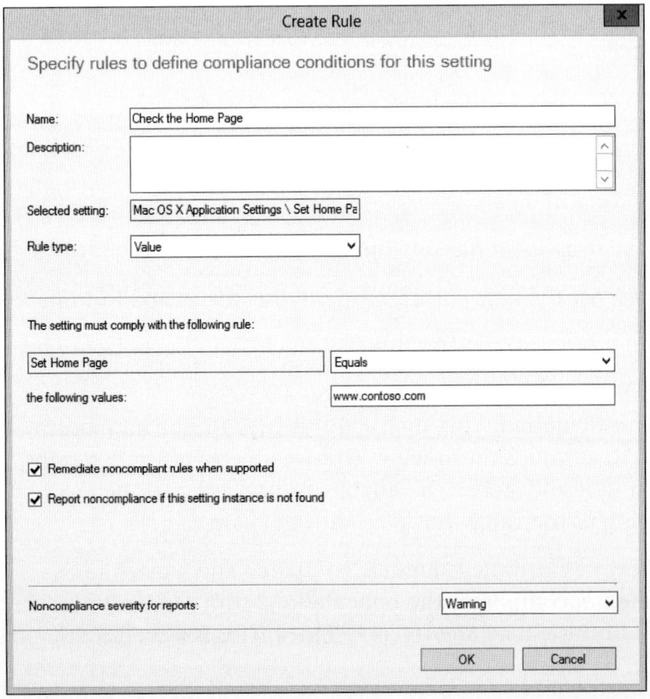

FIGURE 10.6   Mac Create Rule page.

▶ **Name:** Name the condition rule you are creating. Make it meaningful.

▶ **Description:** Explain what the condition rule is for.

▶ **Selected Setting:** Automatically filled out, based on the values in the General page.

▶ **Rule Type:** Define the type of rule. You have two choices:

  ▶ **Value:** Sets up the rule to compare the value returned by the CI or script against a value you specify.

  ▶ **Existential:** Creates a rule that evaluates the setting, depending on whether it exists on the device. Choose one of two comparison settings:

    ▶ The setting must exist on client devices

    ▶ The setting must not exist on client devices

▶ **The Setting Must Comply with the Following Rule:** Set the operator you want to use for the comparison.

▶ **The Following Values:** Enter the value to use for comparison.

▶ **Remediate Noncompliant Rules When Supported:** Turn on or off remediation of the value if the rule determines that the value is noncompliant.

▶ **Report Noncompliance if This Setting Instance Is Not Found:** Check to tell the compliance setting engine to return a value of noncompliance if the value is not found on the device.

▶ **Noncompliance Severity for Reports:** Choose the type of error code returned if the CI is determined noncompliant:

  ▶ None

  ▶ Information

  ▶ Warning

  ▶ Critical

  ▶ Critical with event

The Compliance Rules tab allows you to create new rules, edit rules, and delete rules. If you created a rule as part of the Settings page, it shows up in this page.

The next page is the Summary page. Once you verify that everything looks correct, the last pages are the Progress and Completion pages.

Windows Desktops and Servers (Custom) Configuration Items

This choice applies to Windows desktop and server systems only. An additional option appears on the General page: This configuration item contains application settings. Choosing this option adds a Detection Methods page to the wizard and specifies that this configuration item is an application CI.

Detection Methods   A detection method in ConfigMgr contains rules that detect whether an application is installed on a computer. Use this page to specify the criteria to detect the application this CI targets. This detection occurs before the CI is assessed for compliance. If the application does not exist, the client does not evaluate the CI. There are four possible detection methods:

▶ **Always Assume Application Is Installed:** When this option is selected, the client assumes that the application is installed and does not check for the application.

▶ **Use Windows Installer Detection:** You can select to use information inside an MSI file known as the globally unique identifier (GUID) and version number for the application. To obtain this information, click **Open** and select the MSI file for the application to automatically populate the fields.

REAL WORLD: USING ORCA FOR THE GUID

Depending on how an MSI application was created, it may be difficult to get the product ID. The authors recommend using the Orca program to get this information. Orca is an MSI table editing tool you can use to view information in an MSI file and even change information as needed. For more information about Orca and where to download it, see https://www.geekshangout.com/customising-an-msi-install-using-orca/.

▶ **This Application Is Installed for One or More Users:** Select this check box to detect each user profile on the computer. Use when multiple users using the same computer have installed the same application.

NOTE: MANUALLY DETERMINING A PRODUCT'S GUID

Most applications are installed using an MSI file, which may be wrapped within an executable file. During installation, the MSI is extracted from the executable to a temporary folder and installed from there. An easy method to determine the application's GUID and version if the MSI is hidden in this way is to use the WMI Console (WMIC) after the application is installed on a machine. WMIC, which is part of every Windows installation, is invoked from the command line. Following is an example of a WMIC command line to return the GUID, name, and version of the ConfigMgr client:

```
wmic product where "name like '%Configuration Manager Client%'" get Name,
IdentifyingNumber, version
```

▶ **Detect a Specific Application and Deployment Type:** Use this option to select a previously created application. Clicking **Select** brings up a list of applications and allows you to select the application and deployment type (DT) to use.

▶ **Use a Custom Script to Detect This Application:** Choose between a Windows PowerShell, VBScript, or JScript script to detect the application installed on the machine. A sample PowerShell script to detect if the ConfigMgr console is installed follows:

```
Get-WmiObject -Class Win32_Product | Sort-object Name | select Name | where
{ $_.Name -match "Configuration Manager Console"}
```

NOTE: USING A CUSTOM SCRIPT

When using an application detection script in compliance settings, the detection is considered successful if anything is sent to the standard output, StdOut. When writing your script, make sure to output something only if the application is detected. It does not matter what the output is, as long as there is output. No output means the application was not detected.

Figure 10.7 shows the Detection Methods page with some sample information.

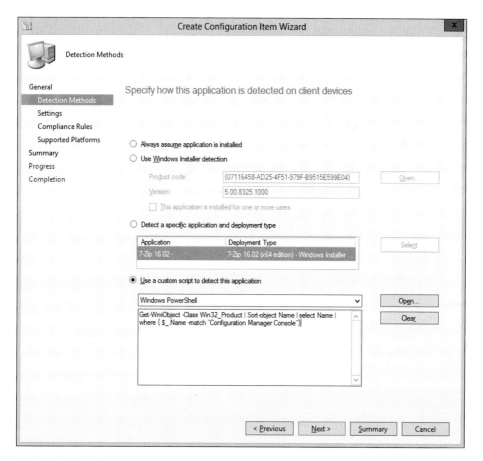

FIGURE 10.7   Detection Methods page.

Settings Evaluating device compliance requires a left and right-hand side of the equation. If the two sides are equal, you have compliance. Settings are the conditions found on the left side. By default, the Settings page is blank when a new CI is created. Click **New** to start creating a setting and then set the following options:

▶ **Name:** Specify the name of the setting you are creating.

▶ **Description:** Explain in detail what the setting is for.

▶ **Setting Type:** Choose from a dropdown menu the type of setting you want to use in the condition statement.

    ▶ **Active Direction Query:** Create an AD query, using the following parameters:

        ▶ **LDAP Prefix:** The prefix to use for your AD query, which would be either LDAP:// or GC:// for a global catalog search.

        ▶ **Distinguish Name (DN):** The DN of the object you want to query. This is the full DN of the object you want to use. An example would be OU=Unleashed, DC=Odyssey, DC=com.

        ▶ **Search Filter:** Specify an additional filter to refine results from the Active Directory Directory Services (ADDS) query. To return all results from the query, enter (objectclass=*). More information about search filters is available at https://msdn.microsoft.com/library/aa746475(v=vs.85).aspx.

        ▶ **Search Scope:** Choose the scope of your search:

            ▶ **Base:** Queries only the specified object. In the example using the DN item in a previous bullet, this queries the Unleashed OU and nothing below it.

            ▶ **One Level:** Not used in ConfigMgr.

            ▶ **Subtree:** Queries the object you specified and anything below it. In the previous example using the DN item, this queries the Unleashed OU and any OU under it.

        ▶ **Property:** Use to define the property of the object you want to query; an example would be pwdLastSet. Find a list of properties at https://msdn.microsoft.com/library/ms675090(v=vs.85).aspx.

        ▶ **Query:** Automatically filled in from the previous items. For the example in this section, the query would read LDAP://OU=Unleashed, DC=Odyssey, DC=com;(objectclass=*);pwdLastSet.

    ▶ **Assembly:** This is a piece of code that can be shared between applications. An assembly has the filename extension .dll or .exe. The global assembly cache (GAC) is a folder named %*systemroot*%\Assembly on client computers, where all shared assemblies are stored.

    Use **Assembly name** to enter the name of the assembly for which you want to search. The name cannot be the same as other assembly objects of the same type and must be registered in the GAC. The name can be up to 256 characters long. An example would be Microsoft.VisualBasic.

▶ **File System:** Allows you to set a file or folder to be used for compliance.

  ▶ **Type:** Choose either File or Folder for this option.

  ▶ **Path:** Define the full path to the location where the file or folder is located. You can use environment variables. Be aware that if you use the *%USERPROFILE%* variable, all user profiles on the machine are searched, which may result in multiple instances of the file or folder being found. UNC paths are not supported.

  ▶ **File or Folder Name:** You can use environment variables and the wildcards * and ? for the file or folder name. Note that using wildcards can cause high resource usage on the client machine.

  ▶ **Include Subfolders:** Enables the search of subfolders under the path destination.

  ▶ **This File or Folder Is Associated with a 64-Bit Application:** If this option is checked, only 64-bit locations like *%ProgramFiles%* are searched on 64-bit systems. If it is unchecked, both 64-bit and 32-bit locations are searched.

▶ **IIS Metabase:** Use to query settings in the IIS metabase and check for compliance. This requires that the IIS 6 metabase compatibility feature be installed.

  ▶ **Metabase Path:** Define the path to the metabase. An example is /LM/ W3SVC/1/ROOT.

  ▶ **Property ID:** IIS metabase properties are identified by numbers. An example is 3001, which would be the property ID of the path of the website, c:\inetpub\wwwroot.

TIP: EXPLORING THE IIS METABASE

You can use the IIS 6.0 Resource Kit to navigate and explore the IIS metabase. By using this kit, you can find the property ID and its data type; you can also find the path of the metabase. Download the resource kit from https://www.microsoft.com/download/ details.aspx?id=17275.

▶ **Registry Key:** Check to see if a certain Registry key exists on devices.

  ▶ **Hive Name:** You can use this dropdown to manually choose a hive, or you can select **Browse** to browse the Registry, looking for the hive and key you want to use for compliance. The following are the hive names:

```
HKEY_CLASSES_ROOT
HKEY_CURRENT_CONFIG
HKEY_CURRENT_USER
HKEY_LOCAL_MACHINE
HKEY_USERS
```

  ▶ **Key Name:** Manually enter the path to the Registry key you want to use for compliance. If you selected Browse, this may already be filled in.

10

▶ **This Registry Value Is Associated with a 64-Bit Application:** Specifies whether to search the 64-bit Registry keys in addition to 32-bit Registry keys when clients are running a 64-bit OS. If the same key exists on both 64-bit and 32-bit Registry hives, both keys are returned.

▶ **Registry Value:** Check to see if a certain value in the Registry exists.

   ▶ **Hive Name:** Choose hives from a dropdown menu. Use the dropdown to manually choose the hive or click **Browse** to browse the Registry, looking for the hive and key you want to use for compliance. The following are the hive names:

```
HKEY_CLASSES_ROOT
HKEY_CURRENT_CONFIG
HKEY_CURRENT_USER
HKEY_LOCAL_MACHINE
HKEY_USERS
```

   ▶ **Key Name:** Specify the path to the Registry key you want to use for compliance. If you selected Browse, this may already be filled in.

   ▶ **Value Name:** Specify the Registry key value you want to use for compliance. If you selected Browse, this may already be filled in.

   ▶ **This Registry Value Is Associated with a 64-Bit Application:** Specify whether to search 64-bit Registry keys in addition to 32-bit keys when clients are running a 64-bit OS. If the same key exists on both 64-bit and 32-bit Registry hives, both keys are returned.

▶ **Script:** Execute a script to return the results needed for the compliance check.

   ▶ **Discovery Script:** This can be a PowerShell, VBScript, or a Microsoft JScript. Click **Open** or just paste in your script. The script must return a value used in the compliance evaluation. For example, if you wanted to check if a service is stopped, your script would return stopped.

   ▶ **Remediation Script (Optional):** Use to fix a noncompliant client. This can be a PowerShell, VBScript, or Microsoft Jscript script. ConfigMgr can pass the compliant value to the script as a parameter, if needed.

   ▶ **Run Scripts by Using the Logged On User Credentials:** Allow the script to be run by the current logged on user instead of using the local system.

   ▶ **Run Scripts by Using the 32-Bit Scripting Host on 64-Bit Devices:** Use the 32-bit script engine to run a script when on a 64-bit device, fixing some issues when trying to run a script with the 64-bit engine.

▶ **SQL Query:** Run a SQL query and use the results as a value for compliance evaluation. You might use this option to determine if all SQL servers are running the same version of SQL:

   ▶ **SQL Server Instance:** The instance of SQL Server to use: the default instance, all instances, or a provided instance name.

▶ **Database:** The SQL Server database to run the query against.

▶ **Column:** The column containing the value you want to use for the compliance evaluation.

▶ **Transact-SQL Statement:** The SQL query to use to return the value for compliance evaluation. Paste in your query or click **Open** to open an existing query.

▶ **WQL Query:** Use to run a query against the local machine's WQL database:

   ▶ **Namespace:** The namespace to use to build out your query. An example would be root\cimv2.

   ▶ **Class:** The name of the class to use to build your query. An example would be Win32_Service.

   ▶ **Property:** The name of the property to use to build your query. An example would be Name.

   ▶ **WQL Query WHERE Clause:** A condition added to the query. An example would be Name=CCMEXEC and StartMode=Auto.

▶ **XPath Query:** Use to query data inside an eXtensible Markup Language (XML) file to use for compliance evaluation:

   ▶ **Path:** The path of the XML file. ConfigMgr supports the use of all Windows system environment variables and the *%USERPROFILE%* user variable in the pathname.

   ▶ **XML Filename:** The filename containing the XML query used to assess compliance on the client computers.

   ▶ **Include Subfolders:** Search subfolders under the specified path.

   ▶ **This File Is Associated with a 64-Bit Application:** Choose if the 64-bit system file location (*%windir%*\System32) should be searched in addition to the 32-bit system file location (*%windir%*\Syswow64).

   ▶ **XPath Query:** Specify a valid full XML path language (XPath) query used to assess compliance on the client computers.

   ▶ **Namespaces:** Open the XML Namespaces dialog box to identify namespaces and prefixes to be used during the XPath query.

▶ **Data Type:** Choose the format of the data the condition returns before the compliance evaluation is made. Certain settings do not have data types, and some settings may not have all of the data types:

   ▶ String

   ▶ Date and time

   ▶ Integer

   ▶ Floating point

   ▶ Version

10

- ▶ Boolean
- ▶ String array
- ▶ Integer array

Compliance Rules   If settings are the left-hand part of the device compliance equation, then compliance rules are the right-hand side of the equation. The settings are compared against compliance rules to verify if the device is in compliance. You may have noticed an additional tab for compliance rules while creating the settings. Create the rules there or click **New** and create your compliance rules in the dialog that appears.

- ▶ **Name:** Name the rule you are creating.

- ▶ **Description:** Explain in detail what the condition rule is for.

- ▶ **Selected Setting:** Pick the setting for which you want to create a compliance rule. Click **Browse** to open the Select Setting dialog box and then select the setting. If the setting you want to use is not there, select **New Setting**. When you are finished, click **Select**. You can also select **Properties** to view a read-only page of the properties of that setting.

- ▶ **Rule Type:** Define what type of rule this will be. You have two choices:

  - ▶ **Value:** Sets up the rule to compare the value returned by the configuration item or script against the value that you specify.

  - ▶ **Existential:** Creates a rule that evaluates the setting depending on whether it exists on the device. If you use this, choose one of three settings:

    - ▶ The setting must exist on client devices
    - ▶ The setting must not exist on client devices
    - ▶ The setting occurs the following number of times

- ▶ **The Setting Must Comply with the Following Rule:** Set the value to make the device compliant. Select an operator to use when the value is assessed for compliance. You can use the following operators:

  - ▶ Equals
  - ▶ Not equal to
  - ▶ Greater than
  - ▶ Less than
  - ▶ Between
  - ▶ Greater than or equal to
  - ▶ Less than or equal to
  - ▶ One of
  - ▶ None of

▶ **Remediate Noncompliant Rules When Supported**: Select this option, and ConfigMgr may be able to automatically remediate the following rule types:

> ▶ **Registry Value:** The Registry value is remediated if it is noncompliant and created if it does not exist.

> ▶ **Script:** If you added a remediation script when the settings item was created, the script is run to remediate the issue.

> ▶ **WQL Query:** The WQL value is set to the value to make it compliant, but only if the operator used is equals.

▶ **Report Noncompliance if This Setting Instance Is Not Found:** Select this option to cause the CI to report noncompliant if the setting is not found on the client system.

▶ **Noncompliance Severity for Reports:** Select this option to create a severity for report purposes when a device is noncompliant. The following severities can be used:

> ▶ None

> ▶ Information

> ▶ Warning

> ▶ Critical

> ▶ Critical with event

Supported Platforms   Use the check box tree on the Supported Platforms page to select the platforms to which this CI applies; all supported versions of Windows are listed. If the client platform does not match, the CI is not evaluated.

Windows application CIs have an additional option at the bottom of this page: This application runs only on computers that have 64-bit hardware. This indicates that the application is 64-bit and will not run on a 32-bit version of Windows, preventing the CI from being applicable and evaluated on 32-bit versions of Windows.

Summary, Progress, Completion   The Summary page summarizes all the choices made in the Create Configuration Item Wizard. Review this page to be sure that each item is correct.

Click **Next**, and you see the Progress page. This page flashes very quickly as the choices made in the wizard are written to the database.

The Completion page shows a success or failure for each item created in the wizard. Pay attention to this page to be sure all items were created successfully. If a failure is shown, review those settings and fix the issue that caused the failure.

Using Devices Without a ConfigMgr Client

To use settings management CIs, you must enroll devices without a ConfigMgr client in Microsoft Intune or manage them on-premise with ConfigMgr. This is accomplished by using the built-in management capabilities of device operating systems that use the Open Mobile Alliance Device Management (OMA DM) standard. This specification is designed to manage mobile devices such as mobile phones, PDAs, and tablet computers. It allows for device configuration, letting you use CIs to change the settings and parameters of a device.

10

Specifying Windows 8.1 and Windows 10 Configuration Items

This selection is for Windows 8.1 tablets, 8.1 RT devices, and all Windows 10 devices, including tablets and phones. Use the Supported Platforms page to select the OS with which to use the CIs. Each OS selection shows different device settings. Figure 10.8 shows these selections on the Device Settings page with all the OS check boxes enabled.

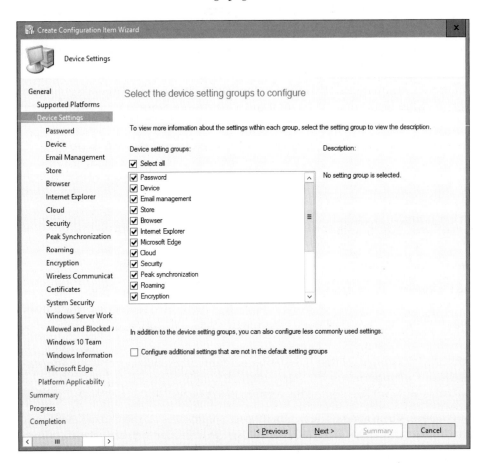

FIGURE 10.8   Windows 8.1 and Windows 10 Device Settings page.

The bottom of the Devices Settings page, displayed in Figure 10.8, shows a check box for some additional settings not included in the default settings groups. If this box is checked, an additional settings page is added. This page is blank by default with an Add option that allows you to choose from several settings. Because the list includes settings from all devices, you may want to sort the list by the supported platforms to narrow down to the setting for which you are looking.

Many settings are common to Windows 8.x devices and Windows 10 devices. Microsoft provides in-depth information on Windows 8.1 and Windows 10 CI settings at https://docs.microsoft.com/sccm/compliance/deploy-use/create-configuration-items-for-windows-8.1-and-windows-10-devices-managed-without-the-client#windows-81-and-windows-10-configuration-item-settings-reference.

Specifying Windows Phone Configuration Items

This selection is for Windows 8.x phones only. The Supported Platforms page allows you to select between Windows Phone 8.0 and 8.1. Available device settings are very similar for the two versions; Figure 10.8 shows the different selections on the Device Settings page. In-depth information on Windows Phone CIs is at https://docs.microsoft.com/sccm/compliance/deploy-use/create-configuration-items-for-windows-phone-devices-managed-without-the-client#windows-phone-configuration-item-settings-reference.

NOTE: THE LIST OF ALLOWED APPS

If you use a list of allowed applications, ensure that the company portal application and any applications you have deployed to Windows Phone devices are in the Allowed Apps list.

Specifying iOS and Mac OS X Configuration Items

The iOS and Mac OS X Configuration Items selection is for iOS devices: iPhones, iPads, and Mac OS X devices. The devices must be enrolled in Microsoft Intune or managed on-premise. The Supported Platforms page allows you to choose iOS 7, iOS 8, or iOS 9. Figure 10.9 shows the selections on this page.

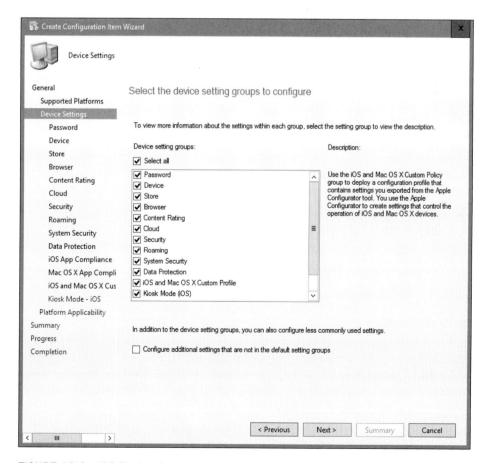

FIGURE 10.9   iOS Device Settings page.

iOS has some of the same settings as the other devices, and it has many more as well. View the full list of settings at https://docs.microsoft.com/sccm/compliance/deploy-use/create-configuration-items-for-ios-and-mac-os-x-devices-managed-without-the-client#ios-and-mac-os-x-configuration-item-settings-reference.

Specifying Android and Samsung Knox Configuration Items

The Android and Samsung Knox Configuration Items selection is for Android and Knox devices, including phones. Knox is a defense-grade security platform built in to certain Samsung devices and phones; for more information, see https://www.samsungknox.com. Android and Knox devices must be enrolled in Microsoft Intune or managed on-premise. Use the Supported Platforms page to choose Android versions 4 and 5 devices as well as Knox Standard 4.0 and higher. Android and Samsung Knox CI settings references are available at https://docs.microsoft.com/sccm/compliance/deploy-use/create-configuration-items-for-android-and-samsung-knox-devices-managed-without-the-client#android-and-samsung-knox-configuration-item-settings-reference.

Use the Certificates page to import a certificate to push down to the device. Selecting **Import** allows you to choose the certificate and the destination store to which you want to import the certificate.

Each page has the check box Remediate noncompliant settings; this allows you to automatically remediate the setting when it is noncompliant. There is also a dropdown for noncompliance severity for reports, which you use to choose the severity to report when the item is noncompliant.

The Platform Applicability page points out settings not supported by all platforms chosen on the Supported Platforms page. These settings are not assessed for compliance on the unsupported platforms. Select **Export report** to export the settings to a comma-separated values (.csv) file.

The Summary page displays a complete summary of the choices made in the Create Configuration Item Wizard. Review this page to confirm that each item is correct.

Click **Next**, and the Progress page flashes by very quickly as the choices made in the wizard are written to the database.

The Completion page shows a success or failure for each item created in the wizard. Pay attention to this page to be sure all items were created successfully. If a failure is shown, review those settings and resolve the issue that caused it to fail.

Creating Baselines

With your CIs created, your next step is to create a baseline. The baseline is a collection of CIs. While a baseline can contain any number of CIs, you will want to create multiple baselines so you can group the CIs that belong together. Multiple baselines make it easier to report compliance or noncompliance and help to troubleshoot errors with the CIs.

To create a baseline, navigate to **Assets and Compliance -> Compliance Settings -> Configuration Baselines**. Select **Create Configuration Baseline** from the ribbon bar or from the right-click context menu to open the Create Configuration Baseline page. Figure 10.10 shows the default page for creating a new baseline.

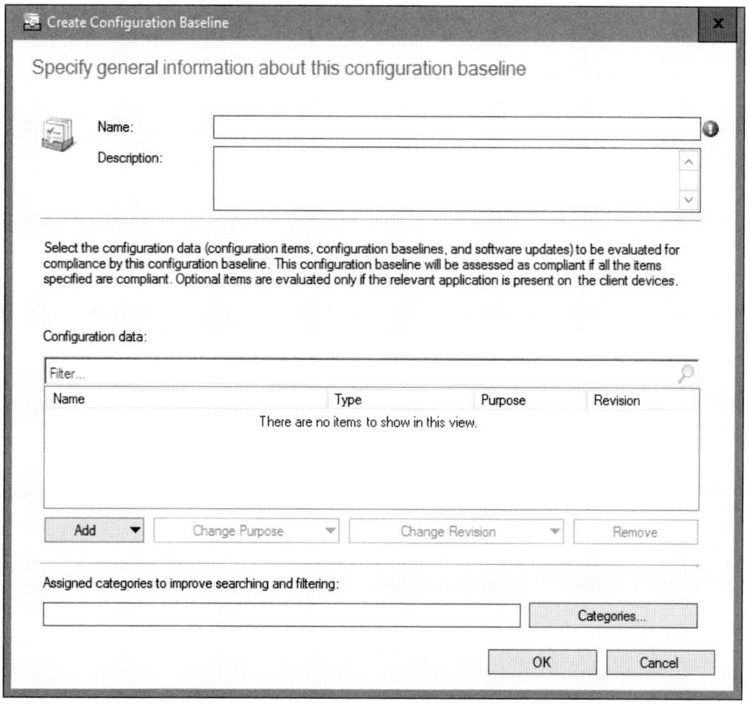

FIGURE 10.10   Create Configuration Baseline page.

Add a name and description for the new baseline at the top of this dialog and pick the desired categories at the bottom by clicking **Categories**. CIs and baselines share the same set of categories from which to choose. Categories have no specific functional purpose outside console organization.

The primary activity when creating a baseline is choosing the configuration data it contains—collectively called *evaluation conditions*. Use the Add menu under the Configuration data list box, which has three choices when selected:

▶ Configuration Items

▶ Software Updates

▶ Configuration Baselines

Each choice results in an object picker dialog, where you select the corresponding type of object to include in the baseline.

Application configuration items can have one of the following purposes:

▶ **Required:** The application defined in the CI must exist on the target system in order to be compliant. All settings in the CI are also evaluated for compliance.

▶ **Optional:** Settings in the CI are evaluated for compliance only if the application defined in the CI exists on a target system.

▶ **Prohibited:** The application defined in the CI must not exist on the target system in order to be compliant. All settings in the CI are ignored.

Change the configuration item revision included in the baseline by selecting the CI in the Configuration data list box and selecting from the Change Revision dropdown menu. This allows you to modify and test a CI without affecting the baselines to which it belongs. The latest revision is included by default. Software updates and baselines always use the latest revision.

Software updates are always set to Required, meaning they must exist on the target system. Baselines are also set to Required, although this has no real substantive meaning other than that the CIs in the baseline will be evaluated according to the evaluation conditions set in that baseline.

To modify a baseline, including its evaluation conditions, select the baseline and choose **Properties** from the ribbon bar or right-click the baseline and choose Properties to see its properties dialog box. The Details pane appears at the bottom of the page when any baseline is selected. The Summary tab lists basic information about the baseline, including deployment status and the following compliance statistics:

▶ Compliance Count

▶ Noncompliance Count

▶ Failure Count

Disabling a baseline prevents its evaluation on target systems even if it is deployed, as discussed in the next section. To disable a baseline, select it and choose **Disable** from the ribbon bar or from the right-click context menu. Choose **Enable** from the same locations to enable it later.

Deploying Baselines

After creating a baseline, you deploy it to a collection of clients. The deployment assigns the baseline to the clients in the collection for evaluation. Each baseline deployment has its own evaluation schedule, set by default to the schedule defined in the default client settings for the hierarchy. To deploy a baseline, navigate to **Assets and Compliance -> Compliance Settings -> Configuration Baselines**. Select the configuration baseline you want to deploy and choose **Deploy** from the ribbon bar or from the right-click context menu to open the Deploy Configuration Baselines dialog box, displayed in Figure 10.11.

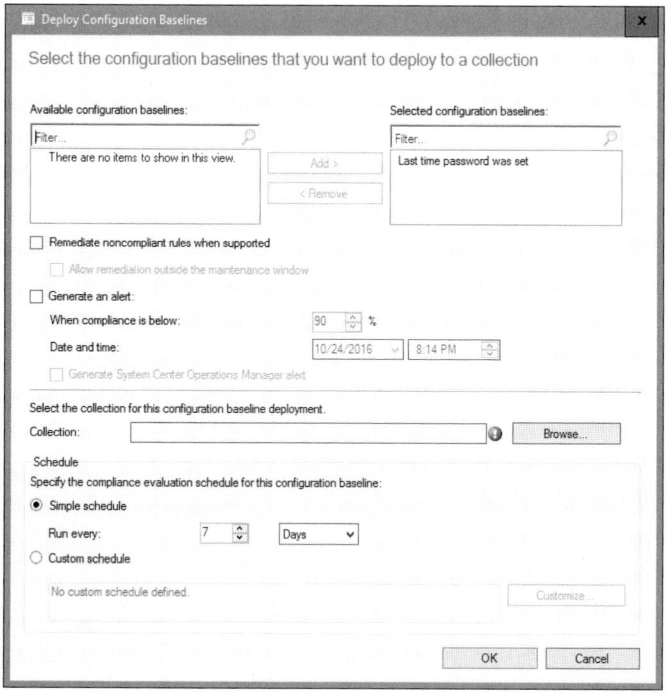

FIGURE 10.11   Deploy Configuration Baseline dialog box.

Configure the following properties for the deployment:

▶ Selected configuration baselines

▶ Remediation for noncompliant rules when supported and remediation is outside maintenance windows

▶ Console alert generation, based on the compliance percentage after a defined date and time

▶ System Center Operations Manager alert using the same criteria

▶ Target collection

▶ Baseline evaluation schedule

You can target baselines to device or user collections. When a baseline is targeted at a user collection, user settings contained in the baseline are evaluated against the currently logged in user. Each baseline chosen has its own deployment created. To view all deployments for a specific baseline, select the baseline in the console. The Details pane has two tabs, one of which is a Deployments tab, which you can select for a list of all deployments for the selected baseline.

To examine or modify baseline deployments, navigate to **Monitoring -> Deployments**, which lists all deployments, not just baseline deployments. Use the console search and filtering capabilities to list or find the deployment you want to view or modify. You cannot delete a baseline deployment from the Monitoring workspace; you must select it in the Assets and Compliance workspace and then delete its deployments from the Deployments tab of the Details pane of the baseline.

To modify a deployment, select it and choose **Properties** from the ribbon bar or from the right-click context menu. You see a dialog nearly identical to the Deploy Configuration Baselines dialog shown in Figure 10.10, where you can refine any of the deployment properties except the targeted collection. To change the targeted collection, you must create a new deployment for the baseline.

REAL WORLD: USING ALERTS WITH COMPLIANCE

It might be tempting to set up alerts when deploying the baseline to a collection. However, the alert will appear in the console when a certain percentage of clients return noncompliant settings. For busy sites that have many deployments and other items that have alerts turned on, a specific alert can get lost in the mix. For these types of environments, the authors recommend creating a rule that generates an email when deploying the baseline creates an alert. This allows ConfigMgr to notify an individual or a small group, rather than requiring an administrator to sift through all alerts to see this particular one.

Developing a Compliance Strategy

Up to this point, the chapter has discussed creating and deploying CIs and baselines. The question now becomes the famous who, what, where, when, and why—in regard to the type of strategy to use to create and deploy those CIs. As with almost all other questions of these types asked in regard to ConfigMgr, the answer is *it depends*. This is more true than ever before with Compliance Settings. While you can create a CI for just about anything, you want to create CIs that make sense for issues you need to monitor. Do not create unnecessary CIs if there is an easier way to get the answers you need; each set of deployed baselines impacts client performance when those baselines are evaluated. You also may find it difficult to locate the results of numerous evaluations.

Do not expect immediate results after developing the process to create your CIs and deploying the baselines. Clients must receive policies for these deployments, evaluate them on the schedule assigned to them, and report the results back to ConfigMgr. Be aware of this time-consuming process so that you are not put in the position of needing results right away.

Obtaining On-Demand Results

ConfigMgr is not designed to deliver real-time results. Compliance results are run on the schedule created with the deployment, which can be annoying if you need to see results quickly. You could change the schedule, but you would have to wait for the client to receive that policy change and incorporate it into the CIs you want to know about. The following sections discuss several approaches to speed up this process.

Using the Client Control Panel Applet

Enabling compliance settings in the console using client settings causes a new tab to become available in the ConfigMgr Control Panel applet on clients where it is enabled. This tab, titled Configurations, is displayed in Figure 10.12.

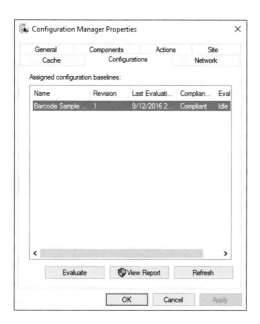

FIGURE 10.12   Configurations tab of the ConfigMgr Control Panel applet.

The list box in Figure 10.12 shows each baseline deployed to that client. Clicking **Evaluate** at the bottom of the page lets users trigger evaluation of selected baselines, enabling you to evaluate baselines in an on-demand environment and get almost instantaneous results when needed. By clicking **View Report**, you can let administrative users display a report that shows the most current evaluation results of the selected baseline. This lets you look at the compliance of a single machine; however, it is not intended be used as a report but rather as a tool to verify that your CIs and baselines are working correctly.

Scripting Client Evaluation

While having a user access the Control Panel applet and manually run an evaluation of the baseline will work, this approach becomes difficult with a collection of more than several users. A better tactic is to implement scripting. Microsoft provides a very rich scripting set in ConfigMgr. The server side has many PowerShell cmdlets available to automate numerous tasks; however, the client side has been, for the most part, neglected. The ConfigMgr software development kit (SDK) includes various client-side scripts you can modify to suit your needs. One of these scripts allows a user with administrative rights on a machine to run that script and cause an evaluation of a baseline, enabling a ConfigMgr administrator to programmatically kick off the evaluation on a mass scale. More information about the SDK can be found at https://docs.microsoft.com/sccm/develop/core/misc/system-center-configuration-manager-sdk. You can search on the Internet for PowerShell scripts that you can use to force a client to run an evaluation. Most of these scripts need to be modified to work for your environment and specific requirements.

Correcting Issues Using Remediation

Getting an alert, viewing a report, and even having someone contact you about a machine or group of machines that are noncompliant notifies you of a problem; however, it does not really help resolve the issue. What you need is the ability to fix the issue as quickly as possible, without human intervention. *Remediation* refers to the process of correcting an identified issue, and auto-remediation is having an issue corrected in an automated manner. For both cases, compliance settings identify the issue, using a baseline assigned to a system in your organization.

ConfigMgr has two built-in strategies for auto-remediation:

▶ **Using Built-in Remediation:** For supported Windows CI setting types, WMI, Registry values, and scripts, you can enable remediation in the compliance rules referencing those settings. All settings in mobile device CIs support remediation, with a similar option in their configurations. Enabling this option causes a baseline evaluation to modify the settings value on the target system to the expected value.

▶ **Creating Collections:** For settings that do not support built-in remediation or require more than correcting a single value, you can build a collection and deploy a program, an application, or a software update to that collection. ConfigMgr conveniently creates the query rule and the collection for you. Perform the following steps:

1. Select the desired baseline from the console.

2. From the Details pane at the bottom, select **Deployments**.

3. Select the appropriate deployment and choose **Create New Collection** from the ribbon bar or from the right-click context menu.

4. From the fly-out menu that appears, with the four compliance statuses as options, choose the desired compliance status for the new collection. The Create Device Collection Wizard appears, offering the same options as when you manually create a new collection except that all of the information, including a query membership rule, is provided.

5. Complete the wizard to create the new collection. After creating the collection, deploy a package, an application, or a software update to correct the issue. The actual actions performed are up to you and should correct any noncompliant issues the baseline can identify. Systems that fail compliance checks in the baseline automatically populate the collection, which in turn deploys your corrective action to those systems, correcting the issue.

Using Reporting to Track Compliance

Once the CIs are created, added to the baseline, and deployed to a target collection, the client evaluates them to determine compliance or noncompliance. The client then returns the results to the site, where they are stored in the site database. While you can view those results inside the Monitoring workspace of the console, reporting allows you to see the results, compare those results, and allow other individuals without access to a console to view the results.

Microsoft provides 22 reports out of the box for compliance settings. Figure 10.13 shows these reports.

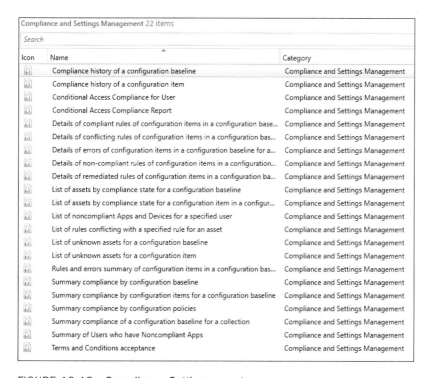

Icon	Name	Category
	Compliance history of a configuration baseline	Compliance and Settings Management
	Compliance history of a configuration item	Compliance and Settings Management
	Conditional Access Compliance for User	Compliance and Settings Management
	Conditional Access Compliance Report	Compliance and Settings Management
	Details of compliant rules of configuration items in a configuration base...	Compliance and Settings Management
	Details of conflicting rules of configuration items in a configuration bas...	Compliance and Settings Management
	Details of errors of configuration items in a configuration baseline for a...	Compliance and Settings Management
	Details of non-compliant rules of configuration items in a configuration...	Compliance and Settings Management
	Details of remediated rules of configuration items in a configuration ba...	Compliance and Settings Management
	List of assets by compliance state for a configuration baseline	Compliance and Settings Management
	List of assets by compliance state for a configuration item in a configur...	Compliance and Settings Management
	List of noncompliant Apps and Devices for a specified user	Compliance and Settings Management
	List of rules conflicting with a specified rule for an asset	Compliance and Settings Management
	List of unknown assets for a configuration baseline	Compliance and Settings Management
	List of unknown assets for a configuration item	Compliance and Settings Management
	Rules and errors summary of configuration items in a configuration bas...	Compliance and Settings Management
	Summary compliance by configuration baseline	Compliance and Settings Management
	Summary compliance by configuration items for a configuration baseline	Compliance and Settings Management
	Summary compliance by configuration policies	Compliance and Settings Management
	Summary compliance of a configuration baseline for a collection	Compliance and Settings Management
	Summary of Users who have Noncompliant Apps	Compliance and Settings Management
	Terms and Conditions acceptance	Compliance and Settings Management

FIGURE 10.13   Compliance Settings reports.

You can access the reports from two places:

- ▶ **ConfigMgr Console:** Navigate to **Monitoring -> Reporting -> Reports -> Compliance and Settings Management**.

- ▶ **SQL Server Reporting Services (SSRS):** SSRS uses the built-in reporting services of Microsoft SQL Server to provide access to the same reports you can see in the ConfigMgr console, plus access to any customized reports that may have been created outside the ConfigMgr reports folder in SSRS.

10

If you need to view the reports on a regular basis, you can create a subscription to a report either in the ConfigMgr console or SSRS, specifying whether the report should be delivered via email or pulled from a common network location. After you set up the subscription, the process is automatic; this saves an administrator the work of delivering the report.

Troubleshooting Settings Management

Compliance settings management is an automated system that works well but sometimes can have problems. When issues arise, troubleshooting is necessary to determine what the issue is, where it might be, and how to fix it.

Troubleshooting compliance settings, like troubleshooting the rest of ConfigMgr, is largely a log file review exercise. Because compliance settings evaluation is a client activity, the logs for compliance setting processing are on the client in the client logs folder (*%SystemRoot%\ CCM\Logs*). Five log files are used by compliance settings to store activity; Table 10.2 describes these files. A complete list of log files is available in Appendix A, "Configuration Manager Log Files."

TABLE 10.2   Compliance Settings Log Files

Filename	Description
CIAgent.log	Provides details about the process of remediation and compliance for compliance settings, software updates, and application management.
CITaskMgr.log	Records information about CI, application, and DT type task scheduling.
DCMAgent.log	Records high-level information about the evaluation, conflict reporting, and remediation of CIs and applications.
DCMReporting.log	Records information about reporting policy platform results into state messages for CIs.
DcmWmiProvider.log	Records WMI information about reading CI synclets.

The Rules and errors summary of configuration items in a configuration baseline for an asset report is another tool to use when troubleshooting an issue, as it should clearly point out why the client is having problems.

In addition, issues involving ConfigMgr's ability to evaluate a baseline or CI are reported through the ConfigMgr status message reporting mechanism. To view these status messages, follow these steps:

1. In the console, navigate to **Monitoring -> System Status -> Status Message Queries**.

2. From the list of status message queries on the right, select **All Status Messages** and then **Show Messages** from the ribbon bar or from the right-click context menu.

3. In the All Status Messages dialog box, enter the desired time frame for which you would like to see status messages.

4. Review the displayed messages, looking for any message IDs listed in Table 10.3.

TABLE 10.3   Compliance Settings Client Status Messages

Message ID	Description
11800	Indicates a download failure for a configuration item.
11801	Indicates a hash failure for a configuration item.
11802	Indicates that .NET Framework 2.0 is not installed.
11850	Indicates a download failure for Service Modeling Language (SML) content.
11851	Indicates that the policy could not be uncompressed.
11853	Indicates that the client computer has evaluated one or more assigned configuration baselines but cannot send the compliance results to its management point.
11854	Indicates a compliance change from noncompliant to compliant or from unknown to compliant.
11855	Indicates a compliance change to noncompliant with a noncompliance severity level of Information.
11856	Indicates a compliance change to noncompliant with a noncompliance severity level of Warning.
11857	Indicates a compliance change to noncompliant with a noncompliance severity level of Error.
11858	Indicates that packages for SML content could not be uncompressed.
11859	Indicates a failure in evaluating a configuration item.
11860	Indicates a failure in evaluating SML content.
11861	Indicates a failure in the SML discovery type process.
11862	Indicates that the SML discovery type is halted.

Using the message IDs listed in Table 10.3 can help narrow down the issues but can also add questions and necessitate research as the message IDs are not user friendly. In these cases, it is useful to gather the client logs referred to in Table 10.3 and find the status message number in the log file. This can help show you what was occurring right before the status message was created and right after it was created. The error or problem may be in that small section of the log files.

These status messages also provide the ability to track and monitor the evaluation status of baselines in your site.

Summary

Compliance Settings is an excellent tool that provides feedback about the configuration and compliance of many different systems. Adding a Microsoft Intune subscription allows you to also include iOS and Android devices, giving your organization the ability to manage most of the devices that users use. Remediation features also enforce compliance, ensuring standard configurations and settings across the enterprise.

Compliance Settings seamlessly integrates with the rest of ConfigMgr, providing a "single pane of glass" to manage all your systems and devices. Just having the ability to provide consistent and timely compliance reports to auditors is critical for any type of review.

ConfigMgr's compliance settings feature efficiently fills a major blind spot in most organizations—configuration and compliance verification and enforcement—without requiring implementation of any additional enterprise tools. Microsoft keeps enhancing this area of ConfigMgr, so look for more great capabilities and supported devices in the future.

CHAPTER 11

Creating and Managing Applications

System Center 2012 Configuration Manager (ConfigMgr) introduced applications and deployment types (DTs) for software deployment, and DTs continue to be enhanced with ConfigMgr Current Branch. Applications include numerous advantages over packages and programs. The client evaluates DTs for applicability at installation, programmatically determining the best preferred command (a DT) to execute. This differs from packages, which use collections for each type of user or system in order to target where to distribute the package, thus requiring multiple collections to distribute a single package.

ConfigMgr applications can associate users with one or more devices, and they can install only when a particular user is logged on to a particular device type. Deployment behavior is controlled by DTs, which means ConfigMgr administrators can control if, when, and how software is installed. Applications also use detection methods to verify that an application installed correctly.

NOTE: CLARIFYING THE TERMS *APPLICATION* AND *PACKAGE*

The term *application* refers to the software application a user installs and executes. It also refers to a ConfigMgr application, which ConfigMgr uses to install an application. As using the same word for two things can be confusing, the authors make a distinction between a software application and a ConfigMgr application.

The same goes for *packages*; there are ConfigMgr packages, referring to the functionality used in ConfigMgr, and you will also see the term *package* used by specific DT variations used in a ConfigMgr application.

This chapter discusses ConfigMgr applications. Chapter 12, "Creating and Using Deployment Types," discusses available DTs and creating new DTs. Chapter 14, "Distributing and Deploying Applications and Packages," describes delivering an application to a device by creating collections, using distribution points (DPs), and creating deployments.

ConfigMgr Applications Overview

A ConfigMgr application is a container that delivers software. It includes a name, a version, an application owner, and localization information describing how the application is displayed in the Software Center and Application Catalog. It also contains information regarding distribution settings and the DPs and DP groups where content is distributed, as well as references and dependencies for other applications, such as whether the application replaces an existing application or is part of a virtual environment.

NOTE: OLD SOFTWARE CENTER AND NEW SOFTWARE CENTER

Several chapters in this book use the terms *old Software Center* and *new Software Center*. These terms refer to two experiences from an end user point of view:

▶ **Old Software Center:** Introduced with ConfigMgr 2012, the old Software Center requires Silverlight on the device and works in conjunction with the Application Catalog. It shows device-targeted deployments, whereas the Application Catalog shows user-targeted deployments.

▶ **New Software Center:** The new Software Center, introduced with ConfigMgr Current Branch version 1511, combines functionality from the old Software Center and Application Catalog into one experience. Silverlight is no longer required.

Applications are shells; installation requires DTs, the key component of the application. Each ConfigMgr application has a minimum of one DT defined.

Following are some actions you can perform on a ConfigMgr application:

▶ Distribute ConfigMgr application content (software) to DPs.

▶ Deploy the application (required or optional) to devices or users.

▶ Create one or more DTs.

▶ Simulate deployment to validate DTs.

▶ Export a ConfigMgr application (with or without content) to import it into a different ConfigMgr environment or save to disk in case it needs to be restored later, as discussed in the "Exporting and Importing Applications" section, later in this chapter.

▶ Create a prestaged content file to transport the content to remote locations (without using wide area network [WAN] connectivity).

11

▶ Set security scopes to ensure that team members have appropriate access to the ConfigMgr application. Chapter 23, "Security and Delegation in Configuration Manager," discusses security scopes.

▶ Monitor content distribution.

▶ Monitor deployment status.

Using a ConfigMgr application is an enhanced technique for delivering software to a user or computer. Applications may contain multiple methods of installation, based on user or computer state. Like packages, applications distribute software, but they include additional information to support smart deployment to different devices and deployment scenarios.

Applications can have multiple DTs. You may have software with different installations for x86, x64, or different versions of Windows. Once the DTs are properly built and the application deployed, the DTs are evaluated using requirement rules to determine the appropriate installation. For example, an x64 Windows 8.1 DT only installs an x64 version of the software.

CAUTION: DEPLOYMENTS UNINSTALLING SOFTWARE DO NOT CHECK REQUIREMENT RULES

Deployments uninstalling applications do not use requirement rules to determine if the uninstall is necessary. The application is always uninstalled on each system for which the deployment is set. For additional information, see https://docs.microsoft.com/sccm/apps/deploy-use/uninstall-applications.

Requirement rules are flexible and can leverage practically anything on a system, as well as Structured Query Language (SQL) or Lightweight Directory Access Protocol (LDAP) queries, primary user information, and more. Applications are deployed to a user or group of users and installed with the applicable DT, depending on the type of device in use and where the device is situated at that time.

At the time of writing this book, 16 types of DTs are available. This chapter discusses the basics of DTs; Chapter 12 provides further detail. Some DTs require the device that executes the DT to be enrolled in Intune; Table 11.1 identifies those types. Intune integration is covered in Chapter 16, "Integrating Intune Hybrid into Your Configuration Manager Environment."

Following is a brief description of the different deployment types:

▶ **Windows Installer:** Executes a Windows Installer file (.msi file).

▶ **Windows Installer Through MDM:** Executes an .msi file using ConfigMgr's mobile device management (MDM) capabilities in combination with Microsoft Intune.

▶ **Microsoft Application Virtualization (App-V):** Deploys virtual application packages created using the Microsoft App-V sequencer. ConfigMgr supports App-V DTs for App-V versions 4 and 5.

▶ **Windows App Package:** Installs a Windows app package (.appx) or Windows app package bundle (.appxbundle) type of application. You can also create a DT that only links to an application in the Windows Store (known as *deeplinking*).

▶ **Windows Phone App Package:** Installs a Windows Phone app package file (.xap). You could also create a link to the application in the Microsoft store for Windows Phone.

▶ **Windows Mobile Cabinet:** Installs a Windows Mobile Cabinet (.cab) file.

▶ **App Package for iOS:** Installs an application package for iOS (.ipa) file or links to an application in Apple's App Store.

▶ **App Package for Android:** Installs an application package for Android (.apk) file or links to an application in the Google Play store.

▶ **Mac OS X:** Deploys applications to Mac OS X using a .cmmac file, created using the CMAppUtil tool on Mac OS X.

▶ **Script Installer:** Specifies a script to deploy to devices running an installation or making specific configuration changes. The script can range from a complex Visual Basic file to a simple batch file. Installations using an executable (.exe, .msu, and so on) are also considered script installers.

▶ **Web Application:** Deploys a link to an uniform resource locator (URL).

TABLE 11.1   Intune Enrollment Requirements for DTs

DT Type	Requires Device to Be Enrolled in Intune?
Windows Installer	No
Windows Installer through MDM	Yes if the device on which you want to install is managed via the Internet; no if managed using its MDM channel through ConfigMgr on-premise
Microsoft Application Virtualization	No
Windows App Package	No
Windows Phone App Package	Yes
Windows Mobile Cabinet	No
App Package for iOS	Yes
App Package for Android	Yes
Mac OS X	No
Web Application	Only if deployed to enrolled devices
Script Installer	No

Using the Requirement Rule Component in a DT

Requirement rules are DT components used to determine if a DT is installable on a system. They are optional; if there is no requirement rule, the DT is applicable to any system evaluating it. Use requirements to determine which DT to install; the first applicable DT is installed.

Requirements are defined using global conditions; they can be based on the operating system (OS) name and/or architecture, total physical memory, free disk space, Active Directory (AD) site, organizational unit (OU), primary user, and more. Global conditions can create requirements for a DT. While requirements are not necessary, the authors recommend using them to ensure that software is delivered to appropriate devices and/or users. The "User Device Affinity" section, later in this chapter, discusses the primary user global condition, which allows the ConfigMgr administrator to specify that the DT may only execute when the primary user of the machine is logged on.

The following is a description of an application with four DTs and their requirements:

▶ Operating system is Windows 8.1 x86 and the primary user is set to True

▶ Operating system is Windows 8.1 x64 and the primary user is set to True

▶ Operating system is Windows 10 x64 and the primary user is set to True

▶ Operating system is Windows 10 x86 or x64

The first three DTs are Windows Installer-based DTs; the final one is an App-V DT. The first three are obvious about whether the DT is installable. Requirements are evaluated by priority, meaning if the OS is Windows 10 x86 and the primary user is set to False, only the fourth DT is installable. The requirements ensure that full installation applies only to systems where the primary user for the device is set to True. If the system is Windows 8.1 x64 and the primary user is set to False, no DTs are applicable; a user attempting to install would receive a message that requirements have not been met to install the application.

Understanding Detection Methods

A detection method must resolve to True for a DT to install on a device. A device evaluates an application using requirement rules to determine which DT to install and uses a detection method to see if the DT is already installed. The detection method could check for a specific Registry key or Registry key value, or it could verify installation of an MSI file by confirming that the MSI product code exists.

If an application is deployed as Required (mandatory), the client agent reevaluates the application installation, based on the requirement rules and detection method. This occurs weekly by default. The reevaluation interval is configured through client settings. Client settings are discussed in Chapter 9, "Client Management."

User Device Affinity

User device affinity allows an administrator to associate a user with his or her primary devices. Primary devices are a user's typical daily work devices, such as a workstation or laptop. Devices can be associated with more than one user, and a user can be associated with more than one device. Chapter 9 discusses configuring client settings for user device affinity.

A huge benefit of user device affinity is that the ConfigMgr administrator can deploy applications to users without knowing the name of the device. Administrators also have more control in deploying the application, as they can create rules related to user device affinity as part of the deployment. Say you have an application for Microsoft Visio with two DTs; the first DT installs Visio with the full MSI file, and the second DT installs the Visio Viewer application:

▶ You create a requirement rule for the full MSI version and require the primary device to be set to True, as displayed in Figure 11.1. You also set this DT as the first DT available, as the first requirement rule valid for the DT is the one executed.

▶ When a user attempts to install the software (or you set it as Required), the application evaluates the first DT, and where the primary user is set to True, the application installs the Windows Installer (.msi) version of Visio. If the primary user is set to False, the Windows Installer application for Visio Viewer is installed.

FIGURE 11.1   Primary device is set to True.

There are many ways to create user device affinity:

▶ Import a comma-separated values (CSV) file that contains two columns: users and devices.

▶ Have the user specify his or her primary device in the Application Catalog or Software Center.

▶ Have the administrator manually select the user and primary device.

▶ Set the user device affinity during operating system deployment (OSD).

▶ Set affinity during mobile device enrollment.

▶ Have the site detect affinities between users and devices based on usage information; the affinity must be approved by an administrator.

Following is information an affinity can hold:

▶ A single user to a single device

▶ A single user to many devices (such as a desktop and a mobile device)

▶ Many users to a single device (such as a desktop shared by the same department)

NOTE: APPLICATIONS ARE NOT ALWAYS THE BEST DEPLOYMENT OPTION

While the authors recommend deploying software using ConfigMgr applications, in some cases—such as the following—implementing packages and programs, task sequences, or PowerShell scripts might be more suitable:

▶ Scripts that do not install an application on a computer (such as a script to defragment a disk drive)

▶ One-off scripts that do not need continual monitoring

▶ Scripts running on a recurring schedule that cannot use global evaluation

▶ Application installations that update frequently

▶ Applications using a complex method to determine if installed correctly

For applications with multiple dependencies on other applications or packages, consider using task sequences to install the application and its dependencies. Task sequence (TS) logic can determine the appropriate prerequisite to install. Task sequences also can combine applications and packages in an installation sequence.

You can migrate existing packages from earlier supported versions of ConfigMgr and deploy them in your ConfigMgr hierarchy. (Only App-V packages from ConfigMgr 2007 migrate automatically to an application.) The packages appear under Software Library -> Packages. You can modify and deploy these packages much as you would by using the ConfigMgr 2007/2012 software distribution.

Three client system logs are used for application monitoring: AppintentEval.log, AppEnforce.log, and AppDiscovery.log. Information on accessing log files is available in Appendix A, "Configuration Manager Log Files" and at https://docs.microsoft.com/sccm/core/plan-design/hierarchy/log-files.

Creating and Modifying Applications

You can create ConfigMgr applications manually by providing all properties and then adding a DT. You could also create an application by specifying its first DT; most application properties are automatically supplied by the information ConfigMgr reads from the installer file that installs the DT.

The following sections introduce the concept of a definitive software library (DSL) and step through the process of creating ConfigMgr applications with the Create Application Wizard. Several properties are available only if the application is created manually or is modified after using the wizard.

Using a Definitive Software Library

The authors recommend using a DSL to host ConfigMgr application source files. A DSL is centrally located, typically on a Distributed File System (DFS) file share. It contains master copies of all software your organization has used, plus modified versions resulting from the application packaging process and used as input to create DTs and programs hosted on the DSL. (For more information about application packaging, see the "Best Practices for Installing Software" section, later in this chapter.) The DSL is often used to store documentation about how to configure applications for use with ConfigMgr, making it a single source of all software being used. Back up the DSL regularly; if something goes wrong, you can then avoid rebuilding your environment from scratch.

Creating a Windows Installer (.msi)-Based Application

The following example shows how to create a Windows Installer-based application, using 7-Zip (available at www.7-zip.org) as a sample ConfigMgr application. The x86 and x64 .msi files are already downloaded and saved to the DSL, \\Odyssey\DSL\Applications\Igor Pavlov\7-Zip\v16.02\Deploy\x86 and \\Odyssey\DSL\Applications\Igor Pavlov\7-Zip\ v16.02\Deploy\x64.

Perform these steps to start the Create Application Wizard:

1. Open the ConfigMgr console and navigate to **Software Library** -> **Application Management**.

2. Right-click **Applications** and select **Create Application**.

The wizard opens to the General page, with two options:

▶ Automatically detect the ConfigMgr application information using existing content

▶ Manually define the information

Follow these steps to create a ConfigMgr application for 7-Zip with existing Windows Installer content:

1. Specify the location or browse to the MSI for the application. The path must be a universal naming convention (UNC). This example creates the x86 DT first: **\\Odyssey\DSL\Applications\Igor Pavlov\7-Zip\v16.02\Deploy\x86\7z1602.msi.**

2. Click **Next**. You may be warned that the .msi could not be verified. Click **Yes** to import this file. The wizard imports the application information from the specified MSI.

3. Click **Next** to see the results. These include the application name and installation program, which is a default command line for a silent, unattended Windows Installer installation. This information is used to create the application's first DT. The information may be minimal, with only the name, installation program, and installation behavior displayed as General Information. This populates the application information and is required for the DT.

4. For 7-Zip, the installation should always install using system rights, so be sure to select **Install for system**. Figure 11.2 shows the outcome of this part of the wizard.

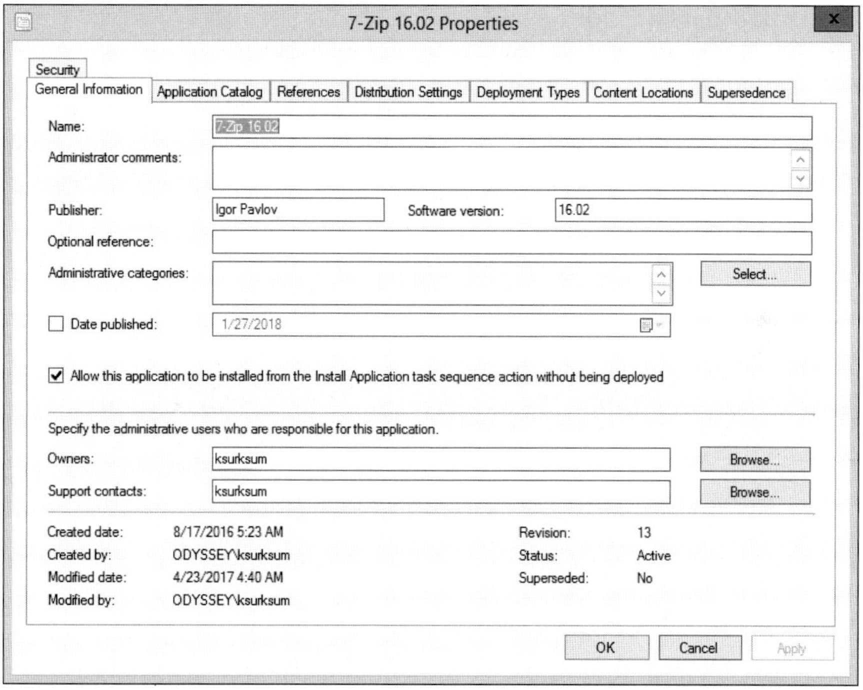

FIGURE 11.2   Specifying application information in the Create Application Wizard.

REAL WORLD: APPLICATIONS OFTEN REQUIRE ADMINISTRATOR RIGHTS FOR INSTALLATION

Most traditional installations, including MSI executables, require that the application be installed with administrator rights. Test applications thoroughly to ensure that you enable the correct installation option.

5. Click **Next** to continue to the Summary page and review the information. Then click **Next** to create the application and DT.

6. On the Completion page, which shows successful completion of the application or details about why the process was not successful, click **Close**.

The wizard provides only several configurable options; other options take defaults. To view the details of this application and its DT to ensure that the defaults are properly configured, select the application in the console and then click **Properties** on the ribbon bar.

Viewing Application Properties

A ConfigMgr application can be more complex than a package and a program, but its benefits significantly compensate for the additional time spent defining the application. Configure settings to provide the best user experience for application delivery. The following sections provide a detailed look at application properties.

General Information Tab

The General Information tab provides basic information about the application. Following is a brief description of each property on this tab. Table 11.2 specifies their locations in the Software Center and Application Catalog:

▶ **Name:** The name is used in the console and for monitoring. Use a generic name, as you may have multiple DTs for specific installation scenarios, such as x86 versus x64. Give your DTs specific names so you can easily identify them in logging and reporting.

▶ **Administrator Comments:** This information is available only in the console. Use this field to add information that is visible only to administrators.

▶ **Publisher:** Specify the software manufacturer, which appears in the Software Center under the Publisher column and in the Application Catalog.

▶ **Software Version:** Use a user-friendly software version, as the end user sees this in the Software Center and Application Catalog.

▶ **Optional Reference:** This property, which is only available to administrators, can be used to add information such as a work order or request ID for software deployment.

▶ **Administrative Categories:** These categories are used in the Application Catalog. An administrator can select existing application categories or create new ones.

▶ **Date Published:** This additional field appears in Software Center. Use this property to timestamp when an application is deployed.

▶ **Allow This Application to Be Installed from the Install Application Task Sequence Action Instead of Deploying It Manually:** Enable this option for installation to occur during an OSD TS.

▶ **Owners:** Enter an optional owner or click **Browse** to select a user or group from AD.

▶ **Support Contacts:** Enter a contact into this field or click **Browse** to select a user or group from AD.

Additional data at the bottom of this tab includes dates created and modified and by whom, current revision, current status (active or retired), and if the application is superseded.

Applications are version controlled. When a new version of an application is created, the previous version is saved and can be restored or revised as needed. Right-click an application and select **Revision History** (or select it and choose **Revision History**) to show or select previous versions.

TABLE 11.2   General Information Tab and End-User Visibility

Description	Visible in Old Software Center?	Visible in Application Catalog?	Visible in New Software Center?
Name	No	No	No
Administrator Comment	No	No	No
Publisher	Yes	Yes	No
Software Version	Yes	Yes	No
Optional Reference	No	No	No
Administrative Categories	No	No	No
Date Published	Yes	No	Yes
Allow Application to be Installed from the Install Application Task Sequence Action Instead of Deploying It Manually	No	No	No
Owners	No	No	No
Support Contacts	No	No	No

Application Catalog Tab

The Application Catalog tab displays all properties used to enhance the user experience when searching for or selecting an application from the Application Catalog. Some properties are also used when the application is visible in Software Center.

Following is a brief description of each property. Table 11.3 specifies their locations in the Software Center and Application Catalog:

▶ **Selected Language:** Multiple languages are supported. If this option is configured, custom language text appears when a user with appropriate language settings in his or her browser launches the Application Catalog using Internet Explorer (IE). If settings are configured for a language not enabled for the application, the user sees the language marked as default (English by default). All items on this tab are localized. Populate the remaining information in the page for each language you support.

▶ **Localized Application Name:** This is the friendly name of the application and appears in the Software Center and Application Catalog. This name is searchable in both locations.

▶ **User Categories:** Use these categories (Web Browsers, Utilities, Human Resources, and so on) to help end users locate software quickly in the Application Catalog. Categories appear in the left-hand frame of the Application Catalog.

▶ **User Documentation:** Enter a web URL or import a file to enable a link to be visible in the Software Center and Application Catalog when viewing application details. Clicking the link launches the web URL or opens the file. If uploading files, use a common file type available on all systems.

▶ **Link Text:** Provide a localized entry of what occurs when a user clicks on the user documentation.

▶ **Privacy URL:** Provide a URL to where privacy information about the application can be found.

▶ **Localized Description:** Populate this field to provide additional details to the user about the application. This field is searchable from the Software Center and Application Catalog.

▶ **Keywords:** Separate keywords with spaces. Add information such as file extensions and generic terms for the product, such as "archive," "word processor," and so on. You can search for these keywords in the Application Center or Software Center.

▶ **Icon:** Click **Browse** to select a standard icon or import an icon from an .ico, .msi, .exe, or .dll file. This icon appears in the Application Catalog and Software Center. Its size is 250 pixels by 250 pixels maximum.

TABLE 11.3   Application Catalog Tab and End-User Visibility

Description	Visible in Old Software Center?	Visible in Application Catalog?	Visible in New Software Center?
Selected Language	Yes	Yes	Yes
Localized Application Name	Yes	Yes	Yes
User Categories	No	Yes	No
User Documentation	Yes	Yes	No
Link Text	No	Yes	No
Localized Description	Yes	Yes	No
Keywords	No	Yes	No
Icon Image	Yes	Yes	Yes

References Tab

The Reference tab displays three types of application relationships, which are self-explanatory:

▶ Applications that depend on this application

▶ Applications that supersede this application

▶ Virtual environments that contain this application

The tab shows whether changes made to the application affect another application. You can also see revisions of the referenced application. You can view the fine print, which tells you that there are no items in the list or that you do not have permission to view all items. Depending on how role-based administration (RBA) is configured, some administrators cannot see all applications based on the configured scopes.

Distribution Settings Tab

The Distribution Settings tab helps you manage how packages are distributed to targeted DP groups and DPs. It offers the following settings:

▶ **Distribution Priority:** Control the order in which multiple packages are sent to DPs. By default, each application has priority Medium, but you can choose Low, Medium, or High. You may want to configure more critical packages (antivirus, security patches, and so on) as High, so they are sent to child sites and DPs faster than those set to Low, such as a portable document format viewer application.

▶ **Distribute the Content for This Package to Preferred Distribution Points:** Preferred DPs exist in the boundary group defined for the boundary matching its location. If a client in a preferred DP boundary requests a package not on the DP, content is automatically deployed to the preferred DP to fulfill the client request. Use this excellent approach for content you do not want to deploy to all DPs, such as a Multi User Interface (MUI) language package.

▶ **Prestaged Distribution Point Settings:** If you select Enable this distribution point for prestaged content check box in the distribution point properties, the following settings affect content distribution:

  ▶ **Automatically Download Content When Packages Are Assigned to Distribution Points:** You can cause the DP to perform normally and not follow prestaged content rules. Content is distributed to any targeted DP.

  ▶ **Download Only Content Changes to the Distribution Point:** Set this option to export and extract content manually on the DP for initial distribution. Subsequent update DP actions send delta updates.

  Say you are ready to deploy the next version of Microsoft Office. The source installation is around 1GB. Due to WAN availability, you may choose to manually transfer content to the DP the first time (by using a WAN file copy or by shipping media that contains content to the remote DP). After prestaging the initial payload, update DPs work normally, as expected.

▶ **Manually Copy the Content in This Package to the Distribution Point:** Prevent ConfigMgr from copying any content to the DP configured for prestaged content, requiring you export content from the console and extract it to the DP *each* time for that package.

Drilldown into the Deployment Types Tabs

DTs are the heart of an application, determining the best method to deploy an application to a system. Each DT contains one source files path and installation command for the deployment.

This section describes the different properties tabs for a DT. Chapter 12 contains information on creating specific DTs. For each DT, select it and click **Edit** to display its properties.

▶ **General Tab:** Table 11.4 describes the properties of this tab.

TABLE 11.4   Deployment Type Properties General Tab

Property	Description
Name	The name is visible in the ConfigMgr client logs, through the console for DT properties and deployment status, and through the reporting services point.
Technology	Specify the technology used to create the DT (Windows Installer, script-based, and so on).
Administrator Comments	Here is where you can add comments about the DT; comments are visible only to ConfigMgr administrators.
Languages	This is another informational box where you can multi-select supported languages for this DT. To actually restrict the application installation to specific languages, use the Requirements tab.

▶ **Content Tab:** Table 11.5 describes the properties of this tab, which contains installation source information and distribution settings.

TABLE 11.5   Deployment Type Properties Content Tab

Property	Description
Content Location	Specify the UNC source path to the content. All files in this path (including subfolders) are captured and stored in the content store, sent to DPs, and downloaded to clients for installation. For content, less is more: Keep the source as small as possible.
Persist content in the client cache	When you enable this setting and deploy the application to a target collection, clients using this DT (based on the requirement rules) download and keep the installation source in the local ConfigMgr cache (%windir%\ ccmcache). Client cache size is limited to 5GB, so use this option sparingly.
Allow clients to share content with other clients on the same subnet	Enable this check box to leverage BranchCache or Peer Cache (provided that they are configured for your environment).
Allow clients to use a distribution point from the default site boundary group	If a client cannot locate content for this deployment on a DP in a current or neighbor boundary group, have the client use the DPs from the default boundary group. See Chapter 14 for more information regarding DPs.
Deployment Options	If the client uses a DP from a neighbor boundary group or the default site boundary group, you can choose to not download content or to download and run locally.

▶ **Programs Tab:** Table 11.6 describes the properties of this tab, which defines the installation/uninstallation properties for a Windows Installer or script-based DT.

TABLE 11.6   Deployment Type Properties Programs Tab

Property	Description
Installation Program	Specify the command line to install the software. This is run from the root of the content source location. Click **Browse** and select the installation program if necessary. The path should be relative to the content source location.
Installation start in	If the installation requires a specific path to run, specify that here. Most modern installations do not require this configuration.
Uninstall program	Specify the unattended uninstall command line. If using the Create Deployment Type Wizard and specifying a Windows Installer program, this command is added automatically. Review and test the command line to verify that the uninstall works as expected. Include the Uninstall command when possible, allowing the user to remove optional software from Software Center, as well as any uninstall deployments from the site. Uninstalling previous applications can also be used with supersedence.
Uninstall start in	If the uninstall requires a specific path to run, specify that here.
Run installation and uninstall program as a 32-bit process on 64-bit clients	Enable this option if the application is a 32-bit installation, meaning it will install to %*Program Files (x86)*%. This setting helps ConfigMgr properly install and uninstall 32-bit applications on a 64-bit system. The ConfigMgr client agent on a 64-bit system will not use the %*Program Files (x86)*% file path or the `HKLM\Software\Wow6432Node` Registry path by default.
Product Code	Used for Windows source management. Specify a Windows Installer product code or click **Browse** and import the .msi file to ensure that the code is accurate.

NOTE: DEFINING WINDOWS SOURCE MANAGEMENT

Many Windows Installer-based applications support self-healing and/or the repair feature. These actions require the original installation files. If installing applications from ConfigMgr, the source location is a subfolder of %*windir*%\ccmcache\ (unless selecting Run from DP, an option only available for packages, which means the DP UNC path is the source location). Neither is ideal in the long term.

Entering a valid product code lets ConfigMgr manage the source location and configure the system to use the closest DP, based on site boundaries. If your network address changes, the client agent verifies that the Windows Installer source is leveraging the closest DP.

▶ **Detection Method Tab:** This tab specifies how ConfigMgr determines whether the software specified in the DT is already installed. When the wizard creates a DT, a detection method is automatically created, based on the MSI product code. A wrapped MSI can cause unwanted side effects; for example, the software may not uninstall, as the product code is from the wrapped MSI and not the actual installed software.

Every DT has a detection method. The application depends on the detection method to provide its proper state. Every seven days (by default), the client performs an application deployment evaluation cycle for required installations. If an application is found required but not installed (based on the detection method), ConfigMgr installs it automatically. For more information on creating detection methods, see the "Creating Detection Methods" section, later in this chapter.

▶ **Deployment Type User Experience Tab:** This tab defines how the installation interacts with the user. Specify user experience settings for the application in the first part of this tab. Make the proper selection to determine the rights used to install the software:

  ▶ **Installation Behavior:** Specify rights used to install the software:

    ▶ **Install for User:** Install using the rights of the current user.

    ▶ **Install for System:** Install using the rights of the SMS Agent Host service (Local System account).

    ▶ **Install for System if Resource Is Device; Otherwise Install for User:** If the application is targeted to a collection of devices, install for system; if targeted to a collection of users or user groups, install for user.

  ▶ **Logon Requirement:** Determine when installation can occur; this will be Only when a user is logged on, Only when no user is logged on, or Whether or not a user is logged on.

  A required (mandatory) deployment waits for the appropriate state before starting the installation.

  ▶ **Installation Program Visibility:** Define how the installation appears to the user during the installation process:

    ▶ **Normal:** Shows the installation program in its intended way, comparable to a normal installation.

    ▶ **Minimized:** Shows the installation program only on the task bar during installation. The window exists on the task bar during the installation process, although it is not the active window maximized on the user's workstation.

    ▶ **Maximized:** Shows the installation program as it would show if executed manually. The authors recommend this setting when installing programs requiring user intervention. It is also useful for package testing.

    ▶ **Hidden:** Hides the program during installation. This option is recommended for fully automated program deployments.

    Installation program visibility settings are effective only if the installation has information to show the user. If you use a Windows Installer command line with the `/passive` switch, an installation progress bar appears during the installation if Installation program visibility is set to

Normal or Maximized. Using /quiet makes the installation completely silent; no information appears during installation, regardless of the property setting. This visibility setting is also dependent on the next check box setting on this tab.

▶ **Allow Users to View and Interact with the Program Installation:** Allow user to see and/or interact with the installation. This is also used for troubleshooting when applications are not installing correctly. You might choose this option if the program requires the user to make a selection or click a button. If a program runs without this option and requires user intervention, it waits for the user interaction (which never occurs) and eventually times out at the maximum allowed runtime. This setting can be enabled only if the Logon requirement is configured to Only when a user is logged on.

The following two settings specify maximum runtime and estimated installation time of the deployment program for the application:

▶ **Maximum Allowed Run Time (Minutes):** Define the maximum time the program is expected to run. There can be considerable variation in how a program runs, due to the speed of the system where it is being installed, program size, and network connectivity between the system and the source files used for the installation. The example in this chapter has the setting defaulted to 120 minutes. However, previous installations of 7-Zip indicate that it should complete within 5 minutes. ConfigMgr requires a setting between 15 and 720 minutes, so set this value to 15 minutes.

▶ **Maximum Run Time Affects Installation:** The client monitors the installation until maximum time is reached. If it does not complete by then, ConfigMgr sends a status message stating the maximum runtime is reached and that ConfigMgr will no longer monitor it, freeing up ConfigMgr to deploy additional software, if required.

Before a program runs, ConfigMgr checks for any defined maintenance windows to verify that the available window is larger than the maximum allowed runtime. If the window is not large enough, the client waits for an available window to deploy, unless the deployment is configured to ignore maintenance windows.

▶ **Estimated Installation Time (Minutes):** This is the expected installation time, and it appears to the user when selecting an application to install from Software Center.

▶ **Should Configuration Manager Enforce Specific Behavior Regardless of the Application's Intended Behavior:** Use this dropdown to specify whether ConfigMgr should manage any operating system restart, providing this information to the user through the Software Center or Application Catalog. Following are the available settings:

▶ **Determine Behavior Based on Return Codes:** Handles reboots based on codes configured on the Return Codes tab. The user sees a message similar to "Might require a reboot" in the Software Center and Application Catalog.

While somewhat vague, this option is the most flexible, as the user is notified that a reboot is required if a defined return code is returned. This is a good user experience.

▶ **No Specific Action:** Tells ConfigMgr and the end user that no reboot should be required after installation.

▶ **The Software Install Program Might Force a Device Restart:** Advises that ConfigMgr is not controlling the reboot, and the actual installation may force a restart without warning. For example, if your Windows Installer command line includes the argument /ForceRestart, the installation process will force a restart. While this is the least desirable outcome, ConfigMgr at least expects a restart to occur. With any other setting, if the application forces a restart, ConfigMgr returns a failure status message about an unexpected system restart.

▶ **Configuration Manager Client Will Force a Mandatory Device Restart:** Use this setting if you know an application requires a restart; make sure the software installation does not force a restart on its own. Once the installation exits, ConfigMgr will notify the user that a restart is required or proceed to restart the computer. This decision is based on the user interaction, configured when you create a deployment (discussed in Chapter 14).

TIP: CONFIGURING THE RESTART OPTION CORRECTLY

Take time to configure the restart option correctly to avoid surprising users with unexpected restarts.

▶ **Requirements Tab:** Defines the required settings for the DT to be installed. For this example (and by default when using the Create Application Wizard), there are no requirements. This tab allows you to specify requirements for an installation to specific operating systems (such as Windows 8.1 x64).

To create the basic requirement for 7-Zip (x64), click **Add** to display and configure the Create Requirement dialog. You can configure this DT to support all Windows 8.1 (64-bit) and all Windows 10 (64-bit) applications. Click **OK** to save the platform restriction. The Requirements tab for an application contains many more features than traditional programs. The "Managing and Creating Global Conditions" section, later in this chapter, discusses creating requirements.

▶ **Return Codes Tab:** Contains defined installation return codes for the DT. Default return codes include the most popular Windows Installer return codes. Update these as required. Click **Add** to create a new return code entry.

▶ **Dependencies Tab:** Specifies required prerequisite applications for the application. See the "Adding Application Dependencies" section, later in this chapter, for more information.

When you are finished setting the properties of the DT, click **OK** to go to the application properties.

Content Locations Tab

The Content Locations tab for the application displays all targeted DPs and DP groups. Content distribution is discussed in detail in Chapter 14.

Supersedence Tab

Use the Supersedence tab to supersede an existing application with a new application or a newer version of the same application. Supersedence can automatically upgrade systems with an existing application or require the latest version on one targeted collection while continuing to support the previous version on a different collection. See the "Superseding Applications" section, later in this chapter, for more information.

The next sections dive a little deeper into some of the components of a ConfigMgr application.

Creating Detection Methods

This section discusses the importance of having a proper detection method and how to create complex detection methods.

Detection methods determine whether software is installed. They do not determine whether ConfigMgr installed the application. Software can be installed and uninstalled in nonstandard ways. When deploying a ConfigMgr application to a collection of devices (either available or required), the application state is evaluated on each targeted system on a regular interval—seven days by default and configurable using client settings. In addition, for user-targeted ConfigMgr applications, when a user installs an application from the Software Center or Application Catalog, the application appears in Software Center and is evaluated on the same interval as device-targeted applications.

The *application deployment evaluation cycle* can be triggered from the client (as with hardware inventory), or it can be configured using client settings. If a ConfigMgr application is deployed as required but not installed when the application deployment evaluation cycle runs, ConfigMgr automatically triggers an install/reinstall. Consider required applications to be a type of desired state. If a required deployment for an application exists, ConfigMgr ensures that the application is installed.

Detection methods are important because they report the current state of the ConfigMgr application (installed, not installed, or required). Correctly configuring detection methods is vital to keeping software from reinstalling.

Automatic software reinstallation can of tremendous benefit; however, if your detection methods are not correct, it can be a nightmare. Incorrect detection methods can cause an incorrect application state (installed or not) and repeated attempts to install the application. Be sure to test thoroughly.

Creating Detection Methods for Windows Installer Applications

ConfigMgr applications using Windows Installer generally use a simple detection method based on the Windows Installer product code. If you use the Create Application Wizard or Create Deployment Type Wizard and select a Windows Installer application, the detection method is automatically configured to use the Windows Installer product code. While this is normally sufficient, there are some caveats:

▶ **Duplicate Product Codes:** MSI product codes should be unique. The authors have encountered duplicate product codes for some repackaged applications. For example, maybe the packager created Package A and then reused Package A to create Package B but failed to generate a new product code. Or perhaps the packager created a major revision to Package A (say from revision 2.1 to revision 3.0) and reused the same product code. In traditional package and program software distribution, these errors would not be as significant. However, with the new application model, using invalid product codes as a detection method could cause an incorrect installation state.

▶ **Repackaged Applications:** When you repackage an application into Windows Installer format, that application will have a product code. This does not always tell you if the actual application is installed, especially if other users installed it with the original source.

▶ **Wrapper Installers:** While similar to a repackaged application, the application installation is usually intact, so the wrapper simply calls the installation executable with the proper command-line arguments. The wrapper may then launch additional actions (such as installing a licensing file) to complete the installation. Wrappers have their place, but not always as a detection method.

While using the wizard to create a Windows Installer DT could save some steps, it might cause additional pain in the future. Be sure you know the origin of the installer (vendor, repackaged, and so on) and are aware of any additional steps the installation performs.

Consider adding additional detection clauses to the detection method when working with these special-case installers. For example, you may want to confirm that a file exists, is a specific version, or uses a specific Registry value. The next section discusses additional detection methods.

Following are the basic steps to add a Windows Installer detection method:

1. From the Deployment Type Properties dialog, select **Detection Method** and click **Add Clause**.

2. Choose the appropriate setting type. In this case, select **Windows Installer** and click **Browse**.

3. Navigate to the desired .msi file and click **Open**. The product code appears. By default, the rule only looks for the product code. You can modify the rule to require a minimum version of the product code.

4. Click **OK** to save the detection rule.

Adding Other Detection Methods

In addition to the Windows Installer detection method, you can use built-in methods based on file system and Registry properties. This section walks through examples of each. Basic steps to add a file-based detection method follow:

1. From the Deployment Type Properties dialog, select **Detection Method** and click **Add Clause**.

2. Choose the appropriate setting type. In this case, select **File System** and click **Browse**. Use the Browse File System dialog to browse the current computer or a different computer (provided that the system is online and you have administrative rights) by entering a computer name and clicking **Connect**. Expand the computer information in the left frame, find the desired file, and click **OK**.

   The Detection Rule dialog appears, with file and folder information populated. The middle section automatically populates based on the file selected. It shows that 7zG.exe will be looked for in *%ProgramFiles%\7-Zip*. An additional file version check was added and is shown in the bottom frame of Figure 11.3.

   Notice the check box This file or folder is associated with a 32-bit application on 64-bit systems. Selecting it enables the DT detection rule to look first in the 32-bit file and Registry location; if not found, it looks in the 64-bit location on 64-bit operating systems. For example, if an application installs in C:\Program Files (X86)\foo\foo.exe on a 64-bit system, enabling this check box causes the rule to check both C:\Program Files (X86)\foo\foo.exe and C:\Program Files\foo\foo.exe.

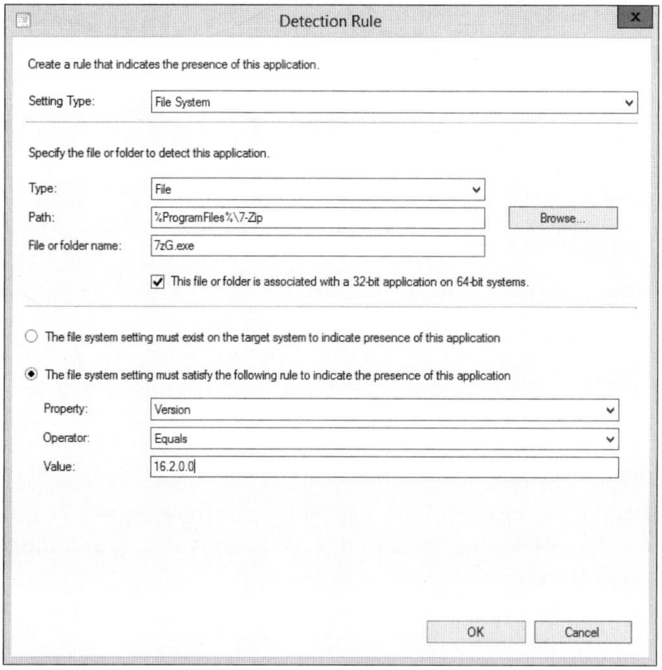

FIGURE 11.3   Creating a file system detection rule.

Following are the basic steps for adding a Registry-based detection method:

1. From the Deployment Type Properties dialog, select **Detection Method** and click **Add Clause**.

2. Choose the appropriate setting type. In this case, select **Registry** and click **Browse**.

3. Select the proper Registry key or value and click **OK**. You could create a basic Registry rule, looking for the existence of the `HKLM\SOFTWARE\Microsoft\Windows\CurrentVersion\Uninstall\{23170F69-40C1-2702-1602-000001000000}` Registry key. As mentioned previously, the check box to include the x86 Registry path on x64 systems is enabled. You can also specify specific Registry name and value properties, if desired, as displayed in Figure 11.4.

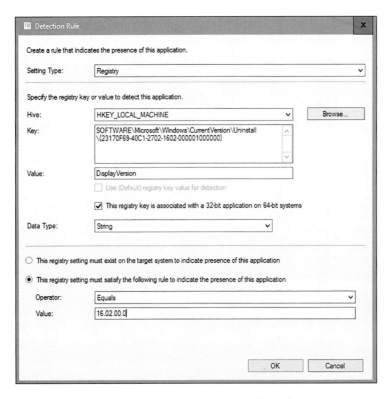

FIGURE 11.4   Creating a Registry-based detection rule.

Creating detection methods is straightforward and similar to creating compliance settings. The challenge is working with your packaging team (or reverse-engineering a product installation) to determine the detection rules needed.

You can also group multiple clauses and change connectors between ANDs and ORs, as shown in Figure 11.5. In the dialog shown in Figure 11.5, select the last two rows in the grid and click **Group** and then toggle the **Or** to an **And**. Also, change the first **And** to an **Or**, as shown in the figure. This enables ConfigMgr to look for either the product code or the combination of Registry key and file path with version. 7-Zip is a good example of why you may want to create a detection method, as shown in this figure: The 7-Zip installer is available as both an .msi and an .exe, so the product code may or may not exist, depending on the installer used.

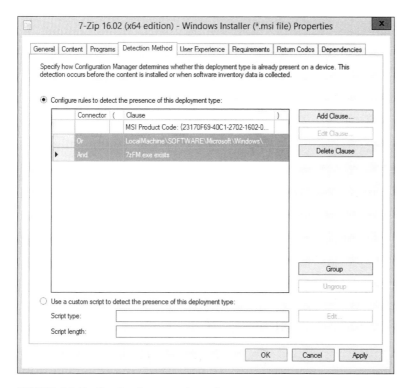

FIGURE 11.5   Configuring grouping rules.

Using Custom Script Detection Methods

The final detection method is to use a custom script, where you can specify any script you want. Most applications use standard detection methods (Windows Installer product code, file, or Registry), but you could encounter an application that requires a more complex way to determine if it is installed.

The custom script detection method requires writing a custom script for ConfigMgr to determine whether the software is installed. Be sure to return text from the script to confirm that the software is installed. If no text is returned, ConfigMgr understands that the software is not installed. The next two sections provide sample scripts to leverage the custom script detection method.

Creating a Custom Detection Method Script with PowerShell

From the Deployment Type Properties dialog, enable **Detection Method** to create a custom script and click **Edit**. Select **PowerShell** as the script type.

TIP: MODIFYING THE POWERSHELL EXECUTION POLICY IF REQUIRED

You may need to use client settings to adjust the PowerShell execution policy (under the Computer Agent group).

Listing 11.1 is a sample PowerShell script that checks for the existence of a file and verifies its version. Note the `write-host Version Exists` line. If all tests pass (that is, the file exists and the version is correct), text is written to standard output, signifying `True` for the script detection. If the script returns text, ConfigMgr considers the application installed.

LISTING 11.1   PowerShell Script to Check for Existence of a File and Its Version

```
$strFilePath = "c:\Program Files\7-Zip\7zG.exe"
if (test-path) ($strFilePath)
{
    $file = get-childitem $strFilePath | select *
    if ($file.VersionInfo.ProductVersion -eq "16.2.0.0")
    {
        write-host "Version Exists"
    }
    else
    {
        #version does not exist
    }
}
else
{
    #file does not exist
}
```

Creating a Custom Detection Method Script with VBScript

Enable the **Detection Method** option and click **Edit**, this time selecting **VBScript** as the script type.

Listing 11.2 is a sample Visual Basic script that checks for the existence of a file and verifies the file version. Notice the `wscript.echo "Proper Version!"` line in the code. If all tests pass (that is, the file exists and the version is correct), text is written to standard output, signaling to ConfigMgr that the application is installed.

LISTING 11.2   Visual Basic Script that Checks for Existence of a File and Verifies the File Version

```vbscript
strFileName = "C:\Program Files\7-Zip\7zG.exe"
Set filesys = CreateObject("Scripting.FileSystemObject")
if filesys.FileExists(strFileName) Then
   'File exists, now let's check version
   if(filesys.GetFileVersion(strFileName) = "16.2.0.0") then
      wscript.echo "Proper Version!"
   else
      'wrong version
   end if
else
'file doesn't exist
End If
```

TIP: AVOIDING SMART QUOTES WITH VBSCRIPT AND POWERSHELL

When you type or paste text into a text editor, you may create "smart quotes," which curve the quotes around whatever is being quoted (both single and double quotes.) Smart quotes cause scripts to break. If you encounter smart quotes, paste the code into a text editor such as Windows Notepad and replace all smart quotes with standard quotes. Remember to replace both single and double quotes.

The Open option in the Script Editor dialog lets you browse to a script file to import it. You can enable scripts to run in the 32-bit environment on a 64-bit system. Some applications install to the 32-bit section of the Registry; this check box allows you to determine the environment where your script will run. The check box has no effect on 32-bit operating systems.

For more information about the application model and how it works, see https://blogs.msdn. microsoft.com/steverac/2015/06/01/configmgr-2012-the-application-model-and-advanced-detection-logic/.

Managing and Creating Global Conditions

Use global conditions to configure DTs to ensure that software only installs on a specific OS and service pack. This way you can deploy software to a collection of all systems, and only the systems that meet the platform requirements actually install the software. Global conditions are requirement rules representing business or technical conditions, and they specify how an application is provided and deployed to client devices. Using global conditions reduces the number of collections needed for software deployment.

TIP: COLLECTIONS VERSUS GLOBAL CONDITIONS

Whereas a deployment requires a target collection, a global condition does not. Say you want to deploy AppA to all systems in the HR organizational unit (OU); you would create requirement rules on the DT in AppA to ensure that it only installs on systems in that OU. You can then target a larger collection of systems than just the HR OU, which means you may not need to create a specific collection for the HR OU.

To review the built-in global conditions, open the Deployment Type properties dialog, select **Requirements**, and then click **Add**. Then choose from one of three categories, discussed in the following sections.

Device Global Conditions

Device conditions contain information specific to the client device. Figure 11.6 shows a built-in device condition with a device requirement where total memory is at least 8GB (8192).

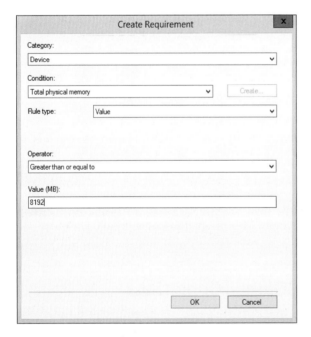

FIGURE 11.6   Specifying a total physical memory requirement.

The following are the built-in device conditions:

▶ **Active Directory Site:** Specifies that the DT can only run for systems that are part of or not part of any specific AD site or sites.

▶ **Configuration Manager Site:** Specifies that the DT can only run for systems that do or do not belong to a specific site code or codes.

▶ **CPU Speed:** Specifies a CPU speed requirement, in megahertz.

▶ **Disk Space:** Specifies an amount of free disk space that must be met to run the DT for the application. Select the system drive, a specific drive, or any drive. The value is specified in megabytes. You can use operators such as Equals, Not equals, Greater than, Less than, Greater than or equal to, and so on.

▶ **Number of Processors:** Specifies the number of processors the device should have to run this DT.

▶ **Operating System:** Specifies that the DT can only run on a specific OS, such as on Windows 7 64-bit operating systems.

▶ **Operating System Language:** Configures the operating system language or languages as a requirement for the DT.

▶ **Organizational Unit (OU):** Specifies that the DT runs only on devices that belong to an OU that you add. To include child OUs, select the Include child OUs option.

▶ **Total Physical Memory:** Specifies how much memory is required to run the DT for the application. The value is entered in megabytes.

User Global Conditions

Only one user global condition currently exists: Primary Device. Set the requirement to True or False so that the appropriate software installs, based on whether the user is considered the primary user of the device.

Creating Custom Global Conditions

Create custom conditions, also known as global conditions, when device and user conditions are inadequate. These can contain LDAP queries, Windows Management Instrumentation (WMI) Query Language (WQL) queries, file and Registry queries, and many other custom configurations. The process is similar to the process of creating configuration items for compliance settings. You can build multiple queries into one custom global condition. Use the Create Deployment Type Wizard or create global conditions from the Global Conditions node under **Software Library -> Application**. Perform the following steps to create a custom condition:

1. In the Create Requirement dialog, select the **Custom** category.

2. Select **Create -> New condition** in the condition field to open a new page to create new custom conditions. The following fields are available in the upper section of this page:

   ▶ **Name:** Specify a name for the global condition.

   ▶ **Description:** Specify a description for the global condition.

   ▶ **Device Type:** Use the dropdown list to specify if the condition is for a Windows, Windows Mobile, or Nokia device.

▶ **Condition Type:** Use the dropdown list to specify if the condition is a single setting or an expression (a group of settings).

Configure the actual condition in the lower section. Based on the settings type, multiple options are available. Available types follow:

▶ **Active Directory Query:** Create an LDAP query condition. For example, the output of the query can be a specific AD group.

▶ **Assembly:** Specify an assembly from the global assembly cache that will be used as the condition for the DT.

▶ **File System:** Specify that a particular file or folder should be present on the device.

▶ **IIS Metabase:** Build a condition based on a specific property ID of an Internet Information Services (IIS) metabase.

▶ **Registry Key:** Specify that a certain Registry key should exist on a device in order to run the application DT. You can specify multiple Registry hives, such as HKEY_LOCAL_MACHINE, or click **Browse** and browse through the local Registry of the system running the console.

▶ **Registry Value:** Similar to the Registry key settings type, this option allows you to specify a key and value requirement.

▶ **Script:** Add a script that queries and returns data to ConfigMgr. Scripts can be in PowerShell, VBScript, or Java.

▶ **SQL Query:** Execute a SQL query against a SQL database. You can specify the SQL instance, the database name, a column, and the actual SQL statement. Click **Open** to upload an existing SQL query file. The query will run under the Local System account.

▶ **WQL Query:** WMI contains information about the OS and where hardware is stored. For example, if your application is software required for a specific video card, you can write a WQL query to query for that card, including type and model.

▶ **XPath Query:** Add an eXtensible Markup Language (XML) script to query and return data to ConfigMgr. You can specify the path for the file and the file-name, along with the XPath query.

3. Select the desired settings and click **OK** to save the global condition.

Global conditions are listed on the Create Requirements page, under Custom. Use this page to specify if the result of the condition should be True, False, or contain a value. Examples of custom global conditions follow:

▶ **File System Condition:** Figure 11.7 demonstrates creating a global condition based on a file system check. The figure shows a global condition using %*ProgramFiles*%\ ACME Corp\Licensefile.lic.

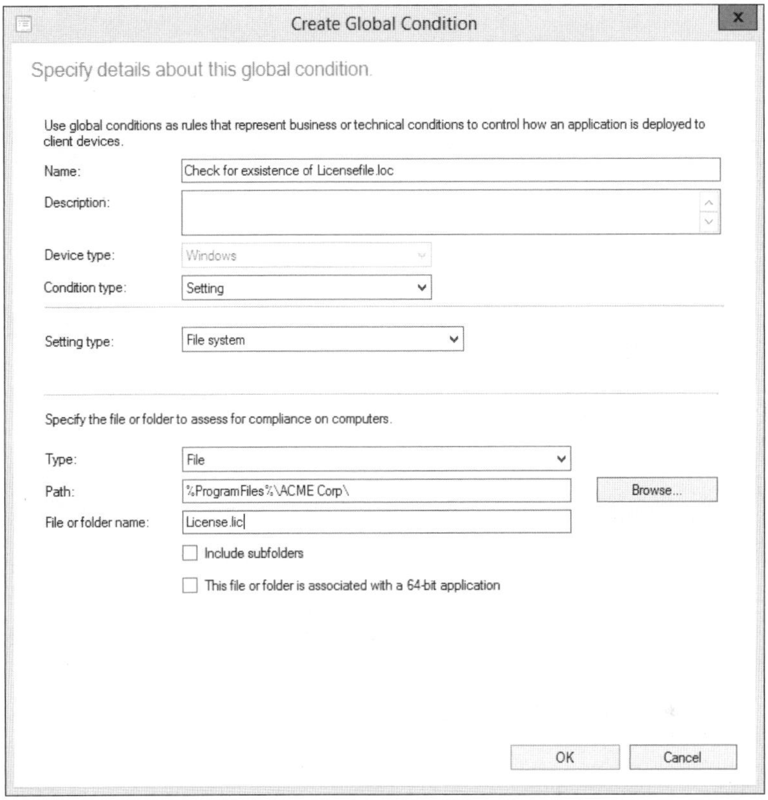

FIGURE 11.7   File system condition.

Add the requirement to your application after saving the global condition. Figure 11.8 shows that the requirement will pass only if the license file has a modified date of 8/22/2016 12:18:23 PM. You can create a requirement to check that a file exists. You can verify more than its existence; following is a list of file properties available for the custom file system global condition:

▶ File Size

▶ File Version

▶ Date Created

▶ Date Modified

▶ Company

▶ Product Name

▶ SHA-1 Hash

▶ File Attributes

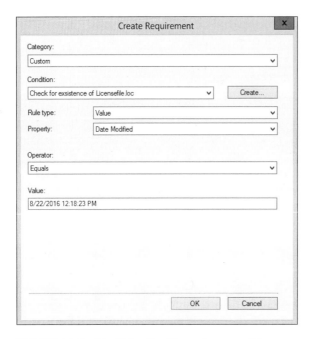

FIGURE 11.8   Modifying the file system condition.

▶ **WQL Query Condition:** WMI queries can add flexibility to global conditions. Figure 11.9 shows how you can create requirement rules to deploy software to specific computer models.

Figure 11.9 shows creating a global condition that dynamically makes the computer model available, based on the Model property of the `Win32_ComputerSystem` WMI class. The condition runs a WQL query in the `root\cimv2` namespace, `Select Model from Win32_ComputerSystem`. Leave the `Where` clause section empty to make the condition dynamic and then create a new requirement for the DT.

Figure 11.10 leverages the global condition created in Figure 11.9. Select the custom condition named Computer Model with the operator Contains followed by the computer model for the value. Note that some computer manufactures pad the Model property with extra spaces, so use Contains instead of Equals when possible. Now this requirement rule will be met only if the computer model property contains HP Elitebook 820 G2.

Global conditions enable targeted software deployments without needing custom collections for each deployment. Test thoroughly to verify that a condition works as expected.

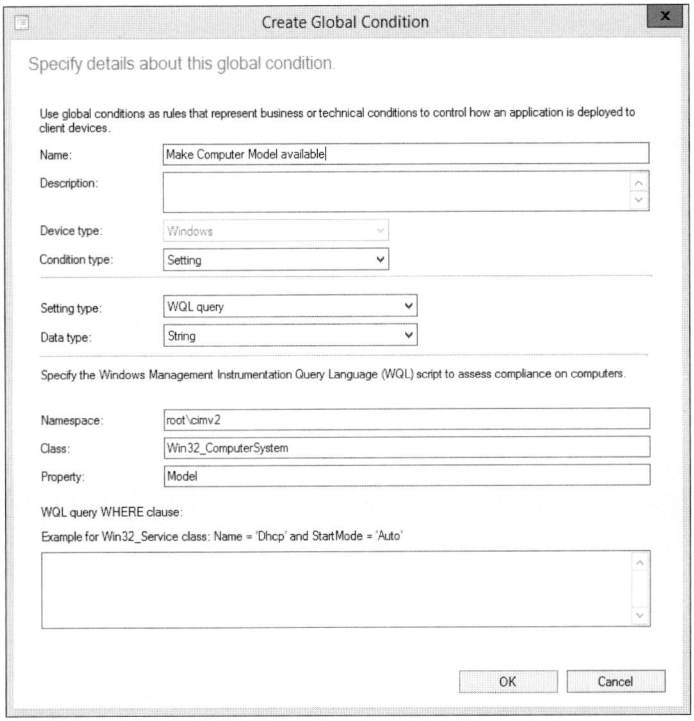

FIGURE 11.9   The Create Global Condition dialog for a WQL query.

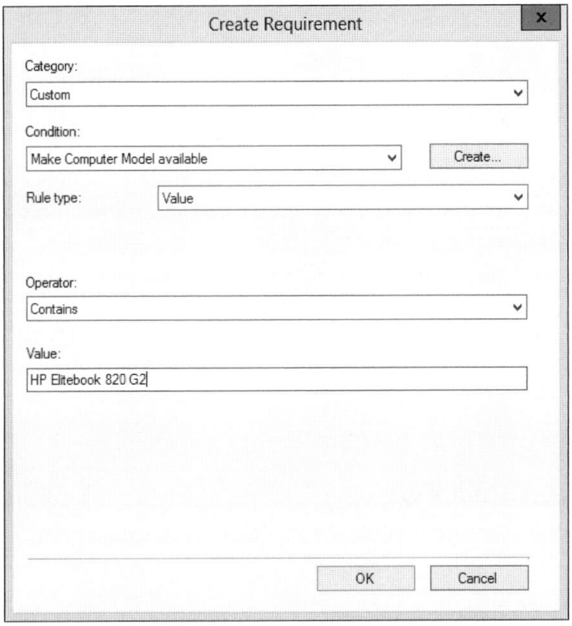

FIGURE 11.10   The Create Requirement dialog for the custom computer model condition.

Managing Application Management, Application Configuration, and Volume License Purchases

You can configure applications or restrict what an application can do by using mobile application management (MAM) policies. ConfigMgr can also manage Internet access for managed browsers and manage volume purchasing of iOS apps or Windows Store for Business apps. These topics are discussed in the following sections.

About Mobile Application Management Policies

MAM policies can modify or restrict app functionality. These policies enable you to restrict copy, cut, and paste operations and ensure that web links within an app are only opened by a managed browser. Currently these policies are supported for Android (version 4 and later) and iOS (version 7 and above).

Not all apps can be managed, as an app must be aware and support manageability by a management platform. To apply restrictions to apps using ConfigMgr with hybrid Intune, the app itself must incorporate the Microsoft Intune software development kit (SDK). This can be done in two ways:

▶ The developer incorporates the Microsoft Intune SDK while developing the app and makes the app publicly available in the app store.

TIP: OVERVIEW OF MANAGEABLE APPS

Available apps built with the Intune SDK are listed in the Microsoft Intune mobile application gallery, at https://www.microsoft.com/cloud-platform/microsoft-intune-partners.

▶ The app is repackaged using a "wrapper" to make it manageable. Wrap Intune apps with the Microsoft Intune App Wrapping Tool, used to process in-house created apps by restricting features of the app without changing any code.

TIP: MORE INFORMATION ABOUT WRAPPING APPLICATIONS

For information about wrapping in-house created apps for iOS, see https://docs.microsoft.com/intune/deploy-use/prepare-ios-apps-for-mobile-application-management-with-the-microsoft-intune-app-wrapping-tool.

For information on wrapping Android in-house created apps, see https://docs.microsoft.com/intune/deploy-use/prepare-android-apps-for-mobile-application-management-with-the-microsoft-intune-app-wrapping-tool.

Creating Application Management Policies

The example in this section shows the different options for an application management policy. Follow these steps:

1. In the ConfigMgr console, navigate to **Software Library -> Application Management -> Application Management Policies**.

2. Select **Create Application Management Policy** in the ribbon bar to start the Create Application Management Policy Wizard.

3. On the General page, provide a name and a description for the application management policy and then click **Next**.

4. On the Policy Type page, select the platform (either iOS or Android) and policy type (either General or Managed Browser) to use.

   Depending on the chosen platform and policy type, the next page displays iOS Policy, Android Policy, or Managed Browser. Figure 11.11 shows the Application management policy for iOS page.

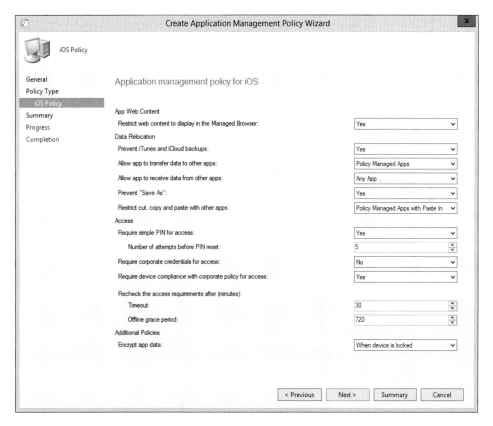

FIGURE 11.11   Application policy for iOS page.

The policy pages provide the following options:

▶ **App Web Content Restrict web content to display in the managed browser:** If this option is enabled, links are opened with the browser.

▶ **Data Relocation Prevent Android Backups:** (Android only) When this option is enabled, backups are disabled.

▶ **Data Relocation Prevent iTunes and iCloud Backups:** (iOS only) When this option is enabled, backups are disabled.

▶ **Data Relocation Allow App to Transfer Data to Other Apps:** Set to none, policy managed apps, or any app.

▶ **Data Relocation Allow App to Receive Data from Other Apps:** Set to none, policy managed apps, or any app.

▶ **Data Relocation Prevent "Save As":** Enable or disable.

▶ **Data Relocation Restrict Cut, Copy and Paste with Other Apps:** Set to none, policy managed apps, policy managed apps with paste in, or any app. Policy Managed Apps with Paste In means that cut or copied data can be pasted into other restricted apps, and the data cut or copied from any app can be pasted into this app.

▶ **Access Require Simple PIN for Access:** When this option is enabled, users must create a personal identification number (PIN) that must be entered before using the app.

▶ **Access Number of Attempts Before PIN Reset:** Specify the number of PIN entry attempts before the user must reset the PIN.

▶ **Access Require Corporate Credentials for Access:** When this option is enabled, requires users enter corporate credentials before using the application.

▶ **Access Require Device Compliance with Corporate Policy for Access:** When this option is enabled, restricts access to apps when device is jailbroken or rooted.

▶ **Access: Recheck the Access Requirements After (Minutes) - Timeout:** Specify the time before access requirements are rechecked (30 minutes by default).

▶ **Access Recheck the Access Requirements After (Minutes) - Offline Grace Period:** Specify the time before access requirements are rechecked if the device is offline (720 minutes by default).

▶ **Additional Policies Encrypt App Data:** When this option is enabled, encrypts all data associated with the app.

iOS data is encrypted using the device-level encryption provided by the OS when the device is at rest; this requires that a device PIN policy be set by the IT administrator.

Android data encryption is provided by Microsoft during file I/O operations, using Advanced Encryption Standard (AES-128) encryption in Cipher Block Chaining (CBC) mode.

▶ **Additional Policies Block Screen Capture:** (Android only) When this option is enabled, blocks screen capture capabilities of the device when using the app.

The Managed Browser page provides two options:

▶ Allow the managed browser to open only the URLs listed below (allow list)

▶ Block the managed browser from opening the URLs listed below (block list)

One option must be used; specify the allow list or block list in the Allowed or blocked URLs section of the Managed Browser page. URLs can be provided using wildcards such as https://*.odessey.com or https://*. *.microsoft.com is always allowed.

5. Check the settings on the Summary page; click **Previous** to reach the page where you want to make modifications. When finished, click **Next** to create the application management policy.

6. On the Completion page, ensure that the application management policy was created successfully and click **Close** to close the wizard.

Associate the application management policy with a DT when creating the deployment defined for a collection. Apps requiring a policy automatically prompt for a policy with which to be associated. When the managed browser is a DT, you must provide a general and managed browser policy, as the managed browser is also a managed app.

If the Intune-managed browser was previously installed, you cannot manage it with ConfigMgr application management policies. The app must be deployed with those policies.

The managed browser app does not open sites with expired or untrusted certificates. It cannot use any settings set for the built-in browser of the device, as it cannot access those settings. The browser cannot block access when intermediate services are used to access the site, such as using the cached or translated version of the page from a search engine. If the Require simple PIN for access or Require corporate credentials for access mobile application management policy setting is set and a user clicks the help link on the authentication page, the help can be used to browse to any Internet site, even sites blocked in the application management policy.

Because application management policy is linked to a DT, conflicts can occur when you apply multiple policies:

▶ The value in conflict is removed and a built-in conflict value of the app is used if the conflict occurs during its first deployment.

▶ If MAM policies are already applied and a conflicting policy is applied with conflicting settings, existing policy settings are retained.

Policy settings are tattooed in the device and not removed when the device is unenrolled from ConfigMgr, even if the app is uninstalled and reinstalled.

Managed browser policies can also conflict; in this case, URLs are not enforced if the modes in each policy are the same or different or when the policy is received for the first time. If a second policy is applied with conflicting policies, these policies are ignored.

Monitor application management policies using the deployment properties for the ConfigMgr application to which the policy is specified. The policy is found under Related Objects.

App Configuration Policies

App configuration policies configure the application with specific settings required when a user runs the app. These could contain language settings, a company logo as branding, and more. Policies are supported on iOS devices running iOS 7 and later and can be configured using individual property list keys and values or with app configuration XML files containing listings of property list keys and values. The format of the XML property list varies, depending on the app you are configuring. Contact the app's supplier for details about the exact format to use.

Intune supports only the following data types in a property list:

- ▶ <integer>
- ▶
- ▶ <string>
- ▶ <array>
- ▶ <dict>
- ▶ <true /> or

Intune supports the following token types (which are placed between the {{ }} characters):

- ▶ {{userprincipalname}}
- ▶ {{mail}}
- ▶ {{partialupn}}
- ▶ {{accountid}}
- ▶ {{deviceid}}
- ▶ {{userid}}
- ▶ {{username}}
- ▶ {{serialnumber}}
- ▶ {{serialnumberlast4digits}}
- ▶ {{udidlast4digits}}

Perform the following steps to create an app configuration policy:

1. In the ConfigMgr console, navigate to **Software Library -> Application Management -> App Configuration Policies.** Click **Create App Configuration Policy** on the ribbon bar to start the Create App Configuration Policy Wizard.

2. On the General page, provide a name and description. You can also assign a category to the policy for searching and filtering afterward by using the ConfigMgr console. Click **Next.**

3. Use the iOS policy page to specify name and value pairs or browse for a property list file. Click **Next**.

Enable the **Specify name and value pairs** option to create pairs. To get there, click **New** to open the Add Name/Value Pair dialog, where you can specify type, name, and value. Browse to a property list file to paste the app configuration policy or click **Select file** to import an XML file with the configuration.

4. On the Summary page, verify the settings and make modifications as needed by clicking **Previous**. When all settings are validated, click **Next** to create the policy.

5. On the Completion page, verify that the policy was created successfully. Click **Close**.

Listing 11.3 is an example of an app configuration XML file.

LISTING 11.3   Sample App Configuration XML File

```
<dict>
 <key>userprincipalname</key>
  <string>{{userprincipalname}}</string>
  <key>mail</key>
  <string>{{mail}}</string>
 <key>partialupn</key>
  <string>{{partialupn}}</string>
  <key>accountid</key>
  <string>{{accountid}}</string>
  <key>deviceid</key>
  <string>{{deviceid}}</string>
  <key>userid</key>
  <string>{{userid}}</string>
  <key>username</key>
  <string>{{username}}</string>
  <key>serialnumber</key>
  <string>{{serialnumber}}</string>
  <key>serialnumberlast4digits</key>
  <string>{{serialnumberlast4digits}}</string>
  <key>udidlast4digits</key>
  <string>{{udidlast4digits}}</string>
</dict>
```

After creating the app configuration policy, associate it with a DT when you create the deployment. Use the App Configuration Policies page of the Deploy Software Wizard, available when deploying Apple DTs.

Apple Volume License Purchasing

ConfigMgr administrators can deploy and manage iOS apps purchased in volume from the Apple App Store, using the Apple Volume Purchase Program (VPP) for Business. This requires ConfigMgr to be configured in hybrid device management mode, using Microsoft Intune. After joining the VPP, you can configure the VPP token to be uploaded into ConfigMgr. The following functionality becomes available:

▶ Purchased apps are displayed in the ConfigMgr console.

▶ Purchased apps can be deployed and monitored for installation and the number of licenses used in ConfigMgr.

▶ Licenses can be reclaimed by uninstalling volume-purchased apps.

▶ Volume purchase change information is synchronized with ConfigMgr twice a day. Full synchronization takes place every seven (7) days, or you can click **Sync** to perform a manual sync.

If you deploy an iOS volume-purchased app to a device without a user, it is not installed. Configure user affinity by using the Device Enrollment Program (DEP) or Apple Configurator from Apple. The VPP token is valid for one year, after which it should be renewed.

Follow these steps to upload the Apple VPP token in ConfigMgr:

1. In the ConfigMgr console, navigate to **Administration -> Cloud Services -> Apple Volume Purchase Program Tokens**.

2. Click **Add Apple Volume Purchase Program Token** in the ribbon bar to start the Add Apple Volume Purchase Program Wizard.

3. Use the General page to configure the following settings:

   ▶ **Name:** Specify the name for the token.

   ▶ **Token:** Click **Browse** to select the token downloaded from Apple.

   ▶ **Description:** Provide a description to help identify the token in the ConfigMgr console.

   ▶ **Assigned Categories to Improve Searching and Filtering:** Specify or assign a category to the VPP token that can be used in searches.

4. Click **Next** to complete the wizard.

View the token's information in the Apple Volume Purchase Program Tokens node. This includes when it was last updated, the expiration date, and when it was last synchronized. Volume-licensed apps are also visible in License Information under **Software Library -> Application Management -> Store Apps**. Select an app and click **Create Application** to create a ConfigMgr application containing the iOS volume-purchased app using deeplinking. When deploying this type of app, Microsoft supports it only as a required app.

11

Integrating Windows Store for Business

Windows Store for Business allows a company to volume purchase or individually purchase Windows apps for Windows 10-based devices. Connecting Windows Store for Business to ConfigMgr lets you synchronize purchased app information, making that information available in the console and for deployment, as in any other ConfigMgr application. Synchronization occurs every 24 hours.

For Windows 10 Azure AD-joined devices, users and devices can connect directly to the store to get the app (called an *online app*) and its license. For all other scenarios, apps can be cached for direct deployment within the on-premise network (an *offline app*); no store or Internet connection is needed.

More information about integrating Windows Store for Business is available at https://technet.microsoft.com/library/mt740630.aspx. This article will be updated after a new ConfigMgr build is released that provides production support for Windows Store for Business integration.

> **TIP: MORE INFORMATION ABOUT WINDOWS STORE FOR BUSINESS**
>
> For information about Windows Store for Business, see https://technet.microsoft.com/itpro/windows/manage/windows-store-for-business-overview.

More About Managing Applications

Applications are a large component of ConfigMgr. The preceding sections provide an extensive discussion about creating applications. The next sections describe additional features that enable you to leverage applications to their fullest potential.

Adding Application Dependencies

Many applications have software prerequisites. For example, the FreeMind application, discussed in Chapter 12, requires the Java Runtime Environment. Package/program deployment incorporates the Run another Program First feature, which works well to install software prerequisites but cannot determine if that software is already installed. ConfigMgr might run the prerequisite software again (depending on advertisement and program rerun properties), even if it is already installed.

ConfigMgr application dependencies are smarter than Run another Program First. When an application has a dependency, detection and requirement rules run to determine which DT needs to be installed, if any. If the dependent application is already installed (per detection rules), ConfigMgr skips that installation, checks additional dependencies, and installs the application. Following are some items to note about application dependencies:

▶ An application can only be dependent on another application (not on a package/program).

▶ A package/program cannot be dependent on an application.

▶ Application dependencies are honored during OSD. (Package/program dependencies are not and must be called out separately in a TS.)

▶ Dependent applications install in a nondeterministic order. If an application requires a specific order, create the dependency for that application rather than creating one application with all dependencies defined.

▶ Create a separate dependency group for each application requirement. When creating a dependency group, only one application from the group must be installed for the requirement to be considered satisfied.

If any of these constraints makes the task more difficult, consider using a TS. You can create a generic TS to install software in a well-defined sequence. However, you can only deploy task sequences to devices.

NOTE: USING A TS TO INSTALL COMPLEX SOFTWARE CONFIGURATIONS

While task sequences are designed primarily for deploying operating systems, they can deploy ConfigMgr applications and packages. This is useful with complex applications or situations, such as when the installation is a combination of ConfigMgr applications and packages.

The following procedure installs FreeMind, which requires Oracle Java. The example uses an Oracle Java ConfigMgr application and the FreeMind ConfigMgr application. Perform the following steps to create the dependency:

1. From the Deployment Type dialog in the ConfigMgr console application, select the **Dependencies** tab. Click **Add** to display the Add Dependency dialog.

2. Enter a group name for the installation (for this example, call it **Oracle Java**) and click **Add** to display the Specify Required Application dialog.

3. Select the required application—in this case, the **Oracle Java JRE 8 Update 11** deployment type—and click **OK**. The Add Dependency dialog displays the dependency information, shown in Figure 11.12. The Auto Install check box is enabled by default, indicating that the software will be automatically installed on targeted systems.

4. Click **OK** in the Add Dependency Wizard and then click **OK** again to save the DT and the application.

Now when you deploy the FreeMind ConfigMgr application, ConfigMgr automatically installs the Oracle Java Runtime Environment requirement first.

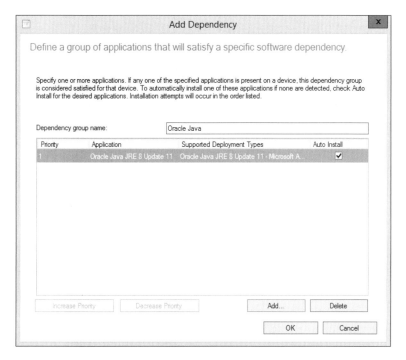

FIGURE 11.12   The Add Dependency dialog for the deployment type.

Managing Revision History

Each time you modify an application, ConfigMgr creates a new revision of that application, allowing you to easily revert to a previous application state. When you restore a revision, ConfigMgr creates a duplicate of the desired revision and assigns it the latest revision number. Figure 11.13 shows a sample application revision history for 7-Zip.

The figure shows that only the last revision is currently referenced. You can select and delete any revision without a reference. A primary site has a site maintenance task, Delete Unused Application revisions, that removes any revision that is not referenced and that is at least 60 days old.

To revert to a previous version, select the desired version and click **Restore**. Notice that newer versions do not disappear. When you select a revision to restore, ConfigMgr clones the desired revision into a new revision.

Older revisions may still have assigned references. View a revision to identify the reference and then go to the reference and reconfigure it to a newer revision, if desired. You cannot delete a revision that has references.

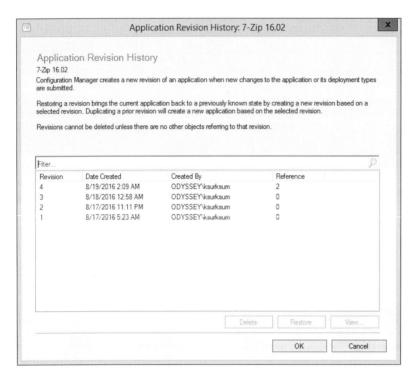

FIGURE 11.13   Viewing application revision history.

CAUTION: REVISIONS AND RELATED CONTENT ON DPS

An important caveat to remember about revision history is that DP content is kept for each revision. Say you have a new application, with a DT that has a content source path. You send that content to the DPs and notice that the size is 8GB. You know this is incorrect and investigate; you discover that you are using the wrong source path, so you change the source path for the DT and, increment the revision history. However, the previous version of the application remains in the revision history, and as long as it is in revision history, that extra 8GB of content remains on the DPs.

When you finish testing and are ready to deploy an application to production, consider implementing a standard process to clean up any old revision history entries so you can start as cleanly as possible in production.

Exporting and Importing Applications

Configuration Manager can export objects from the console and import them into a different infrastructure, enabling you to migrate objects between ConfigMgr environments. Follow these steps to export one or more objects:

1. In the console, navigate to **Software Library -> Applications**. Select one or more applications, right-click, and select **Export**.

2. Enter a path for the destination to export, making sure to include the .zip file extension. Review Figure 11.14 for more information.

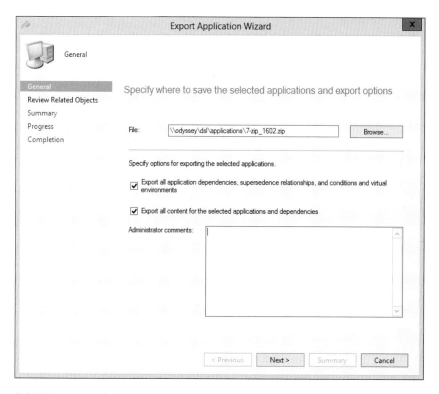

FIGURE 11.14   General page of the Export Application Wizard.

You can choose to export all dependencies, supersedence relationships, and global conditions. You can also choose to export content for the selected applications and dependencies.

3. Continue through the additional pages to complete the wizard.

4. Copy the .zip file to a new infrastructure and import as desired.

If you import a ConfigMgr application that already exists, ConfigMgr adds a revision, unless the action is modified to create a new application.

TIP: MODIFYING THE DEPLOYMENT TYPE PATH AFTER IMPORTING

After importing the exported ConfigMgr application, notice the path of the DT pointing to the location from where you imported the .zip file. The authors recommend that you copy referenced folders to your DSL and ensure that they align with your designed folder structure by modifying the path of the DT.

Superseding Applications

Use supersedence when moving to a new revision of a product. Say you have FooApp version 1.0 and are deploying to multiple collections. When FooApp 2.0 releases, create a new application for FooApp 2.0. When you know it works, supersede FooApp version 1.0 with version 2.0.

Supersedence does not automatically execute an installation. However, if an application was previously deployed as Required, that software can reinstall automatically. Figure 11.15 shows the Uninstall check box enabled, instructing ConfigMgr to uninstall the previous version, based on the uninstall command-line argument in the superseded application, and install the new version. If this option is not enabled, ConfigMgr runs the replacement DT without uninstalling the previous version. Running the replacement DT is expected in some situations, and the installation will upgrade the existing application. As always, test before deploying to production.

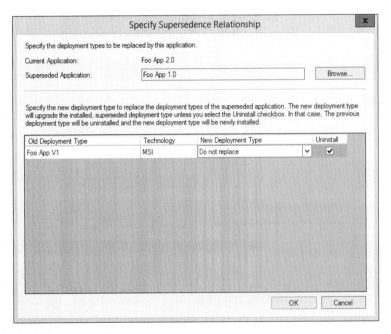

FIGURE 11.15   Specifying the supersedence relationship.

If an application has more than one DT, select the desired old and new DTs to map them to run together. You do not need to re-deploy an old version of software to take advantage of supersedence. Say that myApp version 1.0 has been in production for a year, and you just upgraded to ConfigMgr Current Branch. Create an application for myApp version 1.0, create myApp version 2.0, and supersede myApp 1.0. When you deploy myApp 2.0, ConfigMgr detects that 1.0 is installed and follows supersedence rules.

Retiring and Deleting Applications

When you no longer need to create new deployments for an application, right-click the application and select **Retire**. When an application is retired, you can no longer create deployments or distribute it to DPs unless you reinstate it. Retiring an application does not affect existing deployments; only new deployments.

To delete an application, remove all references to it. References such as dependent applications, active deployments, and dependent task sequences can affect your ability to delete an application.

Remember that you can export an application (with or without associated content) and store it on a file share in case you need to restore it later.

Best Practices for Working with Applications

A common misconception about installing applications is that ConfigMgr supports each installation installer type. This is not true; there are some prerequisites for ConfigMgr to successfully distribute and install software to remote clients. The next sections discuss some best practices for working with applications, including installing software and working with task sequences.

Best Practices for Installing Software

Most software installed with ConfigMgr uses an installer; this could be a Windows Installer (.msi) or third-party installation method such as installers from InstallShield, Wise, Nullsoft, Inno, and so on. You can also use script methods. Keep the following in mind about application installers:

▶ If the installer can install the software unattended (without user interaction), you could use it as a DT within an application or as a program within a package.

▶ If the software cannot be installed with an installer but can be installed unattended or requires company-specific modifications, it uses a *repackaging* process. This process involves capturing a software installation procedure, modifying it, and repackaging the installation to make it repeatable for large-scale rollouts. Microsoft provides the Orca tool to perform some minor adjustments to its Windows Installer .msi installers. However, most organizations repackaging software use third-party tools from InstallShield, Raynet, or Flexera. Repackaging has been used since early versions of Systems Management Server (SMS)/ConfigMgr.

CAUTION: BE CAREFUL WHEN REPACKAGING MICROSOFT INSTALLER FILES.

When repackaging Microsoft Installer files, take care not to change detection settings, uninstallation options, or installation results; such changes could lead to issues when deploying with ConfigMgr. Also make sure that a unique Windows Installer ID is generated for each new packaged .msi.

Before trying to distribute software with ConfigMgr, the authors recommend testing an unattended installation on a nonproduction machine. After confirming that the installation works, define the DT in ConfigMgr.

NOTE: COMMUNITY INFORMATION ABOUT UNATTENDED SOFTWARE INSTALLATION

Testing whether software can be installed unattended is often a matter of finding the right command-line parameters to use with the software installer. The Internet has a valuable community-driven forum for users to share their experiences with software installations. Previously known as AppDeploy.com, the forum now goes by the name AppDetails. See http://www.appdetails.com.

Testing, Testing, Testing

The best way to avoid issues with ConfigMgr packaging is to test as many contingencies as possible. If you create a software package to deploy to 1,000 workstations, you almost certainly will run into unexpected configurations. Effective testing can limit the risks of program failures or unexpected complications.

To test software packages, you need a testing lab (also discussed in Chapter 4, "Architecture Design Planning") that includes computers representative of the systems to which you will deploy the package.

It may be difficult to obtain nonproduction versions of actual systems for testing purposes. Address this issue with a virtual lab. Products such as Hyper-V and VMware let you run multiple systems without using an entire lab of physical hardware. Virtual labs also have smaller physical footprints. You can quickly return a computer to an earlier configuration, which makes it easy to roll back an OS to its previous state (prior to deploying the software). This is useful when testing software packages, as you often need to go through multiple testing iterations. Always build your virtual test systems using the same procedure as with a physical system.

However, physical lab environments provide real examples of systems where you would deploy the package. There are cases in which only a physical environment can identify issues such as a driver conflict between the software package and a set of computers running on a specific hardware platform. These computers should be actual production systems taken from those groups where you are deploying software packages, and they should represent the types of hardware in your environment.

The authors recommend using a hybrid lab environment that includes physical and virtual systems. Using both types of systems minimizes the number of systems required yet provides many of the benefits of a physical lab. Create a set of tests that identify the types of conditions to test before releasing the software package. Following are some examples:

▶ Installing the software package where there is not enough disk space

▶ Deploying to an unsupported platform

▶ Deploying where the software is already installed

▶ Deploying with other software packages installed that may cause conflicts

While tests vary depending on the specific software, identifying potential failure conditions ahead of time and testing for them can significantly increase the likelihood of creating a functional package.

Before ConfigMgr executes a DT, it checks whether the application is already installed, avoiding unnecessary execution. After installation, ConfigMgr checks to verify that the detection method validated successfully. These checks make it important to correctly specify the detection method and understand the process before deploying software to remote agents.

The following occurs when ConfigMgr installs software:

1. ConfigMgr executes the command line specified in the DT.

2. ConfigMgr monitors the process ID of the executable. When the process ID is no longer active, ConfigMgr uses the return code to determine whether installation was successful and whether a reboot is needed. The Maximum allowed runtime value specifies how long the installation may run and is available for DTs and programs. Return codes are specified based on the MSI known return codes, which are as follows:

   ▶ **0:** Successful installation, no reboot is necessary.

   ▶ **1707:** Successful installation, no reboot is necessary.

   ▶ **3010:** Soft reboot required.

   ▶ **1641:** Hard reboot needed.

   ▶ **1618:** Fast retry, meaning another installation is already running.

3. If a reboot is required, users are presented with a popup window asking whether to reboot the machine at this time. Configure the installation such that it utilizes the information that a reboot is needed. Do not let the application reboot the system, as that causes the installation to fail from a ConfigMgr perspective.

CAUTION: POTENTIAL ISSUES WITH SOFTWARE INSTALLATION WRAPPERS

Some organizations use *installation wrappers*, which can be command files or scripts. They typically provide basic logging and determine the required environment for the installation. A wrapper is a template, meaning that individuals creating applications need only fill in the information necessary for the installation.

With packages and programs, wrappers typically were not a problem and could be used to install a 32-bit version of the software on 32-bit systems or a 64-bit version of the software on 64-bit systems. However, installation wrappers often return to ConfigMgr only the return code of the last action performed (such as writing to a log file) and do not take into account the return code of the installer that was executed. For example, if the wrapper logged to a log file as its last action, which was successful, the wrapper would return a return code of success to ConfigMgr even if the installation failed! This can have serious consequences: The detection method executed afterward would determine that the application actually is not installed, causing installation to eventually fail from a ConfigMgr perspective.

ConfigMgr executes the command line specified in the DT or program, waits for the process to finish, and determines whether the installation was successful based on return codes; this means there is time when ConfigMgr logging is unavailable. The authors recommend enabling logging on the installation command line or globally on a per-machine basis. If this is enabled, you can determine why an installation failed.

TIP: SAMPLE APPLICATIONS FROM THE SOFTWARE DEVELOPMENT KIT

The System Center 2012 Configuration Manager SDK includes the Application Model Kit, which contains a set of exported applications demonstrating the use of various features of the application model. Import the .zip file for the kit to create sample applications and some custom global conditions.

The latest version of the SDK is for ConfigMgr 2012 R2 and available at https://www.microsoft.com/download/details.aspx?id=29559. While this version is specifically for an older version of ConfigMgr, the Application Model Kit can still be used with ConfigMgr Current Branch.

Best Practices for Working with Applications in Task Sequences

Although Microsoft recommends that you deploy applications for users, applications could also be included within a TS during OSD. Consider Microsoft Office, which is commonly deployed in a TS because it provides application components such as Word and Excel to end users and also serves as a type of middleware for other applications.

Because of how task sequences run, you must take extra precautions when installing applications in a TS, for several reasons:

▶ The task sequence runs in the context of the Local System account.

▶ The explorer.exe task is not running during a task sequence.

▶ The installer must be fully unattended, and no user interaction is allowed. If the installer requires interaction, the task sequence fails.

Follow these steps to install user-targeted applications after the TS finishes:

1. Define a user device affinity (UDA), filling the SMSTSSUdaUsers variable with the account of the user using the machine. Prompt for its value using a pre-hook execution command or by creating an empty SMSTSUdaUsers variable on the computer object or collection.

2. While deploying the application and specifying the deployment settings, ensure that the purpose is set to **Required** and the **Pre-deploy software to the user's primary device** option is checked.

Support for Write Filters in Windows Embedded

Windows Embedded is designed for use in embedded systems—that is, devices with all-in-one functionality. Microsoft makes Windows Embedded available for original equipment manufacturers (OEMs) to preload on embedded devices.

Operational reasons may make it undesirable to write to storage media in Windows Embedded devices. By redirecting all write requests to a separate disk partition or RAM, a write filter allows the runtime image to maintain the appearance of a writable image without committing changes to the storage media. Changes made to the system are discarded at restart; this is also true for any software installation that occurs while the write filter is enabled.

Microsoft supports write filters with the Commit changes at deadline or during a maintenance window (requires restarts) option (enabled by default) in the Deploy Software Wizard. When this option is enabled, the software is installed when the deadline is reached or when the device enters a maintenance mode time frame defined by the settings for the collection of which it is a member; this is known as *forced persist*. If this option is not enabled, ConfigMgr assumes that you have another process for committing the software; this is called *opportunistically persist*.

When ConfigMgr disables the write filters, the device is put in a servicing lock mode, and only members of the Local Administrators security group are allowed to log on.

Deploying PowerShell Scripts

ConfigMgr Current Branch version 1706 introduced, as a pre-release feature, the ability to deploy PowerShell scripts to collections. This feature allows a ConfigMgr administrator to import PowerShell scripts into ConfigMgr. Scripts can be edited in the ConfigMgr console if they are not signed. The console also provides the ability to approve or deny scripts; this can be done by an approver that is not the author of the script to provide segregation of duties, or it can be done by the author. Scripts can be run targeted at collections, running the script in near real time on client devices. Results returned by a script can be examined in the ConfigMgr console.

PowerShell Script Prerequisites and Configuration

In order to run a PowerShell script on a client, the client must be running ConfigMgr Current Branch version 1706 or newer and have PowerShell version 3.0 or later installed.

By default, the individual who creates the script cannot approve it. You can modify this behavior in the Hierarchy Settings Properties dialog box by clearing the check box at the **Do not allow script authors to approve their own script** option on the General tab.

Creating, Editing, Approving, and Denying Scripts

You can create, edit, approve, and deny scripts in the Scripts section of the Software Library. Perform the following steps to create a script:

1. Open the ConfigMgr console and navigate to **Software Library** -> **Scripts**.

2. Click **Create Script** in the Create group on the Home tab.

3. On the Script page of the Create Script wizard, configure the following settings:

   ▶ **Script Name:** Provide a name for the script.

▶ **Script Language:** For now, there is only one option available (PowerShell), but this may change in the future.

▶ **Script:** Paste the script or click **Import** and browse for a script to import.

Once the script is created, it displays in the script list with the status Waiting for approval. Scripts must be approved before they can be run on a collection.

To approve or deny a script, follow these steps:

1. Open the ConfigMgr console and navigate to **Software Library -> Scripts**.

2. Click on a script that has the Waiting for approval or Approved status and then click **Approve** on the ribbon bar to start the Approve or Deny Script wizard.

3. In the wizard, either approve or deny the script and provide comments for later reference.

Monitoring Scripts

A ConfigMgr administrator can view the results of running scripts from the Monitoring workspace in the ConfigMgr console. Follow these steps:

1. Open the ConfigMgr console and navigate to **Monitoring -> Script Status**.

2. In the Script Status list, view the results of each script that ran on a client device. Exit code 0 typically means that the script ran successfully.

Summary

This chapter discussed creating ConfigMgr applications and explained how applications include DTs. DTs have detection and requirement rules, which you can use to deploy software using fewer collections. This chapter also covered the application state and how to reinstall required applications based on detection rules.

This chapter described how to use custom scripts for detection methods, as well as how to create and leverage global conditions. It covered exporting and importing of applications, revision history, dependency, and supersedence. It also covered deploying PowerShell scripts that run against collections. Chapter 12 shows how to create DTs for different types of applications.

CHAPTER 12

Creating and Using Deployment Types

Chapter 11, "Creating and Managing Applications," introduced applications and deployment types (DTs), showing how to create a System Center Configuration Manager (ConfigMgr) application by specifying its DT. An application must have at least one DT; additional DTs (if the application permits it) can more fully leverage application functionality. ConfigMgr applications enable you to deploy software to users based on device type. You can use DTs to customize deployment based on the device and other requirements.

A ConfigMgr application is a container used to deliver software. It includes basic information regarding the software application, such as name, version, application owner, and localization information that describes how the application is displayed in Software Center and the Application Catalog. It contains information about the distribution settings used and the distribution points (DPs) and DP groups to which the content is distributed, including references/dependencies for other ConfigMgr applications and whether the application replaces an existing ConfigMgr application or is part of a virtual environment. The application is merely a shell; installing software requires a DT.

DTs are functionally similar to ConfigMgr programs that deploy ConfigMgr packages. Just as a program contains an installation command line and any platform requirements (such as Windows 10 x64), a DT contains that same basic information and much more.

Requirement rules, which are used with DTs, are flexible and can leverage just about anything on a system, including SQL or LDAP queries, primary user information, and so on. ConfigMgr applications are deployed to a user or a group of users, with a DT identifying the type of device being used and where the device is situated at that time.

The following is the most important information for DTs:

▶ Content source location (Universal Naming Convention [UNC] path to source installation files).

▶ Install and uninstall command lines.

▶ Detection method(s), used to confirm whether a ConfigMgr application is installed, confirm dependencies, and determine supersedence. Detection methods are applied on a regular interval (every seven days by default) to reevaluate installation status on each system.

▶ End-user experience configuration to determine when to display notifications, logon requirements, and so on.

▶ Requirement rules, used to determine the requirements for a DT to proceed with the installation.

▶ Success and failure return code information, to provide additional control over the installation process.

▶ Dependency information, in case the application requires other applications to be installed first (for example, Java Runtime Environment).

TIP: DEFINITION OF A PRIMARY USER

A *primary user* is the main user using a device; a device can have more than one primary user (for example, a device in a call center that is used on multiple shifts). A primary user can be defined during operating system deployment (OSD), defined manually through the ConfigMgr console, or automatically created based on login events. A ConfigMgr administrator can allow the user to define his or her own association through Software Center, which is installed on the device. For more information about primary users, see Chapter 11.

Creating and Using Windows Installer Deployment Types

DTs are a major component of every application and are required for functional applications. Chapter 11 includes an overview of DTs and discusses creating a new application for a Windows Installer installation, including creating a DT to install 7-Zip for the x86 version of the 7-Zip installation.

Using Windows Installer is Microsoft's preferred method for installing applications. It utilizes MSI file types, which contain installation logic for an application. For information about Windows Installer, see https://msdn.microsoft.com/library/windows/desktop/aa367449(v=vs.85).aspx.

Creating a Windows Installer–Based Deployment Type

This section shows how to create a DT for an x64 installation and use a requirement based on a global condition to ensure that it installs only on x64 platforms. Follow these steps to create the DT:

1. In the ConfigMgr console, navigate to **Software Library -> Application Management**.

2. Click the **Applications** node and select the **7-Zip 16.02** application. Right-click the 7-Zip 16.02 application and select **Create Deployment Type** from the context menu.

3. In the Create Deployment Type Wizard, confirm that Windows Installer (.msi) file is selected as the type. Browse to the .msi, in this case **Odyssey\DSL\Applications\ Igor Pavlov\7-Zip\v16.02\Deploy\x64\7z1602-x64.msi**, and click **Next**.

4. If you receive a warning that the publisher of the .msi could not be verified, click **Yes** to import this file.

5. On the Import Information page, which shows a successful import, click **Next**.

6. Edit the General Information tab, which displays a subset of settings for the DT, as needed. The defaults are modified so the x64 installation is similar to the x86 DT created in Chapter 11. This information is used to populate the minimally required information for the DT. Following is a basic description of the fields:

   ▶ **Name:** Specify the DT's name. This example contains x64 in the name to simplify troubleshooting.

   ▶ **Administrator Comments:** Specify information that is available only in the console.

   ▶ **Languages:** Multi-select supported languages for this DP. To restrict the application installation to specific languages, enable that on the Requirements page.

   ▶ **Installation Program:** Specify the command line to install the software. The default for a Windows installer program uses the /q switch for a quiet installation. Modify this command if you require additional parameters such as public properties or transforms. This command runs from the root of the content source location; the path should be relative to that location.

   ▶ **Run Installation Program as a 32-Bit Process on 64-Bit Clients:** Enable this check box for a 32-bit installation, meaning it will install to %*ProgramFiles (x86)*%. This setting helps ConfigMgr properly install and uninstall 32-bit applications on 64-bit systems. By default, the ConfigMgr client agent on a 64-bit system does not use this path or the HKLM\Software\Wow6432Node Registry path.

   ▶ **Installation Behavior:** Specify the rights used for installation:

     ▶ **Install for User:** Install using the rights of the current user.

     ▶ **Install for System:** Install using the rights of the SMS Agent Host service (Local System account).

▶ **Install for System if Resource Is Device; Otherwise Install for User:** If the application is targeted to a collection of devices, install for system; if targeted to a collection of users or user groups, install for user.

For 7-Zip, the installation should always install using system rights, so be sure to select Install for System.

After making all the appropriate settings, click **Next**.

7. Select the Requirements page, click **Add**, and choose the appropriate supported platforms. As this installation of 7-Zip is for x64, select the desired x64 platforms to support and click **Next**.

8. Leave the Dependencies page blank because 7-Zip does not have dependent applications (such as .NET Framework or Oracle Java) and click **Next**.

9. On the Summary page click **Next** to create the DT. The Completion page confirms success.

As shown on the Deployment Types tab of the 7-Zip 16.02 application in Figure 12.1, you now have two DTs.

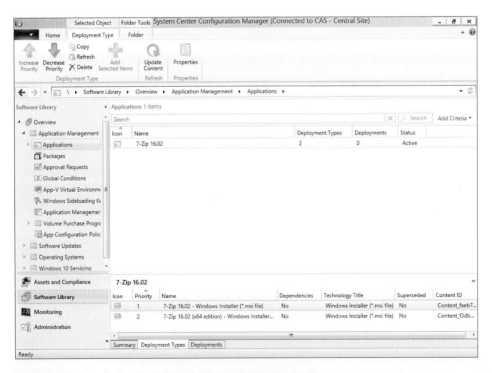

FIGURE 12.1   DTs for the 7-Zip 16.02 ConfigMgr Application.

An additional DT feature is priority. In this case, the x86 installation is priority 1, and x64 is priority 2. When an application deploys, the client evaluates the DTs in order of their priority. In this example, the first priority is the x86 version of the DT; be sure to modify the requirements for the x86 DT so it will only install on x86 platforms, since the first DT that meets the requirements is run. If possible, place the DT you expect will run most as priority 1.

Now that you have created a new DT, review Chapter 11 to determine if you need to make any changes. The wizard shows a limited set of options for the DT. View the properties and make additional changes.

TIP: SPECIFYING EXECUTABLE FILES THAT MUST BE CLOSED BEFORE INSTALLATION

Starting with ConfigMgr Current Branch version 1706, you can specify which executable file(s) must be closed before the installation can run. If the deployment is available, the user will be asked to close the application first; if the deployment is required, ConfigMgr will close the executable before beginning installation of the DT. Specify the executables to be closed on the Install Behavior tab of the Deployment Type properties.

Creating a Windows Installer Through MDM Deployment Type

The Windows Installer through MDM DT allows you to specify a DT to be installed on Windows 10 devices managed via the Open Mobile Alliance (OMA) Device Management (DM) mobile device management (MDM) protocol. (Chapter 17, "Managing Mobile Devices," provides additional information about the OMA DM channel.) Compared to a Windows Installer DT, the Windows Installer through MDM DT has the following limitations:

▶ The default restart behavior of the MSI file will be used; ConfigMgr cannot control restart behavior for this type of DT.

▶ The detection method uses the MSI product code and product version.

▶ You can only use a Windows Installer database file (.msi); no other files can be used (like Windows Installer .mst or .msp file types, or setup.exe).

▶ Per-user MSI files are installed for a single user; per-machine MSIs are installed for all users on a device.

▶ App updates are supported only when the MSI upgrade codes of the versions are the same.

Follow these steps to add a new DT to an existing application:

1. From the application properties, select the Deployment Types tab and click **Add** to create a new DT.

2. For DT type, select **Windows Installer through MDM (*.msi)**. For Location, browse to the .msi by using its UNC path.

3. On the Import Information page, which shows a success message, click **Next**.

4. On the General Information page, modify information, if needed. (This page is similar to the page for the Windows Installer DT, except you cannot modify the Installation Program, Installation Behavior, and Languages fields.) Click **Next** to proceed.

5. On the Requirements page, add a requirement so the DT installs only on 32- or 64-bit versions of Windows 10. Notice in Figure 12.2 that Windows 10 is available as an applicable operating system.

6. Click **Next** on each remaining page to save the DT. When complete, edit the DT. The General, Requirements, and Dependencies pages are similar to those of the Windows Installer DT created in Chapter 11.

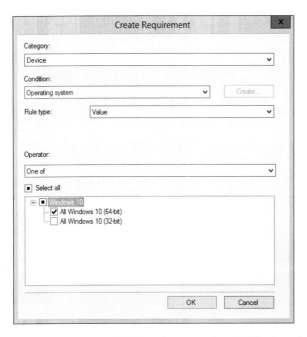

FIGURE 12.2   Available requirements for the Windows Installer through MDM DT.

Creating and Using Application Virtualization Deployment Types

ConfigMgr supports versions 4.6 and 5 of Microsoft App-V. Microsoft completely rewrote App-V with version 5, released in late 2012, introducing the .appv file format for the information formerly contained in the .sft, .ico, .osd, and manifest .xml files, which have been dropped. Due to this major rewrite of the product, Microsoft supports App-V 4.6 and

App-V 5 virtual applications coexisting on the same system to allow a phased migration from App-V 4.6 to App-V 5. (App-V 4.6 applications must be converted or resequenced to be available in App-V 5 format.) ConfigMgr includes support for App-V 4.6 Service Pack 1 and later, App-V 5, and App-V 5.1. Check supported configurations since support could change with a new build of ConfigMgr.

Creating an App-V application requires a sequencer, an application belonging to the App-V product application suite that must be separately installed. The sequencer monitors the application's installation and setup process, recording the information necessary for it to run in a virtual environment. The output of the sequencing process should be copied from the sequencing computer to a definitive software library (DSL) hosting the Config-Mgr application sources. See Chapter 11 for information on DSL.

With App-V 5, the ConfigMgr client uses a Windows PowerShell module to manage App-V objects such as virtual applications, connection groups, and dynamic configuration files.

NOTE: MORE INFORMATION ABOUT INTEGRATING APP-V 5 WITH CONFIGMGR

For additional information about integrating App-V into ConfigMgr, see https://docs.microsoft.com/sccm/apps/get-started/deploying-app-v-virtual-applications.

Creating a Microsoft App-V 4.6 Deployment Type

App-V DTs are probably the easiest DTs to create. Use the Create Application Wizard to create a new application with an App-V DT or choose an existing application and add a DT. Follow these steps to add a new DT to an existing application:

1. From the application properties, select the Deployment Types tab and click **Add** to create a new DT.

2. For DT type, select **Microsoft Application Virtualization**. For location, browse to the .xml file for the App-V package.

3. On the Import Information page, which shows a success message, click **Next**.

4. In the General Information page, notice that the command line is missing. The installation command line is not required for App-V packages. Modify the information as needed and click **Next**.

5. Examine the Requirements page, which already contains requirements for this package. The information is included in the .xml file imported for the DT. Click **Add** to add additional requirements if needed.

6. Click **Next** on each remaining page to save the DT. When complete, edit the DT. The General, Requirements, and Dependencies page are similar to those for the Windows Installer DT created in Chapter 11. The following step review the tabs customized for App-V packages, namely Content and Publishing.

TIP: ENSURING THAT THE APP-V CLIENT IS INSTALLED BEFORE THE APP-V APPLICATION

To ensure that the App-V client is already installed, create an application that installs both the x86 and x64 versions of the App-V client for Windows versions prior to Windows 10 build 1607. Make that application a dependency for this new App-V application. Another option could be to create a global condition that checks whether the App-V client is already installed; this might even be a better option since the App-V client is built in to Windows 10 starting with build 1607.

7. Review the Content tab to ensure that the OS requirements were successfully imported from the manifest. The Content tab for an App-V DT provides the following settings:

▶ **App-V Manifest Location:** Specify the UNC source path to the App-V application manifest. This location is read-only. To update the source location for the manifest file or sequenced application, select Update Content from the Deployment Type properties (either by right-clicking or selecting on the ribbon bar) and walk through the wizard to select a different manifest.

▶ **Persist Content in the Client Cache:** When you enable this setting and deploy the application to a target collection, clients using this DT (based on the requirement rules) download and keep the installation source in the local ConfigMgr cache folder (%*windir*%\ccmcache), which is 5GB by default.

▶ **Enable Peer-to-Peer Content Distribution:** Enable this check box to leverage BranchCache or Peer Cache (provided that they are configured for your environment).

▶ **Load Content into App-V Cache Before Launch:** If this option is disabled and the download content option is configured, a ConfigMgr client downloads the content to its local cache, publishes the icon(s), and exits. If this option is enabled, once content is downloaded, the client calls the App-V command to preload content to the App-V cache immediately (instead of waiting until the first launch). A problem may occur if the check box is cleared. If the software is downloaded to the ConfigMgr cache but the user does not launch the application, the launch will fail if the application is not started until after the cache is cleaned. The authors recommend enabling this check box to pre-cache the application in the App-V cache.

▶ **Deployment Options:** If the client uses a DP located in its current boundary group (defined in the boundary group configuration), you can configure the application to be streamed from the DP or to download the content first. If the client uses a neighbor DP or the default site boundary group, you can choose to not download content, to download and run locally, or to stream content from the DP.

▶ **Allow Clients to Use a Fallback Source Location for Content:** If a client cannot locate content for this deployment in its defined boundary group, select this check box to allow the client to search other locations. To allow clients to access a source from a different boundary group, the boundary group properties must be configured to allow a client outside these boundary groups to fall back and use this site system as a source location for content.

8. Use the Publishing tab, which is also unique to the App-V DT, to determine which icons to publish to the end user. A common scenario to consider is when a user wants to install software on a device that he or she does not use every day. ConfigMgr considers this a device if the user is not considered the primary user. In this example, the DT will only be installed for primary device users.

9. Select the Requirements tab and click **Add** to add a new requirement. In the Create Requirement Dialog, select **User** as the category and verify that Condition is set to **Primary Device equals True**.

Creating a Microsoft App-V 5 Deployment Type

The example in this section shows how to create an App-V 5 DT for the 7-Zip application, which was sequenced with the App-V 5 sequencer. Perform the following steps to create the App-V 5 deployment type:

1. In the console, navigate to **Software Library -> Application Management -> Applications**. Select the application for which you want to add the Windows Store DT and click **Create Deployment Type** on the ribbon bar. The Create Deployment Type Wizard appears.

2. On the General page, select **Microsoft Application Virtualization 5** from the Type dropdown list.

3. Supply the UNC path to the location of the .appv file, created by the App-V sequencer while saving the sequenced application (**\\odyssey\dsl\Applications\Igor Pavlov\ 7-Zip\v16.02\Deploy\Appv5\x64\7 Zip v16.02.appv** in this case). Click **Next**.

4. Verify the information on the Import Succeeded message in the Import Information page. Click **Next**.

5. On the General Information page, modify the name to one that suits your organization's needs. You can also supply administrator comments and select the languages included in this DT. Click **Next**.

6. On the Requirements page, click **Add** to open the Create Requirement dialog and select requirements that must be met to start this application. An example could be a global condition check of whether the App-V 5.0 client is installed on the client. Click **OK** to select the necessary requirements and click **Next**.

7. On the Dependencies page, select dependencies by configuring a dependency group containing the applications on which this application depends. An example would be the App-V client installation.

If you create a requirement based on a global condition that specifies whether the App-V 5 client is installed, the DT dependency is never reached; the App-V 5 client, even though specified as a dependency, is never installed; and the DT is not started.

After creating the dependency group, click **OK** to close the Add Dependency window. Click **Next** to continue.

8. Review the Summary page. Click **Next** to create the DT.

9. Follow the progress and verify that the DT was successfully created in the Completion page. When successful, click **Close** to close the wizard.

Using App-V Virtual Environments

Use App-V's virtual environment functionality in versions 5 and above to define App-V connection groups in ConfigMgr; these are the follow-up to the dynamic suite composition (DSC) functionality that was previously available. Defining interaction between two or more applications using DSC involves editing the OSD file to add a reference to the GUID of the other application, which is error prone.

Applications residing in the same connection group interact and share the file system and Registry on client computers. For example, Microsoft Outlook and a third-party add-in for Outlook could be delivered separately from each other. You can give priority to applications within the connection group, allowing their file system or Registry changes to take precedence over those of an application with lower priority. The next section describes how to create an App-V virtual environment for FreeMind, a mind-mapping tool that requires the Oracle Java Runtime Environment.

Creating an App-V Virtual Environment

The scenario in this section uses two App-V packages created using the App-V 5 sequencer:

▶ **FreeMind version 1.0.1:** This application creates mind maps and depends on the Oracle Java Runtime Environment to be installed on the machine on which it runs.

▶ **Java Runtime Environment:** This is the Java JRE version 8 update 11.

Both applications were sequenced on the App-V sequencing machine and imported using the procedure described in the "Creating a Microsoft App-V 5 Deployment Type" section, earlier in this chapter. Create both applications and then create a dependency between them. Follow these steps:

1. In the ConfigMgr console, navigate to **Software Library** -> **Application Management** -> **App-V Virtual Environments**. Select **Create Virtual Environment** to define a new App-V connection group. The Create Virtual Environment page appears.

2. Specify a name and provide a description for the connection group. In this case, specify **Java 8 Update 11 with FreeMind 1.0.1** as the name and **Connection Group for FreeMind 1.0.1** as a description.

3. Click **Add** to open the Add Applications page. Provide a group name, which in this case is **JRE 8 Update 11**. Click **Add** to open the Specify Application page.

4. Select the **Oracle Java JRE 8 Update 11 - Microsoft Application Virtualization 5** DT and click **OK** to close the page. If you click **Add** again and select an additional application, you can specify another application, creating an OR statement for the specified applications. Click **OK** when finished.

5. Back on the Create Virtual Environment page, click **Add** to again open the Add Applications page. Specify a group name, which in this case is **FreeMind 1.0.1**. Click **Add** to open the Specify Application page.

6. Select the **FreeMind 1.0.1 - Microsoft Application Virtualization 5** DT. Click **OK** to close this page. To select an additional application, if needed, click **Add** again to create an OR statement for the specified applications. Click **OK** when complete.

You now see the two virtual applications added as App-V DTs on the Create Virtual Environment page, as displayed in Figure 12.3. Notice the **AND** statement, which states in this case that FreeMind 1.0.0 and Java 7 update 45 can run in the same virtual environment.

7. Click **OK** to close the Create Virtual Environment page; the Java 7 update 45 with FreeMind 1.0.0 connection group has been created.

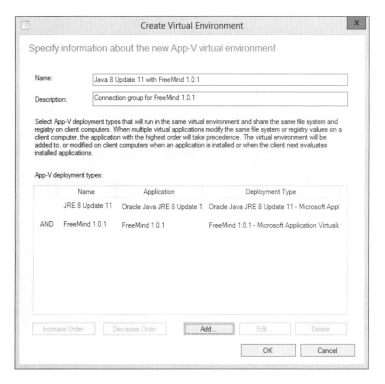

FIGURE 12.3   Creating a virtual environment.

With the App-V virtual environment specified, you can create a deployment for the FreeMind 1.0.1 application. Although you created the App-V virtual environment, you also must specify that the FreeMind 1.0.1 - Microsoft Application Virtualization 5 DT is dependent on the Oracle Java JRE 8 Update 11 - Microsoft Application Virtualization 5 DT.

Check whether the connection group is active on the client by using the Get-AppVClientConnectionGroup PowerShell cmdlet, available on each App-V client after importing the AppvClient.psd1 module and changing the execution policy. Figure 12.4 shows the outcome of running the cmdlet.

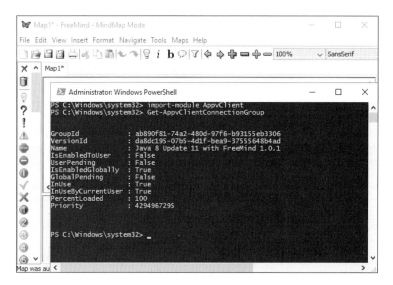

FIGURE 12.4   Output of the Get-AppVClientConnectionGroup cmdlet when the virtual environment is running.

Using Deployment Types for Mobile Devices

ConfigMgr can be integrated with Microsoft's hosted Intune device management solution, using the ConfigMgr console to manage mobile devices connected to Microsoft Intune. Alternatively, you can manage on-premise mobile devices natively through ConfigMgr; in this case, a connection to Intune is required for licensing purposes. Microsoft refers to managing mobile devices through Microsoft Intune as *unified device management*, or *Intune hybrid*. Chapter 16, "Integrating Intune Hybrid into Your Configuration Manager Environment," explains how to set up the integration between Intune and ConfigMgr, and Chapter 17 discusses ConfigMgr MDM when integrated with Microsoft Intune.

After enrolling devices in the hybrid environment, you can manage your Windows-based, Android-based, or iOS devices with ConfigMgr through Intune. You can deploy applications to those devices by using either deeplinking or sideloading; these concepts are explained in the next sections.

Using Sideloading to Distribute Applications

If a company wants to install custom applications on users' mobile devices, it could buy that software from a software development company that develops the application or have in-house developers create an application. These applications are often referred to as line-of-business (LOB) applications; installing these applications on devices is known as *sideloading*.

For each type of application, the vendors of each platform provide a development environment:

▶ Microsoft Visual Studio is a development platform for developing Windows modern applications, applications for Windows Phone, and Universal Windows Platform apps.

▶ The Apple development platform is called Xcode.

▶ Google provides an Android Developer Tools plug-in for Eclipse, which is a platform for developing open source software.

Xamarin, acquired by Microsoft in February 2016, is a tool for writing native Android, iOS, and Windows apps using a shared C# codebase. Other third-party development environments are also available for developers to write software for devices.

All vendors provide methods for developers to test their applications on devices. To prevent mass deployment of these applications, there must be a way to restrict running them:

▶ Running development applications on Apple requires the developer to register the universally unique identifier (UUID) of the device as a development device for testing purposes; a developer can register 100 devices per year. The developer must also create an Apple Developer account.

▶ Microsoft modern and universal applications can be tested on Windows 8.1 domain-joined machines with a Registry key enabled, or the machines can be provisioned with a certificate. The certificate must be renewed every 30 days when using a Microsoft account and every 90 days when using a Store account. For Windows 10, the machine can be put in sideloading or developer mode, as explained in the article at https://msdn.microsoft.com/windows/uwp/get-started/enable-your-device-for-development. For Windows Phone application testing, Microsoft provides an emulator that is available with Visual Studio.

▶ When testing Android applications, enable Developer options to enable installation of applications not coming from Google Play on a per-device basis.

Sideloading applications requires different procedures, depending on the manufacturer of the operating system (OS) on which the mobile device runs. The following scenarios are supported when sideloading applications to mobile devices:

▶ Deploying an application as available to users.

▶ Deploying an application as required to users and devices. This is not supported on Windows Phone 8, and user consent is required for iOS and Android devices.

▶ Uninstalling an application deployed to users and devices. This is not supported on Windows Phone 8; Android devices require user consent.

Chapter 17 provides more information about these scenarios.

Sideloading Windows Modern Applications

With Windows 8, Microsoft introduced a new type of application, known as a metro app. Metro apps were installed from the Windows Marketplace, the first version of what is now known as the Windows Store. Due to a legal dispute with a German company, Microsoft was forced to change that name to Windows 8 style apps and later used the term modern apps.

With the release of Windows 8.1, Microsoft introduced the universal app concept, where an app could be written such that it could be used both on Windows Phone and Windows devices, although it still had to be specifically compiled for each device type. With Windows 10, apps can be written once based on one common application programming interface (API) set and run on all flavors of Windows 10 (Windows Phone, Windows PC, Xbox, Internet of Things [IoT], and Hololens). This simplifies creation from the developer and deployment perspectives. These apps are now called universal Windows apps based on the Universal Windows Platform (UWP); traditional Win32 applications are called Windows desktop apps.

Requirements for installing apps have changed with each evolution of the Windows OS. This can be confusing, particularly if you have multiple versions of Windows in your environment.

A Windows 8/8.1 Enterprise or Windows Server 2012/2012 R2 computer that is domain-joined can use sideloading of trusted applications with the group policy item Allow all trusted applications to install. Sideloading of applications also requires the application to be signed with a trusted certificate, where the publisher name in the certificate matches the publisher name in the package. The certificate can be distributed to your domain-joined clients using group policy or with the Certificate Profiles option in ConfigMgr.

For Windows devices that are not or cannot be joined to a domain, such as Windows RT devices, you must acquire an enterprise sideloading key, which is a special product activation key. Windows 8 and 8.1 Pro, which can be domain-joined, also require a sideloading key. These requirements were changed with Windows 8.1 Update, as domain-joined Pro editions no longer require a sideloading key. As of Windows 10, sideloading keys are no longer necessary.

Apply the sideloading key and reactivate the Windows installation on the device. As of May 1, 2014, Microsoft customers in certain volume licensing programs are provided enterprise sideloading rights at no additional cost. Other customers can purchase enterprise sideloading rights for an unlimited number of devices for as little as $100. (See http://microsoft-news.com/you-can-buy-windows-8-1-enterprise-sideloading-rights-for-an-unlimited-number-of-devices-for-100/ and the volume licensing reference guide at http://download.microsoft.com/download/9/4/3/9439A928-A0D1-44C2-A099-26A59AE0543B/Windows_8-1_Licensing_Guide.pdf.)

Use the slmgr.vbs script for activation with the ConfigMgr client. When managing the client with Microsoft Intune, upload the sideloading key to the ConfigMgr console; it is enrolled during the next maintenance window.

To distribute applications to Windows devices, the application must be signed by a certificate authority (CA) trusted by the device in use. You can obtain a public certificate from a non-Microsoft authority or use your internal organization public key infrastructure (PKI) to generate the code-signing certificate. The certificate can be distributed using the Certificate Profiles functionality in ConfigMgr or with group policy.

Defining the Policy to Enable Sideloading on Domain-Joined Machines   This scenario in this section involves deploying a Windows app to Windows 8.1 and 10 Enterprise domain-joined machines. Configure the necessary group policy object (GPO) setting and distribute the certificate to the machines by using the Certificate Profile option in ConfigMgr. To enable installation of the custom Windows app, modify an already existing group policy, which is applied to your Windows agents. Follow these steps:

1. Start the Group Policy Management Console (GPMC) and browse to the GPO to which you are adding the new policy setting. Right-click the object and select **Edit**.

2. Browse to **Computer Configuration -> Policies -> Administrative Templates -> Windows Components -> App Package Deployment**. Double-click **Allow all trusted apps to install** and modify its setting to **Enabled**.

3. Close the GPMC.

Verify that the policy was applied correctly by opening the local group policy editor on your target machine and browsing for the setting of the group policy that you set using the GPO.

Creating and Deploying a Certificate Profile   If the developer uses an authenticode code-signing certificate from a common CA, such as Symantec or VeriSign, you do not need to deploy a certificate profile, as the root certificates for these authorities are already present in the certificate store. If your own certificate is used, a certificate profile must be created to make the root certificate available in the Trusted Root Certification Authority store. The following steps show how to create a certificate profile, which is distributed to your agents using the compliance settings feature of ConfigMgr. To deploy a certificate to clients managed through MDM, you can also upload the certificate to the ConfigMgr console for the certificate to be automatically installed at enrollment time or during the next maintenance window. Complete the following steps:

1. In the ConfigMgr console, navigate to **Assets and Compliance -> Compliance Settings -> Company Resource Access -> Certificate Profiles**. Select **Create Certificate Profile** on the ribbon bar to start the Create Certificate Profile Wizard.

2. On the General page, provide a name for the certificate profile and an optional description. Confirm that the **Trusted CA certificate** radio button is selected. Click **Next** to continue.

3. On the Trusted CA Certificate page, provide the path to the location where the certificate is stored (in this example, \\odyssey\dsl\Applications\Microsoft\ Barcode Scanner Sample App\v1.0.0.0\BarcodeScannerJS_1.0.0.0_AnyCPU_Debug.cer). Verify that **Computer certificate store - Root** is selected and that the Certificate thumbprint field is filled in after selecting the certificate, as shown in Figure 12.5. Click **Next** to continue.

4. On the Supported Platforms page, confirm that **Windows 8.1** and **Windows 10** are selected and click **Next**.

5. Review the Summary page. Click **Next** to create the certificate profile.

6. On the Completion page, verify that the certificate profile was successfully created. Click **Close** to close the wizard.

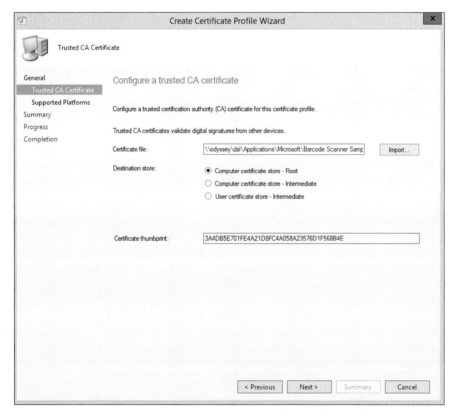

FIGURE 12.5   Configuring a trusted CA certificate page of the Create Certificate Profile Wizard.

You can deploy the certificate profile to a collection containing all the devices to which you want to deploy the application so that they receive the policy. After the machines install the policy with the deployment, the certificate is installed during the next scheduled compliance evaluation.

To check whether the certificate installed successfully, verify that the configuration baseline is compliant on the Configuration tab of the ConfigMgr Control Panel applet, as shown in Figure 12.6, or open Local Computer certificates and browse to **Trusted Root Certification Authorities** -> **Certificates**. The code-signing certificate should be in the list. Use the serial number as the unique identifier to verify that the certificate is present.

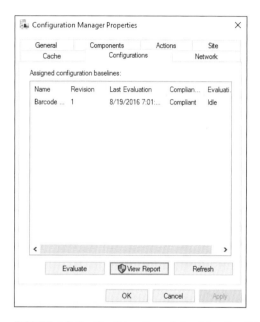

FIGURE 12.6   Configurations tab of the Configuration Manager Control Panel applet.

Creating Windows Modern Deployment Types   Now that the GPO and certificate profile are created and verified as successfully applied, create the DT to distribute the application to users of your Windows 8.1 and Windows 10 machines. Follow these steps:

1. In the console, navigate to **Software Library** -> **Application Management** -> **Applications**. Select the application for which you want to add the Windows Store DT and click **Create Deployment Type** on the ribbon bar to open the Create Deployment Type Wizard.

2. On the General page, select **Windows app package (*.appx, *appxbundle)** as the type from the dropdown list.

3. Provide the UNC path to the .appx file (**\\odyssey\dsl\Applications\Microsoft\ Barcode Scanner Sample App\v1.0.0.0\BarcodeScannerJS_1.0.0.0_AnyCPU_ Debug.appx** in this case) and click **Next**.

4. Confirm that the import succeeded in the Import Information page. If it did not, click **Previous** and verify the information. Click **Next**.

5. On the General Information page, modify the name as desired. You can also provide administrator comments, publisher information, software version, an optional

reference, and administrative categories. Notice that the check box option **Use an automatic VPN connection (if configured)** is available. Click **Next** to continue.

8. On the Summary page, review the information and click **Next**.

9. On the Completion page, shown in Figure 12.7, verify that the DT was created. Click **Close** to close the wizard.

FIGURE 12.7   Completion page of the Create Application Wizard for a Windows App package.

After creating the DT, you can deploy the application to a user collection. If a user is a member of the collection and receives a new user policy, the application becomes available or is installed for the user (depending on the deployment settings). Figure 12.8 shows the BarcodeScanner JS sample application loaded on a Windows 10 device.

If installation fails, check the AppEnforce.log log file, located in the \Logs folder under the ConfigMgr agent installation folder.

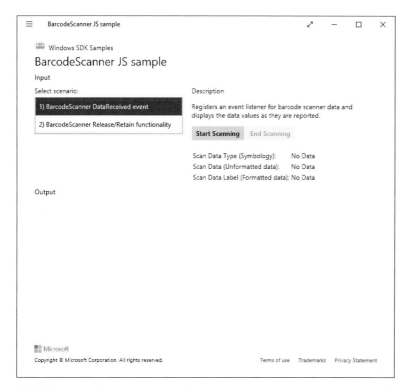

FIGURE 12.8   BarcodeScanner JS sample app loaded on a Windows 10 device.

Sideloading Silverlight-Based Applications for Windows Phone Devices

Silverlight-based applications were introduced with Windows Phone 8.1. Microsoft now recommends that developers port existing Silverlight-based applications to the UWP. Silverlight-based apps are still supported, even on Windows 10. Sideloaded Silverlight-based applications for Windows Phone must be code-signed, which requires a code-signing certificate purchased from Symantec/Digicert. Purchase certificates at http://www.symantec.com/verisign/code-signing/windows-phone.

To create a DT within an application for sideloading on Windows Phone devices, follow these steps:

1. In the console, navigate to **Software Library -> Application Management -> Applications**. Select the application for which you want to add the Windows Phone Store DT and click **Create Deployment Type** on the ribbon bar to open the Create Deployment Type Wizard.

2. On the General page, select **Windows Phone app package (*.xap file)** from the Type dropdown list.

3. Provide the UNC path to the .xap file (**\\odyssey\dsl\Applications\Microsoft\ Windows Phone Sample Apps\Shapes.xap** in this case). Click **Next** to continue.

4. On the Import Information page, verify that the import succeeded. If it did not, click **Previous** and confirm that a valid .xap file is specified. Click **Next**.

5. On the General Information page, modify the name as necessary. You can also provide administrator comments, publisher information, software version, an optional reference, and administrative categories. Click **Next** to continue.

6. Review the information on the Summary page. Click **Next** to create the DT.

7. On the Completion page, shown in Figure 12.9, verify that the DT was created. Click **Close** to close the wizard.

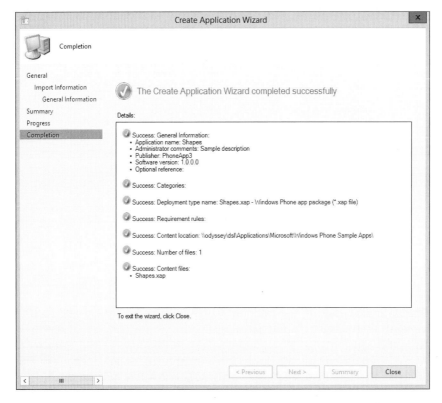

FIGURE 12.9   Completing the Create Application Wizard for Windows Phone app package.

Sideloading Applications for Android Devices

By default, Android devices only install applications from the Google Play store. You can modify the settings of each Android device to enable installation of applications from unknown sources, such as via sideloading (select **Settings -> Applications -> Unknown Sources**). To define applications for sideloading, follow these steps:

1. In the console, navigate to **Software Library -> Application Management -> Applications**. Select the application for which you want to add the Google Play Store DT and click **Create Deployment Type** on the ribbon bar to open the Create Deployment Type Wizard.

2. On the General page, select **App Package for Android (*.apk file)** from the Type dropdown list.

3. Provide the UNC path to the .apk file (**\\odyssey\dsl\Applications\Citrix\ Receiver\v3.9.1\Deploy\Android\CitrixReceiver-v391-373260.apk** in this case). Click **Next** to continue.

4. Verify that the import was successful in the Import Information page. If it was not, click **Previous** and confirm that the correct path is supplied to a location where the .apk file is located. Click **Next** to continue.

5. On the General Information page, modify the name as desired. You can also provide administrator comments and select the languages included in this DT. Click **Next**.

6. If needed, specify a requirement on the Requirements page; in this case, a requirement is already specified: Minimum API Level, which should be greater than or equal to 14. For Android applications, you can only add a requirement based on device ownership. Click **Next** to continue.

7. Review the Summary page. Click **Next** to create the DT.

8. Verify that the DT was created successfully in the Completion page, as shown in Figure 12.10. Click **Close** to close the wizard.

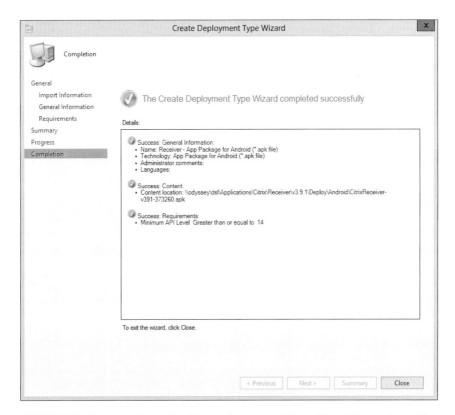

FIGURE 12.10   Completing the Create Deployment Type Wizard for an Android app package.

Sideloading Applications for Apple iPhone, iPod, and iPad Devices

Apple iPhone and iPad devices run the iOS OS. These iOS devices must be contacted by the Apple Push Notification (APN) service to check for policy. An APN certificate is required to communicate with Apple's APN service. When a new policy for iOS devices is created, Intune contacts the APN service for those devices, and the devices in turn check with Intune for their new policy. Configuring the APN service for use with Windows Intune is described in Chapter 16.

NOTE: APPLE ENTERPRISE DEVELOPER LICENSE

Distributing in-house iOS applications requires an Apple Developer license. Alternatively, you could buy applications in volume by using Apple's Volume Purchase Program (VPP). Sideloading applications for iOS devices is accomplished by importing an .ipa file, an application archive that stores the application for the iOS device. The. ipa file is encrypted using Apple's FairPlay digital rights management technology. The Apple Enterprise Developer license costs $299 per year. For information about this license, see http://developer.apple.com/programs/ios/enterprise.

After enrolling an iOS device, a provisioning profile is installed on that device, connecting it to the company's enterprise program membership. Each device has a special profile for the Apple App Store, which cannot be changed. Any application installed on the device is matched against this profile; if profiles do not match, the application is not installed.

Host an .ipa file on the DSL and then follow these steps:

1. In the console, navigate to **Software Library -> Application Management -> Applications**. Select the application for which you want to add the Apple App Store DT and click **Create Deployment Type** on the ribbon bar to open the Create Deployment Type Wizard.

2. On the General page of the wizard, select **App Package for iOS (*.ipa file)** from the Type dropdown list.

3. Provide the UNC path to the .ipa file (in this case **\\odyssey\dsl\Applications\Apple\WireLessAdHocDemo\v.1.0.0\iOS\WirelessAdHocDemo.ipa**). Click **Next** to continue.

4. Confirm that the import succeeded in the Import Information page. If it did not, click **Previous** and confirm that the path is correct. Click **Next** to continue.

5. On the General Information page, modify the name, if needed. You can also provide administrator comments and select the languages included in this DT. Click **Next** to continue.

6. Specify requirements on the Requirements page. Click **Add** to open the Create Requirement dialog box. Select **Operating System** as a condition and specify that the application can only run on **All iOS 7 iPhone and iPod touch devices**. Click **Next** to continue.

7. Review the information on the Summary page. Click **Next** to create the DT.

8. On the Completion page, verify that the DT was successfully created, as shown in Figure 12.11. When successful, click **Close**.

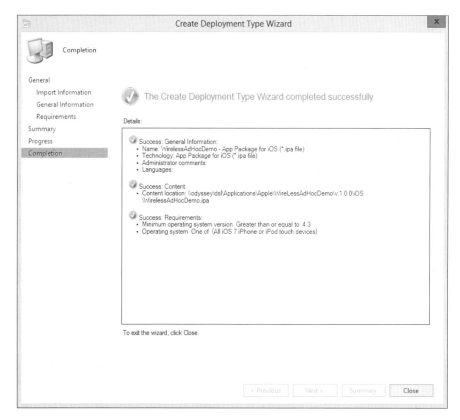

FIGURE 12.11   Completion page of the Create Deployment Type Wizard for an iOS app package.

Unlike with other platforms, installing sideloaded applications for iOS requires the user to access the web version of the company portal. The user should start Safari and browse to https://portal.manage.microsoft.com to log in with his or her Windows Intune account. From there, the user can choose to install the applications that are available for installation on the iOS device.

NOTE: USING VPN PROFILES IN YOUR APPLICATIONS

Defining virtual private network (VPN) profiles in ConfigMgr enables you to deploy VPN settings to different types of devices. The VPN profiles are supported for devices running the following operating systems:

- ▶ Windows 8.1 (32- and 64-bit)
- ▶ Windows RT 8 and Windows RT 8.1
- ▶ Windows Phone 8.1
- ▶ iPhone and iPad devices running iOS 5, iOS 6, iOS 7, and iOS 8
- ▶ Android 4.0 and later

When creating a Windows app package, you can select the option **Use an automatic VPN connection (if configured)** to let the application open the VPN connection automatically. If more than one VPN profile is deployed, using automatic VPN connections is not supported.

Setting up per-app VPNs on iOS devices is supported, although the VPNs must be certificate based. See https://blogs.technet.microsoft.com/karanrustagi/2015/09/21/how-to-set-up-per-app-vpn-using-configuration-manager/ for additional information.

For more information about the prerequisites, how to create and deploy VPN profiles, and how to monitor VPN profiles, see https://technet.microsoft.com/library/mt629185.aspx.

Using Deeplinking with DTs to Distribute Applications

Deeplinking, which refers to creating a direct link to the location of an app in the application store, is quite easy. When you create the DT, browse to the app in the application store of the manufacturer and select the one you want to install. Users are provided with a link they can click to go to a location where they can download and install the app. An Apple, Google, or Windows account is required for the appropriate store. For Windows, Microsoft also provides the Windows Store for Business, which allows users to install company-provided apps, possibly purchased in volume by the company for cost savings.

Creating a Windows Store Deeplinking for the Windows and Windows Phone DT

As Microsoft merged the Windows Phone store into the Microsoft Store, there is no longer a clear distinction between deeplinking for Windows apps and Windows Phone apps. This section shows how to create a DT that provides a link to the Microsoft Store. Clicking the link takes users directly to the app in the store, where they can decide to install the app. Follow these steps:

1. In the ConfigMgr console, navigate to **Software Library -> Application Management -> Applications**. Select the application for which you want to add the Windows app package (in the Windows Store) DT and click **Create Deployment Type** on the ribbon bar to open the Create Deployment Type Wizard.

2. On the General page, select **Windows Phone app package (in the Windows Store)** from the Type dropdown list.

3. Provide a URL to the app or click **Browse** to start the Windows Phone app package browser and search for the application you want to add (in this case, **Instagram**), as shown in Figure 12.12. Click **OK** and then click **Next**.

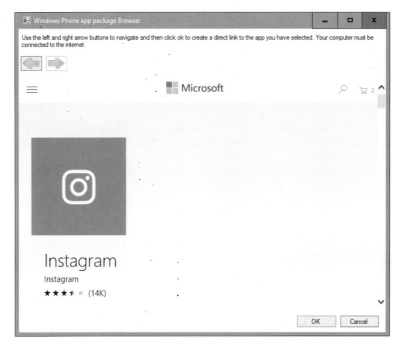

FIGURE 12.12   Windows Phone app package browser.

4. Confirm that the import was successful in the Import Information page. If it was not, click **Previous** and verify that the URL in the Location field is correct. Click **Next** to continue.

5. On the General Information page, modify the name as necessary. You could also provide administrator comments and select languages included in this DT. Click **Next**.

6. On the Requirements page, specify any necessary conditions.

7. Review the information on the Summary page and click **Next**.

8. Follow the progress and verify that the DT was successfully created in the Completion page. When successful, click **Close** to close the wizard.

Creating a Google Play Store Deeplinking Deployment Type

This section shows how to create a DT that provides a link to the Google Play store. Clicking the link takes users directly to the app in the Google Play store, where they can decide to install the app. Follow these steps:

1. In the console, navigate to **Software Library -> Application Management -> Applications**. Select the application for which you want to add the Google Play Store DT and click **Create Deployment Type** on the ribbon bar to open the Create Deployment Type Wizard.

2. On the General page, select **App Package for Android on Google Play** from the Type dropdown list.

3. Provide the URL to the app you want to specify. If you know the URL, paste it into the Location field; otherwise, browse for the URL, using the App Package for Android Browser dialog (which opens https://play.google.com), as shown in Figure 12.13. Click **Next** when the URL is filled in.

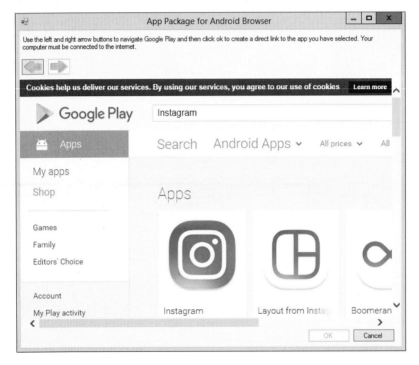

FIGURE 12.13   Selecting Instagram in the Google Play store, using the App Package for Android Browser dialog.

4. Confirm that the import was successful in the Import Information page. If it was not, click **Previous** and verify that the URL in the Location field on the General page is correct. Click **Next** to continue.

5. On the General Information page, modify the name as necessary. You can also provide administrator comments and select the languages included in this DT. Click **Next**.

6. Review the information on the Summary page and click **Next**.

7. Follow the progress and verify that the DT was successfully created in the Completion page. When successful, click **Close** to close the wizard.

Creating an Apple App Store Deeplinking Deployment Type

The procedure in this section shows how to create a DT that provides a link to the Apple App Store. Clicking the link takes users directly to the app in the Apple App Store, where they can decide whether to install it. Some applications may have multiple links, if they are available for both iPhone and iPad. You can specify requirements to ensure that the DT is applicable to the iPhone or the iPad. Follow these steps:

1. In the console, navigate to **Software Library -> Application Management -> Applications**. Select the application for which you want to add the Apple App Store DT and click **Create Deployment Type** on the ribbon bar to open the Create Deployment Type Wizard.

2. On the General page, select **App Package for iOS from App Store** from the Type dropdown list.

3. Supply the URL of the app in the Apple App Store. If you already know the URL, paste it in the **Location** field; otherwise, click **Browse** to open the App Package for iOS dialog and find it there.

4. Click the search icon in the menu bar and type the name of the application you want to add in the search field (in this case **Instagram**). Select the Instagram page, as shown in Figure 12.14, and notice that OK in the lower-right corner is now selectable. Click **OK** to select this application and close the App Package for iOS dialog.

FIGURE 12.14   Selecting Instagram in the Apple App Store, using the App Package for iOS dialog.

TIP: USING THE APPLE VOLUME PURCHASE PROGRAM (VPP)

The App Package for iOS dialog also allows you to select applications from the Apple VPP, which allows customers to purchase applications in volume. For more information, see http://www.apple.com/business/vpp/.

Before selecting an application purchased using Apple VPP, you must upload your VPP token into Intune. Select the **Volume Purchase Program** node under Application Management and then select **Apple** and then **Tokens**. Add your VPP token by selecting **Create Apple Volume Purchase Program Token** and completing the wizard. Once the token is configured, you can manage the apps purchased by using VPP in the Licensed Apps node.

5. Ensure that the URL in the Location field on the General page now contains the Apple App Store location. Click **Next** to continue.

6. Confirm that the import was successful in the Import Information page. If it was not, click **Previous** and verify that the URL in the Location field on the General page is correct. Click **Next** to continue.

7. On the General Information page, modify the name, if needed. You can also enter administrator comments and select the languages to include in this DT. Click **Next**.

8. Specify requirements on the Requirements page. Click **Add** to open the Create Requirement dialog. In this case, select **All iOS 8 iPhone or iPod touch devices, All iOS9 iPhone or iPod touch devices, All iOS 8 iPad devices**, and **All iOS9 iPad devices** as the platform on which this application can run. You can also create a requirement for the ownership of the device as personal or company. Click **Next**.

9. Review the Summary page. Click **Next** to create the DT.

10. On the Completion page, verify that the DT was created successfully. Click **Close** to close the wizard.

Creating and Using Other Deployment Types

Besides Windows Installer, application virtualization, and mobile device-based deployment types, ConfigMgr supports DTs for Mac OS, web applications with links pointing to uniform resource locators, and script-based applications. This provides a way to script applications containing installation methods not covered by other DTs.

Creating a Script-Based Deployment Type

The word *script* typically brings to mind something written in VBScript, PowerShell, or some other scripting language. Script-based installers are commonly used when working with applications. This could be an .exe, .bat, .com, .vbs, or other type of command run from a command line to install software (other than Windows Installer, covered in Chapter 11).

The procedure in this section shows how to add a new DT to an existing application. While it is similar to creating a new Windows Installer–based DT, there are significant differences. Follow these steps to create a script-based DT for the Citrix Receiver application:

1. From the application properties, select the Deployment Types tab and click **Add** to create a new DT.

2. For DT type, select **Script Installer (Native)**.

3. The source location property is disabled because you selected Script Installer (Native) instead of Windows Installer. Click **Next** to display the General Information tab.

4. On the General Information tab, complete as much information as possible and click **Next** to advance to the Content page. If you have previously worked with different types of installations, you know there are no standard installation arguments. For Citrix Receiver, use the arguments `/silent` `/noreboot` when running the CitrixReceiver.exe installer. You should request a Windows Installer package or a document with the correct install/uninstall arguments from the application vendor. As you do not currently know the proper uninstall command, leave it blank.

TIP: ALLOWING USERS TO UNINSTALL APPLICATIONS FROM SOFTWARE CENTER

Include the proper uninstall whenever possible to allow users to leverage Software Center to uninstall an application.

5. On the Detection Method page, specify for a valid detection method. Another advantage of a Windows Installer application is that the detection method is automatically configured when ConfigMgr interrogates an .msi (based on the Windows Installer product code); detection rules must be built for script-based installations. For this step, you will create a basic detection rule. Chapter 11 discusses detection methods. Click **Add Clause** and select **File System** as the setting type; then click **Browse** to browse to **selfservice.exe** on a test system with the Citrix Receiver installed.

TIP: VERIFYING WINDOWS INSTALLER DETECTION METHODS

Some administrators combine multiple applications into a single installer, often referred to as a *wrapper*. Use caution when writing detection methods based on wrapped data; if your wrapper program is a Windows Installer and your detection method looks for that program, you are guaranteeing that the wrapper, not the actual software, is installed on the client!

Check your detection methods to ensure that you are detecting install status. Chapter 9, "Client Management," discusses how the application deployment evaluation cycle validates application installation on a regular interval (seven days by default). If a required application state is evaluated as missing, another application installation is initiated.

Notice that this is a basic rule that checks whether the file exists in the specified path. You could enable the option to look for a specific file date or version, but this example only checks that the file exists. Chapter 11 discusses detection methods.

6. Complete the User Experience page, which provides the standard settings for user experience.

7. Fill out the Requirements page, which is similar to the one discussed earlier in this chapter, in the "Creating a Windows Installer–Based Deployment Type" section. Chapter 11 includes an in-depth look at requirements, also known as *global conditions*. This optional field is blank, implying that the installation will occur on all operating systems and platforms targeted with the installation.

8. Click through the Dependencies, Summary, and Progress pages, which are the same as when creating a DT for a Windows Installer–based application.

As there are no requirements (global conditions), this application is available for any targeted system. If you had a different installation for the server and created a second DT with a priority of 2 for the server DT, it would never run, as DTs are evaluated in priority order. When a system evaluates the requirement rules for a DT, if there are none, that DT is deployed, ignoring all other DTs. Place the least restrictive DT at the lowest priority (that is, with the largest priority number) to ensure that all other DTs are evaluated for applicability first.

Creating a DT for a script-based installer is similar to creating a Windows Installer DT. The challenge is determining the proper detection method and the install and uninstall command-line arguments. Work with your packaging team and third-party application vendors to ensure that your information is correct. And be sure to test!

Creating Deployment Types for Mac OS

Many organizations use non-Windows platforms. To support mobile devices running these operating systems, ConfigMgr uses the Microsoft Intune connector and manages the devices through Microsoft Intune; for in-company devices, ConfigMgr can also support Mac OS. This section describes how to create applications for Mac OS.

ConfigMgr supports the following Mac OS packaging formats:

▶ Apple disk image (*.dmg file)

▶ Meta package file (*.mpkg file)

▶ Mac OS X installer package (*.pkg)

▶ Mac OS X application (*.app)

Before deploying these app packages, gather application information using the CMAppUtil utility, available with the OS X client installation files. Output is a .cmmac file, which must be supplied with the OS X package when importing the DT in ConfigMgr.

Complete the following steps to create a .cmmac file for an Apple Disk Image file you can use to install Acrobat Reader DC:

1. Confirm that the package is copied to the folder that contains the extracted files from the macclient.dmg file used to install the ConfigMgr client.

2. Open a terminal window and navigate to that folder. Type **mkdir AcroReaderDC** to create a subfolder to store the .cmmac file.

3. Execute CMAppUtil by typing `./CMAppUtil -C /users/sysadmin/Downloads/ AcroRdrDC_1501720050_MUI.dmg -o AcroReaderDC`. You now have a AcroRdrDC Installer.pkg.cmmac file in the AcroReaderDC folder.

4. Copy the AcroRdrDC Installer.pkg.cmmac.pkg.cmmac file to the DSL.

After creating the .cmmac file, you can define the application DT for Mac OS X. Follow these steps:

1. In the console, navigate to **Software Library -> Application Management -> Applications**. Select the application for which you want to add the Mac OS X DT and click **Create Deployment Type** on the ribbon bar to open the Create Deployment Type Wizard.

2. On the General page, select **Mac OS X** from the Type dropdown. Provide the UNC path to the .cmmac file (in this case, **\\odyssey\dsl\Applications\Adobe\Reader DC\2015.017.20050\Deploy\MacOS\AcroRdrDC Installer.pkg.cmmac**). Click **Next** to continue.

3. Confirm that the import succeeded in the Import Information page. If it did not, click **Previous** and verify that the correct path is supplied. Click **Next**.

4. On the General Information page, modify the name as needed. You can add administrator comments and select languages as well. Click **Next**.

5. On the Requirements page, click **Add** to open the Create Requirement dialog box. You can select the operating system as a condition to specify the platform on which you can run this application. Click **Next**.

6. Review the Summary page. Click **Next** to create the DT.

7. Verify that the DT was successfully created, as shown in Figure 12.15, and click **Close**.

After a deployment is created, the user receives a popup indicating that new software is available. The user can install the software or let ConfigMgr install it at the specified deadline. Use the CCMClient.log file on that system to troubleshoot any issues.

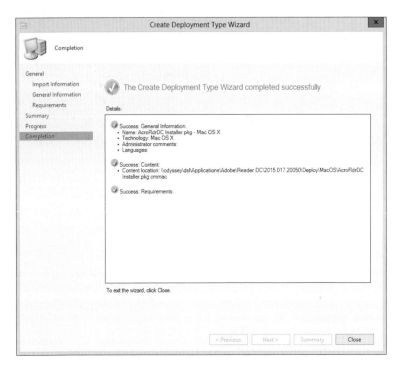

FIGURE 12.15   Completion page of the Create Deployment Type Wizard for a Mac OS X package.

Creating Web Applications

To create a web application, define a link to a URL pointing to an intranet or Internet location. With more and more applications becoming accessible through web browsers, web-based applications are a common requirement. The link is deployed as a shortcut for Windows, a web clip for iOS, and a widget for Android devices. Windows Phone users can launch the link from the company portal. Follow these steps to deploy a web application:

1. In the ConfigMgr console, navigate to **Software Library -> Application Management -> Applications**. Select the application to which to add a Web Application DT. Click **Create Deployment Type** on the ribbon bar to open the Create Deployment Type Wizard.

2. On the General page, select **Web Application** from the dropdown. Specify a URL to the web page hosting the application. Click **Next**.

3. Verify that the import was successful. If it was not, click **Previous** and confirm that the URL for the Location field is correctly formatted. Click **Next**.

4. On the General Information page, modify the name to one that suits your organization's needs. You can provide administrator comments and select the languages included in this DT. Click **Next**.

5. On the Requirements page, click **Add** to open the Create Requirement dialog box and specify any requirements. Click **Next**.

6. On the Dependencies page, define any dependencies. For example, you could specify that Microsoft Silverlight is needed to view the web application. In this case, indicate the necessary Microsoft Silverlight DTs in a dependency group name, if needed, and click **Next** to continue.

7. Review the Summary page. Click **Next** to create the DT.

8. On the Completion page, verify that the DT was successfully created, as shown in Figure 12.16, and click **Close**.

TIP: MORE ABOUT THE END USER EXPERIENCE ON IOS AND ANDROID

Gerry Hampson, one of the authors of this book, provides additional context about app deployment from an end-user perspective. For information about app deployment for Android, see the article at http://gerryhampsoncm.blogspot.ie/2015/07/deploying-apps-to-android-devices-with.html; for information regarding iOS, see http://gerryhampsoncm.blogspot.ie/2015/07/deploying-apps-to-ios-devices-with.html.

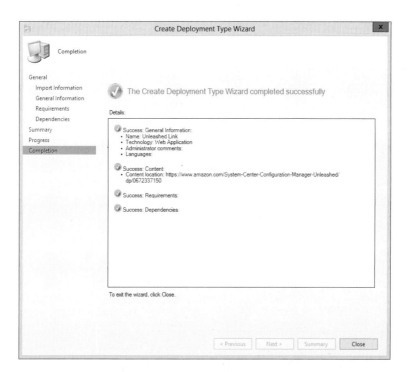

FIGURE 12.16   Completion page of the Create Deployment Type Wizard for a web application.

Synchronizing Apps from the Windows Store for Business

The Windows Store for Business allows companies to purchase individual Windows apps or to purchase apps in volume for use by the company. Connecting Configuration Manager with the Windows Store for Business allows purchased apps to be synchronized; the apps are then accessible in the ConfigMgr console and available for deployment.

In order for synchronization with the Windows Store for Business to work, Azure services must be set up and configured for the Windows Store for Business, as described in Chapter 6, "Installing and Updating System Center Configuration Manager."

Once the Windows Store for Business synchronization is established, the purchased apps become available in the ConfigMgr console. Follow these steps to create an app synchronized from the Windows Store for Business:

1. Open the ConfigMgr console and navigate to **Software Library** -> **Application Management**.

2. Click **License Information for Store Apps** and select the app you want to deploy.

3. Click **Create Application** in the ribbon bar to create a ConfigMgr application.

Summary

This chapter discussed the creation of available DTs for ConfigMgr applications and provided extra context for the options possible when creating a DT. It explained how to create a virtual environment in which you can specify which App-V 5 virtual applications can interact with each other. It described how to deploy and test apps, either provided directly or via the app stores for the different platforms.

Chapter 13, "Creating and Managing Packages and Programs," describes how to create packages and programs.

CHAPTER 13

Creating and Managing Packages and Programs

Applications and deployment types, introduced with System Center 2012 Configuration Manager, are discussed in Chapter 11, "Creating and Managing Applications," and Chapter 12, "Creating and Using Deployment Types." This chapter discusses the packages and programs feature that can also be used to deploy applications. Packages and programs have existed since 1994 with Systems Management Server (SMS), the earlier name for Configuration Manager (ConfigMgr). While the functionality of packages and programs has evolved over the years, their core concepts remain the same.

While Microsoft prefers that you use the application model, in several scenarios, using a package makes more sense or is the only option:

▶ Scripts that do not install an application on a computer (such as a script to defragment a disk drive)

▶ One-off scripts that do not need continual monitoring

▶ Scripts that run on a recurring schedule and cannot use global evaluation

▶ Applications that do not have very good detection methods or that require complex detection methods

▶ Providing just the files to the operating system (OS) and not necessarily having to provide a program (mainly with task sequences during OS deployment [OSD])

This chapter, along with Chapters 11 and 12, focuses on software deployment. It discusses some key terms associated with software deployment using packages and programs, and it provides further detail on how to create and configure packages and programs. Chapter 14, "Distributing and Deploying Applications and Packages," discusses how you can deliver a package to a device by creating collections, using distribution points (DPs), and creating deployments.

Understanding Packages and Programs

A software *package* consists of general information about the software to be deployed, including its name, version, manufacturer, and language, as well as the location of source files for the package (if it has source files). Packages are created manually or from a package definition file such as an MSI, SMS, or PDF file type—discussed in more detail later in this chapter, in the section "Creating Packages Using the Package and Program Wizard and for UNIX and Linux Systems."

ConfigMgr software packages are not actually repackaged vendor software. While ConfigMgr uses the same source files used to install the software, it uses MSI files to automatically populate many of the questions that require answers to create packages and programs. You can also create software packages without package definition files, as you can deploy executables, batch files, VBScript, JavaScript, and command files, among others. If you can execute it, you can design a package to deploy it!

ConfigMgr uses packages to distribute software and to deploy changes (such as Registry changes) to client configurations.

A package may optionally include programs that provide specifics on how the software runs. A package also contains information about who can access it (security) and where it is distributed (DPs). *Programs* are commands specifying what should occur on a client when it receives the package. A program can do just about anything; it can install or uninstall software, distribute data, run antivirus software, or update a client configuration.

While programs are not required, a package must contain at least one program if it is to perform any action other than provide a pointer to source files. A definition file provides answers to the majority of the questions required to create a package. An MSI provided as a package definition file includes six default programs for use with software distribution, each allowing the package to run in different ways:

▶ **Per-System Attended:** This installation causes a program to install and expects user interaction; it runs once for the system on which it is targeted to install.

▶ **Per-System Unattended:** This installation causes a program to install that expects to run without user interaction; it runs once for the system on which it is targeted to install.

▶ **Per-System Uninstall:** This installation performs an uninstallation of the program; it runs once for the system that it is targeted to uninstall.

▶ **Per-User Attended:** This installation causes a program to install and expects user interaction; it runs once for the user for whom it is targeted to install.

▶ **Per-User Unattended:** This installation causes a program to install without user interaction; it runs once for the user for whom it is targeted to install.

▶ **Per-User Uninstall:** This installation performs an uninstallation of the program; it runs once for the user for whom it is targeted to uninstall.

Each program specifies the command line used to run the program in the method described. As an example, a per-system unattended installation includes a switch to run the program without user intervention.

Because this chapter focuses on ConfigMgr packages, the next sections walk through the steps to create a package and provide examples of the process.

Packages can come in many flavors:

▶ **Packages That Use a Definition File:** You can create ConfigMgr packages either with a *definition file* or without. SMS 1.x definition files used an extension of .pdf (package definition file). With SMS 2.0, definition files had either a .pdf or .sms (Systems Management Server) extension. Although these two file types still exist and you can use them with ConfigMgr to create a package, they are relatively uncommon now. Originally, SMS used the .pdf extension; this was later changed to .sms, as the .pdf extension was also used for portable document format files. For information about creating .pdf and .sms definition files, see https://technet.microsoft.com/library/bb632631.aspx.

The package definition file most commonly used by Configuration Manager is a Windows Installer file. Windows Installer (.msi) files are discussed in the next section, "Creating a Package from a Definition File."

▶ **Packages That You Can Create Without a Definition File:** These packages are discussed later in this chapter, in the "Creating a Package Using the New Package Wizard" section.

▶ **A Package That Does Not Even Need to Have Source Files as Part of the Package:** This is often used when ConfigMgr runs a program already stored on the system.

ConfigMgr uses these different flavors of packages to create Configuration Manager packages. To illustrate how this is accomplished, the next sections step through an example that shows how to deploy a relatively simple package.

Creating a Package from a Definition File

This chapter uses the Windows Installer distributable of 7-Zip (which is also used in Chapters 11 and 12) to walk through the process of creating a package from a definition. In this case, the definition is extracted from the .msi, which contains most of the information needed to create the package and programs.

Creating a 7-Zip Package

Creating a ConfigMgr package for 7-Zip is straightforward and requires the following steps:

1. In the ConfigMgr console, navigate to **Software Library** -> **Overview** -> **Application Management** -> **Packages** and select **Create** -> **Create Package from Definition** from the ribbon bar to open the Create Package from Definition Wizard, shown in Figure 13.1.

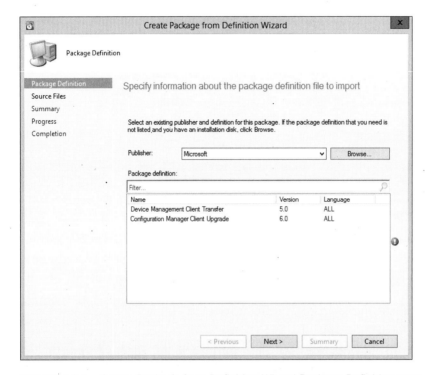

FIGURE 13.1   Create Package from Definition Wizard Package Definition page.

2. Click **Browse** in the wizard and navigate to the .msi. Choose the x86 version for this example. Figure 13.2 shows the imported package definition metadata for 7-Zip version 16.02. Click **Next** to continue.

The next page offers three different ways to manage source files:

▶ **This Package Does Not Contain Any Source Files:** This may be useful when ConfigMgr is running a program already stored on the system.

▶ **Always Obtain Files from a Source Directory:** This is the most commonly used option.

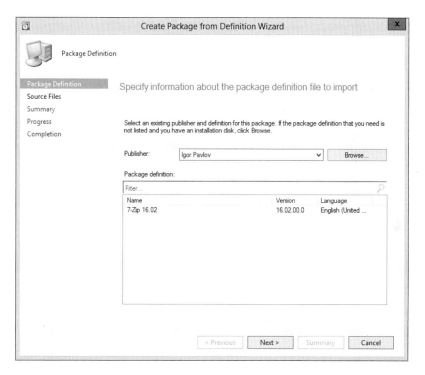

FIGURE 13.2   Create Package from Definition Wizard Package Definition page metadata.

▶ **Create a Compressed Version of the Source Files:** This may be useful when you need to decrease storage requirements or do not expect the package to change.

3. Select the second option for this package—**Always obtain files from a source directory**. Click **Next**. If the option you selected specifies that source files are part of the package, the wizard verifies the location of the source files.

4. Specify the package source location by choosing **Network path** or **Local folder**. As a best practice, always try to use a network path. Applications (as discussed in Chapter 11) require a Universal Naming Convention (UNC) format of \\<servername>\<sharename>\<filename>. A UNC path is required if you convert a package to an application using the Package Conversion Manager (also discussed in Chapter 11). Specify the path to the package source installation folder. As the contents of the selected folder and all subfolders are sent to each targeted DP, try to keep source files organized to reduce any chance of extra files and folders being distributed with a package. Click **Next** to continue.

NOTE: CONFIGMGR PROCESSES USE LOCAL SYSTEM ACCOUNT

ConfigMgr processes run as the Local System account. Ensure that the computer account of the site server has read permissions to the source files share.

5. Review the Summary page of the wizard, which lists the options chosen to create the package, including the name of the package, how to handle source files, and the location of the source directory (folder). Click **Next** to create the package. The Progress page appears briefly and automatically changes to the Completion page.

6. Review the status of this page and then click **Close**. Using the information in the MSI file, the wizard creates a set of installation options for the program, including Per-system attended, Per-system unattended, Per-system uninstall, Per-user attended, Per-user unattended, and Per-user uninstall, as shown in Figure 13.3.

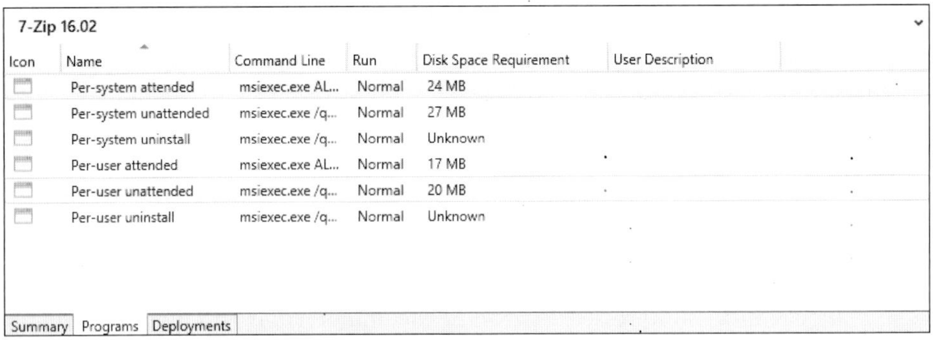

7-Zip 16.02					
Icon	Name	Command Line	Run	Disk Space Requirement	User Description
	Per-system attended	msiexec.exe AL...	Normal	24 MB	
	Per-system unattended	msiexec.exe /q...	Normal	27 MB	
	Per-system uninstall	msiexec.exe /q...	Normal	Unknown	
	Per-user attended	msiexec.exe AL...	Normal	17 MB	
	Per-user unattended	msiexec.exe /q...	Normal	20 MB	
	Per-user uninstall	msiexec.exe /q...	Normal	Unknown	

| Summary | Programs | Deployments |

FIGURE 13.3   Programs for the 7-Zip package.

Advantages of Using an MSI File

Using MSI files for package definition greatly simplifies the process of creating a package because the .msi supplies information that otherwise would be specified manually. Review the Summary and Programs pane for the 7-Zip 16.02 package. The Summary tab shows the package ID (which is helpful for troubleshooting) and content status. You haven't distributed content to any DPs yet, but this summary is helpful when you do.

NOTE: CONTENT AUTOMATICALLY ADDED TO STORE AT CREATION

When you create a new package (manually or with a wizard), files in the content source path are automatically collected and added to the content store on the site that owns the package. You still must send content to the DPs to ensure that content is available for targeted systems.

The Programs tab (refer to Figure 13.3), displays the programs for the selected package. Because you ran the Create Package from Definition Wizard against an MSI file, you can see the six programs automatically created for 7-Zip.

Configuring Package Properties

View the properties of the package and program you created to confirm that all settings are configured as desired. Populate as many fields as possible on the General tab, shown in Figure 13.4. This information can be helpful to a user who needs to choose a software installation from the Software Center or Application Catalog.

Using the Package Properties Data Source Tab

On the Data Source tab, notice the package source location and the current source version. If the contents of the source folder update regularly, consider enabling the Update distribution points on a schedule check box. When a schedule is configured, ConfigMgr re-sends the contents of the package source to the specified DPs. If no changes were detected in the source folder, nothing is re-sent (or refreshed) on the DPs.

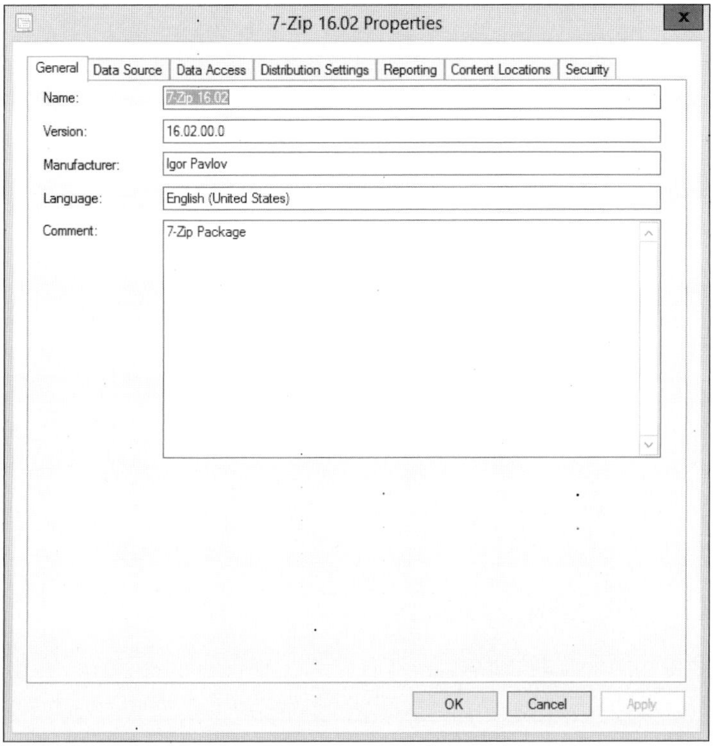

FIGURE 13.4   General tab of package properties.

Enable the following options on the Data Source tab, as required:

▶ **Persist Content in the Client Cache:** Persist content to ensure that the installation source remains in the local cache (%*windir*%\ccmcache). Use this option for software that may need to be rerun regularly but not require content updates. Package source size affects the size of available cache.

▶ **Enable Binary Differential Replication:** Use binary differential replication for packages containing large files, such as the installation .wim file for OSD. These algorithms require additional overhead for calculating which bits need to be transferred to DPs for each file in the package source.

These options should be used sparingly, as they increase overhead.

Using the Package Properties Data Access Tab

The Data Access tab, shown in Figure 13.5, allows you to configure package share settings. Use this tab to configure how the package is stored on DPs.

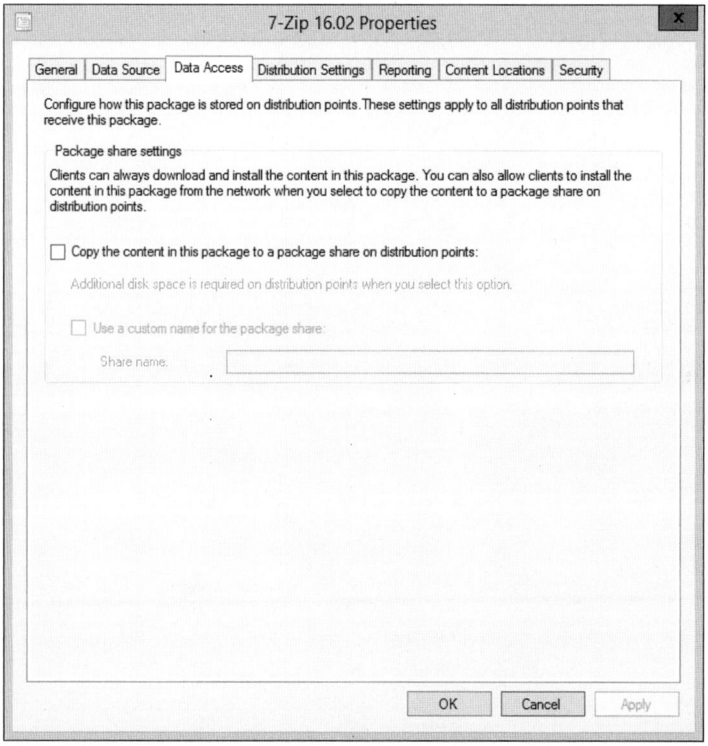

FIGURE 13.5   Data Access tab of package properties.

When the **Copy the content in this package to a package share on distribution points** option is selected, ConfigMgr copies the package contents to the SMSPKG*D*$ share (where *D* is the drive letter for the share). You can also specify a custom-named share to use for the package.

NOTE: PACKAGE SHARE CAUSES DUPLICATE CONTENT ON A DP

One of ConfigMgr's greatest features is its single-instance store for content. When you select the option to copy the content to a package share, ConfigMgr does just that: It copies all required files and places them on the share. All content in package shares is in addition to the content in the content store, which increases the size of your DP. However, the Copy the content in this package to a package share on distribution points check box must be enabled if you plan to configure any deployment to run from a DP.

Using the Package Properties Distribution Settings Tab

The Distribution Settings tab (see Figure 13.6) allows you to specify distribution-specific settings for a package. This tab has the following configurable options:

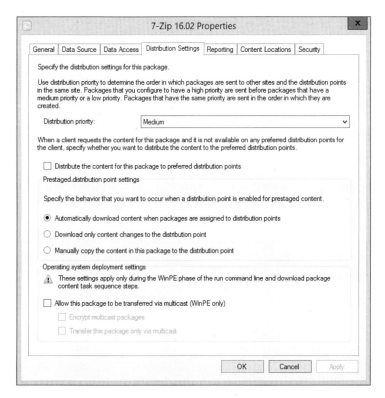

FIGURE 13.6   Distribution Settings tab of package properties.

▶ **Distribution Priority:** Use this option to control the order in which multiple packages are sent to DPs. You may want to configure more critical packages (antivirus, security patches, and so on) to a high priority so they will be sent to child sites and

DPs faster than packages of low priority, such as a portable document format viewer application.

▶ **Distribute the Content for This Package to Preferred Distribution Points:** A client has a "preferred" DP when it is in the boundaries of a defined DP group. If that client requests a package not on the DP, the content is automatically deployed to the preferred DP to fulfill the request for the client. This can useful for content you want to avoid deploying to all DPs, such as a multi user interface (MUI) language package.

▶ **Prestaged Distribution Point Settings:** Selecting the **Enable this distribution point for prestaged content** check box on the properties of the DP causes the following settings that affect content distribution to appear on the Distribution Settings tab:

  ▶ **Automatically Download Content When Packages Are Assigned to Distribution Points:** This setting causes the DP to perform normally and not follow prestaged content rules; content will be distributed to any targeted DP.

  ▶ **Download Only Content Changes to the Distribution Point:** If you select this option, you must export content and then extract content manually on the DP for initial distribution; subsequent update DP actions send delta updates. Say that you are ready to deploy the next version of Microsoft Office, and the source installation is currently around 1GB. Due to WAN availability, you may choose to manually transfer content to the DP the first time (either over a WAN file copy or by shipping media that contains content to the remote DP). After you prestage the initial payload, update DPs work normally, as expected.

  ▶ **Manually Copy the Content in This Package to the Distribution Point:** Selecting this option prevents ConfigMgr from copying any content to the DP, requiring you to export content from the ConfigMgr console and then extract it to a new DP.

▶ **Operating System Deployment Settings:** Use this section to enable multicast, require encryption, and/or allow the package to be transferred only via multicast. This section only applies while the system is running Windows Preinstallation Environment (WinPE).

Using the Package Properties Reporting Tab

The Reporting tab displays status Management Information Format (MIF) matching information. Since the Windows Installer package is now imported, the Use these fields for status MIF matching field is enabled, and all text fields are complete.

The default setting for this dialog is **Use package properties for status MIF matching**. MIF files, which have an extension of .mif, were used in older versions of SMS/ConfigMgr to verify whether software was correctly installed. (For information about MIF files, see https://technet.microsoft.com/library/bb633139.aspx.) Enable the **Use these fields for status MIF matching** radio button only if you can complete the MIF matching information, such as the MIF filename. Choosing the wrong MIF filename (and other text box configurations in the dialog) may cause ConfigMgr to consume the wrong MIF file and incorrectly report installation status to the site server. If you have software that requires a MIF file to correctly report status, consider moving to the application model, discussed in Chapter 11, so you can include additional detection rules to determine whether software is installed.

Using the Package Properties Content Locations Tab

The Content Locations tab enables you to see the targeted DPs and DP groups, as well as the following:

- ▶ **Validate:** Select this option to instruct ConfigMgr to perform a hash check for the desired package on the selected DP. Review SMSDPMon.log on the DP for more information. This option can only be initiated to one DP at a time.

- ▶ **Redistribute:** Use this option to confirm that all packages are on the targeted DPs when needed.

- ▶ **Remove:** This option removes content from selected DPs and from all DPs in a selected DP group.

The Security tab displays all users and user groups with rights to a package, as well as their operational rights. Click **Cancel** to close the dialog (or click **OK** if you have made changes you want to keep) and proceed to view/change the program properties.

Defining Program Properties

After creating a package, next you configure the program the package will use. Notice in Figure 13.3 that a package has six programs. These programs are automatically created by using the Create Package from Definition Wizard and a Windows Installer file. This example requires a system-based unattended installation. The per-system unattended program deploys the7-Zip installation on a per-system basis and runs without user intervention. If you never plan to use some of the programs, such as per-user unattended, consider deleting them to remove clutter.

To set the program properties, right-click the program named **Per-system unattended** (located under **Software Library -> Overview -> Application Management -> Packages**) and then select the 7-Zip package and open the **Properties** page, as shown in Figure 13.7. Properties for each program include the following tabs:

- ▶ General
- ▶ Requirements
- ▶ Environment
- ▶ Advanced
- ▶ Windows Installer
- ▶ OpsMgr Maintenance Mode

These tabs together define how the program will function. The following sections review the content of each, using the 7-Zip package as an example.

Using the Program Properties General Tab

The General tab (shown in Figure 13.7) has a variety of fields automatically populated with information, based on the package definition file used to create the 7-Zip package:

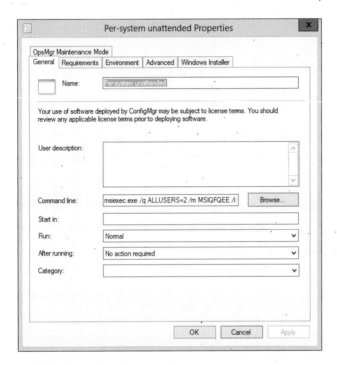

FIGURE 13.7   General tab of the program properties.

▶ **Name:** The Name field is prepopulated and cannot be changed.

▶ **User Description:** This field is a 127-character text field that you use to provide a description of the program.

▶ **Command Line:** This text field can hold up to 255 characters. It provides the command line that installs the application. For the 7-Zip application, the field uses the following syntax:

```
msiexec.exe /q ALLUSERS=2 /m MSIQFQEE /i "7z1602.msi"
```

▶ **Start In:** This optional 127-character text field specifies the absolute path to the program you are installing (such as c:\install_files\program.exe) or the folder relative to the DP you are installing in (such as install_files). This defaults to blank for the 7-Zip installation program.

▶ **Run:** This dropdown specifies whether the program will run normal, minimized, maximized, or hidden:

    ▶ **Normal:** This is the default mode, and it means the program runs based on system and program defaults.

    ▶ **Minimized:** Running minimized shows the program only on the taskbar during installation. The window exists on the taskbar during the installation process; however, it is not the active window maximized on the user's workstation.

    ▶ **Maximized:** Use this option when installing programs that require user intervention. It is also good for package testing.

    ▶ **Hidden:** This mode hides the program during installation and is recommended for fully automated program deployments.

    The 7-Zip installation program defaulted to the Normal configuration.

▶ **After Running:** This dropdown selection determines what occurs after the program completes. The options follow:

    ▶ **No Action Required:** The 7-Zip installation program defaults to this option, which means no restart or logoff is required for the program.

    ▶ **Configuration Manager Restarts Computer:** This option is useful when deploying a program that requires a reboot but the reboot is not initiated as part of the program.

    ▶ **Program Controls Restart:** Select this option if the program requires a reboot and the program will perform the restart program.

    ▶ **Configuration Manager Logs User Off:** Use this option to log off the user after installation.

    Note that both the ConfigMgr restarts computer and ConfigMgr logs user off options take place forcefully, after a grace period. This means that if either of these options is used, any applications running on the clients will not have the opportunity to save their data or state.

▶ **Category:** Category is a dropdown selection used to help find specific programs in ConfigMgr when deployed to the Application Catalog. This field defaults to blank, but you can create a new category by typing in the text for the category's name.

NOTE: USE CARE WHEN ENTERING A NEW CATEGORY

The Category entry is a one-way street. Enter a category and click **Apply**, and that category cannot be removed (at least not in a supported way). Always check to see if a category already exists, and when entering a new category, double-check your spelling! You can remove the category from a program by selecting the blank option from the dropdown.

506 CHAPTER 13 Creating and Managing Packages and Programs

Change the program's configuration on the General tab for the 7-Zip installation, as follows:

▶ **User description:** Add a comment explaining what the program will do

▶ **Command line:** `msiexec.exe /q ALLUSERS="" /m MSIQFQEE /i "7z1602.msi" /l %temp%\7z1602_install.log`

▶ **Run: Hidden**

▶ **After running: No action required**

▶ **Category: Utility**

The command line will run the installation silently and log to *%windir%*\temp\7z1602_ install.log if run using the Local System account.

Using the Program Properties Requirements Tab

This section discusses the Requirements tab for the program. Figure 13.8 shows the default configuration for the 7-Zip program created using the package definition file. This tab is where you tell ConfigMgr the requirements for running the program:

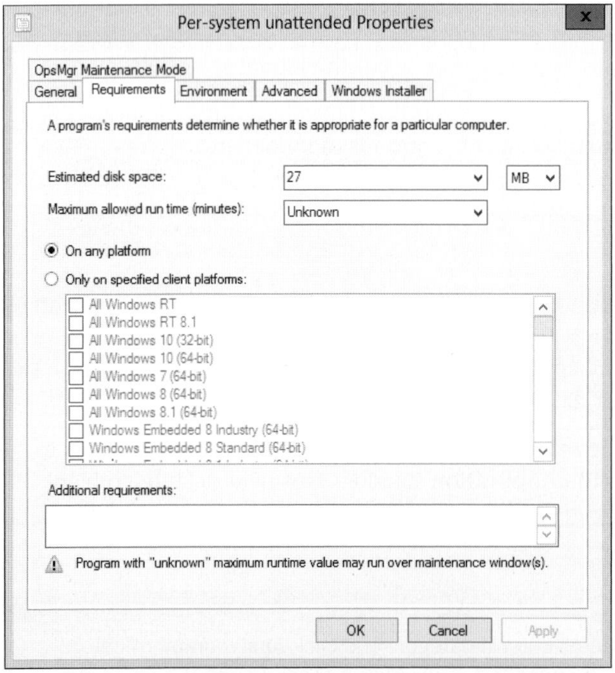

FIGURE 13.8 Program Requirements tab.

▶ **Estimated Disk Space:** Specify the estimated disk space needed to run the program. The setting defaults to 27MB when the package definition file for 7-Zip is used. Although the actual amount of disk space may vary from the amount defined with the package definition file, the default generally provides a good starting point. This setting can be in kilobytes, megabytes, or gigabytes, and it defaults to Unknown for program installations. The setting is for informational purposes only and appears in the properties of the installation in Software Center.

▶ **Maximum Allowed Run Time (Minutes):** Specify the amount of time the program is permitted to run. Enter your worst-case scenario for the time required to install the application. The number should be accurate, as it is used by maintenance windows to determine if the window is large enough to run the installation. With the default setting of Unknown, ConfigMgr monitors the installation for a maximum of 120 minutes; if you have only a 90-minute maintenance window, the program will never run.

The setting defines how long the program is expected to run, which can be quite variable, as it depends on the speed of the system where the program is being installed, program size, and network connectivity between the system and the source files used for the installation. In this example, the setting defaults to Unknown. However, based on previous installations of 7-Zip, the program should complete within 5 minutes. ConfigMgr requires a setting between 15 and 720 minutes (or Unknown), so set this value to 15 minutes. Choose the maximum runtime carefully, as it affects the following:

  ▶ During program installation, the ConfigMgr client monitors the installation until the maximum time is reached. If the installation has not completed by the maximum allowed time, ConfigMgr sends a status message stating that the maximum runtime has been reached and that ConfigMgr will no longer monitor it. (This frees up ConfigMgr to deploy additional software, if required.)

  ▶ Before a program runs, ConfigMgr checks to see if there are maintenance windows defined; if so, it verifies that the available window is larger than the Maximum allowed run time setting. If the window is not large enough, the client will wait for an available window for deployment (unless configured to ignore maintenance windows.)

  ▶ The OpsMgr tab uses the Maximum allowed run time setting as the time-out for the maintenance mode duration.

Two options are available for platforms on which ConfigMgr can run the program:

  ▶ **This Program Can Run on Any Platform:** This default configuration works well for programs that are not platform specific.

▶ **This Program Can Run Only on Specified Client Platforms:** This installation type is for client-specific platforms. For example, the 7-Zip client has two different installation files, based on the client platform (amd64 and i386). In this situation, you would separately package each program type and use this option to allow each program to run only on a specific client platform. It is best to not scope a supported platform down to the service pack level.

If the program can run on only specified platforms, select those platforms. Try to avoid specifying platforms as narrow as Windows 7 Service Pack (SP) 1 (32-bit), unless you know the software will only run on Windows 7 SP 1 and not on RTM. Try instead to use the All Windows 7 (32-bit) platform. Software generally continues to install and execute successfully when an OS upgrades to a new service pack. If you limit your favorite portable document (PDF) utility installation to an All Windows 7 SP 1 collection and then deploy Service Pack 2 (if it is ever released), you could not install the application on the SP 2 system until you modified the supported platforms defined in Figure 13.8.

▶ **Additional Requirements:** Additional text in this box is seen by the user in Software Center. No items are evaluated from this setting.

TIP: HIDING NON-APPLICABLE SOFTWARE WITHOUT CREATING SPECIFIC COLLECTIONS

The **Only on specified client platforms** (also known as *restricted platforms*) setting allows you to control which client systems see a deployment, based on OS and architecture. For machine-targeted deployments, restricted platforms are evaluated when the client receives policy and do not run unless the restrictions are met. The deployment also only appears in Software Center if the current OS meets the required platform restriction. User-targeted software (including software that appears in Application Catalog) is evaluated at runtime. If a user initiates the example described on a Windows 10 system from the Application Catalog, he or she is notified that the requirements were not met to install the software on the computer.

For the 7-Zip program, change the properties on the Requirements tab to set the estimated disk space to **5MB** and the maximum allowed runtime (in minutes) to **15**. Also, specify that this program can only run on the following platforms: **All Windows 7 (32-bit)**, **All Windows 8 (32-bit)**, **All Windows 8.1 (32-bit)**, and **All Windows 10 (32-bit)**. This allows the software to be installed on the described platforms, regardless of service pack.

Using the Program Properties Environment Tab

The Environment tab for this program, shown in Figure 13.9, identifies characteristics about the environment to run the program. Following are options in the Program can run dropdown:

▶ **Only When a User Is Logged On:** Select this option when the program ConfigMgr is installing needs to have the user logged in to install.

▶ **Whether or Not a User Is Logged On:** This is the most common option; it runs the program using the Local System account (run with administrative rights).

▶ **Only When No User Is Logged On:** Selecting this option means the installation does not occur until the user logs out of the system.

The conditions under which a program can run directly tie into the Run mode options:

▶ **Run with User's Rights:** This option is available only if the option **Only when a user is logged on** is chosen for when to run the program.

▶ **Run with Administrative Rights:** This default option is available in any of the three configurations that determine when a program can run. Choosing this option makes a check box available that allows users to interact with the program.

▶ **Allow Users to Interact with This Program:** Use this option when the user needs to interact with the program. This is excellent for troubleshooting when packages are not installing correctly. When this option is selected, the user interface is visible to the logged-in user, and the user can interact with the program. As an example, choose this option if the program requires the user to make a selection or click a button. If a program runs without this option selected and the program requires user intervention, it waits for the user interaction (which never occurs) and eventually times out when the maximum allowed runtime occurs (defined on the Requirements tab of the program; if undefined, the program times out after 12 hours).

TIP: RUNNING DEPLOYMENTS WITH ADMINISTRATIVE RIGHTS

At first glance, running an advertisement with administrative rights seems like a no-brainer. You can use this approach to install the software regardless of the level of permissions available to the logged-in user. However, this can cause some difficulties when installing a program that writes data to the Registry (in HKEY_CURRENT_USER) or if a package tries to access files the account does not have rights to access.

In this situation, try running with the user's rights instead. If that does not work, create two different programs—one running under the user's access and allowing access to the Registry and a second running with administrative rights. Link the programs together with the Run this program first option. This may require repackaging the application to determine the portion of the application that requires administrator rights to install.

Another option involves using the task sequencing engine to deploy packages that need to perform Registry edits or run something in a user context. This can be done by running a command-line task sequence step with a run as statement.

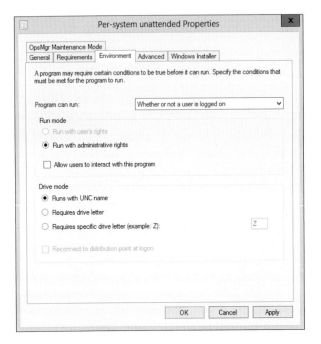

FIGURE 13.9   Program Environment tab.

The Drive mode section includes the following configurations:

▶ **Runs with UNC Name:** This default setting runs the program using the UNC name. A client runs from the UNC path only if the deployment is configured with the Run from Distribution Point option set. By default, content is downloaded from a DP to the client cache and run from there (normally *%windir%*\ccmcache\).

▶ **Requires Drive Letter:** When this option is selected, the program requires a mapped drive to install but allows ConfigMgr to use any available drive letter.

▶ **Requires Specific Drive Letter (Example: Z):** When this option is selected, the program requires a specific drive letter to be mapped for installation. (If you choose this option, an additional box is provided to specify the letter to map.) If the drive letter is not available on the client system, the program will not run.

▶ **Reconnect to Distribution Point at Logon:** This last setting specifies that the client will reconnect to the ConfigMgr DP when logging in to the system. This option is available only if the program runs only when a user is logged on, with the user's rights, and requires either a drive letter or a specific drive letter (such as the drive letter Z).

For 7-Zip, configure the Environment tab as shown in Figure 13.9.

Using the Program Properties Advanced Tab

The Advanced tab for the program, shown in Figure 13.10, allows you to specify a variety of configurations, such as whether other programs run prior to this one, if this program is run once for the computer or for each user, whether program notifications are suppressed, how disabled programs are handled on clients, and how the program integrates with install software task sequences:

▶ **Run Another Program First:** These are program dependencies; selecting this option causes another program to run before this program runs. The check box is cleared by default. Consider a software package with several separate programs requiring installation before the package can be installed: This program has five levels of dependency, and the original program will not run unless program #2 has run, and program #2 will not run unless program #3 has run, and so on.

If you choose this option, you must also specify a package and a program. The option Allow this program to be installed from the Install Software task sequence without being advertised is relevant when discussing task sequences. These are a list of customizable tasks or steps performed sequentially. A task sequence can be deployed to a device collection (for example, advertising a program to a collection). Task sequences provide a more elegant solution than creating dependencies or complex scripts for many situations, including those where multiple dependencies exist for a single program. Task sequences are discussed in detail in Chapter 22, "Operating System Deployment."

If you select Run another program first, the Always run this program first option is also available (unchecked by default). If you check this option, the program it is dependent on will run regardless of whether it previously ran on the same system.

An alternative to using the Run another program first option is to create a task sequence and build in the logic to determine which commands should run. You can also leverage applications with defined dependencies, discussed in Chapter 12, for any prerequisite software.

▶ **When This Program Is Assigned to a Computer:** This dropdown has two choices:

  ▶ **Run Once for the Computer:** This is the default setting.

  ▶ **Run Once for Every User Who Logs In:** This option causes the program to run for each user who logs in to the computer.

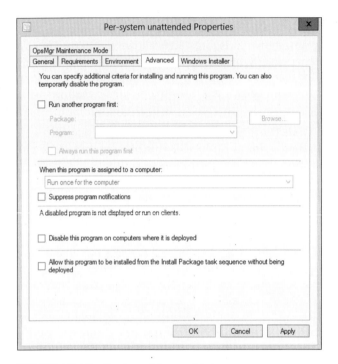

FIGURE 13.10   Program Advanced tab.

▶ **Suppress Program Notifications:** Checking this option causes notification area icons, messages, and countdown notifications to not display for the program. This is useful for programs that may be running when someone is using the system, if there is no requirement to notify that the program is running. Override this setting with the client setting Show notifications for new deployments in the Computer Agent section of the console. Review Chapter 9, "Client Management," for information about customizing client settings.

▶ **Disable This Program on Computers Where It Is Deployed:** This determines how ConfigMgr will handle the program. The default is unchecked; if checked, advertisements containing this program are disabled. When checked, this option also removes the program from the list of available programs the user can run, and it will not run on the systems where it is assigned. This can be useful when there is a need to temporarily halt a deployment because the change applies to all advertisements of the program, and the program is disabled when policies are retrieved by the client.

▶ **Allow This Program to Be Installed from the Install Software Task Sequence Without Being Deployed:** The final check box on the Advanced tab determines how the Install Software task sequence in OSD handles the program. The option is unchecked by default. Check this option for any programs used within an OSD task sequence that are not currently deployed to a collection.

For the 7-Zip program, accept the default configurations.

Program Properties Windows Installer Tab

The Windows Installer tab provides installation source management. If the program requires repair or reinstallation, the MSI file automatically accesses the package files on the DP to reinstall or repair the program.

The available fields shown in Figure 13.11 are Windows Installer product code and Windows Installer file. You can define these by clicking **Import** and specifying the MSI file used for the program. Choosing the MSI file populates both fields.

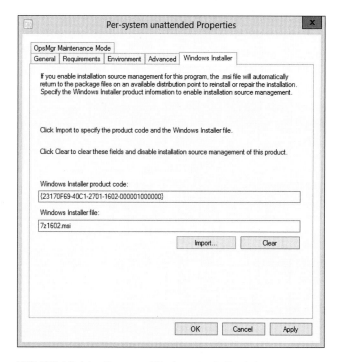

FIGURE 13.11   Program Windows Installer tab.

For the 7-Zip program, click **Import** and select the Windows Installer file used for the installation (in this case, **7z1602.msi**) and click **Open**. The product code and filename are automatically populated, as shown in Figure 13.11.

An added benefit to this feature is that when a device moves to a different location, ConfigMgr automatically modifies the source path on the local system if the system is in a different boundary group with content available for the software.

Program Properties OpsMgr Maintenance Mode Tab

The final program properties tab determines the Operations Manager maintenance mode configurations for the program. Two options are available, as displayed in Figure 13.12:

▶ **Disable Operations Manager Alerts While This Program Runs:** Selecting this option places the computer in OpsMgr maintenance mode while the program is running. The duration of the maintenance mode is defined by the Maximum allowed run time (minutes) setting defined on the Requirements tab (refer to Figure 13.8). In previous versions of OpsMgr, the option did not actually perform the steps required to truly disable Operations Manager alerts while the program ran. This option pauses the OpsMgr health service but does not put everything into maintenance mode, which means heartbeat alerts are still generated. This check box is fully functional with System Center 2012 Operations Manager and higher, enabling full maintenance mode on a system.

▶ **Generate Operations Manager Alert if This Program Fails:** Selecting this option creates an event in the application log containing the package name, program name, advertisement ID, advertisement comment, and failure code or MIF failure description. You can configure the application event to create an Operations Manager alert. The authors recommend using this feature for critical software deployments such as service packs.

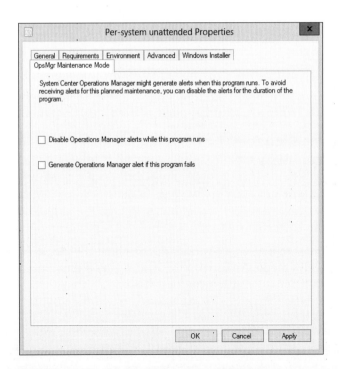

FIGURE 13.12   OpsMgr Maintenance Mode tab.

Packaging the 7-Zip application with a package definition file demonstrates many of the configurations used when manually creating a package and program. While using a package definition file (an MSI, PDF, or MIF file) is recommended, what takes place when one is not available? Drawing on the information used to create the 7-Zip package, the next section discusses the process to create a package and program manually, using the Citrix Receiver installation as an example.

Creating Packages Using the Package and Program Wizard and for UNIX and Linux Systems

The following sections discuss how to create a new package using the Create Package and Program Wizard. You can use this wizard to create a package when a definition file is not available. You also could optionally create a program for a computer or for a device running Windows CE. You can also choose not to define a program, making the files in the package directly available for use. An example of using only a package is the unattended.xml file referenced by the Apply Operating System Image step of OSD.

The sections also discuss how to create a package and program for software that can be deployed to UNIX or Linux systems with an installed ConfigMgr agent. Microsoft does not support deploying ConfigMgr applications to UNIX or Linux systems. Use packages and programs for UNIX and Linux systems to install new software deployments, install updates for software already available, patch a UNIX/Linux computer, or run scripts. ConfigMgr supports maintenance windows to control execution of programs on UNIX and Linux systems.

Creating a Package Using the New Package Wizard

The Citrix Receiver software allows a user to connect to a Citrix environment running either a Virtual Desktop Infrastructure (VDI) or Remote Desktop Services (RDS) workload. Citrix Receiver is available at no charge from https://www.citrix.com/products/receiver/. You can use the Create Package and Program Wizard to create a package for the Citrix Receiver. Follow these steps:

1. As when creating a package using a package definition file, navigate in the console to **Software Library** -> **Overview** -> **Application Management** -> **Packages** and select **Create** -> **Create Package** from the ribbon bar.

2. On the Package page, specify a variety of fields to reflect your personal preferences for the package. These fields are visible in the ConfigMgr console as well as the Software Center and Application Catalog. Enable the check box **This package contains source files** and click **Browse** to select the source files location. From this dialog, you can select a network (UNC) path or a local folder. Select a network path whenever possible so the source files are accessible at all times. The first page of the wizard should look similar to Figure 13.13. When you are finished with this page, click **Next**.

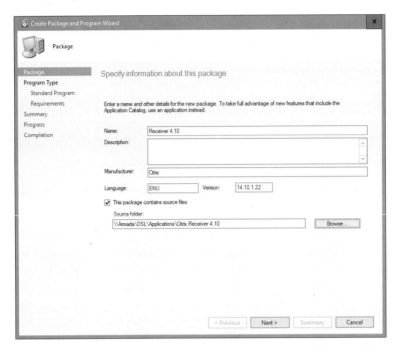

FIGURE 13.13   Package page of the Create Package and Program Wizard.

3. On the Program Type page, select one of three options:

   ▶ **Standard Program:** Specify a standard program used to deploy software to a
   computer system.

   ▶ **Program for Device:** Use this option for creating a package to deploy to
   supported mobile devices running Windows CE.

   ▶ **Do Not Create a Program:** Use this option with a package to access the source
   files on a DP. This type of package (with no program) is often used with OSD
   for running scripts, utilities, and such.

   In this case, select **Standard Program** and click **Next**.

4. On the Standard Program page, enter the required information (the name and command line) and modify any other required settings, as shown in Figure 13.14. Click
   Next to continue.

5. On the Requirements page, select whether another program must run first, any
   platform restrictions, estimated disk space, and maximum allowed runtime, as
   shown in Figure 13.15. For this example, select **All Windows 10 (32-bit)** for the
   specified platforms and click **Next**.

6. Review the Summary page, and if the information looks correct, click **Next**, confirm
   that the wizard completed successfully, and click **Close**.

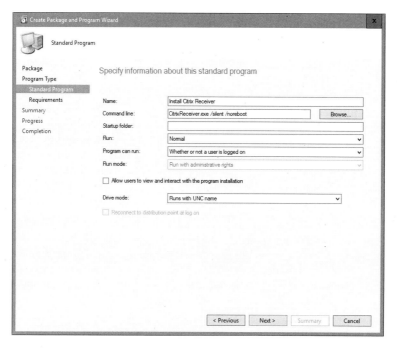

FIGURE 13.14   Standard Program page of the Create Package and Program Wizard.

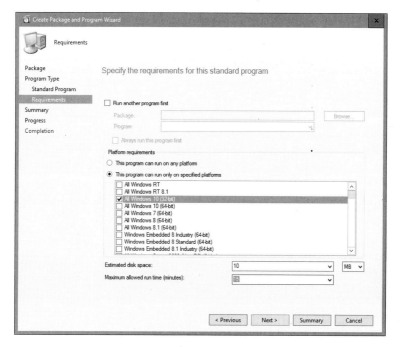

FIGURE 13.15   Requirements page of the Create Package and Program Wizard.

Refer to the section "Creating a Package from a Definition File," earlier in this chapter, for information on how to view and modify properties of the package and program. To create a new program for an existing package, right-click the desired program and select **Create Program** from the context menu.

The majority of packages required by most organizations have existing package definition files because most major packages now install from MSI files. For packages that do not have package definition files but have setup files, the Citrix Receiver client example illustrates that you can manually create packages by performing some additional steps. You can often install simple applications with a batch file or a script. For more complex applications, work with the vendor to find a supported and documented process to perform an unattended deployment of the application.

TIP: SITE FOR SOFTWARE PACKAGING AND DEPLOYMENT GUIDANCE

A great place for general guidance on software deployment is the App Details site (https://www.appdetails.com/). App Details provides information on how to distribute software, including examples for Adobe Reader, Microsoft Office, and Visual Studio .NET. You now can deploy nearly all software using packages that run the various command-line configurations.

Creating Packages for UNIX and Linux Systems

If a Linux or UNIX system is enrolled with a ConfigMgr agent, you can use ConfigMgr's packages and programs software distribution capability to deploy applications to those systems. This functionality works with maintenance windows and provides status messages for centralized reporting. Throttling of network bandwidth while downloading the software is also supported and can be configured using Client Settings.

Complete the following steps to define a package and a program for the Dropbox client version 8.4.19:

1. In the ConfigMgr console, navigate to **Software Library -> Application Management -> Packages**. Select **Create Package** on the ribbon bar to open the Create Package and Program Wizard.

2. On the Package page of the wizard, supply at a minimum a name for the package (see Figure 13.16). In this case, supply the following information:

   ▶ **Name: Dropbox Client 8.4**

   ▶ **Manufacturer: Dropbox**

   ▶ **Language: EN-US**

   ▶ **Version: 8.4.19**

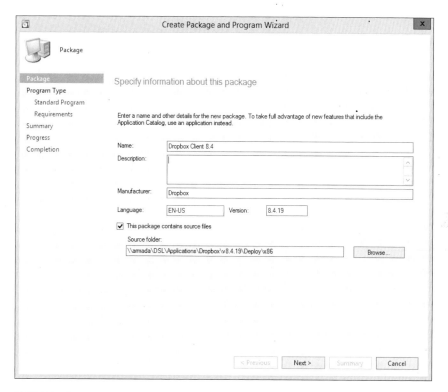

FIGURE 13.16   Package page of the Create Package and Program Wizard.

3. Select **This package contains source files** and click **Browse** to open the Set Source Folder dialog box. Confirm that the radio button for the Network Path (UNC name) is selected and provide the UNC path to the folder where the .rpm file is located (in this case, **\\armada\DSL\Applications\Dropbox\v8.4.19\Deploy\x86**). Click **OK** to close the Set Source Folder dialog box and click **Next** to continue.

4. On the Program Type page, select to create a standard program (for a client computer), select to create a program for a device, or select not to create a program. In this case, confirm that **Standard Program** is selected and click **Next**.

5. On the Standard Program page, provide the information for this specific program (at a minimum, the name and command line). In addition, provide the following information, as shown in Figure 13.17:

   ▶ **Name: Install Dropbox**

   ▶ **Command Line:** `rpm -ivh nautilus-dropbox-2015.10.28-1.fedora.i386.rpm`

   ▶ **Startup Folder:** <none>

▶ **Run: Normal**

▶ **Program Can Run: Whether or not a user is logged on**

▶ **Run Mode: Run with administrative rights**

▶ **Allow Users to View and Interact with the Program Installation:**
   <not selected>

▶ **Drive Mode: Runs with UNC name**

Click **Next** to continue.

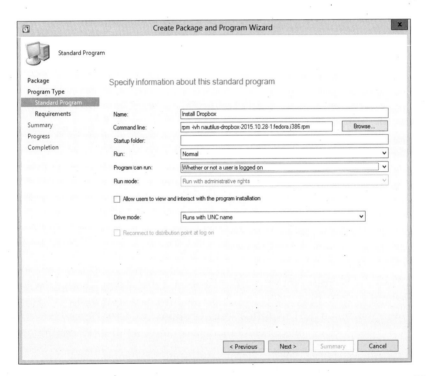

FIGURE 13.17   Standard Program page of the Create Package and Program Wizard.

6. On the Requirements page, specify whether you want to run another program first, which is not necessary in this case. You can also specify platform requirements. Select **This program can run only on specified platforms** and select the x86 versions of RHEL 4, RHEL 5, and RHEL 6 in the list. Also specify the estimated disk space, which is **20MB**, and the maximum allowed runtime, which is **15** minutes in this scenario, as shown in Figure 13.18. When finished, click **Next**.

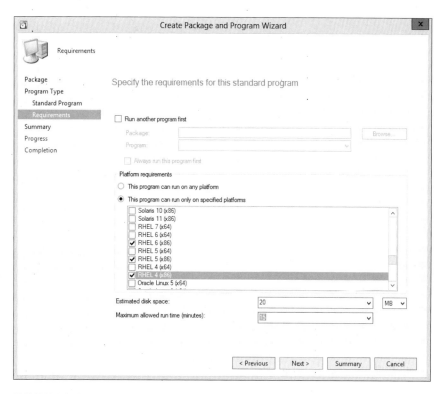

FIGURE 13.18 Requirements page of the Create Package and Program Wizard.

7. On the Summary page of the wizard, verify the information you entered. If everything looks correct, click **Next** to continue.

8. On the Completion page, verify that the package and program were created successfully. When successful, click **Close** to close the wizard.

With the package and program created, you can distribute the files to DPs and deploy the program to a custom collection containing the hosts to which you want to install the Dropbox client.

On the Linux client, you can use the scxcm.log file to troubleshoot package deployment issues. If installation was successful, Dropbox appears under a submenu of Applications.

Summary

This chapter provided examples of creating packages in ConfigMgr both with and without a package definition file. It also discussed programs and packages and available configuration options, as well as tips for avoiding common issues when creating packages. Chapter 14 includes additional details on deploying packages and ConfigMgr applications to users and client systems, and it also discusses the user experience.

CHAPTER 14

Distributing and Deploying Applications and Packages

Chapter 11, "Creating and Managing Applications," Chapter 12, "Creating and Using Deployment Types," and Chapter 13, "Creating and Managing Packages and Programs," discuss applications with deployment types (DTs) and packages with programs; later chapters discuss software updates, mobile device management, endpoint protection, and operating system deployment (OSD). All these object types have at least three things in common:

▶ **Deployable:** All are objects you deploy to one or more systems or users. As you deploy, you also want to monitor the deployment's status.

▶ **Targeted Group:** To leverage any of these objects, you must target a group of systems or users. In Configuration Manager (ConfigMgr) terminology, these target groups are called *collections*.

▶ **Content Availability:** Almost everything you deploy has associated content that must be available for the ConfigMgr client to install.

As an example, deploying Microsoft Office requires a package or ConfigMgr application with the associated content for the installation. This requires sending the content to desired distribution points (DPs), creating a collection of systems or users to target, and creating a deployment. After deployment, you move to monitoring. You may need to monitor the distribution status of content to the DPs, as well as the status of the deployment.

This chapter discusses the features of content distribution in ConfigMgr and using DTs or programs to control deployment behavior. It also discusses interaction with ConfigMgr from an end-user perspective, using the old Software Center, Application Catalog, and new Software Center. This chapter also discusses options for the end user to configure deployment behavior and troubleshooting deployments when something goes wrong.

Creating and Managing Collections

Collections may very well be the most important object type in ConfigMgr. They are used for software distribution, patching, settings management, client settings, power management, and more. ConfigMgr incorporates two distinct types of collections:

▶ Devices: Includes computers and mobile devices

▶ Users: Includes usernames and Active Directory user groups

Collections may also be the most dangerous object type in ConfigMgr. If you modify the rules of a collection, you may significantly increase its number of devices or users. If the collection has mandatory software deployments, settings management configurations, or even OSD mandatory assignments, the ensuing chaos and churn could quickly create a "resume-generating event." Always use extreme caution when modifying collection membership.

NOTE: COLLECTIONS AND DEPLOYMENTS REPLICATE ACROSS ALL PRIMARY SITES

If you have multiple primary sites, you may have noticed that each collection shows the membership information for its site plus a member count showing the total count of members, hierarchy-wide, for this collection. This information is important; when you create collections and target deployments at one site, the collection and rules are updated and evaluated at all primary sites, and the deployment is replicated.

The authors recommend using the central administration site (CAS) to create collections and target deployments. The CAS is the only site that displays complete collection membership.

Creating a Collection

All software deployments except task sequences and software updates can be targeted to user collections. Consider the following when targeting deployments:

▶ User-targeted deployments appear in the Application Catalog.

▶ User-targeted deployments appear in the new Software Center.

▶ Device-targeted deployments appear in both the old and new Software Center.

▶ Deployments that appear in Software Center are evaluated when the policy is downloaded from the management point (MP).

▶ Deployments that appear in the Application Catalog are evaluated only when the user selects the application to be installed.

▶ Application approval requests can be enabled only with user-targeted deployments (through the Application Catalog).

Perform the following steps to create a new collection:

1. In the ConfigMgr console, navigate to **Assets and Compliance**, choose the Devices or Users collection node, and select **Create Device Collection** or **Create User Collection** from the ribbon bar.

2. On the General page of the Create Device Collection Wizard, specify the name of the collection and the limiting collection. (Every collection requires a limiting collection. Specifying a limiting collection filters the collection to ensure that only resources in the limiting collection are available to the current collection.) Click **Next**.

3. On the Membership Rules page, click **Add Rule** to add a collection membership rule. As discussed in the following sections, four types of collection rules are available: Direct, Query, Include, and Exclude. The Membership Rules page shows that you can add membership rules, use incremental updates, and schedule a full collection membership update. (The "Performing Incremental Updates" section, later in this chapter, discusses the difference between full and incremental updates.)

About Direct Rules

A direct rule (also called a *static rule*) is a rule that does not require a collection update schedule. Select **Direct Rule** to open the Create Direct Membership Rule Wizard.

Following is a brief description of each property on the Membership Rules page:

▶ **Resource Class:** For a device collection, select **System Resource** to find devices based on discovery and inventory information.

▶ **Attribute Name:** Choose the desired attribute. For this example, choose **Name**.

▶ **Exclude Resources Marked as Obsolete:** When rebuilding a system or reinstalling the client, you may encounter a duplicate record. This occurs when ConfigMgr marked the old record obsolete, meaning software cannot be deployed to it. Unless you plan to troubleshoot obsolete clients based on a collection, you should exclude obsolete records from your collections. Otherwise, you may see systems in your collection that are no longer valid, which creates extra work when troubleshooting software delivery.

▶ **Exclude Resources That Do Not Have the Configuration Manager Client Installed:** Devices in this category are devices discovered through Active Directory (AD) or some other means that do not appear to have the ConfigMgr client installed. Enable this check box as well.

▶ **Value:** Enter a device name (usually a computer name) or a partial name. You can use the % sign as a wildcard, and you can use the % by itself for a full list of items from which to choose.

Click **Next** to display resources that meet the criteria and then select one or more devices in the Select Resources page. Complete the wizard, and the collection membership appears in the console. You may have to refresh the view to see the new members.

TIP: MULTIPLE PRIMARY SITES CAUSE SLIGHT COLLECTION MEMBERSHIP DELAY

ConfigMgr uses its SQL replication feature to replicate data across a multi-site hierarchy. The collection membership rule is replicated from the CAS to all primary sites so each primary site can evaluate that rule. If the collection membership changes on a primary site (due to the new collection rule or any other reason), that information is replicated back to the CAS. In the authors' experience, the delay in seeing the membership change on the CAS is generally four to five minutes.

Collection membership is not complete on the CAS until the primary sites evaluate the membership rule(s) and replicate the results back to the CAS.

Using Query Rules

A query rule (sometimes called a *dynamic rule*) is a rule requiring a collection update schedule (incremental, full, or both) to update the membership information automatically, based on the criteria of the rule. Selecting Select Query Rule opens a dialog where you can import a query statement from the Available Queries node or select Edit Query Statement to modify the default query rule (this selects all systems, limited to the collection). Chapter 20, "Configuration Manager Queries," discusses queries.

Importing a query copies the query statement to the collection. This means the statement in the collection is not linked to the query rule. If you later modify the query rule (in the query), the query rule for the collection does not change. The example in this section walks through the process of creating a rule for all systems that have 7-Zip installed. Follow these steps:

1. Enter a query rule name and select **Edit Query Statement** to modify the default query.

2. On the Query Rule Properties dialog, select **Criteria** and click the starburst icon to create a new rule.

3. In the Criterion Properties dialog, select **Simple value** as the criterion type and click **Select**.

4. In the Select Attributes dialog, choose **Add/Remove Programs** for the attribute class and **Display Name** as the attribute. Click **OK**.

5. Back in the Criterion Properties dialog, change the Operator dropdown to **is like**.

6. For Value, enter **7-Zip%**, as shown in Figure 14.1. Click **OK**.

FIGURE 14.1   The Criterion Properties dialog.

If you have x64 systems, you may need to create an additional query-based rule, depending on whether the application has a native 64-bit installation or uses x86 installation files. For this example, create a second query rule but select **Installed Applications (64)** for the attribute class.

After saving the rule, the Query Statement Properties dialog displays both rules with an AND join. Select the **AND** join and press **&|** (the second icon from the right) to change it to an OR. You can also see additional actions and parameters you can add to the query criterion. For example, in addition to switching AND to OR, you can group using parentheses or change to a NOT query.

Using Include and Exclude Rules

ConfigMgr allows you to use include and exclude rules:

▶ **Include Rules:** An include rule includes all members of different collections. Say you have two collections: one for all New York systems, and one for all Los Angeles systems. You could create a third collection named All US Systems with two include rules, one for New York and one for Los Angeles and set All US Systems to dynamically update based on rules in the first two collections. The collection membership would update if an included collection's membership changed.

▶ **Exclude Rules:** An exclude rule performs as you would expect, ensuring that systems defined in the desired exclude collection are never members of the collection. Membership of this collection is updated if the membership of the excluded collection changes.

NOTE: EXCLUDE RULES ALWAYS WIN

If you have a collection with both include and exclude rules and a system is in both collections, the exclude collection takes precedence.

Updating Collections

Collections can have membership rules updated as full, manual, incremental, or cascading. Consider this when designing a collection structure, as the rules can negatively impact performance. The next sections discuss these updates.

Performing Full and Manual Updates

When you create a collection, the option Schedule a full update on this collection is enabled by default, and the update occurs every seven days, starting when you create the collection. This option causes the collection membership to be completely reevaluated at the specified interval. You can also select the collection and click **Update Membership** on the ribbon bar. Under the hood, ConfigMgr executes a SQL stored procedure. If a new entry is added during a manual or full collection evaluation, all collections that use the collection are also reevaluated and updated, if applicable (depending on the collection query being used). This occurs even if those collections do not have full or incremental updates enabled.

Performing Incremental Updates

Incremental updates allow you to add systems to a collection quickly, without a full collection membership update. The default is a collection interval update of every seven days with the Use incremental updates for this collection property disabled. The general idea is to use fewer collections and rely more on requirement rules for applications so rules are evaluated at the client. Use incremental updates on collections targeted with deployments to quickly deliver (or make available) software to the user or device. The following classes do not support incremental updates:

- ▶ SMS_G_System_CollectedFile

- ▶ SMS_G_System_LastSoftwareScan

- ▶ SMS_G_System_AppClientState

- ▶ SMS_G_System_DCMDeploymentState

- ▶ SMS_G_System_DCMDeploymentErrorAssetDetails

- ▶ SMS_G_System_DCMDeploymentCompliantAssetDetails

- ▶ SMS_G_System_DCMDeploymentNonCompliantAssetDetails

- ▶ SMS_G_User_DCMDeploymentCompliantAssetDetails (for collections of users only)

- ▶ SMS_G_User_DCMDeploymentNonCompliantAssetDetails (for collections of users only)

- ▶ SMS_G_System_SoftwareUsageData

- ▶ SMS_G_System_CI_ComplianceState

▶ SMS_G_System_EndpointProtectionStatus

▶ SMS_GH_System_*

▶ SMS_GEH_System_*

If you need to use any of these classes, configure the full collection membership update to occur on an interval that meets your requirements.

TIP: BE CONSERVATIVE WITH INCREMENTAL UPDATES

Incremental updates are intended for scenarios where updates need to roll through quickly, such as a collection with devices that were just deployed using OSD. You may encounter evaluation delays if this feature is enabled on a large number of collections. The suggested maximum is approximately 200 collections, but the exact number depends on multiple factors. See https://docs.microsoft.com/sccm/core/clients/manage/ collections/best-practices-for-collections for additional information.

Cascading Updates

When a collection is updated, any collections with incremental updates enabled specifying that collection as a limiting collection are automatically reevaluated, and any collection using that collection as its limiting collection is reevaluated as well.

As reevaluations consume resources, the authors recommend minimizing the use of the All Systems collection as a limiting collection. Because the All Systems collection is updated regularly, its depending collections are re-evaluated each time it is updated.

TIP: MORE INFORMATION ABOUT CASCADING UPDATES

David O'Brien, Microsoft MVP for Cloud and Datacenter Management, provides additional information about how collection updates work. In his blog article at https://david-obrien.net/ 2014/05/configmgr-collection-updates/, he calls cascading updates "indirect updates" and explains why you should minimize using All Systems as a limiting collection. Scott Breen, a Microsoft Premier Field Engineer from Australia, provides an extensive article on update behavior of collections in different scenarios at https://blogs.technet.microsoft.com/ scott/2017/09/13/collection-evaluation-overview-configuration-manager/.

Modifying Collection Properties

After creating a collection, you can modify its properties to further alter its behavior and view information belonging to the collection. Select the collection and click **Properties** in the ribbon bar. For device collections, the following configuration options and information are available:

▶ **General Tab:** View and modify the name and comment for the collection and modify its limiting collection. You can enable the All devices are part of the same server group option; for information about configuring this option, see Chapter 15, "Managing

Software Updates." The tab also shows when the collection was last updated, when the last update occurred, and its Collection ID.

- ▶ **Membership Rules Tab:** Edit or delete membership rules. You can also enable incremental updates and configure the collection update schedule, as discussed in the previous section.

- ▶ **Power Management Tab:** Specify or modify power management settings. Chapter 9, "Client Management," discusses the options.

- ▶ **Deployments Tab:** View deployments assigned to this collection. If many deployments are targeted to the collection, filter as desired.

- ▶ **Maintenance Windows Tab:** View and modify existing maintenance windows and create new windows. The next section discusses configuring maintenance windows.

- ▶ **Collection Variables Tab:** Define collection variables. Chapter 22, "Operating System Deployment," discusses collection variables.

- ▶ **Distribution Point Groups Tab:** View the associated DP and add distribution point groups to the collection. See the "Associating Collections with Distribution Point Groups" section, later in this chapter, for information about associating collections with distribution point groups.

- ▶ **Security Tab:** View current administrative users with permissions on the collection. Chapter 23, "Security and Delegation in Configuration Manager," discusses setting security permissions on collections.

- ▶ **Alerts Tab:** View and add alert thresholds set for endpoint protection (see Chapter 19, "Endpoint Protection").

Using Maintenance Windows

You can use a maintenance window to define the time during which ConfigMgr can apply software deployments to devices in a collection. You can configure one or more maintenance window schedules on a collection.

To configure a maintenance window, open the collection's properties and navigate to the Maintenance Window tab. Add a new maintenance window by clicking on the starburst icon to open the <new> Schedule dialog. This dialog has the following configurable options:

- ▶ **Name:** Provide a name for the schedule; the authors recommend including the purpose of the schedule in the name (for example, 01:00 - 04:00 - Weekly – every 1 weeks - Sunday - All Deployments).

- ▶ **Time:** Specify when the maintenance window should be effective by providing a start and end time. You can also enable the option to use Coordinated Universal Time (UTC).

▶ **Recurrence Pattern:** Configure the recurrence pattern of the maintenance window. By default, this is weekly every 1 week on Sunday, but can be modified to the following:

> ▶ **None:** There is no recurrence; the maintenance window applies only once.

> ▶ **Monthly:** The monthly recurrence is 1 month by default and set to between 1 and 12 months. You can also configure the day of the month. This can be a specific day, the last day of the month, or the first, second, third, fourth, or last Sunday through Saturday.

> ▶ **Weekly:** The weekly recurrence is 1 week by default and set between 1 and 4 weeks. You can configure the day it should occur.

> ▶ **Daily:** The daily recurrence is 1 day by default. This can be set between 1 and 31 days.

▶ **Apply This Schedule To:** Set to All Deployments by default but can be modified to Software Updates or Task Sequences.

CAUTION: OVERLAPPING MAINTENANCE WINDOWS

When a device belongs to multiple collections with maintenance windows, the effective maintenance window is the cumulative window. Say the device is member of collection A with a maintenance window between 1:00 AM and 2:30 AM, and collection B with a window between 2:00 AM and 3:00 AM; the effective maintenance window for that device is 1:00 AM to 3:00 AM. The authors recommend using dedicated collections for maintenance windows and naming them so the defined maintenance window is reflected in the name. Place these collections in a separate folder so they are easy to see.

Using Distribution Points

DPs play a key role in the delivery of packages, programs, endpoint protection updates, applications, software updates, and OSD-related content. You use DPs to make content available to clients. To prevent clients from traversing networks in undesirable paths, leverage boundary groups to help specify the DP (or DPs) a client should use.

The following sections walk through the process of creating DPs and DP groups, sending content to DPs, monitoring DP status, advanced configuration, and troubleshooting.

Installing Distribution Points

Chapter 6, "Installing and Updating System Center Configuration Manager," discusses DP role requirements and how to install and configure DPs with a primary or secondary site. This section describes the process of installing a DP on a remote server or workstation. Follow these steps to create a DP:

1. In the console, navigate to **Administration -> Overview -> Site Configuration**. Select **Servers and Site Systems**. Select **Create Site System Server**.

2. In the Create Site System Server Wizard, enter the fully qualified domain name (FQDN) of the new DP, as well as the site to manage it. (This is the standard wizard page for installing site systems, discussed in Chapter 6.) Click **Next**.

3. If the proxy page appears, provide details of the proxy server configuration for the site system to connect to the Internet. Click **Next**.

4. On the System Role Selection page, select **Distribution Point** and click **Next**.

5. On the Distribution Point page, configure the DP settings for your environment. A brief description of each property on this page follows:

   ▶ **Install and Configure IIS if Required by Configuration Manager:** Enable this option to install Windows components required for a DP automatically. Chapter 6 describes required components.

   ▶ **Enable and Configure BranchCache for This Distribution Point:** Enable this option to have ConfigMgr install and configure BranchCache on the server receiving the new distribution point site system role.

   ▶ **Description:** This is available for later viewing in the properties of the DP in the Distribution Points view under the Administration pane.

   ▶ **Specify How Client Computers Communicate with the Distribution Point:** Choose HTTP or HTTPS for client communication with the DP. Chapter 5, "Network Design," discusses public key infrastructure (PKI) requirements.

   ▶ **Allow Clients to Connect Anonymously:** With HTTP, enable this option if you need anonymous connections. While the ConfigMgr client connects using the local system and network access accounts, there are scenarios in which you may need anonymous access, such as Windows Installer repair functionality on Windows XP and Windows 7, which attempt to connect as anonymous. This is no longer required if the KB2619572 update for Windows 7 is applied; Windows 8 and newer versions use user credentials. See https://docs.microsoft.com/sccm/core/servers/deploy/configure/install-and-configure-distribution-points to determine whether to enable anonymous access.

   ▶ **HTTPS:** Select the HTTPS radio button to enable a dropdown selection, which is set to Allow intranet-only connections by default. If managing Mac computers or mobile devices enrolled by ConfigMgr, select Allow Internet only connections if the DP will serve devices connecting to it over the Internet.

   ▶ **Allow Mobile Devices to Connect to This Distribution Point:** If on-premise MDM is configured (discussed in Chapter 17, "Managing Mobile Devices"), this check box makes content on the DP available to mobile devices.

   ▶ **Create a Self-Signed Certificate or Import a PKI Client Certificate:** The certificate authenticates the DP to an MP so the DP can send status messages to the MP. Clients PXE booting to connect to the MP during OSD also use this certificate. If all your MPs use HTTP, create a self-signed certificate. If they use

HTTPS, import a PKI certificate. See https://docs.microsoft.com/sccm/core/
plan-design/network/pki-certificate-requirements for additional information
about this certificate.

> **Enable This Distribution Point for Prestaged Content:** Enable this check
> box for granular control when content can transfer over a wide area network
> (WAN) link on a per-content package basis (package, application, operating
> system image, and so on). Enabling this option lets you create prestaged con-
> tent files, copy them to a remote location, and import them into the local DP.
> The "Using Prestaged Content" section, later in this chapter, provides addi-
> tional information.

6. On the Drive Settings page, specify the amount of free space to reserve on the disk
   so the content will not completely fill the disks of the DP, as well as the preferred
   primary and secondary drive letter location for the content library and package
   share.

7. Use the Pull Distribution Point page to configure the DP to act as a pull DP, which
   pulls its content from another defined DP (as opposed to a standard DP, which
   receives its content from the site server). Enable the pull DP by selecting the option
   Enable this distribution point to pull content from other distribution points,
   which makes the option to add source DPs available. To add a source DP, click **Add**
   and select DPs from a list of available DPs. After adding source DPs, you can modify
   their priority so that those with the highest priority are used first rather than DPs
   with lower priority.

8. Configure the PXE Settings page, as described in Chapter 22.

9. Configure the Multicast page, as described in Chapter 22.

10. On the Content Validation page, enable content validation and configure a recurring
    schedule for when the server is at low utilization. The time is local to the site server.
    You can review the schedule on the DP from the Control Panel Task Scheduler
    applet. See the "Validating Content" section, later in this chapter, for additional
    information.

11. On the Boundary Groups page, create or add an existing boundary group that will be
    supported by this DP.

12. Complete the wizard to initiate installation of the DP.

Using and Configuring Cloud-Based Distribution Points

Cloud-based distribution points are hosted in Microsoft Azure. The main difference
between installing a VM in Azure and configuring that VM as a DP is that Microsoft
manages the VM for you. The article at https://docs.microsoft.com/sccm/core/
plan-design/hierarchy/use-a-cloud-based-distribution-point discusses configuration
of cloud-based DPs.

Distributing Content

After importing content on a definitive software library (DSL) into ConfigMgr, distribute it to DPs to make it available for clients. Content can be sent to DP groups or individual DPs. After it is sent, it can be validated on a regular schedule on the DPs to verify that it is still the same as its source. When content is updated, it must also be updated on the DPs.

Sending Content to Distribution Points

Several types of content exist in ConfigMgr, such as applications, packages, software updates, and several types of OSD packages (image package, driver package, and so on). Perform the following steps to send content to the DPs:

1. Navigate to the desired object (multi-select if desired), select it, and choose **Distribute Content** from the ribbon bar.

2. On the General page of the Distribute Content Wizard, enable the Detect associated content dependencies check box near the bottom of the page if the object has associated dependencies (such as dependent applications, programs configured to run another program first, and so on).

3. On the Content Distribution page, click **Add** and choose an option:

   ▶ **Collections:** Use this option to select a collection associated with a DP group. Note that you will only see collections associated with the group. Collections associated with DP groups automatically deploy content to those groups when targeted with a deployment, as demonstrated in the "Deploying Applications and Packages" section, later in this chapter.

   ▶ **Distribution Point:** Choose this option to selectively choose one or more DPs. Leverage DP groups when possible.

   ▶ **Distribution Point Group:** Use this option to choose one or more DP groups. If you later add a DP to an existing DP group, all content distributed to that group is automatically distributed to the new DP.

4. Click **Next** on the remaining pages of the wizard to view summary and progress information.

Note that you can add new DPs for a task sequence (TS), which sends all task sequence–associated content to the DP.

Using Distribution Point Groups

DP group configurations are global data that you can manage with scopes to limit visibility of DP groups to different admin roles, if desired. Say you have multiple DPs in Europe and want to ensure that content is available on each DP. Create a DP group named All Europe DPs and add the DPs to the group. As this section discusses, you can send content to a DP group (recommended by the authors) rather than send to individual DPs. Six months later, you have a new DP in Europe. If you add the new DP to the All Europe DPs group, the new DP automatically receives all content previously sent to the group.

A DP can be in multiple DP groups. You may have a DP group called All DPs, which distributes content to all your DPs; and you may also have a group called All Europe DPs, which contains a subset of DPs for Europe. You could add a scope for each DP group to allow the Europe Admins security group to send content only to the All Europe DPs group.

Follow these steps in the ConfigMgr console to create a DP group:

1. Navigate to **Administration -> Overview** and select **Distribution Point Group**. Now select **Create Group**.

2. Enter a name and description in the Create New Distribution Point Group wizard.

3. On the Collections page, click **Add** and select a collection to associate with this DP group (if desired).

4. On the Members page, click **Add** and select DPs to add to the DP group.

5. Click **OK** to save the DP group.

Be aware of the following caveats regarding distribution point groups:

▶ If you distribute content to a DP group and later remove it from a member DP, the association for that content with the DP group is lost. This means that if you later decide to redistribute the content on the DP group, that DP will not get the content even though it is still a member of the group and receives content for new distributions. The only way to re-associate the content with all DPs in the group is to remove the content from the DP group and re-add it.

▶ If you remove a DP from a DP group, the content stays on the DP.

▶ Retired applications stay on the DP but are not distributed to any new DPs added to a DP group. This means that for this specific deployment, you will never reach a 100% success rate on the content status in the Monitoring workspace.

▶ If a DP is a member of several DP groups and those DP groups have overlapping content, the content stays on the DP if you later decide to remove the DP from one of the DP groups.

▶ If you deploy content to both a DP and a DP group and later remove the content from the DP group, it is removed from the members of that group.

Associating Collections with Distribution Point Groups

You can associate collections with DP groups. When distributing content, you can target a collection associated with a DP group (for example, targeting all DPs in the DP group with the content). Say you have an All Devices in Europe collection, which contains all devices in Europe. You also have a DP group for all DPs in Europe, associated with the All Devices in Europe collection. Next, you have an application you need to deploy to the All Devices in Europe collection. When you create the deployment, choose to deploy content automatically to the associated DP group for the target collection. Use this process to ensure that content is distributed to all DPs necessary for the deployment. Review DP and collection association by viewing the properties of the collection or DP.

To associate a DP, view properties for the desired collection and select the Distribution Point Groups tab. Click **Add** and choose the DPs you want to associate to the collection.

You can also view the properties of a DP from the Administration workspace and manage associations on the Group Relationship tab.

Refreshing and Removing Content on Distribution Points

You should not need to refresh content often in ConfigMgr, unless you receive a status message error about a hash value check failure (discussed in the "Validating Content" section, later in this chapter). To refresh, view the package properties, select **Content Locations**, highlight the desired DP, and click **Redistribute**.

Content from DPs is removed automatically when an object is deleted. To remove the content from a defined list of DPs, follow these steps:

1. Right-click the object containing the content (package, deployment type, and so on) and select **Properties**.

2. Click **Content Locations**.

3. Select the desired DP and click **Remove**.

To remove content from multiple DPs, you must follow this process to remove each DP, one at a time. If you deployed content to a DP group, choose the desired DP group and click **Remove** to remove the content from all DPs targeted through the DP group.

Content does not immediately disappear from each DP; ConfigMgr automatically cleans up excess content on a regular interval (approximately every four hours). Note that files from a package or DT may be used in a different package or DT due to the content library. ConfigMgr runs a process to remove content no longer needed by any package.

Validating Content

As Chapter 6 mentions, you can enable content validation on a weekly or daily basis or at multiple intervals. Content is validated by enumerating all content that should be on the DP, performing a hash check for each item on each required file, and comparing that with what is stored in ConfigMgr.

The information is reported to the site server as pass or fail. ConfigMgr only reports the data; there is no built-in method to automate the process to attempt to re-send to DPs or to revalidate. The time you configure for content validation is local to the site server; if your primary server is in Chicago, and you configure content validation for a server in Bangalore to be every day at 6:00 PM, that time is local to Chicago, so the actual run time is at 5:30 AM each day in Bangalore (due to the 12.5-hour time difference). The task is configured as a scheduled task on the DP, and modification of that task should occur from the primary site server through the Content Validation dialog.

Updating Content on Distribution Points

If you modify source content, you must update content on DPs to make it available to clients. A common misconception is that you also must update DPs if you modify metadata for the object. For example, if you modify the command-line arguments of a program or DT, you do not need to update DPs (unless the source was updated with new files.) Update content only if the content source is actually modified. Updating content in ConfigMgr distributes any new files. Recall that due to the content library, a unique binary file is distributed only once.

TIP: UPDATING DISTRIBUTION POINTS

When you create a package or deployment, the content (according to the content source path) is immediately copied into the content library on the CAS or primary site server. Remember to update DPs after making a change to content source, even when you haven't sent content to DPs.

You can update DPs for the following types of objects: packages, DTs, driver packages, OS images, OS installers, and boot images. You cannot update DPs from any properties of an application, as the content source is defined on the DT. You can add DPs for an application. When you need to update a DP, choose the desired DT and click **Update Content**.

Configuring Network Bandwidth for Content Distribution

Configure scheduling and throttling to control when distribution occurs and the bandwidth used. You can configure scheduling and throttling for site-to-site communications if content needs to be transferred between sites or between a site server and a remote DP.

Configuring Network Bandwidth for Content on Distribution Points

Bandwidth settings on a DP are available only when that DP is installed on a server that is not also configured as a site server. The DP Properties page has two tabs you can configure:

▶ **Schedule Tab:** Select a time period and specify its availability settings:

  ▶ **Open for All Priorities:** Data is sent to the DP without restrictions.

  ▶ **Allow Medium and High Priority:** Only medium-priority and high-priority data is sent to the DP.

  ▶ **Allow High Priority Only:** Only high-priority data is sent.

  ▶ **Closed:** ConfigMgr does not send any data to the DP.

▶ **Rate Limits Tab:** Configure rate limits as follows:

  ▶ **Unlimited When Sending to This Destination:** Send content to the DP without rate limit restrictions.

- ▶ **Pulse Mode:** Specify the size of the data blocks sent to the DP. You can specify a time delay between blocks; use this when sending data across a low-bandwidth network connection.

- ▶ **Limited to Specified Maximum Transfer Rates by Hour:** Use this option to have a site send data to a DP using only the configured percentage of time. ConfigMgr will divide the time it can send data; it does not identify the network's available bandwidth. Data is sent for a short block of time, followed by blocks of time when no data is sent. If the maximum rate is set to 50%, ConfigMgr will transmit data for a period of time followed by an equal period of time when no data is sent. The actual amount of data or size of the data block is not managed; only the amount of time is managed.

Configuring Network Bandwidth for Content Between Sites

File replication routes transfer data between sites when content must be sent from a CAS to a DP belonging to a primary site or from a primary site to a DP configured behind a secondary site.

When you create a primary or secondary site, file replication routes are created automatically. A route specifies how data is transferred between sites. Configure routes by navigating to **Administration -> Hierarchy Configuration -> File Replication**. If your hierarchy contains a CAS with primary sites and/or secondary sites, file replication routes should already be available. To create new file replication routes—say to optimize traffic flowing between a CAS and a secondary site behind a primary site—create a direct file replication route between the CAS and the secondary site.

Open file replication route properties to configure the file replication account, which by default is the computer account of the sending site server. You can also specify the schedule and rate limits used, which is similar to the schedule and rate limit settings on a DP, described in the previous section.

See Chapter 5 for more information about file replication routes, configuring the number of threads, and retry settings.

TIP: DISTRIBUTION POINT PROPERTIES ON A SITE SYSTEM

When a DP is installed on a site system, scheduling and throttling options are not available, as they can only be configured on the file replication route.

Monitoring Distribution Point Status

Content is a key element of ConfigMgr. You need to know that content is exactly where you want it to be. Three types of distribution status information are available in the ConfigMgr console:

- ▶ **Content Status:** Focuses on the actual content (a package, an application, a software update package, and so on). Use this information to verify the distribution of one piece of content.

▶ **Distribution Point Group Status:** Focuses on the overall health of a DP group. Use this information to verify the status of all content associated with a DP group.

▶ **Distribution Point Configuration Status:** Focuses on the individual DP. Use this information to verify the state of a single DP.

The following sections provide further information on these types of information.

Content Status Information

Content must be available for clients to install software. Use content status information to view DP status for a specific package, application, or other content. Perform the following steps:

1. In the console, navigate to **Monitoring -> Distribution Status -> Content Status.**

2. In the Details section, which lists all content that has been targeted to any DP, search for specific content or right-click the title bar, select **Group By -> Type,** right-click a type and select **Collapse All** to group content (see Figure 14.2).

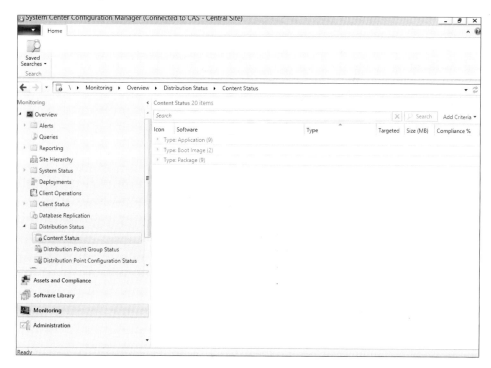

FIGURE 14.2   Content status grouped by type.

3. After selecting the desired content, view the number of DPs targeted, computed size, and compliance for that content state on those DPs. The summary at the bottom shows more information; Figure 14.3 displays an example.

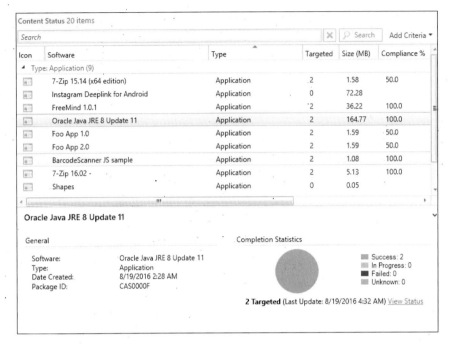

FIGURE 14.3   Content status summary for the Oracle Java application.

The Completion Statistics section in Figure 14.3 gives an overview of content status. The Last Update property displays the last time a status message was received for any DP for that content. Click **View Status** to view details; Figure 14.4 shows an example of the details that appear. Filter the Asset Details frame by entering a DP server name into the filter box in Figure 14.4. Following are brief descriptions for the various states:

▶ **Success:** This can be based on a couple conditions:

  ▶ Content has been distributed successfully to the DP.

  ▶ Content hash has been successfully verified. (If content validation is enabled, a new status message is generated for each validation success or failure.)

▶ **In Progress:** Content is currently being transferred to one or more DPs. (Review details for more information.)

▶ **Error:** Content distribution failed for one or more DPs. (Review details for more information.)

▶ **Unknown:** No status has been reported for one or more DPs.

Content Status   ⟳ Refresh

Content Distribution: Oracle Java JRE 8 Update 11

● Success ● In Progress ● Error ● Unknown

Status	Assets	Status Type
Successfully processed content on distribution point	2	Success

Asset Details

Filter

Device	Last Status Time ▾	Group Targeted	Description
CHARON.ODYSSEY.COM	10/1/2016 4:00 PM	Yes	Package "CAS0000F" on distribution point "["Disp
ATHENA.ODYSSEY.COM	10/1/2016 4:00 PM	Yes	Package "CAS0000F" on distribution point "["Disp

FIGURE 14.4   Completion statistics details.

4. Right-click an asset in the Asset Details section and select **More Details** from the context menu to view additional content status information.

Distribution Point Group Status

DP group status reports overall status for content targeted through a DP group, letting you view the status of all DPs in a group. Figure 14.5 shows group status for three DP groups. Notice that the All Non-Imaging Distribution Points group has eight DPs with 395 items (packages, application content, software update packages, task sequence information, and so on) assigned, and the overall distribution status for the group is Success for 393 items and Failed for 2 items. The Depot DP's and Mac Client DP groups are also displayed.

As with DP status, **View Status** lets you drill down to identify issues.

14

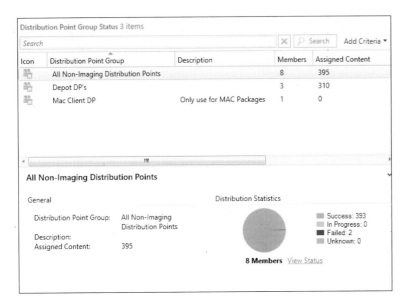

FIGURE 14.5   Distribution point group status.

Distribution Point Configuration Status

Review DP configuration status to review specific information for a single DP. Notice the timestamp associated with each message. If the DP is recently installed, you may find normal warnings/errors that occur during the installation process; these older status messages are eventually purged from the ConfigMgr database. You will find helpful information about hash validation and progress for content sent to DPs.

Using BranchCache and Peer Cache

BranchCache allows you to securely use a peer-to-peer model to share content between systems. This is a Windows OS feature and works for more than just ConfigMgr content, such as transferring huge files from a centrally provided file share. Peer Cache has similar functionality, does not require a BranchCache infrastructure, and works for ConfigMgr-related content only.

Using either cache type or combining both is particularly helpful when you have multiple systems in a remote office without a DP. Enabling BranchCache or Peer Cache reduces the number of systems crossing the WAN link to download source content.

Combine BranchCache and Peer Cache for a best-of-both-worlds scenario. BranchCache can use data deduplication techniques and works even with a local DP on the same subnet, while Peer Cache works over subnets, as it is limited to boundary groups. For information about these cache types and combining them, see http://deploymentresearch.com/Research/Post/608/A-Geek-rsquo-s-Guide-to-reduce-the-network-impact-of-Windows-10-Updates-and-other-packages-with-ConfigMgr. For information about BranchCache, see https://technet.microsoft.com/library/hh831696(v=ws.11).aspx.

After configuring and setting corresponding client settings, as discussed in Chapter 9, there is only one setting you should enable for each deployment. Under Distribution Settings, enable **Allow clients to share content with other clients on the same subnet**.

Using Preferred Distribution Points

Consider a scenario with a large number of DPs and a large amount of content to distribute. You might decide to send everything to all DPs to ensure that content is available when needed. Alternatively, you may have a limited amount of space and might be fairly certain that many packages (or other content) will not be required everywhere.

Say you have packaged all MUI language packs for Windows 7. Rather than distribute all European language MUIs to a Cleveland DP (where it is unlikely most of them would be needed), distribute the content to the parent site of the Cleveland DP and enable the check box **Distribute the content for this package to preferred distribution points**. When this option is enabled, if a client requests content and the content is not available in the boundaries of a DP, ConfigMgr distributes the content to the DP to make it available locally for all managed systems. If you configured the application to allow fallback to a remote DP, this takes precedence over the setting Distribute the content for this package to preferred distribution points.

Using Content

You can reuse content in other ConfigMgr environments by exporting it from one ConfigMgr environment and importing into another. You can also export content for backup purposes.

To distribute large content over low-bandwidth networks, you can use ConfigMgr's prestaging capabilities to save the content on media such as an external hard drive or USB stick and then ship the media to the remote DP and import it. The following sections discuss importing and exporting content, using prestaged content, and using the content library.

Importing and Exporting Content

ConfigMgr allows exporting of objects from one ConfigMgr environment to another or for backup and archival purposes. You can choose to export only the object or the object and the package source.

Perform the following steps to create exported content:

1. Select one or more package objects and choose **Export** from the ribbon bar to start the Export Application Wizard.

2. On the General page, enter a file path for where to store the exported content. Enter the file extension **.zip**, as shown in Figure 14.6.

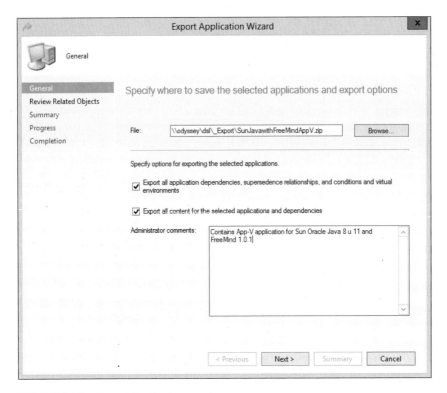

FIGURE 14.6   Export Content example.

Following is a brief description of the other options in Figure 14.6:

▶ **Export All Application Dependencies, Supersedence Relationships, and Conditions and Virtual Environments:** When this option is selected, the export includes all dependence and supersedence information, global conditions, and defined virtual environments for Application Virtualization. For packages, this includes packages referenced with the Run another program first option. For task sequences, it includes all packages, applications, driver packages, and more referenced in a TS (that is, all objects that appear under the References area for a TS). If this check box is not enabled, you only export the selected object.

▶ **Export All Content for the Selected Applications and Dependencies:** This is specific to source files that are referenced by an object. Enabling this check box may significantly increase the size of the exported content.

3. Review the information on the Review Related Objects page and step through the rest of the wizard to completion.

Follow these steps to import content to a different ConfigMgr environment:

1. Select an object node and select **Import** (or **Import Application**, depending on your location) from the ribbon bar.

2. Select the UNC path to the exported content (for example, *<servername>**<sharename>***myExportedApps.zip**).

TIP: ENSURING THAT THE COMPRESSED .ZIP FILE IS IN THE PROPER LOCATION

When you import, content is extracted from the .zip file to the current folder, which becomes the package source location for the object (application, package, program, and so on). Be sure the .zip is in the proper location. Import using the UNC path you want for the content source location or plan to move content and change paths later.

---

3. Review the File Content page. If some content was previously imported, there may be additional options to skip or overwrite.

4. Complete the wizard.

Using Prestaged Content

You may have some locations with very slow connectivity, or even costly connectivity. ConfigMgr allows you to create a prestaged content file on one server, mail it to another server, and import the prestaged content. You can also copy content over the WAN, provided you have adequate throughput. To enable prestaged content, enable the **Enable this distribution point for prestaged content** setting on the properties of the DP. ConfigMgr then obeys the property configurations of the package or application.

Figure 14.7 displays the following package settings available for configuring how prestaged content will be managed:

▶ **Automatically Download Content When Packages Are Assigned to Distribution Points:** When this option is selected, a package works as normally expected. Software is distributed from the ConfigMgr console and arrives on the DPs.

▶ **Download Only Content Changes to the Distribution Point:** When this option is selected, minor updates can occur to the DP, using standard content distribution processes. Say you deploy Office 2016 and later realize you have additional updates to deploy. Using this setting, you could deploy the base install (the largest size for content) of Office 2016 and require the initial package to be installed using prestaged content. Any subsequent changes could be sent using the normal DP process.

▶ **Manually Copy the Content in This Package to the Distribution Point:** When this option is selected, ConfigMgr does not use any WAN for content transfer and relies completely on importing prestaged content.

14

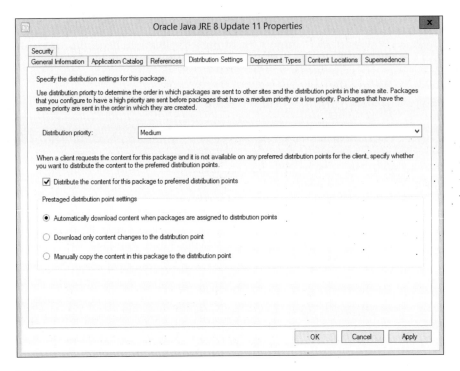

FIGURE 14.7   Distribution Settings tab.

You can use prestaged content to export the package source from the content library. This allows you to manually transfer content from one location to a remote location, insert the media, and import that content into a new DP. Perform the following steps to create the prestaged content file:

1. Select one or more package objects and choose **Create Prestaged Content File** from the ribbon bar to start the Create Prestaged Content File Wizard.

2. On the General page, choose a path to store the compressed content, enable the check box to export all dependencies if desired, and add any additional administrator comments.

3. Review the Content page and confirm that the content you want to prestage is listed. If you need to add or remove content, cancel the wizard and return to step 1. If the content you want prestaged is selected, click **Next**.

4. On the Content Locations page, click **Add** and choose one or more DPs to use as the source for the prestaged content process, shown in Figure 14.8. Select DPs on your local network if possible.

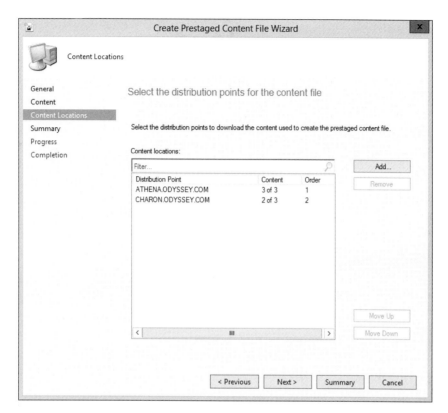

FIGURE 14.8   Create Prestaged Content File Wizard.

Figure 14.8 shows Charon.odyssey.com, which has two of the three desired packages available, and Athena.odyssey.com, which has all three packages. The Charon DP is first in priority, so all content that is available from Charon is collected first, and Athena is used as needed. Click **Next**.

5. Review the Summary page and continue the wizard to completion.

To successfully import prestaged content, first target the desired DPs with the package, using one of the prestaged content settings for the package.

TIP: VERIFYING PRESTAGED CONFIGURATION

Before beginning the import process, verify that the ConfigMgr application properties are configured properly, as described earlier in this section. If an application is configured to automatically download content when packages are assigned to distribution points, the prestage process will not work as expected, as content is sent to the DP without prestaging.

After sending content to the DPs, you will see status messages (under Monitoring -> Distribution Status -> Content Status) that state the DP is waiting for prestaged content. Transport the prestaged content to the desired location by using a simple file copy over the WAN or copy the prestaged content to media and ship it to the remote location. Follow these steps on the DP to import prestaged content:

1. Copy the extracted content to c:\temp\.

2. Open a command prompt and navigate to SMS_DP$\sms\Tools.

3. Run the following command:

```
extractcontent.exe /p:c:\temp\mycontent.pkgx /i
```

4. Review the output (and run extractcontent.exe /? for more options).

About the Content Library

The content library, also informally referred to as the *single-instance store*, is a ConfigMgr feature that adds significant value to your DPs and reduces the need to send duplicate files across the WAN to support different packages. Kent Agerlund has an informative blog post explaining the content library at http://blog.coretech.dk/kea/understanding-the-new-content-library-store-in-5-minutes/.

Troubleshooting Content Distribution

Most content distribution troubleshooting occurs in the ConfigMgr console, as mentioned in the "Monitoring Distribution Point Status" section, earlier in this chapter. You should also review the Software Distribution - Package and Program Deployment and Software Distribution - Content reports for more information. You may need to check the logs to find more information; use the article at https://support.microsoft.com/help/4000401/content-distribution-in-mcm as a guide to find the log files used with content distribution.

Deploying Applications and Packages

Chapters 11 and 12 describe creating applications and DTs, and Chapter 13 discusses creating packages. This chapter discusses creating collections and distributing content to DPs. Now you are ready to deploy software. Both applications and packages use the Deploy Software Wizard. As shown in this section, some options are available only for one type or the other. Follow these steps to deploy a ConfigMgr package or application:

1. In the ConfigMgr console, navigate to **Software Library** -> **Overview** -> **Application Management** -> **Applications** and select an application. Alternatively, navigate to the **Packages** node and select a package.

2. Select **Deploy** from the ribbon bar to start the Deploy Software Wizard. Edit the following properties on the General page as required:

    ▶ **Software:** If deploying a package, click **Browse** and choose the program to deploy. (This is filtered to show only programs for the current package.) If deploying an application, the application name appears in the dialog.

▶ **Collection:** Choose the desired target collection. The Member Count property shows the total count of members in a collection. If you have multiple primary sites, you may not see all collection members from a primary site, although you will see them from the CAS. Thus, when deploying software, you will always see the total member count to know the number of systems impacted.

▶ **Use Default Distribution Point Groups Associated to This Collection:** This option is enabled if you associated a DP group to the targeted collection. Enable the check box to populate the content distribution information automatically on the next page of the wizard.

▶ **Automatically Distribute Content for Dependencies:** Choose this option to distribute all packages required for the Run Another Program First feature for a program. If the program specified references a different package, enable this check box to ensure that the dependent package is distributed. If deploying an application, any dependent application (discussed in Chapter 12) is distributed with the check box enabled. This automatic process only occurs when the deployment is created. If the package is updated later, it must be updated using the Update Content Wizard.

▶ **Comments:** You can optionally specify comments for administrators. Information entered here does not appear to the end user.

3. On the Content page, add additional DPs and DP groups by clicking **Add** and browsing to a DP or DP group. The top frame of this page displays when content is currently distributed. The bottom frame shows any DPs you add. If associated to a collection, the DP group is shown.

4. Fill out the Deployment Settings page as needed. The information on this page varies depending on whether the application is targeted to users or devices, whether it is an application or a package, and whether the software is required or available. All options with explanations follow:

▶ **Action:** For packages, this option is always set to Install. For applications, you can choose Install or Uninstall.

NOTE: ABOUT THE UNINSTALL ACTION

Deploying an uninstall application is similar to deploying a normal application install. There are some differences important enough to document:

▶ Uninstall is only supported through the Application feature.

▶ Uninstall actions can only be deployed as Required.

▶ Dependent applications are not uninstalled.

▶ Requirement rules are not checked for an uninstall; if a detection rule determines that the software is installed, the uninstall rule is initiated, regardless of requirement rules.

▶ If a system is targeted with a required deployment for both install and uninstall, the install occurs.

▶ **Purpose:** Choose Required or Available. This cannot be changed after creating a deployment; if you need a change, you must delete it and create a new one.

▶ **Deploy Automatically According to Schedule Whether or Not a User Is Logged On:** This option applies to required applications targeting a user-based collection and has no impact on packages. The setting instructs ConfigMgr to use the primary user device affinity (discussed in Chapter 12) to target the machine even if no user is logged on. ConfigMgr maps the user to the computer and deploys the required software. It allows you to deploy required software to a user collection, based on the user–primary device association.

▶ **Send Wake-up Packets:** This option is enabled for required deployments; when Wake on LAN is enabled and properly configured, ConfigMgr sends wake-up packets to wake sleeping systems at deployment start time.

▶ **Require Administrator Approval if Users Request This Application:** This option is enabled for available applications that target a user-based collection; it allows the user to see the application in the Application Catalog and submit a request for approval to install. Once an administrator grants approval, the user can navigate to the Application Catalog to install the application.

5. Click **Scheduling** to define when the application should be available and when it will be required, if a required deployment. All times are UTC by default. When configuring this page for a package, you can specify an expiration time. You can select to delay enforcement of the installation deadline according to user-set preferences, up to the grace period defined in the client settings. The user can define this by setting business hours and by specifying that the deployment should occur outside those hours.

TIP: NO EXPIRATION TIME FOR APPLICATIONS

Recall that when you deploy a ConfigMgr application as a required deployment, the intent is for all targeted and applicable systems to have the software installed. Therefore, ConfigMgr applications do not have expiration times.

6. On the User Experience page, configure behavior outside maintenance windows and specify how or if the user is notified of an installation or required restart. These are the options:

▶ **User Notifications:** This option is available for applications. Its settings are self-describing; however, one setting can affect end-user notifications. If the Show notifications for new deployments client setting under Computer Agent (discussed in Chapter 5) is set to False, targeted clients do not receive a system tray notification for new software or system restarts for packages, applications, or software updates.

▶ **Allow the User to Run the Program Independently of Assignments:** This option displays only for packages. If enabled, it allows the deployment to appear in Software Center. To manage notifications for packages, configure a property on the program to deploy. The Advanced tab for the program has a property named Suppress program notifications, which prevents system tray notifications if checked. If unchecked, the end user receives notifications if the Show notifications for new deployments setting is set to True. This same configuration is required for task sequences to handle end-user notifications.

The last two options have to do with managing software installations and system restarts. By default, packages and applications adhere to maintenance windows. Modify these settings to bypass maintenance windows.

7. The packages version of the Deploy Software Wizard has an additional property page for DPs. Use this page to specify how to run the content for the program according to the boundary to which the client is connected, as shown in Figure 14.9.

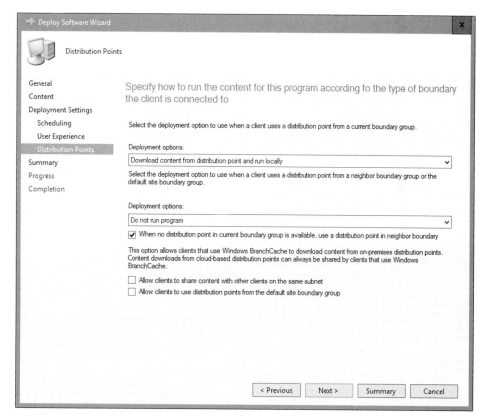

FIGURE 14.9   The Distribution Points tab of the Deploy Software Wizard.

Following is a brief description of each option on that page:

▶ **Deployment Options (Current Boundary Group):** When a system is on a network that can use a DP from its boundary group, the client uses the options defined for this property. By default, content is downloaded from the DP and run from the local cache. You have one additional option: Run program from distribution point. If this is chosen, you must enable the option Copy the content in this package to a package share on distribution points on the Data Access tab for the package, as discussed in Chapter 11. Enabling this option instructs all DPs to copy the required content from the single-instance store to a DP share.

▶ **Deployment Options (Neighbor Boundary):** Specify whether clients should download and install content from a neighbor boundary when no DP in its current boundary group is available or whether to not run the program.

▶ **Allow Clients to Share Content with Other Clients on the Same Subnet:** Set this option to enable the deployment to support BranchCache or Peer Cache (discussed in Chapter 5).

▶ **Allow Clients to Use Distribution Points from the Default Site Boundary Group:** If a client cannot locate content for this deployment in its defined boundary group or a neighbor boundary group (if specified), this allows the client to use the Default-Site-Boundary-Group.

As previously mentioned, the Distribution Points page is available only for packages. DP configuration for applications is part of the application DT. Chapter 12 discusses settings specific to each DT.

8. Continue through the wizard, monitoring progress and viewing completion.

Dealing with High-Risk Deployments

High-risk deployments are deployments where the impact, should something go wrong, is considered high. In such situations, a deployment that is automatically installed could potentially cause unwanted results. To mitigate these types of issues, ConfigMgr offers some precautions to take for collections containing a certain number of clients or collections with site systems. An example of a high-risk deployment is a TS deploying Windows 10 to the All Desktop and Server Clients collection.

High-risk deployment behavior can be configured on the Deployment Verification section of the Site properties for the CAS and primary sites. Perform the following steps to modify settings for high-risk deployments:

1. Navigate to **Administration -> Site Configuration -> Sites** and select the site you want to configure.

2. Select **Properties** from the ribbon bar to open the Site properties. Select the Deployment Verification tab, shown in Figure 14.10.

3. On the Deployment Verification tab, set the following:

▶ **Default Size:** The default size is, by default, set to 100. Modify it to anything between 1 and 1,000,000 to hide collections with memberships that exceed the default size. When 0 is specified, the setting is ignored, meaning all collections are visible.

▶ **Maximum Size:** Modify the maximum size to specify collections that are hidden if they have more members than the maximum size. This option is set to 0 by default, which means it is turned off. The setting can be from 1 to 1,000,000. The value of this setting must be 0 or more than the Default size setting.

▶ **Collections with Site System Servers:** Specify how collections containing site system servers should be treated. You can block these collections, causing the deployment to not be created, or choose to warn, meaning a verification is required before the deployment is created.

After modifying these settings, click **OK** to apply your changes and close the Site Properties dialog.

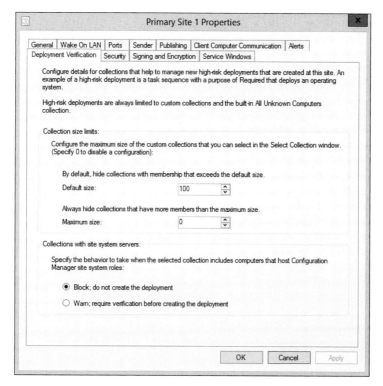

FIGURE 14.10   Deployment Verification tab of Site properties.

When a high-risk deployment is specified, a warning appears, as in Figure 14.11. Click **OK** to continue. To include collections exceeding the specified default size, remove the check box in front of **Hide collections with a member count greater than site's minimum size configuration**, and you can also see collections containing more objects than specified as the default size. You see a warning that you have chosen to display additional collections that exceed the site's default size for deployment verification. Available collections are still restricted by the site's maximum size configuration. A final warning is displayed after the Deployment Settings page of the Deploy Software Wizard, where you must enable the check box **I want to create this high risk deployment. (This will generate an audit status message.)**, shown in Figure 14.12.

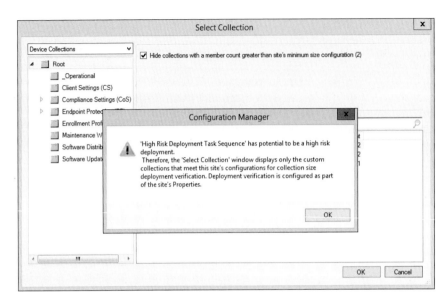

FIGURE 14.11   High-risk collection warning.

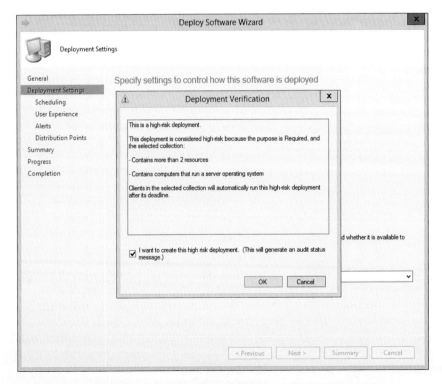

FIGURE 14.12   Deployment verification warning.

When a deployment to a collection containing site systems is created and the setting to block deployments to collections containing site systems is enabled, you receive the error displayed in Figure 14.13.

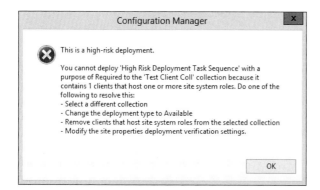

FIGURE 14.13   High-risk deployment warning for a collection containing site system roles.

Simulating Deployments

ConfigMgr allows you to simulate an application deployment. This helps you determine the number of systems that will run each DT. In a simulated deployment, clients download and evaluate policy and return state messages.

To create a simulated deployment, right-click an application and select **Simulate Deployment**. Choose the target collection and the intended action (Install or Uninstall.) No schedule is required; clients download and evaluate policy on their next polling interval.

Understanding the End-User Experience

This section provides a brief overview of the end-user experience on Windows devices. ConfigMgr currently provides two types of end-user experiences:

▶ The first experience, introduced with ConfigMgr 2012, involves Software Center, which the authors will call old Software Center to distinguish it from the new Software Center and the Application Catalog.

▶ The second experience involves the new Software Center, which combines functionality from the old Software Center and the Application Catalog. This section helps you determine the type of end-user experience to use and when to target devices or target users.

There are two main views from the end-user perspective:

▶ **Old Experience:** Old Software Center is a client-based application that can be accessed from **Start -> Programs -> Microsoft System Center -> Configuration Manager -> Software Center**. This application, enabled by default, displays all device-targeted applications that meet the requirements for installation on the system.

The Application Catalog is a rich web-based portal that allows the user to request and install software and manage user–device affinity (if allowed by the administrator). It displays all user-targeted applications. The catalog can be accessed directly by the URL or by clicking **Find additional applications from the Application Catalog** in Software Center (see Figure 14.14).

▶ **New Experience:** To use the new Software Center, enable it using the Computer Agent device client setting. Chapter 9 includes information about client settings and how to enable and deploy them. The new Software Center is a client-based application that can be accessed from the same place as the old Software Center: Select **Start -> Programs -> Microsoft System Center -> Configuration Manager -> Software Center**. The application displays all device and user-targeted applications that meet requirements for installation on that system.

Using the Old Software Center

Figure 14.14 shows an example of software appearing in old Software Center. The Available Software tab shows all available software targeted to the device.

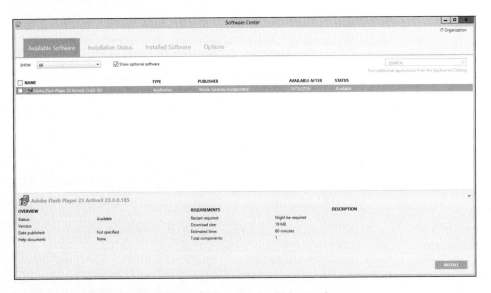

FIGURE 14.14   Showing available software in the Software Center.

This view also shows packages, applications, software updates, and OSD task sequences. You can search, hide optional software, and use the Show dropdown to filter to show only OSD, applications (including packages), or software updates. The user selects the desired application and clicks **Install** to start installation. The Status column shows the status, such as downloading, installing, installed, and so on. Virtually all information on this page is searchable, and if a help document exists for an application, you can link to it directly from here.

The user can also view the Installed Software tab to review installed applications. The Options tab, shown in Figure 14.15, lets the user specify when to install software. The user can specify work hours in the Work information section and enable the check box **Automatically install or uninstall required software and restart the computer outside of the specified business hours**. If this option is enabled, required software with a deadline in the future automatically installs at the next available user-defined window instead of waiting for the deadline, which could cause the installation to occur at a time that is not so convenient for the user. If the user configured a local business hours installation window for 10:00 PM tonight, and the deadline is 5:00 PM today, the software runs at the deadline instead of waiting for the window.

FIGURE 14.15   Options tab in the old Software Center.

TIP: OLD SOFTWARE CENTER IS FOR DEVICE-TARGETED DEPLOYMENTS

All deployments targeted to a device appear in the old Software Center unless configured to not to appear in Software Center in the User Experience tab of the Deploy Software Wizard.

The deployments shown in Software Center have been evaluated based on supported platform rules (for package/program and task sequences) and requirement rules (for ConfigMgr applications.) Consequently, the Software Center view shows only software that has met the requirements for installation on the current system.

Using the Application Catalog

Figure 14.16 shows an example of software appearing in the Application Catalog. You can search, view additional details, and filter by category.

This figure shows that the 7-Zip installation requires approval. If you select the 7-Zip application, the Install button in the bottom frame changes to Request. Clicking **Request** changes the view to allow the user to enter a reason for requesting the software, as shown in Figure 14.17.

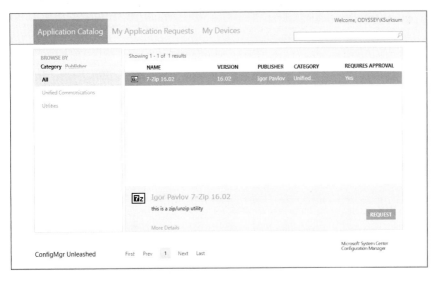

FIGURE 14.16   The Application Catalog.

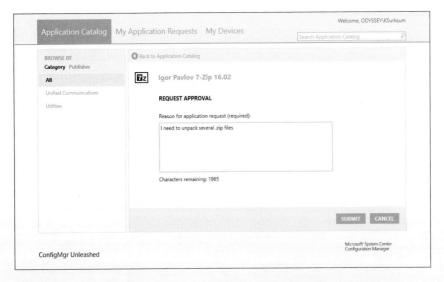

FIGURE 14.17   Request approval in the Application Catalog.

After submitting the request, the user can select the My Application Requests tab to view its status. When a request is submitted, the ConfigMgr administrator (or a delegated authority) can navigate to the **Software Library -> Overview -> Application Management -> Approval Requests** node in the ConfigMgr console and approve the request. If it is approved, the user can install the software on any device, based on the application's requirements.

NOTE: APPLICATION CATALOG IS FOR USER-TARGETED DEPLOYMENTS

All deployments targeted to a user appear in the Application Catalog. Since these deployments target users, no evaluations run in advance to verify that the installation is supported on the current device.

Following is a brief walkthrough of the user experience when installing software from the Application Catalog:

1. The user selects the software and clicks **Install**.

2. The user receives a dialog asking to confirm software installation (see Figure 14.18) and clicks **Yes** to continue.

FIGURE 14.18   Application Installation confirmation dialog in the Application Catalog.

3. Two additional dialogs appear; these are informational only:

   ▶ The first queries the local computer for information.

   ▶ The second appears while evaluating software installation requirements.

   For a package/program, a requirement is as simple as whether the program can run on the current platform (perhaps the program is marked to only run on Windows 10, but the user attempts to install on Windows Server 2016). Alternatively, it can be a complex application requirement rule, such as verifying a specific organizational unit (OU) or requiring a specific amount of memory or disk space.

4. Once the evaluation completes, a dialog notifies that the installation has started. Depending on how notifications are configured, the user may see a system tray notification for installation progress. When the installation completes, a success dialog appears. The Software Center can also be launched to monitor installation status.

5. If a failure occurs during the requirements evaluation step, the end user receives an error dialog, as displayed in Figure 14.19.

FIGURE 14.19   Application Installation failure dialog in the Application Catalog.

As an application can have a large set of complex requirement rules, it can be difficult to inform the user specifically which rule (or rules) failed, so a dialog similar to Figure 14.19 would appear with examples of why the application installation did not start. Note that these are examples and not specific to requirement rules written for the application.

Using the New Software Center

With ConfigMgr Current Branch version 1511, Microsoft introduced a new Software Center, which has a new, modern look and contains applications that previously were visible only in the Application Catalog. A Silverlight-enabled browser is no longer needed to view the new Software Center. Note that both the Application Catalog website point and Application Catalog web service point still must be configured, since the new Software Center uses them to display information in the application.

After enabling the new Software Center, users can start it from the Start menu. The new Software Center has a different layout than the old Software Center, as shown in Figure 14.20.

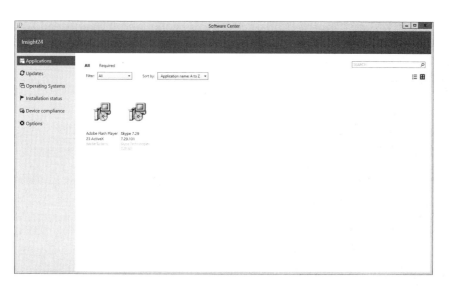

FIGURE 14.20   The new Software Center.

The new Software Center contains several pages:

▶ **Applications:** This page shows all ConfigMgr applications and packages available to the computer and the currently logged-in user. Clicking **Required** makes only required applications available for filtering. Use the filter selections to filter applications based on the User Categories value specified in the Application Catalog tab of the ConfigMgr application properties. Applications can be sorted using the Sort by dropdown box; available options are Application name: A to Z, Application name: Z to A, Oldest, Most recent, Publisher name: A to Z, Publisher name: Z to A, and Status.

▶ **Updates:** This page shows all available and to-be-installed updates; these also can be sorted using the Sort by dropdown box, with the same options available on the Applications page.

▶ **Operating Systems:** This page shows all available and to-be-installed operating systems, which can be sorted using the Sort by dropdown box, with the same options available on the Applications page.

▶ **Installation Status:** This page shows the status of ConfigMgr application installation, including the status of the installation (Installed or Failed). Status can be sorted with the Filter By dropdown box and the Sort By dropdown boxes, using the options specified for the Applications page.

▶ **Device Compliance:** This page shows the status of conditional access compliance, either compliant or non-compliant. Conditional access is described in Chapter 18, "Conditional Access in Configuration Manager." Users can check compliance by clicking **Check Compliance**.

▶ **Options:** This page provides options for Work Information, Power Management, Computer Maintenance, and Remote Control. These options are the same as specified in the old Software Center with one exception: Users can request policy by selecting Sync Policy under Computer maintenance options.

Notifications and Options for Required Deployments

The end user must initiate software installation if using the old Software Center for device-targeted optional deployments. The Application Catalog should be used for user-targeted optional deployments. You can also use the new Software Center for both device and user-targeted optional deployments. If required software is sent to the device or user, the behavior differs depending on settings specified in the deployment.

If a computer receives a policy with a required application that has a scheduled instal-lation deadline and user notification is enabled, the end user receives a notification, as shown in Figure 14.21, that displays the following text: Software Changes are required. Your IT department requires changes to the software on your computer. Click here for options.

FIGURE 14.21   Required software notification.

If the user ignores the notification, it reappears, depending on the specified and active Computer Agent client settings specific to that workstation. An icon also stays active in the system tray. If the user clicks the notification or the View Required Software message from the system tray icon, a Software Center window opens, as shown in Figure 14.22. The user can click the **View details** hyperlink to open the Software Center for more detail regarding the application or package to be installed. The user can also initiate the instal-lation from Software Center. In addition to viewing details, the user can use the following options to control installation behavior:

▶ **Right Now (Recommended):** This is the default option; it initiates installation after the user clicks OK.

▶ **Outside My Business Hours:** This option causes the software to be installed outside user-specified business hours. The Configure my business hours hyperlink takes the user to the Options tab in the Software Center, where business hours can be speci-fied in the Work information section, shown in Figure 14.23. Business hours by default are 05:00 AM to 10:00 PM, Monday to Friday.

▶ **Snooze and Remind Me:** Reminds the user at a later time, where later depends on the specified Computer Agent client settings. The user also can specify to be reminded in 15 minutes, 30 minutes, 1 hour, 4 hours, 12 hours, or 1 day.

The last option the user can specify is whether the software installation is allowed to restart the computer automatically, if needed.

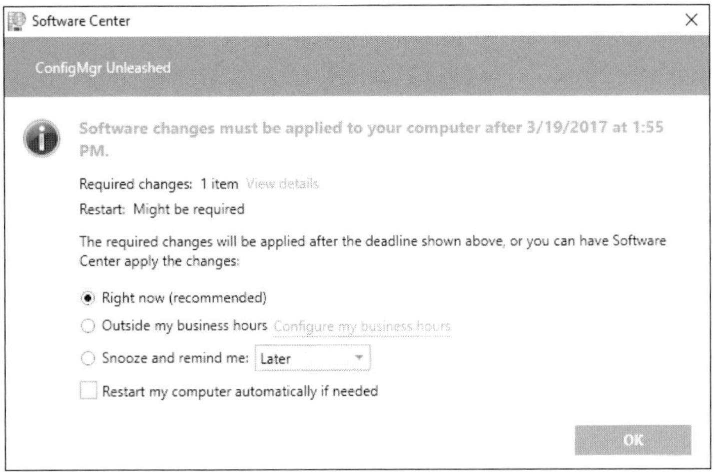

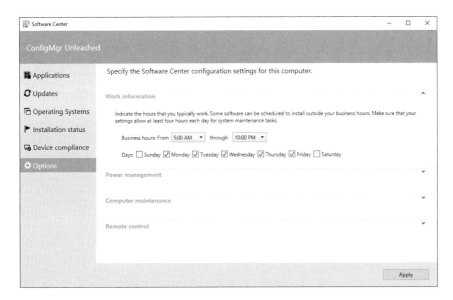

FIGURE 14.22   Software Center installation options.

FIGURE 14.23   Configuring business hours from the Software Center.

Once software installation is initiated, the DT or program is executed on the workstation. If the outcome is successful, the user is notified that the software was successfully installed. If installation fails, the user is also notified. The notification allows the user to view details, opening the Software Center as shown in Figure 14.24, where the user can see when the installation will be retried. The user also can click **Additional**

information to open the window shown in Figure 14.25. While for an end user the message displayed may be very cryptic, the ConfigMgr administrator can determine the cause of the failed installation by looking up the error code using the Error Lookup feature from the Configuration Manager Trace Log Tool (CMtrace.exe). In the example shown in Figure 14.25, the error 0x87D00607 translates to "Content not found".

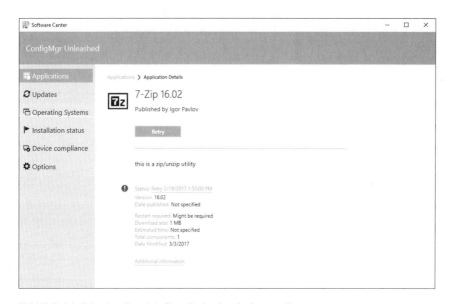

FIGURE 14.24   Application Details in the Software Center.

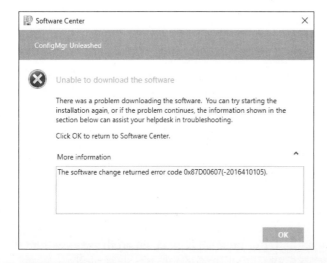

FIGURE 14.25   More information details in the Software Center.

Depending on the error level returned by the installation, the computer may need to be restarted or the user may have to log off to complete installation. In this case, the computer is either rebooted directly (if the option to reboot the computer automatically is selected) or rebooted depending on the specified Device Client Settings for Computer Restart active on the workstation. The user is also notified with a dialog box to reboot the computer to complete installation.

Monitoring and Troubleshooting

Most monitoring and troubleshooting for deployments occurs in the ConfigMgr console. Navigate to **Monitoring** -> **Deployments** to view all deployments. Right-click the header row and choose **Group By** -> **Feature Type** to organize this view by feature. Figure 14.26 shows an example of the Summary page for an application deployment.

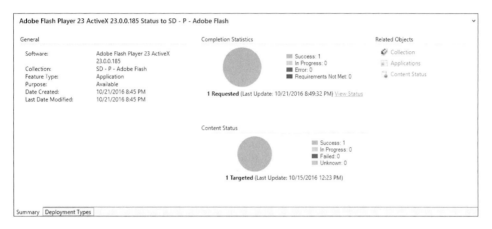

FIGURE 14.26   Summary page for application deployment monitoring.

The information in Figure 14.26 summarizes the deployment status. In one view, you can see the content status (to confirm that content is on the DPs), deployment status, and created and modified dates for the software. The links under Related Objects take you quickly to other areas of the console that you may need for troubleshooting.

Click the Deployment Types tab at the bottom to see the status of each DT if the deployment is for an application. Back on the Summary page, click **View Status** in the Completion Statistics section. A Deployment Status page appears, as shown in Figure 14.27. This page provides a considerable amount of detail. The top-right corner shows the summarization time. If the view is open a long time, click **Refresh** to see if an update summarization occurred. If not, click **Run Summarization** to trigger summarization for this deployment across your hierarchy.

You also see tabs for the following categories:

▶ **Success:** The installation returned a success exit code; for applications, the deployment state is reevaluated on an interval (by default seven days), so you may see many `Already Compliant` messages under Success.

▶ **In Progress:** The installation is currently in progress: downloading, waiting for a maintenance window, or installing.

▶ **Error:** An error occurred during the installation, which could be a failure exit code or a fatal error from the installer.

▶ **Requirements Not Met:** The installation was evaluated against the system and determined that the target system does not meet the platform requirement or the DT requirements.

FIGURE 14.27   Deployment Status details page of application deployment monitoring.

Status information is grouped by category; if there are 500 errors, ConfigMgr groups like errors together to be managed in one view.

The Software Distribution - Package and Program Deployment and Software Distribution - Application Monitoring reports provide additional information.

Summary

This chapter focused on collections, content, deployment, and deployment monitoring. While the previous three chapters discussed ConfigMgr applications and packages, this chapter discussed creating a collection, distributing content, and deploying software. It also described the end-user experience, with both the old and new Software Center applications. The chapter discussed monitoring deployment status, and simulating application deployment.

Another important concept in this chapter is the Application Catalog and Software Center. It is important to know where your deployment will appear and how to configure notifications to work for your environment.

Chapter 15, "Managing Software Updates," discusses distributing software updates to clients using the software update management capabilities of ConfigMgr.

Managing Software Updates

Applying software updates and ensuring patch compliance are important maintenance activities for information technology (IT) organizations. Microsoft first added software updates as an add-on to System Center Configuration Manager (ConfigMgr) in 2003, when it was known as Systems Management Server (SMS); the feature was called the Inventory Tool for Microsoft Updates (ITMU). Software updates was fully embedded beginning with ConfigMgr 2007, and improvements have been made in each new product release. Today software updates is rich in both design and feature sets, providing the ConfigMgr administrator with complete flexibility in deploying updates for supported Microsoft operating systems (OSs), Microsoft server products, selected Microsoft desktop applications such as Microsoft Office, and even cloud-based systems such as Microsoft Office 365. You can also scan and deploy patches for supported third-party products.

What's New with Software Updates in ConfigMgr Current Branch

The core functionality of software updates management in ConfigMgr is largely unchanged from ConfigMgr 2012 R2; however, based on customer feedback and new OSs, Microsoft has incorporated improvements that simplify the process, fill in some gaps, and generally improve the update management experience:

▶ **UseWUServer:** This new attribute differentiates a Windows 10 computer that connects to Windows Update for Business for software update management from computers connected to Windows Server Update

Services (WSUS) for software update management. You can use this attribute, located in the Windows Update section of the Resource Explorer, in a collection to remove these systems from a software update deployment.

▶ **WSUS Clean Up Task:** This new option on the Supersedence Rules tab of the software update point (SUP) properties allows you to run a task that sets the status of expired software updates to Declined on the WSUS server. The Windows Update Agent (WUA) then no longer scans for that update, which causes client scans to run faster.

▶ **Manage Office 365 Client Updates:** This option provides a new product in the Products tab of the SUP properties, named Office 365. Checking the box tells WSUS to sync Office 365 updates from Microsoft Updates; after syncing, updates appear in the Software Updates folder of the console.

▶ **Client Setting to Manage the Office 365 Client Agent:** This is a dropdown menu item in the Software Updates section of the client settings properties. Once this option is enabled and Office 365 client updates are deployed to a client, the ConfigMgr client agent can communicate with the Office 365 client agent to download Office 365 updates from a distribution point (DP) and install them. In ConfigMgr Current Branch version 1706, the client receives a popup and in-app notifications as well as a countdown dialog prior to installing the update. More information can be found at https://docs.microsoft.com/sccm/sum/deploy-use/manage-office-365-proplus-updates#restart-behavior-and-client-notifications-for-office-365-updates.

▶ **Manually Switch Clients to a New Software Update Point:** Use this new option in the client notification area of the console to tell clients to use a new SUP when their active SUP is not working. Once the client gets this policy through the fast policy channel, it looks for another SUP at the next software update scan.

▶ **Restart Options for Windows 10 Clients After Software Update Installation:** This lets Windows 10 clients see the Update and Restart and Update and Shutdown options in the Power menu when there is a pending restart for a ConfigMgr software update.

▶ **Manage Windows as a Service:** This new feature, commonly called *Windows 10 servicing*, allows ConfigMgr to view the status of Windows as a service, create servicing plans to form deployment rings, and view alerts when Windows 10 clients are near the end of support for their build of the Semi-Annual Channel.

▶ **Enforcement Grace Period for Required Application and Software Update Deployments:** This new option allows you to set a period of time between 1 and 120 hours for postponing installation of required deployments, including software updates, after the deadline has passed. It allows end users that have been away for an extended length of time to not have to wait for required deployments to install before using the system.

▶ **Improvements for How Software Update Points Work with Boundary Groups:** With ConfigMgr Current Branch version 1706, the time it takes to fall back to a neighbor boundary group is now configurable. Changes have also been made so that the client, independent of the configurable time, will try for 120 minutes to connect to the last SUP it used. If unsuccessful, the client randomly picks another SUP from the pool of available SUPs and tries to connect to that SUP. After two hours of failing to connect, the client will use a shorter cycle for connecting to a SUP.

▶ **Enable/Disable Support of the Installation of Windows 10 Express Files with Software Updates:** A new setting, located in the Software Updates section of client settings, allows you to enable or disable using Windows 10 Express files with software updates. To use the Express files, enable this setting and change the SUP properties to allow it to synchronize the metadata for the Windows 10 Express files.

▶ **The Ability to Manage Microsoft Surface Driver Updates:** A new pre-release feature with Current Branch version 1706, this capability, if enabled, creates a new classification in the SUP properties that allows the SUP to include metadata for Microsoft Surface drivers and firmware updates. Once the SUP has synchronized this metadata, the ConfigMgr administrator can deploy the drivers and updates through the software updates process. Note that the SUPs must be running Windows Server 2016 for this to work.

▶ **Configuration of Windows Update for Business Deferral Policies:** This new feature in ConfigMgr Current Branch 1706 allows an administrator to create deferral policies for Windows 10 Feature Updates or Quality Updates for Windows 10 devices managed directly by Windows Update for Business. To configure these policies, navigate in the ConfigMgr console to **Software Library** -> **Overview** -> **Windows 10 Servicing** -> **Windows Update for Business Policies**. On the ribbon bar, click **Create Windows Update for Business Policy** to start the wizard. More information about creating the policies can be found at https://docs.microsoft.com/ sccm/sum/deploy-use/integrate-windows-update-for-business-windows-10#configure- windows-update-for-business-deferral-policies.

As you move forward with Windows 10 and Office 365, new software updates features can help improve your overall ConfigMgr experience. This chapter explains how software updates work and how to configure and use this feature to help your overall patching needs.

Creating Your Update Design

Software updates play a critical role in the monthly ConfigMgr and client workstations operations process. It is said that some organizations only deploy ConfigMgr so they can patch their company systems every month. Deploying software updates successfully requires a considerable amount of planning and preparation to develop a process that is usable from month to month and from year to year. There are numerous aspects to consider, many of which depend on individual environmental, user, and even political requirements. Consider the following items when developing the software updates design process:

▶ **Scope:** Determine the systems and applications to patch. Although not updating all systems or applications for a particular flaw may pose a security risk, there may be specific reasons not to patch certain systems or applications.

▶ **Patch Testing:** The authors highly recommend testing patches before deploying them to production systems. If you do not have a full test environment, do not let that deter you from testing. At a minimum, identify a group of systems as your pilot testing group. Deploy patches to these test systems before a production rollout and leave sufficient time to troubleshoot and resolve any problems from the patches.

▶ **Coordination and Scheduling:** Windows patches typically require a reboot after installation, meaning you must schedule a window of time to apply a patch and reboot the system. As you may be patching workstations, servers, or dedicated workstations used in manufacturing or point-of-sale systems that have only a small window to reboot, you must coordinate with other IT staff, server administrators, application administrators, users, and management to establish maintenance windows with acceptable times to reboot these systems. While useful for all types of system maintenance, maintenance windows are a definite requirement for patch management. Many organizations include patch management in their established change control process or create a process to deal with the many ramifications of updates and patches.

▶ **Notification:** If starting a new patching process or changing an old process, always issue fair warning to anyone potentially affected by a patch update or system reboot. Make this notification part of any process documentation. Things will go smoothly once users are used to the new or changed patching process; meanwhile, having proper notifications on a regular basis helps users get accustomed to the new process. Even when coordinating maintenance windows, sending additional notifications to other administrators and users to let them know what will transpire can prevent finger-pointing and many sleepless nights.

▶ **Political Policies and Support:** IT professionals know the risks of not patching systems and applications. Implementing a successful patching strategy requires political support to establish a policy that dictates and enforces applying patches. Without such a top-down policy, you will face opposition to patching, not only from users but also within IT. A policy enforced by your CIO (or equivalent) eliminates any quibbling over patching.

Compliance regulations in the United States such as the Health Insurance Portability and Accountability Act (HIPAA), Sarbanes-Oxley Act of 2002 (SOX), and Gramm-Leach-Bliley Act (GLBA) are also drivers for patching and should eliminate any questions about its necessity. Although none of these compliance laws specifically requires patching, this is one of the first things auditors will check.

▶ **Role-Based Administration:** Consider who needs permission to create patch deployments, download patches, and create deployment packages. Assign permissions based on the role, so only those individuals who need the permissions get them. Some organizations assign different roles to different people to have checks and balances when deploying software updates.

Based on the information in this section, as well as other factors unique to your own organization or environment, consider developing a patch strategy and policy document that includes items such as a time line, a rollback process, and testing procedures. Update it monthly to indicate what patches are in scope and distribute it as part of your notification process.

Planning for Software Updates

Before patching systems or even moving in the direction of doing so, you must first plan your software updates infrastructure. The choices made now allow you to have a successful software updates experience later.

Capacity Planning

Capacity planning is one of the most important items to consider when starting the planning process. You need to know how many systems to patch to determine how much infrastructure you need; too little leads to major issues with performance and customer experience, and too much means capital assets are not fully used—which could mean wasted money. Capacity planning can be broken into two items:

▶ **Number of Clients to Support:** In the planning stage, this should be close to the number of clients you need to support. A single SUP can support 25,000 clients when colocated with another system role and WSUS is installed on the same machine, or it can support up to 150,000 clients on a dedicated machine that meets WSUS requirements to support that number of clients.

▶ **Number of Software Update Objects:** There is a soft limit of 1,000 software updates in a single deployment. Any automatic deployment rules (ADRs) fail if the query returns more than 1,000 updates. While 1,000 may seem high, if you select several products along with different update classifications, you can get to 1,000 very quickly. The 1,000 rule also applies to any manual software update deployments and software updates in configuration baselines.

Planning Your Software Update Point Infrastructure

A SUP is required to deploy software updates to your clients. Every primary site and the central administration site (CAS) must have a SUP, which can be colocated on the site server or installed as remote helper servers. SUPs are optional on a secondary site. The first SUP installed for a site is the synchronization source for all additional installed SUPs. You can install multiple SUPs at a site, which provides for fault tolerance without adding the complexity of a network load balancing (NLB) system. Having multiple SUPs does not mean load balancing for the clients; they are strictly there to be used if the primary SUP the client is using goes down. If you need load balancing, you need to use NLB.

NOTE: SUPS AND NLB

NLB is more robust than SUP failover for pure load balancing. NLB can also increase the reliability and performance of your network, but the trade-off is increased complexity for your ConfigMgr infrastructure. The ConfigMgr console does not allow you to configure the SUP to use NLB; you must use the `Set-CMSoftwareUpdatePoint` PowerShell cmdlet. For more information, see https://technet.microsoft.com/library/jj821938.aspx.

SUP Lists

When multiple SUPs are installed in the same site, the client gets a list of these SUPs when it receives a policy to enable the software updates agent or when it cannot contact the SUP it has been using. The client randomly selects a SUP from the list. Priority is given to SUPs that are in the same forest as the client. The list of SUPs provided to the client is also dependent on the type of client requesting the list:

▶ **Intranet-Based Clients:** These clients receive a list of SUPs configured to allow only connections from the intranet or connections from both intranet and Internet clients.

▶ **Internet-Based Clients:** These clients receive a list of SUPs configured to allow only connections from the Internet or from both intranet and Internet clients.

SUP Failover

The client receives a list of all the SUPs in the site and randomly chooses a SUP to use for scan data. It continues to use this same SUP until it cannot connect to the SUP and the scan fails. Once this happens, the client goes into a retry mode and performs the following steps:

1. When the first scan fails, the client retries in 30 minutes, using the same SUP.

2. If the failure reoccurs, the client tries again four times, with a 30-minute time-out after each retry.

3. After the fourth failure, the client waits an additional two minutes and then tries the next SUP in the SUP list.

4. When the client is successful with the next SUP in the list, that becomes the SUP the client will always use. If connecting to the next SUP in the list fails, the client starts over with step 1.

NOTE: NOT ALL SCAN FAILURES COUNT

If you are off the network when a scan starts and fails, it is not considered a failure that counts toward the four retries. The client knows this is normal because it is not connected to the network. If a scan is started and then the system is powered down before the scan completes, it also is not considered a scan failure and does not count toward the four retries.

If there are problems with the active SUP or you need to take that SUP down for mainte-nance, you can manually fail over the clients to a new SUP, as long as the clients already know that there are multiple SUPs in the site. Navigate in the ConfigMgr console to **Assets and Compliance -> Overview -> Device collections** and select the collection for which you want to switch SUPs. On the ribbon bar, click **Client Notification** and select **Switch to next Software Update Point**. This creates a client notification item sent to the client via the fast channel, telling the client to pick a new SUP from its SUP list.

Switching to a new SUP has a cost, as the SUP's failover design is different from that of DPs or management points (MPs), which affects client and network performance. The client will see an increased size in the catalog when switching, resulting in some performance issues with the network, the client, and the new SUP. This is why when a client successfully scans against a SUP, it preserves that affinity. Take care when failing over clients to a new SUP to avoid causing undue network or client issues.

SUPs in an Untrusted Forest

Due to mergers, acquisitions, or other unforeseen items, you may need to use SUPs in an untrusted forest. In these cases, WSUS must be installed on a server in that forest. When installing the SUP, you also must supply two accounts to be used during installation:

▶ **Site System Install Account:** This account is used during installation to copy over files needed for the install, access the WSUS server in the untrusted forest, and perform the installation of the SUP.

▶ **WSUS Server Connection Account:** This account is used after installation to make ongoing connections to WSUS. These connections are to configure WSUS once changes are made in ConfigMgr, perform a time-out check every 60 minutes to verify that WSUS is still alive, and tell WSUS when to sync with Microsoft Update.

SUPs Without Internet Access

The top-level site, be it a CAS or standalone primary site, is the site configured to synchronize software updates metadata with Microsoft Update. Due to security policies, this site may not have Internet access, which presents a major issue for software updates because it cannot obtain updated metadata. You can configure ConfigMgr to allow a synchronization source at the top-level site to use a WSUS server not in your hierarchy. This server might be in your demilitarized zone (DMZ) or a different data center that allows Internet access. Should you need to use this type of setup, ensure that the WSUS server synchronizes software updates that meet the criteria needed in your ConfigMgr hierarchy; otherwise, the software updates you see in the console will not be what you expect to see. You must also set up the WSUS Server Connection account to communicate with the external WSUS server and open the correct firewall ports for the communication between the two servers—typically port 80 or 8530 and port 443 or 8531 if using Secure Sockets Layer (SSL).

SUPs and Secondary Sites

A SUP is an optional component for secondary sites and is not installed by default. You can install only one SUP at a secondary site. When installing a SUP at a secondary site, the

WSUS database is configured as a replica of the default SUP at the parent primary site. You should need to install a SUP at the secondary site only when bandwidth is very limited between the devices and the SUP at the primary site. After a SUP is successfully installed and configured at the secondary site, a site-wide policy is updated for client computers that are assigned to the site, and they then start to use the new SUP.

Using Windows Software Update Services

A prerequisite of a SUP is that WSUS is installed on the system where the SUP is to be installed. In past versions, WSUS was Microsoft's separate, standalone server-based product for distributing updates to Windows systems. Starting with Windows Server 2012, WSUS is integrated with the OS and is no longer a standalone product. WSUS also uses the WUA to scan for patch applicability and subsequently install updates delivered by WSUS.

ConfigMgr integrates WSUS's update catalog download and distribution capabilities, enabling Microsoft to maintain and support a single update catalog that contains all Microsoft-supported updates used for Windows Update, WSUS, and ConfigMgr, while also allowing each update service to deliver updates in its own way. For ConfigMgr, this means delivering updates to clients through its robust DP capabilities. Once WSUS is integrated, ConfigMgr takes control of WSUS and configures it as needed.

WSUS uses a SQL database to store information. This can be a Windows Internal Database (WID) or a SQL Server database. If you install WSUS using the defaults, the WID is installed. In the case of ConfigMgr, SQL is usually installed on the site server. If installing WSUS on that same site server, you can use SQL Server as your database. If needed, you can create a separate SQL Server instance for ConfigMgr to allow for granular resource control and troubleshooting resource issues; however, this is not required, and WSUS has little overhead on the database server, regardless of the size of the ConfigMgr installation.

WSUS can support up to 25,000 clients if the WSUS server is colocated on the ConfigMgr server. If you need to support a larger number of clients, the authors recommend installing WSUS on a dedicated server. If needed, 150,000 clients can be supported when the SUP is installed on a remote system that meets WSUS requirements to support this number of clients. Rather than using a large single dedicated system, the authors recommend installing multiple WSUS/SUP servers to offset the number of clients reporting to each server.

> **NOTE: USING A SHARED WSUS DATABASE**
>
> When you install more than one SUP at a primary site, it is a best practice to use the same WSUS database for each SUP in the same Active Directory (AD) forest. Sharing the database lets you significantly mitigate the client and network performance impact that can occur when clients switch to a new SUP. When a client switches to a new SUP that shares a database with the old SUP, a delta scan still occurs, but this scan is much smaller than it would be if the WSUS server had its own database. You must also share the local WSUS content folders when using a shared WSUS database for SUPs. See https://docs.microsoft.com/sccm/sum/plan-design/software-updates-best-practices for further information.

Installing WSUS is a wizard-driven process and fairly straightforward. To start, use Server Manager and its Add roles and features section to select the WSUS items that you want to install. Your only real choice here is to use the WID or SQL Server. Your next choice is a bit confusing because the wizard makes it sound like you can uncheck the box to store the updates:

▶ **ConfigMgr:** For ConfigMgr, select to Store updates locally on the system, as shown in Figure 15.1. This setting allows WSUS to download and store license terms for specific software updates in the update content folder that you choose; ConfigMgr handles the download and deployment of updates. During the update synchronization process, ConfigMgr looks for applicable license terms in the content folder. If it cannot find license terms, it does not synchronize the update. In addition, clients must have access to the applicable license terms to scan for update compliance.

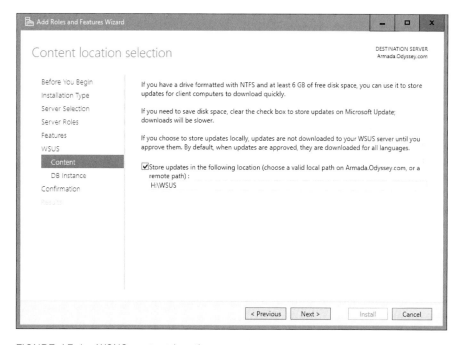

FIGURE 15.1   WSUS content location source.

▶ **SQL Server:** If you selected to use SQL Server and the database is on a remote server, you must enter the machine and instance name (*<machine name\instance name>*) and choose **Check connection** to verify connectivity. If SQL is installed on the same machine and using a default instance, just enter the machine name and select **Check connection** to verify connectivity.

When installation completes, the wizard informs you that configuration is required. Launch the Post-Installation task to finish installation. If something fails or goes wrong, a log file is created in your temp folder. The task details and notifications pane displays the location and name of the log file.

When the post-installation tasks are finished and successful, WSUS is completely installed. The first time you open the WSUS console after installation, it shows a configuration wizard and asks you to configure the settings. It is important to cancel out of the wizard. ConfigMgr configures WSUS based on the settings selected when the SUP is installed.

TIP: USING POWERSHELL TO INSTALL WSUS

Another option for installing WSUS is to use PowerShell commands. You can use several commands, depending on what you want to install:

▶ For a list of the items to install and the name to use to install each item, use this command:

```
get-WindowsFeature update*
```

▶ To use the WID, use this PowerShell command:

```
Install-WindowsFeature -Name UpdateServices -IncludeManagementTools
```

Because WID is a default entry, you do not have specify it on the command line.

▶ To use SQL Server as your database, use this command:

```
Install-WindowsFeature -Name UpdateServices-Services,UpdateServices-DB
-IncludeManagementTools
```

Once the installation is complete, you must run the post-installation tasks. Make sure you are in the %*ProgramFiles*%\Update Services\Tools folder. Assuming that you are still in PowerShell, run one of the following commands:

▶ If you installed WSUS with the WID, run this command:

```
.\wsusutil.exe postinstall CONTENT_DIR=C:\WUS
```

▶ If you installed using SQL Server, use this command:

```
.\wsusutil.exe postinstall SQL_INSTANCE_NAME=ARMADA CONTENT_DIR=C:\WUS
```

Both examples assume that you are using C:\WSUS as the folder to store the WSUS content; change the drive letter and folder as needed. The SQL Server example shows the machine name and assumes the default instance; if using a named instance, change it to <*machine name\instance name*>.

If WSUS is installed on Windows Server 2012 R2, you must apply hotfixes for WSUS to support Windows 10 and Windows Server 2016. Apply these updates before your first sync with Microsoft Updates:

▶ **Windows RT 8.1, Windows 8.1, and Windows Server 2012 R2 Update (April 2014):** If using Windows Server 2012 R2, this rollup hotfix must be applied first. More information about this hotfix can be found at https://support.microsoft.com/kb/2919355.

▶ **Update to Enable WSUS Support for Windows 10 Feature Upgrades:** This hotfix is applied after KB2919355 and allows the Windows 2012 R2 server to sync and distribute feature updates for Windows 10. For more information, see https://support.microsoft.com/kb/3095113.

▶ **Update Enables ESD Decryption Provision in WSUS in Windows Server 2012 and Windows Server 2012 R2:** This update is required to deploy features and upgrades to Windows 10 that released after May 1, 2016. More information is available at https://support.microsoft.com/kb/3159706.

NOTE: SYNCING BEFORE APPLYING UPDATES

If you synchronized the Upgrades classification before installing the hotfixes, the WSUS database is now populated with unusable data that must be cleared out for upgrades to be properly deployed. Find the steps to clear out this data and recover from the synchronization at https://docs.microsoft.com/sccm/sum/plan-design/prerequisites-for-software-updates#BKMK_RecoverUpgrades.

Configuring Components

With WSUS installed and ConfigMgr running, the next step is to prepare ConfigMgr and your Windows infrastructure for software updates functionality. While it is relatively straightforward to install and configure a SUP, this is where all your research and knowledge about your organization will help as you make decisions on the items that need to be updated and what the update schedule should look like.

The configuration process is not difficult, but it has many steps, and it is easy to get confused. With this in mind, the authors have broken down the process in two parts:

▶ Configuring server-side components

▶ Configuring client-side components

The "Configuring Server-Side Components" section describes a wizard with several pages and walks you through the process. The "Configuring Client-Side Components" section is not as clean as there is no wizard, just steps that you need to follow closely so nothing is left out.

Configuring Server-Side Components

The SUP is the site role in ConfigMgr that manages, configures, and communicates with the WSUS server. SUPs are installed on top of the WSUS server and take control of the WSUS settings, changing them back to what has been set in ConfigMgr at every watchdog cycle (usually every hour). To enable software updates functionality, a SUP must be installed at a CAS if it exists and on every primary site with clients that you want to update.

> **NOTE: USING A SUP IS OPTIONAL EXCEPT FOR PATCH MANAGEMENT**
>
> A SUP is not a required site role for ConfigMgr; however, if you want to patch clients, you must install a SUP at every primary site. The clients managed by a primary site without an installed SUP will not scan for update compliance or receive software updates from ConfigMgr.

SUPs should be installed in a top-down fashion, meaning that you start at the CAS, if one exists, and then move to primary sites and then secondary sites, if needed. When installing a SUP, you configure it as part of the installation process; you can edit the configuration after the SUP is installed. To begin installation, navigate in the ConfigMgr console to **Administration -> Overview -> Site Configuration -> Servers and Site System Roles**. Locate the server you want to use as your SUP and select **Add Site System Roles** from the ribbon bar or from the right-click context menu to launch the Add Site System Roles Wizard. If the server is not listed, add it to ConfigMgr by choosing **Create Site System Server** from the ribbon bar.

The General page of the Add Site System Roles Wizard includes the following selections, displayed in Figure 15.2:

- ▶ **Specify an FQDN for This Site System for Use on the Internet:** Check this box if this SUP will be used in a DMZ. This allows you to enter the FQDN to be published to the Internet DNS servers. The client obtains this name when it downloads policy and will try to connect to it when it is an Internet-based client (IBC).

- ▶ **Require the Site Server to Initiate Connections to This System:** By default, site systems initiate connections to the site server to transfer data, which can be a security risk when the connection is initiated from an untrusted network to the trusted network. Check this box when site systems accept connections from the Internet or reside in an untrusted forest so all connections are initiated from the trusted network after installing the site system and any site system roles.

- ▶ **Site System Installation Account:** The default option here is to use the site server's local system account to connect to the remote system to begin installation. If the destination server is in an untrusted forest or if the local system account does not have permissions to access the server, add an account for ConfigMgr to use. Ensure that this account has full administrative permissions on the remote machine.

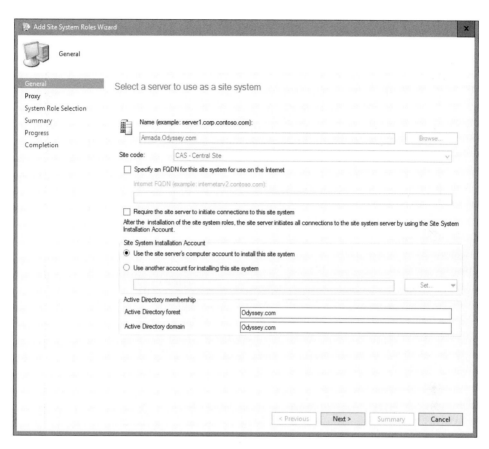

FIGURE 15.2   General Page of the Add Site System Roles Wizard.

Many organizations use a proxy server to control Internet access. The Proxy page of the wizard is where you enter the server name and port number that the proxy server uses. If your organization goes the extra mile and secures access to the proxy server with an account, that information must be entered at bottom of this page also, with the account name in the form *domain\username*, as well as the password. The authors recommend using a separate service account and following the rules of least privilege.

On the System Role Selection page of the wizard, select **Software Update Point** to add several subpages to the wizard. Figure 15.3 shows those subpages, and the next sections describe these subpages in detail.

FIGURE 15.3   Subpages of the Add Site System Roles Wizard.

Software Update Point Page

Since the SUP really interfaces with the WSUS server to configure and manage it, the Software Update Point page allows you to choose the ports your SUP will use to communicate with the WSUS server. There are two options to choose from and a check box to allow for SSL communication:

▶ **WSUS Is Configured to Use Ports 80 and 443 for Client Communication (Default Settings for WSUS 3.0 SP2):** This option is for backward compatibility to WSUS for older versions. It was in common use with Windows Server 2008 R2 and WSUS 3.0 Service Pack (SP) 2. Choose this option if you are using that version of the OS and you accepted the default values when installing WSUS.

▶ **WSUS Is Configured to Use Ports 8530 and 8531 for Client Communications (Default Settings for WSUS on Windows Server 2012):** Microsoft integrated WSUS with the server OS starting with Windows Server 2012, allowing you to install it through Server Manager. As a security precaution, Microsoft changed WSUS to use the default ports 8530 and 8531, which are now the default entries when installing WSUS. The authors recommend that you use this option.

▶ **Require SSL Communication to the WSUS Server:** If you configured your WSUS server to use SSL for communication, you must check this box for ConfigMgr to install and configure the SUP to use SSL. In the default installation, the SUP does not use SSL. When you enable SSL for WSUS that runs on a SUP at a parent site, any WSUS and SUP running on a child site must also be configured to use SSL.

Proxy and Account Settings Page
The previous section discussed access to the proxy server. You also need to tell ConfigMgr when the SUP needs to use those proxy settings. These options are available only if you selected using a proxy server on the Proxy page of the wizard. This page has three items, the first two of which deal with the different times that the SUP needs to use a proxy server and the third of which deals with how to connect to the WSUS server:

▶ **Use a Proxy Server When Synchronizing Software Updates:** If this box is checked, the SUP configures the WSUS server to use proxy settings when connecting to Microsoft Updates to synchronize the metadata for software updates.

▶ **Use a Proxy Server When Downloading Content by Using Automatic Deployment Rules:** If this box is checked, proxy settings are used when an ADR runs and needs to download content from Microsoft Updates.

▶ **Use Credentials to Connect to the WSUS Server:** By default, the SUP connects to the WSUS server using the site server's local system account; check this box if you need to use another set of credentials to make this connection. If you use an account, the authors recommend that it be a separate account and that you follow the rules of least privilege.

NOTE: INSTALL ACCOUNT VERSUS ACCESS CONNECTION ACCOUNT

You may have noticed that there have been two accounts to configure in the install process of a SUP. The first account, on the General page of the Add Site System Roles Wizard, is used only during installation. Once installation completes, that account is not used again unless you remove the SUP role and reinstall it. The account referenced in this section is known as the WSUS server connection account, and it is used every time the SUP or one of its components makes a connection to the WSUS server.

15

Synchronization Source Page

Synchronization is the process of using the choices made in the next few pages of the wizard to determine what software updates metadata needs to be downloaded. This page in the wizard allows you to choose the location to use for retrieving that metadata. There are three options to choose from:

▶ **Synchronize from Microsoft Update:** This is the option that most hierarchies use. It tells the SUP that it needs WSUS to connect to the Microsoft Update website and download the metadata. Internet access at the CAS or the standalone primary site is required for this choice.

▶ **Synchronize from an Upstream Data Source Location:** If your top-level site has no Internet access, this option may be the next best choice. The option allows you to use a top-level WSUS server that is not connected to your ConfigMgr hierarchy as a source for your metadata. You need to use a URL here; for example, https://Armada .odyssey.com:8531.

▶ **Do Not Synchronize from Microsoft Update or Upstream Data Source:** Use this option when you do not have Internet access in your environment; this might be a highly secure area that doesn't allow Internet access. In this case, you would use the import and export functions of WSUS to get the metadata from an outside WSUS server to inside the ConfigMgr server.

TIP: EXPORTING AND IMPORTING THE METADATA

Be sure to use a WSUS server with the same classifications, products, and languages you are using in ConfigMgr. This allows you to see the metadata you are expecting inside ConfigMgr. For in-depth information on how to use the WSUSUtil tool to export and import the metadata for software updates, see https://docs.microsoft.com/sccm/sum/ get-started/synchronize-software-updates-disconnected.

At the bottom of the page, determine what WSUS reporting events to view. These are status messages the WUA creates on the client system to tell WSUS the results of the scan it has run. ConfigMgr does not use these messages; they are only visible inside the WSUS administration console. Your choices follow:

▶ Do not create WSUS reporting events

▶ Create only WSUS status reporting events

▶ Create all WSUS reporting events

The authors recommend keeping the default setting: Do not create WSUS reporting events, as this reduces overhead at the client.

NOTE: SYNCHRONIZATION SOURCE SETTINGS FOR DOWN-LEVEL SITES

Synchronization source settings are only applicable to the top-level site in your ConfigMgr hierarchy (the CAS or a standalone primary site). Sites below the CAS or secondary sites attached to a standalone primary site always sync from their parent and are automatically set to Synchronize from an upstream server when installed from the wizard; this selection is not modifiable.

Synchronization Schedule Page

On the Synchronization Schedule page, set the schedule you want to use for ConfigMgr to synchronize software updates metadata with the Microsoft Update site. The authors recommend using the default setting of once every seven days, which should be sufficient for most organizations. If using Endpoint Protection, set this schedule to run every day to deliver update definition files. Be sure to account for Patch Tuesday, so you have updated metadata right after Microsoft releases its regular security updates. The page has two choices for the schedule and one choice for alerts:

▶ **Simple Schedule:** The simple schedule allows you to set how often the synchronization runs, in days and hours. The recurrence pattern is set to the number you choose, such as every 7 days.

▶ **Custom Schedule:** A custom schedule allows you to choose exactly—down to the day, hour, and minute—when the synchronization runs, as well as the recurrence pattern.

▶ **Alert When Synchronization Fails on Any Site in the Hierarchy:** This option allows an alert to be created when the SUP synchronization fails. When it is enabled, this option is for all SUPs in the hierarchy. The alert can be seen in the console under Monitoring -> Alerts.

NOTE: PATCH TUESDAY

Since 2003, Microsoft has released security and critical updates on the second Tuesday of every month. This has come to be known in the IT industry as *Patch Tuesday*. Although Microsoft occasionally releases updates at other times to fix ultra-critical issues, that is not a regular occurrence and should not directly affect your synchronization schedule. Critical updates not released on Patch Tuesday are often called *out-of-band updates* and typically fix zero-day security holes. To handle out-of-band updates, run a manual update synchronization when appropriate, following the instructions in the "Troubleshooting Software Updates" section, later in this chapter.

Supersedence Rules Page

Supersedence occurs when Microsoft releases a new update to a previously released update. An example of this would be updates for Internet Explorer. Those updates are cumulative, meaning a new update contains all the fixes for the old update plus the new fixes. When a new update is released, it takes the place of (supersedes) the old update. The old update is marked as expired in WSUS and ConfigMgr so it cannot be deployed. The Supersedence Rules page of the wizard allows you to set the supersedence behavior you want to follow when an update is superseded:

▶ **Immediately Expire a Superseded Software Update:** If selected, this option marks the old update as expired immediately in WSUS and all ConfigMgr deployments. Your client can no longer request or install the old update.

▶ **Do Not Expire a Superseded Software Update Until the Software Update Is Superseded for a Specified Period:** This allows you to select a number in months to wait before the old update is marked expired. This is a good option for customers that need extra time to verify that a new update does not break any of their applications. Say an organization has created a custom web page; if a new Internet Explorer patch is released, testing is needed to verify that it works correctly with the custom page before it can be included in deployments for clients to install.

▶ **Run WSUS Cleanup Wizard:** If this check box is checked, at the end of the next sync with WSUS, the ConfigMgr WSUS Sync Manager will run the WSUS Cleanup Wizard and reset the value of the next run time to 30 days. The wizard then runs every 30 days. The Sync Manager checks the last runtime value at the end of every synchronization; when the value is greater than 30 days, it runs the Cleanup Wizard.

Classifications Page

As you might imagine, the overall number of updates for the entire line of products and operating systems is overwhelming. To help manage this massive number of updates, Microsoft divides updates by classifications. The Classifying Updates page allows you to select the type of classifications for which you want updates. There are nine different classifications to choose from, with Security Updates turned on by default:

▶ **Critical Updates:** This specifies a broadly released update for a specific problem that addresses a critical, non-security-related bug.

▶ **Definition Updates:** This is used for updates to antivirus programs and definition update files.

▶ **Feature Packs:** This is for new product features distributed outside a product release and for features that are typically included in the next full product release.

▶ **Security Updates:** This specifies a broadly released update for a product-specific, security-related issue.

▶ **Service Packs:** This is a cumulative set of hotfixes applied to an application. These hotfixes can include security updates, critical updates, software updates, and so on.

▶ **Tools:** This is for a utility or a feature that helps complete one or more tasks.

▶ **Update Rollups:** This is a cumulative set of hotfixes packaged together for easy deployment. These hotfixes can include security updates, critical updates, updates, and so on. An update rollup generally addresses a specific area, such as security or a product component.

▶ **Updates:** This is for an update to an application or a file that is currently installed.

▶ **Upgrades:** This new classification allows you to upgrade the edition of Windows 10 that users have.

NOTE: USING THE UPGRADES CLASSIFICATION

Before enabling the Upgrades classification, be sure you have installed hotfix KB3095113 (https://support.microsoft.com/kb/3095113) on all SUPs in the ConfigMgr hierarchy. This hotfix allows the Windows 10 Servicing feature to work correctly in WSUS and ConfigMgr. Only Windows Server 2012, 2012 R2, and 2016 running WSUS support this classification. To service Windows 10 version 1607 and later, you must also install hotfix KB3159706 from https://support.microsoft.com/kb/3159706. For more information on these updates, see the end of the "Using Windows Software Update Services" section, earlier in this chapter.

When you sync with Microsoft Updates, the classifications are checked to see if they have any new updates. It is a best practice to clear all classifications before synchronizing software updates the first time; once the sync finishes, select the classifications from the properties of the SUP and then re-initiate the sync.

You see this Classifications page of the wizard only when you configure the first SUP at the site, and it is not available if you install additional SUPs. You can change any setting by choosing the properties of the first SUP in the site.

Products Page

The Products page contains the list of products for which you can download related metadata. As the list is very large and an organization may not need all of the updates, Microsoft has broken the list into two types, allowing you to be more selective in the types of products you need updates for:

▶ **Product Families:** This is an option for when you need the updates for everything in the entire family, such as Office. Instead of drilling down and choosing Office 2013, you would check the top box, and all Office products would be checked.

▶ **Products:** This is a specific edition of an OS or product. An example of this would be choosing only the Windows 10 product out of the Windows product family.

Figure 15.4 shows the product families and products, with the Office product family checked and only the Windows 10 product checked in the Windows product family.

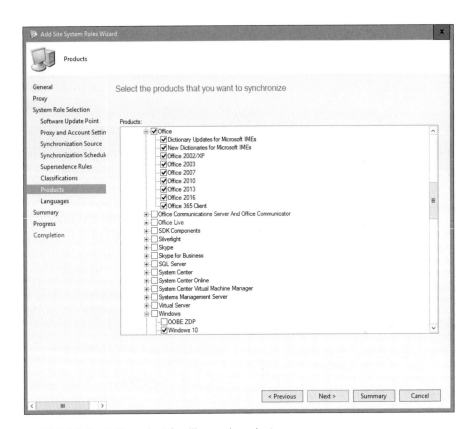

FIGURE 15.4   SUP product families and products.

If a software update selected for synchronization is applicable to multiple products, you will see those multiple products listed in the ConfigMgr console after synchronization completes. For example, if you selected Windows 7, the console would show updates for both Windows 7 and Windows Embedded Standard 7.

Product settings can only be configured at the top-level site. Once the changes are made, the software updates metadata is replicated to all child-level sites. Realize that the more products you sync, the longer the sync with Microsoft Updates takes; there is also a performance hit on the client side, as it takes longer to scan the catalog when more products are in it. The authors recommend selecting only products that are active in your organization.

Languages Page

The Languages page is the last configurable page of the wizard. This page allows you to choose the languages you want the software updates to appear in. There are two choices to select:

▶ **Software Update File:** This item allows you to select the different languages for which you want the software update files to be downloaded. For each language you select, one or more software update files are downloaded. For example, if you select English, French, and Spanish, then for every software update you want to deploy,

ConfigMgr will download the corresponding configured language versions of the software update file. Take care when selecting the languages, as your software update deployment package could be very large. The authors recommend that you select only the languages most often used in your organization. During the download process, you have the option of modifying the number of languages you want to download; this is an option you need to configure for each download.

▶ **Summary Details:** This option allows you to download the software updates metadata in the selected languages you choose. The metadata consists of items such as the name, description, products that the update supports, update classification, article ID, applicability rules, and so on. Because this is metadata, and metadata is replicated to other sites, this option is available only at the top-level site. The authors recommend selecting only the languages most common in your organization, as the more languages that you select, the longer synchronization with Microsoft Updates takes.

TIP: SUMMARY DETAILS LANGUAGE

Select all the needed languages before your first sync; if you select additional languages after synchronizing, then only new or changed updates metadata are downloaded in the new languages. Previously synced updates will not show up in the updated languages.

Verifying SUP Installation

After you complete the wizard, ConfigMgr starts the SUP install process, which you can follow in the SUPSetup.log file. When the install completes, verify that communication between the SUP and WSUS is working correctly. There are three log files to check:

▶ **WCM.log:** This log file is for the SMS WSUS Configuration Manager, which is responsible for connecting to WSUS and configuring it according to the settings selected in the SUP properties. In this log, you are looking for items like the following:

```
Successfully connected to server: Armada.Odyssey.com, port: 8530
Configuration successful. Will wait for 1 minute for any subscription or
proxy changes
Setting new configuration state to 2 (WSUS_CONFIG_SUCCESS)
```

▶ **WSUSCtrl.log:** This log file is for the SMS WSUS Control Manager, which is responsible for connecting to the WSUS server and verifying that connectivity is working correctly and that WSUS is running with the supported version. In this log file, you are looking for things like the following:

```
Checking for supported version of WSUS (min WSUS 3.0 SP2 + KB2720211 +
KB2734608)
Supported WSUS version found
Successfully connected to local WSUS server
There are no unhealthy WSUS Server components on WSUS Server
Armada.Odyssey.com
```

▶ **Wsyncmgr.log:** This log file is for the SMS WSUS Sync Manager. This component is responsible for communicating with WSUS and telling it to sync with Microsoft Updates. When that finishes, it syncs with the WSUS database. In this log, you are looking for items like the following:

```
Synchronizing WSUS server armada.odyssey.com ...
sync: Starting WSUS synchronization
sync: WSUS synchronizing categories
sync: WSUS synchronizing updates
Done synchronizing WSUS Server armada.odyssey.com
Synchronizing SMS database with WSUS server Armada.Odyssey.com
Sync succeeded
```

NOTE: ERROR SYNC FAILED

When looking in the Wsyncmgr.log file right after the SUP install, you might see something like this:

```
Sync failed: WSUS update source not found on site CAS. Please refer to
WCM.log for configuration error details. Source: getSiteUpdateSource
```

This error is caused by a timing issue. Before you can sync updates, WCM must connect to the WSUS server and configure it. This issue will fix itself over time, with the retry in 60 minutes.

Configuring Client-Side Components

To this point, the chapter has been about the server side: installing WSUS and installing and configuring the SUP. It is now time to look at the client side of things. You must configure the client-side settings so that clients can use those settings when scanning for and installing the software updates they need. You also need to look at group policy settings to see those settings for the WUA that are being pushed to clients; these settings may cause some issues with software updates being applied to clients.

Client Settings for Software Updates

The software updates client component is enabled by default; however, several other client settings must be configured for software updates to work correctly. Navigate in the ConfigMgr console to **Administration -> Overview -> Client Settings**. Locate **Default Client Settings** and select **Properties** from the ribbon bar or from the right-click context menu. The Default Settings dialog appears, as shown in Figure 15.5. For additional information about client settings, see Chapter 9, "Client Management."

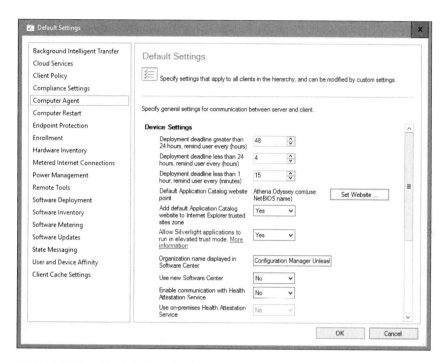

FIGURE 15.5   Client Default Settings.

Several settings in the Default Settings dialog affect how software updates work:

▶ **Computer Agent -> Deployment Deadline Reminders:** The first three options on this page deal with how the user is reminded that a deadline for deployments is about to occur. The first option is the number of hours to remind the user when the deployment is over 24 hours away from beginning. The second option is how often to remind the user when the deadline is less than 24 hours away. The third option is how often to notify the user when the deadline deployment is less than 1 hour away. The defaults for these three options are 48, 4, and 15, respectively.

▶ **Computer Agent -> Grace Period for Enforcement After Deployment Deadline (Hours):** This option allows you to set a period of time, in hours, to postpone the installation of required deployments, including software updates deployments, after the deadline passes. This allows end users who have been away for an extended length of time to not have to wait for required deployments to install before getting to use the system. The grace period value can be between 1 and 120 hours.

▶ **Computer Restart:** There are two options on this page; when a restart is required, the first option is how many minutes before the restart to provide a temporary notification to the user. The second option is the number of minutes before the restart to show a dialog box that cannot be closed by the user; this dialog displays the countdown interval before the user is logged off and the computer restarts.

▶ **Software Updates:** This section of the client settings page includes some key areas that directly affect the software updates component of the ConfigMgr client agent:

   ▶ **Enable Software Updates on Clients:** This option is turned on by default and must remain on for the clients to scan and apply software updates. If it is turned off, ConfigMgr removes existing deployment policies from the clients.

   ▶ **Software Update Scan Schedule:** This option allows you to set the schedule you want to use when the client will again scan the update catalog. The default value is every 7 days, using the simple schedule. The actual start time for the scan on client systems is based on the start time in the schedule plus a random amount of time up to two hours. This prevents all clients from initiating the scan at once.

NOTE: SCAN CATALOG

Client scans have always been a source of confusion. The client receives a policy from ConfigMgr that points it to the WSUS server for the site of which it is a member. The client then connects to the WSUS server and downloads a copy of the updates catalog, which is stored in C:\Windows\SoftwareDistribution\DataStore\DataStore.edb. The first download is large, as it includes the whole catalog; downloads after that are delta changes only. The client then runs its scan against this local catalog. The scan is good for 24 hours, and then the client must scan again for updates.

The client only uses the WSUS server to download the catalog. If a scan determines that a patch is needed, the patch is downloaded from the ConfigMgr package on the DP. The catalog contains only the metadata information about the patch; it does not contain any actual files used to patch systems.

   ▶ **Schedule Deployment Re-evaluation:** This option sets the schedule for when clients re-evaluate the installation status of any previously deployed and installed updates. If any updates are determined to be missing, they are reinstalled from the local ConfigMgr client cache or downloaded again from the DP, if necessary. This occurs once the client is in a maintenance window and free to perform the install. A simple schedule of every 7 days is set by default. The schedule should be set based on the company policy for software update compliance. If the organization is aggressive on compliance, the authors recommend using every 3 days as the schedule; consideration should be taken with a more aggressive schedule as it causes additional network and client CPU activity.

▶ **When Any Software Update Deployment Deadline Is Reached, Install All Other Software Update Deployments with Deadline Coming Within a Specified Period of Time:** This option groups multiple update deployments together into a single deployment if scheduled to occur within the period of time specified by the next setting, minimizing the impact on the end user and decreasing the number of reboots necessary with multiple, separate update deployments.

▶ **Period of Time for Which All Pending Deployments with Deadline in This Time Will Also Be Installed:** This setting is available only if the previous option is enabled by setting it to Yes. This is the period of time to consider update deployments for grouping according to the description of the previous setting.

▶ **Enable Management of the Office 365 Client Agent:** If this option is enabled when Office 365 updates are deployed, the ConfigMgr client agent communicates with the Office 365 client agent to download the Office 365 updates from a DP and install them.

▶ **State Messaging:** Client agent update scan and installation results are returned to the ConfigMgr site using state messages; to minimize network traffic and impact on the site server, state messages are not sent individually but bundled up on the client and sent only on the interval specified here. There is no way to trigger sending of state messages from the client to the server except to restart the client agent.

Group Policy Settings

Sometimes an organization creates several group policies that affect the software updates process on clients. If these policies are not set correctly, the software updates process can fail on clients. There are two areas of group policy to look at with regard to the software updates process:

▶ Specify intranet Microsoft update service location

▶ Configure Automatic Updates

Figure 15.6 shows the settings possible for Specify intranet Microsoft update service location. This group policy object (GPO) allows you to set the internal location of the WSUS server clients will use to scan against and from where they will download updates. If this GPO is being applied to an organizational unit (OU) that contains ConfigMgr clients, the GPO must be set to either Not Configured or Disabled; both settings turn off this GPO.

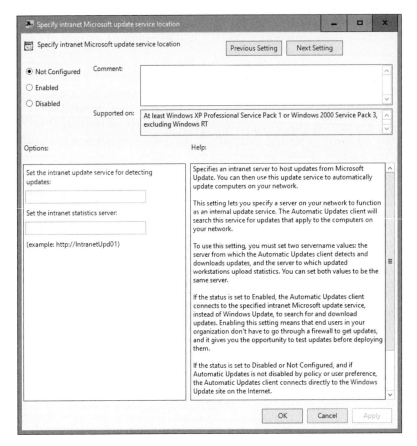

FIGURE 15.6   GPO setting for Specify intranet Microsoft update service location.

ConfigMgr creates a local group policy setting for the client to point to the ConfigMgr SUP with the WSUS server installed. A domain-based GPO overrides the local group policy setting and causes the ConfigMgr client to show this message in its WUAHandler.log file: Group policy settings were overwritten by a higher authority (Domain Controller). The domain GPO causes software updates to fail on the client. If this GPO was enabled, once it is disabled, make sure the clients refresh their domain policy to remove the GPO before retrying software updates.

Figure 15.7 shows the GPO settings for the Windows Update Agent.

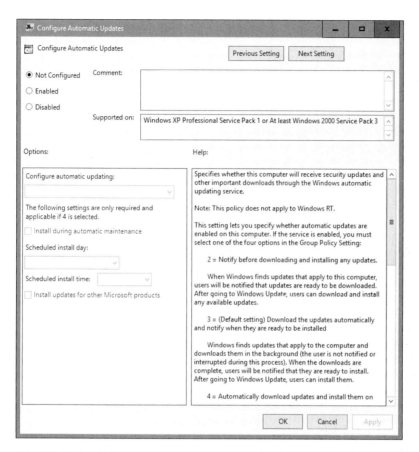

FIGURE 15.7   GPO for Windows Update Agent settings.

Settings in this GPO affect how the WUA works on the client and effectively control how it automatically handles updates, downloads, and installation of those updates. The keyword in the previous sentence is *automatically*; with ConfigMgr, the WUA should not do anything automatically, as the WSUS server itself does not have any updates for the clients; all updates are delivered via the content distribution mechanism in ConfigMgr and not WSUS. When a ConfigMgr client wants to do anything related to software updates, it directly controls the WUA to achieve the desired result; this includes update scans, reevaluations, and installation.

The authors recommend setting this GPO to Disabled. In the past, doing this was a problem because it caused an issue with updates to the WUA itself. Those updates were picked up by WSUS; however, since they were part of the `Infrastructure Updates` class, they were automatically set to approved in WSUS, causing them to be pushed out to all the clients as they connected to the WSUS server. To work around this issue, Microsoft now includes WUA updates in the WSUS catalog, so when ConfigMgr syncs with WSUS, the updates appear in ConfigMgr to be deployed to your clients.

Note that setting this GPO to Disabled doesn't actually disable the WUA service. It does disable all of the automatic functionality of the WUA, including scanning. This means the WUA is not automatically installing any updates or causing any issues with ConfigMgr; the service is there and running when needed but not doing anything until ConfigMgr tells it to through the WUAHandler component.

Creating and Deploying Updates

Previous sections discuss the theory of software updates, how they work with regard to the infrastructure, and how to install all the necessary components. The next sections show how to create and deploy the updates to clients, beginning with what is involved to get software updates into a group and deployed to a collection of machines. The following nodes of the console assist with completing this task; they can all be found in the navigation tree of the ConfigMgr console under Software Library -> Overview -> Software Updates:

- ▶ All Software Updates
- ▶ Software Update Groups
- ▶ Deployment Packages
- ▶ Automatic Deployment Rules
- ▶ Windows 10 Servicing

Using the All Software Updates Node

The All Software Updates node contains a master list of all the updates synchronized with the WSUS server. Clicking **All Software Updates** in the navigation tree causes the right side of the page to list the updates (see Figure 15.8).

FIGURE 15.8   All Software Updates node.

TIP: RETURNING A LARGE NUMBER OF RESULTS

By default, search results include only the top 1,000 items. When syncing software updates, you can easily get thousands or tens of thousands of update results. When you click the All Software Updates node, you may notice a highlight box right above the Search box that says `Configuration Manager returned a large number of results. You can narrow your results by using search. Or, click here to view a maximum of 100,000 results.` To change your search results, click in the Search box and then click **Search Settings** in the ribbon bar and change the results to any number you choose. The authors recommend changing the default from 1,000 to 15,000, as this should work for most organizations.

You may have noticed in Figure 15.8 that some of the updates show different icons. The icons indicate the status of the update. There can be several different statuses for the updates. Table 15.1 lists the different colors of icons and their meanings.

TABLE 15.1   Update Status Icons

Icon Color	Status
Green arrow	Normal software update
Black X	Expired software update
Yellow star	Superseded software update
Red X	Invalid software update
Blue arrow	Metadata-only software update

Table 15.1 is also valid for software update groups and deployment packages. Figure 15.8 shows an extra column added. It is very useful in troubleshooting to add columns to the display. In this case, Unique Update ID is added. In the client logs, updates are referenced by this ID. Add columns by right-clicking a column name, which causes a long list of additional column names to appear; just pick the one you want.

Selecting an update in the list brings up either Summary or Deployment information in the Details pane at the bottom. Double-clicking an update, right-clicking, and choosing Properties or selecting an update and then choosing Properties from the ribbon bar brings up detailed information about that update, organized on six tabs plus the Security tab that is present on every dialog box:

▶ **Software Update Details:** This tab displays information about the update, such as its bulletin ID, article ID, revision date, maximum severity rating, description, and application languages, as well as the affected products.

▶ **Maximum Run Time:** This is a value of time in minutes that the update installation is allowed to run. This number is different for each update; Windows 10 updates are typically 30 minutes, and other OS versions typically run 10 minutes. When using maintenance windows, this value is used to calculate whether there is enough time to install the update within the time remaining in the window.

▶ **Custom Severity:** You can set the custom severity of an update to one of five values, whose meanings you and your organization can define. ConfigMgr does not use these values in any way, but you can use them for filtering purposes:

> ▶ None
>
> ▶ Low
>
> ▶ Moderate
>
> ▶ Important
>
> ▶ Critical

▶ **Content Information:** This read-only tab contains information about the actual update file(s), whether it is downloaded, the size of the update (in megabytes), and the URL from which to download. Normally, ConfigMgr handles the download of the files listed in this tab; however, you can reference this tab if you find you need to review the location ConfigMgr is using or wish to download the file yourself. If you select a line in this list box and press **Ctrl+C**, the entire line is copied to the Windows Clipboard, and you can then paste it into Notepad to extract the URL.

▶ **Custom Bundle Information:** Bundles are groups of updates that are installed together, normally because they are tightly related or have interdependencies. If an update is part of a bundle, that bundle information is listed here.

▶ **Supersedence Information:** This tab lists any updates that this update supersedes or any updates superseding it. When there are multiple versions of an update, this tab is a good source of information for the latest version of the update.

You can select multiple updates to modify either their maximum runtime or custom severity at one time.

Sort the list of updates by clicking on any displayed header. You can also filter the list of updates to display only those you are interested in working with or examining. The first filtering technique is a simple text search: To evaluate and filter content from any displayed column that contains text, type in the word or phrase you want to search for in the Search box above the update list's header and click **Search**. Note that columns such as Required that contain counts, Downloaded that contain Boolean values, and Date released that contain dates are not considered to contain text and thus are not evaluated by the simple text search functionality. To clear the filter, click the **X** next to Search.

You can create advanced filters by combining multiple criteria and columns using **Add Criteria** to the right of Search. This drops down a list where you can select the categories on which you want to filter the list; select the categories and click **Add** to add an advanced filter section underneath the Search input box, where you can define the values for which to search. You can add criteria to the filter by selecting **Add Criteria** from the Search section of the ribbon bar.

Even with advanced filters, you may find that there are so many software updates that you can get lost looking for something. Consider using subfolders of the All Software

Updates node to organize your updates. Create and manage these subfolders by using the Folder tab on the ribbon bar or by right-clicking the All Software Updates node. You can apply filters to any subfolder. You must manually move updates into the subfolders you create. One popular method of using the subfolders is to create one for each year and under the yearly subfolder create each month, then add the month's updates into those subfolders. There are several methods for organizing software updates, but filters remain one of the best choices; they are dynamic, persistent, easily modified, and self-defining. Both filters and subfolders are part of the global data replicated to all sites in a hierarchy, making them available at every site.

TIP: FORCING A MANUAL SYNCHRONIZATION

Sometimes you need a current list of the software updates; in such cases, you must force a manual synchronization with Microsoft Updates. Right-click the **All Software Updates** node in the console and choose **Synchronize Software Updates** to force the WSUS server to sync with Microsoft Updates and cause the SUP to sync with the WSUS server. You can monitor the status in the wsyncmgr.log file.

Using Software Update Groups

When the software updates are available inside the ConfigMgr console, the next step in getting a deployment to clients is to create a software update group (SUG). The SUG is a container that holds a set of software updates you can use to organize the software updates in your environment.

SUGs do not contain actual updates; a SUG contains a reference or pointer to the update. You cannot deploy updates to clients without a SUG. When software updates are deployed to a collection of clients, the list of software updates in the SUG is sent to the client in the form of a client policy authorization list.

Create SUGs by selecting updates from the All Software Updates node or one of its subfolders. Use filters to help narrow down the updates you want to include. After selecting the updates, choose **Create Software Update Group** from the right-click context menu or from the Home tab of the ribbon bar to launch the Create Software Update Group dialog box. In this dialog, shown in Figure 15.9, enter the name and description for the new SUG. New SUGs appear under the Software Update Groups node in the navigation tree of the console.

FIGURE 15.9   Create Software Update Group dialog box.

If a SUG already exists and you want to add or remove software updates from the group, select the updates and choose **Edit Membership** from the right-click context menu or from the Home tab of the ribbon bar to launch the Edit Membership dialog; place a checkmark next to each update you want to add. Remove the checkmark next to any update you want to delete from the SUG. By doing this, you are not actually deleting the update from ConfigMgr; you are just removing the reference to the update in the SUG.

TIP: SOFTWARE UPDATE GROUPS REPLICATION

SUGs are considered part of global data and are replicated up and down the ConfigMgr hierarchy. This means that if you create a SUG on a primary child site, that information is replicated to the CAS. Since many SUGs may be created, the authors recommend always creating SUGs on the CAS. If you are not sure which site actually owns the SUG object, right-click the columns in the **Software Updates** node and add the column source site.

To determine overall compliance either for a set of software updates or all software updates, you could create a compliance group of software updates; this is a SUG without a corresponding deployment. Use this compliance group to evaluate the compliance of a set of updates against all systems in the console or any collection of systems using the built-in reports. New to ConfigMgr is the Software Updates Dashboard, available by selecting **Monitoring -> Overview -> Security -> Software Updates Dashboard**. The dashboard allows you to take a quick look at compliant versus noncompliant systems, and it includes a pie chart of security updates versus critical updates versus update rollups versus others. The Devices Missing Updates chart provides a quick view of the number of systems missing the various updates.

NOTE: 1,000 SOFTWARE UPDATES LIMIT

Software updates are deployed to clients via SUGs. There is a limit of 1,000 software updates for any deployed SUG. This limit exists to prevent performance issues on both the server side (summarizing such large deployments and for rendering reports) and the client side (processing large policy bodies containing more than 1,000 updates). A tremendous amount of SQL processing is required to correlate deployment and compliance states across all updates in a SUG that contains more than 1,000 updates. The authors recommend avoiding frequent modification of deployed update groups by adding/removing updates to them, as this causes significant overhead on the client in terms of policy processing and on the server in terms of SQL processing. You should make changes to software update deployment groups and packages on a monthly maintenance cycle.

Using Deployment Packages

After creating a SUG, download the software updates into a deployment package. Much like a software distribution package, a deployment package is the source location where software updates are downloaded. This can be a local folder on the site server or a network share elsewhere, and it must be created before it can be used as the source location folder. The local computer account of the site server and user downloading the software updates will require read and write permissions to the source local folder. Each deployment package must have its own source location folder; these folders cannot be shared between deployment packages.

It might seem as though the SUG and the deployment package are tied together as one unit. This is not true; the deployment package is not tied to the SUG. A SUG can have software updates that span multiple deployment packages.

Clients install software updates in a deployment by using any DP that has the software updates available, regardless of the deployment package. If a package is deleted for an active deployment, clients can still install the software updates in the deployment as long as each update was downloaded to at least one other deployment package and is available on a DP that is accessible to the client. After the last deployment package containing a software update is deleted, client computers cannot retrieve the software update until the update is again downloaded to a deployment package. Software updates appear with a red arrow in the ConfigMgr console when the software update files are not in any deployment packages. Deployments appear with a double red arrow if they contain any updates in this condition.

You cannot create a deployment package from the console. Use one of two wizards to create the deployment package:

▶ **Download Software Updates Wizard:** Navigate to **All Software Updates** and select a software update or a group of software updates. Choose **Download** from the right-click context menu or from the Home tab of the ribbon bar to access this wizard.

▶ **Deploy Software Updates Wizard:** Navigate to **All Software Updates** and select a software update or group of software updates. Choose **Deploy** from the right-click context menu or from the Home tab of the ribbon bar. When you choose this wizard and the software updates are not yet downloaded, the Download Software Updates Wizard pages are folded into this wizard; you see the pages for both wizards.

The Download Software Updates Wizard, displayed in Figure 15.10, contains six or eight pages, depending on what is selected for a deployment package. If Select a deployment package is selected, there are only six pages; if Create a new deployment package is selected, there are eight pages. In either case, the last three pages are the same as with almost all wizards in ConfigMgr—the Summary, Progress, and Completion pages. The following are the other Download Software Updates Wizard pages:

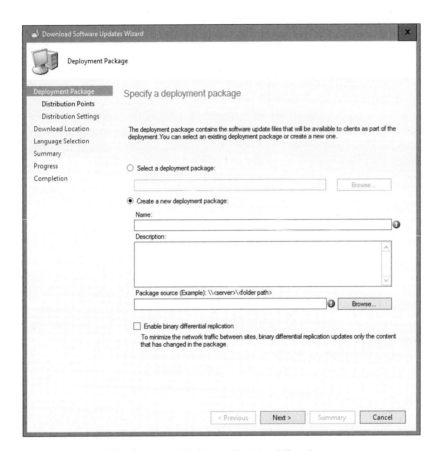

FIGURE 15.10   The Download Software Updates Wizard.

▶ **Deployment Package:** Select an existing deployment package by clicking Browse, or create a new package. If creating a new package, you must provide a name and description for the package; this appears in the Deployment Package node. You also must choose the source location of the package by using a URL path. The location you choose must exist before you run the wizard.

　　▶ **Distribution Points:** Select the DPs to which you want to send this package. You can choose from either a list of DPs or a DP group from a dropdown menu.

　　▶ **Distribution Settings:** Choose the type of settings to use with this distribution. You can choose your priority from a dropdown menu, whether you want to distribute the package to preferred DPs, and the behavior you want to occur when the DP is enabled for prestaged content.

▶ **Download Location:** Choose to use Microsoft Updates or a network share as the location from which to download updates. Most organizations choose to use Microsoft Updates. If your site does not have Internet access, select a network share as the location. This requires preloading the updates from a machine with Internet access and copying them to the network location to be used by the wizard.

▶ **Language Selection:** Choose the language to use when downloading the update files. For example, if you choose English and French, the wizard downloads two files for each update—one in English and one in French.

Monitor the download activity by looking at the PatchDownloader.log file. The downloads run under the current logged-in user running the wizard, so the log is in the temporary folder of that user: C:\users\<*username*>\AppData\Local\Temp. The AppData folder is hidden, so you may not see it until you change display options to show hidden folders.

Deployment packages are similar in nature to software packages but have some distinct differences:

▶ Clients needing to install an applicable update deployed to them using an update deployment would download that update from any available deployment package on any DP in the boundaries for that client.

▶ Deployment packages are not linked to update deployments in any way.

▶ Clients do not need to download an entire deployment package to install the software update; they can download a single update from any deployment package that has the update.

Since there are many software updates across a wide range of operating systems, deployment packages can be very large, which can cause issues when the content is distributed to DPs. A common failure for software updates is not ensuring that all applicable update packages are properly replicated and available on DPs where clients will request the updates. In general, the authors recommend making all your update packages available on every DP unless your DPs are tight on space or you have severe bandwidth limitations. The authors also recommend organizing deployment packages by the release date of updates, such as by year, by half year, or even by quarter, rolling over the updates into the yearly package as needed. This lets you cut down the size of the packages that are most often used.

Creating the Deployment

This section walks through creating the update deployment. An update deployment is the primary, active object in software updates. All other objects are just groupings of other objects or settings and are generally passive in nature. Update deployments are active objects; they assign the updates to clients and cause updates to be installed on managed systems. Without update deployments, software updates is purely a reporting feature set.

There are two methods for creating an update deployment. Both use the Deploy Software Updates Wizard, but one has fewer pages in the wizard than the other:

▶ **Starting with No SUG or Pre-created Deployment Package:** Start this wizard in the All Software Updates node of the console by selecting the software updates you want to deploy and choosing **Deploy** from the right-click context menu or from the Home tab of the ribbon bar. This launches the full wizard, containing all pages, and automatically creates the SUG and deployment package.

15

▶ **Pre-creating the SUG and the Deployment Package:** Launch this version of the wizard in the Software Update Groups node of the console by selecting the SUG you want to deploy and choosing **Deploy** from the right-click context menu or from the Home tab of the ribbon bar. The wizard is launched without the deployment package pages. Because you chose the SUG to deploy, that part of the General page is prefilled.

Figure 15.11 shows the Deploy Software Updates Wizard, launched by deploying an already created SUG and deployment package. The authors recommend first creating your SUG and package and then creating the update deployment by deploying the SUG.

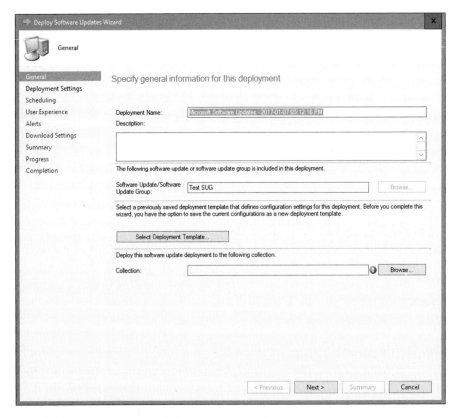

FIGURE 15.11   The Deploy Software Updates Wizard.

This version of the wizard contains nine pages; the last three are the same as with almost all wizards in ConfigMgr (Summary, Progress, and Completion), and the other pages are discussed in the following sections.

General Page

The first page of the wizard has five items to complete, and some of them are required before you can move on to the next page. These are the items on the General page:

▶ **Deployment Name:** This is required and is filled in automatically with the name Microsoft Software Updates - (*current date and time*). Remove this name and add a more meaningful name that describes what the software updates are for (for example, MS Software Updates for 2018).

▶ **Description:** This is an optional field where you can enter a brief description about the deployment.

▶ **Software Update/Software Update Group:** This required field is automatically filled. If you start the deployment by choosing to deploy a SUG, this is filled in with that SUG name and grayed out so you cannot change it. If you are deploying a single software update by selecting the update from the All Software Updates node and choosing **Deploy**, this is the name of that single software update. If you choose several updates from the All Software Updates node and choose **Deploy**, this has a general name filled in but is not grayed out, so you can change the name to be more meaningful. The name you choose will be the name of the SUG it creates.

▶ **Select Deployment Template:** Click this button to bring up a previously saved list of templates. The wizard then uses the pre-created template to show you the pages and settings that are in the template. This allows you to create deployments of the same nature and settings more quickly and also helps avoid human mistakes. To create a deployment template, complete the Deploy Software Updates Wizard and stop on the Summary page. From the top-right side of this page, select **Save As Template**; this allows you to choose the settings on the pages you want to include in the template and a name for the template. Figure 15.12 shows the Save As Template dialog box.

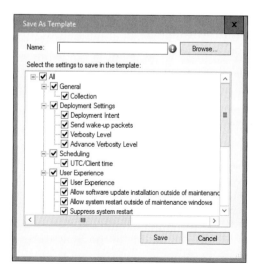

FIGURE 15.12   Save As Template dialog box.

▶ **Collection:** This is a required field. Clicking **Browse** allows you to select a pre-created collection of managed systems to which you want to deploy the software updates. You can only choose device collections; user-based collections cannot be targeted by software update deployments.

Deployment Settings Page

The Deployment Settings wizard page allows you to set the type of deployment you want to use and the level of message details. It provides the following options:

▶ **Type of Deployment:** Use this to select whether the deployment is mandatory. You have two choices from a dropdown menu:

  ▶ Required

  ▶ Available

NOTE: TYPE OF DEPLOYMENT AND DOWNLOADS

If you choose Required as the type of deployment, the client will download the software updates from the DP in the background and honor any Background Intelligent Transfer Service (BITS) settings configured for it. If you choose Available for the deployment type, the client downloads the software updates from the DP in the foreground and ignores any configured BITS settings.

▶ **Use Wake on LAN to Wake Up Clients for Required Deployments:** You can select this check box if the type of deployment is set to Required; it is grayed out if that option is set to Available. If this option is checked, ConfigMgr uses its built-in Wake on LAN functionally to send the magic packet that wakes up the client, and the client then installs the updates. Before using this option, computers and the network must be configured for Wake on LAN.

▶ **Detail Level:** This item allows you to choose the state message detail level that will be returned by the client for the deployment. There are three choices:

  ▶ **All Messages:** This allows all messages from the client to be returned, which is important if you want to view results as soon as the client does something. This is a good option to choose by default, as when someone runs the enforcement states for a deployment report or other compliance reports, he or she will see the detailed information the client has returned.

  ▶ **Only Success and Error Messages:** Use this option to tell the client to only return a state message about success and errors. Running compliance reports with this detail level set may display the last status as unknown. This is because no errors (or success messages) have been returned by the client. Using this option makes troubleshooting very hard if you run into issues.

  ▶ **Only Error Messages:** This option returns a state message only if an error occurs. The same issue applies as with the previous setting, where reports may show as unknown.

Scheduling Page

The Scheduling page allows you to select information about when the deployment will be scheduled to run. The time set here is also the time when end users begin to see notifications of the updates availability if notifications are enabled. If the deployment was set to Required on the previous page, this is the time that updates are available for downloading by the client. There are three options on this page:

▶ **Schedule Evaluation:** This dropdown menu option allows you to set whether a client will use local time or Coordinated Universal Time (UTC). The authors recommend accepting the default value, Client local time.

▶ **Software Available Time:** This radio button allows you to choose when the deployment is available to the client. You have two choices:

  ▶ **As Soon as Possible:** The deployment is available to the client as soon as it receives the policy for the deployment. If you choose Use the client local time in the Schedule evaluation item and choose this option, the current time on the machine where you are running the ConfigMgr console is the time that is set for clients to evaluate when updates are available or when they are installed. If the client is in a different time zone, these actions occur when the client's time reaches the evaluation time.

  ▶ **Specific Time:** If this option is chosen, the two menus below it become available. The first is a dropdown menu for the month and day, and the second is for the time to set.

▶ **Installation Deadline:** This option is available only if Required was chosen in the Deployment Settings page. It allows you to choose a date and time when the required deployment to install the software updates will start automatically. The same two options available in the Software available time are presented here: a dropdown menu for the month and day and the exact time for the deadline.

  The actual installation deadline time is the specific time you configure plus a random amount of time, up to two hours. This reduces the potential impact of all client computers in the destination collection installing the software updates in the deployment at the same time. You can configure the Computer Agent -> Disable deadline randomization setting to disable the installation randomization delay for the required software updates. The authors recommend not disabling randomization, as doing so would have all clients run the software updates installation at the same time.

▶ **Delay Enforcement of This Deployment According to User Preferences, up to the Grace Period Defined in Client Settings:** This option allows the end user to delay the installation of software updates until the grace period set in the client agent becomes applicable. This allows an end user returning from vacation or being away for an extended period from having to wait until all required deployments are installed before being able to use the system. The user can delay the installation until the grace period ends.

User Experience Page

Use the User Experience page to customize the end user's experience with software updates deployments. Some choices are dependent on the Type of Deployment setting. There are three areas to configure:

▶ **User Notifications:** Use this option to choose what you want the user to see when balloons display in the system tray. There are three choices:

  ▶ **Display in Software Center and Show All Notifications:** This option lets the end user see the deployment in Software Center and see all the balloon notifications for the deployment in the system tray.

  ▶ **Display in Software Center, and Only Show Notifications for Computer Restarts:** This choice shows the deployment in Software Center but shows the notification only when the computer needs a restart.

  ▶ **Hide in Software Center and All Notifications:** This hides the deployment from the end user, who will not see anything in Software Center and will not see balloon notifications in the system tray. This can cause issues because the end user is not notified when the reboot occurs and may lose data. This option is not available when Type of Deployment is set to Available.

▶ **Deadline Behavior:** This option allows you to choose what can be done to the system when it is outside the maintenance window. You can choose to install software updates or restart the system. If this option is unchecked, updates are not installed until the maintenance window time starts. This option is grayed out if Type of Deployment is set to Available.

▶ **Device Restart Behavior:** Choose whether to suppress system restart on servers and workstations. Some software updates require a system restart after the install. This option allows you to suppress that restart and have the user restart the system at a convenient time. The authors recommend always suppressing the restart for servers to prevent unplanned outages. This option is grayed out if Type of Deployment is set to Available.

▶ **Write Filter Handling for Windows Embedded Devices:** This option allows you to check the box to commit the changes at the deadline or during a maintenance window. Windows Embedded systems use an overlay to store changes made to the OS; those changes are removed when the device is restarted, restoring the device back to its original state. If deploying software updates to Windows Embedded systems, you should check this box so update installations are not lost. When you do check this box and a Windows Embedded system gets a software updates deployment, the ConfigMgr client requires the Windows Embedded system to reboot; it enters Service mode, allowing only administrators to log in. ConfigMgr then installs the software updates and restarts the Windows Embedded system in Normal mode.

TIP: SOFTWARE UPDATES AND WINDOWS EMBEDDED SYSTEMS

If deploying software updates to Windows Embedded devices, ensure that you are using a maintenance window. The Windows Embedded device should be a member of a collection with an established maintenance window applied. This allows you to manage when the write filter is disabled and enabled, as well as when the device can restart.

▶ **Software Updates Deployment Re-evaluation Behavior Upon Restart:** This item configures the client to run a new software updates compliance scan immediately after it installs software updates and restarts. This allows the client to check for any additional software updates that are applicable after the restart and install them during the same maintenance window.

Alerts Page

Use the Alerts page to configure the criteria to create an alert inside the ConfigMgr console. This page also lets you specify how you want to handle Operations Manager (OpsMgr) alerts when the client has the OpsMgr agent installed. The option for the ConfigMgr alert creation is only available if Type of Deployment is set to Required. The following options are available on the Alerts page:

▶ **Configuration Manager Alerts:** This option starts with a check box that enables the alert to be generated. Checking the box makes two options available for edit:

  ▶ Client compliance is below the following (percent)

  ▶ Offset from the deadline time

  The alert generation time box shows you the day and time the alert will be generated if the criteria are met. This box is not editable. Take care when setting the criteria for the ConfigMgr alert, as incorrect settings could cause false alerts to be generated.

▶ **Operations Manager Alerts:** This allows you to choose what to do with the OpsMgr agent when that agent is installed on the system and software updates need to be installed. There are two check boxes, which are unchecked by default:

  ▶ **Disable Operations Manager Alerts While Software Updates Run:** This check box does not actually put the OpsMgr agent into maintenance mode but suppresses alerts by pausing the OpsMgr health service running on the client. This can be seen by event ID 1217 in the application event log.

  ▶ **Generate Operations Manager Alert When a Software Update Installation Fails:** When a software update fails to install, event ID 11708 is usually generated. When this box is checked, the OpsMgr agent looks for this event ID and generates an OpsMgr alert. The OpsMgr agent is required and must be running on the client for this to occur.

Download Settings Page

The Download Settings Wizard page allows you to customize how the client downloads the software updates from the DP. There are options to deal with slow links, falling back to another content location, BranchCache, and clients that only have Internet connectivity:

▶ **Select the Deployment Option to Use When a Client Uses a DP from a Neighbor Boundary Group or the Default Site Boundary Group:** Choose to download or not download when the client cannot find the content on any DP within its own boundaries. If you allow the download, the client will look at DPs containing the content in a boundary group designated as a neighbor of the client or from the default site boundary group. Following are the two options you can select:

  ▶ Do not install software updates

  ▶ Download software updates from distribution point and install

▶ **When Software Updates Are Not Available on Any DP in the Current or Neighbor Boundary Group, Client Can Download and Install Software Updates from DPs in Site Default Boundary Group:** Choose if you want the client to download the content from the default site boundary when there are no other DPs with the content. You can choose from two options:

  ▶ Do not install software updates

  ▶ Download software updates from distribution point and install

▶ **Allow Clients to Share Content with Other Clients on the Same Subnet:** This option, which is checked by default, tells the clients whether they can use BranchCache for the content downloads. If BranchCache is not set up on the clients, this item has no effect on the content download.

▶ **If Software Updates Are Not Available on DP in Current, Neighbor or Site Boundary Groups, Download Content from Microsoft Updates:** If this option is checked, it allows the client connected to the local intranet to download updates from Microsoft Update if the updates are not found on the DPs. The authors recommend not checking this option.

▶ **Allow Clients on a Metered Internet Connection to Download Content After the Installation Deadline, Which Might Incur Additional Costs:** Select this option to tell the client it can download updates while using a metered Internet connection. Some Internet network providers charge based on the amount of data sent and received with the Internet connection. The authors recommend not enabling this option.

As update deployments only exist in the context of an update group or specific update, to view or edit an existing update deployment, you must first select the update group or update to which that the deployment belongs. Update deployments particular to the update group or update are displayed at the bottom of the Details pane when you select the Deployment tab. After selecting the deployment from the Details pane, you can enable, disable, delete, or view the properties of the deployment by selecting the corre-sponding buttons on the Deployment tab of the ribbon bar or from the right-click context menu of the deployment. The properties displayed in the update deployment's Properties dialog correspond to those configured using the Deploy Software Updates Wizard and are organized on tabs with the same names as the pages of the wizard.

Using Automatic Deployment Rules

Automatic deployment rules are a relatively new concept, introduced in ConfigMgr 2012 and enhanced in some of the latest builds of ConfigMgr Current Branch. An ADR automatically creates an update deployment including the SUG, the download of the updates to a deployment package, and the actual deployment of the SUG to a collection of clients. There are several options for an ADR as well, such as creating everything but not deploying the SUG to clients.

To create an ADR, navigate to **Automatic Deployment Rules** and choose **Create Automatic Deployment Rule** from the ribbon bar or from the right-click context menu to launch the Create Automatic Deployment Rule Wizard, displayed in Figure 15.13.

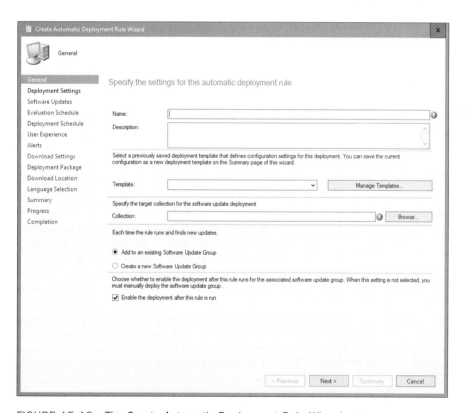

FIGURE 15.13   The Create Automatic Deployment Rule Wizard.

As Figure 15.13 shows, there are several pages to the ADR wizard, most of which you have already seen for creating the SUG, downloading updates, and deploying the updates. The following sections discuss the first four pages, as those are unique to the Create Automatic Deployment Rule Wizard.

General Page

Much like the General pages of other wizards, the General page of the Create Automatic Deployment Rule Wizard is where you start defining the basic items of the ADR, including the following:

▶ **Name:** This is required; unlike with other wizards that automatically fill in the name, the Create Automatic Deployment Rule Wizard leaves it blank. Use a name that is meaningful; it should describe what the ADR is creating.

▶ **Description:** This is an optional field where you can enter a brief description about the deployment.

▶ **Template:** This is a dropdown menu that brings up a list of templates that were previously saved. ConfigMgr also includes four templates for your use. The wizard uses the pre-created template you select to show the pages and settings that are in the template. This allows you to create ADRs of the same nature and settings faster and helps avoid human mistakes. To create a template, complete the Create Automatic Deployment Rule Wizard and stop on the Summary page, which has a Save as Template option on the top-right side. Selecting this option allows you to choose what settings on the pages you want to include in the template and a name for the template (refer to Figure 15.12).

The right-hand side has the option Manage Templates, which allows you to bring up a list of templates, select one, and then either rename the template or delete it.

▶ **Collection:** This is a required field. Click **Browse** and select a collection that will be targeted by this ADR. You can only select device collections.

▶ **Each Time the Rule Runs and Finds New Updates:** Use this item to choose what to do with the SUG if the ADR finds new updates when it runs. You can have the ADR create a new SUG for the new updates or add those to an existing SUG. If you choose to add the updates to a new SUG, beware that a single rule with this option enabled can create hundreds of SUGs in a small amount of time. The authors recommend adding the updates to an existing SUG.

TIP: SOFTWARE UPDATE GROUP NAME

You may notice in the wizard that when you select to use an existing SUG, there is no method for you to choose the SUG to which you want to assign the new updates. The first time the ADR runs, it creates a new SUG, using the same name as the ADR. Each subsequent evaluation of the ADR uses the same SUG.

▶ **Enable the Deployment After the Rule Is Run:** This check box enables the software updates deployment that the rule created after it completes its run. If this option is unchecked, the rule creates the deployment but leaves it disabled. The authors recommend leaving the deployment disabled until you verify that all settings are set correctly. You may want to send the deployment to a test collection to confirm that everything works properly. When the verification is complete, change this setting to enable the deployment.

Deployment Settings Page

The Deployment Settings page has several settings that also appear in other wizards as well as one that is only for ADRs. There are three options to configure on this page:

▶ **Use Wake on LAN to Wake Up Client for Required Deployments:** If this option is checked, ConfigMgr uses its built-in Wake on LAN functionally to send the magic packet that wakes up the client, and the client then installs the updates. Before using this option, computers and the network must be configured for Wake on LAN.

▶ **Detail Level:** Use this item to choose the state message detail level returned by the client for the deployment. There are three choices:

  ▶ All messages

  ▶ Only success and error messages

  ▶ Only error messages

▶ **Software Update License Agreement:** This option deals with software updates for which there are license agreements. A license agreement must be accepted before a software update can be deployed. Since the ADR rule automatically creates the deployment, there is no way to accept the license agreement. This item lets you choose whether to deploy only software updates that do not have a license agreement or those that have the license agreement already approved or deploy all software updates and approve any license agreements. The authors recommend this last option, which is the default.

Software Updates Page

The Software Updates page allows you to set the criteria used by the ADR to find software updates. The software update must meet the criteria defined to be included in the SUG that the ADR creates.

The Property filters section in the top area of this page of the wizard provides several check boxes for the item or items to use for criteria that the software update must meet. You can check as many of these as you like or as few as one of these items. After you select a check box, the bottom area fills with a link that you can select.

Search criteria at the bottom of the page has a link that allows you to fill in the criteria you want to use. The items you check in the Property filters section determine what type

15

of criteria you are allowed to enter (free text, numeric, and product selection). You can use quotes (" ") for an exact string match or the minus sign (-) to indicate that it does not match the item. For example, entering -**Itanium** in the title property criteria will exclude all updates that include Itanium in their title property. Once you have your criteria, click **Add** to add the criteria to the search list.

Evaluation Schedule Page

The Evaluation Schedule page allows you to choose how often the rule will run and evaluate the software updates. It has three options:

- ▶ **Do Not Run This Rule Automatically:** Select this rule when you want to only run the ADR manually. This might be an option when first setting up ADRs to verify that they are selecting the correct software updates.

- ▶ **Run the Rule After Any Software Update Point Synchronization:** This allows the ADR to run after the SUP synchronizes with Microsoft Updates. The authors recommend using this setting, which allows the ADR to truly be automatic and deploys software updates to the clients shortly after they are released.

- ▶ **Run the Rule on a Schedule:** This allows you to set a fixed date and time for the rule to run, such as the second Wednesday of each month at 2:30 PM. Select **Customize** to select a date and time to use. The authors recommend that if you set a schedule for the ADR to run, you should coordinate the time to run after your SUP synchronization time, so you evaluate the latest set of software updates.

When the ADR runs, it logs its information in the RuleEngine.log file. This file is located with the rest of the ConfigMgr logs in the Logs folder.

Understanding Windows 10 Servicing

A new feature in ConfigMgr Current Branch is the ability to service Windows 10 clients. New code is added, allowing older versions of Windows 10 to be upgraded to newer versions using the ConfigMgr software updates process. This new feature makes Windows upgrades much simpler for IT administrators, as the process is very streamlined and acts more like the software update installation process than the process of installing a new version of the OS.

Prior to Windows 10, Microsoft would release new versions or builds of the Windows product line every few years—think Windows XP, Windows Vista, Windows 7, Windows 8, and Windows 8.1. This meant that an organization went through a massive upgrade every several years, after testing the new version of Windows. Large organizations might still be deploying a version of Windows when Microsoft released a newer version. This caused some organizations to skip newer versions and not be current on newer features of the product. Microsoft changed the game with Windows 10; instead of new versions every few years, you will see new functionalities and features in smaller incremental updates two times a year. Microsoft created two ways for Windows 10 to be updated:

▶ **Feature Updates:** These are changes to Windows 10 that add new features and functionalities to the product. These are what previously would have been released in a new version of Windows, such as going from Windows 8 to Windows 8.1.

▶ **Quality Updates:** These are security fixes, product hotfixes, and rollup updates. An example would be the Patch Tuesday security fixes released every month. Another change for organizations is that the quality updates are now released as one cumulative monthly update instead of as several smaller updates.

These changes introduce some new challenges for organizations in how to upgrade or maintain the Windows 10 product being used and the type of support available if they do not upgrade or if they get behind in updating.

Servicing Branches in ConfigMgr

To align with the new approach of delivering feature updates and quality updates in Windows 10, Microsoft introduced the concept of *servicing branches* to allow customers to designate how aggressively their individual devices are updated. Microsoft created two branches:

▶ **Semi-Annual Channel:** This servicing model allows feature updates to be released twice a year, around March and September. This model is typically for consumers and businesses with general-purpose devices running Windows 10. The authors recommend that businesses take a gradual approach to incorporating these releases into their general population. Following this approach would involve a testing phase to see if current applications are compatible with the new release; once that testing is completed, a pilot group would test the update, and the organization would then move to a broader deployment. Each of these twice-a-year releases will be supported by Microsoft for 18 months from the time it is released.

▶ **Long-Term Servicing Channel:** This model is designed for businesses requiring the OS running on a machine to not change and to not have features added. Think of machines controlling medical equipment, point-of-sale (POS) systems, and machines running automation processes in a factory. These systems usually have a financial impact to the organization if they are taken offline or if they fail due to a new feature or update. This channel will see releases approximately every 2 to 3 years. These releases will be supported for 10 years from the date of release.

These new servicing channels mean that you must upgrade your Windows 10 devices at a much faster pace than previously to keep your systems current and keep you in a supported mode. More information about servicing branches and servicing of Windows 10 in general can be found at https://technet.microsoft.com/itpro/windows/manage/waas-overview#servicing-branches.

Table 15.2 shows the servicing options and their life cycles.

TABLE 15.2   Windows 10 Branch Servicing Options

Servicing Branch	Feature Upgrade Availability	Servicing Life Cycle	Supported Editions
Semi-Annual Channel	Twice per year, usually in March and September	Approximately 18 months	Home, Pro, Education, Enterprise
Long-Term Servicing Channel	Every 2 to 3 years	10 years	Enterprise Long-Term Servicing Channel

About Deployment Rings

Deploying previous versions of Windows, regardless of the size of your organization, was a challenge, to say the least. Going forward, deployment rings should make things a bit easier. Deployment rings allow you to group machines together for the purpose of creating a deployment time line. Each deployment ring reduces your risk and exposure to issues from the feature updates by allowing you to gradually deploy the update to rings of users; think of pilot testing groups here, with the difference being that the groups stay fairly consistent.

Microsoft has created a sample of what the deployment rings might look like:

▶ **Preview:** This is a pilot of IT users; users get this release through the Windows Insider Program and the Windows Insider for Business Program.

▶ **Targeted:** This is a pilot of business users; these devices should be across multiple teams and groups. These teams or groups should represent most of the departments in an organization. This ring should be used to test the release before it goes out for deployment to the global set of devices.

▶ **Broad:** This is a deployment to broad IT users; this will be your deployment to the rest of organization.

▶ **Critical:** This for devices that are deemed critical by the business. These devices should receive the update only after the rest of the organization has tested the release and shown that it does not present issues that would affect these critical devices.

CAUTION: RENAMING SERVICING TERMINOLOGY

Microsoft originally used Current Branch (CB), Current Branch for Business (CBB), and Long-Term Servicing Branch (LTSB) when describing Windows 10 servicing. This terminology has recently changed. Semi-Annual Channel takes the place of Current Branch for Business, Semi-Annual Channel (Targeted) replaces Current Branch, and Long-Term Servicing Channel (LTSC) takes the place of Long-Term Servicing Branch.

While Microsoft has publicly released this new terminology, ConfigMgr and several GPOs and other items inside Windows continue to use the terms Current Branch, Current Branch for Business, and Long-Term Servicing Branch. Keep an eye out as you use the current products and newer versions, as the terminology will be mixed until all products are updated with the newer terminology. This section continues to use the newer terminology where appropriate and the older terminology when it relates to ConfigMgr.

While not every organization will use the deployment rings, you should consider how many rings are needed and what users might encompass those rings. This way you can ensure that most issues with deployments of feature updates are found in pre-deployment testing and within the targeted ring.

The deployment rings are based on the servicing branches, so you begin by creating collections of the different servicing branches. This allows you to easily find users for each ring you need to create. The collections of these servicing branches are easily created in ConfigMgr, using an OS property collected as part of the ConfigMgr client discovery inventory, OSBranch. A WQL query that creates the collection follows:

```
select * from SMS_R_System where SMS_R_System.OSBranch = 0 and
SMS_R_System.OperatingSystemNameandVersion like "Microsoft Windows NT
Workstation 10.0%"
```

The values you can use for OSBranch are 0 for Current Branch, 1 for Current Branch for Business, and 2 for Long-Term Servicing Branch; this terminology has been replaced with the Semi-Annual Channel for Current Branch and Current Branch for Business and Long-Term Servicing Channel for Long-Term Servicing Branch. However, ConfigMgr and the OSBranch entries still use the terms Current Branch, Current Branch for Business, and Long-Term Servicing Branch; look for these to change in later releases of ConfigMgr and Windows 10. The second part of the query limits the data returned to only Windows 10 workstations.

Once your servicing branch collections are created, create collections for your rings by using the servicing branch collections as a limiting collection. This should give you a good idea of how many systems are in the different servicing branches and the users you would include in the different rings your deployment process uses.

TIP: WINDOWS INSIDER PROGRAM

The Windows Insider Program is open to anyone; it allows you to see early builds of Windows before they become part of the Semi-Annual Channel. Windows Insider PCs must be enrolled manually on each device and serviced based on the Windows Insider level chosen in the Settings app on that particular PC. Feature update servicing for Windows Insider devices occurs completely through Windows Update. For more information, see https://insider.windows.com. If you have Windows Insider PCs that you manage with ConfigMgr, create a collection for them and use that collection as an exclude collection for all servicing branch collections.

About Windows 10 Servicing Prerequisites

Before you start servicing Windows 10 devices, ensure that ConfigMgr is ready for servicing; this includes information needed to populate the data in the Windows 10 Servicing Dashboard. This is accomplished by implementing several processes you may already have done:

▶ **Software Update Point:** Windows 10 Servicing is delivered and executed by the software updates components on the server and client, so you need to have an installed and working SUP.

▶ **Heartbeat Discovery:** Information from Heartbeat Discovery is used to populate the Windows 10 Servicing Dashboard. The authors recommend setting the frequency of this setting to daily. The information is small and will not cause performance issues.

▶ **WSUS Updates to Support Windows 10 Feature Upgrades:** This is covered in the "Using Windows Software Update Services" section, earlier in this chapter.

▶ **Upgrade Classification and Windows 10 Product:** To deploy upgrades to clients, ensure that for the SUP properties, the **Upgrade** box on the Classification tab is checked and that **Windows 10** is checked on the Products tab. This allows the SUP to synchronize these items with Microsoft Update. These can be seen by navigating to **Software Library -> Overview -> Windows 10 Servicing -> All Windows 10 Updates** in the ConfigMgr console.

▶ **Assign Devices to the Correct Servicing Channel:** As part of the methodology for servicing Windows 10 devices, you must decide what devices to keep at Current Branch and which move to Current Branch for Business. Devices will be at Current Branch by default until moved to Current Branch for Business. A GPO is used to move devices to Current Branch for Business. Two GPOs are used, depending on the version of Windows 10:

  ▶ **Windows 10 Version 1511:** This version can be moved to Current Branch for Business using the GPO located at **Computer Configuration -> Administrative Templates -> Windows Components -> Windows Update -> Defer Upgrades and Updates**. Enable this GPO; no other settings need to be changed. Once the client receives the GPO enabling the setting, the client is considered Current Branch for Business.

  ▶ **Windows 10 Version 1607:** This version can be moved to Current Branch for Business using the GPO located at **Computer Configuration -> Policies -> Administrative Templates -> Windows Components -> Windows Update -> Defer Windows Updates**. Right-click the **Select when Feature Updates are received** settings and select **Edit**. Enable the policy and select the Current Branch for Business branch readiness level. Once the client receives the GPO enabling the setting, it is considered Current Branch for Business. Figure 15.14 shows this GPO setting.

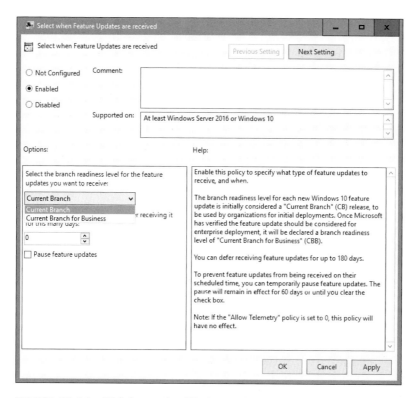

FIGURE 15.14   GPO for setting Windows 1607 to Current Branch for Business.

With the GPOs set and the machines at the correct serving level, when the ConfigMgr client runs the discovery process, the OSBranch property is collected and sent to the ConfigMgr database. This allows you to create your servicing branch collections. Either use GPOs or set a local machine policy for this information to be collected.

TIP: TYPES OF DEPLOYMENT AND DOWNLOADS

To prevent users from enrolling their devices in the Windows Insider program, set a GPO at **Computer Configuration** -> **Administrative Templates** -> **Windows Components** -> **Data Collection and Preview Builds** -> **Toggle user control over Insider builds.** Set this policy to **Disabled.**

Using the Windows 10 Servicing Dashboard

To help determine whether your Windows 10 machines are in Current Branch, Current Branch for Business, or Long-Term Servicing Branch, Microsoft created the Windows 10 Servicing Dashboard, which can be accessed by navigating to **Software Library** -> **Overview** -> **Windows 10 Servicing**. This dashboard shows a quick reference view of the active service plans, compliance for the deployed servicing plans, and life cycle information for Windows 10 versions. The dashboard relies on data from the heartbeat discovery information that clients send in and the service connection point (SCP). The SCP downloads metadata from Microsoft to display in the dashboard. Note that the data is only as good as the last download from the SCP. If the data does not seem right, check the SCP to confirm that it is working properly.

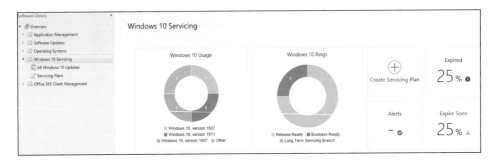

FIGURE 15.15   Windows 10 Servicing dashboard.

Figure 15.15 shows the dashboard with some of its tiles. Eight tiles provide Windows 10 information:

▶ **Windows 10 Usage:** This tile gives a breakdown of the Windows 10 builds managed by ConfigMgr. Each version of Windows shows in the tile below the ring. Moving the mouse over the tile or versions listed at the bottom of the tile highlights that part of the ring and shows the number of Windows 10 devices and their builds.

▶ **Windows 10 Rings:** This tile is by branch and readiness state:

  ▶ **LTSB:** The Long-Term Servicing Branch segment will be all Long-Term Servicing Branch versions, while the first tile breaks down the specific versions, such as Windows 10 2015 Long-Term Servicing Branch.

  ▶ **Release Ready:** This segment corresponds to Semi-Annual Channel, or Current Branch in versions of Windows 10 prior to version 1709.

  ▶ **Business Ready:** This segment is Semi-Annual Channel (targeted), or Current Branch for Business in versions of Windows 10 prior to version 1709.

  Move the mouse over the numbers in the ring or servicing branches at the bottom to highlight the number of machines in that portion of the ring and show a percentage.

▶ **Create Service Plan:** This tile provides a quick way to create a servicing plan (discussed in the "Servicing Plans" section of this chapter). Specify the name, collection (only the top 10 collections display, and they display by size, smallest first), deployment package (only the top 10 packages display, and they display by most recently modified), and servicing ring. Default values are used for the other settings; to change those defaults, click **Advanced Settings** to start the Create Servicing Plan Wizard, where you can configure all the settings, as shown in Figure 15.16.

Create Servicing Plan

Name

Target Collection

Deployment Package

Servicing Ring

Advanced Settings   Create

FIGURE 15.16   Create Servicing Plan tile.

▶ **Expired:** This tile displays the percentage of devices on a build of Windows 10 past its end-of-life. ConfigMgr determines the percentage from the metadata the SCP downloads and compares it against discovery data. A build past its end-of-life no longer receives monthly cumulative updates, including security updates. ConfigMgr rounds up to the next whole number for the percentage, so if the math says that you have 4.5% of machines in this state, the tile will show 5% for the number. This tile provides a good estimate of machines in this state, but you should follow up to obtain the exact number of machines.

▶ **Alerts:** This tile displays any active alerts.

▶ **Expire Soon:** This tile displays the percentage of computers on a build near end-of-life. This would mean that you have about four months before that build of Windows 10 is at end-of-life. As with the Expired tile, ConfigMgr rounds up to the next whole percentage number.

▶ **Service Plan Monitoring:** This tile displays the servicing plans you have created and a compliance chart for each plan, providing a quick overview of the current state of the servicing plan deployments. Clicking **Deploy Now** brings up a dialog box asking to select a collection. Once selected, the highlighted servicing plan is deployed to that collection, creating a basic servicing plan that uses all the default values. Use the ConfigMgr console to create a plan with custom options.

▶ **Windows 10 Builds:** This tile displays a fixed image time line that provides an overview of the Windows 10 builds currently released and gives you a general idea of when builds will transition into different states. This information is gathered by the SCP and should be verified. If the SCP is not working correctly, this information may be out of date.

The dashboard provides a great deal of information in a visual form, giving most users the information they need at a glance. To obtain more information, you need to drill deeper into the Windows 10–managed systems.

Servicing Plans

With the metadata for the Windows 10 upgrade packages inside ConfigMgr, you are ready for the next step: a servicing plan. A servicing plan allows you to upgrade your Windows 10 devices from one build to another. Servicing plans do not allow you to upgrade Windows 7 or Windows 8.1 to Windows 10; those types of upgrades need to use an upgrade sequence as described in Chapter 22, "Operating System Deployment." Servicing plans only use the upgrades software updates classification; other updates, such as cumulative security updates, must still use the software updates workflow.

Servicing plans are created using a wizard and share the same rule engine as the ADR. Some pages in the wizard are the same as the ones covered earlier in this chapter, in the "Using Automatic Deployment Rules" section. To start, open the ConfigMgr console and navigate to **Software Library -> Overview -> Windows 10 Servicing -> Servicing Plans** and choose **Create Servicing Plan** from the ribbon bar or from the right-click context menu to launch the Create Servicing Plan Wizard, displayed in Figure 15.17.

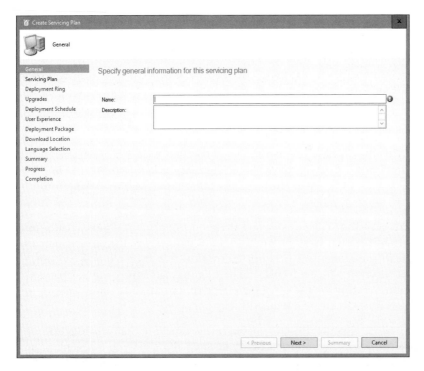

FIGURE 15.17   Create Servicing Plan Wizard.

As Figure 15.17 shows, the wizard has several pages. You may have seen many of these pages when creating the SUG or ADR, downloading updates, and deploying updates. The following are the first four pages, which are unique to the Create Servicing Plan Wizard:

▶ **General:** This page is similar to the General pages of other wizards; add a name that is meaningful and an optional description for this servicing plan.

▶ **Servicing Plan:** This page allows you to select the target collection to use for the servicing plan upgrade. Browse to choose from device collections; user collections are not allowed.

NOTE: HIGH-RISK DEPLOYMENTS

Servicing plans are considered high-risk deployments; if you choose a collection with more members than what is set in the Deployment Verification tab of the site properties, you will see a deployment verification warning message. You must agree to create the high-risk deployment, and an audit status message is created before you can continue. Figure 15.18 shows this message. If you choose a collection containing a machine hosting a site server role, you will receive a critical stop message, as shown in Figure 15.19, and will not be able to continue.

FIGURE 15.18   Deployment Verification warning message.

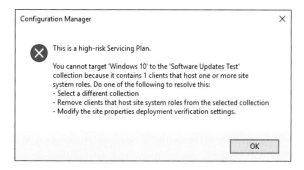

FIGURE 15.19   High-risk error message.

▶ **Deployment Ring:** The top of this page allows you to choose the Windows readiness state for this servicing plan. You can choose between Release Ready (Current Branch) and Business Ready (Current Branch for Business). In the middle of the page, you can select the number of days to delay the deployment after the new upgrade is published by Microsoft. This slider bar goes from 0 to 120 days. ConfigMgr evaluates whether to include an upgrade in the deployment if the current date is after the release date plus the number of days you configure for this setting.

▶ **Upgrades:** This page allows you to set the criteria to be used for the feature updates and upgrades for the deployment.

The Property filters in the top area of the page provide check boxes for Language, Required, and Title that you can use for criteria. Check as many or as few of these items as you want. After selecting a check box, the bottom area fills with a selectable link.

The Search criteria in the bottom of the page has a link allowing you to fill in the actual criteria you want to use. The items you check in the Property filters section determine the type of criteria you are allowed to enter (free text, numeric, and language selection). Use quotes (" ") for an exact string match or the minus sign (-) to indicate that it does not match the item. Once you have your criteria, click **Add** to add the criteria to the search list.

On the bottom-right side is Preview, which allows you to preview what updates and upgrades will be returned, based on the criteria selected. This provides a good opportunity to verify that you used the correct criteria.

After you complete the wizard, the servicing plan will run by default after the next SUP sync; change this by highlighting the servicing plan and choosing **Properties** from the ribbon bar or from the right-click context menu and navigating to the **Evaluation Schedule** tab. Once the rule runs, it adds updates that meet the specified criteria to a SUG, downloads the updates to the deployment package, distributes the updates to the configured DPs, and deploys the SUG to clients in the target collection. The name of the SUG is automatically created and is changeable by choosing the properties of the SUG.

TIP: REQUIRED OR AVAILABLE

The Deployment Schedule page or tab of the servicing plan properties is where you set the available time and installation deadline. As this is an upgrade and will cause an outage for the end user, the authors recommend setting the installation deadline ahead two or three weeks to give sufficient time for the user to prepare for the upgrade or even run it manually.

When the servicing plan rule runs, it downloads the upgrade and/or update packages from Microsoft Update. These packages are in excess of 2GB, and the rule will download x64 and x86 versions of the packages. Once downloaded, the packages are distributed to the DPs. Allow time for the download and content distribution to occur before the deployment becomes available to the end user. The authors recommend setting the available time to four hours or more from the current time of creating the servicing plan.

Since the servicing plan rule and ADR use the same engine, you can monitor the process of the rule running in the RuleEngine.log file. Downloads are logged in PatchDownloader.log.

Client Experience

The discussion so far in this chapter has covered the server side, configuring settings, and creating the deployment. Now it is time to consider the client side of things. What does the user see? What types of notifications take place? Is there any interaction with the user? When does a reboot occur? Many answers to questions such as these are determined by the configured settings and by some of the processes created in your update design.

Almost all client activity for software updates takes place in the background, across multiple client components. These components interact with each other, creating and managing internal jobs to detect the updates needed, scanning to see the state of updates the machine has and needs, downloading the needed updates, installing the updates, and reporting the status of the updates (installed, failed, reboot needed, and so on).

Software update deployments can be created to be totally silent, to notify the user every step of the way, or to do something in between. The following sections point out the differences the user will see but focus mainly on full user notification.

Compliance Scanning

Each computer performs compliance scanning based on the schedule set in the Software Updates section of client settings. The ConfigMgr's client scan agent triggers the client's WUA to download the update catalog from the WSUS instance corresponding to the SUP with which the client is configured to communicate. The catalog is then cached locally, and the system is scanned for update applicability. Note that the entire update catalog is not downloaded each time; only the changed portion of the catalog is downloaded; this is typically called the *delta*. To manually start compliance scanning, initiate a software updates scan cycle from the ConfigMgr Control Panel applet.

Scan results are stored in WMI, using the `ccm_updatestatus` class in the `root\ccm\softwareupdates\updatesstore` namespace. State messages send the results back to the ConfigMgr site. These are XML messages cached on the client for 15 minutes (by default) and submitted in bulk to the client's site MP. They relay point-in-time information about the client to the site.

TIP: DETAIL ABOUT STATE MESSAGES

For a detailed look at the state messaging system in ConfigMgr, see http://blogs.msdn.com/b/steverac/archive/2011/01/07/sccm-state-messaging-in-depth.aspx. This is specific to ConfigMgr 2007 but also applies to ConfigMgr Current Branch. This blog post has a script that allows you to resync the state messages from a client if they get out of sync with the site.

The WUA performs the compliance scan and marks each update with a compliance state. An update can be in one of four states:

▶ **Required:** This means the update is still needed on the client system or that it is installed but requires a restart. If the update needs a reboot, it is not considered installed until that reboot occurs.

▶ **Not Required:** This means the update is not applicable on the local system.

▶ **Installed:** This means the update is already successfully installed on the local system.

▶ **Unknown:** There are many reasons for an unknown update status, including communication issues, client scan issues, and configuration issues. The client's WUAHandler.log is the first place to check to verify proper configuration.

Scan results are good for 24 hours; this is called the time to live (TTL). When the TTL expires, the results are not considered accurate. When the client receives a software updates deployment, the TTL is ignored, and a fresh scan is performed.

Using Notifications

Notifications inform the user of what is occurring on the system. Some users like notifications, and others do not. Some users like to be told what is happening; others do not want to be interrupted with notifications. If notifications are disabled in client settings, no notifications from ConfigMgr are ever displayed on the client machine. If notifications are enabled, there are different levels that can occur, based on settings in the deployment. Table 15.3 shows these different levels and the notifications the user will see.

TABLE 15.3   Software Update Notifications

Level of Notification	Available Deployment	Required Deployment
Display in Software Center and show all notifications	A taskbar notification icon and an initial balloon popup. The notification icon persists as long as the updates are still applicable and available.	A taskbar notification icon and an initial balloon popup. The notification icon persists as long as the updates are still applicable and required. The notification balloon reappears based on the deployment deadline reminders settings on the Computer Agent page of the client settings.
Display in Software Center and only show notifications for computer restarts	No notification is displayed for updates, but notification is displayed according to the restart setting in the client settings page.	No notification is displayed for updates, but notification is displayed according to the restart setting in the client settings page.
Hide in Software Center and all notifications	Not applicable to this state.	No notification is displayed for updates.

Notification is presented by a balloon in the system tray of the machine. Figure 15.20 shows the balloon displayed when the user is notified that updates need to be installed.

FIGURE 15.20   Software updates balloon notification.

TIP: BALLOON DISPLAY TIME

By default, the balloon stays on the screen for five seconds. This often is not long enough for a user to notice that something has changed on the screen. To improve user experience with all balloons on a system, you can change this time to a longer value. In Windows 7, 8.1, and 10, change this by selecting **Control Panel -> Ease of Access -> Use the computer without a display**. Find the dropdown called **How long should Windows notification dialog boxes stay open,** which shows several times to choose from. You can also change this value via the Registry, at `HKEY_CURRENT_USER\Control Panel\ Accessibility\MessageDuration`.

In addition to the balloon, a new item is added to the system tray—a box with a red plus sign. If you right-click this icon and choose **View Required Software**, the dialog box shown in Figure 15.21 appears.

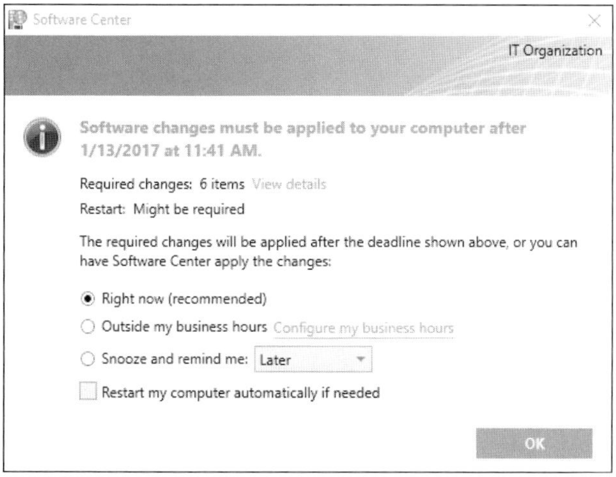

FIGURE 15.21   Software Center Changes dialog box.

This dialog box has several options for the user:

▶ **View Details:** Click this link to open the full Software Center program and see all details for each software update that needs to be installed.

▶ **Right Now (Recommended):** Choosing this option starts the installation immediately.

▶ **Outside My Business Hours:** Each system has a defined set of business hours, found inside Software Center. By default, business hours are set at 5 AM through 10 PM Monday through Friday. Selecting this option causes the software updates to only install outside those hours. Clicking a hyperlink in this option opens Software Center, which shows the business hours.

▶ **Snooze and Remind Me Later:** Select this dropdown to choose to be reminded at a later time.

▶ **Restart My Computer Automatically if Needed:** If this option is checked, the system reboots without warning after installing the software updates, if needed.

The software changes dialog box shown in Figure 15.21 and these options are displayed only when the software updates deployment is set to Available and the deadline has not been reached.

Using Software Center

Software Center is the heart of the user experience for ConfigMgr. Microsoft has redesigned it to be more intuitive and user friendly. In regard to software updates, an Updates section shows the number of updates needed as a quick view. Clicking **Updates** gives you a full list of the updates, their publisher, and the status of each update. The Install All button allows the user to manually install the updates at will. Figure 15.22 shows the new Software Center.

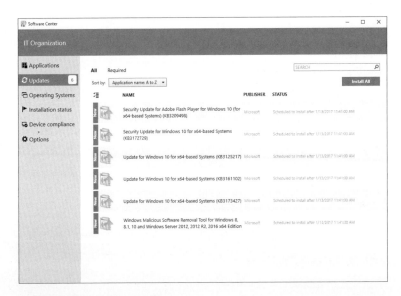

FIGURE 15.22   Software Center.

The Installation status section of the dialog shows the status of the updates or applications as they are being installed. An update can go through several different statuses as the install occurs:

▶ **Available:** The update is available for immediate installation.

▶ **Scheduled to Install After:** This is a required update, scheduled to install after the date and time specified in the status message.

▶ **Past Due - Will Be Installed:** This indicates that a required update is past its scheduled installation time. Updates are often in this status because of maintenance windows or failure to locate content.

▶ **Preparing to Download:** The client agent is finding an available location for the update's content.

▶ **Downloading:** The client agent is downloading the content from an available location. This status also includes a percentage complete.

▶ **Waiting to Install:** The update is preparing to install.

▶ **Installing:** The update is installing.

▶ **Pending Verification:** The update is installed but being verified.

▶ **Installed:** The update is already installed and is verified as installed.

▶ **Requires Restart:** The update requires a reboot to complete installation.

If an update is actively downloading or installing and notifications are enabled, an icon shows in the taskbar icon notification area with a tooltip that reads Downloading and installing software.

Installing Updates and Reporting Status

The next step is installing the updates and reporting status back to ConfigMgr. The user can choose to install the updates using Software Center before the deadline occurs or to wait until the deadline, at which point the installation will occur automatically. If the user chooses to wait, he or she sees the reminders balloon notifications according to the Client Settings -> Computer Agent settings described in the "Configuring Client-Side Components" section, earlier in this chapter.

If the user chooses to install the updates through **Software Center -> Updates**, he or she can click on a single update to display the information about that update and a button that allows for update installation or scheduling of update installation, as shown in Figure 15.23.

A user who wants to install all the updates at once can click **Install All** (refer to Figure 15.22).

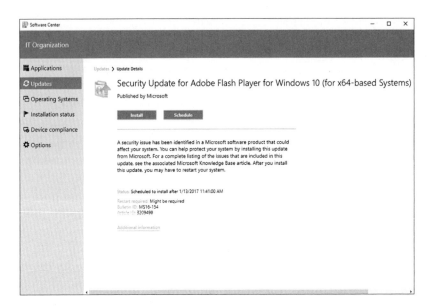

FIGURE 15.23   Software Center Update Details.

Once the updates are installed, if a reboot is needed, a Restart required balloon notification is displayed, as shown in Figure 15.24.

FIGURE 15.24   Software updates Restart required balloon.

Since the user may not be ready to reboot at that specific time, ConfigMgr places an icon in the system tray, as shown in Figure 15.25, to remind the user to reboot.

FIGURE 15.25   Software updates Restart icon.

If the user chooses not to reboot before the deadline, the icon remains in the system tray, and the user is notified with balloon notifications according to the reminders set up in Client Settings -> Computer Restart.

At each step, state messages are sent to the MP with which the client is communicating. These state messages help track the installation status of the updates and can be seen in the console by navigating to **Monitoring -> Overview -> Deployments**. If a reboot is needed, the update is not considered installed until it occurs. After the reboot, there may be a delay in reporting that the update is installed. To prevent this delay, Microsoft added a check box forcing a software updates deployment reevaluation upon restart to the User Experience tab of the software updates deployment. If this option is checked, after the reboot occurs, the ConfigMgr client runs the reevaluation, sees that the update is installed, creates a state message, and sends it to the MP, where it is processed into the database.

Troubleshooting Software Updates

There are many points where the software update process can break down. Multiple components coordinate their efforts to make the process work normally. When something goes wrong, your first step is to identify the component having issues. Depending on the exact failure point, you can review a variety of log files for error messages. It is also important to track and report on the status of software updates for everyone to know the organization's compliance level and to find failures or unpatched machines quickly. The next sections discuss how to monitor software updates as well as areas that typically have issues and how to diagnose and (hopefully) fix them.

In addition to the information presented here, four excellent blog posts are available that review and step through the in-depth minutia of the software update process, as viewed through the log files. Some of these are older posts but still can be applied to ConfigMgr Current Branch:

▶ https://blogs.msdn.microsoft.com/steverac/2011/04/10/software-updatesinternals-mms-2011-sessionpart-i/

▶ https://blogs.msdn.microsoft.com/steverac/2011/04/16/software-updatesinternals-mms-2011-sessionpart-ii/

▶ https://blogs.msdn.microsoft.com/steverac/2011/04/30/software-updatesinternals-mms-2011-sessionpart-iii/

▶ https://blogs.technet.microsoft.com/configurationmgr/2016/08/25/software-updates-in-configuration-manager-current-branch-deep-dive-client-operations/

Monitoring the Updates Process

To monitor the updates process, navigate to **Monitoring -> Overview -> Deployments**. Find your software updates deployment in the list and select it. At the bottom of the page, a pie chart shows the current summarization status of the deployment, which can be useful for a quick update. Choose **View Status** from the ribbon bar or from the right-click context menu to open the Deployment Status page, where you can see the following five states that the deployment could be in:

▶ **Success:** Machines listed here have successfully completed the software updates deployment. They report in green.

▶ **In Process:** These are machines currently running the software updates deployment but have not yet finished. These are reported in yellow.

▶ **Error:** These are machines that received the software updates deployment but ran into an error when trying to download the content or execute the deployment. Dig deeper by looking at the lower part of the page, at Asset Details. One of the details is the error code returned from the client. This can give you an idea of where to start looking for the issue with that client.

▶ **Requirements Not Met:** Machines in this state received the deployment but did not meet the rules that allow the deployment to run.

▶ **Unknown:** All systems appear in this state once the deployment is created. When a system returns a state message, it moves out of this state. If you see machines in this state after the deployment has been running a while, they did not receive the deployment and could be broken clients.

Another area in Monitoring that can be helpful is Software Update Point Synchronization Status. This section allows you to see the current status of the SUPs, when their last synchronization attempt was, the status of that attempt, and the catalog version on each SUP. This lets you quickly see if there are sync problems or if the SUPs are using old catalog versions. If a client is saying that it doesn't need an update, it may be that it is scanning against an older version of the catalog.

WSUS and SUP in Software Updates

The first component in software updates is WSUS. WSUS is significant because it acquires all information about available software updates and distributes that catalog of software updates to clients. ConfigMgr takes over control of WSUS by using a SUP, and it creates detailed log files of the WSUS operation. Following are the three main log files, located in *<ConfigMgrInstallPath>*\Logs, to look at for issues with your WSUS and SUP:

▶ **WCM.log:** This component provides information about the SUP configuration and connecting to the WSUS server for subscribed update categories, classifications, and languages. When changes are made to the SUP's settings, this component connects to WSUS and makes the changes. If you change your settings on WSUS, this component will connect to WSUS and overwrite those changes.

▶ **WSUSCtrl.log:** This log file provides information about the configuration, database connectivity, and health of the WSUS server for the site. Once an hour, this component connects to the WSUS website to verify that connectivity is working. If your SUP is remote, this log file is located on the remote SUP.

▶ **wsyncmgr.log:** This component synchronizes WSUS with Microsoft Updates and then synchronizes ConfigMgr with WSUS; it is a two-part process.

Most errors experienced with WSUS are configuration errors, including not matching the ports configured during installation of WSUS and then configured in the SUP. Remember that with WSUS 4.0 and above, the default port is 8530.

Also common are Internet connectivity issues due to firewalls, proxy servers, and other mitigating factors. Confirm that the system running WSUS has Internet connectivity if you are downloading the update catalog directly from Microsoft and ensure that you have properly configured the proxy account if one is required.

TIP: WSUS IIS APPLICATION POOL MEMORY

One issue the authors have seen is when the IIS application pool for the WSUS website is set to the default memory amount. With the larger number of updates in WSUS, there are more download trips from the clients, which uses a larger amount of memory from the IIS application pool. To fix this issue, the authors recommend increasing the WSUS IIS application pool memory. What you increase it to depends on the number of clients using that SUP and how many updates you are synchronizing. The default amount of memory is set to 1.8GB; the authors suggest changing this to 4GB to start and increasing by 2GB from there if problems occur. The blog post at https://blogs.technet.microsoft.com/configurationmgr/2015/03/23/configmgr-2012-support-tip-wsus-sync-fails-with-http-503-errors/ explains more about this issue and how to increase the memory.

Downloading Updates

Update downloads from Microsoft can fail. Recall that WSUS does not download the updates in ConfigMgr; you must manually initiate download of all updates when not using ADRs. This is an interactive process; ConfigMgr initiates a connection to the Microsoft download servers using credentials of the user currently logged in to the console. Test connectivity for that user by opening Internet Explorer and navigating to http://www.microsoft.com/downloads. (If a proxy server is required to connect to the Internet, configure the settings in Internet Explorer.) If the logged-in user does not have permission to perform the action, the download does not occur.

For ADRs, the site server hosting the SUP downloads the updates for you. This uses that system's local system account, which in turn uses that system's AD computer account for its identity on the network.

The PatchDownloader.log file logs download activity for updates and contains information about the update download process. The file is located in different places, depending on who is running the downloads:

▶ **SMS_CCM\Logs:** When the ADR runs, it runs as Local System and creates the log file in this folder.

▶ **%User%\AppData\Local\Temp:** When downloading updates, the file is created under the user's temp folder. Some folders are hidden, so make sure you are viewing hidden files to see them.

Troubleshooting Client Scanning and Update Deployment

WUA on the local system handles the process of scanning a client for applicable updates. The ConfigMgr agent initiates the scanning according to the defined schedules or any on-demand requests; the WUA in turn reports to the ConfigMgr agent. The WUA connects to the WSUS/SUP server and downloads an updated catalog to scan against; this is the only time the client uses the WSUS server. The following client log files, located in the %*windir*%\CCM\logs folder, can help when investigating failures:

▶ **ScanAgent.log:** Provides information about the scan requests for software updates, the tool requested for the scan, and the WSUS location. If your clients do not seem to be requesting the newer software updates, it could be that the scan has failed or the scan is not getting a current copy of the catalog. This log is a good place to start.

▶ **UpdatesDeployment.log:** Provides information about the deployment on the client. This includes software update activation, evaluation, and enforcement. This log also shows all the software updates deployments the client has received. You can also see the downloads of the updates in this log.

▶ **UpdatesHandler.log:** Provides information about software update compliance scanning as well as download and installation of software updates on the client.

▶ **UpdatesStore.log:** Provides information about the compliance status for software updates assessed during the compliance scan cycle.

▶ **WUAHandler.log:** Provides information regarding when the WUA on the client searches for software updates. One of the main issues that can affect the scanning process is a domain-based GPO overriding the Windows Updates settings. The WUAHandler.log file clearly indicates if this issue exists in your environment.

Troubleshooting Software Updates

Most of the time WSUS works fine; it works so well that most folks forget about it, which is when problems start to form. You won't see them right away, but after a while, they can creep up on you. You should be doing four items as part of your weekly or monthly maintenance process:

▶ **Back Up the WSUS Database:** You may ask why, as there is nothing in the database that you cannot recover by rebuilding the SUP or synchronizing with Microsoft Updates. While this is true, why waste the time to resync everything when you can restore a small backup and be up and running again quickly? Plus, if you are using System Center Update Publisher (SCUP), a lot of custom information will be lost if you lose the SUSDB. Use SQL backup or any other backup program that works with SQL databases. This can even be set up as an automated process using a SQL job and the SQL agent.

▶ **Run the WSUS Server Cleanup Wizard:** ConfigMgr now provides a check box for this in the Supersedence Rules tab of the SUP properties of a site. However, this is only run every 30 days. In some organizations, it should be run every week. If it has been a long time since this was last run—or perhaps has never run—the wizard may time out. The fix is to run it repeatedly until it stops timing out.

▶ **Decline Superseded Updates:** Since the client downloads the entire catalog the first time and then delta updates afterward to scan against, that catalog will contain any superseded updates that have not been declined. Declining the superseded updates reduces the size of the catalog and the amount of time the client needs to complete a scan.

▶ **Re-index the WSUS Database:** An index allows the database to be read faster, giving results quicker. Over time, with updates and deletions, the index can become out of date and may actually cause a slowdown in reading data. For optimal performance, re-index the database monthly or every week, if possible.

Most of these steps can be scripted and automated. See https://blogs.technet.microsoft .com/configurationmgr/2016/01/26/the-complete-guide-to-microsoft-wsus-and-configuration-manager-sup-maintenance/ for additional information.

Microsoft has released some best practices for software updates with ConfigMgr, which can help give the best performance overall:

▶ Use a shared WSUS database for SUPs.

▶ When ConfigMgr and WSUS use the same SQL Server instance, configure one of them to use a named instance and the other to use the default instance of SQL Server.

▶ Specify the Store updates locally setting for the WSUS installation.

▶ Limit software updates to 1,000 in a single software updates deployment.

▶ Create a new SUG each time an ADR runs for Patch Tuesday and for general deployment.

▶ Use an existing SUG for ADRs for Endpoint Protection definition updates.

In-depth information for these items can be found at https://docs.microsoft.com/sccm/ sum/plan-design/software-updates-best-practices.

Using the System Center Update Publisher

One issue organizations have with the software update process is that it only allows deployment of Microsoft updates. What happens when you need to deploy a third-party update? One approach is to use the System Center Update Publisher. This tool from Microsoft allows you to publish items to a WSUS server. When ConfigMgr synchronizes with that WSUS server, the published item appears in the Software Updates section of the console. SCUP also allows third parties, including vendors and administrators, to publish their own catalogs for use with ConfigMgr software updates.

SCUP is not included with ConfigMgr but is a separate and free download from Microsoft, available at http://www.microsoft.com/download/details.aspx?id=11940. The tool lets you import updates from non-Microsoft products into ConfigMgr or define your own for third-party products or in-house applications; these non-Microsoft updates sit side-by-side with the Microsoft updates in the ConfigMgr console and are managed and deployed exactly the same way as Microsoft updates contained in the WSUS catalog. Many administrators have also used SCUP to deploy Microsoft updates not included in the WSUS catalog. Updates are updates, and managing them the same way regardless of their source has great value.

Installing SCUP

Windows Server 2008 R2 is removed for use as a SUP with all publicly released ConfigMgr builds after ConfigMgr Current Branch version 1610, and since SCUP does not yet support the WSUS version released with Windows Server 2016, you must use Windows Server 2012 R2 for your SUP role if you need to use SCUP. SUP servers running WSUS 4.1, which is included with Windows Server 2012 R2, are not able to communicate with WSUS versions 3.0, 3.2, and 4.0. As SCUP is very tightly integrated with WSUS, the machine you install SCUP on must have the same 4.1 version of the WSUS console installed on it as the SUP to which you want to publish. If you try to use a different version of WSUS on the SCUP machine, you will get an error when trying to publish to the WSUS server. This error shows up in the SCUP log file as a version mismatch: `Publish: A fatal error occurred during publishing: Publishing operation failed because the console and remote server versions do not match`. Because of this issue with the version mismatch, there are only two operating systems you can use to install SCUP:

▶ Windows 8.1

▶ Windows Server 2012 R2

You can install SCUP on any system with connectivity to your top-level SUP, including the site server or a remote workstation that also has the WSUS administration console installed (or full WSUS) and is one of these listed operating systems.

NOTE: USING SERVER 2016 FOR YOUR SITE SERVER

If your site server is running Windows Server 2016, you must install your first active SUP on a remote Windows Server 2012 R2 machine. This allows the machine you install SCUP on to use the same WSUS version as your SUP. This is needed only if you plan to use SCUP with ConfigMgr.

If using Windows 8.1 for you SCUP workstation, install the Remote Server Administration Tools (RSAT) for Windows 8.1. Part of the RSAT installation also installs the WSUS 4.1 console and binary files that allow the SCUP application to connect to the Windows Server 2012 R2 WSUS server. This in turn allows the Windows 8.1 workstation to publish items into the WSUS server. Download the RSAT tools from http://www.microsoft.com/download/details.aspx?id=39296. If using a Windows 2012 R2 SUP server for the SCUP install, the WSUS server is already installed on that machine.

No matter which OS you choose for SCUP installation, you still must complete a workaround to allow local administrators to publish updates from SCUP to the Windows Server 2012 R2 WSUS server. This workaround involves editing the Registry and DCOM permissions. Details are at https://technet.microsoft.com/library/hh134747.aspx#PublishToServer2012. (This site talks about Windows Server 2012 but is also relevant for Windows Server 2012 R2.)

NOTE: WSUS NO LONGER ISSUES SELF-SIGNED CERTIFICATES

The updated version of WSUS for Windows Server 2012 R2 no longer issues self-signed certificates. This is explained in a blog post by the WSUS Product Team at https://blogs .technet.microsoft.com/wsus/2013/08/15/wsus-no-longer-issues-self-signed-certificates. At this point, you should be thinking about using a certificate authority (CA) to generate a signing certificate for your organization. There is a workaround described in the blog post but also a warning that it may not function with future Windows releases.

SCUP uses a local SQL Server Compact Edition database, so there is no need to provide permissions or connectivity to a full SQL Server instance. SQL Server Compact Edition is a local, single-user, Microsoft Access-like database engine that is automatically installed with SCUP. For more information on SQL Server Compact Edition, see http://technet.microsoft.com/library/ms173037(v=sql.105).aspx.

SCUP installation is straightforward: Launch the downloaded Windows Installer MSI package and follow the wizard. The install requires administrator rights, so on a machine with User Account Control (UAC) settings enabled, open an administrator command prompt, navigate to where the MSI is located, and launch it from the command prompt window. Figure 15.26 shows the second page of the installation program, where you might run into issues.

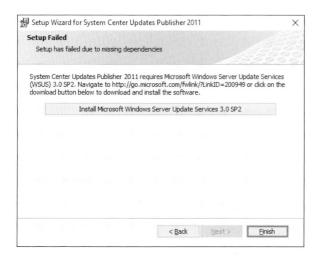

FIGURE 15.26   Second page of SCUP install.

If the correct version of the WSUS console and binaries are not installed on your machine, you will not be able to click Next to move forward. Installing the 3.0 SP 2 version of WSUS is not an option at this point; you must install the RSAT tools for Windows 8.1 on the workstation and restart the SCUP installation.

Configuring SCUP

Once the installation is complete, you can launch SCUP and start the configuration. It is important with UAC enabled that SCUP is always launched as an administrator. SCUP includes its own separate console and requires a small amount of initial configuration. Figure 15.27 shows the SCUP console.

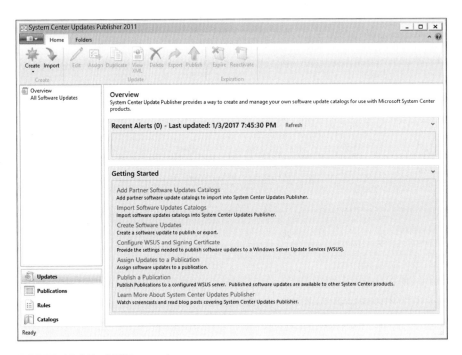

FIGURE 15.27   SCUP console.

After launching the SCUP console, select the **Application** menu from the ribbon bar and choose **Options**. There are five sections in the resulting Options dialog:

▶ **Update Server:** On this page, shown in Figure 15.28, enable update publishing and configure the options SCUP uses to connect to the SUP so it can publish updates. Specify the top-level site in your hierarchy and be sure to set the correct port. The default of port 80 is no longer used by WSUS 4.1; the default now is 8530. If your test connection fails, check that the port is set to the correct value.

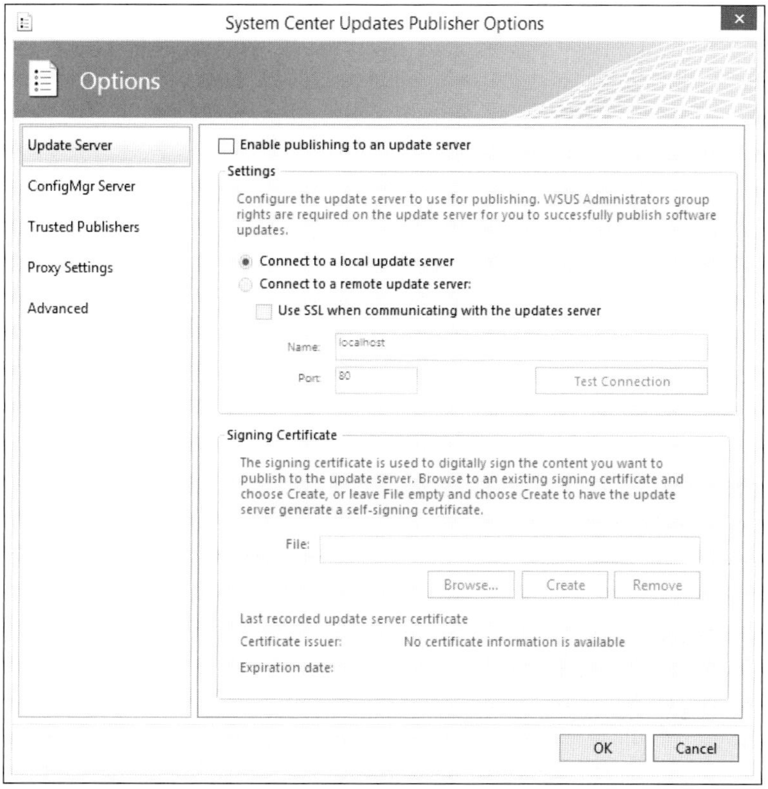

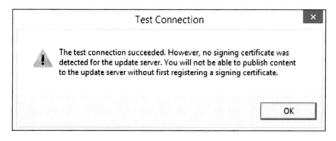

FIGURE 15.28   SCUP update options configuration.

Publishing updates into a SUP also requires a code-signing certificate so clients can verify the source of updates delivered to them. In past versions of WSUS, you could create a self-signed certificate by clicking Create on this page. When clicking Test Connection or Create, you now see a warning message, as shown in Figure 15.29, as you cannot publish content to the WSUS server until the certificate is in place.

FIGURE 15.29   SCUP update options certificate warning.

To work around this issue and restore the legacy ability to create the self-signed certificate, add a Registry key to the machine SCUP is installed on; the location of the Registry key is `HKEY_LOCAL_MACHINE\Software\Microsoft\Update Services\Server\Setup\`. Next, create a new DWORD value called `EnableSelfSignedCertificates` and set the value to `1`. The authors recommend restarting the SCUP application if it was running when you made the Registry change. Once the Registry change is in place, click **Test Connection** and **Create** to create the self-signed certificate. Note that because this is a legacy operation that has been removed from the GUI, there is no guarantee that this will continue to work with updated versions of WSUS.

You will find this self-signed certificate in the SUP's local computer store, under the WSUS folder. You need to export the certificate; to do so, follow these steps:

1. Open a new or existing instance of the Microsoft Management Console (MMC). To open a new instance, launch mmc.exe.

2. On the MMC File menu, choose **Add/Remove Snap-in**.

3. On the resulting Add or Remove Snap-ins dialog, choose **Certificates** in the Available snap-ins list box on the right and click **Add**.

4. In the Certificates snap-in dialog, choose **Computer account**, click **Next**, leave **Local computer** selected on the next page, and click **Finish**.

5. Click **OK** on the Add or Remove Snap-ins dialog.

6. In the tree on the left, expand **Console Root -> Certificates (Local Computer) -> WSUS** and select the resulting **Certificates** node.

7. Right-click the certificate generated by SCUP (named WSUS Publishers Self-signed) in the Details pane on the right, and choose **All Tasks -> Export** to launch the Certificate Export Wizard.

8. Chose **Next** on the first page of the wizard. On the second page chose **No, do not export the private key**; on the third page choose **DER encoded binary X.509 (.CER)** and click **Next**.

9. Enter an appropriate filename and click **Next** to reach the final page of the wizard. Click **Finish** to complete exporting the certificate.

Figure 15.28 shows two other selections that are grayed out: Browse and Remove. These buttons work only if you connected to the WSUS server using SSL and port 8531. You must set up WSUS to use certificates and SSL before making the connection in SCUP. Once this connection is made, you can use a certificate generated by an internal public key infrastructure (PKI) or a public CA such as VeriSign. The only requirement is that the certificate be a code-signing certificate. Some public CAs call these types of certificates *Microsoft Authenticode certificates*. Click **Browse** to import an externally generated certificate. To use an internal PKI-generated certificate with SCUP, see https://blogs.technet.microsoft.com/jasonlewis/2011/07/12/system-center-updates-publisher-signing-certificate-requirements-step-by-step-guide, which documents the process for creating that certificate. Once the certificate is created, use a GPO to deploy it to all clients, including the SCUP and the WSUS server to which you will be publishing. (The article explains how to use a GPO to deploy the certificate.)

If using a public CA, ensure that you are very explicit when requesting the certificate and that you thoroughly test the certificate. Special use certificates like the one required for SCUP may require extra steps when using a public CA, depending on the CA. For in-depth information on how to use public certificates with SCUP, see https://blogs.msdn.microsoft.com/steverac/2011/09/17/using-system-center-update-publisher-2007-with-verisign-certificates.

It does not matter what type of certificate you use, as they all work the same inside SCUP. After choosing the certificate type, confirm that the certificate is added to Trusted Publishers and that the Trusted Root Publishers certificate store is on all systems, including the machine running SCUP and the WSUS/SUP server to which SCUP is trying to publish. Publishing the update will fail if the certificates are not in the correct stores. When an update is published, it is signed with the certificate inside SCUP; when the client receives the policy to execute this update, it verifies that the certificate used to sign the update is trusted by checking the Trusted Publishers and Trusted Root Publishers certificate stores. If the certificate is not found in both stores, the update is not allowed to execute.

15

TIP: DISTRIBUTING THE CERTIFICATE

When using self-signed and public certificates, you must manually install the certificates in the correct stores. This can easily be done using a deployment package and ConfigMgr. Use the application certutil.exe in a script, in a batch file, or standalone to install the certificate. Confirm that the package source files include your script or batch file, the certutil. exe program, the certadm.dll file, and your certificate. The certutil.exe and certadm.dll files can be found in the Windows\System32 folder of any Windows machine. Use the files from the highest version Windows machine that you have; they are downward compatible with lower versions of Windows but not upward compatible. A sample command line for installing the certificate in the Trusted Root Publishers store is `certutil.exe -addstore Root Certificate Name`. Install the certificate in the Trusted Publishers store with `certutil.exe -addstore TrustedPublisher Certificate Name`. Since you must run both programs, the authors recommend using a script or batch file so you need only one program in your ConfigMgr package. If using certutil.exe standalone, you must use two programs in a single package and link the programs together; it does not matter which command is run first. For more information on certutil.exe, see https://technet.microsoft.com/library/cc732443(v=ws.11).aspx.

One last requirement on any client where you wish to deploy updates published using SCUP is to enable the **Allow signed content from intranet Microsoft update service location policy**. This is typically set using a GPO and can be found under **Computer Configuration -> Administrative Templates -> Windows Components -> Windows Update** in the group policy object editor.

▶ **ConfigMgr Server:** Use this tab to enable the integration with ConfigMgr. Make sure you connect to your top-level site. Use the FQDN as the name and click

Test Connection to verify connectivity. If using automatic publishing, enabling ConfigMgr integration allows SCUP to query the compliance status of updates and fully publish them in ConfigMgr only if actually requested by clients and they fall under a particular size. Prior to fully publishing updates, the two thresholds at the bottom of this page are checked:

▶ **Requested Client Count (Threshold):** This is the minimum number of clients that must request an update. If this number is not met, SCUP only publishes the metadata for the update.

▶ **Package Source Size Threshold (MB):** This is the maximum size of the content for an update. If the size of the update is over this number, only the metadata for the update is published.

▶ **Trusted Publisher:** This tab allows you to see the publishers trusted by SCUP, view the certificate of the trusted publishers, and remove a publisher from the list. Publishers are added to the Trusted Publishers list when a catalog is imported into SCUP and when publishing a software update. You cannot add certificates here; you can only remove or view them.

▶ **Proxy Settings:** This tab allows you to configure the proxy settings, if necessary, for SCUP to download third-party update catalogs. If your organization requires access to the Internet to go through a proxy server using username and password credentials, you must enable these settings and add the correct information before you can download any third-party catalogs.

▶ **Advanced:** The options on this tab allow you to view the location of the SCUP repository, enable some general settings, enable certificate revocation, set the location for local source publishing, and run the Software Updates Cleanup Wizard.

▶ **Database File:** This is the location of the SQL Compact Edition database file used by SCUP; it is read-only and user specific, meaning that each user can have specific settings and software updates to publish. The authors recommend using only one user, as using multiple users tends to complicate the process more than help it.

▶ **Add Timestamp When Signing Updates:** This adds a timestamp from an authoritative Internet source when signing updates, which is useful because it makes updates deployable even after the certificate used to sign them has expired. With this option enabled, the updates are always deployable, as long as the updates were signed during the valid lifetime of the signing certificate. If this option is not chosen, updates signed by an expired certificate cannot be deployed.

▶ **Check for New Catalog Alerts on Startup:** This option enables alerts on console startup to notify you of updated update catalogs. When enabled, the startup of SCUP is delayed for a small amount of time, which can make it look like SCUP is hung.

▶ **Enable Certificate Revocation Checking for Digitally Signed Catalog Files:** This option verifies that the certificates used to sign imported update catalogs have not been revoked.

▶ **Always Check the My Documents\LocalSourcePublishing Folder for Software Update Content Before Attempting to Download from the Specified Download URL:** Using this option enables you to manually download content referenced in update catalogs instead of SCUP automatically downloading the content. This option is useful for SCUP consoles that are not connected to the Internet.

▶ **Use a Custom Local Source Path:** Use this option to specify a custom local path for manually downloaded content.

▶ **Software Update Cleanup Wizard:** This option launches a wizard that searches for updates published in ConfigMgr that are not in the default WSUS catalog or the SCUP repository. These are updates previously published by SCUP that were deleted from SCUP and thus orphaned in ConfigMgr. If any updates meeting these criteria are found, you can select them to be cleaned up. Cleaning up an update expires it in ConfigMgr, making it no longer deployable. This operation is irreversible and should be performed only on updates that are no longer needed.

Using SCUP Catalogs

Catalogs in SCUP contain the updates you import and publish into ConfigMgr. You do not actually publish whole catalogs into ConfigMgr using SCUP; they are containers that make it easy to import and export groups of related updates from or to other SCUP publishers or users. These are managed from the Catalogs workspace in the SCUP console.

Third-party vendors can use SCUP to create update catalogs for their own products and then make these catalogs available to you for direct import and use in ConfigMgr using SCUP. There are two types of catalogs: those from Microsoft partners and directly listed in SCUP and those from other sources.

Directly import catalogs from Microsoft partners in the SCUP console by going to the Catalogs workspace and choosing **Add Catalogs** from the ribbon bar to launch the Add Partners Software Updates Catalogs dialog, which lists available catalogs that you can pick for import into SCUP. The list of catalogs also includes download URLs, support URLs, and descriptions. Importing a catalog into SCUP is not the same as actually publishing the updates into ConfigMgr, so this step is harmless and reversible with respect to ConfigMgr.

Catalogs from other sources can be some of the following:

▶ Commercial catalogs for third-party products

▶ Community catalogs

▶ Your own organization's internal catalogs

To import one of these types of catalogs, navigate to the Catalogs workspace and click **Add** on the ribbon bar to launch the Add Software Update Catalog Wizard, where you input five pieces of information:

▶ **Catalog Path:** The path to the CAB file containing the catalog. This can be a local path, a UNC, or a URL.

▶ **Publisher:** The name of the publisher of the catalog. You can use the name entered here to sort and filter updates in the SCUP console as well as the ConfigMgr console.

▶ **Name:** The name of the catalog.

▶ **Description:** An applicable description for the catalog.

▶ **Support URL:** A URL where support information for the catalog can be accessed.

After adding a catalog to SCUP, you must import the updates in that catalog into SCUP to use them. Select or multi-select the update catalogs listed in the Catalogs workspace and choose **Import** from the ribbon bar or from the right-click context-menu to launch the Import Software Updates Catalog Wizard. There are no real options in this wizard except selecting additional or deselecting chosen catalogs for import.

During the update import process, you may be presented with a Security Warning dialog asking you to accept content from the publisher. Choosing Always Accept content from the publisher trusts the publisher and accepts all future content from that publisher. You can view or remove the code signing certificate from that publisher in the Trusted Publishers page of the Options dialog.

Also available from the Catalogs workspace are options to edit and remove a catalog from the ribbon bar or from the right-click context menus of the catalogs. You cannot edit a vendor-signed catalog; selecting **Edit** displays a dialog box with read-only information about the catalog. Removing a catalog does not remove the updates imported from that catalog.

Using SCUP Publications

Publications are group updates for mass publishing into ConfigMgr, enabling their use and deployment, or for export to a catalog that you can distribute to others. Using publications is optional; they allow you to logically group published updates. Publications can be created based on vendors, periods, or whatever makes sense for your environment.

View existing publications from the Publications workspace in the console. To create a publication, choose the Publication tab in the ribbon bar and choose **Create**. You can also create publications from selected updates in the Updates workspace by selecting updates and choosing Assign or Publish from the ribbon bar or from the right-click context menu.

Existing publications are listed in the navigation list box on the left; this is a simple list rather than a tree, as there is no hierarchy with publications. Selecting a publication displays the list of updates it contains. Additional options available from the Home tab of the ribbon bar for a selected publication include the following:

▶ **Export:** This option exports all of the selected publication's updates to a catalog in the form of a CAB file that you can provide to other SCUP users.

▶ **Publish:** This option publishes the selected publication's updates into ConfigMgr, making them available for compliance scanning or installation, depending on publication type.

▶ **Automatic:** Use this option to allow SCUP to query ConfigMgr to determine whether the selected software update or software update bundle is published with full content or only metadata. In this mode, software updates are published only when meeting the client request count and package size thresholds specified on the ConfigMgr Server page of the Options dialog box. Automatic mode is available only if ConfigMgr integration is selected in the SCUP configurations options.

▶ **Full Content:** Use this option when you are sure that you want to deploy the software update by using ConfigMgr. When selected, SCUP publishes the binary of the software update and the metadata of the software update.

▶ **Metadata Only:** Use this option when you only want to gather compliance information for software updates. When selected, SCUP publishes only the definition of the software update but does not publish the software update binaries.

▶ **Remove:** Use this option to remove the software update(s) from the publication.

The following options are available on the Publication tab of the ribbon bar for a select publication:

▶ **Create:** Use this option to create a new blank publication.

▶ **Edit:** Displays a simple dialog box where you can change the name of a publication.

▶ **Delete:** Deletes the selected publication.

Once you publish information into WSUS, you may find it takes two ConfigMgr synchronization cycles before your update appears in the ConfigMgr console. For example, say you have published a group of Adobe Reader updates to WSUS. When ConfigMgr synchronizes with WSUS, it learns that a new product is available. That new product appears under the Products tab of the top-level site's SUP properties. Figure 15.30 shows the list with the new product in it.

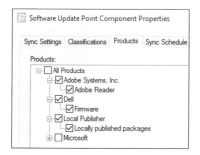

FIGURE 15.30   SCUP product added to a list.

You must check the box under the Adobe product list that so that on the next synchronization of ConfigMgr with WSUS, the product is added to the list of software updates that it synchronizes. If you don't check the box, your SCUP-published software updates will not appear in the ConfigMgr console.

SCUP Updates

All updates imported into SCUP and ready for publication into ConfigMgr are listed in the Updates workspace. Updates are organized under the All Software Updates node in the navigation tree by publisher first and then by their applicable product. Use the Search box on the upper right of the update list to filter the list of updates currently displayed.

The Details pane at the bottom displays detailed information about the selected update from the update list. If you select multiple updates, information from the first update selected is displayed in the pane.

For each update, you can choose one of several different operations from the ribbon bar or the update's right-click context menu; most of these operations are valid and available when multiple updates are selected. The options follow:

▶ **Create:** This allows you to create a custom software update or custom software update bundle. In-depth information about creating these items can be found in the "Using SCUP Custom Updates" section, later in this chapter.

▶ **Import:** This item allows you to import one or more catalogs listed in the My Catalogs section into SCUP. It also allows you to import a custom catalog by providing the full path to the CAB file.

▶ **Edit:** This option, also accessible by double-clicking any update, displays the Edit Software Update Wizard, where you can edit all aspects of the update. A detailed description of the many options available in this wizard is provided in the "Using SCUP Custom Updates" section, later in this chapter. The authors do not recommend modifying any updates from third-party vendors; if you must modify one, make a copy of the update and then change the copy, leaving the original intact.

▶ **Assign:** This option adds an update or update bundle to an existing publication or a new publication. Adding an update to a publication does not publish it to ConfigMgr.

▶ **Duplicate:** As its name implies, this option creates an exact replica of an update; the new update's name is prefixed with Copy of. Use this option to create a copy of a third-party vendor update so that you can edit the update, if needed.

▶ **View XML:** This option shows the raw XML that defines an update. It is sometimes useful to see raw XML for updates to view hidden options and identifiers not displayed in SCUP or ConfigMgr. Another benefit of this option is that you can review all the rules associated with an update.

▶ **Delete:** This option deletes an update from SCUP. If the update is published into ConfigMgr, this orphans the update and makes it unmanageable. Use the Software Update Cleanup Wizard to clean up orphaned updates. This option is not recommended for updates in a catalog supplied by a third-party vendor; rather, the vendor should do this cleanup for its catalog.

▶ **Export:** This option exports the selected updates to a catalog in the form of a CAB file that you can provide to other SCUP users.

▶ **Publish:** This option publishes an update directly to ConfigMgr, using one of the three publication types. Note that the update is not placed into a publication.

▶ **Expire:** This option expires updates so they can no longer be deployed by ConfigMgr. Once published to the SUP, it is irreversible, and your only course of action is to create a new update, possibly using the Duplicate option, if the update is still needed.

▶ **Reactivate:** This option reactivates updates expired in SCUP that have not been published to ConfigMgr. Some vendors include expired updates in their catalogs so you can use them if the newer updates have not yet been approved for use in your organization. In this case, use this option to reactivate and then publish them. As mentioned with the Expire option, once an update is published as Expired to the SUP, it cannot be reactivated, so you must reactivate an update before initially publishing it.

CAUTION: EXPIRING UPDATES

Before expiring any update, understand the caveats listed in this section. Specifically, the Reactivate option is not applicable to published updates that are expired: Expiring published updates closes the door on using them again.

Updates must be published either directly using the Publish option from the All Software Updates list in the Updates workspace or the Publish option available in the Publications workspace. Adding an update to a publication does not publish the update in ConfigMgr.

Updates can exist in multiple publications or none at all, but they are published only once to ConfigMgr, if at all. Every occurrence of an update in a publication or the All Software Updates list shares the same publication type and date.

Using SCUP Custom Updates

A primary use of SCUP is for creating custom updates that sit alongside Microsoft's updates for your own line-of-business applications or third-party applications in your environment. To create your own custom updates, first create the folder structure in the navigation tree on the Updates workspace, beginning with the vendor at the top level and then adding a folder for the product. Use the following steps as a guide to creating your custom vendor and product names:

1. Select the All Software Updates node and choose **Create Vendor** from the right-click context menu or choose the Folders tab and select **Create -> Vendor** from the dropdown menu. Enter the vendor name in the resulting dialog box.

2. Select the new vendor folder you just created and choose **Create Product** from the right-click context menu or choose the Folders tab and select **Create -> Product** from the dropdown menu. Enter the product name in the resulting dialog box.

Alternatively, you can use an existing vendor or product folder; vendor folders may contain multiple product folders, and products may contain multiple updates. Updates are displayed in the Updates view on the right when a product folder is selected in the navigation tree.

Delete and Edit options are available from the right-click context menu of a selected vendor or product folder and the ribbon bar; Edit shows a dialog box, where you can rename the folder.

After creating your vendor and product names, you are ready to proceed with creating your custom updates. Updates must be one of the following file types:

▶ Windows executable (.exe)

▶ Microsoft Installer file (.msi)

▶ Microsoft Installer Patch file (.msp)

Windows Update (.msu) files are not directly supported because WSUS does not support them by design; they are typically associated with hotfixes that are not really intended for mass distribution. If you find that you need to use an MSU file, a workaround is explained in depth at https://blogs.technet.microsoft.com/dominikheinz/2011/10/17/deploying-custom-msu-updates-with-sccm-and-scup.

To create a new custom software update, choose **Create** from the Home tab of the ribbon bar and then select **Software Update** from the resulting dropdown. You do not have to select any specific node or node type in the navigation tree for this option to work. This launches the Create Software Update Wizard, which has 10 pages; 7 of the pages require information to be entered, and the last 3 are the standard Summary, Progress, and Confirmation pages. The following are the 7 pages where you need to enter information:

▶ **Package Information:** This page contains the following information about the update package you are creating:

  ▶ **Package Source:** This is the location of the actual update file and must be a valid type previously listed in this section. This file is used only as a point of reference and to establish a filename; it is not actually captured or placed in the update.

  ▶ **Use a Local Source to Publish Software Update Content:** If selected, this option designates that the content source used by ConfigMgr to download the actual software update file specified in the Package source option is a local folder rather than a location specified by the next option. The local folder is the current logged-in user's Documents\LocalSourcePublishing folder by default, but this is configurable on the Advanced page of the Options dialog.

This option is useful when creating updates for your own internal use and the SCUP console is installed on your site server.

▶ **Download URL (or UNC):** This field specifies the content source location used by ConfigMgr to download the update file specified in the Package source option. If the previous option is selected, this field is grayed out and is not fillable.

▶ **Binary Language:** This is the language of the update file specified in the Package source field. It usually is listed as Language Neutral. If using a different language, choose the correct language to use from the dropdown.

▶ **Success Return Codes:** Codes are returned from the update installation file upon a successful installation. A typical success return code is 0, but this may vary; manually test the update or consult the documentation of the vendor that created the update file to ensure that you have accounted for all valid success return codes.

▶ **Success Pending Reboot Codes:** Similar to the Success return codes, these codes are returned from a successful update installation that requires a reboot. This code is usually 3010. Updates should never reboot the system on their own.

▶ **Command Line:** This is the actual command line options and properties used to run the update on a target system. The specified options should suppress reboots and all user interaction, and they should be fully automated. Consult the vendor's documentation for information on how to achieve this and then verify by manually testing the complete command line. Do not include the update filename in this field; include only the options or properties. For MSIs and MSPs, the proper options to make them silent and unattended are added automatically and should not be specified.

If the package source is an MSI or MSP, these last four fields are automatically populated, as the values are standard or extractable from the source file.

▶ **Required Information:** This information defines the metadata published into WSUS, displayed in the ConfigMgr console, and used by ConfigMgr to determine if the update should be included in the catalog, including the following:

▶ Language

▶ Title

▶ Description

▶ Classification

▶ Vendor

▶ Product

▶ More Info URL

NOTE: VENDOR NAMES

When choosing vendor names, you can use anything except the following names, as they are already used: Microsoft Corporation, Microsoft, Update, Software Update, Tools, Tool, Critical, Critical Updates, Security, Security Updates, Feature Pack, Update Rollup, Service Pack, Driver, Driver Update, Bundle, and Bundle Update.

▶ **Optional Information:** Additional metadata is specified on this page. This information is displayed in the ConfigMgr console and can be used for filtering and sorting in the console but is not directly used by ConfigMgr. Each field's definition is subjective, and you can define each for your own needs. Fields on this page include the following:

  ▶ Bulletin ID

  ▶ Article ID

  ▶ CVE IDs

  ▶ Support URL

  ▶ Severity

  ▶ Impact

  ▶ Restart behavior

▶ **Prerequisites:** On this page, define the prerequisites that must already be in place on a target system for an update to be scanned for compliance. Valid prerequisites include other updates from SCUP and detectoids. *Detectoids* are high-level rules that the WUA can evaluate quickly. You can choose from a set of well-known WSUS detectoids but cannot create your own in SCUP. There are two groups of well-known WSUS detectoids: CPU Architecture and OS language.

▶ **Superseded Updates:** On this page, select which updates, if any, are superseded by this new update. You can only choose updates in SCUP.

▶ **Installable Rules:** This page defines the update applicability rules; these rules are used by the WUA to scan the local system and determine if it requires the update. You combine rules on this page by using typical Boolean logic constructs such as AND, OR, and NOT. For a brief discussion of rules, see the next section, "Using SCUP Rules." Using prerequisites is preferred to using installable rules when possible, as prerequisites are essentially pre-evaluated and thus incur very little overhead.

▶ **Installed Rules:** Similar to installable rules, these rules define how the WUA verifies that the update is installed. In some cases, these rules may be identical to the installable rules; this is perfectly valid. Ensure that these rules evaluate to True after the software update is installed; otherwise, you can end up in a loop when software updates evaluation runs.

In addition to doing individual updates, you can create software update bundles. Although not very common, software update bundles ensure that specific software updates are deployed at the same time. The WUA handles software update bundles very much like it handles software updates.

Create a software update bundle by selecting **Create** from the Home tab of the ribbon bar and then selecting **Software Update Bundle** from the resulting dropdown. You do not have to select any specific node or node type in the navigation tree for this option to work. This launches the Create Software Update Bundle Wizard, whose pages are mostly identical to those in the Create Software Updates Wizard, with the exception of the following:

- ▶ **Optional Information:** This page only differs because of the lack of the Impact and Restart behavior options.

- ▶ **Bundle Updates:** This page allows you to select the updates you wish to include in the bundle. You can choose from any updates inside SCUP.

Using SCUP Rules

The rules used by SCUP are similar to the rules you create in compliance settings. Rules are the checks the WUA uses to determine if an update is required on a system and verify that an update has been successfully installed.

The Rules workspace lists all previously saved rules. Just because a rule is used by an update does not mean it is saved. You must explicitly save a rule before it appears in this workspace; there are no default saved rules in SCUP.

Use the Rules workspace to construct and save reusable rules for use with the installable and installed rule definitions in updates. You can also create rules directly in the Software Update Wizard on the Installable Rules and Installed Rules pages by using the small disk icon. To load a previously saved rule on these pages, click the yellow starburst icon and choose **Saved Rule** from the **Rule type** dropdown.

You can create four different rule types:

- ▶ File
- ▶ Registry
- ▶ System
- ▶ Windows Installer

Each rule type is self-explanatory to configure and not covered in depth here. However, because they are nearly identical to the rules used in compliance settings, you can reference Chapter 10, "Managing Compliance," for detailed explanations.

Summary

There are many options for deploying software updates to Windows systems, but when you combine the power of ConfigMgr with proven tools like WSUS and WUA, none of those tools can compare to the power and options available with ConfigMgr. ConfigMgr gives you the flexibility to update single systems, groups of systems, or all systems in a single user-friendly tool. Add to that the ability to service the new Windows 10 systems with core updates to move them from current state to CB or CBB, and there really is no other choice.

SCUP provides a method to patch your third-party products and any homegrown applications your organization may have created. Wrap all this together, and you have a tool that provides the comfort of safely delivering software updates, Windows 10 core updates, and third-party updates with the ability to customize your settings and have a user-friendly experience.

The next chapter explains how you can integrate Intune with ConfigMgr to provide hybrid management of on-premise and mobile devices using a single console.

CHAPTER 16

Integrating Intune Hybrid into Your Configuration Manager Environment

The past several years have seen dramatic changes in the information technology (IT) landscape. To meet the shift toward mobile devices, enterprises are recognizing the "consumerization of IT" and incorporating consumer devices into their IT infrastructure. This movement is being led by tech-savvy users demanding the ability to use the latest devices to access corporate resources from any location. To facilitate this access, employees must allow some control over their devices, and they must agree for their devices to be enrolled in a management solution.

Intune is Microsoft's mobile device management (MDM, sometimes called modern device management) and mobile application management (MAM) solution. You can integrate Intune with System Center Configuration Manager (ConfigMgr) to provide hybrid management of on-premise and mobile devices using a single console.

Introducing Microsoft Intune

Microsoft Intune is a cloud-based device management solution. It can be deployed in a standalone or hybrid configuration (for more information, see the next section, "Hybrid Versus Standalone"). This chapter focuses on hybrid integration of Intune with ConfigMgr, which enables administrators to manage mobile devices (Android, iOS, Windows Phone, and Windows 8.1 and above) using the ConfigMgr console. This integration was introduced in ConfigMgr 2012 Service Pack (SP) 1 and enhanced with the

2012 Release 2 (R2) version. ConfigMgr previously provided MDM using the Exchange Connector. However, this capability was limited to the basic management features supported by Exchange ActiveSync.

Using Intune provides the following features:

▶ Secure management of personal and corporate-owned devices across popular mobile platforms

▶ Self-enrollment of devices

▶ Hardware and software inventory

▶ Mobile device configuration (for example, Wi-Fi profiles, email profiles, certificates, and virtual private networks [VPNs])

▶ MAM policies, including integration with Office mobile apps

▶ Application deployment (required or available via the Intune company portal)

▶ Conditional access, which prevents access to email and other services on devices that are not enrolled with Microsoft Intune

Hybrid Versus Standalone

There has been a considerable amount of debate on the subject of using Intune hybrid versus standalone since Intune was first integrated with ConfigMgr 2012 several years ago. Which approach should you use? Which one is better?

Intune standalone means that mobile device management is carried out using a cloud portal. A hybrid solution involves integrating Intune and ConfigMgr, which makes it possible to manage your mobile and on-premise devices using the ConfigMgr console. The best solution— and the one you should use—is the one that works best for your organization. Do note that, as of the time this book was published, Microsoft has stated that Intune standalone is their recommended deployment topology. Microsoft has also developed migration strategies for customers to migrate from Intune hybrid to Intune standalone. With that said, Microsoft has also committed to supporting customers using Intune hybrid.

Intune hybrid and standalone both have pros and cons; however, the rapid cadence of releases from Microsoft constantly changes the advantages of each solution, making it futile to even attempt to provide a comparison table in this book, as it would be obsolete before the book is even published. For more information on choosing between the models, see https://docs.microsoft.com/sccm/mdm/understand/choose-between-standalone-Intune-and-hybrid-mobile-device-management.

As ConfigMgr is the industry standard for computer management, it is great that you can now use it to manage all your devices through a single console. However, historically there was always one major disadvantage: Microsoft would regularly release new Intune features that could be immediately utilized by standalone users, while hybrid customers would have to wait for the changes to be integrated with ConfigMgr, as it was challenging to quickly add new features to this massive on-premise solution.

The wait was quite frustrating for customers, and they often chose to implement stand-alone Intune as a result. With the release of ConfigMgr Current Branch, Microsoft has committed to upgrading the entire ConfigMgr solution at a rapid rate, using the new servicing model. This makes it easier to add new features in a reasonable time frame.

Microsoft's Enterprise Mobility + Security

The advent of mobile devices has blurred corporate security boundaries, increasing potential risks. An organization needs an effective strategy to manage the mobile workforce. It is not enough to manage devices; to adhere to strict security and compliance policies, you must adopt an end-to-end management strategy. Microsoft has identified this need and taken a holistic view with the introduction of Enterprise Mobility + Security (EMS). The EMS suite is a licensing bundle that consists of the following products:

- ▶ **Azure Active Directory (AD) Premium:** Enables user identity management

- ▶ **Microsoft Intune:** Provides mobile device and application management

- ▶ **Azure Information Protection:** Enables data protection

- ▶ **Cloud App Security:** Manages cloud app usage and shadow IT

- ▶ **Advanced Threat Analytics:** Provides breach and threat identification

While this book is concerned with Microsoft Intune, it is important to know about EMS and how it fits into the total solution.

16

Purchasing Microsoft Intune

Microsoft Intune is a subscription-based service, licensed on a per-user basis, with each user entitled to enroll 15 devices. While Intune can be licensed as a single product, purchasing EMS is a more cost-effective approach. The suite can be purchased through an Enterprise Agreement (EA) with Microsoft and became available for purchase through the open licensing model as of March 1, 2015.

If you are unsure whether the product is an appropriate fit for your organization, you can sign up for a trial in one of two ways. Note that you can transition your trial to production in each case:

- ▶ To sign up for a 30-day Intune trial, go to https://docs.microsoft.com/intune/free-trial-sign-up and click **Try now**.

  Click **Sign in** if you wish to add the trial to an existing Office 365 subscription. Otherwise, enter your information to sign up.

  To extend the trial an additional 30 days, contact Intune support. Local support telephone numbers are available in the TechNet documentation at https://technet.microsoft.com/jj839713.aspx.

NOTE: SELECTING AN AZURE DOMAIN NAME

During the sign-up process you must choose a new Azure domain name in the format *mydomain*.onmicrosoft.com.

Choose wisely, as this name cannot be changed later, and it is for all your Microsoft cloud services—Intune, Office 365, and so on. You are notified immediately if the domain name is available, and you can then continue the process by selecting a username. The username and domain name combine to generate a user ID for the first global administrator account, in the format admin@*mydomain*.onmicrosoft.com.

Use this account to sign in to the Office 365, Intune, and Azure portals.

▶ Existing Microsoft cloud customers can sign up for a 90-day EMS trial through the FastTrack program, at http://fasttrack.microsoft.com/ems. This program allows customers to explore new resources at their own pace. It helps with planning for successful rollouts and onboarding of new users.

Using the Management Portals

At the time this book was published, Intune was being migrated from a Silverlight-based portal to the Azure portal. The classic Intune admin portal was being discontinued, and Intune management is now available via the Azure portal. Currently the following can be used to manage the various configurations and features of Microsoft Intune:

▶ **Office 365 Admin Center (https://portal.office.com):** You can use the Office 365 admin center to carry out some preliminary configuration for the hybrid solution. Use it to add and verify a custom domain, as described in the "Preparing Your Environment for Intune" section, later in this chapter.

The admin center can also be used to access the Intune admin console. Navigate to **Admin Centers -> Intune**.

▶ **Intune Admin Portal (https://manage.microsoft.com):** The Intune admin portal is currently used only for day-to-day management of computers. Mobile device management using Intune standalone has been migrated to the Azure portal. In a hybrid environment, most management activities are performed using the Configuration Manager console. This is discussed further in Chapter 17, "Managing Mobile Devices."

▶ **Azure Portal (https://portal.azure.com):** Intune management is carried out using the Azure portal. Navigate to **More Services -> Monitoring and Management -> Intune** to access the Intune tiles, as shown in Figure 16.1.

NOTE: SINGLE IDENTITY ACROSS MICROSOFT CLOUD SERVICES

Azure Active Directory (Azure AD) is the primary directory that provides access to Microsoft cloud services such as Office 365, Azure, and Intune. It is vitally important to link these services together correctly. For example, if you use Office 365, you already use Azure AD (even though you do not manage your users via the Azure portal). In this case, do not create a new tenant if you purchase Intune or Azure services.

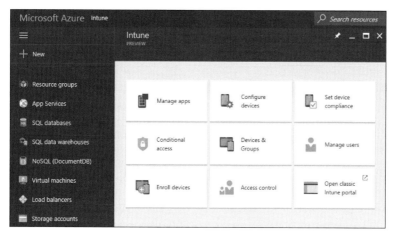

FIGURE 16.1   Managing Intune via the Azure portal.

Using Intune Storage

When you create a paid Intune subscription, you are allocated 20GB of Azure cloud storage. This storage is only used for line-of-business applications to be deployed to mobile
devices. It is not required for store apps or for compliance and configuration policies.

Use the Intune admin console to check how much storage you are using. Navigate to
Admin -> Storage Use. You can purchase additional storage as needed.

A trial Intune subscription entitles you to 2GB of Azure storage.

User Identity Options

User accounts and groups are utilized to manage and secure access to corporate resources.
Azure AD is a comprehensive identity and access management solution that Microsoft
leverages for authentication to online services (including Intune and Office 365). Microsoft provides three user identity models:

▶ Cloud identity

▶ Synchronized identity

▶ Federated identity

Each model presents varying levels of complexity, and it is important to choose the model
that works best for your business. The following sections discuss these models in more detail.

Cloud Identity

The cloud identity model is not commonly used in an enterprise environment. The model
uses Azure AD to create and manage users. Azure AD verifies passwords, and on-premise
identity configuration is not required.

This model is normally used only in small organizations that do not have on-premise AD.

Synchronized Identity (Password Synchronization)

In the synchronized model, user identity is managed on-premise using AD. Selected user accounts and password hashes are synchronized to Azure AD. Passwords are verified by Azure AD to provide a "same sign-on" experience.

Various tools are available to synchronize the user accounts and password hashes. Azure AD Connect was the recommended tool at the time this book was published, and it is the only tool currently undergoing Microsoft development. Azure AD Connect is discussed in the "Synchronizing Active Directory" section, later in this chapter.

Federated Identity

The federated identity model requires a synchronized identity model to be in place already. However, unlike with the synchronized identity model, the password hash is not synchronized to Azure AD, as passwords are verified by on-premise AD to provide a single sign-on experience.

This model typically uses Active Directory Federation Services (ADFS) and is the most complex model to implement. Additional network and server infrastructure is required to achieve high availability.

> **NOTE: THE IDENTITY MODEL USED IN THIS BOOK**
>
> This book uses the synchronized identity model. ADFS configuration is beyond the scope of the book.
>
> You can easily switch from synchronized identity to federated identity at a later stage, if required.

Preparing Your Environment for Intune

After purchasing Intune (or EMS), there are a number of tasks required to prepare your on-premise and cloud environments:

▶ Adding and verifying a custom domain

▶ Creating Domain Name System (DNS) records

▶ Adding a user principal name (UPN)

▶ Synchronizing Active Directory

▶ Creating an alternate login ID (optional)

This work will already have occurred if you are using Office 365 services. The following sections describe these tasks in detail.

Adding and Verifying a Custom Domain

The first task in preparing your environment for Intune is to create a custom domain. For enterprise production environments, the authors recommend adding a custom domain name with which your users are familiar and comfortable. Add this custom domain prior to synchronizing your user accounts so that the users can receive a custom UPN and then can access resources using credentials they recognize. Typically, this will be their primary Simple Mail Transfer Protocol (SMTP) email address.

Follow these steps to add a custom domain:

1. Log in to the Office 365 portal (https://portal.office.com) using the global administrator account.

2. Navigate to **Settings -> Domains**. Initially you see only your onmicrosoft.com domain. Configuring the custom domain in advance simplifies management of user identities. (UPNs are discussed in the section "Adding a User Principal Name," later in this chapter.)

NOTE: CUSTOM DOMAINS

Your custom domain must be an Internet-routable domain, and you need to verify your ownership of this domain. This custom domain is then added as an alternative UPN suffix in Active Directory.

3. Select **Add Domain** and enter your custom domain name. This book uses the domain EMSlab.ie.

4. The next screen of the wizard, shown in Figure 16.2, presents instructions to verify your ownership of this domain. You must add a specific record to the DNS records of the domain, and Microsoft verifies that new record. This action does not affect any existing DNS records.

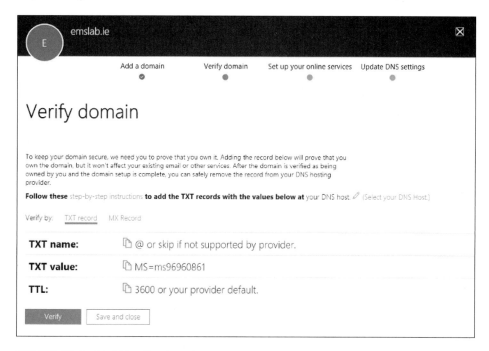

FIGURE 16.2   Verifying the domain.

Two verification methods are available:

▶ Adding a TXT record (preferred)

▶ Adding an MX record (alternative)

Adding a TXT record is the easiest option. Follow the hyperlink in the wizard for additional information on this process with the various domain name registrars.

The DNS record can take up to 24 hours to propagate fully after being added, although it is normally available within an hour. Once the record is propagated, click **Verify**. You will receive the error "Verification DNS record not found" if you have not waited a sufficient amount of time before verification. Once the domain is verified, its status changes in the portal.

Creating DNS Records

The authors recommend that you create DNS records to assist with enrolling Windows devices. While doing so is optional, it provides a better support experience.

You create a CNAME record for your domain that redirects EnterpriseEnrollment-s .yourdomain.com to manage.microsoft.com. When the MDM agent in Windows starts the enrollment process, it examines the email address provided and searches the DNS records for that domain for this CNAME value.

▶ If the CNAME is found, the enrollment is redirected to Microsoft servers, and the process continues without any further user intervention.

▶ If the CNAME value is not found, you are prompted to enter the server name (manage.microsoft.com) to continue.

Creating a CNAME record helps ensure seamless enrollment of Windows devices in a production environment. You also could create a CNAME record that redirects to Enterprise-Registration.windows.net to support Windows 8.1 and Windows 10 mobile devices that register with Azure AD.

Adding a User Principal Name

A UPN is a login name for an Active Directory user, based on Internet standard RFC 822. The UPN usually maps to the user's primary SMTP address.

The "Adding and Verifying a Custom Domain" section, earlier in this chapter, discusses adding to Intune a custom domain name that is verified by Microsoft. This section shows how to add that domain as a UPN suffix in Active Directory.

To add a UPN, log on to a domain controller (DC) and perform the following steps:

1. Open Active Directory Domains and Trusts. Right-click **Active Directory Domains and Trusts** and choose **Properties**.

2. Add an alternative UPN suffix (that is, a custom domain name), as shown in Figure 16.3.

FIGURE 16.3   Adding an alternative UPN suffix.

3. You can now change the UPN for your users so it matches the primary SMTP address. Using Active Directory User and Computers, open the properties of a user account and then select the **Account** tab.

4. Using the dropdown arrow, select the alternate UPN suffix and ensure that the logon name matches the primary SMTP address, as shown in Figure 16.4.

It would be inefficient to perform this procedure manually for a large number of users. Community-developed scripts are available, and several tools exist to make bulk changes.

FIGURE 16.4   Changing the user UPN.

> **TIP: THE ADMODIFY TOOL**
>
> ADModify is a recommended tool for making mass changes of UPNs in Active Directory. The Microsoft TechNet library has detailed instructions on the correct usage of this tool. See https://technet.microsoft.com/library/aa996216(v=exchg.65).aspx for additional information.

Synchronizing Active Directory

After adding the custom domain to both on-premise Active Directory and Azure Active Directory, you can synchronize your user accounts with Microsoft Azure.

This book uses the commonly implemented synchronized user identity model (password synchronization). Azure AD Connect is the recommended tool for integrating your on-premise AD with Azure AD; it replaces older directory synchronization tools such as DirSync and Azure AD Sync, both of which reached end-of-support in April 2017.

> **NOTE: ABOUT PASSWORD SYNCHRONIZATION**
>
> Password synchronization involves synchronizing the hashes of user passwords from your on-premise AD to Azure AD. It allows users to log on to Microsoft Online services using the same password they use to access local network resources. This is not a single sign-on solution, as there is no token sharing or exchange in the process.

At the time this book was published, Azure AD Connect 1.1 was the current version of the tool. This version has new and improved features, including the following:

▶ **Automatic Upgrades:** Previous upgrades of DirSync, Azure AD Sync, and Azure AD Connect were manual.

▶ **More Frequent Synchronizations:** Previous synchronization intervals were three hours. Azure AD Connect 1.1 supports synchronization intervals of 30 minutes.

▶ **Multi-factor Authentication (MFA):** Azure AD Connect 1.1 now natively supports MFA.

Table 16.1 shows the prerequisite requirements for Azure AD Connect.

TABLE 16.1   Azure AD Connect Software Prerequisites

Component	Prerequisite	Details
Accounts	Azure User ID (Global Administrator)	Created when signing up for Microsoft Intune.
	Local Active Directory	Must be enterprise administrator.
Azure AD	Custom domain	Added to Azure and verified.
On premise infrastructure	Minimum AD schema and forest functional level	Windows Server 2003.
	For password writeback	DCs must be Windows Server 2008 (with SP 2) or later. Windows Server 2008 DCs must have KB2386717 applied.

Component	Prerequisite	Details
	Domain controller	A writable DC must be available. Read-only DC is not supported.
	Firewall ports	Communication between Azure AD Connect and on-premise AD. 53 (TCP/UDP): DNS 88 (TCP/UDP): Kerberos 135 (TCP/UDP): RPC 389 (TCP/UDP): LDAP 636 (TCP/UDP): LDAP/SSL 1024–65353 (TCP/UDP): Random high RPC Port Communication between Azure AD Connect and Azure AD. 80 (TCP/UDP): HTTP 443 (TCP/UDP): HTTPS
Azure AD Connect server	In order to use password synchronization	Windows Server 2008 R2 SP 1 Standard or later.
	.NET Framework	4.5.1 or later.
	Microsoft PowerShell	3.0 or later.
Database	SQL Server 2012 Express	Installed automatically with express installation. Supports approximately 100,000 objects. Full SQL Server version for more than 100,000 objects.

NOTE: USE THE LATEST VERSION OF WINDOWS SERVER

Table 16.1 lists the minimum requirements. However, the authors recommend installing Azure AD Connect on the latest available Windows Server operating system.

Table 16.2 lists the minimum hardware requirements for the Azure AD Connect server.

TABLE 16.2   Azure AD Connect Minimum Hardware Requirements

Number of Active Directory Objects	CPU (GHz)	RAM (GB)	Hard Disk (GB)
Fewer than 50,000	1.6	4	70
50,000–100,000	1.6	16	100
100,000–300,000	1.6	32	300
300,000–600,000	1.6	32	450
More than 600,000	1.6	32	500

Download AzureADConnect.msi from the Microsoft Download Center, at https://www.microsoft.com/download/details.aspx?id=47594.

Two installation methods exist for Azure AD Connect:

▶ **Express:** Supports the most common implementation scenarios

▶ **Custom:** For more advanced options (recommended by the authors, so that you can choose which organizational units [OUs] to synchronize to Azure)

This book assumes that you are using the most common topology, which is a single on-premise forest with one or more domains and a single Azure AD. This scenario is supported by the Azure AD Connect express installation.

Before installing Azure, AD Connect, examine the official Microsoft Azure documentation to discover the differences and the details of each option. In particular, you should understand the expected behavior when you make specific choices.

TIP: USING A DEDICATED SERVER FOR AZURE AD CONNECT

In an enterprise environment, you should install Azure AD Connect on a dedicated server. Although it supports an express installation, the authors recommend choosing a custom installation for control over many important aspects of the implementation, including the following:

▶ Filtering to synchronize only the OUs you require

▶ Using a dedicated SQL instance (rather than SQL Server Express)

Follow these steps to install Azure AD Connect:

1. Log on to the server as a local administrator.

2. Launch the installer to start the Microsoft Azure Active Direct Connect installation wizard.

3. Check the box to agree to the license terms and privacy notice and click **Continue**.

4. Choose between an express or custom installation. Choose **Customize** if you want to make any changes to the default installation (such as selecting which user accounts to synchronize). This is the recommended option.

5. When you are presented with the choices for installing required components, choose whether to accept the default configuration. If you do, the wizard installs a local SQL Server 2012 Express instance. The wizard also creates the appropriate security groups and assigns the correct permissions. Remember that the authors recommend using an existing SQL Server instance for advanced management purposes. Click **Install** to continue. The required components are installed.

6. When prompted to do so, choose the single sign-on method you want for your users, as shown in Figure 16.5. If you are not federating with ADFS, choose **Password Synchronization**. Click **Next** to continue.

FIGURE 16.5   Selecting the user sign-in method.

7. Enter your Azure Active Directory credentials. (You must be global administrator on the tenant; this process creates an Azure AD account that is used for subsequent synchronizations.) If this account has multi-factor authentication enabled, you need to complete the MFA challenge. Click **Next** to commence the Microsoft Online verification process.

8. Provide details for your on-premise Active Directory. (You must be an enterprise administrator.) Choose your forest and select **Active Directory** as the directory type. Enter your on-premise AD account and click **Add Directory**. After the directory is configured, click **Next** to continue.

9. By default, all domains and OUs are synchronized. This is not recommended. You should deselect domains and OUs as required. Click **Next** to continue.

10. When you are asked how your users should be uniquely identified, accept the default settings, which are appropriate for most scenarios, or change them. Click **Next** to continue.

11. On the next page, which gives you the option to filter users and devices, filter by AD group if this installation is part of a pilot project. If you wish to synchronize all user accounts in the selected OUs, accept the default and click **Next** to continue.

12. When you are presented with some optional features, check the box for any features you want and click **Next**. You are informed that you have completed the wizard and are ready to configure Azure AD Connect.

13. Choose to start the synchronization process as soon as the configuration completes and click **Install** to finish.

14. Verify that the users have synchronized to Azure AD. Log in to the Azure or Office 365 portal to view the synchronized accounts. Note that the user format matches the UPN configured in AD.

Although Azure AD Connect supports synchronization intervals of 30 minutes, you may want to use PowerShell to manually force the synchronization. Follow these steps:

1. Launch PowerShell as administrator.

2. Navigate to the *%ProgramFiles%*\Microsoft Azure AD Sync\bin folder.

3. Execute **DirectorySyncClientCmd.exe** with the delta parameter.

Implementing an Alternate Login ID (Optional)

The "Adding a User Principal Name" section discusses the most common approach to enabling user account synchronization to Azure AD so that users can be authenticated for access to one of the associated services (for example, Intune, Office 365). As part of this process, you modified the UPN to use an Internet-routable domain name and configured it to match the user's primary SMTP address. However, this is not always possible, as in some organizations you may not be allowed or able to alter the existing UPN.

This problem is resolved by implementing alternate login ID functionality, which enables you to configure the sign-in experience to use an alternative user attribute in Active Directory Domain Services rather than using the usual UPN.

TIP: USING THE MAIL ATTRIBUTE

The authors highly recommend using the mail attribute as the alternate login ID.

You can use the alternate login ID functionality in conjunction with each of the three user identity models. You must configure how your users are identified during Azure AD Connect installation. You cannot edit or repair this configuration afterward. More information on configuring an alternate login ID can be found at https://technet.microsoft.com/library/dn659436.aspx.

Integrating Intune with Configuration Manager

With the on-premise and cloud environments prepared and the on-premise user accounts synchronized with Azure AD, you can now integrate Microsoft Intune with ConfigMgr. This is achieved by adding an Intune subscription in the ConfigMgr console.

NOTE: LICENSING USERS

Microsoft Intune is a subscription cloud service. If Intune is deployed in a standalone model, you must assign Intune (or EMS) licenses to users via Azure or Office 365 portals. This entitles them to enroll up to 15 mobile devices.

When you integrate Intune with ConfigMgr, the behavior is different. You license users by adding them to the Configuration Manager collection configured in the Intune subscription. This is described in the "Creating a User Collection" section, later in this chapter.

A number of tasks are required to integrate Intune and Configuration Manager:

▶ Configure user discovery

▶ Create a user collection

▶ Add an Intune subscription

▶ Add the service connection point

These tasks are discussed in the following sections. After ConfigMgr and Intune are integrated, you will be able to manage mobile devices. This is described in detail in Chapter 17.

NOTE: DESKTOP COMPUTER MANAGEMENT WITH INTUNE

Microsoft Intune also allows you to manage desktop computers if you install and configure an Intune agent. However, when ConfigMgr and Intune are integrated, it is expected that the computer management is provided by ConfigMgr, which provides a much more comprehensive management solution.

Configuring User Discovery

ConfigMgr does not discover AD users by default; Active Directory User Discovery must be enabled. Follow these steps to enable Active Directory User Discovery:

1. In the console, navigate to **Administration -> Discovery Methods -> Active Directory User Discovery**.

2. Check the box **Enable Active Directory User Discovery**, as shown in Figure 16.6. Click the yellow starburst icon and select the OUs you require. Only users in these OUs will be discovered. If you selected specific OUs when configuring Azure AD Connect, remember to include them. Click **Apply**.

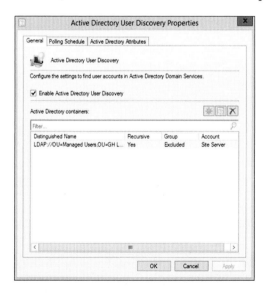

FIGURE 16.6   Enabling Active Directory User Discovery.

3. When you are prompted to run full discovery as soon as possible, click **Yes** and monitor the progress by using the ADUSRDIS.LOG file.

The discovery agent contacts a DC to locate the user resources. It discovers user accounts from the specified OUs in Active Directory Domain Services and creates discovery data records (DDRs) when sufficient resource information can be found. The users are then available in the ConfigMgr console.

NOTE: VERIFYING THE UPN

Use the following SQL query to verify that the UPN of the discovered users is consistent with the custom domain added to Intune (replacing P01 with your site code):

```
SELECT UserPrincipalName,
    COUNT(*) AS NumOfOccurances FROM (SELECT
    RIGHT(User_Principal_Name0,
    LEN(User_Principal_Name0)-PATINDEX('%@%',
    User_Principal_Name0)) AS UserPrincipalName FROM CM_P01.dbo.v_R_User)
AS sub GROUP BY UserPrincipalName
```

Creating a User Collection

You should create a user collection before adding a Microsoft Intune subscription. You will be prompted to select this collection when adding the subscription. Users who will be entitled to enroll devices for management should be added to this collection.

TIP: INCREMENTAL USER COLLECTIONS

The authors recommend creating an incremental collection so that users are added as quickly as possible.

Adding an Intune Subscription

The Microsoft Intune subscription allows you to specify your configuration settings for the Microsoft Intune service. This includes specifying which collection of users can enroll their devices and defining the mobile device platforms to manage. You can also customize the look and feel of the Intune company portal by adding contact information and branding with a company logo.

The Intune subscription is responsible for the following:

▶ Retrieving the certificate needed to connect to Intune

▶ Enabling users to enroll devices

▶ Configuring the supported mobile platforms

NOTE: SERVER BROWSER ISSUES

The security restrictions on the browser of a server operating system can cause issues with connecting to or authenticating with the Intune service. Disable Internet Explorer Enhanced Security Configuration before adding the Intune subscription.

Figure 16.7 shows another typical issue. This particular issue can be solved by enabling scripting in the security settings of the Internet zone.

FIGURE 16.7   Server browser issues.

To add an Intune subscription to Configuration Manager, follow these steps:

1. In the ConfigMgr console, navigate to **Administration -> Overview -> Hierarchy -> Cloud Services**. Right-click **Microsoft Intune Subscriptions**, and choose **Add Microsoft Intune Subscription**, as shown in Figure 16.8.

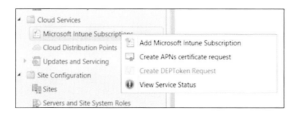

FIGURE 16.8   Adding an Intune subscription.

2. In the first dialog of the Create Microsoft Intune Subscription Wizard that appears, read the steps to complete the wizard and the prerequisites for managing the following platforms, as shown in Figure 16.9:

   ▶ **Windows:** Sideloading keys

   ▶ **Windows Phone 8:** Code-signing certificate

   ▶ **Windows Phone 8.1:** Sideloading keys

   ▶ **iOS:** Apple Push Notification Service certificate

   Click **Next** to continue.

FIGURE 16.9   The Create Microsoft Intune Subscription Wizard.

3. Select **Sign In** to sign in to Microsoft Intune (see Figure 16.10).

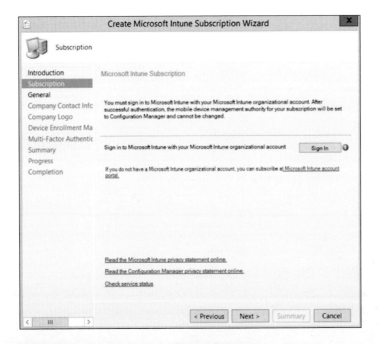

FIGURE 16.10   Signing in to Microsoft Intune.

4. Confirm that you want to set Configuration Manager to be the mobile device management authority, as shown in Figure 16.11.

NOTE: MICROSOFT MDM AUTHORITIES

A mobile device management authority is the management service that has permission to manage a set of devices. Microsoft has MDM authorities for the following:

▶ Intune

▶ Configuration Manager with Intune

▶ Office 365

Understand the consequences of setting this authority: If the MDM authority was previously set to Intune or Office 365, the ConfigMgr integration will fail.

FIGURE 16.11   Setting the mobile device management authority.

5. Enter your Intune credentials and click **Sign In**. This account must be a global administrator on the tenant. The account is authenticated and the Intune screen disappears.

6. Click **Next** to continue creating the subscription.

7. Complete the general configuration of the Intune Subscription, shown in Figure 16.12:

▶ Select the ConfigMgr collection configured earlier in this chapter, in the "Creating a User Collection" section. (Members of this collection are entitled to enroll devices.)

▶ Specify how you would like your company name to appear on the company portal on your managed mobile devices. You can also provide a URL to company privacy documentation.

▶ Choose the color scheme for the company portal. You can choose standard colors or customize the color using the palette.

▶ Verify the Configuration Manager site code.

▶ Use the dropdown to select a device enrollment limit, from 1 to 15. This limit defines the maximum number of devices a user can enroll and is optional. Note that an Intune license entitles a user to enroll a maximum of 15 devices.

Click **Next** to continue.

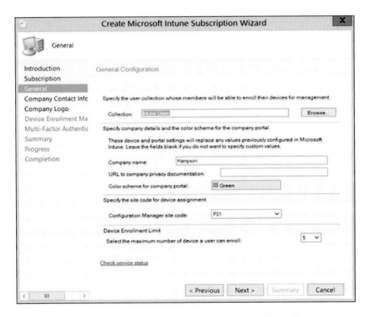

FIGURE 16.12   Intune subscription general configuration.

8. Specify the company contact information for the company portal, as shown in Figure 16.13. Enter the following information, which will be displayed to the user:

▶ IT department contact name

▶ IT department phone number

▶ IT department email address

▶ Website name

▶ Additional information

Click **Next** to continue.

9. Customize the company portal by adding the company logo (see Figure 16.14). Click **Next** to continue.

NOTE: COMPANY LOGO SPECIFICATIONS

The company logo can be added as a JPEG or PNG file type. The maximum allowed file size is 750KB, and the maximum resolution is 400×100 pixels.

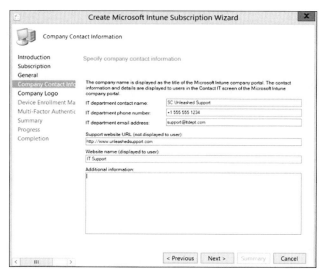

FIGURE 16.13   Specifying company contact information.

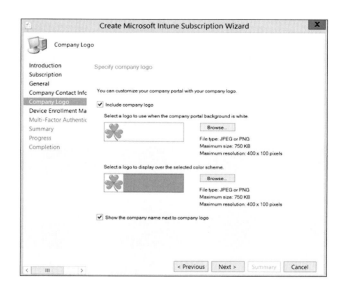

FIGURE 16.14   Specifying your company logo.

10. Add device enrollment managers, if required, and click **Next** to continue.

NOTE: DEVICE ENROLLMENT MANAGER

A standard user can enroll a maximum of 15 devices (depending on the device enrollment limit that is configured). A device enrollment manager does not have this limitation and can enroll more than this number. This is a special Intune account and is suitable when you want to enroll many shared user-less devices.

All of the device enrollment manager's devices are enrolled as company owned. This is discussed in more detail in Chapter 17.

11. Check the box to enable multi-factor authentication, if required. (There are several methods of configuring MFA, but they are beyond the scope of this book. See https://docs.microsoft.com/azure/multi-factor-authentication/multi-factor-authentication for more information.) Click **Next** to continue.

12. Review the configuration in the Summary dialog box and click **Next** to configure the Intune subscription.

13. Close the wizard.

The Intune Subscription is now added, and you can verify that a new site system is created (manage.microsoft.com). This is the cloud distribution point.

You can now configure management of the various platforms (see Figure 16.15), as discussed in Chapter 17.

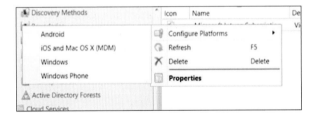

FIGURE 16.15   Configuring platforms.

Adding the Service Connection Point

In previous versions of ConfigMgr, when you added the Intune subscription, you were immediately informed that you were not finished with the Intune integration and still needed to add the Intune connector role. This connector was responsible for low-level communication with the Intune service.

The Intune connector role is not present in ConfigMgr Current Branch, and the service connection point (SCP) is now responsible for this functionality. This site system role is discussed in Chapter 6, "Installing and Updating System Center Configuration Manager."

The authors recommend adding the SCP during ConfigMgr installation. This is actually the default action. If you skipped this step during installation, you must add the role now.

The role can only be added on a central administration site (CAS) or standalone primary site. Follow these steps:

1. In the ConfigMgr console, navigate to **Administration -> Site Configuration -> Servers and Site System Roles**.

2. Right-click the server you require and select **Add Site System Roles**. The Add Site System Roles Wizard is launched.

3. Specify the service connection point role and click **Next** to continue.

4. Choose the device connection mode. **Online** is the recommended setting.

5. Click **Next** to continue.

6. Confirm your settings on the summary screen and click **Next** to add the role.

NOTE: SERVICE CONNECTION POINT MODES

Figure 16.16 shows the service connection point modes. Online mode is a persistent connection and the recommended setting. This mode is required if you configure an Intune subscription. If you create the Intune subscription while the service connection point is in Offline mode, it is automatically changed to Online.

FIGURE 16.16   Service connection point modes.

Removing an Intune Subscription

You can switch to a different Intune subscription. This may be necessary, for example, if you configured a trial subscription and want to move to a different paid subscription. Begin by performing the following steps to delete the subscription:

1. In the Configuration Manager console, navigate to **Administration -> Overview -> Cloud Services** and select **Microsoft Intune Subscription**.

2. Right-click **Microsoft Intune Subscription** and select **Delete**.

3. Navigate to **Administration -> Overview -> Site Configuration** and select **Servers and Site System Roles**.

4. Highlight the server with the service connection point.

5. Right-click **Service connection point** in the Site System Roles pane and select **Remove Role**.

6. Confirm that you wish to remove the role.

Now, create a new subscription. Follow these steps:

1. Create a new service connection point.

2. Add a new Intune subscription.

3. Set Configuration Manager to be the MDM authority.

CAUTION: DELETING A SUBSCRIPTION DELETES ALL ASSOCIATED INFORMATION

Enrollments, policies, and deployments associated with a deleted subscription are lost, and you must re-enroll all devices.

Removal of Intune Extensions

Earlier versions of ConfigMgr used Intune extensions to deliver new features out of band so they could be delivered at a more rapid cadence than service packs or cumulative updates. These extensions are no longer required in ConfigMgr Current Branch. New features are now delivered through regular Configuration Manager upgrades.

Troubleshooting Intune Hybrid

Configuration Manager is a very stable solution. However, sometimes things go wrong, and you need to be able to troubleshoot and resolve these issues. ConfigMgr administrators are generally very skilled at troubleshooting by analyzing the huge number of log files at their disposal. However, when you add and configure an Intune subscription, you add to the complexity of integration with a cloud service.

There are a number of tools available to troubleshoot Intune integration, discussed in the next sections.

Viewing Site and Component Status

To view site and component status, in the ConfigMgr console, navigate to **Monitoring -> System Status**. Using **Site Status** and **Component Status** provides a good overview of the health of the ConfigMgr servers and components. Figures 16.17 and 16.18 provide examples.

Right-click any component and choose **Messages -> All** to see detailed information, including errors and warnings.

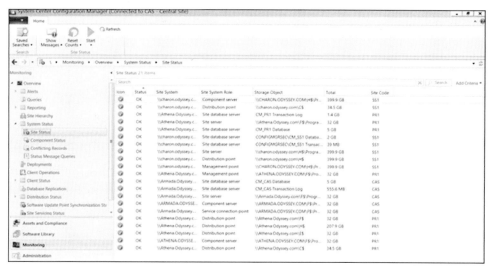

FIGURE 16.17   Configuration Manager Site Status.

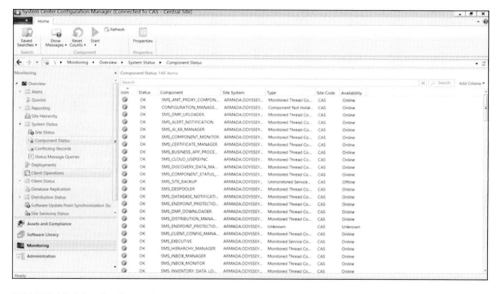

FIGURE 16.18   Configuration Manager Component Status.

For Intune integration, concentrate on the following components:

▶ SMS_Cloud_Services_Manager

▶ SMS_CloudUserSync

▶ SMS_DMP_Downloader

▶ SMS_DMP_Uploader

Using Log Files

ConfigMgr is well known for having extensive logging capabilities. Find the log files in the installation folder at *%ProgramFiles%*\Microsoft Configuration Manager\Logs.

Table 16.3 describes log files that are useful in troubleshooting Intune integration issues.

TABLE 16.3   Log Files for Intune Integration Troubleshooting

Log File	Purpose
CloudUserSync.log	Records license enablement for users. (Figure 16.19 shows an example.) Ensure that Intune licensed user accounts have been synchronized.
Dmpdownloader.log	Records details on downloads from Microsoft Intune. Review it for communication errors.
Dmpuploader.log	Records details for uploading database changes to Microsoft Intune. Review it for communication errors.
Outgoingcontentmanager.log	Records content uploaded to Microsoft Intune. Review it for errors.

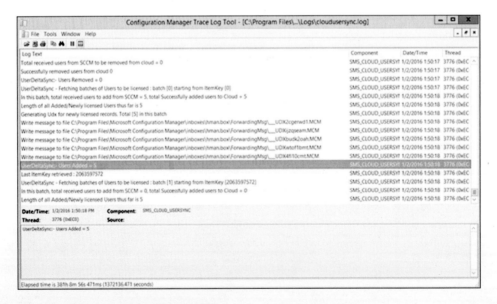

FIGURE 16.19   CloudUserSync.log file.

You can enable verbose logging for any of the components (but do not forget to turn it off again). Follow these steps:

1. Open the registry on the Configuration Manager server and navigate to `HKEY_LOCAL_MACHINE\SOFTWARE\Microsoft\SMSCOMPONENTS`.

2. Select the component for which you need to enable verbose logging.

3. If there already is a DWORD key called `Verbose Logging`, change the value.

4. If the key is not there, create it and change the value.

Table 16.4 lists verbose logging values.

TABLE 16.4   Verbose Logging Values

Value	Definition
0	Default value; displays errors and important information
1	Displays errors, important information, warnings, and general information
2	All logging

Viewing Intune Status

To view Intune status, open the Intune Subscription properties. Note the link in the bottom-left corner: **Check service status**. Clicking this link brings you to the Current Status page, shown in Figure 16.20, where you can see details of any current issues or outages on your tenant. You can access this page directly by using the URL https://status .manage.microsoft.com/StatusPage/ServiceDashboard.

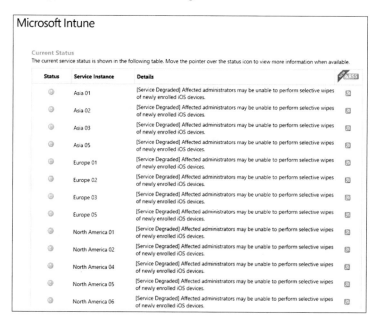

FIGURE 16.20   Intune service current status.

NOTE: INTUNE SERVICE DASHBOARD

The Intune Service Dashboard has been migrated to the Office 365 management portal.

Troubleshooting Directory Synchronization

Directory synchronization can be a complex operation with many moving parts, many of which may be out of your control. It is difficult to troubleshoot an issue without full visibility of all the elements.

Several online documents are available to assist you, including the following:

▶ **Troubleshoot Azure AD Connect Installation Issues:** https://support.microsoft
.com/kb/3121701

▶ **Troubleshoot Connectivity Issues with Azure AD Connect:** https://azure.microsoft
.com/documentation/articles/active-directory-aadconnect-troubleshoot-connectivity/

Utilizing Microsoft Support for Intune

At the time this book was published, Microsoft offered free support for Intune-related issues—for both trial and production environments.

For urgent issues, you can contact Microsoft by telephone. You can find a full list of local numbers for Intune support in the TechNet library. Local language is supported in most locations, and English is supported in all locations. See https://technet.microsoft.com/library/jj839713.aspx for further information.

For a less urgent issue, you can create an online support request through the Office 365 admin center, at https://portal.office.com. Follow these steps:

1. Navigate to **Support -> Service Requests**.

2. In the Create a service request page, which presents a list of support options, click **More** to see more options.

3. Select **Mobile Device Management**. You are presented with two dropdown boxes to identify the issue.

4. Make a selection in the **Feature** box. You can choose **Intune: Service Administration**, for example.

5. Select a symptom. This is a dynamic portal, and different choices are available, depending on the feature you select. You can choose **Subscriptions and licenses**, for example.

6. In the **Issue Summary** box, summarize your issue in one sentence.

7. Enter further details in the **Issue details** box. Click **Next** to continue. Microsoft provides hyperlinks to some documentation that may assist you.

8. If you still need to create a service request, click **Yes, continue**.

9. Add further details about the service affected. You can attach log files or screenshots if you wish. Click **Next** to continue.

10. Confirm your contact details and click **Submit request**.

Accessing the Microsoft TechNet Forum

The Intune TechNet forum is a useful free troubleshooting tool. You can search for issues similar to yours to see if a solution already exists. Create a new thread if you cannot find a suitable answer. The Microsoft community is very strong in this area, and questions are typically answered very quickly. To use the forum, open an Internet browser and go to https://social.technet.microsoft.com/Forums/home?category=microsoftintune& filter=alltypes&sort=lastpostdesc.

Using the Configuration Manager Hybrid Diagnostics Tool

Microsoft's System Center Configuration Manager Hybrid Diagnostics tool checks for a number of issues related to Intune integration; Figure 16.21 shows an example. Download the tool from https://www.microsoft.com/download/details.aspx?id=53306.

The current version of the tool performs the following checks:

▶ Verifies that the SMSExec service is running

▶ Verifies the service connection point certificate

▶ Checks for potential conflicts between service connection point certificates

▶ Verifies the DNS CNAME entry for the specified UPN

▶ Verifies device type enablement in Configuration Manager

▶ Looks for known errors in status messages

▶ Verifies UPN synchronization in Azure AD

▶ Verifies that the specified user is a member of the cloud user collection

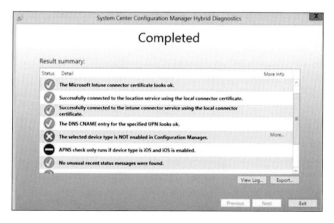

FIGURE 16.21   Hybrid Diagnostics tool.

Summary

This chapter described the tasks you need to perform to integrate Configuration Manager and Intune in a hybrid solution. It discussed a number of choices that need to be made during the process.

After providing an overview of Intune, this chapter introduced user identity, including a description of each method to assist with deciding which is right for your organization. The chapter discussed the preparation of AD and Azure AD prior to integration. Remember that Azure AD Connect is now the only recommended tool for directory synchronization.

The integration is relatively straightforward. This chapter showed how to add the service connection point and Intune subscription. Configuring the Intune subscription enables you to customize the Intune company portal on the clients.

Finally, this chapter looked at some useful troubleshooting techniques and showed the values in log files and the status in the Configuration Manager console.

Chapter 17 discusses managing mobile devices. It walks through the enrollment of each of the device types and then shows the management possibilities provided by the Intune-integrated hybrid solution.

Chapter 17 also focuses on Windows 10. Windows 10 mobile and desktop devices can be enrolled for MDM management using the Intune hybrid integration. Standalone Intune also provides computer management with the Intune client. However, if possible, the authors recommend managing Windows 10 desktops using the full ConfigMgr client, as it provides a more comprehensive management experience.

Managing Mobile Devices

As discussed in Chapter 16, "Integrating Intune Hybrid into Your Configuration Manager Environment," you can integrate System Center Configuration Manager (ConfigMgr) with Microsoft Intune to provide a solution for managing mobile devices, and you can set ConfigMgr as the mobile device management authority. Chapter 16 also describes the process of synchronizing user accounts from on-premise Active Directory (AD) to Azure AD.

This chapter focuses on configuring this hybrid solution to manage mobile devices. It describes the steps to enroll devices and the features available for managing the supported platforms.

> **NOTE: MANAGING ACCESS TO CORPORATE RESOURCES**
>
> Conditional access prevents access to corporate resources when a device is not enrolled in ConfigMgr. It is implemented through compliance policies and conditional access policies. This major feature of the hybrid solution is discussed in Chapter 18, "Conditional Access in Configuration Manager."

Table 17.1 lists the devices supported for management by ConfigMgr and Intune.

TABLE 17.1   Devices Supported for Management

Platform	Version
Google Android	Version 4.0 and later (including Samsung Knox)
Apple iOS	Version 8.0 and later
Windows Phone	Version 8.0 and later
Windows	Windows RT, Windows 8.1 RT, Windows 8.1 and later (managed as mobile devices)
Mac OS X	Version 10.9 and later

Enabling Devices for Management

Each platform listed in Table 17.1 is managed differently. Android and iOS users download the Intune Company Portal app from Google Play and the Apple App Store, respectively. Once the app is installed, users log in to Microsoft Intune to enroll the device. However, Windows devices do not require the Intune Company Portal.

Each platform has different prerequisites. For example, only iOS devices require that you create and install an Apple Push Notification (APN) certificate before enrolling those devices. Further information is available in the "Enabling iOS Devices for Management" section, later in this chapter.

Various enrollment scenarios exist, including the two primary ones:

▶ Bring your own device (BYOD)

▶ Choose your own device (CYOD)

Enrolling devices is a user process with BYOD. For CYOD, an administrator or device manager can enroll devices as well.

Enabling Android Devices for Management

Android device management can be challenging, as management capabilities are not consistent across all Android devices. Samsung Knox extends the management capabilities in some Android devices. To manage Android devices, you must enable Android support in the ConfigMgr console (with an Intune subscription). There are no prerequisite tasks for Android support. To enroll an Android device, a user or an administrator must download and install the Intune Company Portal app for Android, which is available from the Google Play store. The user is prompted to log in to Intune, and the device is subsequently enrolled for management.

Enabling Android Devices in Configuration Manager

Enabling Android support in ConfigMgr is straightforward. Follow these steps:

1. In the console, navigate to **Administration -> Overview -> Cloud Services -> Microsoft Intune Subscription**.

2. Right-click the Microsoft Intune subscription you created in Chapter 16.

3. Select **Configure Platforms -> Android**.

4. Enable the check box **Enable Android enrollment**.

5. Click **OK** to finish enabling Android support.

Enrolling Android Devices

Use the Intune Company Portal for Android to enroll Android devices. You can download this portal, released in December 2013, from the Google Play Store, at https://play.google.com/store/apps/details?id=com.microsoft.windowsintune.companyportal. The process of enrolling an Android device follows. This example uses a Samsung Galaxy tablet:

1. Open Google Play on the Android device.

2. Search for **Intune Company Portal app**. Download and install the app.

3. When you are presented with a list of features that the Intune Company Portal needs to access, such as device and app history, identity, contacts, photos/media/files, Wi-Fi connection information, device ID, and call information, click **Accept** to continue (see Figure 17.1).

FIGURE 17.1   Intune Company Portal access required.

4. After the Company Portal completes installing, open the app.

5. Click **Sign in** to continue. You are redirected to an Intune login page.

6. Enter an account that has permission to enroll devices and select **Sign in** to sign in using the UPN you configured in Chapter 16.

7. Note on the Company Access Setup page that Device Enrollment and Device Compliance require attention. Select **Begin**.

8. On the Why enroll your device? page, which describes the benefits of enrolling your device, click the hyperlink for more information and then click **Continue**.

9. When you are presented with privacy information, listing items that an information technology (IT) administrator can and cannot see on the device, click **Continue**.

10. On the next page, which includes a description of what comes next, click **Enroll**.

11. For Android devices, you must activate the device administrator, so review the list of operations the Company Portal can perform and click **Activate**.

12. Check the box to accept the Samsung Knox terms and conditions (assuming a Knox-enabled Android device). Click **Confirm** to continue.

13. If you are asked to configure screen unlock settings, enter a pattern, PIN, or password and then confirm your choice.

14. When you are redirected back to the Company Access Setup page, note that the green checkmarks show that Device Enrollment and Device Compliance no longer require attention. Select **Continue**.

15. When you are informed that the company access setup is complete, click **Done**. The Android device is enrolled (see Figure 17.2), and you can see apps available in the Company Portal.

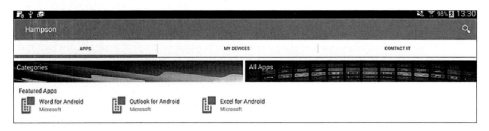

FIGURE 17.2   Intune Company Portal with an Android device enrolled.

The device, highlighted in Figure 17.3, is now available for management in the ConfigMgr console. Note the automatic naming convention for Android devices: *Username*_Android_Enrollment_*Date_Time*.

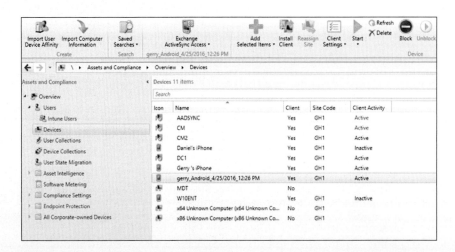

FIGURE 17.3   Viewing an Android device in the Configuration Manager console.

TIP: TROUBLESHOOTING WITH THE HYBRID DIAGNOSTICS TOOL

Use the Configuration Manager Hybrid Diagnostics tool to troubleshoot issues with enrolling devices. Chapter 16 provides additional information.

Enabling iOS Devices for Management

The process of enabling and enrolling iOS devices is similar to the process for Android devices. First, enable iOS support in the ConfigMgr console, which requires configuring an APN certificate. A user or an administrator can then download and install the Intune Company Portal app for iOS, which is available from the Apple App Store. During that process, the device is enrolled for management.

NOTE: ENABLING MAC OS X ENROLLMENT

In ConfigMgr 2012 you could manage Apple Mac OS X devices by installing the Mac Client for ConfigMgr. In ConfigMgr Current Branch you manage Mac devices by enrolling them as MDM clients in the same way as with iOS devices. It is no longer required to configure an HTTPS infrastructure to support Mac OS X devices.

Enabling iOS support in ConfigMgr automatically enables support for Mac OS X devices enrolled in MDM.

Enabling iOS Devices in Configuration Manager

Enrolling iOS devices for management requires additional configuration. Follow these steps:

1. In the ConfigMgr console, navigate to **Administration -> Overview -> Cloud Services -> Microsoft Intune Subscription**.

2. Highlight the Microsoft Intune subscription.

3. Select **Create APNs certificate request** from the Ribbon.

4. In the Request Apple Push Notification Service Certificate Signing Request dialog box, enter the path for downloading the certificate signing request (.csr file) and click **Download** to create the CSR.

5. Click the **Apple Push Certificate Portal** hyperlink or browse to https://identity.apple.com.

6. Click **Sign in** and sign in to the portal, using an Apple ID. (Note that you can now create an Apple ID without adding credit card information.)

TIP: USING AN ORGANIZATION APPLE ID

The authors recommend creating an organization Apple ID to enroll iOS devices for management. If the APN certificate is not renewed every 12 months using the same ID, the iOS devices must be re-enrolled.

Avoid this situation by using an organization Apple ID rather than personal Apple IDs with your APN certificate.

17

7. Select **Create a Certificate** on the Get Started page.

8. Check the **Accept** box to accept the terms and conditions.

9. Browse to your CSR file on the Create a New Push Certificate page and click **Upload**.

10. Depending on the browser used for this part of the process, you may be asked to download a .json file. This file is not required and should be ignored. Cancel the download and log out of the portal.

11. Log back into the portal and your new certificate will be visible. Select **Download** to retrieve the MDM_Microsoft Corporation_Certificate.pem file (see Figure 17.4).

FIGURE 17.4   Apple Push Certificates Portal.

12. Back in the ConfigMgr console, right-click the Microsoft Intune subscription.

13. Select **Configure Platforms -> iOS and Mac OS X (MDM)**.

14. Check the box **Enable iOS and Mac OS X (MDM) enrollment**. Click **Browse** and locate the .pem certificate file you downloaded earlier (see Figure 17.5).

15. Click **Apply** to enable enrollment of these devices. Click **OK** to finish.

The next time you open the properties page, you do not see the path to the APN certificate; it is replaced by the text <Certificate on file>.

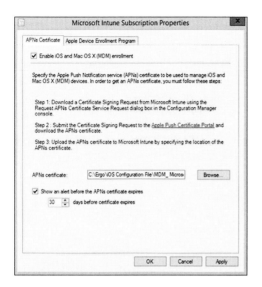

FIGURE 17.5   Enabling iOS devices.

Enrolling iOS Devices

This section uses an iPhone 6 to illustrate enrolling an iOS device. The Intune Company Portal for iOS is used for device enrollment. Download the portal from the Apple App Store at https://itunes.apple.com/app/microsoft-intune-company-portal/id719171358?mt=8 and perform the following steps:

1. Search for the **Intune Company Portal** app in the Apple App Store and then download and install the app.

2. Launch the app and log in to Intune with your user account, using the UPN configured in Chapter 16.

3. The first steps of this wizard are the same as when enrolling an Android device. Follow the wizard through the Company Access Setup, Why enroll your device, We care about privacy, and What comes next pages. Click **Enroll** to enroll your device.

4. Click **Install** to install Management Profile, as shown in Figure 17.6. This profile contains the Device Enrollment Challenge and is signed and verified by IOSProfileSigning.manage.microsoft.com.

17

FIGURE 17.6 Installing the iOS Management Profile.

5. After the enrolling certificate is installed, again click **Install** to install the mobile device management profile.

6. Click **Trust** to verify that you trust the profile's source.

7. Click **Open** when prompted to open the page in the Company Portal.

8. Company Access Setup requires no more attention, so click **Continue** and then click **Done** on the next page. The Intune Company Portal for iOS is installed, and the device is enrolled.

9. Select **Rate App** if you wish to give feedback on the setup experience.

The device is now available for management in the ConfigMgr console. The automatic naming convention for iPhones is *Name_iPhone.*

TIP: PREVENTING DUPLICATE DEVICE NAMES

The authors recommend renaming iOS devices before enrollment to avoid duplicate device names in the ConfigMgr console.

Enterprise enrollment of corporate iOS devices is discussed in the "Managing Company Devices" section, later in this chapter.

Enabling Windows Phone Devices for Management

Enabling support to manage Windows mobile devices in ConfigMgr is more involved than with the other platforms, and different configurations are required depending on the type of device you wish to manage. For example, for Windows Phone 8.0, you must sign the

Company Portal app (ssp.xap) with a Symantec Enterprise Code Signing certificate. Enrolling Windows Phone 8.1 and Windows 10 Mobile devices is more straightforward. This book uses Windows 10 Mobile as an example.

Enabling Windows Phone Devices in Configuration Manager

To enable support for Windows Phone in the ConfigMgr console, perform the following steps:

1. Navigate to **Administration -> Overview -> Cloud Services -> Microsoft Intune Subscription**.

2. Right-click on the Microsoft Intune subscription.

3. Select **Configure Platforms -> Windows Phone**.

4. Check the box **Windows Phone 8.1 and Windows 10 Mobile**, as shown in Figure 17.7.

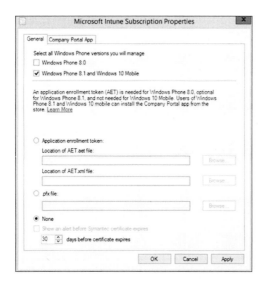

FIGURE 17.7   Enabling Windows Phone devices.

Automatic Intune Enrollment

There are many more options for enrolling Windows 10 Mobile devices than with other platforms. Windows 10, Intune, and Azure are closely integrated to provide a holistic solution.

At this point, the device could be enrolled in Intune by navigating to **Settings -> Accounts -> Work access** and choosing **Enroll in device management**. However, it is more useful to integrate with Microsoft Azure during this process. Performing an Azure AD join of the device lets you take advantage of advanced Azure features such as multi-factor authentication (MFA). You can configure Azure so that automatic Intune enrollment is part of the process.

NOTE: AUTOMATIC INTUNE ENROLLMENT

Automatic Intune enrollment refers to a process in which a device enrolls with Intune automatically after it has been joined to Azure AD.

The term *automatic* can be confusing in this scenario as it is not a fully automatic process. User input is still required to join the device to Azure AD.

NOTE: AZURE AD PREMIUM LICENSE

An Azure AD Premium license is required for each user who will have Azure AD-joined devices automatically enrolled in Microsoft Intune. This license is included with an Enterprise Mobility + Security (EMS) license.

The process of configuring automatic Intune enrollment for Azure AD-joined devices follows:

1. Assign an EMS license to the global administrator account.

2. Log in to the Azure portal (https://manage.windowsazure.com) using the global administrator account.

3. Access the **Azure Active Directory** namespace.

4. Click on the **Mobility (MDM and MAM)** tab and select **Microsoft Intune**.

5. Select **Configure** to open the Intune properties.

6. Verify that the **MDM Discovery URL**, **MDM Terms of Use URL**, and **MDM Compliance URL** fields are prepopulated. You do not have to change these URLs.

7. Select the groups of users to configure automatic enrollment to Intune.

8. Save the configuration.

Enrolling Windows 10 Mobile Devices

After Intune auto-enrollment is configured, perform the following steps to join a Windows 10 Mobile device to Azure AD:

NOTE: JOINING WINDOWS 10 MOBILE TO AZURE AD

For Windows 10 Mobile, you must perform the configuration to join Azure AD during the initial setup of the device (out-of-box experience). It is not possible to do so afterward without resetting the device.

This is different with Windows 10 computers, for which you can join Azure AD in the context of the operating system.

1. Start the initial setup of a Windows 10 Mobile device. Continue through the out-of-box experience until you get to the Who owns the device? page, shown in Figure 17.8.

2. Under My work or school owns it, click **Set up for work**.

3. Read the information on the What happens next page and click **Next** to continue.

4. On the Let's get you signed in page, sign in with your user account (UPN) and password.

5. If MFA is configured, and you are prompted to verify your identity, choose your preferred verification method and continue through the wizard. You may also be prompted to provide a work PIN if Passport for Work is enabled on your Azure tenant.

The wizard informs you "You're all set!" This means the device has been added to Azure AD and enrolled in Intune.

FIGURE 17.8   Joining Windows 10 Mobile to Azure AD.

The device is now available for management in the ConfigMgr console. Figure 17.9 shows the automatic naming convention for Windows Phone devices: *Username_WindowsPhone_Enrollment_Date_time*.

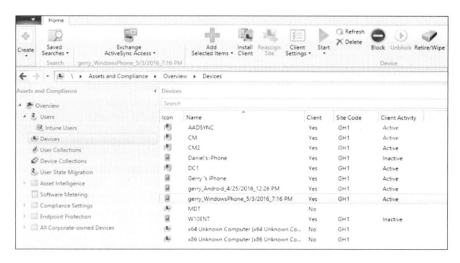

FIGURE 17.9   Windows 10 Mobile in the Configuration Manager console.

Using Windows Computers as Mobile Devices

Beginning with Windows 8.1, Windows computers can be enrolled and managed as mobile devices in Microsoft Intune through the Open Mobile Alliance Device Management (OMA DM) channel. This chapter uses Windows 10 as an example.

The prerequisites for enrolling and managing Windows computers are the same as those for Windows mobile devices, as already discussed in this chapter, in the context of Windows Mobile. Intune auto-enrollment is discussed in the "Automatic Intune Enrollment" section, earlier in this chapter, and Chapter 16 discusses external DNS records.

Enabling Windows Computers in Configuration Manager

Enabling enrollment of Windows computers in Configuration Manager is straightforward; no special prerequisites are required. Follow these steps:

1. In the ConfigMgr console, navigate to **Administration -> Overview -> Cloud Services -> Microsoft Intune Subscription**.

2. Right-click the Microsoft Intune subscription.

3. Select **Configure Platforms -> Windows**.

4. Enable the check box **Enable Windows enrollment**, as shown in Figure 17.10.

NOTE: ENTERPRISE CODE-SIGNING CERTIFICATE

An enterprise code-signing certificate is required to deploy apps to Windows computers managed through OMA DM.

FIGURE 17.10   Enabling Windows enrollment in the ConfigMgr console.

Enrolling Windows 10 Computers

The process of enrolling a Windows 10 computer is slightly different from that for Windows 10 Mobile. You can join the device to Azure AD during the out-of-box experience. However, you can also perform this step within the context of the OS. This is described in the following steps, using a Windows 10 v1607 computer:

1. In Windows, navigate to **Start -> Settings -> Accounts -> Access work or school**.

2. Under Connect to work or school, select **Connect**.

3. On the Set up a work or school account page, click **Join this device to Azure Active Directory** (see Figure 17.11).

4. Sign in with your user account (UPN) and password.

5. If MFA is configured, and you are prompted to verify your identity, choose your preferred verification method, and continue through the wizard. You may also be prompted to provide a work PIN if Passport for Work is enabled on your Azure tenant.

17

Set up a work or school account

You'll get access to resources like email, apps, and the network. Connecting means your work or school might control some things on this device, such as which settings you can change. For specific info about this, ask them.

someone@example.com

Alternate actions:

Join this device to Azure Active Directory

Join this device to a local Active Directory domain

Next

FIGURE 17.11   Joining a Windows 10 computer to Azure AD.

The wizard informs you that You're all set! This means that the device is added to Azure AD and enrolled in Intune.

6. In **Access work or school**, verify that the computer is connected to Azure AD.

The computer is now available for management in the ConfigMgr console. Notice that Windows computers retain their system name but are enrolled as mobile devices, as displayed in Figure 17.12.

Icon	Name	Client	Site Code	Client Activity	Client Type	Device Owner
	AADSYNC	Yes	GH1	Active	Computer	Company
	CM	Yes	GH1	Active	Computer	Company
	CM2	Yes	GH1	Active	Computer	Company
	Daniel's iPhone	Yes	GH1	Inactive	Mobile	Personal
	DC1	Yes	GH1	Active	Computer	Company
	Gerry 's iPhone	Yes	GH1	Active	Mobile	Personal
	gerry_Android_4/25/2016_12:26 PM	Yes	GH1	Active	Mobile	Personal
	gerry_WindowsPhone_5/3/2016_7:16 PM	Yes	GH1	Active	Mobile	Personal
	MDT	No			None	
	W10ENT	Yes	GH1	Inactive	Mobile	Company
	W10PRO	Yes	GH1	Active	Mobile	Personal
	x64 Unknown Computer (x64 Unknown Co...	No	GH1		None	
	x86 Unknown Computer (x86 Unknown Co...	No	GH1		None	

FIGURE 17.12   Windows 10 computer available as a mobile device.

NOTE: WINDOWS 10 PROVISIONING PACKAGES

Administrators can use provisioning packages to automate the configuration of Windows 10 devices. This automation includes the steps to join the device to Azure AD.

Managing Company Devices

Mobile devices are automatically categorized as personal devices when enrolled into Intune and ConfigMgr. You can easily change a personal device to a company device by right-clicking the device and selecting **Change Ownership** and then selecting from the dropdown shown in Figure 17.13. You can also multi-select devices and then follow the same process to change ownership.

FIGURE 17.13   Changing ownership of a mobile device.

There are several differences in the way that ConfigMgr manages personal and company devices:

▶ The inventory data collected is different for personal and company devices. For example, for iOS and Android devices, all software is inventoried for company devices, while the inventory for personal devices shows managed apps only.

▶ You can use device ownership as a global condition when targeting a policy or an app to a group of devices.

There are a number of methods to enroll company-owned devices for MDM with Intune and ConfigMgr, discussed in the following sections. Some of these methods are dependent on the device type and how it was purchased.

Device Enrollment Program (iOS Only)

To use the Device Enrollment Program, organizations must first join the Apple Device Enrollment Program (DEP) and receive a DEP token. iOS devices must be purchased through DEP. The Intune enrollment profiles can then be uploaded to Apple and assigned to these devices.

The high-level process for enabling DEP enrollment follows:

1. In the ConfigMgr console, create a DEP token request by navigating to **Administration -> Overview -> Cloud Services -> Microsoft Intune Subscription**, selecting your subscription, and clicking **Create DEP token request** from the ribbon bar (see Figure 17.14).

17

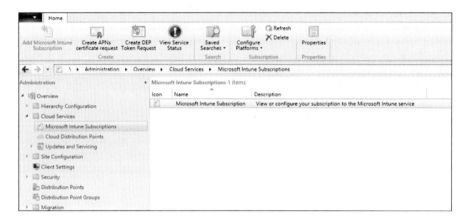

FIGURE 17.14   Creating a DEP token request.

2. Get a DEP token from Apple and add it to ConfigMgr.

3. Add a corporate device enrollment profile.

4. Assign DEP devices for management.

5. Synchronize DEP-managed devices.

See https://technet.microsoft.com/library/mt706231.aspx for further information on configuring DEP.

Apple Configurator (iOS Only)

The Apple Configurator tool is an Apple-developed solution to assist administrators in deploying corporate iOS devices. It can be downloaded from the Mac App Store and can be installed only on Apple operating systems.

The high-level process for iOS enrollment using the Apple Configurator follows:

1. Add a corporate device enrollment profile. In the ConfigMgr console, navigate to **Assets and Compliance -> Overview -> All Corporate-owned devices -> iOS -> Enrollment Profiles.**

2. Add iOS devices to enroll with the Setup Assistant.

3. Select devices to enroll.

4. Assign a profile.

5. Select a profile to deploy to iOS devices.

6. Prepare the device with the Apple Configurator.

See https://technet.microsoft.com/library/mt706232.aspx for full details on device enrollment with the Apple Configurator.

Device Enrollment Manager

From a licensing perspective, a user is entitled to enroll a maximum of 15 devices in the hybrid Intune/ConfigMgr solution. The maximum of 15 devices is configured by default in the General tab of the Intune subscription properties. You can set this maximum value to any number between 1 and 15.

The devices are enrolled as user specific, and you can target these devices with apps and policies based on the user. However, sometimes app deployment to specific users is not required, and you may want to quickly bulk-enroll many devices that will be shared by users. The device enrollment manager is a special Intune account with permission to enroll more than 15 devices.

Device enrollment managers cannot be Intune administrators. Assign this role as follows:

1. In the ConfigMgr console, navigate to **Administration** -> **Overview** -> **Cloud Services** -> **Microsoft Intune Subscription**.

2. Right-click the Microsoft Intune subscription and select **Properties**.

3. Choose the Device Enrollment Manager tab.

4. Select **Add/Remove** to add the managers.

NOTE: DEVICE ENROLLMENT MANAGERS

Device enrollment managers can enroll devices and log in to the Company Portal to install and uninstall apps. However, these devices cannot be workplace or Azure AD joined; therefore, they are not subject to conditional access policies.

See Chapter 18 for information regarding conditional access.

17

Protecting Mobile Devices

ConfigMgr provides a number of options should one of your devices be lost or stolen. It can also assist if a device no longer needs to be managed or is no longer accessible. In the console, right-click a mobile device to see available options, shown in Figure 17.15. Notice the Retire/Wipe feature.

FIGURE 17.15   Viewing mobile device options.

Click on **Remote Device Actions** to view further options, shown in Figure 17.16.

FIGURE 17.16   Viewing remote device actions.

The following sections examine some of these options.

Retiring and Wiping Mobile Devices

You can retire a device if you no longer want to manage it with ConfigMgr. Right-click the device and choose **Retire/Wipe**. You are asked whether to wipe company content or the entire device when it is retired from ConfigMgr, as shown in Figure 17.17.

FIGURE 17.17   Options for retiring a device.

Select **Wipe company content and retire the mobile device from Configuration Manager** if you require a selective wipe. This is useful in a BYOD scenario if the user is leaving the company. In this scenario, the device is no longer managed, and corporate data is removed. Personal data is not affected by a selective wipe.

There is an additional consideration regarding retiring and wiping Windows 10 devices. Joining devices to Azure AD is discussed earlier in this chapter, in the "Enrolling Windows 10 Mobile Devices" section. Joining devices to Azure AD is typically used to enroll corporate devices. The selective wipe option may be grayed out and unavailable for these devices. This is by design as executing a full wipe on a corporate device is the required action.

Workplace joining a device is an alternative method of enrolling a device and is the preferred option in a BYOD scenario. For these personal devices, both selective and full wipe options are available. (Workplace join steps for personal devices are beyond the scope of this book.)

Tables 17.2 and 17.3 list the company data removed for each platform when retiring a device and choosing selective wipe.

TABLE 17.2   Data Removed with Selective Wipe (Windows)

Content	Windows 8.1 and Later	Windows Phone 8.1 and Windows Mobile 10
Company apps and associated data	Apps are uninstalled, and side-loading keys are removed. Data will no longer be accessible.	Apps are uninstalled. App data is removed.
Virtual private network (VPN) and Wi-Fi profiles	Removed.	Removed.
Certificates	Removed and revoked.	Removed.
Settings	Removed.	Mostly removed (review TechNet documentation).
Email profiles	Email and attachments are removed from Outlook and the Mail app for Windows.	Removed.

TABLE 17.3   Data Removed with Selective Wipe (iOS and Android)

Content	iOS	Android	Samsung Knox
Company apps and associated data	Apps are uninstalled. App data is removed.	Apps and data remain installed.	Apps are uninstalled.
VPN and Wi-Fi profiles	Removed.	Removed.	Removed.
Certificates	Removed and revoked.	Revoked.	Revoked.
Settings	Mostly removed (review TechNet documentation).	Removed.	Removed.
Management agent	Management profile is removed.	Device administrator privilege is revoked.	Device administrator privilege is revoked.
Email profiles	For email profiles provisioned by Microsoft Intune, the email account and email are removed.	N/A	For email profiles provisioned by Microsoft Intune, the email account and email are removed.

Select **Wipe the mobile device and retire it from Configuration Manager** if a full wipe is required. This action restores the device to factory defaults; all data, applications, and settings are removed. This option is useful when a device is stolen or lost.

NOTE: PERFORMING RETIRE/WIPE

Administrators perform the Retire/Wipe operations in the ConfigMgr console. Users can also perform these operations on their own devices by using the Company Portal app.

Resetting Passcodes

Passcode Reset is one of the additional remote device actions that you can perform (refer to Figure 17.16). If a user forgets the passcode for his or her device, you can provide assistance by removing the passcode or forcing a new temporary passcode. The behavior is platform dependent (see Table 17.4).

TABLE 17.4   Password Reset Behavior

Platform	Passcode Reset
iOS	Clears the passcode from a device. Does not create a new temporary passcode.
Android	Supported; a temporary passcode is created.
Windows Phone 8 and later	Supported.
Windows 8.1 and later	Not supported.

You can view the state of a passcode reset by selecting **View Passcode State** (refer to Figure 17.16). You can also select this from the Remote Device Actions menu.

TIP: ANDROID TEMPORARY PASSWORDS

Android temporary passwords are long and complex. You should warn your users in advance.

Remotely Locking a Device

You can lock a device remotely if it is lost. The behavior is platform dependent (see Table 17.5).

TABLE 17.5   Remote Lock Support, by Platform

Platform	Remote Lock
iOS	Supported.
Android	Supported.
Windows Phone 8 and later	Supported.
Windows 8.1 and later	Supported if the current user of the device is the same user who enrolled the device.

You can view the state of a remote lock by selecting **View Remote Lock State** or by using the Remote Device Actions menu.

Accessing Activation Lock Bypass (iOS Only)

iOS Activation Lock is a feature of the Find My iPhone app for iOS 7.1 and later versions. It is automatically enabled when the Find My iPhone app is used on a device. When it is enabled, the user's Apple ID and password are required for the following actions:

▶ Turning off Find My iPhone

▶ Erasing the device

▶ Reactivating the device

If a user sets up Activation Lock on a device and then leaves the company without resetting this option, the device cannot be reactivated without the user's Apple ID and password. Activation Lock Bypass overcomes this problem, and this feature is now supported in Configuration Manager.

To use this feature, select **Activation Lock Bypass** from the Remote Device Actions menu.

> **NOTE: ACTIVATION LOCK WARNING**
>
> Microsoft issues a strong warning related to using this feature: "After you bypass the Activation Lock on a device, it will automatically apply a new Activation Lock if the Find My iPhone app is opened. Because of this, **you should be in physical possession of the device before you follow this procedure.**"

Configuring Mobile Devices

Devices can be managed after they are enrolled in Intune and ConfigMgr. This includes many platform-dependent features and settings. Those options are not listed here as there are many of them, and they change at a rapid pace. You can find details at https://docs.microsoft.com/sccm/mdm/deploy-use/manage-compliance-settings.

Define the settings you require by creating configuration items and adding them to a configuration baseline. You apply the settings to mobile devices by deploying the baseline to a collection of devices. This process is discussed in the next section, "Creating Configuration Items and Baselines."

The settings are not supported on all platforms. The settings that are available are categorized. Select the required categories when working through the wizard.

Creating Configuration Items and Baselines

You can create a configuration item (CI) in order to apply some configuration settings to mobile devices. Follow these steps to create a CI:

1. In the ConfigMgr console, navigate to **Assets and Compliance -> Overview -> Compliance Settings**.

2. Right-click **Configuration Items** and select **Create Configuration Item**.

3. In the first screen of the Create Configuration Item Wizard, enter a descriptive name and choose the device type for the CI you want. You can choose devices with or without the full ConfigMgr client. This section is concerned with devices enrolled with Intunc (without the ConfigMgr client). Choose one of the following (see Figure 17.18):

▶ Windows 8.1 and Windows 10

▶ Windows Phone

▶ iOS and Mac OS X

▶ Android and Samsung Knox

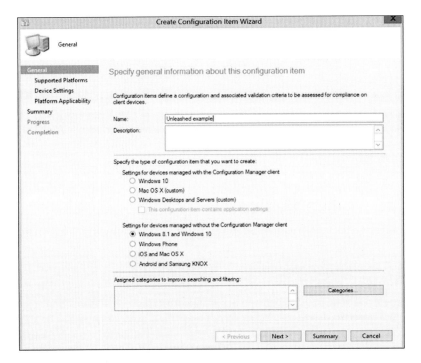

FIGURE 17.18   Choosing a device type for the CI.

4. To view the available configuration options, it would be useful to select the various devices and run through the wizard. This example deploys password settings to Windows 10 devices, so select **Windows 8.1 and Windows 10** and click **Next**.

5. Specify the support platforms for this configuration item. In this case, choose **Windows 10** only and click **Next** to continue.

6. Select the device setting groups you wish to configure. If you select all the options, you can see that these options become available to you in the left side of the wizard, as shown in Figure 17.19. For this example, you only need the Password group, so check only the box beside **Password** and click **Next** to continue.

7. On the next page of the wizard, configure the required password settings. Continue through the wizard, configuring the settings for each group you selected, checking the box **Remediate noncompliant settings** on each page.

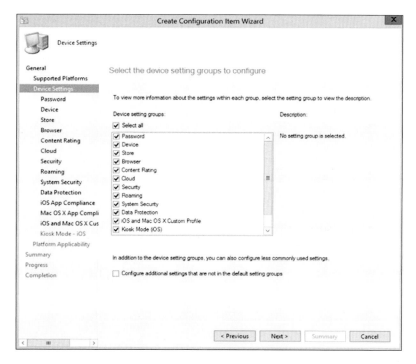

FIGURE 17.19   Selecting the device setting groups.

8. On the Platform Applicability page, which contains a list of the settings that are not supported by all the platforms you selected, choose whether to export this list to a CSV file for review. Click **Next** to continue.

9. Review the Summary and click **Next** to create the CI.

10. Click **Close** to finish the wizard.

Now you need to create a configuration baseline, adding the CIs so they can be deployed to a collection of devices. Follow these steps:

1. In the ConfigMgr console, navigate to **Assets and Compliance -> Overview -> Compliance Settings**.

2. Right-click **Configuration Baselines** and select **Create Configuration Baseline**.

3. Enter a descriptive name. Click **Add** and choose **Configuration Items**, as shown in Figure 17.20. Choose the CIs you previously created and click **Add**. Click **OK** to add the CIs to the baseline.

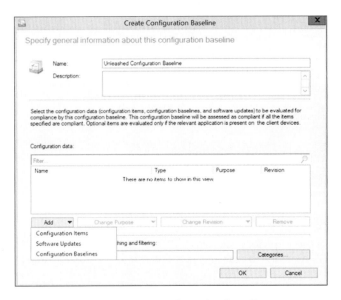

FIGURE 17.20   Creating a configuration baseline.

4. Click **OK** to create the configuration baseline containing your configured settings.

The last step in this process is to deploy the configuration baseline to a collection of devices. Perform the following steps:

1. Right-click the configuration baseline and select **Deploy**.

2. Ensure that the correct baseline is selected in the **Selected configuration baselines** box, shown in Figure 17.21.

3. Enable the option **Remediate noncompliant rules when supported**. You may also choose to allow remediation outside the maintenance window. You can choose to generate an alert based on a compliance level or at a specific date and time.

4. Select the collection for the baseline deployment.

5. Choose the compliance evaluation schedule. The default interval is every seven days.

6. Click **OK** to deploy the configuration baseline to the members of your selected collection.

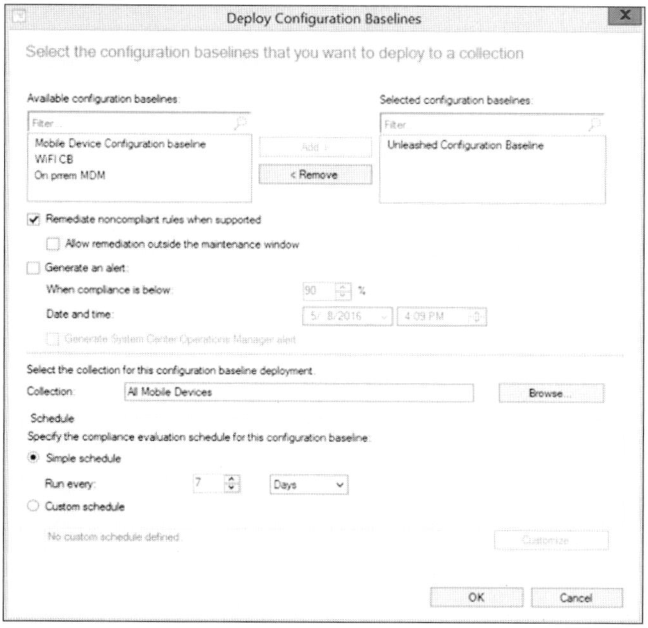

FIGURE 17.21   Deploying a configuration baseline.

Using Custom Configuration Items

The OMA DM standard is designed for managing mobile devices such as mobile phones and tablets. It is a lightweight specification and is designed to manage small-footprint devices, where memory, storage space, and bandwidth could be limited. Devices that use this standard are referred to as *modern devices*.

OMA DM uses Open Mobile Alliance-Unified Resource Identifier (OMA-URI) values; these can be used to enhance mobile device management capabilities in Configuration Manager.

Microsoft has led the way in publishing OMA-URI values that can be used to manage devices. Useful examples of custom URI settings for Windows 10 are available at https://docs.microsoft.com/intune/deploy-use/windows-10-policy-settings-in-microsoft-intune.

NOTE: CUSTOM OMA-URI EXAMPLE

Following is an example of a custom URI value for Windows 10:

▶ **Setting:** AllowDateTime

▶ **URI Full Path:** ./Vendor/MSFT/Policy/Config/Settings/AllowDateTime

▶ **Data Type:** Integer

▶ **Allowed Values:** 0—not allowed, 1—allowed (default)

You can create a CI with a custom OMA-URI. Follow these steps:

1. In the ConfigMgr console, navigate to **Assets and Compliance -> Overview -> Compliance Settings -> Configuration Items**.

2. Create the CI, as discussed earlier in this chapter, in the "Creating Configuration Items and Baselines" section. Ensure that you select the check box **Configure additional settings that are not in the default setting groups** on the Select the device setting groups to configure page. This allows you to add custom settings to the CI.

3. Click **Add** on the Configure additional mobile device settings page.

4. When you are presented with a list of existing settings, click **Create Setting** to add your own.

5. Enter your OMA-URI settings as shown in Figure 17.22 and click **Apply** and then **OK**.

> **NOTE: OMA-URI SETTINGS**
>
> Remember that OMA-URI settings are case sensitive.

6. Highlight the setting you just created and choose **Select**.

7. Enter a value on the Create Rule page, such as 0 for not allowed. Check the box **Remediate noncompliant rules when supported** and click OK.

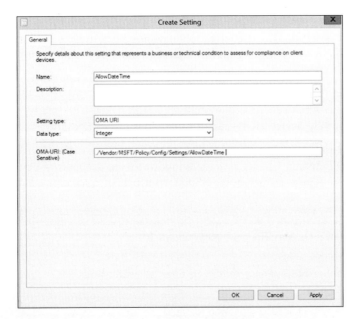

FIGURE 17.22   Creating a custom configuration item.

8. Click **Close** to close the Browse Settings page. The OMA-URI setting is now created and added to the CI wizard.

9. Complete the wizard and add the CI to a baseline to be deployed.

About Device Policy Refresh Intervals

Intune notifies a device almost immediately when a policy or an app is deployed— typically within 5 minutes. The device then checks in with the Intune service to retrieve the policy or app. If the device does not check in after the first notification, three additional attempts are made to contact the device. If the device is offline, it may not receive these notifications and will get the policy or app on the next scheduled check-in.

The scheduled check-in intervals for the various platforms are as follows:

▶ **iOS:** Every 6 hours

▶ **Android:** Every 8 hours

▶ **Windows Phone:** Every 8 hours

▶ **Windows Computers Enrolled as Mobile Devices:** Every 24 hours

Users can also manually sync a device at any time to immediately check for policy, using the Company Portal app.

Check-in is more frequent if the device has just been enrolled:

▶ **iOS:** Every 15 minutes for 6 hours and then every 6 hours

▶ **Android:** Every 3 minutes for 15 minutes then every 15 minutes for 2 hours, and then every 8 hours

▶ **Windows Phone:** Every 5 minutes for 15 minutes then every 15 minutes for 2 hours, and then every 8 hours

▶ **Windows Computers Enrolled as Mobile Devices:** Every 3 minutes for 30 minutes, and then every 24 hours

Inventorying Mobile Devices

A mobile device reports its discovery data record (DDR) and inventory to Intune after the enrollment process. This data is then downloaded via the service connection point (SCP) and written to the ConfigMgr database. After this initial inventory, the devices report their inventory according to the schedule defined in the client settings.

Inventory classes reported by the devices are platform specific; Figure 17.23 shows an example. Mobile devices report full inventory each time. Right-click a device in the console and select **Start -> Resource Explorer** to view the inventory data.

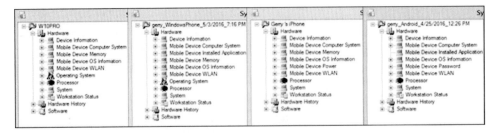

FIGURE 17.23   Inventory collection from various personal devices.

As discussed earlier in this chapter, in the section "Managing Company Devices," the app inventory reported depends on the ownership of the device, according to Table 17.6.

TABLE 17.6   App Inventory, by Platform

Platform	Personal Devices	Company Devices
Windows 8.1 and later	For enrolled (OMA DM), only managed apps	For enrolled (OMA DM), only managed apps
Windows Phone 8.1 and later	Only managed apps	Only managed apps
iOS	Only managed apps	All apps
Android	Only managed apps	All apps

Figure 17.24 shows the inventory of all the apps that are collected on a Windows 10 computer enrolled as a company device.

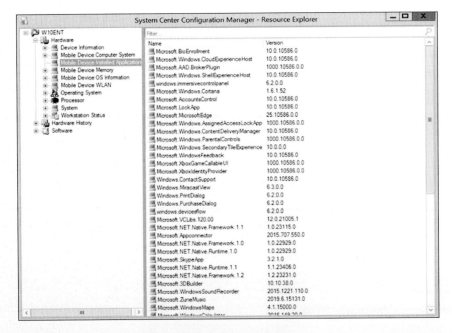

FIGURE 17.24   App inventory for a company device.

Numerous reports are available in the (mobile) device management category. Many reports present the data collected through inventory; see Figure 17.25 for an example. Navigate to **Monitoring -> Overview -> Reports** in the ConfigMgr console to view the available reports.

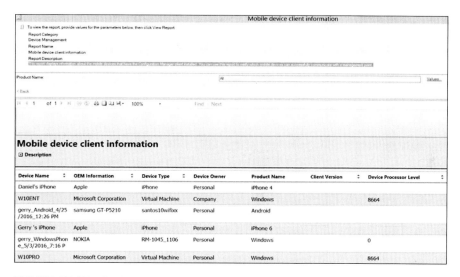

FIGURE 17.25   Device management report.

Deploying Apps

Chapter 11, "Creating and Managing Applications," and Chapter 12, "Creating and Using Deployment Types," describe how to create and manage applications and deployment types (DTs). This section concentrates specifically on deploying apps to mobile devices. The process is the same as with other devices: Use the Create Application Wizard to create an application and use the Deploy Software Wizard to deploy it to a collection of mobile devices.

The following application types can be deployed to modern mobile devices:

▶ Windows app package (*.appx, *.appxbundle) (Windows 8.1 or later)

▶ Windows app package (in the Windows Store)

▶ Windows Phone app package (*.xap file) (Windows Phone 8.1)

▶ Windows Phone app package in the Windows Phone Store

▶ App package for iOS (*.ipa file)

▶ App package for iOS from the App Store

▶ App package for Android (*.apk file)

▶ App package for Android on Google Play

▶ Web application

▶ Windows installer through MDM (*.msi) (on-premise MDM)

In general, there are three types of apps you can deploy to mobile devices, each of which behaves differently when deployed to a device:

▶ **Store Apps (Google Play, App Store, Windows Store):** The user uses a link to the app in the store to download and install the app. The user must have a store account to download the app (with the exception of a Microsoft Store for Business app).

▶ **Line-of-Business Apps (.xap, .appx, .ipa, .apk):** These are apps developed in-house, and they must be side-loaded to the devices.

▶ **Web Applications:** These are deployment types that specify a link to a web application. The deployment type adds an icon for the web application on the user's device. The icon type varies per platform.

  ▶ Web clip (iOS)

  ▶ Widget (Android)

  ▶ Shortcut (Windows)

Table 17.7 lists the app deployment scenarios.

TABLE 17.7   App Deployment Scenarios

Deployment Scenario	iOS	Android	Windows Phone 8.1 and Later	Windows 8.1 and Later
Available install (to users)	Yes	Yes	Yes	Yes
Required install of side-loaded apps (to users or devices)	User prompted to accept the installation	User prompted to accept the installation	N/A	Automatically installed
Remote uninstall of side-loaded apps (to users or devices)	Yes	User prompted to accept the uninstall	N/A	Automatically uninstalled

Leveraging Mobile Application Management (MAM)

ConfigMgr leverages Intune's MAM capabilities to enable the deployment of MAM policies to MAM-managed apps. MAM policies allow administrators to modify the functionality of apps to conform to a security policy. You can control operations such as cut, copy, and paste by restricting data transfer only to other managed apps. You can also configure a MAM-managed app to open all web links inside the Intune Managed Browser app, as this app is a MAM-managed app.

MAM policies are supported on iOS (versions 8.1 and later) and Android (version 4 and later) only. Follow these steps to create a MAM policy and associate it with the DT of an app:

1. In the ConfigMgr console, navigate to **Software Library -> Overview -> Application Management -> Application Management Policies.**

2. Right-click **Application Management Policies** and select **Create Application Management Policy.**

3. Enter a name and description and click **Next.**

4. On the Specify the type of application management policy page, choose the required platform (iOS or Android) and policy type (General or Managed Browser). Click **Next.**

5. Enter your application management policy selections (see Figure 17.26 for an iOS example) and click **Next.**

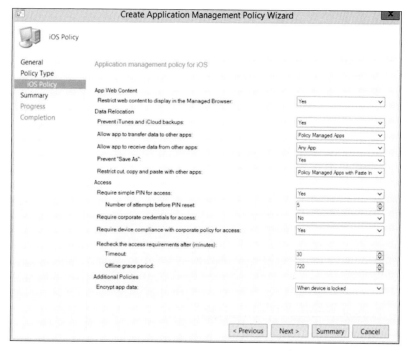

FIGURE 17.26   Specifying an iOS MAM policy.

6. Review the summary and click **Next** to create the MAM policy.

7. Click **Close** to complete the wizard.

NOTE: DEPLOYING MAM POLICIES

MAM policies are not deployed to collections; they are associated with the deployment type of a MAM-managed app. You configure this in the Deploy Software Wizard.

Import a MAM-managed app into the ConfigMgr console and deploy it as normal. The Deploy Software Wizard asks you to select the MAM policy you want to associate with the MAM app DT, as shown in Figure 17.27.

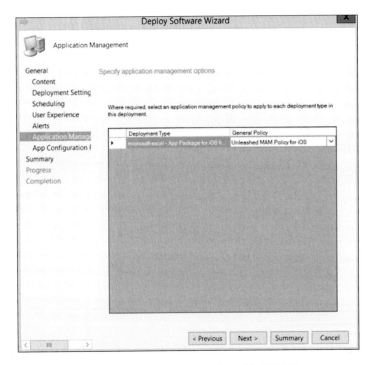

FIGURE 17.27   Associating a MAM policy with iOS DT.

Microsoft publishes details of MAM-capable apps in the Intune mobile application gallery at https://www.microsoft.com/cloud-platform/microsoft-intune-apps. This list of apps is increasing rapidly.

TIP: INTUNE APP WRAPPING TOOLS

You can use the Intune app wrapping tools for iOS and Android to convert your own line-of-business apps to be capable of MAM management.

Creating Mobile Device Collections

You may want to target specific device platforms with app or policy deployments. Do so by creating target collections using dynamic queries. Examples follow:

▶ Listing 17.1 creates a collection of Windows Phone 8.1 devices.

▶ Listing 17.2 creates a collection of iPhones.

▶ Listing 17.3 creates a collection of iPads.

▶ Listing 17.4 creates a collection of Android devices.

LISTING 17.1   Creating a Collection of Windows Phone 8.1 Devices

```
SELECT SMS_R_System.ResourceId,SMS_R_System.ResourceType,SMS_R_System.Name,
    SMS_R_System.SMSUniqueIdentifier,
    SMS_R_System.ResourceDomainORWorkgroup,
    SMS_R_System.Client
FROM SMS_R_System
    INNER JOIN SMS_G_System_DEVICE_OSINFORMATION ON
    SMS_G_System_DEVICE_OSINFORMATION.ResourceID = SMS_R_System.ResourceId
WHERE
    SMS_G_System_DEVICE_OSINFORMATION.Platform like "Windows Phone" and
    SMS_G_System_DEVICE_OSINFORMATION.Version like "8.1%"
```

LISTING 17.2   Creating a Collection of iPhones

```
SELECT SMS_R_SYSTEM.ResourceID,SMS_R_SYSTEM.ResourceType,SMS_R_SYSTEM.Name,
    SMS_R_SYSTEM.SMSUniqueIdentifier,SMS_R_SYSTEM.ResourceDomainORWorkgroup,
    SMS_R_SYSTEM.Client
FROM SMS_R_System
    INNER JOIN SMS_G_System_DEVICE_COMPUTERSYSTEM ON
    SMS_G_System_DEVICE_COMPUTERSYSTEM.ResourceId
    = SMS_R_System.ResourceId
WHERE
    SMS_G_System_DEVICE_COMPUTERSYSTEM.DeviceModel like "%iphone%"
```

LISTING 17.3   Creating a Collection of iPads

```
SELECT SMS_R_SYSTEM.ResourceID,SMS_R_SYSTEM.ResourceType,
    SMS_R_SYSTEM.Name, SMS_R_SYSTEM.SMSUniqueIdentifier,
    SMS_R_SYSTEM.ResourceDomainORWorkgroup, SMS_R_SYSTEM.Client
FROM SMS_R_System INNER JOIN SMS_G_System_DEVICE_COMPUTERSYSTEM ON
    SMS_G_System_DEVICE_COMPUTERSYSTEM.ResourceId
    = SMS_R_System.ResourceId
WHERE
    SMS_G_System_DEVICE_COMPUTERSYSTEM.DeviceModel like "%ipad%"
```

LISTING 17.4   Creating a Collection of Android Devices

```
SELECT SMS_R_System.ResourceId,SMS_R_System.ResourceType,SMS_R_System.Name,
    SMS_R_System.SMSUniqueIdentifier, SMS_R_System.ResourceDomainORWorkgroup,
    SMS_R_System.Client
FROM SMS_R_System
    INNER JOIN SMS_G_System_DEVICE_OSINFORMATION
    ON SMS_G_System_DEVICE_OSINFORMATION.ResourceID =
    SMS_R_System.ResourceId
WHERE
    SMS_G_System_DEVICE_OSINFORMATION.Platform like "Android%"
```

Using the Company Resource Access Workspace

View company resource access in the ConfigMgr console by navigating to **Assets and Compliance -> Overview -> Compliance Settings -> Company Resource Access**. This area provides tools that allow users to access company resources from remote locations. Four options are available to deploy configuration profiles to mobile devices:

▶ Certificate profiles

▶ Email profiles

▶ VPN profiles

▶ Wi-Fi profiles

These options are described in the following sections.

NOTE: COMPANY RESOURCE ACCESS MANAGER

Company Resource Access Manager is a security role in ConfigMgr. This role is assigned to an administrative user to create and deploy resource profiles.

Using Certificate Profiles

Certificate profiles integrate with Active Directory Certificate Services (ADCS) and Network Device Enrollment Services (NDES) to provision certificates for authentication of mobile devices. (A full description of certificates and Certificate Services is beyond the scope of this book.)

You can deploy three certificate types:

▶ **Trusted CA Certificates:** Deploy a trusted root or intermediate CA certificate.

▶ **Certificates Issued via Simple Certificate Enrollment Protocol:** Request a certificate by using SCEP and NDES.

▶ **Personal Information Exchange (PFX) Certificates:** Deploy certificates that support user-based public key infrastructure (PKI) communication.

In the ConfigMgr console, navigate to **Assets and Compliance -> Overview -> Compliance Settings -> Company Resource Access**. Right-click **Certificate Profiles** and select **Create Certificate Profile** to open the dialog displayed in Figure 17.28. Select the type of profile you want to create and enter the required details to complete the wizard. Deploy the profile to a collection of users or mobile devices as normal.

Certificate profiles are supported on all device types that can be enrolled in Intune.

> **NOTE: SCEP CERTIFICATE PREREQUISITES**
>
> Before you can create a SCEP certificate profile, you must implement a PKI and NDES infrastructure. To deploy profiles that use SCEP, you also must install the certificate registration point on a site system and deploy the Configuration Manager Policy Module for NDES.

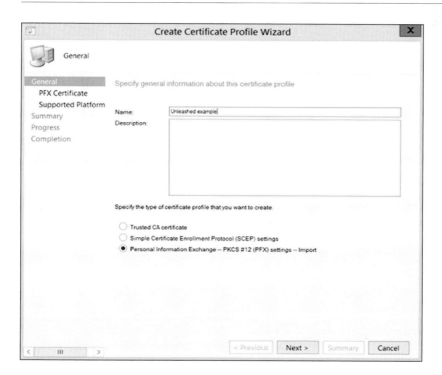

FIGURE 17.28   Types of certificate profiles.

Using Email Profiles

Email profiles allow you to enable access to corporate email with minimal user input by deploying Exchange ActiveSync settings.

In the ConfigMgr console, navigate to **Assets and Compliance -> Overview -> Compliance Settings -> Company Resource Access**. Right-click **Email Profiles** and select **Create Exchange ActiveSync Profile** to open the dialog displayed in Figure 17.29. Enter a name for the profile and the required details to complete the wizard. Deploy the profile to a collection of users or devices.

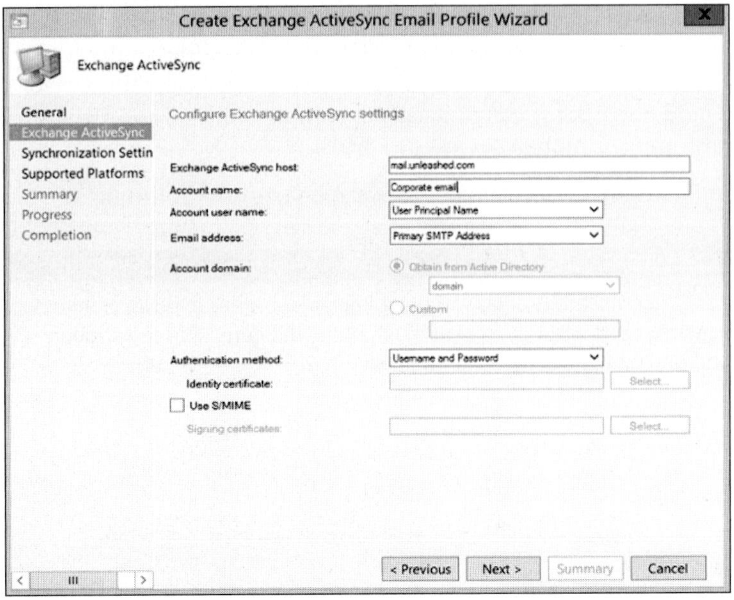

FIGURE 17.29   Configuring email profiles.

There are a number of options to specify when configuring the email profile:

▶ **Email Address:** Primary SMTP address/user principal name

▶ **Authentication Method:** Username and password/certificate

▶ **Synchronization Schedule:** Manual, as messages arrive or at interval

▶ **Content Type to Synchronize:** Email/contacts/calendar/tasks/notes

Email profiles are supported on all device types that can be enrolled in Intune.

NOTE: EMAIL PROFILE DEPLOYMENT

Email profiles can only be deployed to the native mail app on a device. They cannot be deployed to the Outlook app, for example. A user could therefore end up with two email profiles if a device has already been configured manually with a profile for the same account.

Deploying VPN Profiles

To minimize the effort required for users to remotely access corporate resources, you can deploy VPN profiles to iOS, Android, Windows Phone, and Windows devices when they are enrolled into Microsoft Intune.

In the ConfigMgr console, navigate to **Assets and Compliance -> Overview -> Compliance Settings -> Company Resource Access**. Right-click **VPN Profiles** and select **Create VPN Profile**. Enter a name for the profile and enter the required details to complete the wizard. Deploy the profile to a collection of users or devices.

Table 17.8 lists currently supported VPN connection types.

TABLE 17.8   Supported VPN Connection Types

Connection Type	iOS	Android	Windows 8.1 and Later	Windows Phone 8.1 and Later
Cisco AnyConnect	Yes	Yes	No	No
Pulse Secure	Yes	Yes	Yes	Yes
F5 Edge Client	Yes	Yes	Yes	Yes
Dell SonicWALL Mobile Connect	Yes	Yes	Yes	Yes
Check Point Mobile VPN	Yes	Yes	Yes	Yes
Microsoft SSL (SSTP)	No	No	Yes	No
Microsoft Automatic	No	No	Yes	No
IKEv2	No	No	Yes	Yes
PPTP	Yes	No	Yes	No
L2TP	Yes	No	Yes	No

Using Wi-Fi Profiles

Wi-Fi profiles, used to deploy wireless network settings to users, are supported on all device types that can be enrolled in Intune. You can create Wi-Fi profiles to use certificates previously provisioned by certificate profiles.

In the ConfigMgr console, navigate to **Assets and Compliance -> Overview -> Compliance Settings -> Company Resource Access**. Right-click **Wi-Fi Profiles** and select **Create Wi-Fi Profile**. Enter a name for the profile and the required details to complete the wizard. Deploy the profile to a collection of users or devices.

Configuration Manager offers the following Wi-Fi security types:

▶ No authentication (open)

▶ WPA-Personal

▶ WPA2-Personal

▶ WPA-Enterprise

▶ WPA2-Enterprise

▶ WEP

▶ 802.1X

17

Each security type offers different encryption options. Note that all types may not be supported on all platforms.

> **NOTE: PRE-SHARED KEYS**
>
> At the time this book was published, it was not possible to deploy a Wi-Fi profile with a pre-shared key using ConfigMgr, although the authors expect this feature to be available soon. You can create a custom profile by using the Apple Configurator tool and deploy it to iOS devices.

On-Premise Mobile Device Management

On-premise MDM is a new solution released with ConfigMgr Current Branch version 1511. It differs from traditional hybrid MDM (ConfigMgr integrated with Intune) in that managed devices do not have to be enrolled in Microsoft Intune. This feature supports Windows 10 devices only (mobile or desktop) and uses the on-premise ConfigMgr infrastructure and the built-in OMA DM capabilities of the device.

On-premise MDM enables you to manage mobile devices without synchronizing user accounts to Azure AD. Although devices are not managed by Intune directly, an Intune subscription and licenses are still required. The following sections describe management capabilities, advantages and disadvantages, and on-premise MDM requirements.

Management Capabilities

The following features are available for management with on-premise MDM:

- ▶ Hardware and software inventory
- ▶ The Retire/Wipe feature
- ▶ App deployment, which supports web applications from the Windows Store, 32-bit MSI apps, and line-of-business apps (.appx)
- ▶ Configuration of devices using OMA DM policies
- ▶ Leverage of Windows 10 provisioning packages

Advantages and Disadvantages of On-Premise MDM

For some organizations, a huge advantage to using on-premise MDM is that all management and data is maintained on-premise. The solution is also easier to maintain, as there is no additional client to install, and all functionality is built into the operating system.

Disadvantages include limited device support (only Windows 10 desktop and Windows 10 mobile are supported at this time), and there is currently less client management functionality. However, this is a new feature and a work in progress.

On-Premise MDM Configuration

A number of prerequisites must be fulfilled before an on-premise MDM solution can be implemented with ConfigMgr. Many of these prerequisites should be familiar to those who have previously implemented a solution for managing Apple Mac devices:

▶ **Intune Subscription and Service Connector Role:** Although this is an on-premise solution, you must configure an Intune subscription and add the Service Connector role.

▶ **PKI with Certificate Revocation List (CRL) and CRL Distribution Point:** A PKI infrastructure is required with the following role services: Certification Authority (CA), CA Web Enrollment, and CA Web Service.

When Windows 10 clients communicate over HTTPS, they automatically check to see if the certificate they are using has been revoked. They find this information in the CRL, which is two files stored in a virtual folder that is accessible to the Windows 10 clients (full and delta CRL files).

The CRL location (CRL distribution point) must be configured in the CA so that it is included in all issued certificates.

▶ **ConfigMgr Management Point (MP) Configured to Communicate via HTTPS:** This requires a web certificate assigned in Internet Information Services (IIS) and bound to HTTPS. The MP must be configured with a fully qualified domain name (FQDN).

▶ **ConfigMgr Distribution Point (DP) Configured to Communicate via HTTPS:** This requires a web certificate assigned in IIS and bound to HTTPS. The DP must be configured to allow intranet and Internet connections and to allow mobile devices to connect, as shown in Figure 17.30.

▶ **Trusted Root CA:** After adding secure MP and DP, navigate to **Administration -> Site Configuration -> Sites**. Right-click your site and choose **Properties**. Select the **Client Computer Communications** tab and set the **Trusted Root CA**.

▶ **Client Certificate:** This certificate, installed on Windows 10 clients, is generated from the client certificate template.

▶ **Enrollment Point (EP):** This site system role is added in the default configuration.

▶ **Enrollment Proxy Point (EPP):** This site system role is added in the default configuration. The EP and EPP roles can be installed on the same site system and can coexist with the secure MP and DP.

▶ **Certificate Profile and Enrollment Profile:** Navigate to **Assets and Compliance -> Compliance Settings -> Company Resource Access**. Right-click **Certificate Profiles** to launch the Create Certificate Profiles wizard. Navigate to **Administration -> Site Configuration -> Client Settings**. Open your client settings and choose the **Enrollment** section. Select **Allow users to enroll modern devices** and set the modern device enrollment profile.

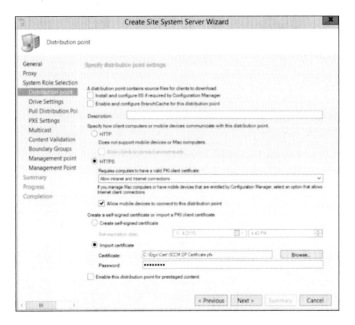

FIGURE 17.30   DP configured for HTTPS.

On-Premise MDM Client Configuration

When the on-premise MDM prerequisites are satisfied, you are ready to enroll devices. Note that you can use provisioning packages to automate the client configuration. Follow these steps to enroll a Windows 10 client in the ConfigMgr on-premise MDM solution:

1. Import the trusted root certificate and client certificate discussed in the previous section.

2. Navigate to **Settings** -> **Accounts** -> **Work access** and select **Connect to work or school**.

3. Enter your local domain credentials. The first attempt fails, as Windows attempts to authenticate with Azure AD and is unable to do so as you are using local credentials.

4. When you are prompted to enter a server name, enter the FQDN of the enrollment point. You are then connected to the ConfigMgr enrollment point.

5. When you are prompted to authenticate, enter your local domain credentials.

The device is now connected and available in ConfigMgr, where it has been enrolled as a mobile device.

Summary

This chapter discussed managing mobile devices. It described how to enroll the various device types (Android, iOS, Windows Phone, and Windows) with Microsoft Intune so that they can be managed using the Intune/ConfigMgr hybrid solution. The enrollment process is slightly different for each platform. The chapter also discussed the difference between personal and company devices and described some ways to assist administrators with the enrollment of company-owned devices.

Protection and configuration of mobile devices are important parts of an administrator's role. The chapter discussed features such as remote wipe, password reset, remote lock, and activation lock bypass. It demonstrated how to configure devices using configuration items and configuration baselines.

It also described the different management features offered by the hybrid solution— inventory, app deployment, certificate profiles, email profiles, VPN profiles, and Wi-Fi profiles.

Chapter 18 discusses conditional access, including how you can protect access to corporate resources by forcing users to enroll their devices.

17

CHAPTER 18

Conditional Access in Configuration Manager

IN THIS CHAPTER

- Understanding Modern Authentication
- Implementing Configuration Manager Policies
- Enabling Conditional Access for Exchange Online
- Enabling Conditional Access for SharePoint Online
- Enabling Conditional Access for Skype for Business Online
- Enabling Conditional Access for Exchange On-Premises
- Monitoring and Troubleshooting Conditional Access

As described in Chapter 16, "Integrating Intune Hybrid into Your Configuration Manager Environment," System Center Configuration Manager (ConfigMgr) can be integrated with Microsoft Intune. This integration provides many powerful new features for ConfigMgr. One of the most widely deployed of those features, *conditional access*, involves securing access to corporate resources from mobile devices and is the focus of this chapter.

One of the greatest challenges for today's information technology (IT) professionals is the elimination of corporate boundaries. The advent of bring your own device (BYOD) requires IT to adapt its security policies to control a myriad of devices and security settings. Administrators previously could protect corporate devices and data from the outside world by hiding them behind many layers of security. That is no longer possible; IT must allow external access to data as users are demanding total flexibility in managing their professional and personal business wherever they are and on their devices of choice.

At the time this book was published, ConfigMgr's conditional access feature could secure access to the following services:

- Microsoft Exchange Online
- SharePoint Online
- Skype for Business Online
- Microsoft Exchange On-Premises

This chapter provides an overview of modern authentication and describes the steps to implement conditional access for each of these services.

Understanding Modern Authentication

Modern apps use modern authentication. This Microsoft solution is utilized during the conditional access workflow. Modern authentication is based on the Active Directory Authentication Library (ADAL) and OAuth 2.0 (an open standard for authorization). ADAL is a code library, designed to allow secure access for client applications to resources via security tokens. ADAL works with OAuth 2.0 to enable advanced authentication and authorization scenarios; this includes multi-factor authentication (MFA) and additional forms of Security Assertion Markup Language (SAML) Authentication.

ADAL assists developers in easily obtaining access tokens from Azure Active Directory (AD) and Windows Server Active Directory Federation Services (ADFS) for Windows Server 2012 R2, which can be used to request access to protected resources.

ADAL removes the need for modern apps to use basic authentication protocols and allows them to use browser-based authentication (known as *passive authentication*), where the user is directed to an identity provider's web page to authenticate.

Apps that act as clients can leverage modern authentication. Modern authentication conversations have the following features:

▶ A client app, which makes a request to access a resource (for example, Outlook for iOS) and attempts to access Exchange Online

▶ A resource to which the client needs a specific level of access, and this resource is secured by a directory service (such as Exchange Online)

▶ An OAuth connection, which authorizes a user to access a resource

Table 18.1 shows the current availability of modern authentication across Office applications.

TABLE 18.1   Modern Authentication in Office Apps

Client App	Windows	Windows Phone	iOS	Android
Office	Available in Office 2013 and Office 2016	Not available	Available in Word, Access, and PowerPoint	Available in Word, Access, and PowerPoint
Outlook	Included with Office 2013 and 2016	Not available	Available	Available
Skype for Business	Included with Office 2013 and 2016	Not available	Available	Available
OneDrive for Business	Included with Office 2013 and 2016	Available for Windows Phone 8.1 and later	Available	Available

Modern authentication may not turned on by default for all services. For example, Table 18.2 shows the default modern authentication states for Office 365 services.

TABLE 18.2   Modern Authentication States for Office 365 Services

Service	Default State	Details
Exchange Online	Off	Turn on with PowerShell; see http://social.technet.microsoft.com/wiki/contents/articles/32711.exchange-online-how-to-enable-your-tenant-for-modern-authentication.aspx.
SharePoint Online	On	Not available.
Skype for Business Online	Off	Turn on with PowerShell; see http://social.technet.microsoft.com/wiki/contents/articles/34339.skype-for-business-online-enable-your-tenant-for-modern-authentication.aspx.

NOTE: MODERN AUTHENTICATION STATES

Table 18.2 shows the modern authentication state of the services for all tenants created before August 1, 2017. The services are turned on by default for all tenants created after that time.

NOTE: MODERN AUTHENTICATION

Conditional access requires modern authentication for use with modern apps. However, you can also implement conditional access without modern authentication by using other supported apps, such as built-in mail clients for iOS and Android, which use basic authentication.

Implementing Configuration Manager Policies

There are two policy types for implementing conditional access in ConfigMgr:

▶ **Compliance Policies:** These policies contain the rules and settings used to determine whether a device is compliant. Compliance rules include advanced password settings, encryption, whether a device is jailbroken or rooted, and whether email on the device is managed by an Intune policy. Rules can also check for minimum and maximum operating system (OS) versions.

▶ **Conditional Access Policies:** Conditional access policies are used to enable conditional access for a particular service. These policies define which user groups are targeted or exempt. A conditional access policy permits only devices deemed compliant (that is, satisfying the compliance policy) to access a service.

NOTE: ABOUT COMPLIANCE POLICIES

Compliance policies are optional. If no compliance policy is configured, all devices are deemed compliant by the conditional access policies.

Supported Compliance Policy Settings

Table 18.3 and Table 18.4 list the compliance policy settings for Windows, iOS, and Android, showing supported settings for these systems. These tables also show how non-compliant settings are managed when a policy is used with a conditional access policy.

TABLE 18.3   Supported Compliance Settings and Noncompliant Device Management in Windows

Compliance Setting	Windows 8.1 and Later	Windows Phone 8.1 and Windows Mobile 10
PIN or password configuration	Remediated	Remediated
Device encryption	N/A	Remediated
Jailbroken or rooted device	N/A	N/A
Email profile	N/A	N/A
Minimum OS version	Quarantined	Quarantined
Maximum OS version	Quarantined	Quarantined

TABLE 18.4   Supported Compliance Policy Settings and Noncompliant Device Management in iOS and Android

Compliance Setting	iOS	Android	Samsung Knox
PIN or password configuration	Remediated	Quarantined	Quarantined
Device encryption	Remediated	Quarantined	Quarantined
Jailbroken or rooted device	Quarantined	Quarantined	Quarantined
Email profile	Quarantined	N/A	N/A
Minimum OS version	Quarantined	Quarantined	Quarantined
Maximum OS version	Quarantined	Quarantined	Quarantined

Noncompliant settings are managed as follows:

▶ **Remediated:** The device OS is capable of enforcing compliance.

▶ **Quarantined:** The device OS is not capable of enforcing compliance. The device is blocked, and the user is notified about the non-compliance.

NOTE: DEPLOYING COMPLIANCE POLICIES TO USERS

Compliance policies are deployed to user collections. The policies are then evaluated on all devices enrolled by those users.

Creating a Compliance Policy

Follow these steps in the ConfigMgr console to create a compliance policy:

1. Navigate to **Assets and Compliance -> Compliance Settings -> Compliance Policies**.

2. Right-click **Compliance Policies** and select **Create Compliance Policy**. The Create Compliance Policy Wizard is launched, as displayed in Figure 18.1.

FIGURE 18.1   The Create Compliance Policy Wizard.

3. Enter a suitable name and description for the policy. Select to create a policy for devices with or without the ConfigMgr client. For this example, choose **Compliance rules for devices managed without the Configuration Manager client** for mobile devices.

4. Select the device type. Figure 18.1 shows iOS chosen.

5. Specify the severity level to be reported in ConfigMgr reports if a device is deemed noncompliant with this policy. (The default setting is Warning.) Click **Next** to continue.

6. Select the platforms to be provisioned with this policy. The choices presented are dependent on the device type chosen on the previous page. Click **Next**.

7. Specify the rules for evaluating a compliant device. Some rules are specified by default. You can edit or delete these rules. Click **New** for additional rules, shown in Figure 18.2. After completing the Add Rule page, click **Next** to continue. Table 18.5 provides examples of compliance policy rules and the supported platforms.

FIGURE 18.2   Additional compliance policy rules.

TABLE 18.5   Compliance Policy Rules

Rule	Details	Supported Platforms
Require password settings on mobile device	Forces users to enter a password on the device. Enabled by default.	iOS 8.0 and later Android 4.0 and later Samsung Knox Standard 4.0 and later Windows Phone 8 and later
Minimum password length	Six characters by default.	iOS 8.0 and later Android 4.0 and later Samsung Knox Standard 4.0 and later Windows Phone 8 and later Windows 8.1 and later
Allow simple passwords	Simple passwords have repeated or consecutive numbers, for example. Disabled by default.	iOS 8.0 and later Windows Phone 8 and later
File encryption on mobile device	Requires device encryption. Enabled by default. (See the note "iOS Encryption" in this section.)	Android 4.0 and later Samsung Knox Standard 4.0 and later Windows Phone 8 and later (automatically encrypted) Windows 8.1 and later

Rule	Details	Supported Platforms
Device is jailbroken or rooted	Jailbroken (iOS) or rooted (Android) devices will be non-compliant. Disabled by default.	iOS 8.0 and later Android 4.0 and later Samsung Knox Standard 4.0 and later
Minimum operating system version	Earlier operating system versions will be non-compliant.	iOS 8.0 and later Android 4.0 and later Samsung Knox Standard 4.0 and later Windows Phone 8 and later Windows 8.1 and later
Maximum operating system version	Later operating system versions will be non-compliant.	iOS 8.0 and later Android 4.0 and later Samsung Knox Standard 4.0 and later Windows Phone 8 and later Windows 8.1 and later
Email profile must be managed by Intune	Device must use the email profile deployed to the device by Intune. Disabled by default.	iOS 8.0 and later

NOTE: IOS ENCRYPTION

iOS devices are encrypted when you configure the setting **Require password settings on mobile devices**.

8. Review the details on the Summary page. Click **Next** to complete the wizard. The compliance policy is now created.

9. Click **Close** to close the wizard.

NOTE: EDITING COMPLIANCE POLICY SETTINGS

Note that you cannot just turn some compliance settings on and off by toggling between True and False because this value is grayed out, as shown in Figure 18.3. You must remove the setting and add it again with a different value.

18

FIGURE 18.3   Compliance value grayed out.

Deploying a Compliance Policy

To view a compliance policy, navigate to **Assets and Compliance -> Compliance Settings -> Compliance Policies** in the console. To deploy a policy to a user collection, follow these steps:

1. Right-click the policy and choose **Deploy**.

2. In the Deploy Compliance policy page, click **Browse** and select a user collection (see Figure 18.4).

FIGURE 18.4   Deploying a compliance policy.

3. Optionally choose to generate an alert when policy compliance falls below a defined amount (percentage).

4. Configure the policy evaluation schedule. Click **OK** to deploy the policy.

You now can use the compliance policy in conjunction with conditional access policies to control access to corporate services, as described in the following sections.

Enabling Conditional Access for Exchange Online

One of the most common use cases for conditional access is to protect and secure access to corporate email. This section demonstrates securing access to Exchange Online. Use the ConfigMgr console to begin the process of configuring a conditional access policy, which launches the Intune console to complete the operation.

Figure 18.5 shows the flow that conditional access policies for Exchange Online use to evaluate whether to allow or block devices.

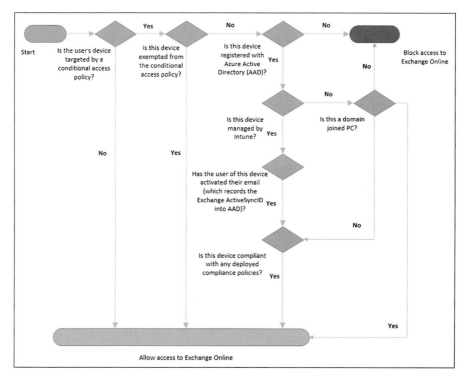

FIGURE 18.5   Conditional access policy flow for Exchange Online.

Requirements for Exchange Online

There are a number of prerequisites to meet before implementing conditional access for Exchange Online. Only specific mail apps on specific devices are supported. There are also some Azure and Exchange requirements. Finally, modern authentication must be turned on for Exchange Online. These requirements are described in the following sections.

Exchange Online Supported Platforms and Apps

It is possible to control access to Exchange Online from the built-in Exchange ActiveSync mail client on the platforms and versions listed in Table 18.6. These clients use basic authentication.

The Microsoft Outlook app for iOS and Android is also supported for conditional access for Exchange Online (see Table 18.7). These are modern apps and require modern authentication to be turned on for Exchange Online.

TABLE 18.6   Exchange Online Conditional Access: Supported Built-in Mail Clients

Platform	Supported Versions
Google Android	Version 4.0 and later (including Samsung Knox)
Apple iOS	Version 8.0 and later
Windows Phone	Version 8.1 and later
Windows	Windows 8.1 and later (managed as mobile devices)

TABLE 18.7   Exchange Online Conditional Access: Additional Supported Apps

App	Supported Platforms
Microsoft Outlook	Android and iOS
Outlook 2013 and 2016	Windows desktop

Additional Requirements for Exchange Online

Support for conditional access to Exchange Online depends on the following additional requirements:

▶ Devices must be workplace joined or enrolled with Intune. Devices must also be registered with the Azure Active Directory Device Registration Service. This is automatic when a device is enrolled or workplace joined.

▶ Exchange Online subscription is required.

▶ Users must each be assigned an Exchange Online license.

Turning on Modern Authentication for Exchange Online

Exchange Online must be configured to accept a modern authentication connection from modern apps. This is achieved by running PowerShell commands on the tenant:

1. Connect to Exchange Online by using remote PowerShell. For details, see https://technet.microsoft.com/library/jj984289(v=exchg.160).aspx.

2. Run the following command:

```
Set-OrganizationConfig -OAuth2ClientProfileEnabled:$true
```

3. Verify that the change was successful by running the following command:

```
Get-OrganizationConfig | ft name, *OAuth*
```

Enabling Conditional Access for Exchange Online

After all prerequisites are in place, conditional access can be enabled. A number of phases are involved, as discussed in the following sections:

▶ Evaluating the effect of the conditional access policy (optional but recommended)

▶ Configuring Azure AD security groups (targeted and exempted)

▶ Configuring the conditional access policy

Evaluating the Effect of the Conditional Access Policy for Exchange Online

In the ConfigMgr console, navigate to **Monitoring -> Reporting -> Reports**. Under Device Management, run the report List of Devices by Conditional Access State to identify devices that will be blocked from Exchange Online when you enable conditional access. Select the collection to be evaluated and choose **View Report**. Figure 18.6 shows a sample report. Notice that one of the devices shown is not compliant, so email access to this device will be blocked. Notify affected users to remediate their devices before enabling conditional access; otherwise, they will not have access to email.

						Microsoft System Center Configuration Manager	

List of devices by Conditional Access State

Device Name	Operating System	Primary User	Management Channel	Registered with AAD	EAS Activated	Compliant	Last Evaluation Date and Time (UTC)
Daniel's iPhone	iOS		Microsoft Intune	Yes	Yes	Yes	03/22/2016 20:09:01.696
W10ENT	Windows		Microsoft Intune	No	No	Unknown	
gerry_Android_4/25/2016_12:	Android	GH\gerry	Microsoft Intune	Yes	Yes	Yes	04/26/2016 13:43:11.867
Gerry 's iPhone	iOS	GH\gerry	Microsoft Intune	Yes	Yes	Yes	05/23/2016 22:55:15.709
gerry_WindowsPhone_5/3/201	Windows	GH\gerry	Microsoft Intune	Yes	Yes	Yes	05/09/2016 22:16:24.574
W10PRO	Windows	GH\gerry	Microsoft Intune	Yes	Yes	Yes	05/07/2016 15:08:19.226

FIGURE 18.6   Conditional access evaluation report.

Configuring Security Groups for Exchange Online

Two group types can be specified when enabling conditional access. The conditional access policy is applied to targeted groups and is not applied to exempted groups.

> **NOTE: TARGETED AND EXEMPTED GROUPS**
>
> A user in both groups is exempt from the conditional access policy.

These groups are Azure AD security user groups and can be configured in one of two portals:

▶ Office 365 admin center

▶ Azure portal

Configuring the Conditional Access Policy for Exchange Online
Follow these steps to enable conditional access for Exchange Online:

NOTE: ENABLING CONDITIONAL ACCESS

The technique described in this section is the supported method for enabling conditional access at the time this book was published. The ConfigMgr console provides a link that directs you to the conditional access node in the Intune portal. However, the authors anticipate that the mobile device management component of the Intune portal will be deprecated later in 2018.

Should that occur, the authors recommend that conditional access be enabled using the Azure portal.

---

1. In the ConfigMgr console, navigate to **Assets and Compliance -> Compliance Settings -> Conditional Access**.

2. Select **Exchange Online**. You are notified that conditional access policies for Exchange Online must be configured through the Intune console, as shown in Figure 18.7. Select **Configure conditional access policy in the Intune console**.

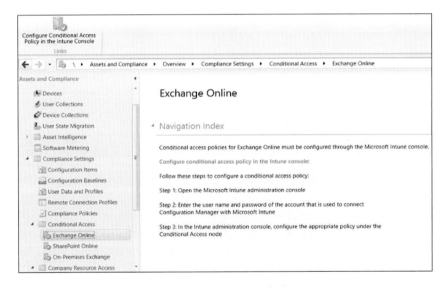

FIGURE 18.7   Conditional access for Exchange Online.

3. The Intune administration console is launched. Log in with the user account previously used to create the Intune subscription in ConfigMgr. You are immediately directed to the Exchange Online Policy page in the Intune console, shown in Figure 18.8.

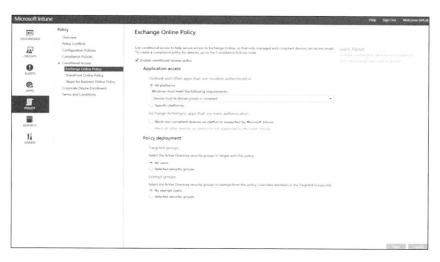

FIGURE 18.8   Enabling conditional access for Exchange Online in the Intune portal.

4. Check the box **Enable conditional access policy**.

5. Choose to restrict all noncompliant devices or select the specific platforms.

6. Select whether to allow access to email in cases where Intune cannot manage the device.

7. Select the required targeted and exempt groups.

8. Click **Save** to save the policy, and it takes effect immediately.

NOTE: CONDITIONAL ACCESS POLICY DEPLOYMENT

A conditional access policy does not have to be deployed to users or devices. It takes effect immediately and is automatically applied when it is created.

Exchange Online End-User Experience

When conditional access is enabled, if a user tries to add an email account on an unmanaged or noncompliant device, the device is immediately blocked. The built-in mail client on an iPhone 6 is used in the example shown in Figures 18.9 and 18.10.

The user successfully added an Exchange Online mail account but sees only a single email, shown in Figure 18.9, warning that further action is required. This notification email cannot be customized.

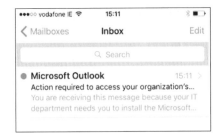

FIGURE 18.9   Conditional access action email.

The email contains further instructions and explains that the device must be enrolled with Intune before corporate email can be accessed. The user can click the **Get started now** hyperlink shown in Figure 18.10, which directs the user to download and install the Intune company portal. See Chapter 17, "Managing Mobile Devices," for information on device enrollment.

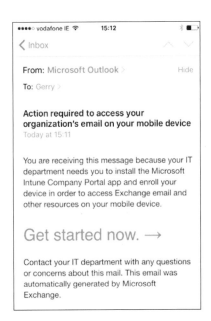

FIGURE 18.10   Conditional access: Getting started.

Once the device is enrolled and compliant, the user can access his or her corporate email.

> **NOTE: CONDITIONAL ACCESS EMAIL BLOCKING INTERVALS**
>
> If a device is blocked (meaning it is not enrolled or is noncompliant), it is unblocked within two minutes if the user enrolls or remediates the device.
>
> If the user subsequently un-enrolls a device, email is blocked after approximately six hours.

Enabling Conditional Access for SharePoint Online

Enabling conditional access for SharePoint Online is very similar to the process for Exchange Online, described in the preceding section. Conditional access for SharePoint Online allows you to control access to OneDrive for Business files located on SharePoint Online. Use the ConfigMgr console to begin the process of configuring a conditional access policy, which launches the Intune console, where you can complete the operation.

Figure 18.11 shows the flow used by conditional access policies for SharePoint Online when a targeted user attempts to connect to a file using a supported app such as OneDrive.

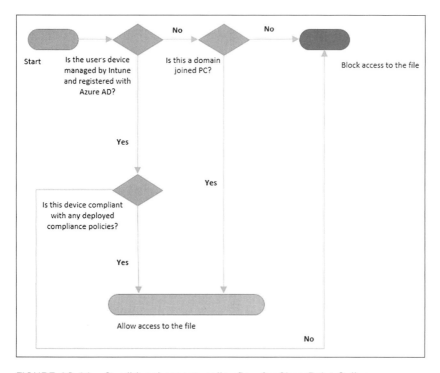

FIGURE 18.11   Conditional access policy flow for SharePoint Online.

Requirements for SharePoint Online

A number of prerequisites must be in place before you can enable conditional access for SharePoint Online. Only specific platforms, browsers, and apps are supported. There are also additional Azure and SharePoint requirements, described in the following sections.

Supported Platforms for SharePoint Online

You can control access to SharePoint Online from the platforms listed in Table 18.8. The built-in browsers on these devices use basic authentication.

TABLE 18.8   SharePoint Online Conditional Access: Supported Devices

Platform	Supported Versions
Google Android	Version 4.0 and later (including Samsung Knox)
Apple iOS	Version 8.0 and later
Windows Phone	Version 8.1 and later
Windows	Windows 8.1 and later (managed as mobile devices)

You can control access to SharePoint Online from the apps listed in Table 18.9. These apps require modern authentication, which is turned on by default for SharePoint Online.

NOTE: SHAREPOINT ONLINE DEFAULT STATE

For tenants created before August 1, 2017, SharePoint Online is the only Office 365 service for which modern authentication is turned on by default.

TABLE 18.9   SharePoint Online Conditional Access: Supported Apps

Apps	Supported Platforms
Microsoft Office Mobile	Android
Microsoft OneDrive	Android and iOS
Microsoft Word	Android and iOS
Microsoft Excel	Android and iOS
Microsoft PowerPoint	Android and iOS
Microsoft OneNote	Android and iOS

Additional Requirements for SharePoint Online

Additional requirements to support conditional access to SharePoint Online follow:

▶ Devices must be workplace joined or enrolled with Intune. Devices must also be registered with the Azure Active Directory Device Registration Service. This is automatic when a device is enrolled or workplace joined.

▶ A SharePoint Online subscription is required.

▶ Users must each be assigned a SharePoint Online license.

Enabling Conditional Access for SharePoint Online

Evaluating the effect of the SharePoint Online conditional access policy in advance is the same as for Exchange Online, discussed earlier in this chapter, in the section "Evaluating the Effect of the Conditional Access Policy for Exchange Online." The configuration of the targeted and exempted groups is also the same; see the earlier section "Configuring Security Groups for Exchange Online."

Evaluating the Effect of the Conditional Access Policy for SharePoint Online

In the ConfigMgr console, navigate to **Monitoring -> Reporting -> Reports**. Under Device Management, use the List of Devices by Conditional Access State report to identify devices that will be blocked from SharePoint Online when you enable conditional access. Select the collection to evaluate and choose **View Report**. As shown in Figure 18.6, earlier in this chapter, one of the devices shown is not compliant, and access to protected corporate files by that device will be blocked. Notify affected users to remediate their devices before enabling conditional access; otherwise, they will not be able to access corporate SharePoint resources.

Configuring Security Groups for SharePoint Online

Two group types can be specified when enabling conditional access. The conditional access policy is applied to targeted groups and is not applied to exempted groups. These groups are Azure AD security user groups and can be configured in one of two portals:

▶ Office 365 admin center

▶ Azure portal

Configuring the Conditional Access Policy for SharePoint Online

Follow these steps to enable conditional access for SharePoint Online:

1. In the ConfigMgr console, navigate to **Assets and Compliance -> Compliance Settings -> Conditional Access**.

2. Select **SharePoint Online**. You are notified that conditional access policies for SharePoint Online must be configured through the Intune console.

3. Select **Configure conditional access policy in the Intune console**. The Intune administration console is launched.

4. Log in with the user account used to create the Intune subscription in ConfigMgr. You are immediately directed to the Exchange Online Policy page in the Intune console.

5. Switch to **Policy -> Conditional Access -> SharePoint Online Policy** (see Figure 18.12).

FIGURE 18.12   Enabling conditional access for SharePoint Online.

6. Check the box **Enable conditional access policy**.

7. Choose the specific platforms for the policy.

8. Select the required targeted and exempted groups.

9. Click **Save** to save the policy, and it takes effect immediately.

The SharePoint Online End-User Experience

When conditional access is enabled, a user cannot open a SharePoint document on an unmanaged or a noncompliant device. The following example uses an iPhone 6 with Word for iOS installed.

The user opens a browser and navigates to the SharePoint site. The user wants to open a Word document, as shown in Figure 18.13.

FIGURE 18.13   Word document on SharePoint Online.

However, the device has not been enrolled, so the user cannot open the document and is notified that this SharePoint site is secured by conditional access, as shown in Figure 18.14.

FIGURE 18.14   Message that This SharePoint Site is secured by conditional access.

The user must enroll the device in order to proceed.

Enabling Conditional Access for Skype for Business Online

The process of enabling conditional access for Skype for Business Online is similar to the process for other services and is carried out using the Intune console. See the "Enabling Conditional Access for Exchange Online" and "Enabling Conditional Access for Share-Point Online" sections, earlier in this chapter, for details. Modern authentication must be enabled before you can implement conditional access for the Skype for Business app.

Figure 18.15 shows the flow used by conditional access policies when a targeted user attempts to use Skype for Business Online on his or her device. The following sections describe the prerequisites and steps for enabling conditional access.

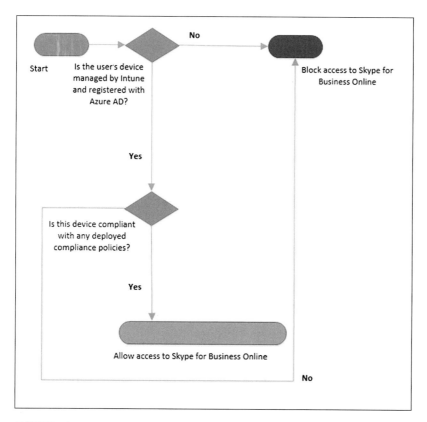

FIGURE 18.15   Conditional access policy flow for Skype for Business Online.

Requirements for Skype for Business Online

Certain prerequisites must be fulfilled before you can enable conditional access for Skype for Business Online. Only specific platforms and apps are supported. There are also specific Azure and Skype for Business Online requirements. Finally, modern authentication must be turned on. The following sections describe the various requirements.

Supported Platforms for Skype for Business Online

You can control access to Skype for Business Online from the platforms listed in Table 18.10.

TABLE 18.10   Skype for Business Online Conditional Access: Supported Devices

Platform	Supported Versions
Google Android	Version 4.0 and later (including Samsung Knox)
Apple iOS	Version 8.0 and later

You can also control access to Skype for Business Online from the Skype for Business apps for Android and iOS.

Additional Requirements for Skype for Business Online

Additional requirements to support conditional access to Skype for Business Online include the following:

▶ Devices must be workplace joined or enrolled with Intune. Devices must also be registered with the Azure Active Directory Device Registration Service. This is automatic when a device is enrolled or workplace joined.

▶ Skype for Business Online must be enabled for modern authentication (see the earlier section, "Understanding Modern Authentication").

Turning on Modern Authentication for Skype for Business Online

Skype for Business Online must be configured to accept a modern authentication connection from modern apps. This is achieved by running PowerShell commands on the tenant. Follow these steps to configure Skype for Business Online:

1. Connect to Skype for Business Online by using remote PowerShell. For more information, see https://technet.microsoft.com/library/dn362795.aspx.

2. Run the following command:

```
Set-CsOAuthConfiguration -ClientAdalAuthOverride Allowed
```

3. Verify that the change was successful by running the following command:

```
Get-CsOAuthConfiguration
```

> **TIP: ORDER OF TURNING ON MODERN AUTHENTICATION**
>
> The authors recommend turning on modern authentication for Exchange Online prior to turning on modern authentication for Skype for Business Online.

Configuring Conditional Access for Skype for Business Online

Evaluating the effect of the Skype for Business Online conditional access policy in advance is the same as for Exchange Online; refer to the section "Evaluating the Effect of the Conditional Access Policy for Exchange Online," earlier in this chapter. Configuration of the targeted and exempted groups is also the same. The section "Configuring Security Groups for Exchange Online," earlier in this chapter, provides additional information.

Evaluating the Effect of the Conditional Access Policy for Skype for Business Online

To evaluate the effect of the conditional access policy, navigate to **Monitoring -> Reporting -> Reports** in the ConfigMgr console. Under Device Management, run the report List of Devices by Conditional Access State to identify devices blocked from Skype for Business Online when you enable conditional access. Select the collection to evaluate and choose **View Report**. As shown earlier in Figure 18.6, one of the devices shown is not compliant, and access to Skype for Business will be blocked for that device.

Notify affected users to remediate their devices before enabling conditional access; otherwise, they will not be able to access Skype for Business Online.

Configuring Security Groups for Skype for Business Online

You can specify two group types when enabling conditional access. The conditional access policy is applied to targeted groups and is not applied to exempted groups.

These groups are Azure AD security user groups and can be configured in one of two portals:

▶ Office 365 admin center

▶ Azure portal

Configuring the Conditional Access Policy for Skype for Business Online

All configurations for Skype for Business Online are carried out directly using the Intune portal, https://manage.microsoft.com. Follow these steps:

1. Launch the portal and log in with a global administrator account.

2. Navigate to **Policy -> Conditional Access -> Skype for Business Online Policy**, as shown in Figure 18.16.

18

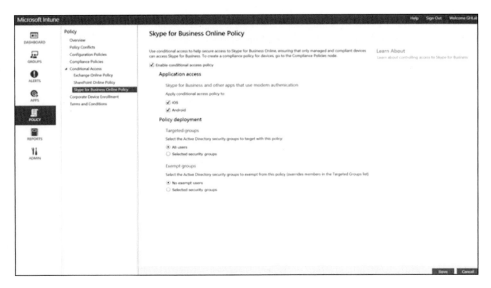

FIGURE 18.16   Enabling conditional access for Skype for Business Online.

3. Check the box **Enable conditional access policy**.

4. Choose the specific platforms for the policy.

5. Select the required targeted and exempted groups.

6. Click **Save** to save the policy, and it takes effect immediately.

Enabling Conditional Access for Exchange On-Premises

Enabling conditional access for Exchange On-Premises is a very different process from the scenarios already described in this chapter for Exchange Online, SharePoint Online, and Skype for Business Online. In the case of Exchange On-Premises, all configurations are carried out using the ConfigMgr console rather than the Intune console. You must add an on-premise Exchange Server connector and configure a conditional access policy.

Several technologies are combined in the implementation of this solution:

▶ **Microsoft Intune:** Manages the compliance and conditional access policies for the device.

▶ **Microsoft Azure AD:** Authenticates the user and provides device compliance status.

▶ **Configuration Manager:** Manages device enrollment and provides reporting.

▶ **Exchange On-Premises:** Enforces access to email, based on the device state.

Figure 18.17 shows the flow that conditional access policies for Exchange On-Premises use to evaluate whether to allow or block devices. The following sections describe the process.

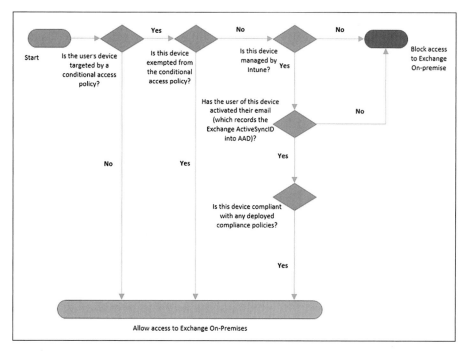

FIGURE 18.17   Conditional access policy flow for Exchange On-Premises.

Requirements for Exchange On-Premises

A number of prerequisites must be in place before you can enable conditional access for Exchange On-Premises. Only specific devices and versions of Exchange are supported. Also, the on-premise Exchange connector must be deployed. These requirements are described in the following sections.

Supported Platforms for Exchange On-Premises

You can control access to Exchange On-Premises from the default mail client on the platforms listed in Table 18.11.

TABLE 18.11   Exchange On-Premises Conditional Access: Supported Devices

Platform	Supported Versions
Google Android	Version 4.0 and later (including Samsung Knox)
Apple iOS	Version 8.0 and later
Windows Phone	Version 8.1 and later
Windows	Windows 8.1 and later (managed as mobile devices)

Additional Requirements for Exchange On-Premises

Additional requirements to support conditional access to Exchange On-Premises include the following:

▶ The On-Premises Exchange version must be Exchange 2010 or later.

▶ The On-Premises Exchange connector must be deployed (as discussed in the next section, "Implementing the Exchange Server connector").

Implementing the Exchange Server Connector

To implement the Exchange Server connector, first create an AD account and configure it to run the following Exchange cmdlets:

▶ Clear-ActiveSyncDevice

▶ Get-ActiveSyncDevice

▶ Get-ActiveSyncDeviceAccessRule

▶ Get-ActiveSyncDeviceStatistics

▶ Get-ActiveSyncMailboxPolicy

▶ Get-ActiveSyncOrganizationSettings

▶ Get-ExchangeServer

▶ Get-Mailbox

▶ Get-Recipient

▶ Get-User

▶ Set-ADServerSettings

▶ Set-ActiveSyncDeviceAccessRule

▶ Set-ActiveSyncMailboxPolicy

▶ Set-CASMailbox

▶ New-ActiveSyncDeviceAccessRule

▶ New-ActiveSyncMailboxPolicy

▶ Remove-ActiveSyncDevice

This account will be used as the Exchange Server connector account.

Follow these steps in the ConfigMgr console to add the Exchange Server connector:

1. Navigate to **Administration -> Overview -> Exchange Server Connectors**.

2. Right-click and select **Add Exchange Server**. The Add Exchange Server Wizard, shown in Figure 18.18, launches.

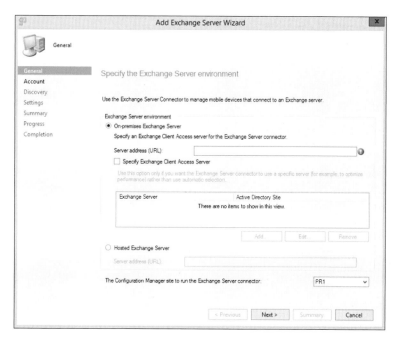

FIGURE 18.18   The Add Exchange Server Wizard.

3. Specify the server address of an on-premise Exchange client access server and click **Next** to continue.

4. Specify the Exchange Server connector account. Also set an account to be used to send quarantine email notifications to clients that are blocked by conditional access. This account must have a valid mailbox on the Exchange server. If you do not specify both accounts, conditional access will fail. Click **Next** to continue.

5. Specify when and how to find the mobile devices to be managed using the Exchange Server connector. Choose whether the connector will discover all devices (the default) or just those in a specified organizational unit (OU). Set a synchronization schedule and click **Next** to continue. The Exchange ActiveSync policies already deployed on the Exchange Server are displayed.

6. Set the **External mobile device management** option to **Allowed** to ensure that mobile devices continue to receive email from Exchange after Configuration Manager enrolls them. Click **Next** to continue.

7. Review the Summary page and click **Next** to add the Exchange Server connector.

NOTE: EXCHANGE SERVER CONNECTOR SUPPORT

ConfigMgr supports a single connector per Exchange organization.

Configuring Conditional Access for Exchange On-Premises

When all the prerequisites are in place, conditional access can be enabled. There are a number of phases to follow, discussed in the following sections:

▶ Evaluating the effect of the conditional access policy (optional but recommended)

▶ Creating ConfigMgr user collections (targeted and exempted)

▶ Configuring the conditional access policy

Evaluating the Effect of the Conditional Access Policy for Exchange On-Premises

To evaluate the effect of the conditional access policy, navigate to **Monitoring -> Overview -> Reporting -> Reports** in the ConfigMgr console and run the report List of Devices by Conditional Access State to identify devices that will be blocked from accessing Exchange after you configure the conditional access policy.

Select the collection to be evaluated and choose **View Report**. As shown earlier in Figure 18.6, one of the devices shown is not compliant, and email access will be blocked.

Creating User Collections

Two collections can be specified when enabling conditional access. The conditional access policy is applied to targeted collections and is not applied to exempted collections.

NOTE: TARGETED AND EXEMPT COLLECTIONS

A user in both collections is exempt from the conditional access policy.

Navigate to **Assets and Compliance -> Overview -> User Collections** in the ConfigMgr console to create these collections.

Configuring the Conditional Access Policy for Exchange On-Premises

Follow these steps to enable conditional access for Exchange On-Premises:

1. In the ConfigMgr console, navigate to **Assets and Compliance -> Compliance Settings -> Conditional Access**.

2. Right click **On-Premises Exchange** and select **Configure Conditional Access Policy** to launch the Configure Conditional Access Policy Wizard, shown in Figure 18.19.

3. When you are presented with details on how the policy works, decide whether to select the **Default rule override** check box, which allows Intune enrolled and compliant devices to access Exchange. Click **Next** to continue.

4. Specify the targeted collection and click **Next** to continue.

5. Specify an exempted collection (optional).

6. Create custom text for the email Exchange sends to the users of blocked devices. You could also accept the default text, displayed in Figure 18.20.

FIGURE 18.19   The Configure Conditional Access Policy Wizard.

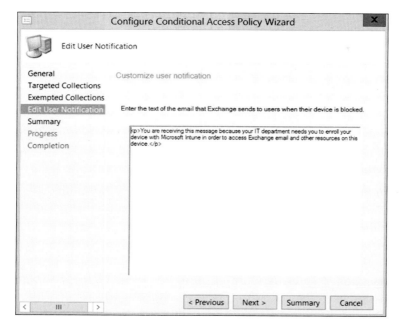

FIGURE 18.20   Customizing the notification email.

7. Review the Summary page and click **Next** to create the policy to enable conditional access.

The conditional access policy does not have to be deployed. It takes effect immediately.

The Exchange On-Premises End User Experience

When conditional access is enabled, if a user tries to add an email account on an unmanaged or a noncompliant device, the device is immediately blocked.

Refer to Figures 18.9 and 18.10, earlier in this chapter, which show that the user successfully added a mail account but sees only a single email warning that further action is required. The email contains instructions and explains that the device must be enrolled with Intune before corporate email can be accessed.

The end-user experience for conditional access with Exchange On-Premises is slightly different than the experience for Exchange Online users:

▶ When a user sets up an Exchange ActiveSync profile on a supported device, it may take from one to three hours for the device to be blocked if it is not compliant or enrolled with Intune.

▶ If a blocked user enrolls the device (or remediates non-compliance), email access is unblocked within two minutes.

▶ If the user un-enrolls a device from Intune, it could take from one to three hours for the device to be blocked.

Monitoring and Troubleshooting Conditional Access

Conditional access involves many components working together to protect corporate resources. Because many of the components are out of your control, it can sometimes be difficult to understand why a solution is not performing as you expect it should.

Conditional access is also a work in progress with significant development focus at this time. New functionality is being released rapidly and published on the Microsoft blogs. Refer to the following blogs for new information:

▶ **ConfigMgr Team Blog:** https://blogs.technet.microsoft.com/configmgrteam/

▶ **Intune Team Blog:** https://blogs.technet.microsoft.com/microsoftintune/

The following sections discuss what you can do to monitor and troubleshoot conditional access issues.

Monitoring Conditional Access Compliance

Use the ConfigMgr console to view the compliance status of conditional access policies. Follow these steps:

1. Navigate to **Monitoring** -> **Overview** -> **Deployments** and select a compliance policy deployment to review.

2. Right-click the policy and select **View Status**.

Figure 18.21 shows an example of a compliance policy deployment status.

FIGURE 18.21   Viewing compliance policy deployment status.

The deployment status page contains the following compliance states:

▶ Compliant

▶ Error

▶ Non-compliant

▶ Unknown

3. Double-click a user or device in the Asset Details pane for more details on the asset message. Figure 18.22 shows an example.

18

FIGURE 18.22   Viewing a compliance policy asset message.

Troubleshooting Conditional Access

Troubleshooting conditional access is not as straightforward as troubleshooting other ConfigMgr features. ConfigMgr administrators are typically provided with many log files and error messages to investigate. However, because conditional access integrates with so many external services (mostly cloud based), it does not have the same extensive logging available. The exception is easdisc.log, which records the activities and the status of the Exchange Server connector for Exchange On-Premises access.

Troubleshoot conditional access by walking through each step of the solution to determine what was overlooked. Consider the following:

▶ **Client Side:** What client is configured in your solution? Are you using a modern app or a built-in mail client? Remember that not all combinations are supported. For example, modern apps are not supported for implementing conditional access with Exchange On-Premises.

▶ **Server Side:** If you are using modern apps, remember that modern authentication may not be turned on by default for Exchange Online or Skype for Business Online.

▶ **Compliance Policy:** Compliance policies are optional. However, have you deployed a policy that includes the settings you require?

▶ **Conditional Access Policy:** Has conditional access been enabled for the service you require? Have you configured your targeted and exempted users correctly?

At the time this book was published, you could create free Microsoft support requests for all Intune-related activities. If you have difficulties with troubleshooting, locate your local number for Intune support at http://technet.microsoft.com/jj839713.aspx.

Summary

This chapter described conditional access, one of the most widely implemented features of the hybrid ConfigMgr and Intune solution. It discussed how conditional access ensures that access to corporate data can be limited to devices that are managed and compliant. This chapter talked about modern authentication, the cornerstone for conditional access for modern apps, and explained terms such as ADAL and OAuth.

The chapter introduced compliance and conditional access policies. It demonstrated how to configure and deploy these policies to control access to corporate services: Exchange Online, SharePoint Online, Skype for Business Online, and Exchange On-Premises. It also discussed monitoring the compliance of the conditional access policies on corporate devices.

Chapter 19, "Endpoint Protection," discusses endpoint protection—that is, how to protect endpoints from malware. Beginning with ConfigMgr 2012, this feature, formerly called System Center Endpoint Protection, is now an integrated component of ConfigMgr.

18

CHAPTER 19

Endpoint Protection

This chapter discusses Microsoft's antimalware platform and enterprise management of that platform using System Center Endpoint Protection (SCEP). The chapter also covers the cloud-based capabilities provided with built-in features of SCEP/Windows Defender, along with the advanced additional features in Windows Defender Advanced Threat Protection (ATP).

The chapter includes an extensive presentation of Microsoft's protection technologies, including a detailed breakdown of the internal capabilities of SCEP/Defender. The chapter also discusses the protection capabilities of Windows itself. These generic capabilities are included in this chapter because SCEP/Defender does not replace any Windows capabilities.

A concise planning and requirements gathering discussion is provided to help you understand how to select a definition distribution methodology and how to use ConfigMgr to get the most out of SCEP/Defender. The chapter discusses deployment, configuration, monitoring/reporting, and actions/alerts, including information on how to configure the various definition distribution methods along with how to distribute the Endpoint Protection (EP) client. Information is provided regarding how best to leverage the ConfigMgr console to monitor SCEP/Defender.

The chapter concludes by discussing Windows Defender ATP, a cloud service that enhances and extends the protection capabilities of Defender on Windows 10. It is licensed separately from SCEP and ConfigMgr, but the agent can be onboarded by ConfigMgr through client policy.

Protection Capabilities of Microsoft's Antimalware Platform

SCEP and Windows Defender in Windows 10 provide solid antimalware capabilities that are directly integrated into ConfigMgr's console and infrastructure. The following sections introduce the antimalware platform and protection technologies included within SCEP and Windows Defender in Windows 10. They explain Microsoft's technology and design in developing its common antimalware platform, which is shared by Windows Defender and SCEP. This overview of protection technologies can help you better understand SCEP and Windows Defender's antimalware technologies, enabling their successful deployment, configuration, and operation.

Understanding these antimalware capabilities is important, as they are often delivered as part of a simple toggle in the user interface, and in some cases multiple features are included in a single toggle. Other antimalware solutions often provide these capabilities in a much more verbose fashion.

Key antimalware capabilities built into Windows 10 are also discussed. These capabilities leverage Windows Defender, the default antimalware solution for Windows 10. Microsoft does not intend to replace the security capabilities of Windows with Defender/SCEP. Keep this in mind if you have many legacy systems to manage or maintain.

Using Antimalware as a Service

Consider Microsoft's antimalware platform as a service. This antimalware solution was intentionally designed to provide simple and direct protection, in contrast with other antimalware solutions that provide advanced capabilities but often require specialists with antimalware knowledge. To achieve this simplicity, Microsoft leverages its monthly engine updates and multiple daily definition updates to introduce new signatures and additional protection technologies, delivered in the engine updates or via platform updates if more substantial changes are required, such as reporting or enterprise controls.

These capabilities are defined based on information gathered by a global network of telemetry, which includes the following:

▶ **Email Services:** Specifically, Microsoft offers the consumer cloud email service Hotmail/Outlook.com along with Office 365. These services are often the frontline for spreading malware.

▶ **Consumer Microsoft Antivirus (AV) Installations:** This telemetry data is from non-commercial users of Microsoft's antimalware platform. It includes Windows Defender on Windows 10 and Windows 8/8.1, as well as Microsoft Security Essentials on Windows 7 and below.

▶ **Microsoft Malicious Software Removal Tool:** This telemetry data is reported back from execution of the Malicious Software Removal Tool (MSRT). New versions of MSRT are released each Patch Tuesday.

▶ **Enterprise Microsoft AV Installations:** These installations include SCEP, Azure Endpoint Protection, and Windows Defender in Windows 10, which apply only when cloud protection is enabled; see the "Dynamic Signatures Service and Behavior Monitoring" section, later in this chapter.

This network of millions of endpoints lets Microsoft respond and prioritize efforts based on real-world evolution and development of malware so it can respond to trends as well as to completed malware. For an example of the type of telemetry to which Microsoft has access, review the Microsoft Security Intelligence Report, published quarterly at https://www.microsoft.com/security/intelligence-report. Microsoft is less focused on investigating malware that *might* cause a problem and instead focuses on malware that *is* causing a problem.

This strategy often means that Microsoft's antimalware platform lags in lab testing due to the use of real-world prevalence-based telemetry. In addition, Microsoft focuses heavily on preventing false positives across its antimalware development life cycle, and it has one of the industry's lowest false positive rates. Given the number of devices in the world running Microsoft Security Essentials and Windows 10 Windows Defender, Microsoft needs to ensure that its false positives are extremely low.

In addition, Microsoft does not provide controls and settings to define different thresholds based on process "risk," as defined by an administrator or similar advanced controls. Instead, Microsoft makes these determinations based on its malware research and telemetry. The response is then codified into the definition updates. When a new threat creates a need for a new way to protect systems, Microsoft releases a change into its engine or the platform itself—again, based on the complexity of the change.

The telemetry, dynamic definition distribution, and settings design discussed in this section show that you could consider Microsoft antimalware a Software as a Service (SaaS) solution. Similar to the desktop client or app portion of a SaaS solution, SCEP is regularly updated and limits customization, but the trade-off is easier configuration and quicker releases. As an administrator, your role is to keep each client as current as possible without interrupting your business rather than making low-level configuration changes. As you can see, leveraging the cloud protection and dynamic update capabilities of SCEP and Windows Defender is critical to delivering the best protection Microsoft's antimalware platform provides.

Understanding Microsoft's Core Protection Technologies

The following sections discuss the key protection technologies included in SCEP and Windows Defender. As just discussed in the "Using Antimalware as a Service" section, many of these capabilities are not settings or features you can toggle or enable; they are part of enabling real-time protection (RTP) and regular scans and are provided as a reference to understand that a simple switch has many moving parts beneath it.

Antimalware, Generics, and Heuristics

Antimalware is the core RTP and scanning included with any antimalware/antivirus product. In SCEP/Defender, this includes file, process, Registry, and network watchers.

19

SCEP/Defender also includes a cache to ensure that unmodified files are not needlessly rescanned; this is accomplished via low-level integration with the file system.

SCEP/Defender also automatically enables generics and heuristics as part of protection, using emulated behavior and/or decrypted binary characteristics, which helps in detecting malware revisions or new malware variants.

In addition, SCEP/Defender's dynamic translation capability uses virtualization to cause potential malware to run against safe virtualized resources, allowing SCEP/Defender to observe that behavior before it can affect key system resources. This was built into the product because with polymorphic malware, often the only commonality between two samples of malicious code is their behavior, and the binaries are completely different.

Using Antirootkits

Antirootkit and diagnostic scanning address the growing dangers of rootkits and other complex malware (*complex* referring to malware that has a deep understanding of its target operating system and how to obfuscate itself from detection). To address the threat posed by rootkits and other complex threats, SCEP/Defender includes kernel support libraries, which allow it to detect initial attempts of obfuscation or already obfuscated code. SCEP/Defender can hook into the Windows boot process to remove malware during the next restart prior to the kernel loading; this process is similar to the process by which kernel binaries are updated. It also provides the ability to perform low-level scans. See the section "Using Windows Defender Offline," later in this chapter, for more information.

Diagnostic Scanning

SCEP/Defender's quick scan is often assumed to be inferior to a full scan. The quick scan should be named *intelligent scan*, though, because its diagnostic scanning capability allows SCEP/Defender to automatically vary the scan intensity. By default, if RTP has been constantly enabled and there has been no malware activity, the quick scan is low intensity, and many low-level/expensive elements are disabled.

If RTP is disabled, if other suspicious activity occurs, or if there are known malware incidents, the scan intensity ramps up accordingly. SCEP/Defender also signals administrators when a full scan is required to fully remediate malware. This is only triggered when SCEP/Defender finds specific malware that requires remediation through a full scan.

Dynamic Signature Service and Behavior Monitoring

SCEP/Defender provides two seemingly unrelated features: Dynamic Signature Service (DSS) and Behavior Monitoring (BM). These two features are intrinsically linked. DSS isn't directly called out in documentation or the console settings, and it receives mention only at tradeshows and during events. However, the description of Microsoft Active Protection Service (MAPS) in SCEP and the description of cloud protection in Defender include a description of DSS. DSS essentially allows SCEP/Defender to pull down late-breaking malware signatures. These are not general-purpose definition updates designed to run against a system that may not be infected; they are designed to protect a machine that has definite signs of infection. The following explains how DSS and BM work:

▶ **DSS:** DSS addresses unknown software or previously known good software compromises. An example of this is freeware network configuration utilities that promise to increase network performance by tweaking the Windows TCP/IP configuration. While these utilities are of dubious value, they are not outright malicious; however, they require administrative rights, which makes them prime targets for attackers. In some cases, mirror websites hosting these utilities are attacked, allowing the attacker to post compromised versions of the utilities. The compromised versions are used to provide a Trojan attack, where the utility downloads malware and then configures it to automatically launch with the next run. DSS allows Microsoft to instruct SCEP/Defender to block the compromised utility and thus the channel used to deliver the malware.

▶ **BM:** BM helps determine when to invoke DSS. RTP within the engine is constantly looking at file, process, Registry, and network activity; it compares this activity against the definitions provided. RTP blocks the compromised utility from writing or launching the malware. In addition to providing active protection, RTP forwards key events to another queue, which BM then analyzes in the background. This occurs because RTP can block processing of the file system and other activities, which dramatically affects system performance. BM determines from where malware has been downloaded to the system; in this example, it is the compromised network utility.

BM and DSS are intrinsically linked because BM triggers DSS to report the compromised network utility binary to Microsoft's Windows Defender cloud protection (formerly MAPS). DSS then receives a response from Microsoft, confirming that the network utility is compromised. This response takes the form of a new micro-definition that instructs RTP to prevent the compromised network utility from launching. Windows Defender refers to the combination of MAPS and DSS settings as *cloud-based protection*. Ensure that MAPS/cloud protection is enabled to be able to receive the high level of protection and the most responsive protection. For more information on cloud-based protection, see https://cloudblogs.microsoft.com/microsoftsecure/2015/01/14/maps-in-the-cloud-how-can-it-help-your-enterprise/.

Understanding Windows Antimalware Capabilities

SCEP/Defender does not replace the security features of Windows itself. Instead, SCEP/Defender leverages the capabilities Windows provides to antimalware vendors to their fullest. This means that SCEP/Defender does not perform as well as other products on older Windows operating systems compared to products that attempt to replicate some of the latest Windows security capabilities and features on those operating systems. It is therefore important to consider the intrinsic Windows capabilities discussed in the next sections when evaluating SCEP/Defender.

Early Launch Antimalware and Measured Boot

Windows 8 and Windows Server 2012 introduced two key capabilities to the Windows security stack: Early Launch Antimalware (ELAM) and Measured Boot. SCEP/Defender takes advantage of both operating system (OS) capabilities to ensure secure transition between device firmware, the OS boot process, and the running OS. The following explains how ELAM and Measured Boot work:

▶ **ELAM:** ELAM was specifically designed to help address rootkits, which tend to attempt to masquerade as system processes or low-level drivers to avoid detection by antimalware products running inside the OS. Secure Boot enables ELAM, which is implemented as a driver, to kick in during the boot process. The ELAM driver starts before other boot drivers, allowing antimalware products to evaluate those drivers and detect malware in the boot process and remediate it prior to initialization.

ELAM also allows SCEP/Defender to remove any malicious changes at the next reboot. This is important as you may find that a restart is required after malware remediation. The reason for this is often to remove rootkit-type infections from the boot process using ELAM.

▶ **Measured Boot:** Whereas ELAM is about prevention, Measured Boot provides remediation, measuring each boot-critical component, which includes everything from the Unified Extensible Firmware Interface (UEFI) firmware through boot start drivers. The measurement is stored in the device's Trusted Platform Module (TPM). Storing the boot attestation in the TPM provides a log that is resistant to spoofing and tampering. This log contains a trace of all software that loaded prior to the antimalware software, allowing the antimalware software to determine whether those components are infected with malware or are trustworthy.

Windows 10 and Windows Server 2016 Antimalware Technologies

Windows 10 and Server 2016 further enhance the native security capabilities that Windows Defender can leverage. The Windows Defender name takes on a broader meaning in the latest versions of Windows and Windows Server, as it now refers to the set of security-related capabilities built in to Windows and not just traditional antimalware. These capabilities include the following:

▶ **Application Control (Windows 10 Version 1709 and later) and Device Guard:** For more information, reference https://docs.microsoft.com/sccm/protect/ deploy-use/use-device-guard-with-configuration-manager.

▶ **Application Guard:** For additional information, see https://docs.microsoft.com/ sccm/protect/deploy-use/create-deploy-application-guard-policy.

▶ **Exploit Guard:** For more information, see https://docs.microsoft.com/sccm/protect/ deploy-use/create-deploy-exploit-guard-policy.

ConfigMgr Current Branch version 1710 can configure these security features. This chapter does not focus on these technologies; rather, it focuses on the antimalware capabilities of Windows Defender, given the change in ConfigMgr from managing SCEP on Windows 7 and earlier versions to Windows Defender on Windows 10. For general information on the overall capabilities of Windows Defender outside antimalware and Windows 10 threat protection capabilities, see https://docs.microsoft.com/windows/threat-protection/.

Windows Defender is specifically called out in this section rather than SCEP in Windows 10 and Windows Server 2016 because it is built in and enabled by default rather than being an add-in, as with previous versions of Windows. SCEP on Windows 10 and Windows Server 2016 acts a management and monitoring layer on top of Windows Defender. In contrast, previous versions of SCEP installed a complete standalone instance of the Microsoft Common Antimalware Platform.

A new element of Windows Defender is *local context*, which provides Defender with the specific context of files to use in subsequent analysis and detection. These contexts include the following:

- ▶ **Entry Point Context:** This context is about malware infiltration. It enables Defender to do advanced scanning at higher-risk entry points. For example, Defender uses the Mark of the Web feature (see https://msdn.microsoft.com/library/ms537628.aspx) to determine if a file was obtained from an external system (such as the Internet) and local context to ensure that this information is available during file use, even if the file is used after it was obtained.

- ▶ **Elevation Change Context:** Windows Defender now has synchronous scan hooks into User Account Control (UAC) elevation requests, allowing it to understand when a process is elevated. Defender then applies additional scanning to such processes, as they can impact the running system. This also hooks into Smart UAC. As part of the scan, if Defender determines that a process is malicious, the UAC message is altered to explain that Windows Defender blocked the process from executing.

- ▶ **Secure Persisted Context:** The context elements discussed in the previous two bullets are now stored securely in a persisted store, which allows the live context obtained via real-time protection components to be persisted for later use. Following is an example from Microsoft:

  1. An email with an attachment arrives via Outlook, and the user saves the attachment.

  2. Days later, the user attempts to execute the attachment.

  3. During execution, the attachment requires administrative rights (via a UAC prompt).

  4. Defender is both able to determine the level of scanning that needs to be done because of the persisted context and gets the immediate context regarding the UAC prompt.

The final element is the Antimalware Scan Interface (AMSI). This generic interface is designed to allow applications to integrate with the antimalware product present on a device. AMSI is intended to tackle the problem of script obfuscation by malware writers. As scripts and automation code are non-executable and instead leverage script engines for execution, they are good targets for delivering obfuscated payloads. These obfuscated payloads must be deciphered to their native format prior to execution by the script engine.

19

AMSI allows script engines including PowerShell and VBScript, along with other applications, the ability to submit deciphered code to the antimalware engine on the system prior to execution. As the code is now deciphered, it becomes easier for signatures to catch the malicious code. For more information and detailed examples of how AMSI works, see https://cloudblogs.microsoft.com/microsoftsecure/2015/06/09/windows-10-to-offer-application-developers-new-malware-defenses/.

Using Windows Defender Offline

The final protection capability is Windows Defender Offline (WDO). WDO, which has been available as a separate download since Forefront Endpoint Protection 2010, is designed to address rootkits and other malware that either obfuscate from or embed themselves within the Windows OS, preventing complete removal. WDO is based on the Windows Preinstallation (WinPE) version of Windows, which is designed to run directly from boot media rather than having to be installed, and commonly used by ConfigMgr's operating system deployment (OSD) and Windows Setup to install Windows itself.

By leveraging WinPE, WDO can scan and clean files that would normally not be accessible on a running system. It can also perform raw disk scans to identify malware that uses slack space, providing remediation against some of the more complex varieties of malware and rootkits.

NOTE: MALWARE THAT USES SLACK SPACE

Slack space refers to space marked as deleted by a file system. This is a perfectly normal design that improves performance, as file systems should only mark data as deleted without overwriting the deleted data. Once the data is marked as deleted, the underlying physical storage units/sectors can be reused to write new data.

Malware can use this slack space to obfuscate itself from protection software running inside the OS. This is usually done by corrupting the boot process, allowing the malware to launch prior to the OS and make changes to the boot order and gain privileged access to low-level application programming interfaces (APIs). The malware can then repeatedly infect a supposedly clean machine with each restart. An example of malware using this technique is Alureon.

SCEP and Windows Defender both attempt to notify the user and the administrator that malware requiring a WDO scan (or offline) scan has been found. SCEP and Defender always attempt to remove what is accessible in the running OS or during a restart. When this is not possible, their state is changed to indicate that an offline scan is required.

In versions prior to Windows 10 and Windows Server 2016, a user or local on-site PC support technician would have to download a version of WDO and install it on a clean PC, as the installation process would obtain the latest drivers and create boot media. The user or technician would then have to use that boot media to boot the infected PC into WDO and allow a scan to complete. The duration of the scan would depend on the malware and whether raw disk scanning was required. Raw disk scanning allows WDO to ignore disk locations marked as free or unpartitioned and scan them as though they were formatted. With Windows 10, WDO is now built in to the main Defender settings and can be launched directly from the Windows Settings app.

WDO is freely available for Windows 7 and later operating systems at http://windows.microsoft.com/windows/what-is-windows-defender-offline.

Microsoft's Approach to Antimalware

The previous sections provide an overview of the protection capabilities of Windows Defender in Windows 10 and SCEP. Many of these advanced capabilities are enabled simply by enabling RTP and running regular quick scans. SCEP and Defender are designed to provide antimalware as a service, where Microsoft drives both the most appropriate response to malware through telemetry and dedicated researchers. Keep this in mind when determining whether to deploy SCEP/Defender in your organization.

Prerequisites for Endpoint Protection

There are certain prerequisites to meet before deploying EP. These are a combination of external and ConfigMgr-specific dependencies, as follows:

▶ External dependencies:

   ▶ If you choose to deliver updates via Microsoft Update (MU) and/or the Microsoft Malware Protection Center (MMPC), you must ensure that your client computers have Internet access. As the MMPC download can be quite large, sufficient bandwidth should be available.

NOTE: MMPC NOW WINDOWS DEFENDER SECURITY INTELLIGENCE

Microsoft has renamed MMPC to the Windows Defender Security Intelligence (WDSI). The content remains the same: malware research, SCEP/Defender definition downloads, and a cleanup tool. The WDSI site is at https://www.microsoft.com/wdsi. Depending on your version of ConfigMgr, you may still find references to the MMPC in your console.

   ▶ Microsoft requires that you license Endpoint Protection to use it in your hierarchy. While it is often bundled alongside ConfigMgr client licenses, this technically is a separate license.

   ▶ Ensure that the clients where SCEP is to be deployed are running a Microsoft-supported OS. At the time this book was published, this included Windows 7, Windows Server 2008, and later OSs. SCEP is not supported on any older versions of Windows because SCEP does not replace or replicate Windows-based innovations in older OSs.

▶ ConfigMgr dependencies:

   ▶ The Endpoint Protection site system role must be deployed on your central administration site (CAS) or standalone primary site and prior to configuring any EP policies or client settings.

19

▶ If you intend to leverage ConfigMgr's infrastructure to deliver definition updates, you must have a software update point (SUP) on your standalone primary site or SUPs deployed in your hierarchy.

▶ Ensure that appropriate permissions are granted. EP includes a specific security role in ConfigMgr called Endpoint Protection Manager. You can use this role to delegate permissions to EP functions rather than rely on built-in permissions.

Planning and Considerations

The following sections provide an overview of the key planning areas and considerations for deploying EP. They provide a good starting point for an overall design that includes EP or for deploying EP into an existing hierarchy.

The following sections include guidelines on the general requirements for an EP solution. These are not specifically SCEP related, but are high-level items to discuss at the start of a project to deploy an antimalware solution. There is also information regarding the key design decisions prior to starting a SCEP configuration and deployment.

Gathering Requirements for Endpoint Protection

The first step in any EP deployment is gathering requirements. It is important to understand the driver behind the selection of Endpoint Protection versus other antimalware products. Following is a list of key questions to address as part of the requirements-gathering process:

▶ **Does Endpoint Protection Replace an Existing Solution?** If so, understand how EP implements your existing solution's protection features and how you will migrate settings to EP.

▶ **What Is the Primary Business Driver for Endpoint Protection?** As with most other infrastructure deployments, this often comes down to cost. Understanding the primary business driver helps weigh the cost of design decisions. For example, having to create loads of manual processes to replace existing automation built up over time may negate savings from reduced licensing costs.

▶ **Where Are Client Computers Located?** Distributing update definitions can cause a significant amount of bandwidth usage.

▶ **Who Will Require Access to Configure Settings from and View Data for Endpoint Protection?** Consider to whom you will need to provide access. Will users need to read monitoring data or create and modify policy? Will the built-in security role meet their requirements?

▶ **Will You Need to Consider Mac OS X and Linux Clients?** These clients require separate agents. They also obtain updates directly from the Internet and do not support centralized management.

▶ **What Are Your Organization Security Policies Regarding Antimalware?** Most organizations maintain standards around general configuration of antimalware products (real-time protection enablement, regular on-demand scanning). This may also include guidance on exclusions and any banned exclusion types. Microsoft's guidance for Windows and Windows Server is found at https://support.microsoft. com/kb/822158. The Microsoft IT Pro community also maintains an index of other Microsoft product recommendations, at http://social.technet.microsoft.com/wiki/ contents/articles/953.microsoft-anti-virus-exclusion-list.aspx.

▶ **What Are Your Organization's Antimalware Processes and Procedures?** Knowledge and documentation of the IT operational guides and processes helps ensure that you can deploy a solution that fits nicely into existing processes and procedures. This helps minimize any resistance to change, allows you to determine large-scale malware incident response plans, and ensures that your EP implementation matches those plans.

Determining Definition Update Sources

There are multiple options for delivering EP definitions, covered more fully in the "Delivery of Definition Updates" section, later in this chapter. Following are several key design considerations:

▶ Leveraging ConfigMgr as an update source allows you to utilize its infrastructure for software updates and content distribution.

▶ Microsoft releases updates three times a day (exact timings are not published). At a minimum, plan to synchronize your SUP at least once a day and at most every eight hours.

▶ The Windows Server Update Services (WSUS) and file server (or UNC) definition sources require you to provision additional servers or server storage. The UNC method requires developing scripts to update the file share hosting the updates.

▶ Always enable the MMPC update source if there is client Internet connectivity. This method is used only after 14 days of definition update failures. It is designed to address malware that attempts to disable the Windows Update Agent (WUA) on clients. Disabling the WUA, especially on Internet-connected laptops, is not recommended.

Leveraging ConfigMgr's Capabilities

One important capability available to Endpoint Protection infrastructures is ConfigMgr itself. ConfigMgr is a highly capable PC management solution. Because all EP data flows through ConfigMgr, you can use its management capabilities to drastically enhance antimalware capabilities. Following are several examples of how to leverage EP with ConfigMgr capabilities:

▶ Build a collection that finds all clients in a Full scan required state and target them with a more aggressive scan policy that requires a daily full scan during lunch hours.

▶ Build a collection that targets a simple package and program that restarts the client computer (perhaps an existing restart wrapper from software distribution). The collection can include clients in the Restart required antimalware state.

Using System Center Endpoint Protection with Windows 10

Windows Defender in Windows 10 and Windows Defender in Windows Server 2016 are based on the same common antimalware platform as SCEP. Windows Defender is also the default antimalware shipped and enabled by default on both operating systems. It is also serviced by updates to Windows 10 and Windows Server 2016.

For these reasons, SCEP does not supplant Windows Defender on these systems. Instead, it provides enterprise management and monitoring capabilities on top of Windows Defender. The underlying client user interface remains unchanged and continues to refer to Windows Defender. This is important, as it may require any end-user guidance to address both SCEP and Windows Defender when multiple Windows versions are in use.

Figure 19.1 shows the Windows Defender user interface on a SCEP-managed PC.

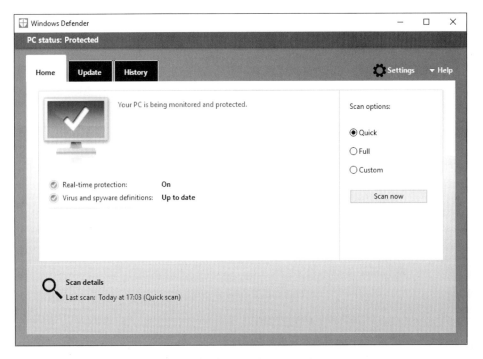

FIGURE 19.1   Windows Defender on Windows 10.

Deployment Best Practices

Certain best practices can help ensure a successful EP deployment. The authors provide the following best practices to help you avoid common pitfalls with SCEP/Defender. Like any other best practices, they should be compared to the business requirements and technical constraints of your environment. Following are general best practices for deploying SCEP:

▶ **Test Uninstallation of Third-Party Antivirus Solutions:** SCEP can uninstall certain third-party antivirus solutions as part of installation. However, this is version and product specific. Uninstallation may require restarts, disabling password protection features, or removing other agents (for example, management agents). These actions may require use of application management in ConfigMgr or a task sequence (TS), depending on the complexity of the third-party solution.

▶ **Always Have Multiple Update Methods:** Multiple redundant definition update deployment methods are critical to a successful deployment. This may be as simple as ensuring that multiple SUPs and distribution points (DPs) are available for clients. It may also include allowing fallback to Microsoft Update for Internet-connected systems. It could also include creating and using a UNC location for updates. ConfigMgr Current Branch version 1706 includes enhanced fallback capabilities for SUPs both within and between boundary groups. This includes a more aggressive failover if the first backup SUP cannot be contacted within a boundary group. You can also now configure the failover time-out from one boundary group to another neighboring boundary group.

▶ **Do Not Disable the MMPC Update Source:** This location is designed as a fallback update source to use when the client has not been able to update definitions for 14 days. It is designed to address scenarios where malware or other issues impact the WU agent (Windows Update) or its service (wuauserv) on a SCEP/Defender client or server.

Deploying and Configuring Endpoint Protection

The next sections focus on deploying and configuring SCEP. They cover server-side activities along with configuring policies and deploying SCEP agents using various methods. They do not include monitoring, alerts, reporting, or other areas of SCEP. Those topics are discussed in the sections "Enabling Alerts for a Collection" and "Monitoring and Reporting in Endpoint Protection," later in this chapter.

Deploying and configuring SCEP from a server point of view is relatively simple, requiring a single site system to be deployed. Policy and client distribution is also straightforward when you plan ahead and document each team's requirements. The update definition process is the most complex of these processes.

Installing the Endpoint Protection Point Role

Deploying SCEP throughout your hierarchy or site requires deploying the Endpoint Protection Point (EPP) site system role. The role should be deployed to a site system server, either the CAS or your primary site. The EPP needs to be installed on only a single site system, and it can be installed on only one site system.

Deploying the site system role requires the following:

▶ Accepting the end user licensing agreement (EULA) for SCEP

▶ Selecting the default MAPS (formerly SpyNet) configuration for all antimalware policies (which can be overridden on a policy-by-policy basis)

▶ Installing the SCEP agent on the site system server hosting the role

NOTE: THE SCEP AGENT ON THE ENDPOINT PROTECTION POINT

Deploying the EPP on a site system server causes the SCEP agent to be deployed to that server as part of the process of installing the site system role. The agent is installed to allow the EPP components to access the definition update metadata and store it in the site database, allowing easier reporting and monitoring. The agent is not configured to perform real-time protection or scheduled scans.

In environments where SCEP is not deployed to servers, this instance of the SCEP client can coexist with other antimalware solutions. When SCEP is deployed to servers, this instance of the SCEP client may have its protection technologies enabled.

The installation process on a hierarchy and a standalone primary site is the same (barring the selection of servers/sites available). The following steps can be used to deploy the EPP (in this case, on the CAS):

1. In the ConfigMgr console, navigate to **Administration -> Site Configuration -> Servers and Site System Roles.**

2. Right-click the server where you want to install the EPP role and select **Add Site System Roles** to launch the Add Site System Roles Wizard, shown in Figure 19.2.

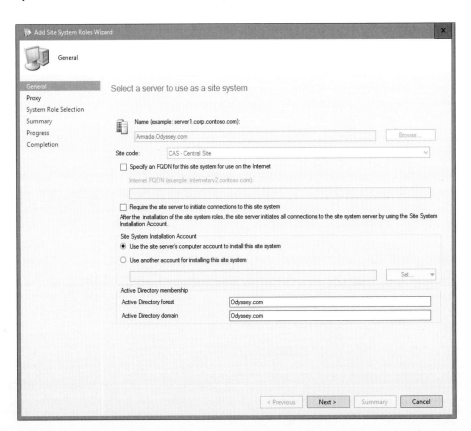

FIGURE 19.2   The Add Site System Roles Wizard.

3. Continue through the wizard. At the System Role Selection page, select the **Endpoint Protection Point**. If the SUP role is not already installed and configured, you are warned that you should configure it prior to enabling the EPP. If you continue, you must adjust the default antimalware policy to not receive updates from ConfigMgr.

4. On the Endpoint Protection page, displayed in Figure 19.3, accept the EULA and click **Next**. SCEP has a separate license from ConfigMgr, although the two are often bundled together. If you need clarification regarding your organization's licensing, speak to your Microsoft reseller or representative.

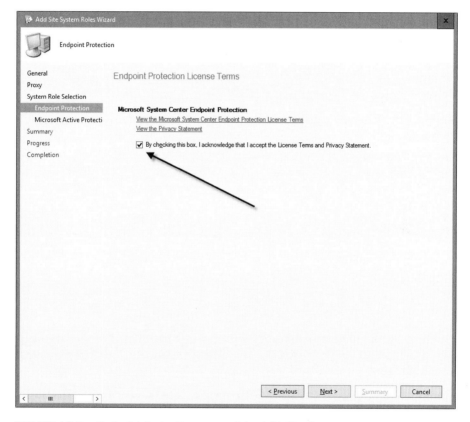

FIGURE 19.3   Endpoint Protection page of the Add Site System Roles Wizard.

5. On the Microsoft Active Protection Service page, shown in Figure 19.4, select the appropriate MAPS level for your organization. Prior to selecting an option, review the "Dynamic Signatures Service and Behavior Monitoring" section, earlier in this chapter. Choosing to disable MAPS may reduce the security protection provided by SCEP. This page of the wizard alters the default settings for all antimalware policies created in the hierarchy or standalone site.

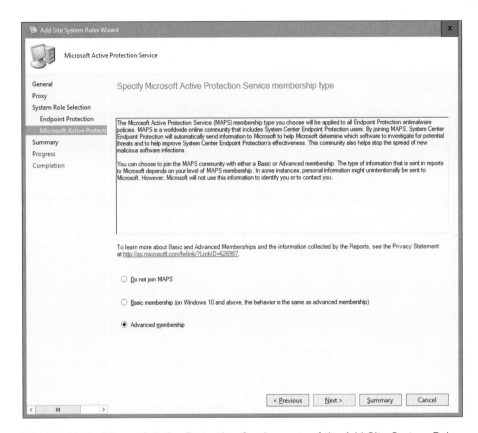

FIGURE 19.4   Microsoft Active Protection Service page of the Add Site System Roles Wizard.

By using MAPS, SCEP can send information to Microsoft to enable dynamic delivery of micro-signatures in response to BM-gathered data. The basic membership option causes SCEP to attempt to obfuscate from known locations. Advanced membership causes additional data to be sent to Microsoft for more comprehensive responses to malicious behavior.

On Windows 10/Windows Server 2016, there is no difference between basic and advanced settings, and MAPS is represented in the UI by the Cloud-based Protection setting, shown in Figure 19.5.

6. Continue through the rest of the Add Site System Roles Wizard.

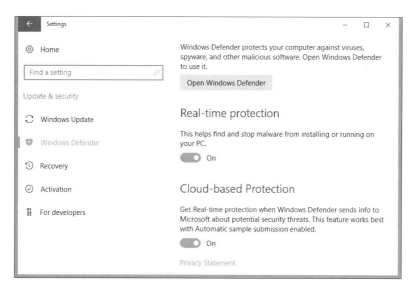

FIGURE 19.5   Cloud-based Protection setting in Windows Defender.

When the wizard completes, ConfigMgr installs the EPP role. To modify the default behavior of the MAPS membership settings, navigate to **Administration -> Overview -> Site Configuration -> Server and Site Systems**. Double-click the **Endpoint Protection Point** role and then access the MAPS tabs to make changes.

Confirm installation of the EPP role by reviewing the EPSetup.log file in the site server's log files folder. The log should end with the line "Installation was successful."

Delivery of Definition Updates

Keeping SCEP/Defender current with definition updates is a critical element for a successful deployment. As discussed earlier in this chapter, in the "Protection Capabilities of Microsoft's Antimalware Platform" section, you should view SCEP/Defender as a service. The key component powering this "service" is definition updates, which provide standard antimalware detection rules, engine updates, and improvements to the core protection capabilities in response to malware advancements.

Much like a cloud-based service's code, SCEP/Defender's definition updates are updated regularly. Microsoft publishes SCEP/Defender updates three times a day to accommodate its worldwide customer base and meet the rapidly evolving threats of the online world. This frequency can change, based on evolving malware conditions reported through telemetry and research.

SCEP/Defender provides multiple methods for updating definition updates. ConfigMgr's software updates feature is typically used to deliver updates to SCEP/Defender, as discussed later in this chapter, in the "ConfigMgr Software Update Management Source" section.

19

You can also leverage WSUS, Microsoft Update, or UNC file share sources, although they are less commonly used. For completeness and because you can use these options as backup definition update methods, the other methods are covered in the sections after the "ConfigMgr Software Update Management Source" section of this chapter. Review the various options to determine which source or set of sources would work best for your environment.

Definition Updates Architecture

SCEP/Defender definition updates are composed of multiple components. The definition updates are composed of antimalware virus definition modules (VDMs) and the malware protection engine, which contains the core protection technologies and capabilities of SCEP/Defender. The VDMs contain the rules and metadata required to detect and remediate malware infections.

The VDMs are four separate files, as follows:

▶ **MpAvBase.vdm:** This is the largest VDM; it contains antivirus metadata and rules. It is generally updated monthly by Microsoft as part of the baselining process (see the "Definition Rebase Process" section of this chapter). This VDM provides the starting point for that month's subsequent delta updates. It enables any new SCEP/Defender clients to get set up or clients who haven't received definitions for a month or more to get running again.

▶ **MpAvDlta.vdm:** This file is the antivirus delta VDM. It is updated with each definition update release multiple times a day. It contains all changes since the last base (MpAvBase.vdm) was created, and enables any client with that month's base to get up to date with that release's definitions. This file becomes progressively larger with each release, until the monthly baselining process occurs, discussed in the following section, "Definition Rebase Process."

▶ **MpAsBase.vdm:** This file contains the antispyware base rule set for the month. It contains base spyware software metadata and rules, along with other potentially unwanted software information. Like the antivirus base VDM (MpAvBase.vdm), it is designed to get new clients set up and to get clients out of date by a month or more updated to that month's baseline.

▶ **MpAsDlta.vdm:** This file is the antispyware delta VDM. Like the antivirus delta VDM (MpAvDlta.vdm), this delta VDM updates the month's antispyware baseline to that definition update's release of the antispyware rule set and metadata.

The final file included in a definition update release is the Microsoft malware protection engine, MpEngine.dll. The engine uses the VDMs described in these bullets to scan and protect against malware, including viruses and spyware. The engine is generally updated once a month, along with the baseline. The engine often gains new protection capabilities in response to advancements and innovations made by malware authors.

Definition Rebase Process

Throughout the month, the delta VDMs (MpAvDlta.vdm and MpAsDlta.vdm) grow larger with each definition update release, which increases the size of the definition updates. The increase in size occurs as new malware is discovered and rules to combat it are added. The rebase process occurs monthly. At that time, delta definitions released throughout that month are reviewed, and any opportunity for deduplication is taken and added to the base VDMs. While this slightly increases the size of the baseline VDM files, the delta VDMs are significantly reduced in size.

Over the next month, the delta VDM files slowly grow until the next rebaseline. In terms of file size, Microsoft publishes guidance in KB article 977939 (https://support.microsoft.com/kb/977939) as follows:

▶ **New Agent Installation:** Approximately 40–70MB

▶ **Agent with Previous Month's Definitions:** 1–15MB

▶ **Agent with Recent Definitions:** 50KB–15MB

These values will vary based on malware activity and when in the rebase cycle they are viewed. For example, at the time this book was published, the following file sizes were obtained from the 64-bit version of the definition updates toward the end of month's rebase cycle, downloaded from https://www.microsoft.com/wdsi/definitions:

▶ **MpEngine.dll:** 14MB

▶ **MpAvBase.vdm:** 58MB

▶ **MpAvDlta.vdm:** 28MB

▶ **MpAsBase.vdm:** 36MB

▶ **MpAsDlta.vdm:** 4MB

You can repeat this process by decompressing mpam-fe.exe using 7-zip (http://www.7-zip.org/) or another decompression utility. The files are directly viewable and are not further encoded.

ConfigMgr Software Update Management Source

The method of definition updates described in this section leverages the software updates feature and package distribution infrastructure of ConfigMgr to deliver definition updates. The process relies on having an automatic deployment rule (ADR) configured. For more information on software updates and ADRs, see Chapter 15, "Managing Software Updates." The first step in configuring this update method is configuring ConfigMgr to synchronize the definition update updates into the site database, using these steps:

1. In the ConfigMgr console, navigate to **Administration -> Site Configuration -> Sites**.

2. Select the CAS or your standalone primary site. Click **Configure Site Components** in the ribbon bar and select **Software Update Point**.

3. On the Classifications tab of the Software Update Point Component Properties window, check the **Definition Updates** update classification check box, highlighted in Figure 19.6.

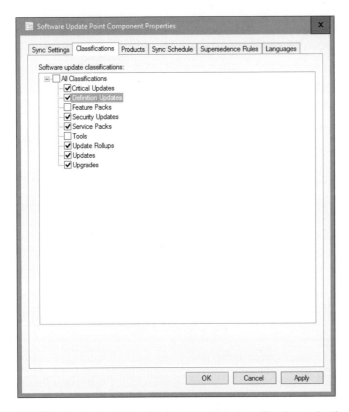

FIGURE 19.6   Definition Updates update classification selection.

4. On the Products tab, select the following based on the client OS where SCEP/ Defender will run, as displayed in Figure 19.7:

▶ For Windows 8.1/Windows Server 2012 R2 and earlier, check the **Forefront Endpoint Protection 2010** product check box.

▶ For Windows 10/Windows Server 2016, check the **Windows Defender** product check box.

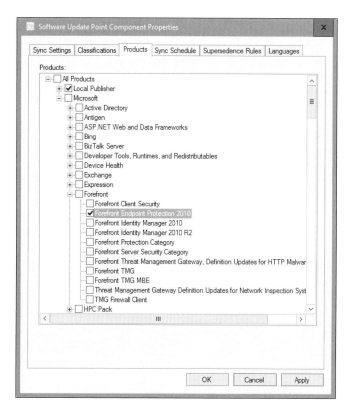

FIGURE 19.7   Definition Updates products selection.

5. Click **OK** to close the dialog box and commit your changes.

6. Wait for ConfigMgr to complete the next scheduled SUP synchronization. It may be necessary to change the SUP synchronization schedule to daily to ensure that definition update metadata is synchronized in a timely manner.

Once synchronization of the definition updates completes successfully and you confirm that definition updates are visible in the ConfigMgr console as software updates, create an ADR. Using an ADR allows you to save time and prevents you from having to manually approve and distribute the updates. Following are several recommendations to consider prior to creating the ADR:

▶ Place definition updates for SCEP/Defender in their own software update package. This keeps the size of the package smaller than it would be if it included other software updates, allowing for faster replication to targeted DPs.

▶ Select the **Only error messages** detail level for deployment state reporting. This helps reduce the number of state messages sent as part of definition update deployment, reducing the processor load on the site servers.

▶ Set the ADR to run with scheduled SUP synchronizations; this helps reduce the lag time between the synchronization process and definition update ADR execution.

19

Follow these steps to configure the ADR to push definition updates to SCEP/Defender agents:

1. In the ConfigMgr console, navigate to **Software Library -> Software Updates -> Automatic Deployment Rules**.

2. Select **Create Automatic Deployment Rule**.

3. Enter the following information on the General page of the wizard:

   ▶ **Name:** Any descriptive name for the ADR

   ▶ **Collection:** The device collection where you want to deploy the definition updates

4. Click **Add to an existing software update group** and select the software update group where you want to group the definition updates. If one does not exist, create one.

5. Check the **Enable the deployment after this rule is run** check box.

6. Review the configuration, as shown in Figure 19.8, and then click **Next**.

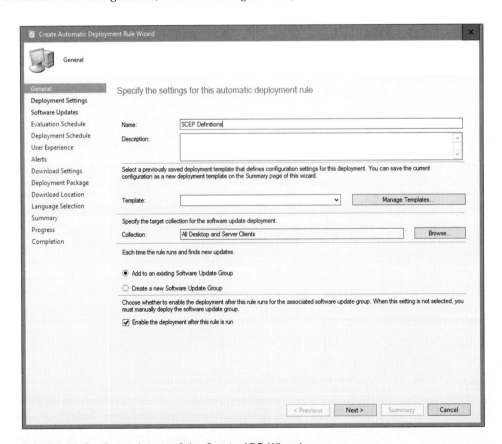

FIGURE 19.8   General page of the Create ADR Wizard.

7. On the Deployment Settings page, set the **Detail level** list and select **Only error messages**.

8. In the Property filters list, set the following (Figure 19.9 shows the end result of filter configuration):

   ▶ Check the **Product** check box to enable the filter and then set the filter to one or both of the following:

      ▶ Forefront Endpoint Protection 2010 for Windows 8.1 and earlier

      ▶ Windows Defender for Windows 10 and later

   ▶ Check the **Superseded** check box to enable the filter and then select **No**.

   ▶ Check the **Update Classification** check box to enable the filter and then select **Definition Updates**.

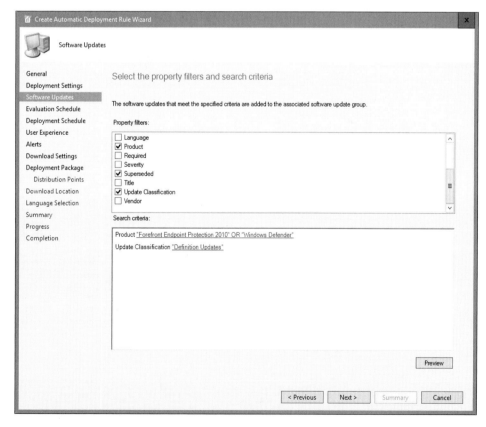

FIGURE 19.9   Deployment page of the ADR wizard.

9. In the Evaluation Schedule page, select **Run the rule after any software update point synchronization**, as shown in Figure 19.10. Click **Next**.

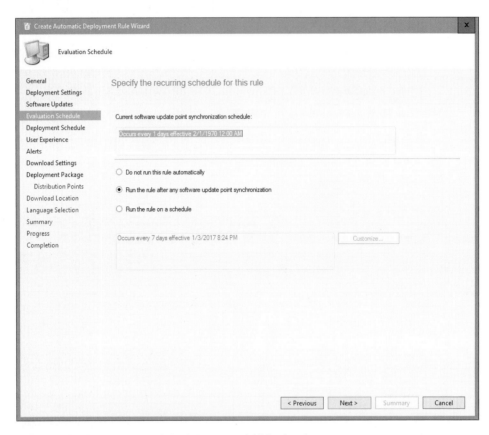

FIGURE 19.10   Evaluation Schedule page of ADR wizard.

10. On the Deployment Schedule page, shown in Figure 19.11, set the following configurations:

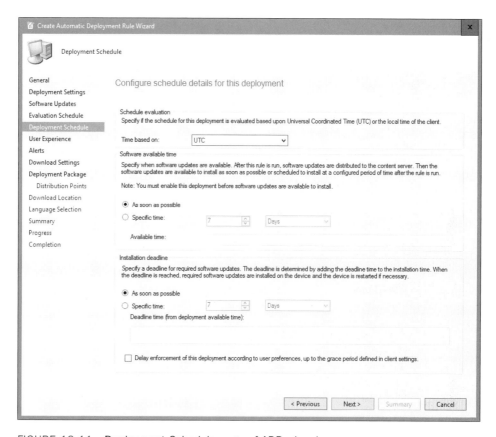

FIGURE 19.11   Deployment Schedule page of ADR wizard.

▶ **Time Based On:** Select **UTC**, as installation is automatically randomized within a two-hour window.

▶ **Software Available Time:** Specify the available time that allows for the definition update content to replicate to the DPs in your hierarchy. If the hierarchy has DPs that take a very long time to receive content, consider deploying definitions to those locations via a separate ADR.

▶ **Installation Deadline:** Select **As soon as possible**.

Click **Next**.

11. On the User Experience page, set the users notification list to **Hide in Software Center and all notifications** and click **Next**.

12. At the Alerts page, click **Next** because there is no need to generate alerts as the SCEP/Defender clients will send up state messages based on their definition update status independently as part of SCEP/Defender monitoring.

19

13. On the Download Settings page, select the required software updates download behavior for the clients, based on the network topology where they are located, and then click **Next**.

14. On the Deployment Package page, select an existing deployment package used only to store definition updates or create a new deployment package to store only definition updates. Click **Next**.

15. On the Distribution Points page, select one or more DPs that will host the definition updates for the clients targeted by this ADR. Click **Next**.

16. On the Download Location page, select **Download software updates from the Internet** and then click **Next**.

17. On the Language Selection page, select the languages required for your organization and then click **Next**.

18. Close the wizard to finish creating the ADR.

Confirm that the ADR was created successfully. The authors recommend testing the ADR by running it manually once to validate that it is working as expected. Ensure that when you test, you use a test collection rather than the production device collection.

Microsoft Malware Protection Center Source

The MMPC is Microsoft's central location for publishing antimalware information and resources. It also hosts Microsoft's threat encyclopedia (https://www.microsoft.com/security/portal/threat/Threats.aspx), which contains information on all the malware that SCEP/Defender protects against.

The MMPC also hosts definition updates that are available for direct download (https://www.microsoft.com/security/portal/definitions/adl.aspx). These cover not just SCEP/Defender but all Microsoft antimalware products. The definition updates contain complete definitions and thus are quite large. At the time this book was published, the 64-bit definitions were between 111MB to 124MB. Sizes vary constantly, based on when the updates are in the rebase cycle (see the "Definition Updates Architecture" section, earlier in this chapter) and malware activity.

The MMPC update method is used only if the SCEP/Defender client cannot obtain definitions for at least 14 days. This helps protect against scenarios where malware may have disabled WU components or convinced the user to do so. This is an automated process with no configuration or setup required; the SCEP/Defender client simply downloads the definitions directly from the MMPC. However, because it is automated and unmanaged, there is no protection against wide area network link usage. As this method is used as a last resort, it should be enabled wherever possible.

WSUS and Microsoft Update Sources

Using the WSUS and Microsoft Update definition update method causes the SCEP/Defender client to directly request definition updates from the WUA service. This method circumvents ConfigMgr's software update management feature and DPs, instead causing the client to directly request the update from the SUP. It is useful in the following scenarios:

▶ As a backup definition update method (although it is dependent on the same SUPs used by software update management)

▶ For use in environments that do not use ConfigMgr for software update management

▶ For scenarios where the ConfigMgr client is not deployed, such as server management where the System Center Operations Manager agent is used alongside WSUS for update management

There are no steps to configure this process for Microsoft Update. The SCEP/Defender client calls out to WUA and requests a scan directly against MU. (WUA can communicate with WSUS and MU simultaneously.) However, configuring this process for WSUS requires that you perform specific configuration steps:

▶ If using a WSUS server that is a SUP, follow the steps in the "ConfigMgr Software Update Management Source" section, earlier in this chapter—specifically those that configure software update synchronization to include the products and classifications for definition updates.

▶ If using a standalone WSUS server, follow the steps in this section to configure the products and classifications for definition updates.

▶ Regardless of whether you are using a standalone or SUP-enabled WSUS server, you must configure WSUS approval rules in the WSUS console to enable WSUS to supply the definition updates when requested by WUA clients.

To enable the required products and classifications for definition updates to be synchronized into the WSUS database, perform the following steps:

1. In the WSUS administration console, select **Options -> Products and Classifications**.

2. Select the following products accordingly:

▶ For SCEP running on Windows 8.1 and earlier, select **Forefront Endpoint Protection 2010**.

▶ For Windows Defender running on Windows 10 and later, select **Windows Defender**.

3. On the Classifications tab, select the **Definition Updates** and **Updates** check boxes.

Follow these steps to create an automatic approval rule in WSUS, which automatically deploys the latest definitions to clients:

1. In the WSUS administration console, select **Options -> Automatic Approvals**.

2. On the Update Rules tab, select **New Rule**.

3. Select the following check boxes, as shown in Figure 19.12:

> ▶ For the When an update is in a specific classification setting, select **Definition Updates.**

> ▶ For the When an update is in a specific product setting, select **Forefront Endpoint Protection 2010** and **Windows Defender.**

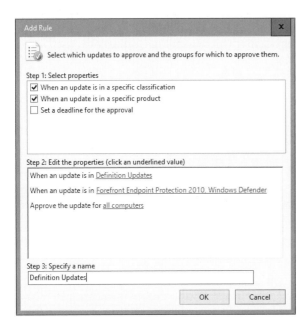

FIGURE 19.12   WSUS Automatic Approval Rule for Definition Updates.

4. Enter a descriptive name in the **Step 3: Specify a name** text box and click **OK.**

CAUTION: MAINTAINING THE WSUS DATABASE

Definition updates are regularly updated and generate a large amount of metadata in the WSUS database. This makes maintaining the WSUS database critical to the long-term health and availability of the WSUS server. Microsoft provides guidance on how to ensure the performance of WSUS servers in KB articles 938947 (https://support.microsoft.com/kb/938947) and 2517455 (https://support.microsoft.com/kb/2517455).

File Shares (UNC) Source

The final definition update method available is the network share or UNC path update option. This option is the most complex to implement, as it requires using scripts to populate the share and a method of distributing the content to multiple locations.

Microsoft does not provide any official guidance on how to automate this process. However, this is the only method with no dependencies on the WSUS/SUP infrastructure or Internet downloads. The ConfigMgr community has produced multiple guides and sample scripts for configuring this method, listed here for reference:

▶ https://www.niallbrady.com/2013/02/22/how-can-i-deploy-system-center-2012-endpoint-protection-definition-updates-from-a-unc-file-shares/

▶ https://blogs.technet.microsoft.com/charlesa_us/2015/05/20/configmgr-2012-how-to-deploy-scep-definition-updates-via-unc-share-for-isolated-environment/

▶ https://blog.thesysadmins.co.uk/sccm-2012-scep-unc-definition-updates-automation-powershell.html

Working with Antimalware Policies

After selecting one or more methods of definition update distribution, your next step is determining that policy configuration. Policies in SCEP/Defender define the configuration of the protection agent installed on the device. They are distributed as a client policy, like ConfigMgr client settings, and are deployed to collections in a similar fashion. As with ConfigMgr client settings, there is a default policy available to any client without requiring deployment of that policy to specific collections. You can modify the default policy as required to define an organization-wide baseline.

This section covers the various antimalware settings contained in an antimalware policy object in the console. Key settings are provided, along with descriptions and recommendations. For brevity and simplicity, the following are major settings for endpoint protection (those settings not covered are documented at https://docs.microsoft.com/sccm/protect/deploy-use/endpoint-antimalware-policies):

▶ **Scan Type:** There are two types of scans in SCEP/Defender:

▶ **Full Scan:** A full scan is a traditional antivirus scan. It covers files, folders, running processes, memory, and the Registry, scanning the system completely with each execution, without any optimizations. A full scan consumes significant resources and time.

▶ **Quick Scan:** A quick scan dynamically alters the depth of the scan based on the machine's state, skipping steps not required on healthy systems but becoming increasingly aggressive on unhealthy or suspect systems.

If a quick scan or real-time protection determines that malware is detected and requires a full scan for removal, an in-console alert is generated. You should leverage quick scans wherever possible. In most cases, a quick scan has a light enough touch to run daily without impacting the user experience. SCEP/Defender can also be configured to run a daily quick scan and a weekly full scan, if required.

19

▶ **Scan Settings:** In addition to setting the type of scan, you can control the configuration of the scan itself. The following settings are available:

   ▶ **Check for the Latest Definition Updates Before Running a Scan:** Selecting this setting causes SCEP/Defender to trigger a definition update prior to executing a scan. This only applies if the WSUS, MU, or network share/UNC definition update sources are configured, as those methods cause the SCEP/ Defender client to reach out directly to the source. The Configuration Manager definition update source causes SCEP/Defender to rely on ConfigMgr to push definitions to it; this setting does not apply if only Configuration Manager is set as a definition update source.

   ▶ **Start a Scheduled Scan Only When the Computer Is Idle:** This setting causes a scan to trigger only when the computer is determined to be idle. The idle detection method varies by OS version. For information on the exact idle detection method for your OS, see https://msdn.microsoft.com/library/ windows/desktop/aa383561(v=vs.85).aspx. Enable this setting only if using full scans, as a quick scan has low enough impact not be noticed in most cases.

   ▶ **Force a Scan of the Selected Scan Type if Client Computer Is Offline During Two or More Scheduled Scans:** This setting is self-explanatory. In general, you should enable this setting to ensure that multiple scans are not missed due to the machine being consistently offline during the scheduled times.

   ▶ **Scan Network Files:** This setting causes scans to remotely scan network locations from the client during a scheduled scan. This may be desired, but it is often more efficient to run a scan on the server itself.

   ▶ **Scan Mapped Network Drives When Running a Full Scan:** Exercise caution when selecting this setting, as it causes any client machine with a mapped network drive to scan the file server hosting that network drive, which may cause repeated redundant scanning of the same files and increased resource usage on the server and network. For increased granularity, this setting does allow for the **Scan network files** setting to be enabled while this setting is disabled.

   ▶ **Scan Archived Files:** This setting causes a scheduled scan to extract compressed files and scan their contents. It should be noted that SCEP/ Defender scans more than traditional compressed files (.zip, .rar, .cab); it also includes container formats such as ISO files. The list of container formats is varied through engine and definition updates.

▶ **Real-Time Protection:** Multiple settings are included in real-time protection, as follows:

   ▶ **Monitor File and Program Activity on Your Computer:** This setting controls the core RTP capabilities. While it is possible to enable other components of real-time protection, in most environments, this setting should be enabled.

▶ **Enable Behavior Monitoring:** In most organizations, this setting should be enabled to improve protection performance. However, if cloud protection/ MAPS is disabled, enabling Behavior Monitoring provides little value. See the section "Dynamic Signatures Service and Behavior Monitoring," earlier in this chapter, for information on how cloud protection/MAPS and Behavior Monitoring work together.

▶ **Enable Protection Against Network-Based Exploits:** This setting augments BM and causes network traffic to act as an additional sensor for behavior monitoring. It does so by duplicating network traffic and performing asynchronous scanning. This method of scanning reduces the impact of a scan. For more information about this feature, see the blog post at https:// cloudblogs.microsoft.com/enterprisemobility/2013/06/24/enhancements-to-behavior-monitoring-and-network-inspection-system-in-the-microsoft-anti-malware-platform/.

▶ **Enable Protection Against Potentially Unwanted Applications at Download and Prior to Installation:** This setting protects the system against potentially unwanted applications (PUAs). PUAs are not malware or malicious software but software that may detrimentally impact the user experience. This impact may involve a lack of choice/control, inability to remove/uninstall, performance impact, advertising, and privacy concerns. For more information on how Microsoft classifies PUAs and malicious software, see https://www.microsoft.com/wdsi/antimalware-support/malware-and-unwanted-software-evaluation-criteria.

▶ **Exclusion Settings:** These settings support standard file and folder exclusions, process exclusions, and file type exclusions. When using process or file and folder exclusions, ensure that file system permissions to modify or replace the process binaries or file/folders are restricted to trusted persons. As of ConfigMgr Current Branch version 1602, excluding files and folders can also be specified for Windows device names (for example, \Device\HarddiskVolume2) and environmental variable paths (for example, *%ExchangeInstallPath%*).

▶ **MAPS/Cloud Protection Service:** As discussed in the "Dynamic Signatures Service and Behavior Monitoring" section, earlier in this chapter, enabling MAPS/cloud protection service is critical for allowing SCEP/Defender to react quickly to evolving malware incidents using cloud-based telemetry. Relying purely on scheduled definition pull reduces the overall protection for your devices. For these reasons, the authors recommend that you enable this setting.

NOTE: WINDOWS FIREWALL POLICIES

In addition to configuring SCEP/Defender, you can configure Windows Firewall policies via ConfigMgr. Capabilities with Windows Firewall policies are limited to simply enabling or disabling the firewall for each profile. In most cases, leveraging group policy provides more granular control and includes additional features. Find information on how to deploy Windows Firewall configurations and settings using group policy at https://docs.microsoft.com/windows/security/identity-protection/windows-firewall/windows-firewall-with-advanced-security.

Installing the Endpoint Protection Client

Once you have created antimalware policies, the next step in deploying SCEP/Defender is installing the client. ConfigMgr provides multiple methods to deploy the SCEP/Defender client. Usually deployment with ConfigMgr is simplest. The other methods accommodate more advanced scenarios.

Installing Endpoint Protection Using ConfigMgr Client Settings

To deploy SCEP using ConfigMgr client settings, the authors recommend creating a custom client device setting and deploying that to clients in a device collection. The same process is used for Windows Defender, except with Windows 10/Windows Server 2016, where the core antimalware components continue to be Windows Defender. On Windows 10/Windows Server 2016 and later, a thin management layer is installed to allow ConfigMgr to manage Windows Defender. For either scenario, perform the following steps:

1. Navigate to **Administration -> Client Settings**.

2. From the ribbon bar, select **Create -> Create Custom Client Settings**.

3. In the Create Custom Client Device Settings dialog, provide a name for the custom settings and then select **Endpoint Protection**.

4. Select the Endpoint Protection client settings, as required. Following are key settings for any SCEP/Defender deployment (see Figure 19.13):

   ▶ **Manage Endpoint Protection Client on Client Computers:** This setting causes SCEP/Defender installations to be managed by ConfigMgr and is required to install the client. It can also be used to manage clients installed through other methods.

   ▶ **Install Endpoint Protection Client on Client Computers:** This setting causes ConfigMgr to deploy SCEP to ConfigMgr computers. On systems running Windows 10 and later, this installs a management layer between Windows Defender and the ConfigMgr client. This setting has no effect on computers where the client is already installed. Disabling or setting this to false/no does not uninstall SCEP.

   ▶ **Disable Alternate Sources (Such as Windows Update, Microsoft Windows Server Update Services or UNC Shares) for the Initial Definition Update on Client Computer:** This setting is important where multiple definition sources are defined in the default or a custom antimalware policy, as it helps prevent those sources from being used. Instead, the SCEP client relies on ConfigMgr to deploy definition updates after its installation, helping reduce network bandwidth consumption by leveraging the ConfigMgr infrastructure. This setting does not apply to Windows Defender, as the client is running by default in Windows 10/Windows Server 2016 and later.

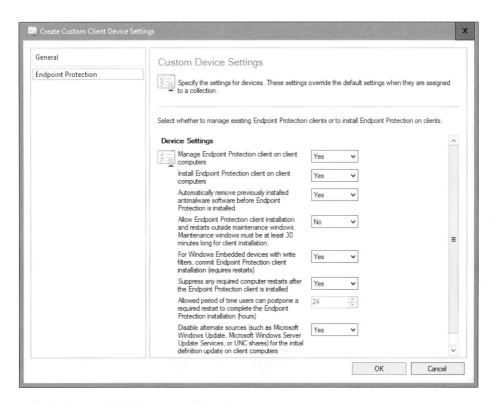

FIGURE 19.13   SCEP/Defender Client Settings dialog.

Installing Endpoint Protection Using Application Management or the Command Line

Sometimes a complex uninstallation routine is required for an existing antimalware product prior to installation of SCEP. In such cases, you can deliver the uninstallation routines either by an application or task sequence (depending on the uninstall routine's complexities and requirements). You can also use the command-line method to deploy SCEP outside ConfigMgr, such as where server software distribution is managed via a different product.

This method relies on executing scepinstall.exe from an application, a TS, or the command line. The scepinstall.exe file is located in the Client folder on the ConfigMgr media. A complete list of command-line switches is available at https://docs.microsoft.com/sccm/protect/deploy-use/endpoint-protection-configure-client#to-install-the-endpoint-protection-client-from-a-command-prompt.

Installing Endpoint Protection in an Image

To include SCEP in an image, the SCEP agent must be prepared for imaging. Follow these steps on the reference computer to prepare the SCEP agent:

1. Obtain psexec.exe from https://live.sysinternals.com/.

19

2. From an elevated command prompt, use psexec.exe to launch `regedit` as a local
system:

```
Psexec.exe -s -i regedit.exe
```

3. From the Registry Editor, delete the following keys and then immediately shut down
the computer:

```
HKEY_LOCAL_MACHINE\SOFTWARE\Microsoft\Microsoft Antimalware\InstallTime
HKEY_LOCAL_MACHINE\SOFTWARE\Microsoft\Microsoft Antimalware\Scan\LastScanRun
HKEY_LOCAL_MACHINE\SOFTWARE\Microsoft\Microsoft Antimalware\Scan\LastScanType
HKEY_LOCAL_MACHINE\SOFTWARE\Microsoft\Microsoft Antimalware\Scan\LastQuickScanID
HKEY_LOCAL_MACHINE\SOFTWARE\Microsoft\Microsoft Antimalware\Scan\LastFullScanID
HKEY_LOCAL_MACHINE\SOFTWARE\Microsoft\RemovalTools\MRT\GUID
```

4. Shut down the reference computer (if you have not already) and capture the reference computer for imaging.

Endpoint Protection for Linux and Mac

Endpoint Protection is available for both Linux and Mac. Documentation and installation
media are available at the Microsoft Volume Licensing Service Center as a separate download and are restricted to Microsoft Volume Licensing.

Monitoring and Reporting in Endpoint Protection

ConfigMgr provides multiple methods for monitoring SCEP/Defender. This section
explains how to monitor SCEP/Defender operations. It also explains how to provide
reports on SCEP/Defender to audiences other than ConfigMgr/SCEP IT administrators.
Monitoring involves both in-console monitoring from the SCEP dashboard and drilldown
into ConfigMgr device collections to view the device state. Operationally, ConfigMgr also
provides alerts for complex malware incidents; the "Endpoint Protection Actions and
Alerts" section, later in this chapter, provides information on alerts.

SCEP/Defender delivers a set of reports that leverage the same reporting capabilities as the
rest of ConfigMgr. While there are only four reports, far fewer than with other ConfigMgr
features, they are designed for drilldown inside and between the reports rather than being
isolated individual reports. For this reason, it is often useful to grant access to the specific
reports rather than email copies of them.

As with all other ConfigMgr data, you can extract SCEP/Defender data for use in other
systems. This may include security information and event management (SIEM) solutions
to provide a data feed into a security operations center (SOC). It also enables integration
with service management solutions to automatically trigger tickets for malware response
by security administrators or local desktop support technicians.

Operational Status of Endpoint Protection Clients

To see the primary operational views for Endpoint Protection, navigate to **Monitoring ->** **Security** and then expand **Endpoint Protection Status** to view the individual items:

- ▶ **System Center Endpoint Protection Status:** This is the primary view and is generally used for most daily in-console monitoring.

- ▶ **Malware Detected:** This simpler view provides a list of all malware by collection and a count of infected machines. This view is typically used for secondary analysis after a malware incident has been identified.

By default, the All Desktop and Server Clients collection appears in the Status view. Perform the following steps to add more collections to this view:

1. Open the properties of the collection you want to include in the dashboard.

2. Click the **Alerts** tab in the Properties dialog box.

3. Check the **View this collection in the Endpoint Protection dashboard** check box and click **OK**.

The dashboard views do not pull live data for scalability and performance reasons. They are based on summarized data, refreshed every 20 minutes by default. You can increase or decrease the frequency by going to the Endpoint Protection Status view (the node directly above the two dashboard views), clicking **Schedule Summarization**, and configuring an appropriate summarization interval. Take care when setting a more frequent summarization, as doing so increases the load on your ConfigMgr site infrastructure (primarily the site database).

The various elements of the Status view are designed to provide actionable information to a ConfigMgr administrator or security professional. The remainder of this section explains the expected actions for each element of the view. They are grouped into two areas: Security State (see Figure 19.14) and Operational State (see Figure 19.15).

The Security State group is composed of two elements. This section of the view is designed to provide information about security-related incidents where either SCEP/Defender has detected malware, SCEP/Defender requires additional steps to remediate malware, or SCEP/Defender itself is not running/installed. The following are the various elements in this group:

- ▶ **Endpoint Protection Client Status:** This element is designed to provide a view of all clients where SCEP/Defender is not installed, is inactive, is pending installation, or cannot be installed. Active clients at risk count is the sum of all clients in these states. The core action here is to investigate the installation failures and disablements of SCEP/Defender on those clients, as those clients will not report any antimalware status to the other elements in the view.

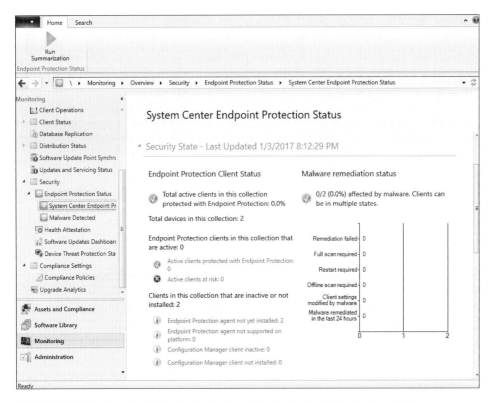

FIGURE 19.14   Security State in the System Center Endpoint Protection Status view.

▶ **Malware Remediation Status:** This element provides a view of the malware remediation status. It begins by providing a total number of computers that are in one or more malware remediation statuses. If a computer is in multiple statuses, it is counted only once. Remediation statuses are as follows:

   ▶ **Remediation Failed:** SCEP/Defender was unable to remove the malware in question. The administrator should investigate the failure and re-attempt remediation via SCEP/Defender or take manual remediation steps. The most common reason for this is malware found on read-only removal storage (CD/DVD or write-protected USB/SD card memory devices).

   ▶ **Full Scan Required:** SCEP/Defender determined that the client is infected by malware that requires a full scan to completely remove it rather than relying on the detections from real-time protection. This is triggered in response to Microsoft's analysis of the malware and is stored in the definition updates. The administrator should trigger a full scan either via the ConfigMgr console (including automation), manually on the client itself, via software distribution, or by waiting for a full scan scheduled in an antimalware policy to trigger.

▶ **Restart Required:** Clients in this state are impacted by malware that cannot be removed without a restart. This is usually due to rootkit or similar complex manipulation of the OS. The administrator should restart the machine via software distribution (for example, a simple shutdown.exe execution) or manually by restarting the computer.

▶ **Offline Scan Required:** Clients in this state require a comprehensive scan outside the running OS. This requires running Windows Defender Offline (regardless of whether the client has SCEP or Windows Defender installed). For more information, see the "Using Windows Defender Offline" section, earlier in this chapter. The administrator should manually run Windows Defender Offline for clients running SCEP or run Windows Defender Offline from the Settings app for clients running Windows 10 and later. For information on automating this and other actions, see the "Scripting Endpoint Protection Actions" section in this chapter.

▶ **Client Settings Modified by Malware:** Clients in this state have had one or more settings modified by malware. In cases where there is a clear way to determine the previous state, SCEP/Defender restores the setting. An example would be malware that disables a component of Windows that is always running. However, it is not always possible to determine what the setting should be. For example, it could be a setting that is not configured by default but may have been enabled before the malware disabled it. The administrator should review the information provided on the malware in the MMPC Threat Encyclopedia and take the required steps. This requires understanding what the intended configuration of the setting should be.

▶ **Malware Remediated in the Last 24 Hours:** Largely informational in nature, this state allows the administrator to know how many malware incidents have been remediated and understand the environment and number of infections occurring. There is no specific action expected of the SCEP administrator.

The Operational state, shown in Figure 19.15, is focused on maintenance and operation of SCEP/Defender clients in the selected collection. The objective of this section of the dashboard is to ensure that SCEP/Defender is running as efficiently as possible. It is also composed of two distinct elements:

▶ **Operational Status of Clients:** This element contains SCEP-specific issues related to the SCEP/Defender client itself rather than malware events. It is broken down into specific states that relate to the health of the SCEP/Defender client infrastructure.

▶ **Definition Status on Computers:** This element contains information about the state of definition updates in the collection in question. A large group of out-of-date clients may indicate a problem with the definition update source.

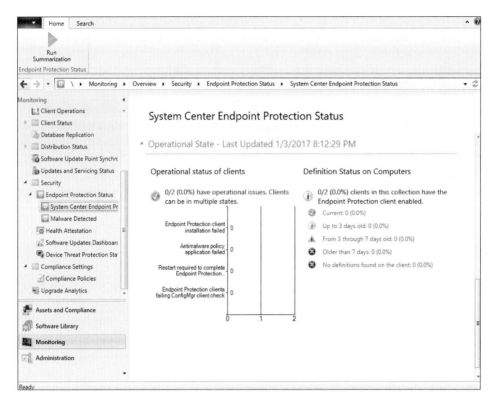

FIGURE 19.15   Operational State in the System Center Endpoint Protection Status view.

Reports Available for Endpoint Protection

In addition to in-console monitoring available in the ConfigMgr console, SCEP provides a set of reports. These reports operate on the same data sources from the in-console monitoring. The reports provide the ability to create subscriptions to have SQL Server Reporting Services (SSRS) email the reports to a set of recipients on a regular basis. For more information on ConfigMgr reporting, see Chapter 21, "Configuration Manager Reporting."

The reports also provide historical information, like the hardware inventory reports. However, the SCEP historical data defaults to 365 days, as opposed to 90 days for hardware inventory. You can reduce this value by modifying the Delete Aged Endpoint Protection Health Status History Data maintenance tasks on the primary sites that manage SCEP/Defender clients. For more information on site maintenance, see Chapter 24, "Backup, Recovery, and Maintenance."

The following are the reports and the recommended usage of each one:

▶ **Antimalware Overall Status and History:** This is the primary report. Generally, it should be the first report shared outside the antimalware/security administration team. It provides similar data to the in-console data by surfacing both security (malware and protection states) and operational (definition updates and SCEP deployment) information. It also provides a historical view of the same data, which the in-console monitoring does not provide. It is run on a per-collection basis and requires start and end dates for historical data.

▶ **Antimalware Activity Report:** This report provides high-level counts of malware remediation activities on a per-collection basis. Each count links to the Infected Computers report, with a different value for Infection Status based on the column selected in the Antimalware Activity report.

▶ **Infected Computers:** This report provides details on computers that have suffered malware infection. It lists each infected computer. It allows filtering by Threat Name (name of malware), Cleaning Action (Cleaned/Quarantined/Removed/ Allowed/User Specified/No Action/Blocked), Infection Status (outcome of remediation attempt), and User Name.

▶ **Top Users by Threats:** This report provides a user-based view per collection of users with the most malware incidents. It lists the users whose behavior and actions appear to result in more malware incidents. It may be that a malware dropper is downloading or dropping other malware on the system, and the incidents are not due to any action of the user running the dropper. This report is useful for end-user outreach and education to help alter behavior and make systems safer. It can also be used for remedial actions such as revoking administrative rights from users that repeatedly install malware.

▶ **User Threat List:** This report provides a list of all malware incidents filtered on a specific user. It acts as a useful drilldown from the Top Users by Threats report.

▶ **Computer Malware Details:** This report provides a list of all malware incidents, filtered on a specific user. It acts as a useful drilldown from the Infected Computers report.

Integrating Report Data with Other Systems

As with all other ConfigMgr site database information, you can use SQL Server views to extract EP data. These views use the ConfigMgr 2012 schema; the ConfigMgr 2012 R2 documentation on Endpoint Protection views, located at https://technet.microsoft.com/ library/dn581986.aspx, is still valid. An example of how to use SCEP/Defender data from the ConfigMgr database is available with the Power BI dashboards at https:// cloudblogs.microsoft.com/enterprisemobility/2016/04/01/exploring-your-system-center- configuration-manager-and-microsoft-intune-hybrid-data-on-power-bi-dashboard/.

Following are the top views to leverage when extracting data for use with other systems:

▶ `v_OverallThreatActivity`: This view contains the same data as the in-console dashboard's Security State groups Malware remediation status element. This is essentially data on malware activity and remediation of that malware for the selected collection. Only collections that appear in the dashboard and have the View this collection in the Endpoint Protection dashboard check box checked in their collection properties appear in this view. There is also a history table, `v_OverallThreatActivityHistory`, to access one year of historical information (by default).

▶ **`v_EndpointProtectionHealthStatus`:** This view contains the same data as the in-console dashboard across the Endpoint Protection client status, Operational status of clients, and Definition status on computers elements. As with `v_OverallThreatActivity`, only Endpoint Protection collections appear in this view. There is also a history view, `v_EndpointProtectionHealthStatusHistory`.

▶ **Client-Specific Views:** Several client-specific views surface information on a per-client basis rather than summarized data. In general, you should use the client views to return per-client data. Avoid aggregating this data on the fly, as built-in summarization processes for SCEP/Defender data feed the `v_OverallThreatActivity` and `v_EndpointProtectionHealthStatus` views and their respective history views. These are the client-specific views:

   ▶ `v_GS_AntimalwareHealthStatus`

   ▶ `v_GS_AntimalwareInfectionStatus`

   ▶ `v_GS_Threats`

   ▶ `v_EndpointProtectionStatus`

NOTE: ENDPOINT PROTECTION `v_GS` VIEWS

ConfigMgr sends all Endpoint Protection data from SCEP/Defender clients as state messages. Traditionally, `v_GS` views store current hardware inventory data. (`v_HS` views store hardware inventory history data.)

Endpoint Protection data stored in these views is not sent via hardware inventory. As part of processing the state message, an additional step populates the tables backing these views. This enables some backward compatibility scenarios for Forefront Endpoint Protection (FEP) and ConfigMgr 2007 reporting and data access scenarios. To verify that this data is not processed by hardware inventory, track the state messages processed by statsys.log and review the associated SQL operations performed during the processing of SCEP/Defender state messages. This also explains why there are no historical tables/views and why this data does not appear in the Hardware Inventory setting under Client Settings.

Endpoint Protection Actions and Alerts

A key activity for a SCEP/Defender administrator is responding to malware activities and incidents. Individual malicious activities often occur across multiple devices throughout an organization. The authors refer to such an activity as a *malware incident* (adopting the ITIL [Information Technology Information Library] definition of multiple individual events combining to an incident). ConfigMgr's Alerts feature notifies SCEP/Defender administrators of these incidents. The alerts enable administrators to respond to those incidents. This is especially important for environments without a SIEM solution or other advanced security operational processes.

In most cases, SCEP/Defender automatically handles remediation of malware activities. In some cases, remediation requires that an administrator intervene either because the remediation is disruptive to an end user (for example, an offline scan) or requires additional information (for example, restoration of corrupted settings). Most actions can be triggered from within the console; however, some require either user interaction or automation/scripting.

The next sections explain the available alerts and configuration, available actions, and how to use those actions. They also provide a brief overview of automating alerts and actions. The automation topics are meant to provide guidance on what interfaces and classes/views/cmdlets to use rather than in-depth or prescriptive guidance on building scripts or software development kit (SDK) solutions.

Overview of Endpoint Protection Alerts

ConfigMgr provides four SCEP/Defender-specific alerts. Each alert is configured on one or more collections, and any configurable settings are per collection. This allows you to use ConfigMgr's dynamic rules to create alert targeting based on AD data, installed software, hardware, operating system, ConfigMgr compliance settings, or anything stored in the Registry or Windows Management Instrumentation (WMI). This is a key capability of merging antimalware management with PC management.

The following are the SCEP/Defender alert types:

▶ **Malware Detected:** This is the simplest type of alert for SCEP/Defender. It is triggered whenever malware is found on a computer. The Malware detection threshold controls the specific conditions in which an alert is triggered. High, medium, and low refer to the frequency or volume of alerts. Use this threshold to target alerts based on the criticality of the computers in a collection. For example, a server that processes credit card payments is a high risk to the business if compromised; being high risk means it may need high thresholds set. This is based on the following logic:

  ▶ **High – All Detection:** This alert level causes any detection of malware to trigger an alert. Use this level for systems where any malware detection should trigger an alert, regardless of SCEP/Defender action or response.

  ▶ **Medium – Detected, Pending Action:** This alert level triggers an alert when malware removal requires manual action. It is useful for invoking help desk processes for desktops. It is also useful on most servers.

  ▶ **Low – Detected, Still Active:** This alert level triggers an alert only when malware removal failed and malware is still active. This generally warrants immediate follow-up, except with malware stored on read-only media.

19

NOTE: MALWARE DETECTED ALERT ON READ-ONLY MEDIA (CDS, DVDS, AND SO ON)

You may find that SCEP/Defender reports malware remediation failures for malware that the MMPC Threat Encyclopedia says SCEP/Defender can remove. This is most commonly caused by read-only media, typically optical media (CD, DVD, or Blu-ray discs), but may also include portal flash memory with write protection. When SCEP/Defender or any other program attempts to write to read-only media, Windows returns an access denied error (error code 5). SCEP/Defender has no specific way of knowing why its system-level permissions failed to access the file. In practice, SCEP/Defender is blocking the malware but cannot remove the malware from storage attached to the computer, and hence it reports the failure.

Keep this scenario in mind when building processes around SCEP alert handling and choosing where to enable these alerts.

▶ **Malware Outbreak:** This alert level allows you to define a custom threshold on when to trigger the alert; the threshold is defined using a percentage of ConfigMgr clients in a collection where malware was detected. The percentage includes computers that do not yet have the SCEP client installed. This is useful in triggering malware/security incident response processes.

▶ **Repeated Malware Detection:** This alert is triggered when the same malware is detected between 2 and 32 times in an interval (1 to 168 hours) across all computers in a collection. This alert is useful for finding malware infections caused by repeated user actions or other actions. Detections may be on the same computer or different computers in the collection; this in contrast to the malware outbreak alert, which tells you that multiple computers are infected.

▶ **Multiple Malware Detection:** This alert is triggered when between 2 and 32 different malwares are found on computers within an interval (1 to 168 hours). This differs from the repeated malware detection level in that different malware is found. This provides a similar ability to detect suspicious actions on computers that may be causing multiple infections.

NOTE: AUTOMATING ENDPOINT PROTECTION ALERTS

It is possible to programmatically access SCEP alerts. Doing so is useful when you want to extract alerts into other systems, such as ticketing systems to trigger local IT technicians to visit users or IT process automation workflow tools.

There are various methods to extract alerts, including using PowerShell, T-SQL, or WMI:

▶ **PowerShell:** Get-CMAlert allows you to get a ConfigMgr alert to use within PowerShell directly. You can also leverage PowerShell's ability to call .NET or VBScript interfaces as a means to move alerts into other systems. You can also use the Suspend-CMAlert and Disable-CMAlert cmdlets to suppress or close an alert in the console for roundtrip automation workflows. For more information on Get-CMAlert, see the ConfigMgr cmdlet documentation at https://docs.microsoft.com/powershell/sccm/configurationmanager/vlatest/get-cmalert.

▶ **T-SQL:** If you need to extract information directly from the ConfigMgr database using T-SQL, two key views are `v_Alert` and `vex_Alert`. The `v_Alert` view contains all alerts generated across the hierarchy and the state of each. This includes multiple timestamp values to aid in filtering results (`SkipUntil`, `CreationTime`, `LastChangeTime`, and `AlertStateChangeTime`). You can only use the T-SQL views to pull data from ConfigMgr, not to write or change alert data. *Microsoft does not support writing directly to the ConfigMgr database.*

▶ **WMI:** The ConfigMgr provider provides the `SMS_Alert` and `SMS_EPAlert` WMI classes, enabling you to both export alert information and alter alert states. `SMS_Alert` returns all ConfigMgr alerts, while `SMS_EPAlert` filters only to SCEP-related alerts. The `Close` method of `SMS_EPAlert` can be used to close alerts. For more information, see https://docs.microsoft.com/sccm/develop/reference/core/servers/manage/sms_epalert-server-wmi-class.

Enabling Alerts for a Collection

After determining which alerts to configure, the next step is to enable them on a collection of computers you want to monitor for malware activity or incidents. You will want to leverage the dynamic nature of collections to get the maximum value out of SCEP/Defender. This could include monitoring critical servers by type based on the Windows services they run rather than using a static list or server naming standard. It can also include building a collection based on compliance settings. Compliance settings–based collections would allow you to determine, for example, if the membership of the local administrators group deviates from the organizational standards for local admin rights. Computers with deviations (authorized or unauthorized) may require closer monitoring, as malware is more likely to be running with administrative rights on these computers.

Perform the following steps to enable a collection for SCEP/Defender alerts:

1. In the console, navigate to **Assets and Compliance -> Device Collections**.

2. Select the collection where you want to configure an alert; open its properties by right-clicking the collection and selecting **Properties**.

3. If the **View this collection in the Endpoint Protection dashboard** check box is unchecked, check it to ensure you can review the collection in the SCEP section of the Monitoring workspace.

4. Click **Alerts** and then click **Add**.

5. Select the type of alerts you want to configure, input the desired configuration, and provide an alert name and severity, as shown in Figure 19.16.

19

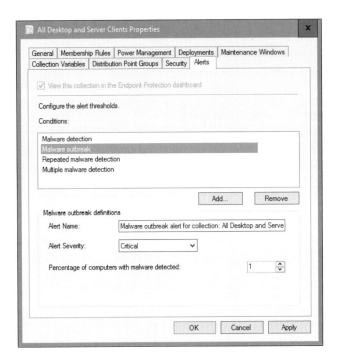

FIGURE 19.16   SCEP alert dialog box.

On-Demand Actions Related to Endpoint Protection

In addition to alerting on malware activity, it is often necessary to act on monitoring information. ConfigMgr provides SCEP/Defender administrators with multiple built-in capabilities to trigger actions against systems. The on-demand actions allow an administrator to respond quickly to situations remotely. There are two types of targets for actions: specific clients and detected malware.

Client actions cause clients to download new definitions, run scans, download policy, and/or evaluate software updates. These actions are delivered using either standard client policy (by default, once an hour) or client notifications (immediately). You can also use the download policy client notification action to cause standard client policy to be processed sooner. Client actions are triggered by right-clicking a client from a device collection and selecting either **Client Notification** or **Endpoint Protection** from the menu.

The following are the client actions related to SCEP/Defender:

▶ **Download Definition:** Delivered using standard ConfigMgr client policy. This causes the client to trigger the SCEP/Defender built-in update methods (that is, not the Configuration Manager definition update source). It is equivalent to using the SCEP/Defender user interface to trigger a definition update.

▶ **Full Scan/Quick Scan:** Delivered using standard ConfigMgr client policy. This causes the client to trigger a quick or full scan within SCEP/Defender.

▶ **Evaluate Software Update Deployments:** Delivered using client notification (immediate push of policy to clients). This action is useful in environments where software update management is used to deliver SCEP/Defender definition updates and can be used in place of the Download Definitions action.

▶ **Switch to Next Software Update Point:** Delivered using client notification. This action is useful when definition source is set to ConfigMgr software update deployments or WSUS (when the WSUS server is also used as a SUP). It can be used to rapidly switch clients between SUPs to ensure that the definition updates can be delivered to clients.

▶ **Download Computer Policy:** Delivered using client notification. You can use this to force immediate delivery of all SCEP policies and actions (Download Definition, Full Scan, or Quick Scan). This can be useful when an urgent change of policy is required—for example, in response to a malware outbreak or when a false positive is encountered.

Detected malware actions allow you to override detections (for example, to mitigate false positives), restore quarantined files, or exclude files/paths from scanning. This is accomplished by creating client policy and delivery to the client via the normal computer policy polling cycle (by default, hourly). The actions can be accessed as follows:

1. In the ConfigMgr console, navigate to **Monitoring-> Security** and select **Endpoint Protection Status**.

2. Click the **Malware Detected** node.

3. Select one of the available actions to respond to the malware.

Following are the potential actions you can take on malware:

▶ **Allow This Threat:** This action creates an antimalware policy that allows the selected malware to run. The created policy is deployed to the All Systems collection. This action allows you to respond to false positives or allow potentially unwanted programs (PUPs). Use the Download Computer Policy client notification action to cause impacted clients to immediately process this policy.

▶ **Restore Files Quarantined by This Threat:** This action allows you to restore quarantined files associated with this malware. Like the previous action, it allows you to respond to false positives or PUPs. The action allows you to only restore the files or restore the files and add an exclusion for the files. If you choose not to exclude the files, they are quarantined when next scanned by SCEP/Defender.

19

▶ **Exclude Selected Files or Paths from Scan:** This action creates a policy that excludes the selected paths from malware scanning. This also excludes the path for all SCEP/Defender real-time and schedule scan activities. If responding to a false positive, using the Allow this threat action may be more appropriate.

CAUTION: REPORTING FALSE POSITIVES AND FALSE NEGATIVES

If you run into a false positive or a false negative in SCEP/Defender, report it to Microsoft via your organization's Microsoft support channel to enable Microsoft to issue a revised definition. Microsoft may also be able to provide prerelease definitions prior to a public release or other workarounds. If you don't have a commercial support channel with Microsoft, you can submit malware samples directly via the Windows Defender Security Intelligence site at https://www.microsoft.com/wdsi/filesubmission.

Scripting Endpoint Protection Actions

Your organization may require that you automate SCEP actions—either due to limited administrative resources to monitor and trigger these actions or to expedite response to malware. Automated activities can include triggering a full scan, restarting the client, triggering policy polling, and offline scans. These activities rely on building a list of clients that require one or more of those activities to be executed on them.

To build a collection, create a query-based rule to identify the client in the respective states. The attribute class required is Endpoint Protection Status, which includes attributes that represent the various states where additional action is required: AmFullscanRequired, AmRestartRequired, and AmOfflineScanRequired. Each attribute is a Boolean value. Create one collection per attribute and set the query to look for devices where the attributes are true.

After creating these collections, use the Get-CMDevice PowerShell cmdlet to obtain a list of the clients. You can use the following methods to trigger each action against the collection in question:

▶ **Full Scan Required:** Use the Invoke-CMEndpointProtectionScan cmdlet to invoke a full scan. Run this cmdlet using the -DeviceCollectionId parameter. Specify the collection ID for the collection of devices where the AmFullscanRequired property is true. This queues up an instruction for the next time the client polls for policy. If you need to trigger this more quickly, you can use Invoke-CMClientNotification with the -DeviceCollectionId parameter to issue a client notification.

▶ **Restart Required:** This requires building the collection and deploying a program to restart the client system. You can reuse existing restart scripts, if available. If one isn't available, create a ConfigMgr program object that runs cmd /c (which opens and closes the command prompt instantly). Set this program to have ConfigMgr restart the computer.

> ▶ **Offline Scan Required:** This is the most complex of the three actions. It requires leveraging a script for Windows 10 (1607/Anniversary Update and later). The script can be deployed as a package/program in ConfigMgr. For information on this scripting interface, see https://docs.microsoft.com/windows/security/threat-protection/windows-defender-antivirus/windows-defender-offline. To execute an offline scan on SCEP clients and Windows 10 devices prior to Windows 10 1607/Anniversary Update, see the ConfigMgr product team blog post at https://cloudblogs.microsoft.com/enterprisemobility/2012/04/12/launching-a-windows-defender-offline-scan-with-configuration-manager-2012-osd/.

Using these scripting methods to automate EP action can significantly improve the security of your environment. As with any other automation and scripting, be sure to fully test prior to deploying in production.

Windows Defender Advanced Threat Protection

Windows Defender ATP is a cloud-based security service provided by Microsoft. It enables Windows 10 to send endpoint behavioral telemetry from Windows Defender and other Windows security components to an organization's unique and isolated cloud tenant. Endpoint behavior sensors include process, Registry, file, and network communication patterns. These are some of the sample behavior monitoring capabilities discussed in the "Protection Capabilities of Microsoft's Antimalware Platform" section, earlier in this chapter. Each endpoint is onboarded to Windows Defender ATP, and its telemetry is delivered securely to the organization's online tenant for processing. This telemetry is then combined with cloud-based security analytics and threat intelligence:

> ▶ **Cloud-Based Security Analytics:** Cloud-based security analytics are driven through a combination of big data and machine-learning tools, fed unique information from the Windows and Microsoft ecosystems. This data includes telemetry from the Microsoft Malicious Software Removal Tool, Windows Defender telemetry (both enterprise and consumer data), Office 365 behavioral data, and consumer cloud systems such as Bing and SmartScreen.

> ▶ **Threat Intelligence:** Threat intelligence is generated by Microsoft in cooperation with antimalware partners. It is used to develop analysis models that enable identification of malware along with attacker techniques and procedures. This threat intelligence modeling is then used as the lens to interpret and analyze endpoint telemetry and cloud security analytics. The result is provided to organizations via the Windows Defender ATP online portal.

ConfigMgr allows you to easily onboard Windows 10 managed clients onto Windows Defender ATP. This significantly eases rollout and configuration of the endpoint behavioral sensors and ensures that their telemetry is delivered to the Windows Defender ATP tenant. Windows Defender ATP can also be used with non-Microsoft endpoint

19

protection technologies by running Windows Defender in passive mode. For more information, see the "Prerequisites for Windows Defender ATP" section, later in this chapter.

Windows Defender ATP Capabilities

Windows Defender ATP has various features available to use with data gathered and processed within an organization's tenant, including the following:

▶ **Post-Breach Detection:** Enables you to find both known and unknown attackers in an actionable alert. This enables a last line of defense and mitigation capability.

▶ **Timeline for Forensic Investigation:** Enables you to scope a breach or suspicious behaviors to any onboarded machine via a time line. This can be pivoted across file, URLs, and network connections.

▶ **Deep Analysis of Files and URLs:** Allows you to request further analysis by Microsoft of files or URLs. Files can be manually submitted in the portal or automatically collected by Windows Defender.

Prerequisites for Windows Defender ATP

The first step in using Windows Defender ATP is to subscribe to the service. For information on how to subscribe, see https://docs.microsoft.com/windows/security/threat-protection/windows-defender-atp/windows-defender-advanced-threat-protection. This site also provides information about how to sign up for a free trial of Windows Defender ATP.

In addition to subscribing to the service, the following prerequisites must be met:

▶ **Windows Editions:** Computers must be running Windows 10 Enterprise, Windows 10 Education, Windows 7 SP1, Windows 8.1, Windows Server 2016 or Windows Server 2012 R2. (Windows Defender ATP also supports non-Windows clients through 3rd party integration.) ATP is not supported on Windows 10 Mobile.

▶ **Connectivity:** Each computer will send approximately 5MB per day to the Windows Defender ATP service. Telemetry components need network access to submit information to the service. For information on connectivity requirements, see https://docs.microsoft.com/windows/security/threat-protection/windows-defender-atp/configure-proxy-internet-windows-defender-advanced-threat-protection.

▶ **Windows Telemetry Service:** The Connected User Experiences and Telemetry (diagtrack) service must be running on monitored enrollments and set to start automatically.

▶ **Windows Defender Signatures:** The Windows Defender ATP agent relies on Windows Defender to perform file scans and return data from those scans. Signatures must be up to date even if Windows Defender is not used in your organization. Windows Defender runs in passive mode in this scenario.

▶ **Windows Defender ELAM Driver:** The Windows Defender ELAM driver must be enabled. If Windows Defender is your antimalware solution, this driver is enabled by default. If you are running a non-Microsoft antimalware solution, the ELAM driver must be enabled to successfully onboard Windows Defender ATP. For more information on ELAM, see the "Early Launch Antimalware and Measured Boot" section, earlier in this chapter. For information on how to enable the Windows Defender ELAM driver when Windows Defender is not the antimalware solution of choice, see https://docs.microsoft.com/windows/security/threat-protection/windows-defender-atp/troubleshoot-onboarding-windows-defender-advanced-threat-protection#ensure-that-windows-defender-antivirus-is-not-disabled-by-a-policy.

Configuring Windows Defender ATP Using ConfigMgr

To configure Windows Defender ATP, you must first obtain an onboarding configuration file from the Windows Defender ATP portal. This file enables Windows Defender ATP to access the organization's tenant and securely submit telemetry data. Take care to ensure that the onboarding configuration file is kept securely, as it contains sensitive information. Perform the following steps to obtain the onboarding configuration file:

1. Log on to the Windows Defender ATP portal at https://securitycenter.windows.com/.

2. Click **Endpoint Management**.

3. Select the link **System Center Configuration Manager (current branch)** and then click **download package**.

4. Decompress the .zip file and place it in a secure location.

When the file is ready, you can use ConfigMgr to distribute it and onboard clients. This process is simple and involves supplying the onboarding file as part of the policy wizard. The policy can then be deployed and monitored like any other ConfigMgr policy. To create the Windows Defender ATP onboarding policy, follow these steps:

1. In the ConfigMgr console, navigate to **Assets and Compliance -> Endpoint Protection -> Windows Defender ATP Policies**. Right-click and select **Create Windows Defender ATP Policy**.

2. Enter a name and a description and then select **Onboarding**. Click **Next**.

3. Click **Browse** and navigate to the onboarding configuration file you downloaded from the Windows Defender ATP portal. Click **Next**.

4. Determine whether you want file samples collected for analysis from managed devices. This can expedite the response to an attack by eliminating the need to gather sample files from impacted machines and submitting them manually to the Windows Defender ATP portal.

5. Complete the wizard and deploy the newly created policy to a collection of clients. You can choose to phase the rollout prior to a mass rollout.

Summary

This chapter provided an in-depth look at the protection technologies and capabilities of SCEP/Defender and Windows. It also provided a guide to designing SCEP deployment, along with configuration and monitoring of that deployment. The chapter covered more advanced topics around programmatic access to EP data across alerts and reporting data, providing a look into how to integrate EP into security event management solutions.

The chapter explained how to leverage ConfigMgr's device management capabilities to significantly enhance and automate SCEP/Defender antimalware protection. This combination of PC management and antimalware adds tremendous value and is achieved by using simple ConfigMgr automation to drive antimalware responses.

The chapter also discussed the cloud-backed features of SCEP/Defender and the cloud-based nature of Windows Defender Advanced Threat Protection. The purpose is to give you an understanding of the benefits that come from opting into the cloud-based system and provide you with the ability to weigh the costs of sending telemetry to Microsoft against the gains from opting in.

CHAPTER 20

Configuration Manager Queries

Queries were mentioned briefly in Chapter 3, "Looking Inside Configuration Manager," as a means for retrieving information from the ConfigMgr database. You can use the information retrieved in a variety of ways—from something as simple as creating an ad hoc list of clients with a specific operating system (OS) to areas as complex as listing devices missing a certain type of software. However, queries are not just about hardware and software information. You can use queries to easily access information regarding component status and activity audits.

While ConfigMgr comes with a handful of predefined queries, the goal of this chapter is to help you become comfortable writing your own—first by using the ConfigMgr query builder and then, with enough practice, by hand. This chapter provides information on objects, classes, and attributes, as well as descriptions of criterion types, operators, and joins to provide insight for you to build your own queries.

Queries can be the basis of any well-constructed collection, helping to narrow the target of a deployment to the right set of devices. While application intelligence reduces the necessity for intricate collections to deploy software in ConfigMgr, you still must generate a target list of devices for other purposes—such as applying power management, maintenance windows, and endpoint protection settings.

NOTE: USING QUERIES TO CREATE COLLECTIONS

Queries are useful for testing desired criteria for a collection. Simply build the query and review your results; when you create a collection, select the query as a basis for your query-based collection rule. Consider this a one-time copy of the query to the collection; modifying a query or a collection rule initially created from a collection does not update or affect the collection.

Introducing the Queries Node

As introduced in Chapter 8, "Using the Configuration Manager Console," you manage and run queries by using the Queries node of the Monitoring workspace, shown in Figure 20.1.

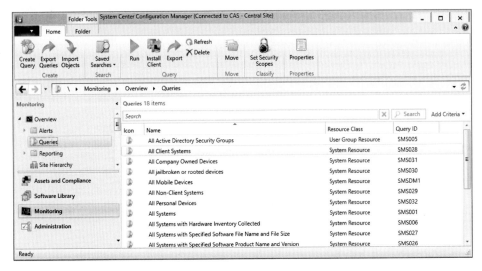

FIGURE 20.1   The Queries node of the Monitoring workspace.

When you select a query in the List pane, the ribbon bar displays the following set of options, also shown in Figure 20.1:

▶ **Create Query:** Creates a new query.

▶ **Export Queries:** Exports queries to other ConfigMgr environments.

▶ **Import Objects:** Imports queries.

▶ **Run:** Executes the selected query.

▶ **Install Client:** Initiates the Install Client Wizard, targeting the objects of the selected query.

▶ **Refresh:** Refreshes the selected query.

▶ **Delete:** Deletes the selected query.

▶ **Move:** Moves the selected query to a different folder.

▶ **Set Security Scopes:** Associates the selected query to one or more security scopes.

▶ **Properties:** Displays the properties of the selected query.

Organizing the Query List Pane

When you select the Queries node, the List pane displays the icon, name, resource class, and query ID of each query. You can add or remove columns to customize this pane to fit your environment. For example, if your environment utilizes comments heavily, you may want to include the Comments column in your list. Following are the available columns:

▶ **Icon:** Specifies the icon assigned to the query.

▶ **Name:** Specifies the name assigned to the query.

▶ **Resource Class:** Indicates the type of object returned in the result set.

▶ **Query ID:** Shows the unique ID assigned by the system to the query. Default queries begin with SMS, while custom queries begin with the site code.

▶ **Comments:** Provides a comment about the query, often to help identity the query.

▶ **Expression:** Specifies the Windows Management Instrumentation (WMI) Query Language (WQL) statement inside the query.

▶ **Limit to Collection ID:** Specifies to retrieve only values that match the query and exist in the specified collection if you specified a collection ID in the Collection Limiting section.

To select additional columns, right-click a column header (see Figure 20.2), and select a column.

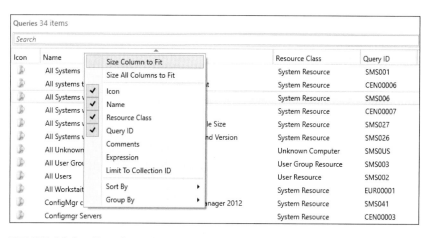

FIGURE 20.2   Choosing columns in the Queries node.

If you find that adding and removing columns adds excessive white space between column values, you can resize the columns to overlap data or fit them in. To resize columns, choose the separator bar between the column headers and drag it to the left or right. To resize a column to fit the contents automatically, right-click the column header and choose **Size Column to Fit**. Optionally, resize all columns to fit by right-clicking and choosing Size All Columns to Fit.

While viewing all columns of interest is useful, it may be difficult to sort through the number of queries in the List pane. Clicking any column header sorts the List pane results in the order of the arrow: up for ascending or down for descending. Sorting is also accessible via the menu by right-clicking the column header area.

You can also sift through queries by grouping them by type. You can group queries by any column if the column has been selected for display. To group by a column, right-click in the column header area, choose **Group By**, and select the column. Figure 20.3 shows how the List pane looks when grouping by the Resource class. Grouping queries together lets you collapse and expand groups.

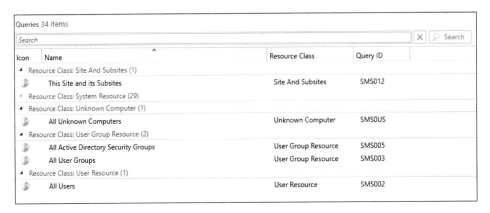

FIGURE 20.3   The List pane when grouping by the `Resource` class.

TIP: USING GROUPING

Grouping is not just for managing queries; you can use it to manage the set of results returned from a query, using any of the available columns referenced in the query.

Query objects also benefit from the organizational use of folders and search capabilities inherent in the ConfigMgr console. Well-organized queries in structured folders not only make searching faster, they provide fellow administrators with a structure to look for items even if they do not know exactly what they are looking for! Take time to plan your folders to suit the way your organization uses queries in ConfigMgr.

Viewing Queries and Query Results

To view a query, you must first run it. The easiest way to run a query is to double-click the query you are interested in. Alternatively, you can either select the query and click **Run** in the toolbar or right-click it and choose **Run**.

If running a query results in many returned objects, you can use the search bar to narrow the results. This makes finding information extremely fast, as it does not require sorting the results or scrolling up and down to find a particular object.

Once you have a result set from your query, you can perform the following actions, also shown in Figure 20.4, against any of the objects in the set (provided that the resource class is a system resource):

▶ **Install Client:** Launches the Install Client Wizard.

▶ **Client Settings -> Resultant Client Settings:** Helps you easily see the resultant set of client settings for a specific device.

▶ **Start -> Resource Explorer:** Displays all hardware and software inventory information for the selected device.

▶ **Start -> Remote Control:** Initiates remote control process, enabling you to view and control users' desktops.

▶ **Start -> Remote Assistance:** Initiates remote assistance, the built-in remote feature for Windows.

▶ **Start -> Remote Desktop Client:** Initiates the standard remote desktop client, allowing you to remotely log in to a server.

▶ **Refresh:** Refreshes the current query results.

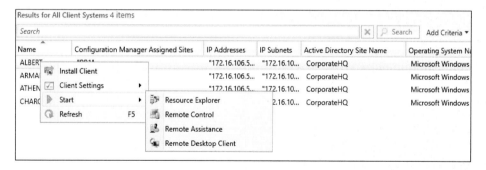

FIGURE 20.4   Available actions for system resource objects.

Creating Queries

ConfigMgr comes with a handful of queries out of the box that illustrate a very small subset of the rich amount of data available. Consider them a starting point; take time to review these queries to understand the available query properties.

Using the query builder is a safe way to retrieve data from ConfigMgr. Since class joins are built automatically behind the scenes, there is less concern that an improper query will be resource intensive (although this is not entirely mitigated). The next sections provide insights into WQL, the available object types to query, use of the query builder, and available operators.

Building Queries Using the WMI Query Language

ConfigMgr query expressions are written in WQL. Using WQL lets you gather information from the site database by accessing information through the WMI provider. If you are familiar with Structured Query Language (SQL) queries, the format of WQL queries should look familiar, as WQL is a subset of SQL.

WQL is a Microsoft implementation of the CIM Query Language (CQL). CQL is a query language designed for the Common Information Model (CIM), which is a standard created by the Distributed Management Task Force (DMTF). (That is quite a few acronyms!)

Following is an example of a WQL query that lists devices with more than 1,024MB of RAM:

```
select * from  SMS_R_System inner join SMS_G_System_X86_PC_MEMORY on
SMS_G_System_X86_PC_MEMORY.ResourceID = SMS_R_System.ResourceId where
SMS_G_System_X86_PC_MEMORY.TotalPhysicalMemory >= 1048576
```

> **NOTE: MORE ABOUT WMI QUERY LANGUAGE**
>
> If you are familiar with SQL, you may notice that this query looks very similar to a SQL query. However, rather than querying tables, WQL queries classes and returns instances instead of rows. Another distinction is that WQL is strictly a retrieval language. WQL cannot create, delete, or modify classes or instances.

Understanding Query Objects, Classes, and Attributes

Before building your own queries, you should understand some of the terminology behind the technology. As discussed in the following sections, a query always consists of the following:

▶ An object type

▶ One or more attribute classes

▶ One or more attributes

Object Types

An *object type* is a set of attributes representing a ConfigMgr database object. Such objects include applications, deployments, devices, and so on. Table 20.1 lists commonly used object types and their descriptions.

TABLE 20.1   Commonly Used Object Types

Object Type	Description
IP Network	A single attribute class containing data related to subnet addresses.
Package	A single attribute class that contains data in a ConfigMgr package, such as description, language, manufacturer, priority, programs, version, and so on.

Object Type	Description
Program	A single attribute class containing data relevant to programs, such as command line, description, space requirements, runtime, and so on.
Security Roles	A single attribute class containing information specifically for security roles, such as role name, created by, and users in the role.
Security Scopes	A single attribute class that contains data specifically related to security scopes, such as scope name, creator, and category ID.
Site	A single attribute class holding data related to site information, such as site code, server name, version, state, and so on.
Software Metering Rule	A single attribute class containing data specific to software metering rules, such as filename, file version, date modified, and so on.
System Resource	The only multi-attribute class object type containing data from ConfigMgr devices, such as hardware, software, and discovery. This is the object type most often used when writing ConfigMgr queries.
Unknown Computer	A single attribute class containing unknown computer data, such as CPU type, agent site, name, description, and so on.
User Group Resource	A single attribute class containing discovery data related to user groups, such as domain, organizational unit, SID, group name, and so on.
User Resource	A single attribute class that contains the discovery data related to users, such as name, SID, mail, user account control, and so on.

Attribute Classes

An *attribute class* is a container object that groups related attributes together. Use the example in the "Building Queries Using the WMI Query Language" section to examine the Memory attribute class, which contains attributes such as AvailableVirtualMembory, TotalPageFileSpace, TotalVirtualMemory, TotalPhysicalMemory, and so on. As all these attributes are logically related to memory, they are grouped into the Memory attribute class.

Most attribute classes exist as part of the System Resource object type. Information in these attributes is provided by hardware inventory. If the available information is inadequate, you can extend the hardware inventory, which enables you to add even more attribute classes to the System Resource object type. Extending hardware inventory is discussed in online-only Appendix E, "Extending Hardware Inventory," which you can download from the book's companion website, at http://www.informit.com/title/9780672337901, on the Downloads tab.

Attributes

An *attribute* is a property in an attribute class that is used for displaying or filtering data. For example, the TotalPhysicalMemory attribute of the Memory attribute class contains the total amount of RAM available, expressed in kilobytes. Figure 20.5 illustrates the relationship of an object type to an attribute class and an attribute class to an attribute.

20

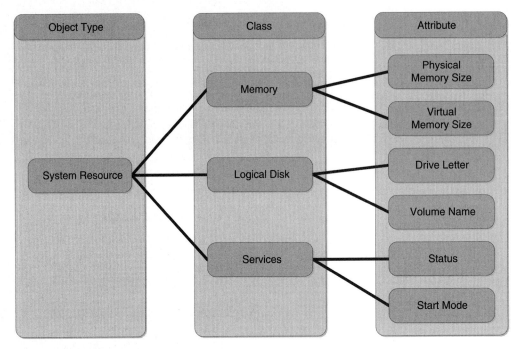

FIGURE 20.5   The relationship of an object type to an attribute class and an attribute class to an attribute.

The next query removes the WHERE clause and modifies the first line to display the Name and the TotalPhysicalMemory attribute as part of the result set:

```
select SMS_R_System.Name, SMS_G_System_X86_PC_MEMORY.TotalPhysicalMemory
from SMS_R_System inner join SMS_G_System_X86_PC_MEMORY on
SMS_G_System_X86_PC_MEMORY.ResourceID = SMS_R_System.ResourceId
```

This query returns all devices and their total physical memory. To return only a certain set of results, use attributes as a part of the criteria set to filter data based on an expression. The example in the "Building Queries Using the WMI Query Language" section uses the TotalPhysicalMemory attribute to specify that the query should bring back only information from devices with over 1024MB of RAM. The query is next modified to add criteria specifying the memory requirements:

```
select SMS_R_System.Name, SMS_G_System_X86_PC_MEMORY.TotalPhysicalMemory
from SMS_R_System inner join SMS_G_System_X86_PC_MEMORY on
SMS_G_System_X86_PC_MEMORY.ResourceID = SMS_R_System.ResourceId where
SMS_G_System_X86_PC_MEMORY.TotalPhysicalMemory >= 1048576
```

Using the ConfigMgr Query Builder

This section shows how to create the query used in the previous section. The ConfigMgr query builder has two modes of operation:

- ▶ **Design View:** The design view is where you are likely to spend most of your time as it simplifies the query building process.

- ▶ **Language View:** The language view provides enhanced query writing capability, discussed in the "Writing Advanced Queries" section, later in this chapter.

The easiest way to create a new query is with the Create Query Wizard. Perform the following steps to launch the wizard and create the query:

1. Click the **Queries** node and choose the **Create Query** action to launch the wizard.

2. On the first page, the General Query Settings page, fill in the name of the query. For this example, use the name **Systems with Minimum 4GB RAM**. Following are some other fields on this page:

    - ▶ **Comment:** This field is optional, but as a best practice you should use it to help identify the query and indicate its purpose. Fill in the comment with **Systems with Minimum 4GB (4194304KB) RAM.**

    - ▶ **Import Query Statement:** Use this field to browse through existing queries and use one as a starting point for building a query. As this query is built from scratch, do not use this feature at this time.

    - ▶ **Collection Limiting:** This feature limits results to objects that exist as members of a specified collection. You can specify the collection in the dialog as part of the query properties or have it prompt for a collection each time the query executes. Do not use collection limiting at this time.

3. Create a new query statement by clicking **Edit Query Statement**. The Create Query Wizard now displays the Query Statement Properties dialog box.

    To display device names and their associated total physical memory, add the attributes to the Results section. Click **New** to display the Result Properties dialog box. Click **Select** to bring up the Select Attribute dialog box and add the following paired values:

    - ▶ **Attribute Class:** System Resource

        Attribute: Name

    - ▶ **Attribute Class:** Memory

        Attribute: Total Physical Memory (KB)

    When completed, the General tab of the Query Statement Properties dialog box should look as shown in Figure 20.6.

20

4. Now that you have defined the attributes you want to see in your query results, the next step is to specify criteria to display systems that match the requirements. In the Query Statement Properties dialog box, choose the **Criteria** tab. Click **New** to display the Criterion Properties dialog box.

Leave the default criterion type (discussed later in this chapter, in the "Understanding Criterion Types, Operators, and Values" section) as Simple value. Click **Select** to display the Select Attribute dialog box and add the **Memory** class and the **Total Physical Memory (KB)** attribute.

Click **OK** to return to the Criterion Properties dialog box and set Operator to **is greater than or equal to**. Specify **4194304KB** (4GB, expressed in kilobytes) as the value, as shown in Figure 20.7.

TIP: FILLING IN VALUES

If you are unsure of the types of values to use in the Value box, click the **Value** button. The Values dialog box returns a list of values that you can use.

Click **OK** to close the Criterion Properties dialog box. Notice that the Criteria tab is now filled with the criterion properties you just created, as shown in Figure 20.8. Click **OK** to close the Query Statement Properties dialog box and return to the General Query Settings page.

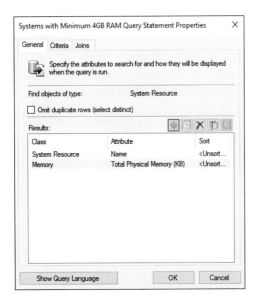

FIGURE 20.6   Attributes added to the General tab.

FIGURE 20.7   Criterion Properties.

FIGURE 20.8   Memory expression in the Criteria tab.

5. Click **Next** to move to the Summary page, which displays the query properties for review, as shown in Figure 20.9. Click **Next** again to move through the Progress page and bring up the Completion page, which provides details. Click **Close** to complete the wizard.

FIGURE 20.9   The Summary page of the Create Query Wizard.

TIP: USING TOOLS TO CREATE WMI QUERIES

There are times when creating WMI queries through the wizard or by hand can be quite cumbersome. Several no-cost tools are available to help ease the process. Following is a list of some popular ones:

▶ **WMI Code Creator:** https://www.microsoft.com/download/details. aspx?displaylang=en&id=8572

▶ **WMI Code Generator:** http://www.robvanderwoude.com/wmigen.php

▶ **Scriptomatic:** https://docs.microsoft.com/previous-versions/windows/it-pro/ windows-powershell-1.0/ff730935(v=technet.10)

Understanding Criterion Types, Operators, and Values

In the "Using the ConfigMgr Query Builder" section, you learned a little about types, operators, and values that are essential components of building criteria to filter data. To illustrate this, the query discussed in that section follows:

```
select SMS_R_System.Name, SMS_G_System_X86_PC_MEMORY.TotalPhysicalMemory
from SMS_R_System inner join SMS_G_System_X86_PC_MEMORY on
SMS_G_System_X86_PC_MEMORY.ResourceID = SMS_R_System.ResourceId where
SMS_G_System_X86_PC_MEMORY.TotalPhysicalMemory >= 1048576
```

The criteria of the query follow after the word where. This is known as a WHERE clause, and it is made up of a property, an operator, and a value, closely matching the focus of this section. The query uses the following as the property, operator, and value:

▶ **Property:** SMS_G_System_X86_PC_MEMORY.TotalPhysicalMemory

▶ **Operator:** >= (greater than or equal to)

▶ **Value:** 1048576

A WHERE clause limits the scope of data returned. The WHERE clause illustrated in this section returns devices with greater than 1024MB of physical RAM. The next sections examine these elements in more detail.

Filtering Queries with Criterion Types

Six different criterion types are used in ConfigMgr queries, all serving the purpose of narrowing the amount of data returned by a query. While all criterion types are used to limit data, each has a different function:

▶ **Null Value:** This criterion type compares an attribute to null. One such use of this criterion type would be to search for devices where the Active Directory (AD) Domain Name value is unknown.

   To search for devices where the value is missing, the criteria can be set to **is NULL**. Inversely, the criteria can also search for where the value is present (or **is not NULL**).

▶ **Simple Value:** This criterion type compares an attribute to a constant value. This is the most basic and yet widely used type of criterion. This is the type used in the memory query example in the previous section.

▶ **Prompted Value:** This criterion type prompts for the value to compare against at runtime. As an example, using the memory query, instead of specifying 1048576, the criterion type can be left as *<prompted value>*, providing the administrative user executing the query the ability to populate the value to something else. If 2048MB were more desirable, the administrative user would enter the value **2097152** at runtime.

> **NOTE: PROMPTED VALUES NOT SUPPORTED IN COLLECTIONS**
>
> Though the prompted value type exists in queries, you cannot use it in collections. Collections do not provide an interactive interface to prompt a user at runtime. All other criterion types are usable for query-based collections.

▶ **Attribute Reference:** To compare two values from the ConfigMgr database, use the attribute reference criterion type. One example of such a use is to locate systems where the current processor clock speed is less than the maximum processor clock speed.

20

▶ **Subselect Value:** When the queried attribute is multi-valued and the operator to use is a type of NOT (not like, not equal to, and so on), you must use a subselect value criterion type. Otherwise, a condition to match something such as all devices where Microsoft Visio 2016 is not installed would not work correctly, as every computer would have at least one entry in the Add/Remove Programs class that did not match the criteria. A query such as that would return every device, installed or not.

If you are unfamiliar with subselect queries, it can be a challenge to write one for the first time. Check the "Examples of Advanced Queries" section, later in this chapter, for a sample query.

CAUTION: BE CAREFUL WHEN RUNNING SUBSELECT QUERIES

Using subselect queries is not necessarily a bad thing. However, they are expensive to run. Because a subselect query is effectively running two queries—one to return all matching objects and another to return subselect objects—if there is a high count for the number of objects, it can take a while for the query to complete. Of course, this is subjective, based on the performance of your server hardware.

▶ **List of Values:** This criterion type compares the value to a list of constant values. A useful example is when searching for devices that match a certain chassis type. To find devices that match a desktop profile, you could use the values 3, 4, 6, and 7 as a starting point. Figure 20.10 shows the properties of the list of values criterion type when constructing such a query. Note that while you can add multiple values, you are restricted to using one operator type.

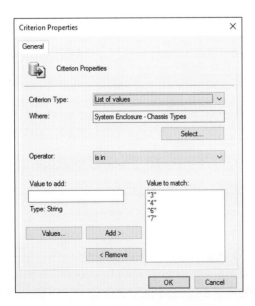

FIGURE 20.10   Using a list of values to select certain chassis types.

TIP: INFORMATION ON CHASSIS TYPES

For more information on chassis types, research the `Win32_SystemEnclosure` class. You can find other useful information in this class, such as serial number, manufacturer, model, and so on. The MSDN article at http://msdn.microsoft.com/library/aa394474. aspx provides additional information.

Using Relational and Logical Operators

Some operators indicate how to assess a value, while others are used to join expressions together. A relational operator indicates how to compare a value against a certain type of data. A logical operator, on the other hand, indicates how to join multiple expressions together. These are discussed in the following sections.

Relational Operators

Depending on the criterion and data type, you will find that certain operators may not be available. Because operators in ConfigMgr are relational in nature, the available operators depend on the data type of the specified attribute. For example, whenever a date value is used, such as Workstation Status - Last Hardware Scan, additional operators become available that are specifically designed to query dates and parts of dates.

Following are the three types of relational operators:

▶ **Date and Time Operators:** This type of operator requires a value that matches the specified date/time operator. The operators match those found for the other criterion types (with the exception of NULL), prepended with one of the following: day, day of week, day of year, hour, millisecond, minute, month, quarter, second, week of year, or year.

▶ **Numerical Operators:** This type of operator requires a numerical value; otherwise, the query fails. The numerical operator consists of the following: is equal to, is greater than, is greater than or equal to, is less than, is less than or equal to, and is not equal to.

▶ **String Relational Operators:** This type of operator requires a string to evaluate against the operator. Operators such as `LIKE` are available with strings.

Table 20.2 lists available operators for each criterion type when using the string data type.

TABLE 20.2   Operators for Each Criterion Type for Strings

Criterion Type(s)	Operators
NULL value	is NULL
	is not NULL
Simple value, prompted value, attribute reference	is equal to
	is greater than
	is greater than or equal to
	is less than

20

Criterion Type(s)	Operators
	is less than or equal to
	is like
	is not equal to
	is not like
	lowercase is equal to
	lowercase is greater than
	lowercase is greater than or equal to
	lowercase is less than
	lowercase is less than or equal to
	lowercase is like
	lowercase is not equal to
	lowercase is not like
	uppercase is equal to
	uppercase is greater than
	uppercase is greater than or equal to
	uppercase is less than
	uppercase is less than or equal to
	uppercase is like
	uppercase is not equal to
	uppercase is not like
Subselect value, list of values	is in
	is not in
	lowercase is in
	lowercase is not in
	uppercase is in
	uppercase is not in

Logical Operators

Sometimes a query with a single expression will have insufficient criteria to return the correct set of data. For example, say that the criterion is more than simply looking for devices with greater than 1024MB of RAM, and you are also interested in devices that have more than 800MB of free disk space. You can join the expressions together by using the logical AND operator to cause both expressions to evaluate.

ConfigMgr has three types of logical operators to manage multiple expressions:

▶ **AND:** Finds all objects that match both expressions joined by AND. This is illustrated with the RAM and free space example in the "Building Queries Using the WMI Query Language" section of this chapter.

▶ **OR:** Finds all objects that match either expression joined by OR. An example of an OR expression is to search for ConfigMgr client versions that match 5.00.7561.0000 OR 4.00.6487.2157.

▶ **NOT:** Finds all objects that do not match the expression the NOT operator is applied to. For example, using NOT on an expression looking for ConfigMgr client version 5.00.7561.0000 would return any object with a different version of the client installed.

Operator Precedence Order

When you were in math class, your teacher may have talked about something called order of operations. This is a rule that defines which procedures go first. ConfigMgr query evaluations also follow this process. When writing queries that use logical operators, it is important for you to understand the order of operations that is followed to accurately predict the outcome of the query. (And you thought you would never need to know what you learned in school!)

Here is the order in which expressions are evaluated:

1. Any expressions inside parentheses

2. Any expressions using NOT

3. Any expressions using AND

4. Any expressions using OR

To change the order of operations, use parentheses to force a certain expression to evaluate first. For example, if you have multiple AND statements, placing one of the AND statements inside parentheses will cause it to evaluate first. Parentheses are also useful for breaking up complex expressions so that they are easier to understand.

Specifying or Selecting Values

You can specify a value by entering it into the Value field. Clicking **Values** queries ConfigMgr for data from the specified attribute. The console will display a list of possible values, which is helpful for viewing a sampling of the content of data. If a value that is useful for the query appears, you can select it to automatically insert it into the Value field. If the values returned are larger than 2,000 entries, the list of values is truncated. Keep in mind that there is no specifiable sort order for the list of values.

The Value field also accepts wildcards to help shape the query correctly. Wildcards work with operators that use the LIKE clause. Any other operators assume that the wildcard is a literal character. Table 20.3 details available wildcards and their functions.

20

TABLE 20.3   Available Wildcards and Their Functions

Wildcard	Function	Example(s)
_ (underscore)	Matches any single character (can be used more than once)	_eek matches geek, meek, peek, seek, week
		__eek matches Greek, cheek, sleek
		_ea_ matches beak, leaf, seal
		se__ matches seal, seek
% (percent)	Matches any zero or more characters	%eek matches Greek, geek, peek, sleek, eek
		g%eek matches geek, Greek
[x] (bracketed character)	Matches any specified literal character once	[%]eek matches %eek
		[?]eek matches ?eek
		[_]eek matches _eek
		[gps]eek matches geek, peek, seek
		[gm]eek matches geek, meek
		[w]eek matches week
[x-x] (bracketed range)	Matches a range of specified characters once	[g-s]eek matches geek, meek, peek, seek
[^x] (bracketed range with a caret)	Matches any single character not in the bracket once	[^m]eek matches geek, peek, seek, week

You can mix and match wildcards together to create more definitive filters in order to match widely and narrowly at the same time. For example, say that you want to find the names Apollo, Ares, Artemis, Athena, Erebos, and Hermes. The following are wildcards you can use to find them:

▶ **Apollo and Athena:** A%[ao]

▶ **Erebos and Hermes:** [EH]%s

▶ **Ares, Artemis, and Erebos:** _r%s

Writing Advanced Queries

Until this point, the only type of query illustrated in this chapter has been a simple value query to look for computers with more than 1024MB of RAM. However, the complexity in writing queries for ConfigMgr can grow to be quite challenging. Not only does ConfigMgr support a number of different criterion types, it supports some hidden functions that are not readily exposed in the console.

Using the query builder is a much simpler process than writing WQL queries by hand. However, the query builder is limited in the options it displays in Design view. ConfigMgr supports the use of Extended WQL for query writing, which supports SELECT clauses such as

COUNT, DISTINCT, ORDER BY, DATEPART, and so on. Some of these options, such as DISTINCT and ORDER BY, are exposed, as shown in Figure 20.11. Other equally useful syntax must be manually entered—specifically the date and time functions.

Writing queries with certain criterion types, such as a subselect value query, is considered advanced because the process of writing such queries is not particularly straightforward. This type of query is extremely helpful when querying multi-valued attributes such as Add/Remove Programs.

The next section considers several of the restrictions of the Extended WQL implementation as used in ConfigMgr to help understand what is available when writing advanced queries.

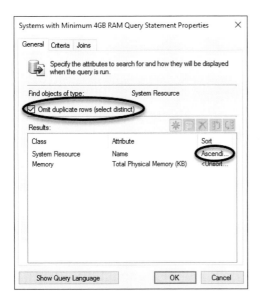

FIGURE 20.11   SELECT DISTINCT and ORDER BY exposed in the query builder.

Limitations of Extended WQL in ConfigMgr

Extended WQL has certain limitations in Configuration Manager (either inherently or because of the SMS provider) to be aware of when writing queries. The following list explains these limitations:

▶ The results of COUNT do not display properly and are therefore not useful for querying through the ConfigMgr console.

▶ COUNT and DISTINCT cannot be used together in a WQL query.

▶ While supported, UPPER and LOWER are not helpful because WQL is entirely case-insensitive.

▶ The SMS provider does not support querying against system properties. These properties are easily identifiable as they all begin with a double underscore—for example, __CLASS, __NAMESPACE, __PATH, and so on.

20

▶ If the query is using the collection limiting option, the ORDER BY clause will not work.

▶ You cannot use date and time functions in the query following the SELECT clause. However, they can be used as a part of the WHERE clause, as shown in the next section.

Utilizing the Date and Time Functions in WQL Queries

In many situations, applying a date filter to a query is quite useful. For example, when creating queries, it is often helpful to know that the information retrieved is the most current information available. An example is pulling changes to hardware inventory that occurred sometime in the past week. ConfigMgr queries support the use of the following functions:

▶ **Dateadd():** Returns a specified date value with a specified interval added to it. The following is an example:

```
DateAdd ( datepart, number, date )
```

> ▶ **Datepart:** This parameter specifies the portion of the date to add the number to.
>
> ▶ **Number:** This integer value is added to the specified datepart.
>
> ▶ **Date:** This is the initial date value to which to add the integer. For example, the following query looks for 30 days ago from July 20, 2017
>
> ```
> DateAdd(DD,-30,"7/20/2017")
> ```

▶ **Datediff():** Returns the difference between two date values in the increment of the datepart specified. The following is an example:

```
DateDiff ( datepart, startdate, enddate )
```

> ▶ **Datepart:** This parameter specifies the portion of the date to calculate the difference against.
>
> ▶ **Startdate:** This is the starting date to use in the calculation. Startdate is subtracted from enddate.
>
> ▶ **Enddate:** This is the ending date to use in the calculation. The following example looks for the difference between July 20, 2017, and today, in days:
>
> ```
> DateDiff(DD,"7/20/2017",Getdate())
> ```

▶ **Getdate():** Returns the current date value of the system executing the command. Following is an example that looks for 30 days ago from today:

```
DateAdd(DD,-30,GetDate())
```

Table 20.4 illustrates the components of Datepart and their relative abbreviations.

TABLE 20.4   Components of DatePart

Datepart	Abbreviations
Year	year, yy
Month	month, mm
Day	day, dd
Hour	hour, hh
Minute	minute, mi
Second	second, ss

TIP: SAMPLE DATE AND TIME QUERY

For an example of a query that uses the date and time functions, refer to the query in the "Querying for Devices with a Hardware Scan in the Past 15 Days" section, later in this chapter.

The next section explores some different advanced queries. Understanding them can assist in broadening your query writing ability.

Examples of Advanced Queries

It is true that WMI queries are limited in functionality compared to SQL queries. However, combining all the query elements discussed in this chapter enables you to produce queries of certain complexity. These queries often cannot be displayed in the ConfigMgr console because the graphical user interface (GUI) simply lacks the capability to show all the components.

The next sections provide examples of advanced queries, which you should find useful as a basis for constructing your own queries. You can use them as-is to tease out data for quick reporting, or you can apply a complex filter to isolate clients for targeting.

Querying for Devices with a Hardware Scan in the Past 15 Days

The following query retrieves any device that has reported a hardware scan within the past 15 days:

```
select SMS_R_System.Name, SMS_G_System_WORKSTATION_STATUS.LastHardwareScan
from  SMS_R_System
inner join SMS_G_System_WORKSTATION_STATUS on
SMS_G_System_WORKSTATION_STATUS.ResourceId = SMS_R_System.ResourceId
where DateDiff(dd,SMS_G_System_WORKSTATION_STATUS.LastHardwareScan,GetDate()) <= 15
```

Look closely at the WHERE clause. The DateDiff function is used to calculate the difference between the last hardware scan date and the current date. If the calculated difference is less than or equal to 15 days, the device is included in the results.

This example uses `DateDiff`, but you can accomplish the same result with `DateAdd`. `DateAdd` can manipulate the current date (`GetDate`) into a date 15 days ago. By comparing the hardware scan date against the `DateAdd` manipulated date, you can bring back only devices that match the criterion, as illustrated here:

```
select SMS_R_System.Name, SMS_G_System_WORKSTATION_STATUS.LastHardwareScan
from SMS_R_System inner join SMS_G_System_WORKSTATION_STATUS on
SMS_G_System_WORKSTATION_STATUS.ResourceId = SMS_R_System.ResourceId
where SMS_G_System_WORKSTATION_STATUS.LastHardwareScan > DateAdd(DD,- 15,GetDate())
```

Querying for Devices Newly Discovered in the Past Day

To locate recently discovered devices, query against the record creation date. Calculating the creation date against the current date will produce devices that are recently discovered. In this case, the value supplied, `1` (following the `DateDiff` function), looks for creation dates as recently as a day ago:

```
select SMS_R_System.Name, SMS_R_System.CreationDate from  SMS_R_System where
DateDiff(dd,SMS_R_System.CreationDate,GetDate()) <= 1
```

Querying for Devices Without Microsoft Silverlight Installed

With this query, using the subselect criterion type, you can draw out devices that do not have Microsoft Outlook installed:

```
select SMS_R_System.ResourceId, SMS_R_System.ResourceType, SMS_R_System.Name,
SMS_R_System.SMSUniqueIdentifier, SMS_R_System.ResourceDomainORWorkgroup,
SMS_R_System.Client from  SMS_R_System where SMS_R_System.ResourceId not in
(select distinct SMS_R_System.ResourceId from  SMS_R_System inner join
SMS_G_System_ADD_REMOVE_PROGRAMS on SMS_G_System_ADD_REMOVE_PROGRAMS.ResourceID =
SMS_R_System.ResourceId where SMS_G_System_ADD_REMOVE_PROGRAMS.DisplayName =
"Microsoft Outlook") and SMS_R_System.Client = 1
```

When writing a subselect query, a query is embedded inside another query.

The query in the WHERE clause creates a list of computers that match the criterion of having Microsoft Silverlight installed (see Figure 20.12). The outer query uses an IS NOT IN operator to list any computers that are not in the initial query. Finally, this query uses another criterion to qualify that the query should be limited to information where the resource is a ConfigMgr client.

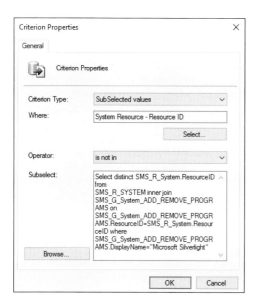

FIGURE 20.12   Subselect query that looks for all clients without Microsoft Silverlight.

Querying for Computers and Logical Disks with a Prompted Value

This query displays the logical disk(s) of a specified computer:

```
select SMS_R_System.Name, SMS_G_System_LOGICAL_DISK.DeviceID,
SMS_G_System_LOGICAL_DISK.FileSystem, SMS_G_System_LOGICAL_DISK.Description,
SMS_G_System_LOGICAL_DISK.Size from  SMS_R_System inner join
SMS_G_System_LOGICAL_DISK on SMS_G_System_LOGICAL_DISK.ResourceID =
SMS_R_System.ResourceId where SMS_G_System_LOGICAL_DISK.Description =
"Local Fixed Disk" and SMS_R_System.Name like ##PRM:SMS_R_System.Name##
```

Because it uses a prompted value, the query prompts the user to provide a computer name at execution. Because the LIKE operator is in use for the prompted value, you can use a wildcard to mask part of the computer name and potentially return more than one computer.

Querying for Devices Not in a Specified Collection

This query is designed to show devices that are not in a collection that you specify:

```
select sms_r_system.resourceid, sms_r_system.name
from sms_r_system
where resourceid not in
    (
    select sys.resourceid
    from SMS_CM_RES_COLL_PR10000A AS coll, sms_r_system as sys
    where sys.resourceid = coll.resourceid
    )
```

The collection is referred to by the `collection ID`. In this example, the `collection ID` is PR10000A. When using this query, simply change the `collection ID` to one in your environment.

Much like the earlier example with Microsoft Outlook (see the section "Querying for Devices Without Microsoft Outlook Installed"), this is a subselect query. However, this query statement uses a class that, while it is not exposed in the query builder's design mode, can be pasted or typed into the query language window.

For additional information about this query, see http://marcusoh.blogspot.com/2007/08/sms-selecting-objects-not-in-collection.html.

Converting WQL to SQL

By now, you are probably writing queries you find useful enough that you want to move them into a SQL Server Reporting Services (SSRS) report to leverage all the formatting, sharing, and scheduling capabilities! Chapter 21, "Configuration Manager Reporting," discusses SSRS in depth.

Let's examine the query used earlier in this chapter, in the section "Querying for Devices with a Hardware Scan in the Past 15 Days." To quickly convert this query to SQL, look at the ConfigMgr logs. Open smsprov.log and execute the query you want to convert. Look for a line that begins with `Execute WQL`. This entry displays the actual WQL query issued:

```
Execute WQL  =
select SMS_R_System.Name, SMS_G_System_WORKSTATION_STATUS.LastHardwareScan
from  SMS_R_System inner join SMS_G_System_WORKSTATION_STATUS on
SMS_G_System_WORKSTATION_STATUS.ResourceId = SMS_R_System.ResourceId
where DateDiff(dd,SMS_G_System_WORKSTATION_STATUS.LastHardwareScan,GetDate())

<= 15
```

The query in the log matches the referenced query! The next line in the log that begins with `Execute SQL` contains the SQL query:

```
Execute SQL =
select  all SMS_R_System.Name0,___System_WORKSTATION_STATUS0.LastHWScan
from vSMS_R_System AS SMS_R_System INNER JOIN WorkstationStatus_DATA AS
___System_WORKSTATION_STATUS0 ON ___
System_WORKSTATION_STATUS0.MachineID = SMS_R_System.ItemKey
where DATEDIFF (day,___System_WORKSTATION_STATUS0.LastHWScan,GETDATE ()) <= 15
```

> **CAUTION: MICROSOFT DOES NOT SUPPORT QUERYING CONFIGMGR TABLES**
>
> Though extracting the SQL query from smsprov.log is a very useful trick, using ConfigMgr tables in a SQL query is not considered a best practice. Microsoft may alter the database schema between versions to add functionality or improve performance. For this reason, Microsoft does not publish a database schema, as it would imply that the schema is static. Wherever possible, use the provided ConfigMgr database views.

Understanding Relationships, Operations, and Joins

Until now, there has been no discussion of relationships. It has not been a necessary conversation, as the ConfigMgr query builder manages this dynamically as you create a query. Earlier in this chapter, in the section "Using the ConfigMgr Query Builder," you used the General and Criteria tabs to build a query for finding devices with greater than 1024MB of RAM. Figure 20.13 shows that the query builder also has a Joins tab. The lower pane in Figure 20.13 shows the content of the Joins tab.

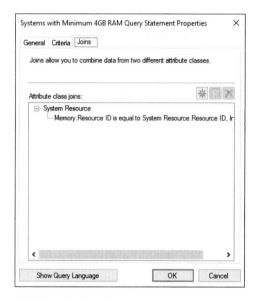

FIGURE 20.13   The Joins tab.

In most scenarios, `Resource ID` is used as the attribute for joining classes together. Notice that in Figure 20.13, both the join and base attributes are set to `Resource ID`. This is because `Resource ID`, a unique value that represents a ConfigMgr client resource, is in nearly every class.

The diagram in Figure 20.14 helps illustrate how two classes such as `System Resource` and `Workstation Memory` are joined together. Figure 20.15 is a graphic display of the join for System Resource and Memory (on Resource ID), providing combined results from both tables.

As discussed earlier in this chapter, in the "Writing Advanced Queries" section, ConfigMgr uses Extended WQL. Through Extended WQL support, ConfigMgr can provide two kinds of join operations: inner and outer. An inner join is limited to a single type of the same name—inner. Inner join types are the most common type of join used in WQL. (This is also the case with SQL.)

20

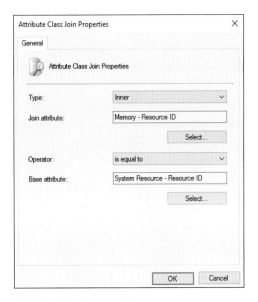

FIGURE 20.14   The Attribute class join properties.

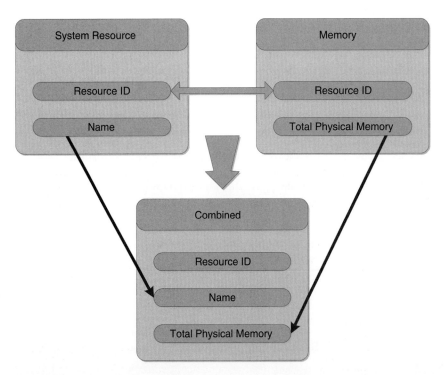

FIGURE 20.15   Diagram of joins.

Outer joins, on the other hand, include full, left outer, and right outer. Queries are often optimized based on the join type selected. Depending on the join, this may mean the difference between pulling some select records and pulling every record in the joined classes. Here is how data is brought together based on the join used:

▶ **Inner:** All joins created in the ConfigMgr Query Builder automatically use the inner join when the join type is not specified. The inner join will only provide matching results.

▶ **Full:** In contrast to the inner join, the full join type displays all the results for the base and the join attribute.

▶ **Left:** When using a left join type, all the results from the base attribute are displayed. In addition, the matching results from the join attribute are displayed.

▶ **Right:** The right outer join type is exactly the opposite of the left outer join type. The matching results from the base attribute are displayed, along with all the results from the join attribute.

When might you deviate from the default? Say that you want to retrieve a list of all your devices as well as the name and version number of internally developed software. The developer who wrote that software did not always populate the version number correctly. Such a query with the default inner join type would bring back only records where the device name, the software name, and the software version exist. Because you need to see the devices where the software is installed but the version value is potentially empty, you switch the join type to a left join to include all records.

To demonstrate, consider this simple query that retrieves system enclosure information:

```
select SMS_R_System.Name, SMS_G_System_SYSTEM_ENCLOSURE.ChassisTypes
from  SMS_R_System inner join SMS_G_System_SYSTEM_ENCLOSURE on
SMS_G_System_SYSTEM_ENCLOSURE.ResourceID = SMS_R_System.ResourceId
```

If you use the default join, only devices with a chassis type will be displayed. By switching the join type to left, all devices are displayed, with a blank value for chassis type. The next query, where the inner join has been replaced with a left join, shows the join type modified to left:

```
select SMS_R_System.Name, SMS_G_System_SYSTEM_ENCLOSURE.ChassisTypes
from SMS_R_System left join SMS_G_System_SYSTEM_ENCLOSURE on
SMS_G_System_SYSTEM_ENCLOSURE.ResourceID = SMS_R_System.ResourceId
```

Querying Discovery Data

Three different types of discovery data are available for use in a query: `system resource`, `user resource`, and `user group resource`. As some discovery data is captured through ConfigMgr discovery methods, this information is available even before the device has a ConfigMgr client installed.

20

Each of these classes provides information discovered through the ConfigMgr discovery methods:

▶ `System Resource`: Use this class to draw out ConfigMgr information about the device, such as the assigned, installed, or resident site; the client version; and so on. Other information, such as the system name, IP address, subnets, and security identifier (SID), is also available. Finally, you can also query AD information about the device, such as the system organizational unit (OU) name, the system container name, and the system group name, and so on.

▶ `User Resource`: Use this class to obtain information about user accounts from attributes such as the full username, mail, unique user name, user account control (disabled, enabled, and so on), and such. In addition, AD information about the user account, such as the distinguished name, user OU name, and user container name, is available.

▶ `User Group Resource`: This class contains attributes related to AD user group properties, such as the `domain`, `organizational unit`, `unique user group name`, `group name`, and so on.

With information available regarding AD accounts, you can use discovery data to build collections to support your ConfigMgr deployment. Collections can be created to group AD computer accounts together to install the ConfigMgr agent.

Querying Inventory Data

The `System Resource` class, discussed earlier in this chapter, in the "Understanding Query Objects, Classes, and Attributes" section, contains discovered attributes about an object. However, this class contains more than just discovered data.

All queries requiring data from hardware or software inventory need to utilize the `System Resource` class. In fact, most of the queries covered in this chapter use the `System Resource` class, which shows how prevalent this class is! Table 20.5 illustrates some popular hardware and software inventory classes.

TABLE 20.5   Useful Hardware and Software Inventory Classes

Class	Description
Add/Remove Programs	Based on `Win32Reg_AddRemovePrograms`. Now referred to as Programs and Features in newer operating systems (Windows Vista and above). Holds the same type of software information found in the Add/Remove Programs Control Panel applet. Systems running x64 hold data in the equivalent `Add/Remove Programs_(64)` class.
Computer System	Based on `Win32_ComputerSystem`. An eclectic class with information including hardware manufacturer and model. Also includes time zone data, domain role, and so on.

Class	Description
Disk Drives	Based on `Win32_DiskDrive`. Contains information about disk drives, such as manufacturer, drive size, and count of partitions.
Logical Disk	Refer to `SMS_LogicalDisk`. Contains information related to logical disks, such as drive letter, file system, size, and volume name.
Memory	Refer to `CCM_LogicalMemoryConfiguration`. Displays information for page file size, physical memory size, and virtual memory size.
Network Adapter Configuration	Based on `Win32_NetworkAdapterConfiguration`. Contains IP configuration such as the IP address, default gateway, subnet mask, and so on.
Operating System	Based on `Win32_OperatingSystem`. Contains details about the operating system, such as the name, build number, version, last boot-up time, and so on.
Power Configuration	Refer to `CCM_PowerConfig`. Displays information such as peak and non-peak power plan names, wake-up time, and so on.
Processor	Refer to `SMS_Processor`. Contains information about clock speed, number of cores, 64-bit capability, and so on.
Recently Used Applications	Refer to `CCM_RecentlyUsedApps`. Displays information about recent application usage, including the last user, last used time, the application, and so on.
Server Feature	Based on `Win32_ServerFeature`. Displays installed server features.
Services	Based on `Win32_Service`. Displays information about services, such as name, description, start mode, and status.
Shares	Based on `Win32_Share`. Displays configured shares of the operating system.
Software Files	Contains file information collected from `Software Inventory`.
Software Products	Contains information from file headers from `Software Inventory`.
Virtual Machine	Based on `Win32Reg_SMSGuestVirtualMachine`. Displays information related to the virtual machine host. Systems running x64 hold data in the Virtual Machine (64) class.
System Enclosure	Based on `Win32_SystemEnclosure`. Contains useful hardware information, such as manufacturer, model, chassis type, and serial number.
Workstation Status	Refer to this class to query the last hardware inventory scan date.

20

This is just a small list of the rich amount of inventory data that ConfigMgr provides. Over time, as your environment changes, inventoried classes also change. ConfigMgr is flexible enough to evolve with these changes. Refer to Chapter 9, "Client Management," for information on modifying hardware inventory classes.

If you find that a device does not contain the expected inventory class, the device may not be healthy. In such circumstances, the device may be incapable of running the inventory scan or sending the inventory to the site server, and the expected information may never reach the site server.

Using Query Results

Queries are excellent resources for administrators. They provide a means to view data in an ad hoc manner from ConfigMgr. Such sources of data include discovery, inventory, advertisement, and site status information. Queries can also be the basis of collections that dynamically update. You could also export queries to text files for use in other ways. The next sections discuss these topics.

Exporting Query Results to a Text File

Earlier versions of ConfigMgr included the ability to export query results to a text file. This option was available as a part of the MMC (Microsoft Management Console) functionality, but Microsoft did not port it to Configuration Manager 2012 and newer versions. However, copy and paste can be used as a viable replacement for this functionality. Even though there is no option in the ribbon bar or the right-click context menu, highlighting results and using **Ctrl+C** will store the results in memory. You can then paste these results into any text editor.

Importing and Exporting Queries between Sites

Unlike some previous versions, ConfigMgr Current Branch no longer requires movement of queries between sites to share them, as the queries are globally available in a hierarchy. However, this function remains available, as it is still useful to export queries to share them with other hierarchies or in community groups with other administrators.

To export a query object, perform the following steps:

1. Select the Queries node and click **Export Queries** in the ribbon bar.

2. In the Export Objects Wizard, click **Next**.

3. Select the queries you wish to export, as displayed in Figure 20.16, and click **Next**.

4. Enter a valid path and filename for the export and ensure that it ends with a .mof extension. Click **Next**.

5. Confirm the settings and click **Next**. Click **Close** to exit the wizard.

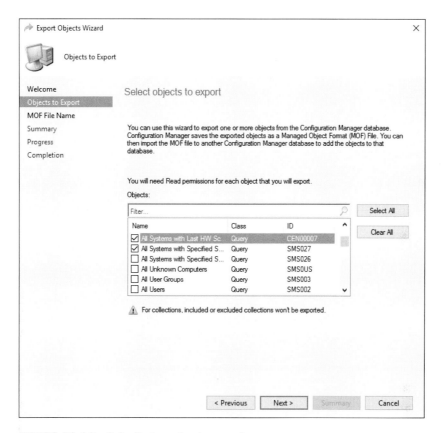

FIGURE 20.16   Selecting queries to export.

When these steps are complete, you can copy or move the file to a suitable location for importing into a different hierarchy. Before looking at the import steps, let's examine the file content of a sample export, which is based on the query built earlier in this chapter, in the "Querying for Devices with a Hardware Scan in the Past 15 Days" section. The content of the file follows:

```
// ****************************************************************************
//
//     Created by SMS Export object wizard
//
//     Tuesday, August 09, 2016 created
//
//     File Name: C:\Queries\HardwareScan.MOF
//
// Comments :
//
//
// ****************************************************************************
```

```
// ***** Class : SMS_Query *****
[SecurityVerbs(-1)]
instance of SMS_Query
{
    Comments = "";
    Expression = "select SMS_R_System.Name,
SMS_G_System_WORKSTATION_STATUS.LastHardwareScan from  SMS_R_System inner join
SMS_G_System_WORKSTATION_STATUS on SMS_G_System_WORKSTATION_STATUS.ResourceId =
SMS_R_System.ResourceId where
DateDiff(dd,SMS_G_System_WORKSTATION_STATUS.LastHardwareScan,GetDate()) <= 15";
    LimitToCollectionID = "";
    LocalizedCategoryInstanceNames = {};
    Name = "Recent Hardware Scan (15 days)";
    QueryID = "";
    ResultAliasNames = {"SMS_R_System", "SMS_G_System_WORKSTATION_STATUS"};
    ResultColumnsNames = {"SMS_R_System.Name",
 "SMS_G_System_WORKSTATION_STATUS.LastHardwareScan"};
    TargetClassName = "SMS_R_System";
};
// ***** End *****
```

The query remains intact in the expression line.

Importing queries is just as easy as exporting queries. For example, perform the following steps to import a query object:

1. Right-click the Queries node and choose **Import Objects**. The Import Objects Wizard launches.

2. In the wizard, click **Next**.

3. Supply the path and name of the file to import. Click **Next**.

4. Review the name (or names) of the object(s) to import. Click **Next** and review the comments. Click **Next** when complete.

5. Confirm the settings on the summary screen and click **Next**. Click **Close** to exit the wizard.

> **CAUTION: DUPLICATE NAMED QUERIES ARE OVERWRITTEN**
>
> Review your existing objects carefully to ensure that the query to import does not use an existing name. Any existing objects with duplicate names are overwritten.

Creating a Collection Based on Query Results

Before creating a collection that uses a query rule, examine the results in a query. This provides an opportunity to view attributes, as a collection only shows a default set of attributes. The authors recommend creating a query first, verifying that the results are as you expect, and then using the query as the basis of your collection.

When you import a query into a collection, the additional attributes specified in your query are ignored and replaced with a default set. This also occurs if you paste the WQL from a query to the collection rule directly. Looking at the previous memory query, first examined earlier in this chapter, in the "Building Queries Using the WMI Query Language" section, note the attributes requested in the `select` statement below:

```
select SMS_R_System.Name, SMS_G_System_X86_PC_MEMORY.TotalPhysicalMemory
from SMS_R_System inner join SMS_G_System_X86_PC_MEMORY on
SMS_G_System_X86_PC_MEMORY.ResourceID = SMS_R_System.ResourceId
```

The following shows how the query is modified after it is imported or pasted into a collection:

```
select SMS_R_SYSTEM.ResourceID, SMS_R_SYSTEM.ResourceType, SMS_R_SYSTEM.Name,
SMS_R_SYSTEM.SMSUniqueIdentifier, SMS_R_SYSTEM.ResourceDomainORWorkgroup,
SMS_R_SYSTEM.Client from SMS_R_System inner join SMS_G_System_X86_PC_MEMORY on
SMS_G_System_X86_PC_MEMORY.ResourceID = SMS_R_System.ResourceId
```

Notice that while `SMS_R_SYSTEM.Name` still exists, the attribute for memory, `SMS_G_System_X86_PC_MEMORY.TotalPhysicalMemory` has been replaced with other values.

Using Status Message Queries for In-Depth Analysis

Status message queries provide deeper insight into component-level activity and audit messages. Details such as user activity (changes to the hierarchy, sites, or client settings), deployed program messages, collection modifications, deployment, remote control, and even query activity are tracked and reported in status messages. You can find status message queries under Monitoring -> System Status.

ConfigMgr comes stocked with more than 60 different status messages. If one of the standard status messages does not contain the information you are seeking, you can create a custom status message. There currently is no documentation that provides a translation between the status message IDs and their meanings. It is best to build your queries from the existing queries as much as possible, since the criteria may list the necessary message ID values. For example, Figure 20.17 shows the query criteria for the query titled Deployments Created, Modified, or Deleted.

20

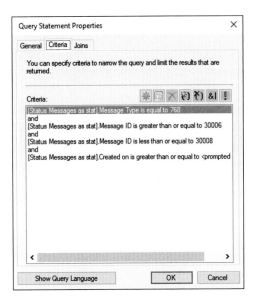

FIGURE 20.17   Status message criteria, displaying message IDs and types.

Viewing Status Messages

Executing status message queries is a straightforward process; the only caveat is that they often prompt for information with a dialog you may not be familiar with. Most times, status message queries filter by a date range so that the amount of information returned is not overwhelming and does not take a long time to execute.

For example, examine the following default status message query, titled Remote Control Activity Initiated by a Specific User:

```
select stat.*, ins.*, att1.*, att1.AttributeTime from SMS_StatusMessage as stat left
join SMS_StatMsgInsStrings as ins on stat.RecordID = ins.RecordID left join
SMS_StatMsgAttributes as att1 on stat.RecordID = att1.RecordID inner join
SMS_StatMsgAttributes as att2 on stat.RecordID = att2.RecordID where
stat.MessageType = 768 and stat.MessageID >= 30069 and stat.MessageID <= 30087 and
att2.AttributeID = 403 and att2.AttributeValue = "ODYSSEY\\MOh" and
att2.AttributeTime >= '2018/01/08 01:47:23.000' order by att1.AttributeTime desc
```

This query requests two pieces of information: property value and time. When using a query to look for a property value, the value can be manually entered or selected from a dropdown list. If you are not familiar with the data or the format, it is often easier to use the dropdown. Once the dialog is loaded, the dropdown list is filled with values.

NOTE: MANUALLY ENTER THE VALUE IF KNOWN

The disadvantage to using dropdown lists is time. As the option suggests, the option **Load Existing** will query the ConfigMgr database to retrieve a list of values.

You can enter time values by using the **Specify date and time** option, which provides a calendar view as well as a time frame. If the specific date and time are unknown, use the **Select date and time** option, which provides some generic values to use as a date, such as 1 hour ago, 12 hours ago, 2 weeks ago, 1 year ago, and so on. View the query information after executing the query to confirm what was entered if you use the values as expressed in Figure 20.18, including a date and time value of 1 hour ago.

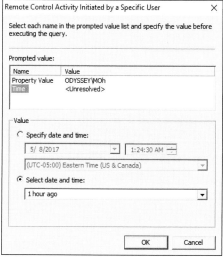

FIGURE 20.18   Using date and time in a status message query.

Creating Status Message Queries

In the list of status message queries, there is a query titled Clients That Received a Specific Deployed Program and another titled Clients That Rejected a Specific Deployed Program. To view both statuses in the same list, you must create a custom status message query (or sift through hundreds of records in the All Status Message query). To create a new status message query, perform the following steps:

1. Launch the Create Status Message Query Wizard. Give the query a name such as Clients That Received and Rejected a Specific Deployed Program.

2. To make it easier to create the new query, click **Import Query Statement** and select the query titled Clients That Received a Specific Deployed Program. Click **OK**.

3. Click **Edit Query Statement**. Note that the contents of the selected query are imported.

4. Switch to the Criteria tab and highlight the line labeled **[Status message as stat]. Message ID is equal to 10002**. Double-click the line or select the properties icon to bring up the Criterion Properties dialog.

5. As shown in Figure 20.19, change Criterion Type to **List of values** and Operator to **is in** and add the following to the Value to match section: **10002**, **10018**, and **10019**.

6. Click **OK** to commit the changes and close all the dialog windows.

7. After returning to the Create Status Message Query Wizard, click **Next** to view the summary. Click **Next** again to create the query. Finally, click **Close** to end the wizard.

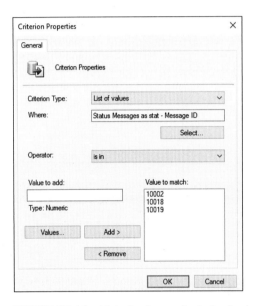

FIGURE 20.19   List of values criteria to display selected status message IDs.

TIP: LEARNING ABOUT CRITERION PROPERTIES

For a refresher on criterion properties, review the "Using the ConfigMgr Query Builder" section, earlier in this chapter.

Most status message queries are named descriptively enough to identify their purpose. However, it is helpful to point out some of the more useful queries. Table 20.6 lists some useful queries and helps you understand the various sources of data from which these queries can draw information.

TABLE 20.6   Useful Status Message Queries

Status Message Query	Description
All Audit Status Messages for a Specific User	Shows the activity of a specific user.
Client Configuration Requests (CCRs) Processed Unsuccessfully	Allows for tracking of failures related to processing client configuration requests (CCR).

Status Message Query	Description
Collections Created, Modified, or Deleted	Displays audit messages related to collection modification, displaying collections that have been modified or deleted and by whom.
Deployments Created, Modified, or Deleted	Displays audit messages related to creation, modification, and deletion of deployments.
Remote Control Activity Initiated by a Specific User	Shows the activity of any remote control sessions started by a specified user.
Server Component Configuration Changes	Tracks changes made to any of the myriad ConfigMgr server components.
Server Components Experiencing Fatal Errors	Shows fatal errors displayed by any Configuration Manager server component.

Summary

Queries are an excellent means of gathering data, testing results for collections, and understanding the requirements of creating reports. This chapter discussed using the ConfigMgr query builder to construct queries. It showed how to use advanced functions to create complex queries when the query builder does not suffice. This chapter covered the fundamentals of classes and operators to equip you to build your own queries. In addition, the chapter showed how to convert WQL to SQL, as well as examples of advanced queries, and it discussed creating status message queries.

20

CHAPTER 21

Configuration Manager Reporting

Reporting is often an overlooked feature in System Center Configuration Manager (ConfigMgr). Many ConfigMgr administrators focus on deploying operating systems, software updates, or applications. It is not until management asks questions such as "Who has Office 2010 installed?" or "What was the success rate for Office 2016 deployment?" that ConfigMgr's reporting capabilities are considered. ConfigMgr reporting then becomes important, and this is also where ConfigMgr shines. If you had to manually inventory and report on several thousand computers by walking to each computer and collecting its inventory, it would take days if not weeks to collect and report this information. However, performing this same task using ConfigMgr could take only several hours.

Configuration Manager allows you to collect vast amounts of information about your servers, computers, mobile devices, and users. However, displaying the information contained within the ConfigMgr database would not be possible without both SQL Server Reporting Services (SSRS) and the ConfigMgr Reporting Point (RP) role. While both SSRS and RP are optional components for a ConfigMgr environment, the authors strongly recommend that you install and configure them to leverage the built-in reports in ConfigMgr. After installing these components, you can also create custom reports to meet your organization's business needs.

Overview of SSRS and Configuration Manager Reporting

With the ConfigMgr RP installed, you have access to more than 400 built-in reports. These reports provide information regarding computer hardware, ConfigMgr site details, software licensing, and much more. The best part is that you do not need to access these reports with the ConfigMgr console; you can use a standard web browser.

Although many reports are available out of the box, at some point you will need additional information, either within an existing report or in a completely new one. This is when you will want to create your own reports to leverage the information collected by ConfigMgr. The next sections introduce you to SSRS, the ConfigMgr RP, and the optional features that are installed to enable ConfigMgr reporting.

Using SQL Server Reporting Services

SSRS is a server-based reporting platform that allows for comprehensive reports to be created and displayed to end users. In addition, SSRS allows you to schedule reports, enabling them to be saved to a file share or emailed to end users. The SSRS feature is typically installed on the SQL Server at the same time SQL Server is installed for ConfigMgr. For details about installing SSRS, access the SQL online books at https://docs.microsoft.com/sql/reporting-services/install-windows/install-reporting-services or see Chapter 1 of *System Center Configuration Manager Reporting Unleashed* (Sams Publishing, 2016).

Using the ConfigMgr Reporting Point Role

For ConfigMgr to leverage SSRS, you must install the ConfigMgr RP on the SSRS server. Prior to this, you must create an SSRS execution account, which SSRS uses to access the ConfigMgr database and schedule reports. The authors recommend that this account be used for SSRS only and that it be a low-rights user within Active Directory (AD). As part of the RP setup, the execution account is granted the appropriate permissions within both ConfigMgr and SSRS. Settings for the reporting point should look similar to Figure 21.1.

As part of the RP installation, the default ConfigMgr SSRS reports are created on the SSRS website. Because the appropriate security permissions are applied to each report during this time, this process can take several minutes to complete.

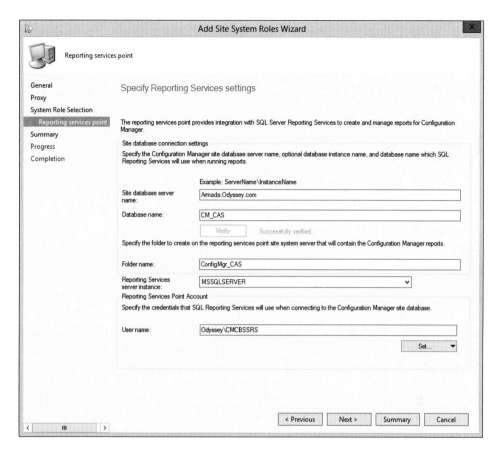

FIGURE 21.1   A completed Reporting services point page.

Notable Reporting Point Information

As a single chapter could not possibly cover all options for reporting point and report creation, the authors call attention to the following items:

▶ For performance reasons, the authors recommend that reports be accessed via the SSRS website rather than the ConfigMgr console. This reduces the workload on your ConfigMgr Site server and RP server. It also has an added benefit: You no longer need to install the ConfigMgr console for end users to only view reports.

▶ To help with troubleshooting report errors, enable Remote Errors on your SSRS website to gather more details about errors. For more information, see http://www.enhansoft.com/blog/turn-on-remote-error-reporting.

Understanding Configuration Manager Data

Before you can start writing reports for Confirmation Manager, you should understand where and how the information is stored within the ConfigMgr site database. The next sections introduce you to the locations of various types of information stored in the ConfigMgr database. They discuss how each SQL view relates to the ConfigMgr client and cover the most common SQL view classes. Following is where you can find Microsoft documentation on SQL schemas for the various versions of Configuration Manager:

▶ **ConfigMgr Current Branch:** At the time this book was published, Configuration Manager Current Branch version 1710, Microsoft had not released official SQL schemas. However, you can use the ConfigMgr 2012 and ConfigMgr 2007 schemas as a reference.

▶ **ConfigMgr 2012:** The ConfigMgr 2012 SQL schema can be referenced at http://technet.microsoft.com/library/dn581954.aspx.

▶ **ConfigMgr 2007:** Information on the ConfigMgr 2007 SQL schema is available at http://technet.microsoft.com/library/dd334611.aspx.

NOTE: MICROSOFT QUERY SUPPORT

Microsoft supports querying only from the SQL views. Directly querying the base SQL tables is unsupported, as the underlying table structure may change between versions of Configuration Manager.

Using Discovery Classes

The following ConfigMgr discovery tasks populate the SQL views that start with either `v_R_*` or `v_RA_*` (see Table 21.1):

▶ Active Directory System Discovery

▶ Active Directory User Discovery

▶ Heartbeat Discovery

▶ Network Discovery

For more information about ConfigMgr discovery, see Chapter 9, "Client Management."

TABLE 21.1   Discovery Data Views

SQL View	Description
v_R_System	Lists all systems discovered by ConfigMgr.
v_R_User	Lists all users discovered by ConfigMgr.
v_R_System_Valid	Lists all active clients within ConfigMgr. This is a subset of v_R_System.

Using Hardware Inventory Classes

You would think, based on the name alone, that hardware inventory classes would provide only details about the physical computer. This actually is not the case, as hardware inventory classes collect information from Windows Management Instrumentation (WMI) and the Windows Registry, as well as the actual hardware details for each ConfigMgr client. This class is therefore used within most queries, as it provides the widest range of information available about individual computers, from software installed to free disk space. ConfigMgr asset intelligence information falls into this class as well.

These inventory classes also maintain history data that you can use in your reports. No other inventory classes maintain history data. As a general rule, there are two SQL view name identifiers for these items:

▶ The SQL view names starting with v_GS_* identify the latest and current hardware inventory data.

▶ The v_HS_* views identify history data for the hardware inventory.

Table 21.2 and Table 21.3 provide listings of hardware data views.

TABLE 21.2   Current Hardware Data Views

SQL View	Description
v_GS_COMPUTER_SYSTEM	Lists basic details about a computer, such as manufacturer, model, and username.
v_GS_DISK	Provides details about hard drives attached to a computer.
v_GS_ADD_REMOVE_PROGRAMS	Provides details about 32-bit Add/Remove Programs data for computers.
v_GS_ADD_REMOVE_PROGRAMS_64	Provides details about 64-bit Add/Remove Programs data for computers.

TABLE 21.3   History Hardware Data Views

SQL View	Description
v_HS_COMPUTER_SYSTEM	Provides history data for the basic details of a computer.
v_HS_DISK	Provides history data for the hard drives attached to a computer.
v_HS_ADD_REMOVE_PROGRAMS	Provides history data for the 32-bit Add/Remove Programs data for computers.
v_HS_ADD_REMOVE_PROGRAMS_64	Provides history data for the 64-bit Add/Remove Programs data for computers.

In addition to these SQL views, there is one very important SQL view that does not follow the naming rules in this section: the v_ADD_REMOVE_PROGRAMS SQL view. This SQL view provides the combined details of the `v_GS_ADD_REMOVE_PROGRAMS` and `v_GS_ADD_REMOVE_PROGRAMS_64` views. This view is extremely helpful for viewing both 32-bit and 64-bit Add/Remove Programs entries.

ConfigMgr Software Inventory Classes

The software inventory class SQL views are mislabeled, as they do not provide a software inventory; they are actually file inventories. The software inventory provides header details about the files inventoried. This feature is not enabled by default, and even after being enabled, it must be configured in order for those files and locations to be inventoried. Unlike the other inventory methods, the authors generally do not recommend that this inventory method be enabled, due to its overhead and the limitations imposed. Limitations include the following:

▶ A four-hour runtime limit on the software inventory cycle before the inventory is terminated (without an error message returned to ConfigMgr)

▶ Incomplete inventory (Although it is not obvious, not all folders would be inventoried on a client due to file encryption, file security, deliberate exclusions by the ConfigMgr client, and so on.)

Table 21.4 lists the two SQL views where most information is located when this inventory collection method is enabled and configured correctly.

TABLE 21.4   Current Software Data Views

SQL View	Description
`v_GS_LastSoftwareScan`	Provides status details about the last software scan cycle.
`v_GS_SoftwareFile`	Provides details about all inventory files.

Using Software Update Inventory Classes

Software update details for a computer are found in the two SQL views listed in Table 21.5. It can be difficult to write software update SQL queries and correctly report the software update details. Care should be taken to confirm the results prior to creating a report.

TABLE 21.5   Software Update Data Views

SQL View	Description
`v_UpdateComplianceStatus`	Provides compliance status details for each PC's software update.
`v_CategoryInfo`	Provides details about software update categories.

About Software Metering Inventory Classes

Software metering is an optional component in ConfigMgr. Once enabled and configured, the ConfigMgr client can collect software usage information for the rules you configure. Software metering can help you understand the software being used in your environment. Table 21.6 lists the software metering data views.

TABLE 21.6   Software Metering Data Views

SQL View	Description
v_MeterData	Lists all gathered software metering data.
v_MeteredProductRule	Lists all software metering rules.

About Status Message Classes

Status messages provide details about the status of ConfigMgr client/server actions. For example, when a deployment is sent to a ConfigMgr client, the client sends a status message to the ConfigMgr server, saying that it has received the deployment notice. When the ConfigMgr client starts to download an application, it sends a status message indicating that the download has started. Table 21.7 lists the common status message classes.

TABLE 21.7   Status Message Data Views

SQL View	Description
v_StatusMessage	Provides status messages. This view is generally used in conjunction with v_StatMsgAttributes and v_StatMsgInsStrings to get the complete status message information.
v_StatMsgAttributes	Lists the attributes for a status message.
v_StatMsgInsStrings	Lists status messages.

About State Messages Classes

Similar to status messages, state messages provide the state of items such as client health, configuration items, and software updates. State messages are broken into topic types that identify the client component, and the StateID, which identifies a specific status for the component. Each topic type contains multiple state IDs. The v_StateName SQL view maps topic types and their respective state IDs to a descriptive state name. Table 21.8 lists the state message views.

TABLE 21.8   State Message Views

SQL View	Description
v_StateName	Maps topic types and their state IDs to descriptive names.
v_ClientHealthState	Provides the last client health state reported by ConfigMgr clients.
v_CIAssignmentStatus	Provides the evaluation state messages for assigned configuration items (CIs).
v_UpdateComplianceStatus	Provides the compliance state for software updates scanned by ConfigMgr clients.

Using Collection Data Classes

Table 21.9 lists the collection data classes, which are popular SQL views because most objects (users, computers, mobile device, and AD security groups) in ConfigMgr are listed within collections. These SQL views are generally used to limit the results to a particular collection.

TABLE 21.9   Collection Data Views

SQL View	Description
v_Collection	Lists all collections and the CollectionID of each one.
v_FullCollectionMembership	Lists the membership of each collection (user account/computer/security group).

Introducing Transact-SQL

SQL Server uses Transact-SQL, also referred to as SQL or T-SQL, to query SQL databases. The language will be familiar to many ConfigMgr administrators, as it is the parent language to WMI Query Language (WQL), which is used to create collections in ConfigMgr.

It is important to have a good understanding of how to create T-SQL queries, as a poorly designed query can be a significant impact on a SQL database. This section provides basic information about T-SQL and discusses how to execute a T-SQL query prior to using the query in a report. This section only covers the basics needed for creating reports; be aware that there is significantly more to T-SQL than what is discussed in this chapter.

Introducing SQL Server Management Studio

A number of tools are available for executing T-SQL queries against a SQL database; the most popular one is SQL Server Management Studio, introduced in Chapter 3, "Looking Inside Configuration Manager." This GUI tool allows you to interface with SQL Server and execute queries against the ConfigMgr database. As a best practice, you should not execute T-SQL queries against a production database; use a copy of the ConfigMgr database or execute queries in your development environment. Avoiding running against production helps prevent any issues that might arise from poorly written T-SQL queries. The authors also recommend that SQL Server Management Studio be installed locally on ConfigMgr administrators' workstations when they need to create reports, as Microsoft does not recommend building or creating queries and reports on your ConfigMgr site server. This allows the ConfigMgr administrator the option of using a copy of the database on his or her local computer or connecting to the development environment.

To get started with SQL Server Management Studio, launch the tool, log on to your ConfigMgr SQL Server, and then change the database to the ConfigMgr database.

Basic SQL Sections in a Query

SQL queries are composed of four major sections:

- ▶ SELECT
- ▶ FROM
- ▶ WHERE
- ▶ ORDER BY

These sections form the basic core of a SQL query. Not all these sections are mandatory to obtain results from a query; however, they are recommended to produce clear and easy-to-read results.

To help better explain each section, Listing 21.1 shows the breakdown of these sections.

LISTING 21.1   SQL Query to Locate All Computers Within the Odyssey Domain

```
SELECT
  RV.Netbios_Name0,
  RV.Operating_System_Name_and0,
  RV.AD_Site_Name0
FROM
  dbo.v_R_System RV
WHERE
  RV.Resource_Domain_OR_Workgr0 = 'Odyssey'
ORDER BY
  RV.Netbios_Name0,
  RV.Operating_System_Name_and0,
  RV.AD_Site_Name0
```

Using the SELECT Statement

A T-SQL query starts with the SELECT section. This section indicates the columns within a SQL view(s) that will be included in the results of your query.

Listing 21.2 shows the lines comprising the SELECT section. The Netbios_Name0, Operating_System_Name_and0, and AD_Site_Name0 columns are identified in Listing 21.2. Notice that they are separated by commas.

LISTING 21.2   SELECT Section of a T-SQL Query

```
SELECT
  RV.Netbios_Name0,
  RV.Operating_System_Name_and0,
  RV.AD_Site_Name0
```

About the FROM Statement

The FROM section tells SQL Server Management Studio where in the ConfigMgr database to find the information used within the query, as shown in Listing 21.3. It is also in the FROM section that you can join multiple SQL views together by defining a common column between the SQL views.

LISTING 21.3   FROM Section of a T-SQL Query

```
FROM
  dbo.v_R_System RV
```

The WHERE Statement

The WHERE section is an optional section in a T-SQL query that T-SQL uses to limit the results of the query. This is useful when you want to see just a small portion of the information. The sample query in Listing 21.4 limits the results to displaying only computers with the computer domain 'Odyssey' instead of all computers.

LISTING 21.4   WHERE Section of a T-SQL Query

```
WHERE
  RV.Resource_Domain_OR_Workgr0 = 'Odyssey'
```

Using ORDER BY

The T-SQL section shown in Listing 21.5 allows for the column results to be sorted; the default sort order is alphabetical. Sorting the results makes them easier to read. Very much like the WHERE statement, this is an optional component. For performance reasons, the authors recommend that sorting be done within T-SQL on the server rather than within reports.

LISTING 21.5   ORDER BY Section of a T-SQL Query

```
ORDER BY
  RV.Netbios_Name0,
  RV.Operating_System_Name_and0,
  RV.AD_Site_Name0
```

Using Operators

With any computer language, there are a number of operators that allow you to perform operations on SQL data. T-SQL is no exception; Table 21.10 lists the common SQL operators.

TABLE 21.10   Common SQL Operators

Operator	Description
+	Addition
−	Subtraction
*	Multiplication

Operator	Description
/	Division
=	Equals
>	Greater than
<	Less than
%	String wildcard, used in LIKE statements
AND	Logical AND, identifies multiple conditions that must be met
OR	Logical OR, identifies multiple conditions where one must be met
NOT	Logical NOT, opposite of the value or condition
LIKE	Logical LIKE, value matches a portion or pattern, used with wildcards
IN	Logical IN, equal to one of a list of values

TIP: COMPLETE LIST OF OPERATORS

For a complete list of available operators, see the "Operators (T-SQL)" section in the T-SQL online help, available at https://docs.microsoft.com/sql/t-sql/language-elements/operators-transact-sql.

Building a Report Design

This section discusses the importance of report design, styles, and consistency throughout your reports. These concepts are important as following them can help you project a professional look and feel for all your reports. If your reports lack a consistent look and feel, they appear disjointed and, therefore, unprofessional.

The key to ensuring a useful report or dashboard is to ensure that you are consistent with report styles and appearance. When you take time to ensure that you are consistent—with your T-SQL query, the report style, with colors and fonts, and even with report titles—your reports can't help but look and feel professional.

About Report Series

As a general rule, there is a flow to reports and dashboards:

▶ You start by creating a summary report or dashboard that shows the overall status of what it is you are reporting.

▶ You then allow the users to drill though to a list report that provides more details about the computers or objects.

▶ Finally, you drill through to the details about the specific computer or object.

This flow provides a natural progression from summary information to full details for a computer. In report terminology, this would be the Dashboard/Count, List, and Details report types.

Following is an example of a sample report series:

▶ **Overall Software Update Status:** This count report (dashboard) shows the overall software update status for a company.

▶ **List of PCs by Missing Software Updates:** This report provides a list of computers missing one or more software updates.

▶ **Software Update Details for a Computer:** This report shows a detailed list of all software updates for a specific computer.

Incorporating a general report series design provides value for everyone from your chief technology officer (CTO) to your help desk staff. Here's how:

▶ The CTO can see high-level information needed to make upgrade/purchase decisions about the environment.

▶ The service desk manager can drill down to see additional details such as the computers or users that will be affected.

▶ A frontline service desk technologist can view what software products are installed on a specific computer he or she is troubleshooting or upgrading.

Creating Consistent Reports

Designing consistent-appearing reports ensures that your dashboards and reports look professional. While it might seem like a lot of work initially to make sure all your reports look similar, the payback comes when users actually use your reports. Figure 21.2 shows the areas where you should be consistent with your reports. Table 21.11 provides details about the options to use for your reports to appear consistent, with the numbers in the table corresponding to the numbers in Figure 21.2.

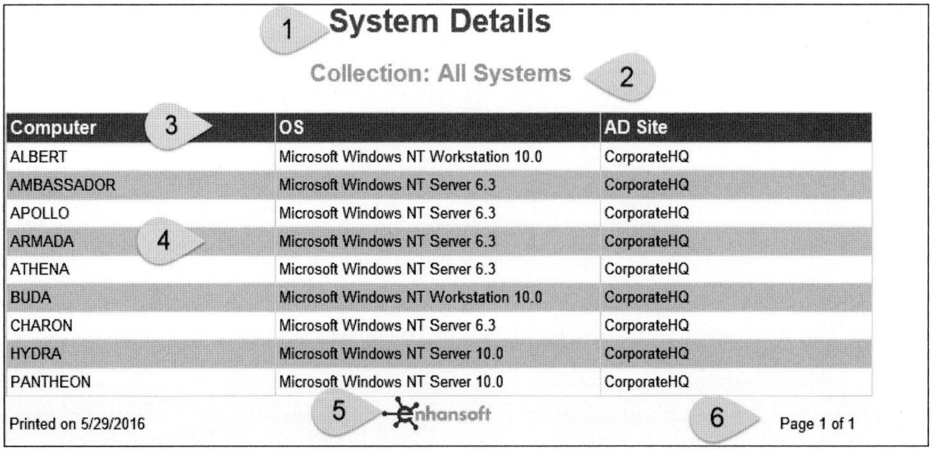

FIGURE 21.2   Report style locations.

TABLE 21.11   Consistent Report Options

Item	Object	Elements
1	Header	Text Color, Font, Size, Background Color
2	Sub-Header	Text Color, Font, Size, Background Color
3	Table Header	Text Color, Font, Size, Background Color
4	Row	Text Color, Font, Size, Alternating Row Colors
5	Logo	Image Type, Size, URL
6	Footer	What should be included in the footer, including Page Number, Logo, Date & Time, Background Color, and so on.

The authors suggest that when you define style guides for your reports, you should start with your company's graphic designer or webmaster. These individuals should be able to provide you with your organization's style guide. If your company does not have a graphic designer or webmaster, use Table 21.11 to define your own report style guide.

Building a Basic Report

This section discusses a number of items, from report design to creating a basic report. It begins by discussing report creation tools and then moves on to report design and then finally to creating a report.

Understanding how to build a basic report is important, as this report type is the foundation on which all reports are created. It does not matter if the report is a simple report or a very complex dashboard with multiple distinct areas. Much as you need a strong foundation for a house, you need to have a good understanding of how to create a basic report, or you will have difficulty creating complex reports.

Tools for Creating Reports

Two primary tools exist to create SSRS reports for ConfigMgr:

▶ SQL Server Data Tools-Business Intelligence (SSDT-BI) for Visual Studio 2013

▶ Report Builder

These tools are also used to design SSRS reports for other System Center products, such as Operations Manager and Service Manager. All examples in this chapter use SSDT-BI 2014 for Visual Studio 2013, which the authors suggest you use for creating reports. Table 21.12 lists some of the reasons for this recommendation.

TABLE 21.12   Comparing SSDT and Report Builder

SSDT	Report Builder
Can open and work on multiple reports at one time.	Only able to work on a single report at once.
Can cut/copy and paste between reports.	Because only one report can be open at once, copy and paste is not available.
Can easily create drill-down links in reports.	Although it is possible to create drill-down links, it is very cumbersome.
Can control every feature and setting within the report.	Some features are missing and cannot be modified or controlled in Report Builder.

Note that there are multiple versions of report authoring tools available, including several versions of SSDT and Business Intelligence Development Studio (BIDS), as well as multiple versions of the Report Builder tool. It can be challenging to understand report compatibility for the different versions of Reporting Services. Table 21.13 identifies the different SSRS versions and their compatible Report Definition Language (RDL), generated from the various tools. It is important to create reports using a tool that generates files supporting the installed SSRS version in your environment.

TABLE 21.13   SSRS-Compatible Reports

SSRS Version	SSDT and BIDS Versions	Report Builder Versions
SQL Server 2016	SSDT-BI 2016 for Visual Studio 2015 SSDT-BI 2014 for Visual Studio 2013 SSDT-BI 2012 for Visual Studio 2012 BIDS 2008 R2 or BIDS 2008 or BIDS 2005	Report Builder 1.0, 2.0, 3.0
SQL Server 2014	SSDT-BI 2014 for Visual Studio 2013 SSDT-BI 2012 for Visual Studio 2012 BIDS 2008 R2 or BIDS 2008 or BIDS 2005	Report Builder 1.0, 2.0, 3.0
SQL Server 2012	SSDT-BI 2014 for Visual Studio 2013 SSDT-BI 2012 for Visual Studio 2012 BIDS 2008 R2 BIDS 2008 BIDS 2005	Report Builder 1.0, 2.0, 3.0
SQL Server 2008 R2	SSDT-BI 2014 for Visual Studio 2013 SSDT-BI 2012 for Visual Studio 2012 BIDS 2008 R2 BIDS 2008 BIDS 2005	Report Builder 1.0, 2.0, 3.0
SQL Server 2008	BIDS 2008 BIDS 2005	Report Builder 1.0, 2.0

Getting Started with SSDT-BI

Before creating your first SSRS report, you need to create a project (or a project within a solution) in SSDT-BI. Perform the following steps to create a new project for a fictional company named Odyssey:

1. From the Windows Start menu, navigate to **Microsoft SQL Server 2014 -> SQL Server Data Tools for Visual Studio 2013**.

2. At the Microsoft Visual Studio start page, click **File -> New -> Project** to create a new project.

3. In the New Project window, shown in Figure 21.3, select **Report Server Project** from the Business Intelligence node under Templates. At the bottom of the window, enter a name for the project—which automatically populates the Solution name field—and specify a location to store the project.

   Notice that the Create directory for solution check box is checked by default. This option creates a folder under the location you have specified to contain the project files, configuration, and reports. Click **OK** to create the project.

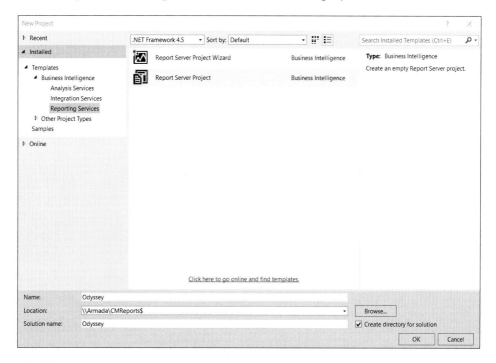

FIGURE 21.3   Creating a report project.

> **TIP: RECOMMENDED PROJECT LOCATION**
>
> The authors recommend storing your project on a network share where all ConfigMgr administrators and report creators can access the project. This enables all report creators to share already created reports as well as report templates.
>
> The authors also suggest including this network share in any backup solution to ensure that it is recoverable if the data is lost or corrupt.

4. Once the project is created, add a new shared data source. Under the Solution Explorer window, on the top-right side of the Visual Studio window, right-click **Shared Data Sources** and select **Add New Data Source**.

5. On the Shared Data Source Properties window, specify a name for the shared data source and click **Edit** to configure a connection string.

6. In the Connection Properties window, specify the server name of the server containing the ConfigMgr database and then use the dropdown to specify the ConfigMgr database name under the **Select or enter a database name** field.

7. Click **Test Connection** to ensure that the connection is successful and then click **OK** to close the Connection Properties window.

8. Confirm that the settings for the shared data source properties are correct and click **OK**.

After the solution/project and share data source have been created, they can be used by multiple reports moving forward. This is where SSDT-BI shines: It allows you to work on multiple reports at the same time or just copy and paste between reports to reduce duplication of effort.

Creating a Basic Report

With the prerequisites in place, you can create reports and dashboards based on your needs. Use the following steps to create a report:

1. From the Solutions Explorer window, on the far right side of SSDT, right-click the **Reports** folder and select **Add -> New Item**.

2. In the Add New Item window, select **Report** from the list of items, specify a name for the report, such as **System Details**, and click **Add**.

The center window of SSDT now contains a new blank report that is ready to be populated.

Creating a Data Source

In order for a report to query the ConfigMgr database, the report must know which shared data source to use. You identify this by linking the project shared data source to the report itself. Follow these steps to create a data source within the report:

1. In the Report Data window, on the left side of SSDT, right-click the **Data Sources** folder and select **Add Data Source** (see Figure 21.4).

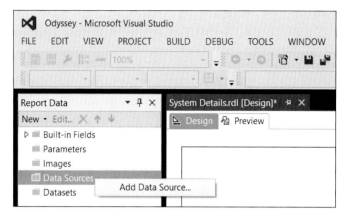

FIGURE 21.4   Selecting **Add Data Source**.

2. In the Data Source Properties window, specify a name for the data source and select **Use shared data source reference**. From the dropdown, select the shared data source added in the Getting Started with SSDT-BI section (**OdysseyReportDS**) and click **OK**.

Creating a Dataset

After the data source is linked to the shared data source, you need to create a dataset. The dataset is where you insert the T-SQL query that you created for this report. A report can have more than one dataset; for example, you might have one dataset to populate a prompt and another dataset for the report itself. Follow these steps to create a dataset:

1. In the Report Data window, on the left side of SSDT, right-click the **Datasets** folder and select **Add Dataset** (see Figure 21.5).

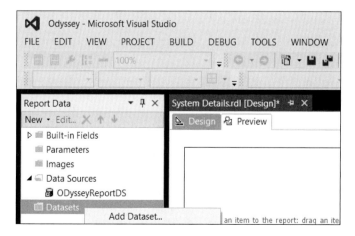

FIGURE 21.5   Adding a dataset.

2. In the Dataset Properties window, specify a name for the dataset and then select **Use a dataset embedded in my report**. From the **Data source** dropdown, select the data source you created in the "Creating a Data Source" section of this chapter. In the **Query** field, paste the query previously created in SQL Server Management Studio. (This example uses the query in Listing 21.1, 21list01_System Details.sql, which is included in the online content for this book. For additional information, see Appendix D, "Available Online.") Click **OK** to create the dataset.

Accessing the Toolbox

On the far left side of SSDT is the Toolbox menu, which includes items such as tables, charts, and text boxes. By default, the Toolbox menu is automatically hidden when not in use, and it is displayed only when you click the tab shown in Figure 21.6. You can use the pin feature to pin open the toolbox while working on a report.

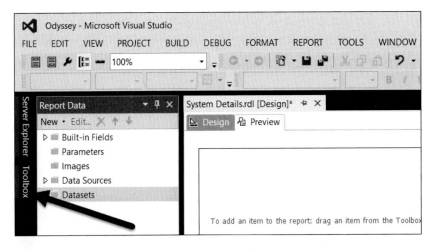

FIGURE 21.6   Opening the Toolbox menu to display report items.

Many report items are available to add to your reports:

▶ **Pointer:** The pointer is the default selected item when using SSDT. This is the simple mouse pointer that allows you to select items within a report.

▶ **Textbox:** This item allows you to enter simple text for your report, such as a label, or specify expressions to be populated when the report is executed, such as the current date or page number.

▶ **Line:** The line item adds a simple line to your report for visual effect. It can be used to separate sections or information.

▶ **Table:** The table item is similar to the properties of an Excel spreadsheet. In an SSDT table, you can group data together, identify header columns and rows, and more. Tables are some of the most popular items used in reporting.

▶ **Matrix:** A matrix is a special type of table similar to a pivot table in Microsoft Excel. Data in a matrix can be grouped together and can grow both by columns and rows.

▶ **Rectangle:** The rectangle item allows you to group other report objects together and treat them as a single object within a report.

▶ **List:** A list is a grouping of report items. It allows you to add items from other reports in the list and display them in free form instead of within a grid.

▶ **Image:** The image item allows you to import images or pictures into a report. This item is commonly used to display a company logo in the header or footer sections of a report.

▶ **Subreport:** This item allows you to embed another report within the current report. The body section of the targeted report will be displayed within this item when the report is executed.

▶ **Chart:** This item creates a chart within the report to represent your data. Various kinds of charts that can be selected, such as a bar, line, pie, or pyramid charts.

▶ **Gauge:** The gauge item can display a value, an expression, or a field in either a radial or linear type of gauge. Gauges are similar to charts; however, they are intended to display summary data.

▶ **Map:** This item allows you to display data against a map. There are two types of map charts:

   ▶ **Marker Map:** This type of map allows you to pinpoint a location.

   ▶ **Bubble Map:** A bubble map shows the number of items for a given area.

▶ **Data Bar:** This item displays a visual indicator of a value. It tends to be used within a table item.

▶ **Sparkline:** Similar to a data bar, a sparkline is often used within a table. This is a miniature line chart without any labels.

▶ **Indicator:** An indicator is similar to a gauge; it displays minimal information so that at a quick glance, a user can determine the value that is represented. In most cases, indicators are used within tables.

Adding a Table to a Report

In most cases, the results of a report query (dataset) are displayed as either a table or chart within a report. This section shows you how to add a table to a report.

Tables can be used to display the results of a query (dataset) in a report. Within the table, you can add the individual columns you want to display. When the report is executed, the query results populate the table item. Follow these steps to add a table and populate the query columns to the report:

   1. From the toolbox, drag the table item to the blank report. Notice that, by default, the table item creates three columns, as displayed in Figure 21.7.

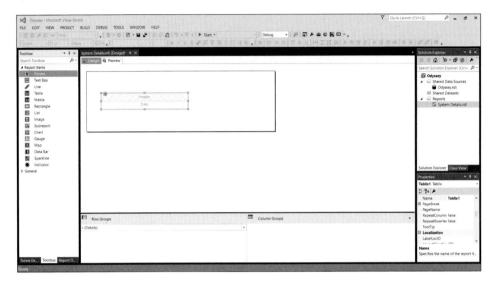

FIGURE 21.7   A table item added to a report.

2. Now add the dataset to the table. In the Report Data window, expand the **Datasets**
   folder and expand the dataset you created (in this case, SystemDetailsDS). Drag each
   column from the dataset into the corresponding column in the table. When this is
   complete, your table will be similar to the one shown in Figure 21.8.

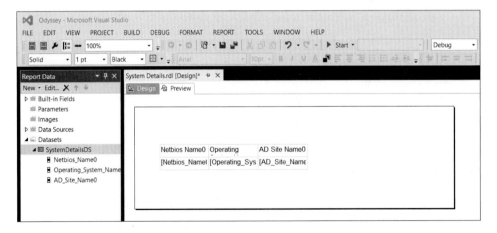

FIGURE 21.8   Dataset columns added to a table item in a report.

3. With the dataset added to the table item, you can properly format the table. To do
   so, make the following changes to the table:

   ▶ Modify the labels of the headers in the first row to appropriate titles that represent
     the data. Accomplish this by double-clicking each header cell and replacing the
     text Netbios Name0, Operating System Name and0, and AD Site Name0.

▶ Set the font style of the header row to **bold**.

▶ Adjust the widths of the table columns to an appropriate size for the data to be displayed. Avoid cutting off information or having the row expand vertically to fit the data output.

▶ Adjust the table size to have it stretch the width of the entire page—but ensure that it does not affect the width of the page. The page width should not exceed 8 inches.

Previewing a Report

SSDT-BI lets you preview a report to see how it will look on your SSRS server. To preview a report, perform the following steps:

1. Click **Preview** (see Figure 21.9) at the top of the report to view the end product. The preview action executes the query in the dataset and populates the report items with data.

2. Ensure that everything displays as intended and that the columns are appropriate widths, such that no information is cut off or missing. If additional changes are required, make any necessary adjustments and preview your report again to ensure that those items are resolved. To return to Design mode after previewing is complete, click **Design** at the top of the report.

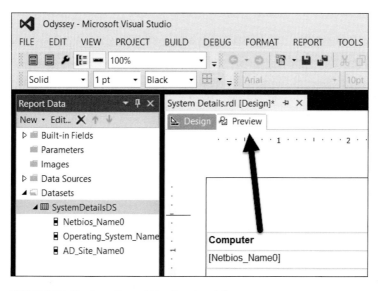

FIGURE 21.9   Location of the Preview tab.

Publishing a Report

Once you have created a report, you can publish it to the ConfigMgr folder on your SSRS server. It takes approximately 10 minutes for ConfigMgr to evaluate the new report and make it available within the console. The authors recommend that reports be accessed from the website instead of the console for performance reasons, as discussed earlier in this chapter, in the "Notable Reporting Point Information" section. Using the SSRS website also allows non-ConfigMgr administrators to access a report without the need to access the ConfigMgr console.

There are two methods to publish a report: manually adding a report to SSRS and publishing a report from SSDT-BI to the SSRS website. These are discussed in the following sections.

Manually Adding a Report to SSRS

A simple method of adding a report to SSRS is to manually browse to the SSRS website and upload a report by browsing for the .rdl file. The downside of this method is that it allows you to upload only one report at a time. To manually add a report to the SSRS website, follow these steps:

1. Open a web browser and browse to your SSRS report website, **http://armada/Reports**.

2. On the SQL Server Reporting Services home page, click the ConfigMgr Reporting Services Point folder (**ConfigMgr_CAS**). You now see a list of ConfigMgr folders, which were created during the installation of the reporting services point in ConfigMgr. These contain the out-of-box reports.

3. Create a new folder to store your custom created reports by clicking **New Folder**.

4. Specify a name for the new folder and click **OK**. A description for the folder can also be specified, although it is not required.

5. From the list of folders, click the folder created in step 4.

6. In the new folder, click **Upload File**. In the Upload File page, click **Browse** next to the **File to upload** field. Browse to your SSDT project location, select a report RDL file to upload, and then click **Open**. The Name field for the report is populated by default with the name of the RDL file, and it can be changed if desired. Click **OK** to upload the selected report.

7. When you are redirected to the folder view where the report was uploaded, click the newly added report to execute it.

8. When you receive the error shown in Figure 21.10, indicating that the shared data source is not valid for use from the SSRS website, resolve this error by updating the report's data source in the properties of the report on the website. To do this, go back to the folder view, hover the cursor over the report name, click the downward-pointing arrow that appears, and select **Manage**, as shown in Figure 21.11.

FIGURE 21.10   SSRS invalid source error.

FIGURE 21.11   Editing the properties of a report by selecting the **Manage** option.

9. In the report's properties page, select the **Data Sources** tab from the left pane. Click **Browse** next to the **Select a shared data source** option. Under the location field, expand the ConfigMgr folder, scroll to the bottom of the list, and select the data source item (the last item identified by the long unique ID between curly braces), as shown in Figure 21.12. Click **OK**.

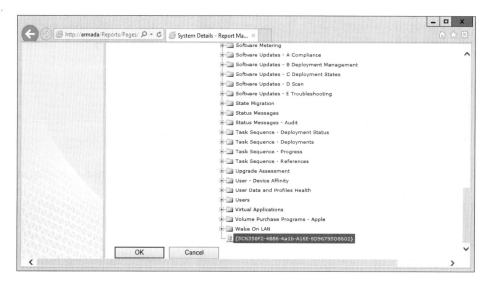

FIGURE 21.12   Selecting the data source item from the list and clicking **OK**.

10. Back in the Data Sources page, click **Apply** at the bottom of the page to save the changes.

11. To test the changes and run the report, click the report name at the top of the page or go back to the folder view and click the report. Confirm that the report now runs without errors and displays properly.

12. To add additional reports now that you have created a folder, repeat steps 6 through 11.

Publishing Reports from SSDT to the SSRS Website

Manually adding each individual report to the SSRS website may be acceptable when you have a small number of reports; however, it can be time-consuming when there are dozens of custom created reports. SSDT provides an option to publish reports directly to the SSRS website; it refers to this process as *deploying*. Perform the following steps to configure the required deployment options and publish reports from SSDT without having to manually upload each report:

1. In SSDT, open the SSRS project that contains your custom reports.

2. From the SSDT menu at the top, select **PROJECT** and click **Properties**, shown in Figure 21.13.

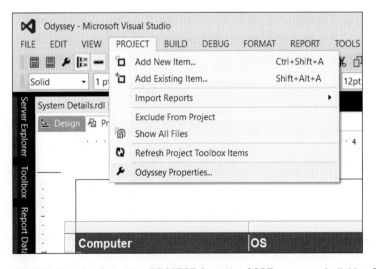

FIGURE 21.13   Selecting **PROJECT** from the SSDT menu and clicking **Properties**.

3. In the project's properties page, click **Configuration Manager** at the top right of the page.

4. In the Configuration Manager page, in the Configuration column of the project row, use the dropdown list to change the value to **Release**, as shown in Figure 21.14. Ensure that the Build and Deploy column values are checked and click **Close**.

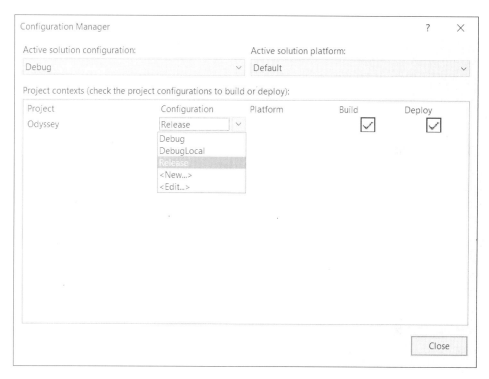

FIGURE 21.14   Setting the project configuration to **Release**.

5. In the properties page, under the Deployment section, enter the SSRS virtual directory URL under the TargetServerURL value. For this example, the value is **http://armada/ReportServer**. Optionally, to set the folder in SSRS to store your reports, set the folder path as the TargetReportFolder value. The value is set to **ConfigMgr_CAS/Odyssey** to store the reports under the same folder created in the "Manually Adding a Report to SSRS" section, earlier in this chapter. Click **OK** when complete as shown in Figure 21.15 to apply your changes, and then close the Property window.

TIP: TARGETSERVERURL VALUE

To get the proper TargetServerURL value, find the web service URL in the Reporting Services configuration on the SSRS server. By default, this path is http://<servername>/ReportServer.

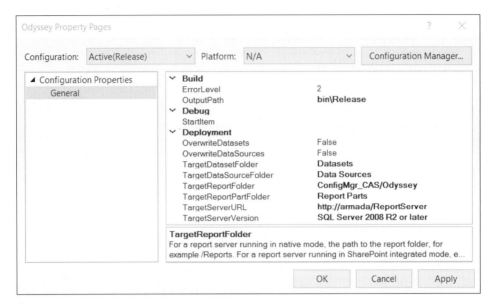

FIGURE 21.15   Completed properties page for deploying reports.

6. Before publishing a report to SSRS, you must publish the shared data source created in SSDT. To publish the data source, expand the Shared Data Source folder in the Solution Explorer window, right-click the .rds object, and select **Deploy**.

7. When the shared data source is deployed to SSRS, right-click a report in the Solution Explorer window and select **Deploy**.

8. To confirm that the report is deployed, use a web browser to navigate to the SSRS website and browse to the folder identified in the TargetReportFolder value from step 5. Verify that the report is listed in the folder and runs successfully, without errors.

TIP: DEPLOYING AN ENTIRE PROJECT

Rather than deploying one report at a time, you can deploy an entire project to SSRS by right-clicking the project name in the Solution Explorer and selecting **Deploy**. All shared data sources and all reports will be published to SSRS. Once all reports are deployed, any actions set on objects to go to a report will function as they did in SSDT Preview mode.

NOTE: PUBLISHING REPORTS WITH SSDT

Using the deployment method described in this section means your custom reports are *not* using the default ConfigMgr data source. You must therefore update this data source any time the execution account username and password change. Alternatively, you could manually reset all reports to use the default ConfigMgr data source, as outlined in steps 6–10 in the "Manually Adding a Report to SSRS" section, earlier in this chapter.

Advanced Reporting Concepts

There are many aspects to creating reports for ConfigMgr SSRS; this chapter only touches on the basics of writing ConfigMgr SSRS reports. Considerably more could be discussed but, due to space limitations, could not be included in this book. The following are some Advanced Reporting topics you might want to explore:

▶ Installing SSRS

▶ Installing the ConfigMgr RP

▶ Additional SQL details:

  ▶ Explaining More operators (DISTINCT, GROUP BY, and so on)

  ▶ Explaining SQL functions (COUNT, MAX, MIN, GETDATE, CASE, and so on)

  ▶ Explaining SQL joins (LEFT OUTER JOIN, RIGHT OUTER JOIN, and so on)

  ▶ Providing Examples for the various configuration items

▶ Installing SSDT-BI and SQL Server Management Studio tools

▶ More in-depth discussion on report series

▶ Additional SSRS report features:

  ▶ Adding prompts to a report

  ▶ Interactive sorting

  ▶ Report templates

  ▶ Report drillthrough

  ▶ Custom color palettes

  ▶ Custom code in an SSRS report

▶ SSRS website features:

  ▶ Emailing reports

  ▶ Exporting reports

▶ Role-based administration (RBA) and reporting

  ▶ How to update an existing T-SQL query to become an RBA query

  ▶ Updating reports for RBA

  ▶ Creating RBA roles within ConfigMgr for reporting

▶ Troubleshooting tips

All these topics and more are covered in the deep dive provided by *System Center Configuration Manager Reporting Unleashed* (Sams Publishing, 2016).

TIP: BEST PRACTICES

Following are some best practices when creating reports:

► Use only SQL views within your T-SQL queries.

► Use SSDT-BI to create reports and dashboards.

► Create a common look and feel for reports and dashboards.

Summary

ConfigMgr provides a number of reports; however, they never seem to answer the questions asked by management, service desk managers, and end users. Therefore, being able to create meaningful custom reports is truly beneficial to any company.

This chapter touched on where information can be found in the ConfigMgr database. It discussed the basic structure of a T-SQL query that can be used in ConfigMgr SSRS reports. It also discussed the importance of a report series and having a consistent report look and feel to provide more professional ConfigMgr reports. The chapter showed that by using SSDT-BI, you can create meaningful custom reports that will benefit your management, service desk managers, and end users. This chapter also showed how to publish reports to ConfigMgr.

CHAPTER 22

Operating System Deployment

One of an organization's most difficult information technology (IT) tasks is managing operating systems (OSs); this includes upgrading to new versions, migrating to new hardware, performing clean installs, and more. To help address these needs, Microsoft includes operating system deployment (OSD) components in System Center Configuration Manager (ConfigMgr). ConfigMgr first included OSD components with ConfigMgr 2007. OSD was refined in ConfigMgr 2012 and continues to be enhanced with ConfigMgr Current Branch to meet today's many needs from an OSD perspective.

OSD involves delivering a mass deployment of a new instance of the Windows OS to compatible devices. While that may seem simple, due to the philosophy and architecture of Windows, it is not always as easy as it sounds. Mass delivery of the Windows OS is nothing new; enterprises have been creating an image of a single system and copying it to other systems since Windows became the de facto standard OS for businesses.

Following are some reasons OSD is the tool to use for this task:

▶ OSD is about automating the entire process, from image creation and image maintenance to actual image deployment.

▶ OSD is not just about creating and deploying an image. It is an entire process that allows you to define actions before the image is applied to a system. This includes partitioning and formatting the drive or even BIOS upgrades and actions after applying the image, such as software update installation or application deployment.

▶ OSD is dynamic, enabling different yet automatic deployment time behavior based on an unbounded set of criteria, including hardware type, location, and intended user or system roles.

▶ OSD is extensible to meet the needs of any organization. The Microsoft Deployment Toolkit (MDT) and its subset feature, User Driven Installation (UDI), are excellent examples of this extensibility.

▶ OSD is integrated into ConfigMgr, enabling you to utilize the other powerful features of the product, including software distribution, software updates, and reporting, all from a single management console in a seamless manner.

This chapter covers OSD in depth, including applicable scenarios, detailed use, guidance, best practices, and troubleshooting. This single chapter cannot and does not cover the complete range of information and knowledge required to deploy Windows fully in an enterprise environment, nor does it cover supplemental tools such as MDT.

What's New with OSD in Current Branch

While OSD has not changed much from its original concept, each new version of ConfigMgr fixes issues, adds new features, and has tweaks to code so that it performs better. These new features give OSD a rich set of commands, variables, and task sequence (TS) items. The following items are new to ConfigMgr Current Branch:

▶ **Upgrade an Operating System from an Upgrade Package:** This TS type, found in the Create Task Sequence Wizard, creates steps to upgrade systems from Windows 7, 8, and 8.1 to Windows 10.

▶ **WinPE Peer Cache:** This allows systems running a TS to download content from a local peer machine while in Windows Preinstallation Environment (WinPE).

▶ **Windows 10 Servicing:** While not completely an OSD item, Windows 10 servicing allows you to upgrade Windows 10 devices from one version of the Semi-Annual Channel to another version, using the software updates feature. For a complete overview of this process, which can help keep your Windows 10 devices current, see Chapter 15, "Managing Software Updates."

▶ **Evaluate Software Updates from Cached Scan Results:** This is a check box in the Install Software Updates TS step. If it is unchecked, the system can connect to the software update point (SUP) and download the latest software updates catalog to scan against and determine what software updates are needed.

▶ **The `SMSTSSoftwareUpdateScanTimeout` Variable:** This TS variable controls the timeout for the software updates scan during the install software updates TS step.

▶ **`OSDPreserveDriveLetter` Variable Has Been Deprecated:** This TS variable allowed you to choose the drive letter to use during OSD; this is now automatically determined by Windows Setup.

▶ **Customize the RamDisk TFTP Window Size:** You can customize the window size for the RamDisk Trivial File Transfer Protocol (TFTP) when using Preboot eXecution Environment (PXE), so you can optimize the traffic across the network.

▶ **The `TSUEFIDrive` Variable:** This variable allows you to customize an OSD TS so the restart computer step prepares a FAT32 partition on the hard drive for transition to Unified Extensible Firmware Interface (UEFI).

▶ **Prepare ConfigMgr Client for Capture TS Step:** This step now completely removes the Configuration Manager client instead of only removing key information.

▶ **Secure Boot Information Is Now Collected with Hardware Inventory:** There is a new WMI class called `SMS_Firmware`, which allows ConfigMgr to collect the UEFI and secure boot information from machines that have these newer updates to their hardware. This class is enabled by default in the hardware inventory classes.

▶ **Collapsible Task Sequence Groups:** This new item allows you to collapse or expand groups with a TS. This can be a big benefit for large TSs with many groups inside them. Collapsing allows the user to more easily focus on specific areas of the TS. The groups can be expanded or collapsed all at once with buttons at the top of the TS, or they can be expanded or collapsed individually with the plus (+) or minus (-) on the left-hand side of the TS.

▶ **Reload Boot Images with the Current WinPE Version:** The 1706 version of ConfigMgr Current Branch provides the option to reload the latest version of WinPE installed on the machine with the Windows Assessment and Deployment Kit (ADK) when you update your distribution points (DPs). When choosing to update the boot image on the DPs, a new wizard page is displayed that shows the current version of the boot image, OS version, and ConfigMgr client version, as well as the installed version of the ADK. To update to the newer ADK version, select the check box at the bottom of the screen, and the boot image will be updated using the ADK version that is installed.

OSD Deployment Scenarios

Microsoft defines four Windows deployment scenarios, which generally encompass how to deploy Windows to any organization. Minor variations are possible, and implementation details may vary depending on the tools used or your deployment goals. These are the four scenarios:

▶ **Upgrade:** Involves an in-place upgrade of the current OS to a new OS. It preserves user data and applications, and some consider it the best choice when moving an organization to a new OS. The downside is it preserves misconfigurations, unauthorized software, and any existing malware.

▶ **New Computer:** This name is a little misleading as it can apply to new systems out of the box or to those that are being completely reloaded. Its distinguishing factor is that any user data and applications on an existing system are ignored. Often referred to as *bare-metal* or *wipe-and-load*, this scenario assumes that nothing on the system is valid, and the system should be built from scratch or bare metal.

▶ **Refresh:** Involves installing a fresh, new OS on an existing system while preserving applicable user data and reinstalling authorized applications—in effect refreshing just the OS. This reload can result in a variety of situations:

▶ The version of Windows is updated from an older version to a newer version.

▶ The current OS installation is broken beyond repair.

▶ The OS installation does not meet current standards.

TIP: CONFUSING UPGRADE AND REFRESH SCENARIOS

The upgrade and refresh scenarios sound similar and even have similar results; however, they are very different. The upgrade scenario literally runs setup.exe in the existing OS, with Windows Setup upgrading the OS in-place. The refresh scenario backs up the user data, wipes the disk (not necessarily formatting it), installs a clean version of Windows, and adds back the user data.

▶ **Replace:** While similar to the refresh scenario, the replace scenario involves replacing the physical system. It also preserves applicable user data and reinstalls authorized applications.

NOTE: ORIGINAL EQUIPMENT MANUFACTURER IMAGES

Another scenario is similar to the new computer scenario in that the current user state is not involved. However, this scenario is explicitly for new systems delivered from the original equipment manufacturer (OEM)/vendor. It involves delivering a seed image to the OEM for use during the factory's system build process. Because the OEM cannot join a system to your domain or install applications from your internal network, the seed image, once booted, kicks off the rest of the process when the system is physically on your internal network, finishing the deployment. The disadvantage is that you will probably end up maintaining at least two sets of images: one for in-house scenarios, and one for the OEM scenario. Each vendor may also have varying states of support, procedures, and supplemental tools for this method. Contact your vendor for guidance and recommendations before pursuing this option.

Tools Used with OSD

OSD relies on additional tools to help complete the process of deploying the Windows OS. Some are built into OSD; others are installed as part of prerequisites to installing ConfigMgr Current Branch. Knowing how OSD uses these tools and each tool's function is beneficial—perhaps even critical—for setting up a deployment and troubleshooting any problems. Tools include System Preparation (Sysprep), the Windows Assessment and Deployment Kit (ADK), and the User State Migration Tool (USMT), covered in the next sections.

Using Sysprep to Assist with Imaging

The Microsoft tool Sysprep removes system-specific information from the OS so it can be used to image multiple devices. It also configures the installation to run the GUI-based mini-setup when the system restarts. The mini-setup does the following:

▶ Generates new and unique identifiers for the system

▶ Enables the input of a new Windows product key

▶ Reruns the plug-and-play hardware detection

▶ Reruns the driver installation process

OSD fully automates the mini-setup process with the unattend.xml configuration file. It builds the appropriate file or uses one that is supplied, inserting information automatically into the file, including the product key, organization name, networking information, and domain credentials. Incorporating this functionality increases OSD's flexibility by eliminating the need to maintain multiple Sysprep files supporting multiple deployment scenarios.

Incorporating the Windows ADK

The Windows ADK, a prerequisite to installing ConfigMgr, is a set of tools designed to automate a Windows installation. It is a separate download and includes the WinPE 10 boot images. ConfigMgr automatically uses some of these tools (such as ImageX and the Deployment Image Servicing and Management [DISM] tool) during the deployment process. The ADK includes user guides on how to use these tools, reference documents on the unattended setup file, and WinPE.

Using OSD fully automates and completely integrates the many details of using the tools in the ADK. You can also use it to manipulate images outside OSD. The tools in the ADK follow:

▶ **WinPE:** A mini-operating system based on Windows 10, WinPE includes support for networking, Windows Management Instrumentation (WMI), VBScript, batch files, and database access. Its advantage is that it is much smaller than the full-blown OS, loads from a read-only disk, and runs in a RAM disk (a minimum of 512MB of memory is required for the version of WinPE included with and used by OSD in ConfigMgr) suitable for booting from a CD/DVD or over the network using PXE. OSD uses WinPE as a boot environment, ensuring that the currently installed operating system will not interfere with the deployment process.

▶ **Windows System Image Manager (WSIM):** This GUI tool builds unattended answer files for Windows. You do not need to worry about the syntax of the answer file because WSIM graphically presents all available options and generates the unattend. xml file for you. This same file format is utilized for Sysprep files used by the mini-setup to complete setup of Windows systems.

▶ **Deployment Image Servicing and Management:** This command-line tool manually services and manages Windows and WinPE images. Servicing changes an image's content; managing involves listing the content of the image file or combining two image files together. Servicing specifically includes adding updates and drivers to the image; OSD uses DISM for both. Images can be offline or online; offline can be in a Windows Imaging (WIM) file or extracted to disk, making managing many aspects of Windows seamless, regardless of where the OS is located or its state.

Microsoft ties the ADK to the version of Windows you are using but makes it backward compatible; for example, the Windows 8 version of the ADK works with Windows 8 and Windows 7, so the question is when to upgrade the ADK. The authors recommend upgrading when you upgrade Windows; this lets you keep everything tightly integrated with support for the current version and backward compatibility with older versions of Windows that are not yet upgraded.

Using the User State Migration Tool

USMT is an extensive tool that searches a system for all user data and settings and packages them into a single archive file for import onto another system, restoring user data and settings. USMT's default configuration captures all known Microsoft-centric settings and data, such as wallpaper, color scheme, Microsoft Office documents, favorites, and all files in the user's Documents folder. You can customize these defaults based on your requirements. USMT is part of the Windows 10 ADK and is installed when the ADK is installed. It is also a prerequisite for ConfigMgr installation. Microsoft provides documentation on USMT at https://technet.microsoft.com/itpro/windows/deploy/usmt-reference.

The information USMT captures is highly customizable by modifying or creating a series of Extensible Markup Language (XML) configuration files that describe the files, folders, and Registry entries to capture; you can specify exact filenames and Registry locations or perform wildcard searches to locate data or settings in these files. USMT uses these configuration files to capture all specified data and settings and place them into an archive used to restore to a destination system. To accomplish this, USMT uses the following tools:

▶ LoadState.exe

▶ ScanState.exe

As their names imply, ScanState.exe captures the data and settings whereas LoadState.exe restores them.

Planning for OSD

Planning is key to the success or failure of OSD. The old saying *An ounce of prevention is worth a pound of cure* is extremely accurate here. If not planned and tested thoroughly, OSD can be a major problem instead of a cost-saving move for your organization. Planning involves defining the who, what, and when of Windows deployment for your organization. The answers to the following questions will guide how you go about technically implementing the process and making it work.

▶ **Who:** Who are you deploying Windows to—or for? To your entire organization or a subset? Who initiates deployment to each system? End users, field technicians, you, or someone else?

▶ **What:** What OS are you deploying? What version and edition? Do different users or systems get different versions or editions? What applications will be deployed with the OS? Will they differ for different user or system roles? Are there other customizations to make to the OS or applications? To which hardware models are you deploying?

▶ **When:** When will you deploy? Do you need to meet a deadline? Are you going to deploy during the day or after hours?

▶ **Other:** Do you care about user data? How does your organization update Windows and other software? What other desktop standards must be part of a Windows deployment?

These questions and their answers will guide your efforts; the answers provide a blueprint for your Windows rollout. Depending on your organization, you may not be able to answer all these questions yourself, and it may take time to gain consensus from all the key players. Knowing the answers ahead of time will save you work or rework later.

When you understand the requirements and are equipped with the answers to the previous questions, you can move forward. The following items may assist in this planning process:

▶ **Preparation:** You need to start gathering the needed resources, importing them into your ConfigMgr lab, and performing any necessary ConfigMgr changes to meet those requirements. Resources include OS source media, application source files, drivers, configuration scripts, test systems, and storage space. Many of these must be imported into ConfigMgr for use in OSD. Based on your organization's physical nature, you may need to add site systems or modify current site systems. For example, to support PXE, you may need to add that role to your DPs as well as modify the network to allow PXE packets to cross routers.

▶ **Creation:** The core of the OSD process is putting in place all the requirements to deploy Windows. This part of the process is usually the second-most time-consuming step. It involves taking all the information gathered so far and putting it together to form a Windows image you can use for testing. This is often a repetitive process, involving building a basic structure, testing, adding to the basic structure, testing again, and so on. As requirements change, the repetitive process continues even after implementing OSD into production.

▶ **Testing:** This is the most time-consuming process of OSD. It is a self-explanatory step that is often overlooked and rarely given the time or attention it deserves. So many different permutations and factors exist even in smaller and simpler environments that you can probably never test all of them; however, not properly and thoroughly testing as many as possible results in poor results, lost data, and sleepless nights. Test against every scenario and hardware model possible for your organization. While it may seem that much of your time is watching progress bars or waiting for the OS image to download, without this testing, you will never actually know if your design work will result in the desired outcome of properly deployed Windows that meets all your requirements.

Be sure to perform all your imports and testing in a lab environment. You may find that you did not need all those drivers after all, or maybe you do not need to modify your WinPE image. Once testing is complete and you have a successful image, move all the needed items over to your production hierarchy.

Using the Console

The ConfigMgr console has many sections that form the OSD area. Knowing these sections and how they are used can help you understand how to fit them together to create and deploy your image. To access the OSD area of the console, navigate to **Software Library** -> **Overview** -> **Operating Systems**. Several sections are listed in this area, as shown in Figure 22.1.

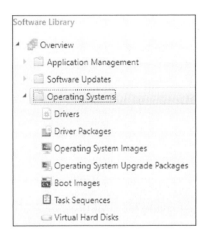

FIGURE 22.1   OSD section of the console.

Using Drivers and Driver Packages

Windows setup is very good at installing the correct drivers needed for Windows OS deployment; however, certain hardware components require a manufacturer's driver to function correctly. You must import these drivers into the ConfigMgr driver catalog in order for them to be available to OSD. Each imported driver must be part of a driver package distributed to the DPs, where the OSD process downloads the driver. The driver package can be pre-created before the driver import or as part of the import. Not all drivers added to the catalog are used; Windows setup makes the ultimate decision about which of them to install and use. The process of importing the drivers into Config-Mgr is handled by the Import New Driver Wizard, accessed by navigating to **Software Library** -> **Overview** -> **Operating Systems** -> **Drivers** and choosing **Import Driver** either from the ribbon bar or after right-clicking **Drivers**. Figure 22.2 displays the Import New Driver Wizard.

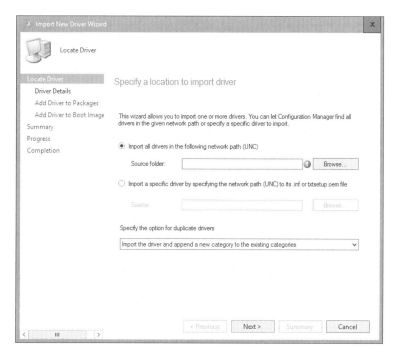

FIGURE 22.2   The Import New Driver Wizard.

The wizard has seven pages, three of which are the standard Summary, Progress, and Completion pages included in all ConfigMgr wizards. The following sections cover the pages that are unique to this wizard.

Locate Driver Page

The Locate Driver page of the wizard has three options for the user to complete:

▶ **Import All Drivers in the Following Network Path (UNC):** Use this radio button to import a number of drivers at once. The path you specify to the folder containing the drivers must be in Universal Naming Convention (UNC) format; you cannot specify a drive letter. Some hardware manufacturers create a file with all the drivers for a specific model of their hardware; once this file is expanded to a folder containing all the drivers, you can use this option to import all those drivers at once.

▶ **Import a Specific Driver by Specifying the Network Path (UNC) to its .inf or txtsetup.oem File:** If you need to test a specific driver and not a whole package, use this option to import that single driver. Again, the path must be a UNC path and point to an .inf file or a .txtsetup.oem file. These two file types are part of the driver files you download.

▶ **Specify the Option for Duplicate Drivers:** This dropdown menu allows you to select how the import wizard should handle a duplicate driver. These are the options:

   ▶ Import the driver and append a new category to the existing categories.

   ▶ Import the driver and overwrite the existing categories.

   ▶ Do not import the driver.

Driver Details Page

After selecting the correct information in the "Locate Driver Page" section, click **Next** to display the Validate Driver Information box. The ConfigMgr provider reads the folder location, validates file permissions, and reads driver attributes; this may take some time, depending on the number of drivers to import. If you think this process might be hung, check the SMS_Prov log file, where this information is logged. Once ConfigMgr has the driver information, the Driver Details page appears, shown in Figure 22.3.

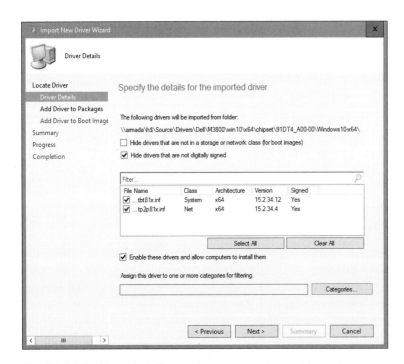

FIGURE 22.3   Driver Details page.

This page includes a lot of information, and the more drivers you add, the busier it looks. The first part of the page shows the path location from where the drivers will be imported. Two check boxes follow:

▶ **Hide Drivers That Are Not in a Storage or Network Class (for Boot Images):** Select this check box to allow the user to filter out drivers that would not be used in a boot image.

▶ **Hide Drivers That Are Not Digitally Signed:** This is checked by default. If a driver is not digitally signed, it should not be loaded; this is a security precaution.

The middle of the page contains a list box listing the drivers found by the wizard. If you chose to install a single driver, details are shown for that driver only. There is a check box beside each driver; all are checked by default. To skip importing a driver, uncheck its box. The list box also shows the class, architecture, version, and whether the driver is signed.

The following options are available at the bottom of the page:

▶ **Enable These Drivers and Allow Computers to Install Them:** This check box determines if the driver is enabled or disabled after the import completes. Uncheck the box to disable the drivers so they are not usable when the import finishes.

▶ **Assign This Driver to One or More Categories for Filtering:** This option allows you to choose an existing category or create a new one to which to add the drivers. You can either create a new category or click **Categories** to see categories already created and choose one.

Add Driver to Packages Page

Before drivers can be used by OSD, they must be part of a driver package. You can add them to an existing package or create a new package. Figure 22.4 shows this page, which allows you to choose between existing packages and creating a new one.

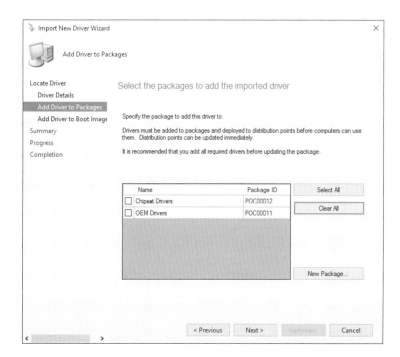

FIGURE 22.4   Add Driver to Packages page.

The driver packages are in the list box; choose one or more or all. At the bottom of the list box, click **New Package** to create a new package if you are not using any existing packages.

TIP: IDENTIFYING DRIVER PACKAGES

When creating driver packages, either before the driver import or as part of the import, the authors recommend creating a folder structure that starts with the system manufacturer name, model number, and folders for each component of that model number for which you will need a driver. Doing so creates many driver packages but allows you to keep the drivers in separate folders, which makes maintenance and upkeep easier.

Pre-create a driver package by navigating to **Software Library** -> **Overview** -> **Operating Systems** -> **Driver Packages** and choosing **Create Driver Package** from the ribbon bar or after right-clicking **Driver Package**. You get a dialog box where you enter a name, comment, and the path of the package, using UNC format. The path specified must be an empty folder. This is not the path you imported the drivers from or will import them from; it is the source location used to populate the DPs. From the same menu, you can also choose to import a driver package.

Add Driver to Boot Images Page

The Add Driver to Boot Images page, shown in Figure 22.5, allows you to inject drivers into the boot images, which may be necessary if the driver is for a network card or mass storage driver that allows access to a disk drive. You must have these drivers at boot time to complete the OSD TS steps to deploy the OS.

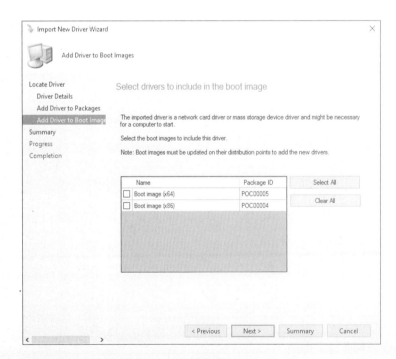

FIGURE 22.5   Add Driver to Boot Images page.

The middle of the page displays a list box showing all boot images. None are checked by default. Place a checkmark next to each image into which you want to inject the drivers. You can choose more than one boot image. If you do not want to inject drivers into a boot image, leave its check box unchecked.

After importing the drivers, you must distribute the driver package or packages; if you are injecting drivers into the boot image or images, they also must be distributed to DPs. Right-click the driver package or boot image and choose **Distribute Content** to open the Distribute Content Wizard, where the only page allows you to choose the DPs to which to distribute the content. The authors recommend choosing all DPs if using OSD in multiple locations.

Using Operating System Images

The Operating System Images console node lists all OS images imported into ConfigMgr. OS images are captured images in the form of a WIM file, used to mass-deploy Windows. This node also lists data images. These WIM files do not contain an installed OS; they are a collection of files stored in the WIM that you would like to deploy to a system. Add an OS image by navigating to **Software Library -> Overview -> Operating Systems -> Operating System Images**. Choose **Add Operating System Image** from the ribbon bar or after right-clicking **Operating System Images** to launch a wizard that has five pages. The last three pages are the standard Summary, Progress, and Completion pages. The other two have items you must complete:

▶ **Data Source:** Enter the full path to the OS image you want to add. The path must be a UNC path that points all the way to the .wim file. You do not need to create a unique folder for each WIM file, as the path must point to the actual file. If you are not using unique folders, the authors recommend assigning a complete and descriptive name for each .wim file so you can distinguish between them.

▶ **General:** Define the name, version, and comments about the WIM image you are adding. The name is automatically filled in based on what is in the WIM; change it to anything you want.

After adding the OS image to ConfigMgr, you must distribute it to your DPs to be available for use in OSD. Right-click the image and choose **Distribute Content** to open the Distribute Content Wizard; the only page asks you to choose DPs to which you want to distribute the content. The authors recommend choosing all DPs if using OSD in multiple locations.

NOTE: USING A DEFAULT OS IMAGE

While this is not a preferred option, rather than capture a reference system and use it as your OS image, you can use the default OS image included with the Windows OS media, located in <operating system source path>\Sources\ and named install.wim. This image installs a basic vanilla OS; you must customize each deployed OS for your environment and install any needed applications and software updates. For these reasons, the authors recommend creating a reference image with all needed customizations, applications, and software updates and then capturing that reference system and using it to deploy images.

Using Operating System Upgrade Packages

An OS update package contains all the source files that come with your Windows media, which are imported into a package inside ConfigMgr and distributed to your DPs. The files are used to upgrade a Windows OS from one version to another, such as from Windows 7 to Windows 10. Your upgrade package must be the same edition, architecture, and language as the clients you are upgrading. Add the package to ConfigMgr by navigating to **Software Library -> Overview -> Operating Systems -> Operating System Upgrade Packages**. From the ribbon bar or after right-clicking on **Operating System Upgrade Packages**, choose **Add Operating System Upgrade Package** to launch a five-page wizard. The last three pages of the wizard are the standard Summary, Progress, and Completion pages; the other two include items you must complete:

▶ **Data Source:** Enter the path to the Windows source files used for the upgrade. These should be the files from your Windows install media. The path must be a UNC and point to the folder containing setup.exe.

▶ **General:** Define the name, version, and comments about the upgrade package you are adding. The name is automatically filled in, based on the name of the source folder name; you can change this to anything you want for the name.

When the OS upgrade package is added to ConfigMgr, distribute it to your DPs to be available for use in OSD. Right-click the package and choose **Distribute Content** to open the Distribute Content Wizard; the only page allows you to choose the DPs to which to distribute the content. The authors recommend choosing all DPs when using OSD in multiple locations.

After adding your OS images and/or OS upgrade packages to ConfigMgr, you must update them when new security updates are released. The authors recommend updating quarterly. Navigate to **Software Library -> Overview -> Operating Systems -> Operating System Images** or **Software Library -> Overview -> Operating Systems -> Operating System Upgrade Packages**. Select the image or upgrade package and choose **Schedule Updates** to launch the Schedule Updates Wizard, shown in Figure 22.6. This wizard has five pages, the last three of which are the standard Summary, Progress, and Completion pages. You must complete two pages:

▶ **Choose Updates:** This page is filled in automatically, though it might take several seconds or longer for this to occur. ConfigMgr opens the image or update package and compares it with known software updates. It determines which updates are needed and shows them in the list box on this page. Uncheck any of them that you do not want to apply.

▶ **Set Schedule:** Decide when to apply the software updates; either select to apply them as soon as possible or set a custom date and time. You can also choose to stop applying updates if an error occurs or continue regardless of errors, and you can update the DPs after the process has completed.

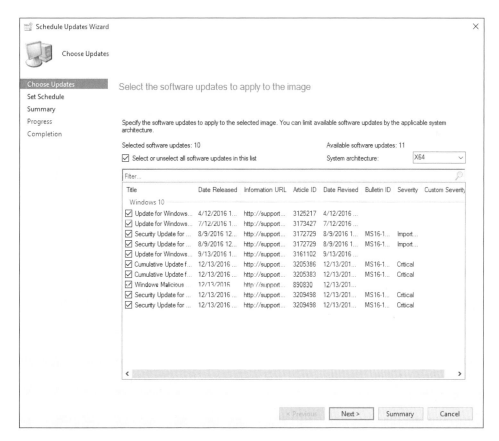

FIGURE 22.6   Schedule Updates Wizard.

Using Boot Images

A ConfigMgr boot image is a WinPE image used during OSD to start a computer; this is a minimal operating system with limited components and services that prepares the destination computer for Windows installation. Two boot images are supplied by default when ConfigMgr is installed: one to support x86 platforms, and one for x64. These are the basic boot images installed with the Windows 10 ADK. These images are required because the main operations of the deployment cannot occur within a full install of Windows;

formatting the disk and applying an image file cannot happen while the target disk drive is in use and must be initiated from something that does not live on or run from that disk.

WinPE is ideal because it is small, easy to deliver, and fast, and it runs from a RAM disk without needing persistent storage. It also shares the core kernel and driver model with Windows itself, can run any valid native Windows executable, and provides much of the same automation-enabling functionality, including batch scripting and VBScript.

The default boot images work for most organizations for OSD requirements, but there may be a time when you need to add a separate boot image to ConfigMgr. This is fully supported—but only when you use a boot image based on a supported version of WinPE:

- ▶ **WinPE 10:** This version of WinPE is part of the Windows 10 ADK and installed as a prerequisite for ConfigMgr. It is also the version of WinPE on which the default boot images are based. This version is customizable from within the ConfigMgr console.

- ▶ **WinPE 5:** This version comes from the Windows 8.1 ADK. It cannot be customized from the ConfigMgr console. The boot images are supported but must be customized elsewhere, using the version of DISM installed with the Windows 8.1 ADK.

- ▶ **WinPE 3.1:** From the Windows Automated Installation Kit (AIK) supplement for Windows 7 Service Pack (SP) 1, this version is an upgrade to the Windows 7 AIK. You cannot customize it in the ConfigMgr console.

For complete information on how to customize older versions of WinPE, see https://docs.microsoft.com/sccm/osd/get-started/customize-boot-images.

To add a boot image to ConfigMgr, navigate to **Software Library** -> **Overview** -> **Operating Systems** -> **Boot Images**. Choose **Add Boot Image** from the ribbon bar or after right-clicking **Boot Images** to launch a five-page wizard. The last three wizard pages are the standard Summary, Progress, and Completion pages. The other two pages have items you must fill in:

- ▶ **Data Source:** Enter the path to the boot image you want to add. The path must be in UNC format and point to the actual .wim file.

- ▶ **General:** Define the name, version, and comments about the boot image you are adding. The name and version are filled in automatically, although you can change the name to anything you want. The authors recommend adding comments to explain what this boot image is for, to avoid confusion with other boot images.

After adding or customizing a boot image, it must be distributed before being used by OSD. Right-click an image and choose **Distribute Content** to open the Distribute Content Wizard, whose only page allows you to choose the DPs to distribute the content. The authors recommend choosing all DPs if you plan to use OSD in multiple locations.

View a boot image's properties by right-clicking it and choosing **Properties** to open the Boot Image Properties dialog box. Figure 22.7 displays the Customization tab selected.

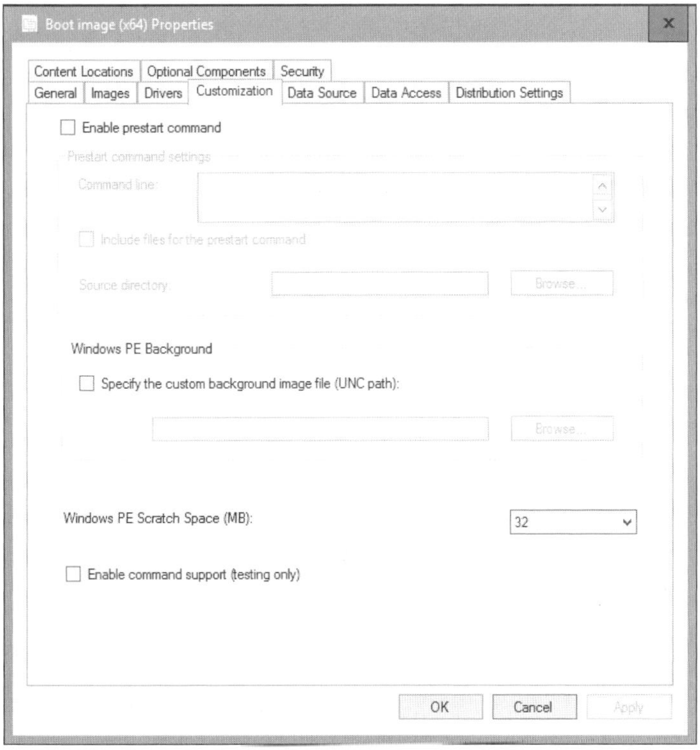

FIGURE 22.7   Viewing boot image properties.

While you can create completely custom boot images from scratch, this generally is not necessary as the built-in boot images are sufficiently customizable to meet nearly any need. The following customizations are available in the Customization tab shown in Figure 22.7:

▶ **Prestart Commands:** Prestart commands run before the OSD process. They are typically used to display information and prompt the interactive user for input such as the system's location, desired name, or role. There are no predefined prestart commands; this type of customization is completely up to your needs and abilities. In general, any valid Windows script (batch, VBScript, Jscript, or PowerShell script) will work. Prestart commands often require additional files, such as executables or scripts that are not part of the default boot image. Add these files by specifying the folder containing them in the Properties dialog. Using this section to add files to the boot image is helpful even if not using a prestart command; these could be diagnostic scripts that help in troubleshooting. Add cmd/c to the start of the command line that runs any program; otherwise, the command will not close after it runs, forcing the deployment to wait for the command to finish and putting you in a loop where nothing else starts.

You can also enter prestart commands when you create specific boot media, which means you can create the media and commands at the same time. More information about the prestart commands can be found at https://docs.microsoft.com/sccm/osd/understand/prestart-commands-for-task-sequence-media.

▶ **Windows PE Background:** Specify an image to use as the background during OSD instead of the default provided by Microsoft. You can customize the background to your organization's logo and color scheme, for example, so users know the OSD process is from your organization.

▶ **Windows PE Scratch Space (MB):** This is temporary RAM-based storage used by WinPE applications that need to write temporary files. WinPE points the application to this area, and the application sees it as a hard drive to write the files it needs.

▶ **Enable Command Support (Testing Only):** Check this check box to launch a command prompt anytime during the OSD process by pressing F8. This is useful for troubleshooting. When the process is working correctly, the authors recommend unchecking this box so users are not able to open the command prompt.

The Drivers tab is another area you might want to customize in the Boot Image Properties dialog. It allows you to inject drivers into the image so they can be used at boot time. Click the yellow starburst icon to bring up the Select a driver dialog box, which lists all the drivers imported into ConfigMgr and allows you to pick drivers to add to the image. The authors recommend using only boot-critical drivers, such as network and mass storage drivers. Ensure that the drivers you are adding match the architecture of the boot image: x64 drivers for an x64 image, x86 drivers for an x86 boot image.

NOTE: USING A BOOT IMAGE WITH PXE

When users PXE boot, they must use a boot image that matches the system's architecture, so if you use PXE, ensure that the x86 and x64 boot images allow PXE boots. This is configured on the Data Source tab of the Boot Image Properties dialog: Check the check box **Deploy this boot image from a PXE enabled distribution point**. It is checked by default, but the authors recommend verifying that it is selected.

After making any changes to your boot images, update the DPs by right-clicking the boot image and choosing **Update Distribution Points**; if the boot images have not been distributed to the DPs, choose **Distribute Content**.

Using Task Sequences

Task sequences (TSs) are the heart of OSD. A TS is a series of customizable tasks or sequentially performed steps. With OSD you build steps into the TS to accomplish deployment, application installation, software update installation, application of drivers, and so on to create an OS for your users. ConfigMgr comes with several standard TSs built in to allow you to perform a variety of functions; it also includes the capability to create a custom TS to use for OSD or non-OSD applications. (For more about using TSs for non-OSD applications, see Chapter 13, "Creating and Managing Packages and Programs.") Access the TS menu by navigating to **Software Library -> Overview -> Operating Systems -> Task Sequences** and choosing **Create Task Sequence** from the ribbon bar or after right-clicking **Task Sequences**. Figure 22.8 shows the Task Sequence menu.

FIGURE 22.8   Task Sequence menu.

Figure 22.8 shows several different TSs you can choose from. Each presents some different pages as well as some of the same pages as in the Create Task Sequence Wizard.

Install an Existing Image Package

Use this TS to deploy an OS added to the Operating System Images section of the ConfigMgr console. This wizard has 10 pages, with the last 3 being the standard Summary, Progress, and Completion. These are the other 7 pages:

▶ **Task Sequence Information:** Provide a name and description. The page also allows you to pick a boot image; click **Browse** to bring up a list of boot images to choose from. Select a boot image whose architecture will work on the destination hardware, such as an x64 boot image for x64 hardware; do not pick an x64 boot image for x86 hardware.

▶ **Install Windows:** Choose an OS image package to deploy, the image index if the image has more than one, and whether to partition and format the target computer before installing the OS. A check box allows you to configure the TS for use with BitLocker encryption software. Enter your product key and server licensing mode. At the bottom, choose to use a randomly generated password for the administrator account and disable the account or enter a password and enable the account.

▶ **Configure Network:** Specify your connection to a domain or a workgroup. If choosing a workgroup, enter its name; for a domain, enter the domain and organizational unit (OU) in which to create the computer account. Click **Browse** to select these settings if you do not want to enter them manually. The last option is to enter an account with permissions to join the machine to the domain. Use **Set** to search for an account to use or enter it manually in the format *domain\user*.

▶ **Install Configuration Manager Client:** Enter the parameters needed to install the ConfigMgr client. There are two settings: Package and Installation properties. The information is prepopulated from the site's client push settings; change these to any valid settings you like.

▶ **State Migration:** Specify some of the basic configuration for using the state migration tools. Use a check box to capture users' settings or not; if this box is checked, choose the USMT package to use (this is prepopulated). You can also specify using a state migration point (SMP) to save user files and settings, or you can capture and store it locally by using hard links. Choose whether to capture network and Windows settings.

▶ **Include Updates:** Specify whether to have software updates installed as part of the OSD process. Choose to install the required mandatory software updates only, to install all software updates, or not to install any software updates.

▶ **Install Applications:** Add applications to install into the TS. Use the yellow starburst icon to select from a list of applications; choose as many as needed. A check box allows the TS to continue installing applications if one of the applications fails to install.

After creating your TS, edit its properties to verify that the correct boot image is selected, among other items. Edit the properties by right-clicking the TS and choosing **Properties** or highlighting the TS and then choosing **Properties** from the ribbon bar.

▶ **General:** Use this tab to change the name of the TS, add a description for the TS, add a category for the TS, and choose between using the default text Running: *<task sequence name>* or creating a custom text entry to show the user when the TS is executing.

▶ **Advanced:** This tab has several options you can select:

    ▶ **Run Another Program First:** This check box is valid only for TSs started while in an existing OS. It runs the specified program from the specified package before executing the TS if the program has not been previously run on the system. If the Always run this program first option is selected, the specified program is always run, regardless of its previous run status or result.

    ▶ **Suppress Task Sequence Notifications:** Checking this check box turns off any notifications to the user that the TS is available for execution.

    ▶ **Disable Task Sequence on Computers Where It Is Deployed:** You can select this option to disable the TS.

▶ **Maximum Allowed Run Time (Minutes):** The number of minutes specified for this option is used when calculating whether a TS should run in an available maintenance window. If a TS exceeds this time, it is terminated.

▶ **Use a Boot Image:** Choose the boot image to use for this TS. For non-OSD TSs, such as those used to deploy applications or a complex series of ordered tasks that may involve some advanced conditional logic available in a TS, you can choose to use no boot image.

▶ **Run on Any Platform or Run Only on the Specified Platforms:** Use this option to limit the platforms on which a TS can run. Choose from a series of Windows versions or choose to run on any platform.

Build and Capture a Reference Operating System Image

Use this TS to build a new reference system and capture that system to use as the image to deploy out to new machines. A reference system is sometimes referred to as a *gold image*. It is a system customized with your organization's color schema, Windows settings, applications, and office productivity software. You can capture that image and use it as your corporate image to deploy. Start the process by confirming that you added a default install.wim file from valid Windows media. You can then use this WIM file as the basis for your reference image. The wizard that builds these TSs has some of the same pages used by the TS in the previous section, as well as the following three different pages:

▶ **System Preparation:** Select the package that contains the appropriate version of Sysprep to use to capture the reference computer's settings. This page is grayed out for Windows Vista or later because Vista was the first version of Windows to automatically include Sysprep as part of the OS.

▶ **Image Properties:** Add information about the image in terms of who created it, what version it is, and a description of the image.

▶ **Capture Image:** Enter the details of where the captured image is stored. The path is entered as a UNC (\\<*servername*>\<*sharename*>\<*filename*>); click **Browse** to select the path to avoid entering it manually. The account you enter must have permissions to access the share and the folder where the image is created. Full admin permissions are not required but suggested by the authors to help prevent problems with the capture process.

TIP: CAPTURING A REFERENCE SYSTEM

If you previously created a reference system and just want to capture that system, you can create a custom TS, edit it, and add a step to capture the system. If the system has a ConfigMgr client installed, add a step in the TS that prepares the ConfigMgr client for capture. This step must be added before the step to capture the system. If you would rather not use a TS, you can use the DISM tool from the ADK to capture the image.

Install an Existing Image Package to a Virtual Hard Disk

This TS enables ConfigMgr to deploy Windows to a new virtual hard disk (VHD) and update an existing instance of Windows within a VHD it previously created. It also directly uploads a VHD to an instance of Virtual Machine Manager (VMM) for use within your enterprise. To utilize this new feature set, install the ConfigMgr console on a 64-bit Windows 8 or 8.1 system or on Windows Server 2012 R2 or 2016 where Hyper-V is fully enabled and operational. To upload the VHDs to VMM, you must also install the VMM console on a system where the ConfigMgr console is loaded. This does not need to be the same system where you are creating and maintaining VHDs. All VHD management is performed from the Virtual Hard Disks node under **Software Library -> Overview -> Operating Systems**. This node is visible on all systems running the console; however, if a system does not meet the necessary OS requirements, the Virtual Hard Disks nodes actions are grayed out.

These TSs use the same pages that the Install an existing image package page uses except for the following pages that are removed from the TS:

▶ State Migration

▶ Include Updates

For more in-depth information on this TS and about how to use VHDs within ConfigMgr, reference https://docs.microsoft.com/sccm/osd/deploy-use/use-a-task-sequence-to-manage-virtual-hard-disks.

Upgrade an Operating System from an Upgrade Package

Use this TS to upgrade a Windows 7, 8, or 8.1 system to Windows 10 and take advantage of the OS upgrade packages in ConfigMgr. The TS wizard automatically creates the steps needed to perform the upgrade, with one page different from those of the other TSs.

Use the Upgrade the Windows Operating System page to select an upgrade package to use; the middle of the page then shows the package's OS version, edition, language, and architecture. This allows you to verify that you selected the correct upgrade package to use. At the bottom of the page is a dropdown menu to choose the correct index of the Windows edition you want to use. You can enter your product key as well. Figure 22.9 shows the upgrade TS created with this wizard in Edit mode.

The TS adds in a Pre-Upgrade group and a Post-Upgrade group that allow the upgrade to Windows 10 to occur with checks and balances:

▶ **Prepare for Upgrade:** This adds the step Check readiness for upgrade to the TS to ensure the target system has enough memory, processor speed, and free disk space to meet Windows 10 prerequisites. If the target system does not meet these standards, the TS fails. You may need to modify the settings for your organization's standards. You can add additional steps to uninstall applications, drivers, or other items known to not be compatible with Windows 10.

▶ **Post-Processing:** Add applications, drivers, or other items to install after the upgrade finishes.

▶ **Rollback:** This is added by default and should not be removed. If an error occurs during the upgrade, the TS variable _SMSTSSetupRollback is set to True. This step has a condition to check that variable; if it is set to True, the TS rolls back the upgrade to the previously installed OS. If there are additional steps you need to take after that rollback occurs, add them to this group.

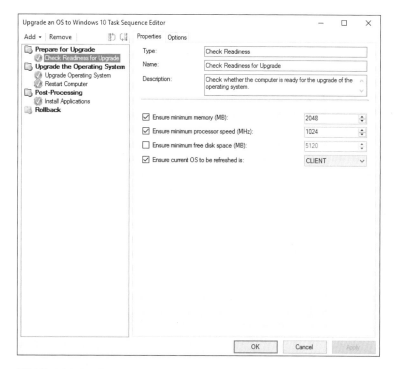

FIGURE 22.9   The Upgrade to Windows 10 TS page.

Create a New Custom Task Sequence

This TS wizard creates a blank TS with no steps, allowing you to create your own custom-ized TS from scratch. The only page is the Task Sequence Information page, which allows you to name the TS, provide a description, and choose a boot image if you need to use one.

These custom TSs are usually created for non-OSD tasks that typically must be executed in a particular set of steps. These TSs are the perfect solution for those deployments. For more information about steps to add to these custom TSs, see https://docs.microsoft.com/sccm/osd/understand/task-sequence-steps.

Using Tasks and Variables in a Task Sequence

With your TS created and its properties defined, you may find that you need to add or delete tasks in the TS through the edit process. ConfigMgr provides a very rich set of tasks you can add to the TS to provide it with more flexibility. These tasks and TSs are similar to a macro-based programming language or a storyboard where you put together high-level steps and instructions using a graphical tool, without having to know or learn the syntax of the underlying language to fully take advantage of it.

To edit a TS, navigate to **Software Library -> Overview -> Operating Systems -> Task Sequences** and right-click the TS, or select the TS, and from the ribbon bar choose **Edit** to launch the TS editor. Figure 22.10 shows the TS editor for a TS created using the Install an Existing Image Package Wizard.

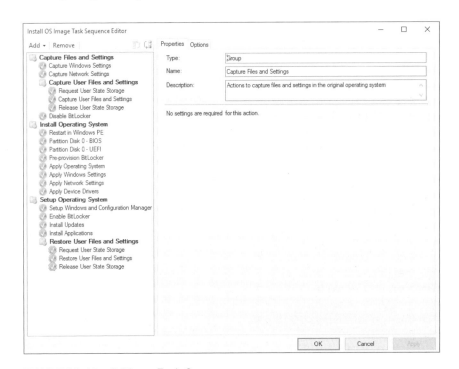

FIGURE 22.10   Editing a Task Sequence.

Using Tasks

The wizard creates a very basic TS, which you must customize for your organization. You can add, delete, or move steps in the TS. To delete a step or group from the TS, highlight the item and choose **Remove** from the menu; to move an item up or down in the TS list, highlight the item and then click the **Move up** or **Move down** icon on the menu.

To add a group or a task, select the **Add** menu item. Tasks are divided into seven categories, with tasks under each one. Figure 22.11 shows the first of these built-in categories and the tasks in the General category.

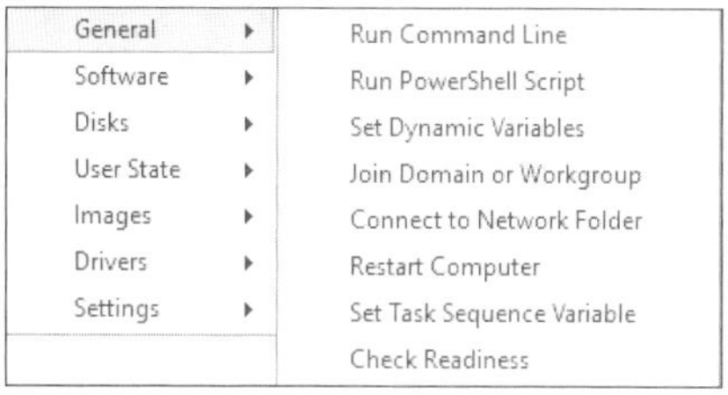

General ▶	Run Command Line
Software ▶	Run PowerShell Script
Disks ▶	Set Dynamic Variables
User State ▶	Join Domain or Workgroup
Images ▶	Connect to Network Folder
Drivers ▶	Restart Computer
Settings ▶	Set Task Sequence Variable
	Check Readiness

FIGURE 22.11   General Group of Tasks.

When you add a task to the TS (see the "Add Condition" bullet in the Options tab discussion that follows), the editor adds the task below the current highlighted step. Each task has its own set of parameters that must be filled for the task to execute correctly. When a task is added to the TS, it shows an icon with a red X beside the name, indicating that it has a required parameter that must be completed; once all parameters are filled in, the icon turns into a green checkmark, indicating that the step is ready to execute. Each task has two tabs:

▶ Properties

▶ Options

The Properties tab contains all parameters that must be completed for the task to become execution ready. In-depth information on each task and its parameters can be found at https://docs.microsoft.com/sccm/osd/understand/task-sequence-steps.

The Options tab generally has the same settings for each task; sometimes there is an additional parameter, but none are required. The Options tab always has the following items:

▶ **Disable This Step:** Allows you to disable the step so it is not performed when the TS executes. A common use for this is when you are creating a TS and are not sure if all steps need to be performed.

▶ **Continue on Error:** Allows the TS to continue running if the step that is running fails. The error is logged in the SMSTS.log file, and the TS continues to the next step. This is handy for troubleshooting issues when a step in the TS keeps failing but you need to execute the rest of the TS.

▶ **Add Condition:** Allows you to add logical conditions to the step. If a condition evaluates to true, the step executes; if the condition is false, the step is skipped. The most common use for conditions is when installing drivers. For example, you may have a driver package for each model of system you are deploying. You would want to check the model number of the system to see if the drivers should be applied.

Conditions can be combined by using `If` statements to form a master conditional statement. This is a collection of substatements that evaluate to either True or False, based on the logical evaluation of those substatements. There are three types of master statements, and each type of evaluation affects how the master statement is evaluated:

▶ All child statements must be true.

▶ Any child statement is true.

▶ No child statements are true.

You can chain `If` statements together to form complex logical statements. `If` statements in this context closely resemble the traditional logical operators AND/OR, and can be used in a similar way.

Using Variables

A major advantage of TSs over ConfigMgr's traditional software delivery mechanism is that they maintain state between steps. This state is embodied in a series of built-in variables and custom variables that survive reboots because they are stored in a locally persistent file, allowing you to pass data or configuration items from one step to the next. In fact, the task the TS is currently executing is also part of the state of the TS. Variables are encrypted for security when transmitted between ConfigMgr and the target system. Three types of variables are available:

▶ **Action:** These variables specify parameters for specific tasks. The variable is used by a single step in the TS and is initialized before the step is run and is only available while the step is running. The value for the variable is removed after the step finishes. Nearly all action variables are directly editable using the task sequence editor.

▶ **Custom:** This is a simple name/value pair that you can define as you see fit.

▶ **Built-in:** These variables are almost always read-only. They start with an underscore and are automatically generated by the TS; they generally describe the environment where the TS executes. The value of the variable is available throughout the entire TS.

Find a full list of TS action variables at https://docs.microsoft.com/sccm/osd/understand/task-sequence-action-variables and a list of the built-in variables at https://docs.microsoft.com/sccm/osd/understand/task-sequence-built-in-variables.

Each GUI field shown in a task in the TS editor has a corresponding TS variable. Setting these values in the GUI defines the action's runtime behavior, making your TS static for the most part. Setting TS variables based on collection membership or using a script while executing the TS makes your TSs dynamic, performing tasks differently or even performing different tasks based on runtime conditions. You can set action variables and custom variables in a number of ways:

▶ Use a Set Task Sequence Variable task.

▶ Statically assign one to a specific computer resource.

▶ Statically assign one to a collection.

▶ Use the Microsoft.SMS.TSEnvironment COM object in a script or other COM-aware tool, development environment, or language. See http://msdn.microsoft.com/library/cc145669.aspx for more information on using this COM object; the page refers to ConfigMgr 2007 but also applies to ConfigMgr Current Branch.

You can also set a TS variable on a device collection or computer resource in the ConfigMgr console. For device collections, open the collection's Properties page and navigate to the Collection variables tab; for computer resources, open the resource's Properties page and select the Variables tab. TSs initiated on applicable resources will have all variables initially set. If you leave the value of a collection or computer variable blank, the built-in TS UI prompts the user for values for these empty variables.

Finally, there is an order to the precedence of TS variables:

1. Task sequence variables set at runtime (using a Set Task Sequence Variable task or the Microsoft.SMS.TSEnvironment COM object)

2. Task sequence variables set on computer resources

3. Task sequence variables set on collections

4. Task sequence variables set at design time in the GUI

Site System Roles for OSD

Depending on the choices made within a TS, some tasks will require adding additional site system roles; for example, you would need an SMP if you used the state migration package and needed a place to store the users' data other than locally. Following are additional site system roles that play a part in the OSD process, some of which you may use and some of which you may not. These are discussed in the next sections.

▶ Distribution Point

▶ PXE Point (part of the DP role)

▶ Multicast (part of the DP role)

▶ State Migration Point

Using Distribution Points

You probably already have a DP that is used for software distribution. OSD uses the DP in the same manner—as a storage place for content needed for OSD and for the client to download the content when needed while deploying the OS. Following are types of software stored on the DP for use in OSD:

▶ Applications

▶ Boot images

▶ Driver packages

▶ Operating system images

▶ Operating system upgrade packages

▶ Software distribution packages

▶ Software update deployment packages

While the system is executing the TS, it requests these types of content as needed. The content is downloaded from the DP to the local client and processed according to the step in the TS. Not all of the package may be used; it depends on the tasks in the TS.

Using a PXE Point

In simple terms, PXE is a standard client/server environment that allows a machine to boot an OS that is retrieved from the network. The client side must have a network interface card (NIC) that is PXE-boot capable; the server side handles a process that intercepts the PXE packet, reads it, and delivers the OS to the client requesting it. PXE is not a ConfigMgr concept or even a Microsoft concept; it is more of an industry-wide concept implemented in different flavors across a wide multitude of server OSs. For in-depth information on PXE, see https://en.wikipedia.org/wiki/Preboot_Execution_Environment. ConfigMgr uses PXE in conjunction with Windows Deployment Services (WDS) on Windows Server.

Starting with ConfigMgr 2012, the PXE point is included as part of the DP properties. Install PXE and configure it by navigating to **Administration** -> **Overview** -> **Distribution Points**; then either right-click the DP name and select **Properties** or select the DP and from the ribbon bar, choose **Properties**, and click the PXE tab. Figure 22.12 shows the PXE tab of a DP's properties.

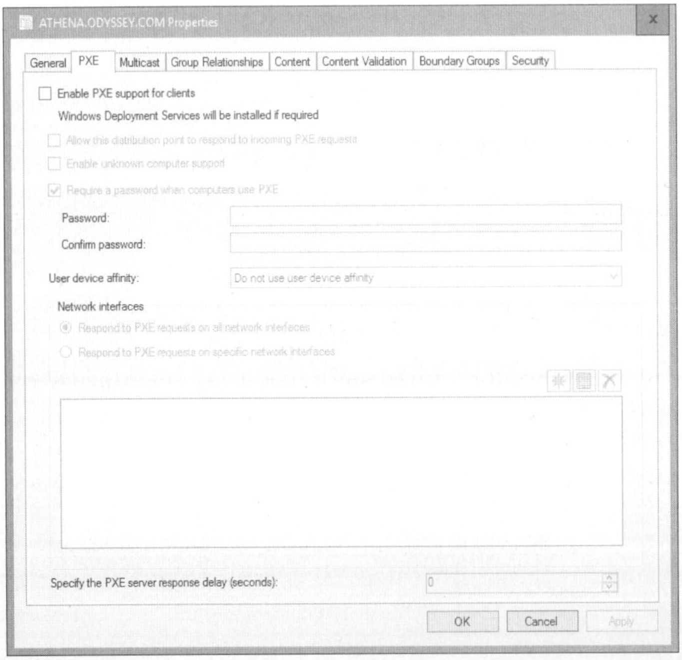

FIGURE 22.12   PXE tab of a DP's properties.

The first step in installing and configuring the PXE point is to check the box **Enable PXE support for clients**. You see a warning popup dialog box, as shown in Figure 22.13. The warning explains that PXE uses certain ports to transfer packets across the network. These ports must be open to allow traffic through the firewall on systems and routers for PXE to work correctly. If you are using a Windows firewall, ConfigMgr opens the ports for you. Click Yes in the warning dialog box to be presented with the PXE tab to configure; click No, and the checkbox remains unchecked with the rest of the PXE tab grayed out.

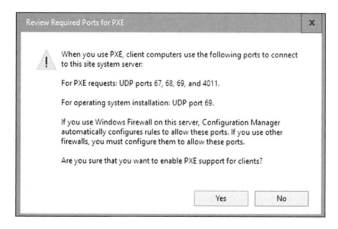

FIGURE 22.13   PXE port warning message.

NOTE: WINDOWS DEPLOYMENT SERVICES

ConfigMgr takes full advantage of WDS to implement PXE services. In prior versions, WDS installed separately, which could cause issues in terms of how it was configured. ConfigMgr now installs WDS during the PXE point install and configures it as needed to work correctly with ConfigMgr and PXE. Smaller organizations that might have WDS and Dynamic Host Configuration Protocol (DHCP) on the same machine must configure WDS to use a different port. For more information on WDS, see https://docs.microsoft.com/sccm/osd/plan-design/infrastructure-requirements-for-operating-system-deployment#BKMK_WDS.

The PXE tab has several other items to complete:

▶ **Allow This Distribution Point to Respond to Incoming PXE Requests:** Checking this box sets up WDS on this DP/PXE point to respond to any incoming PXE requests. Unchecking it stops or disables the ability to answer incoming PXE requests.

▶ **Enable Unknown Computer Support:** Checking this option allows the WDS/PXE server to respond to incoming requests from systems not managed by ConfigMgr. A system without the ConfigMgr client installed or discovered by ConfigMgr is an *unknown system*. In OSD terms, these typically are bare-metal systems without an installed OS. If this option is checked, you see a warning popup dialog box, as shown in Figure 22.14, explaining that when these types of systems PXE boot, they can run any of the deployed TSs to the unknown computer collection. This could result in formatting the hard drive and losing data. Click **OK** to turn on this support.

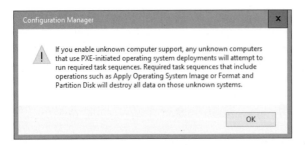

FIGURE 22.14   Unknown computer support warning message.

▶ **Require a Password When Computers Use PXE:** Selecting this option requires a password for the system to complete a PXE boot; the boot aborts if the password is not returned by the user of the system. If this option is enabled, you must enter your password and confirm it in the second box. This is a good way to prevent users from PXE booting and running a TS that is not meant for them.

▶ **User Device Affinity:** For this option, you can select one of three options: Do not use device affinity, Allow user device affinity with manual approval, or Allow user device affinity with automatic approval. Device affinity allows you to marry a user to a single device. For more about this, see https://docs.microsoft.com/sccm/osd/get-started/associate-users-with-a-destination-computer.

▶ **Network Interfaces:** This option allows you to specify that either all NICs respond to the PXE requests or only specific NICs respond, assuming that you have multiple NICs on this DP/PXE server. If you choose to use specific NICs, use the yellow star-burst icon to open a dialog box where you can enter the media access control (MAC) addresses of the NICs you want to respond.

▶ **Specify the PXE Server Response Delay (Seconds):** Use this option to delay the response from this PXE point to the incoming PXE request. If you have multiple DP/PXE servers, you might want to establish a precedence for which responds first. This setting allows you to tune the response from each DP/PXE server. It is not an exact way to set prioritization, but it does work.

TIP: EXCLUDING SYSTEMS FROM PXE BOOTING

There may be specific systems you do not want to PXE boot; these could be systems from executive employees, point-of-sale systems, or systems in charge of manufacturing plants. You can create an exclusion list for such devices. Create a text file on the DP/PXE point and add to it the MAC address of each system you want to exclude. Use colons to separate the MAC address values and put each MAC address on a separate line. Save the text file to any location on the system. Next, navigate to the HKLM\Software\Microsoft\SMS\DP Registry key on the DP/PXE server. Create a new string value called MACIgnoreListFile and set its value to the full path of your exclusion text file. You must do this on all DP/PXE points if you have multiple DP/PXE systems.

How exactly does PXE work? At a high level, the steps are as follows:

1. The system boots, and because no OS is installed or the user presses the **F12** key, the NIC attempts to get a DHCP address and start the process of PXE booting; the PXE packet is sent to the DHCP server.

2. The PXE-enabled DP sends back a packet that contains the boot filename and location along with the WDS network boot program.

3. The client opens a session and starts transferring boot files from the server.

4. The system boots into WinPE, and the TS boot shell is started from the SMS folder that is in the WinPE image.

For more detailed information about how PXE works and several processes in-between these steps, see the complete walkthrough at https://support.microsoft.com/help/10082/ troubleshooting-pxe-boot-issues-in-configuration-manager-2012. This article is for ConfigMgr 2012 but also applies to ConfigMgr Current Branch.

Using Multicast

Multicast is group communication in which information is simultaneously addressed to a group of destination computers. Say you have 10 systems that need to download an OSD image; normally each system downloads the image, for a total of 10 downloads. Multicasting means only one image is downloaded for all 10 systems, assuming that they all need the same image. Note that multicasting requires considerable network configuration and bandwidth tuning. In addition, OSD imaging packages and packages included as part of the TS are the only items that can use multicasting in ConfigMgr, and it occurs only inside WinPE. This section does not cover multicasting in depth—just enough to set it up. For complete information, see https://blogs.msdn.microsoft.com/steverac/2008/10/18/ setting-up-multicasting-in-sccm. While written for ConfigMgr 2012 R2, this blog post also applies to ConfigMgr Current Branch.

Multicasting is configured as part of the DP properties; you can install multicasting and configure it by navigating to **Administration -> Overview -> Distribution Points** and right-clicking the DP name and selecting **Properties** or selecting the DP and from the ribbon bar choosing **Properties** and clicking the Multicast tab. Figure 22.15 shows the Multicast tab of a DP's properties.

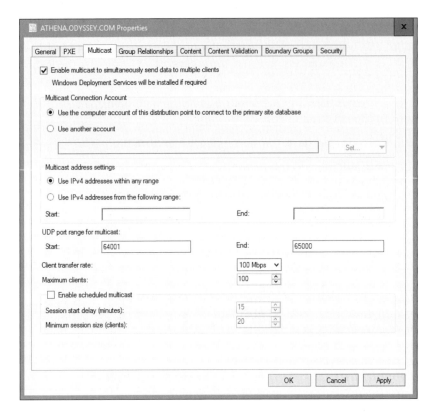

FIGURE 22.15   Multicast tab of a DP's properties.

Once the box is checked to enable multicast to simultaneously send data to multiple clients, the following options are available:

▶ **Multicast Connection Account:** This account, which by default is the local machine account, is used to communicate with the site database. If you choose to use a different account, Set becomes available, and you can select between using an existing account ConfigMgr already knows about or using a new account.

▶ **Multicast Address Settings:** Use the default range of IPv4 addresses from a DHCP server or enter an IPv4 address range to use.

▶ **UDP Port Range for Multicast:** Choose the User Datagram Protocol (UDP) range of ports you want to use. The default set of ports is entered automatically but can be changed. Remember that no matter what ports you set, they must be allowed through any firewalls or routers.

▶ **Client Transfer Rate:** Set the speed at which the content is downloaded. Take care to ensure that not all of the bandwidth is consumed on the network.

▶ **Maximum Clients:** Set the maximum number of clients that can download content at the same time.

▶ **Enable Schedule Multicast:** Control the schedule at which systems are allowed to download the content. When this option is checked, you can set the session start delay time, which is 15 minutes by default. This is the amount of time set aside before the first clients start to download the content. The minimum session size also becomes available; it is 20 by default but can be changed. This is the number of clients that must request the content before it is available for download.

While there are many options on this page, most organizations can enable multicasting and leave all settings at their default values.

If you intend to use multicasting, the next step in the process is to enable the OS image packages and any packages used during WinPE to use multicast. Navigate to **Software Library -> Overview -> Operating Systems -> Operating System Images** and select your OS image. Then choose **Properties** either from the ribbon bar or after right-clicking on the OS image. Select the Distribution Settings tab of the properties dialog that appears. At the bottom of the page, look for the Operating system deployment settings section, which offers these options:

▶ **Allow This Package to Be Transferred via Multicast (WinPE Only):** Allows the OS image package to be transferred to the client by multicast. If this option is unchecked, multicast is not used.

▶ **Encrypt Multicast Packages:** Allows ConfigMgr to encrypt the data in packages sent by multicast. Packages sent via multicast go over the network in clear text; if they have any sensitive information, the authors recommend checking this box.

▶ **Transfer This Package Only via Multicast:** Allows the package to be transferred only via a multicast session. The image package cannot be downloaded by any other method.

Using State Migration Points

If a user is having severe problems with his or her system; it might be determined that rather than spend too many hours trying to fix it, it is best to reimage the system and format the hard drive. Or perhaps a user gets a new bare-metal system and needs his or her data transferred to the new system and a new OS installed. In these types of cases, you may find that you need a place to store the user's data and settings so you can restore them after the machine is reimaged or the new OS installed. You can use an SMP to store this information securely.

SMPs can be installed on new servers added to the ConfigMgr hierarchy or on existing servers such as DPs that are already part of the hierarchy. There are some considerations to take into account when deciding where to put your SMP:

▶ **User State Size:** User state data usually consists of the user's data stored in the Documents folder. This is a mix of documents, pictures, music, and other data, and it could be quite large, depending on the organization's policy for user data. For example, if you include Outlook Personal Store (PST) files, this can be many gigabytes of data. How many migrations will occur at the same time? These all must be taken into account when considering the amount of space to allocate for the SMP.

▶ **Retention Policies:** These policies deal with the amount of time to keep user data on the SMP. It may not be as simple as capture the data, restore the data, and then delete it. What happens if a user has issues a day or a week after the data was deleted? How do you deal with a user who says not all the data has been restored to the new system? Consider these questions when determining how much space is needed and how long that space will be in use on an SMP; you may determine that you need to place SMPs in different locations or even on separate servers.

After gathering the SMP information, answering the questions, creating the policies, and creating the SMP's server layout, you can install the SMP. Navigate to **Administration -> Overview -> Site Configuration -> Servers and Site System Roles**. If adding the role to an existing server, highlight that server and either right-click it and choose **Add Site System Roles** or from the ribbon bar choose **Add Site System Roles**. If adding the SMP role to a new server to the ConfigMgr hierarchy from the ribbon bar, choose **Create Site System Server**. Both options launch a wizard with very similar pages:

▶ **General:** Click **Browse** and select the FQDN name, add a site code from a drop-down list, select an FQDN for the system to use if it will be on the Internet, define whether the site server will initiate connections to this site system, and choose what site system installation account to use. If adding the SMP role to an existing server, some fields are grayed out.

▶ **Proxy:** This page allows you to define what proxy to use if one is needed.

▶ **System Role Selection:** This page lists all roles that can be installed on this server. If using an existing server, roles that are already installed on the server do not display. Place a checkmark in the box for State Migration Point.

▶ **State Migration Point:** As shown in Figure 22.16, this page allows you to configure options for the SMP. You must complete three options:

  ▶ **Folder details:** Define the folder to use for SMP data. Clicking the yellow starburst icon allows you to choose a folder location, which must already exist. You can also select the maximum number of clients and the minimum amount of free disk space.

  ▶ **Deletion Policy:** Select when you want to remove the SMP data marked for deletion: immediately or after a certain number of days or hours.

  ▶ **Restore-Only Mode:** Set the SMP in a restore-only mode so no new SMP data can be written to it. This might be useful when disk space is filling up. You can turn this on, wait for data to be restored, and delete the data and turn it back off.

▶ **Boundary Groups:** This page allows you to associate an SMP to a boundary group so clients know which SMP to use. The Add and Create choices allow you to add a previously created boundary group or create a new boundary group.

The final three pages of this wizard are the standard Summary, Progress, and Completion pages.

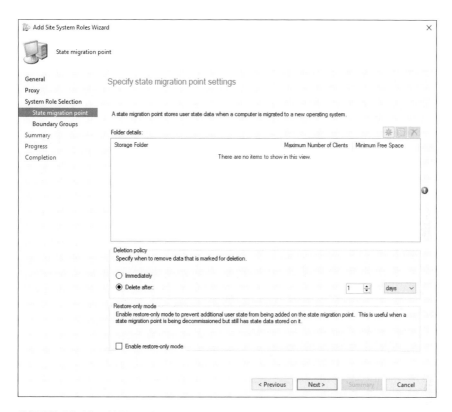

FIGURE 22.16   SMP settings page.

TIP: USING THE USER STATE MIGRATION TOOL

After configuring and installing the SMP, you will want to look at USMT in depth. There are many layers to USMT, its tools, the configuration files, gathering the user's data, storing the data, restoring the data, and marking data for deletion. This chapter does not go into detail on USMT or using it; for more information on USMT, see https://docs.microsoft.com/sccm/osd/get-started/manage-user-state and see https://technet.microsoft.com/library/hh397289.aspx for a flowchart on user state capture and restore. This last link refers to ConfigMgr 2012 R2 and USMT 5.0 but also applies to ConfigMgr Current Branch and USMT 10.0.

Getting Ready for Deployment

With everything set up and configured and the TS created, the next steps are to distribute the content and deploy the TS. As the TS executes, each step may require some form of content from a DP. If the content is not found on the DPs, that step in the TS fails, which could lead to a complete failure of the TS and, ultimately, the OS imaging process. Before executing the TS, you must deploy it to a collection of systems. After booting into WinPE, the TSs deployed to this system are downloaded and shown to the user; once the user selects a TS to execute, the OSD process begins.

Distributing the Content

Some of the content your TS uses may have to be distributed. If you reference applications or packages previously used in software distribution, that content may already be on the DPs. You could edit the TS and get a list of all content needed and then use the console to check each of those items and distribute those that need it, but there is an easier way. Navigate in the ConfigMgr console to **Software Library** -> **Overview** -> **Operating Systems** -> **Task Sequences** and select your TS, then either from the ribbon bar or after right-clicking the TS, choose **Distribute Content** to launch the Distribute Content Wizard. Figure 22.17 shows the Content Destination page of this wizard.

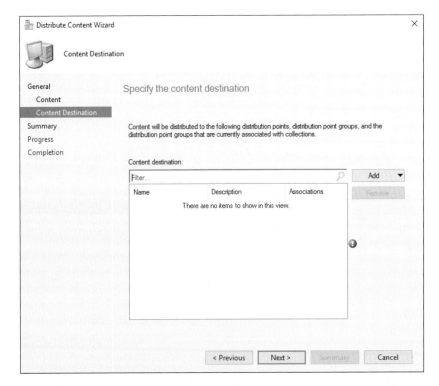

FIGURE 22.17   TS Distribute Content Wizard.

There are six pages to the wizard; the last three are the standard Summary, Progress, and Completion pages. The following are the unique pages:

▶ **General:** This page provides information only, and there is really nothing to configure. It shows the TS you selected, and at the bottom a check box is automatically checked to allow detection of any associated content dependencies to the TS.

▶ **Content:** This is another information-only page. You might notice a slight delay in moving from the General page to this page; this is because of the content detection occurring in the background. This page shows all the content associated with the TS, and this content is now added to the distribution, which means you can distribute all the content at one time.

▶ **Content Destination:** Select a collection, a DP, or a DP group to which to send the content by using the dropdown menu under Add. If you have DP groups, the authors recommend using that as your choice, to get the content to every DP in the group.

Depending on the content already distributed, the number of DPs to which you are sending content, the size of the content, and how many sites are in the hierarchy, it may take some time to finish distributing the content to the DPs. It is not unusual for a TS to need over 10GB of content. The images can be quite large, depending on what is actually in them. Before proceeding to the next step of deploying the TS, the authors recommend waiting for all the content to be distributed.

You may run into an issue with a low-bandwidth site where it takes too long for content to reach the DP. Solve this by prestaging the content. Select the TS in the console and choose **Create Prestaged Content File** from the ribbon bar to bring up a wizard that walks you through creating the prestaged content file. After creating the file, use other means to get the content copied over to the DP. When the file is on the DP, use the Extract Content tool to add the content to your DP. For more information about prestaging content, see https://docs.microsoft.com/sccm/core/servers/deploy/configure/deploy-and-manage-content#a-namebkmkprestagea-use-prestaged-content.

To monitor distribution status, navigate to **Monitoring-> Overview -> Distribution Status** and choose Content Status or Distribution Point Group Status. If you choose Content Status, you must search each content item and check its status. If you choose Distribution Point Group Status, highlight the DP group you select and choose View Status from the ribbon bar to open a status window where you see a pie chart, a list of content, and current status.

Deploying the Task Sequence

To execute the TS, you must deploy it to a collection of machines. If the TS is for new systems only, it is deployed to the unknown computer collection; if for refresh scenarios, the collection might be a query-based collection to determine the age of the systems and those that might fall out of support and need to be refreshed. Whatever the collection is, the TS must be deployed to it. To deploy a TS, navigate to **Software Library -> Overview -> Operating Systems -> Task Sequences** and select your TS, and then either from the ribbon bar or after right-clicking the TS, choose **Deploy** to launch the Deploy Software Wizard. This wizard has nine pages, of which the last three are the standard Summary, Progress, and Completion pages. The following sections describe the other pages of this wizard, and Figure 22.18 shows the Deployment Settings page of this wizard.

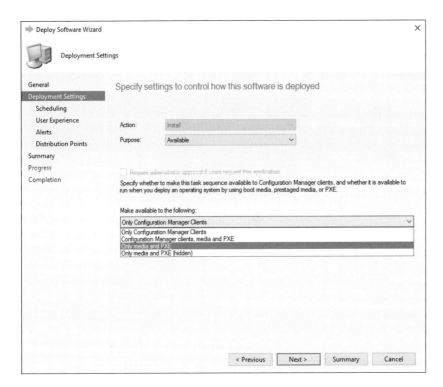

FIGURE 22.18   Task Sequence Deploy Software Wizard.

TIP: DEPLOY IS GRAYED OUT

When trying to deploy the TS, you may find that the Deploy option is grayed out. This occurs when the TS has a reference to a task, an application, a package, a driver, a boot image, or something else that is invalid. For example, if you import a TS created in your lab or in another ConfigMgr hierarchy, that TS will have references to the old environment and must be edited. If you find yourself in such a situation, edit the TS to find the invalid item, fix it, and then save your TS and retry the deployment option.

General Page

The first page of the wizard, General, has five items to complete, and some of them are required before moving to the next page:

▶ **Task Sequence:** Filled automatically with the name of the TS you selected to deploy. Change the default by clicking **Browse**.

▶ **Collection:** Required; allows you to select the collection to which you want to deploy the TS. Click **Browse** to select a collection from the list. You can select only one collection.

CAUTION: HIGH-RISK DEPLOYMENTS

A TS that deploys an OS is considered a high-risk deployment. Clicking **Browse** to select a collection brings up a high-risk warning message, as shown in Figure 22.19. The message explains that these types of deployments can be high risk, so it only shows you collections that have members that are greater than what is set in the Deployment Verification tab of the site properties. Click **OK** to continue. Notice at the top of the General page the check box to hide collections with a member count greater than the site's minimum site configuration; this check box is checked by default. The authors recommend that you not uncheck this box.

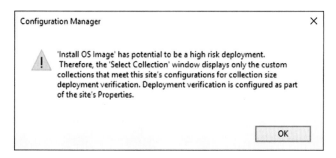

FIGURE 22.19   High-risk warning message.

▶ **Use Default Distribution Point Groups Associated to This Collection:** This option is grayed out unless the collection you chose has been associated with a DP group. Associate a collection to a DP group by navigating to **Administration -> Overview -> Distribution Point Groups** and selecting the DP group, and then either from the ribbon bar or after right-clicking the DP group, choose **Properties**. In the Collections tab of the properties dialog, click **Add** to choose the collection to associate with this DP group. You can add as many collections as you like.

▶ **Automatically Distribute Content for Dependencies:** This option is grayed out unless applications in the TS have a dependency assigned to them.

▶ **Comments:** This is an optional field for entering comments about the deployment.

Deployment Settings Page
On the Deployment Settings page, the Action menu dropdown is grayed out and always set to Install; you cannot uninstall an OS deployment. The page offers different options if Purpose is set to Required. The Deployment Settings offers the following options:

▶ **Purpose:** Select whether the deployment is mandatory. There are two choices from a dropdown menu:

  ▶ Required

  ▶ Available

▶ **Require Administrator Approval if Users Request This Application:** This option appears only when Purpose is set to Available. This option is usually grayed out for TSs that are imaging a device.

▶ **Send Wake-up Packets:** This option appears only when Purpose is set to Required. If this option is checked, ConfigMgr uses its built-in Wake on LAN functionally to send the magic packet that wakes up the client. Before using this option, computers and the network must be configured for Wake on LAN.

▶ **Allow Clients on a Metered Internet Connection to Download Content After the Installation Deadline, Which Might Incur Additional Costs:** This option appears only when Purpose is set to Required. Checking this option tells the client it can download content while using a metered Internet connection. Some Internet network providers charge based on the amount of data you send and receive with your Internet connection. The authors recommend that you not enable this option.

▶ **Make Available to the Following:** This option allows you to choose to whom the TS is available. There are four choices:

    ▶ **Only Configuration Manager Clients:** With this choice selected, any ConfigMgr client in the collection can see this deployment in Software Center. TS media and PXE booting systems are not able to see this deployment.

    ▶ **Configuration Manager Clients, Media, and PXE:** With this choice selected, ConfigMgr clients can see the deployment in Software Center, and TS media and PXE-booted machines can also see the deployment.

    ▶ **Only Media and PXE:** With this choice selected, TS media and PXE-booted systems can see the deployment, and ConfigMgr clients do not see the deployment.

    ▶ **Only Media and PXE (Hidden):** With this choice selected, the deployment is hidden from the TS media and PXE-booted systems, making it an automated TS. You must set up your TS to be completely automated if you want to use this option.

For most OS imaging deployments, the authors recommend using the option Only Media and PXE to make the deployment available to TS media and PXE-booted systems only.

Scheduling Page

The Scheduling page allows you to select information about when the deployment will be scheduled to become available or executed. It has four options:

▶ **Schedule When This Deployment Will Become Available:** Select the day and time for the TS deployment to become available.

▶ **Schedule When This Deployment Will Expire:** Select the day and time when this TS deployment will expire.

▶ **Assignment Schedule:** This option is available only if Purpose on the Deployment Settings page is set to Required. It allows you to set a schedule for when the TS deployment becomes mandatory. You can choose an exact date and time, or you can assign it to become mandatory as soon as possible, after a logon event, or after a logoff event.

▶ **Rerun Behavior:** This option is available only if Purpose on the Deployment Settings page is set to Required. It provides a dropdown menu that allows you to choose how ConfigMgr will handle reruns of the deployment. These are the options:

   ▶ Never rerun deployed program

   ▶ Always rerun program (default option)

   ▶ Rerun if failed previous attempt

   ▶ Rerun if succeeded on previous attempt

User Experience Page

Use the User Experience page to customize the end user's deployment experience. Some choices are dependent on the Purpose setting on the Deployment Settings page. These are the areas to configure:

▶ **Notification Settings:** Choose what the user can see and run. There are two choices:

   ▶ **Allow Users to Run the Program Independently of Assignments:** This option is available only if the Purpose setting on the Deployment Settings page is set to Required. If this option is checked, the end user can see this TS deployment in Software Center and run it at will.

   ▶ **Show Task Sequence Progress:** This option allows the user to see the progress bar the TS shows when running each step of the TS. Unchecking this box allows the non-OSD TS to run silently.

▶ **Activities Performed Outside of the Maintenance Window:** This option allows you to select between allowing software installation and system restarts to occur if the available time of the deployment falls outside a scheduled maintenance window assigned to the collection.

▶ **Write Filter Handling for Windows Embedded Devices:** Check this box to commit the changes at the deadline or during a maintenance window. Windows Embedded Systems (WES) use an overlay to store changes made to the OS; those changes are removed when the device is restarted, and the device is restored back to its original state. When you check this box and the WES gets a TS deployment, the ConfigMgr client requires the WES to reboot and enter service mode, allowing only administrators to log in. ConfigMgr then executes the TS and restarts the WES back into normal mode.

▶ **Allow Task Sequence to Run for a Client on the Internet:** This option allows a non-OSD TS to run on an Internet-based client. OSD imaging is not supported on these clients.

Alerts Page

Use the Alerts page to configure the criteria to create an alert inside the ConfigMgr console when the threshold is met. Two options are available:

▶ **Threshold for Successful Deployment:** This option is available only if the Purpose setting on the Deployment Settings page is set to Required. If this option is checked, you must choose the percentage amount that must be successful by a date and time you choose. If the percentage is not met by that time, an alert is generated inside the ConfigMgr console.

▶ **Threshold for Failed Deployment:** When this option is checked, you can pick a percentage number for the failed deployments. When the deployments reach that failed percentage, an alert is generated inside the ConfigMgr console.

Distribution Points Page

Use the Distribution Points page to customize how the client downloads the content from the DP. There are options to deal with no local DP with content, boundary groups, and BranchCache:

▶ **Download Content Locally When Needed by the Running Task Sequence:** This option appears in a dropdown menu but is the only item on the menu. TS deployments always require the content to be downloaded locally to the machine running the TS.

▶ **When No Local Distribution Point Is Available Use a Remote Distribution Point:** Selecting this option allows you to have the TS download content from a remote DP if the content is not found on a DP within its boundary. The authors recommend considering this setting carefully. OSD imaging content can be very large—10GB or greater in some cases. If the remote DP is across a slow network link, this could cause network errors.

▶ **Allow Clients to Use Distribution Points from the Default Site Boundary Group:** Selecting this option allows the system to fall back to the default site boundary group to find and download content when a local DP within its own boundary group does not have the content available.

▶ **Allow Clients to Share Content with Other Clients on the Same Subnet:** Selecting this option allows clients to use BranchCache for content downloads. If BranchCache is not installed on the clients, this item does not affect the content download.

Creating the TS Media

The next step in deploying your OS is creating TS media. Unless you plan to PXE boot all the systems on which you are going to use OSD TSs, you must have some type of TS media to start the process. TS media lets you boot the machine into WinPE so the TSs available for use can be shown to the user. There are four types of TS media you can create:

▶ Stand-alone media

▶ Bootable media

▶ Capture media

▶ Prestaged media

To create the TS media, navigate in the console to **Software Library** -> **Overview** -> **Operating Systems** -> **Task Sequences** and either from the ribbon bar or by right-clicking Task Sequences, choose **Create Task Sequence Media** to launch the Create Task Sequence Media Wizard. This wizard has different pages, depending the type of media you choose to create; in all cases, the last three pages are the standard Summary, Progress, and Completion. Figure 22.20 shows the wizard.

FIGURE 22.20   The Create Task Sequence Media Wizard.

Creating Stand-alone Media

Use stand-alone media when you have systems without a network connection or with a very slow connection and no local DP from which to pull content. Creating stand-alone media involves copying your entire OS deployment with content to the media of your choice, allowing the system to be booted with a USB stick or DVD, and enabling the OSD process to complete without a network connection. If your TS includes tasks that require a network connection, such as joining a domain, those tasks will fail. Using the wizard to create this type of media includes five pages that require user input, discussed in the next sections.

Media Type Page

Use the Media Type page to select the type of media to which you want to write the content:

▶ **Removable USB Drive:** Create media using a USB drive plugged into the machine running the console; if you remoted into the site server, the USB drive must be plugged into that site server. Selecting this option makes the Drive box available so you can select the USB drive. You can also format the drive and make it bootable. One caution on using a USB drive: Be sure it is large enough to hold the full set of media. Stand-alone media includes all drivers, packages, applications, boot images, and the OS image. It is not unheard of for the stand-alone media to be 32GB or more.

▶ **CD/DVD Set:** Choose the media size from a dropdown menu; 650MB, 4.7GB, 8.5GB, or unlimited. The sizes correspond to sizes of CD and DVD media. The thought is that you write the information to an ISO file and then burn the ISO file to CD or DVD for the machine to be booted with it. Before choosing the media size, have a good estimate of the content size. If the content is more than 8.5GB, you can make multiple files of the size you choose, or you can choose unlimited and create only one file.

▶ **Media File:** This option, which is available when the CD/DVD set is chosen, allows you to click Browse and select a folder and filename to use. You can also enter the path and filename (ending with .iso) in the list box. If you did not start the ConfigMgr console with the Run as Administrator option and UAC is enabled, you may receive an error saying you do not have write permissions to the location. Solve this by right-clicking the console icon and choosing Run as Administrator.

Security Page

Stand-alone media contains everything needed to deploy an organization's image, and it is possible that some sensitive information may be contained on the device where the media is being written. The Security page allows you to require a password to be entered before someone can start the OSD process once WinPE boots. If you check the box Protect media with a password, you must enter and confirm the password.

Stand-Alone CD/DVD Page

On the Stand-Alone CD/DVD page, choose the TS to use for this stand-alone media selection. You can choose only one TS per stand-alone media. Click **Browse** to see a list of all TSs and then choose one from the list. The middle of the page then shows the content associated with that TS, allowing you to see all of the content items on one page. The check box at the bottom of the page, Detect associated application dependencies and add them to this media, is checked by default. This box checks any applications in the content list and adds any dependencies the applications have to the content list. Unchecking the box could mean that those dependencies are not included in the stand-alone media, which may cause application installations to fail. The authors recommend leaving this box checked.

Distribution Points Page

The upper section of the Distribution Points page shows a list of DPs with the content needed to create the stand-alone media. The list contains any DPs that have any part of the content stored on the DP. It also shows you how many packages of the total number of packages are on the DP (for example, 8 of 10 packages).

The purpose of this page is to select the DP or DPs with all the packages you need to create the stand-alone media. It may be that all packages are distributed to all the DPs; in this case, you might end up selecting multiple DPs so that all of the content is covered.

TIP: CHOOSING THE CORRECT DPS

As the list on the Distribution Points page is in no particular order, take note of the DPs since you will want to select those with the fastest link or DPs that are local to your location. Stand-alone media is created by copying the content in the list from the DP or DPs to the local machine where the console is running. If you pick a DP across a slower network link, it takes much longer to create the media.

Customization Page

Use the Customization page to add any custom commands (which run before the TS begins) to the stand-alone media:

▶ **Variables:** At the top of the page, add any OSD variables you want to use. Clicking the yellow starburst icon launches a dialog box that allows you to add the variable name and value and then confirm the value. There is also a box that allows you to hide the value from the ConfigMgr console. For a refresher on OSD variables, see the "Using Variables" section, earlier in this chapter.

▶ **Enable Prestart Command:** Checking this box enables a text box where you enter the command you want to run before the TS begins. There is also a check box to include any files you might need for the prestart command. Check this box to select the package that the files are in by using the Set option; click Browse to choose what DP that package is on so it can be downloaded by the stand-alone media installer. An example might be that you need to run a script to check the ConfigMgr database to see if the machine running the stand-alone media is already in the database. You might need to delete that entry for the TS to run correctly. More in-depth information is available at https://blogs.msdn.microsoft.com/steverac/2015/04/22/power-belongs-to-youthe-osd-prestart-command/.

Creating Bootable Media

When you create bootable media, you create an ISO file or a USB drive that allows the system to boot into WinPE. Bootable media contains only the files needed to boot the system; it does not contain any content or image files. Those files must be downloaded across the network from a DP. Using bootable media means that the systems being imaged require network connections. Most of the pages in the wizard for creating bootable media are the same as for creating stand-alone media; the following sections describe those that are different.

Media Management Page

Use the Media Management page to choose how clients will find a management point (MP) so they can download information about the deployment that points them to the correct DPs. Since this is bootable media, no content is included with the media. There are two options:

▶ **Dynamic Media:** Allows the media to query MPs to find the correct MP, based on the site boundary for the IP address of that system.

▶ **Site-Based Media:** Allows you to pick an MP to use during the OSD process. That MP will be used until the ConfigMgr client is installed, at which point it will find an MP based on the site boundary information.

Security Page

The Security page for bootable media is similar to the Security page in the stand-alone media in that you can choose a password to protect the media; you can also select the certificate you want to use. These are the available options on the page:

▶ **Enable Unknown Computer Support:** Checking this option allows the bootable media to work with an unknown computer. In ConfigMgr, an unknown computer is any system without the ConfigMgr client installed or a system that has not been discovered.

▶ **Create Self-Signed Media Certificate:** Checking this option allows the Create TS Media Wizard to create a self-signed certificate using the date and time you choose for the start and expiration dates. This certificate is included with the boot media used to authenticate the system running the bootable media with the MP, telling the MP this is a real client that needs access and not a rogue client. The default length of time for the certificate is one year; when the certificate expires, the boot media will no longer work. Using this option allows communication over HTTP.

▶ **Import PKI Certificate:** Select this option to import a certificate from your organization's certificate authority. Browse to select the certificate to import. You must include the password associated with the certificate you want to import. Using this option allows communication over HTTPS.

▶ **User Device Affinity:** Use this option to choose how to set up device affinity for the user. User device affinity is the ability for ConfigMgr to understand which device is the user's primary device. When this option is set for a device, that device becomes the user's primary device. Applications or other items can then be targeted to the primary device. There are three options to choose from:

    ▶ Do not allow user device affinity (default option)

    ▶ Allow user device affinity pending administrator approval

    ▶ Allow user device affinity with auto-approval

Boot Image Page

Use the Boot Image Page to choose what boot image, DP, and MPs to use for this media. If you chose Site based media in the Media Management page, this option changes, and you can only pick one MP to use. The following options are available on this page:

▶ **Boot Image:** Pick the boot image you want to use for this media creation. Choose the boot image that will work with the systems you are imaging; for example, if imaging x86 systems, pick an x86 boot image.

▶ **Distribution Point:** Choose the DP from which the wizard will download the boot image. When creating the boot media, the wizard must download the boot image to a local folder on the system running the console. If no DPs are shown when you click **Browse**, you must distribute the boot image content to your DPs.

▶ **Associated Management Points:** The option varies depending on the option you selected on the Media Management page. If you choose Dynamic Media, a list box appears, allowing you to click Add to select multiple MPs for the boot media to use when starting communication. If you choose Site Media, the box is a single list box where you can click **Browse** to select a single MP to use for that initial communication.

22

NOTE: IMAGING SYSTEMS WITHOUT A WIRE-BASED NIC

The increase in systems like Microsoft Surface without a wire-based connection to the network make it harder to successfully image these devices from a bare-metal framework or as a reimage. To solve these issues, a ConfigMgr administrator can use a dongle that allows for a network connection using a USB port on the device. This works great as long as the drivers for the dongle are injected into the boot image. The problem has long been with ConfigMgr and its ability to manage hardware identifiers. The issue occurs when the dongle is moved from machine A to machine B. ConfigMgr would now consider machine B to be a known machine, causing issues with OSD when TSs were only targeted to the unknown computers collection. The ConfigMgr administrator would then have to delete the entry from the database so the machine would again become unknown. ConfigMgr Current Branch fixes this problem by allowing you to add hardware identifiers to a list so ConfigMgr will ignore them, allowing you to move dongles from machine to machine without any issues. Access this list by navigating to **Administration** -> **Overview** -> **Site Configurations** -> **Sites** and then either from the ribbon bar or after right-clicking Sites, choose **Hierarchy Settings**. In the dialog that appears, choose the Client Approval and Conflicting Records tab. At the bottom of the tab, in the Duplicate hardware identifiers section, click **Add** to enter the MAC address or SMBIOS GUID of the hardware you want to ignore.

Creating Capture Media

Capture media is created and used when you need to capture an entire image from a *reference* computer. The reference system is a clean system that has been installed from scratch, configured with the organization's settings, installed with the appropriate applications, and updated with the current software updates. The capture media allows you to boot into WinPE and capture this image into a WIM file so it can be added into ConfigMgr and used to deploy the OS to other systems.

The wizard has only two pages besides the standard Summary, Progress, and Completion pages—the Media type and Boot image pages. These pages are described earlier in this chapter for other media creations. The capture media contains the ConfigMgr binary files as well as the boot image that you selected in the wizard.

Creating Prestaged Media

Prestaged media allows you to create an image to be used by an OEM to image devices your organization purchases before they leave the manufacturer. Prestaged media is used at large organizations that have a staging center in place but no access to ConfigMgr. Prestaged media contains the boot and OS image; the TS you use with this type of media is not included in the WIM file the wizard creates. An example of how this would work follows: You deliver the WIM file to the OEM, which applies it to the bare-metal machine, which is then sent to the end user or staging center and plugged into the network and turned on. The machine locates an MP from where it will download the TS and starts executing the remaining tasks, eventually completing and giving the end user or staging center a completely imaged corporate machine.

The wizard has several pages, some of which have been discussed before. The Task Sequence page of this wizard is the same page as the Stand-Alone CD/DVD seen in the wizard for stand-alone media. The following sections discuss pages of the wizard that are different.

Media Properties Page

Use the Media Properties page to define the following properties for this WIM file and the actual filename to use:

▶ Created by

▶ Version

▶ Comment

▶ Media file

Images Page

Use the Images page to choose the image you want to use for the prestaged media. It is automatically populated from the TS chosen in earlier pages of the wizard. It provides the following options:

▶ **Image Package:** Click Browse and select the image package that you want to use with this media.

▶ **Image Index:** Sometimes an image WIM file contains multiple images, which are separated in the WIM file by different indexes. You see this mostly on OS images that come from the OS manufacturer. An example is the Windows 10 image file, which can contain the Home, Professional, and Enterprise versions in the same WIM file. Use this option to choose the index you want to use from a dropdown menu.

▶ **Distribution Point:** Click Browse and choose the DP you want the wizard to use to pull the content from when creating the prestaged media WIM file.

Select Application, Select Package, and Select Driver Package Pages

Three pages are discussed in this section because they are all very similar in layout and in terms of what needs to be entered:

▶ Select Application

▶ Select Package

▶ Select Driver Package

Each page has a list box with Add and Remove choices to select from a list of applications, packages, and driver packages, allowing you to add those items to the WIM file. This allows the content to be stored locally in the WIM file so that if a step in the TS references it, the content is pulled from the local store and not from a DP across the network. It allows you to add tasks into the TS that will install applications, packages, and drivers without having the system connected to the network.

NOTE: ALLOWING UNATTENDED OPERATING SYSTEM DEPLOYMENT

At the bottom of the Select Media Type page in the Create Task Sequence Media Wizard, shown in Figure 22.20, is a check box that allows you to set up the media for an unattended deployment of the OS. If you check this box, the user running the OS deployment is not prompted for any network configuration information or any optional TSs. The required TS runs automatically. The user is still prompted to enter a password if that option was selected when the TS media was created.

Troubleshooting OSD Deployments

OSD is one of the more complex areas of ConfigMgr. It includes several parts: the OS image, drivers, boot images, TSs, and TS media. It has many steps and places where things can and do go wrong. Most of the time, the components and processes work together to complete an OS deployment. When things go wrong or when the completed process is not what you thought it should be, there are places to look, logs to review, steps to monitor, and reports that explain what did not go as expected. The next sections discuss how to monitor and troubleshoot OSD, with some tips to make the experience better for all.

Monitoring OSD

In past versions of ConfigMgr, monitoring could be a difficult and clumsy task. Starting with ConfigMgr 2012 and more so in ConfigMgr Current Branch, monitoring involves a rich set of tools an administrator can use to understand where a system is in the process and what has occurred with that system. The first step to monitoring the OSD process is to navigate to **Monitoring -> Overview -> Deployments**. Find your OSD deployment in the list and select it. If it is difficult to find the OSD deployment among all the other deployments in this list, sort the list by feature type: Just click the Feature Type column. When you find your OSD deployment and select it, the bottom of the page shows a pie chart with the current summarization status of the deployment, which can provide a quick update. Choose **View Status** from the ribbon bar or from the right-click context menu to open the Deployment Status page, which shows the following five states possible for the deployment:

▶ **Success:** Machines listed here are those that have successfully completed the OSD deployment. They report in green.

▶ **In Process:** These machines are currently running the OSD deployment but are not yet finished. These are reported in yellow.

▶ **Error:** These machines received the OSD deployment but ran into an error when trying to download the content or execute the deployment. Dig deeper by looking at the lower part of the page to see the asset details. One of the details is the error code returned from the client; use this as a starting point to look for the issue with that client.

▶ **Requirements Not Met:** Machines in this state received the deployment but did not meet the rules that allow the deployment to run.

▶ **Unknown:** All systems appear in this state after the deployment is created. When a system returns a state message, it moves out of this state. If you see machines in this state after the deployment runs for some time, they did not receive the deployment and could be broken clients.

The Monitoring view can help you understand the deployment status and where machines are in the process (successful or still work in progress), but if you need to dig a little deeper, reporting might be your next step. ConfigMgr has an extensive report library you can access by navigating to **Monitoring -> Overview -> Reporting -> Reports**.

With each version of ConfigMgr, the number of reports has increased, and Current Branch has 478 reports. Of these reports, 28 of them deal specifically with OSD and TSs. By default the reports are sorted by the Name column in the ConfigMgr console. To focus solely on OSD reports, click the Category column and look for Task Sequence. If using the SQL Server Reporting Services (SSRS) web interface, you see the reports divided between four categories:

▶ Task Sequence-Deployment Status

▶ Task Sequence-Deployments

▶ Task Sequence-Progress

▶ Task Sequence-References

Some of the 28 reports are more helpful than others. The authors recommend looking at the following 3 reports as a starting point:

▶ **Status Summary of a Specific Task Sequence Deployment:** This report provides an overall summary of all resources targeted by the deployment.

▶ **History of a Task Sequence Deployment on a Computer:** Use this report to view what the TS executed on the target system and the output or exit code. This is a good report when you are seeing issues with the TS running tasks on the target system, as it shows what tasks were completed and the status message IDs.

▶ **Summary Report for a Task Sequence Deployment:** This report summarizes the number of systems that executed the TS, start and end times, and how many failed. While more of a 30,000-foot view, it is a great overall report if you just want a quick summary.

Boot Image Command-Line Support

When problems occur inside WinPE or before the OS image is applied, you may feel like you are inside a black box without knowing where to look. Enabling command-line support inside the boot image can help ease the burden of the black box. To enable this feature, navigate to **Software Library -> Overview -> Operating Systems -> Boot Images**, select the boot image, and choose **Properties** from the ribbon bar or after right-clicking Boot Images. Select the **Customization** tab (refer to Figure 22.7). For more information on the settings in this tab, see the "Using Boot Images" section, earlier in this chapter.

To enable command support, ensure that the box Enable command support (testing only) is checked. If you change the boot image here or in one of the other tabs, you must redistribute the boot image to your DPs before the change becomes active in WinPE. Once the box is checked and a system boots that boot image, pressing the F8 key on the keyboard opens a command window where you can run commands. For example, if you need to verify the IP address, you can run `ipconfig /all` in the window to return the IP information. A command that administrators commonly run to test network connectivity is the `ping` command. Use this command to verify that you can reach other network locations.

CAUTION: COMMAND SUPPORT SECURITY RISK

You cannot restrict access to the command line during a TS once it is enabled in a boot image. Internals of the OSD and Windows deployment process are accessible from the command line, including certain passwords stored in clear text.

In general, most organizations consider enabling command line support an acceptable risk as it is relatively hidden and obscure. And without command line support, there is no way to troubleshoot connectivity or other startup issues experienced in the OSD process. If you follow sound security practices, the accounts used and embedded in the process should be least-privilege accounts that can only do their specific tasks.

Using OSD Log Files

When monitoring and reporting is not enough to narrow down the issue, you can dig into the logs. Logging for the OSD process can occur in many places, depending on the process you are looking for and where the TS is in that process.

When creating TS media, the log file is CreateTsMedia.log, found on the site server in the ConfigMgr installation folder \AdminConsole\AdminUILog. If on a remote machine running the console, the log is located in %ProgramFiles(x86)%\Microsoft Configuration Manager\AdminConsole\AdminUILog. The filename is the same.

The log file when using TSs for deployments is SMSTS.log. This log file lives in different places, depending on the stage of the deployment process. It contains a detailed record of every TS-related action on the target system and usually contains any error that occurred as well as successful executions of TS steps. Referencing this file is the single most important step for troubleshooting a TS and should be the first thing you ask for when troubleshooting. Press the **F8** key to open the command window to obtain the log. Table 22.1 shows the location of the log, depending the state of the TS.

TABLE 22.1   SMSTS.log File Locations

Deployment Complete	TS Status	ConfigMgr Client Installed	SMSTS.log Location
No	WinPE Running	N/A	Windows temp folder in WinPE X:\Windows\Temp\SMSTS.log
No	Deployed OS Running with a TS running	Yes	SMSTSLog subfolder in the ConfigMgr client logs folder: C:\Windows\CCM\Logs\ SMSTSLog\SMSTS.log
No	OS Setup running	No	SMSTSLog folder C drive: %_SMSTSMDataPath%\Logs\ SMSTSLog\smsts.log
Yes	Deployed OS Running no TS is running	Yes	ConfigMgr client logs folder: C:\Windows\CCM\Logs\SMSTS.log

You may need to check the SMSTS.log if the TS fails, but you may discover that the target system rebooted before you could access the file. An example of this might be when you are testing your TS; you initiate the sequence and then go home for the night, expecting to check it in the morning, only to find the system rebooted and is sitting at the network page. This probably means that the TS encountered an error, the machine waited the default 15-minute timeout and then rebooted, WinPE loaded, and you lost everything in the log about the error. The authors suggest that in such a situation, you reset the default time-out for when an error occurs. You can do this by adding a step to your TS that changes the value of the SMSTSErrorDialogTimeout variable. Figure 22.21 shows an example where the value is set to 86,400 seconds (24 hours). Changing the value for this setting should give any administrator adequate time to see the error and collect the logs for review.

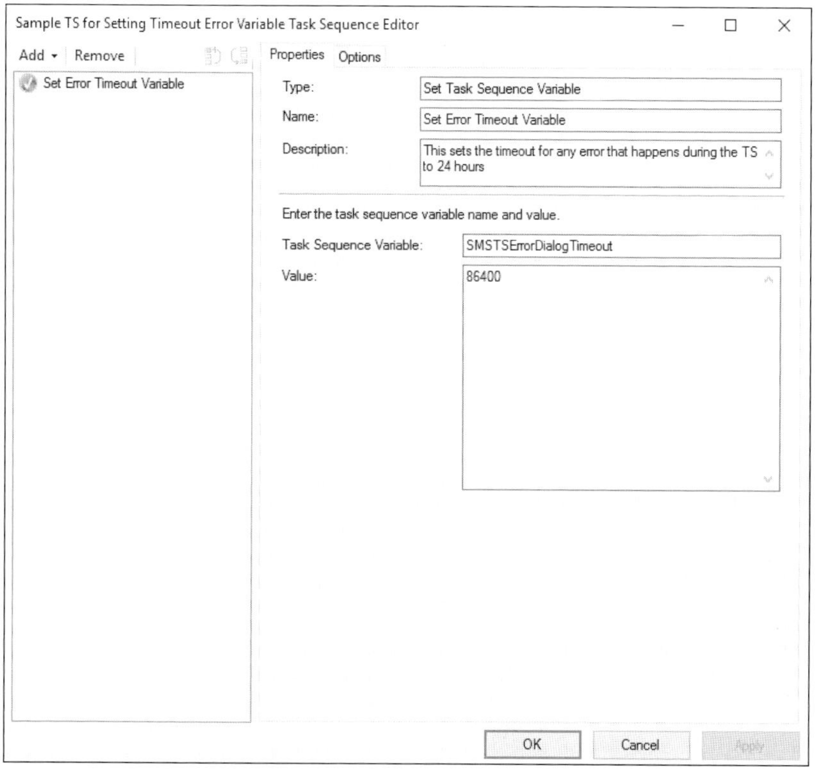

FIGURE 22.21   Setting the `SMSTSErrorDialogTimeout` variable.

TSs can get very long (200 steps are more); if this occurs, the log file rolls over, and you lose valuable information that might be needed for troubleshooting. You are left trying to reproduce the issue and catch log files before they roll over. You can change the parameters of the SMSTS.log file, which are hard-coded by default when WinPE boots. They are set in the WinPE Registry; press the F8 key to open the command window and type **regedit.exe**. In the Registry editor, navigate to `HKLM\Software\Microsoft\CCM\Logging\` `TaskSequence`, which shows you the following values about the logging for SMSTS.log:

▶ `LogDirectory=X:\Windows\Temp`

▶ `LogEnabled=1`

▶ `LogLevel=0`

▶ `LogMaxHistory=2`

▶ `LogMaxSize=2097152`

These values turn on logging and set the values; the ones you will want to change are `LogMaxHistory` and `LogMaxSize`, which modify the number of rollover logs and the size of a log. If you change these in the Registry, they will not take effect. The authors recommend changing the values using the SMSTS.ini file; this text file contains the settings you want for those Registry values. SMSTS.ini is read at WinPE boot time, before any TS runs and before the TS environment is built. The settings are usually the first line in your SMSTS.log file. Changing the values here allows your settings to be in place from the very beginning. The format of the file is very simple, just the settings you want to change:

```
[Logging]
LOGMAXSIZE=5120000
LOGMAXHISTORY=6
DEBUGLOGGING=1
```

Create a text file named SMSTS.ini, edit the file to include these options using the values you want to set, and save the file. Be sure the file is named SMSTS.ini, as sometimes when creating text files, the file may end up with an extra .txt extension (for example, SMSTS.ini.txt). Once the file is created, copy the file to the following two locations on your ConfigMgr site server:

▶ *<ConfigMgr_install_directory>*\OSD\bin\i386

▶ *<ConfigMgr_install_directory>*\OSD\bin\x64

Now navigate to **Software Library** -> **Overview** -> **Operating Systems** -> **Boot Images**, select the boot image, and choose **Update Distribution Points** from the ribbon bar or after right-clicking Boot Images to start the process of creating an updated boot image. The process injects SMSTS.ini into the WinPE image and distributes the image to your DPs. If you have set up PXE booting with WDS, the image used when a machine PXE boots is also updated. If using more than one boot image, you must update the others as well. When the log values are working the way you want, you must still collect them. The blog entry at https://blogs.msdn.microsoft.com/steverac/2008/07/15/capturing-logs-during-failed-task-sequence-execution can help automate part of that process. Be aware that no matter how much automation you have, there will still be times when you must collect the files manually.

The SMSTS.log file is not the only log file created or updated during the OSD process. The Setup Windows and ConfigMgr task runs the Windows Setup program, which creates and keeps several logs updated throughout the process. The following logs are some of the ones that may be of importance when looking for solutions to problems:

▶ *%SystemRoot%*\Panther\setuperr.log

▶ *%SystemRoot%*\Logs\DISM\dism.log

▶ *%SystemRoot%*\Logs\CBS\CBS.log

▶ *%SystemRoot%*\Debug\NetSetup.log

For more information about the Windows Setup logs, see https://support.microsoft.com/help/927521/windows-vista,-windows-7,-windows-server-2008-r2,-windows-8.1,-and-windows-10-setup-log-file-locations.

Once you have a log file, you need to view it. As it is a text file, you can use Notepad, but it will not be formatted for the best viewing. The preferred tool to view all ConfigMgr log files is CMTrace.exe, found in *<ConfigMgr_install_directory>*\Tools. CMTrace was built by the ConfigMgr product team and is updated with each version of ConfigMgr. It is designed to present the ConfigMgr logs in a more readable format, showing the log text, component, date and time, and the thread that wrote the log entry, which is valuable because many ConfigMgr components are multithreaded. You can search up or down the log for information. Errors are highlighted in red and warnings in yellow. You can also choose your own words and colors to highlight those words. The error lookup tool, accessed from the **Tools** menu or by pressing **Ctrl+L**, allows you to enter the error code and returns the text message associated with that error.

A very useful but often overlooked feature of CMTrace is its ability to open multiple log files and merge them chronologically. This can be helpful if you need to trace the flow of an object across multiple components. Access the feature by opening CMTrace without any log files open and then select the open folder icon or choose File -> Open to see the list of log files; at the bottom of the page, select the **Merge selected files** check box to open the files as a single file and then arrange the lines by their date and time values.

Understanding the PXE Boot Process

Networks that use PXE booting make life much easier for an OSD administrator. No more dealing with boot media or USB sticks or having to update them when a change is made to the boot image, although the authors recommend having these items available as a backup in case PXE does not work. However, this easier process has its drawbacks. PXE booting is prone to issues from network, routing, and DHCP problems—components external to ConfigMgr. The first stop for PXE boot issues is the PXE log file, SMSPXE.log, located on the system running WDS and PXE and usually in the SMS_DP$\SMS\Logs folder. The log file provides information about the system that is PXE booting, its MAC address, whether the system is known or unknown, the lookup reply, the package ID of the boot image it is looking for, and any errors that occur. These all could be pieces of the puzzle to help fix the error that is occurring. The following are common issues with PXE booting:

▶ IP address helper services are not running.

▶ Ports on the routers or firewalls are not open to allow PXE packets across the network.

▶ DHCP servers are not configured to process PXE boot packets.

▶ Domain Name System (DNS) resolution is not working correctly.

▶ The DHCP address pool is exhausted.

The PXE boot screen on the target system may also contain some valuable information. Figure 22.22 shows the boot screen for a virtual machine.

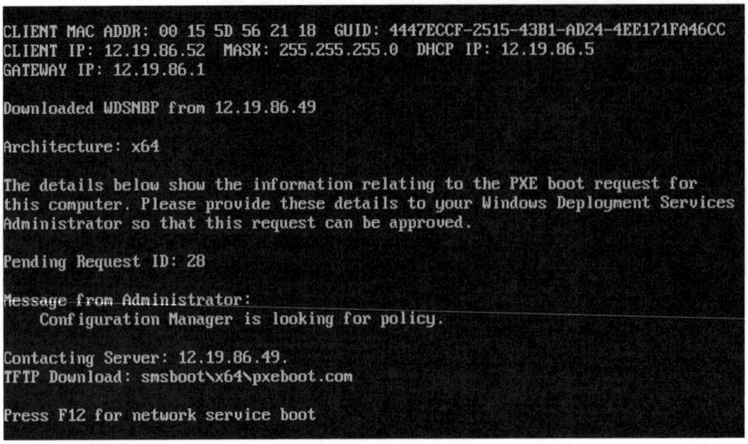

```
CLIENT MAC ADDR: 00 15 5D 56 21 18  GUID: 4447ECCF-2515-43B1-AD24-4EE171FA46CC
CLIENT IP: 12.19.86.52  MASK: 255.255.255.0  DHCP IP: 12.19.86.5
GATEWAY IP: 12.19.86.1

Downloaded WDSNBP from 12.19.86.49

Architecture: x64

The details below show the information relating to the PXE boot request for
this computer. Please provide these details to your Windows Deployment Services
Administrator so that this request can be approved.

Pending Request ID: 28

Message from Administrator:
    Configuration Manager is looking for policy.

Contacting Server: 12.19.86.49.
TFTP Download: smsboot\x64\pxeboot.com

Press F12 for network service boot
```

FIGURE 22.22   PXE boot screen for a virtual machine.

One often overlooked issue with clients having PXE boot failures is the IP address. A quick look at the PXE boot screen shows whether the client obtained a DHCP IP address. This screen also gives the IP address of the DHCP server it is talking to, its default gateway, the IP address of the WDS server, and the MAC address and GUID of the client system. Notice that it also says that ConfigMgr is looking for a policy. This is important because it determines whether the client is known or unknown to ConfigMgr. This is where the hardware identifier explained in the "Boot Image Command-Line Support" section, earlier in this chapter, comes in to play and allows you to PXE boot or not.

Many PXE issues are related to the network. One item that helps with some network issues is being able to change the default TFTP block and window size. If the default sizes are not working because of custom network changes, you may encounter time-out errors when trying to download the boot image. ConfigMgr now allows you to customize two settings:

▶ **TFTP Block Size:** This is the size of the data packets sent by the server to the client downloading the file. A larger block size allows the server to send fewer packets, meaning fewer round-trip delays between the server and the client. However, large block sizes lead to fragmented packets, which are unsupported by most PXE client implementations. Change this value by locating the following Registry key on the PXE-enabled DP: `HKLM\Software\Microsoft\SMS\DP\RamDiskTFTPBlockSize`; the default value is `4096 (4K)`. (If the key does not exist and you need to change the block size, you must create the key.)

▶ **TFTP Window Size:** TFTP requires an acknowledgment (ACK) packet for each block of data sent. The server does not send the next block until it receives an ACK for the previous block. TFTP windowing is a feature in WDS that allows you to define how many data blocks fill a window. The server sends the data blocks back-to-back until the window fills, and then the client sends an ACK packet. Increasing this window size reduces the number of round-trip delays between the client and server, decreasing the overall time for downloading a boot image. To change this value, locate the following Registry key on the PXE-enabled DP: `HKLM\Software\Microsoft\SMS\DP\RamDiskTFTPWindowSize`; the default value is `1`. (If the key does not exist and you need to change the block size, you must create the key.)

Updating Your OS Images

As you deploy OSs to new machines and even old ones, it is important to keep your images current with new security updates. It does not matter which OS is deployed, new or old: They all need to be updated. The authors recommend that you update each image on a quarterly basis. Offline servicing is an easy way to accomplish this process as Config-Mgr has built offline servicing of OS images into the console. To get started, navigate to **Software Library -> Overview -> Operating Systems -> Operating System Images**, select the OS image, and choose **Schedule Updates** either from the ribbon bar or after right-clicking the OS image to launch the Schedule Updates Wizard, shown in Figure 22.23.

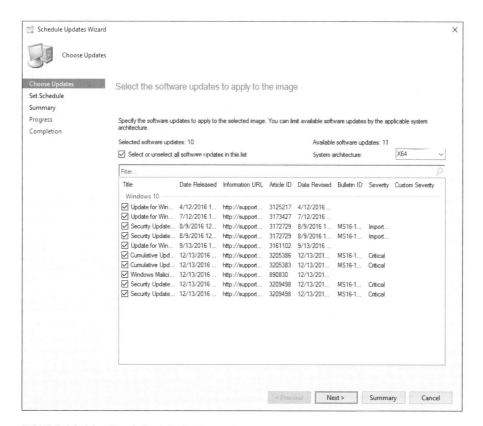

FIGURE 22.23   The Schedule Updates Wizard.

The wizard may take several minutes to populate the page of updates, as it must scan the image to get the list of updates needed. This process relies on a working Software Updates installation in ConfigMgr. The wizard uses the synchronized software updates as a baseline to scan against so it knows what updates can be applied. It is key to synchronize the updates for the OS versions of the images being used. The offline servicing process works only for security updates for the OS; Microsoft Office updates are not applied. The wizard has the standard Summary, Progress, and Completion pages as well as two pages for user input:

▶ **Choose Updates:** The list box in the middle of this page is populated with the updates applicable to the image you selected. How many are listed depends on how long ago the image was last updated. The older the image, the more updates it will need. Beside each update is a check box for you to select or deselect that update. By default all updates are selected. Above the list box are two options: a check box to select or unselect all updates at one time and a dropdown that allows you to choose between x64 and x86 architectures.

▶ **Set Schedule:** Select the schedule to use to update the image. Choose **As soon as possible** or pick an exact date and time to use. Two check boxes are checked by default: Continue on error, and Update distribution points with the image. Sometimes an error will occur when trying to apply the update to the image; the Continue on error option allows the process to continue and not stop on that error. The Update distribution points with the image check box allows DPs to be updated with the newly updated image when the process is finished.

The process is fairly simple: The image is copied to a temporary location on the machine running the console, the image is mounted, updates are applied using the DISM tool, the image is saved as it is unmounted, the old image is renamed, and the new image is copied back to its permanent location. The DPs are then updated if the box was checked in the wizard. The entire process is logged in the OfflineServicingMgr.log file located in the *<ConfigMgr_install_directory>*\Logs folder.

Summary

OSD is a large topic that cannot really be covered in a single chapter. If you search, you will find entire books dedicated to OSD and the deployment of OSs in general. Many organizations have dedicated deployment experts whose only job is deploying Windows and implementing OSD. Good or bad, you will be learning OSD and deployment techniques as long as you are in the business of Windows deployment.

OSD continues to be a primary reason for many organizations to implement ConfigMgr. Once set up and configured correctly, ConfigMgr becomes a workhorse that reduces the workload of IT administrators, engineers, and architects while also improving user satisfaction and overall effectiveness of the IT department. With Windows 10 Servicing inside ConfigMgr and the ability to create a streamlined upgrade TS, Microsoft has committed to enhancing OSD even more with ConfigMgr Current Branch, allowing the deployment and overall Windows experience to become as painless as possible.

The next chapter discusses security issues you should consider when implementing System Center Configuration Manager.

PART IV

Configuration Manager Administration

IN THIS PART

Security and Delegation in Configuration Manager

The rising number of high-profile data breaches in recent years has increased awareness of the importance of security in information technology (IT). This chapter discusses security issues to consider when implementing System Center Configuration Manager (ConfigMgr). It includes a detailed discussion of how to safeguard Configuration Manager workflows and protect ConfigMgr from compromise. The chapter begins with a discussion of how to address security requirements during ConfigMgr design and planning. Configuration Manager is a powerful platform you can use to implement core security controls. This chapter includes an overview of those controls. It presents ConfigMgr role-based administration (RBA), which allows you to assign access to IT support personnel on a least-privilege basis. The chapter also discusses how to prevent unauthorized administrative access to Configuration Manager and takes a deep dive into options for hardening your ConfigMgr environment against malicious attack.

Planning for Security and Delegation

Consider security requirements throughout the ConfigMgr deployment life cycle. In the design and planning phases, ensure that you have a basic understanding of security principles, involve the right personnel, and address aspects of your solution that are fundamental to security. Following is a brief overview of security concepts.

Security Planning Overview

As you begin planning for security, consider these basic questions:

▶ What am I trying to protect?

▶ From what do I need to protect it?

▶ How can I implement the required protection?

Much of this chapter focuses on the last question. This section looks at the first two, discussing things to consider as you think about what you are protecting and from what you are protecting it.

You need to protect the data stored in the ConfigMgr site database. The site database contains extensive information about your environment. An attacker could use this information to learn about your systems, networks, and applications, as well as your organization's security posture. Many ConfigMgr features collect and store user information. Recently there has been increased emphasis on securing personally identifiable information (PII). PII is any data about an individual that can be used to establish his or her personal identity. PII is highly regulated in many jurisdictions, most notably in the European Union (EU); be aware of those privacy regulations. Engage with the persons responsible for privacy in your organization to learn what requirements are in place for personal user data. You may need to limit the data you collect or implement additional controls to protect user data.

NOTE: ABOUT DIAGNOSTIC USAGE DATA

ConfigMgr collects data about product usage and functioning that it sends to Microsoft for product improvement. You can configure the level of data collected. At basic and enhanced levels, Microsoft does not intentionally collect IP addresses, user or computer names, physical addresses, or email addresses, which may be PII data. If you change the collection level from enhanced (default) to full, these items may be included in advanced diagnostics information such as log files. For detailed information about Microsoft's data collection and usage, see https://docs.microsoft.com/sccm/core/plan-design/diagnostics/levels-of-diagnostic-usage-data-collection-1710.

Protect your site systems and the services they provide. A ConfigMgr service failure could affect normal operations, user productivity, and security; users could lose access to applications, and administrators could be unable to patch systems efficiently.

In addition to protecting ConfigMgr itself, plan your solution with a view toward protecting your larger environment. The "ConfigMgr Security Solutions" section, later in this chapter, discusses how to use ConfigMgr to protect systems and data. Realize that a ConfigMgr security breach or an administrator's mistake could compromise the security of managed systems.

Most large organizations have teams dedicated to security, regulatory compliance, and privacy. Involve these teams in the design and planning phases of your deployment, make them aware of the security and compliance solutions ConfigMgr offers, and help them recognize the criticality of the ConfigMgr infrastructure and the threats to that infrastructure. Understand your organization's security policies and the business drivers for security as they relate to your deployment, as this will help focus your efforts on the highest-priority security and compliance objectives.

Working with the security team can help avoid costly delays and poorly planned security controls. During design and planning, work with your security group to identify threats to each ConfigMgr service you plan to provide and select risk management strategies to deal with those threats. Most threat actors have a financial motivation. In the past, payment card and banking information was commonly targeted for financially motivated cyber-crime. Recent trends include using extortion and increased targeting of intellectual property and health information. In addition to financially motivated cyber-criminals, significant threat actors include disgruntled employees and others with personal animosity toward an organization, political "hacktivists" seeking to promote some cause, and nation-states seeking economic or military advantage. Following are some important changes to the threat landscape since the publication of *System Center 2012 Configuration Manager (SCCM) Unleashed* (Sams Publishing, 2013):

▶ **Emergence of Ransomware as a Primary Security Concern:** Ransomware typically encrypts data using keys known only to the attackers, who demand bitcoin payment for the keys to decrypt that data. Ransomware attacks against consumers have become very common. A recent development has been ransomware attacks on enterprise servers. Some attackers also threaten to expose sensitive data or to exfiltrate and monetize the data in other ways.

▶ **PowerShell as a Weapon:** Systems administrators understand that PowerShell is a highly capable and flexible tool for managing all resources in the Windows environment. Attackers are aware of this, and toolkits such as PowerSploit and PowerShell Empire have made PowerShell the weapon of choice to attack Windows systems.

▶ **Digitally Signed Malware:** Digital signatures provide a foundation of trust that files come from a trusted publisher and have not been tampered with. Attackers gain access to code-signing certificates by various means, such as by stealing them from developer workstations or purchasing them from legitimate certificate authorities (CAs).

The number of known digitally signed malicious binaries as of the 4th quarter of 2017 is well over 20 million. Code signing as a service is now available in the underground economy.

▶ **Rise in Cryptographic Attacks:** While there were earlier exploits based on flaws in cryptographic technology, the number of exploits directed against the cryptographic methods at the core of Internet security has risen dramatically since the disclosure of the Heartbleed vulnerability in April 2014.

▶ **Slash and Burn:** Traditionally, attackers attempted to cover their tracks using techniques such as deleting log files. More recently, attackers have tried to do as much damage as possible after achieving their initial objectives.

Many companies and government agencies have become victims of a class of attacks known as *advanced persistent threats* (APTs) from sophisticated, well-financed hacker groups, often backed by nation-states. Targets include virtually every type of business, with a general objective of stealing valuable intellectual property and business secrets for military or economic advantage. APTs often take advantage of user mistakes, such as clicking links or opening attachments sent though social media or phishing emails. Once in the door, they spread laterally from machine to machine, seeking to find high-value targets. These attackers often attempt to compromise domain controllers as a control point to reach systems across the enterprise. As companies use increasing vigilance to secure domain controllers, management systems become the next logical point of attack. Defending against APT attacks requires different approaches from defending against traditional malware and hackers. Make your security team aware that ConfigMgr site systems are potential targets for these attacks.

The next section introduces security concepts and terminology used throughout the chapter. If already familiar with concepts such as the CIA (confidentiality, integrity, availability) triad, risk management, and layered defense, you may choose to skim this section briefly or skip it altogether.

A Security Primer

The principal objectives of information security are to protect data confidentiality and integrity, as well as service availability. It is also essential to maintain a reliable audit trail of actions taken on the system. Following is a description of these objectives:

▶ **Confidentiality:** Keeping secret information you are responsible for secret.

▶ **Integrity:** Protecting information and systems from unauthorized modification.

▶ **Availability:** Keeping systems and services running.

▶ **Accountability:** Maintaining effective audit logs to track security-sensitive operations on a per-user basis. The completeness and integrity of audit logs is essential in demonstrating regulatory compliance. Audit logs are also an integral part of the incident response and forensic investigation processes.

A guiding principle in security is the concept of risk management. No organization can keep its assets completely secure. Organizations must therefore implement strategies to prioritize and deal with risks. Following are some essential terms used in risk management:

▶ A *vulnerability* is a weakness that could result in compromise of the confidentiality, integrity, or availability of information or systems.

▶ A *threat* is a potential danger to information systems. Threats include malicious and inadvertent actions. Good security helps protect against honest mistakes by users and deliberate breaches by hackers and malware creators.

▶ A *risk* is the likelihood of a threat being realized and the associated business impact.

Effective risk management depends on understanding the risks to your systems and data and making appropriate business decisions on how to deal with each set of risks. Following are some approaches for dealing with risk:

▶ **Risk Avoidance:** You might decide that the business value of undertaking a technology initiative does not justify the risk. As an example, you might determine that the value to your company of Internet-based client management (IBCM) is not sufficient to justify exposing your ConfigMgr infrastructure to the Internet.

▶ **Risk Mitigation:** You might decide to implement countermeasures to address potential threats to reduce risk. Much of the material in this chapter relates to risk mitigation strategies.

▶ **Risk Acceptance:** You might decide to accept certain risks if the business value of the activity and cost of implementing additional controls to mitigate risk outweigh the potential losses posed by the risk. As an example, say that you determine that using a file server running an older version of Windows as a distribution point (DP) provides sufficient business value to justify the risk, while the cost of providing a more secure system is not justified by the risk mitigation it would provide.

Leading security organizations, such as the following, publish lists of critical controls to help you prioritize your security efforts:

▶ **Center for Internet Security (CIS):** Leading industry and government stakeholders in information security support this not-for-profit organization. CIS publishes extensive guidance on cyber-defense, including the *CIS Controls for Effective Cyber Defense*. See https://www.cisecurity.org.

▶ **Information Assurance Directorate (IAD):** Part of the National Security Agency (NSA), IAD shares its expertise with other government agencies, industry, academia, and the public. Its valuable publications include *IAD's Top 10 Information Assurance Mitigation Strategies*. See https://www.iad.gov/iad. Note that the iad.gov website uses TLS 1.2, supported by a Department of Defense (DoD) PKI certificate. Website users will need to have the current DoD Root and Intermediate CAs loaded into their browsers to avoid receiving untrusted website notifications.

▶ **Australian Signals Directorate (ASD):** ASD is the Australian authority for information security. It provides leading cybersecurity research, including *Top 4 Strategies to Mitigate Targeted Cyber Intrusions*. The Australian government's information security manual is at https://www.asd.gov.au/infosec/ism/index.htm.

Microsoft has worked with CIS and IAD to develop best practices for Windows operating systems, Active Directory (AD), and other Microsoft products. Microsoft provides a free tool, Microsoft Security Compliance Manager (https://www.microsoft.com/ download/ details.aspx?id=16776), for use in comparing your systems against baseline Microsoft recommendations. You can customize the baselines to the needs of your organization and export them to use in ConfigMgr compliance settings, AD group policy, and other security tools.

Security experts generally advocate implementing controls throughout your environment—addressing threats to the network perimeter, internal network, system hardware, OS, applications, human resources, and so on. This method, known as the *layered security model* or *defense in depth*, recognizes that while any single control can fail, it is difficult for an attacker to defeat controls at every layer of the computing stack.

Traditional risk mitigation strategies focused on preventing known threats. Security experts now teach that no organization should expect to prevent every attempt to gain unauthorized access to their networks and systems. It is therefore important to adopt a "prevent, detect, respond" model, in which you prevent as many intrusions as you can but are prepared to detect and respond to compromise when it occurs. The first indication of compromise is often unexpected system behavior, such as crashes or degraded performance. Make sure systems administrators consider the possibility of system compromise when troubleshooting stability and performance issues. If they are unable to determine the root cause, involve the incident response team to check systems for indicators of compromise (IOCs).

Designing Your Hierarchy for Security

When designing your hierarchy, consider the following:

▶ **Active Directory:** Although ConfigMgr sites and hierarchies can span more than one AD forest, such an arrangement might compromise your AD security design. The forest is a security boundary in AD. Weigh the importance of maintaining the strongest possible security boundary between forests against the possible administrative advantages of a single ConfigMgr hierarchy to manage multiple forests.

▶ **ConfigMgr Site Selection:** The fewer sites you have, the easier it is to maintain site security. Additional sites increase the number of site servers, site databases, and intersite communications links to administer and secure. However, in some cases you might require additional sites. Chapter 4, "Architecture Design Planning," discusses reasons to deploy additional sites.

▶ **Site System Role Assignment:** You should move client-facing roles, such as the management point (MP) and DP, off the site server. The risk of a network attack is greatly reduced if you restrict client access to only server roles that require it. The site server and site database server are the most important roles in your site; opening network access required for clients to establish a connection to these systems is a risk you should consider eliminating.

Separating server roles generally reduces the requirement for services and open network ports on each system, which reduces the system attack surface. Weigh this advantage against the effort required to support and secure additional site systems. As installing Internet Information Services (IIS) on a server greatly increases its attack surface, you should generally separate server roles requiring IIS from those that do not. You also should separate the Fallback Status Point (FSP) server role from all other system roles. The FSP must accept unauthenticated client data, presenting a risk to which you would want to avoid exposing other site roles.

Perhaps the most important security consideration for assigning system roles is to avoid using systems hosting other applications as site systems, especially those with applications based on IIS or SQL Server. Poorly written or vulnerable web and database applications are favorite targets of attackers and could be exploited to gain control of a site system. Placing a DP on a server that provides file and print services presents a much lower risk.

▶ **Server Placement:** Deploy site systems in locations that are as secure as possible in terms of physical and network access. An attacker with physical access to a site system could compromise your system by installing a hardware device such as a keystroke logger or booting the system to an insecure operating system (OS). Restrict network traffic to that which is necessary for ConfigMgr operations and basic server functions. Using a host-based firewall or taking advantage of the microsegmentation capabilities available through network virtualization provides the most granular control of network traffic. If possible, place the site server and site database server in a secure network zone, isolated from systems with lower security requirements, such as user workstations.

▶ **Managing Clients on the Internet:** If you plan to manage clients on the Internet, consider using a cloud management gateway for managing Internet-based clients. Doing so eliminates some security challenges associated with Internet-based client management, especially the need to expose your on-premise infrastructure to the Internet.

▶ **Administrative Workstations:** If administrators must reach site systems from less-secure network zones, have them use a virtual private network (VPN) to connect to systems in the higher-security zone. Consider providing an extra measure of security by using a "jump box." In this scenario, administrators establish a Remote Desktop Protocol (RDP) session to the jump box to run the console and other tools rather than connect directly to site systems.

Planning for Secure Administration

To mitigate the risk of someone with ConfigMgr administrative access misusing her privileges, follow these principles when developing ConfigMgr administrative models and procedures:

▶ Grant the least privilege necessary for each administrator to carry out his or her responsibilities. Assigning overly broad privileges to users or administrators greatly increases the chances of compromising systems or data. Review permissions in the built-in roles; consider customizing the roles by removing permissions not required in your administrative model.

▶ Employ separation of duties wherever possible to make it more difficult to abuse administrative access. When a person carries out improper activity on his or her own, the level of effort and risk of detection are much lower than when the person colludes with others. For example, a user with the Application Administrator role could introduce unauthorized code into an application and then target specific systems for attack. Assigning the Application Author role and the Application Deployment Manager role to separate individuals can mitigate this risk. The extent to which you choose to separate responsibilities for related tasks depends on your security requirements and available resources.

The "About Role-Based Administration in ConfigMgr" section, later in this chapter, explains how to use RBA to assign ConfigMgr administrative permissions.

Several ConfigMgr features can provide significant risk mitigation for your managed systems. The next section reviews these features.

ConfigMgr Security Solutions

Configuration Manager can play a major role in supporting your security program. Previous chapters present a number of ConfigMgr features you can use to enhance the security of your environment. Following are some of them:

▶ **Patch Management:** A large number of exploits take advantage of unpatched systems that remain vulnerable even after a fix is available from the software vendor. ConfigMgr facilitates patch management for Microsoft operating systems and applications through its software updates feature set. Chapter 15, "Managing Software Updates," discusses patch management.

▶ **Conditional Access:** Keeping unpatched or otherwise inadequately protected devices and systems from accessing services such as SharePoint and email provides a strong line of defense against threats that might use these systems to compromise data. Chapter 18, "Conditional Access in Configuration Manager," discusses conditional access.

▶ **Compliance Settings:** Misconfigured systems are another major category of vulnerabilities. The ConfigMgr compliance settings feature supports enforcement of configuration standards and reporting on system compliance. Chapter 10, "Managing Compliance," describes how to use ConfigMgr to enforce consistent, secure system configuration based on best practices and organizational standards.

▶ **Certificate Profiles:** ConfigMgr can deploy and manage certificates profiles used for secure access to resources such as a VPN or wireless access point.

▶ **Endpoint Protection:** ConfigMgr can provide centralized management of Windows Firewall policies and Microsoft Endpoint Protection antimalware policies. Endpoint protection also allows you to manage the Microsoft Endpoint Protection engine update and signature file distribution. Chapter 19, "Endpoint Protection," discusses endpoint protection.

New ConfigMgr functionality includes integration with Windows 10 security features such as Device Health Attestation and Passport for Work. Device Health Attestation provides strong, hardware-enabled security to ensure the integrity of the OS and other core system components. ConfigMgr provides extensive reporting on Device Health Attestation status and allows you to use health status in compliance rules for conditional access. Passport for Work eliminates the need for password-based authentication across the network, as the user authenticates to the local device using Hello biometric authentication or a locally stored PIN. Digital certificates then provide access to network resources. ConfigMgr allows you to control passport policies in your organization.

> **NOTE: NETWORK ACCESS PROTECTION DEPRECATED IN CONFIGMGR CURRENT BRANCH**
>
> Network Access Protection (NAP), a security feature in ConfigMgr 2012, has been deprecated in the current version of ConfigMgr and is no longer supported. NAP is a complex technology and seldom used. If you require the protection NAP provided, consider DirectAccess, Windows Web Application Proxy, or various third-party network access control solutions.

Beyond these specific features, well-managed environments are inherently more secure than less-well-managed environments. Central management of day-to-day IT functions such as software installation, OS upgrades, and troubleshooting reduces the need for large numbers of privileged users and provides better auditing and control. Comprehensive inventory and reporting are essential to security planning. Much of this chapter focuses on potential misuse or compromise of the ConfigMgr infrastructure; the risks of not having effective configuration management are much greater.

The next section describes how to assign the appropriate ConfigMgr administrative access.

About Role-Based Administration in ConfigMgr

RBA allows you to manage administrative rights efficiently so that each user has only the access required for his or her job function. An administrator with full access to the ConfigMgr hierarchy can perform an almost unlimited range of actions within your managed environment. Following are some examples of what a person with the requisite permissions could do:

▶ Execute arbitrary code on any ConfigMgr client system, in the context of the privileged system account or the logged-on user.

▶ Collect and view any file from client systems.

▶ Interact directly with client systems through remote tools.

Misuse of administrative rights can occur in three ways:

▶ An authorized ConfigMgr administrator can deliberately abuse his or her privileges.

▶ An attacker can gain access to the administrator's account.

▶ An administrator might make an honest mistake.

The ConfigMgr RBA security model is similar to that of other System Center components. Sets of related administrative tasks are grouped together to define roles. ConfigMgr administrators are assigned roles based on job function. The roles provide the minimum privilege required to carry out the user's responsibilities. The next section shows how ConfigMgr administrators in the Odyssey domain provide the web server administrators with the minimum permissions necessary to manage the specific servers for which they are responsible.

Managing Administrative Users

Before assigning a user or group to a role, you must add the user or group as an administrative user. Do not confuse administrative users with administrators; administrative users only have the rights provided by their specific roles. To add administrative users, perform the following steps:

1. In the ConfigMgr console, navigate to **Administration** -> **Security** -> **Administrative Users** -> **Add User or Group**.

2. Click **Browse** and select a user or group from the Select User, Computer, or Group dialog. As a best practice, assign roles to AD groups rather than to individual users. Figure 23.1 shows the Add User or Group dialog.

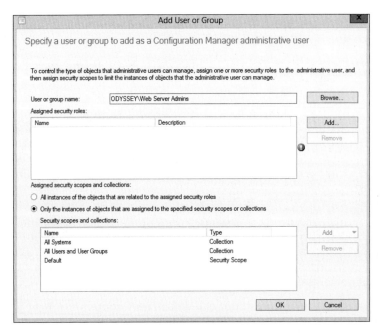

FIGURE 23.1   Adding the Web Server Admins group as a ConfigMgr administrative user.

3. Click **Add** and select one or more roles from the Add Security Role dialog. Figure 23.2 shows this dialog with roles selected for web server administrators. (The following section, "Security Roles," describes security roles.)

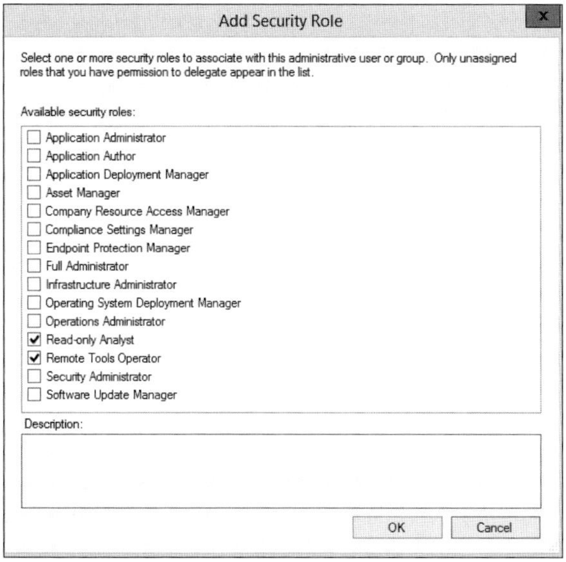

FIGURE 23.2   Associating roles with an administrative group.

4. Optionally, restrict the account to assigned security scopes or collections. The "Using Security Scopes" section, later in this chapter, discusses these options.

POWERSHELL RBA CMDLETS

The examples in this chapter show how to manage RBA using the ConfigMgr console. You can also use PowerShell for RBA management. For example, to add the Remote Tools Operator role to the Web Server Admins, execute the cmdlet
`Add-CMSecurityRoleToAdministrativeUser -AdministrativeUserName "ODYSSEY\ Web Server Admins" -RoleName "Remote Tools Operator"`.

See https://docs.microsoft.com/powershell/sccm/overview?view=sccm-ps for instructions on getting started with PowerShell to administer ConfigMgr. See https://docs.microsoft.com/ powershell/module/configurationmanager/?view=sccm-ps as a reference for available cmdlets.

Security Roles

A security role consists of a set of related permissions that allow a user to perform specific tasks. Configuration Manager provides several built-in roles that address common administrative responsibilities. You can create additional roles and customize them to the particular needs of your organization. Security roles are hierarchy-wide and replicate to all sites.

Using Built-in Roles

The built-in security roles represent typical sets of job responsibilities for IT administrators needing access to ConfigMgr. If these roles meet your requirements, you can assign them to administrative users. You can view the properties of each built-in role, but you cannot modify them. The following section, "Creating Custom Roles," describes how to use these roles as templates to create custom roles.

To view the roles and their descriptions, navigate to **Administration -> Security -> Security Roles**. The Full Administrator role provides unrestricted access to all ConfigMgr operations. If your organization separates security administration from operational duties, you might assign the Security Administrator and Operations Administrator roles to separate users; however, you must have at least one user with the Full Administrator role. The "Auditing ConfigMgr Administrative Actions" section, later in this chapter, explains how auditors or security personnel can keep an eye on all administrative users, including full administrators.

Creating Custom Roles

Create a custom role by copying an existing role and editing the copy's permissions. For example, the Asset Manager role includes rights to read, create, delete, and modify mobile device enrollment profiles. If asset managers in your organization are not responsible for managing these profiles, you may want to create a custom role without this access. Follow these steps to create a customized role:

1. Navigate to **Administration -> Security -> Security Roles**.

2. Right-click the role you want to customize and choose **Copy**.

3. On the Copy Security Role page, enter the name and an optional description for the new role. Figure 23.3 shows the Copy Security Role dialog for the Asset Manager role without access to manage mobile device enrollment profiles.

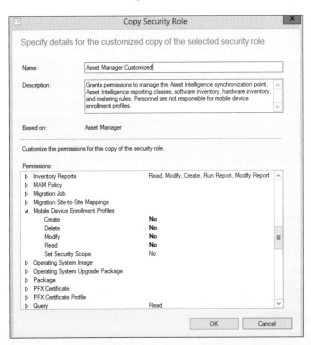

FIGURE 23.3   Duplicating and customizing the Asset Manager role by removing permissions on mobile device enrollment profiles.

You can export a custom role and import it into a different hierarchy. For example, you might develop and test all custom roles in your lab environment and import them in production. After creating a custom role, you can edit its permission set and other properties on the role's property sheet. Built-in roles and roles imported from other hierarchies are not editable.

Using Security Scopes

Security roles define the operations a user can perform on each class of securable objects. You can further limit an administrative user's access rights to a subset of the securable objects of each class. Depending on the class of securable object, you could accomplish this through collections or security scopes:

▶ **Collections:** To specify the set of devices and users an administrator can manage, assign specific device collections or user collections to the administrator. You can assign one or more collections to each user. By default, each administrative user is assigned the All Systems and All Users collections.

▶ **Security Scopes:** To specify other sets of objects an administrator can manage, assign specific security scopes to the administrator. A *security scope* is essentially a container that contains one or more types of securable objects. You can assign one or more security scopes to each administrative user. By default, each administrative user is assigned the Default security scope.

Permissions on some types of objects apply to all type instances, and you cannot restrict these by collection membership or security scope.

You can associate objects of the following types with security scopes:

▶ Antimalware settings

▶ Application

▶ Authorization lists

▶ Boot image packages

▶ Boundary groups

▶ Client settings

▶ Configuration items

▶ Configuration policies

▶ Device enrollment profiles

▶ Device setting items

▶ Device setting packages

▶ Distribution point groups

▶ Distribution point info

▶ Driver packages

▶ Firewall policies

▶ Global conditions

▶ Image packages

▶ Metered product rules

▶ Migration jobs

▶ Operating system install packages

▶ Packages

▶ Queries

▶ Sites

▶ Software updates packages

▶ Subscriptions

▶ Task sequence packages

▶ Virtual hard disk (VHD) packages

▶ Virtual environments

There are two built-in security scopes: All and Default. Administrative users assigned the All security scope can administer all objects related to their role. Built-in instances and newly created instances of securable objects are assigned the Default security scope. Perform the following steps to create additional security scopes:

1. Navigate to **Administration -> Security** and right-click **Security Scopes**.

2. Choose **Create Security Scope**.

3. In the Create Security Scope dialog, enter the security scope name and an optional description and then click **OK**. Figure 23.4 shows the Create Security Scope dialog for the Web Server Resources scope.

FIGURE 23.4   Creating a security scope for objects available to web server admins.

After creating a new securable object, set its security scopes. Follow these steps:

1. Locate and right-click the object in the ConfigMgr console. Use the standard Ctrl and Shift options to multi-select objects for which you want to specify the same scopes.

2. Choose **Set Security Scopes**.

3. In the Set Security Scopes dialog, select one or more scopes to associate with the objects and then click **OK**. Figure 23.5 shows the Set Security Scopes dialog.

FIGURE 23.5   Associating the Web Server Resources security scope with an object.

By default, all administrative users have permissions on the All Systems and All Users collections. You may choose to remove these default permissions. If you do, users can only see and manage resources in collections to which you explicitly grant access. This practice minimizes the chance a user could accidentally gain access to resources he or she does not need to see. Allowing access to All Systems and All Users collections simplifies administration by eliminating the requirement to grant access explicitly to individual collections. Note that when you create a collection, you can base the new collection on an existing collection. Users with access to the original collection inherit access to collections based on the original one.

Associating Security Scopes and Collections with Individual Roles

An administrative user assigned more than one role may have the same security scopes and collections available for all roles or may have different security scopes and collections available for each role. For example, the Web Server Admins group has the Compliance Settings Manager role but only manages compliance settings for web servers. To prevent users in this group from modifying compliance settings designed for other systems, remove the default security scope and add the web server resources scope. To prevent the group from deploying compliance settings to systems other than web servers, remove the All Systems and All Users collections and assign a collection consisting of web servers only. Follow these steps:

1. Navigate to **Administration -> Security -> Administrative Users**.

2. Double-click the user or group you want to customize to open the Properties page.

3. On the Security Scopes tab, select **Associate assigned security roles with specific security scopes and collections**. Select the role you want to edit and click **Edit** to open the Edit Security Scope dialog. Figure 23.6 shows the Security Scopes tab for the Odyssey\Web Server Admins Security group with the Compliance Setting Manager role selected.

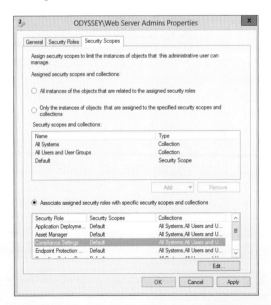

FIGURE 23.6   Editing the Web Server Admins security scopes.

4. In the Edit Security Scope dialog, select the **All Systems** collection and the **Default** security scope and click **Remove**. Then click **Add** and choose **Collection**. Select **Device Collections** from the upper-left dropdown and check the box for the appropriate collection. Click **OK**. Click **Add** and choose **Security Scope**, select the appropriate scope, and click **OK**. Figure 23.7 shows the edited list of security scopes for the Web Server Admins group.

FIGURE 23.7   Specifying the security scope for which a group has a specific role.

Using Administrative Security Reports

ConfigMgr provides several reports related to security administration. To view these reports in the Odyssey environment, open http://armada/reports in a web browser, click the **ConfigMgr_CAS** folder, and then click the **Administrative Security** folder. For example, Figure 23.8 shows the configuration items associated with the Web Server Resources security scope. You can also create custom security reports. Chapter 21 discusses developing custom reports.

The Configuration Manager Toolkit, available at https://www.microsoft.com/download/details.aspx?id=50012, includes the Role Based Administration Modeling and Auditing Tool (RBAViewer.exe), which simplifies the customization and auditing of security roles. RBAViewer allows you to create a new role based on one or more existing security role(s) and provides a tree control for viewing and editing permissions for the newly created role. When your customization is complete, you can save the role as an eXtensible Markup Language (XML) file and import it using the ConfigMgr console. RBAViewer also provides a consolidated view of RBA objects. Figure 23.9 shows an RBA Administration Modeling and Auditing Tool view of the web server admins.

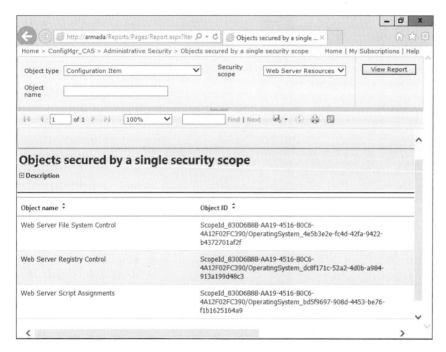

FIGURE 23.8   The objects secured by a single security scope report for configuration items with security scope Web Server Resources.

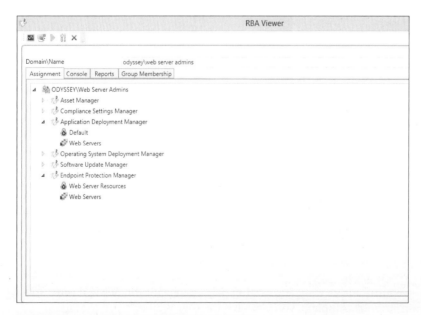

FIGURE 23.9   RBAViewer showing roles held by a user with associated security scopes and collections.

> **RBA UNDER THE HOOD**
>
> ConfigMgr stores data defining securable objects, administrative users, security roles, and other RBA constructs in the site database. While you will not work directly with RBA data in the site database, looking at its inner workings in a lab environment can help you understand its concepts more fully.
>
> The `RBAC` prefix identifies database tables containing RBA security objects and related data. For example, the `RBAC_Admins` table contains the AD identity and other metadata for each administrative user. The `vRBAC` prefix identifies RBA-related database views. Querying these tables and views can provide insight into some RBA features. For example, selecting the rows from the `vRBAC_SecuredObjectTypes` database view where the `IsTypeWideClass` column is `False` generates the list shown earlier in this chapter of object types you can associate with security scopes.

Securing Administrative Access to ConfigMgr

In addition to assigning authorized users to appropriate roles, it is important to prevent unauthorized or inappropriate use of administrative access. Following are some ways an attacker could gain unauthorized ConfigMgr rights:

▶ An attacker could alter ConfigMgr security through AD. ConfigMgr roles are assigned to AD users and groups. Anyone who gains the requisite AD privileges could add himself or herself to a group with access to ConfigMgr.

▶ An attacker with access to modify the site database could alter ConfigMgr security by directly modifying the RBA objects in the site database.

▶ An attacker could steal the credentials or hijack the session of a legitimate administrator.

Protecting against these risks requires effective security at the AD and database layers; it also depends on maintaining a strong auditing policy. The following sections address these issues.

Securing Access at the Active Directory Level

Following are some ways to protect groups and user accounts with privileged access to ConfigMgr:

▶ Restrict rights to manage ConfigMgr administrative accounts and groups to a small group of senior administrators and remove any delegated rights to groups such as help desk personnel. Consider moving administrative accounts and groups to specific organizational units (OUs) to simplify security management.

▶ Set auditing to record any changes to these user accounts and groups and monitor such changes.

▶ Provide ongoing education for administrators on security best practices. Some of the highest-profile security breaches have targeted administrators using phishing or other social engineering methods. A hacker who tricks an administrator into clicking the wrong link or attaching the wrong device to a system has a good chance of compromising your network.

▶ Pay extra attention to securing administrative workstations and other systems where the console is installed. The security practices discussed in the "Securing Site Systems" section, later in this chapter, apply to administrative workstations and to servers. It is especially important to disable password caching on administrative workstations and locate these systems in areas that are physically secure and not easily accessible for shoulder surfing. Windows 10 Credential Guard technology uses hardware-assisted virtualization to protect the Local Security Authority Subsystem Service (LSASS). Credential Guard and Passport are both able to take advantage of a hardware Trusted Platform Module (TPM) if available. The authors recommend that all administrator workstations run Windows 10, have hardware TPM (preferably version 2.0), and have the Credential Guard and Passport features configured though group policy.

This section described some specific AD security practices that are particularly relevant to ConfigMgr administrative access. Microsoft provides guidance on AD security best practices at https://technet.microsoft.com/library/dn487446.aspx.

Securing Site System Local Administration

The built-in local Administrators group on any Windows system has complete and unrestricted access to the computer. Even without specific administrative rights within ConfigMgr, a member of this group on a ConfigMgr site system could potentially alter files, Registry settings, or other items related to system configuration in ways that would affect ConfigMgr services. By default, the Domain Admins group for the local domain is part of the local Administrators group. Consider removing the Domain Admins group and replacing it with the appropriate AD group having direct responsibility for server administration of the site system. For non-client-facing site systems, consider removing the Domain Users group from the local Users group. The remaining built-in groups, such as Backup Operators and Power Users, should not contain any members unless required for your administrative processes. You should generally not create local users or groups on site systems other than those required by ConfigMgr. As with all Windows systems, best practice is to rename the built-in Administrator account, set a strong password for that account, and use appropriate procedures to manage access to the account password. You should also disable the built-in Guest account. You can configure most of these settings locally or through group policy. Although Microsoft does not supply a tool to automate changes to the local Administrator account password across multiple systems, a number of third-party tools and scripts provide this functionality.

CAUTION: ADMINISTRATION OF MACHINES DISJOINED FROM THE DOMAIN

The local Administrator account is often needed to log on to a machine that was removed from the domain. In such a case, the account name reverts to its state before domain group policy was applied. Maintain accurate records of the local Administrator account name on each system independent of the group policy setting.

The Just Enough Administration (JEA) Security Feature

Just Enough Administration is one of several important security features in Windows Management Framework (WMF) 5.0, which includes PowerShell 5.0. WMF 5.0 is native on Windows 10 and Windows Server 2016. Download WMF 5.0 for Windows 2007/ Windows Server 2008 R2 and all newer Windows versions at https://www.microsoft.com/ download/details.aspx?id=50395. The "Hardening PowerShell" section, later in this chapter, describes other security enhancements in PowerShell 5.0.

JEA provides role-based administration for anything you can manage through PowerShell, including Windows, AD, and various applications. It allows you to provide users with access to specific administrative tasks on designated systems without adding them to the administrators group. JEA uses PowerShell Desired State Configuration (DSC) to enable centralized administration of task delegation. It does not work with traditional graphical user interface (GUI)-based administrative tools. If you require use of the GUI tools by administrators with limited, delegated permissions, consider third-party role-based access control products.

Securing Access at the Database Level

ConfigMgr supports SQL Server in either mixed-mode or Windows-only authentication; you should use Windows-only authentication for all site database servers. Windows authentication provides much stronger account controls and authentication mechanisms than are available for mixed-mode accounts defined in SQL Server. As with any other administrative access, assign SQL Server access on a least-privilege basis. It is particularly important to limit access to privileged server roles such as sysadmin and securityadmin, as there generally is no reason to assign database roles for the site database directly to users. If possible, use a dedicated SQL Server that is not shared with other applications. This reduces the number of users needing access to the server as well as the overall attack surface of the database server.

Microsoft provides guidance on security considerations for SQL Server at http://msdn. microsoft.com/library/ms144228.aspx. SQL Server Reporting Services (SSRS) implements its own role-based access control model. Learn about SSRS security in another book in this series, *System Center Configuration Manager Reporting Unleashed* (Sams Publishing, 2016).

Auditing ConfigMgr Administrative Actions

Maintain and regularly review audit trails for all security-sensitive actions. Although you cannot block administrators from all opportunities to misuse their authority, monitoring their actions increases the possibility of detecting misuse or compromise of administrative accounts.

ConfigMgr generates status messages of type Audit to provide an audit record of certain security-sensitive operations. The SMS provider generates an audit message when a user creates, modifies, or deletes a ConfigMgr object or changes the associated security scopes for an object. Remote control of client systems also generates audit messages. Audit messages for object modifications indicate the user making the change, the target object class and object ID, and details about when and how the change occurred. The specific attributes changed are not included.

Chapter 20, "Configuration Manager Queries," describes how to run status message queries and create custom status message queries. Many of the built-in status message queries display audit messages. You can use these queries as is and as a basis for creating your own queries. Following are the built-in status message queries you can use to audit administrative activity:

▶ All Audit Status Messages from a Specific Site

▶ All Audit Status Messages for a Specific User

▶ Boundaries Created, Modified, or Deleted

▶ Client Component Configuration Changes

▶ Collection Member Resources Manually Deleted

▶ Collections Created, Modified, or Deleted

▶ Deployments Created, Modified, or Deleted

▶ Packages Created, Modified, or Deleted

▶ Programs Created, Modified, or Deleted

▶ Queries Created, Modified, or Deleted

▶ Remote Control Activity Initiated at a Specific Site

▶ Remote Control Activity Initiated by a Specific User

▶ Remote Control Activity Initiated from a Specific System

▶ Remote Control Activity Targeted at a Specific System

▶ Security Roles/Scopes Created, Modified, or Deleted

▶ Server Component Configuration Changes

▶ Site Addresses Created, Modified, or Deleted

An important auditing consideration is the audit records retention period. You may be required to retain audit data for a specified time to meet regulatory requirements. Chapter 24, "Backup, Recovery, and Maintenance," discusses audit message retention policy.

ConfigMgr provides several reports based on audit messages. Table 23.1 lists reports you can use to audit sensitive actions.

TABLE 23.1   Reports Displaying Audit Messages

Report Folder	Report Name	Description
Status Messages - Audit	All audit messages for a specific user	Displays a summary of all audit status messages for a single user. Audit messages describe actions taken in the ConfigMgr console that add, modify, or delete objects in ConfigMgr.
Status Messages - Audit	Remote Control - All computers remote controlled by a specific user	Displays a summary of status messages indicating remote control of client computers by a single specified user.
Status Messages - Audit	Remote Control - All remote control information	Displays a summary of status messages indicating remote control of client computers.
Administrative Security	Administration Activity Log	Shows the log of administrative changes made for administrative users, security roles, security scopes, and collections.

Many organizations use a security information and event management (SIEM) solution to aggregate and correlate data from various security information and event sources. SIEM solutions monitor activity in real time and allow rapid detection and response to suspicious activity. If you have such a system available, it is desirable to connect all audit data feeds to the SIEM solution. Most SIEM solutions have facilities to extract event data from database sources. The site database stores status messages in the `StatusMessages` and `StatusMessageInsStrs` tables. Audit messages can be distinguished by the condition `[StatusMessages.Type] = 768`.

It is important to log and audit sensitive actions at every layer of the infrastructure. In addition to the auditing described in this section, auditing of the following systems and services will help protect your ConfigMgr environment:

▶ Active Directory

▶ Site systems

▶ SQL Server activity

▶ Network infrastructure devices

Microsoft provides extensive guidance on auditing AD, Windows, and SQL Server in its learning centers for each product. Some specific events you should consider incorporating into your organization's incident response plan follow:

▶ **Changes to Active Directory Groups with ConfigMgr Access:** Administrators responsible for ConfigMgr security should review these changes.

▶ **Changes to Local Users and Groups on ConfigMgr Site Systems and the Site Database Server:** These events should rarely occur.

▶ **Changes to the Local Security Policy on ConfigMgr Site Systems and the Site Database Server:** These events should rarely occur.

▶ **Changes to the SQL Server Security Configuration on the Site Database Server:** These events should rarely occur.

Securing the ConfigMgr Infrastructure

While effective management and monitoring can greatly enhance the security of your environment, potential compromise of a management application is a threat you cannot afford to ignore. After all, why should an attacker go to the trouble of deploying and managing malware agents in your environment if he or she can just use the highly capable agents you have already deployed? Critical infrastructure components that could be subject to attack include ConfigMgr site systems, accounts used by ConfigMgr, intersite and intrasite communications, and the file base and infrastructure services that ConfigMgr depends on for its operations.

Securing Site Systems

Your ConfigMgr site server, site database server, and site systems are among the most security-sensitive assets in your organization, on a par with domain controllers. All basic controls applicable to such systems should be applied to your site systems. The next sections discuss some of the types of controls you can use to protect site systems.

Threats to systems generally fall into one or more of the following categories:

▶ *Fingerprinting* is an attempt to enumerate and gather information about resources on the network. Typically, the attacker tries to discover system characteristics such as operating system, open ports, and installed applications in order to determine what vulnerabilities may be present. Fingerprinting is generally a precursor to a more serious attack. Detecting an attack at this stage may enable you to prevent the attack from progressing.

▶ *Execution attacks* are the greatest threat to systems. Execution attacks are attempts to execute unauthorized code on the system. These attacks use methods such as malware, application layer attacks, and network-based exploits of remote code execution vulnerabilities.

▶ *Identity-based attacks* are another major threat to systems. These attacks involve stealing a legitimate user's credentials or bypassing authentication or access controls. The "Securing Administrative Access to ConfigMgr" section, earlier in this chapter, discusses mitigation strategies for identity-based attacks.

▶ *Denial-of-service attacks* are attempts to bring down or disrupt essential IT services.

The following sections discuss methods to mitigate these risks through secure design supplemented by security technology.

Implementing Physical Security and Carefully Selecting Hardware

Choose the most secure location and hardware available for your site systems. Locate site servers and site database servers in secure datacenters. Balance security concerns with your other requirements as you consider placement of client-facing systems such as DPs. Server-class hardware often provides functionality such as alarms that alert when detecting an open chassis or modifications to hardware. Just as Microsoft continues to enhance the security of Windows, semiconductor manufacturers are adding security features into their chip designs; consider these features in your hardware specifications. If possible, use hardware with a physical TPM and enable boot integrity checking to verify that there has not been tampering with critical OS files and other system components. Choose hardware with maximum reliability and redundancy for systems with high availability requirements. If you run site systems as virtual machines (VMs), similar considerations apply to the physical hosts they run on. Windows Server 2016 Hyper-V and other virtualization environments provide attestation mechanisms to protect VMs by ensuring that they run on approved hosts with verified identity and code integrity.

Using System Software Security

Choose the most recent version of Microsoft Windows consistent with your system requirements and stay current on all service packs and security patches. Microsoft makes it a priority to incorporate the latest security awareness and technology into Windows on an ongoing basis. Each version of Windows contains numerous security enhancements over its predecessor. Often the accumulation of small enhancements can make as much or more difference compared to the more highly publicized features. In addition to OS patches, keep system components such as the basic input/output system (BIOS) and firmware current and regularly update all drivers and applications installed on your systems.

Reducing the Attack Surface and Hardening Servers

A basic principle for securing any system is to reduce the number of potential vulnerabilities by eliminating unnecessary services, accounts, applications, network shares, open network ports, and so on. The key to reducing the attack surface without reducing required functionality is determining if any features are unnecessary on a particular system so you can turn them off. You can also harden the server, modifying default settings such as requiring the use of more secure network protocols and limiting access to certain GUI features. Microsoft provides tools that greatly simplify attack surface reduction and server hardening for the Windows OS and for ConfigMgr and SQL Server systems. The Windows Security Configuration Wizard (SCW) is an attack surface reduction tool for Windows Server. Use SCW to configure individual systems or use group policy to deploy SCW-generated configurations. The System Center Configuration Manager template for SCW is included as part of the Configuration Manager Toolkit. The authors recommend using this tool to configure all applicable site system roles. Use the ConfigMgr compliance settings feature to ensure continuous compliance of system components such as IIS. Chapter 10 describes compliance settings.

Hardening PowerShell

Attackers generally gain initial access to systems by exploiting some weakness such as a software vulnerability or a careless user. Once on the box, the attacker can use

PowerShell to access data and other system resources or to attack other systems on the network. Set the strictest execution policy consistent with your operational requirements to guard against administrators accidentally running dangerous scripts; however, an attacker can easily bypass the execution policy after the initial compromise. Microsoft has responded to the increase in malicious use of PowerShell by delivering several new or enhanced security features in PowerShell 5.0. Consider taking advantage of each of these features:

▶ Constrained language mode limits PowerShell access to features such as the Win32 API, .NET framework, and COM objects that can invoke unverified code. AppLocker integration enforces PowerShell constrained language mode when AppLocker is in allow mode. If you have scripts requiring extended language support, use a mechanism such as a trusted enterprise-signing certificate allowed by AppLocker policy to run those scripts.

▶ Utilize Windows 10 Antimalware Scan Interface (AMSI) integration. PowerShell submits all script content to the registered antimalware service on the system. Traditional scanning based on file access might miss PowerShell scripts that exist only in memory and never touch the disk. No special configuration is required.

▶ Use group policy, Registry settings, or PowerShell commands to enable and configure PowerShell logging. As with other security logging, use a SIEM or Windows Event Forwarding to store log data off the box. PowerShell 5 includes the following logging:

  ▶ System-wide transcript logging provides a record of commands entered in each session.

  ▶ Deep script block logging provides execution details of all script activity on the system. Use Windows 10 Protected Event Logging to protect sensitive data stored in logs, such as credentials used by PowerShell.

Implementing Security Software

Antivirus (AV) software provides basic protection against viruses and other types of malware. Run AV software on all your systems and update virus signatures regularly. Traditional AV software compares files and processes against a database of signatures used to recognize known malware. Signature-based malware detection is reasonably effective against widely deployed viruses, spyware, and other malware, and it is an essential part of antimalware strategy. Some AV programs also use behavioral characteristics and cloud-based reputation services to identify suspicious files. Files determined to be suspicious are sent to network- or cloud-based advanced threat detection systems for further analysis. Even with these enhancements, traditional malware protection is largely ineffective in detecting targeted threats, including APTs, for which signatures are unlikely to exist.

Many organizations are incorporating application whitelisting programs into their malware protection strategies. The IAD and ASD top controls lists, referenced in the section "A Security Primer," earlier in this chapter, both list application whitelisting as the number-one control. Whitelisting allows only "known good" programs to run, as opposed to signature-based antimalware that eliminates "known bad." AppLocker provides application whitelisting technology. Use the Group Policy Management Microsoft Management Console (MMC) snap-in or PowerShell to manage AppLocker. AppLocker can allow or ban executable code by attributes such as publisher, product, and filename. Some application whitelisting programs allow implementation of policies to allow software updates made through specific methods. For example, your policy might allow the ConfigMgr agent and Windows Update executables to add or modify software and block other processes from making such changes. While such dynamic whitelisting reduces administrative overhead by eliminating the need to manage the whitelist manually, expect to spend time tuning the rules for each distinct system build. Application whitelisting is best suited to relatively static environments with effective change management and consistent processes, as should be the case with production servers. It is more difficult to implement in highly dynamic environments such as development environments and end-user systems.

Software firewalls, including Windows Firewall, provide protection against network-based attacks. In high-security environments, consider using specialized host intrusion prevention (HIP) software to provide an additional layer of protection by detecting and blocking a more extensive range of suspicious process activity, such as nonstandard memory access methods. The latest versions of Windows have impressive built-in memory protection. HIP software may supplement Windows memory protection by providing signatures to block known memory-based attacks such as those exploiting known application vulnerabilities. File integrity monitoring (FIM) software protects critical files from alteration. Consider using FIM to alert you if changes occur to key ConfigMgr files such as the service executables, site control file, and client source files.

Endpoint detection and response (EDR) is one of the hottest new security technologies. Working with preventive technologies such as traditional antimalware and application whitelisting, EDR implements a prevent, detect, respond approach to security, described earlier in this chapter, in the section "Planning for Security and Delegation." EDR software monitors endpoints (including end-user systems and servers) for suspicious or anomalous activity, correlates detections across the enterprise, and enables administrative or automated responses.

Security programs are intrusive by nature, often consuming significant amounts of system resources and sometimes blocking legitimate activity. Test and adjust your security software settings in your proof of concept environment and monitor the impact of security software in production. To improve system performance and availability, you may decide to create exceptions, such as excluding certain folders from virus scanning. Exclusions typically apply to files locked during normal operations, such as database files, or to files that are frequently accessed and that are not common vectors for introducing malware, such as log files. Any exclusions you create can introduce potential weaknesses in your protection framework that could be exploited by malware. Follow your organization's risk policy when considering any exclusions or other exceptions in your controls. Microsoft TechNet Wiki provides a comprehensive list of resources for related to AV exclusions at http://social.technet.microsoft.com/wiki/contents/articles/953.microsoft-anti-virus-exclusion-list.aspx. This includes recommendations for software on site systems including ConfigMgr, Windows, SQL Server, and IIS. Major AV vendors also provide guidance on the use of their products on Microsoft systems. Also, consider any vendor-recommended exclusions for installed components such as backup software or host-based adapters (HBAs). Note that vendors are typically more concerned with the functioning of their products than with the security of your systems and might publish overly broad recommendations for excluding their software.

CAUTION: DO NOT DOWNLOAD FILES DIRECTLY TO EXCLUDED FOLDERS

With any exclusion, be sure to scan all downloaded files for malware before copying them to locations where they are excluded from scanning.

Create a process to respond to events from security software such as malware detections and blocked activity. If you find false positives, evaluate the impact on system functionality and modify security software settings as required. Process Monitor is a Windows monitoring tool that shows detailed process-related activity; it is available for download at https://technet.microsoft.com/sysinternals/processmonitor.aspx. If you suspect that virus scanning is affecting system or application stability or performance, Process Monitor can help determine what files are being opened. If you see files that are frequently scanned, you might consider them for exclusions. Some antivirus applications allow you to apply different on-access scanning exclusions based on the process accessing files. For example, a file modification by the Windows Module Installer (TrustedInstaller.exe) might be considered a low-risk event and may not trigger a scan, whereas a file modification by Internet Explorer would be far more likely to introduce malware and warrant an immediate scan. Using this type of feature is safer than allowing all processes to read from or write to the excluded files without scanning. If your antivirus software supports it, designate ConfigMgr processes as low risk and apply exclusions for specific site roles only to low-risk processes. Some processes you might want to designate as low risk follow:

- ▶ ccmexec.exe (on management points)
- ▶ sitecomp.exe
- ▶ smsexec.exe
- ▶ smswriter.exe
- ▶ sqlservr.exe (on site database servers)
- ▶ sqlwriter.exe (on site database servers)

Securing the Site Database

The site database server is the heart of your ConfigMgr site, and its security is at least as important as that of the site server. Use a dedicated SQL Server for each primary site or colocate the database on the site server. Microsoft continues to improve SQL Server security. The authors recommend using the latest version of SQL Server supported by ConfigMgr for site database servers and updating it with all service packs and security updates. At secondary sites, apply the latest updates to your instance of SQL Server Express.

Configure SQL Server to use Windows authentication only and enable logging at least for failed logon attempts. Use a low-privilege domain account rather than Local System for the

SQL Server startup account. When you run SQL Server in a low-privilege account context, you must register the service principal name (SPN) manually for the server in AD. Clients use the SPN to locate SQL services. Use the procedure described at http://technet.microsoft.com/library/hh427336.aspx#BKMK_ManageSPNforDBSrv to register the SPN.

Securing Additional Site Systems

Microsoft provides guidance for securing specific site system servers at https://docs.microsoft.com/sccm/core/plan-design/hierarchy/security-and-privacy-for-site-administration. Microsoft provides specific recommendations for the following site systems:

- ▶ Site servers

- ▶ Site database servers

- ▶ Site systems that run IIS

- ▶ Management points

- ▶ Fallback status point

About ConfigMgr Cryptographic Controls

Cryptography is the science of using secrets to protect information. Cryptographic methods are an essential part of information security. ConfigMgr uses cryptography to support the following goals:

- ▶ **Confidentiality:** ConfigMgr uses encryption to prevent disclosure of sensitive data. Encryption converts data into a form that only parties with access to a secret key can read.

- ▶ **Authentication:** ConfigMgr uses digital certificates to authenticate the identity of systems during network communications and to sign sensitive files exchanged between systems. ConfigMgr can use either public key infrastructure (PKI) certificates or self-signed certificates. Chapter 4 introduces the certificates used in ConfigMgr.

- ▶ **Integrity:** ConfigMgr uses hashing and digital signatures to protect the integrity of data such as the content used in software distribution. A hash is generated by applying a hashing algorithm to a file. The receiving system re-creates the hash and compares it to the hash value provided by the policy provider. Any alteration of the file also alters the hash and causes the comparison to fail. This protection does not apply to App-V streamed content or to certain mobile device and non-Windows clients.

The authors highly recommend using PKI certificates rather than self-signed certificates wherever possible. The following features require PKI:

- ▶ HTTPS communications

- ▶ Support for clients on the Internet

- ▶ The Microsoft Intune connector for mobile device management

> **NOTE: ABOUT CRL CHECKING**
>
> Certificate revocation list (CRL) checking increases security by preventing systems from accepting a certificate that is known to have been compromised and has been revoked. CRL checking requires planning to minimize performance and availability issues. Find information about planning for CRL checking and other considerations for deploying AD certificate services at https://technet.microsoft.com/library/hh831574(v=ws.11).aspx.

There are no silver bullets in security. Security researchers have recently discovered several flaws in cryptographic methods that have been Internet standards for many years. If you haven't already, you should disable SSL 3.0 and enable TLS 1.1 and 1.2, as described at https://support.microsoft.com/kb/245030. In addition, at least one major certificate vendor has had its root CA canceled. This does not detract from the importance of cryptographic controls in securing your data. However, it underscores the importance of using multiple layers of security and keeping systems up to date on all security patches.

The next sections discuss the two principal scenarios where ConfigMgr uses cryptographic controls: securing network communications and securing content distribution.

Securing Network Communications

Network-based attacks are commonly used to steal data or carry out other malicious objectives. Following are some types of network attacks that could be launched against ConfigMgr sites, site systems, and clients:

▶ **Misdirection Attacks:** In this type of attack, a client or site system is provided with the wrong name, Internet Protocol (IP) address, or MAC address for the partner with which it needs to communicate. Secure service advertisement and name resolution services to avoid misdirection attacks.

▶ **Spoofing Attacks:** In this type of attack, a rogue system impersonates the actual system with which a client or site system needs to communicate. All communications must be properly authenticated to defeat these attacks.

▶ **Eavesdropping or Sniffer-Based Attacks:** This type of attack involves an attacker intercepting network communications and gaining access to confidential information. Data encryption is the primary defense against breach of confidential communications.

▶ **Man-in-the-Middle (MITM) Attacks:** These attacks occur involve an attacker stealing, altering, or interrupting communications by routing data through an intermediate node under his or her control. You can often defeat MITM attacks by using mutual authentication. Digitally signing files can help detect alterations due to MITM attacks.

▶ **Denial-of-Service (DoS) Attacks:** In this type of attack, an attacker uses large amounts of data or malformed data packets to crash systems or clog communication links. A resilient network infrastructure and fault-tolerant service delivery design are the best defenses against DoS attacks.

Microsoft provides several security features to protect the confidentiality, integrity, and availability of ConfigMgr communications. The next sections discuss using these features to secure communications between ConfigMgr clients and their site and communications between ConfigMgr sites and site systems.

> **CAUTION: DON'T LET ATTACKERS USE ENCRYPTION TO BYPASS OTHER SECURITY CONTROLS**
>
> Cryptographic controls such as encryption and digital signatures are among the most important security mechanisms for protecting the confidentiality and integrity of data. Encryption can be a double-edged sword, as many other security controls do not work on encrypted data. Antivirus programs are typically unable to scan encrypted files. Similarly, network intrusion detection systems (IDSs) or intrusion prevention systems (IPSs) cannot inspect encrypted packets for attack signatures. Consider implementing procedures to ensure that any files and packets that bypass one control are inspected by another, such as quarantining inbound encrypted files until they can be decrypted and scanned or using a host-based IDS or IPS at each endpoint of an encrypted tunnel.

23

Client-to-Server Communications Security

Clients communicate with most site systems using either HTTP or HTTPS. Chapter 5, "Network Design," provides details on ConfigMgr network protocols. A client configured to support HTTPS will select a site system using HTTPS if one is available. Principal advantages of HTTPS follow:

▶ Most ConfigMgr HTTPS traffic is encrypted. This prevents an attacker eavesdropping on client communications from gaining access to sensitive data such as vulnerability data that could be used to attack the client. Even with HTTPS, state messages sent to the FSP, PXE requests to a PXE-enabled DP, and notification data to an MP are not encrypted.

▶ ConfigMgr HTTPS implements mutual authentication. Authentication protects the client from being redirected to a rogue site system. With HTTP communication, the MP is authenticated using a self-signed certificate; however, other site systems are not authenticated. As HTTP clients do not authenticate themselves to MPs, you accept either the risk of untrusted clients joining your site or the added effort of managing client approval.

▶ Mutually authenticated HTTPS prevents an attacker from impersonating the client in order to carry out MITM attacks, which may be used to tamper with and access data.

> **CAUTION: NOT ALL HTTPS COMMUNICATION IS MUTUALLY AUTHENTICATED**
>
> Do not assume that you are safe from MITM attacks when using HTTPS to access systems such as Internet servers. Unlike ConfigMgr, most Internet sites using HTTPS do not implement mutual authentication. Microsoft Intune is not able to deploy client certificates to mobile devices locked by the carrier. These devices do not support mutual authentication.
>
> For maximum security, always choose HTTPS communications between clients and servers. HTTPS is required for mobile device clients and Internet-based clients.

Server-to-Server Communications Security

All communication between site systems within a site uses certificate-based authentication. Intrasite server communication is not encrypted. If you require encryption for server-to-server communications, consider using IPsec encryption.

The site server should have the highest level of system, network, and physical security you can provide. There may be instances in which you cannot provide the same level of security for all site systems. In such instances, consider enabling the Require the site server to initiate connections to this site system setting on the less secure systems. To enable this setting, check the appropriate box on the General page of the Add Site System Roles Wizard. This site system setting protects the site server by preventing less secure systems from initiating communication to the site server.

Site-to-Site and Communications Security

Sites share data using database replication and file-based replication, discussed in Chapter 5. Database replication uses self-signed certificates to authenticate replication connections and to sign and encrypt data. The certificate trust mechanism ensures that only ConfigMgr database servers can participate in database replication for the hierarchy. File-based replication implements data signing but does not provide encryption. Consider implementing IPsec communications between site servers to encrypt file-based replication traffic.

ConfigMgr Content Security

The integrity of the policy and content your clients receive is of paramount importance when considering client-to-server communications. An attacker who could directly tamper with client policy could instruct the ConfigMgr agent to execute instructions of the attacker's choosing. Similarly, an attacker who could cause clients to use forged or altered software packages, OS images, or other content could gain control of client systems. ConfigMgr uses cryptographic controls to protect against such attacks. You should also use appropriate settings and procedures to ensure policy and content integrity.

Security in Policy and Software Distribution

To protect against policy tampering, the site server signs all client policy assignments using a self-signed certificate. Policy assignment tells the client which policies apply to it and contains a hash of each policy. After downloading the assigned policies, the client generates a hash for each applicable policy, compares it with the hash in the signed policy assignment, and applies the policy if the hash matches. In some cases, client policy may contain sensitive or confidential information. You may optionally encrypt policy to protect such information. Each policy includes a hash for packages referenced in the policy. The client validates the hash before installing the software in a package. If you configure a deployment to run from a DP rather than using the Download and run option, the client is not able to verify the hash before running content, making the Run from distribution point option a less secure software distribution method.

The application catalog represents another potential point of attack against clients. Configure the application catalog website to use HTTPS rather than HTTP. The authors recommend separating the Application Catalog website and the Application Catalog web services role, particularly if the website can accept connections from the Internet.

Another important consideration for software distribution is preventing users from leveraging deployments to gain elevated privileges. Avoid configuring both the Allow users to view and interact with the program installation and Run with administrative rights program options. These options enable the user to influence the execution of a program running in an administrative context, generally Local System. In some cases, the user might break out of the user interface provided by the setup program and spawn another program, such as a command shell, providing unlimited access to the system. You can specify these options for software distribution packages on the Standard Program page of the Create Program Wizard. For Windows Installer applications, you can control user interaction through the `msiexec /q` command line switch; group policy or registry settings govern whether or not Windows Installer runs packages with elevated rights.

ConfigMgr can only protect the content you provide; you must ensure the integrity of the source files. Download software only from trusted sources and verify the files after download. Similarly, inspect any physical media used to receive files for a certificate of authenticity and tamper-resistant packaging.

Scan all source files for malware and keep them on a secure network share or storage system. Consider using file integrity monitoring software to prevent alterations.

Security for Operating System Deployment

ConfigMgr uses certificates to authenticate both the clients and servers during operating system deployment (OSD). Following are some points regarding secure OSD:

▶ Secure the reference computer by placing it in a secure network environment, blocking unauthorized access, and keeping patches and antivirus software current.

▶ Secure all boot images, OS images, drivers, and driver packages as you would secure package source files.

▶ Password protect all boot media and keep media physically secure.

▶ Use a secure network channel such as IPsec to protect private or confidential data during user state migration. Secure user data on the user state migration point and delete all user content that is no longer needed. Use the latest version of the User State Migration Tool (USMT) supported by ConfigMgr.

▶ Enable encryption for all multicast packages to prevent tampering and exclude rogue computers from multicast sessions.

Securing ConfigMgr Accounts

ConfigMgr uses a variety of accounts as part of its operating framework. Many of these accounts are required in specific situations, such as to support clients or site systems in untrusted domains. Other accounts are required to provide a security context for specific operations, such as task sequences. Use only the accounts required by your environment or those necessary to support specific ConfigMgr features you use. Follow best practices for configuring and managing accounts. Some principles for managing ConfigMgr accounts follow:

▶ Use strong passwords and change those passwords regularly.

▶ Enable the Password never expires and User cannot change password options for Windows and AD accounts used by ConfigMgr.

▶ Use a password management application to secure ConfigMgr passwords. Restrict access to administrators on a need-to-know basis and track who knows those passwords. If a person with access to ConfigMgr passwords leaves the company or if you suspect that a password is compromised, change the affected passwords immediately.

▶ Keep track of which accounts are used where and deprovision any accounts no longer needed.

▶ Configure each account with the minimum rights to accomplish its job.

▶ When you use AD accounts, allow time for newly created accounts to replicate throughout the domain before adding them to ConfigMgr.

▶ Do not grant the interactive logon right. You may need to grant it to an account temporarily so the account can be used for troubleshooting purposes. An exception is the Task Sequence Run As account, which needs interactive logon rights on systems where a task sequence configured to use this account runs.

Microsoft provides detailed descriptions of all ConfigMgr accounts in the online documentation. To help you sort out these accounts, the next sections present ConfigMgr accounts organized into functional groups. Find additional details about ConfigMgr accounts at https://technet.microsoft.com/library/mt627794.aspx.

Accounts to Support ConfigMgr Infrastructure

ConfigMgr uses accounts to install components on site systems. Within the site server's AD forest or in domains trusting that domain, use the site server machine account for these purposes rather than configuring separate accounts.

TIP: ASSIGNING RIGHTS TO MACHINE ACCOUNTS

Any time you use the site server machine account for ConfigMgr operations, ensure that it has the required access rights for the task. In most cases, you can provide rights by adding accounts to groups. When you use Active Directory Users and Computers (ADUC) to add users to groups, by default only users, groups, and other objects such as contacts are available through the user interface. To add machine accounts to groups using ADUC, click **Object Types** in the Select Users, Computers, or Groups dialog, and check the selection next to **Computers**. You can also specify machine accounts when using command line tools or scripts by entering the computer name with a $ appended to the end.

Following are the accounts used for installation purposes:

▶ Site system installation accounts are used to install and configure site systems.

▶ Client push installation accounts are used to install and configure client systems when using the client push installation method. Client push is less secure than other client installation methods; avoid using it if possible.

Chapter 6, "Installing and Updating System Center Configuration Manager," discusses site server installation. Chapter 9, "Client Management," discusses client installation methods. Use AD or local accounts for site system installation and client push. These accounts must be in the local Administrators group on the target systems. Do not add these accounts to the Domain Admins group because it provides excessive privileges to the accounts. Create groups that include the appropriate accounts and use group policy or local computer management to add those groups to the local Administrators group. To limit the administrative scope of these accounts, consider using multiple accounts and granting each account access only on the systems where it is used.

Database Connection Accounts

If you have site systems in a different AD forest from the site database server and the site database server's domain does not trust the site system's domain, you must configure accounts these systems can use to connect to the database. Within the site database server's AD forest or in trusted domains, use site system machine accounts for database connectivity. If you need database connection accounts, create these accounts as low-privilege local accounts on the database server and do not grant them interactive logon rights. Specify a database connection account by using the Add Site System Roles Wizard or on the site system role Properties page. Chapter 7, "Upgrading and Migrating to ConfigMgr Current Branch," describes the configuration and use of the source site database account. Add the connection accounts to predefined database roles to provide the access they require. Table 23.2 lists these accounts and the database roles they require.

TABLE 23.2   Database Roles for Connection Accounts

Account Name	Database Role
Management point connection account	smsdbrole_MP
Certificate registration point account	db_datareader
Enrollment point connection account	smsdbrole_EnrollSvr
Multicast connection account	smsdbrole_MCS
Source site database account	db_datareader and smsschm_users on the source (ConfigMgr 2007) site database during migration
Reporting services point account	Administrative rights on the SSRS instance

Accounts Used for OSD and Software Distribution

ConfigMgr OSD requires accounts to carry out several specific task sequence actions. These accounts are specified in the task sequence properties. Chapter 22, "Operating System Deployment," discusses task sequence configuration. Table 23.3 displays the task sequence accounts, with information about their usage and required permissions.

TABLE 23.3   Accounts Used in Task Sequences

Account Name	Where Used	How Used	Required Permissions
Capture operating system image account	Task sequences with the Capture Operating System Image step	To access the folder where captured images are stored	Read/write permissions on the network share where the captured image is to be stored
Task sequence editor domain joining account	Apply Network Settings task sequence or Join Domain or Workgroup task sequence	To join newly imaged computers to the domain	Right to join computers to the target domain
Task sequence editor network folder connection account	Connect to Network Folder task sequence	To connect to network shares	Access to content
Task sequence run as account	Run Command Line task sequence	To provide a context for running commands during a task sequence	Interactive logon rights and other rights required by the specific command

OSD accounts are generally AD domain accounts, although you can use local accounts for the capture operating system image account and the task sequence run as account.

In addition to the accounts listed in Table 23.3, OSD and software distribution use the network access account to access network resources when the client computer account and/or current user does not have access. This account typically is used for client computers in workgroups or untrusted domains or during OSD before the computer joins the domain. Grant the account domain user permissions only.

For granular access to packages, specify one or more package access accounts on a per-package basis. Package access accounts can be any Windows user or group. Generally use existing groups as package access accounts rather than creating accounts for this purpose. The default package access permissions are assigned to the local Users group with read permission and local Administrators with full control. In general, you change these defaults only to restrict those packages that you do not want all users to be able to access. Occasionally you might grant modify permission for package access accounts if a setup program needs to write back to the source folder.

Accounts Used for Software Updates

ConfigMgr uses two accounts to authenticate in order to access content for software updates:

▶ **Software Update Point Proxy Server Account:** The software update point (SUP) uses this account to authenticate to a proxy server or firewall to synchronize with Microsoft Updates or an upstream Windows Server Update Services (WSUS) server. Use any account that can authenticate to your proxy server or firewall and access the site for WSUS synchronization for this account.

▶ **Software Update Point Connection Account:** WSUS services use this account to configure settings and request synchronization. This account is required only if the SUP role is assigned to a remote server or a network load balancing (NLB) cluster. The account must be a member of the local Administrators group on the SUP.

Chapter 15 describes the Software Updates feature.

Accounts Used for Active Directory Discovery and Publishing

If possible, use the site server's computer account to perform AD discovery and publish site data to AD. For forests that do not trust the site server's forest, running the AD discovery methods or publishing to AD requires an account in the target forest. Following are the accounts ConfigMgr uses for AD discovery and publishing:

▶ **Active Directory Group Discovery Account:** ConfigMgr uses this account to discover AD security groups and group memberships.

▶ **Active Directory System Discovery Account:** ConfigMgr uses this account to discover computer objects.

▶ **Active Directory User Discovery Account:** ConfigMgr uses this account to discover user accounts.

▶ **Active Directory Forest Account:** ConfigMgr central and primary sites use this account to publish data to AD. ConfigMgr also uses this account for AD network infrastructure discovery.

Each discovery account requires read access to the AD containers specified for discovery. The Active Directory forest account also requires full control permissions to the System Management container to publish to AD.

Proxy Server Accounts

Following are the accounts ConfigMgr uses to connect to a proxy server or firewall when required for Internet connections:

▶ **Asset Intelligence Synchronization Point Proxy Server Account:** The Asset Intelligence synchronization point uses this account for proxy authentication when connecting to System Center Online.

▶ **Exchange Server Connector Proxy Server Account:** Exchange uses this account for proxy authentication when connecting to the Internet.

Configure proxy server accounts with the minimum permissions required to authenticate to the proxy server.

Miscellaneous Accounts

Following are some additional accounts that ConfigMgr uses:

▶ **Exchange Server Connection Account:** The site server uses this account to connect to the Exchange server for mobile device management. Chapter 15 discusses how to configure this account and the permissions it requires.

▶ **Remote Tools Permitted Viewer Accounts:** Any Windows users or group can be included in the permitted viewers list to allow remote control access to clients. Chapter 9 describes how to configure permitted viewer accounts. Under most scenarios, it is better to use RBA to delegate remote control access than to use permitted viewers.

▶ **SMTP Server Connection Account:** The site server uses this account to authenticate the mail server using Simple Mail Transfer Protocol (SMTP) to send email alerts for Endpoint Protection.

▶ **Source Site Account:** ConfigMgr Current Branch uses the source site account to connect to ConfigMgr 2007 sites during migration. This account requires read access on the source site and all objects to be migrated. Chapter 7 describes the configuration and use of this account as well as the source site database account.

Summary

This chapter discussed infrastructure security considerations for ConfigMgr and the appropriate delegation of administrative access. It described the RBA model, ConfigMgr cryptographic controls, and security accounts. The chapter also provided general considerations for secure hierarchy design, audit support, and server configuration and placement. Chapter 24 describes ConfigMgr backup, recovery, and maintenance.

Backup, Recovery, and Maintenance

This chapter discusses some very important aspects of a Configuration Manager (ConfigMgr) implementation that are often overlooked.

A critical piece of maintaining a healthy and functional system is to ensure its integrity through backup and recovery processes. Organizations often do not test backup and recovery procedures until there is an outage—only to discover too late that the process was not set up properly. All production systems, including ConfigMgr, should have established backup and recovery procedures in place.

Disaster recovery is the ability to recover a service from catastrophic failure in the least possible time with minimal data loss. Backup and recovery procedures should be integral components in any organization's disaster recovery plan. These procedures are vital to maintaining the integrity of the infrastructure and should be tested on a regular basis. This is a very important function of a ConfigMgr administrator.

The maintenance of the solution is also often disregarded. You must maintain data integrity and currency, and ConfigMgr provides a number of maintenance tasks to assist with this. In addition to backup and recovery, this chapter discusses the regular tasks you should perform in order to guarantee a healthy ConfigMgr environment. It also describes configuring the built-in maintenance tasks. Optimizing SQL Server and Windows Server Update Services (WSUS) are more advanced tasks, but they can drastically improve the performance of the infrastructure.

A ConfigMgr site is quite robust; however, occasionally problems can occur. It is crucial to be proactive rather than reactive. This chapter describes how to implement monitoring in the ConfigMgr environment.

NOTE: SYSTEM CENTER OPERATIONS MANAGER

The authors recommend deploying Microsoft System Center Operations Manager (OpsMgr) to monitor ConfigMgr sites and site systems. For more information, see the "Using System Center Operations Manager" section, later in this chapter.

Implementing Configuration Manager Backup

With ConfigMgr 2007, the native Backup Site Server maintenance task was the only Microsoft-supported method to back up and restore a site. ConfigMgr 2012 Service Pack (SP) 1 introduced another method: Microsoft now supports recovering a ConfigMgr site using only a SQL database backup.

TIP: MIGRATING CONFIGURATION MANAGER

Site backup and restoration are not just specific to disaster recovery. They can also be used when migrating a ConfigMgr site to a new environment. In addition, backup and restoration can be useful for upgrading the site server hardware.

This chapter describes how to implement a backup solution using both methods. However, the SQL backup method is the recommended approach. Some of the considerations follow:

▶ The Backup Site Server maintenance task backup merely copies the database, log files, and other system files to the backup folder location. A SQL database backup compresses the files, which could result in a massive reduction in disk space requirements for larger sites.

▶ SQL database backups utilize advanced features such as retention periods and data integrity checks.

▶ SQL database backups allow you to back up other important databases at the same time (such as ReportServer, ReportServerTempdb, and SUSDB).

▶ The Backup Site Server maintenance task backup stops ConfigMgr services before copying the database, log files, and system files. SQL backups do not require loss of service while performing backups.

▶ SQL database backups allow configuration of email notifications on success or failure.

▶ SQL database backups provide more granular control over scheduling.

▶ ConfigMgr Current Branch backup routines must now include the CD.Latest folder, which is required for site recovery. The folder is automatically included as part of the Backup Site Server maintenance task backup, but this folder must be backed up separately if you implement a SQL database backup.

▶ For organizations employing dedicated ConfigMgr and database administrators, the advantage to utilizing the Backup Site Server maintenance task backup is that it provides the ConfigMgr administrator with full control over the backup process.

NOTE: CHOOSING A BACKUP METHOD

Choose the backup method that fits best into your organization. It is possible to implement both methods as long as the backup schedules do not overlap and sufficient storage is available. Such an approach provides more options for site recovery in the event of disaster.

Configuring the Backup Site Server Maintenance Task

The Backup Site Server maintenance task is the traditional backup method and is disabled by default. This maintenance task provides an automated method to back up the entire site. The backup routine includes the site database, ConfigMgr files, Registry keys, and system configuration information.

In the ConfigMgr console, follow these steps to enable and configure site backup:

1. Navigate to **Administration** -> **Overview** -> **Site Configuration** -> **Sites**.

2. Right-click the site to back up and select **Site Maintenance** from the menu.

3. The Site Maintenance dialog box, shown in Figure 24.1, displays a list of maintenance tasks for the site. Select **Backup Site Server** and click **Edit**.

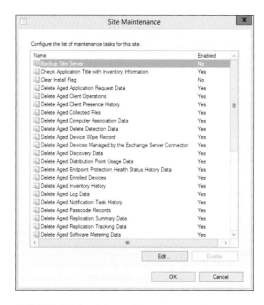

FIGURE 24.1   Site maintenance tasks.

4. On the Backup Site Server Properties page, check the box **Enable this task**.

5. Click **Set Paths** to configure a backup destination. You can choose a network location or a local drive on the site server.

NOTE: CHOOSING A BACKUP LOCATION

The authors do not recommend using a local drive as the location for the backed-up files. If the system hosting the site server failed, the ConfigMgr site and the backup would be lost.

If you use a local drive, supplement this approach by including these files in your overall backup strategy.

---

6. Configure the backup schedule (days of the week, start time, and latest start time).

7. Choose **Enable alerts for backup task failures**. These failure alerts are available in the Alerts node of the Monitoring workspace.

8. Monitor backup progress with the Smsbkup.log file. This log file is useful when troubleshooting failed backups. Figure 24.2 shows backed-up files.

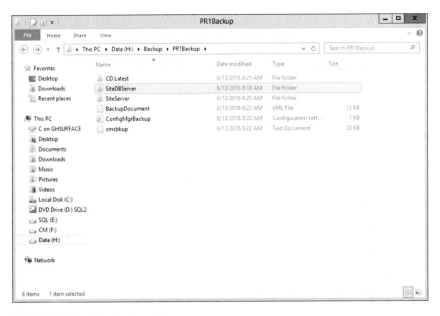

FIGURE 24.2   Site backup files.

Follow these steps to run a backup that starts immediately:

1. Navigate to **Monitoring -> System Status -> Component Status**.

2. Right-click any component and then select **Start -> Configuration Manager Service Manager**.

3. In the Configuration Manager Service Manager, expand your site code and choose **Components**, as shown in Figure 24.3.

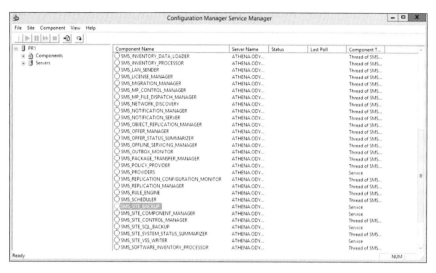

FIGURE 24.3   Configuration Manager Service Manager.

4. Right-click the **SMS_SITE_BACKUP** component and select **Query**. The component displays as stopped. This is the default state unless a backup is running.

5. Right-click the **SMS_SITE_BACKUP** component and select **Start**. The backup task runs when the component starts.

6. Monitor progress of the backup by using the Smsbkup.log file.

CAUTION: BACKUPS ARE OVERWRITTEN

The maintenance task backup creates a new backup each time it runs, overwriting the previous backup.

Backed-Up Files (ConfigMgr Maintenance Task)

The backup creates a folder called *<site code>*Backup at the destination location (see Figure 24.2). This folder contains the following subfolders and files:

▶ **CD.Latest:** This folder contains the ConfigMgr source installation files for the currently installed version. Each time an update is applied to the ConfigMgr site, the files in this folder are updated as well.

▶ **SiteDBServer:** This folder contains a copy of the ConfigMgr database and log files (CM_*<site code>*.mdf and CM_*<site code>*.ldf).

▶ **SiteServer:** This folder contains SMSbkSiteRegSMS.dat. It also contains a subfolder called SMSServer, with four additional folders (data, inboxes, Logs, and srvscct) and the install.map file.

▶ **Files:** The files are BackupDocument.xml, ConfigMgrBackup.ini, and Smsbkup.log.

NOTE: THE CD.LATEST FOLDER

The source files in the CD.Latest folder are required for the following situations:

▶ **Site Recovery:** The installation files in the folder are required for the recovery of a site. These files cannot be copied from an external source.

▶ **Child Primary Site:** The installation files in the folder must match the central administration site (CAS) version if you need to reinstall a child primary site.

▶ **Expand Existing Site:** The installation files in the CD.Latest folder are required to install the CAS if you need to expand the hierarchy.

Customizing Backups

You can customize ConfigMgr maintenance task backups by using the following files:

▶ **Smsbkup.ctl:** The ConfigMgr backup service follows instructions defined in this backup control file (located in the *<ConfigMgrInstallPath>*\Inboxes\Smsbkup.box folder). This file can be edited, but there are clear instructions about which parts can be edited. Remember to make a copy of the file before performing any edits.

▶ **Afterbackup.bat:** This file allows you to automatically perform post-backup actions after a successful backup (such as archiving or versioning the backup). The file must be created and placed in the *<ConfigMgrInstallPath>*\inboxes\Smsbkup.box folder.

About SMS Writer

The SMS_SITE_VSS_WRITER service (smswriter.exe) must be running to perform a successful backup. This service carries out the following tasks:

▶ Interacts with the Volume Shadow Copy Service (VSS)

▶ Reads instructions from the backup control file (Smsbkup.ctl)

▶ Prepares the environment for the backup

▶ Stops the ConfigMgr services

▶ Restarts the ConfigMgr services after the backup

Using SQL Backup

As previously discussed in the "Implementing Configuration Manager Backup" section, the authors recommend using a SQL backup of the ConfigMgr site as a core component of any disaster recovery plan. That section also noted that the CD.Latest folder is vital in a site recovery but is not automatically backed up by a SQL backup.

This section describes how to create a backup task in which SQL Server backs up the core items required for a successful ConfigMgr site recovery. This procedure, which was developed by Steve Thompson, MVP, consists of these tasks:

▶ Configure the SQL Server Agent task to back up the CD.Latest folder.

▶ Configure a SQL Server maintenance plan to back up the databases.

Begin by choosing the location of the backup and creating a folder to hold the backup files (H:\SQLBackup for the purposes of this book). Also, create a CD.Latest folder within the backup location.

Backing Up the CD.Latest Folder

Follow these steps to create a SQL Server Agent task to back up the CD.Latest folder:

1. Launch SQL Server Management Studio and expand the **SQL Server Agent** node.

NOTE: SQL SERVER AGENT NODE

The SQL Server Agent node may not be visible in SQL Server Management Studio. This normally means that your user account does not have the required SQL permissions. Resolve this by launching the tool as administrator.

2. Right-click **Jobs** and select **New Job**.

3. Enter a suitable name in the New Job dialog box, such as **Backup CDLatest**.

4. Select **Steps** in the Select a page workspace. Click **New** to open a new job step.

5. Enter a suitable name for the job step. Select **Operating system (CmdExec)** as the type.

6. Copy and paste the PowerShell command shown in Listing 24.1 into the New Job Step dialog, as shown in Figure 24.4. (Modify the paths in this listing to match your environment).

LISTING 24.1   PowerShell Command to Back Up CD.Latest

```
powershell.exe -command "Get-ChildItem -Path 'H:\SQLBackup\CDLatest\
*.zip' | Where-Object
{$_.CreationTime -lt (Get-Date).AddDays(-7)} | Remove-Item | Add-Type -Assembly
'System.IO.Compression.FileSystem' -PassThru | Select -First 1 | % {
[IO.Compression.ZIPFile]::CreateFromDirectory('f:\program files\
microsoft configuration
manager\cd.latest', 'H:\SQLBackup\CDLatest\CDLatestArchive'
+ (Get-Date -format 'yyyyMMddHHmm') + '.zip') }"
```

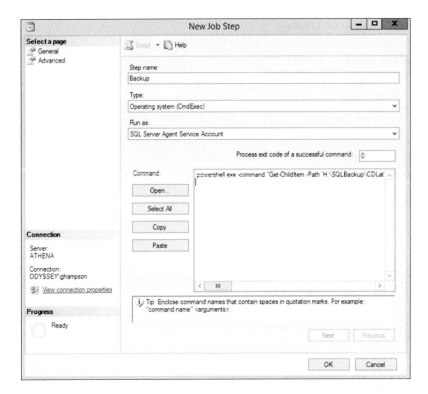

FIGURE 24.4   SQL Server Agent job step.

7. Click **OK** to create the job step.

8. Click **OK** to complete the SQL Server Agent job. This job is selected as an additional task in the SQL maintenance plan, created in the next section.

Creating a Maintenance Plan for a Database Backup

Using SQL Server Management Studio, follow these steps to create a SQL Server maintenance plan to back up the ConfigMgr site database and other associated databases:

1. Navigate to the **Management** node and right-click **Maintenance Plans**. Select **Maintenance Plan Wizard**. Click **Next** to launch the SQL Server Maintenance Plan Wizard.

2. Enter a suitable name in the Select Plan Properties dialog box. Click **Change** to configure a backup schedule.

3. Enter the schedule details as shown in Figure 24.5 and click **OK** to create the schedule.

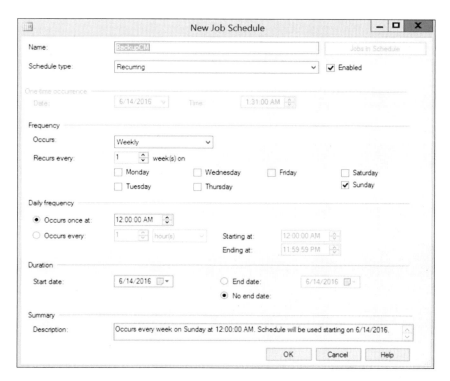

FIGURE 24.5   Database backup schedule.

4. Select the following maintenance tasks:

   ▶ Clean Up History

   ▶ Execute SQL Server Agent Job

   ▶ Back Up Database (Full)

   ▶ Maintenance Cleanup Task

   Click **Next**.

5. Change the maintenance task order by selecting the **Execute SQL Server Agent Job** and clicking **Move Down** until this task is listed last. Click **Next** to continue.

6. On the General tab of the Define Back Up Database (Full) Task dialog box, click the dropdown arrow beside **Databases** and choose **All user databases**. Click **OK**.

NOTE: NOT INCLUDED WITH ALL USER DATABASES

Selecting All user databases excludes master, model, msdb, and tempdb.

7. Select the **Destination** tab of the Define Back Up Database (Full) Task dialog box (see Figure 24.6).

FIGURE 24.6   Selecting the database backup destination.

8. Check the **Create a backup for every database** and **Create a sub-directory for each database** check boxes.

9. Type the backup destination folder name and type **bak** as the Backup file extension, as shown in Figure 24.6.

10. Select the **Options** tab of the Define Back Up Database (Full) Task dialog box. Click the **Set backup compression** dropdown arrow and select **Compress Backup**. Click **Next** to continue.

11. Perform the following tasks on the Define Maintenance Cleanup Task page, as shown in Figure 24.7.

   ▶ Type the backup destination folder name.

   ▶ For the file extension, type **bak**.

   ▶ Check the box **Include first-level subfolders**.

   ▶ In the File age section, select how long to retain the backup files.

   Click **Next** to continue.

FIGURE 24.7   Defining the maintenance cleanup task.

12. Select the **Backup CDLatest SQL Agent task** on the Define Execute SQL Server Agent Job Task page. This is the SQL Server Agent task that was created earlier, in the "Backing Up the CD.Latest Folder" section. Click **Next** to continue.

13. Choose a location for reports and click **Next**.

14. On the Complete the Wizard page, verify your choices and click **Finish** to create the maintenance plan.

Backed Up Files (SQL Maintenance Plan)

The backup creates a folder structure at the destination location, as shown in Figure 24.8. Following is information about that structure:

▶ CD.Latest contains the ConfigMgr source installation files for the currently installed version.

▶ The other folders contain compressed copies of SQL databases.

FIGURE 24.8   SQL backup folder structure.

Additional Files to Back Up

In the event of a disaster, a site can be fully recovered using a backup of the databases and the CD.Latest folder. However, this recovers only the site infrastructure. There are other aspects to consider when planning a disaster recovery strategy, including the content library, source files, and SQL Server Reporting Services (SSRS), as discussed in the following sections.

About the Content Library

The content library was introduced in ConfigMgr 2012. It is designed to optimize disk storage and to avoid duplication by not distributing files to distribution points (DPs) if they already exist. A copy of the single-instance store is kept on the site server as the source for the distribution points. The content library must be backed up using your regular backup routines, as it is not automatically included in any of the methods previously discussed in this chapter. The content library must be restored before content can be redistributed to distribution points.

> **NOTE: CONTENT REDISTRIBUTION**
>
> When you redistribute content in ConfigMgr, the files are copied from the content library on the site server to the distribution points.

The content library location is the SCCMContentLib folder on the site server. It is normally found on the disk drive that had the most available space when the site was installed.

You should back up the following folders:

▶ SCCMContentLib

▶ SMSPKG

▶ SMSPKGSIG

▶ SMSSIG$ (primary site only)

▶ SMSPKG*X*$ (where *X* is the drive letter; primary site only)

About Source Files
Package source files can be located anywhere and often are placed on a highly available remote file share. Regardless of location, they should be included in every organization's backup routine. The source files must be restored to allow content to be updated on DPs. After any content update, ConfigMgr first copies the updated files from the source location to the content library. The updated content is subsequently copied to the DPs.

Recovering SQL Server Reporting Services
There are several additional required tasks to facilitate the recovery of SSRS:

▶ Back up encryption keys using the SQL Server Reporting Services Configuration Manager.

▶ Back up the ReportServer and ReportServerTempDB databases. This is straightforward using the SQL maintenance plan discussed in the "Using SQL Backup" section, earlier in this chapter.

▶ Back up SSRS configuration files, which are typically found in *<SQL Server installation folder>*\MSRS12.MSSQLSERVER\Reporting Services. Table 24.1 lists the locations of these files.

TABLE 24.1   Reporting Service Configuration Files

Filename	Location
Rsreportserver.config	*<SQL Server installation folder>*\MSRS12.MSSQLSERVER\ Reporting Services\ReportServer
Rssvrpolicy.config	*<SQL Server installation folder>*\MSRS12.MSSQLSERVER\ Reporting Services\ReportServer
Rsmgrpolicy.config	*<SQL Server installation folder>*\MSRS12.MSSQLSERVER\ Reporting Services\ReportManager
ReportingServicesService. exe.config	*<SQL Server installation folder>*\MSRS12.MSSQLSERVER\ Reporting Services\ReportServer\bin
RSWebApplication.config	*<SQL Server installation folder>*\MSRS12.MSSQLSERVER\ Reporting Services\ReportManager

Recovering Configuration Manager Sites

Configuration Manager includes multiple recovery options. The option you choose varies depending on what has occurred and the backup types available.

ConfigMgr site recovery may be required in three scenarios:

▶ Site server operating system (OS) failure

▶ Site failure

▶ Site database failure

NOTE: SITE DATABASE RECOVERY

When you recover a site database, you must use the same version and edition of SQL Server.

Selecting Recovery Options

When you run the wizard to recover a site, you are presented with recovery options that fall into two distinct categories, as shown in Figure 24.9 and discussed in the following sections:

FIGURE 24.9   Selecting ConfigMgr recovery options.

▶ Site server recovery

▶ Site database recovery

Site Server Recovery Options

Site server recovery is required if the site server has failed (due to OS failure or ConfigMgr environment failure). The wizard presents two options:

▶ **Recover the Site Server Using an Existing Backup:** Select this option to reinstall the site using a backup that was created by the ConfigMgr Backup Site Server maintenance task (before the failure).

▶ **Reinstall the Site Server:** Use this option when no backup exists. You must use the server name, site code, and database name of the failed site.

NOTE: EXISTING SITE SERVER

Choosing the Recovery option during ConfigMgr setup on an existing site server enables recovery of the site database. However, the option to recover the site server is disabled.

Site Database Recovery Options

Three options are available if you need to recover the site database only:

▶ **Recover the Site Database Using a Backup Set:** Use this option if you have a backup of the site database created by the ConfigMgr Backup Site Server maintenance task prior to the failure.

▶ **Create a New Database for This Site:** Use this option when there is no database backup. It is only useful in a hierarchy when data can be replicated from the CAS.

▶ **Use a Site Database That Has Been Manually Recovered:** Use this option when you have already restored the SQL database and now must complete the recovery process.

NOTE: ADDITIONAL RECOVERY OPTION

There is a fourth option in the database recovery category. Use the **Skip database recovery option** when no data loss has occurred on the ConfigMgr site database server. This option is valid when the database is located on a remote server.

Restoring a Failed Site

When you have a site failure, follow these steps to recover the site:

1. Navigate to the location of the backed-up files (in the CD.Latest folder). Extract the files, if required. If recovering the entire server, copy the files to the new site server.

2. Launch setup by double-clicking **splash.hta** in the root of the CD.Latest folder.

3. In the Microsoft System Center Configuration Manager Setup Wizard, click **Install** to continue.

4. Read and ensure that you understand the notes on the Before You Begin page. Click **Next** to continue.

5. Select **Recover a site** on the Available Setup Options page, shown in Figure 24.10. Click **Next**.

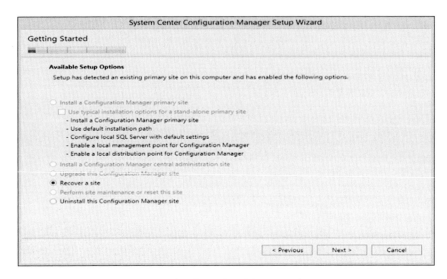

FIGURE 24.10   Recovering a Configuration Manager site.

The Site Server and Database Recovery Options page presents recovery options (refer to Figure 24.9). This particular example demonstrates database recovery from existing ConfigMgr backup.

6. Setup will detect an existing site installation and site server recovery settings will be disabled. Choose **Recover the site database using the backup at the following location** and click **Browse** to enter the path to the backed up files. Click **Next** to continue.

7. If restoring a primary site, you do not need to select any options on the Site Recovery information page. Recover primary site is pre-selected and the options are grayed out. Click **Next**.

8. Enter the product license key or choose to install a 180-day evaluation. If you choose the 180-day option, the wizard informs you that you can enter the product key from the Site Maintenance option in setup to upgrade the evaluation edition to the licensed edition. Click **Next**.

9. On the Product License Terms page, read the license terms and privacy statement. Check the box **I accept these License Terms and Privacy Statement**.

10. Accept the prerequisite license terms by selecting **I accept the License Terms** for Microsoft SQL Server Express and Microsoft SQL Server Native Client, and click **I accept the License Terms, Privacy Statement and automatic updates of Silverlight**. Click **Next**.

11. Select **Download required files** and enter a path to save these prerequisite files. You can alternatively choose **Use previously downloaded files** to use files downloaded previously. Click **Next** to continue.

NOTE: PREREQUISITE DOWNLOAD REQUIREMENTS

An Internet connection is required to download the prerequisite files. Optionally, you can download the files offline in advance, using setupDL.exe. For more information, see Chapter 6, "Installing and Updating System Center Configuration Manager."

The site code and site name on the Site and Installation Settings page is prepopulated and grayed out. This information is derived from the backup files specified in step 6.

12. Verify or browse to choose an alternative installation folder. You can optionally install the ConfigMgr console during the restore by checking the option **Install the Configuration Manager console**. Click **Next** to continue.

13. In the Database Information page, which is also prepopulated with information taken from the backup files, specify the SQL Service Broker (SSB) port or accept the default and click **Next** to continue.

14. On the second Database Information page, select paths for the SQL Server database and log files or accept the default locations. Click **Next** to continue.

15. Accept the ConfigMgr terms on the Usage Data page. (See Chapter 6 for details.) Click **Next**.

16. Review the settings summary and click **Next** to begin the prerequisite check. The wizard runs the prerequisite checker and identifies any prerequisite issues. Errors and warnings are displayed on the Prerequisite Check page. All activities are logged to C:\ConfigMgrPrereq.log.

17. Select **Begin Install** to start the recovery process. The restore may take a considerable amount of time, depending on the size of the database to be restored and server performance. You can monitor the process on the Install page of the wizard. Full details of the recovery process are also available in C:\ConfigMgrSetup.log.

The following post-recovery tasks may be required:

▶ Re-entering user passwords

▶ Re-entering side-loading keys

▶ Re-creating the Microsoft Intune subscription

▶ Configuring SSL for site system roles

▶ Reinstalling hotfixes in the recovered server

▶ Recovering custom reports

▶ Recovering content files

▶ Re-creating and exchanging SQL broker certificates (for multisite hierarchies)

NOTE: VERIFYING SITE RECOVERY

To verify the recovery, examine the ConfigMgr status messages, the site and component status, and the event log to verify that no errors have occurred and that the site is functioning normally.

Maintaining a Configuration Manager Site

Maintaining a ConfigMgr site is one of the primary functions of a ConfigMgr administrator. This involves working with many technologies to ensure optimal performance of the site. A conscientious administrator should constantly review event logs, queues, status messages, and log files to monitor how well the site is performing and to detect any issues before they cause poor performance or even a loss of service.

An administrator should also carry out regular tasks to maintain and optimize the environment:

▶ Configuring built-in maintenance tasks

▶ Monitoring and optimizing SQL

▶ Maintaining WSUS

The following sections discuss these tasks in detail. Site maintenance options that are required under specific circumstances are also described.

Configuring Built-in Maintenance Tasks

ConfigMgr includes predefined maintenance tasks to assist with maintaining the health of the ConfigMgr database. Most of these tasks are designed to remove obsolete data, which reduces the database size and improves performance.

In the ConfigMgr console, follow these steps to configure the maintenance tasks:

1. Navigate to **Administration** -> **Overview** -> **Site Configuration** -> **Sites**.

2. Right-click the site to be maintained and select **Site Maintenance** from the menu. The Site Maintenance dialog box displays a list of maintenance tasks for the site (refer to Figure 24.1).

NOTE: AVAILABLE MAINTENANCE TASKS

Not all maintenance tasks are available for each type of site.

Optimizing SQL Server

The "Using SQL Backup" section, earlier in this chapter, discusses the importance of backing up the SQL database. Additional SQL maintenance is required to ensure optimal database performance.

Fragmented indexes cause performance issues with SQL databases, and this gets worse over time. It is crucial to perform regular re-indexing of the ConfigMgr database. Execute the following T-SQL command on a database to establish whether there is excessive fragmentation.

DBCC Showcontig

Figure 24.11 shows the results of running this command in a test lab, where some of the tables have extensive fragmentation. If the site database is fragmented more than 10%, action is required to rebuild the indexes.

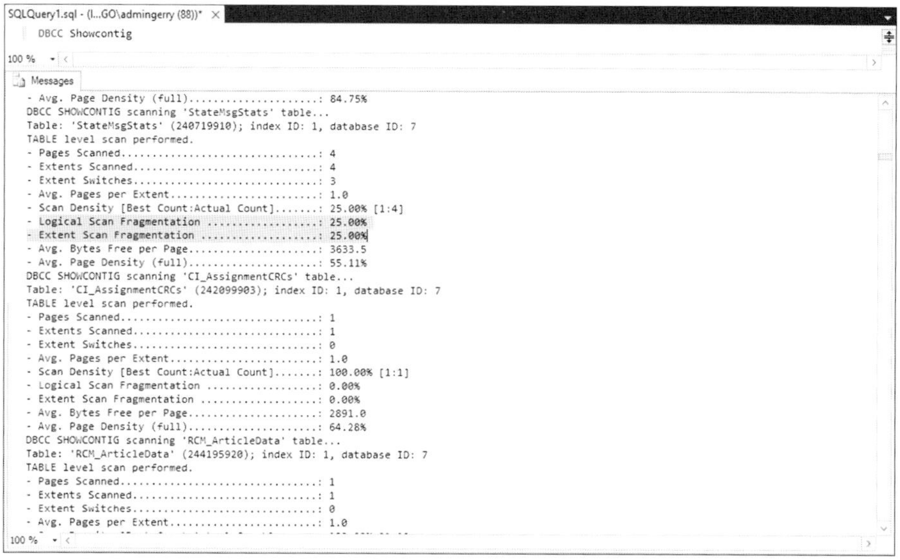

FIGURE 24.11   Displaying the level of database fragmentation.

Microsoft provides two ConfigMgr maintenance tasks to assist administrators:

▶ **Monitor Keys:** The ConfigMgr database uses primary keys to quickly identify unique records in a table. This task monitors the integrity of these keys within the ConfigMgr database. The task is enabled by default and runs Sunday mornings between 12 AM and 5 AM.

NOTE: DEFINITION OF THE CONFIGMGR PRIMARY KEY

A *primary key* is a column (or multiple columns) that uniquely identifies one row from any other row in a database.

▶ **Rebuild Indexes:** Much like database applications, ConfigMgr uses indexes to speed up data retrieval. The data in the ConfigMgr database constantly changes, and the Rebuild Index task improves performance by creating indexes on database columns that are at least 50% unique. The task also drops indexes on columns that are less than 50% unique and rebuilds all existing indexes to maximize the performance when accessing these columns. By default, the task is not enabled. If it is enabled, it runs every Sunday between 12 AM and 5 AM.

While rebuilding indexes is a useful method for re-indexing the database, it is not the most reliable method. The authors recommend using a SQL maintenance plan for re-indexing. Using SQL Server Management Studio, follow these steps to create a SQL maintenance plan to re-index the site database and other associated databases.

1. Navigate to the **Management** node and right-click **Maintenance Plans**. Select **Maintenance Plan Wizard**. Click **Next** to launch the SQL Server Maintenance Plan Wizard.

2. Enter a suitable name in the Select Plan Properties dialog box. Click **Change** to configure a backup schedule.

3. Enter the schedule details and click **OK** to create the schedule.

4. Select the following maintenance tasks, as shown in Figure 24.12:

   ▶ **Reorganize Index**

   ▶ **Rebuild Index**

   ▶ **Update Statistics**

   ▶ **Clean Up History**

   Click **Next**.

FIGURE 24.12   Database re-index maintenance tasks.

5. Accept the default task execution order and click **Next** to continue.

6. On the Define Reorganize Index Task page, use the database dropdown arrow to select **All user databases**. Accept the other configuration settings and click **Next**.

7. On the Define Rebuild Index Task page, use the database dropdown arrow to select **All user databases**. Accept the other configuration settings and click **Next**.

8. On the Define Update Statistics Task page, use the database dropdown arrow to select **All user databases**. Accept the other configuration settings and click **Next**.

9. Accept the default settings on the Define History Cleanup Task page and click **Next** to continue.

10. Select the location to save the report. Alternatively, enter an email recipient. Click **Next**.

11. Review the wizard summary and click **Finish** to create the maintenance plan.

NOTE: ADVANCED SQL OPTIMIZATION

Steve Thompson, MVP, is an expert in SQL Server optimization. He has proposed an alternative database optimization method that is widely accepted to be the optimal solution for optimizing ConfigMgr database performance. For more information, see https://stevethompsonmvp.wordpress.com/2013/05/07/optimizing-configmgr-databases/.

Maintaining Windows Server Update Services

As discussed in detail in Chapter 15, "Managing Software Updates," WSUS is a prerequisite component for implementing a software updates solution with ConfigMgr. WSUS can become problematic over time if it is not regularly maintained.

A WSUS maintenance routine should include the following:

▶ Backing up the WSUS database

▶ Running the WSUS Server Cleanup Wizard

▶ Re-indexing the WSUS database

Backing Up the WSUS Database

Back up the WSUS database using any method available to you. Database backup using a SQL maintenance plan is discussed earlier in this chapter, in the "Using SQL Backup" section.

Running the WSUS Server Cleanup Wizard

The WSUS Server Cleanup Wizard allows administrators to remove the following items from the WSUS database:

▶ Out-of-date update files

▶ Unused update files

▶ Old revisions of update files

▶ Superseded updates

▶ Expired updates

▶ Inactive computers

NOTE: WSUS CLEANUP TASK

You can now run and schedule the WSUS cleanup task from the ConfigMgr console. Configure this in the Software Update Point properties, and the task runs at the next software updates synchronization.

Follow these steps to manually run the wizard:

1. From the **Tools** menu of Server Manager, open the Windows Server Update Services (WSUS) console and select **Options -> Server Cleanup Wizard** (see Figure 24.13).

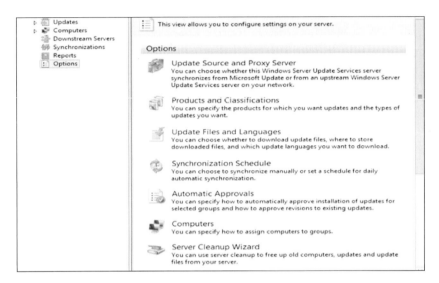

FIGURE 24.13   Selecting WSUS options.

2. In the WSUS Server Cleanup Wizard, select the items you would like to clean up and click **Next** to begin the cleanup. This process may take some time to complete.

NOTE: WSUS CLEANUP WIZARD TIMES OUT

If the WSUS Server Cleanup Wizard has never run and WSUS has been in production some time, the cleanup may time out. In that case, run the cleanup with only the top selection (**Unused updates and updates revisions**). This may require several passes. If it times out, run again until it completes and then run each of the other options, one at a time. Finally, make a "full pass" with all options checked.

Re-indexing the WSUS Database

To re-index the WSUS database, download the WSUSDBMaintenance T-SQL script from the TechNet gallery at https://gallery.technet.microsoft.com/scriptcenter/ 6f8cde49-5c52-4abd-9820-f1d270ddea61.

This script re-indexes the WSUS database. The steps to execute it vary, depending on whether you installed SUSDB on SQL Server or a Windows Internal Database (WID). The link provided in the previous paragraph also contains instructions for use.

The authors recommend using this script if WSUS has been installed using the WID. For re-indexing the WSUS database using SQL, refer to the "Advanced SQL Optimization" note earlier in this chapter.

Using ConfigMgr Site Maintenance Options

The ConfigMgr site maintenance wizard performs a site reset, which re-applies default file and Registry permissions on a primary or central administration site server.

Launch the site maintenance wizard by running Configuration Manager setup from the Microsoft System Center apps menu, as shown in Figure 24.14. Choose **Perform site maintenance or reset this site** on the first page of the wizard.

FIGURE 24.14   Running Configuration Manager setup.

Four site maintenance options are available, as shown in Figure 24.15 and described in the following sections:

▶ Reset site with no configuration changes

▶ Modify SQL Server configuration

▶ Modify SMS provider configuration

▶ Modify language configuration

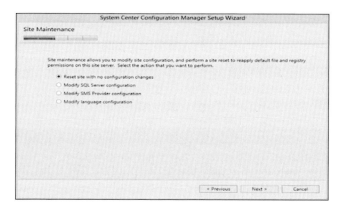

FIGURE 24.15   Configuration Manager site maintenance options.

Resetting a Site with No Configuration Changes

In addition to reapplying the default file and registry permissions on a primary or central administration site server, a site reset reinstalls all site system roles on the site. A site reset can be performed manually, using the ConfigMgr site maintenance wizard. ConfigMgr also runs a site reset automatically when required after a configuration change.

Modifying the SQL Server Configuration

The Modify SQL Server configuration option enables you to modify the configuration of the site database and site database server. ConfigMgr restarts or reinstalls services on the site server and remote site system servers that communicate with the database.

The following site database configurations can be changed:

▶ Windows server hosting the site database

▶ SQL Server instance

▶ Database name

▶ SQL Server port

▶ SQL Server Service Broker port

NOTE: SQL SERVER MODIFICATION FOR SECONDARY SITES

Microsoft does not support modifying the database configuration for a secondary site.

Modifying the SMS Provider Configuration

The SMS provider is a Windows Management Instrumentation (WMI) provider that assigns read and write access to the ConfigMgr database at a site. The ConfigMgr console, Resource Explorer, tools, and custom scripts use the SMS provider so that ConfigMgr administrative users can access information stored in the database.

The Modify SMS provider configuration option lets you change the SMS provider configuration for a site by adding a new provider or uninstalling an existing provider.

Modifying Language Configuration

During ConfigMgr site installation, you are prompted to choose the server and client languages to be supported. Use the Modify language configuration option if you wish to add or remove supported languages.

NOTE: MODIFYING LANGUAGE CONFIGURATION

Selecting the Modify language configuration option initiates a prerequisite download. An Internet connection is required (or you can run setupdl.exe to download the files to an alternate location).

Monitoring Configuration Manager

Use the Monitoring workspace in the ConfigMgr console, displayed in Figure 24.16, to monitor the hierarchy and associated operations. The navigation index contains links to the various monitoring sections. Table 24.2 lists these resources.

FIGURE 24.16   Configuration Manager monitoring.

TABLE 24.2   Configuration Manager Monitoring Resources

Resource	Description
Alerts	View and manage alerts.
Reporting	View and manage reports and report subscriptions and configure report options.
System Status	View and manage site status, component status, conflicting records, and status message queries.
Client Operations	View client operation details.
Database Replication	View site-to-site link status.
SUP Synchronization Status	View SUP synchronization status across the hierarchy.
Security	View endpoint protection and health attestation details.
Queries	View and manage ConfigMgr queries.
Site Hierarchy	View and manage the status of all sites in the hierarchy, using a hierarchy diagram or geographic view.
Deployments	View information about the status of deployed software.
Client Status	View and configure options for client status.
Distribution Status	View content status, DP status, and DP configuration status.
Site Servicing Status	View the status of ConfigMgr updates installed in the hierarchy.

Many reports and log files are designed to assist with maintaining a healthy environment. Consider the following when monitoring a ConfigMgr hierarchy:

▶ Status messages with errors and warnings

▶ Event log errors on site systems

▶ SQL errors

▶ Poor SQL performance

▶ Excessive file backlog on site systems

▶ Network issues

▶ Inactive clients

Monitoring Site Replication

Data Replication Service (DRS) was introduced in ConfigMgr 2012 to manage replication between sites. DRS is responsible for replicating the following data types:

▶ **Global Data:** This is administrator-created data (such as packages, applications, and collections), which is common across the hierarchy and shared between the CAS and all primary sites.

▶ **Site Data:** This data is generated by clients reporting directly to a primary site and is shared between the CAS and the respective primary sites.

The integrity of replication between sites is essential to ensure a healthy ConfigMgr environment. Replication status can be monitored in the ConfigMgr console. Follow these steps:

1. Open the console and navigate to **Monitoring -> Database Replication** (see Figure 24.17).

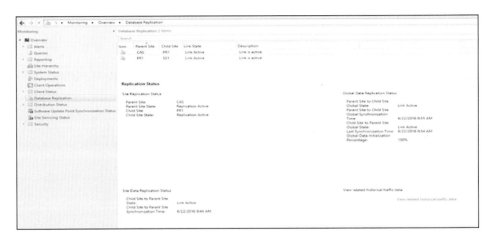

FIGURE 24.17   Configuration Manager Database Replication monitoring.

2. Highlight a set of replication partners to obtain a detailed status summary of several replication types:

▶ **Site Replication Status:** Lists the sites and their replication state.

▶ **Global Data Replication Status:** Lists the status for parent-to-child and child-to-parent replication with the timestamp of the last synchronization time and the global data initialization percentage.

▶ **Site Data Replication Status:** Lists the status for child-to-parent replication with the timestamp of the last synchronization time.

3. Right-click a site to view additional options, shown in Figure 24.18.

Choose **Save Diagnostics File** to view more detailed information on replication status.

Select **Replication Link Analyzer** to assist with the detection, analysis, and remediation of replication-related issues in a ConfigMgr hierarchy. Figure 24.19 shows a successful result after running this tool.

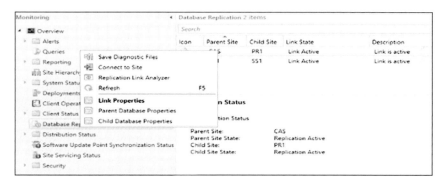

FIGURE 24.18   Configuration Manager Database Replication monitoring options.

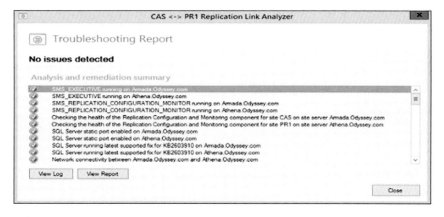

FIGURE 24.19   Viewing Replication Link Analyzer results.

Using System Center Operations Manager

Operations Manager (OpsMgr) is a robust monitoring solution. It can be deployed as highly available and provides comprehensive monitoring for critical systems. It uses a single interface that shows state, health and performance information of the server estate, and utilizes management packs that contain monitoring settings for different applications and services. Microsoft has developed a management pack that monitors the health of the ConfigMgr environment. Versions are also available for previous versions of ConfigMgr.

Download the System Center Monitoring Pack for Configuration Manager at https://www.microsoft.com/download/details.aspx?id=34709. The following very detailed and informative documents can also be downloaded from the same location:

▶ **Monitoring Pack Contents for System Center Configuration Manager:** This guide includes a detailed list of the monitors, rules, and reports available for the various Configuration Manager components.

▶ **Guide for System Center Monitoring Pack for System Center Configuration Manager:** This guide provides general information on monitoring scenarios and configuration options.

Summary

This chapter discussed backup, recovery, and maintenance of ConfigMgr. It described the different ways to implement backup solutions and the various scenarios for recovering sites.

Maintaining and monitoring a hierarchy is a vital part of a ConfigMgr administrator's role. This chapter explained that many components must be considered to maintain a healthy environment. Even though ConfigMgr has its own built-in maintenance tasks, components such as SQL Server and WSUS can and should be maintained using their native tools.

This chapter also discussed monitoring ConfigMgr hierarchies and introduced useful tools such as the Replication Link Analyzer and System Center Operations Manager.

PART V

Appendixes

IN THIS PART

Configuration Manager Log Files

ConfigMgr has historically used comprehensive logging throughout the product. The level of logging means that there are lots of log files. This appendix provides information on how to easily view the log files and increase the logging levels to provide more details. This can often be helpful when troubleshooting an issue and when initially learning how ConfigMgr works, as you can see low-level details and behaviors. The appendix ends with a list of core client and site server logs. Logs that are commonly used for troubleshooting have been tagged with **(Frequently used.)**.

Viewing Log Files

ConfigMgr logs files are all written in plain text, as are most of the other log files listed in this appendix. This means you can view them using various tools, including the Windows Notepad program. ConfigMgr also provides its own log file viewer, called *CMTrace*. CMTrace is included on the ConfigMgr installation media and is installed on the central administration site (CAS) and primary site servers under *<ConfigMgrInstallPath>*\tools. The CMTrace.exe file is portable and can be copied to workstations rather than having to view log files on ConfigMgr servers. CMTrace allows you to merge multiple log files into a single window, and it updates the logs in real-time. It also supports highlighting specific lines.

CMTrace provides the following ConfigMgr-specific benefits:

▶ CMTrace can automatically highlight errors and warnings in ConfigMgr logs. This is primarily for the components that have existed since Systems Management Server (SMS) 2.0 and SMS 2003. For newer log files, log lines are highlighted in yellow if they contain the word *warning* and in red if they contain the word *error*.

▶ ConfigMgr log files are in a ConfigMgr-specific tagged format. This can cause them to appear unclear when using Notepad. CMTrace automatically suppresses the tagging and moves tagged data into individual columns.

▶ CMTrace provides a built-in Error Lookup component, which is accessed from the Edit menu. You can use it to look up Windows hexadecimal and decimal error codes to provide documented error messages.

Configuring Logging

Most ConfigMgr logs are enabled by default. As part of troubleshooting, it may be necessary to enable additional debug or verbose logging. In production, you should not configure additional logging on an ongoing basis; it should be enabled only to trouble-shoot a specific issue. This is because the additional detail in those logs can consume a large amount of disk space. Those additional details may also obscure normal operational information, hampering identification of more mundane operational issues day-to-day.

In addition to troubleshooting, enabling debug/verbose logging is an excellent method to learn the internals and product architecture of ConfigMgr. If you or someone on your team is learning about ConfigMgr, turning on debug/verbose logging while walking through various features and scenarios provides an excellent learning experience.

Server-Side Logging Levels

The following are the various Registry values where additional logging can be configured on the ConfigMgr server-side components (except the management point [MP], covered in the next section):

▶ **Site Server SMSExec Component Logs:** Verbose logging needs to be enabled on a per-component basis for each component/thread of SMSExec (smsexec.exe). To enable verbose logging, set the following Registry value (a DWORD value) to 1 on the components that support the level of detail:

```
HKLM\Software\Microsoft\SMS\Components\<component_name>\Verbose Logging
```

▶ **SQL Logging:** SQL Server trace logging causes ConfigMgr components to log any Transact-SQL (T-SQL) queries/statements to the ConfigMgr log files. To enable SQL logging in ConfigMgr, set the following Registry value (a DWORD value) to 1:

```
HKLM\Software\Microsoft\SMS\Tracing\SQLEnabled
```

SQL statements may be truncated in the log file. Tracing those long statements requires the use of SQL Server Profiler.

▶ **NAL Logging:** Network Abstraction Layer (NAL) logging can be useful when troubleshooting file share access issues. It provides low-level information on file share login and access attempts. To enable NAL logging, set the following Registry value (a DWORD value) to 7:

```
HKLM\SOFTWARE\Microsoft\NAL\Logging\Verbosity
```

Set the following Registry value (a DWORD value) to 3:

```
HKLM\SOFTWARE\Microsoft\NAL\Logging\LogTo
```

MP/Client and Console Logging Levels

The following are the various Registry values where additional logging can be configured on the ConfigMgr client-side components:

▶ **Client and MP Logs:** Perform the following steps to enable debug logging:

1. Create the DebugLogging key:

```
HKLM\Software\Microsoft\CCM\Logging\DebugLogging
```

2. Set the following Registry value (a DWORD value) to 0:

```
HKLM\Software\Microsoft\CCM\Logging\@Global\Loglevel
```

Client and MP logs are configured the same way as they share a common framework and hosting process (ccmexec.exe). For more information on ccmexec, see Chapter 3, "Looking Inside Configuration Manager."

▶ **Admin Console Logs:** Perform the following steps to enable debug logging:

1. Open the following file in Notepad:

```
%ProgramFiles%\Microsoft Configuration Manager\AdminConsole\bin\
Microsoft.ConfigurationManagement.exe.config
```

2. Search for `switchValue="Error"` and change it to `switchValue="Verbose"`.

3. Restart the console.

Client Logs

Client logs are located under %windir%\CCM\Logs. If the ConfigMgr client is installed on an MP after the MP is installed, the logs will be located under %ProgramFiles%\ SMS_CCM\Logs. The following are the ConfigMgr core client log files (with logs often/ commonly used for troubleshooting marked **(Frequently Used.)**). For a comprehensive list of client log files by ConfigMgr functionality, see https://docs.microsoft.com/sccm/core/ plan-design/hierarchy/log-files#BKMK_FunctionLogs.

▶ **CAS.log (Content Access Service):** Responsible for package/content caching. **(Frequently used.)**

▶ **Ccm32BitLauncher.log:** Responsible for executing applications marked as run as 32-bit.

▶ **CcmEval.log:** Responsible for ConfigMgr client health evaluation.

▶ **CcmEvalTask.log:** Responsible for invocation of the CcmEval process.

▶ **CcmExec.log:** Core log file for the ccmexec.exe process. Main component of the ConfigMgr client.

▶ **CcmMessaging.log:** Responsible for communication (or messaging) between the client and management points.

▶ **CcmNotificationAgent.log:** Responsible for client push notification and waking up the ConfigMgr client in response to a client notification channel event.

▶ **CcmPerf.log:** Responsible for ccmexec.exe Windows performance counters.

▶ **CcmRestart.log:** Responsible for any ConfigMgr client-initiated restarts.

▶ **CcmSdkProvider.log:** Logs client software development kit (SDK) interfaces usage.

▶ **CcmSetup.log:** Logs high-level client installation process and result. **(Frequently used.)**

▶ **ccmsetup-ccmeval.log:** Logs activities performed by ccmsetup.exe related to client status and remediation.

▶ **CertificateMaintenance.log:** Logs Active Directory (AD) and MP certificate operations and trust between client and MP.

▶ **CIAgent.log:** Provides details about the process of remediation and compliance for compliance settings, software updates, and application management.

▶ **CiDownloader.log:** Logs details about configuration item (CI) definition downloads. CIs underpin software updates, application management, compliance settings, drivers, and resource profile management.

▶ **CiTaskMgr.log:** Logs scheduling tasks for each action, such as content download or installation, for applications and their deployment types. **(Frequently used.)**

▶ **Client.msi.log:** Logs details of the client installation process. Triggered by ccmsetup.exe (described above). **(Frequently used.)**

▶ **ClientAuth.log:** Logs authentication and signing activity for messages sent to the MP.

▶ **ClientIdManagerStartup.log:** Part of the client registration process.

▶ **CmHttpsReadiness.log:** Log for the ConfigMgr HTTPS Readiness Assessment Tool.

▶ **CmRcService.log:** Logs remote control activities on the device.

▶ **ContentTransferManager.log:** Logs the scheduling of Service Message Block (SMB) access or Background Intelligence Transfer Service (BITS) download of package content. This is the component responsible for content download. **(Frequently used.)**

▶ **DataTransferService.log:** Logs all BITS job management activities for both policy and package download. **(Frequently used.)**

▶ **DcmAgent.log:** Records high-level information about the evaluation, conflict reporting, and remediation of configuration items and applications.

▶ **DcmReporting.log:** Records information about reporting policy platform results into state messages for configuration items.

▶ **DcmWmiProvider.log:** Records information about reading configuration item synclets from Windows Management Instrumentation (WMI).

▶ **EndpointProtectionAgent.log:** Logs installation of System Center Endpoint Protection (SCEP) client and Endpoint Protection policy deployment.

▶ **execmgr.log:** Logs details about legacy packages and program deployment along with task sequences. **(Frequently used.)**

▶ **ExpressionSolver.log:** Logs details about the detection method used when verbose or debug logging is enabled.

▶ **ExternalEventAgent.log:** Logs details about gathering of SCEP malware detection from the event log.

▶ **FileBITS.log:** Logs information related to package access for content hosted on SMB shares.

▶ **FileSystemFile.log:** Logs file collection and software inventory activities from the WMI provider.

▶ **FSPStateMessage.log:** Logs all activity for state messages that are sent to the fallback status point (FSP).

▶ **InternetProxy.log:** Logs proxy configuration and usage by the ConfigMgr client.

▶ **InventoryAgent.log:** Logs heartbeat discovery along with hardware and software inventory activities. **(Frequently used.)**

▶ **LocationCache.log:** Logs actions related to maintenance and use of the location cache.

▶ **LocationServices.log:** Logs client actions related to locating MPs, software update points (SUPs), and content on distribution points (DPs). Useful for troubleshooting why a client cannot locate content or the MP/SUP. Shows the network details sent by the client to the MP to locate a SUP or DP. **(Frequently used.)**

▶ **MaintenanceCoordinator.log:** Logs the actions for client maintenance tasks.

▶ **Mifprovider.log:** Logs the actions related to the WMI provider that processes Management Information Format (MIF) files. This is a legacy method of extending hardware inventory.

▶ **mtrmgr.log:** Logs actions related to software metering.

▶ **PolicyAgent.log:** Logs requests for policy. The Policy Agent makes these requests using the Data Transfer Service. **(Frequently used.)**

▶ **PolicyAgentProvider.log:** Logs policy storage and changes after Policy Agent receives changes to client policy.

▶ **PolicyEvaluator.log:** Logs details about the evaluation of policies after Policy Agent receives those policies.

▶ **PolicyPlatformClient.log:** Logs remediation and compliance of Microsoft Policy Platform providers, except the file provider. These providers underpin application management, software update management, and compliance policies.

▶ **PolicySdk.log:** Logs activities for the policy system's software development kit (SDK) interfaces.

▶ **Pwrmgmt.log:** Logs information about configuring, enabling, and disabling wake-up proxy client settings.

▶ **PwrProvider.log:** Logs activities of the power management provider in WMI. This provider gathers the current settings and power usage activities on client computers and applies power plan settings.

▶ **SCClient_*domain@username*_1.log:** Logs activities related to the SCClient.exe (Software Center) for the specified user. *domain@username* will match each Software Center user that has logged on to the client.

▶ **Scheduler.log:** Logs all scheduled activities on the client, with the exception of client health operations, which are handled by the Windows Task Scheduler. **(Frequently used.)**

▶ **SCNotify_*domain@username*_1.log:** Logs activity related to Software Center-generated notifications to the client for the user specified by *domain@username*. Historic log files are stored with the name format SCNotify_*domain@username*_1-*<date_time>*.log.

▶ **SetupPolicyEvaluator.log:** Logs initial creation of the configuration and inventory policy in WMI.

▶ **SleepAgent_*domain*@SYSTEM_0.log:** Logs main wake-up proxy activities.

▶ **SmsCliUi.log:** Logs ConfigMgr Control Panel applet usage.

▶ **SrcUpdateMgr.log:** Logs activity for Windows Installer installations when they are updated with current DP source locations.

▶ **StatusAgent.log:** Logs status message creation and submission by other client components.

▶ **SwMtrReportGen.log:** Logs software metering report generation based on data gathered by the metering agent (MtrMgr.log).

▶ **UserAffinity.log:** Logs the processing of logon/logoff activity to generate automatic user–device affinity.

▶ **VirtualApp.log:** Logs details related to the management of Microsoft Application Virtualization (App-V) deployment types and inventory of App-V sequenced applications.

▶ **WedmTrace.log:** Logs configuration, disablement, and enablement of the Windows Embedded write filters.

▶ **WakePrxy-Install.log:** Logs installation status when the wake-up proxy is enabled on a client.

▶ **WakePrxy-Uninstall.log:** Logs uninstallation status when the wake-up proxy is disabled on a client.

NOTE: THE WINDOWSUPDATE.LOG FILE IN WINDOWS 10 VERSION 1607 DIFFERS FROM PREVIOUS VERSIONS

In versions of Windows prior to Windows 10, the Windows Update log is in cleartext and can be viewed with CMTrace, like any other ConfigMgr log file. The log file itself, WindowsUpdate.log, is documented in the Microsoft support article at https://support.microsoft.com/kb/902093. Starting with Windows 10 Version 1607, the Windows Update client now uses Event Tracing for Windows (ETW) for logging instead of cleartext. A human-readable log file can be generated by running `Get-WindowsUpdateLog` PowerShell command. The resulting WindowsUpdate.log is written to the current user's desktop. For more information on the changes in Windows 10 Version 1607 and later, see https://support.microsoft.com/kb/3036646.

Server Logs

The following sections group log files based on their server function: site server, server installation and update logs, site system logs, and cloud management gateway logs (in Azure). Microsoft has published a list of log files that is scenario based; see the ConfigMgr documentation at https://docs.microsoft.com/sccm/core/plan-design/hierarchy/log-files.

Site Server Logs

Site Server Logs are located under the *%ProgramFiles%*\Microsoft Configuration Manager\Logs folder by default. The following are the site server log files (with logs often/commonly used for troubleshooting marked **(Frequently Used.)**):

▶ **adctrl.log:** Logs enrollment processing activities.

▶ **AdForestDisc.log:** Logs processing of AD Forest Discovery and generation of data discovery record (DDR) files. **(Frequently used.)**

▶ **AdService.log:** Logs core Active Directory discovery engine work. **(Frequently used.)**

▶ **adsgdis.log:** Logs AD Group Discovery processing of group objects in AD and generation of associated DDR files. **(Frequently used.)**

▶ **adsysdis.log:** Logs AD System Discovery processing of computer objects in AD and generation of associated DDR files. **(Frequently used.)**

▶ **adusrdis.log:** Logs AD User Discovery processing of user objects in AD and generation of associated DDR files. **(Frequently used.)**

▶ **bgbMgr.log:** Logs details about the site server activities related to client notifications.

▶ **ccm.log:** Logs client push installation actions and results. Useful for troubleshooting failed client push installation as you can see each action performed in push installation. **(Frequently used.)**

▶ **CertMgr.log:** Logs certificate-related activities for intrasite communication and setup of certs required for the certificate registration points (CRPs).

▶ **chmgr.log:** Logs client health manager activities, including processing of incoming client health information.

▶ **Cidm.log:** Logs changes to the client settings by the Client Install Data Manager (CIDM).

▶ **CloudDP-<*ServiceName*>.log:** Logs details for a specific cloud-based DP. This includes information about storage and content access and transaction data pulled from Microsoft Azure.

▶ **CloudMgr.log:** Logs deployment of the cloud management gateway service to Azure, service status, and use data. Also logs content provisioning and collects storage and bandwidth statistics, along with admin actions to stop/start the cloud service for cloud-based DPs.

▶ **CloudUserSync.log:** Logs synchronization and licensing of users from the site database to Microsoft Intune. Used only in an Intune hybrid environment.

▶ **colleval.log:** Logs information related to collection evaluation, including when collections are created, changed, and deleted. Useful for troubleshooting collection membership updates. **(Frequently used.)**

▶ **compmon.log:** Logs the status of components monitored by the site server.

▶ **compsumm.log:** Logs the summarization of the data processed by CompMon.log.

▶ **ComRegSetup.log:** Logs the results of COM registrations during setup and maintenance (site reset) of a site server.

▶ **dataldr.log:** Logs information related to processing of the hardware inventory (including MIF files) by Data Loader (DataLdr) and update of the ConfigMgr site database. **(Frequently used.)**

▶ **ddm.log:** Logs information related to the processing of discovery information in the form of DDR files by Data Discovery Manager (DDM). Useful when troubleshooting discovery processing issues. **(Frequently used.)**

▶ **despool.log:** Logs information related to the processing on incoming intersite replication by the receiving site. This is useful for troubleshooting package replication. **(Frequently used.)**

▶ **distmgr.log:** Logs details of package storage in the content library from content source locations and packages that content for replication to other sites. **(Frequently used.)**

▶ **dmpDownloader.log:** Logs details about data coming from Microsoft Intune and information on ConfigMgr releases (and content for those releases). Useful for troubleshooting Intune mobile device management (MDM) inventory, state, and device discovery.

▶ **Dmpuploader.log:** Transmits policy and targeting information from the site database to Microsoft Intune, along with any line-of-business (LOB) mobile apps deployed using enterprise sideloading in Intune. Useful for troubleshooting Intune MDM policy deployment and targeting.

▶ **EpCtrlMgr.log:** Logs information related to syncing of malware threat data from the Endpoint Protection Point to the site server and ultimately the site database.

▶ **EPMgr.log:** Logs the status of the Endpoint Protection Point site system role.

▶ **EPSetup.log:** Logs information during the installation of the Endpoint Protection Point site system role.

▶ **EnrollSrv.log:** Logs activities of the enrollment service. This is the back-end component for Windows Mobile/CE and Windows 10 devices managed via the on-premise MDM component.

▶ **EnrollWeb.log:** Logs activities of the enrollment website. This is the front-end component to the enrollment service (see EnrollSrv.log).

▶ **fspmgr.log:** Logs activities of the FSP.

▶ **hman.log:** Logs information about site configuration change, publishing of site information in AD, and routes incoming Intune hybrid device data to the correct site in the hierarchy. **(Frequently used.)**

▶ **inboxmgr.log:** Logs file transfer actions between inboxes.

▶ **inboxmon.log:** Logs statistics regarding the processing on inbox files and the updating of corresponding performance counters on the site server.

▶ **invproc.log:** Logs the forwarding of MIF files from a secondary site to its parent primary site.

▶ **migmctrl.log:** Logs information on migration job actions, DP sharing, and DP upgrades. Runs on the CAS in a hierarchy; runs on the primary site server in a stand-alone primary environment.

▶ **mpcontrol.log:** Records the availability of the MP every 10 minutes.

▶ **netdisc.log:** Logs the processing of Network Discovery using SNMP, DHCP, and the Computer Browser service, along with the generation of associated DDR files.

▶ **ntsvrdis.log:** Logs the discovery process of site system servers; this is generally performed during installation and maintenance (site reset) of site system instances.

▶ **Objreplmgr.log:** Logs the object change notifications for file-based replication.

▶ **offermgr.log:** Logs processing of legacy package/program advertisements.

▶ **offersum.log:** Logs the summarization of software distribution status messages.

▶ **OfflineServicingMgr.log:** Logs activities related to application of software updates to operating system image files.

▶ **outboxmon.log:** Logs statistics regarding the processing of outbox files along with the updating of corresponding performance counters.

▶ **PerfSetup.log:** Logs installation results of performance counters installed on the site server.

▶ **PkgXferMgr.log:** Logs content distribution activity from the site server's content library to remote DPs and cloud DPs. Useful for troubleshooting package replication and content distribution issues. **(Frequently used.)**

▶ **policypv.log:** Logs creation, update, and deletion to client policy by the policy provider (hence PolicyPv). These are the policies stored in the site database and distributed to clients by the MP. This includes client settings and deployment.

▶ **rcmctrl.log:** Logs high-level information related to the Data Replication Service (DRS) that replicates data between site databases. Useful for initial troubleshooting of DRS but often needs to be followed up with reviewing the vLogs view in the site database for each site. **(Frequently used.)**

▶ **replmgr.log:** Logs details of movement of files between various site components and the Scheduler component (in preparation for intersite replication).

▶ **ruleengine.log:** Logs automatic deployment rule (ADR) activity relating to updating software update groups and packages with new software updates. Also responsible for Windows 10 servicing plans. **(Frequently used.)**

▶ **schedule.log:** Logs details about scheduling file-based intersite replication of content and files by the Scheduler component. Jobs are passed to Sender component for actual transmission. Useful for troubleshooting replication schedule configuration. **(Frequently used.)**

▶ **sender.log:** Logs details about transfer activity during file-based intersite replication by the Sender component. The Scheduler component handles when replication occurs. Useful for troubleshooting content transmission to destination sites. **(Frequently used.)**

▶ **sinvproc.log:** Logs information related to the processing of software inventory into the site database.

▶ **sitecomp.log:** Logs information about installation and maintenance of site components on all site system servers and the site server within a site. Runs in its own Windows process (sitecomp.exe) and is not part of SMSExec (smsexec.exe). **(Frequently used.)**

▶ **sitectrl.log:** Logs site setting changes made by the site settings.

▶ **sitestat.log:** Logs results of availability and disk space monitoring for all site systems.

▶ **smsbkup.log:** Logs actions and results of the site backup process.

▶ **smsdbmon.log:** Logs database changes. Useful for detecting SQL Server access and site maintenance task issues.

▶ **smsexec.log:** SMSExec is the main site server process in ConfigMgr. This file logs the start and stop of ConfigMgr components that run as threads under smsexec.exe and SMSExec's own activity. **(Frequently used.)**

▶ **SMS_Cloud_ProxyConnector.log:** Logs connections between the cloud management gateway in Azure and the cloud management gateway connection point on-premise.

▶ **SMSProv.log:** Logs WMI provider access to the site database. Useful for troubleshooting console issues that occur on multiple machines and for tracing console interactions at the WMI level.

▶ **statesys.log:** Logs state message processing. State messages are used across application management, settings management, and software update management to record the states of individual application deployment types, settings, and updates.

▶ **statmgr.log:** Logs processing of status messages. Status messages are used for ConfigMgr server and client status along with task sequences and package/program deployments.

▶ **swmproc.log:** Logs the processing of software metering data files and settings.

▶ **WCM.log:** Logs remote configuration by the site server of Windows Server Update Services (WSUS) on SUPs. Useful for troubleshooting initial deployment of a SUP.

▶ **WsfbSyncWorker.log:** Logs synchronization of app data and purchases from the Windows Store for Business (WSFB).

▶ **WSUSCtrl.log:** Logs monitoring of the SUPs within a site as a status message.

▶ **wsyncmgr.log:** Logs the synchronization process performed by the site server. This process moves metadata from WSUS to the site database. Used to troubleshoot that sync process and software update deployment. **(Frequently used.)**

Server Installation and Update Logs

The following logs are created during server installation, maintenance, and version updates:

▶ **CMUpdate.log:** Logs activities related to ConfigMgr version updates triggered from the Updates and Servicing node of the console. Useful for troubleshooting an unresponsive update process. Located under the ConfigMgr installation folder on the CAS and all primary site servers.

▶ **ConfigMgrPrereq.log:** Logs evaluation of prerequisites for ConfigMgr setup. Used to troubleshoot installations that will not start due to missing prerequisites. Located on the root of C:\ on all site servers.

▶ **ConfigMgrSetup.log:** Logs actions of ConfigMgrSetup.exe. Used to troubleshoot failed site server installation and complex ConfigMgr version updates. Located on the root of C:\ on all site servers.

▶ **ConfigMgrSetupWizard.log:** Logs information related to the setup wizard. Does not contain actual setup process information. Located on the root of C:\ on all site servers.

▶ **sitecomp.log:** Logs information regarding post-ConfigMgrSetup.exe bootstarting and component installation throughout a site. Used during initial installation, site maintenance (a.k.a. site reset), and version updates. Located under the ConfigMgr installation folder on all site servers.

▶ **SMS_BOOTSTRAP.log:** Logs information about remotely launching (that is, boot-strapping) a secondary site installation. Hands off to ConfigMgrSetup.exe, and the actual setup process can be seen in ConfigMgrSetup.log on the secondary site server.

Site System Logs

The following section contains information about the MP, software update point (SUP), and FSP log files. Distribution points are not covered as their logging is hosted on the site server—in the distMgr.log and PkgXferMgr.log files. For a list of other site system role log files, see https://docs.microsoft.com/sccm/core/plan-design/hierarchy/log-files.

The following are the MP logs, which are stored under the *%ProgramFiles%*\SMS_CCM folder:

▶ **CcmExec.log:** Log file for the main process (ccmexec.exe) that hosts all MP components as threads. Used to trace overall service and individual component startup/termination.

▶ **CcmIsapi.log:** Log file for the MP ISAPI (Internet Server Application Programming Interface) extension used to process incoming client requests sent to the \CCM_System URL subpath on the MP.

▶ **MP_CliReg.log:** Log file for client registration activities. Useful for troubleshooting failed client registration.

▶ **MP_Ddr.log:** Logs the conversion of XML client-generated .ddr files into site server format .ddr files. Copied by MP File Dispatch Manager (MpFdm.log) to the site server for processing by DDM (ddm.log).

▶ **MP_Framework.log:** Logs core activities of the MP components that run under ccmexec.exe.

▶ **MP_GetAuth.log:** Logs client authorization activities.

▶ **MP_GetPolicy.log:** Logs client requests for policy. By default, it only logs the start/stop of the component and not individual client requests. For temporary debugging purposes, enable policy request logging by creating the LogPolicyRequests DWORD value and setting the decimal value to 1 in the following Registry key:

HKLM\Software\Microsoft\SMS\MP

Be sure to set `LogPolicyRequests` to 0 to stop logging after you gather the data you need.

▶ **MP_Hinv.log:** Logs the conversion of XML client-generated hardware inventory files into site server format files. Copied by MP File Dispatch Manager (MpFdm.log) to the site server for processing by Data Loader (DataLdr.log).

▶ **MP_Location.log:** Logs client location requests for content and site systems.

▶ **MP_Policy.log:** Logs information related to policy retrieval from the site database.

▶ **MP_Relay.log:** Logs transfer of files from the MP to the site server.

▶ **MP_Retry.log:** Logs hardware inventory retry processes.

▶ **MP_Sinv.log:** Logs the conversion of XML client-generated software inventory files into site server format files. Copied by MP File Dispatch Manager (MpFdm.log) to the site server for processing by the Software Inventory Processor (sInvProc.log).

▶ **MP_SinvCollFile.log:** Logs details about file collection by software inventory.

▶ **MP_Status.log:** Logs the conversion of XML client-generated status messages files into site server format files. Copied by MP File Dispatch Manager (MpFdm.log) to the site server for processing by Status Manager (statmgr.log).

▶ **mpcontrol.log:** Logs the availability of MPs in the site every 10 minutes. Runs under smsexec.exe and not ccmexec.exe, like other log files previously listed in this section.

▶ **mpfdm.log:** Logs activities of the MP File Dispatch Manager (MP FDM). MP FDM copies site server–formatted client files to their corresponding inbox folders on the MP's site server.

▶ **mpMSI.log:** Logs details about the MP installation. MSI installation is triggered by MPSetup.exe.

▶ **MPSetup.log:** Logs the initialization of MP installation. This component invokes the MP .msi installer.

The SUP and FSP logs are in the SMS\Logs folder on one of the remote site systems and in the same folder as the Site Server logs when the SUP is installed on the site server. They are the SUP log files:

▶ **SUPSetup.log:** Logs details about the SUP's installation. Used to troubleshoot failed SUP installations.

▶ **WSUSCtrl.log:** Logs details about the SUP configuration, database connectivity, and availability of the WSUS components.

▶ **wsyncmgr.log:** Logs details about software update sync process.

The following are the FSP log files:

▶ **FspIsapi.log:** Logs details about communication to the FSP by client computers. These messages traverse the FSP ISAPI extension in Internet Information Services (IIS).

▶ **fspMSI.log:** Logs details of the installation by the FSP Windows Installer package.

▶ **fspmgr.log:** Logs activities of the FSP.

Cloud Management Gateway Logs in Azure

ConfigMgr Current Branch version 1610 introduced the cloud management gateway (CMG). The CMG runs in Microsoft Azure Cloud Services virtual machines (VMs). Cloud Services is Azure's Platform as a Service (PaaS) offering. Logging is generated on each Cloud Services VM and then copied to Azure storage.

CMGs push logs to Azure storage every five minutes. To aid with troubleshooting, the Cloud Service Manager (CloudMgr.log) syncs the log files down from Azure storage every five minutes to the site server. This is important if there are connectivity issues from the site server to Azure storage, as it may be necessary to access logs directly on the Azure VMs used by the CMG.

To access the logs on the Azure VMs, access the *%approot%*\logs folder on the CMG VMs. The AppRoot environment variable is part of the Azure PaaS app deployment model. It is where Azure Cloud Services deploys an Azure app, and the folder is the root folder of the app.

The following log files can be used to troubleshoot the CMG:

▶ **CloudMgr.log:** Logs details about the deployment of the CMG, ongoing service status, and usage data associated with the service.

▶ **CMGSetup.log:** Logs details about the Azure portion of deployment after CloudMgr has completed its work. This log file's name is used on the Azure VM itself. On the CMG's site server, the format is CMG-*<RoleInstanceId>*-CMGSetup.

▶ **CMGHttpHandler.log:** Logs details related to the CMG HTTP handler binding in IIS in the Azure VMs. Used to troubleshoot client traffic and communications. On the CMG's site server, the format is CMG-*<RoleInstanceId>*-CMGHttpHandler.

▶ **CMGService.log:** Logs details about the CMG service's core components in Azure. Used to troubleshoot service health along with client communications. This log file's name is used on the Azure VM itself. On the CMG's site server, the format is CMG-*<RoleInstanceId>*-CMGService.

▶ **SMS_Cloud_ProxyConnector.log:** Logs details about connection setup between the CMG and the CMG connection point (an on-premise site system role). Used to troubleshoot service health along with client communications.

APPENDIX B

Co-Managing Microsoft Intune and ConfigMgr

Windows 10 introduces new and streamlined methods for managing Windows, which Microsoft refers to as *modern management*. There are multiple paths to modern management, depending on where an organization is on its Windows 10 journey and the constraints of that organization's environment and infrastructure. The main component of modern management is the use of Windows 10's built-in mobile device management (MDM) agent instead of additional management agents.

This appendix discusses modern management and what it brings to Windows management. It also explains how you can leverage and configure Configuration Manager (ConfigMgr) to create a pathway to modern management. This pathway allows moving workloads from ConfigMgr to Microsoft Intune (and thus the Windows 10 MDM agent) once you have qualified those workloads and are confident they will meet your organization's requirements.

Modern Management in Windows 10

Windows has historically relied on additional agents to manage PCs. For organizations with ConfigMgr, this is the ConfigMgr agent. Windows has also had basic management capabilities in group policy and Windows Server Update Services (WSUS). These capabilities have not undergone major changes since Windows XP; rather, there have been incremental advances over time through Windows 8.1.

Beginning with Windows 10, Microsoft has significantly increased the release cadence of Windows. Windows now receives approximately two major feature updates every year. This cadence is referred to as the *Semi-Annual Channel*, and it replaces earlier Current Branch and Current Branch for Business release channels. Since the initial release of Windows 10, these updates have included Windows 10 Anniversary Update (1607), Windows 10 Creators Update (1703), and Windows 10 Fall Creators Update (1709). The four-digit number refers to the year (for example, 17 refers to 2017) and month (for example, 09 refers to September) in which the release's development was finalized.

The revised release cadence creates a need for equivalent releases of management tools. This is one of the reasons ConfigMgr Current Branch adopted a regular release cadence that aligns to Windows 10 releases. In addition, Windows 10 has a significant investment in MDM as a management method. In Windows 10, the MDM stack has the ability to configure device encryption (BitLocker), take hardware and app inventory, and configure Windows Update for Business, among other enhancements. In addition, with feature updates, or major releases, Windows 10 has received significant enhancements to MDM capabilities. For a comprehensive list of all the management capabilities available in Windows 10 MDM, see the list of configuration service providers (CSPs) at https://docs.microsoft.com/windows/client-management/mdm/configuration-service-provider-reference.

Modern management was introduced as a new way to think about managing Windows. It was meant to enable information technology (IT) to consume Windows regularly—moving away from 3- to 10-year deployments of Windows as large capital expenditure projects and to regular annual or semi-annual operational tasks. The intent is to look at servicing (including updating), application management, security, provisioning, and settings management in new ways, including:

▶ **Modern Servicing:** Moving to Windows Update for Business and leveraging ring-based release models.

▶ **Modern Provisioning:** Moving from custom images to a clean "signature" image.

▶ **Modern Settings:** Moving from group policy objects (GPOs) to MDM policy.

▶ **Modern Authentication:** Moving from Kerberos to Windows Hello for business and modern authentication (OAuth in Azure Active Directory [Azure AD]).

▶ **Modern Security:** Leveraging Windows Information Protection (WIP), Windows Defender Advanced Threat Protection (ATP; discussed in Chapter 19, "Endpoint Protection"), and other Windows Defender capabilities, such as SmartScreen, Device Guard, Credential Guard, and so on.

▶ **Modern Apps:** Moving from legacy .exe/.msi installers to Universal Windows Platform apps, converting to Store format (.appx) using the Desktop Conversion Tool, Office 365 Pro Plus, and Software as a Service (SaaS) web apps.

Modern management is the evolution of the last 10 years of user-centric computing in Windows management.

Defining Co-Management

While many architects and decision makers may have an aspirational or strategic goal to move to modern management, there is significant effort in moving an entire company from traditional agent-based PC management to modern management. There are also human aspects to change to address, and an organization will typically need to create operational roles and move away from a project-based Windows deployment mindset.

There are parallels between moving to modern management and the challenges that Exchange administrators went through when their organizations moved to Exchange Online. Instead of managing an Exchange upgrade every few years, Exchange administrators now consume multiple changes to Exchange Online and Office 365 Pro Plus's version of Outlook each year. New capabilities must be understood, articulated, determined if they should be used, and then configured; a Windows client administrator now needs to think in a similar fashion.

From a technology standpoint, this transformation is also difficult to accomplish without the ability to have traditional and modern methods co-exist—something ConfigMgr has historically blocked by disabling the MDM agent in Windows when the ConfigMgr agent is installed.

Co-management alleviates this issue by enabling side-by-side management of Windows 10 by the ConfigMgr agent and MDM management via Microsoft Intune. It requires the use of Microsoft Intune standalone rather than the hybrid mode of Intune integrated with ConfigMgr. Using Intune standalone allows you to maintain your ConfigMgr Current Branch environment while obtaining the rapid advancements of the cloud-only version of Intune, without binding Intune to ConfigMgr. Standalone is also Microsoft's recommended method for deploying Intune.

Co-management also enables a company to evaluate modern management in its own time and control the rollout to its environment. You can choose which workloads to move to co-management. For example, you could move only Windows Update for Business from ConfigMgr update management. Alternatively, you could enable resource profile distribution so that Intune deploys certificates and Wi-Fi profiles to your devices.

In addition, co-management enables Intune-specific scenarios, such as device compliance conditional access. This allows Intune to validate device compliance and write that compliance state to Azure AD for use in conditional access, while continuing to leverage existing ConfigMgr policies to configure and control devices. This allows you to build compliance rules that target a specific month's patches (using the Windows 10 version number) as part of compliance or require BitLocker prior to allowing access to Office 365 or another SaaS app protected by Azure AD. This control can apply from any location from which a user logs in.

For more information on co-management, see the ConfigMgr documentation at https://docs.microsoft.com/sccm/core/clients/manage/co-management-overview.

Why Co-Management?

One question that often comes up is *why is there co-management*? Microsoft built co-management based on customer feedback that modern management was on customer roadmaps but had not been heavily investigated or had hit some sort of blocker. However, this feedback was never in-depth because the customer was unable to pilot modern management without completely disabling ConfigMgr.

In addition, countless ConfigMgr environments exist, and loads of effort has been invested in them over the years. Co-management provides the ability to leverage your ConfigMgr investment while making a gradual and controlled move, on your terms, to modern management across all workloads, without a "big bang" migration or a rush to ramp up on modern management and the MDM stack.

For example, consider the complexity of legacy application deployment, which includes multiple application model deployments with supersedence logic and dependencies. Those types of applications are not modern in nature but will continue to exist until they are replaced by newer apps or moved to SaaS solutions or web-based systems. An entire environment should not hinge on those apps, nor should they block your company's investigation into modern management. Co-management provides the ability to continue to deliver those apps via the ConfigMgr application model while shifting other workloads to Intune. Continuing to deliver those apps via ConfigMgr also allows you to leverage the investment in packaging and testing those apps while examining modern app packaging methods and development methods.

Choosing Where to Start with Co-Management

A major element of any deployment of new technology is choosing where to begin the initial rollout. The following are potential areas you can review as starting points for co-management. This list is not exhaustive; it is meant to provide ideas for low resistance that are relatively easy options:

▶ **Securing Your Office 365 Access Using Azure AD Conditional Access:** Enabling co-management allows you to configure conditional access for Windows 10 PCs with Microsoft Intune, so you can require that PCs are managed, encrypted with BitLocker, and up-to-date with the latest features and cumulative updates for Windows 10. ConfigMgr continues to enable and deploy the configuration. This helps prevent access to unmanaged PCs, such as a home PC, from Office 365. Compliance policies should be the first workload to consider moving from ConfigMgr to Intune.

▶ **Enabling Your Remote Workers to Setup PCs over the Internet:** You can combine co-management with Windows AutoPilot and/or Azure AD Join automatic MDM enrollment. This combination allows you to leverage AutoPilot or Azure AD Join to automate provisioning of off-the-shelf devices during the Windows 10 out of box experience (OOBE). Azure AD Join, either manually or via AutoPilot, during OOBE causes the PC to register with Microsoft Intune. You can configure Intune as part of co-management to install the ConfigMgr agent and thus light up co-management, combining the flexibility of MDM with the detailed control of ConfigMgr.

▶ **Piloting Highly Mobile Users Who Use SaaS Apps:** Most organizations have a set of users who are primarily mobile or remote workers in a field role. If you use Office 365 and other SaaS solutions for these users, they might be a good fit for initial co-management of devices with minimal workloads delivered from ConfigMgr. Office 365 ProPlus (a.k.a. Click2Run) can be delivered directly via Intune over the MDM channel in Windows 10, and most SaaS apps rely on web-based portals or simply client apps that self-update. In addition, SaaS solutions do not require intranet connectivity.

▶ **Leveraging Intune to Provision Wi-Fi Profile and Associated Certs:** Organizations requiring WPA2-Enterprise or 802.1x using x.509 certificates for access are often challenged with issuing certificates, as certificates must be issued and renewed to devices over a wired network while on-premise or via a virtual private network (VPN). Co-management enables you to leverage Intune's ability to deploy certificates using Personal Information Exchange (PFX) (or Public Key Cryptography Standards #12 [PKCS#12]). This negates the need to stand up a Simple Certification Enrollment Protocol (SCEP) Connector and Network Device Enrollment Service (NDES) server. Intune can then bind the issued certificates to a Wi-Fi profile issued by Intune. This means those devices can be ready to use the corporate Wi-Fi as soon as users get to work.

Configuring Co-Management in ConfigMgr

The following sections discuss the configuration and the multiple enablement methods of co-management. The first section describes the prerequisites within ConfigMgr for co-management, assuming that Microsoft Intune standalone is configured and ready for Windows 10 devices to enroll. If Microsoft Intune is already configured in a hybrid setup with ConfigMgr and you want to move from hybrid to standalone, see the documentation at https://docs.microsoft.com/sccm/mdm/deploy-use/change-mdm-authority. Note that as of ConfigMgr Current Branch 1610, you can change MDM authority to standalone from hybrid without contacting Microsoft support.

Subsequent sections explain how to configure co-management on Windows 10 devices. Each is based on the starting states of those clients: existing Intune clients, existing ConfigMgr clients, or new devices. Use one or more of these sections to move your selected clients to co-management.

The final section explains how to select and transition workloads from ConfigMgr to Intune. This should be performed when you are ready to move those workloads. You do not need to move all clients when you move a workload; you can phase out that change across a group of client devices.

Co-Management Prerequisites

Multiple simple prerequisites—both ConfigMgr and Intune prerequisites—are required for co-management:

▶ **ConfigMgr Version:** Configuration Manager Current Branch version 1710.

▶ **Licenses:** Microsoft Enterprise Mobility + Security (EMS) license for users or Microsoft Intune and Azure AD Premium. While Azure AD Premium is not strictly required for co-management, it is required for conditional access to Office 365 and other SaaS apps protected by Azure AD, MDM auto-enrollment, self-service BitLocker recovery, and Enterprise State Roaming.

▶ **Microsoft Intune Tenant Authority:** The Microsoft Intune tenant should be set to a standalone authority and configured via the Microsoft Azure portal. The documentation at https://docs.microsoft.com/sccm/mdm/deploy-use/change-mdm-authority discusses moving from hybrid to standalone. The tenant should also be configured for Windows 10 device enrollment. For details on how to configure Intune for Windows 10 device enrollment, see https://docs.microsoft.com/intune/windows-enroll.

▶ **Windows 10 Version:** Windows 10 devices should be running the Fall Creators Update or later (version 1709 or later).

▶ **Configure Hybrid Azure AD Join:** To join existing ConfigMgr clients, you must set up hybrid Azure AD Join in your Active Directory environment. The Azure AD documentation discusses how to do so at https://docs.microsoft.com/azure/active-directory/device-management-hybrid-azuread-joined-devices-setup.

▶ **Cloud Management Gateway (Optional):** Installing ConfigMgr clients from the Internet using Microsoft Intune requires that you deploy a cloud management gateway (CMG). The CMG site system acts as a Microsoft Azure hosted channel for Internet-connected ConfigMgr clients. You cannot use an Internet-based client management (IBCM) management point (MP), as that requires the client to be on-premise for initial installation. You do not require a CMG to enable co-management; however, it does enable ConfigMgr to manage co-managed clients on the Internet. For more information on the CMG, see Chapter 4, "Architecture Design Planning," and Chapter 9, "Client Management."

▶ **Cloud Distribution Point (Optional):** To leverage the CMG and fully manage ConfigMgr clients, consider deploying a cloud distribution point (DP), which you can use to deploy complex applications to co-managed Windows 10 devices.

Enabling Devices for Co-Management

This section covers the ways to enable existing Microsoft Intune or ConfigMgr clients for co-management. You need to configure one or more of these onboarding options, although you do not have to enable all options. For more information, see the co-management documentation at https://docs.microsoft.com/sccm/core/clients/manage/co-management-prepare.

Windows 10 Devices with ConfigMgr Clients

The approach described in this section is the simplest way to enable co-management. Essentially, ConfigMgr uses a new feature of Windows 10 version 1709 (Windows 10 Fall Creators Update) to trigger an automated enrollment into MDM enrollment. This can be enabled from the Co-management Onboarding Wizard. Perform the following steps to launch the wizard:

1. In the ConfigMgr console, navigate to **Administration -> Overview -> Cloud Services -> Co-management**. Choose **Configure co-management** to launch the wizard.

2. On the Subscription page, click **Sign In** and enter the credentials of an Intune service administrator or a tenant global administrator. Click **Next**.

3. On the Staging page, choose how you want to enable co-management on your ConfigMgr clients:

    ▶ **Pilot group:** This is the inclusive method of enabling co-management, where you must include each collection where you want to enable co-management. This allows you to granularly control enabling co-management. You can either change the definition of the collections as required or change the pilot group collections by using the co-management properties.

    ▶ **Production:** This is an exclusive method of enabling co-management, where you must exclude each collection in which you do not want to enable co-management. This allows you to automatically opt in any new Config-Mgr clients for co-management, regardless of their collection membership, while excluding any Windows 10 devices where you do not want to enable co-management.

4. On the Enablement page, choose either Pilot or All, depending on what you chose on the Staging page in step 3. This triggers the configured enablement of co-management of Windows 10 devices with the ConfigMgr agent.

Windows 10 Devices Enrolled in Intune

For devices enrolled in Intune, you can configure Intune to install the ConfigMgr client via Intune's Windows Installer software distribution method. This is accomplished using the traditional ccmsetup.msi installation method, along with additional command-line options to enable the location and authentication to the CMG. Chapter 9 discusses how to enable this method. To obtain the required command-line parameters, perform the following steps:

1. In the ConfigMgr console, navigate to **Administration -> Overview -> Cloud Services -> Co-management**.

2. Select **Configure co-management** to launch the wizard.

3. On the Subscription page, click **Sign In** to sign in as an Intune service administrator or tenant global administrator.

4. In the Enablement page, see the Devices enrolled in Intune section of the wizard for the command line required to install the client from Intune.

New Windows 10 Devices

If you have new Windows 10 devices that are being built not using operating system deployment (OSD) but using a modern provisioning method, you can use this method to enable co-management. This method is essentially a variation of the method described in the "Windows 10 Devices Enrolled in Intune" section, earlier in this appendix, and uses either the AutoPilot service or Azure AD Join via OOBE to trigger MDM enrollment in Microsoft Intune. Once you are enrolled in Intune, Intune can push the ConfigMgr client via ccmsetup.msi installation.

To enable this method, follow these steps:

1. Configure AutoPilot for new Windows 10 devices with the help of the documentation at https://docs.microsoft.com/windows/deployment/windows-10-auto-pilot.

2. Have AutoPilot trigger Azure AD Join automatically by following the documentation at https://docs.microsoft.com/intune/windows-enroll#enable-windows-10-automatic-enrollment. This also causes manually configured Azure AD Join to be automatically enrolled in Microsoft Intune. Manual Azure AD Join can be triggered during OOBE, when the user selects **My work or school owns it** when asked who owns the PC; in this case, the user can select **Join Azure AD**. Azure AD Join can also be performed on an existing Windows 10 device by using the Settings app: Go to **System** -> **About** and select **Join Azure AD**.

3. Configure Intune to install the ConfigMgr agent by following the steps outlined earlier in this appendix, in the "Windows 10 Devices Enrolled in Intune" section.

Moving Workloads from ConfigMgr to Intune

When co-management is enabled, you can use the co-management settings to choose which workloads are enabled. This can be done from the Co-management Onboarding Wizard or the co-management properties after completing the wizard. It is anticipated that Microsoft will continue to invest in adding support for transitioning new workloads with each new release of ConfigMgr. The following are workloads you can move from ConfigMgr to Intune:

▶ **Compliance Policies:** Moving this workload to Intune enables you to leverage Intune to assess device compliance for the purposes of Azure AD conditional access. For more information, refer to the "Choosing Where to Start with Co-Management" section, earlier in this appendix. For information on how to configure compliance policies for Windows 10 devices in Microsoft Intune, see https://docs.microsoft.com/intune/compliance-policy-create-windows.

▶ **Resource Access Profiles:** Moving this workload to Intune enables you to push resource access profiles to Windows 10 via MDM. Resource access profiles include VPN, certificate, Wi-Fi, or email account (for the Mail Universal Windows Platform [UWP] app) profiles. For information on how to configure resource profiles for Windows 10 devices in Microsoft Intune, see the following links:

   ▶ **Certificates:** https://docs.microsoft.com/intune/certificates-configure

► **Wi-Fi Profiles:** https://docs.microsoft.com/intune/wi-fi-settings-configure

► **VPN Profiles:** https://docs.microsoft.com/intune/vpn-settings-configure

► **Windows Update for Business Policies:** Moving this workload to Intune enables you to move to modern servicing, where you define deferral policies for Windows 10 feature and/or quality updates. This is accomplished by configuring Windows 10 update rings in Microsoft Intune. For more information, see https://docs.microsoft.com/intune/windows-update-for-business-configure. These updates are then delivered directly from Windows Update for Business.

You can switch workloads from ConfigMgr to Intune by modifying the properties of the co-management configuration at **Administration -> Overview -> Cloud Services -> Co-management**. For more details on how to switch workloads from ConfigMgr, see the co-management documentation at https://docs.microsoft.com/sccm/core/clients/manage/co-management-switch-workloads.

TIP: MONITORING CLIENT-SIDE CO-MANAGEMENT STATES

ConfigMgr provides a SQL Server view (`v_ClientCoManagementState`) and a site provider Windows Management Instrumentation (WMI) class (`SMS_Client_CoManagementState`) to monitor the client-side rollout of co-management. You can use the `v_ClientCoManagementState` view to build reports to track the enablement of co-management and the automatic MDM enrollment into Intune triggered by ConfigMgr. The `SMS_Client_CoManagementState` class can be used to create collections in ConfigMgr, which can be used for monitoring or to target deployments based on MDM state.

Note that for a client to be co-managed, both the `MDMEnrolled` column/property and the `CoMgmtPolicyPresent` column/property must be set to a value of `1`.

In addition to these workloads, you can also trigger remote actions on Windows 10 devices co-managed with Intune and ConfigMgr. These actions are triggered from the Microsoft Intune blade in Azure Portal:

► Factory reset

► Selective wipe (not applicable for Azure AD Join devices)

► Delete device

► Restart device

► Fresh start

Reference URLs

This appendix includes a number of reference URLs associated with System Center Configuration Manager (ConfigMgr) Current Branch. URLs do change, so although the authors have made every effort to verify the references here as working links, there is no guarantee that they will remain current. It is quite possible some will change or be dead by the time you read this book. Sometimes the Wayback Machine (http://www.archive.org/index.php) can rescue you from dead or broken links. This site is an Internet archive, and it can sometimes take you back to an archived version of a site.

The links listed in this appendix are also available "live" at Pearson's InformIT website, at http://www.informit.com/title/9780672337901, on the Downloads tab. Look for and select Appendix C, "Reference URLs."

General Resources

A number of websites provide excellent resources for Configuration Manager. This section lists some of the general resources available:

► myITforum—http://myitforum.com—is a community of worldwide information technology (IT) professionals established in 1999 by Rod Trent. myITforum includes topics on System Center and IT.

The list of blogs and other ConfigMgr-related articles at myITforum.com is enormous. This appendix includes some specific links and pertinent information, but it does not include everything.

► See http://myitforum.com for the Windows IT Pro forums.

▶ IT Pro publishes online articles about System Center and other topics. See http://www.itprotoday.com for information.

▶ A source of information for all things System Center related, including Configuration Manager, is System Center Central (http://www.systemcentercentral.com).

▶ FAQShop.com, published by Enterprise Client Management (ECM) MVP Cliff Hobbs at http://www.faqshop.com/, provides hints, tips, and answers to frequently asked questions (FAQs) related to Microsoft's various systems management technologies.

▶ People-centric IT enables each person you support to work from virtually anywhere, on any device, and gives you a consistent way to manage and protect it all (see http://download.microsoft.com/download/1/3/7/137B2CF6-79FE-438B-BA00-F343022C3CE3/Enabling_Enterprise_Mobility_white_paper.pdf).

▶ The Windows Server technical library is located at https://docs.microsoft.com/windows-server/windows-server.

▶ Microsoft's white paper on performance tuning guidelines for Windows Server 2016 is at https://docs.microsoft.com/windows-server/administration/performance-tuning/. The following are links to previous versions of performance tuning guidelines:

    ▶ Guidelines for Windows Server 2012 R2 are at http://msdn.microsoft.com/library/windows/hardware/dn529133.aspx.

    ▶ Download performance tuning guidelines for Windows Server 2012, 2008 R2, and 2008 from https://msdn.microsoft.com/library/windows/hardware/dn529134.

▶ The Microsoft System Center website is at https://www.microsoft.com/cloud-platform/system-center, and Microsoft's jumping-off point for System Center technical resources is at http://technet.microsoft.com/systemcenter/.

▶ Read about monitoring and tuning SQL Server for performance at http://technet.microsoft.com/library/ms189081.aspx.

▶ Find guidance on security considerations for SQL Server at http://msdn.microsoft.com/library/ms144228.aspx.

▶ To learn about moving databases configured for SQL Server AlwaysOn, see http://blogs.msdn.com/b/sqlserverfaq/archive/2014/02/06/how-to-move-databases-configured-for-sql-server-alwayson.aspx.

▶ Review the process of upgrading the SQL Server test database at https://docs.microsoft.com/sccm/core/servers/manage/test-database-upgrade.

▶ For a complete list of available operators, see the SQL Operators section within the T-SQL online help at http://msdn.microsoft.com/library/ms174986(v=SQL.110).aspx.

▶ Find information about SQL Server 2017, 2016, and 2014 at https://docs.microsoft.com/sql/sql-server/sql-server-technical-documentation.

- ▶ Use the SQL Server Profiler to view SQL requests sent to an SQL Server database. See http://msdn.microsoft.com/library/ms187929.aspx for information.

- ▶ Read about the SQL Server Service Broker at http://social.technet.microsoft.com/wiki/contents/articles/6598.sql-server-service-broker-at-a-glance.aspx and https://docs.microsoft.com/sql/database-engine/configure-windows/sql-server-service-broker.

- ▶ Find information about SQL Server Compact Edition (CE) at http://technet.microsoft.com/library/ms173037(v=sql.105).aspx.

- ▶ See http://technet.microsoft.com/ff657833.aspx for information on SQL Server Reporting Services (SSRS). Installation information is at http://msdn.microsoft.com/library/ms143711.aspx.

- ▶ Mike Pearson discusses SSRS recovery planning at http://www.sqlservercentral.com/columnists/mpearson/recoveryplanningforsqlreportingservices.asp. Register with SQLServerCentral to view the full article.

- ▶ http://technet.microsoft.com/library/ms156421.aspx discusses moving the SSRS databases to another computer.

- ▶ Want to create drilldown SSRS reports? See http://technet.microsoft.com/library/dd207042.aspx.

- ▶ http://msdn.microsoft.com/library/ms157403.aspx provides a complete listing of SSRS log files.

- ▶ Leading security organizations include:

    - ▶ **Center for Internet Security (CIS):** https://www.cisecurity.org

    - ▶ **Information Assurance Directorate (IAD):** https://www.iad.gov/iad/

    - ▶ **Australian Signals Directorate (ASD):** http://www.asd.gov.au

- ▶ Find the Microsoft Malware Protection Center (MMPC) at http://www.microsoft.com/wdsi.

- ▶ Microsoft's antimalware guidance for security policies for Windows and Windows Server is at https://support.microsoft.com/kb/822158.

- ▶ Windows Defender Offline (WDO) is available at no cost for Windows 7 and later operating systems at http://windows.microsoft.com/windows/what-is-windows-defender-offline.

- ▶ Information about servicing branches and servicing of Windows 10 in general is at https://technet.microsoft.com/itpro/windows/manage/waas-overview#servicing-branches.

- ▶ Feature update servicing for Windows Insider devices occurs completely through Windows Update; see https://insider.windows.com.

- ▶ Download the Windows Management Framework (WMF) from https://www.microsoft.com/download/details.aspx?id=50395.

▶ Windows Firewall logs and settings are described at http://technet.microsoft.com/network/bb545423.aspx.

▶ A bit dated but still useful International Data Corporation whitepaper sponsored by Microsoft quantifies how businesses can reduce costs by managing the Windows desktop. This whitepaper is available for download at http://download.microsoft.com/documents/australia/government/desktop_optimization_wp.pdf.

▶ Read about WunderBar trivia at http://blogs.msdn.com/b/jensenh/archive/2005/10/07/478214.aspx.

▶ Information about the Windows setup logs is at https://support.microsoft.com/help/927521/windows-vista,-windows-7,-windows-server-2008-r2,-windows-8.1,-and-windows-10-setup-log-file-locations.

▶ According to the SANS Institute (https://www.computerworld.com/article/2565944/security0/sans-unveils-top-20-security-vulnerabilities.html), the threat landscape is increasingly dynamic, making efficient and proactive update management more important than ever before.

▶ Symantec's 2017 Internet Security Threat Report concluded that the cyber-criminals revealed new levels of ambition in 2016, causing unprecedented levels of disruption with relatively simple IT tools and cloud services (https://www.symantec.com/security-center/threat-report).

▶ Microsoft provides guidance on Active Directory (AD) security best practices at https://technet.microsoft.com/library/dn487446.aspx.

▶ For information on the impact of AD schema extensions and modifications, see https://msdn.microsoft.com/library/ms677103.aspx.

▶ For information on how to perform schema changes, see https://msdn.microsoft.com/library/windows/desktop/ms676929.aspx.

▶ A complete list of Active Directory supportability requirements is at https://technet.microsoft.com/library/mt617258.aspx.

▶ Information about search filters for AD Directory Services is at https://msdn.microsoft.com/library/aa746475(v=vs.85).aspx.

▶ https://msdn.microsoft.com/library/ms675090(v=vs.85).aspx lists attributes defined by Active Directory.

▶ Find information on LDIFDE at http://technet.microsoft.com/library/cc731033.aspx. ConfigMgr-specific instructions are at https://technet.microsoft.com/library/mt345589.aspx.

▶ http://support.microsoft.com/kb/555636 describes exporting and importing objects using LDIFDE.

▶ An overview of Windows Azure Active Directory is at http://www.windowsazure.com/services/active-directory/.

▶ Troubleshoot Azure AD Connect installation issues with help from https:// support.microsoft.com/kb/3121701 and connectivity issues with help from https://azure.microsoft.com/documentation/articles/active-directory-aadconnect-troubleshoot-connectivity/.

▶ Read about directory integration at http://technet.microsoft.com/library/jj573653.aspx.

▶ Prepare for directory synchronization with Azure Active Directory by reading http://technet.microsoft.com/library/jj151831.aspx, which discusses architecture and deployment considerations.

▶ Information on password synchronization between on-premise directories and Azure Active Directory is available at http://technet.microsoft.com/library/dn246918.aspx.

▶ Information on Windows Deployment Services (WDS) is at https://docs.microsoft .com/sccm/osd/plan-design/infrastructure-requirements-for-operating-system-deployment#BKMK_WDS.

▶ https://en.wikipedia.org/wiki/Preboot_Execution_Environment provides in-depth information on the Preboot eXecution Environment (PXE). A troubleshooting guide for boot issues is at https://support.microsoft.com/help/10082/troubleshooting-pxe-boot-issues-in-configuration-manager-2012.

▶ Device affinity allows you to marry a user to a single device; for more on this, see https://docs.microsoft.com/sccm/osd/get-started/associate-users-with-a-destination-computer.

▶ Requirements for Windows To Go are at http://technet.microsoft.com/library/ hh831833.aspx#wtg_hardware.

▶ Interested in learning more about the Microsoft Operations Framework (MOF)? See https://technet.microsoft.com/library/dd320379.aspx.

▶ Information on the MOF Deliver Phase is at http://technet.microsoft.com/library/ cc506047.aspx.

▶ You can read about the MOF Envision SMF at http://technet.microsoft.com/library/ cc531013.aspx.

▶ Infrastructure and operations maturity refers to an organization's capability to take on new challenges. Gartner recognizes five levels of infrastructure and opera-tions maturity and has developed a self-assessment tool that organizations can use to understand their level of maturity, available at https://www.gartner.com/ doc/2481415/itscore-overview-infrastructure-operations.

▶ For a full discussion of infrastructure and operations maturity, see https://www.savision.com/resources/blog/how-mature-your-it-department.

▶ See https://msdn.microsoft.com/library/windows/desktop/aa367449(v=vs.85).aspx for information about the Windows Installer.

▶ To learn about Service Modeling Language (SML), see http://www.w3.org/ TR/sml/. For additional technical information on SML from Microsoft, visit http://technet.microsoft.com/library/bb725986.aspx.

▶ Usage data collection provides information to the product group on your use of ConfigMgr, allowing them to better understand how ConfigMgr is used and ensure that their testing emulates real-world scenarios. For more information, see https://docs.microsoft.com/sccm/core/servers/deploy/install/setup-reference#bkmk_usage and https://docs.microsoft.com/sccm/core/plan-design/diagnostics/diagnostics-and-usage-data.

▶ By November 2016, more than 50 million devices were being actively managed by Configuration Manager Current Branch (see https://blogs.technet.microsoft.com/enterprisemobility/2016/11/18/configmgr-current-branch-surpasses-50m-managed-devices/).

▶ A list of cryptographic controls maintained by Microsoft is available at https://docs.microsoft.com/sccm/protect/deploy-use/cryptographic-controls-technical-reference. In-depth information about cryptographic controls for ConfigMgr can be found at https://technet.microsoft.com/library/mt629331.aspx. Required certificate properties for Internet-based client management (IBCM) are at https://docs.microsoft.com/sccm/core/plan-design/security/plan-for-security#BKMK_PlanningForCertificates.

▶ Microsoft's Sysinternals website is at http://technet.microsoft.com/sysinternals/default.aspx.

▶ Silect Software (http://www.silect.com) offers CP Studio. CP Studio, like Security Compliance Manager (SCM), enables authoring of configuration baselines and configuration items (CIs) outside the ConfigMgr console.

▶ Configuring multi-factor authentication (MFA) is discussed at https://docs.microsoft.com/azure/multi-factor-authentication/multi-factor-authentication.

▶ Find an overview of Windows 8.1 sideloading enhancements at https://www.eightforums.com/threads/windows-8-1-update-sideloading-enhancements.43788/.

▶ The group behind the Web-Based Enterprise Management (WBEM) standard is the Distributed Management Task Force (DMFT); for information on WBEM and the DMTF, see http://www.dmtf.org/standards/wbem.

▶ A complete description of Web Services Management (WS-Man) and related specifications is at http://www.dmtf.org/standards/wsman.

▶ Information on Windows Management Instrumentation (WMI) is available at http://msdn.microsoft.com/library/aa394582.aspx.

▶ http://msdn.microsoft.com/library/aa394564.aspx discusses WMI logging.

▶ See http://msdn.microsoft.com/library/aa394603(v=vs.85).aspx, http://technet.microsoft.com/library/cc180763.aspx, and https://blogs.technet.microsoft.com/askperf/2007/06/22/basic-wmi-testing/ for information on WMI troubleshooting.

▶ For a discussion of User Account Control and WMI, see http://msdn.microsoft.com/library/aa826699.aspx.

► Command-line tools for managing WMI can be downloaded from http://msdn.microsoft.com/library/aa827351.aspx.

► A list of Microsoft-supplied WMI providers is available at https://msdn.microsoft.com/library/aa394570.aspx.

► For information regarding WMI Query Language (WQL), see http://msdn.microsoft.com/library/aa394606.aspx.

► Learn about USMT at https://docs.microsoft.com/windows/deployment/usmt/usmt-topics. You will also want to see https://docs.microsoft.com/sccm/osd/get-started/manage-user-state; also visit https://technet.microsoft.com/library/hh397289.aspx for a flowchart on user state capture and restore.

► Learn about classless interdomain routing (CIDR) and supernetting to define IP subnets at https://technet.microsoft.com/library/cc958837.aspx. Note that ConfigMgr does not support these methods.

► Microsoft provides solution accelerators, which are guidelines and tools to leverage the full functionality of Microsoft usage within your organization. They are available for download at no cost at http://technet.microsoft.com/solutionaccelerators/dd229342.

► Learn about using the Visual Studio Report Designer at http://msdn.microsoft.com/library/bb558708.aspx.

► See https://docs.microsoft.com/intune-classic/deploy-use/manage-windows-pcs-with-microsoft-intune for information on Windows Intune for cloud PC management.

► The Windows Intune administrator console is located at https://manage.microsoft.com.

► Purchase a code-signing certificate for sideloading Windows Phone applications for Windows Phone from Symantec at http://www.symantec.com/verisign/code-signing/windows-phone.

► Information about the Apple Enterprise Developer license is at http://developer.apple.com/programs/ios/enterprise.

► The Apple Volume Purchase Program (VPP) is described at http://www.apple.com/business/vpp/.

► How to set up per-app VPN using ConfigMgr is described at https://blogs.technet.microsoft.com/karanrustagi/2015/09/21/how-to-set-up-per-app-vpn-using-configuration-manager/. Additional information is at https://technet.microsoft.com/library/mt629185.aspx.

► Trying to understand Microsoft licensing? See the following:

   ► General licensing information is at https://www.microsoft.com/licensing.

   ► https://www.microsoft.com/en-us/licensing/product-licensing/client-access-license.aspx discusses client access licenses (CALs) and the suites they may be included on.

▶ System Center 2016 volume licensing is discussed at https://www.microsoft. com/en-us/licensing/product-licensing/system-center-2016.aspx. The Configuration Manager licensing page is at https://www.microsoft.com/cloud-platform/ system-center-configuration-manager-licensing.

▶ Learn about Samsung Knox at https://www.samsungknox.com/en.

▶ Information on Kerberos is at https://msdn.microsoft.com/library/bb742516.aspx.

Microsoft's Configuration Manager Resources

The following list includes some general Microsoft resources available for System Center Configuration Manager Current Branch:

▶ Microsoft's Configuration Manager website is located at https://www.microsoft.com/ cloud-platform/system-center-configuration-manager, and the TechNet main library page is at https://docs.microsoft.com/sccm/index.

▶ For a list of recommended hardware for ConfigMgr, see https://docs.microsoft.com/ sccm/core/plan-design/configs/recommended-hardware.

▶ https://docs.microsoft.com/sccm/core/plan-design/configs/size-and-scale-numbers discusses current ConfigMgr scaling numbers.

▶ Identify the latest baseline version at https://docs.microsoft.com/sccm/core/servers/ manage/updates#baseline-and-update-versions.

▶ For a list of changes from ConfigMgr 2012 to version 1511, the first release of ConfigMgr Current Branch, see https://docs.microsoft.com/sccm/core/plan-design/ changes/what-has-changed-from-configuration-manager-2012.

▶ Version 1602 introduced features to caution administrators with high-risk deployments; https://docs.microsoft.com/sccm/protect/understand/settings-to-manage-high-risk-deployments provides information.

▶ See what other changes were made in version 1602 at https://docs.microsoft.com/ sccm/core/plan-design/changes/whats-new-in-version-1602.

▶ Microsoft's support policy for ConfigMgr Current Branch versions is at https://docs.microsoft.com/sccm/core/servers/manage/current-branch-versions-supported.

▶ Native support for Active Management Technology (AMT)–based computers is deprecated in Current Branch, but they can still be managed using the Intel add-on for ConfigMgr, located at https://www.intel.com/content/www/us/en/software/ setup-configuration-software.html.

▶ Stay informed about new updates in ConfigMgr by checking the article at https://docs.microsoft.com/sccm/core/plan-design/changes/whats-new-incremental-versions. https://docs.microsoft.com/sccm/core/plan-design/changes/removed-and-deprecated-features provides information on deprecated items.

▶ Learn how clients find site resources and services for ConfigMgr at https://docs.microsoft.com/sccm/core/plan-design/hierarchy/understand-how-clients-find-site-resources-and-services.

▶ Command-line options and usage examples for ccmsetup.exe are described at https://docs.microsoft.com/sccm/core/clients/deploy/about-client-installation-properties.

▶ The number of clients supported by ConfigMgr sites is at https://docs.microsoft.com/sccm/core/plan-design/configs/supported-operating-systems-for-site-system-servers, which also reviews supported operating systems for ConfigMgr Current Branch.

▶ Find a three-part series on upgrading ConfigMgr 2012 to Current Branch at https://blogs.technet.microsoft.com/systemcenterpfe/2017/08/16/lift-shift-configmgr-2012-to-configmgr-1702-current-branch-part-1-the-upgrade/.

▶ The migration process is documented at https://docs.microsoft.com/sccm/core/migration/migrate-data-between-hierarchies.

▶ The Automated Installation Kit (AIK) is backward compatible with Windows 7. Ensure that you are on a supported version of the AIK for Current Branch, as shown at https://docs.microsoft.com/sccm/core/plan-design/configs/support-for-windows-10.

▶ Boundary behavior depends on the Current Branch version you are running:

　　▶ For information on the 1610 and later boundary models (including 1706 SUP failover changes), see https://docs.microsoft.com/sccm/core/servers/deploy/configure/define-site-boundaries-and-boundary-groups.

　　▶ For legacy information on pre-1610 ConfigMgr behavior, refer to https://docs.microsoft.com/sccm/core/servers/deploy/configure/boundary-groups-for-1511-1602-and-1606.

　　　Also check https://docs.microsoft.com/sccm/core/servers/deploy/configure/define-site-boundaries-and-boundary-groups#a-namebkmkboundarygroupsa-boundary-groups.

▶ For a list of reserved names to avoid using as site codes, see https://msdn.microsoft.com/library/aa365247.aspx.

▶ The Windows 10 CI settings reference is at https://docs.microsoft.com/sccm/compliance/deploy-use/create-configuration-items-for-windows-10-devices-managed-with-the-client#windows-10-configuration-item-settings-reference.

▶ Information about Windows 8.1 and Windows 10 CI settings is at https://docs.microsoft.com/sccm/compliance/deploy-use/create-configuration-items-for-windows-8.1-and-windows-10-devices-managed-without-the-client#windows-81-and-windows-10-configuration-item-settings-reference.

▶ The full list of iOS and Mac OS X compliance settings is at https://docs.microsoft.com/sccm/compliance/deploy-use/create-configuration-items-for-ios-and-mac-os-x-devices-managed-without-the-client#ios-and-mac-os-x-configuration-item-settings-reference.

▶ See https://docs.microsoft.com/sccm/compliance/deploy-use/create-configuration-items-for-windows-phone-devices-managed-without-the-client#windows-phone-configuration-item-settings-reference for information on Windows Phone CIs.

▶ An Android and Samsung Knox CI settings reference is available at https://docs.microsoft.com/sccm/compliance/deploy-use/create-configuration-items-for-android-and-samsung-knox-devices-managed-without-the-client#android-and-samsung-knox-configuration-item-settings-reference.

▶ ConfigMgr Current Branch is supported in Microsoft Azure. For information, review https://docs.microsoft.com/sccm/core/understand/configuration-manager-on-azure.

▶ Azure offers ExpressRoute as an alternative to using VPNs over the Internet. For information about ExpressRoute, including costs and availability, see https://azure.microsoft.com/services/expressroute/.

▶ Configuration Manager Current Branch supports hosting ConfigMgr servers in Azure Infrastructure as a Service (IaaS) virtual machines (VMs). Information about Azure storage scalability and performance is at https://azure.microsoft.com/documentation/articles/storage-scalability-targets/. For information about Azure Premium Storage, see https://azure.microsoft.com/documentation/articles/storage-premium-storage/. A complete list of current Azure VM sizes, processor performance, and VM-level network bandwidth limits is at https://azure.microsoft.com/documentation/articles/virtual-machines-windows-sizes/.

▶ To learn about Azure AD Join and hybrid Azure AD join, see https://docs.microsoft.com/azure/active-directory/device-management-introduction.

▶ When using Azure AD for authentication, you need the app ID to install Windows 10 clients. This is found in the App Registrations part of Azure AD. More information on how to find the ID is available at https://docs.microsoft.com/azure/azure-resource-manager/resource-group-create-service-principal-portal#get-application-id-and-authentication-key.

▶ For information about installation properties published to AD, see https://docs.microsoft.com/sccm/core/clients/deploy/about-client-installation-properties-published-to-active-directory-domain-services.

▶ Following is where to find Microsoft documentation on SQL schema for the various versions of Configuration Manager:

   ▶ **ConfigMgr Current Branch:** At the time this book was published, Microsoft had not released an official SQL schema. However, you can use the ConfigMgr 2012 and ConfigMgr 2007 schemas, listed next, as a reference.

> ► **ConfigMgr 2012:** Reference the ConfigMgr 2012 SQL schema at
> https://technet.microsoft.com/library/dn581978.aspx.

> ► **ConfigMgr 2007:** Information on the ConfigMgr 2007 SQL schema is available
> at http://technet.microsoft.com/library/dd334611.aspx.

► Information about the different versions of Background Intelligent Transfer Service
(BITS) is available at https://msdn.microsoft.com/library/aa363167.aspx.
Read about the different BITS settings at https://msdn.microsoft.com/library/
aa362844(v=VS.85).aspx.

► See https://docs.microsoft.com/powershell/module/configurationmanager/?view=
sccm-ps for a complete list of ConfigMgr PowerShell cmdlets. The System Center
Configuration Manager Cmdlet Library download and usage instructions are at
https://www.microsoft.com/download/details.aspx?id=46681. Find documentation at https://docs.microsoft.com/powershell/sccm/configurationmanager/vlatest/
configurationmanager.

► Read about planning for communications in Configuration Manager, including the
wake-up proxy for clients, at http://technet.microsoft.com/library/gg712701.aspx.

► Information about implementing wake-up proxy functionality is at https://
docs.microsoft.com/sccm/core/clients/deploy/plan/plan-wake-up-clients.

► If you have WSUS installed on Windows Server 2012 R2, you must apply hotfixes for
WSUS to support Windows 10 and Windows Server 2016:

> ► **Rollup hotfix for Windows RT 8.1, Windows 8.1, and Windows Server
> 2012 R2 update (April 2014):** https://support.microsoft.com/kb/2919355

> ► **Update to enable WSUS support for Windows 10 feature upgrades:** https://
> support.microsoft.com/kb/3095113

> ► **Update to enable ESD decryption provision in WSUS in Windows Server
> 2012 and 2012 R2:** https://support.microsoft.com/kb/3159706

> If the updates classification is synchronized before installing these hot-
> fixes, you must clear out the data and recover from the synchronization.
> Follow the steps at https://docs.microsoft.com/sccm/sum/plan-design/
> prerequisites-for-software-updates#BKMK_RecoverUpgrades.

► Information on using WSUSUtil to export and import the metadata for
software updates is at https://docs.microsoft.com/sccm/sum/get-started/
synchronize-software-updates-disconnected.

► Read about certutil.exe at https://technet.microsoft.com/library/cc732443(v=ws.11).
aspx.

► To use an MSU file with ConfigMgr (and System Center Updates Publisher
[SCUP]), see https://blogs.technet.microsoft.com/dominikheinz/2011/10/17/
deploying-custom-msu-updates-with-sccm-and-scup.

▶ See https://technet.microsoft.com/itpro/windows/deploy/usmt-reference to customize boot images with ConfigMgr. Information about the prestart commands is at https://docs.microsoft.com/sccm/osd/understand/prestart-commands-for-task-sequence-media.

▶ Read about prestaging content at https://docs.microsoft.com/sccm/core/servers/deploy/configure/deploy-and-manage-content#a-namebkmkprestagea-use-prestaged-content (Scroll down the page to find the prestaged content section).

▶ You can script report backups using RS.exe. Documentation is available at http://msdn.microsoft.com/library/ms162839.aspx and http://msdn.microsoft.com/library/ms159720.aspx.

▶ Verify your reporting services installation before installing the reporting services point. https://docs.microsoft.com/sql/reporting-services/install-windows/verify-a-reporting-services-installation discusses the steps to take.

▶ Supported OS versions may change with each new build; check https://docs.microsoft.com/sccm/core/plan-design/configs/supported-operating-systems-for-site-system-servers#bkmk_ClientOS for current information. Check supported configurations for ConfigMgr at https://docs.microsoft.com/sccm/core/plan-design/configs/supported-configurations.

▶ The ConfigMgr client agent installation process automatically installs necessary prerequisites, although you may want to preinstall if a reboot is required. Prerequisite software is at https://docs.microsoft.com/sccm/core/clients/deploy/prerequisites-for-deploying-clients-to-windows-computers.

▶ Learn how to prevent client software from being installed on specific computers from the article at https://technet.microsoft.com/library/bb693996.aspx.

▶ Configuring a service principal name (SPN) for SQL Server site database servers is discussed at http://technet.microsoft.com/library/bb735885.aspx. For site systems that require Internet Information Services (IIS), if the system is registered in the Domain Name System (DNS) using a CNAME (a DNS alias rather than the actual computer name), you must register the SPN using the procedure described at http://technet.microsoft.com/library/bb694288.aspx.

▶ To identify the Windows groups and accounts used in Configuration Manager and any requirements, see https://docs.microsoft.com/sccm/core/plan-design/hierarchy/accounts.

▶ Download the Configuration Manager Vulnerability Assessment configuration pack at https://www.microsoft.com/download/details.aspx?id=51948.

▶ Guidance for security site system servers is at https://docs.microsoft.com/sccm/core/plan-design/hierarchy/security-and-privacy-for-site-administration.

▶ Find information about planning for certificate revocation list (CRL) checking and other considerations for deploying AD certificate services at https://technet.microsoft.com/library/hh831574(v=ws.11).aspx.

▶ Security researchers recommend disabling Secure Socket Layer (SSL) 3.0 and enabling Transport Layer Security (TLS) 1.1 and 1.2, as described at https://support.microsoft.com/kb/245030.

▶ For information about remote WMI security requirements, see https://docs.microsoft.com/sccm/core/plan-design/hierarchy/plan-for-the-sms-provider.

▶ Read about group policy and WMI filtering at https://docs.microsoft.com/windows/security/identity-protection/windows-firewall/create-wmi-filters-for-the-gpo.

▶ To configure proxies for site server roles, see http://technet.microsoft.com/library/gg712282.aspx#BKMK_PlanforProxyServers.

▶ http://technet.microsoft.com/library/gg712321.aspx discusses the automatic retry settings for a pull DP.

▶ Information on the `ClientSDK` namespace is available in the ConfigMgr software development kit (SDK) in MSDN, at https://msdn.microsoft.com/library/jj874139.aspx.

▶ The `Win32_SystemEnclosure` WMI class represents the properties associated with a physical system enclosure. Properties are listed at https://msdn.microsoft.com/library/aa394474(v=vs.85).aspx.

▶ See https://docs.microsoft.com/sccm/core/plan-design/network/pki-certificate-requirements for ConfigMgr PKI certificate requirements.

▶ Read about integrating App-V into ConfigMgr at https://technet.microsoft.com/library/jj822982.aspx. While written for ConfigMgr 2012, this white paper is valid for ConfigMgr Current Branch.

▶ Read about enabling your device for development at https://msdn.microsoft.com/windows/uwp/get-started/enable-your-device-for-development.

▶ Use a task sequence to manage virtual hard disks in ConfigMgr; read https://docs.microsoft.com/sccm/osd/deploy-use/use-a-task-sequence-to-manage-virtual-hard-disks.

▶ To understand task sequence (TS) steps, see https://docs.microsoft.com/sccm/osd/understand/task-sequence-steps.

▶ Find the full list of TS action variables at https://docs.microsoft.com/sccm/osd/understand/task-sequence-action-variables and a list of the built-in variables at https://docs.microsoft.com/sccm/osd/understand/task-sequence-built-in-variables.

▶ How to use TS variables in a running ConfigMgr TS is documented at https://msdn.microsoft.com/library/cc145669.aspx.

▶ Although written for ConfigMgr 2007, KB925282 (http://support.microsoft.com/kb/925282) includes a good overview of the client push installation process and what can go wrong.

▶ Learn about the health checks performed by the Client Manager Health Evaluation scheduled task at https://docs.microsoft.com/sccm/core/clients/manage/monitor-clients#BKMK_ClientHealth.

▶ Find information about Windows 10 health attestation at https://docs.microsoft. com/windows/device-security/protect-high-value-assets-by-controlling-the-health-of-windows-10-based-devices.

▶ Creating and issuing a Mac client certificate template on a certification authority (CA) is described at https://docs.microsoft.com/sccm/core/plan-design/network/example-deployment-of-pki-certificates. Before installing the agent, download the program installation files and make them available on the Mac system. Obtain these files by installing the ConfigMgrMacClients.msi file on a Windows system. Download the MSI file from https://www.microsoft.com/download/details.aspx?id=47719. Also use this link to download client installation files for UNIX/Linux systems.

▶ You can modify keychain access as described at https://docs.microsoft.com/sccm/core/clients/deploy/deploy-clients-to-macs.

▶ Command-line properties for the installation scripts on UNIX/Linux systems are described at https://docs.microsoft.com/sccm/core/clients/deploy/deploy-clients-to-unix-and-linux-servers.

▶ Many reports analyze power consumption and check applied power settings. See https://docs.microsoft.com/sccm/core/clients/manage/power/monitor-and-plan-for-power-management for information.

▶ Use profiles to set up connections for devices to remotely connect to your network. For information, see https://docs.microsoft.com/sccm/compliance/deploy-use/create-remote-connection-profiles.

▶ https://docs.microsoft.com/sccm/apps/deploy-use/uninstall-applications discusses uninstalling ConfigMgr applications.

▶ Read about how the application model works at https://blogs.msdn.microsoft.com/steverac/2015/06/01/configmgr-2012-the-application-model-and-advanced-detection-logic/.

▶ Information on Microsoft Intune is available at https://www.microsoft.com/cloud-platform/microsoft-intune-features. To learn how to get started with a free 30-day trial, see https://docs.microsoft.com/intune/understand-explore/get-started-with-a-30-day-trial-of-microsoft-intune. You can extend the trial for an additional 30 days by contacting Intune support; find the support numbers at https://technet.microsoft.com/jj839713.aspx.

▶ Existing Microsoft cloud customers can sign up for a 90-day Enterprise Mobility + Security (EMS) trial through the FastTrack program, at http://fasttrack.microsoft.com/ems.

▶ The following management portals are available to manage the various configurations and features of Microsoft Intune:

  ▶ **Office 365 Admin Center:** https://portal.office.com

  ▶ **Intune Admin Portal:** https://manage.microsoft.com

  ▶ **Azure Portal:** https://portal.azure.com

▶ For information on iOS Device Enrollment Program (DEP) enrollment for hybrid deployments with ConfigMgr, see https://docs.microsoft.com/sccm/mdm/ deploy-use/ios-device-enrollment-program-for-hybrid.

▶ Download the Apple Configurator from https://itunes.apple.com/app/apple-configurator-2/id1037126344?mt=12. Details on device enrollment with the Apple Configurator are at https://technet.microsoft.com/library/mt706232.aspx.

▶ The Intune status page is at https://status.manage.microsoft.com/StatusPage/ ServiceDashboard.

▶ Available apps built with the Intune SDK are listed in the Microsoft Intune mobile application gallery at https://www.microsoft.com/cloud-platform/ microsoft-intune-apps.

▶ For information about wrapping in-house created apps for iOS, see https:// docs.microsoft.com/intune/deploy-use/prepare-ios-apps-for-mobile-application-management-with-the-microsoft-intune-app-wrapping-tool.

▶ https://docs.microsoft.com/intune/deploy-use/prepare-android-apps-for-mobile-application-management-with-the-microsoft-intune-app-wrapping-tool discusses wrapping Android in-house created apps.

▶ Read about integrating Windows Store for Business at https://technet.microsoft. com/library/mt740630.aspx, https://technet.microsoft.com/itpro/windows/manage/ windows-store-for-business-overview, and https://technet.microsoft.com/library/ mt740630.aspx.

▶ Find the Configuration Manager SDK at https://docs.microsoft.com/sccm/develop/ core/misc/system-center-configuration-manager-sdk.

▶ For information about creating PDF and SMS definition files, see https://technet.microsoft.com/library/bb632631.aspx.

▶ Information about MIF files is at https://technet.microsoft.com/library/ bb633139.aspx.

▶ Find best practices for collections at https://docs.microsoft.com/sccm/core/clients/ manage/collections/best-practices-for-collections.

▶ For information about serialized editing of distributed objects (SEDO), see https://msdn.microsoft.com/library/hh949794.aspx.

▶ Settings for mobile devices in ConfigMgr are described at https:// docs.microsoft.com/sccm/mdm/deploy-use/manage-compliance-settings.

▶ Examples of custom URI settings for Windows 10 are available in the document at https://docs.microsoft.com/intune/deploy-use/ windows-10-policy-settings-in-microsoft-intune.

▶ Microsoft publishes details of mobile application management (MAM)–capable apps in the Intune mobile application gallery at https://www.microsoft.com/ cloud-platform/microsoft-intune-apps.

▶ To enable modern authentication for Exchange Online, see http://social.technet. microsoft.com/wiki/contents/articles/32711.exchange-online-how-to-enable-your-tenant-for-modern-authentication.aspx; for Skype for Business Online, see http://social.technet.microsoft.com/wiki/contents/articles/34339.skype-for-business-online-enable-your-tenant-for-modern-authentication.aspx.

▶ Connect to Exchange Online using remote PowerShell. See https://technet.microsoft. com/library/jj984289(v=exchg.160).aspx.

▶ Information on installing the ConfigMgr client using Intune MDM-managed Windows devices can be found at https://docs.microsoft.com/intune-classic/deploy-use/set-up-windows-device-management-with-microsoft-intune#azure-active-directory-enrollment. You may also want to check https://docs.microsoft.com/sccm/core/clients/deploy/deploy-clients-to-windows-computers#how-to-install-clients-to-intune-mdm-managed-windows-devices.

▶ For information on the cloud management gateway (CMG), supported scenarios, costs, and Azure requirements, see https://docs.microsoft.com/sccm/core/clients/manage/plan-cloud-management-gateway.

▶ Information on planning for IBCM is at https://docs.microsoft.com/sccm/core/clients/manage/plan-internet-based-client-management.

▶ See https://docs.microsoft.com/sccm/core/servers/deploy/configure/install-and-configure-distribution-points to determine whether to enable anonymous access for clients.

▶ Find an overview of cloud DPs at https://docs.microsoft.com/sccm/core/plan-design/hierarchy/use-a-cloud-based-distribution-point.

▶ See https://technet.microsoft.com/library/hh831696(v=ws.11).aspx for information about BranchCache.

▶ Learn about Peer Cache at https://docs.microsoft.com/sccm/core/plan-design/hierarchy/client-peer-cache.

▶ For a complete breakdown of the latest information on choosing between hybrid and standalone Intune, see https://docs.microsoft.com/sccm/mdm/understand/choose-between-standalone-intune-and-hybrid-mobile-device-management.

▶ Download the System Center Monitoring Pack for ConfigMgr at https://www.microsoft.com/download/details.aspx?id=34709.

▶ The Windows Update log, Windowsupdate.log, is documented at https://support. microsoft.com/kb/902093. For information on the changes in Windows 10 version 1607, see https://support.microsoft.com/kb/3036646.

▶ Find information on server log files at https://docs.microsoft.com/sccm/core/plan-design/hierarchy/log-files.

▶ Information on site system log files is at https://docs.microsoft.com/sccm/core/plan-design/hierarchy/log-files.

▶ Use the article at https://support.microsoft.com/help/4000401/content-distribution-in-mcm as a guide to find the log files used with content distribution.

▶ Learn how to script WSUS and ConfigMgr SUP maintenance at https://blogs.technet.microsoft.com/configurationmgr/2016/01/26/the-complete-guide-to-microsoft-wsus-and-configuration-manager-sup-maintenance/. You will also want to read https://docs.microsoft.com/sccm/sum/plan-design/software-updates-best-practices.

▶ To publish SCUP updates to WSUS on Windows Server 2012, see the requirements at https://technet.microsoft.com/library/hh134747.aspx#PublishToServer2012.

▶ Read about co-management at https://docs.microsoft.com/sccm/core/clients/manage/co-management-overview.

▶ If you have already configured Microsoft Intune in a hybrid setup with ConfigMgr, see https://docs.microsoft.com/sccm/mdm/deploy-use/change-mdm-authority for moving from hybrid to standalone.

▶ To configure Intune for Windows 10 device enrollment, see https://docs.microsoft.com/intune/windows-enroll.

▶ To join existing ConfigMgr clients to co-management, you must set up hybrid Azure AD Join in your AD environment, as discussed in the Azure AD documentation at https://docs.microsoft.com/azure/active-directory/device-management-hybrid-azuread-joined-devices-setup.

▶ Read how to enable existing Intune or ConfigMgr clients for co-management at https://docs.microsoft.com/sccm/core/clients/manage/co-management-prepare.

▶ Read about Windows AutoPilot at https://docs.microsoft.com/windows/deployment/windows-10-auto-pilot and https://docs.microsoft.com/intune/windows-enroll#cnable-windows-10-automatic-enrollment.

▶ Information about configuring compliance policies for Windows 10 devices in Microsoft Intune is at https://docs.microsoft.com/intune/compliance-policy-create-windows.

▶ Read https://docs.microsoft.com/intune/windows-update-for-business-configure for information on configuring Windows 10 update rings in Microsoft Intune.

▶ Following is where to find information about configuring resource profiles for Windows 10 devices in Microsoft Intune:

    ▶ **Certificates:** https://docs.microsoft.com/intune/certificates-configure

    ▶ **Wi-Fi Profiles:** https://docs.microsoft.com/intune/wi-fi-settings-configure

    ▶ **VPN Profiles:** https://docs.microsoft.com/intune/vpn-settings-configure

▶ For details on how to switch workloads from ConfigMgr, see https://docs.microsoft.com/sccm/core/clients/manage/co-management-switch-workloads.

Other Configuration Manager Resources

Microsoft of course is not the only organization to discuss Configuration Manager. A number of websites provide excellent resources for Configuration Manager. Here are several you may want to investigate:

- ▶ Looking for training? Check out the following options:

    - ▶ Microsoft provides two courses on System Center Configuration Manager:

        - ▶ "Administering System Center Configuration Manager," 20703-1A=: Information on this five-day class is available at https://www.microsoft.com/learning/course.aspx?cid=20703-1.

        - ▶ "Integrating MDM and Cloud Services with System Center Configuration Manager," 20703-2: Information on this three-day class is at https://www.microsoft.com/learning/course.aspx?cid=20703-2.

    - ▶ A great ConfigMgr trainer who teaches the ConfigMgr MOC is Michael Head. His current course schedule is located at http://www.HeadSmartGroup.com/.

    - ▶ Microsoft Virtual Academy provides a course on updating, servicing, and telemetry in Configuration Manager Current Branch at https://mva.microsoft.com/training-courses/updates-servicing-and-telemetry-in-configuration-manager-current-branch-16596.

- ▶ https://www.windows-noob.com/forums/topic/13288-step-by-step-guides-system-center-configuration-manager-current-branch-and-technical-preview/ provides guides on new versions of ConfigMgr Current Branch or Technical Preview and how they incorporate with Microsoft Intune.

- ▶ Information about optimizing ConfigMgr database performance is at https://stevethompsonmvp.wordpress.com/2013/05/07/optimizing-configmgr-databases/.

- ▶ To help with troubleshooting report errors, enable Remote Errors on your SSRS website to gather more details. See http://www.enhansoft.com/blog/turn-on-remote-error-reporting.

- ▶ To re-index the WSUS database, download the WSUSDBMaintenance T-SQL script from the TechNet gallery at https://gallery.technet.microsoft.com/scriptcenter/6f8cde49-5c52-4abd-9820-f1d270ddea61.

- ▶ For information about BranchCache and Peer Cache and combining them, see http://deploymentresearch.com/Research/Post/608/A-Geek-rsquo-s-Guide-to-reduce-the-network-impact-of-Windows-10-Updates-and-other-packages-with-ConfigMgr.

- ▶ Find a list of resources related to AV exclusions at http://social.technet.microsoft.com/wiki/contents/articles/953.microsoft-anti-virus-exclusion-list.aspx.

- ▶ Read about how collection updates work at https://david-obrien.net/2014/05/configmgr-collection-updates/. In addition, Scott Breen, a Microsoft Premier Field Engineer, provides an extensive article on update behavior of collections in different scenarios at https://blogs.technet.microsoft.com/scott/2017/09/13/collection-evaluation-overview-configuration-manager/.

▶ Don Jones discusses defining parameters in PowerShell scripts at http://technet.microsoft.com/magazine/jj554301.aspx.

▶ Read about using PowerShell to troubleshoot and repair WMI errors by the Scripting Guy at http://blogs.technet.com/b/heyscriptingguy/archive/2012/03/29/use-powershell-to-troubleshoot-and-repair-wmi-errors.aspx.

▶ The Microsoft IT Pro community maintains an index of antimalware security policy recommendations for Microsoft products at http://social.technet.microsoft.com/wiki/contents/articles/953.microsoft-anti-virus-exclusion-list.aspx.

▶ CIM is the Common Information Model component that WMI is based on. To learn more about CIM, see the tutorial at http://www.wbemsolutions.com/tutorials/CIM/index.html.

▶ Need help with troubleshooting client push installation? Check out http://blogs.technet.com/b/sudheesn/archive/2010/05/31/troubleshooting-sccm-part-i-client-push-installation.aspx. Although this post is written for ConfigMgr 2007, the concepts are still valid.

▶ A step-by-step guide on using software metering is available at http://blogs.msdn.com/b/minfangl/archive/2011/04/29/step-by-step-on-how-to-use-software-metering.aspx. Although written for ConfigMgr 2007, the article is still valid for ConfigMgr Current Branch.

▶ Steve Rachui discusses state messaging in depth at http://blogs.msdn.com/b/steverac/archive/2011/01/07/sccm-state-messaging-in-depth.aspx.

▶ Read about the software updates process as viewed through the log files. See the following sites:

  ▶ http://blogs.msdn.com/b/steverac/archive/2011/04/10/software-updates-internals-mms-2011-session-part-i.aspx

  ▶ https://blogs.msdn.microsoft.com/steverac/2011/04/16/software-updatesinternals-mms-2011-sessionpart-ii/

  ▶ https://blogs.msdn.microsoft.com/steverac/2011/04/30/software-updatesinternals-mms-2011-sessionpart-iii/

  ▶ https://blogs.technet.microsoft.com/configurationmgr/2016/08/25/software-updates-in-configuration-manager-current-branch-deep-dive-client-operations/

▶ Coauthor Gerry Hampson provides additional context about app deployment from an end-user perspective. For information about app deployment for Android, see the article at http://gerryhampsoncm.blogspot.ie/2015/07/deploying-apps-to-android-devices-with.html; for information regarding iOS, see http://gerryhampsoncm.blogspot.ie/2015/07/deploying-apps-to-ios-devices-with.html.

▶ Use the Intune Company Portal for Android to manage Android devices. Download the portal from the Google Play Store at https://play.google.com/store/apps/details?id=com.microsoft.windowsintune.companyportal&hl=en.

▶ The Intune Company Portal for iOS can be downloaded from the Apple App Store at https://itunes.apple.com/us/app/microsoft-intune-company-portal/id719171358?mt=8.

▶ The Apple Push Certificates Portal is at https://identify.apple.com.

▶ Kent Agerlund has an informative blog post explaining the content library, at http://blog.coretech.dk/kea/understanding-the-new-content-library-store-in-5-minutes/.

▶ Deploying Endpoint Protection through the network share option does not have any dependencies on the WSUS/SUS infrastructure or Internet downloads. Following are guides and sample scripts for deploying Endpoint Protection through the network share option:

  ▶ https://www.niallbrady.com/2013/02/22/how-can-i-deploy-system-center-2012-endpoint-protection-definition-updates-from-a-unc-file-shares/

  ▶ https://blogs.technet.microsoft.com/charlesa_us/2015/05/20/configmgr-2012-how-to-deploy-scep-definition-updates-via-unc-share-for-isolated-environment/

  ▶ https://blog.thesysadmins.co.uk/sccm-2012-scep-unc-definition-updates-automation-powershell.html

  ▶ http://richardbalsley.com/using-sccm-distribution-points-for-forefront-endpoint-protection-2010-definition-updates

▶ http://blogs.msdn.com/b/steverac/archive/2014/03/29/the-suite-spot-of-imaging.aspx discusses using OSD for imaging.

▶ http://www.appdetails.com provides general guidance on software deployment and a forum for users to share their experiences testing whether software can be installed unattended.

▶ WSUS no longer issues self-signed certificates; see the WSUS Product Team posting at https://blogs.technet.microsoft.com/wsus/2013/08/15/wsus-no-longer-issues-self-signed-certificates/.

▶ To use an internal PKI-generated certificate with SCUP, see https://blogs.technet.microsoft.com/jasonlewis/2011/07/12/system-center-updates-publisher-signing-certificate-requirements-step-by-step-guide. Information on how to use public certificates is at https://blogs.msdn.microsoft.com/steverac/2011/09/17/using-system-center-update-publisher-2007-with-verisign-certificates.

▶ Read about Open Management Infrastructure (OMI) at http://www.opengroup.org/software/omi. Find in-depth information on OMI and how it works at https://collaboration.opengroup.org/omi/. The OMI getting started guide can be downloaded from https://collaboration.opengroup.org/omi/documents.php.

▶ Steve Rachui discusses operating system deployment to Linux/UNIX operating systems (which is not supported by Microsoft) at http://blogs.msdn.com/b/steverac/archive/2014/01/02/osd-for-linux-imaging-yes-really.aspx.

▶ For information on setting up multicasting, see https://blogs.msdn.microsoft.com/steverac/2008/10/18/setting-up-multicasting-in-sccm.

▶ To enable the prestart command for a TS, see https://blogs.msdn.microsoft.com/steverac/2015/04/22/power-belongs-to-youthe-osd-prestart-command/.

▶ To capture logs during failed TS execution, see https://blogs.msdn.microsoft.com/steverac/2008/07/15/capturing-logs-during-failed-task-sequence-execution/.

▶ Marcus Oh writes about retrieving objects into a collection that does not exist in another collection at http://marcusoh.blogspot.com/2007/08/sms-selecting-objects-not-in-collection.html.

▶ Beginning with ConfigMgr 2007 R2, ConfigMgr has the ability to define a task sequence variable on a collection or individual resource without a value. Read about it in a posting by Jason Sandys at http://blog.configmgrftw.com/?p=44.

▶ Flexera's AdminStudio is a popular software packaging suite. See http://www.flexerasoftware.com/products/adminstudio-suite.htm.

▶ Adaptiva Software (http://www.adaptiva.com) extends Microsoft's technologies to enhance PC power management. 1E (http://www.1e.com) also has a number of products to assist with sustainability and energy efficiency.

▶ Symantec offers mobile device management software for iOS, Android, and Windows Phone devices; http://www.symantec.com/mobile-management#sccm provides details.

Blogs

Here are some blogs the authors have used. Some are more active than others, and new blogs seem to spring up overnight!

▶ Microsoft's Enterprise Mobility and Security Blog is at https://cloudblogs.microsoft.com/enterprisemobility/.

▶ The ConfigMgr Team blog is at https://blogs.technet.microsoft.com/configmgrteam/.

▶ See the Intune Team blog at https://blogs.technet.microsoft.com/microsoftintune/.

▶ http://bink.nu is managed by Steven Bink, former MVP for Windows Server Technologies. According to the blog, it "watches Microsoft like a hawk."

▶ Garth Jones, ECM MVP and contributing author to this book, is affiliated with the SMS User Group in Canada, whose blogs are at http://smsug.ca/blogs/.

▶ http://sms-hints-tricks.blogspot.com is by Matthew Hudson, ECM MVP.

▶ Ronni Pederson's blog is at http://ronnipedersen.com.

▶ Sherry Kissinger, former ECM MVP, blogs at https://mnscug.org/blogs/sherry-kissinger.

▶ http://systemscentre.blogspot.com is maintained by MVP Steve Beaumont.

▶ The OSD Support Team blog is at http://blogs.technet.com/b/system_center_configuration_manager_operating_system_deployment_support_blog/.

▶ Microsoft's hybrid cloud blog is at https://cloudblogs.microsoft.com/hybridcloud/.

▶ The Microsoft Deployment Guys have a blog at http://blogs.technet.com/deploymentguys/default.aspx.

▶ Kevin Sullivan is a Technology Specialist at Microsoft focusing on Azure Site Recovery. His blog is at https://blogs.technet.com/kevinsul_blog/.

▶ http://marcusoh.blogspot.com is a blog by former MVP Marcus Oh.

▶ http://stefanschorling.azurewebsites.net is Stefan Schörling's blog on Microsoft system and cloud management. Stefan is a former ECM MVP.

▶ Niall Brady, ECM MVP, blogs at http://www.niallbrady.com.

▶ Samuel Erskine, Cloud and Datacenter Management MVP, blogs at www.itprocessed.com.

▶ Torsten Meringer, ECM MVP, manages the German ConfigMgr blog, at http://www.mssccmfaq.de.

▶ https://stevethompsonmvp.wordpress.com is the blog for Steve Thompson, ECM MVP.

▶ Greg Ramsey, ECM MVP and a coauthor for this book, blogs at http://gregramsey.wordpress.com.

▶ Coauthor Kenneth van Surksum blogs at http://www.vansurksum.com.

▶ Coauthor Michael Wiles blogged at http://blogs.technet.com/b/mwiles/ while at Microsoft.

▶ Steve Rachui is a CSS guru on ConfigMgr and our technical editor. Check out his blog at http://blogs.msdn.com/steverac/.

Public Forums

If you need an answer to a question, the first place to check is the Microsoft public forums. A list of available TechNet forums is maintained at http://social.technet.microsoft.com/Forums/home. It is best to see if your question has already been posted before you ask it yourself!

▶ For the Configuration Manager—General forum, see https://social.technet.microsoft.com/Forums/en-US/home?forum=ConfigMgrCBGeneral.

▶ For the Configuration Manager Servicing forum, see https://social.technet.microsoft.com/Forums/en-US/home?forum=configmgrservicing.

▶ For the Configuration Manager Site and Client Deployment forum, see https://social.technet.microsoft.com/Forums/en-US/home?forum=ConfigMgrDeployment

▶ For the Configuration Manager Migration forum, see https://social.technet.microsoft.com/Forums/en-US/home?forum=ConfigMgrMigration

▶ For the Configuration Manager SDK and PowerShell forum, see https://social.technet.microsoft.com/Forums/en-US/home?forum=ConfigMgrPowerShell

▶ For the Configuration Manager Application Management forum, see https://social.technet.microsoft.com/Forums/en-US/home?forum=ConfigMgrAppManagement

▶ For the Configuration Manager Security, Updates, and Compliance forum, see https://social.technet.microsoft.com/Forums/en-US/home?forum=ConfigMgrCompliance

▶ For the Configuration Manager Operating System Deployment forum, see https://social.technet.microsoft.com/Forums/en-US/home?forum=ConfigMgrCBOSD

▶ For the Configuration Manager Mobile Device Management forum, see https://social.technet.microsoft.com/Forums/en-US/home?forum=ConfigMgrMDM

▶ For the Intune forum, see https://social.technet.microsoft.com/Forums/en-US/home?category=microsoftintune.

▶ myITforum also has a discussion list for Configuration Manager, along with a number of other discussion lists; see http://myitforum.com/newsletter/email-lists-2/.

Utilities

Here are some utilities, both Microsoft and third party:

▶ The WMI Diagnosis Utility (WMIDiag) is available at the Microsoft download site, https://www.microsoft.com/download/details.aspx?id=7684. For more information about WMIDiag and the team that wrote it, see https://blogs.technet.microsoft.com/askperf/2015/05/12/wmidiag-2-2-is-here/. The team also published a list of recommended WMI hotfixes for Windows 7/Server 2008 R2 and older versions at https://blogs.technet.microsoft.com/askperf/2011/08/05/suggested-hotfixes-for-wmi-related-issues-on-windows-platforms-updated-august-9th-2013/.

▶ ADModify is recommended for making mass changes of UPNs in AD. See https://technet.microsoft.com/library/aa996216(v=exchg.65).aspx for information.

▶ Download AzureADConnect.msi to quickly onboard to Azure AD and Office 365 from https://www.microsoft.com/download/details.aspx?id=47594. You can configure an alternate login ID by using the information at https://technet.microsoft.com/library/dn659436.aspx.

▶ The `Nslookup` command is described at http://support.microsoft.com/kb/200525. To troubleshoot NetBIOS name resolution using `Nbtstat` and other methods, see KB article 323388, at http://support.microsoft.com/kb/323388.

▶ To get the WMI Explorer (PowerShell version), written by Marc van Orsouw, see http://powershell.org/wmi-explorer/.

▶ The WMI Explorer (.NET-version) is available at https://github.com/vinaypamnani/wmie2/releases.

▶ `PSExec` is available at https://docs.microsoft.com/sysinternals/.

▶ Process Monitor can capture detailed process activity on Windows systems. https://technet.microsoft.com/sysinternals/processmonitor.aspx provides information and a download link.

▶ `NetDiag` is a diagnostic tool that helps isolate networking and connectivity problems. For information, see http://technet.microsoft.com/library/Cc938980.

▶ `Netperf` is a benchmarking tool that can be used to measure performance of many types of networking. It provides tests for both unidirectional throughput and end-to-end latency. For more information and to download the tool, see http://www.netperf.org/netperf/.

▶ The Configuration Manager Toolkit is available at https://www.microsoft.com/download/details.aspx?id=50012.

▶ Download the 7-Zip decompression utility at http://www.7-zip.org/.

▶ Microsoft Security Compliance Manager (https://www.microsoft.com/download/details.aspx?id=16776) can be used to compare your systems against baseline Microsoft recommendations.

▶ Troubleshoot port status issues using `PortQry` and `PortQryUI`, downloadable from http://www.microsoft.com/downloads/details.aspx?familyid=89811747-C74B-4638-A2D5-AC828BDC6983&displaylang=en and http://www.microsoft.com/downloads/details.aspx?FamilyID=8355E537-1EA6-4569-AABB-F248F4BD91D0&displaylang=en, respectively. Going to http://www.microsoft.com/downloads and searching for PortQry brings up links for each tool.

▶ `Orca` is an MSI table editing tool you can use to view and change information in an MSI file. Information about Orca and where to download it is at https://msdn.microsoft.com/library/windows/desktop/aa370557%28v=vs.85%29.aspx.

▶ SCUP is not included with ConfigMgr but is a separate and free download from Microsoft, available at http://www.microsoft.com/download/en/details.aspx?id=11940.

▶ The Remote Server Administration Tools for Windows 8.1 (RSAT) can be utilized if using Windows 8.1 for your SCUP workstation. Download the tools from http://www.microsoft.com/download/details.aspx?id=39296.

▶ XML Notepad 2007 is an intuitive tool for browsing and editing XML documents. Read about it at http://msdn2.microsoft.com/library/aa905339.aspx and download the tool from http://www.microsoft.com/downloads/details.aspx?familyid=72d6aa49-787d-4118-ba5f-4f30fe913628&displaylang=en.

▶ Microsoft's Configuration Manager Hybrid Diagnostics tool checks for a number of issues related to Intune integration. Download the tool at https://www.microsoft.com/download/details.aspx?id=53306.

▶ Use the Microsoft Assessment Planning Toolkit (MAP) to help plan client agent deployment. MAP is available at http://www.microsoft.com/download/en/details.aspx?id=7826. For frequently asked questions on MAP, see http://social.technet.microsoft.com/wiki/contents/articles/1643.aspx.

▶ At times, creating WMI queries can be quite cumbersome. A number of tools are available for free to help ease the process. Some popular ones follow:

> ▶ **WMI Code Creator:** https://www.microsoft.com/download/en/details.aspx?displaylang=en&id=8572

> ▶ **WMIGen Code Generator:** http://www.robvanderwoude.com/wmigen.php

▶ RegKeyToMOF, which can assist in using hardware inventory to inventory a specific Registry key, is available at http://mnscug.org/images/Sherry/RegKeyToMOFv33a.zip. You can also read about this utility at https://www.enhansoft.com/blog/how-to-use-regkeytomof.

APPENDIX D

Available Online

Online content is available to provide add-on value to readers of *System Center Configuration Manager Current Branch Unleashed*. You can download this material, organized by chapter. First, register your book at informit.com/register. You will then be able to download content from http://www.informit.com/title/9780672337901.

This content is not available elsewhere. Note that the authors and publisher do not guarantee or provide technical support for the material.

Configuration Manager Reporting

Chapter 21, "Configuration Manager Reporting," discusses where Configuration Manager (ConfigMgr) stores its inventory data and how to find that information. It also explains the different types of reports within a series and basic design rules, such as having a consistent look and feel across all reports. Chapter 21 also illustrates how to create and use a report. The following related online content is available:

▶ **21list01_System Details.sql:** This SQL query was used to create the report in Chapter 21. It returns the computer name, operating system name, and Active Directory site details.

▶ **21list06_Alternate row color expression.txt:** This expression allows for alternating colors within a table.

▶ **21list07_Expression to display the date.txt:** This expression displays today's date within the report.

▶ **21list08_Expression to add the page number.txt:** This expression displays page x of y within the report.

▶ **System Details.rdl:** This is the sample report created in Chapter 21, in .rdl format.

▶ **System Details Chart.rdl:** This is the sample chart report created in Chapter 21.

Live Links

Reference URLs (see Appendix C, "Reference URLs") are provided as live links. These include nearly 400 clickable hypertext links and references to materials and sites related to Configuration Manager.

A disclaimer and unpleasant fact regarding live links: URLs change! Companies are subject to mergers and acquisitions, pages move, changes are made on websites, and so on. Although these links were accurate at the time this book was published, it is possible that some will change or be "dead" by the time you read this book. Sometimes the Wayback Machine (http://www.archive.org/) can rescue you from dead or broken links. The Wayback Machine site is an Internet archive that can take you back to an archived version of a site—sometimes.

Extending Hardware Inventory—Online Only

Appendix E, "Extending Hardware Inventory," is a bonus appendix you can download from the book's website after you register your book at informit.com/register. It discusses how to extend hardware inventory, which queries Windows Management Instrumentation (WMI) on each ConfigMgr-managed client to gather data about that device. What is queried depends on what WMI classes are enabled. Two files referenced in Appendix E are available as online content:

▶ CM12Config.mof

▶ CM12Import.mof

Use these files to assist in extending hardware inventory.

Index

Numbers

A

D

N

P

R

U

V

X-Y-Z